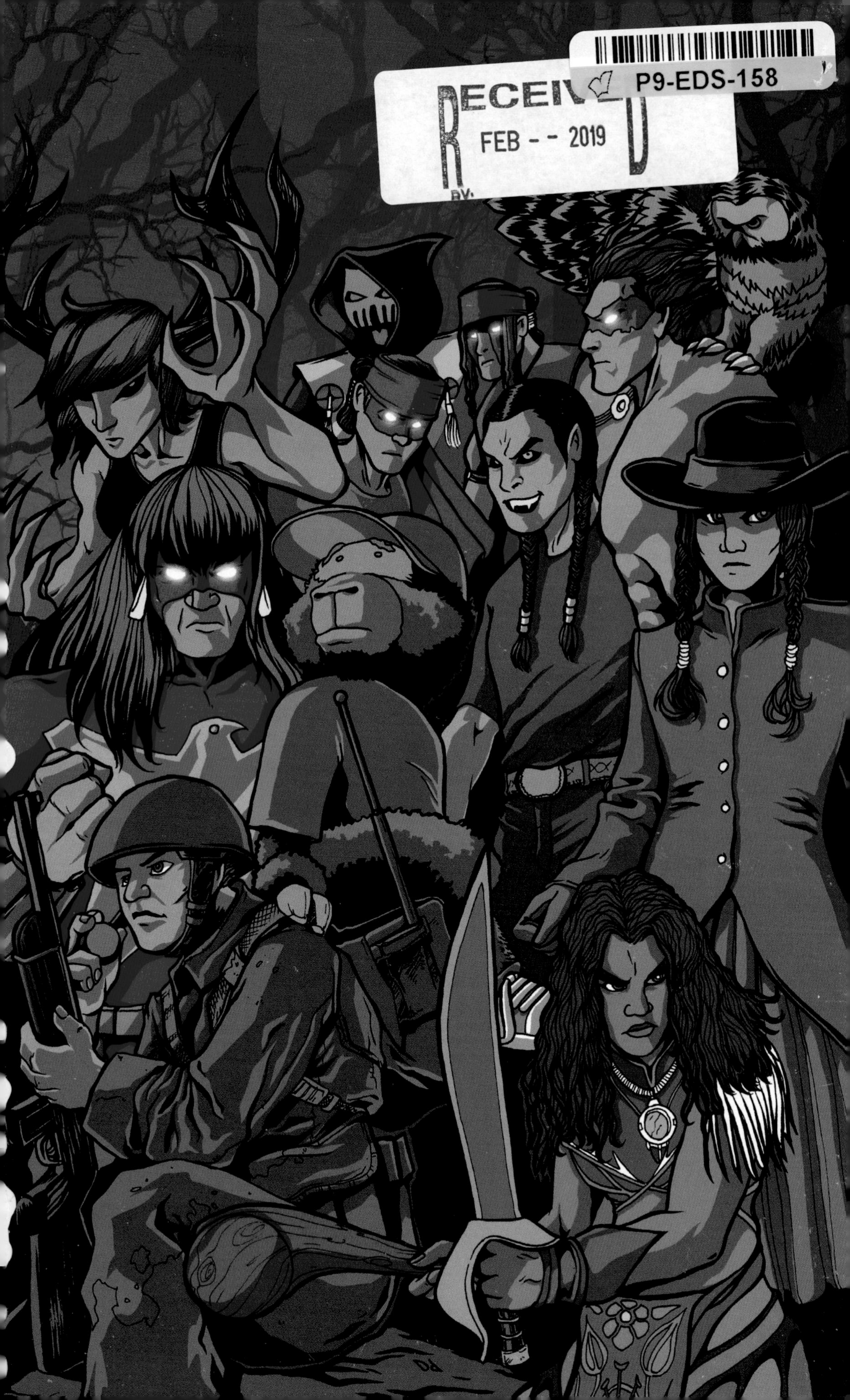

native realities anthology:one

LEE FRANCIS IV
CEO/PUBLISHER

AARON CUFFEE
CCO/EDITOR

NEZ EVANS
DISTRIBUTION MGR

KENN RODRIGUEZ-REED
MEDIA MANAGER

table of contents

introduction   6

the wool of jonesy   8

code: love   35

tribal force #1   47

asdzą́ą́ changing   59

hero twins #1   71

upcoming releases   87

from the editor

In 2015, we published our first comic book - Annumpa Luma - the first issue of the Tales of the Mighty Code Talkers. Our goals was to tell authentic and dynamic stories of Native and Indigenous people through comic books and graphic novels. The need for these kinds of stories has been well documented, especially for Native communities where there is little to no literature that portrays the positive realities of those communities.

This anthology is a collection of several of our original comics as well as teasers for current and upcoming books we intend to produce in the near future. They present a range of stories, from sheep to superheroes, and highlight the incredible work that Native comic book artists are accomplishing. It is this work that provides insight into the creative expression and the dynamic interpretations of modern Native and Indigenous identity that goes beyond the historical and stereotypical images associated with our people for over three hundred years. With these efforts, we hope to undo some of the damage that has been done to Native people through popular culture and forge a new path of Indigenous portrayals that give hope and healing to our youth and communities.

What you will find here is an exceptional representation of the Native and Indigenous imagination. Rather than

continue to perpetuate a tragic existence, these stories look to inspire and illuminate the beautiful and hopeful within our Native people. These stories hold their own power: the power to change, the power to inspire, the power to respond in a creative manner to the imagery usually associated with Native people. This power is prevalent in each of the works contained. Most importantly they evoke a sense of joy and wonder. Even when dealing with difficult topics - abuse, despair, tragedy - the spirit of the work shines through in a way that is undeniably celebratory, something often overlooked in popular media portrayals of Native people. As such we consider this anthology to be an act of resilience and healing, as well as a celebration of the Indigenous creative capacity.

We are thrilled to present this work and want to offer a huge thank you to all those who have supported us and our efforts to make positive change on behalf of Native and Indigenous people world-wide. Without your support we would not have been able to produce the number of books and continue to do this important work. Da'wah'eh - thank you!

lee francis iv, publisher and ceo
native realities publishing and media

the wool of jonesy #1

Written and illustrated by
Jonathan Nelson

Life in Hogback can have its challenges. But for
Jonesy the world is waiting. As his high school
journey is over, there are new adventures are
about to begin.

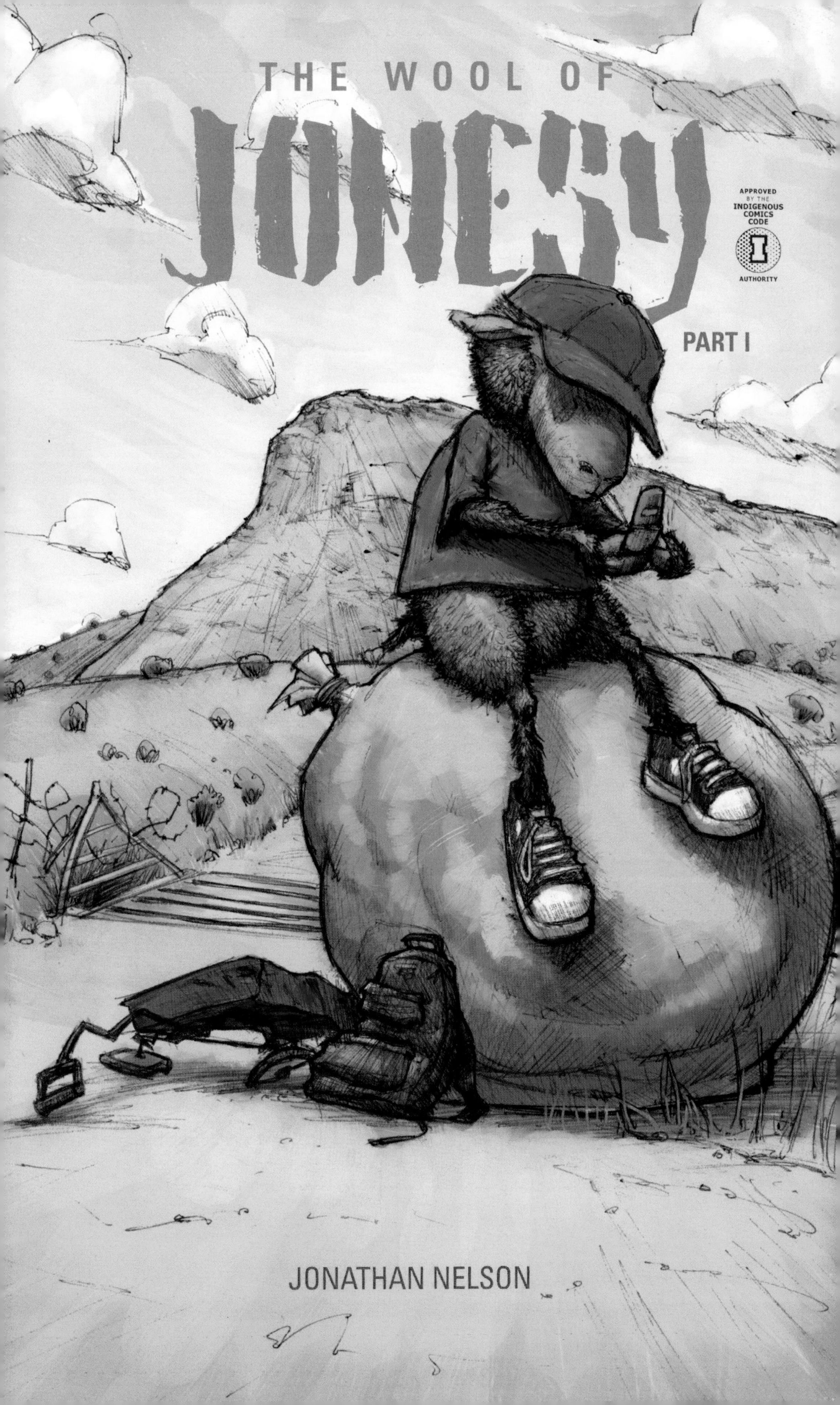
THE WOOL OF
JONESY
APPROVED BY THE INDIGENOUS COMICS CODE AUTHORITY
PART I
JONATHAN NELSON

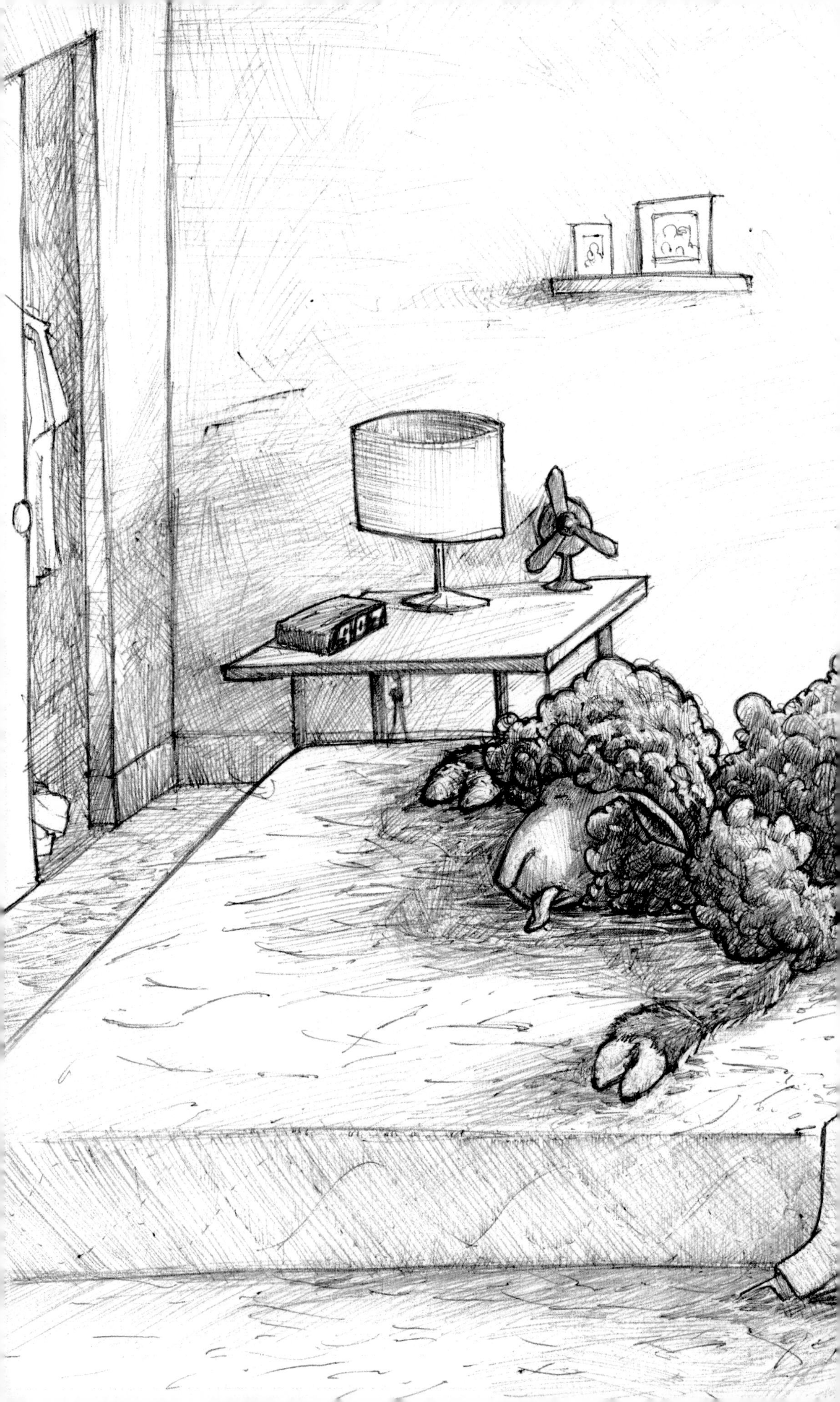

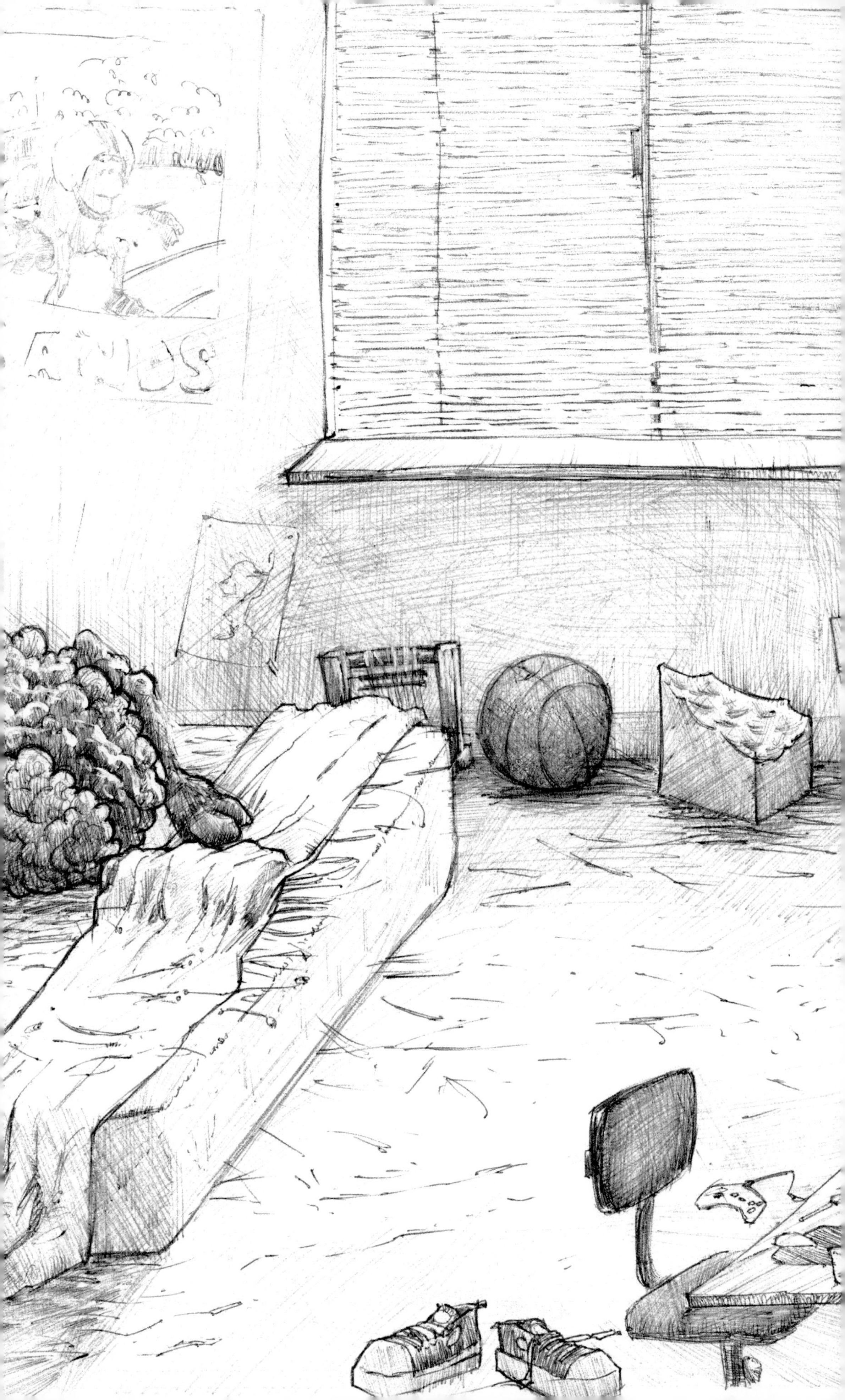

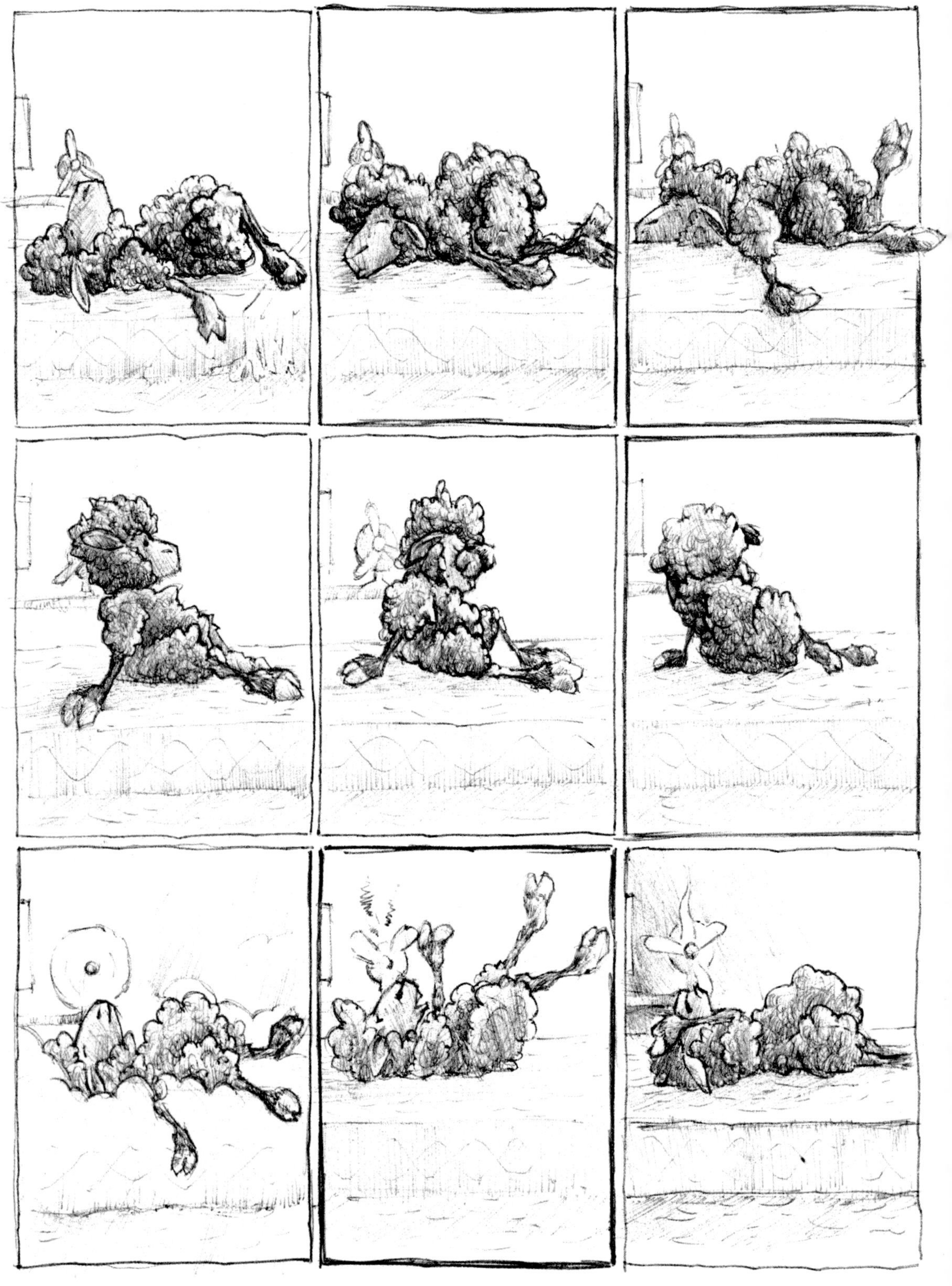

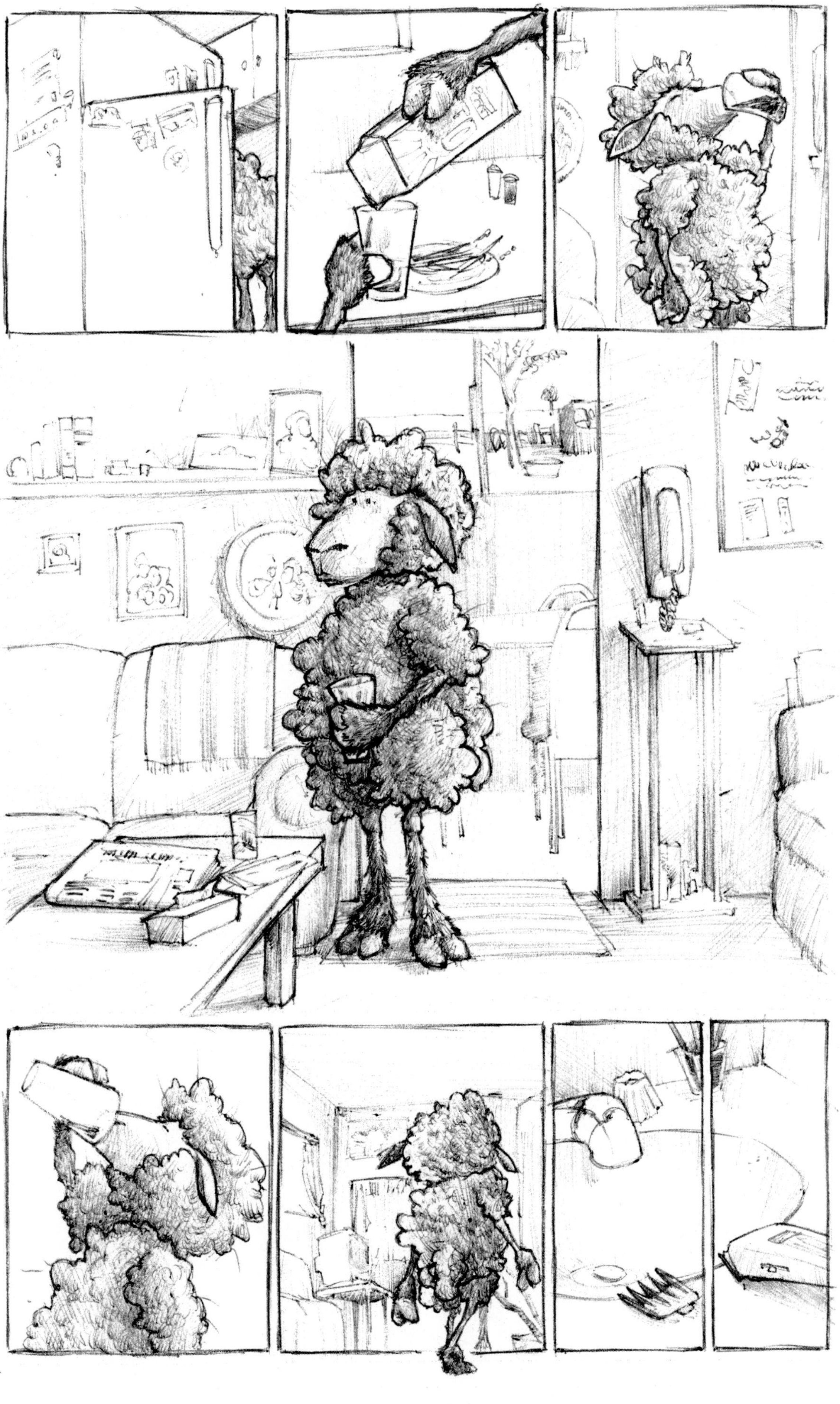

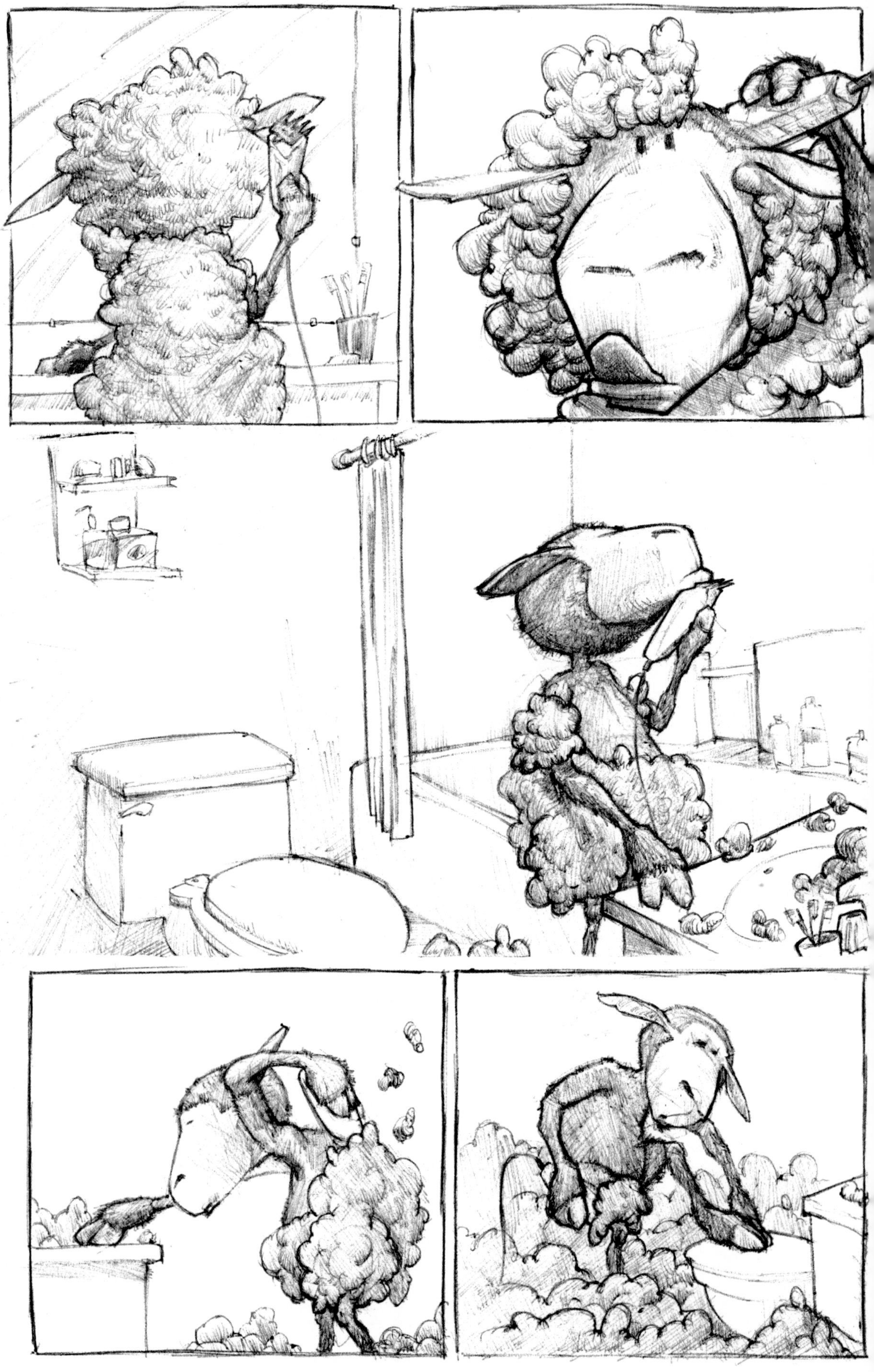

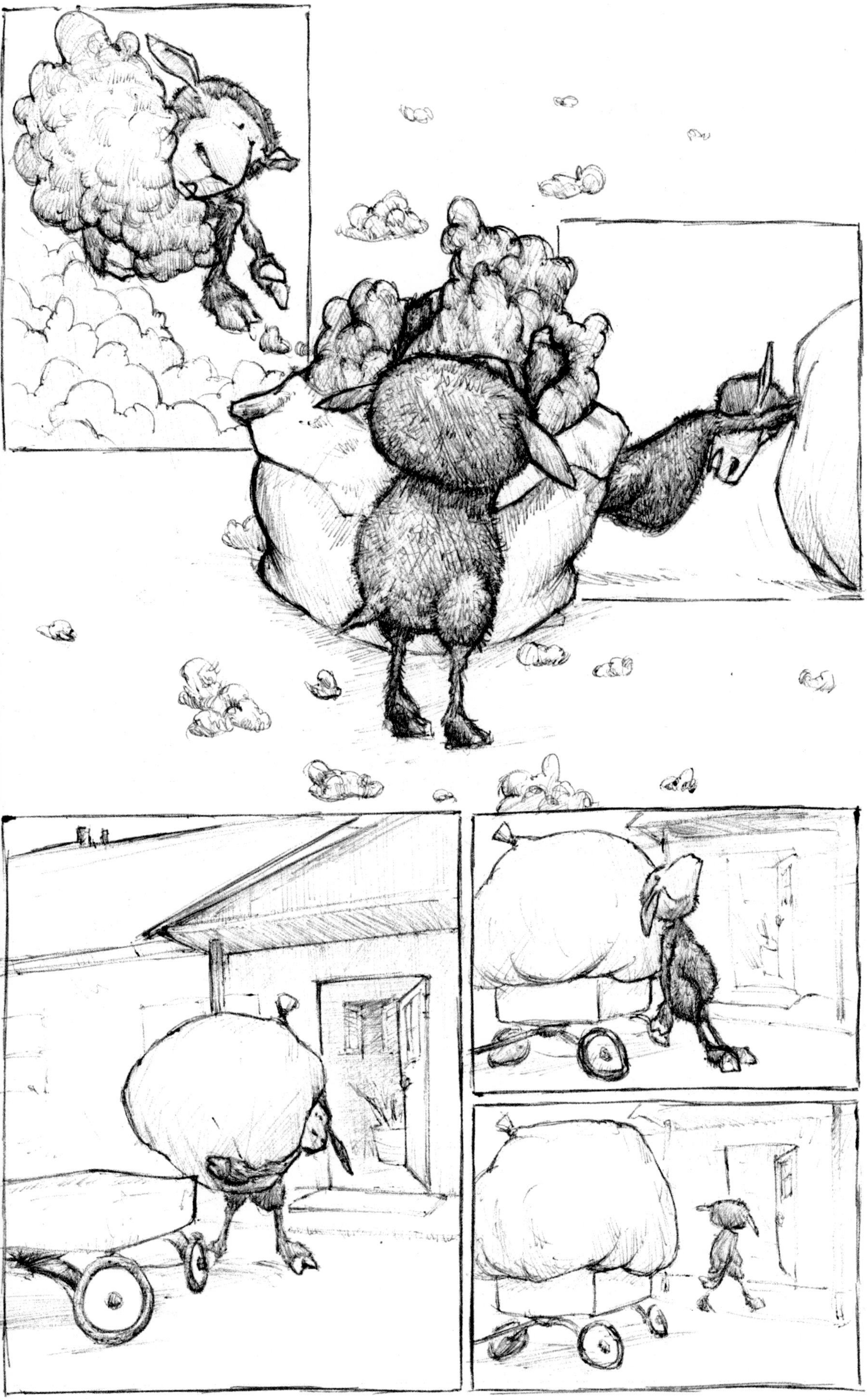

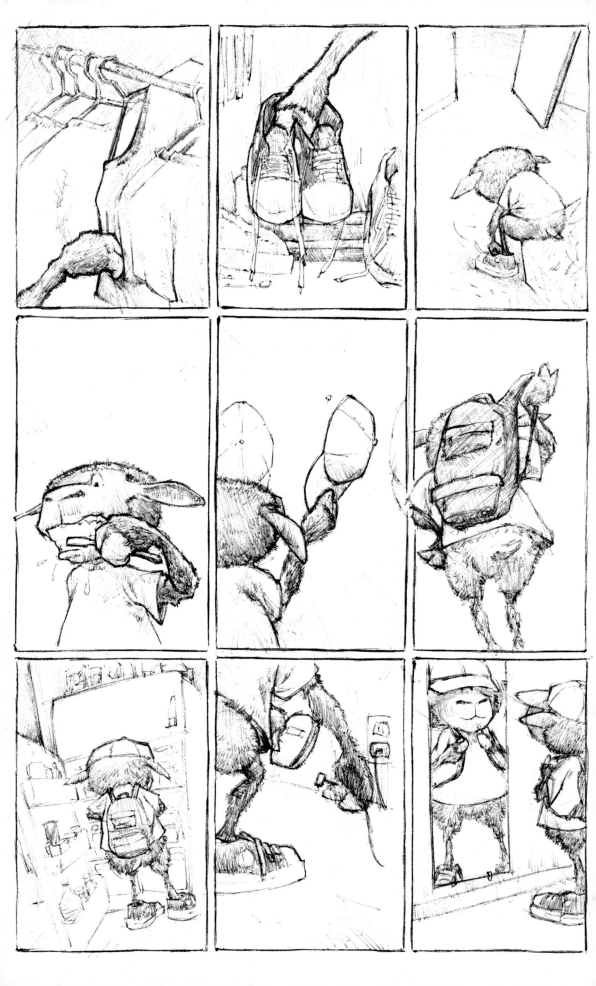

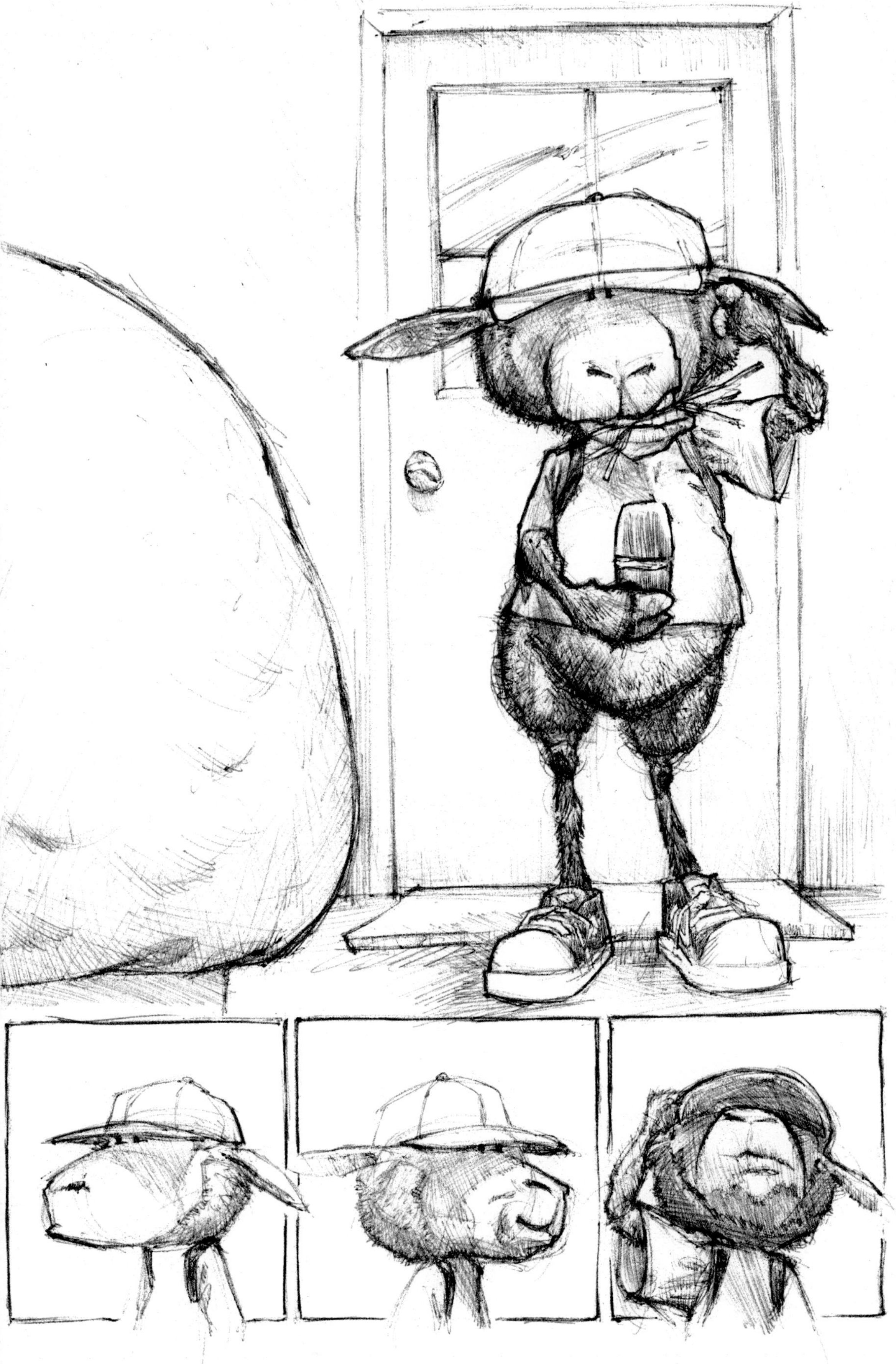

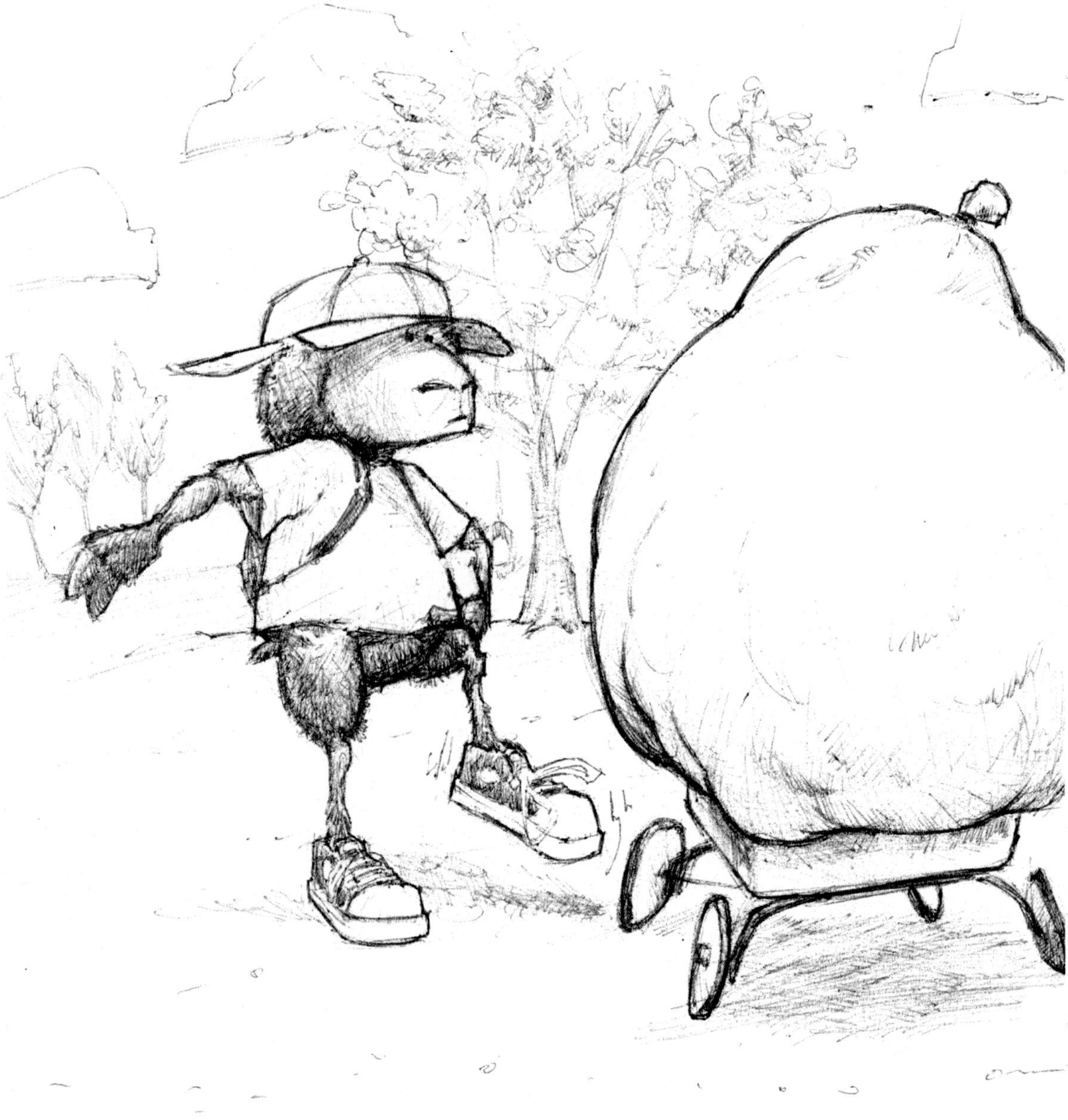

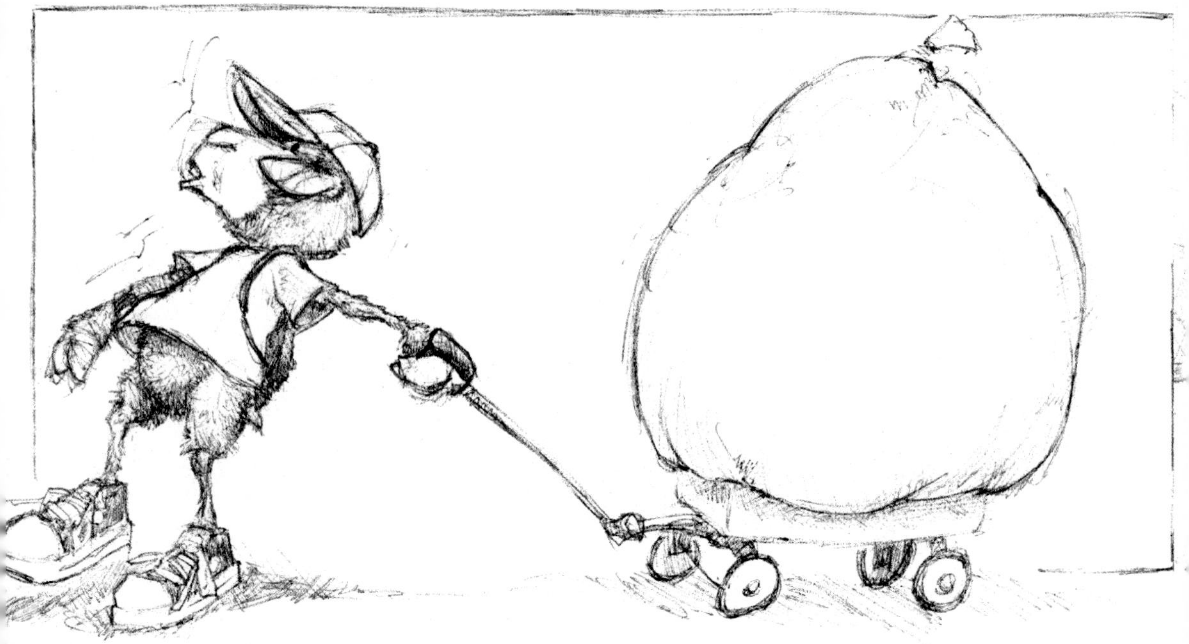

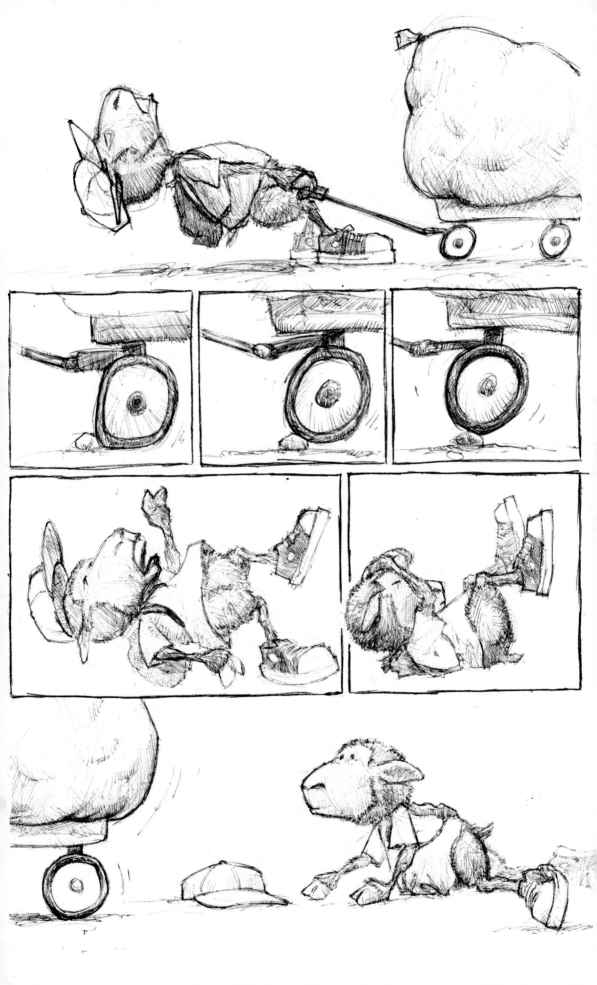

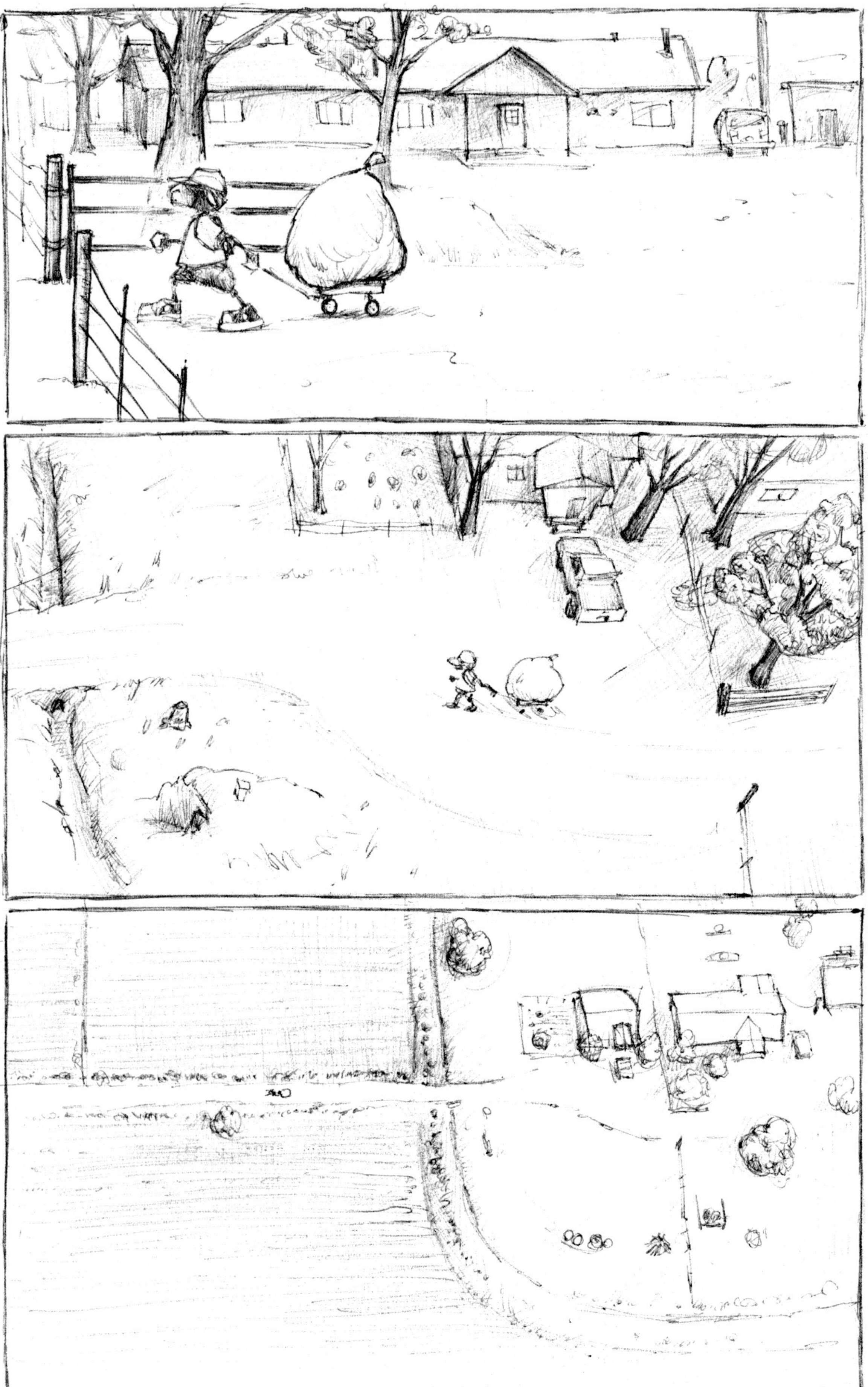

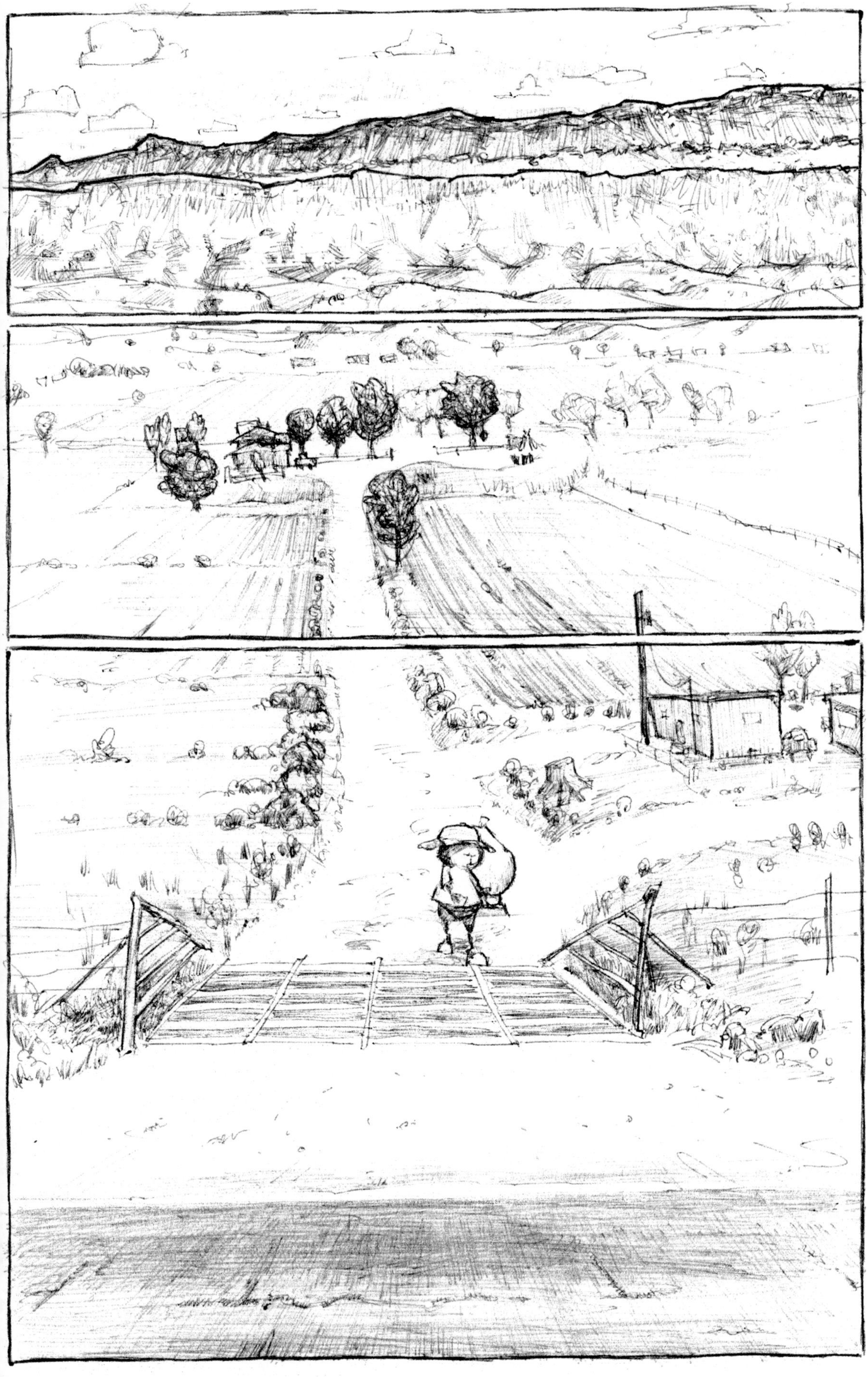

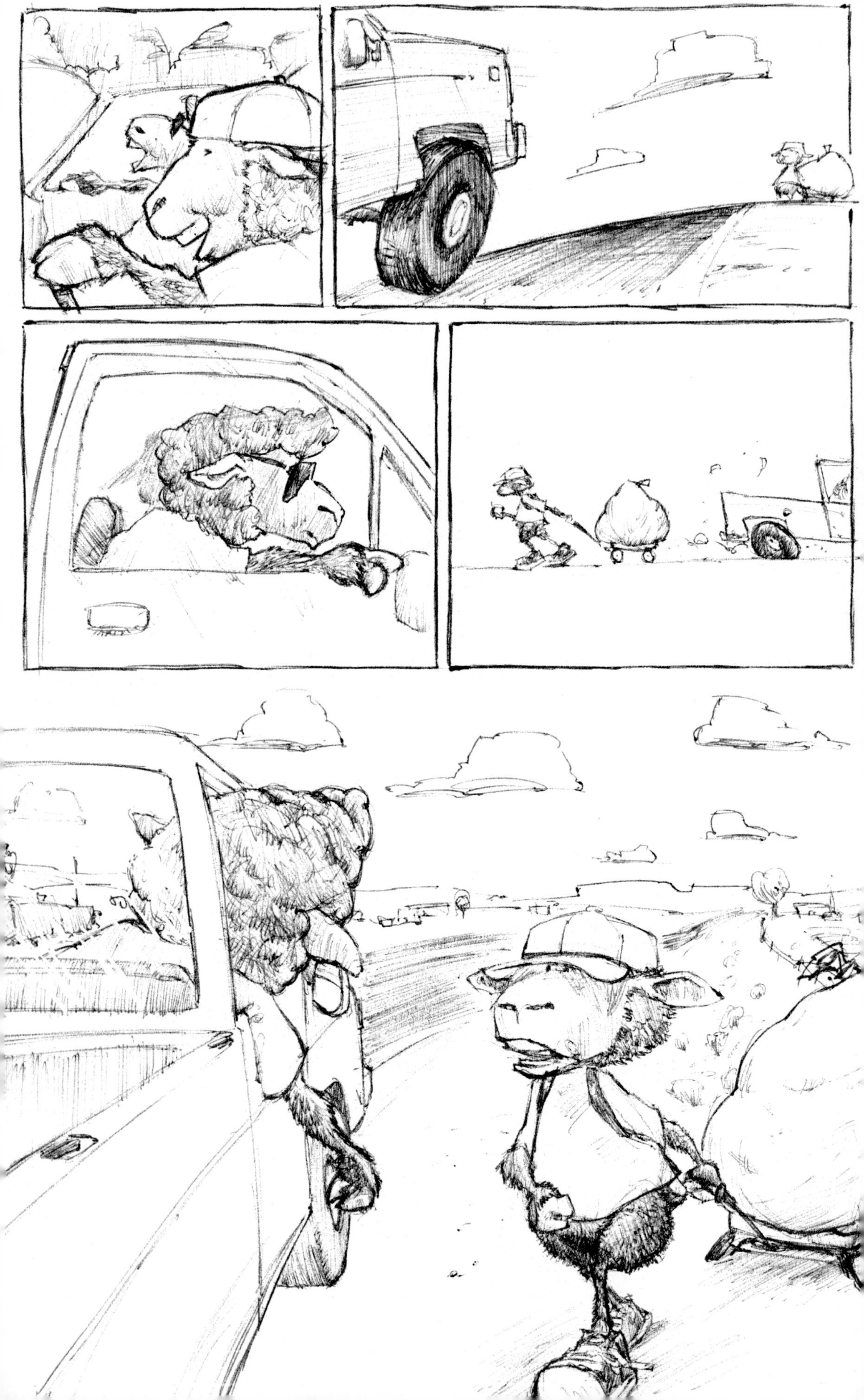

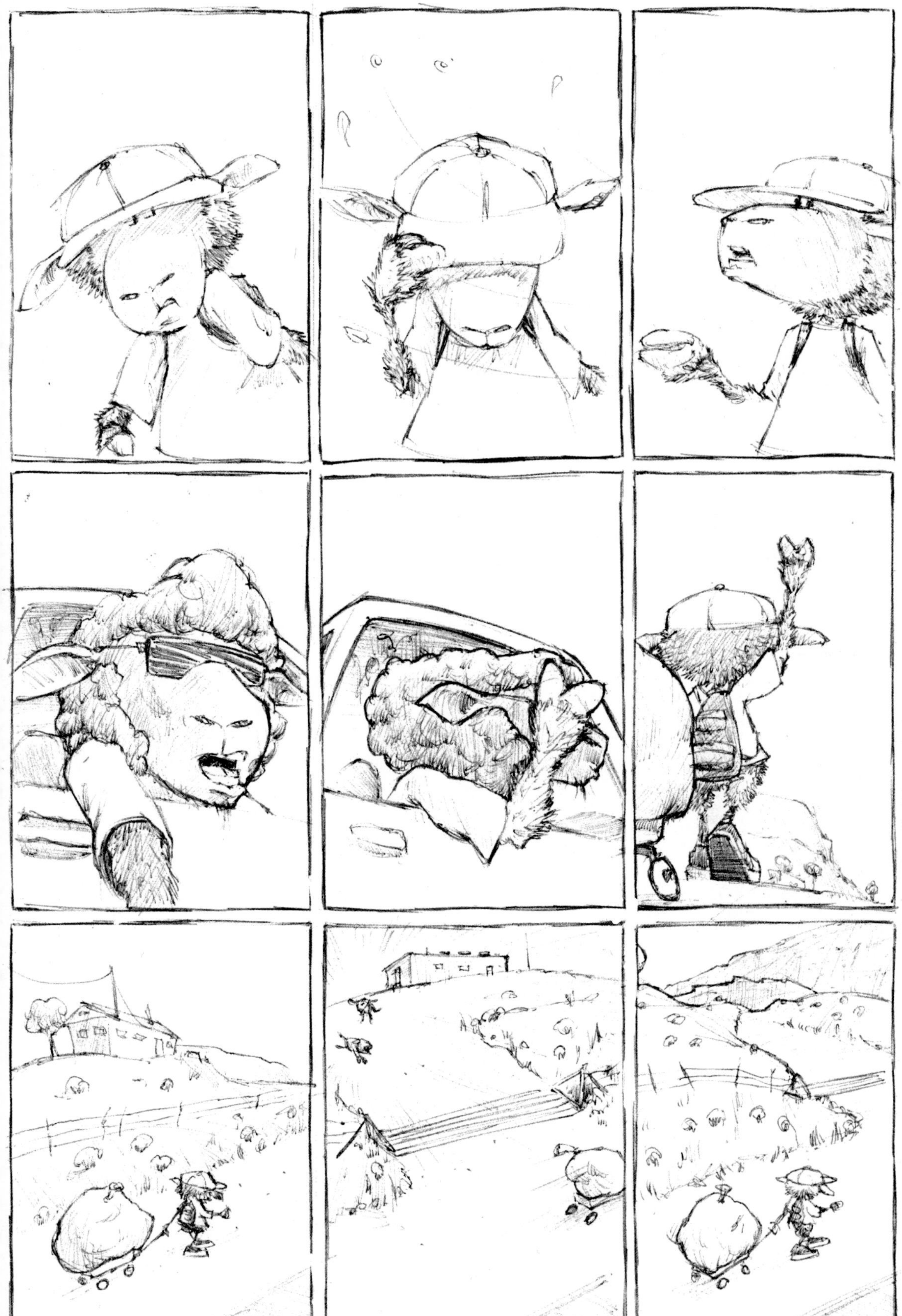

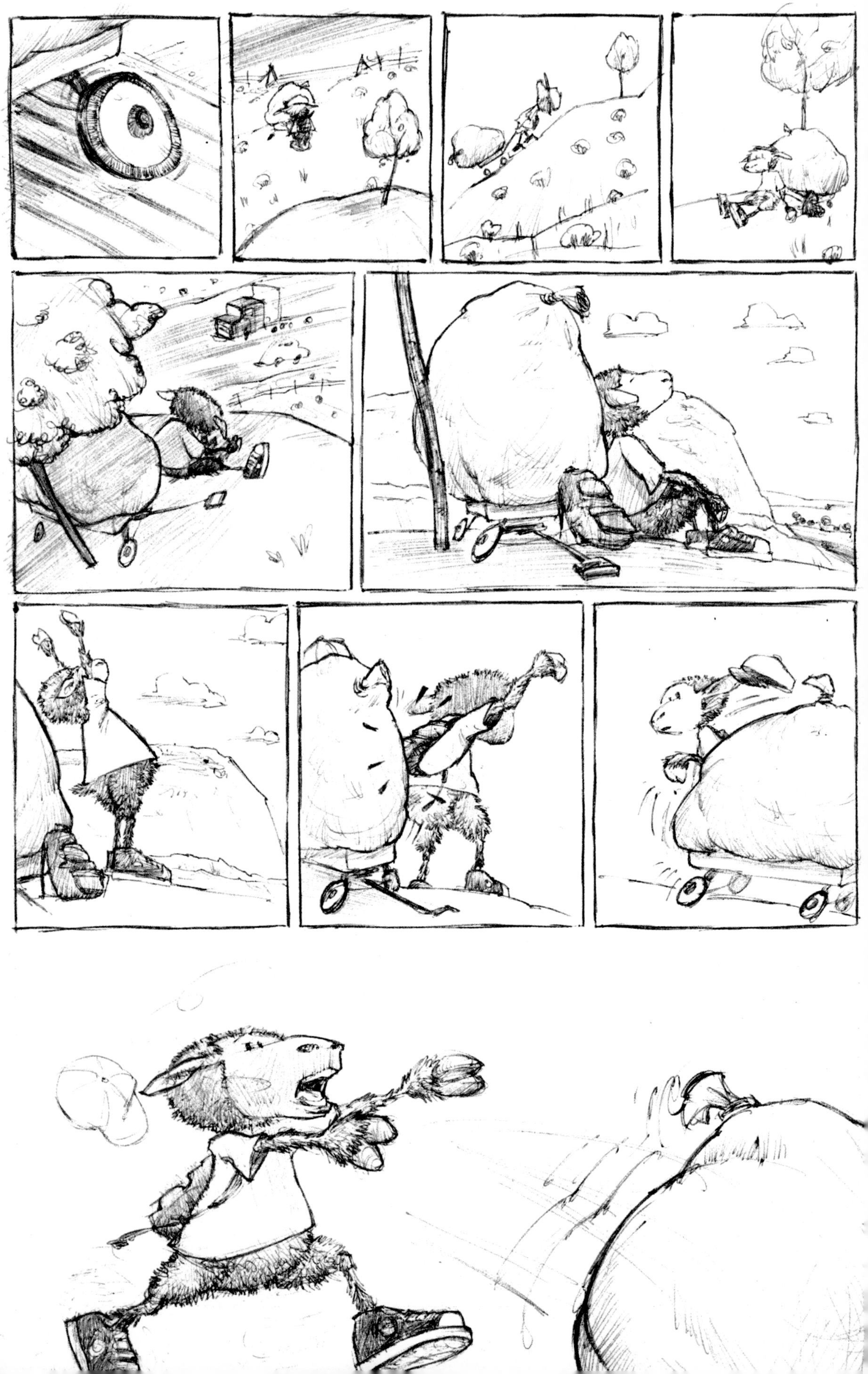

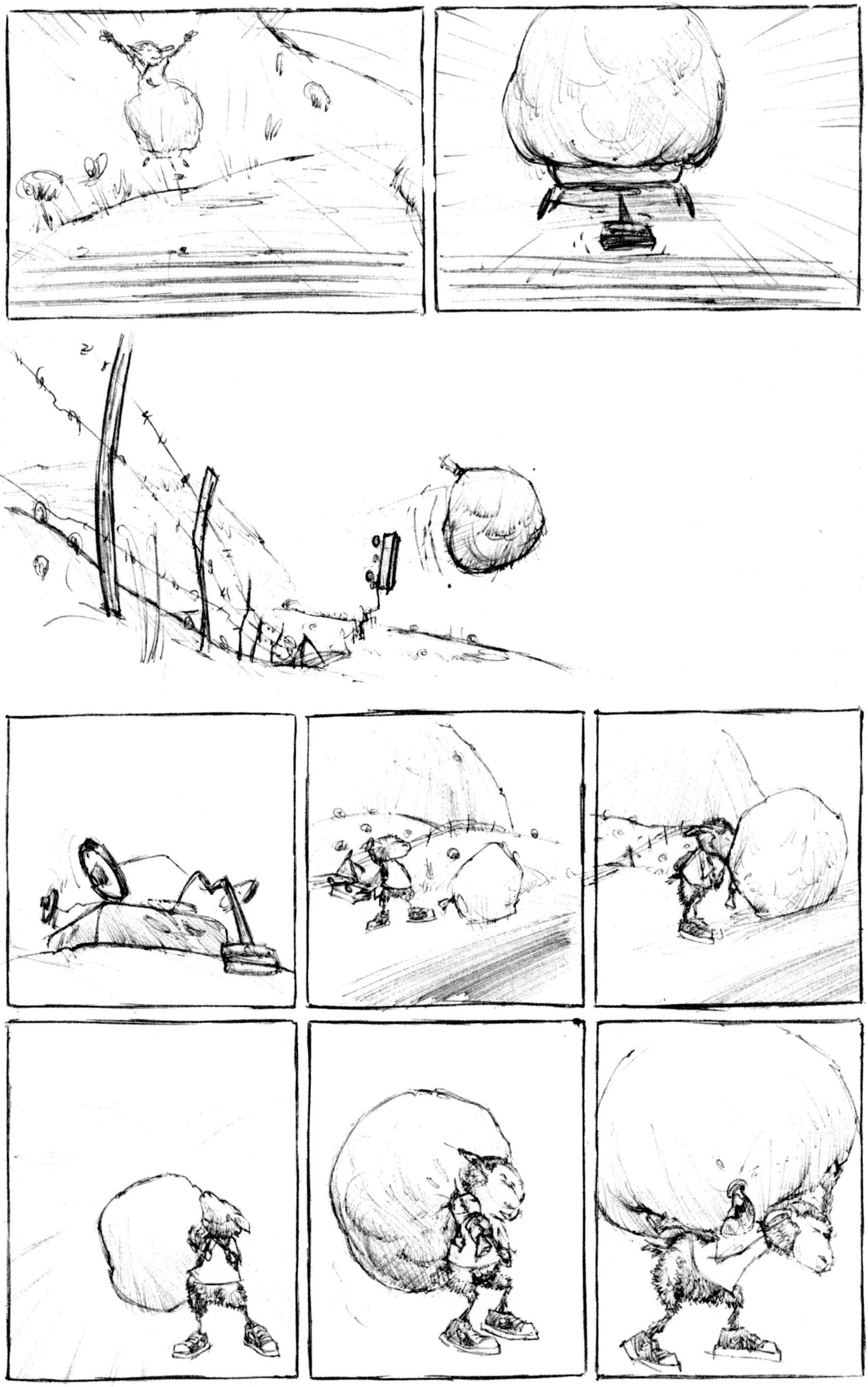

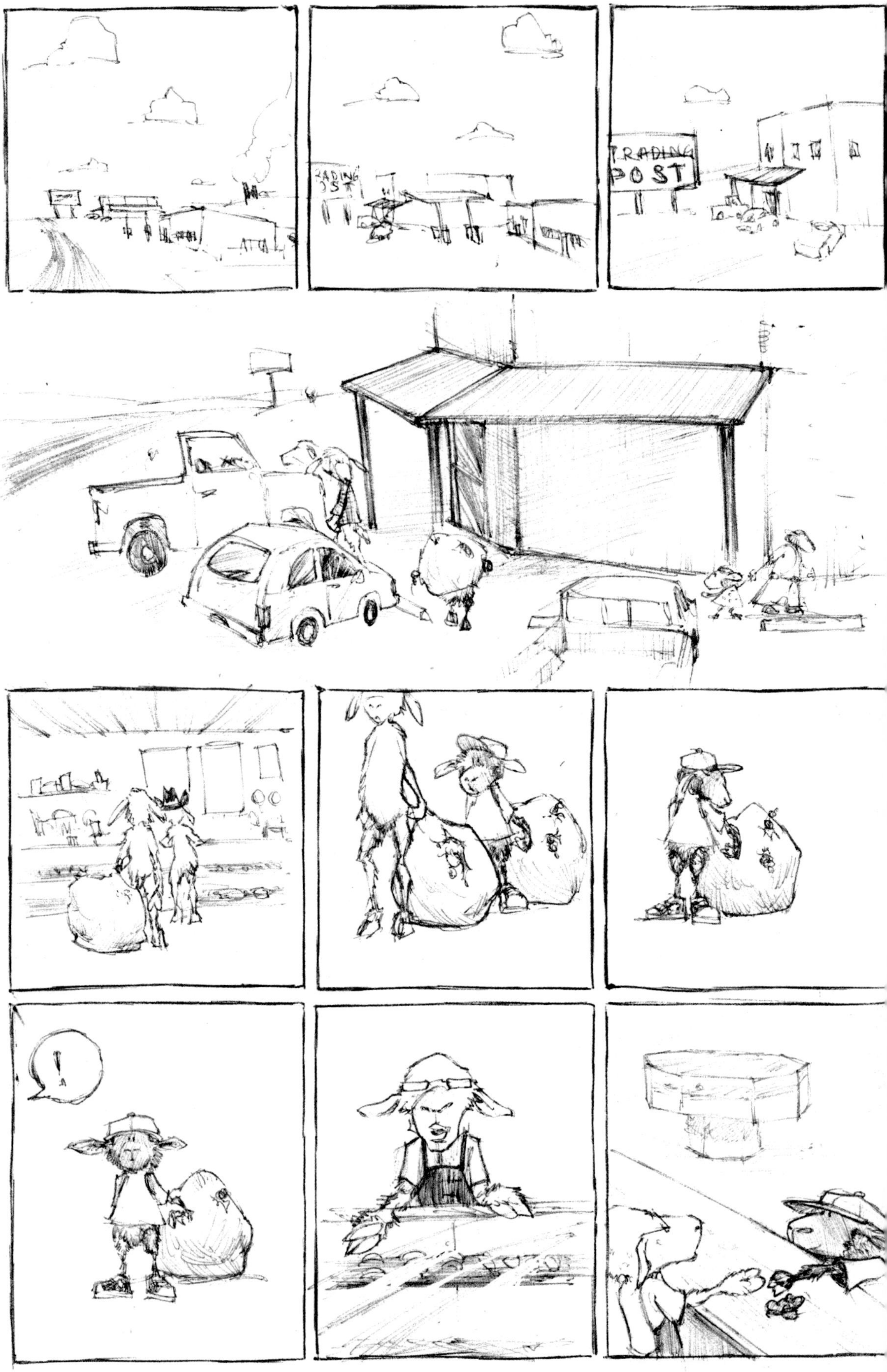
TRADING POST
!

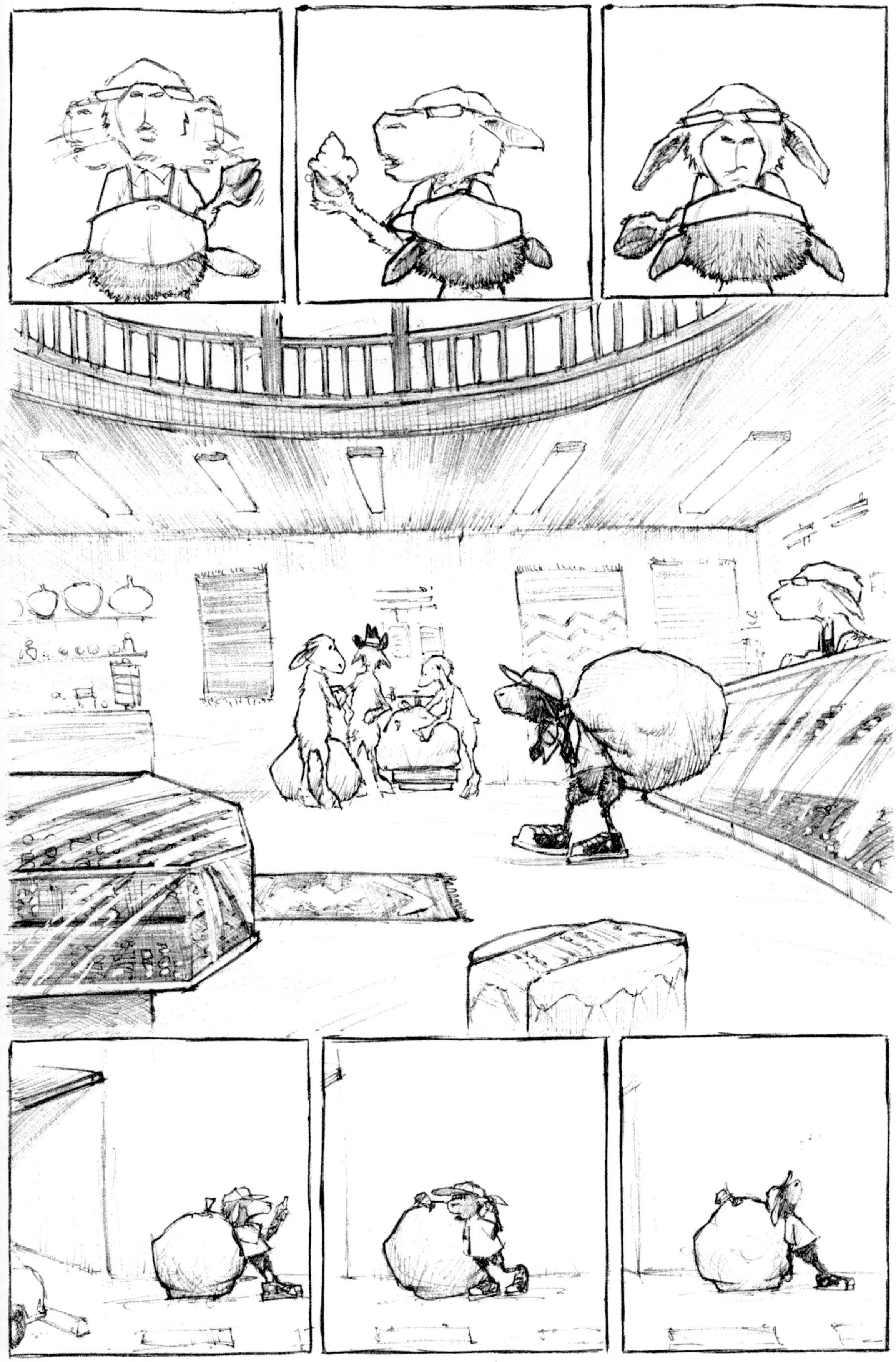

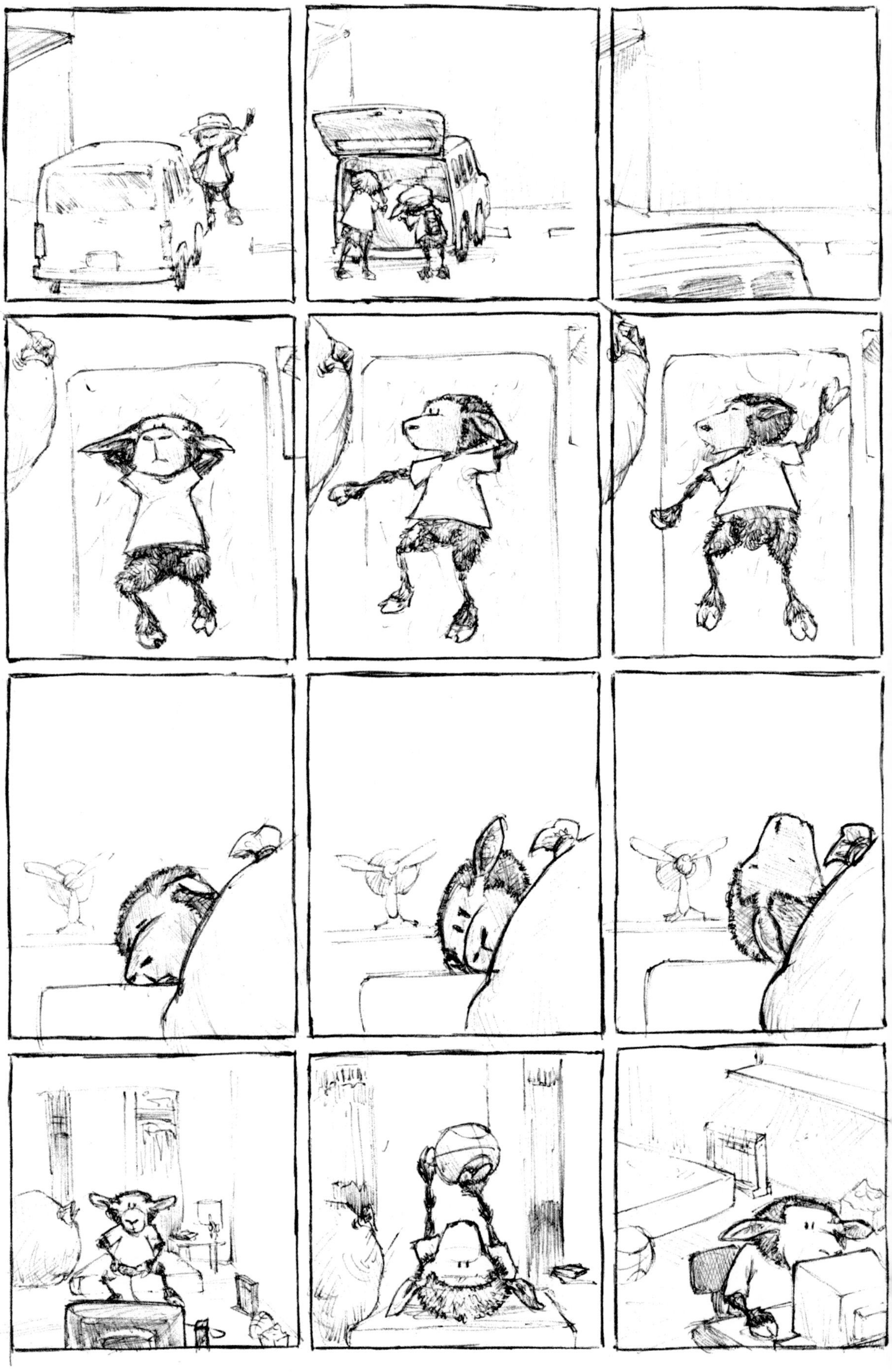

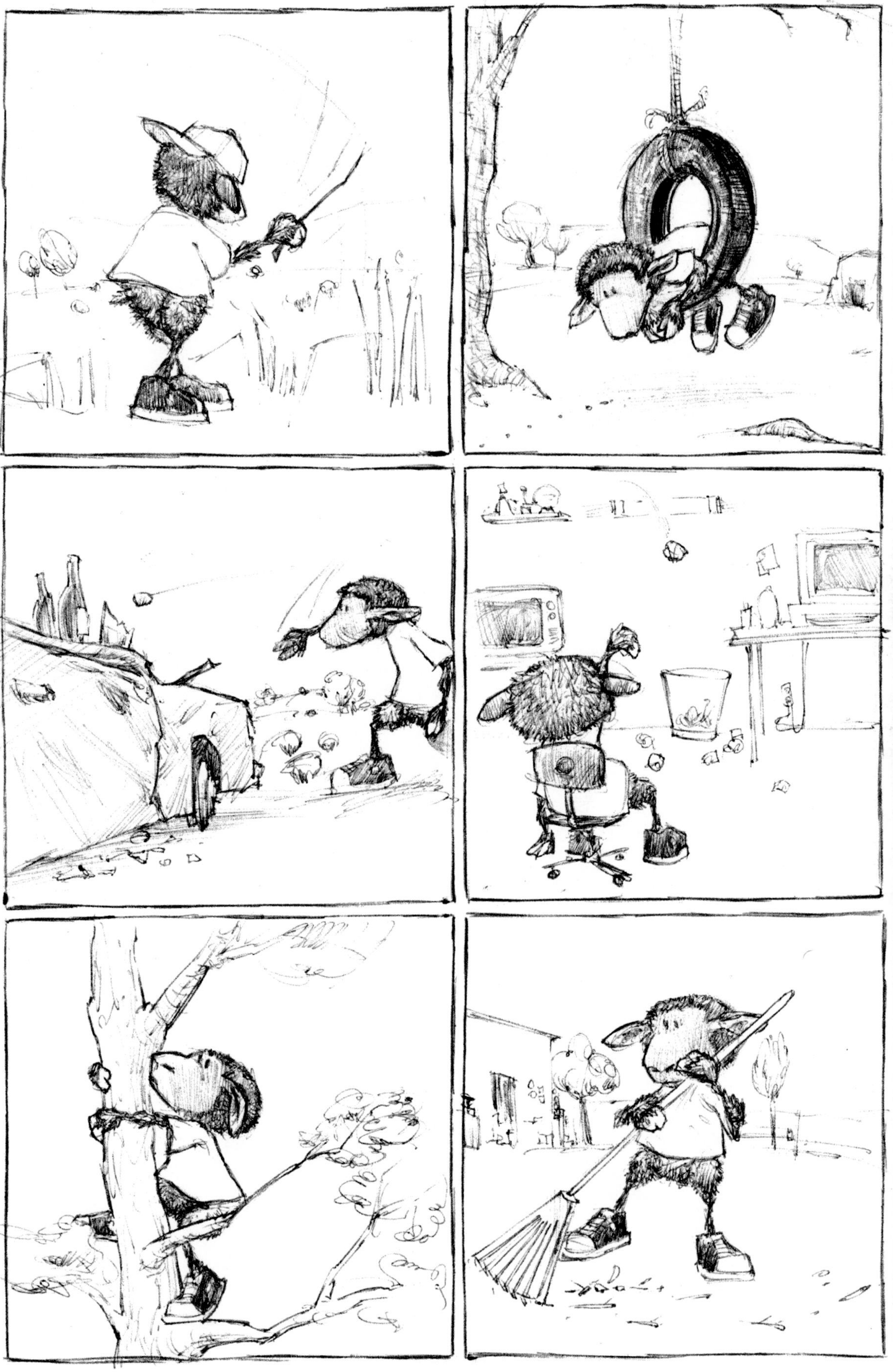

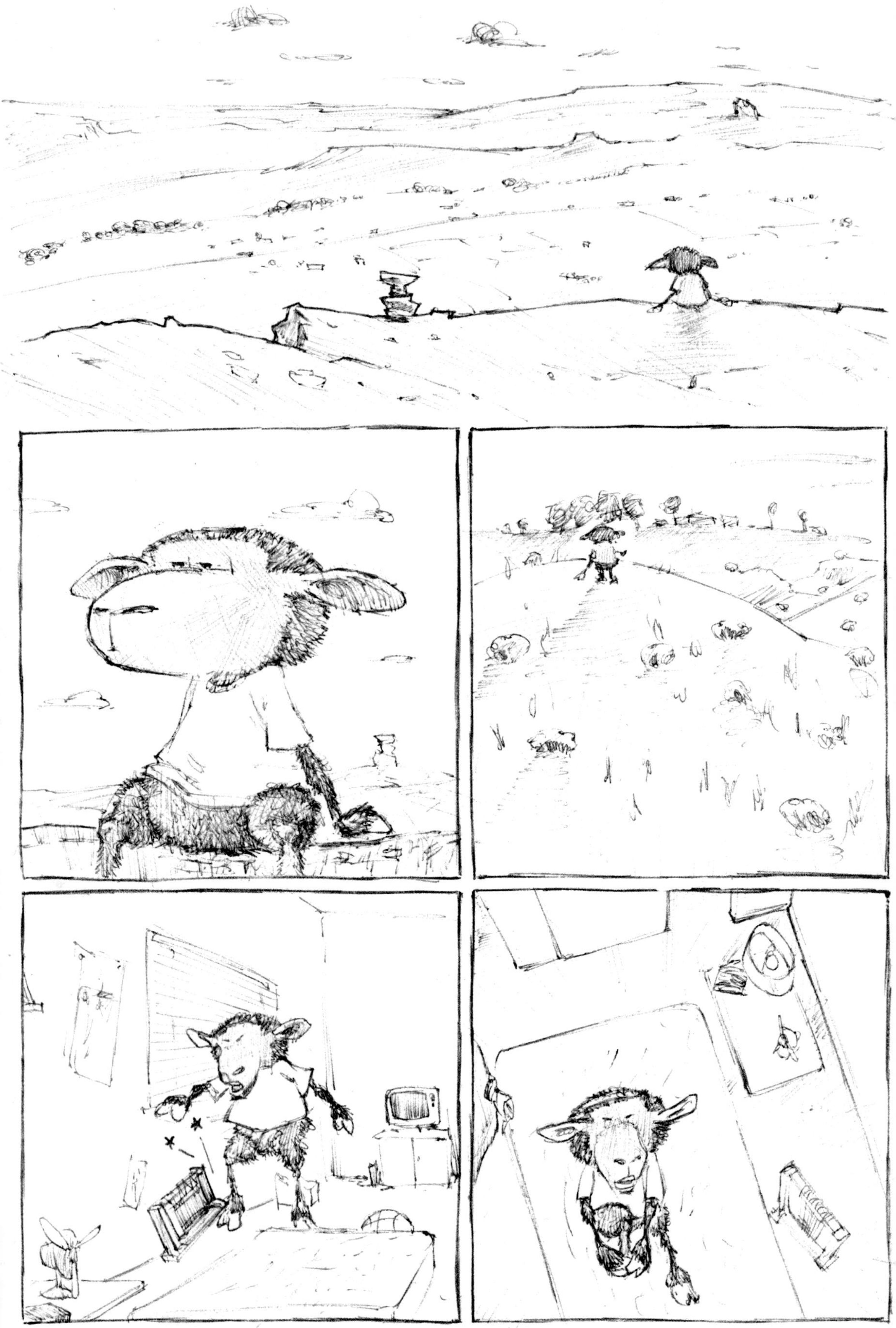

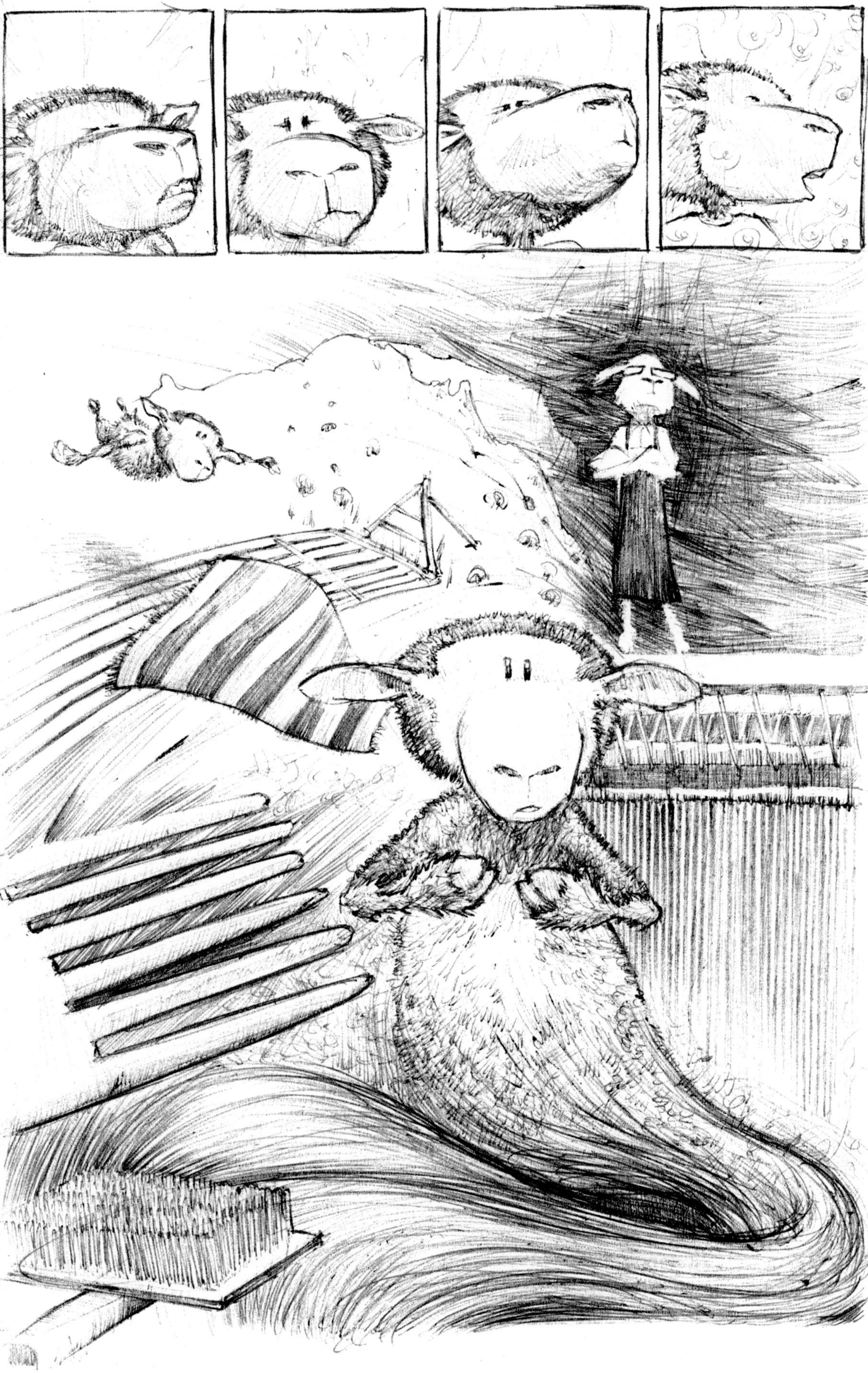

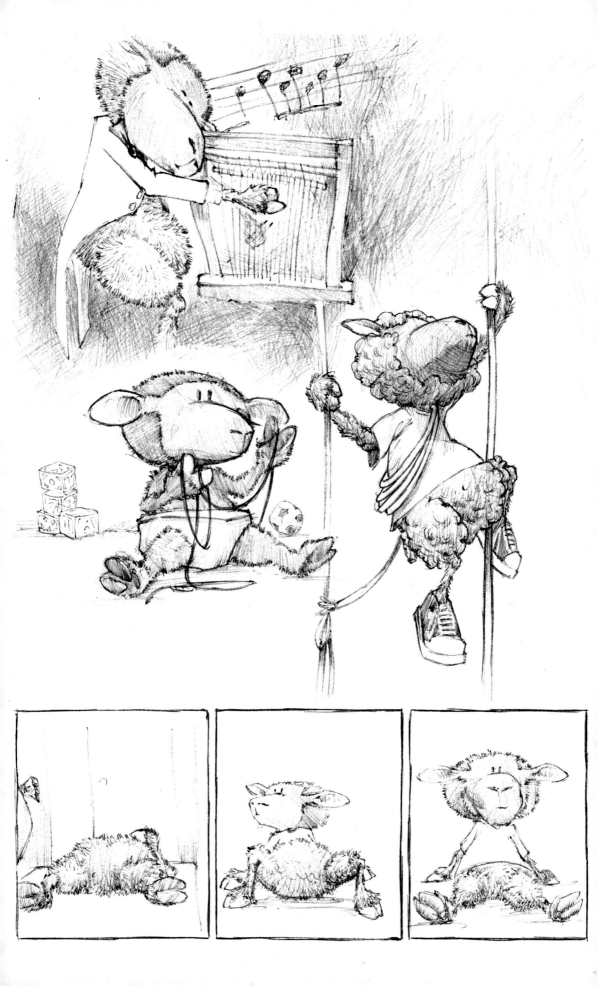

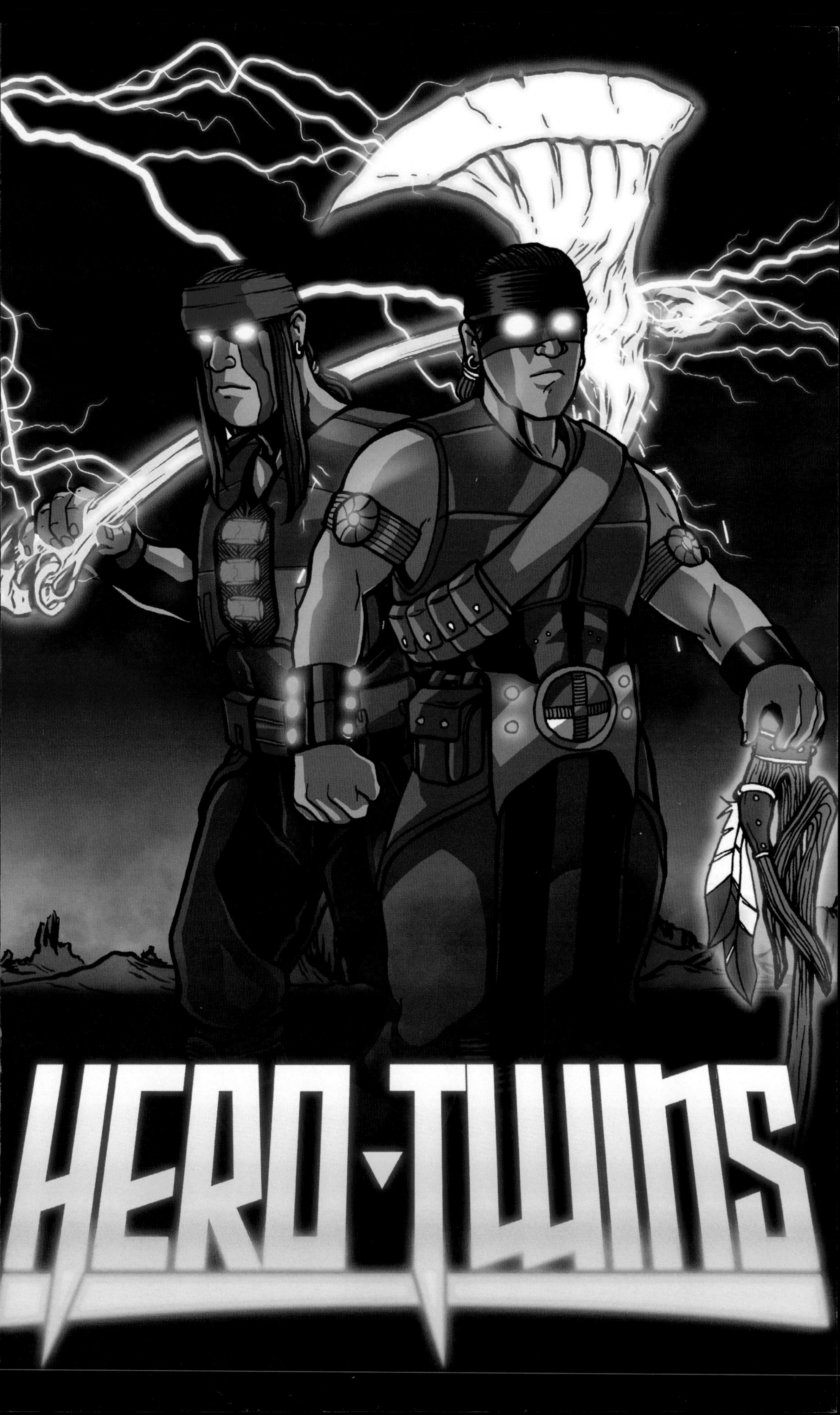
HERO TWINS

code: love

Written by Lee Francis IV
Illustrated by Arigon Starr

from tales of the mighty code talkers, vol. 1
Edited by Arigon Starr

Every code talker felt the suffering of war. Even
those not on the front lines. But sometimes a
small gesture could heal wounds, especially those
hidden beneath the surface.

"CODE: LOVE"

Words
by
Lee Francis IV

Art, Color and Letters
by
Arigon Starr

ANADARKO GAZETTE

ANADARKO GIRLS AID WAR EFFORT

Our fierce fighting boys now have local allies beside them, including an Indian maiden, Sheila Tstoke. Miss Tstoke is from the Kiowa Tribe and serves as a nurse behind enemy lines in Europe. She is one of many area girls who volunteered to aid our heroes across the sea.

She is one of the many young ladies who abandoned dance socials, church recitals and summer picnics for army fatigues. Miss Tstoke, a dark beauty, is an employee of J.F. Johnson at Johnson's General Store. She has been in contact with Mrs. Marie Kientah of Kientah Farm. "Sheila is known for her compassion and holding her head high," said Mrs. Kientah.

Prominent citizen, Miss June Ryan has written letters to her father, Rev. O.P. Ryan of the First Presbyterian Church. None will forget her stirring declamation given at the annual contest on the subject of "The Blessed Damozel," by Rosetti. "We are the most proud parents in Caddo County," exclaimed Rev. Ryan.

Miss Ryan wasted no time in joining the Army Nurse Corps. She used her oratory skills to recruit her fellow classmates and other talented ladies in her university class.

Another local beauty, Evelyn Kunkel joins the war effort by way of her father's dairy farm. Ed Kunkel, owner of Daisy Dairy, cherishes each letter from his daughter. "She is a championship milker and will return to claim her title as Caddo County Dairy Queen when the war is won," he said.

LOCAL BEAUTIES. Miss June Ryan and her local 'recruits' relax behind enemy lines. Not pictured, Miss Sheila Tstoke.

WEATHER.

For Anadarko and vicinity: Unsettled weather with probably local thunder storms this afternoon or evening, followed by fair weather Sunday; cooler tonight.

Weather conditions.
Scattered showers and thunderstorms have occured in Minnesota, the Dakotas, Nebraska, western Kansas,

WRITE STORIES FOR MOVING PICTURE PLAYS

Owing to the large number of new motion picture theatres which are being opened throughout the country, there is offered to the men and women of to-day a new profes-

Sheila:

Did you forget your lipstick?

Love,

Mom

November 1944, 59th Evac Field Hospital, Eastern France, Winter

YOUR NUMBERS LOOK GOOD TODAY, PRIVATE JACKSON. YOU'LL BE HOME IN NO TIME.

WE GOT ONE HERE! HE'S STABLE BUT HE NEEDS ATTENTION.

MOVE HIM OVER THERE.

I'LL GET A LINE INTO HIM. HMMM...

DOESN'T LOOK *TOO* BAD...

I'LL MAKE A FEW ROUNDS THEN CHECK BACK ON HIM. THANKS, FELLAS. THAT SHOULD DO IT.

TOHN... ⟨WATER⟩

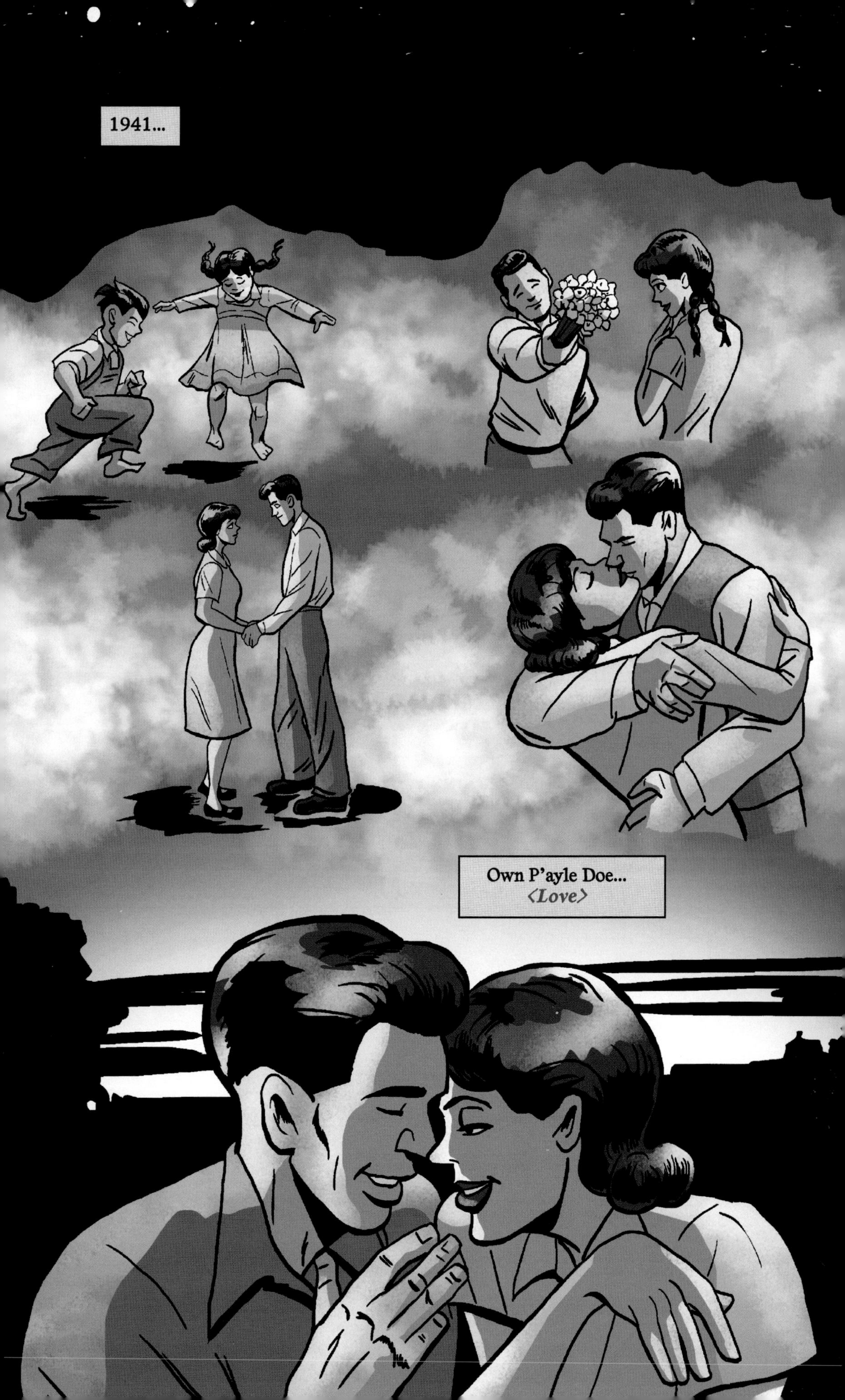
1941...
Own P'ayle Doe...
‹Love›

SORRY, MA'AM. THIS GUY IS SPECIAL ARMY. DOCTORS ONLY.

WHAT DOES HE DO?

DON'T KNOW MUCH. SOME SORT OF RADIO MAN. COMMAND WANTS HIM UNDER GUARD.

TOHN... ⟨WATER⟩

1941. Anadarko, OK. Johnson's General Store.

...THE NEWS COMING OUT OF HAWAII. THE UNITED STATES HAS BEEN *ATTACKED* BY THE NATION OF JAPAN.

PEARL HARBOR IS UNDER ASSAULT...WITH HUNDREDS *DEAD* OR MISSING...

WELL, THAT'S IT THEN. WE'LL BE AT WAR BY NEXT WEEK.

WHAT DOES THAT *MEAN*, THOMAS?

NOT SURE, YET. WE'LL *KNOW* IN THE NEXT COUPLE OF DAYS WHAT'S GONNA HAPPEN. FOR *SURE* THERE'LL BE FIGHTING.

DON'T WORRY, EVERYTHING WILL BE OKAY.

AIM OWN P'AYLE DOE. ⟨I LOVE YOU.⟩

TOHN!!! ⟨WATER!⟩

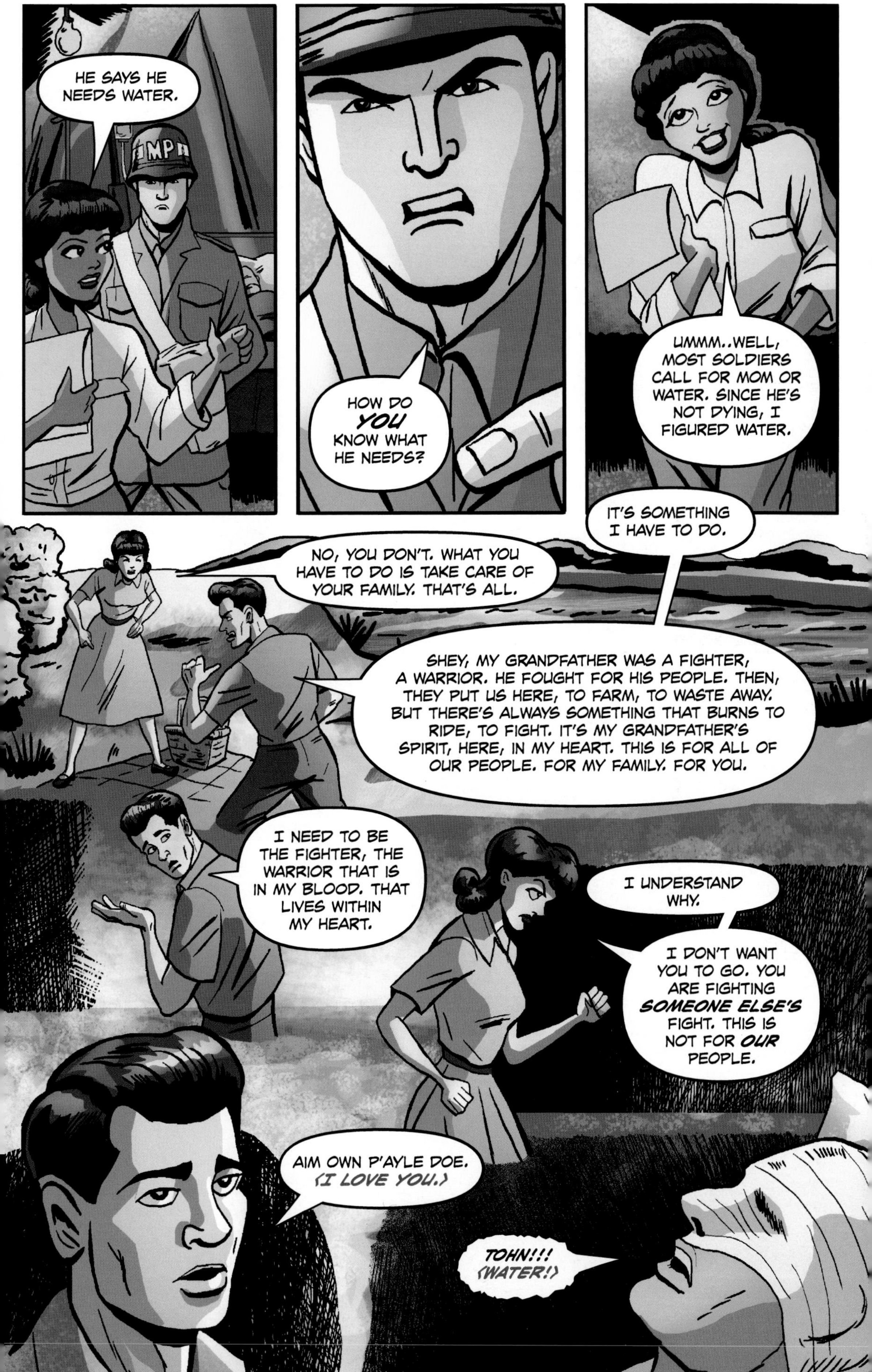
HE SAYS HE NEEDS WATER.
MP
HOW DO ***YOU*** KNOW WHAT HE NEEDS?
UMMM..WELL, MOST SOLDIERS CALL FOR MOM OR WATER. SINCE HE'S NOT DYING, I FIGURED WATER.
IT'S SOMETHING I HAVE TO DO.
NO, YOU DON'T. WHAT YOU HAVE TO DO IS TAKE CARE OF YOUR FAMILY. THAT'S ALL.
SHEY, MY GRANDFATHER WAS A FIGHTER, A WARRIOR. HE FOUGHT FOR HIS PEOPLE. THEN, THEY PUT US HERE, TO FARM, TO WASTE AWAY. BUT THERE'S ALWAYS SOMETHING THAT BURNS TO RIDE, TO FIGHT. IT'S MY GRANDFATHER'S SPIRIT, HERE, IN MY HEART. THIS IS FOR ALL OF OUR PEOPLE. FOR MY FAMILY. FOR YOU.
I NEED TO BE THE FIGHTER, THE WARRIOR THAT IS IN MY BLOOD. THAT LIVES WITHIN MY HEART.
I UNDERSTAND WHY.
I DON'T WANT YOU TO GO. YOU ARE FIGHTING ***SOMEONE ELSE'S*** FIGHT. THIS IS NOT FOR ***OUR*** PEOPLE.
AIM OWN P'AYLE DOE. *‹I LOVE YOU.›*
TOHN!!! ‹WATER!›

WAIT A MINUTE... DID YOU WASH UP?

EXCUSE ME, MA'AM?

CORPORAL, THIS IS A MEDICAL FACILITY. WE HAVE A LOT OF PATIENTS AND *YOU* ARE A RISK FOR INFECTION.

WASH UP NOW.

MA'AM, I ALREADY TOLD YOU, I'M NOT ALLOWED TO LEAVE THIS MAN UNATTENDED.

CONSIDER THIS AN ORDER FROM A RANKING OFFICER...AND I DO OUTRANK YOU. WASH UP. *NOW.*

February 1943...

MRS. KIENTAH, JOHNSON'S DIDN'T HAVE ANY PLUM JAM. HE SAID TO CHECK BACK NEXT TUESDAY...

WESTERN UNION

TOHN KXAW AH TDAW.
⟨A GLASS OF
WATER FOR YOU.⟩

February 1943...

SHEILA AH KHAUN.
KHOIYE YAWKOYE AH DAW.
HAW AIM PEYOAM DAW?
⟨MY NAME IS SHEILA.
I'M A KIOWA LADY.
ARE YOU FEELING
BETTER?⟩

You can find more of the Tales of the Mighty Code Talkers at nativerealities.com.

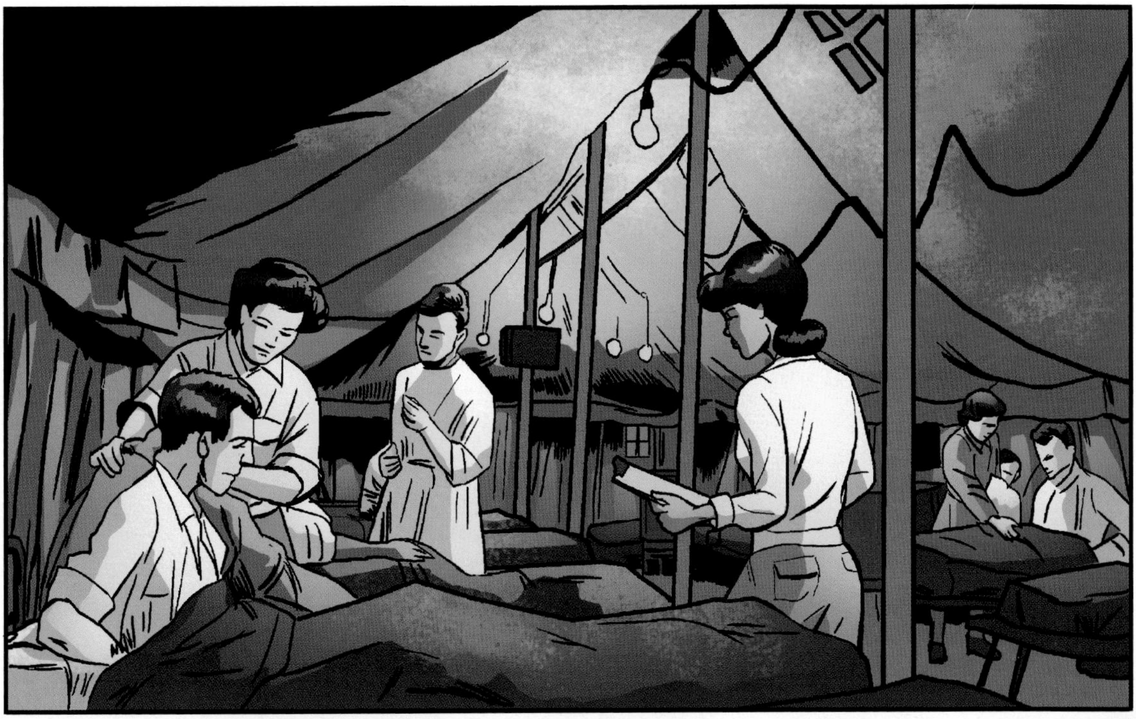

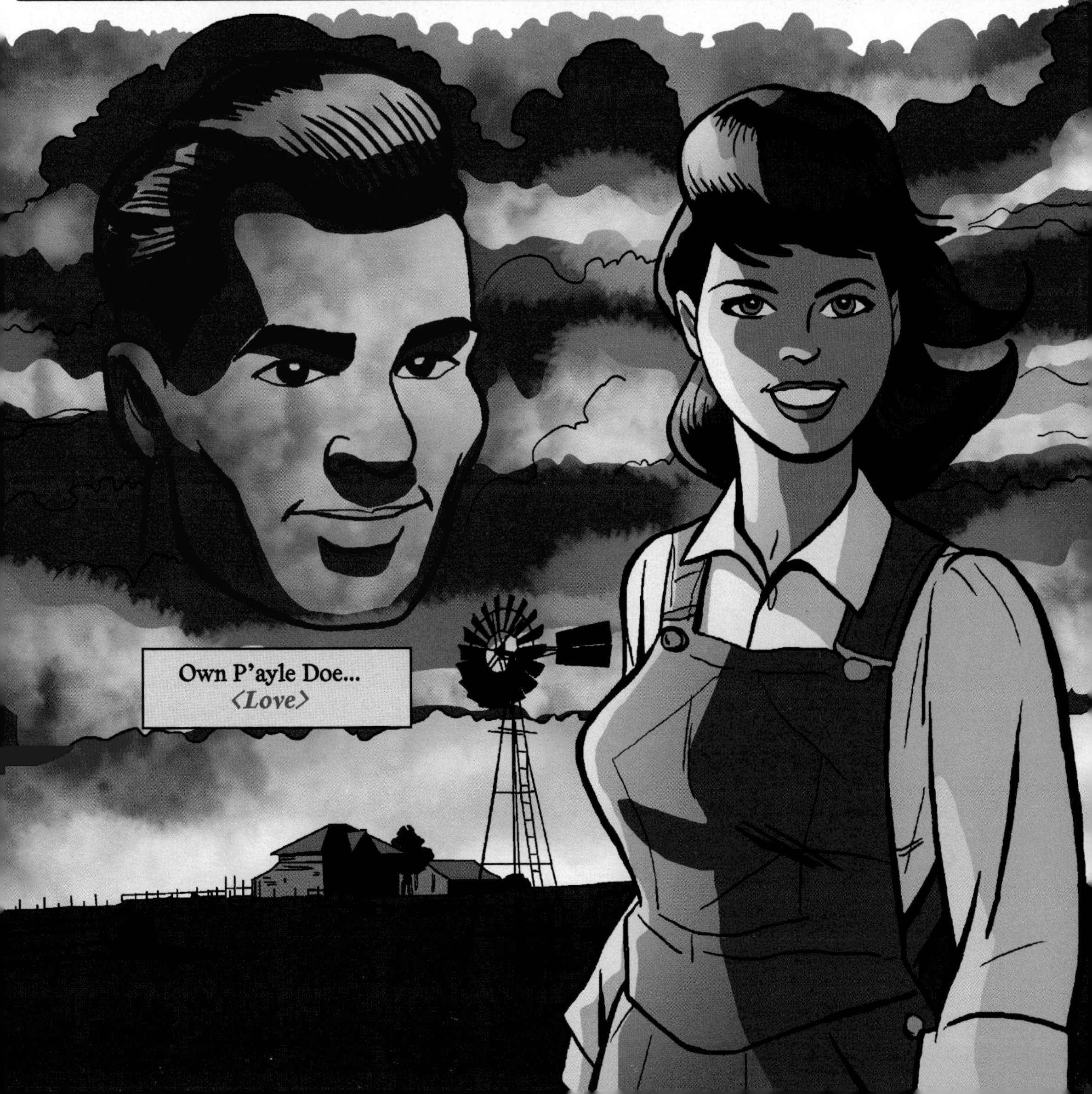
Own P'ayle Doe...
⟨Love⟩

tribal force #1 (excerpt)

Written and created by Jon Proudstar
Illustrated by Ron Joseph
Cover and colors by Weshoyot Alvitre

First published in 1996, Tribal Force was the first
Native American centric comic book ever created.
The story follows the action of Thunder Eagle and
the Tribal Force as they set out to save a young
woman who is the key to saving the world.

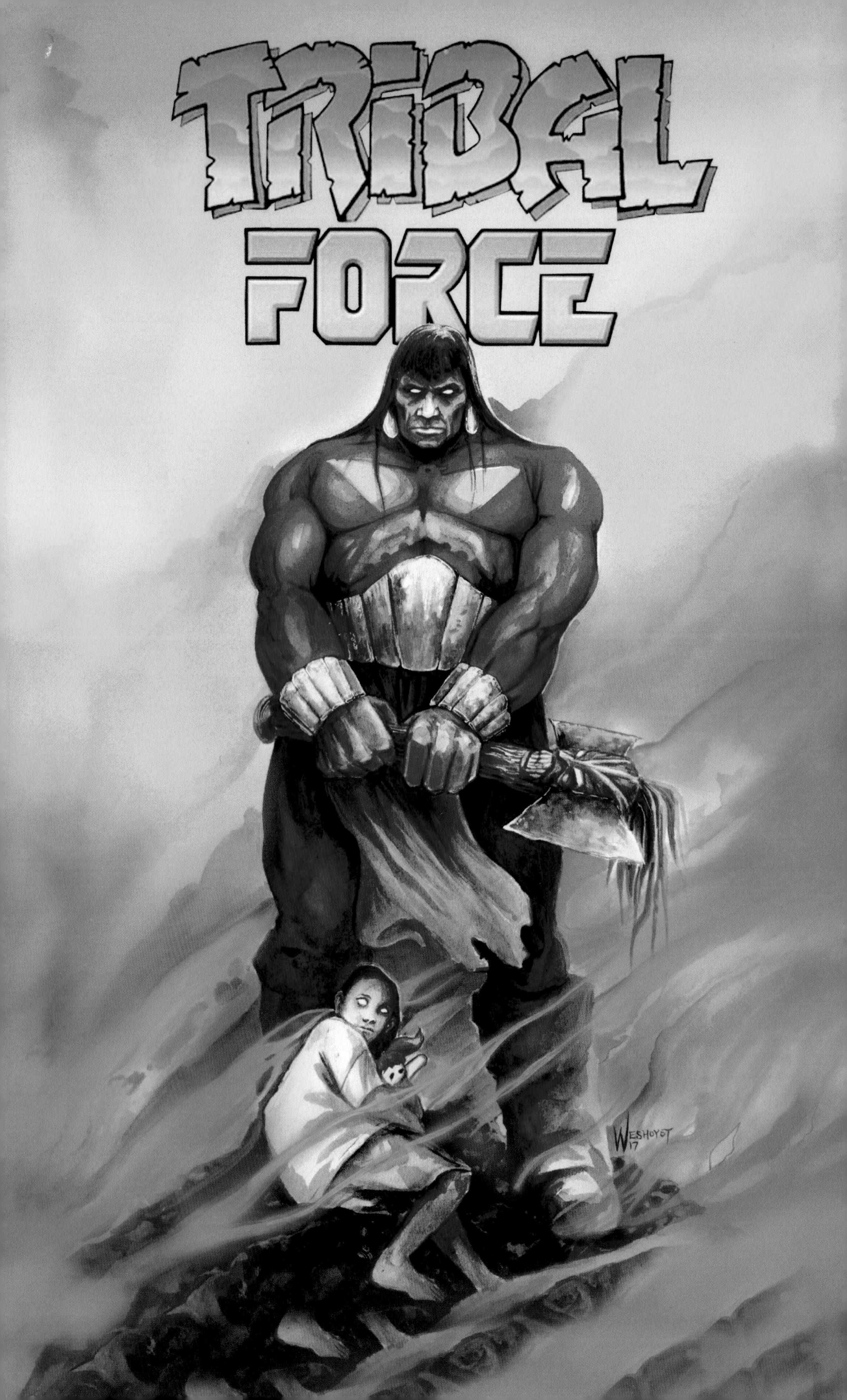
TRIBAL
FORCE
WESHOYOT
17

IN THE DINÉ BELIEF THERE ARE FIVE
WORLDS OF EXISTENCE. THESE WORLDS ARE BARRED
FROM MORTALS. NITA NITAAL NAKIA IS THE FIRST TO BREAK THE
BOUNDARIES PLACED BY THE GODS.

WHAT SHE SEES AS DREAMS OR NIGHTMARES ARE GLIMPSES INTO POSSIBLE FUTURES,
PARALLEL REALITIES, MIRRORS OF UNCOUNTABLE EXISTENCES.

THE DREAMS BEGAN SOON AFTER THE DEATH OF NITA'S MOTHER. BUT ALONG WITH THE DREAMS
CAME THE UNIMAGINABLE ASSAULTS OF HER FATHER.

THE STORY YOU ARE ABOUT TO READ HAS HAPPENED HUNDREDS OF THOUSANDS OF TIMES BEFORE.
WITH AN INEXHAUSTIBLE ARRAY OF POSSIBLE ENDINGS, THE UNIQUE FACTOR PRESENTED BEFORE US IS
THAT THIS IS THE LAST SPOKE IN THE WHEEL OF REALITY. THE LAST CHANCE FOR EVERYTHING TO GO
RIGHT. THE WRONG OUTCOME IS THE END OF HUMAN CIVILIZATION AS WE KNOW IT.

WILL THE HEROES OF TRIBAL FORCE OVERCOME THE DARKNESS WHICH HAS PERMEATED THE LAST
BASTION OF HOPE FOR MANKIND? FOLLOW WITH GREAT TREPIDATION FELLOW ADVENTURER, FOR
YOU ARE NOW ENTERING THE WORLD OF TRIBAL FORCE WHERE THE SPIRITUAL
FORCES OF THE NATIVE PANTHEON WILL FACE TERRA FIRMA'S MIGHTIEST HEROES
AND DEADLY TECHNOLOGY.

FOR WHERE DOES THE EAGLE LAND WHEN THE WORLD IS ON FIRE?

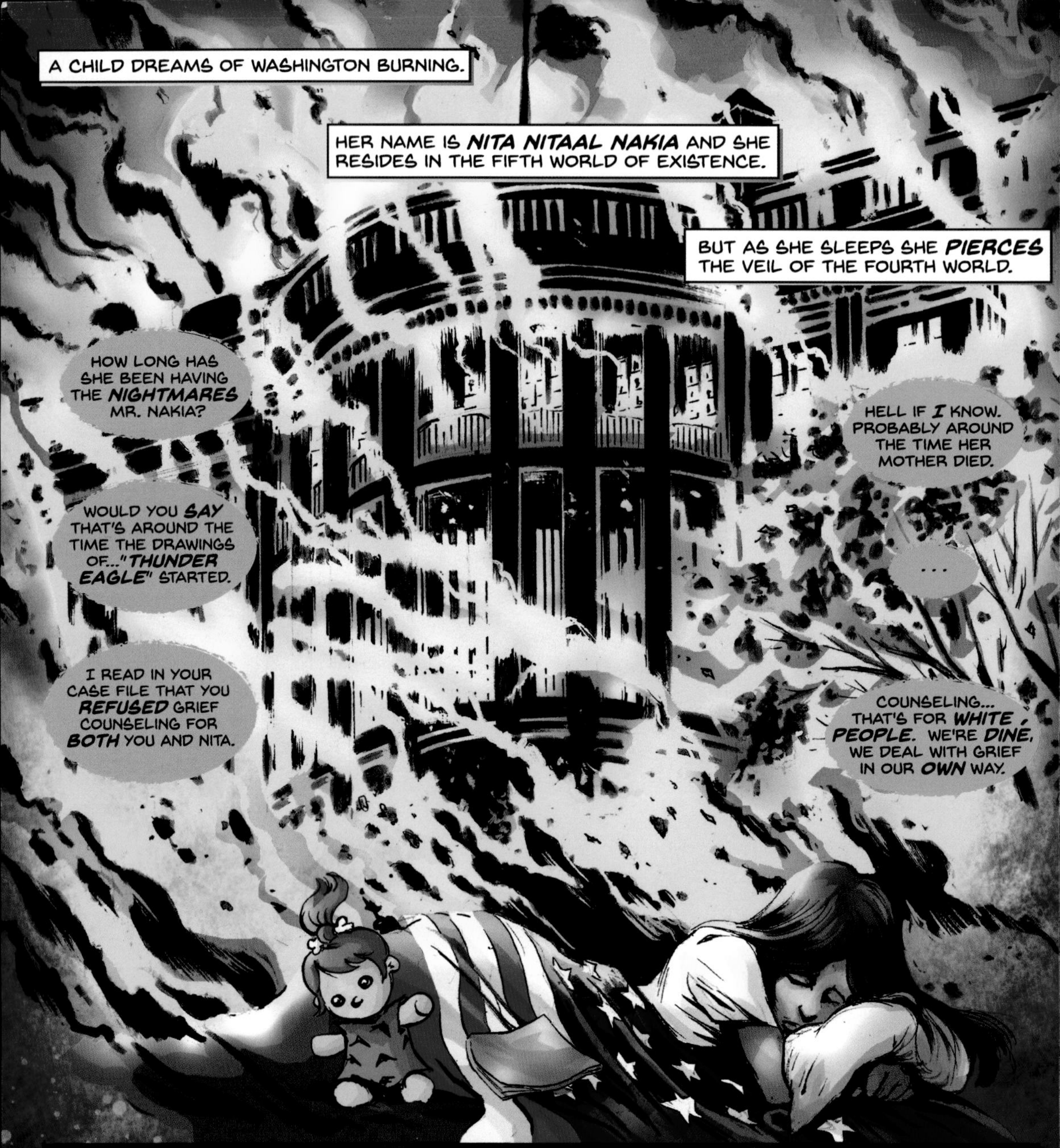
A CHILD DREAMS OF WASHINGTON BURNING.
HER NAME IS NITA NITAAL NAKIA AND SHE RESIDES IN THE FIFTH WORLD OF EXISTENCE.
BUT AS SHE SLEEPS SHE PIERCES THE VEIL OF THE FOURTH WORLD.
HOW LONG HAS SHE BEEN HAVING THE NIGHTMARES MR. NAKIA?
HELL IF I KNOW. PROBABLY AROUND THE TIME HER MOTHER DIED.
WOULD YOU SAY THAT'S AROUND THE TIME THE DRAWINGS OF..."THUNDER EAGLE" STARTED.
...
I READ IN YOUR CASE FILE THAT YOU REFUSED GRIEF COUNSELING FOR BOTH YOU AND NITA.
COUNSELING... THAT'S FOR WHITE PEOPLE. WE'RE DINE, WE DEAL WITH GRIEF IN OUR OWN WAY.

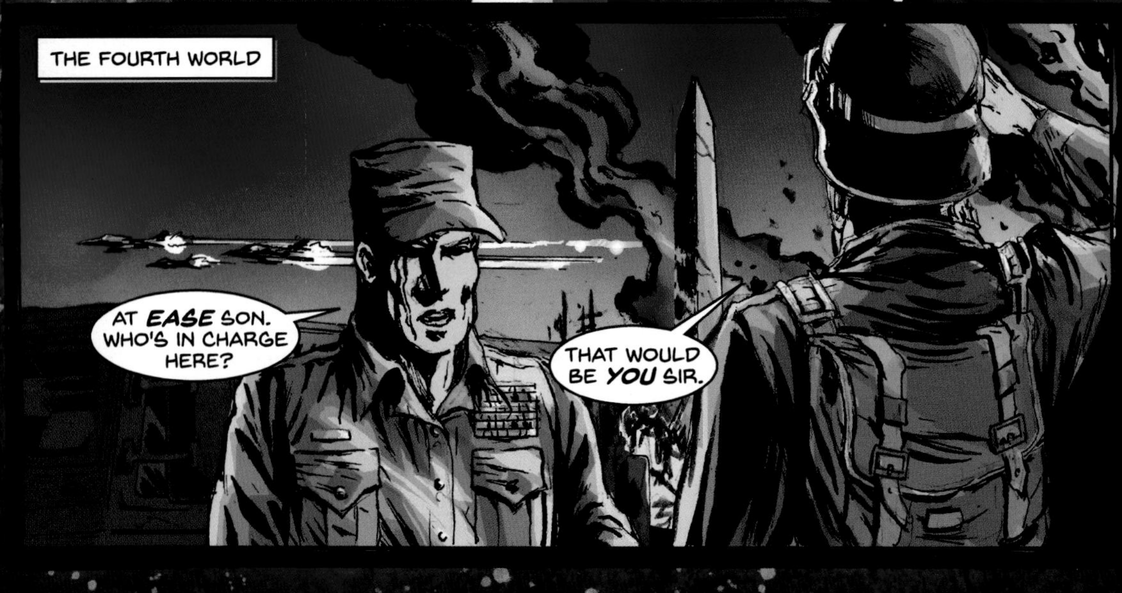
THE FOURTH WORLD
AT EASE SON. WHO'S IN CHARGE HERE?
THAT WOULD BE YOU SIR.

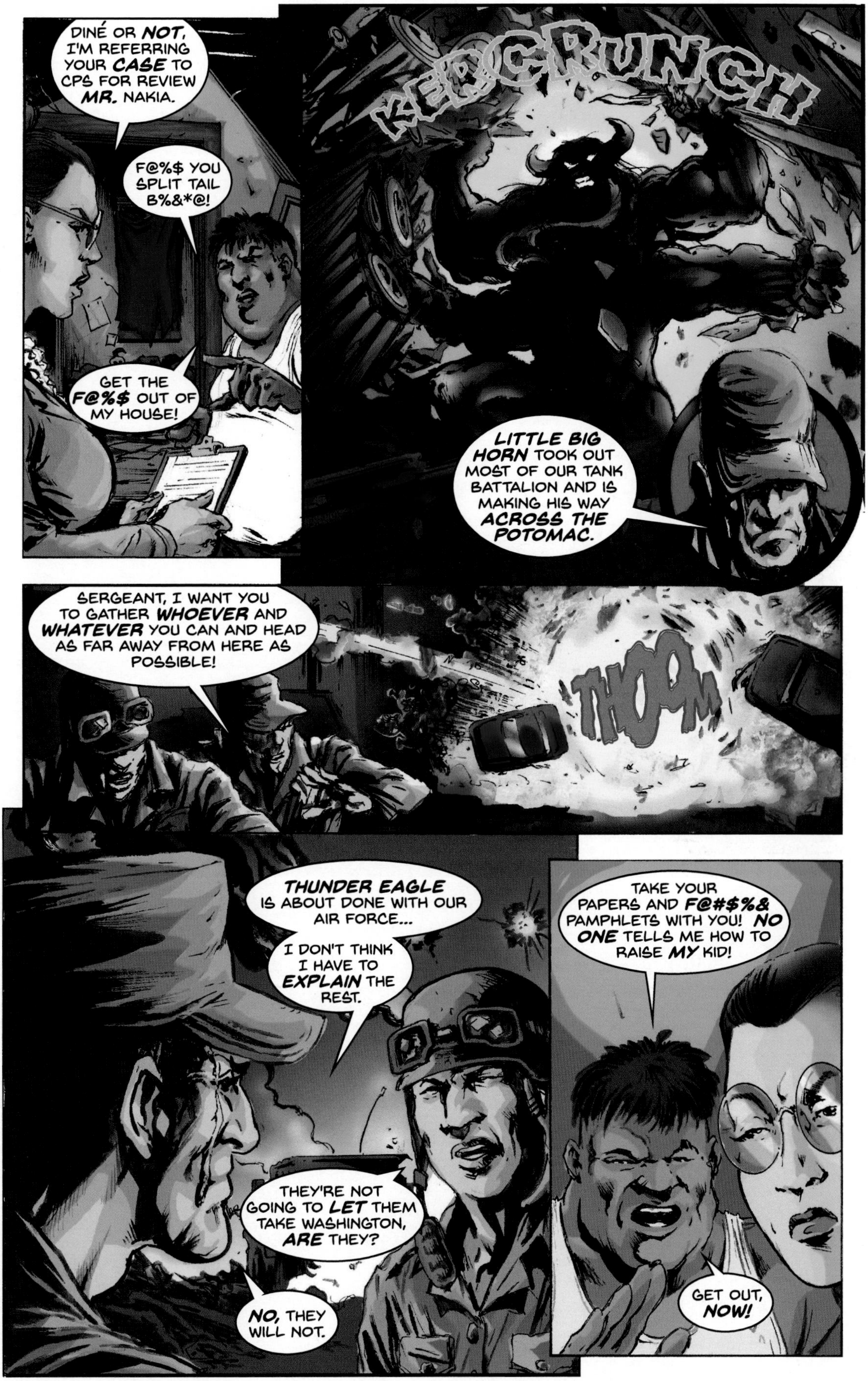
DINÉ OR NOT, I'M REFERRING YOUR CASE TO CPS FOR REVIEW MR. NAKIA.
F@%$ YOU SPLIT TAIL B%&*@!
GET THE F@%$ OUT OF MY HOUSE!
KERCRUNCH
LITTLE BIG HORN TOOK OUT MOST OF OUR TANK BATTALION AND IS MAKING HIS WAY ACROSS THE POTOMAC.
SERGEANT, I WANT YOU TO GATHER WHOEVER AND WHATEVER YOU CAN AND HEAD AS FAR AWAY FROM HERE AS POSSIBLE!
THOOM
THUNDER EAGLE IS ABOUT DONE WITH OUR AIR FORCE...
I DON'T THINK I HAVE TO EXPLAIN THE REST.
THEY'RE NOT GOING TO LET THEM TAKE WASHINGTON, ARE THEY?
NO, THEY WILL NOT.
TAKE YOUR PAPERS AND F@#$%& PAMPHLETS WITH YOU! NO ONE TELLS ME HOW TO RAISE MY KID!
GET OUT, NOW!

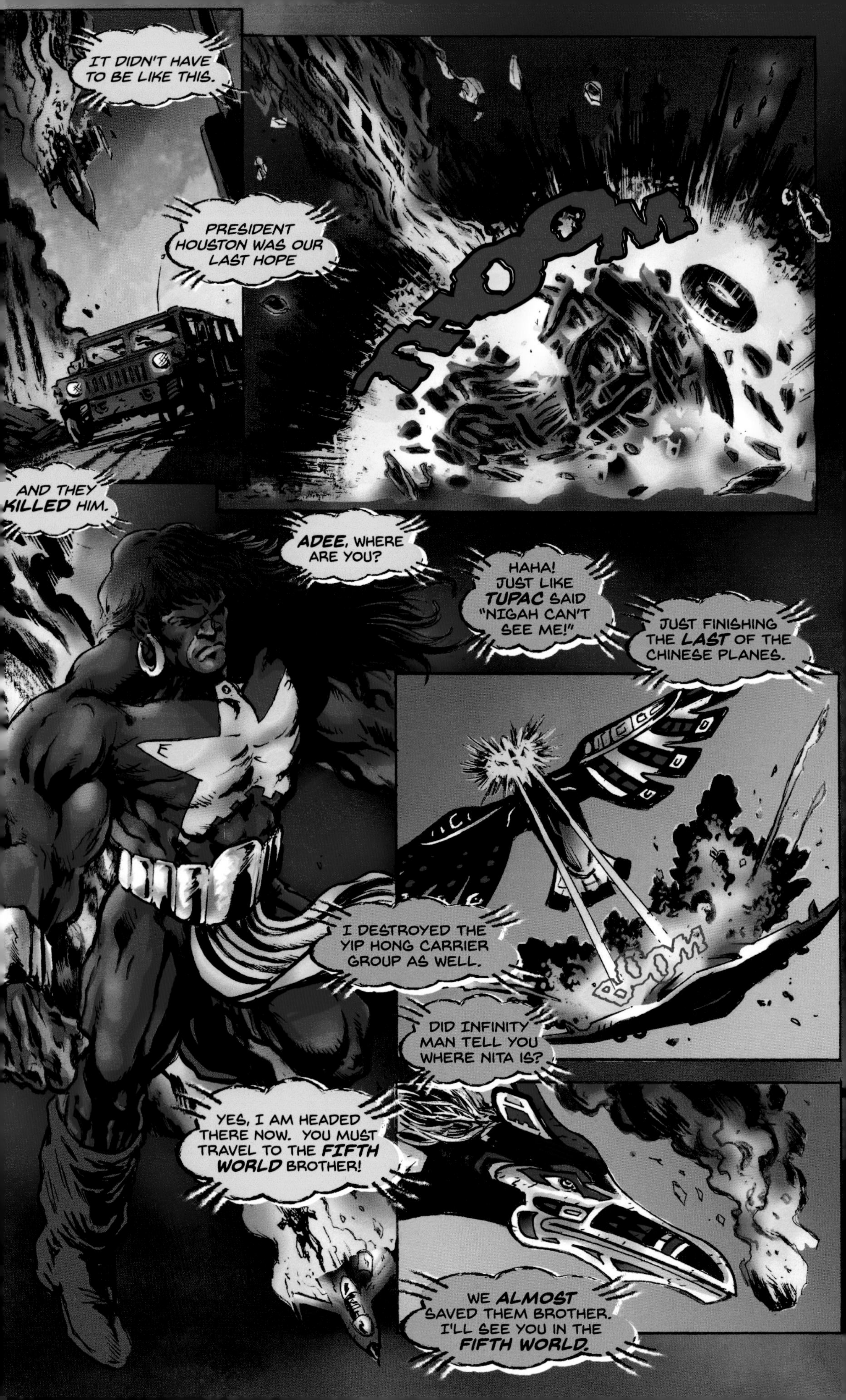
IT DIDN'T HAVE TO BE LIKE THIS.
PRESIDENT HOUSTON WAS OUR LAST HOPE
THOOM
AND THEY KILLED HIM.
ADEE, WHERE ARE YOU?
HAHA! JUST LIKE TUPAC SAID "NIGAH CAN'T SEE ME!"
JUST FINISHING THE LAST OF THE CHINESE PLANES.
I DESTROYED THE YIP HONG CARRIER GROUP AS WELL.
BOOM
DID INFINITY MAN TELL YOU WHERE NITA IS?
YES, I AM HEADED THERE NOW. YOU MUST TRAVEL TO THE FIFTH WORLD BROTHER!
WE ALMOST SAVED THEM BROTHER. I'LL SEE YOU IN THE FIFTH WORLD.

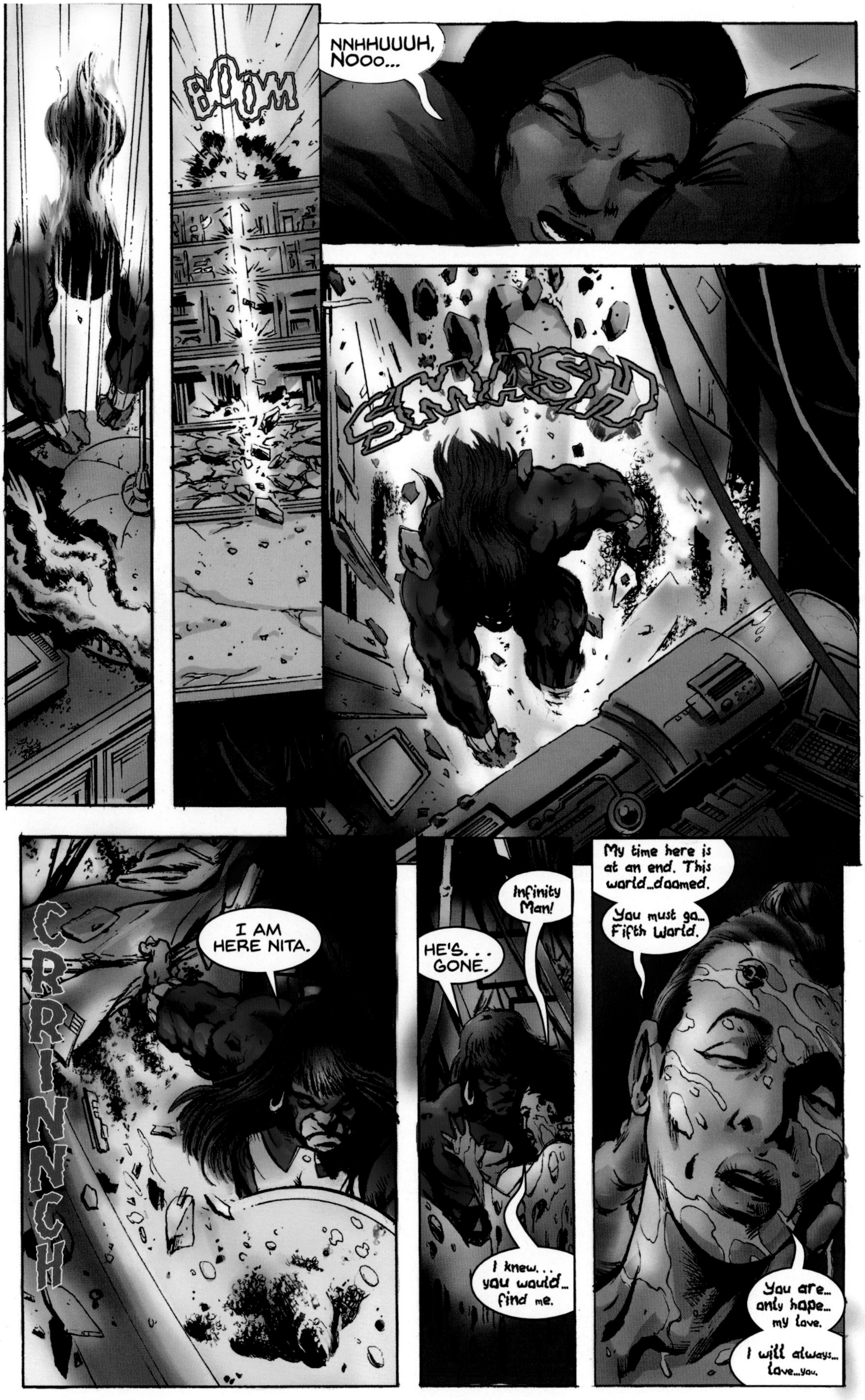
BOOM
NNHHUUUH, NOOO...
SMASH
CRRINNCH
I AM HERE NITA.
Infinity Man!
HE'S. . . GONE.
I knew... you would... find me.
My time here is at an end. This world...doomed.
You must go... Fifth World.
You are... only hope... my love.
I will always... love...you.

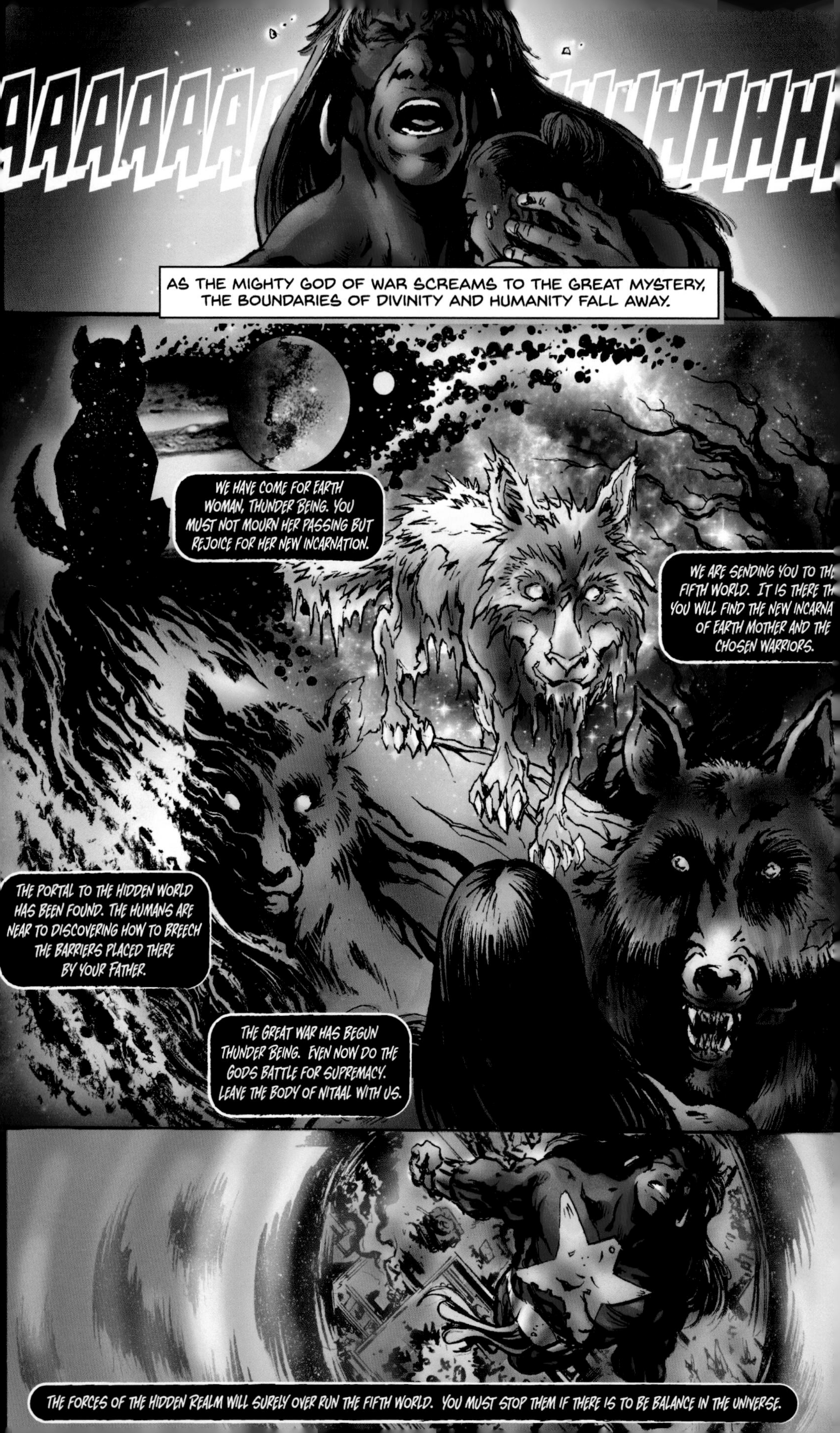
AS THE MIGHTY GOD OF WAR SCREAMS TO THE GREAT MYSTERY, THE BOUNDARIES OF DIVINITY AND HUMANITY FALL AWAY.
WE HAVE COME FOR EARTH WOMAN, THUNDER BEING. YOU MUST NOT MOURN HER PASSING BUT REJOICE FOR HER NEW INCARNATION.
WE ARE SENDING YOU TO TH FIFTH WORLD. IT IS THERE TH YOU WILL FIND THE NEW INCARNA OF EARTH MOTHER AND THE CHOSEN WARRIORS.
THE PORTAL TO THE HIDDEN WORLD HAS BEEN FOUND. THE HUMANS ARE NEAR TO DISCOVERING HOW TO BREECH THE BARRIERS PLACED THERE BY YOUR FATHER.
THE GREAT WAR HAS BEGUN THUNDER BEING. EVEN NOW DO THE GODS BATTLE FOR SUPREMACY. LEAVE THE BODY OF NITAAL WITH US.
THE FORCES OF THE HIDDEN REALM WILL SURELY OVER RUN THE FIFTH WORLD. YOU MUST STOP THEM IF THERE IS TO BE BALANCE IN THE UNIVERSE.

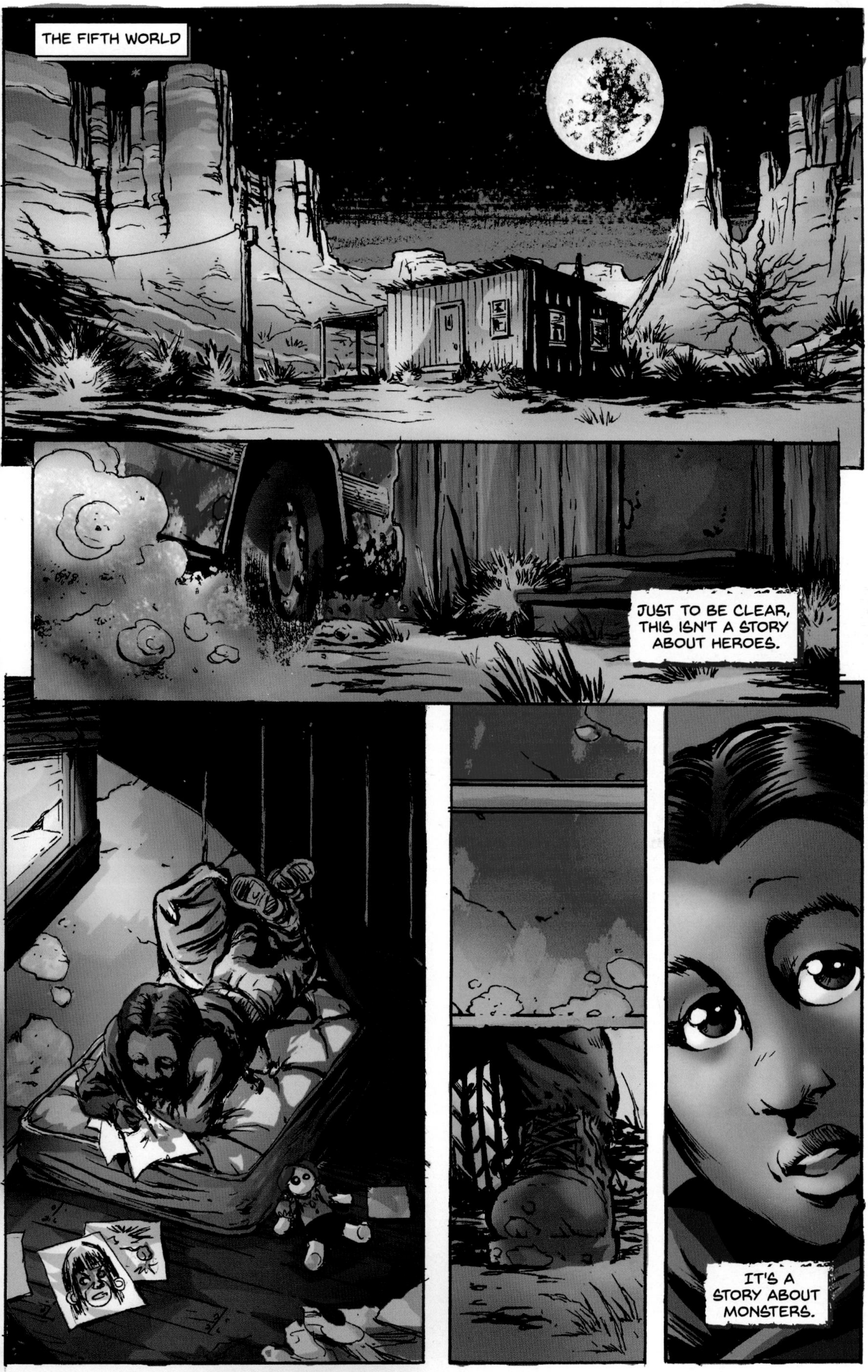
THE FIFTH WORLD
JUST TO BE CLEAR, THIS ISN'T A STORY ABOUT HEROES.
IT'S A STORY ABOUT MONSTERS.

You can find the rest of the story in Tribal Force #1 at nativerealities.com.

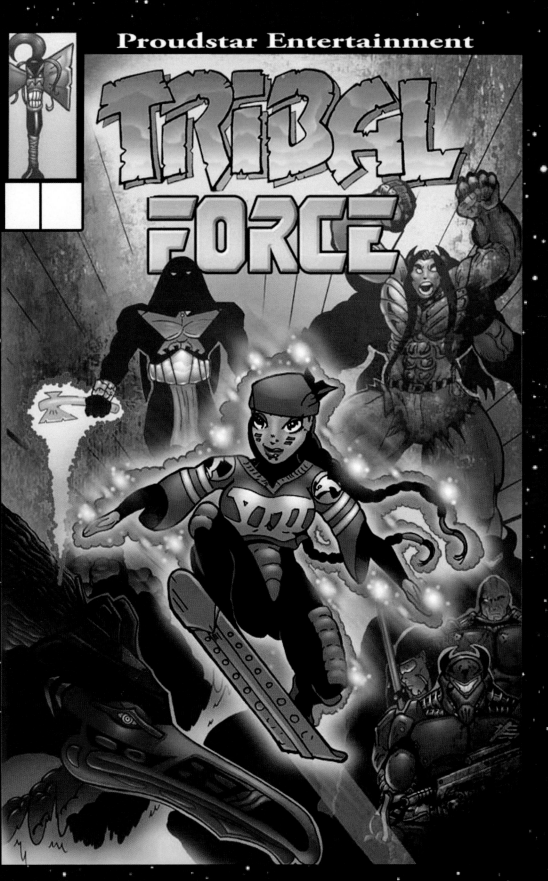

Original Tribal Force cover issue #0

asdzą́ą́ changing

Written and illustrated by
Tatum Bowie

from deer woman: an anthology
Edited by Elizabeth LaPensée & Weshoyot Alvitre

Strength and healing can often come from a
place of remebrance. When we take the time to
listen, learn, and change then the values instilled
in us from the long ago time can shine through.

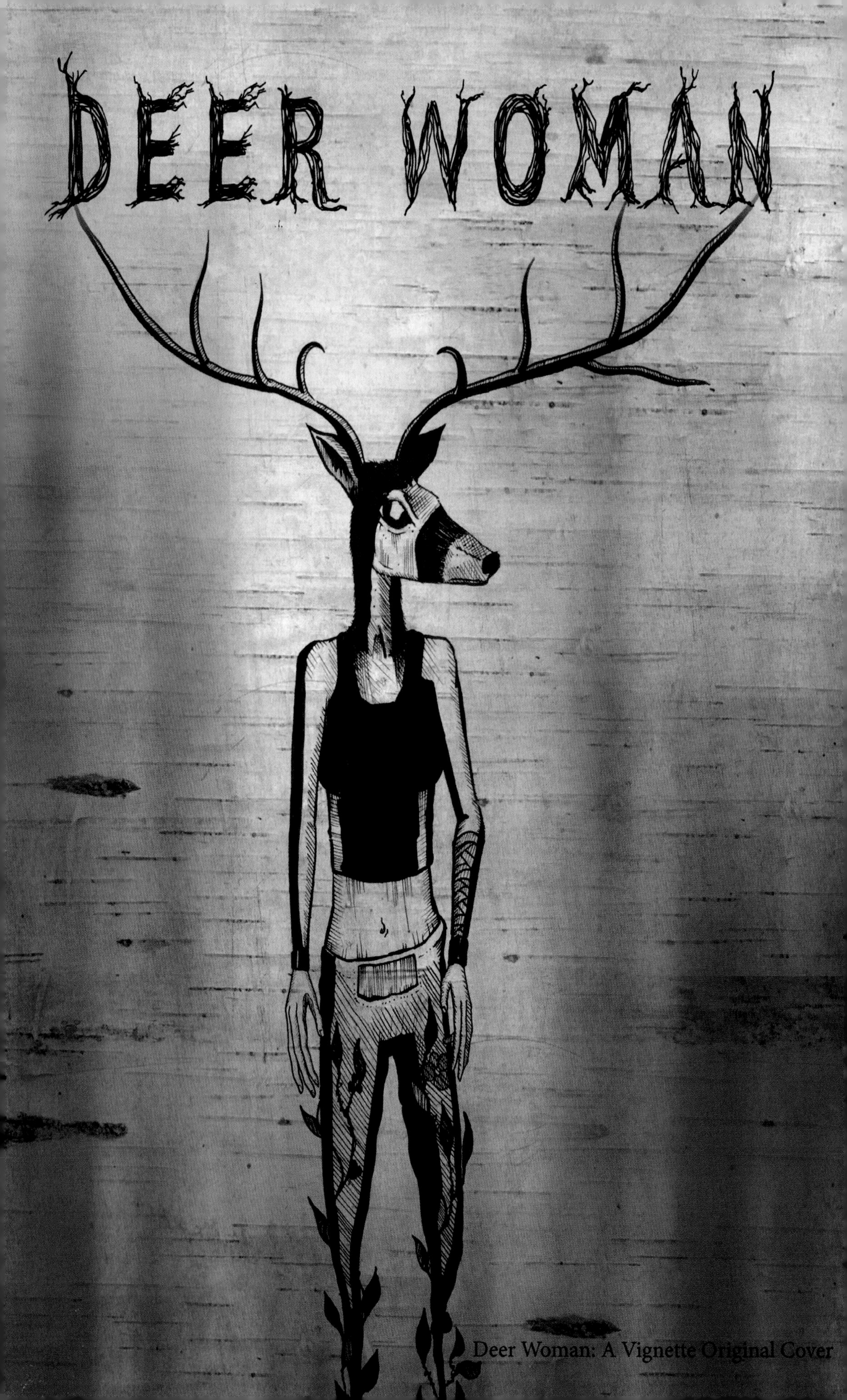
DEER WOMAN

Deer Woman: A Vignette Original Cover

Asdzą́ą́ Changing

story and art by

Tatum Bowie

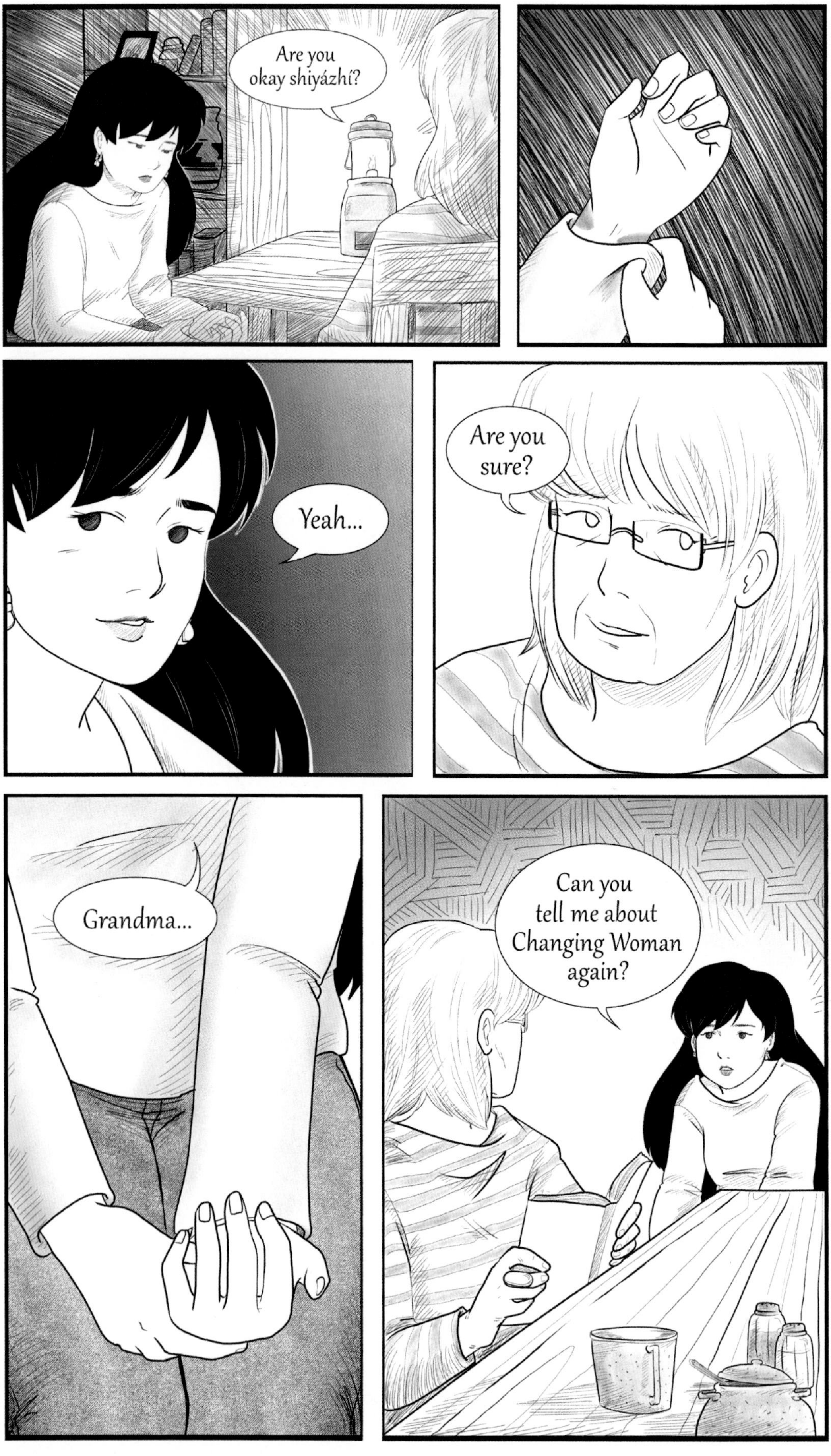
Are you okay shiyázhí?
Yeah...
Are you sure?
Grandma...
Can you tell me about Changing Woman again?

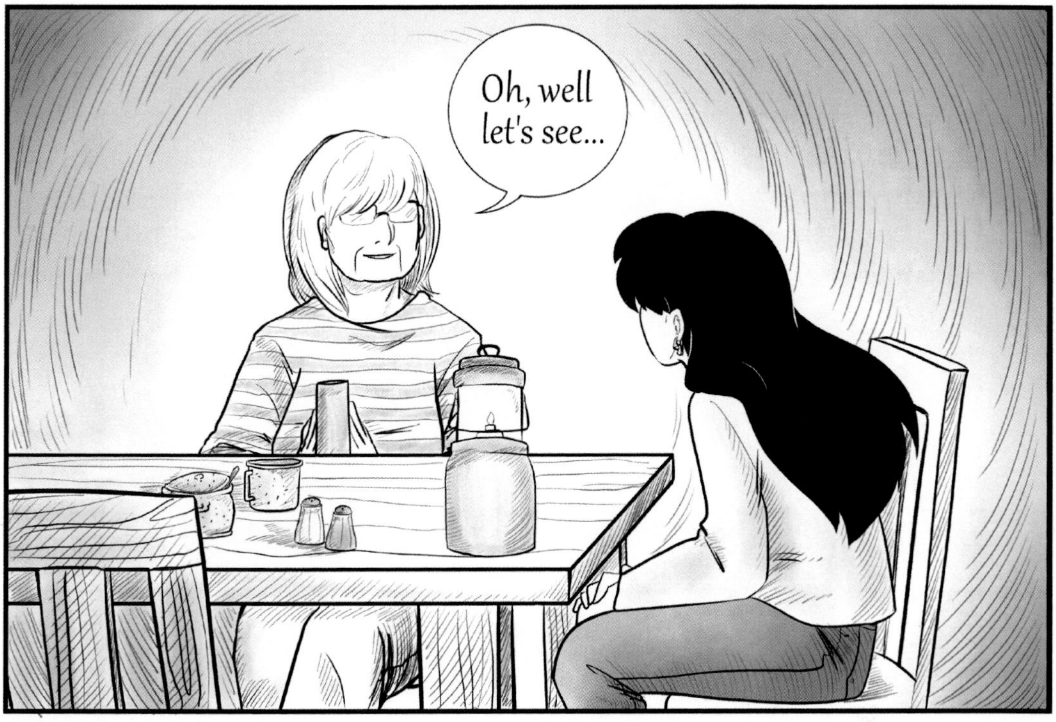
Oh, well let's see...

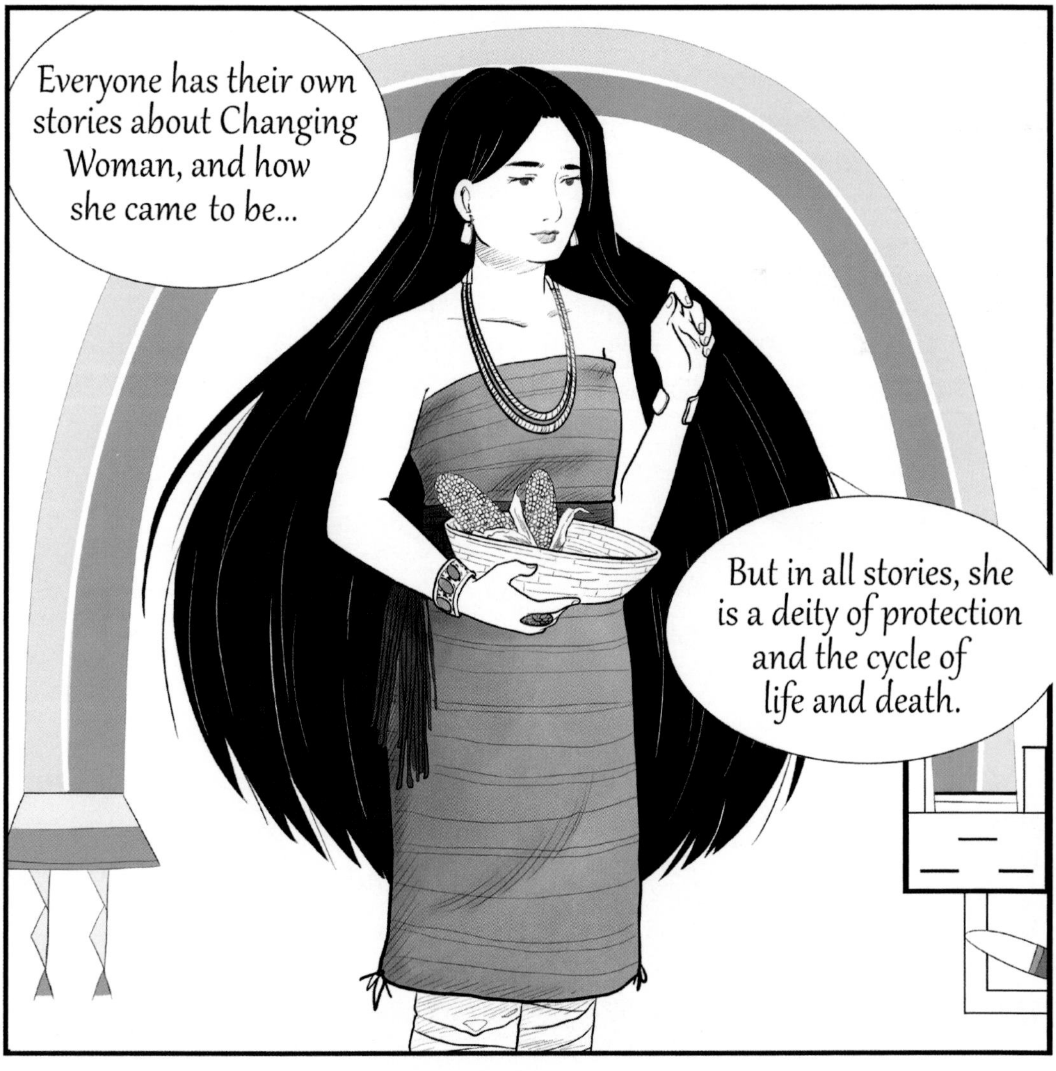
Everyone has their own stories about Changing Woman, and how she came to be...
But in all stories, she is a deity of protection and the cycle of life and death.

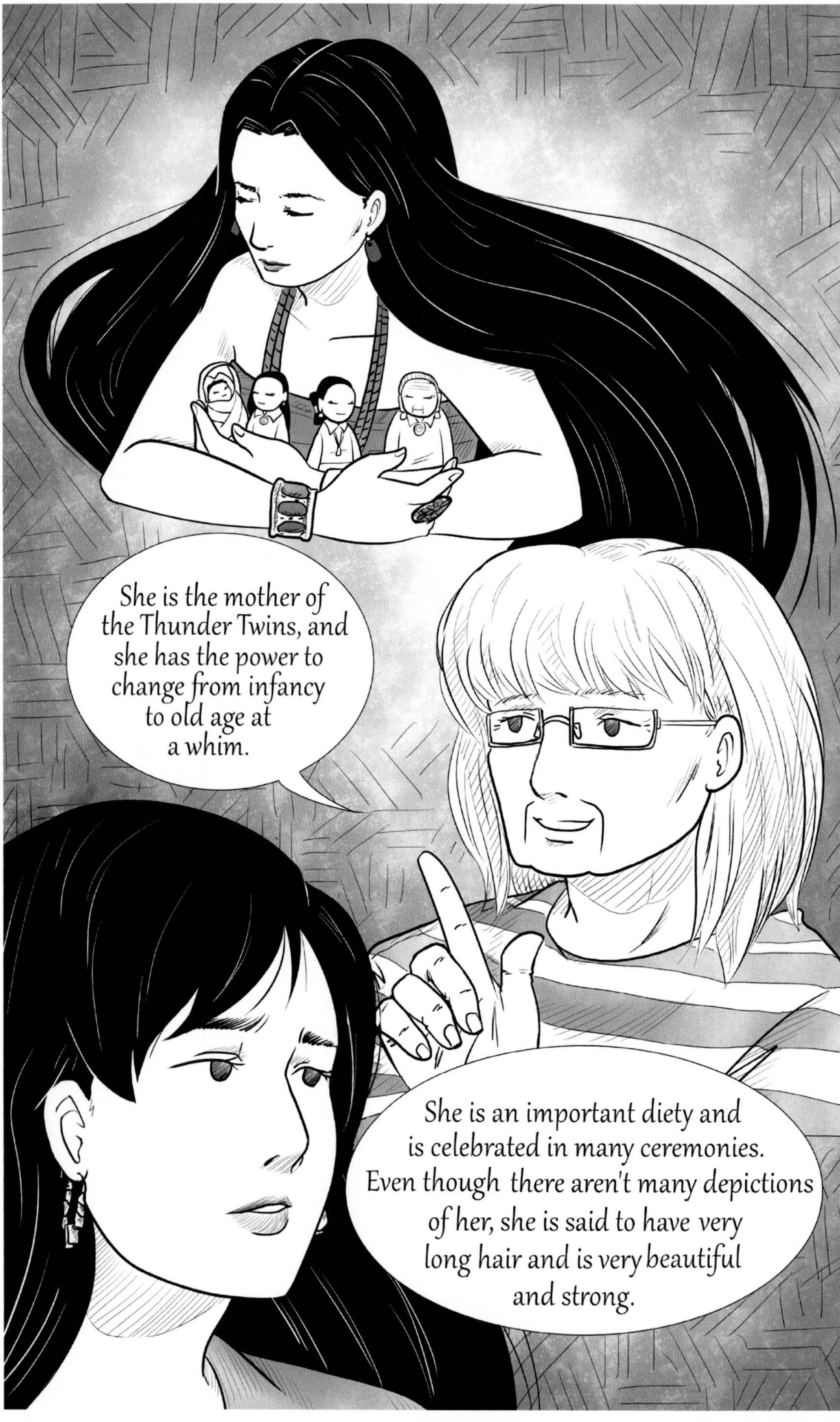
She is the mother of the Thunder Twins, and she has the power to change from infancy to old age at a whim.
She is an important diety and is celebrated in many ceremonies. Even though there aren't many depictions of her, she is said to have very long hair and is very beautiful and strong.

Is it even possible to be as strong as her though? I mean, to change too?

It seems too scary...

Of course it's scary, change isn't easy.

But Changing Woman didn't get her name by staying the same...

And you can't change by letting things stay as they are!

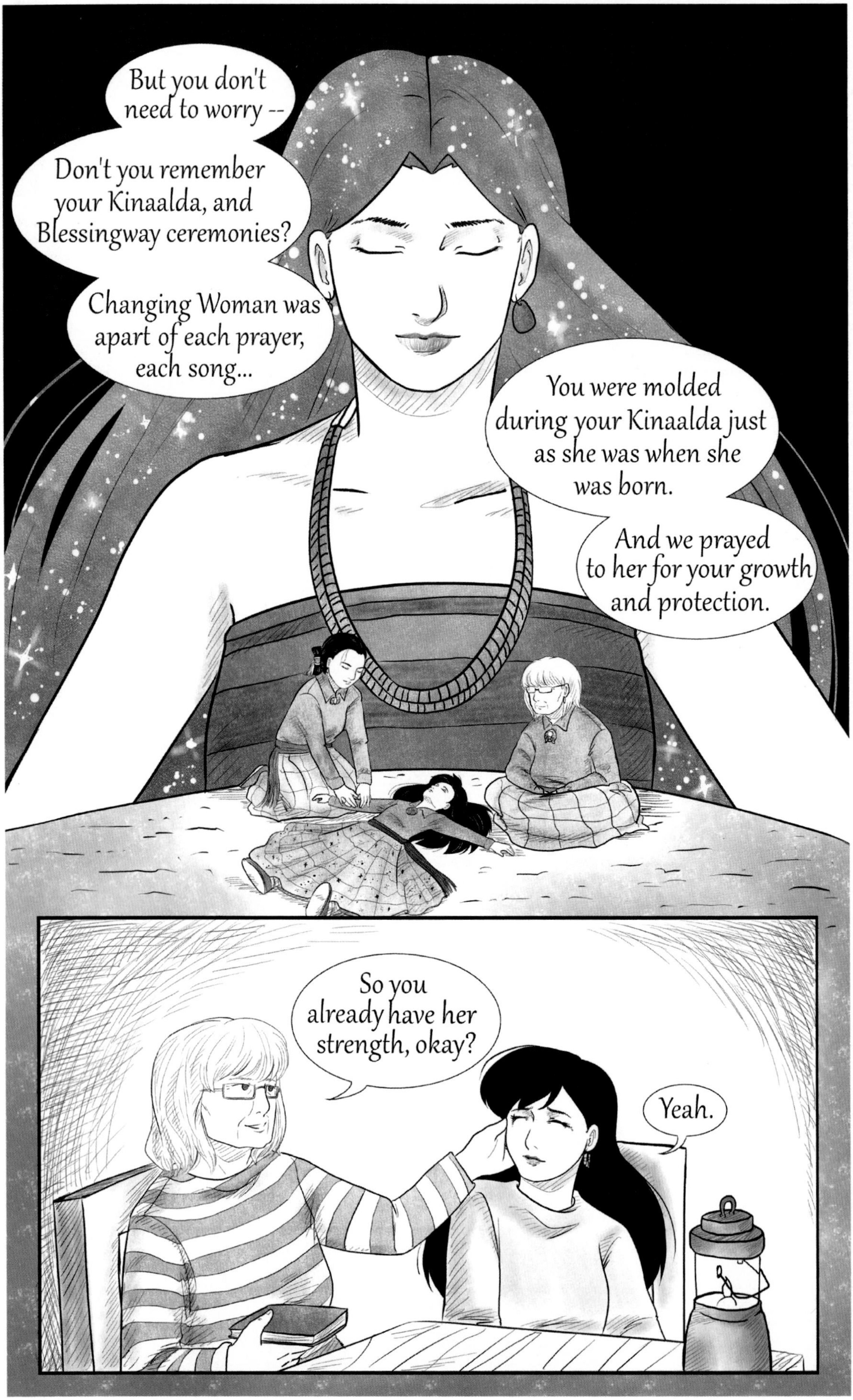
But you don't need to worry --
Don't you remember your Kinaalda, and Blessingway ceremonies?
Changing Woman was apart of each prayer, each song...
You were molded during your Kinaalda just as she was when she was born.
And we prayed to her for your growth and protection.
So you already have her strength, okay?
Yeah.

Greyhills High School

HONK!
HONK!

We'll wait for you by my car.

I wish you would stop hanging out with that guy...

Don't worry, I'll be back in a sec.

You can find more Deer Woman stories at nativerealities.c

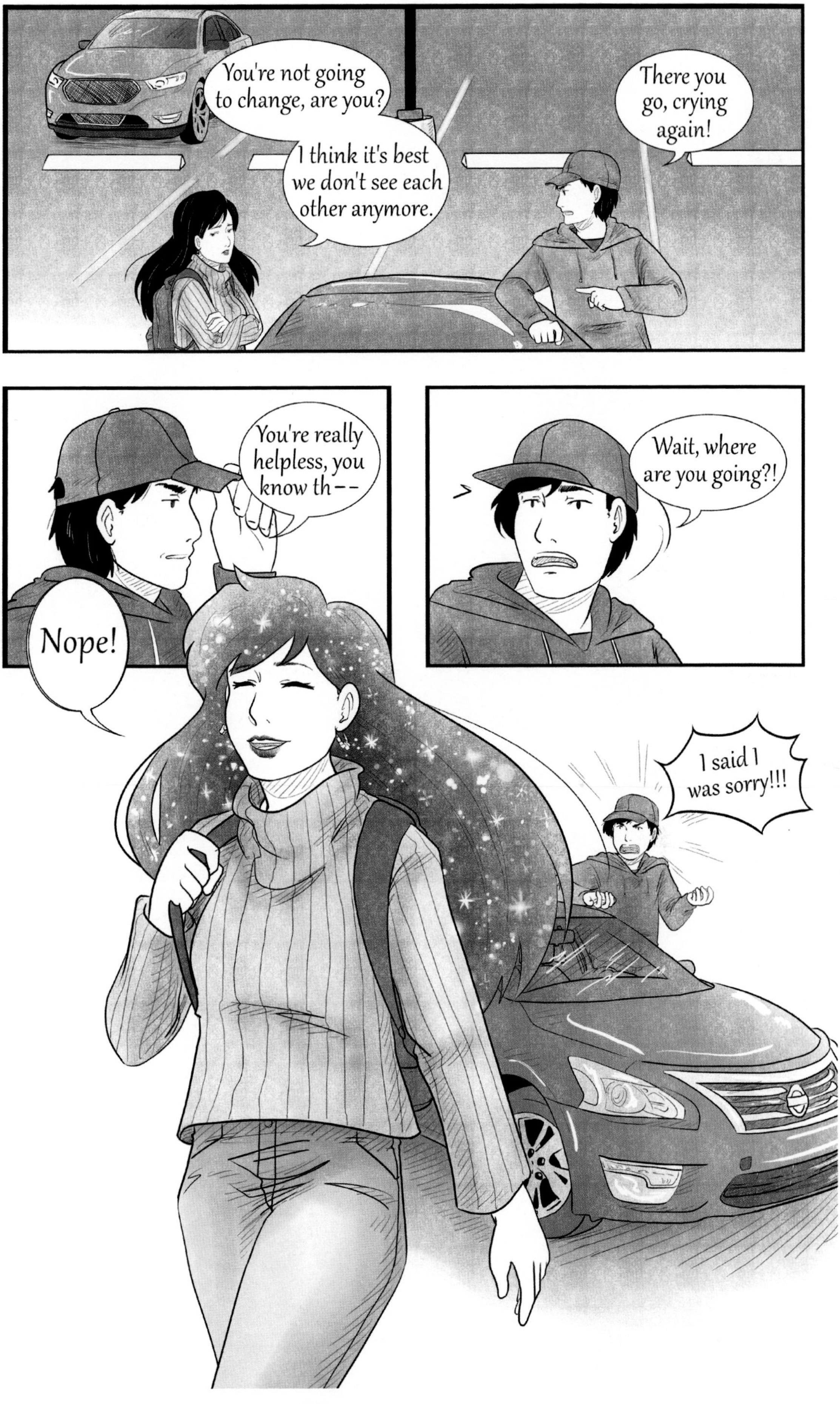
You're not going to change, are you?
I think it's best we don't see each other anymore.
There you go, crying again!
You're really helpless, you know th--
Nope!
Wait, where are you going?!
I said I was sorry!!!

hero twins #1 (excerpt)

**Written and illustrated by
Dale Deforest**

In 1860 as a calvary unit is sent to investigate a
threat. While a winter storm rages around the
unit, a mysterious officer makes a world-changing
discovery. Meanwhile, banished from the spirit
realm, Changing Woman must find a way to
protect her newborn children so they may fulfill
their destiny and bring light to the world.

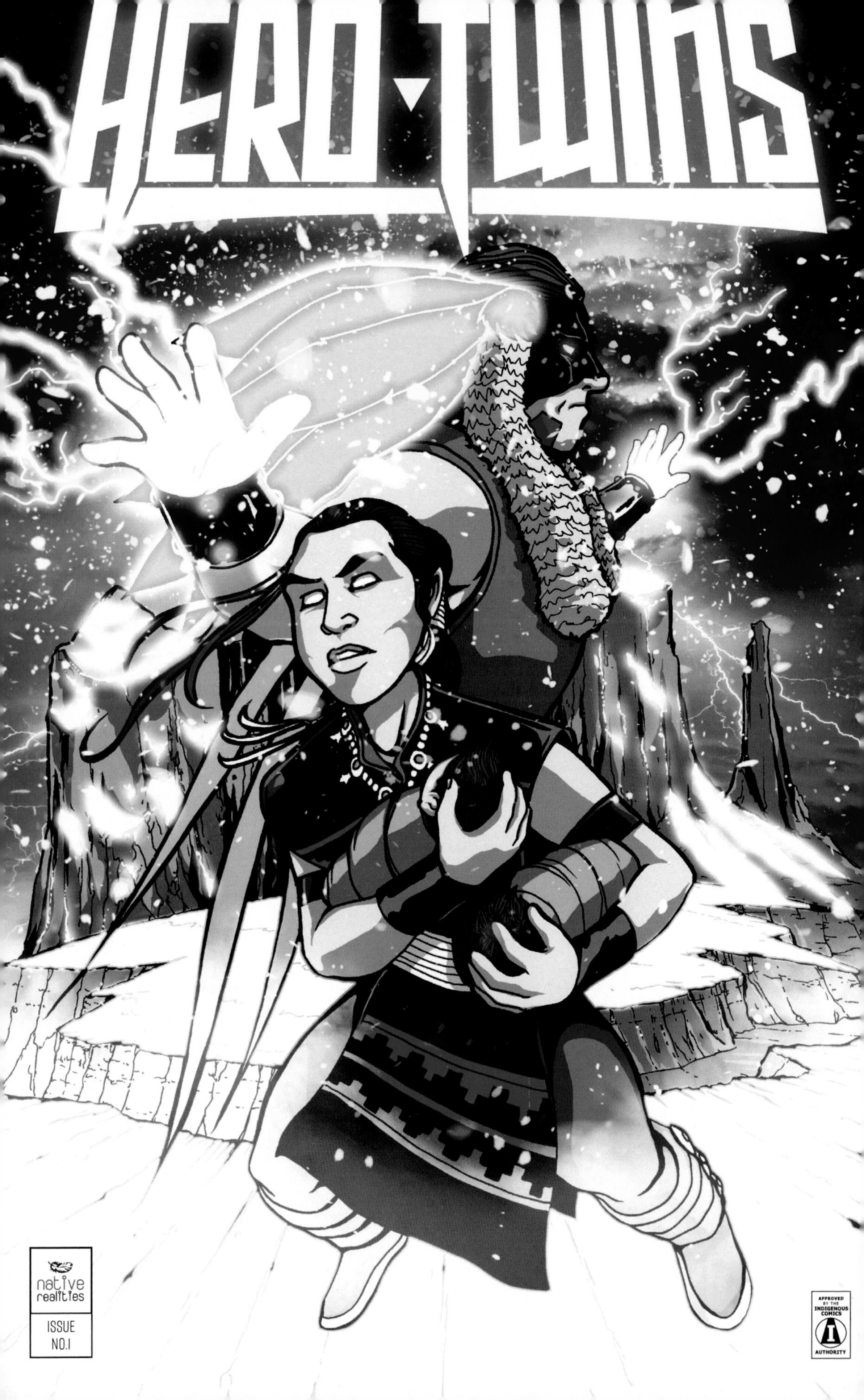
HERO TWINS
native realities
ISSUE NO.1
APPROVED BY THE INDIGENOUS COMICS AUTHORITY

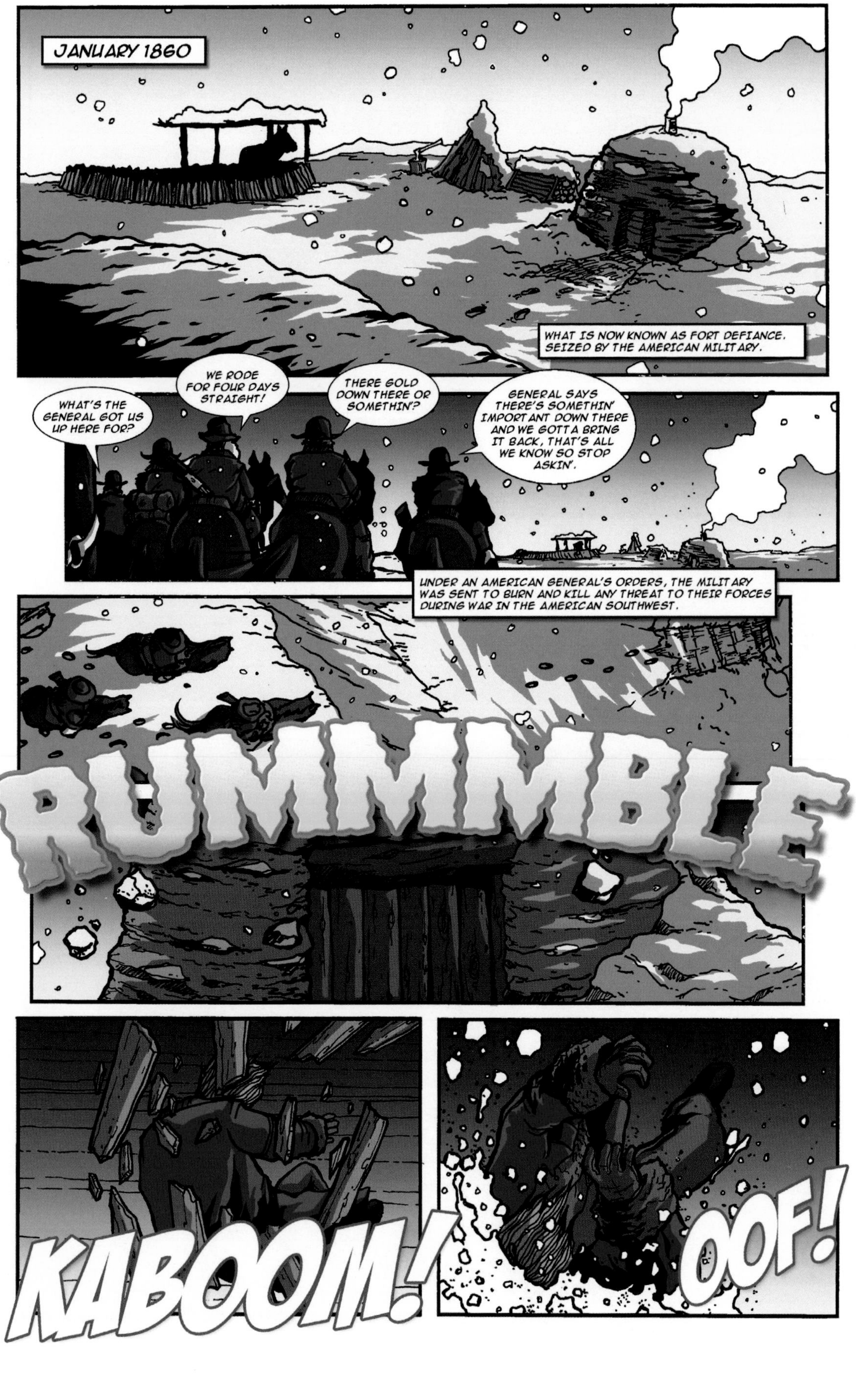
JANUARY 1860
WHAT IS NOW KNOWN AS FORT DEFIANCE. SEIZED BY THE AMERICAN MILITARY.
WHAT'S THE GENERAL GOT US UP HERE FOR?
WE RODE FOR FOUR DAYS STRAIGHT!
THERE GOLD DOWN THERE OR SOMETHIN'?
GENERAL SAYS THERE'S SOMETHIN' IMPORTANT DOWN THERE AND WE GOTTA BRING IT BACK, THAT'S ALL WE KNOW SO STOP ASKIN'.
UNDER AN AMERICAN GENERAL'S ORDERS, THE MILITARY WAS SENT TO BURN AND KILL ANY THREAT TO THEIR FORCES DURING WAR IN THE AMERICAN SOUTHWEST.
RUMMMBLE
KABOOM!
OOF!

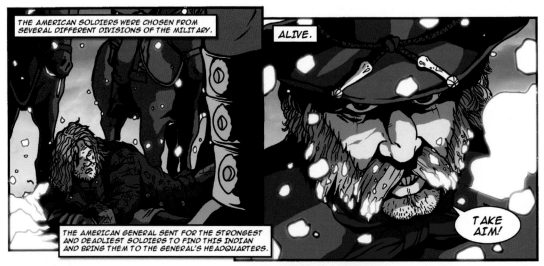

THE AMERICAN SOLDIERS WERE CHOSEN FROM SEVERAL DIFFERENT DIVISIONS OF THE MILITARY.

THE AMERICAN GENERAL SENT FOR THE STRONGEST AND DEADLIEST SOLDIERS TO FIND THIS INDIAN AND BRING THEM TO THE GENERAL'S HEADQUARTERS.

ALIVE.

TAKE AIM!

FIRE!

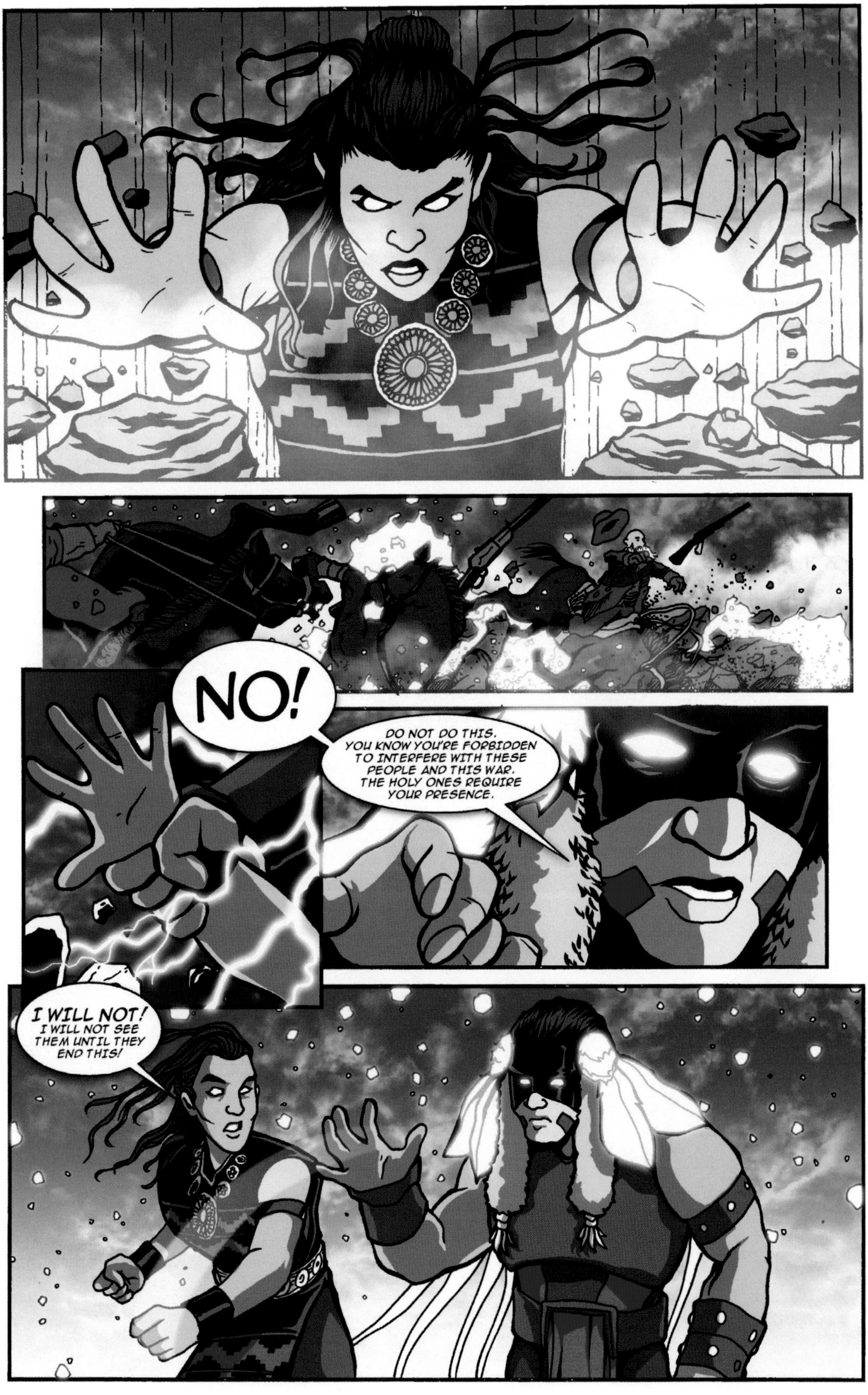
NO!
DO NOT DO THIS. YOU KNOW YOU'RE FORBIDDEN TO INTERFERE WITH THESE PEOPLE AND THIS WAR. THE HOLY ONES REQUIRE YOUR PRESENCE.
I WILL NOT! I WILL NOT SEE THEM UNTIL THEY END THIS!

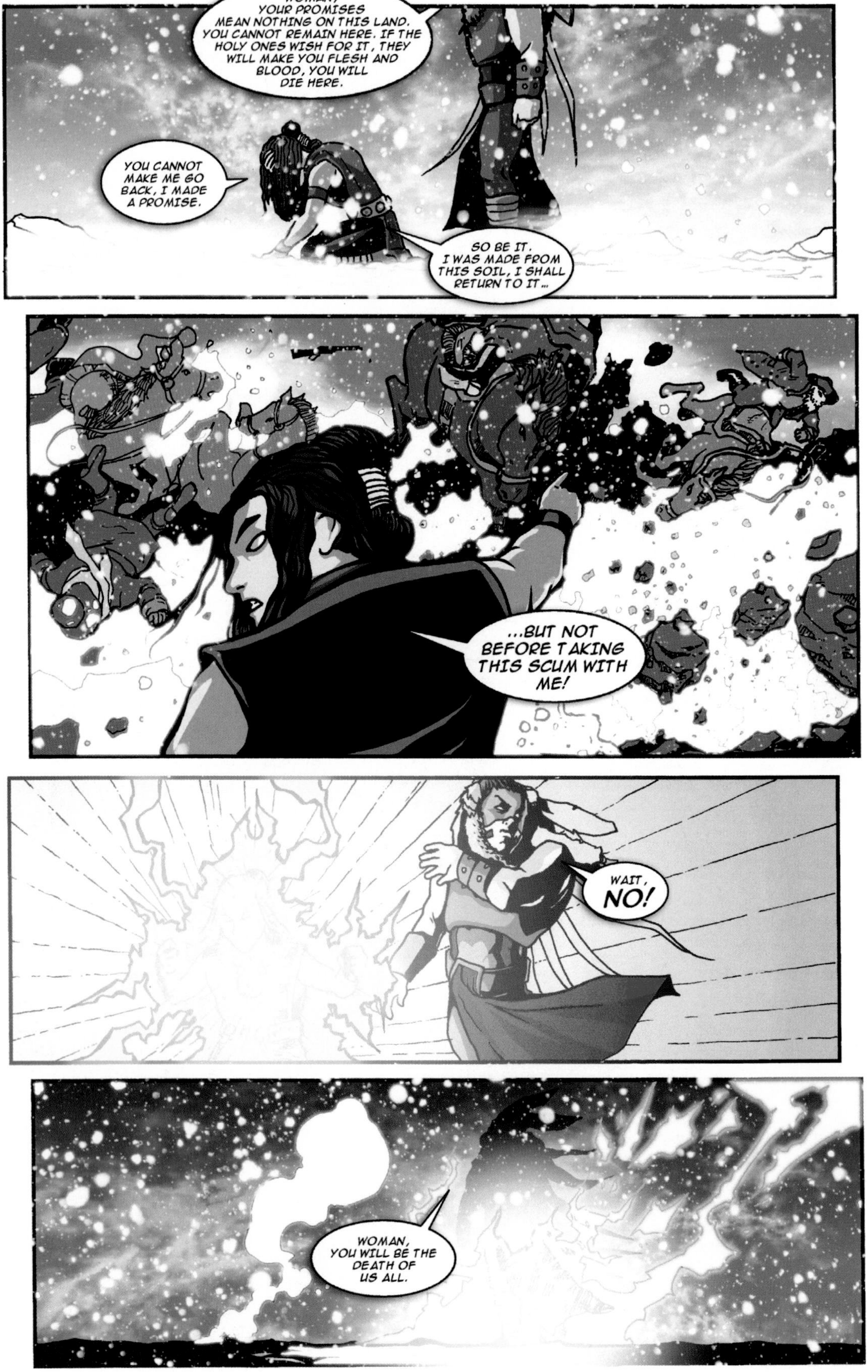
WOMAN, YOUR PROMISES MEAN NOTHING ON THIS LAND. YOU CANNOT REMAIN HERE. IF THE HOLY ONES WISH FOR IT, THEY WILL MAKE YOU FLESH AND BLOOD, YOU WILL DIE HERE.
YOU CANNOT MAKE ME GO BACK, I MADE A PROMISE.
SO BE IT. I WAS MADE FROM THIS SOIL, I SHALL RETURN TO IT...
...BUT NOT BEFORE TAKING THIS SCUM WITH ME!
WAIT, NO!
WOMAN, YOU WILL BE THE DEATH OF US ALL.

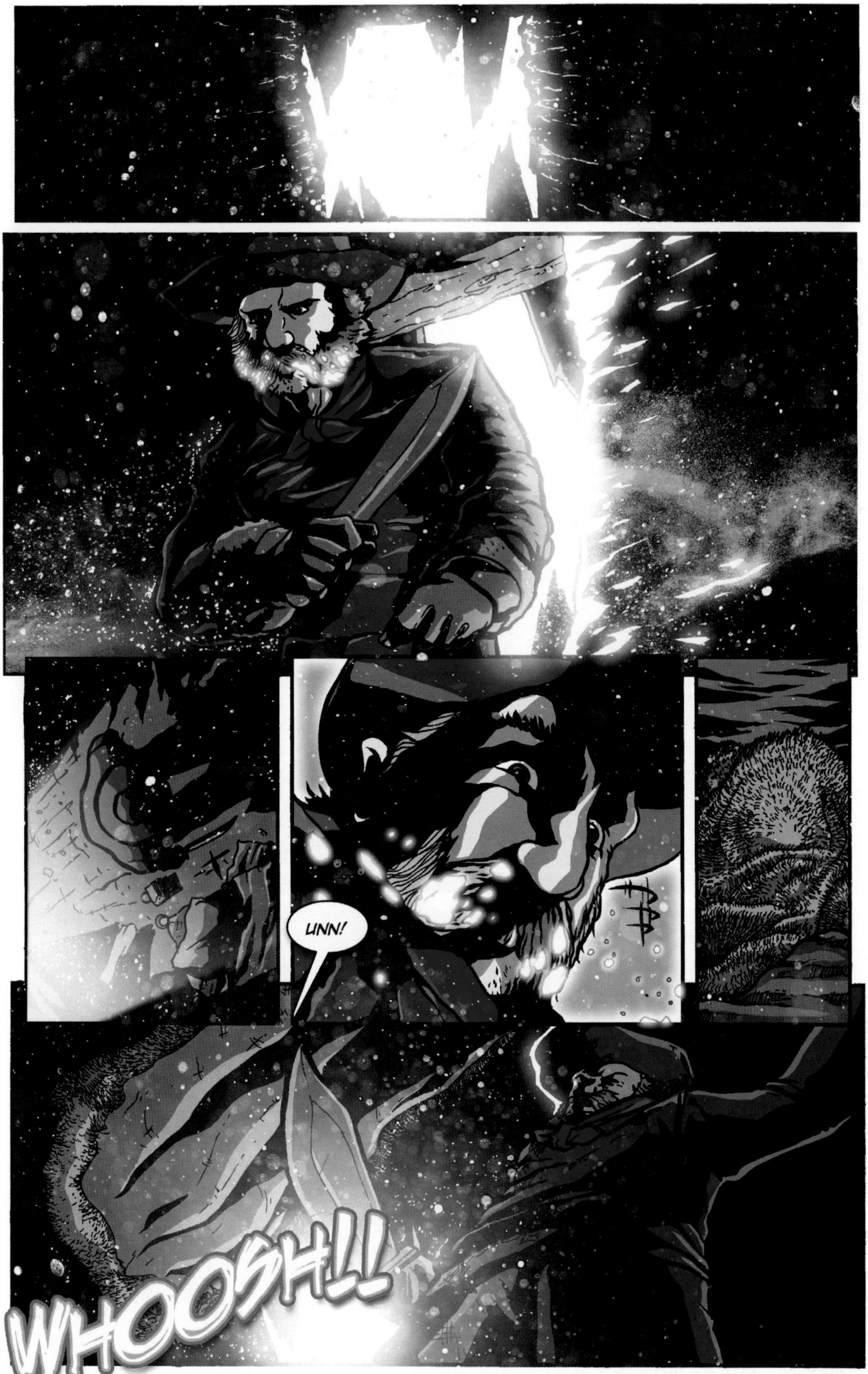
UNN!
WHOOSH!!

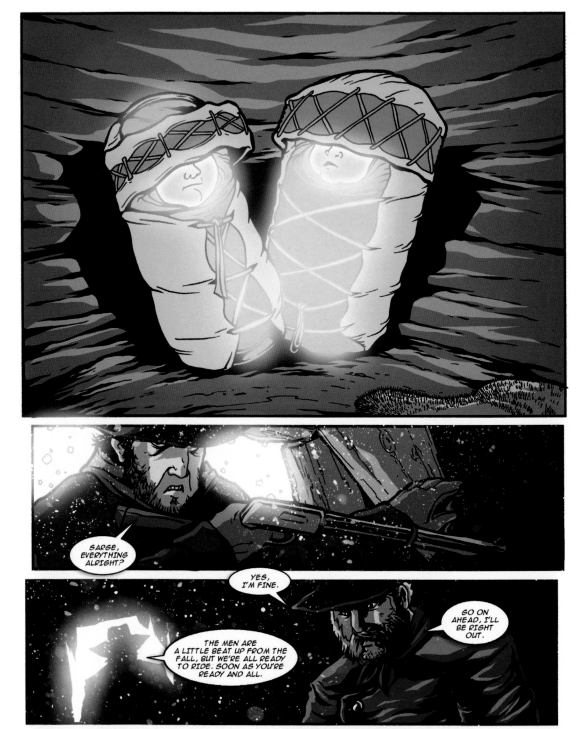

SARGE, EVERYTHING ALRIGHT?

YES, I'M FINE.

THE MEN ARE A LITTLE BEAT UP FROM THE FALL, BUT WE'RE ALL READY TO RIDE. SOON AS YOU'RE READY AND ALL.

GO ON AHEAD, I'LL BE RIGHT OUT.

SADDLE UP! WE RIDE!

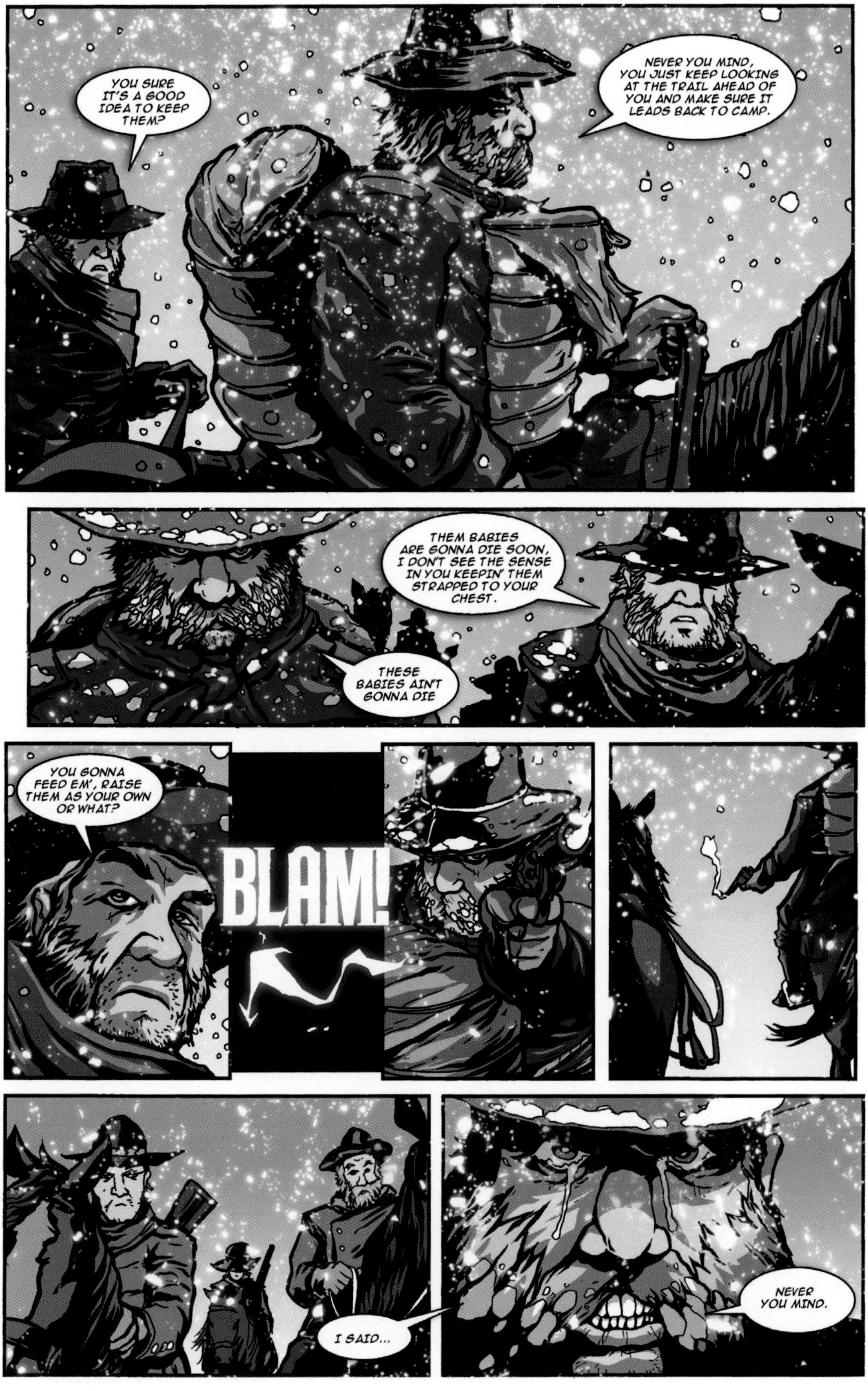
YOU SURE IT'S A GOOD IDEA TO KEEP THEM?
NEVER YOU MIND, YOU JUST KEEP LOOKING AT THE TRAIL AHEAD OF YOU AND MAKE SURE IT LEADS BACK TO CAMP.
THEM BABIES ARE GONNA DIE SOON, I DON'T SEE THE SENSE IN YOU KEEPIN' THEM STRAPPED TO YOUR CHEST.
THESE BABIES AIN'T GONNA DIE
YOU GONNA FEED EM', RAISE THEM AS YOUR OWN OR WHAT?
BLAM!
I SAID...
NEVER YOU MIND.

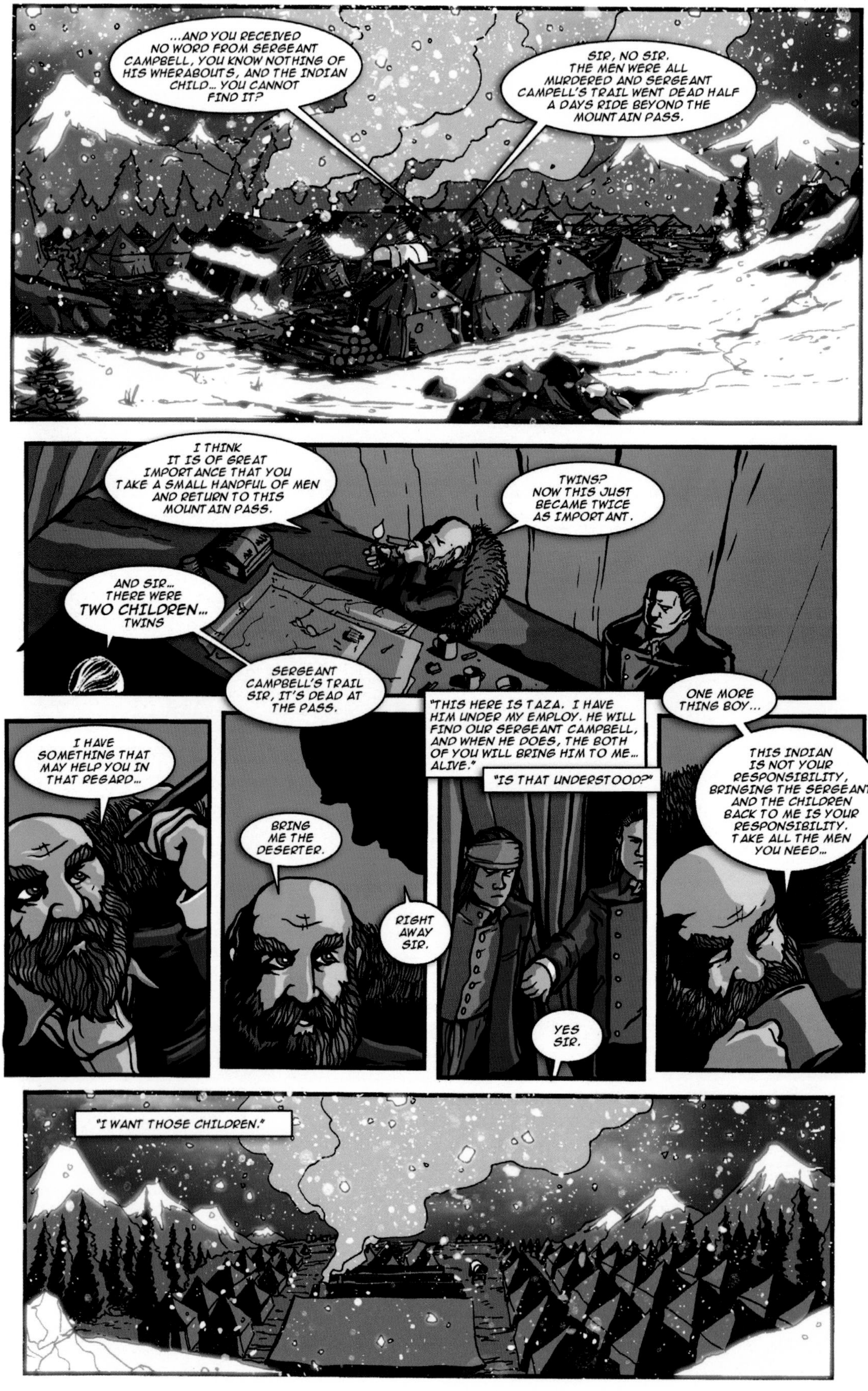

...AND YOU RECEIVED NO WORD FROM SERGEANT CAMPBELL, YOU KNOW NOTHING OF HIS WHERABOUTS, AND THE INDIAN CHILD... YOU CANNOT FIND IT?
SIR, NO SIR. THE MEN WERE ALL MURDERED AND SERGEANT CAMPELL'S TRAIL WENT DEAD HALF A DAYS RIDE BEYOND THE MOUNTAIN PASS.
I THINK IT IS OF GREAT IMPORTANCE THAT YOU TAKE A SMALL HANDFUL OF MEN AND RETURN TO THIS MOUNTAIN PASS.
AND SIR... THERE WERE TWO CHILDREN... TWINS
TWINS? NOW THIS JUST BECAME TWICE AS IMPORTANT.
SERGEANT CAMPBELL'S TRAIL SIR, IT'S DEAD AT THE PASS.
I HAVE SOMETHING THAT MAY HELP YOU IN THAT REGARD...
BRING ME THE DESERTER.
RIGHT AWAY SIR.
"THIS HERE IS TAZA. I HAVE HIM UNDER MY EMPLOY. HE WILL FIND OUR SERGEANT CAMPBELL, AND WHEN HE DOES, THE BOTH OF YOU WILL BRING HIM TO ME... ALIVE."
"IS THAT UNDERSTOOD?"
YES SIR.
ONE MORE THING BOY...
THIS INDIAN IS NOT YOUR RESPONSIBILITY, BRINGING THE SERGEANT AND THE CHILDREN BACK TO ME IS YOUR RESPONSIBILITY. TAKE ALL THE MEN YOU NEED...
"I WANT THOSE CHILDREN."

SOLDIERS PACK FOOD, SUPPLIES AND AMMO. ENOUGH FOR 30 DAYS OF HUNTING.

THEY WILL COMB THE ENTIRE NAVAJO NATION FOR AS LONG AS THE UNITED STATES MILITARY IS IN POWER.

THE UNITED STATES ARMY GENERAL HAS GIVEN THE ORDER.

FOR MONTHS THEY WILL SEARCH.

MANY WILL LOSE THEIR LIVES BY MOTHER NATURE'S HAND.

MANY WILL DIE IN BATTLE.

THE GENERAL'S ORDERS ARE TO KILL ANY SAVAGE ATTEMPTING TO ATTACK OR FLEE.

THESE MEN WILL RIDE TO THEIR DEATHS.

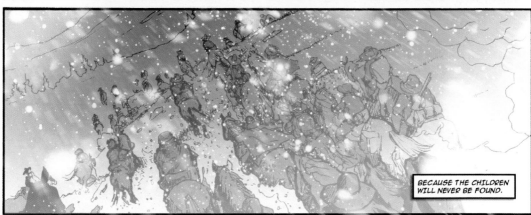

BECAUSE THE CHILDREN WILL NEVER BE FOUND.

WEAK MINDED PEOPLE CAN OFTEN BE THE MOST SECURE OF VESSELS.

INSTINCT IS WHAT HAS DRIVEN THEM TO THIS LOCATION.

NAATSISAAN, WHAT IS KNOWN AS NAVAJO MOUNTAIN. THE HIGHEST PEAK ON THE NAVAJO NATION, A SANCTUARY FOR THOSE TRAPPED OUTSIDE THE SPIRIT WORLD, LOOKING FOR REDEMPTION.

THEY WILL BE SAFE HERE.

FOUR HOURS LATER.

HOO BOY.

THE FIRST WOMAN WAS BORN FROM TIME AND LIGHT. SHE WAS BROUGHT INTO BEING FROM THE DIYN DINE'E (HOLY PEOPLE) BECAUSE THEIR VISION OF VARIOUS TIMELINES DEMANDED THEY HAVE AN AMBASSADOR FOR ALL FACETS OF LIFE, THE FIRST WOMAN WAS MEANT TO BE THEIR AMBASSADOR FOR HUMANITY.

THE DIYIN DINE'E BELIEVED THAT ONLY A BEING CAPABLE OF CARRYING LIFE ITSELF WAS A PROPER AMBASSADOR FOR OTHER SENTIENT BEINGS THAT WILL INHABIT WORLDS THAT WILL NURTURE HUMANITY AS WELL AS OTHER FORMS OF LIFE.

HEAR MY PRAYER, HEAR MY VOICE, HEAR MY HEART. THE CHILDREN SHALL LIVE, THEIR BIRTH IS THE COMING OF A NEW LIGHT, NEW HOPE AND A STRONGER PEOPLE.

I DO NOT COME HERE FOR REDEMPTION. I COME HERE SO THAT THE CHILDREN MAY FULFILL THEIR PURPOSE. THEY MUST LIVE TO PROTECT LIFE.

You can find the rest of the story in Hero Twins #1 at nativerealities.com.

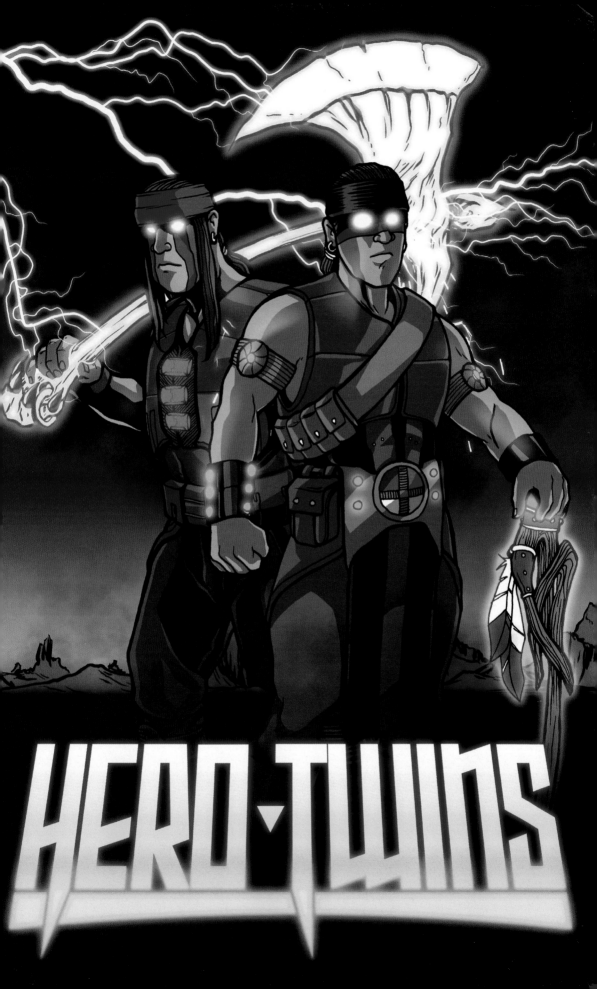

HERO·TWINS

upcoming releases

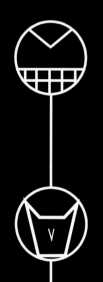

sixkiller
Written by Lee Francis IV
Illustrated by Weshoyot Alvitre

ghost of the green
Written by Richard Davis & Lee Francis IV

liminality
Written by Migizi Pensoneau
Illustrated by Bobby Wilson

demicon
Written & illustrated by
Jeffrey Veregge

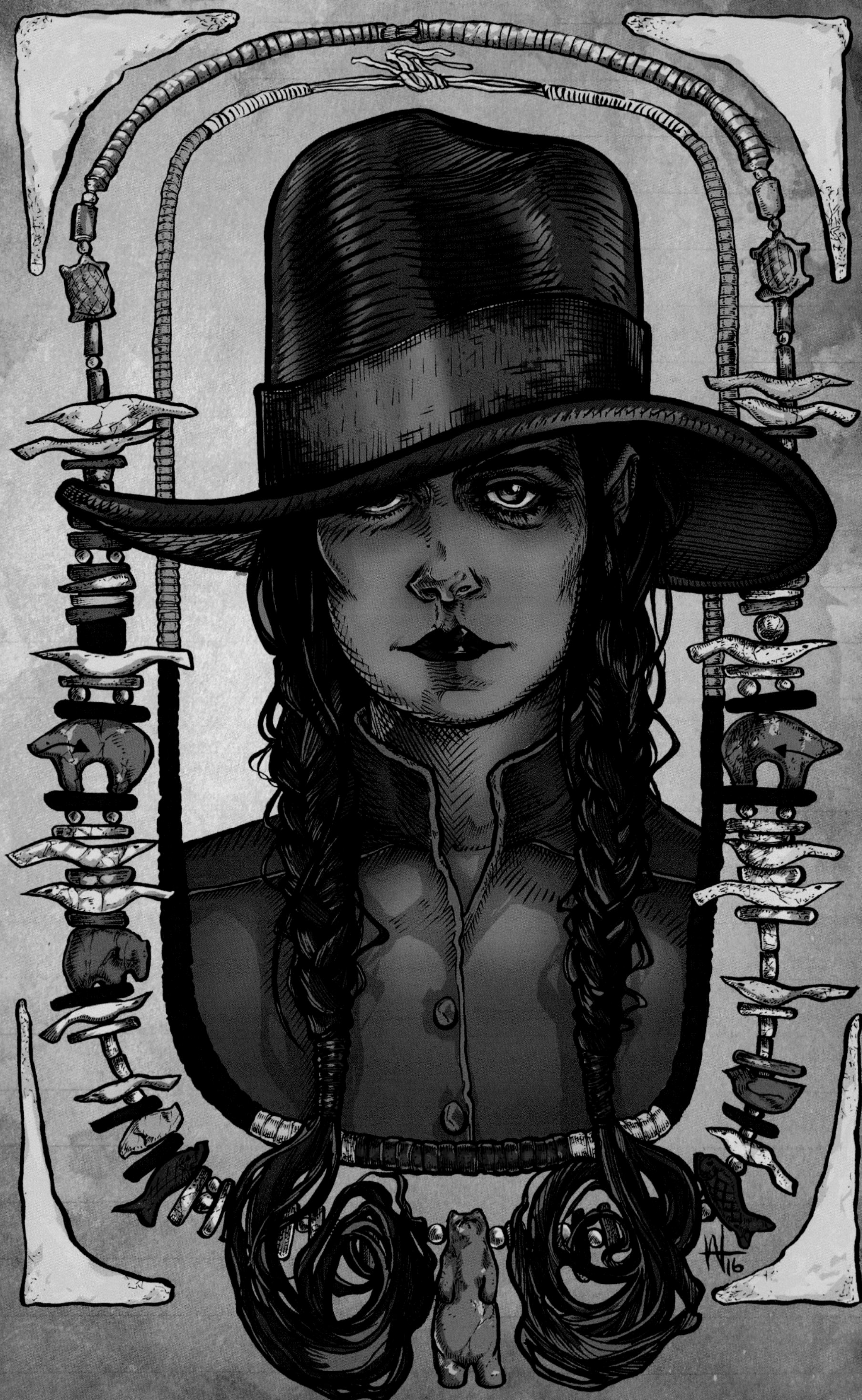

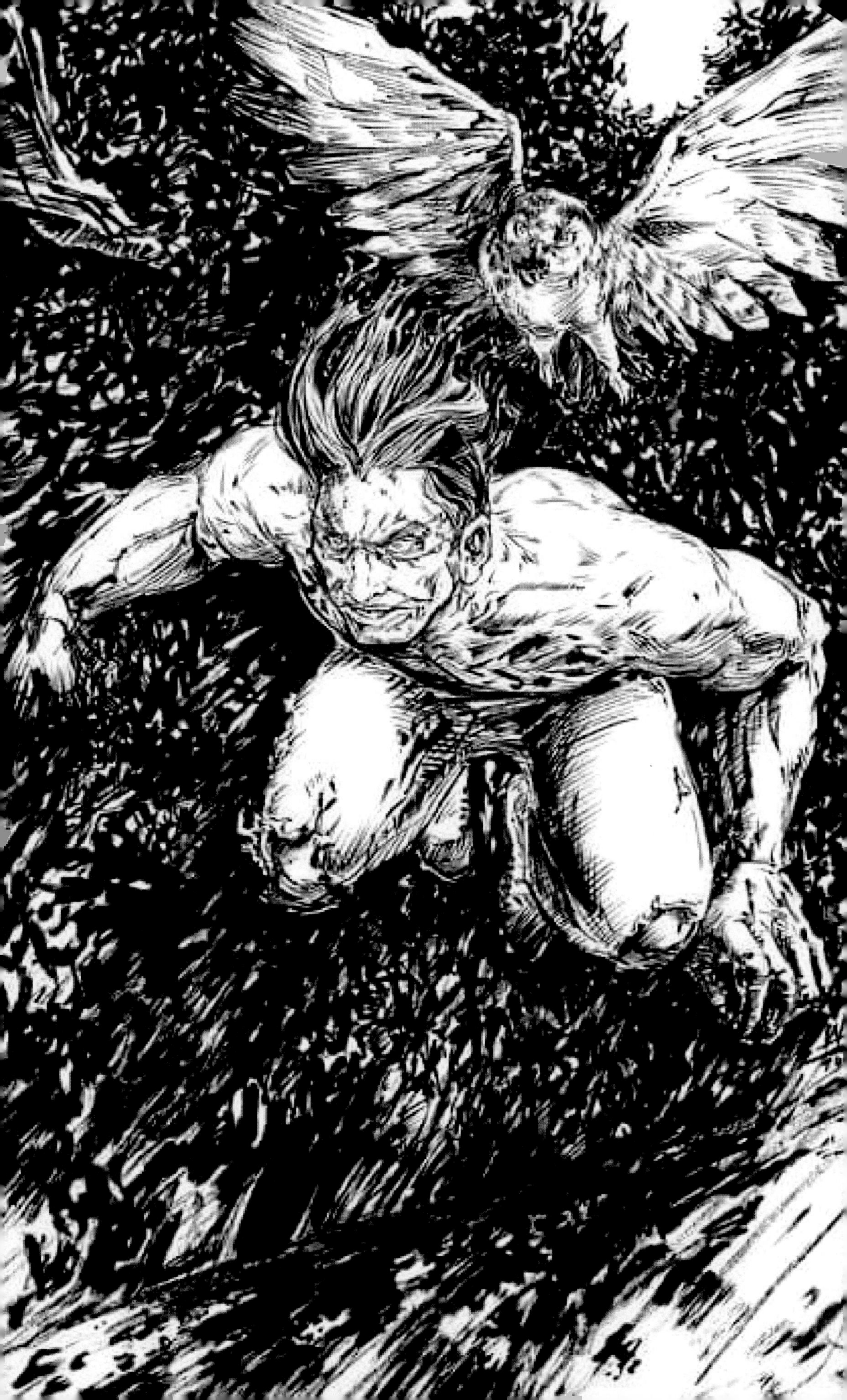

LIMINALITY

2017

DEMiCON ™

VOLUME 1: BIRTHRIGHT

VEREGGE | ISSUE 1

Indigenous Comic Con 2017

November 10 - 12, 2017
Isleta Resort & Casino
www.indigenouscomiccon.com

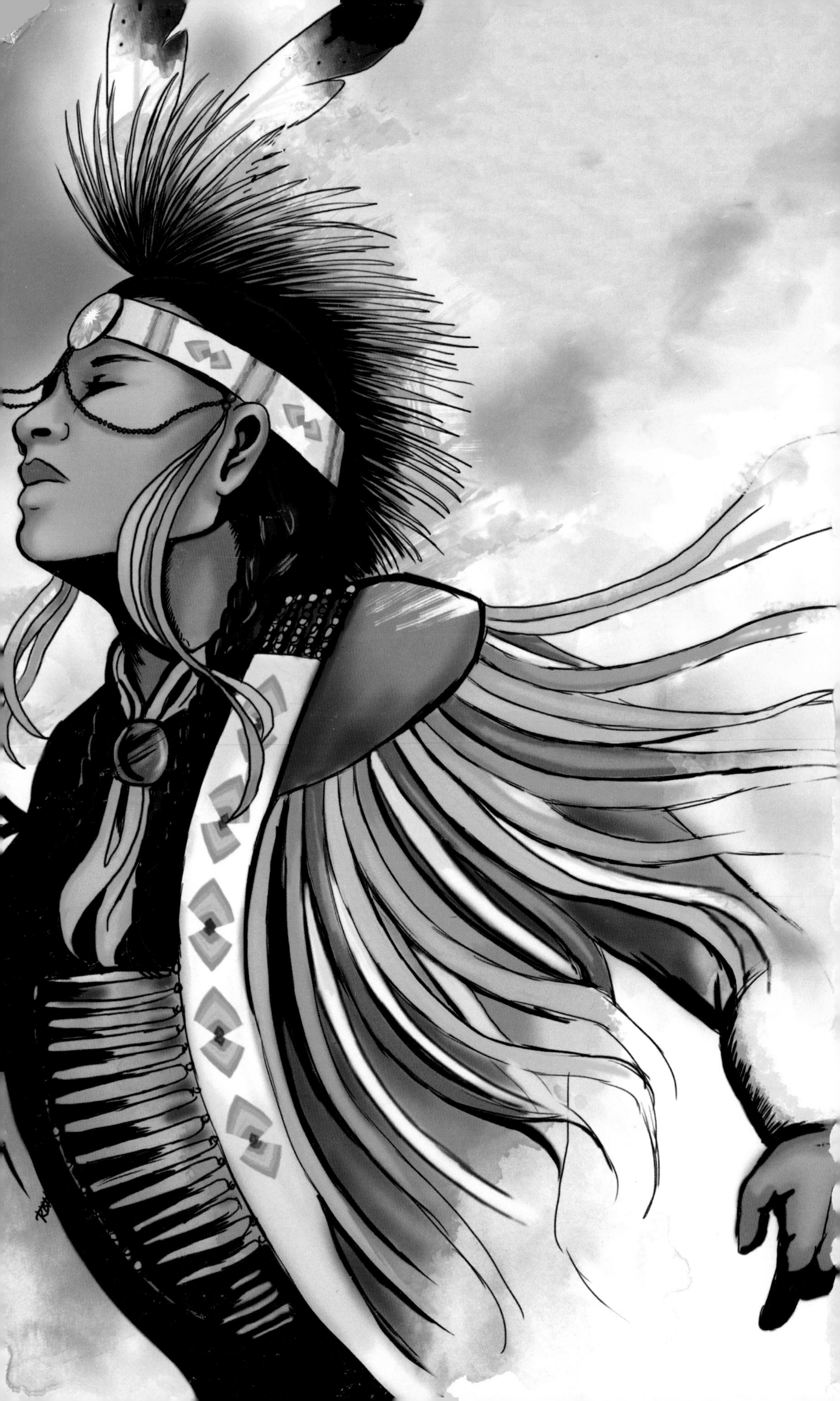

GENKI PLUS

KANJI
LOOK AND LEARN
512 Kanji with Illustrations and Mnemonic Hints
イメージで覚える[げんき]な漢字512

坂野永理
Eri Banno

池田庸子
Yoko Ikeda

品川恭子
Chikako Shinagawa

田嶋香織
Kaori Tajima

渡嘉敷恭子
Kyoko Tokashiki

the japan times

［著者紹介］

坂野　永理　　岡山大学言語教育センター教授

池田　庸子　　茨城大学留学生センター教授

品川　恭子　　カリフォルニア大学サンタバーバラ校東アジア学科講師

田嶋　香織　　関西外国語大学外国語学部非常勤講師

渡嘉敷　恭子　関西外国語大学外国語学部教授

KANJI LOOK AND LEARN

2009 年 5 月 20 日　初版発行
2017 年 11 月 5 日　第 20 刷発行
著　者：坂野永理・池田庸子・品川恭子・田嶋香織・渡嘉敷恭子
発行者：堤 丈晴
発行所：株式会社 ジャパンタイムズ
　　　　〒108-0023 東京都港区芝浦 4 丁目 5 番 4 号
　　　　電話 （03）3453-2013 （出版営業部）
ISBN978-4-7890-1349-9

First edition: May 2009
20th printing: November 2017

Illustrations: Noriko Udagawa
Layout design and typesetting: DEP, Inc.
Cover design: Nakayama Design Office
　　　　　　　Gin-o Nakayama and Kenji Sugiyama
Published by The Japan Times, Ltd.
5-4, Shibaura 4-chome, Minato-ku, Tokyo 108-0023, Japan
Phone: 03-3453-2013
http://bookclub.japantimes.co.jp/

ISBN978-4-7890-1349-9

Printed in Japan

はじめに

　本書は非漢字圏の日本語学習者を対象にした、初〜中級レベルの漢字教材です。漢字を習っているけれどもっと楽しく勉強したい人、漢字について全く知らないけれど漢字の勉強を始めたいと思っている人のために作りました。

　日本語学習者にとって漢字習得は一朝一夕にいかないものです。「漢字が苦手」「覚えられない」「覚えてもすぐ忘れてしまう」と感じてしまう人も多いでしょう。本書はこのような学生と向き合っている教師5人が、日々の漢字指導で生み出したアイディアを集め、検討・改良を重ねて作ったものです。学習者が楽しく学べるように、512字すべての漢字をイラストで表し、覚えやすくするためにストーリーを付けました。この教材を手にした学習者が、楽しみながら少しでも多くの漢字を学んでくれることを望みます。また、漢字指導に携わる先生方にも、漢字を教える際の参考にしていただければ幸いです。

　この本の完成には構想から5年余りの時間を要しました。本の出版にあたり、編集に労を注いでくださったジャパンタイムズ出版編集部の関戸千明さん、イラストを描いてくださった宇田川のり子さんに、著者一同心より感謝いたします。また、教材作成に協力してくださった大野裕さん、この教材を作るきっかけを与えてくれた学生たちに、心よりお礼を申し上げます。

2009年4月

著者一同

Preface

This book is a beginning- to intermediate-level kanji textbook for Japanese-language learners from cultures that do not use Chinese characters. It is designed for basically two types of students—those who have already begun to learn kanji but want to have more fun in their studies, and those without any background in kanji who want to start learning these characters.

Kanji cannot be mastered overnight, and many learners find the characters to be intimidating, tricky to memorize, and easy to forget. We, the authors of this book, have frequently worked with such learners in our roles as Japanese-language instructors, so we decided to pool together ideas from our daily teaching experiences to create a tool for helping students to tackle kanji. By carefully selecting and refining our ideas, we came up with a book that makes kanji learning fun and easy through illustrations and mnemonic hints for each of the 512 characters presented. We hope that this book will enable students to enjoyably learn many kanji and that it will serve as a handy reference for Japanese-language instructors when they teach kanji.

We wish to express our deep appreciation to everyone who assisted us during the five years it took to bring this book to completion. We especially thank Chiaki Sekido of the Japan Times Publications Department for painstakingly editing our work, Noriko Udagawa for drawing the illustrations, Yutaka Ono for aiding our development of the material, and our students for inspiring us to create this book.

April 2009
The Authors

 # Contents

はじめに／Preface ·· [3]

この教材の内容と使い方／About This Book ································ [8]

漢字の基本／Kanji Basics ··· [16]

おもな構成要素／Kanji Parts ·· [26]

Part 1

第1課	1 一	2 二	3 三	4 四	5 五	6 六	7 七	8 八	9 九	10 十	11 百	12 千	13 万	14 円	15 口	16 目
	p.2			p.3			p.4			p.5			p.6			p.7

第2課	17 日	18 月	19 火	20 水	21 木	22 金	23 土	24 曜	25 本	26 人	27 今	28 寺	29 時	30 半	31 刀	32 分
	p.8			p.9			p.10			p.11			p.12			p.13

第3課	33 上	34 下	35 中	36 外	37 右	38 工	39 左	40 前	41 後	42 午	43 門	44 間	45 東	46 西	47 南	48 北
	p.14			p.15			p.16			p.17			p.18			p.19

第4課	49 田	50 力	51 男	52 女	53 子	54 学	55 生	56 先	57 何	58 父	59 母	60 年	61 去	62 毎	63 王	64 国
	p.20			p.21			p.22			p.23			p.24			p.25

第5課	65 見	66 行	67 米	68 来	69 良	70 食	71 飲	72 会	73 耳	74 聞	75 言	76 話	77 立	78 待	79 周	80 週
	p.26			p.27			p.28			p.29			p.30			p.31

第6課	81 大	82 小	83 高	84 安	85 新	86 古	87 元	88 気	89 多	90 少	91 広	92 早	93 長	94 明	95 好	96 友
	p.32			p.33			p.34			p.35			p.36			p.37

第7課	97 入	98 出	99 市	100 町	101 村	102 雨	103 電	104 車	105 馬	106 駅	107 社	108 校	109 店	110 銀	111 病	112 院
	p.38			p.39			p.40			p.41			p.42			p.43

第8課	113 休	114 走	115 起	116 貝	117 買	118 売	119 読	120 書	121 帰	122 勉	123 弓	124 虫	125 強	126 持	127 名	128 語
	p.44			p.45			p.46			p.47			p.48			p.49

第9課	129 春	130 夏	131 秋	132 冬	133 朝	134 昼	135 夕	136 方	137 晩	138 夜	139 心	140 手	141 足	142 体	143 首	144 道
	p.50			p.51			p.52			p.53			p.54			p.55

第10課	145 山	146 川	147 林	148 森	149 空	150 海	151 化	152 花	153 天	154 赤	155 青	156 白	157 黒	158 色	159 魚	160 犬
	p.56			p.57			p.58			p.59			p.60			p.61

Part 2

	161	162	163	164	165	166	167	168	169	170	171	172	173	174	175	176
第11課	料	理	反	飯	牛	豚	鳥	肉	茶	予	野	菜	切	作	未	味
	p.64			p.65			p.66			p.67			p.68			p.69

	177	178	179	180	181	182	183	184	185	186	187	188	189	190	191	192
第12課	音	楽	歌	自	転	乗	写	真	台	央	映	画	羊	洋	服	着
	p.70			p.71			p.72			p.73			p.74			p.75

	193	194	195	196	197	198	199	200	201	202	203	204	205	206	207	208
第13課	家	矢	族	親	兄	姉	弟	妹	私	夫	妻	主	住	糸	氏	紙
	p.76			p.77			p.78			p.79			p.80			p.81

	209	210	211	212	213	214	215	216	217	218	219	220	221	222	223	224
第14課	教	室	羽	習	漢	字	式	試	験	宿	題	文	英	質	問	説
	p.82			p.83			p.84			p.85			p.86			p.87

	225	226	227	228	229	230	231	232	233	234	235	236	237	238	239	240
第15課	遠	近	者	暑	寒	重	軽	低	弱	悪	暗	太	豆	短	光	風
	p.88			p.89			p.90			p.91			p.92			p.93

	241	242	243	244	245	246	247	248	249	250	251	252	253	254	255	256
第16課	運	動	止	歩	使	送	洗	急	開	閉	押	引	思	知	考	死
	p.94			p.95			p.96			p.97			p.98			p.99

	257	258	259	260	261	262	263	264	265	266	267	268	269	270	271	272
第17課	医	始	終	石	研	究	留	有	産	業	薬	働	員	士	仕	事
	p.100			p.101			p.102			p.103			p.104			p.105

	273	274	275	276	277	278	279	280	281	282	283	284	285	286	287	288
第18課	図	官	館	昔	借	代	貸	地	世	界	度	回	用	民	注	意
	p.106			p.107			p.108			p.109			p.110			p.111

	289	290	291	292	293	294	295	296	297	298	299	300	301	302	303	304
第19課	頭	顔	声	特	別	竹	合	答	正	同	計	京	集	不	便	以
	p.112			p.113			p.114			p.115			p.116			p.117

	305	306	307	308	309	310	311	312	313	314	315	316	317	318	319	320
第20課	場	戸	所	屋	堂	都	県	区	池	発	建	物	品	旅	通	進
	p.118			p.119			p.120			p.121			p.122			p.123

Part 3

	321	322	323	324	325	326	327	328	329	330	331	332	333	334	335	336
第21課	丸	熱	冷	甘	汚	果	卵	皿	酒	塩	付	片	焼	消	固	個
	p.126			p.127			p.128			p.129			p.130			p.131

	337	338	339	340	341	342	343	344	345	346	347	348	349	350	351	352
第22課	笑	泣	怒	幸	悲	苦	痛	恥	配	困	辛	眠	残	念	感	情
	p.132			p.133			p.134			p.135			p.136			p.137

	353	354	355	356	357	358	359	360	361	362	363	364	365	366	367	368
第23課	覚	忘	決	定	比	受	授	徒	練	復	表	卒	違	役	皆	彼
	p.138			p.139			p.140			p.141			p.142			p.143

		369	370	371	372	373	374	375	376	377	378	379	380	381	382	383	384
第24課		全	部	必	要	荷	由	届	利	払	濯	寝	踊	活	末	宅	祭
		p.144		p.145			p.146			p.147			p.148			p.149	

		385	386	387	388	389	390	391	392	393	394	395	396	397	398	399	400
第25課		平	和	戦	争	政	治	経	済	法	律	際	関	係	義	議	党
		p.150		p.151			p.152			p.153			p.154			p.155	

		401	402	403	404	405	406	407	408	409	410	411	412	413	414	415	416
第26課		遊	泳	疲	暖	涼	静	公	園	込	連	窓	側	葉	景	記	形
		p.156		p.157			p.158			p.159			p.160			p.161	

		417	418	419	420	421	422	423	424	425	426	427	428	429	430	431	432
第27課		吉	結	婚	共	供	両	若	老	息	娘	奥	将	祖	育	性	招
		p.162		p.163			p.164			p.165			p.166			p.167	

		433	434	435	436	437	438	439	440	441	442	443	444	445	446	447	448
第28課		取	最	初	番	歳	枚	冊	億	点	階	段	号	倍	次	々	他
		p.168		p.169			p.170			p.171			p.172			p.173	

		449	450	451	452	453	454	455	456	457	458	459	460	461	462	463	464
第29課		勝	負	賛	成	絶	対	続	辞	投	選	約	束	守	過	夢	的
		p.174		p.175			p.176			p.177			p.178			p.179	

		465	466	467	468	469	470	471	472	473	474	475	476	477	478	479	480
第30課		飛	機	失	鉄	速	遅	駐	泊	船	座	席	島	陸	港	橋	交
		p.180		p.181			p.182			p.183			p.184			p.185	

		481	482	483	484	485	486	487	488	489	490	491	492	493	494	495	496
第31課		申	神	様	信	調	査	相	談	案	内	君	達	星	雪	降	直
		p.186		p.187			p.188			p.189			p.190			p.191	

		497	498	499	500	501	502	503	504	505	506	507	508	509	510	511	512
第32課		危	険	拾	捨	戻	吸	放	変	歯	髪	絵	横	当	伝	細	無
		p.192		p.193			p.194			p.195			p.196			p.197	

画数さくいん (Stroke Count Index) ………… 198

音訓さくいん (*On-Kun* Reading Index) ………… 200

字形さくいん (Kanji Shape Index) ………… 209

語彙さくいん (Vocabulary Index) ………… 217

この教材の内容と使い方

1. 対象とねらい

　この教材は、主に非漢字圏の学習者を対象に、初級〜中級レベルの漢字512字の形と意味を、イラストとストーリーを使って無理なく楽しく覚えられるようにした教材です。テキストで漢字について学習し、ワークブックで練習することで、初中級の漢字を文章の中で理解し、書けるようになることを目標としています。

2. 漢字の選定と構成

　この教材では、日本語能力試験のN5とN4で出題頻度の高い漢字、及び他の漢字の構成要素となっている漢字を含めた、512字の漢字を選びました。現在の日本語能力試験では、レベルごとの漢字や語彙の基準は公開されていないため、旧日本語能力試験の出題基準を参考にしています。そして、これらの漢字を1課16字ずつ、全32課に分け、能力試験N5レベル相当の漢字から、N4、N3相当へと段階的に導入していきます。全体は以下のように、Part 1からPart 3までの3レベルに分けています。

	課	漢字
Part 1	1−10課	N5 レベル 160 字（日本語能力試験旧4級漢字をすべて含む）
Part 2	11−20課	N4 レベル 160 字（日本語能力試験旧3級漢字をすべて含む）
Part 3	21−32課	N3 レベル 192 字（日本語能力試験旧2級漢字を中心とする）

3. 教材の特徴

●楽しいイラストとストーリーで簡単に漢字を覚えられる

　学習者は、テキストの各漢字に提示されたイラストとストーリーを通して、漢字の形と意味を関連づけて楽しく覚えることができます。イラストは、象形文字をもとにしたものもあれば、字源とは関係なく作成したものもあります。

●漢字辞書のように使えるテキスト

　各漢字では、イラスト以外に、漢字の意味、読み方、画数、書き順、その漢字の構成要素や間違えやすい漢字、その漢字を使った語彙が一目で参照できるようにしました。巻末のさまざまなさくいんを合わせて利用することで、初級学習者が漢字辞書のように使えます。

●ワークブックでより深く漢字が身につく

　ワークブック（別売）といっしょに学ぶことで、漢字や単語レベルだけでなく、文や文章の中で漢字が学習できます。

●効率よく自習ができる

　テキストに収録した漢字語彙は、日本語能力試験の語彙レベルを参考にして、学習者が覚えるべき語彙に印をつけ、自習しやすくしました。ワークブックでもこれらの語彙を練習するので、初中級の学習者が必要な漢字と語彙を効率よく学習できます。

1. Targeted Users and Purpose

This book is designed primarily for learners from cultures that do not use Chinese characters. It presents 512 beginning- and intermediate-level kanji along with illustrations and mnemonic hints that make it fun and easy to learn the characters. By studying with this textbook and practicing with the companion workbook, users should become able to comprehend beginning- and intermediate-level kanji they come across in reading, and to write those characters from memory.

2. Selection and Composition of Kanji Presented

The 512 kanji presented in this book were selected on the basis of several factors, such as their having a higher frequency of appearance in levels N4 and N5 of the Japanese Language Proficiency Test (JLPT), and their use as parts of other kanji. Reference was made to the pre-revision JLPT's test material selection criteria, since the criteria for the current format are not published. This book is divided into 32 lessons, each of which covers 16 kanji. The characters are presented in order of their JLPT classification, starting with those equivalent to level N5 and gradually working up to those equivalent to level N3. The lessons are grouped into three parts according to their JLPT level, as indicated below.

	Lessons	Kanji
Part 1	1–10	160 characters, including all former JLPT level 4 kanji
Part 2	11–20	160 characters, including all former JLPT level 3 kanji
Part 3	21–32	192 characters, mainly from former JLPT level 2

3. Features of This Book

● **Kanji can be easily learned through fun illustrations and mnemonic hints**

The fun illustrations and mnemonic hints that accompany the kanji presented in this book provide a link between each character's shape and its meaning, making it easier for users to commit the kanji to memory. Some illustrations are based on pictograms, while others were freely created with no relationship to the character's origin.

● **The book doubles as a kanji dictionary**

This book is designed to allow users to readily look up the meaning, readings, stroke count, and stroke order of kanji, as well as the kanji that form part of other characters, easily confused kanji, and words incorporating particular kanji. By referring to the various indexes included at the end of the book, beginning learners can use this book like a kanji dictionary.

● **Workbook helps users to gain a firmer grasp of kanji**

Using the companion workbook (sold separately) in conjunction with this book enables users to learn kanji not only at the level of characters and words, but also in the context of sentences and longer text.

● **Kanji can be learned efficiently**

The kanji vocabulary in this book that should be studied for particular levels of the JLPT have been shaded to make it easier for learners to focus on them. These expressions are also practiced in the workbook to allow beginning and intermediate students to efficiently learn the necessary kanji.

4. 漢字表の見方

各漢字の表は以下のようになっています。

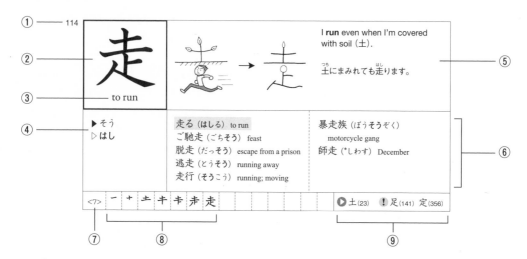

①**漢字番号**　本書での漢字の通し番号です。

②**漢字**

③**漢字の意味**（英語）

④**漢字の読み方**

・　▶がついているのは「音読み」、つまり中国語から伝わった読み方です。▷がついているのは「訓読み」、つまり漢字の持つ意味を日本の言葉に当てはめた読み方です。

・　読みは、▶▷ごとに、語彙リスト（⑥）の順番に合わせて提出されています。

・　ここに挙げた読みには、常用漢字表に示された読みがすべて含まれています。

・　漢字の読み方は、音読みも訓読みも、語彙の中で使われる時、促音や濁音などに音が変化する場合があります。⑥にそのような語彙が載っている場合は、その読み方もこの部分に表示しています。

・　太字の読みは、この課で覚えたほうがいい読み方です。これは、⑥で網がけになっている語彙（覚えたほうがいい語彙）で使われる読み方です。

⑤**ストーリー**

・　漢字の関連づけを助けるストーリーです。英語の説明文の中で太字になっている言葉は、その漢字の意味にあたる言葉です。イラストを見ながらこの文を読むことで、漢字の字形と意味を結びつけ、覚えやすくなります。また、文の中で（　）で示した漢字は、その漢字の構成要素、または関連のある漢字です。すでに学習した漢字と関連づけることによって新しい漢字が容易に覚えられるように配慮しています。

・　日本語訳もつけました。

⑥**語彙リスト**

　その漢字を含んだ語彙のうち、よく使われるものと多様な読み方をするものをリストアップして、読み方と英訳を示しました。網がけの語彙はその課で覚えたほうがいいもので、これらの語彙はワークブックで練習します。網がけの基準は以下のようになっています。

　　Part 1（第 1 課 – 第 10 課）： 主に日本語能力試験の N5 相当の語彙
　　Part 2（第 11 課 – 第 20 課）： 主に日本語能力試験の N5〜N4 相当の語彙
　　Part 3（第 21 課 – 第 32 課）： 主に日本語能力試験の N5〜N2 相当の語彙

　*がついている語彙は、④に挙げた漢字の読み方にない、特別な読み方をしているものです。

4. Kanji Tables

Each target kanji is presented in a table formatted as follows.

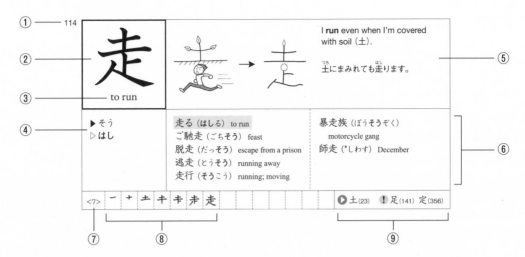

① **Entry number**   The target kanji are numbered in order of their appearance in the book.

② **Kanji**

③ **Meaning** (in English)

④ **Readings**

· Readings marked with ▶ are *on-yomi*, or readings derived from the Chinese pronunciation of the character. Those marked with ▷ are *kun-yomi*, or readings that represent the native Japanese word for the concept expressed by the character.

· Both *on-yomi* and *kun-yomi* readings are arranged in the order of their appearance in the vocabulary list (⑥) of the table.

· Each table presents all readings included in the Jōyō Kanji list (a list of 1,945 standard kanji issued by Japan's Ministry of Education in 1981).

· *On-yomi* and *kun-yomi* readings sometimes change to assimilated or voiced sounds when the kanji appears in the middle or end of a compound. Such phonetically shifted readings are also included if the table's vocabulary list contains words with those readings.

· Readings listed in bold are ones that should be studied as part of the lesson. These are readings that appear in the shaded expressions (focus words) of the table's vocabulary list.

⑤ **Mnemonic hint**

· This is a short description or scenario designed to facilitate memorization of the character. The word in bold indicates the kanji's meaning. Reading the mnemonic hint while looking at the accompanying illustration allows the user to form a mental link between the kanji's form and meaning, making it easier to remember them. Also, kanji enclosed in parentheses in the mnemonic hint are a part of the target kanji, or are related to the target kanji. This feature was added to make new kanji easier to remember by tying them to kanji already learned.

· A Japanese translation is provided for each hint.

⑥ **Vocabulary list**

This section lists expressions containing the target kanji that are frequently used or represent various readings of the target kanji. Shaded expressions are focus words that should be memorized, and are included in the workbook drills. The levels of the shaded expressions are as follows.

⑦漢字の総画数
⑧漢字の筆順
⑨その他の情報
・**参考情報**：▶は、その漢字の部分になっている漢字や要素、またはストーリーで言及している漢字です。単独の漢字の場合はその漢字の通し番号を、Kanji Parts の要素の場合は Kanji Parts での記号を提示しています。(Kanji Parts については次項を参照)
・**間違えやすい漢字**：❗には、形が似ていて学習者が混乱しやすい漢字を挙げています。誤用をしないためにも、字形の違いを意識することが大切です。

5. Kanji Parts について

　p. [26]−[27] に「Kanji Parts」のリストがあります。Kanji Parts は漢字の一部分 (構成要素) であり、それ自体で意味を持つものです。一般的には「部首」と呼ばれます。部首の数は非常に多くありますが、ここでは本書で勉強する際に知っておいたほうがいいものとして、16 の構成要素を紹介しています。

　16 の Kanji Parts には、画数順に A〜P の記号をつけました。イラストとともにその意味と筆順を提示し、本書の漢字のうちその部分を持つすべての漢字とその漢字番号を示してあります。

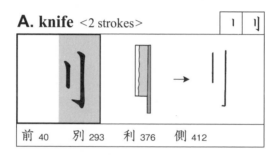

6. さくいんについて

●画数さくいん (p.198〜p.199)
　漢字の総画数の少ないものから並んでいます。同じ画数内では漢字の提出順になっています。漢字番号が示されていますので、その漢字を参照してください。漢字の総画数がわかっている場合は、このさくいんを使います。

●音訓さくいん (p.200〜p.208)
　漢字の読み方があいうえお順に並んでいます。漢字番号が示されていますので、その漢字を参照してください。漢字の読み方がわかっている場合は、このさくいんを使います。

●字形さくいん (p.209〜p.216)
　漢字はさまざまな構成要素から成っていますが、その構成要素ごとに漢字を並べたのが字形さくいんです。このさくいんは、構成要素の画数順に並んでいます。まず、調べたい漢字の構成要素をリストから探します。その構成要素を持つ漢字が漢字番号順に並んでいるので、そこから該当する漢字を見つけます。このさくいんを使えば、漢字の一部分がわかっている場合に、それを手がかりに探している漢字が見つけられます。

●語彙さくいん (p.217〜p.244)
　本書に掲載されているすべての漢字語彙が、あいうえお順に並んでいます。漢字番号が示されていますので、その漢字を参照してください。

Part 1 (Lessons 1–10):   Mainly words equivalent to JLPT level N5
Part 2 (Lessons 11–20): Mainly words equivalent to JLPT levels N4 and N5
Part 3 (Lessons 21–32): Mainly words equivalent to JLPT levels N2 to N5

Vocabulary marked with * are words in which the target kanji has an unusual reading not listed in the readings section (④) of the table.

⑦ **Stroke count**

⑧ **Stroke order**

⑨ **Additional information**

- *Reference information*: Items marked with ▶ are kanji or components that form part of the target kanji, or are kanji included in the mnemonic hint. If the item is an independent character, the entry number is given. If the item is a kanji part, the corresponding kanji part code is listed (see the following section, "Kanji Parts," for details).

- *Easily confused kanji*: Items marked with an exclamation mark (!) are kanji that are easily confused with the target kanji due to their similarity in form. It's important to take notice of the differences in shape so in order to avoid using the wrong kanji.

5. Kanji Parts

Pages [26]–[27] list kanji parts, which are components of kanji that hold meaning of their own. They are often referred to as "radicals." There are many radicals, but the kanji parts list presents just sixteen that should be memorized by users of this book. These sixteen kanji parts are arranged according to stroke order, and are coded with letters A to P. Each is presented along with its meaning, stroke order, an illustration, and all kanji in this book that incorporate the same part (the entry numbers of these kanji are also given).

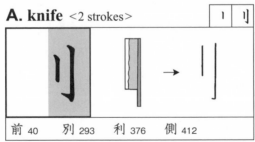

6. Indexes

● **Stroke Count Index** (pp.198-199)

The target kanji are indexed according to their stroke count, from lowest to highest. Kanji with the same stroke count are listed in their order of appearance in the book. The entry number of each kanji is also given so that users can look up a character when they know its stroke count.

● *On-Kun* **Reading Index** (pp.200-208)

This index contains kanji readings arranged in *a-i-u-e-o* order, so it can be used to look up a particular kanji when you know at least one of its readings. The corresponding kanji and its entry number are listed next to each reading.

● **Kanji Shape Index** (pp.209-216)

Kanji are made up various parts. This index arranges the target kanji according to their key parts. To look up a particular kanji, first find its key part in the kanji parts list preceding the kanji shape index (the parts are listed in stroke-count order). Next, look for the kanji in its kanji part group in the index. Kanji

7. 本教材を使った勉強の仕方

(1) 漢字の形と意味を覚える

　本書で漢字の絵とストーリーを確認しながら、それぞれの漢字の形と意味を勉強します。一見複雑に見える漢字も、部分に分ければそれほど難しくありません。わかりにくい漢字は、本書に示されている漢字の構成要素を参照して、それぞれの部分をよく見てから、全体の形をつかむようにしてみましょう。

　次に、本書の筆順を参考にしながら、漢字を書いてみましょう。ワークブックの漢字練習用のマスに書いて練習することもできます。

(2) 漢字語彙を覚える

　個々の漢字を覚えたら、漢字語彙を覚えましょう。漢字には複数の読み方を持つものが多くありますが、語彙によって読み方が違うので、漢字は語彙とともに覚えることが必要です。語彙リストで網がけになっている語彙は、その課までに習った漢字で構成されていて、かつよく使われる語彙です。これらの語彙はしっかり覚えてください。網がけされた語彙の一覧がワークブックでまとめて提示されるので、もう一度確認をするといいでしょう。

(3) 文や文章の中で読み書きする

　漢字語彙を覚えたら、語彙を使いこなせるように、ワークブックを使って、文の中で読んだり書いたりする練習をしましょう。また、ワークブックの各課には読み物があり、文章の中で漢字を読み書きする練習もできます。

(4) 繰り返し覚える

　一度覚えた漢字も使わなければ、忘れてしまいます。次の課に進むことも大切ですが、前の課に戻って何度も繰り返し見て思い出すことも、同様に大切です。ワークブックでは前に習った漢字が後の課の練習に出てくるので、学習した漢字を復習することができます。

in the same group are listed in the order of their entry number. This index allows learners to use kanji parts as a reference tool for finding specific kanji.

● **Vocabulary index** (pp.217-244)

This index lists all kanji vocabulary presented in this book, in *a-i-u-e-o* order. The details of the word's kanji can be looked up by referring to the entry number listed alongside it.

7. Methods for Studying with This Book

(1) Learning kanji shapes and meanings

Study the shape and meaning of each kanji presented by going over the illustration and mnemonic hint provided for it. Even kanji that seem dauntingly complex can be readily digested when broken down into their various parts. When faced with a troublesome kanji, get a better idea of its overall form by looking up its components in this book and closely examining their features.

After learning a kanji, practice writing it while referring to its stroke order shown in this book. The workbook has rows of squares that are handy for writing practice.

(2) Studying kanji vocabulary

After learning a particular kanji, study the accompanying list of vocabulary. Many kanji have multiple readings, and the reading used varies with the word in which the kanji appears. This means that it is necessary to learn the accompanying vocabulary in order to gain a full grip on the character's different readings. The shaded words in each vocabulary list are frequently used expressions made up of kanji that have been studied up to that point. Please be sure to solidly learn them. Also, the shaded vocabulary of each lesson are recompiled into lists in the workbook, so go over the words once more to firm up your understanding of them.

(3) Reading/writing kanji in context

In order to fully master the kanji vocabulary studied, use the workbook to practice reading and writing them as part of sentences. The workbook lessons also include reading material for practicing kanji reading and writing in the context of longer text.

(4) Reviewing

Kanji can be easily forgotten if not used regularly. While it is important to keep advancing to each new lesson, it is equally essential to frequently go back over past lessons. In the workbook, previously studied kanji reappear in the drills of later lessons, enabling users to review those characters.

漢字の基本

漢字について

　漢字は中国で作られた文字です。その起源にはいろいろな説があるようですが、紀元前 1500 年ごろには使われていたようです。漢字の特徴は、アルファベットのような表音文字とは異なり、意味も表す表語文字である点です。漢字は今から 1500 年以上前、中国から朝鮮半島を経て、日本に伝わったと考えられています。当時日本には文字がなかったので、日本語を書き表すために漢字が使われるようになりました。現在は日本語を書き表すのに、漢字、ひらがな、カタカナ、アルファベットが使われています。

漢字の数

　漢字はいくつあるのでしょうか。約 5 万の漢字が収められている辞典もありますが、この中には現在ほとんど使われなくなった漢字も多く含まれています。実際に新聞や雑誌で使われる漢字は 3,000 字ぐらいです。その中でも特に日常的に使うものとして政府が定めたものが常用漢字 (2,136 字) です。日本の小学校ではその中の 1,006 の漢字 (教育漢字) を学び、中学校で残りの常用漢字のほぼすべてを学びます。

　新聞や雑誌で使われる漢字の約 99％が常用漢字です。よく使う常用漢字の上位 500 字が、新聞の漢字の 8 割近くを占めています。ちなみに上位 1,000 字だと 9 割以上になります。

漢字のなりたち

　漢字はどのように作られたのでしょうか。漢字のなりたちを考えていくと、大まかに 4 種類に分類することができます。

●象形文字

　物の形を表した絵から作られた漢字です。数は多くありませんが、他の漢字の部分として多く使われるため、漢字の基本ともいえる文字です。

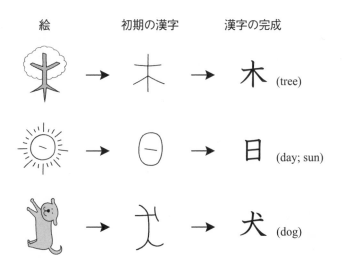

絵	初期の漢字	漢字の完成
		木 (tree)
		日 (day; sun)
		犬 (dog)

What are kanji?

Kanji are characters that were created in China. While there are various theories on their origin, the general consensus is that they were already in use by 1,500 B.C. Kanji (the Chinese characters) differ from the alphabet and other phonographic writing systems in that they are logograms, meaning that each character holds meaning in addition to expressing sound. They are believed to have been introduced to Japan via Korea more than 1,500 years ago. At that time, Japan did not have a writing system of its own, so the Chinese characters were adopted to write Japanese. Today, Japanese is written using a mixture of kanji, *hiragana*, *katakana*, and the alphabet.

How many are there?

Just how many kanji exist? There are Chinese character dictionaries that list roughly 50,000 characters, but most of them have fallen out of common use. Japanese newspapers and magazines employ about 3,000 kanji. Of that number, 2,136 were designated by the Japanese government as commonly used kanji—the Jōyō Kanji. A total of 1,006 Jōyō Kanji are taught at the elementary school level (referred to as Kyōiku Kanji), and most of the remainder are taught in junior high school.

Nearly 99% of the kanji appearing in newspapers and magazines are Jōyō Kanji. The 500 most frequently used kanji account for almost 80% of all newspaper kanji, and the 1,000 most frequently used kanji cover more than 90%.

Types of Kanji

How were kanji created? They can be largely divided into the following four types based on their formation.

● **Pictograms**

Some kanji are pictograms, which are characters that pictorially represent certain things. While few in number, pictographic kanji are frequently used as parts of other kanji, so they can be considered fundamental characters.

Picture	Early kanji	Modern kanji
	→ 十 →	木 (tree)
	→ ⊝ →	日 (day; sun)
	→ 尤 →	犬 (dog)

●指事文字
絵にすることが難しい抽象的な概念や数字を点や線を使って表した漢字です。

三 → 三 (three)　　　ヽ → 上 (up)

●会意文字
2つ以上の漢字を組み合わせて作った漢字です。

木 (tree)　　＋　　木 (tree)　　＝　　林 (small forest)

日 (day; sun)　　＋　　月 (moon)　　＝　　明 (bright)

●形声文字
　意味を示す部分と音を示す部分を組み合わせて作った漢字です。現在使われている漢字の8割以上が形声文字だとも言われています。

意味を示す部分	音を示す部分	音読み
日 (day; sun) ＋	寺〈ジ〉(temple) ＝	時〈ジ〉(time)
扌 (hand) ＋	寺〈ジ〉(temple) ＝	持〈ジ〉(to hold)
言 (to say) ＋	寺〈ジ〉(temple) ＝	詩〈シ*〉(poem)

＊このように同じ音でなく、似ている音になる場合も多く見られます。

部首
　一見複雑そうな漢字でも、よく見てみるといくつかの部分に分けられることがわかります。実際、多くの漢字は部分の組み合わせでできています。その部分のうち、漢字の意味と関わりの深い部分を「部首」(radical) と呼びます。部首は漢字の中の位置により、7つに分けることができます。「人」や「木」など、それ自体が部首でもあり、単独の漢字でもあるものと、「亻」や「宀」など、単独では漢字にならないものがあります。

① 偏（へん：left）一番多いのがこのタイプです。　　体 校 話

② 冠（かんむり：top）　　字 今 答

③ 脚（あし：bottom）　　見 買 然

④ 構（かまえ：enclosure）　　国 聞 医 凶

⑤ 垂（たれ：upper left）　　広 病 屋

⑥ 繞（にょう：lower left）　　道 建 起

⑦ 旁（つくり：right）　　別 都 頭

• Simple ideograms

These are kanji that use dots and lines to represent numbers and abstract concepts that would be difficult to depict with pictograms.

三 → 三 (three)　　　　　　　∴ → 上 (up)

• Compound ideograms

These are kanji formed from the combination of two or more kanji.

木 (tree)　　+　　木 (tree)　　=　　林 (small forest)

日 (day; sun)　+　月 (moon)　=　明 (bright)

• Phonetic-ideographic characters

These kanji are made up of an element that expresses meaning and an element that represents a sound. It is said that more than 80% of the kanji used today fall into this category.

Meaning part		Sound part		On-yomi
日 (day; sun)	+	寺 <ji> (temple)	=	時 <ji> (time)
扌 (hand)	+	寺 <ji> (temple)	=	持 <ji> (to hold)
言 (to say)	+	寺 <ji> (temple)	=	詩 <shi*> (poem)

*This is an example of the many cases where the sound part of a phonetic-ideographic kanji is used to represent a slightly different sound.

Radicals

Close inspection of even the most intricate kanji reveals that they are made up of several simpler parts. In fact, the vast majority of kanji are combinations of various subunits. The part that is most closely tied to the character's meaning is called a radical. Depending on their position within a kanji, the radicals are classified into the seven categories indicated below. Some radicals can stand on their own as kanji, such as 人 and 木, while others like 彳 and 宀 are not used as independent characters.

① Left (*hen*)　This is the most common type of radical.　　体 校 話

② Top (*kanmuri*)　　字 今 答

③ Bottom (*ashi*)　　見 買 然

④ Enclosure (*kamae*)　　国 聞 医 凶

⑤ upper left (*tare*)　　広 病 屋

⑥ Lower left (*nyō*)　　道 建 起

⑦ Right (*tsukuri*)　　別 都 頭

漢字の読み方

中国で使われている漢字の場合、基本的に一つの漢字は一つの読みしか持っていません。しかし、日本語の漢字の多くは複数の読みを持っています。漢字の読みには「音読み（Chinese readings）」と「訓読み（Japanese readings）」の2種類あります。

音読み：音読みはずっと昔、古くは千数百年前に中国で読まれていた読み方がもとになっています。複数の音読みを持つ漢字があるのは、中国国内で時代または地域差により変化してきた漢字の読みを、日本ではそのまま受け継いでいるからです。たとえば、「人」の音読みには「ニン」と「ジン」がありますが、「ジン」は「ニン」よりも後になって中国から伝わった読み方です。

訓読み：日本に漢字が伝わった当時、漢字は音読みで読まれていました。一方、それだけでは不便なため、日本語本来の言葉も漢字を使って記そうとした結果、生まれたのが訓読みです。たとえば「人」は "ひと（person）" という意味の漢字なので、この漢字を「ひと」とも読むようになりました。

漢字の書き方

●書き方の基本　横の線を書くときは左から右へ、縦の線を書くときは上から下へ書きます。

① 左から右へ

② 上から下へ

●筆の終わり方の基本

① とめ（stop）　　　　　ペンをしっかりと止めます。

② はらい（stretch）　　　ペンを止めずに自然にはらいます。

③ はね（hook）　　　　　ペンを止めて反対方向にはねます。

●書き順の基本

① 上から下へ　　　　　　　　　　　　三（一 二 三）

② 左から右へ　　　　　　　　　　　　川（丿 川 川）

③ 交差する場合は横が先　　　　　　　十（一 十）

④ 左右対称は中が先　　　　　　　　　小（丿 小 小）

⑤ 囲むときは外が先、ただし下の線は一番最後　回（丨 冂 冂 冋 回 回）

⑥ 貫くときは最後　　　　　　　　　　中（丨 冂 口 中）

上記6つの基本に当てはまらないものもあります。書き順は右手で書く場合に一番書きやすいとされてきた順番です。漢字の形を整えるためにも、画数を数えるためにも、筆順は大切です。気をつけて一つ一つの漢字を正しい書き順で書くように心がけましょう。

Kanji Readings

Chinese characters as used in China generally have one reading. In contrast, most Japanese kanji possess multiple readings, which are divided into *on-yomi* (Chinese readings) and *kun-yomi* (Japanese readings).

On-yomi: These readings are derived from the pronunciations used in China in the distant past, more than a millennium ago in some cases. The reason why certain kanji have multiple *on-yomi* is that temporal and regional variances in the Chinese pronunciation were imported along with the characters. For example, the *on-yomi* of 人 are *nin* and *jin*; *nin* was the reading initially introduced to Japan, while *jin* was adopted in a later era.

Kun-yomi: When Chinese characters were transplanted to Japan, they were read with only the Chinese pronunciations at first. Since this limited the range of expression for the Japanese language, kanji started to also be used for writing native Japanese words corresponding to the characters' meaning, marking the birth of the *kun-yomi*. As one example, the kanji 人 means "person," so it came to also be read as *hito*, the corresponding Japanese word.

Writing Kanji

• Basic stroke directions

Horizontal strokes are written from left to right. Vertical strokes are written from top to bottom.

① Left to right

② Top to bottom

• Basic stroke endings

① Stop (*tome*)　　　The pen is stopped sharply.

② Stretch (*harai*)　　The pen is gently lifted to create a sweeping stroke end.

③ Hook (*hane*)　　　The pen is stopped and then pulled backward to make a hook.

• Basic stroke order

① Top to bottom　　　　　　　　　　　　　三 （ 一 二 三 ）

② Left to right　　　　　　　　　　　　　川 （ 丿 川 川 ）

③ Horizontal strokes precede intersecting vertical strokes　十 （ 一 十 ）

④ Center strokes precede smaller side strokes　　　小 （ 亅 小 小 ）

⑤ Enclosures come first, but the bottom stroke is written last　回 （ 丨 冂 冂 冋 同 回 ）

⑥ Piercing strokes are written last　　　　　　中 （ 丶 冂 口 中 ）

There are some exceptions to the six rules noted above. The stroke orders are considered the easiest way to write kanji right-handed, and a proper knowledge of them is important for writing well-structured characters and counting strokes. Try to learn each kanji in its correct stroke order.

フォントによる字形の違い

フォントによって漢字が違って見えるときがあります。また、手書きの場合も、人によっては崩したり、省略したりして、本来の漢字と少し違う場合があります。

教科書体	明朝体	ゴシック体	手書き
道	道	道	道
北	北	北	北
長	長	長	長
入	入	入	入
心	心	心	心

漢字の辞書の使い方

辞書で漢字を調べるには、以下の三つの方法があります。

1. **読み方から調べる** 調べたい漢字の読み方（音読みでも、訓読みでもかまいません）がわかれば、その読み方から漢字を調べることができます。
2. **部首から調べる** 漢字の部首がわかれば、その部首を持つ漢字のリストから調べたい漢字を探すことができます。
3. **画数から調べる** 読み方も部首もわからないときは、漢字の総画数から調べることができます。総画数を数えて、画数ごとのリストから調べたい漢字を見つけます。

電子辞書によっては、調べたい漢字を付属のペンで書けばその漢字を調べることができるものもあります。

＜例：「姓」という字を調べてみましょう＞

1. **読み方から** 「セイ」という読み方がわかれば、それから調べられます。（読み方を知らなくても、推測できる場合もあります。「姓」の右側の部分「生」は学生「ガクセイ」の「セイ」です。この漢字も「セイ」と読みます。）
2. **部首から** この漢字の部首は「女」（おんなへん）でその画数は3です。この部首を、画数3の部首リストの中から探し出します。そして、「姓」は「女」の部首を含む漢字のリストから見つけられます。
3. **画数から** 総画数を数えます。「姓」は8画ですから、8画の漢字の中から「姓」を探し出します。

送り仮名

形容詞や動詞などの活用する語は、漢字とひらがなで書きます。そのひらがなの部分を「送り仮名」と言います。たとえば、「食べます」の「べます」が送り仮名です。漢字を覚えるとき、「食」の漢字の読みが「た」か「たべ」なのか、注意して覚える必要があります。送り仮名になる部分は漢字によって違うので、漢字を覚えるときに注意して覚えましょう。

動詞：	行く	行かない	形容詞：	大きい	大きくない
	食べる	食べない		長い	長くない

Font-based Variations in Form

The shape of kanji in print often varies according to the font used, sometimes to the point that the same kanji can appear to be a completely different character. Also, handwritten kanji may diverge slightly from their printed form, as some writers tend to use cursive styles or abbreviate parts of characters.

Kyōkasho font	*Minchō* font	*Goshikku* font	Handwriting
道	道	道	道
北	北	北	北
長	長	長	長
入	入	入	入
心	心	心	心

Using Kanji Dictionaries

There are three keys for looking up characters in a kanji dictionary, as described below.

1. **Reading**   If you know at least one of the target character's readings (*on-yomi* or *kun-yomi*), you can use it to find the character in the dictionary's reading index.

2. **Radical**   If you know character's radical, you can search for the target character in the dictionary's listings of kanji with the same radical.

3. **Stroke count**   In cases where you don't know the target character's reading or radical, count its strokes and look for it in the dictionary's listings of kanji with the same stroke count.

Some electronic dictionaries have a stylus that allows the user to look up kanji by writing it on the screen.

<Kanji search example: Finding 姓>

1. **Reading**   If you know that 姓 is read *sei*, you can use this clue to find the character in the dictionary's reading index. Even if you don't know the reading of a certain kanji, you may be able to guess it sometimes. In this example, the right part of 姓 is the same 生 found in 学生 (*gakusei*). Since 生 is usually read as *sei*, you could infer that 姓 is also read *sei*.

2. **Radical**   The radical of 姓 is 女 (*onna-hen*), which consists of three strokes. Look for this radical in the dictionary's index of three-stroke radicals in order to locate the listing of all kanji with the *onna-hen* radical. Next, go to that group and scan for 姓.

3. **Stroke count**   Count the number of strokes. 姓 is made up of eight strokes, so you would search for it among the dictionary's listing of 8-stroke kanji.

Okurigana

Adjectives, verbs, and other conjugated words are written with kanji and *hiragana*. The *hiragana* portion is called *okurigana*. For instance, the *okurigana* of 食べます is べます. When learning kanji, you need to pay attention to the extent of their readings, such as whether 食 is read as *ta* or as *tabe*. This point needs to be kept in mind for each kanji, since the extent of the *okurigana* portion of conjugated words varies with every kanji.

動詞：	い 行く	行かない		形容詞：	おお 大きい	大きくない
	た 食べる	食べない			なが 長い	長くない

漢字を読むヒント

　多くの漢字は、意味を表す部分と音読みの音を表す部分を持っています。知らない漢字を見たときは、その中に含まれている、音を表す部分を探してみましょう。同じ音読みをする場合があります。

＜同じ音を表す部分を持つ漢字の例＞

　　生　姓　性　星 ………… 音読みはすべて「セイ」

　　寺　時　持　侍 ………… 音読みはすべて「ジ」

　　青　晴　静　精 ………… 音読みはすべて「セイ」

　熟語の場合、「音楽（オン・ガク）」のようにどちらの漢字も音読みにすることが多いですから、読み方がわからないときは、まず音読みしてみるといいでしょう。しかし下の例のように、両方の漢字を訓読みで読む場合や、音読みと訓読みが混ざる場合もあります。

＜訓＋訓＞	名前（な・まえ）	手紙（て・がみ）
＜音＋訓＞	本屋（ホン・や）	駅前（エキ・まえ）
＜訓＋音＞	場所（ば・ショ）	古本（ふる・ホン）

熟語の中での音の変化

　日本語では、二つ以上の語をつなげて複合語を作る場合、後にくる音が「゛」のつく音、つまり濁音になる場合があります。また、「〜つ」「〜く」「〜き」などの音の後に別の語がくると、「つ」「く」「き」が小さい「っ」に変わる場合もあります。これらの変化がどんなときに起こるか、はっきりとした規則はありません。ほとんどの辞書では、漢字の「読み方」にこれらの変化した音は書いてありません。

「゛」に変化する場合：

　　旅行（りょこう）　＋　会社（かいしゃ）　→　旅行会社（りょこうがいしゃ）

　　勉強（べんきょう）　＋　机（つくえ）　→　勉強机（べんきょうづくえ）

「っ」に変化する場合：

　　百（ひゃく）　＋　回（かい）　→　百回（ひゃっかい）

　　別（べつ）　＋　世界（せかい）　→　別世界（べっせかい）

Reading Unfamiliar Kanji

● Single kanji

Most kanji combine a part that indicates meaning and a part that represents sound. Whenever you come across an unfamiliar kanji, try to pinpoint its sound part. You might be able to figure out the character's reading if you know the reading of other kanji with the same part.

<Examples of kanji with the same sound part>

生　姓　性　星　·········· All are read *sei* in their *on-yomi*.

寺　時　持　侍　·········· All are read *ji* in their *on-yomi*.

青　晴　静　精　·········· All are read *sei* in their *on-yomi*.

● Kanji compound

Both characters in a kanji compound are usually read in their *on-yomi*, such as the reading *on-gaku* of 音楽, so when you don't know the reading of a compound, first try the *on-yomi* of its kanji. However, note that there are compounds in which one or both kanji are read with the *kun-yomi*, as seen in the examples below.

kun + *kun*:　名前 (*na · mae*)　手紙 (*te · gami*)

on + *kun*:　本屋 (*HON · ya*)　駅前 (*EKI · mae*)

kun + *on*:　場所 (*ba · SHO*)　古本 (*furu · HON*)

Phonetic Shifts in Compounds

In compound words, the component words that do not come at the start of the compound sometimes shift to voiced sounds—that is, the diacritical mark (゛) is added to the component's first syllable. Also, certain sounds like *tsu*, *ku*, and *ki* sometimes become a small *tsu* when they end a component word preceding another component word. However, there are no clear rules for when these phonetic shifts occur. Most kanji dictionaries do not list the shifted pronunciations among the character's readings.

Examples of shifting to voiced sounds (゛)

旅行 (*ryokō*)　+　会社 (**kaisha**)　→　旅行会社 (*ryokōgaisha*)
travel　　　　　　company　　　　　　　travel agency

勉強 (*benkyō*)　+　机 (**tsukue**)　→　勉強机 (*benkyōzukue*)
study　　　　　　desk　　　　　　　　study desk

Examples of shifting to small *tsu* (つ)

百 (**hyaku**)　+　回 (*kai*)　→　百回 (*hyakkai*)
one hundred　　　~ times　　　　one hundred times

別 (**betsu**)　+　世界 (*sekai*)　→　別世界 (*bessekai*)
different　　　　world　　　　　　another world

KANJI PARTS（おもな構成要素）

A. knife <2 strokes>

	リ

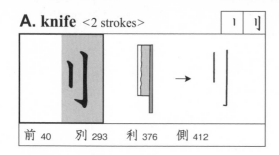

前 40	別 293	利 376	側 412

B. person <2 strokes>

ノ	イ

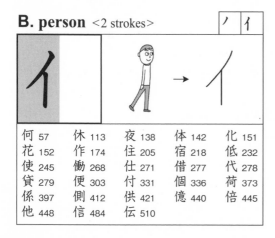

何 57	休 113	夜 138	体 142	化 151
花 152	作 174	住 205	宿 218	低 232
使 245	働 268	仕 271	借 277	代 278
貸 279	便 303	付 331	個 336	荷 373
係 397	側 412	供 421	億 440	倍 445
他 448	信 484	伝 510		

C. human legs <2 strokes>

ノ	儿

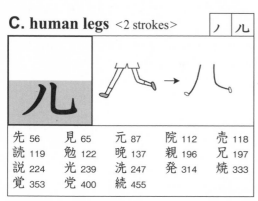

先 56	見 65	元 87	院 112	売 118
読 119	勉 122	晩 137	親 196	兄 197
説 224	光 239	洗 247	発 314	焼 333
覚 353	党 400	続 455		

D. street <3 strokes>

ノ	ク	彳

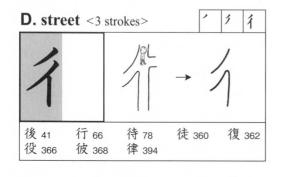

後 41	行 66	待 78	徒 360	復 362
役 366	彼 368	律 394		

E. enclosure <3 strokes>

｜	冂	口

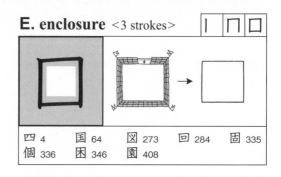

四 4	国 64	図 273	回 284	固 335
個 336	困 346	園 408		

F. road <3 strokes>

`	⻌	辶

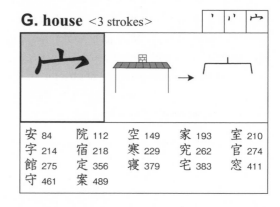

週 80	道 144	遠 225	近 226	運 241
送 246	通 319	進 320	違 365	遊 401
込 409	連 410	選 458	過 462	速 469
遅 470	達 492			

G. house <3 strokes>

`	⼍	宀

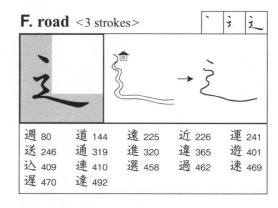

安 84	院 112	空 149	家 193	室 210
字 214	宿 218	寒 229	究 262	官 274
館 275	定 356	寝 379	宅 383	窓 411
守 461	案 489			

H. roof <3 strokes>

`	一	广

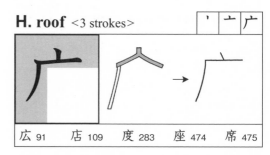

広 91	店 109	度 283	座 474	席 475

I. hand <3 strokes>

| | | ─ | 十 | 扌 |

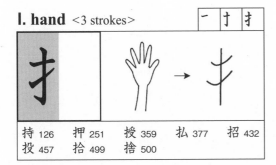

| 持 126 | 押 251 | 授 359 | 払 377 | 招 432 |
| 投 457 | 拾 499 | 捨 500 | | |

M. altar <4 strokes>

| | | ` | ラ | ネ | ネ |

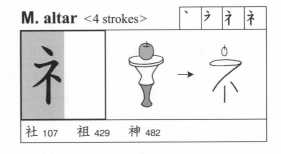

| 社 107 | 祖 429 | 神 482 |

J. water <3 strokes>

| | | ` | ; | シ |

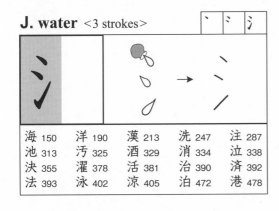

海 150	洋 190	漢 213	洗 247	注 287
池 313	汚 325	酒 329	消 334	泣 338
決 355	濯 378	活 381	治 390	済 392
法 393	泳 402	涼 405	泊 472	港 478

N. fire <4 strokes>

| | | ' | '' | ''' | ''''|

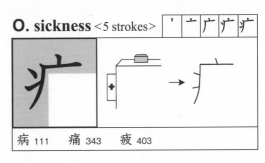

| 黒 157 | 魚 159 | 熱 322 | 点 441 | 無 512 |

O. sickness <5 strokes>

| | | ` | 亠 | 广 | 广 | 疒 |

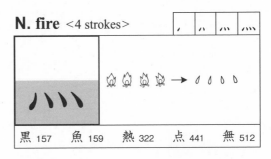

| 病 111 | 痛 343 | 疲 403 |

K. grass <3 strokes>

| | | ─ | 十 | 艹 |

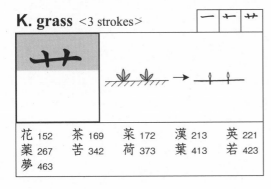

花 152	茶 169	菜 172	漢 213	英 221
薬 267	苦 342	荷 373	葉 413	若 423
夢 463				

P. rice plant <5 strokes>

| | | ノ | 二 | 千 | 禾 | 禾 |

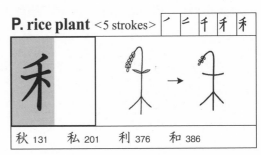

| 秋 131 | 私 201 | 利 376 | 和 386 |

L. heart <3 strokes>

| | | ' | '' | 忄 |

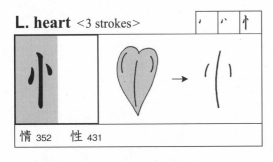

| 情 352 | 性 431 |

Part 1

第1課 － 第10課
_{だい} _か _{だい} _か

（漢字番号 1-160)
_{かん じ ばん ごう}

第　1　課

●この課の漢字

一	二	三	四	五	六	七	八
1	2	3	4	5	6	7	8

九	十	百	千	万	円	口	目
9	10	11	12	13	14	15	16

1

一

one

One is represented by **one** finger.

一本の指で示したのが「一」です。

▶いち　いっ
　いつ
▷ひと

一（いち）one
一つ（ひとつ）one
一時（いちじ）one o'clock
一分（いっぷん）one minute
一月（いちがつ）January

一日（いちにち）one day
一日（*ついたち）
　　the 1st (of the month)
一人（ひとり）one person
一番（いちばん）number one

<1>

2

二

two

Two is represented by **two** fingers.

二本の指で示したのが「二」です。

▶に
▷ふた

二（に）two
二つ（ふたつ）two
二時（にじ）two o'clock
二月（にがつ）February
二人（ふたり）two people

二日（*ふつか）the 2nd (of the month);
　　two days
二十日（*はつか）20 days; the 20th
　　(of the month)
二十歳（*はたち／にじゅっさい）
　　20 years old

<2>

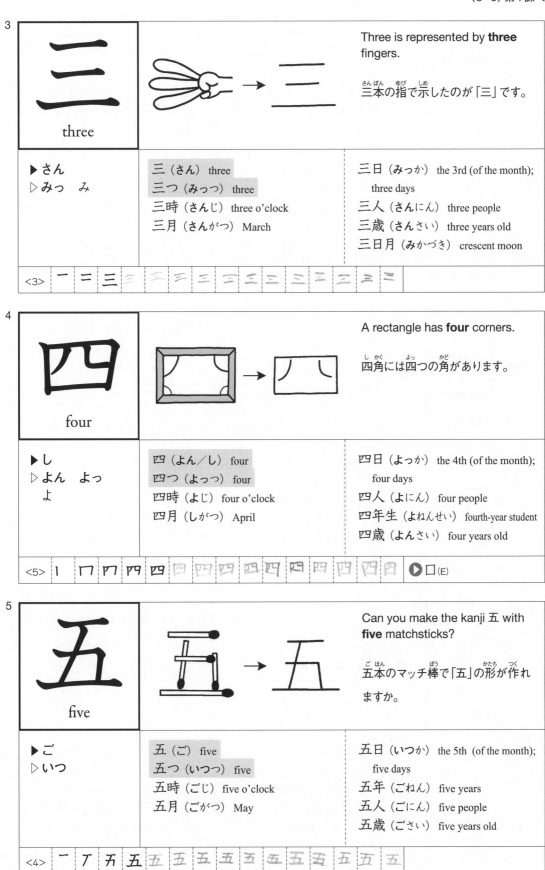

3

三
three

Three is represented by **three** fingers.

三本の指で示したのが「三」です。

▶ さん
▷ みっ　み

三（さん）three
三つ（みっつ）three
三時（さんじ）three o'clock
三月（さんがつ）March

三日（みっか）the 3rd (of the month); three days
三人（さんにん）three people
三歳（さんさい）three years old
三日月（みかづき）crescent moon

<3> 一 二 三

4

四
four

A rectangle has **four** corners.

四角には四つの角があります。

▶ し
▷ よん　よっ
　よ

四（よん／し）four
四つ（よっつ）four
四時（よじ）four o'clock
四月（しがつ）April

四日（よっか）the 4th (of the month); four days
四人（よにん）four people
四年生（よねんせい）fourth-year student
四歳（よんさい）four years old

<5> 丨 冂 冈 四 四　⏵ 口 (E)

5

五
five

Can you make the kanji 五 with **five** matchsticks?

五本のマッチ棒で「五」の形が作れますか。

▶ ご
▷ いつ

五（ご）five
五つ（いつつ）five
五時（ごじ）five o'clock
五月（ごがつ）May

五日（いつか）the 5th (of the month); five days
五年（ごねん）five years
五人（ごにん）five people
五歳（ごさい）five years old

<4> 一 丆 五 五

6

六
six

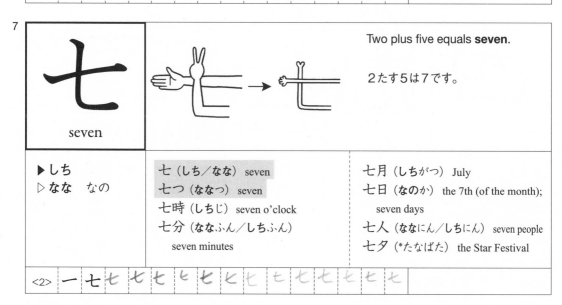

This is how Chinese people show **six** with their fingers.

中国の人は、6をこうやって表します。

▶ろく　ろっ
▷むっ　むい
　む

六 (ろく) six
六つ (むっつ) six
六百 (ろっぴゃく) six hundred
六時 (ろくじ) six o'clock
六分 (ろっぷん) six minutes

六月 (ろくがつ) June
六日 (むいか) the 6th (of the month); six days
六人 (ろくにん) six people

<4>　、　一　亠　六　六　六　六　六　六　六　六　六　六　六

7

七
seven

Two plus five equals **seven**.

2たす5は7です。

▶しち
▷なな　なの

七 (しち／なな) seven
七つ (ななつ) seven
七時 (しちじ) seven o'clock
七分 (ななふん／しちふん) seven minutes

七月 (しちがつ) July
七日 (なのか) the 7th (of the month); seven days
七人 (ななにん／しちにん) seven people
七夕 (*たなばた) the Star Festival

<2>　一　七　七　七　七　七　七　七　七　七　七　七　七　七

8

八
eight

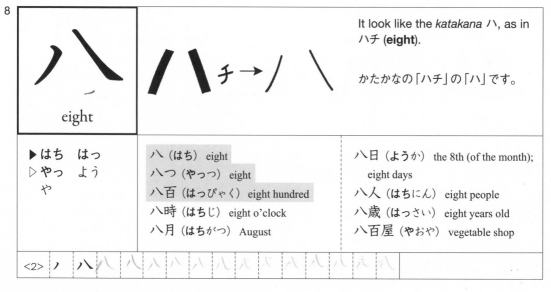

It look like the *katakana* ハ, as in ハチ (**eight**).

かたかなの「ハチ」の「ハ」です。

▶はち　はっ
▷やっ　よう
　や

八 (はち) eight
八つ (やっつ) eight
八百 (はっぴゃく) eight hundred
八時 (はちじ) eight o'clock
八月 (はちがつ) August

八日 (ようか) the 8th (of the month); eight days
八人 (はちにん) eight people
八歳 (はっさい) eight years old
八百屋 (やおや) vegetable shop

<2>　ノ　八　八　八　八　八　八　八　八　八　八　八　八　八

9

九
nine

"Can you do ten push-ups?"
"Seven, eight, **nine** … No."

「10回腕立て伏せができますか。」
「7、8、9……だめだ。」

▶ きゅう　く
▷ ここの

九（きゅう／く）nine
九つ（ここのつ）nine
九時（くじ）nine o'clock
九月（くがつ）September

九日（ここのか）the 9th (of the month); nine days
九年（きゅうねん／くねん）nine years
九歳（きゅうさい）nine years old
九人（きゅうにん／くにん）nine people

<2>　ノ　九　九　九　九　九　九　九　九　九　九　九　　！丸（321）

10

十
ten

Let's bind **ten** of these.

10本を束ねましょう。

▶ じゅう　じっ
　じゅっ
▷ とお　と

十（じゅう／とお）ten
十時（じゅうじ）ten o'clock
十分（じっぷん／じゅっぷん）
　ten minutes
十月（じゅうがつ）October

十日（とおか）the 10th (of the month); ten days
十人（じゅうにん）ten people
十歳（じっさい／じゅっさい）
　ten years old
十分（じゅうぶん）enough

<2>　一　十　十　十　十　十　十　十　十　十　十　十

11

百
hundred

Turn "**100**" 90 degrees to the right and it looks like 百.

100を90度右へ回転すると、「百」のようになります。

▶ ひゃく　びゃく
　ぴゃく　ひゃっ

百（ひゃく）hundred
二百（にひゃく）two hundred
三百（さんびゃく）three hundred
六百（ろっぴゃく）six hundred
八百（はっぴゃく）eight hundred

八百屋（*やおや）vegetable shop
百科事典（ひゃっかじてん）
　encyclopedia
百貨店（ひゃっかてん）
　department store

<6>　一　一　丆　丆　百　百　百　百　百　百　百　百　百　　▶ 白（156）

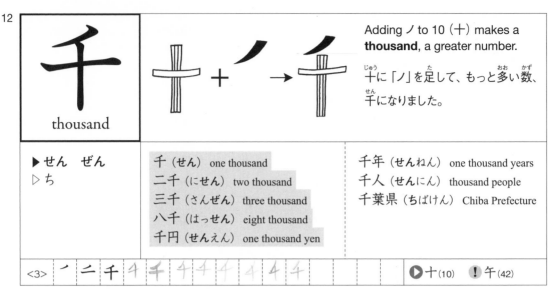

12

千

thousand

Adding ノ to 10 (十) makes a **thousand**, a greater number.

十に「ノ」を足して、もっと多い数、千になりました。

▶ せん　ぜん
▷ ち

千 (せん)　one thousand
二千 (にせん)　two thousand
三千 (さんぜん)　three thousand
八千 (はっせん)　eight thousand
千円 (せんえん)　one thousand yen

千年 (せんねん)　one thousand years
千人 (せんにん)　thousand people
千葉県 (ちばけん)　Chiba Prefecture

<3>　ノ　二　千

▶十(10)　!午(42)

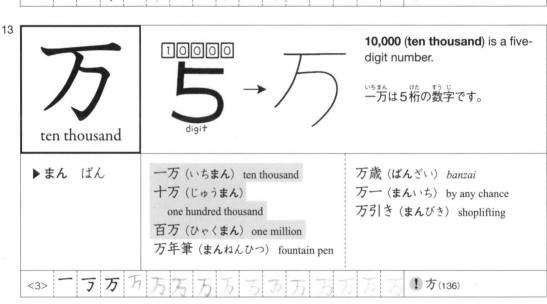

13

万

ten thousand

10,000 (ten thousand) is a five-digit number.

一万は5桁の数字です。

▶ まん　ばん

一万 (いちまん)　ten thousand
十万 (じゅうまん)
　　one hundred thousand
百万 (ひゃくまん)　one million
万年筆 (まんねんひつ)　fountain pen

万歳 (ばんざい)　*banzai*
万一 (まんいち)　by any chance
万引き (まんびき)　shoplifting

<3>　一　フ　万

!方(136)

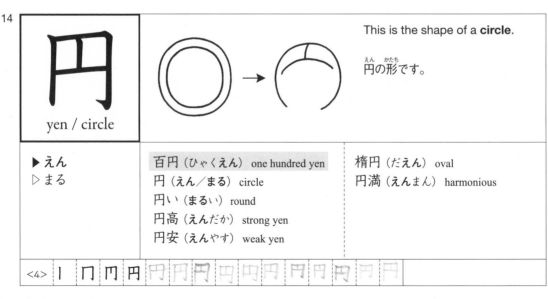

14

円

yen / circle

This is the shape of a **circle**.

円の形です。

▶ えん
▷ まる

百円 (ひゃくえん)　one hundred yen
円 (えん／まる)　circle
円い (まるい)　round
円高 (えんだか)　strong yen
円安 (えんやす)　weak yen

楕円 (だえん)　oval
円満 (えんまん)　harmonious

<4>　丨　冂　冂　円

15

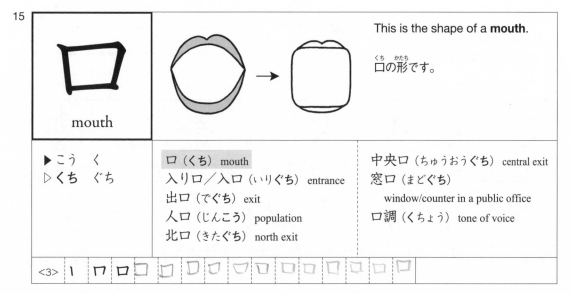

口 mouth	This is the shape of a **mouth**. 口（くち）の形（かたち）です。	

▶ こう　く
▷ くち　ぐち

口（くち）mouth
入り口／入口（いりぐち）entrance
出口（でぐち）exit
人口（じんこう）population
北口（きたぐち）north exit

中央口（ちゅうおうぐち）central exit
窓口（まどぐち）
　　window/counter in a public office
口調（くちょう）tone of voice

<3> 丨 冂 口 口 口 口 口 口 口 口 口 口 口 口 口

16

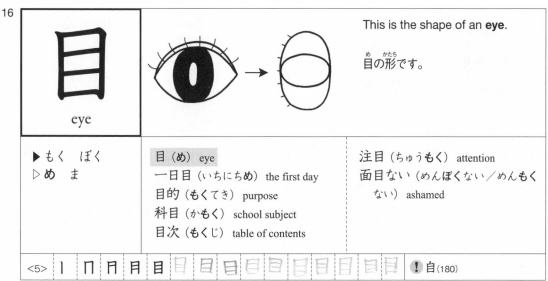

目 eye	This is the shape of an **eye**. 目（め）の形（かたち）です。	

▶ もく　ぼく
▷ め　ま

目（め）eye
一日目（いちにちめ）the first day
目的（もくてき）purpose
科目（かもく）school subject
目次（もくじ）table of contents

注目（ちゅうもく）attention
面目ない（めんぼくない／めんもく
　　ない）ashamed

<5> 丨 冂 冂 目 目 目 目 目 目 目 目 目 目 目　　❗自(180)

7

第 2 課

● この課の漢字

日	月	火	水	木	金	土	曜
17	18	19	20	21	22	23	24
本	人	今	寺	時	半	刀	分
25	26	27	28	29	30	31	32

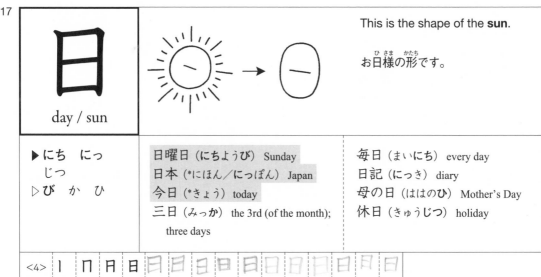

17

日
day / sun

This is the shape of the **sun**.
お日様の形です。

▶ にち　にっ
　　じつ
▷ び　か　ひ

日曜日（にちようび）Sunday
日本（*にほん／にっぽん）Japan
今日（*きょう）today
三日（みっか）the 3rd (of the month);
　　　　　three days

毎日（まいにち）every day
日記（にっき）diary
母の日（ははのひ）Mother's Day
休日（きゅうじつ）holiday

<4>　｜　冂　月　日

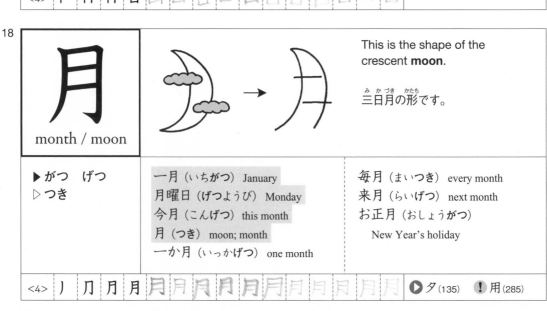

18

月
month / moon

This is the shape of the
crescent **moon**.
三日月の形です。

▶ がつ　げつ
▷ つき

一月（いちがつ）January
月曜日（げつようび）Monday
今月（こんげつ）this month
月（つき）moon; month
一か月（いっかげつ）one month

毎月（まいつき）every month
来月（らいげつ）next month
お正月（おしょうがつ）
　　New Year's holiday

<4>　丿　几　月　月　　　　▶ 夕(135)　❗ 用(285)

19

火
fire

This is the shape of **fire**.

火の形です。

▶ か
▷ ひ び ほ

火曜日（かようび）Tuesday
火（ひ）fire
火事（かじ）fire
火山（かざん）volcano
花火（はなび）fireworks

火星（かせい）Mars
消火器（しょうかき）fire extinguisher
火災（かさい）fire disaster

<4> 丶 丷 少 火

20

水
water

The **water**fall splashes around.

滝が水しぶきをあげています。

▶ すい
▷ みず

水曜日（すいようび）Wednesday
水（みず）water
水泳（すいえい）swimming
水道（すいどう）water supply
海水浴（かいすいよく）sea bathing

水着（みずぎ）bathing suit
香水（こうすい）perfume
鼻水（はなみず）snivel

<4> 丿 才 水 水

21

木
tree

This is the shape of a **tree**.

木の形です。

▶ もく ぼく
▷ き こ

木曜日（もくようび）Thursday
木（き）tree
木綿（*もめん）cotton
木村さん（きむらさん）
Mr./Ms. Kimura

木星（もくせい）Jupiter
大木（たいぼく）big tree
材木（ざいもく）lumber
木陰（こかげ）shade of a tree

<4> 一 十 才 木

！本(25) 不(302)

22

金
gold

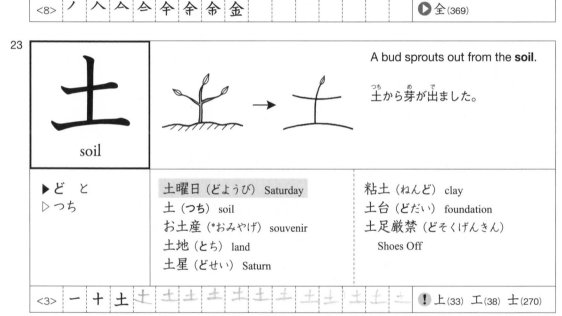

People say that there is **gold** under the mountain.

山の下に金があるそうです。

▶ きん　こん
▷ かね　かな

金曜日（きんようび）Friday	現金（げんきん）cash
お金（おかね）money	税金（ぜいきん）tax
お金持ち（おかねもち）rich person	金づち（かなづち）hammer
料金（りょうきん）charge	
奨学金（しょうがくきん）scholarship	

<8> ノ 𠆢 𠆢 合 全 全 金 金　　▶ 全(369)

23

土
soil

A bud sprouts out from the **soil**.

土から芽が出ました。

▶ ど　と
▷ つち

土曜日（どようび）Saturday	粘土（ねんど）clay
土（つち）soil	土台（どだい）foundation
お土産（*おみやげ）souvenir	土足厳禁（どそくげんきん）
土地（とち）land	Shoes Off
土星（どせい）Saturn	

<3> 一 十 土 土 土 土 土 土 土 土 土 土 土　　! 上(33) 工(38) 士(270)

24

曜
weekday

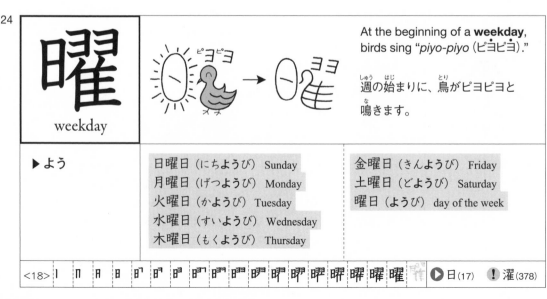

At the beginning of a **weekday**, birds sing "*piyo-piyo*（ピ˙ヨピ˙ヨ）."

週の始まりに、鳥がピヨピヨと鳴きます。

▶ よう

日曜日（にちようび）Sunday	金曜日（きんようび）Friday
月曜日（げつようび）Monday	土曜日（どようび）Saturday
火曜日（かようび）Tuesday	曜日（ようび）day of the week
水曜日（すいようび）Wednesday	
木曜日（もくようび）Thursday	

<18> l 冂 月 日 日' 日' 日' 日' 日' 日' 日' 日' 日' 晔 晔 曜 曜　　▶ 日(17)　! 濯(378)

25

本
book / base

Here is the **base** of a tree (木).
Let's mark it with "一."

ここが木(き)のもとです。「一」で
しるしをつけましょう。

▶ ほん　ぽん
　 ぼん
▷ もと

本 (ほん)　book
日本 (にほん／にっぽん)　Japan
一本 (いっぽん)　one (long object)
二本 (にほん)　two (long objects)
三本 (さんぼん)　three (long objects)

日本語 (にほんご)　Japanese language
山本さん (やまもとさん)
　　Mr./Ms. Yamamoto

<5>　一　十　才　木　本　本　本　本　本　本　本　本　本　本　▶ 木(21)

26

人
person

A **person** is standing with two
legs.

人(ひと)が二本(にほん)の足(あし)で立(た)っています。

▶ じん　にん
▷ ひと

人 (ひと)　person
日本人 (にほんじん)　Japanese people
一人 (*ひとり)　one person
二人 (*ふたり)　two people
三人 (さんにん)　three people

一人で (*ひとりで)　alone
大人 (*おとな)　adult
女の人 (おんなのひと)　woman

<2>　ノ　人　人　人　人　人　人　人　人　人　人　人　人　⚠ 入(97)

27

今
now

"What are you doing **now**?"
"I am singing la la la (ラララ) in
my house."

「今(いま)何(なに)をしているの?」
「家(いえ)でラララと歌(うた)っているの。」

▶ こん　きん
▷ いま

今 (いま)　now
今月 (こんげつ)　this month
今日 (*きょう)　today
今晩 (こんばん)　tonight
今週 (こんしゅう)　this week

今年 (*ことし)　this year
今朝 (*けさ)　this morning
今度 (こんど)　near future; next time

<4>　ノ　ハ　ム　今　今　今　今　今　今　今　今　今　今

28

寺
temple

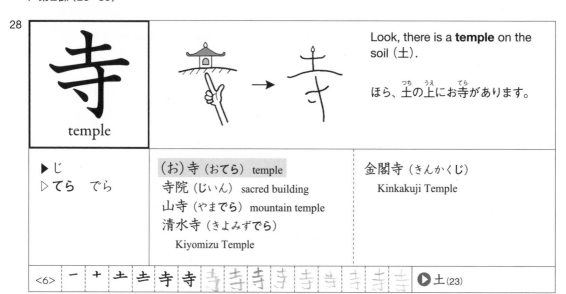

Look, there is a **temple** on the soil (土).

ほら、土の上にお寺があります。

▶ じ
▷ てら　でら

（お）寺（おてら）temple	金閣寺（きんかくじ）
寺院（じいん）sacred building	Kinkakuji Temple
山寺（やまでら）mountain temple	
清水寺（きよみずでら）	
Kiyomizu Temple	

<6>　一　十　土　圥　寺　寺　寺　寺　寺　寺　寺　寺　寺　▶ 土(23)

29

時
time

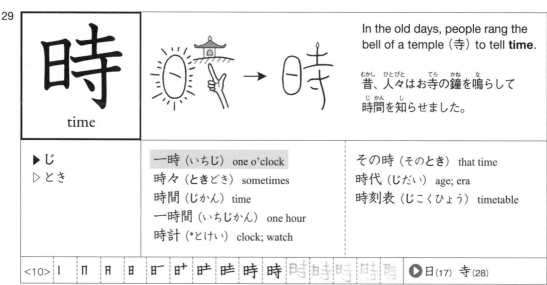

In the old days, people rang the bell of a temple (寺) to tell **time**.

昔、人々はお寺の鐘を鳴らして時間を知らせました。

▶ じ
▷ とき

一時（いちじ）one o'clock	その時（そのとき）that time
時々（ときどき）sometimes	時代（じだい）age; era
時間（じかん）time	時刻表（じこくひょう）timetable
一時間（いちじかん）one hour	
時計（*とけい）clock; watch	

<10>　丨　冂　月　日　旷　旷　昿　旹　時　時　時　時　時　時　時　▶ 日(17)　寺(28)

30

半
half

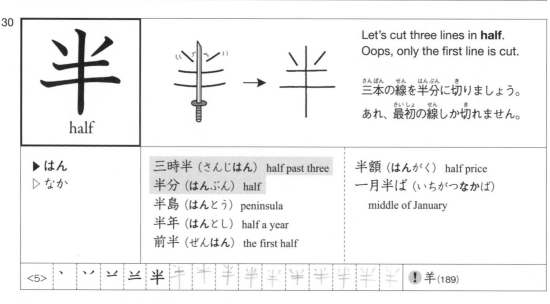

Let's cut three lines in **half**. Oops, only the first line is cut.

三本の線を半分に切りましょう。あれ、最初の線しか切れません。

▶ はん
▷ なか

三時半（さんじはん）half past three	半額（はんがく）half price
半分（はんぶん）half	一月半ば（いちがつなかば）
半島（はんとう）peninsula	middle of January
半年（はんとし）half a year	
前半（ぜんはん）the first half	

<5>　丶　丷　丷　业　半　半　半　半　半　半　半　半　半　⚠ 羊(189)

31

| 刀 sword | 口 → 刀 | This is the shape of a **sword** (knife).

かたな かたち
刀の形です。 |

| ▶ とう
▷ かたな | 刀（かたな） sword
日本刀（にほんとう） Japanese sword
短刀（たんとう） dagger | |

| <2> | フ 刀 刀 刀 刀 刀 刀 刀 刀 刀 刀 刀 刀 | ❗ 力 (50) |

32

| 分 minute / to divide | → 分 | Let's **divide** it in half with a knife（刀）.

かたな はんぶん き
刀で半分に切りましょう。 |

| ▶ ふん　ぷん
　　ぶん　ぶ
▷ わ | 五分（ごふん） five minutes
十分（じっぷん／じゅっぷん）
　　ten minutes
半分（はんぶん） half
分かる（わかる） to understand | 自分（じぶん） oneself
気分（きぶん） feeling
十分（じゅうぶん） enough
分ける（わける） to divide |

| <4> | ノ 八 分 分 分 分 分 分 分 分 分 分 分 | ▶ 刀 (31) |

第 3 課

●この課の漢字

上	下	中	外	右	工	左	前
33	34	35	36	37	38	39	40
後	午	門	間	東	西	南	北
41	42	43	44	45	46	47	48

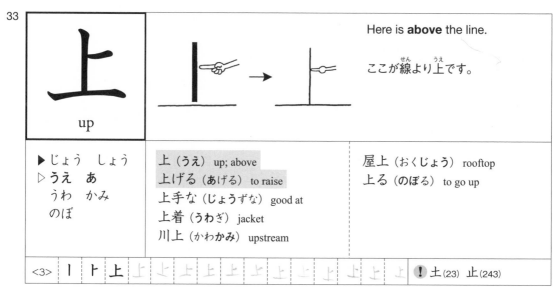

33

上
up

Here is **above** the line.
ここが線より上です。

▶ じょう　しょう
▷ うえ　あ
　うわ　かみ
　のぼ

上（うえ）up; above
上げる（あげる）to raise
上手な（じょうずな）good at
上着（うわぎ）jacket
川上（かわかみ）upstream

屋上（おくじょう）rooftop
上る（のぼる）to go up

<3>　｜ 卜 上　上 上 上 上 上 上 上 上 上 上　❗ 土(23) 止(243)

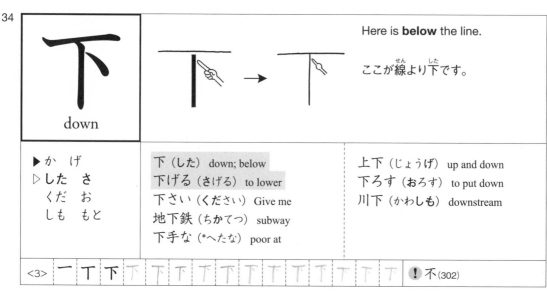

34

下
down

Here is **below** the line.
ここが線より下です。

▶ か　げ
▷ した　さ
　くだ　お
　しも　もと

下（した）down; below
下げる（さげる）to lower
下さい（ください）Give me
地下鉄（ちかてつ）subway
下手な（*へたな）poor at

上下（じょうげ）up and down
下ろす（おろす）to put down
川下（かわしも）downstream

<3>　一 丁 下　下 下 下 下 下 下 下 下 下 下　❗ 不(302)

35

中 middle

Here is the **center** of a circle.

ここが円の真ん中です。

▶ ちゅう　じゅう
▷ なか

中（なか）middle; inside
中国（ちゅうごく）China
一年中（いちねんじゅう）
　　all year round
中学校（ちゅうがっこう）
　　junior high school

世界中（せかいじゅう）
　　throughout the world
背中（せなか）back (of a body)
中止（ちゅうし）cancellation
中級（ちゅうきゅう）intermediate

<4> 丨 口 口 中

36

外 outside

You should smoke tobacco
（タバコ）**outside**.

タバコは外で吸いましょう。

▶ がい　げ
▷ そと　ほか
　 はず

外（そと）outside
外国（がいこく）foreign country
外国人（がいこくじん）foreigner
外の（ほかの）another; other
海外（かいがい）overseas

意外な（いがいな）unexpected
外す（はずす）to take off; to remove
外科（げか）surgery

<5> ノ ク タ タ 外

37

右 right

I eat with my **right** hand.

右手で食べます。

▶ ゆう　う
▷ みぎ

右（みぎ）right
右手（みぎて）right hand
右足（みぎあし）right foot
右側（みぎがわ）right side
左右（さゆう）right and left

右翼（うよく）right wing

<5> ノ ナ ナ 右 右　　▶ 口（15）　❗ 石（260）

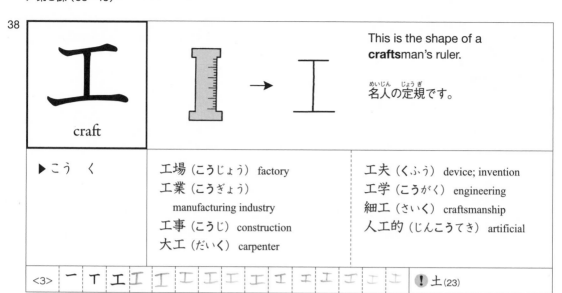

38 工 craft

This is the shape of a **crafts**man's ruler.

名人の定規です。

▶ こう く

工場（こうじょう）factory
工業（こうぎょう）manufacturing industry
工事（こうじ）construction
大工（だいく）carpenter

工夫（くふう）device; invention
工学（こうがく）engineering
細工（さいく）craftsmanship
人工的（じんこうてき）artificial

<3> 一 丁 工 工 工 工 工 工 工 工 工 工 工 ！土(23)

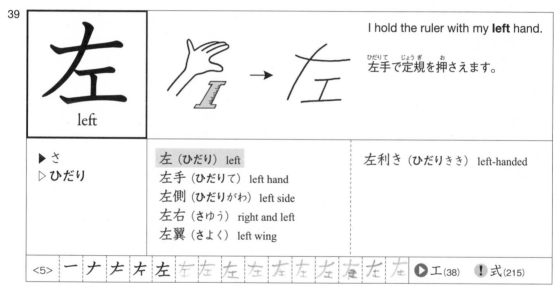

39 左 left

I hold the ruler with my **left** hand.

左手で定規を押さえます。

▶ さ
▷ ひだり

左（ひだり）left
左手（ひだりて）left hand
左側（ひだりがわ）left side
左右（さゆう）right and left
左翼（さよく）left wing

左利き（ひだりきき）left-handed

<5> 一 ナ ナ 左 左 左 左 左 左 左 左 左 左 ▶工(38) ！式(215)

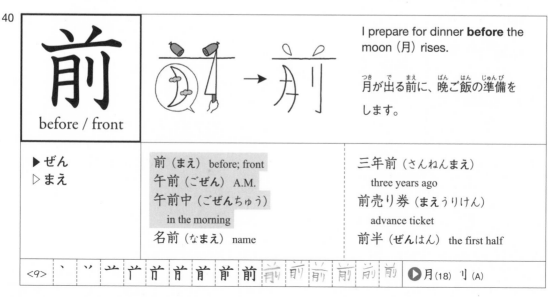

40 前 before / front

I prepare for dinner **before** the moon（月）rises.

月が出る前に、晩ご飯の準備をします。

▶ ぜん
▷ まえ

前（まえ）before; front
午前（ごぜん）A.M.
午前中（ごぜんちゅう）in the morning
名前（なまえ）name

三年前（さんねんまえ）three years ago
前売り券（まえうりけん）advance ticket
前半（ぜんはん）the first half

<9> 丶 丷 计 产 斉 首 首 前 前 前 前 前 前 前 前 ▶月(18) 刂(A)

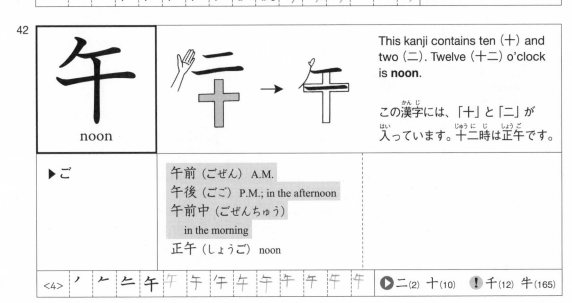

41

後
back / after

A person is walking **back**ward on a street.

道を後ろ向きに歩いています。

▶ ご　こう
▷ うし　あと
　のち　おく

後ろ（うしろ）back; behind
クラスの後（クラスのあと）
　　after class
後で（あとで）later
午後（ごご）P.M.; in the afternoon

最後（さいご）last
後半（こうはん）latter half
後ほど（のちほど）later
後れる（おくれる）to be behind

<9>　ノ　ク　イ　彳　彳　彳　彳　後　後　▶ 彳(D)

42

午
noon

This kanji contains ten（十）and two（二）. Twelve（十二）o'clock is **noon**.

この漢字には、「十」と「二」が入っています。十二時は正午です。

▶ ご

午前（ごぜん）A.M.
午後（ごご）P.M.; in the afternoon
午前中（ごぜんちゅう）
　　in the morning
正午（しょうご）noon

<4>　ノ　ト　二　午　▶ 二(2)　十(10)　❗千(12)　牛(165)

43

門
gate

This is the shape of **gates**.

門の形です。

▶ もん
▷ かど

門（もん）gate
専門（せんもん）major; speciality
正門（せいもん）front gate
部門（ぶもん）division; section
入門（にゅうもん）introduction

門松（かどまつ）
　　pine branch decoration for the New Year
名門（めいもん）distinguished family

<8>　Ｉ　Ｆ　Ｆ　Ｆ　Ｆ　門　門　門

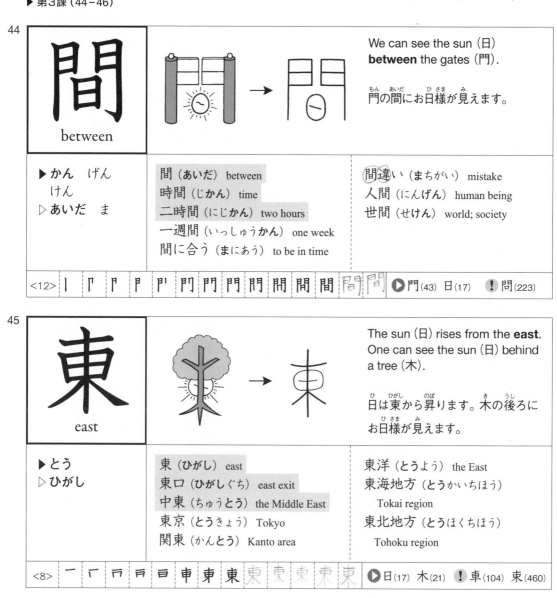

44

間
between

▶ かん げん
　けん
▷ あいだ ま

間（あいだ） between
時間（じかん） time
二時間（にじかん） two hours
一週間（いっしゅうかん） one week
間に合う（まにあう） to be in time

間違い（まちがい） mistake
人間（にんげん） human being
世間（せけん） world; society

We can see the sun （日）
between the gates （門）.
門の間にお日様が見えます。

<12> 丨 冂 冂 冃 冃 門 門 門 門 間 間 間 間 ▶門(43) 日(17) ！ 問(223)

45

東
east

▶ とう
▷ ひがし

東（ひがし） east
東口（ひがしぐち） east exit
中東（ちゅうとう） the Middle East
東京（とうきょう） Tokyo
関東（かんとう） Kanto area

東洋（とうよう） the East
東海地方（とうかいちほう）
　Tokai region
東北地方（とうほくちほう）
　Tohoku region

The sun （日） rises from the **east**.
One can see the sun （日） behind
a tree （木）.
日は東から昇ります。木の後ろに
お日様が見えます。

<8> 一 厂 冂 日 車 車 東 東 東 東 東 東 ▶日(17) 木(21) ！ 車(104) 束(460)

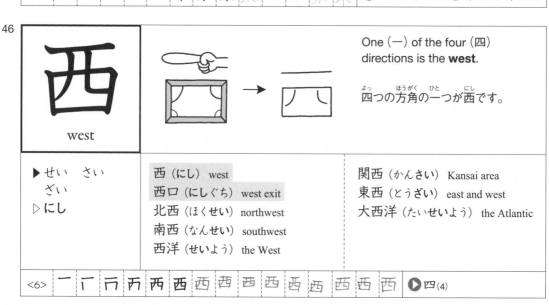

46

西
west

▶ せい さい
　ざい
▷ にし

西（にし） west
西口（にしぐち） west exit
北西（ほくせい） northwest
南西（なんせい） southwest
西洋（せいよう） the West

関西（かんさい） Kansai area
東西（とうざい） east and west
大西洋（たいせいよう） the Atlantic

One （一） of the four （四）
directions is the **west**.
四つの方角の一つが西です。

<6> 一 厂 冋 西 西 西 西 西 西 西 西 西 西 ▶四(4)

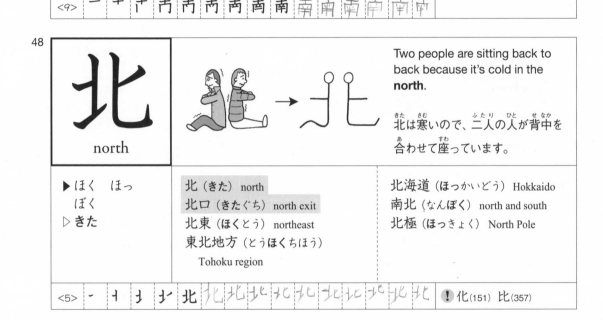

47

南
south

Two plants grow in the garden facing the **south**.

二つの植物が南向きの庭で育っています。

▶ なん　な
▷ みなみ

南（みなみ）south
南口（みなみぐち）south exit
東南アジア（とうなんアジア）
　　Southeast Asia
南東（なんとう）southeast

南北（なんぼく）north and south
南米（なんべい）South America
南極（なんきょく）Antactica

<9> 一 十 十 方 内 内 南 南 南

48

北
north

Two people are sitting back to back because it's cold in the **north**.

北は寒いので、二人の人が背中を合わせて座っています。

▶ ほく　ほっ
　 ぼく
▷ きた

北（きた）north
北口（きたぐち）north exit
北東（ほくとう）northeast
東北地方（とうほくちほう）
　　Tohoku region

北海道（ほっかいどう）Hokkaido
南北（なんぼく）north and south
北極（ほっきょく）North Pole

<5> 一 寸 丬 扌 北　❗ 化(151) 比(357)

第 4 課

●この課の漢字

田	力	男	女	子	学	生	先
49	50	51	52	53	54	55	56
何	父	母	年	去	毎	王	国
57	58	59	60	61	62	63	64

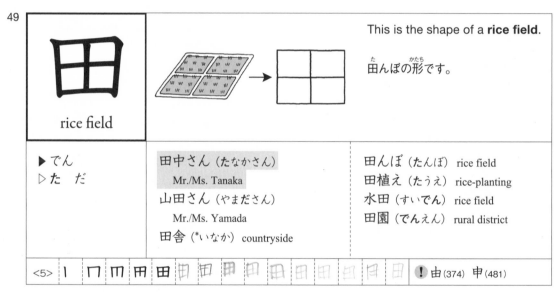

49

田

rice field

This is the shape of a **rice field**.

田んぼの形です。

▶ でん
▷ た　だ

田中さん（たなかさん）
　Mr./Ms. Tanaka
山田さん（やまださん）
　Mr./Ms. Yamada
田舎（*いなか）countryside

田んぼ（たんぼ）rice field
田植え（たうえ）rice-planting
水田（すいでん）rice field
田園（でんえん）rural district

| <5> | 丨 | 冂 | 皿 | 甲 | 田 | | | | | | | | | | ！由(374)　申(481) |

50

力

power

A muscular man has **power**.

筋肉質の男の人は力持ちです。

▶ りょく　りき
▷ ちから

力（ちから）power
学力（がくりょく）academic ability
電力（でんりょく）electric power
重力（じゅうりょく）gravity

協力する（きょうりょくする）
　to cooperate
努力（どりょく）effort
力学（りきがく）dynamics
視力（しりょく）eyesight

| <2> | フ | 力 | 力 | 力 | | | | | | | | ！刀(31) |

51

男
man

A **man** works powerfully（力）in the rice field（田）.

おとこ ひと ちから だ た
男の人が力を出して、田んぼで
はたら
働いています。

▶ だん　なん
▷ おとこ

男の子（おとこのこ）boy
男の人（おとこのひと）man
男性（だんせい）male
男子学生（だんしがくせい）
　　　male student

長男（ちょうなん）the eldest son

<7> 　丨　冂　冊　冊　田　甼　男

▶ 田(49)　力(50)

52

女
woman

This is the shape of a **woman**.

おんな ひと かたち
女の人の形です。

▶ じょ　にょう
　　にょ
▷ おんな　め

女の子（おんなのこ）girl
女の人（おんなのひと）woman
女性（じょせい）female
長女（ちょうじょ）the eldest daughter
少女（しょうじょ）girl

彼女（かのじょ）she; girlfriend
女房（にょうぼう）wife
女神（めがみ）goddess

<3> 　く　夕　女

53

子
child

This is the shape of a **child**.

こ ども かたち
子供の形です。

▶ し　す
▷ こ

女の子（おんなのこ）girl
男の子（おとこのこ）boy
子供（こども）child
電子辞書（でんしじしょ）
　　　electronic dictionary

女子学生（じょしがくせい）
　　　female student
男子学生（だんしがくせい）
　　　male student
様子（ようす）condition

<3> 　了　了　子

54	学 *learning*	Children（子）**learn** in school.

子供は学校で学びます。

▶ がく　がっ ▷ まな	学生（がくせい）student 大学（だいがく）college 学校（がっこう）school 学部（がくぶ）department; faculty 学習（がくしゅう）learning	学者（がくしゃ）scholar 文学（ぶんがく）literature 学ぶ（まなぶ）to study

<8>	丶 ⺌ ⺍ ⺌ ⺍ 学 学 学	▶子(53)　❗字(214)

55	生 *birth*	A plant is **born** from the ground（土）.

植物が土から生まれます。

▶ せい　じょう しょう ▷ う　い　は なま　き　お	学生（がくせい）student 先生（せんせい）teacher 生まれる（うまれる）to be born 生きる（いきる）to live 誕生日（たんじょうび）birthday	生える（はえる）to come out; to grow 生（なま）raw 一生（いっしょう）one's whole life

<5>	ノ ⺧ 牛 牛 生	▶土(23)

56	先 *ahead*	That person is running **ahead** of everyone.

だれよりも先を走っています。

▶ せん ▷ さき	先生（せんせい）teacher 先月（せんげつ）last month 先週（せんしゅう）last week 先輩（せんぱい）senior member 先日（せんじつ）the other day	先祖（せんぞ）ancestor 先に（さきに）ahead

<6>	ノ ⺧ 牛 生 先 先	▶儿(C)

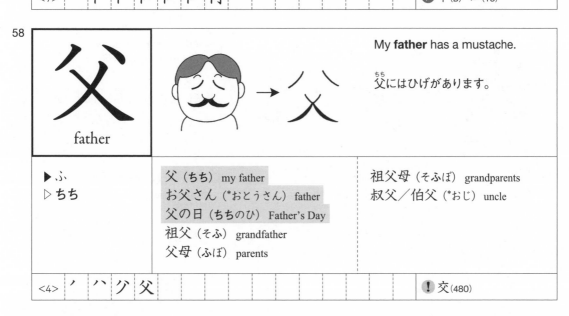

57

何
what

A person is carrying something.
"**What**'s that?"

人が何か運んでいます。
「それは何？」

▶ か
▷ なに　なん

何（なに／なん）what
何か（なにか）something
何人（なんにん）how many people
何時（なんじ）what time
何でも（なんでも）anything

何度（なんど）
　how many times/degrees
幾何学（きかがく）geometry

<7>　ノ　イ　イ　仁　仃　何　何　　　　　▶ イ (B)　口(15)

58

父
father

My **father** has a mustache.

父にはひげがあります。

▶ ふ
▷ ちち

父（ちち）my father
お父さん（*おとうさん）father
父の日（ちちのひ）Father's Day
祖父（そふ）grandfather
父母（ふぼ）parents

祖父母（そふぼ）grandparents
叔父／伯父（*おじ）uncle

<4>　ノ　ハ　グ　父　　　　　　　　　　! 交(480)

59

母
mother

This is the shape of a **mother**.

お母さんの形です。

▶ ぼ
▷ はは

母（はは）my mother
お母さん（*おかあさん）mother
母の日（ははのひ）Mother's Day
祖母（そぼ）grandmother
父母（ふぼ）parents

祖父母（そふぼ）grandparents
母語（ぼご）mother tongue
叔母／伯母（*おば）aunt

<5>　ㄥ　口　口　母　母

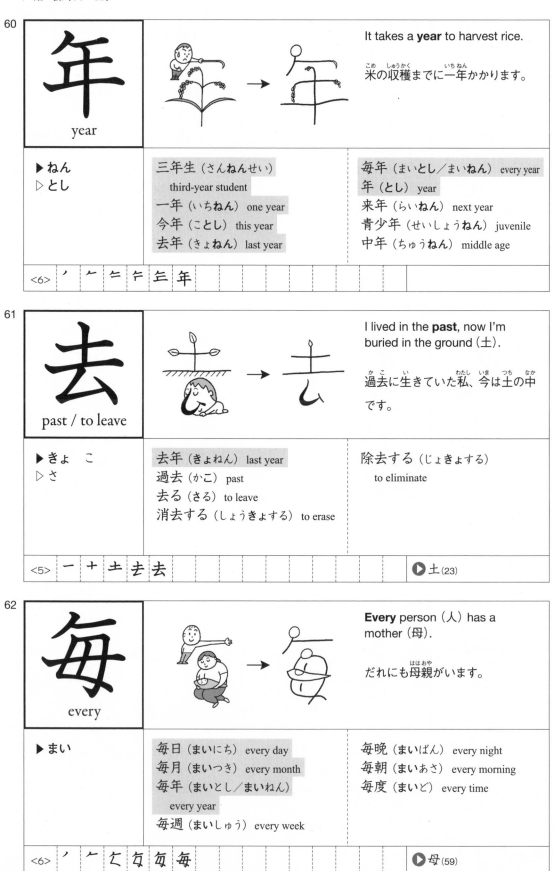

60 年 year

It takes a **year** to harvest rice.

<ruby>米<rt>こめ</rt></ruby>の<ruby>収穫<rt>しゅうかく</rt></ruby>までに<ruby>一年<rt>いちねん</rt></ruby>かかります。

▶ ねん
▷ とし

三年生 (さんねんせい) third-year student
一年 (いちねん) one year
今年 (ことし) this year
去年 (きょねん) last year

毎年 (まいとし／まいねん) every year
年 (とし) year
来年 (らいねん) next year
青少年 (せいしょうねん) juvenile
中年 (ちゅうねん) middle age

<6> ノ ヒ ヒ ケ 年 年

61 去 past / to leave

I lived in the **past**, now I'm buried in the ground (土).

<ruby>過去<rt>かこ</rt></ruby>に<ruby>生<rt>い</rt></ruby>きていた<ruby>私<rt>わたし</rt></ruby>、<ruby>今<rt>いま</rt></ruby>は<ruby>土<rt>つち</rt></ruby>の<ruby>中<rt>なか</rt></ruby>です。

▶ きょ　こ
▷ さ

去年 (きょねん) last year
過去 (かこ) past
去る (さる) to leave
消去する (しょうきょする) to erase

除去する (じょきょする)
　　to eliminate

<5> 一 十 土 去 去 　　▶ 土(23)

62 毎 every

Every person (人) has a mother (母).

だれにも<ruby>母親<rt>ははおや</rt></ruby>がいます。

▶ まい

毎日 (まいにち) every day
毎月 (まいつき) every month
毎年 (まいとし／まいねん)
　　every year
毎週 (まいしゅう) every week

毎晩 (まいばん) every night
毎朝 (まいあさ) every morning
毎度 (まいど) every time

<6> ノ ヒ ヒ 与 毎 毎 　　▶ 母(59)

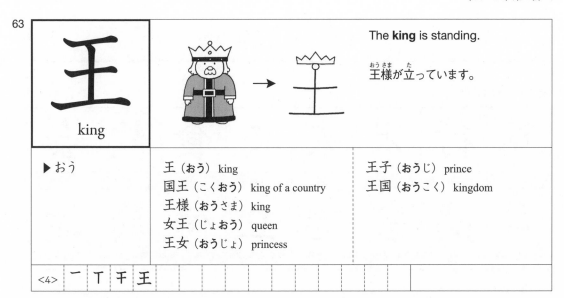

The **king** is standing.

王様（おうさま）が立（た）っています。

▶ おう

王（おう）king
国王（こくおう）king of a country
王様（おうさま）king
女王（じょおう）queen
王女（おうじょ）princess

王子（おうじ）prince
王国（おうこく）kingdom

<4> 一 丁 千 王

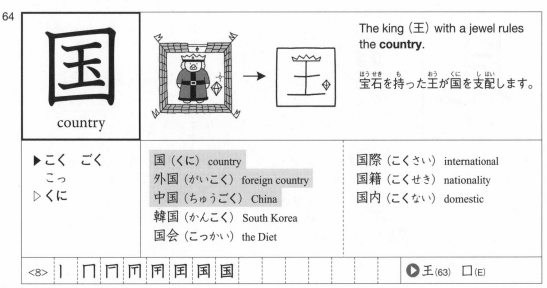

The king（王）with a jewel rules the **country**.

宝石（ほうせき）を持（も）った王（おう）が国（くに）を支配（しはい）します。

▶ こく　ごく
　こっ
▷ くに

国（くに）country
外国（がいこく）foreign country
中国（ちゅうごく）China
韓国（かんこく）South Korea
国会（こっかい）the Diet

国際（こくさい）international
国籍（こくせき）nationality
国内（こくない）domestic

<8> 丨 冂 冂 冃 冃 国 国 国

▶ 王(63) 口(E)

第 5 課

●この課の漢字

見	行	米	来	良	食	飲	会
65	66	67	68	69	70	71	72
耳	聞	言	話	立	待	周	週
73	74	75	76	77	78	79	80

65

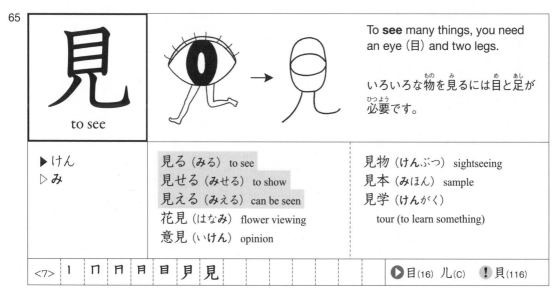

見 to see

To **see** many things, you need an eye（目）and two legs.

いろいろな物を見るには目と足が必要です。

▶ けん
▷ み

見る（みる）to see
見せる（みせる）to show
見える（みえる）can be seen
花見（はなみ）flower viewing
意見（いけん）opinion

見物（けんぶつ）sightseeing
見本（みほん）sample
見学（けんがく）
　tour (to learn something)

<7> 丨 冂 冃 月 目 貝 見 　 ▶目(16) 儿(C) ！貝(116)

66

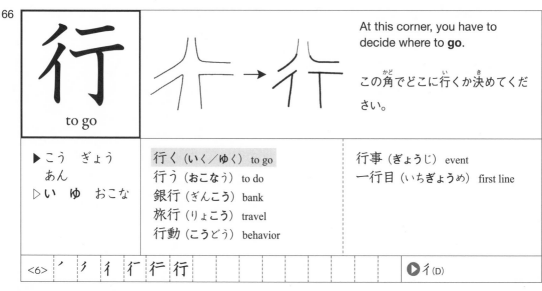

行 to go

At this corner, you have to decide where to **go**.

この角でどこに行くか決めてください。

▶ こう ぎょう
　 あん
▷ い ゆ おこな

行く（いく／ゆく）to go
行う（おこなう）to do
銀行（ぎんこう）bank
旅行（りょこう）travel
行動（こうどう）behavior

行事（ぎょうじ）event
一行目（いちぎょうめ）first line

<6> ノ ン 彳 彳 行 行 　 ▶彳(D)

67

米
rice

This is the shape of **rice** plants.

稲の形です。

▶ べい　まい
▷ こめ

(お)米 （おこめ）　rice
米屋 （こめや）　rice merchant
米国 （べいこく）　U.S.A.
欧米 （おうべい）　Europe and America
南米 （なんべい）　South America

北米 （ほくべい）　North America
新米 （しんまい）　new rice

<6> 丶 丷 一 丷 米 米　　　❗来(68)

68

来
to come

When October **comes**, rice （米）
is ready for harvest.

十月が来ると米が収穫できます。

▶ らい
▷ く　き　こ
　　きた

来る （くる）　to come
来ます （きます）　to come
来ない （こない）　not to come
来年 （らいねん）　next year
来週 （らいしゅう）　next week

将来 （しょうらい）　future
来学期 （らいがっき）　next semester
来る （きたる）　this coming…

<7> 一 ー 一 一 平 来 来　　　▶十(10)　米(67)

69

良
good / well

Everyone feels **good** on a full
stomach.

だれでもおなかがいっぱいの時は
気分がいいです。

▶ りょう
▷ よ

良い （よい）　good
良心 （りょうしん）　conscience
不良 （ふりょう）　delinquent
奈良県 （*ならけん）　Nara Prefecture

<7> 丶 ⼎ ⼎ ⺕ 自 自 良

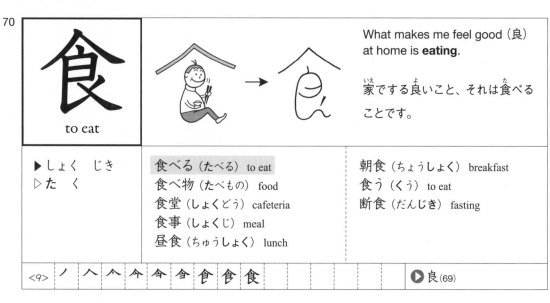

70 食 to eat

What makes me feel good (良) at home is **eating**.

家でする良いこと、それは食べることです。

| ▶ しょく じき
▷ た く | 食べる （たべる） to eat
食べ物 （たべもの） food
食堂 （しょくどう） cafeteria
食事 （しょくじ） meal
昼食 （ちゅうしょく） lunch | 朝食 （ちょうしょく） breakfast
食う （くう） to eat
断食 （だんじき） fasting |

<9> ノ 人 𠆢 今 今 今 食 食 食　　▶ 良(69)

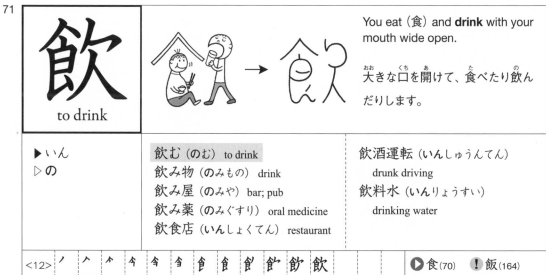

71 飲 to drink

You eat (食) and **drink** with your mouth wide open.

大きな口を開けて、食べたり飲んだりします。

| ▶ いん
▷ の | 飲む （のむ） to drink
飲み物 （のみもの） drink
飲み屋 （のみや） bar; pub
飲み薬 （のみぐすり） oral medicine
飲食店 （いんしょくてん） restaurant | 飲酒運転 （いんしゅうんてん）
　 drunk driving
飲料水 （いんりょうすい）
　 drinking water |

<12> ノ 人 𠆢 今 今 今 𩙿 𩙿 𩙿 飲 飲 飲　　▶ 食(70)　! 飯(164)

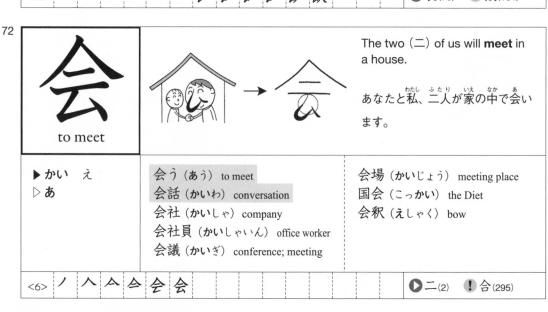

72 会 to meet

The two (二) of us will **meet** in a house.

あなたと私、二人が家の中で会います。

| ▶ かい え
▷ あ | 会う （あう） to meet
会話 （かいわ） conversation
会社 （かいしゃ） company
会社員 （かいしゃいん） office worker
会議 （かいぎ） conference; meeting | 会場 （かいじょう） meeting place
国会 （こっかい） the Diet
会釈 （えしゃく） bow |

<6> ノ 人 𠆢 会 会 会　　▶ 二(2)　! 合(295)

73

耳
ear

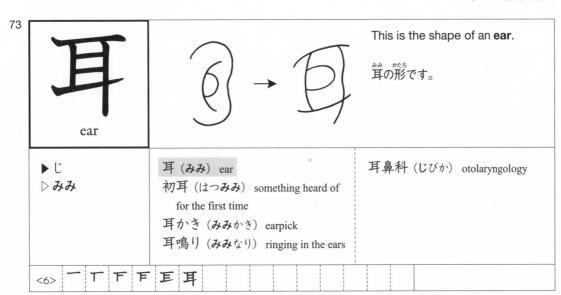

This is the shape of an **ear**.

耳の形です。

▶ じ
▷ みみ

耳 (みみ) ear	耳鼻科 (じびか) otolaryngology
初耳 (はつみみ) something heard of for the first time	
耳かき (みみかき) earpick	
耳鳴り (みみなり) ringing in the ears	

<6> 一 丁 丌 丌 耳 耳

74

聞
to listen

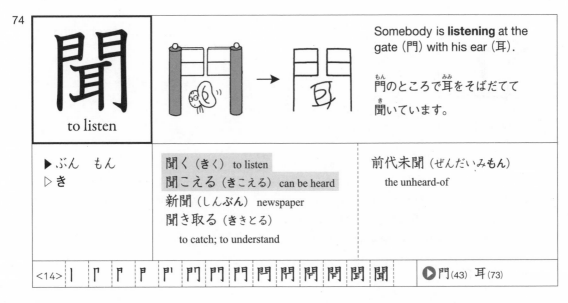

Somebody is **listening** at the gate (門) with his ear (耳).

門のところで耳をそばだてて聞いています。

▶ ぶん もん
▷ き

聞く (きく) to listen	前代未聞 (ぜんだいみもん) the unheard-of
聞こえる (きこえる) can be heard	
新聞 (しんぶん) newspaper	
聞き取る (ききとる) to catch; to understand	

<14> 丨 冂 冂 冂 冂 門 門 門 門 門 門 門 聞 聞   ▶ 門(43) 耳(73)

75

言
to say

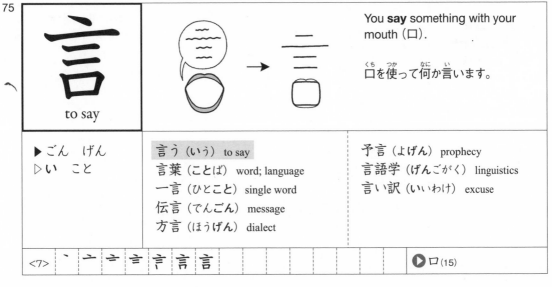

You **say** something with your mouth (口).

口を使って何か言います。

▶ ごん げん
▷ い こと

言う (いう) to say	予言 (よげん) prophecy
言葉 (ことば) word; language	言語学 (げんごがく) linguistics
一言 (ひとこと) single word	言い訳 (いいわけ) excuse
伝言 (でんごん) message	
方言 (ほうげん) dialect	

<7> 丶 一 二 三 言 言 言   ▶ 口(15)

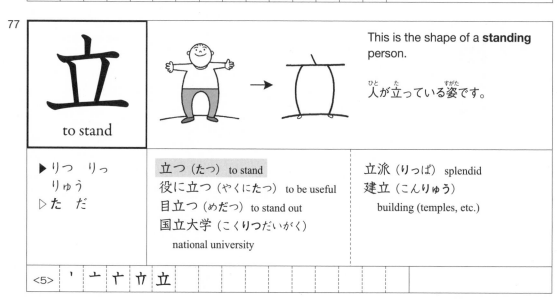

76

話
to speak

People **speak** using thousands (千) of words.

何千もの単語を使って話します。

▶ わ
▷ はな　はなし

話す（はなす）to speak
話（はなし）talk; story
会話（かいわ）conversation
電話（でんわ）telephone
世話（せわ）care

話題（わだい）topic of conversation
話し合う（はなしあう）to discuss
手話（しゅわ）sign language

<13>　丶　亠　≥　≥　言　言　言　訁　訁　訐　許　話　話

▶ 言(75)　千(12)　！語(128)

77

立
to stand

This is the shape of a **standing** person.

人が立っている姿です。

▶ りつ　りっ
　りゅう
▷ た　だ

立つ（たつ）to stand
役に立つ（やくにたつ）to be useful
目立つ（めだつ）to stand out
国立大学（こくりつだいがく）
　　national university

立派（りっぱ）splendid
建立（こんりゅう）
　　building (temples, etc.)

<5>　丶　亠　亠　立　立

78

待
to wait

I will **wait** for you on the street in front of the temple (寺).

お寺の前の道で待っています。

▶ たい
▷ ま

待つ（まつ）to wait
招待する（しょうたいする）to invite
待合室（*まちあいしつ）waiting room
待ち合わせる（まちあわせる）
　　to arrange to meet

期待する（きたいする）to hope for
待望（たいぼう）long-awaited

<9>　丿　夕　彳　彳　彳　彳　待　待

▶ 彳(D)　寺(28)　！持(126)　特(292)

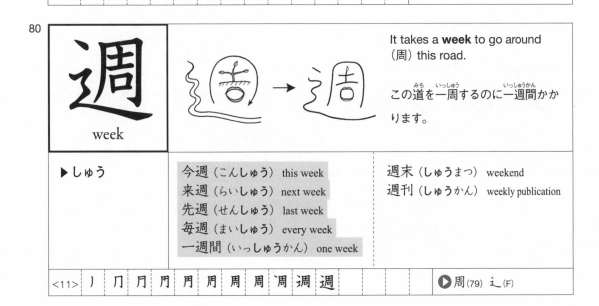

79

周
to go around

What you eat returns to the soil （土）. Everything **goes around**.

食べたものは土に返ります。
すべてのものは循環します。

▶ しゅう
▷ まわ

周り（まわり） surrounding
周辺（しゅうへん） surrounding
周期（しゅうき） cycle
世界一周（せかいいっしゅう）
　　around the world

一周年（いっしゅうねん）
one-year anniversary

<8> 丿 冂 刀 冂 冃 用 周 周

▶ 土(23)　ロ(15)　❗同(298)

80

週
week

It takes a **week** to go around （周）this road.

この道を一周するのに一週間かかります。

▶ しゅう

今週（こんしゅう） this week
来週（らいしゅう） next week
先週（せんしゅう） last week
毎週（まいしゅう） every week
一週間（いっしゅうかん） one week

週末（しゅうまつ） weekend
週刊（しゅうかん） weekly publication

<11> 丿 冂 刀 冂 冃 用 周 周 冐 涓 週

▶ 周(79)　辶(F)

第 6 課

● この課の漢字

大	小	高	安	新	古	元	気
81	82	83	84	85	86	87	88
多	少	広	早	長	明	好	友
89	90	91	92	93	94	95	96

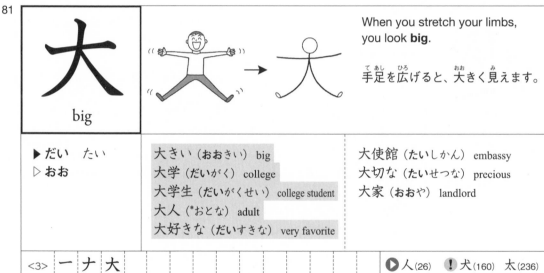

81

大
big

When you stretch your limbs, you look **big**.

手足を広げると、大きく見えます。

▶ だい　たい
▷ おお

大きい（おおきい）big
大学（だいがく）college
大学生（だいがくせい）college student
大人（*おとな）adult
大好きな（だいすきな）very favorite

大使館（たいしかん）embassy
大切な（たいせつな）precious
大家（おおや）landlord

<3> 一 ナ 大　　　　　　▶人(26) ！犬(160) 太(236)

82

小
small

When you bend your limbs, you look **small**.

手足を曲げれば、小さく見えます。

▶ しょう
▷ ちい　こ　お

小さい（ちいさい）small
小学生（しょうがくせい）
elementary school student
小学校（しょうがっこう）
elementary school

小説（しょうせつ）novel
小包（こづつみ）parcel
小麦（こむぎ）wheat
小川（おがわ）small stream

<3> 亅 小 小　　　　　　！少(90)

83

高
high

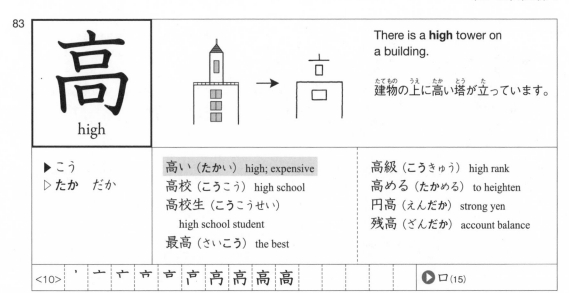

There is a **high** tower on a building.

たてもの うえ たか とう た
建物の上に高い塔が立っています。

▶ こう
▷ たか　だか

高い（たかい）high; expensive
高校（こうこう）high school
高校生（こうこうせい）
　high school student
最高（さいこう）the best

高級（こうきゅう）high rank
高める（たかめる）to heighten
円高（えんだか）strong yen
残高（ざんだか）account balance

<10> 亠 亠 亠 亠 古 古 高 高 高 高 | ▶ 口 (15)

84

安
cheap / ease

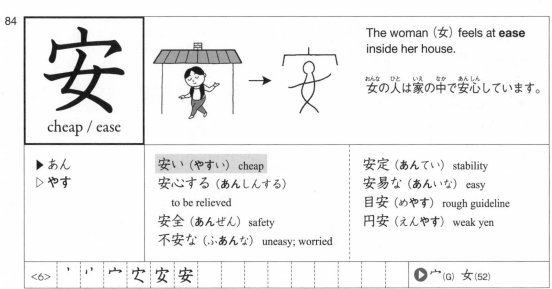

The woman（女）feels at **ease** inside her house.

おんな ひと いえ なか あんしん
女の人は家の中で安心しています。

▶ あん
▷ やす

安い（やすい）cheap
安心する（あんしんする）
　to be relieved
安全（あんぜん）safety
不安な（ふあんな）uneasy; worried

安定（あんてい）stability
安易な（あんいな）easy
目安（めやす）rough guideline
円安（えんやす）weak yen

<6> 丶 䒑 宀 安 安 安 | ▶ 宀 (G) 女 (52)

85

新
new

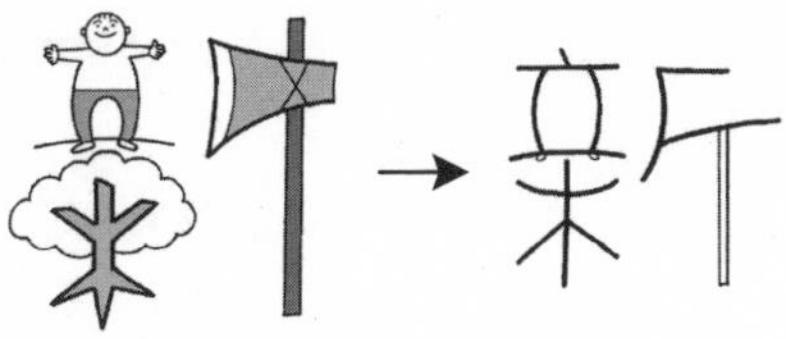

To start something **new**, you stand up（立）, and cleave through woods（木）with an ax.

あたら はじ た
新しいことを始めるには、立って、
みち き ひら
おので道を切り開きます。

▶ しん
▷ あたら　あら
　にい

新しい（あたらしい）new
新聞（しんぶん）newspaper
新幹線（しんかんせん）bullet train
新年（しんねん）new year
新鮮な（しんせんな）fresh

新たな（あらたな）new
新潟（にいがた）Niigata

<13> 丶 亠 亠 立 立 辛 辛 亲 亲 新 新 新 | ▶ 立 (77) 木 (21) ❗親 (196)

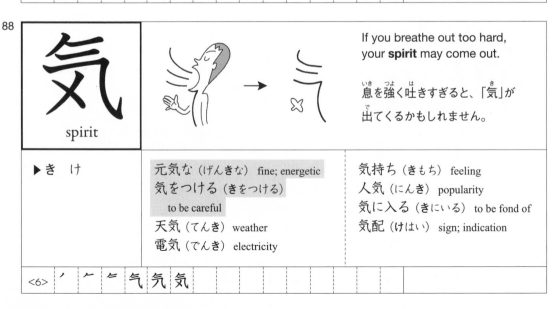

86

古 old

When you hear the same story ten (十) times, it sounds **old**.

同じ話を十回聞くと、その話は
古くなります。

▶ こ
▷ ふる

古い (ふるい) old
中古 (ちゅうこ) secondhand
古本 (ふるほん) old book
使い古す (つかいふるす)
　　to wear out

考古学 (こうこがく) archaeology
古代 (こだい) ancient times
古都 (こと) old capital

<5> 一 十 十 古 古　　　　　　　　▶十(10) 口(15)

87

元 origin

If two (二) people run together, they will be more **genki**.

二人で走れば、もっと元気になり
ます。

▶ げん　がん
▷ もと

元気な (げんきな) fine; energetic
元日 (がんじつ) the first day of the year
足元 (あしもと) at one's feet
地元 (じもと) local
三次元 (さんじげん) three dimensions

元 (げん)
　　yuan (Chinese monetary unit)
紀元前 (きげんぜん) B.C.

<4> 一 二 テ 元　　　　　　　　▶二(2) 儿(C)

88

気 spirit

If you breathe out too hard, your **spirit** may come out.

息を強く吐きすぎると、「気」が
出てくるかもしれません。

▶ き　け

元気な (げんきな) fine; energetic
気をつける (きをつける)
　　to be careful
天気 (てんき) weather
電気 (でんき) electricity

気持ち (きもち) feeling
人気 (にんき) popularity
気に入る (きにいる) to be fond of
気配 (けはい) sign; indication

<6> ノ 𠂉 气 気 気 気

89 多 many / much

There are **many** "タ."

「タ」がたくさんあります。

▶ た
▷ おお

多い（おおい）many
多分（たぶん）probably
多少（たしょう）a little; somewhat
滅多に（めったに）rarely

多数決（たすうけつ）
  decision by majority
多数（たすう）large number
多量（たりょう）large quantity

<6> ノ　ク　タ　タ　多　多

90 少 little

When you cut a small（小）thing, you can get only **little**.

小さいものを分けると、少ししかもらえません。

▶ しょう
▷ すこ　すく

少し（すこし）a little
少ない（すくない）few
少年（しょうねん）boy
少女（しょうじょ）girl
少々（しょうしょう）a little

減少（げんしょう）decrease
少量（しょうりょう）small amount

<4> 丿　丿　小　少　　　▶小(82)

91 広 spacious

"It's my house. **Spacious**, isn't it?"

「私の家です。広いでしょ。」

▶ こう
▷ ひろ　びろ

広い（ひろい）wide; spacious
広島（ひろしま）Hiroshima
広告（こうこく）advertisement
広場（ひろば）square; open space
広がる（ひろがる）(something) spreads

広める（ひろめる）
  to spread (something)
広さ（ひろさ）width
背広（せびろ）business jacket

<5> 丶　亠　广　広　広　　　▶广(H)

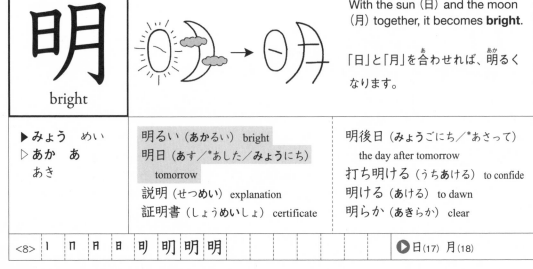

92

早　early

It is too **early** to get up at ten
（十）on Sundays （日）.

日曜日に十時に起きるのは早すぎ
ます。

▶ さっ　そう
▷ はや　ばや

早い （はやい）　early
早く （はやく）　early
早口 （はやくち）　fast talker
素早い （すばやい）　quick
早送り （はやおくり）　fast forward

早める （はやめる）　to hasten
早速 （さっそく）　at once
早朝 （そうちょう）　early morning

<6>　丿　⼍　甲　曰　旦　早

▶日(17)　十(10)

93

長　long

This is the shape of a person
with **long** hair.

髪が長い人の姿です。

▶ ちょう
▷ なが

長い （ながい）　long
社長 （しゃちょう）　company president
部長 （ぶちょう）　department head
身長 （しんちょう）　height
長所 （ちょうしょ）　good point

長男 （ちょうなん）　the eldest son
長方形 （ちょうほうけい）　rectangle
長さ （ながさ）　length

<8>　丨　⼡　⼫　⺕　⻑　⻑　⻑　長

94

明　bright

With the sun （日）and the moon
（月）together, it becomes **bright**.

「日」と「月」を合わせれば、明るく
なります。

▶ みょう　めい
▷ あか　あ
　 あき

明るい （あかるい）　bright
明日 （あす／*あした／みょうにち）
　　　 tomorrow
説明 （せつめい）　explanation
証明書 （しょうめいしょ）　certificate

明後日 （みょうごにち／*あさって）
　　　 the day after tomorrow
打ち明ける （うちあける）　to confide
明ける （あける）　to dawn
明らか （あきらか）　clear

<8>　丨　⼌　⽇　日　旳　明　明　明

▶日(17)　月(18)

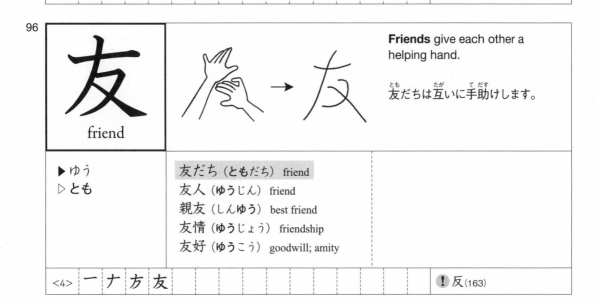

95

好
to like

▶こう
▷す　この

好きな（すきな）favorite
大好きな（だいすきな）very favorite
好み（このみ）liking; taste
好む（このむ）to like

お好み焼き（おこのみやき）
　okonomiyaki; Japanese pancake
好意（こうい）fondness
好感（こうかん）good feeling

The woman（女）**likes** children
（子）.

その女の人は子供が好きです。

<6>　く　夕　女　好　好　好

▶女(52)　子(53)

96

友
friend

▶ゆう
▷とも

友だち（ともだち）friend
友人（ゆうじん）friend
親友（しんゆう）best friend
友情（ゆうじょう）friendship
友好（ゆうこう）goodwill; amity

Friends give each other a
helping hand.

友だちは互いに手助けします。

<4>　一　ナ　方　友

❗反(163)

第 7 課

●この課の漢字

入	出	市	町	村	雨	電	車
97	98	99	100	101	102	103	104
馬	駅	社	校	店	銀	病	院
105	106	107	108	109	110	111	112

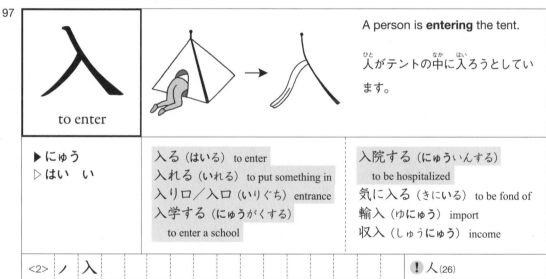

97

入

to enter

A person is **entering** the tent.

<ruby>人<rt>ひと</rt></ruby>がテントの<ruby>中<rt>なか</rt></ruby>に<ruby>入<rt>はい</rt></ruby>ろうとしています。

▶ にゅう
▷ はい　い

入る（はいる）to enter
入れる（いれる）to put something in
入り口／入口（いりぐち）entrance
入学する（にゅうがくする）
　　to enter a school

入院する（にゅういんする）
　　to be hospitalized
気に入る（きにいる）to be fond of
輸入（ゆにゅう）import
収入（しゅうにゅう）income

<2>　ノ　入　　　　　　　　　❗人(26)

98

出

to exit

The **exit** is this way.

EXIT

<ruby>出口<rt>でぐち</rt></ruby>はこちらです。

▶ しゅつ　しゅっ
　　すい
▷ で　だ

出る（でる）to exit
出かける（でかける）to go out
出す（だす）to take something out
出口（でぐち）exit
思い出す（おもいだす）to recall

輸出（ゆしゅつ）export
出席（しゅっせき）attendance
提出する（ていしゅつする）
　　to submit

<5>　丨　中　中　出　出

99

市
city / market

People go to a **market** for shopping.

人々が市場に買い物に行きます。
<small>ひとびと いちば か もの い</small>

▶ し ▷ いち	つくば市 （つくばし） Tsukuba City 市長 （しちょう） mayor 市民 （しみん） citizen 市役所 （しやくしょ） city hall 都市 （とし） metropolis	市場 （しじょう） market for stocks, etc. 市場 （いちば） market 朝市 （あさいち） morning market

<5> ` 一 广 方 市

100

町
town

There used to be rice fields （田） and roads in the **town**.

町には田んぼと道がありました。
<small>まち た みち</small>

▶ ちょう ▷ まち	町 （まち） town 北山町 （きたやまちょう／きたやままち） Kitayama Town 町長 （ちょうちょう） mayor of a town 町民 （ちょうみん） townspeople	城下町 （じょうかまち） castle town 港町 （みなとまち） port town

<7> 丨 冂 冂 田 田 町 町　　　　　▶田(49)

101

村
village

There is a **village** beyond the tree （木）.

木の向こうに村があります。
<small>き む むら</small>

▶ そん ▷ むら	村 （むら） village 田村さん （たむらさん） 　　Mr./Ms. Tamura 村長 （そんちょう） village chief 村民 （そんみん） village people	農村 （のうそん） farm village 市町村 （しちょうそん） municipality 漁村 （ぎょそん） fishing village

<7> 一 十 オ 木 村 村 村　　　　▶木(21)　！付(331)

102

雨
rain

This is the shape of clouds and **rain**drops.

雲と雨粒から、この漢字ができました。

| ▶ う
▷ あめ　あま | 雨（あめ）rain
梅雨（*つゆ／ばいう）rainy season
　（of early summer）
大雨（おおあめ）heavy rain
雨季（うき）rainy season | 暴風雨（ぼうふうう）windy rainstorm
雨水（あまみず）rainwater |

<8> 一 厂 冂 币 币 雨 雨 雨

103

電
electricity / lightning

It is raining （雨） and **lightning** flashes on a rice field （田）.

雨の中、田んぼに稲妻が光っています。

| ▶ でん | 電気（でんき）electricity
電車（でんしゃ）train
電話（でんわ）telephone
電力（でんりょく）electric power
電子（でんし）electron | 電池（でんち）battery
停電（ていでん）blackout
電源（でんげん）power source |

<13> 一 厂 冂 币 币 币 雨 雨 雫 雫 雪 電　　▶ 雨(102) 田(49)

104

車
car

This is the shape of a **car**.

車の形です。

| ▶ しゃ
▷ くるま | 車（くるま）car
電車（でんしゃ）train
自動車（じどうしゃ）automobile
自転車（じてんしゃ）bicycle | 駐車場（ちゅうしゃじょう）
　parking area
救急車（きゅうきゅうしゃ）
　ambulance
車いす（くるまいす）wheelchair |

<7> 一 厂 冂 冇 盲 亘 車　　! 東(45)

105

馬
horse

This is the shape of a **horse**.

馬（うま）の形（かたち）です。

▶ ば
▷ うま　ま

馬（うま）horse
子馬（こうま）pony
馬小屋（うまごや）stable
馬車（ばしゃ）horse-drawn carriage
乗馬（じょうば）horseback riding

競馬（けいば）horse racing
馬鹿（ばか）fool

<10> 丨 厂 冂 厈 馬 馬 馬 馬 馬 馬

106

駅
station

There are horses（馬）and people carrying luggage at the **station**.

駅（えき）には、馬（うま）や、荷物（にもつ）を持（も）った人（ひと）がいます。

 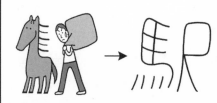

▶ えき

駅（えき）station
東京駅（とうきょうえき）
　Tokyo Station
駅員（えきいん）station staff
駅前（えきまえ）in front of the station

<14> 丨 厂 冂 厈 馬 馬 馬 馬 馬 馬 馬 馬 駅 駅　▶ 馬(105)　❗ 験(217)

107

社
company / shrine

People offer things and pray for rich harvest at a **shrine**.

神社（じんじゃ）で人（ひと）はお供（そな）えをして豊作（ほうさく）を祈（いの）ります。

 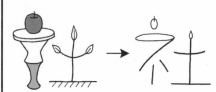

▶ しゃ　じゃ
▷ やしろ

会社（かいしゃ）company
社会（しゃかい）society
社長（しゃちょう）company president
神社（じんじゃ）shrine
社会学（しゃかいがく）sociology

社会主義（しゃかいしゅぎ）
　socialism
社（やしろ）shrine
商社（しょうしゃ）trading firm

<7> 丶 ㇀ ネ ネ ネ 社 社　▶ ネ(M) 土(23)　❗ 仕(271)

108 校 school

My father (父) came to **school** to pick me up.

父が私を学校に迎えに来ました。

▶ こう

学校 (がっこう) school
高校 (こうこう) high school
中学校 (ちゅうがっこう)
    junior high school

小学校 (しょうがっこう)
    elementary school
校長 (こうちょう) principal
校舎 (こうしゃ) school building
校歌 (こうか) school song

<10> 一 十 才 才 才゙ 朾 朾 杧 杧 校

▶ 木(21) 交(480) 父(58)

109 店 shop

At the **shop**, tomatoes (トマト) are piled on a box.

店先の台に、トマトが積んであります。

▶ てん
▷ みせ

店 (みせ) shop
喫茶店 (きっさてん) café
店員 (てんいん) store clerk
書店 (しょてん) book store
売店 (ばいてん) stand; kiosk

店長 (てんちょう) store manager
本店 (ほんてん) main office
支店 (してん) branch office

<8> ` 一 广 广 广 庄 店 店

▶ 广(H) 口(15)

110 銀 silver

Silver is not as good as gold (金).

銀は金ほど良くありません。

▶ ぎん

銀行 (ぎんこう) bank
銀 (ぎん) silver
水銀 (すいぎん) mercury
銀色 (ぎんいろ) silver (colored)
銀河 (ぎんが) galaxy

<14> ノ ハ ム 스 牟 牟 余 金 釒 釒 釒 鈤 鈤 銀

▶ 金(22)

111

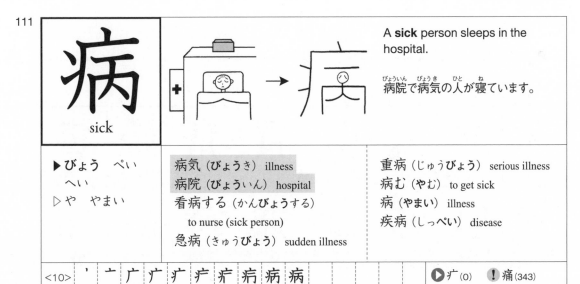

病
sick

A **sick** person sleeps in the hospital.

病院で病気の人が寝ています。

▶びょう　ぺい
　へい
▷や　やまい

病気（びょうき）illness
病院（びょういん）hospital
看病する（かんびょうする）
　　　to nurse (sick person)
急病（きゅうびょう）sudden illness

重病（じゅうびょう）serious illness
病む（やむ）to get sick
病（やまい）illness
疾病（しっぺい）disease

<10>　丶　一　广　广　疒　疒　疒　疒　病　病

▶广(0)　❗痛(343)

112

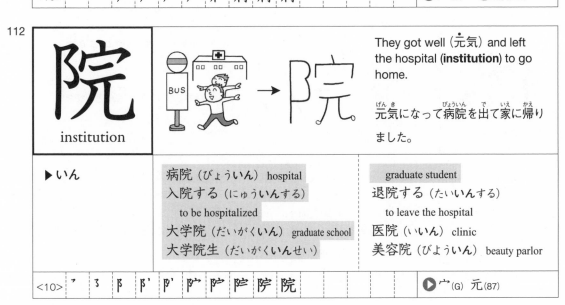

院
institution

They got well (元気) and left the hospital (**institution**) to go home.

元気になって病院を出て家に帰りました。

▶いん

病院（びょういん）hospital
入院する（にゅういんする）
　　　to be hospitalized
大学院（だいがくいん）graduate school
大学院生（だいがくいんせい）

graduate student
退院する（たいいんする）
　　　to leave the hospital
医院（いいん）clinic
美容院（びよういん）beauty parlor

<10>　⻖　阝　阝　阝'　阝'　阝宀　阝宁　阝宇　阝完　院

▶宀(G)　元(87)

第 8 課

● この課の漢字

休	走	起	貝	買	売	読	書
113	114	115	116	117	118	119	120
帰	勉	弓	虫	強	持	名	語
121	122	123	124	125	126	127	128

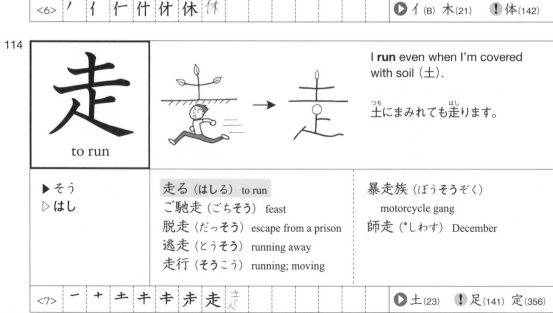

113

休
to rest

A person is **resting** by a tree（木）.

人（ひと）が木（き）のところで休（やす）んでいます。

▶ きゅう
▷ やす

休む（やすむ） to rest; to be absent
休み（やすみ） holiday; absence
夏休み（なつやすみ） summer vacation
昼休み（ひるやすみ） lunch break
休日（きゅうじつ） holiday

休講（きゅうこう）
　　cancellation of lecture
定休日（ていきゅうび）
　　holiday (of a store)

<6> ノ　イ　イ　仁　什　休　休　休

▶ イ (B)　木(21)　！体(142)

114

走
to run

I **run** even when I'm covered with soil（土）.

土（つち）にまみれても走（はし）ります。

▶ そう
▷ はし

走る（はしる） to run
ご馳走（ごちそう） feast
脱走（だっそう） escape from a prison
逃走（とうそう） running away
走行（そうこう） running; moving

暴走族（ぼうそうぞく）
　　motorcycle gang
師走（*しわす） December

<7> 一　十　土　キ　キ　走　走

▶ 土(23)　！足(141)　定(356)

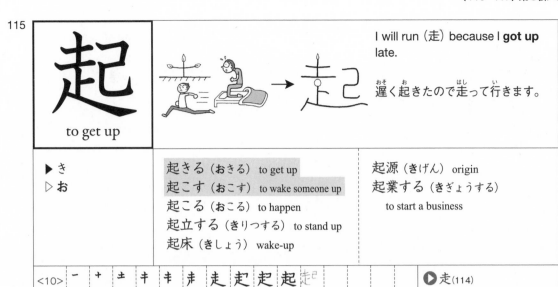

115 起 to get up

I will run（走）because I **got up** late.

<ruby>遅<rt>おそ</rt></ruby>く<ruby>起<rt>お</rt></ruby>きたので<ruby>走<rt>はし</rt></ruby>って<ruby>行<rt>い</rt></ruby>きます。

▶ き
▷ お

起きる（おきる）to get up
起こす（おこす）to wake someone up
起こる（おこる）to happen
起立する（きりつする）to stand up
起床（きしょう）wake-up

起源（きげん）origin
起業する（きぎょうする）
　to start a business

<10> 一 十 土 キ キ 非 走 起 起 起 起

▶走(114)

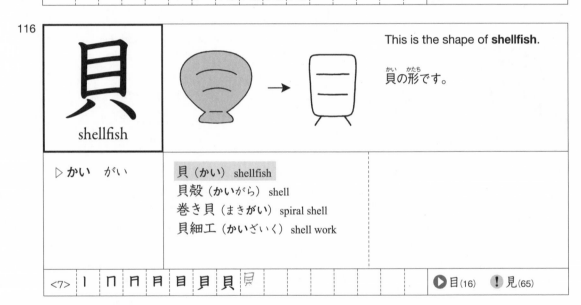

116 貝 shellfish

This is the shape of **shellfish**.

<ruby>貝<rt>かい</rt></ruby>の<ruby>形<rt>かたち</rt></ruby>です。

▷ かい　がい

貝（かい）shellfish
貝殻（かいがら）shell
巻き貝（まきがい）spiral shell
貝細工（かいざいく）shell work

<7> 丨 冂 冂 月 目 貝 貝

▶目(16)　！見(65)

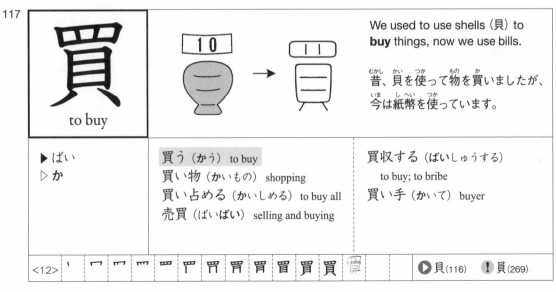

117 買 to buy

We used to use shells（貝）to **buy** things, now we use bills.

<ruby>昔<rt>むかし</rt></ruby>、<ruby>貝<rt>かい</rt></ruby>を<ruby>使<rt>つか</rt></ruby>って<ruby>物<rt>もの</rt></ruby>を<ruby>買<rt>か</rt></ruby>いましたが、<ruby>今<rt>いま</rt></ruby>は<ruby>紙幣<rt>しへい</rt></ruby>を<ruby>使<rt>つか</rt></ruby>っています。

▶ ばい
▷ か

買う（かう）to buy
買い物（かいもの）shopping
買い占める（かいしめる）to buy all
売買（ばいばい）selling and buying

買収する（ばいしゅうする）
　to buy; to bribe
買い手（かいて）buyer

<12> 丶 冂 冂 罒 罒 罒 甼 胃 胃 買 買 買

▶貝(116)　！貫(269)

118

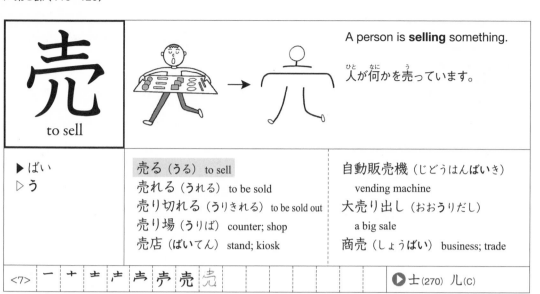

売 to sell		A person is **selling** something.

人が何かを売っています。
<ruby>人<rt>ひと</rt></ruby>が<ruby>何<rt>なに</rt></ruby>かを<ruby>売<rt>う</rt></ruby>っています。

▶ばい
▷う

売る（うる）to sell
売れる（うれる）to be sold
売り切れる（うりきれる）to be sold out
売り場（うりば）counter; shop
売店（ばいてん）stand; kiosk

自動販売機（じどうはんばいき）
　vending machine
大売り出し（おおうりだし）
　a big sale
商売（しょうばい）business; trade

<7> 一 十 土 士 声 声 売 *売*

▶ 士(270) 儿(C)

119

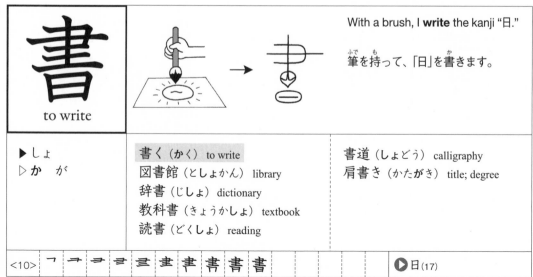

読 to read		He said（言），"**Read** this best-selling（売）book."

「このベストセラーの<ruby>本<rt>ほん</rt></ruby>を<ruby>読<rt>よ</rt></ruby>んでください」と<ruby>彼<rt>かれ</rt></ruby>は<ruby>言<rt>い</rt></ruby>いました。

▶どく　とう
　とく
▷よ

読む（よむ）to read
読み物（よみもの）reading matter
読書（どくしょ）reading
読者（どくしゃ）reader
句読点（くとうてん）punctuation

愛読書（あいどくしょ）
　one's favorite book

<14> 丶 亠 亠 亖 言 言 言 訁 計 計 誌 誌 読

▶ 言(75) 売(118) ! 続(455)

120

書 to write		With a brush, I **write** the kanji "日."

<ruby>筆<rt>ふで</rt></ruby>を<ruby>持<rt>も</rt></ruby>って、「日」を<ruby>書<rt>か</rt></ruby>きます。

▶しょ
▷か　が

書く（かく）to write
図書館（としょかん）library
辞書（じしょ）dictionary
教科書（きょうかしょ）textbook
読書（どくしょ）reading

書道（しょどう）calligraphy
肩書き（かたがき）title; degree

<10> 丁 丆 ヨ ヨ 聿 聿 書 書 書

▶ 日(17)

121

帰

to return

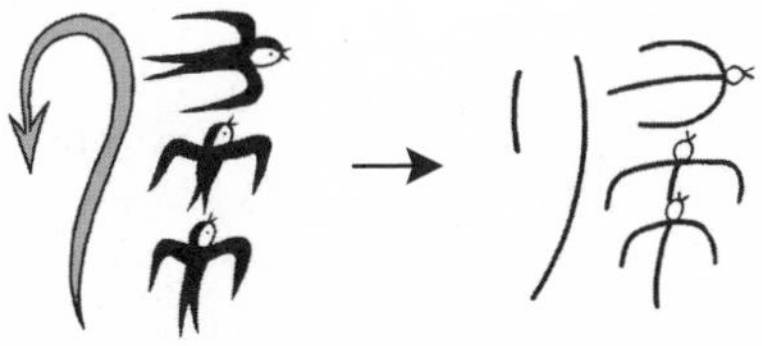

Swallows **return** to their nests.

つばめが巣に帰ります。

▶ き
▷ **かえ**　がえ

- 帰る（かえる） to return
- 帰国（きこく） returning to one's home country
- 帰り（かえり） return
- 行き帰り（いきかえり） way to and from
- 日帰り旅行（ひがえりりょこう） day trip
- 帰宅（きたく） returning home
- 帰化（きか） naturalization

<10> 丨 刂 刂ㄱ 刂ㅋ 刂ヨ 刂冖 刂⺕ 刂帚 帰 帰

122

勉

to make efforts

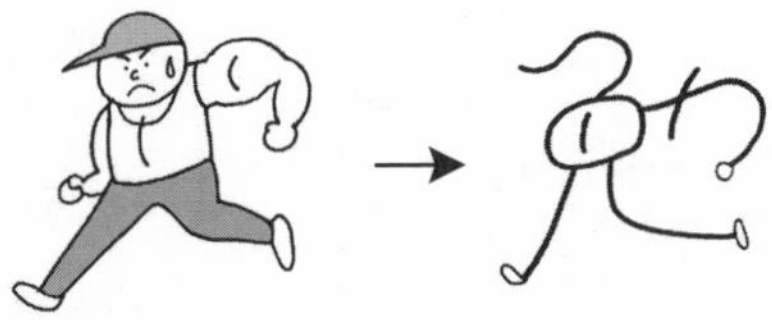

A man is **making an effort** with all his strength (力).

男の人が、力いっぱいがんばっています。

▶ べん

- 勉強する（べんきょうする） to study
- 勤勉な（きんべんな） diligent
- 勉学（べんがく） study

<10> ノ ク ケ 各 缶 缶 争 免 勉 勉

▶ 儿(c) 力(50)　! 晩(137)

123

弓

bow

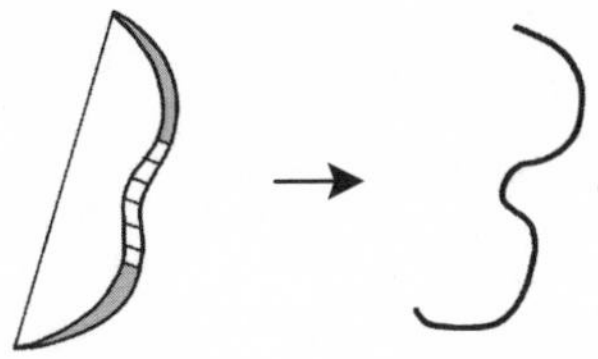

This is the shape of a **bow**.

弓の形です。

▶ きゅう
▷ ゆみ

- 弓（ゆみ） bow
- 弓矢（ゆみや） bow and arrow
- 弓道（きゅうどう） *kyudo*; Japanese archery

<3> ㇆ ㇆ 弓

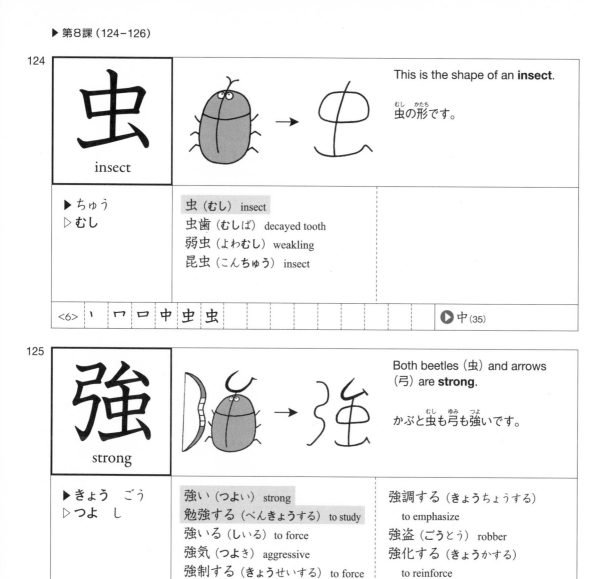

124

虫 insect

This is the shape of an **insect**.

虫の形です。

▶ ちゅう
▷ むし

虫 (むし) insect
虫歯 (むしば) decayed tooth
弱虫 (よわむし) weakling
昆虫 (こんちゅう) insect

<6> 丨 口 口 中 虫 虫

▶ 中 (35)

125

強 strong

Both beetles (虫) and arrows (弓) are **strong**.

かぶと虫も弓も強いです。

▶ きょう ごう
▷ つよ し

強い (つよい) strong
勉強する (べんきょうする) to study
強いる (しいる) to force
強気 (つよき) aggressive
強制する (きょうせいする) to force

強調する (きょうちょうする)
　　 to emphasize
強盗 (ごうとう) robber
強化する (きょうかする)
　　 to reinforce

<11> フ ユ 弓 弘 弘 弘 弘 強 強 強 強

▶ 弓 (123) 虫 (124)

126

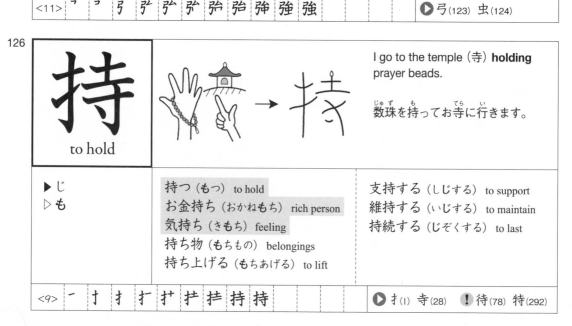

持 to hold

I go to the temple (寺) **holding** prayer beads.

数珠を持ってお寺に行きます。

▶ じ
▷ も

持つ (もつ) to hold
お金持ち (おかねもち) rich person
気持ち (きもち) feeling
持ち物 (もちもの) belongings
持ち上げる (もちあげる) to lift

支持する (しじする) to support
維持する (いじする) to maintain
持続する (じぞくする) to last

<9> 一 十 才 扌 扩 扩 拌 持 持

▶ 扌 (1) 寺 (28) ❗ 待 (78) 特 (292)

127

名
name

His **name** is Taro (タロ).

名前はタロです。

▶ めい　みょう
▷ な

名前 (なまえ) name
有名な (ゆうめいな) famous
平仮名 (ひらがな)
　　hiragana (a Japanese syllabary)
名刺 (めいし) name card

氏名 (しめい) full name
名字 (みょうじ) surname
名詞 (めいし) noun

<6> ノ ク タ タ 名 名 ▶タ(135) 口(15)

128

語
word / language

They talk (言) in five (五) **languages**.

彼らは五つの言葉で話します。

▶ ご
▷ かた

日本語 (にほんご) Japanese language
中国語 (ちゅうごくご)
　　Chinese language
英語 (えいご) English
敬語 (けいご) honorific language

外国語 (がいこくご)
　　foreign language
単語 (たんご) vocabulary
語る (かたる) to talk
主語 (しゅご) subject of a sentence

<14> 丶 亠 亖 亖 亖 言 言 訂 訂 評 語 語 語 語 ▶言(75) 五(5) 口(15) ❗話(76)

第 ９ 課

●この課の漢字

春	夏	秋	冬	朝	昼	夕	方
129	130	131	132	133	134	135	136
晩	夜	心	手	足	体	首	道
137	138	139	140	141	142	143	144

129

春
spring

Spring has come. Three（三）people（人）look at the sun（日）.

春が来ました。三人の人がお日様を見ています。

▶ しゅん
▷ はる

春（はる）spring
春休み（はるやすみ）spring vacation
春学期（はるがっき）spring semester
春巻（はるまき）spring roll
春分（しゅんぶん）vernal equinox

青春（せいしゅん）youth
春夏秋冬（しゅんかしゅうとう）
　four seasons

<9> 一 ニ 三 丰 夫 表 春 春 春

▶ 三(3) 人(26) 日(17) ！ 青(155)

130

夏
summer

It's so hot in **summer**. A person collapses in the shade.

夏は暑いので、人が日陰でぐったりしています。

▶ か げ
▷ なつ

夏（なつ）summer
夏休み（なつやすみ）
　summer vacation
夏服（なつふく）summer clothes
真夏（まなつ）midsummer

初夏（しょか）early summer
夏至（げし）summer solstice
春夏秋冬（しゅんかしゅうとう）
　four seasons

<10> 一 一 一 ア 万 百 百 夏 夏 夏

▶ 自(180)

131

秋 autumn

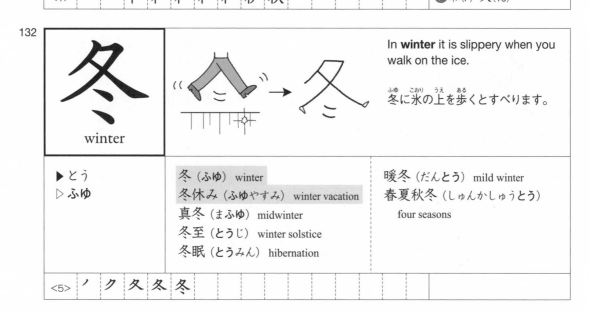

In **autumn**, rice plants bear grain and leaves turn into the color of fire (火).

秋になると、稲が実り、葉は火の色になります。

▶ しゅう
▷ あき

秋 (あき) autumn; fall
秋学期 (あきがっき) fall semester
秋風 (あきかぜ) autumn breeze
秋分 (しゅうぶん) autumnal equinox
晩秋 (ばんしゅう) late autumn

春夏秋冬 (しゅんかしゅうとう)
　four seasons

<9> ノ 二 千 千 禾 禾 利 秒 秋 ▶ 禾 (P) 火 (19)

132

冬 winter

In **winter** it is slippery when you walk on the ice.

冬に氷の上を歩くとすべります。

▶ とう
▷ ふゆ

冬 (ふゆ) winter
冬休み (ふゆやすみ) winter vacation
真冬 (まふゆ) midwinter
冬至 (とうじ) winter solstice
冬眠 (とうみん) hibernation

暖冬 (だんとう) mild winter
春夏秋冬 (しゅんかしゅうとう)
　four seasons

<5> ノ ク 冬 冬 冬

133

朝 morning

It is the **morning** of October 10th (十月十日).

十月十日の朝です。

▶ ちょう
▷ あさ

朝 (あさ) morning
毎朝 (まいあさ) every morning
今朝 (*けさ) this morning
朝ご飯 (あさごはん) breakfast
朝食 (ちょうしょく) breakfast

朝寝坊する (あさねぼうする)
　to sleep in
朝刊 (ちょうかん) morning paper
北朝鮮 (きたちょうせん)
　North Korea

<12> 一 十 十 古 吉 古 直 卓 朝 朝 朝 朝 ▶ 十 (10) 日 (17) 早 (92) 月 (18)

134

昼
daytime

We hang shades in **daytime** when the sun (日) is high.

昼、日が高くなると、日よけをつるします。

| ▶ ちゅう
▷ ひる | 昼 (ひる)　noon; daytime
昼間 (ひるま)　daytime
昼休み (ひるやすみ)　lunch break
昼ご飯 (ひるごはん)　lunch
昼食 (ちゅうしょく)　lunch | 昼寝 (ひるね)　nap |

<9>　一　一　尸　尺　尺　尺　尽　昼　昼　　▶日(17)

135

夕
early evening

In the **early evening**, you see the moon and birds.

夕方、月と鳥が見えます。

| ▶ せき
▷ ゆう | 夕方 (ゆうがた)　early evening
夕日 (ゆうひ)　setting sun
夕食 (ゆうしょく)　evening meal
七夕 (*たなばた)　the Star Festival
夕刊 (ゆうかん)　evening newspaper | 夕立 (ゆうだち)　evening shower
一朝一夕 (いっちょういっせき)
　in a very short time |

<3>　ノ　ク　夕　　❗月(18)

136

方
direction / person

Please go to the **direction** of that flag.

旗のある方へ行ってください。

| ▶ ほう
▷ かた　がた | 読み方 (よみかた)　way of reading
夕方 (ゆうがた)　early evening
あの方 (あのかた)　that person
　[polite expression]
両方 (りょうほう)　both (sides) | 方法 (ほうほう)　method
方向 (ほうこう)　direction
方言 (ほうげん)　dialect
長方形 (ちょうほうけい)　rectangle |

<4>　丶　一　方　方　　❗万(13)

137

晚
evening

A child hurries home before **evening** comes.

晚にならないうちに、急いで家に帰ります。

▶ ばん

晚（ばん） evening; night
今晚（こんばん） tonight
毎晚（まいばん） every night
晚ご飯（ばんごはん） dinner
晚婚（ばんこん） a late marriage

晚年（ばんねん） one's later years

<12> 丨 冂 冂 日 日' 日勹 日勹 昨 昢 晚 晚 晚

▶日(17) 儿(C) ❗勉(122)

138

夜
night

At **night**, a person with a hat is watching the moon and a cloud.

夜、帽子をかぶった人が月と雲を見ています。

▶ や
▷ よる　よ

夜（よる） night
今夜（こんや） tonight
夜中（よなか）
　　midnight; middle of the night
夜明け（よあけ） dawn

深夜（しんや） late at night
夜食（やしょく） night snack
徹夜する（てつやする）
　　to stay up all night

<8> 丶 亠 广 广 疒 疒 夜 夜

▶イ (B)

139

心
heart

My **heart** beats.

心臓が動いています。

▶ しん
▷ こころ

心（こころ） heart
安心する（あんしんする）
　　to be relieved
心配する（しんぱいする） to worry
中心（ちゅうしん） center

熱心な（ねっしんな） enthusiastic
感心する（かんしんする）
　　to be impressed
心理学（しんりがく） psychology

<4> 丶 心 心 心

❗必(371)

140

手
hand

This is the shape of a **hand**.

手の形です。

▶ しゅ
▷ て　た

手（て）hand
下手な（へたな）poor at
上手な（*じょうずな）good at
手紙（てがみ）letter
お手洗い（おてあらい）restroom

切手（きって）postage stamp
手伝う（てつだう）to help
歌手（かしゅ）singer

<4> 一 二 三 手

141

足
foot / leg

Stretch your **legs** and run.

足を伸ばして走りましょう。

▶ そく　ぞく
▷ あし　た

足（あし）foot; leg
足りる（たりる）to be sufficient
足す（たす）to add
一足（いっそく）one pair of shoes
水不足（みずぶそく）water shortage

遠足（えんそく）one-day excursion
満足（まんぞく）satisfaction
足音（あしおと）sound of footsteps

<7> 丶 冖 口 口 口 尸 尸 足

▶ 口 (15)　！走 (114)

142

体
body

When your **body** is injured, apply a bandage and rest（休）.

体にけがをしたら、包帯を巻いて休みましょう。

▶ たい　てい
▷ からだ

体（からだ）body
体重（たいじゅう）body weight
体操（たいそう）gymnastics
体温（たいおん）body temperature
全体（ぜんたい）the whole

団体（だんたい）group
世間体（せけんてい）reputation
体調（たいちょう）physical condition

<7> ノ イ 仁 什 什 休 体

▶ 休 (113)　本 (25)

143

首

neck / head

This is the shape of a person who has a long **neck**.

首の長い人の形です。
<ruby>首<rt>くび</rt></ruby> <ruby>長<rt>なが</rt></ruby> <ruby>人<rt>ひと</rt></ruby> <ruby>形<rt>かたち</rt></ruby>

▶ しゅ
▷ くび

首（くび）neck
首になる（くびになる）to get fired
手首（てくび）wrist
首相（しゅしょう）prime minister
首都（しゅと）capital

首位（しゅい）top position
部首（ぶしゅ）radical (of kanji)

<9> 丶 丷 丷 丷 产 首 首 首 首 ！自(180)

144

道

road

He is craning his neck（首）as he waits for someone on the **road**.

道で首を長くしてだれかを待っています。
<ruby>道<rt>みち</rt></ruby> <ruby>首<rt>くび</rt></ruby> <ruby>長<rt>なが</rt></ruby> <ruby>待<rt>ま</rt></ruby>

▶ どう　とう
▷ みち

道（みち）road
片道（かたみち）one way
書道（しょどう）calligraphy
柔道（じゅうどう）judo
北海道（ほっかいどう）Hokkaido

道具（どうぐ）tool
歩道（ほどう）sidewalk
近道（ちかみち）shortcut

<12> 丶 丷 丷 丷 产 首 首 首 首 首 道 道 ▶首(143) 辶(F)

第 10 課

● この課の漢字

山	川	林	森	空	海	化	花
145	146	147	148	149	150	151	152
天	赤	青	白	黒	色	魚	犬
153	154	155	156	157	158	159	160

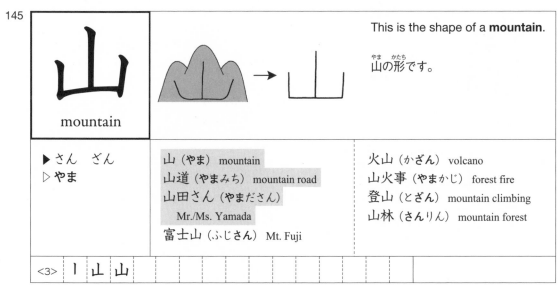

145

山
mountain

This is the shape of a **mountain**.

山の形です。

▶ さん　ざん
▷ やま

山（やま） mountain
山道（やまみち） mountain road
山田さん（やまださん）
　 Mr./Ms. Yamada
富士山（ふじさん） Mt. Fuji

火山（かざん） volcano
山火事（やまかじ） forest fire
登山（とざん） mountain climbing
山林（さんりん） mountain forest

<3>　１　山　山

146

川
river

The **river** runs through it.

川が流れていきます。

▶ せん
▷ かわ　がわ

川（かわ） river
小川さん（おがわさん）
　 Mr./Ms. Ogawa
ナイル川（ナイルがわ） the Nile
天の川（あまのがわ） the Milky Way

川岸（かわぎし） riverside
川遊び（かわあそび）
　 outing to the riverside
河川（かせん） rivers

<3>　丿　刂　川

147

林
small forest

Two trees (木) become a **small forest**.

二本の木が林になります。

▶ りん
▷ はやし　ばやし

林 (はやし)　small forest; grove
小林さん (こばやしさん)
　Mr./Ms. Kobayashi
森林 (しんりん)　forest
山林 (さんりん)　mountain forest

林業 (りんぎょう)　forestry
松林 (まつばやし)　pine forest
林道 (りんどう)　path through forest
密林 (みつりん)　dense forest

<8>　一　十　才　木　村　村　材　林　　▶ 木(21)

148

森
forest

Three trees (木) become a **forest**.

三本の木が森になります。

▶ しん
▷ もり

森 (もり)　forest
森田さん (もりたさん)
　Mr./Ms. Morita
森林 (しんりん)　forest

<12>　一　十　才　木　木　杏　杏　柔　森　森　森　森　　▶ 木(21)

149

空
sky / empty

Open the window and measure the **sky** with a craftsman's ruler (工).

窓を開けて、空を定規で測ってください。

▶ くう
▷ そら　から
　あ　ぞら

空 (そら)　sky
空気 (くうき)　air
空港 (くうこう)　airport
航空便 (こうくうびん)　airmail
空手 (からて)　karate

空く (あく)　to be vacant
空っぽ (からっぽ)　empty
大空 (おおぞら)　big sky

<8>　丶　丷　宀　宀　空　空　空　空　　▶ 宀(G) 工(38)　! 究(262)

150

海
sea

We go to the **sea** and swim every（毎）day.

毎日、海に行って泳ぎます。

▶ かい
▷ うみ

海（うみ）sea	海賊（かいぞく）pirates
北海道（ほっかいどう）Hokkaido	海藻（かいそう）seaweed
海外（かいがい）overseas	海水（かいすい）seawater
エーゲ海（エーゲかい）the Aegean Sea	
海岸（かいがん）seashore	

<9> 丶 氵 氵 氵 汇 洺 洧 海 海　　　▶ 氵（J）毎（62）

151

化
change

A person stands up and sits down. He **changes** his position.

人が立ったり座ったりして、姿勢を変えます。

▶ か　け
▷ ば

化学（かがく）chemistry	変化（へんか）change
文化（ぶんか）culture	進化（しんか）evolution
お化け（おばけ）ghost	
化粧（けしょう）makeup	
民主化（みんしゅか）democratization	

<4> ノ イ 仁 化　　　▶ イ（B）　! 北（48）

152

花
flower

Grass changes（化）into **flowers**.

草が変化して花になります。

▶ か
▷ はな　ばな

花（はな）flower	生け花（いけばな）
花見（はなみ）flower viewing	flower arrangement
花火（はなび）fireworks	花瓶（かびん）flower vase
花屋（はなや）flower shop	花粉症（かふんしょう）hay fever
花嫁（はなよめ）bride	

<7> 一 十 艹 艹 苁 花 花　　　▶ 艹（K）化（151）

153

天

heaven

→

I look up to **heaven** with my hands wide open.

両手を大きく広げて、天を見上げます。

▶ てん
▷ あま　あめ

天気 （てんき）　weather
天気予報 （てんきよほう）
　　　　　weather forecast
天国 （てんごく）　heaven
天皇 （てんのう）　emperor

天使 （てんし）　angel
天才 （てんさい）　genius
天の川 （あまのがわ）　the Milky Way
天文学 （てんもんがく）　astronomy

<4> 一 二 チ 天 　　　　　　　▶大(81) ❗夫(202)

154

赤

red

→

You put soil （土）over the fire to make **red** bricks.

火の上に土を置いて、赤いレンガを作ります。

▶ せき　しゃく
▷ あか

赤 （あか）／赤い （あかい）　red
赤ちゃん （あかちゃん）　baby
赤字 （あかじ）　deficit
真っ赤 （*まっか）　deep red
赤十字 （せきじゅうじ）　the Red Cross

赤道 （せきどう）　the equator
赤飯 （せきはん）　festive red rice
赤外線 （せきがいせん）　infrared rays

<7> 一 十 土 サ 赤 赤 赤 　　　　▶土(23)

155

青

blue

→

Blue grass and a blue moon （月）.

青い草と青い月。

▶ せい　しょう
▷ あお

青 （あお）／青い （あおい）　blue
青空 （あおぞら）　blue sky
青信号 （あおしんごう）　green light
青森 （あおもり）　Aomori
青年 （せいねん）　youth

真っ青 （*まっさお）　deep blue
青春 （せいしゅん）　youth

<8> 一 十 キ 圭 青 青 青 青 　　▶月(18) ❗春(129)

156

白
white

There is a **white** building.

白い建物があります。
しろ　たてもの

▶ はく　びゃく
▷ しろ　しら

白（しろ）／白い（しろい）　white
白黒（しろくろ）　black and white
面白い（おもしろい）　interesting
白髪（しらが／はくはつ）
　　　white (gray) hair

真っ白（まっしろ）　snow-white
白紙（はくし）　blank sheet
白鳥（はくちょう）　swan
白夜（びゃくや）　white nights

<5>　ノ　イ　ウ　白　白

▶ 日(17)　！ 百(11)　自(180)

157

黒
black

The rice field（田）was burned
and the soil（土）turned **black**.

田んぼが焼けて、土が黒くなりま
た　　　や　　　つち　くろ
した。

▶ こく
▷ くろ

黒（くろ）／黒い（くろい）　black
白黒（しろくろ）　black and white
黒猫（くろねこ）　black cat
黒板（こくばん）　blackboard
真っ黒（まっくろ）　pitch-black

黒字（くろじ）　surplus

<11>　丨　冂　冃　日　甲　甲　里　里　黒　黒　黒

▶ 田(49)　土(23)　灬(N)　！ 魚(159)

158

色
color

This is the shape of a swirl of
two **colors**.

二つの色のうずまきの形です。
ふた　いろ　　　　　かたち

▶ しき　しょく
▷ いろ

色（いろ）　color
色々な（いろいろな）　various
水色（みずいろ）　light blue
灰色（はいいろ）　gray
色鉛筆（いろえんぴつ）　color pencils

景色（けしき）　scenery
特色（とくしょく）　characteristic
脱色（だっしょく）　bleaching

<6>　ノ　ク　ク　ム　色　色

159

魚

fish

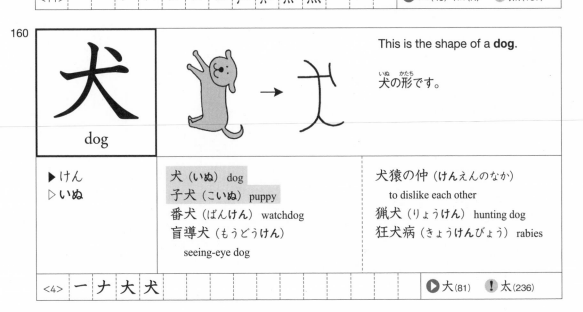

This is the shape of **fish**.

魚の形です。

▶ ぎょ
▷ さかな　ざかな
　 うお

魚（さかな）fish
魚屋（さかなや）fish shop
小魚（こざかな）small fish
魚市場（うおいちば）fish market
金魚（きんぎょ）goldfish

人魚（にんぎょ）mermaid
熱帯魚（ねったいぎょ）tropical fish
魚介類（ぎょかいるい）seafood

<11> ノ ク 几 凢 命 免 角 鱼 魚 魚 魚

▶ 田(49) 灬(N)　！黒(157)

160

犬

dog

This is the shape of a **dog**.

犬の形です。

▶ けん
▷ いぬ

犬（いぬ）dog
子犬（こいぬ）puppy
番犬（ばんけん）watchdog
盲導犬（もうどうけん）
　 seeing-eye dog

犬猿の仲（けんえんのなか）
　 to dislike each other
猟犬（りょうけん）hunting dog
狂犬病（きょうけんびょう）rabies

<4> 一 ナ 大 犬

▶ 大(81)　！太(236)

Part 2

第11課 — 第20課
（漢字番号 161-320）

第　11　課

● この課の漢字

料	理	反	飯	牛	豚	鳥	肉
161	162	163	164	165	166	167	168
茶	予	野	菜	切	作	未	味
169	170	171	172	173	174	175	176

161

料

ingredients / fare

You measure rice （米） and other **ingredients** on a scale.

はかりで米やそのほかの材料を量ります。

▶ りょう

料理 （りょうり） cooking; dish
食料品 （しょくりょうひん） groceries
無料 （むりょう） free of charge
料金 （りょうきん） charge
授業料 （じゅぎょうりょう） tuition

給料 （きゅうりょう） salary
材料 （ざいりょう） material
資料 （しりょう） documents; data

<10> 丶 ⺌ ⺍ ⺥ 半 米 米 米 米 料　　▶ 米(67)

162

理

logic

The king （王） **logically** thought and made the rice fields （田）.

王様は論理的に考えて、田んぼを作りました。

▶ り

料理 （りょうり） cooking; dish
無理な （むりな） impossible
理由 （りゆう） reason
地理 （ちり） geography
修理 （しゅうり） repair

理想 （りそう） ideal
理解 （りかい） understanding
心理学 （しんりがく） psychology

<11> ⁻ ⊺ ㆗ 王 玊 玕 玾 珄 理 理 理　　▶ 王(63)　田(49)　土(23)

163

反

to oppose

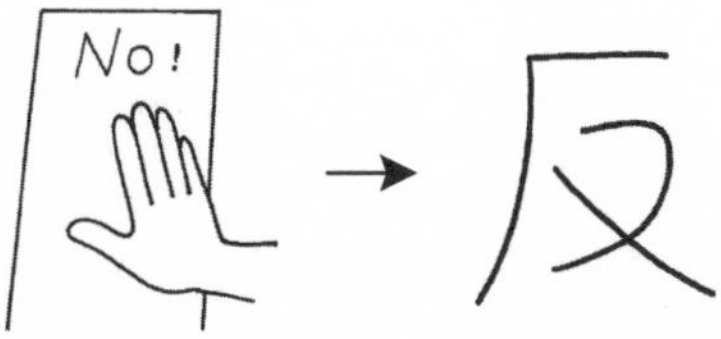

I **oppose** it.

私(わたし)は反対(はんたい)です。

▶はん　たん
　ほん
▷そ

反対する（はんたいする） to oppose
違反（いはん） violation
反省（はんせい） reflection
反抗（はんこう） resistance
反る（そる） to bend
反応（はんのう） reaction
反物（たんもの） cloth
謀反（むほん） rebellion

<4> 一 厂 万 反 ｜ ❗友(96)

164

飯

meal / cooked rice

They oppose (反) my habit of eating (食) too much **rice**.

皆(みな)は私(わたし)がご飯(はん)ばかり食(た)べるのに反対(はんたい)です。

▶はん
▷めし

ご飯（ごはん） cooked rice; meal
朝ご飯（あさごはん） breakfast
昼ご飯（ひるごはん） lunch
晩ご飯（ばんごはん） dinner
飯（めし） meal [vulgar expression]
炊飯器（すいはんき） rice cooker

<12> ノ 𠆢 𠆢 今 今 今 食 食 食 飣 飯 飯 ｜ ▶食(70) 反(163) ❗飲(71)

165

牛

cow

This is the shape of a one-horned **cow**.

角(つの)が一本(いっぽん)しかない牛(うし)の形(かたち)です。

▶ぎゅう
▷うし

牛（うし） cow; bull
牛肉（ぎゅうにく） beef
牛乳（ぎゅうにゅう） milk
子牛（こうし） calf; veal
牡牛座（おうしざ） Taurus
水牛（すいぎゅう） buffalo
牛丼（ぎゅうどん） beef rice bowl
闘牛（とうぎゅう） bullfight

<4> ノ 𠂉 𠂉 牛 ｜ ❗午(42)

| 166 | 豚
pig | | A **pig** is looking at the moon （月）.
ぶた　つき　み
豚が月を見ています。 |

| ▶ とん
▷ ぶた | 豚（ぶた）pig
豚肉（ぶたにく）pork
子豚（こぶた）piglet
豚カツ（とんカツ）pork cutlet | |

| <11> |) 刀 月 月 尸 尸 尸 肝 肝 肝 豚 | | ▶ 月(18) |

| 167 | 鳥
bird | | This is the shape of a **bird**.
とり　かたち
鳥の形です。 |

| ▶ ちょう
▷ とり | 鳥（とり）bird
小鳥（ことり）little bird
鳥肉（とりにく）chicken
白鳥（はくちょう）swan
焼き鳥（やきとり）grilled chicken | 鳥居（とりい）shrine gate
一石二鳥（いっせきにちょう）
to kill two birds with one stone |

| <11> | ' 亻 亣 户 户 皀 鸟 鳥 鳥 鳥 鳥 | | ! 島(476) |

| 168 | 肉
meat | | This is the shape of **meat**.
にく　かたち
肉の形です。 |

| ▶ にく | 肉（にく）meat
牛肉（ぎゅうにく）beef
豚肉（ぶたにく）pork
鳥肉（とりにく）chicken
肉屋（にくや）meat shop | 筋肉（きんにく）muscle
皮肉（ひにく）irony; sarcasm |

| <6> | l 冂 内 内 肉 肉 | | ▶ 内(490) |

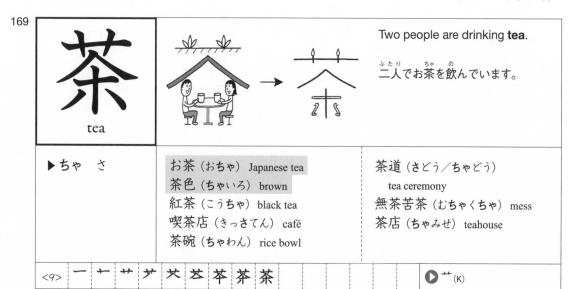

169

茶
tea

Two people are drinking **tea**.

二人でお茶を飲んでいます。
ふたり　ちゃ　の

▶ちゃ　さ

お茶 （おちゃ） Japanese tea
茶色 （ちゃいろ） brown
紅茶 （こうちゃ） black tea
喫茶店 （きっさてん） café
茶碗 （ちゃわん） rice bowl

茶道 （さどう／ちゃどう）
　　tea ceremony
無茶苦茶 （むちゃくちゃ） mess
茶店 （ちゃみせ） teahouse

<9> 一 十 サ ザ 大 大 苯 茶 茶　　⟳ 艹 (K)

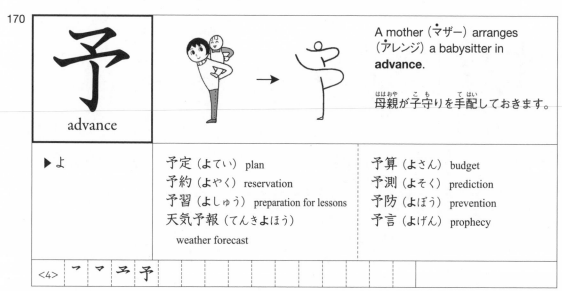

170

予
advance

A mother （ᴍᴀᴢᴀᴀ マザー） arranges
（ᴀʀᴇɴᴊɪ アレンジ） a babysitter in
advance.

母親が子守りを手配しておきます。
ははおや　こも　　てはい

▶よ

予定 （よてい） plan
予約 （よやく） reservation
予習 （よしゅう） preparation for lessons
天気予報 （てんきよほう）
　　weather forecast

予算 （よさん） budget
予測 （よそく） prediction
予防 （よぼう） prevention
予言 （よげん） prophecy

<4> フ フ マ 予 予

171

野
field

They go to the **field** in advance
（予）.

野原に行って耕しておきます。
のはら　い　　たがや

▶や
▷の

野菜 （やさい） vegetable
長野 （ながの） Nagano
小野さん （おのさん） Mr./Ms. Ono
野球 （やきゅう） baseball
分野 （ぶんや） realm; field

野党 （やとう） opposition party
野原 （のはら） field; plain

<11> 丨 冂 冂 日 甲 甲 里 野 野 野 野　　⟳ 田(49) 予(170)

172

菜
vegetable

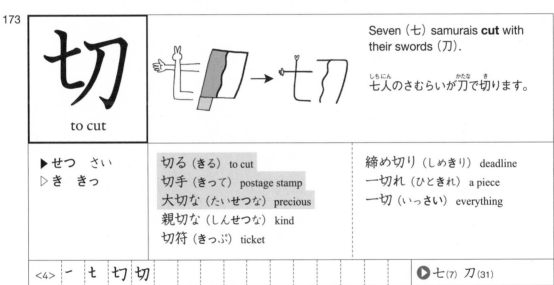

You pick **vegetables** from grasses and trees (木).

草や木の中から野菜を摘み取り
ます。

▶ さい
▷ な

野菜 (やさい) vegetable
菜園 (さいえん) vegetable garden
菜の花 (なのはな) rape blossom
白菜 (はくさい) Chinese cabbage
山菜 (さんさい) edible wild plants

菜食主義 (さいしょくしゅぎ)
vegetarianism

<11> 一 十 艹 サ 艿 艾 菜 芝 茉 苹 菜

▶ サ (K) 木 (21)

173

切
to cut

Seven (七) samurais **cut** with
their swords (刀).

七人のさむらいが刀で切ります。

▶ せつ さい
▷ き きっ

切る (きる) to cut
切手 (きって) postage stamp
大切な (たいせつな) precious
親切な (しんせつな) kind
切符 (きっぷ) ticket

締め切り (しめきり) deadline
一切れ (ひときれ) a piece
一切 (いっさい) everything

<4> 一 七 切 切

▶ 七 (7) 刀 (31)

174

作
to make

A person with a saw **makes**
something.

人がのこぎりを持って、何かを
作ります。

▶ さく さっ
　　さ
▷ つく づく

作る (つくる) to make
手作り (てづくり) handmade
作文 (さくぶん) composition
作品 (さくひん) artistic piece
作家 (さっか) novelist; writer

操作 (そうさ) operation
名作 (めいさく) masterpiece
動作 (どうさ) movement

<7> ノ イ 亻 仁 作 作 作

▶ イ (B)

175

未
not yet

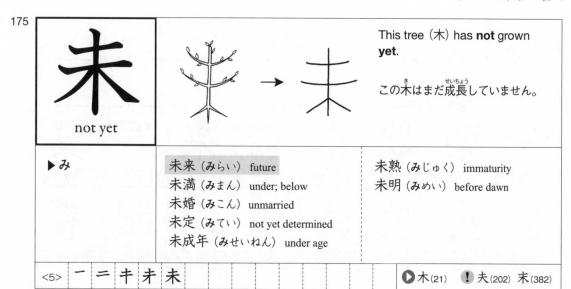

This tree（木）has **not** grown **yet**.

この<ruby>木<rt>き</rt></ruby>はまだ<ruby>成長<rt>せいちょう</rt></ruby>していません。

▶み

未来（みらい） future	未熟（みじゅく） immaturity
未満（みまん） under; below	未明（みめい） before dawn
未婚（みこん） unmarried	
未定（みてい） not yet determined	
未成年（みせいねん） under age	

<5> 一 二 キ 未 未　　　▶木(21)　❗夫(202) 末(382)

176

味
taste

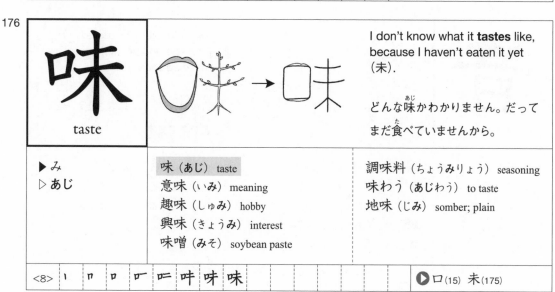

I don't know what it **tastes** like, because I haven't eaten it yet （未）.

どんな<ruby>味<rt>あじ</rt></ruby>かわかりません。だって まだ<ruby>食<rt>た</rt></ruby>べていませんから。

▶み
▷あじ

味（あじ） taste	調味料（ちょうみりょう） seasoning
意味（いみ） meaning	味わう（あじわう） to taste
趣味（しゅみ） hobby	地味（じみ） somber; plain
興味（きょうみ） interest	
味噌（みそ） soybean paste	

<8> 丨 冂 口 口 吁 呀 呋 味　　　▶口(15) 未(175)

第　12　課

● この課の漢字

音	楽	歌	自	転	乗	写	真
177	178	179	180	181	182	183	184
台	央	映	画	羊	洋	服	着
185	186	187	188	189	190	191	192

177

音
sound

When the sun（日）rises, people stand up（立）and make **sounds**.

日が昇ると、人々は立ち上がって音をたてます。

▶ おん　いん
▷ おと　ね

音楽（おんがく） music
音（おと） sound
発音（はつおん） pronunciation
録音（ろくおん） recording
音量（おんりょう） volume

母音（ぼいん） vowel
子音（しいん） consonant
本音（ほんね） real intention

<9> 　 ' 　 一 　 ナ 　 ウ 　 立 　 产 　 音 　 音 　 音

▶立(77) 日(17) ❗昔(276)

178

楽
fun / comfortable

Let's have **fun** beating the white（白）drum on the wooden（木）stand.

木の上の白い太鼓をたたいて楽しもう。

▶ がく　らく
　 がっ
▷ たの

音楽（おんがく） music
楽しい（たのしい） enjoyable
楽しみ（たのしみ） fun
楽しむ（たのしむ） to have fun
楽な（らくな） easy; comfortable

楽器（がっき） musical instrument
娯楽（ごらく） entertainment

<13> 　 ' 　 ′ 　 ⺮ 　 ⺤ 　 白 　 泊 　 泊 　 泊 　 淅 　 渔 　 楽 　 楽 　 楽

▶白(156) 木(21)

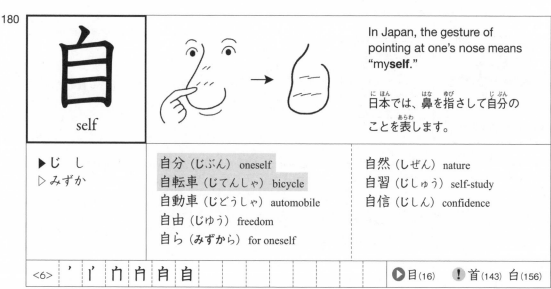

179

歌
to sing

People (人) are **singing** with their mouths (口) wide open.

大きい口を開けてみんなで歌っています。

▶ か
▷ うた

歌（うた）song
歌う（うたう）to sing
歌手（かしゅ）singer
歌詞（かし）lyrics
短歌（たんか）*tanka* (poem)

国歌（こっか）national anthem
校歌（こうか）school song

<14> 一 厂 厂 冎 匞 哥 哥 哥 哥 哥 歌 歌 歌 ▶ 口(15) 人(26)

180

自
self

In Japan, the gesture of pointing at one's nose means "my**self**."

日本では、鼻を指さして自分のことを表します。

▶ じ し
▷ みずか

自分（じぶん）oneself
自転車（じてんしゃ）bicycle
自動車（じどうしゃ）automobile
自由（じゆう）freedom
自ら（みずから）for oneself

自然（しぜん）nature
自習（じしゅう）self-study
自信（じしん）confidence

<6> ' 丨 冂 冃 自 自 ▶ 目(16) ❗ 首(143) 白(156)

181

転
to roll over

I fell off the car (車) **rolling**.

車から転がり落ちました。

▶ てん
▷ ころ

自転車（じてんしゃ）bicycle
運転（うんてん）driving
運転手（うんてんしゅ）driver
転ぶ（ころぶ）to tumble
転がる（ころがる）to roll

回転ずし（かいてんずし）
　conveyor-belt sushi bar
転職（てんしょく）changing jobs
転校（てんこう）changing schools

<11> 一 厂 厅 亘 亘 車 車 軒 軒 転 転 ▶ 車(104)

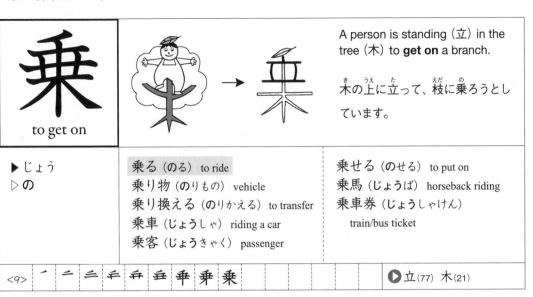

182

乗
to get on

A person is standing (立) in the tree (木) to **get on** a branch.

木の上に立って、枝に乗ろうとしています。

▶ じょう
▷ の

乗る（のる）　to ride
乗り物（のりもの）　vehicle
乗り換える（のりかえる）　to transfer
乗車（じょうしゃ）　riding a car
乗客（じょうきゃく）　passenger

乗せる（のせる）　to put on
乗馬（じょうば）　horseback riding
乗車券（じょうしゃけん）
　　train/bus ticket

<9>　一　二　三　千　千　垂　垂　乗　乗　　　● 立(77)　木(21)

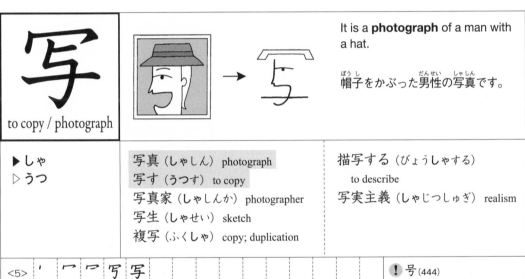

183

写
to copy / photograph

It is a **photograph** of a man with a hat.

帽子をかぶった男性の写真です。

▶ しゃ
▷ うつ

写真（しゃしん）　photograph
写す（うつす）　to copy
写真家（しゃしんか）　photographer
写生（しゃせい）　sketch
複写（ふくしゃ）　copy; duplication

描写する（びょうしゃする）
　　to describe
写実主義（しゃじつしゅぎ）　realism

<5>　丶　冖　冖　写　写　　　　　！ 号(444)

184

真
true

The television shows the **true** image.

テレビは本当のイメージを映し出します。

▶ しん
▷ ま

写真（しゃしん）　photograph
真ん中（まんなか）　center
真っ黒（まっくろ）　pitch-black
真っ白（まっしろ）　snow-white
真夜中（まよなか）　midnight

真剣（しんけん）　serious
真実（しんじつ）　truth

<10>　一　十　广　内　南　育　盲　直　真　真　　　！ 直(496)

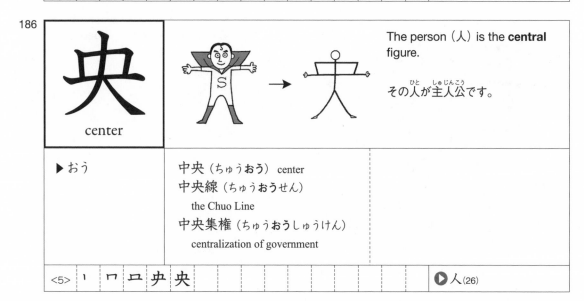

185

台
stand

I am on the **stand**.

私は台の上にいます。

▶ だい　たい

二台（にだい）two (machines)
台所（だいどころ）kitchen
台風（たいふう）typhoon
台（だい）stand; board
舞台（ぶたい）stage

台湾（たいわん）Taiwan
台本（だいほん）script; scenario

<5> ㇐ ㇂ 厶 台 台　　　　▶口 (15)　❗合 (295)

186

央
center

The person（人）is the **central** figure.

その人が主人公です。

▶ おう

中央（ちゅうおう）center
中央線（ちゅうおうせん）
　　the Chuo Line
中央集権（ちゅうおうしゅうけん）
　　centralization of government

<5> 丶 冂 口 央 央　　　　▶人 (26)

187

映
to project

The central（央）figure of the movie was **projected** on the screen.

映画の主人公が映し出されました。

▶ えい
▷ うつ　は

映画（えいが）movie
映画館（えいがかん）movie theater
映る（うつる）to be projected
映す（うつす）to project
反映する（はんえいする）to reflect

放映する（ほうえいする）
　　to televise
映える（はえる）to stand out against
上映する（じょうえいする）
　　to show films

<9> 丨 冂 日 日 旷 明 叩 映 映　　　▶日 (17) 央 (186)　❗英 (221)

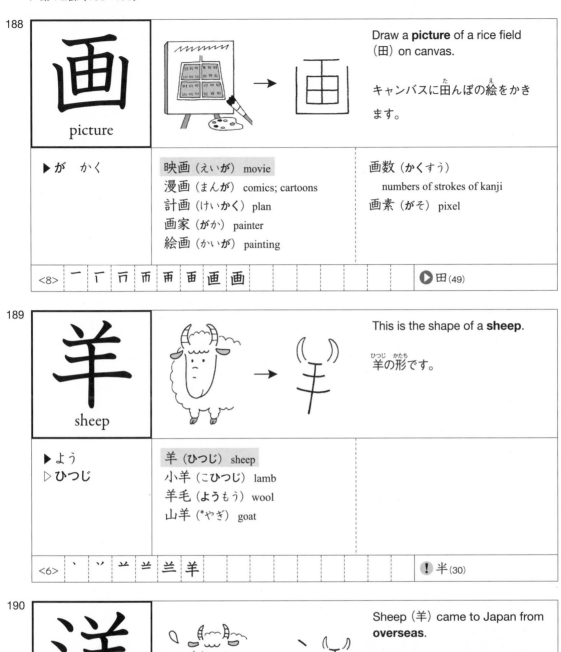

188

画

picture

Draw a **picture** of a rice field（田）on canvas.

キャンバスに田んぼの絵をかきます。

▶ が　かく

映画（えいが）movie
漫画（まんが）comics; cartoons
計画（けいかく）plan
画家（がか）painter
絵画（かいが）painting

画数（かくすう）
　　numbers of strokes of kanji
画素（がそ）pixel

<8>　一　厂　冂　币　雨　面　画　画　　　　　　　　▶ 田 (49)

189

羊

sheep

This is the shape of a **sheep**.

羊の形です。

▶ よう
▷ ひつじ

羊（ひつじ）sheep
小羊（こひつじ）lamb
羊毛（ようもう）wool
山羊（*やぎ）goat

<6>　丶　丷　半　兰　兰　羊　　　　　　　　　　　　! 半 (30)

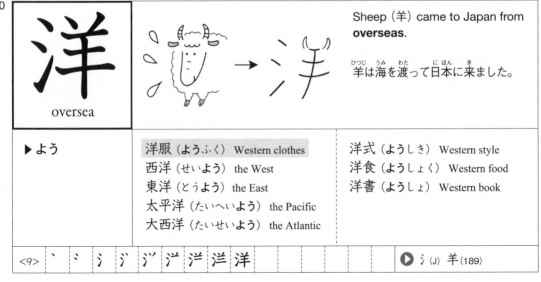

190

洋

oversea

Sheep（羊）came to Japan from **overseas**.

羊は海を渡って日本に来ました。

▶ よう

洋服（ようふく）Western clothes
西洋（せいよう）the West
東洋（とうよう）the East
太平洋（たいへいよう）the Pacific
大西洋（たいせいよう）the Atlantic

洋式（ようしき）Western style
洋食（ようしょく）Western food
洋書（ようしょ）Western book

<9>　丶　冫　氵　汁　汁　洋　洋　洋　洋　　　　　▶ 氵 (J) 羊 (189)

191

服

clothes / to submit

Under the moon（月）, you hang your **clothes**.

月の下で服をかけます。

▶ ふく

服（ふく）clothes
洋服（ようふく）Western clothes
和服（わふく）Japanese clothes
服装（ふくそう）costume

克服する（こくふくする）
　　to overcome
制服（せいふく）uniform
喪服（もふく）mourning dress
征服（せいふく）conquest

<8>) 刀 月 月 肝 朋 服 服 ｜ ｜ ｜ ｜ ▶ 月（18）

192

着

to reach / to wear

I saw a sheep（羊）**wearing** a sweater.

セーターを着ている羊を見ました。

▶ ちゃく じゃく
▷ き ぎ つ

着る（きる）to wear
上着（うわぎ）jacket
下着（したぎ）underwear
着く（つく）to arrive
着物（きもの）kimono

到着（とうちゃく）arrival
落ち着く（おちつく）to calm down
水着（みずぎ）bathing suit

<12> 、 ゛ ソ ヤ 芏 羊 差 羊 荠 着 着 着 ｜ ｜ ▶ 羊（189）目（16）

第 13 課

●この課の漢字

家	矢	族	親	兄	姉	弟	妹
193	194	195	196	197	198	199	200
私	夫	妻	主	住	糸	氏	紙
201	202	203	204	205	206	207	208

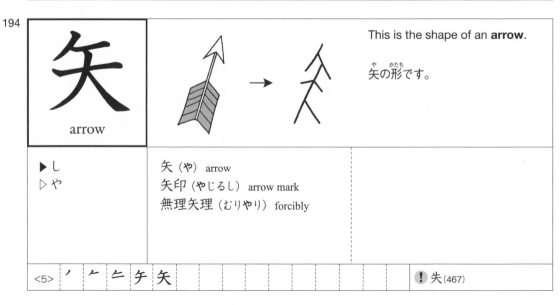

193

家
house

In the old times, people kept pigs in the **house**.

昔、家で豚を飼いました。
<small>むかし いえ ぶた か</small>

▶ か け
▷ いえ や

家（いえ） house
家族（かぞく） family
家庭（かてい） home; family
家内（かない） my wife
家事（かじ） housework

大家（おおや） landlord
家賃（やちん） (house) rent
山田家（やまだけ） Yamada family

<10> ＇ ＂ 宀 宁 宇 守 宇 宇 家 家　　▶宀(G)

194

矢
arrow

This is the shape of an **arrow**.

矢の形です。
<small>や かたち</small>

▶ し
▷ や

矢（や） arrow
矢印（やじるし） arrow mark
無理矢理（むりやり） forcibly

<5> ノ ヒ 匕 午 矢　　❗矢(467)

195

族
family / tribe

Under the flag, people protect their **family** with their arrows (矢).

旗<ruby>旗<rt>はた</rt></ruby>の<ruby>下<rt>した</rt></ruby>、<ruby>矢<rt>や</rt></ruby>で<ruby>家族<rt>かぞく</rt></ruby>を<ruby>守<rt>まも</rt></ruby>ります。

▶ ぞく

家族（かぞく）family
親族（しんぞく）relatives
貴族（きぞく）aristocracy
民族（みんぞく）ethnic group
水族館（すいぞくかん）aquarium

<11> ' 亠 宁 方 扩 扩 扩 扩 斿 斿 族 族

▶ 方(136) 矢(194) ！旅(318)

196

親
parent / intimacy

A **parent** is standing (立) on top of a tree (木) to look at (見) his/her child.

<ruby>木<rt>き</rt></ruby>の<ruby>上<rt>うえ</rt></ruby>に<ruby>立<rt>た</rt></ruby>って、<ruby>子供<rt>こども</rt></ruby>を<ruby>見守<rt>みまも</rt></ruby>っているのが<ruby>親<rt>おや</rt></ruby>です。

▶ しん
▷ おや　した

親（おや）parent(s)
親切な（しんせつな）kind
両親（りょうしん）parents
親友（しんゆう）best friend
父親（ちちおや）father

母親（ははおや）mother
親子（おやこ）
　　parent(s) and child(ren)
親しい（したしい）intimate

<16> ' 亠 十 立 立 立 辛 辛 亲 亲 新 新 新 新 親 親

▶ 立(77) 木(21) 見(65) ！新(85)

197

兄
older brother

My **older brother** is a walking big mouth (口).

<ruby>兄<rt>あに</rt></ruby>は<ruby>大口<rt>おおぐち</rt></ruby>をたたきます。

▶ きょう　けい
▷ あに

兄（あに）my older brother
お兄さん（*おにいさん）older brother
兄弟（きょうだい）siblings
義兄（ぎけい）older brother-in-law

<5> ' 口 口 尸 兄

▶ 口(15) 儿(C)

198

姉
older sister

My **older sister** is a woman（女）who lives in a city（市）.

姉は都市に住んでいます。

▶ し
▷ あね

姉（あね）my older sister
お姉さん（*おねえさん）older sister
姉妹（しまい）sisters
姉妹都市（しまいとし）sister city

<8> く　く　女　女'　女゛　女゛　妒　姉

▶ 女(52)　市(99)

199

弟
younger brother

My **younger brother** plays with the bow（弓）.

弟は弓で遊びます。

▶ だい　で
　　てい
▷ おとうと

弟（おとうと）younger brother
兄弟（きょうだい）siblings
弟子（でし）apprentice; disciple
義弟（ぎてい）younger brother-in-law

<7> 丶　ゝ　ソ　ソ　ゞ　弟　弟

▶ 弓(123)

200

妹
younger sister

A woman（女）and the tree that has not yet（未）grown. It means "a **younger sister**."

女とまだ若い木、つまり妹のことです。

▶ まい
▷ いもうと

妹（いもうと）younger sister
姉妹（しまい）sisters

<8> く　く　女　女　女=　妹　妹　妹

▶ 女(52)　未(175)

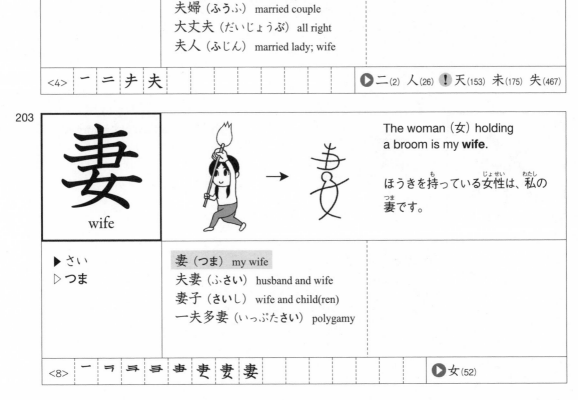

201

私
I / private

▶ し
▷ わたくし
　 わたし

This is the rice plant that **I** raised.

これは私が作った稲です。

私（わたくし／わたし）I
私立大学（しりつだいがく）
　　private university
私鉄（してつ）private railroad
私用（しよう）personal use

私有（しゆう）private ownership
私生活（しせいかつ）private life
私書箱（ししょばこ）post-office box

<7> ノ 二 千 禾 禾 私 私 　　　▶禾 (P) ！払(377) 和(386)

202

夫
husband

▶ ふ　ふう　ぶ
▷ おっと

My **husband** and I are always two （二）people （人）together.

私はいつも夫と二人でいます。

夫（おっと）my husband
夫妻（ふさい）husband and wife
夫婦（ふうふ）married couple
大丈夫（だいじょうぶ）all right
夫人（ふじん）married lady; wife

工夫（くふう）device; invention
丈夫な（じょうぶな）strong

<4> 一 二 ナ 夫 　　　▶二(2) 人(26) ！天(153) 未(175) 失(467)

203

妻
wife

▶ さい
▷ つま

The woman （女）holding a broom is my **wife**.

ほうきを持っている女性は、私の妻です。

妻（つま）my wife
夫妻（ふさい）husband and wife
妻子（さいし）wife and child(ren)
一夫多妻（いっぷたさい）polygamy

<8> 一 ⇁ ⇒ ⇒ 妻 妻 妻 妻 　　　▶女(52)

204

主
main

The man with a hat is the master (**main** person).

帽子をかぶった男性が主人です。

▶ しゅ　す
▷ おも　ぬし

主人 (しゅじん) my husband
主婦 (しゅふ) housewife
主語 (しゅご) subject of a sentence
主義 (しゅぎ) principle; -ism
主題 (しゅだい) topic

主食 (しゅしょく) staple food
主に (おもに) mainly
持ち主 (もちぬし) owner

<5> 丶 二 十 キ 主　　　▶ 王(63)

205

住
to live

The master (主) **lives** with someone.

主人はある人と住んでいます。

▶ じゅう
▷ す

住む (すむ) to live
住所 (じゅうしょ) address
住民 (じゅうみん) resident
住宅 (じゅうたく) house

衣食住 (いしょくじゅう)
　food, clothing and shelter
移住する (いじゅうする)
　to immigrate

<7> ノ イ イ゛ 仁 仁 住 住　　　▶ イ (B) 主(204)　！ 注(287)

206

糸
thread

This is the shape of the **thread** on a spool.

糸巻きの形です。

▶ し
▷ いと

糸 (いと) thread
毛糸 (けいと) woolen yarn
釣り糸 (つりいと) fishing line
抜糸 (ばっし) removing stitches

<6> く 幺 幺 糸 糸 糸

207

氏
surname

My **surname** is on the name tag.

名札に名前が書いてあります。

▶ し
▷ うじ

氏名 (しめい) full name
彼氏 (かれし) boyfriend
大野氏 (おおのし) Mr./Ms. Ohno
摂氏 (せっし) centigrade
華氏 (かし) Fahrenheit

氏神 (うじがみ) guardian god

<4> ノ 厂 氏 氏

! 民(286)

208

紙
paper

Write your surname (氏) on the **paper**, and put the thread (糸) through.

紙に名前を書いて、糸で縫い付けましょう。

▶ し
▷ かみ　がみ

紙 (かみ) paper
手紙 (てがみ) letter
表紙 (ひょうし) cover page
紙幣 (しへい) bill (paper money)
和紙 (わし) Japanese paper

紙くず (かみくず) wastepaper
折り紙 (おりがみ) origami
紙コップ (かみコップ) paper cup

<10> 乡 幺 幺 糸 糸 糸 糸 紅 紙 紙

▶ 糸(206) 氏(207)

第 14 課

● この課の漢字

教	室	羽	習	漢	字	式	試
209	210	211	212	213	214	215	216
験	宿	題	文	英	質	問	説
217	218	219	220	221	222	223	224

209

教
to teach

Old people **teach** a child（子）.

老人が子供を教えます。

▶ きょう
▷ おし　おそ

教える（おしえる）to teach
教室（きょうしつ）classroom
教会（きょうかい）church
教育（きょういく）education
教授（きょうじゅ）professor

教師（きょうし）teacher
教科書（きょうかしょ）textbook
宗教（しゅうきょう）religion
教わる（おそわる）to be taught

<11> 一 十 土 耂 耂 孝 孝 孝 孝 教 教 ▶ 子(53)

210

室
room

I stay in my **room** on Saturdays（土）.

土曜日はいつも室内にいます。

▶ しつ
▷ むろ

教室（きょうしつ）classroom
研究室（けんきゅうしつ）
　　research room
会議室（かいぎしつ）conference room
待合室（まちあいしつ）waiting room

温室（おんしつ）greenhouse
地下室（ちかしつ）basement
和室（わしつ）Japanese-style room
浴室（よくしつ）bathroom

<9> ' 宀 宀 宀 宁 室 室 室 室 ▶ 宀(G) 土(23) ！屋(308)

211

羽
wing

This is the shape of **wings**.

羽の形です。

▶ う
▷ はね　は　ば

羽 （はね）　wing; feather
羽根 （はね）　wing; feather
一羽 （*いちわ）　one bird
千羽 （せんば）　one thousand birds
羽毛 （うもう）　feather

<6> ］ ］ ヲ 习 羽 羽

212

習
to learn

Birds flap their wings （羽）
above a white （白） building
and **learn** to fly.

鳥は白い建物の上で羽を動かして、
飛び方を習います。

▶ しゅう
▷ なら

習う （ならう）　to learn
練習 （れんしゅう）　practice
習慣 （しゅうかん）　habit; custom
復習 （ふくしゅう）　review

予習 （よしゅう）
　　preparation for lessons
学習 （がくしゅう）　learning
自習 （じしゅう）　self-study
習字 （しゅうじ）　calligraphy

<11>]] ヲ 习 羽 羽 羽 羽 習 習 習　　▶ 羽(211) 白(156)

213

漢
China

A **Chinese** husband （夫） is
crossing a river with grass on
his head.

中国人の夫が草を頭の上に載せて
川を渡っています。

▶ かん

漢字 （かんじ）　Chinese character
漢和辞典 （かんわじてん）
　　Japanese dictionary of Chinese characters
漢方薬 （かんぽうやく）
　　Chinese herbal medicine

漢文 （かんぶん）　Chinese classics

<13> ` ⺀ 氵 汁 汁 浐 浐 浐 浐 浐 漢 漢　　▶ 氵(J) ⺾(K) 夫(202)

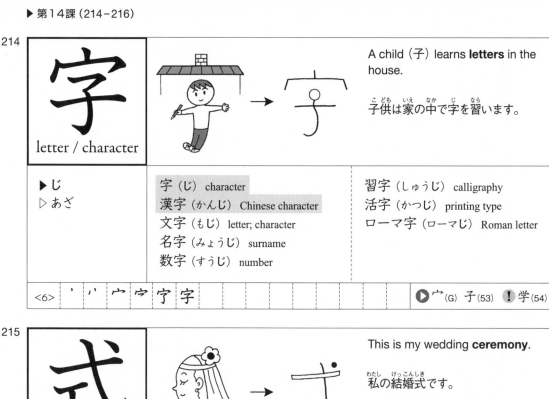

214

字

letter / character

A child（子）learns **letters** in the house.

子供は家の中で字を習います。

▶ じ
▷ あざ

字（じ）character
漢字（かんじ）Chinese character
文字（もじ）letter; character
名字（みょうじ）surname
数字（すうじ）number

習字（しゅうじ）calligraphy
活字（かつじ）printing type
ローマ字（ローマじ）Roman letter

<6> ｀ ｀ 宀 字 宁 字　　　▶ 宀(G) 子(53) ！学(54)

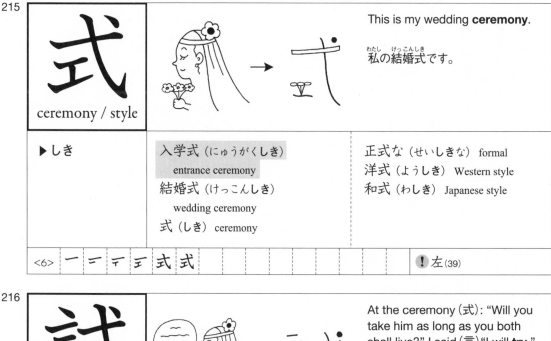

215

式

ceremony / style

This is my wedding **ceremony**.

私の結婚式です。

▶ しき

入学式（にゅうがくしき）
entrance ceremony
結婚式（けっこんしき）
wedding ceremony
式（しき）ceremony

正式な（せいしきな）formal
洋式（ようしき）Western style
和式（わしき）Japanese style

<6> 一 二 テ 王 式 式　　　！左(39)

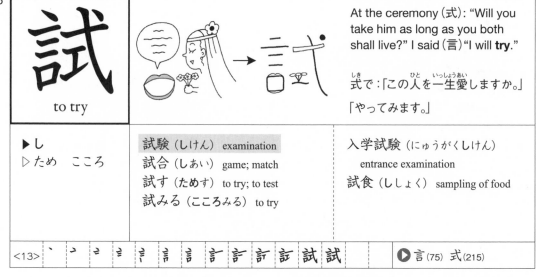

216

試

to try

At the ceremony（式）: "Will you take him as long as you both shall live?" I said（言）"I will **try**."

式で：「この人を一生愛しますか。」
「やってみます。」

▶ し
▷ ため こころ

試験（しけん）examination
試合（しあい）game; match
試す（ためす）to try; to test
試みる（こころみる）to try

入学試験（にゅうがくしけん）
entrance examination
試食（ししょく）sampling of food

<13> ｀ ｀ ｀ ｀ ｀ 言 言 訂 訂 訂 訂 試 試　　　▶ 言(75) 式(215)

217

to examine

Before climbing up a mountain, a person（人）**examines** the horse（馬）.

山に登る前に、馬を調べます。

▶ けん　げん

試験（しけん）examination
経験（けいけん）experience
実験（じっけん）experiment
受験（じゅけん）taking an examination
体験（たいけん）experience

<18> l Γ Γ F F 馬 馬 馬 馬 馬 馬 駧 駧 駼 駼 験 験 験　▶ 馬(105) 人(26) ❗ 駅(106)

218

宿

inn

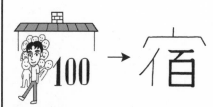

This **inn** can accommodate 100（百）people.

この宿は百人泊まれます。

▶ しゅく
▷ やど

宿題（しゅくだい）homework
下宿（げしゅく）boarding house
宿泊（しゅくはく）lodging
宿（やど）inn
民宿（みんしゅく）tourist home

雨宿り（あまやどり）
　　take shelter from the rain

<11> ' '' 宀 宀 宀 宀 宀 宿 宿 宿 宿　▶ 宀(G) イ(B) 百(11)

219

題

topic

Journalists look for a **topic**, using their head（頭）and feet（足）.

記者は頭と足を使って題材を探します。

▶ だい

宿題（しゅくだい）homework
問題（もんだい）problem; question
題（だい）title
題名（だいめい）title
話題（わだい）topic of conversation

議題（ぎだい）topic for discussion
課題（かだい）task; assignment
主題（しゅだい）topic

<18> l Π Ħ 日 旦 早 早 昇 是 是 是 匙 題 題 題 題 題 題　▶ 日(17) 足(141) 頭(289)

220

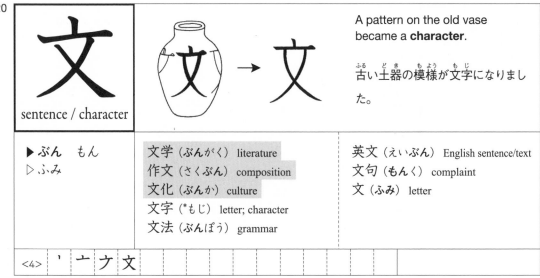

文

sentence / character

A pattern on the old vase became a **character**.

古い土器の模様が文字になりました。

▶ ぶん　もん
▷ ふみ

文学（ぶんがく）literature
作文（さくぶん）composition
文化（ぶんか）culture
文字（*もじ）letter; character
文法（ぶんぽう）grammar

英文（えいぶん）English sentence/text
文句（もんく）complaint
文（ふみ）letter

<4> 丶 一 ナ 文

221

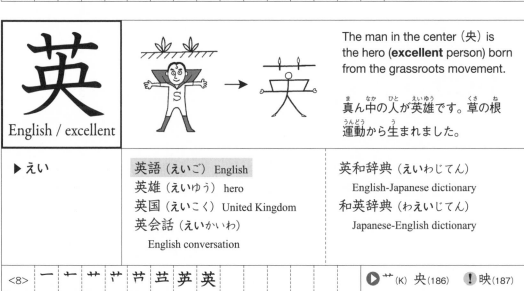

英

English / excellent

The man in the center（央）is the hero（**excellent** person）born from the grassroots movement.

真ん中の人が英雄です。草の根運動から生まれました。

▶ えい

英語（えいご）English
英雄（えいゆう）hero
英国（えいこく）United Kingdom
英会話（えいかいわ）English conversation

英和辞典（えいわじてん）
English-Japanese dictionary
和英辞典（わえいじてん）
Japanese-English dictionary

<8> 一 十 艹 艹 艻 苃 苹 英

▶ 艹（K）央(186)　! 映(187)

222

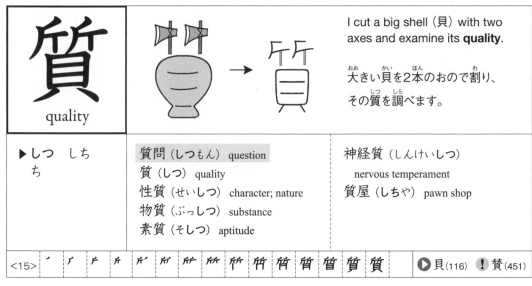

質

quality

I cut a big shell（貝）with two axes and examine its **quality**.

大きい貝を2本のおので割り、その質を調べます。

▶ しつ　しち
　ち

質問（しつもん）question
質（しつ）quality
性質（せいしつ）character; nature
物質（ぶっしつ）substance
素質（そしつ）aptitude

神経質（しんけいしつ）
nervous temperament
質屋（しちや）pawn shop

<15> 丶 厂 斤 斤 斤 斦 斦 斦 斦 斦 質 質 質 質 質

▶ 貝(116)　! 賛(451)

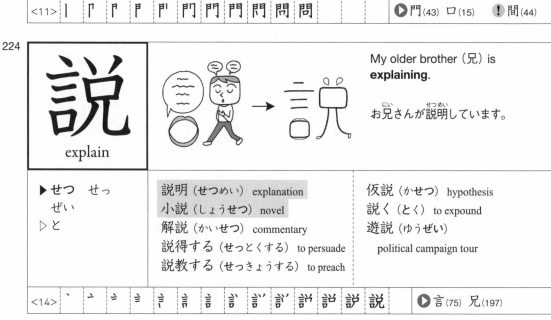

223

問
question

At a gate (門), I ask **questions**.

門のところで質問します。

▶ もん
▷ と　とん

問題 (もんだい) problem; question
質問 (しつもん) question
問い (とい) question
問い合わせ (といあわせ) inquiry
訪問 (ほうもん) visit

疑問 (ぎもん) question; doubt
学問 (がくもん) learning
問屋 (とんや) wholesale store

<11> 丨 冂 冂 冂 冃 門 門 門 問 問 問

▶ 門 (43) 口 (15) ⚠ 間 (44)

224

説
explain

My older brother (兄) is **explaining**.

お兄さんが説明しています。

▶ せつ　せっ
　 ぜい
▷ と

説明 (せつめい) explanation
小説 (しょうせつ) novel
解説 (かいせつ) commentary
説得する (せっとくする) to persuade
説教する (せっきょうする) to preach

仮説 (かせつ) hypothesis
説く (とく) to expound
遊説 (ゆうぜい)
　　 political campaign tour

<14> 丶 亠 三 言 言 言 訁 訁 訁 訅 訬 説 説

▶ 言 (75) 兄 (197)

第 15 課

● この課の漢字

遠	近	者	暑	寒	重	軽	低
225	226	227	228	229	230	231	232
弱	悪	暗	太	豆	短	光	風
233	234	235	236	237	238	239	240

225

遠
far

On Saturday（土）, I go **far** away.

土曜日に遠くまで出かけます。

▶ えん　おん
▷ とお

遠い（とおい）far
遠く（とおく）far place
遠慮する（えんりょする）
　　　　to be reserved
遠足（えんそく）one-day excursion

望遠鏡（ぼうえんきょう）telescope
永遠の（えいえんの）eternal
遠方（えんぽう）distant place

<13> 一 十 土 士 吉 吉 声 声 幸 袁 袁 遠 遠　　　▶ 土(23) 口(15) 辶(F)

226

近
near

Cut trees with an ax and your destination will become **nearer**.

おので木を切ると、目的地が近くなります。

▶ きん
▷ ちか

近い（ちかい）near
近く（ちかく）nearby
近所（きんじょ）neighborhood
最近（さいきん）recently
近ごろ（ちかごろ）recently

近代的な（きんだいてきな）modern
近視（きんし）near-sighted
中近東（ちゅうきんとう）
　　　the Middle East and Near East

<7> ' ⺁ ⼳ 斤 斤 近 近　　　▶ 辶(F)

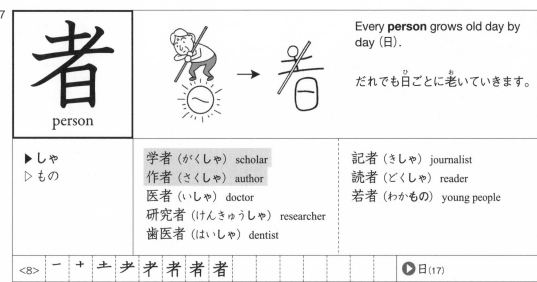

227

者
person

▶ しゃ	学者（がくしゃ）scholar	記者（きしゃ）journalist
▷ もの	作者（さくしゃ）author	読者（どくしゃ）reader
	医者（いしゃ）doctor	若者（わかもの）young people
	研究者（けんきゅうしゃ）researcher	
	歯医者（はいしゃ）dentist	

<8> 一 十 土 少 耂 者 者 者　　▶ 日(17)

228

暑
hot

A person（者）under the sun（日）feels **hot**.

太陽の下の人は暑いです。

▶ しょ	暑い（あつい）hot	避暑地（ひしょち）summer resort
▷ あつ	蒸し暑い（むしあつい）humid	
	暑中見舞い（しょちゅうみまい）	
	summertime greeting card	
	残暑（ざんしょ）late summer heat	

<12> 丶 口 曰 日 旦 早 旱 昇 昇 暑 暑 暑　　▶ 日(17) 者(227)

229

寒
cold

On a **cold** day, I came to your house leaving footsteps on the snow.

寒い日に、雪の上に足跡を残してあなたの家まで来ました。

▶ かん	寒い（さむい）cold
▷ さむ	寒気（さむけ）chill
	寒気（かんき）the cold
	寒帯（かんたい）frigid zone
	寒風（かんぷう）cold wind

<12> 丶 ｼ 宀 宀 宀 宒 宑 宲 寒 寒 寒　　▶ 宀(G)

230

重

heavy / to pile up

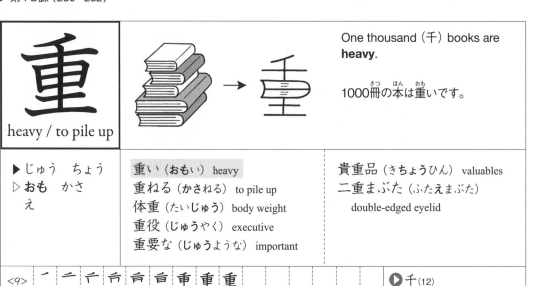

One thousand (千) books are **heavy**.

1000冊(さつ)の本(ほん)は重(おも)いです。

▶ じゅう ちょう
▷ おも かさ
　　え

重い (おもい) heavy
重ねる (かさねる) to pile up
体重 (たいじゅう) body weight
重役 (じゅうやく) executive
重要な (じゅうような) important

貴重品 (きちょうひん) valuables
二重まぶた (ふたえまぶた)
　 double-edged eyelid

<9> 一 二 三 三 三 亘 亘 重 重

▶千(12)

231

軽

light

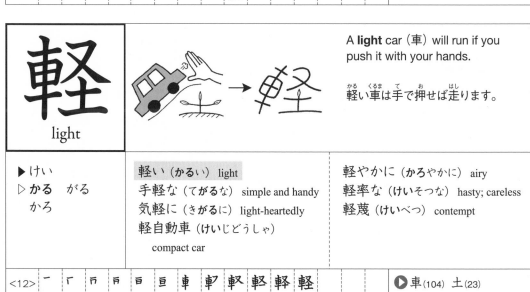

A **light** car (車) will run if you push it with your hands.

軽(かる)い車(くるま)は手(て)で押(お)せば走(はし)ります。

▶ けい
▷ かる がる
　　かろ

軽い (かるい) light
手軽な (てがるな) simple and handy
気軽に (きがるに) light-heartedly
軽自動車 (けいじどうしゃ)
　　compact car

軽やかに (かろやかに) airy
軽率な (けいそつな) hasty; careless
軽蔑 (けいべつ) contempt

<12> 一 一 一 一 戸 戸 車 車 車 軽 軽 軽

▶車(104) 土(23)

232

低

low

“Why did I get my surname (氏) underlined?” “Because your grade was **low**.”

「どうして私(わたし)の名前(なまえ)に下線(かせん)をつけたんですか。」「点数(てんすう)が低(ひく)かったからです。」

▶ てい
▷ ひく

低い (ひくい) low
最低 (さいてい) the lowest
低下 (ていか) decline
低温 (ていおん) low temperature
低気圧 (ていきあつ) low pressure

高低 (こうてい) high and low

<7> ノ イ イ 仁 仟 低 低

▶イ (B) 氏(207)

233

弱
weak

Baby birds are **weak**.

小鳥（ことり）は弱（よわ）いです。

▶ じゃく
▷ よわ

弱い（よわい） weak
弱点（じゃくてん） weakness
弱る（よわる） to weaken
病弱（びょうじゃく） physically weak

弱肉強食（じゃくにくきょうしょく）
   the law of the jungle
弱気（よわき） weakness

<10> 　 　 弓 弓 弓 弱 弱 弱 弱 弱

▶ 弓(123)

234

悪
bad

Bad feelings are in their hearts （心）.

彼（かれ）らはお互（たが）いに悪（わる）い感情（かんじょう）を持（も）っています。

▶ あく　お
▷ わる

悪い（わるい） bad
悪口（わるくち／わるぐち） slander
意地悪な（いじわるな） mean-spirited
最悪（さいあく） the worst
悪者（わるもの） villain

悪魔（あくま） devil
悪（あく） evil
悪寒（おかん） chills

<11> 一 ⼁ 一 亘 亜 亜 亜 悪 悪 悪

▶ 心(139)

235

暗
dark

Inside is **dark** and one can hear the sound （音）.

中（なか）は暗（くら）く、音（おと）だけ聞（き）こえます。

▶ あん
▷ くら

暗い（くらい） dark
真っ暗（まっくら） complete darkness
暗記する（あんきする）
   to learn by heart

暗殺（あんさつ） assassination
暗証番号（あんしょうばんごう）
   personal identification number

<13> 丨 冂 冃 日 日' 旷 旷 旷 晖 晖 暗 暗 暗

▶ 日(17) 音(177)

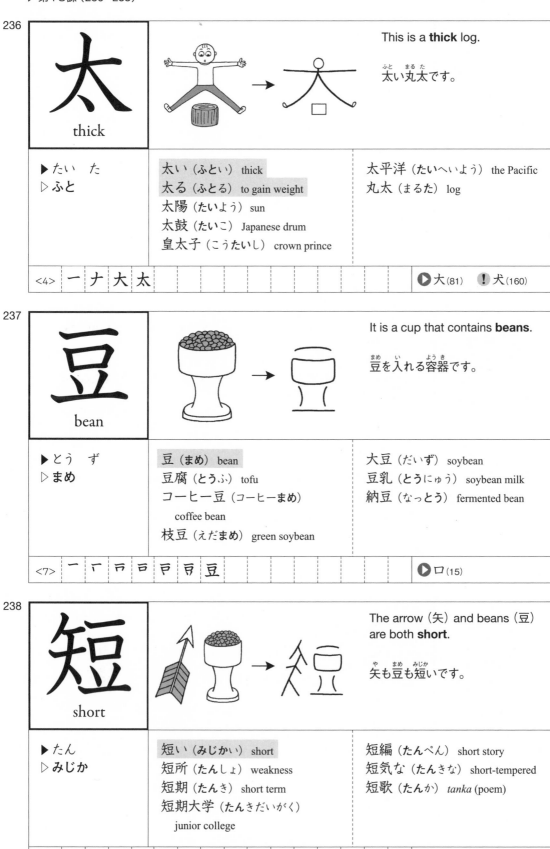

236

太

thick

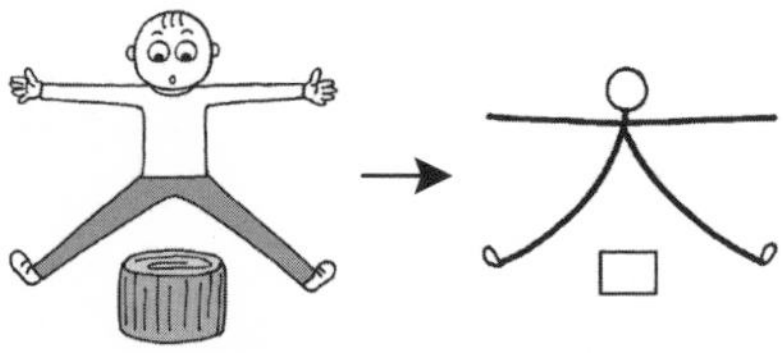

This is a **thick** log.

太(ふと)い丸太(まるた)です。

▶ たい　た
▷ ふと

太い（ふとい） thick
太る（ふとる） to gain weight
太陽（たいよう） sun
太鼓（たいこ） Japanese drum
皇太子（こうたいし） crown prince
太平洋（たいへいよう） the Pacific
丸太（まるた） log

<4> 一 ナ 大 太

▶ 大（81）　！ 犬（160）

237

豆

bean

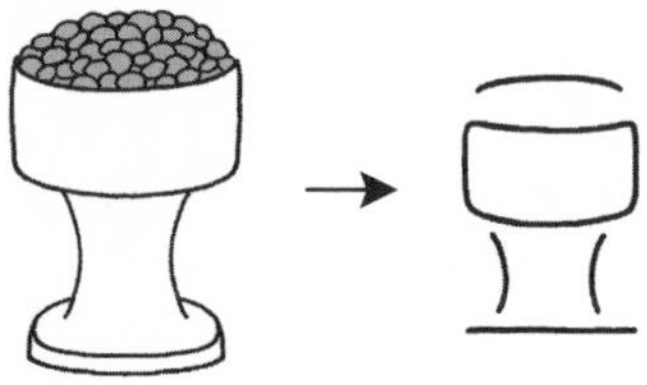

It is a cup that contains **beans**.

豆(まめ)を入(い)れる容器(ようき)です。

▶ とう　ず
▷ まめ

豆（まめ） bean
豆腐（とうふ） tofu
コーヒー豆（コーヒーまめ） coffee bean
枝豆（えだまめ） green soybean
大豆（だいず） soybean
豆乳（とうにゅう） soybean milk
納豆（なっとう） fermented bean

<7> 

▶ 口（15）

238

短

short

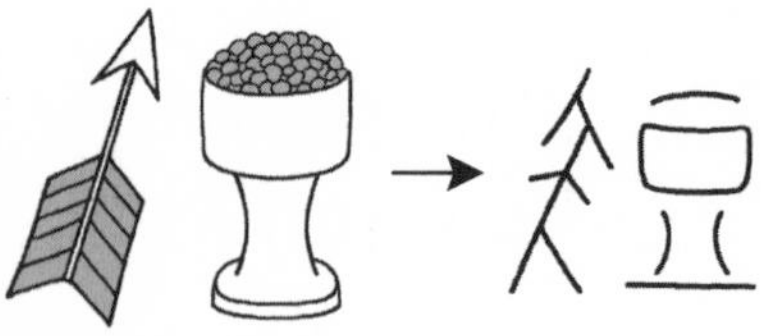

The arrow（矢）and beans（豆）are both **short**.

矢(や)も豆(まめ)も短(みじか)いです。

▶ たん
▷ みじか

短い（みじかい） short
短所（たんしょ） weakness
短期（たんき） short term
短期大学（たんきだいがく） junior college
短編（たんぺん） short story
短気な（たんきな） short-tempered
短歌（たんか） *tanka* (poem)

<12> 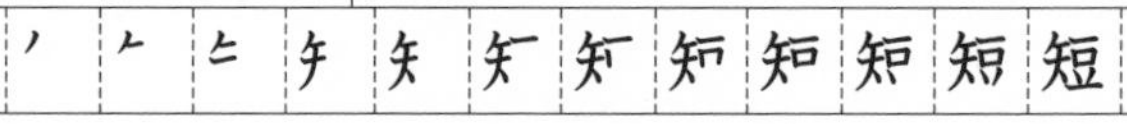

▶ 矢（194）　豆（237）

239

光
light

This is the shape of rays of **light**.

太陽の光線の形です。

▶ こう
▷ ひかり　ひか

光（ひかり）light
光る（ひかる）to shine
観光（かんこう）sightseeing
日光（にっこう）sunshine
光線（こうせん）ray

光景（こうけい）sight
光熱費（こうねつひ）
　　heating and lighting expenses

<6>　丿　丶　⺌　⺌　⺌　光　　　　　▶ 儿(C)

240

風
wind

An insect（虫）is blocking the
wind with the leaf.

虫が葉っぱで風をよけています。

▶ ふう　ふ
▷ かぜ　かざ

風（かぜ）wind
台風（たいふう）typhoon
風邪（*かぜ）common cold
お風呂（おふろ）bath
風船（ふうせん）balloon

風景（ふうけい）scenery
洋風（ようふう）Western style
和風（わふう）Japanese style

<9>　丿　几　几　凡　凡　凬　風　風　風　　　　　▶ 虫(124)

第　16　課

●この課の漢字

運	動	止	歩	使	送	洗	急
241	242	243	244	245	246	247	248
開	閉	押	引	思	知	考	死
249	250	251	252	253	254	255	256

241

運

to transport / luck

A car（車）**transports** a mattress.

車がマットレスを運びます。

▶ うん
▷ はこ

運ぶ（はこぶ）to carry
運転（うんてん）driving
運転手（うんてんしゅ）driver
運動（うんどう）physical exercise
運がいい（うんがいい）lucky

不運（ふうん）unlucky
運命（うんめい）fate
運賃（うんちん）fare

<12>　 ` 　 冖 　 冖 　 冖 　 尸 　 写 　 自 　 宣 　 軍 　 軍 　 運 　 運

▶ 車(104) ⻌(F)　❗ 連(410)

242

動

to move

A man **moves** the heavy（重）books with power（力）.

力を入れて重い本を動かします。

▶ どう
▷ うご

動く（うごく）to move
運動（うんどう）physical exercise
自動車（じどうしゃ）automobile
動物（どうぶつ）animal
活動（かつどう）activity

感動する（かんどうする）
　to be moved; to be touched
動詞（どうし）verb
自動ドア（じどうドア）
　automatic door

<11>　 ` 　 二 　 仁 　 듬 　 듬 　 盲 　 重 　 重 　 重 　 動 　 動

▶ 重(230) 力(50)　❗ 働(268)

243

止
to stop

The traffic light is red. **Stop**!

信号は赤です。止まれ！
しんごう　あか　　　　　と

▶ し
▷ と

止まる（とまる）(something) stops
止める（とめる）to stop (something)
中止（ちゅうし）cancellation
止まれ（とまれ）Stop [street sign]
禁止する（きんしする）to prohibit

停止する（ていしする）
　　to come to a stand
廃止する（はいしする）to abolish
防止する（ぼうしする）to prevent

<4> 丨 ㇏ 止 止　　▶ 上(33)　❗ 正(297)

244

歩
to walk

Stop（止）a little（少）and then **walk** again.

少し止まって、また歩きましょう。
すこ　と　　　　　　　ある

▶ ぽ　ほ　ぶ
　 ふ
▷ ある　あゆ

歩く（あるく）to walk
散歩する（さんぽする）to stroll
一歩（いっぽ）one step
進歩（しんぽ）progress
歩道（ほどう）sidewalk

歩み（あゆみ）walking
歩合（ぶあい）
　　percentage commissions
歩行者（ほこうしゃ）pedestrian

<8> 丨 ㇏ 止 止 步 步 歩 歩　　▶ 止(243) 少(90)

245

使
to use

He **uses** people.

人を使います。
ひと　つか

▶ し
▷ つか

使う（つかう）to use
大使館（たいしかん）embassy
大使（たいし）ambassador
使用中（しようちゅう）"Occupied"
使命（しめい）mission

天使（てんし）angel
お使い（おつかい）errand

<8> ノ イ 仁 仁 仨 伊 使 使　　▶ イ(B) ❗ 便(303)

246

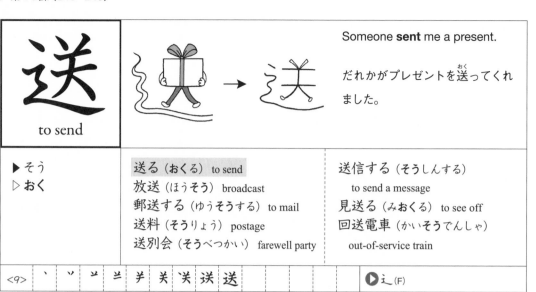

送
to send

Someone **sent** me a present.

だれかがプレゼントを送ってくれ
ました。

▶ そう ▷ おく	送る（おくる）to send 放送（ほうそう）broadcast 郵送する（ゆうそうする）to mail 送料（そうりょう）postage 送別会（そうべつかい）farewell party	送信する（そうしんする） 　to send a message 見送る（みおくる）to see off 回送電車（かいそうでんしゃ） 　out-of-service train
<9>	丶 ソ ⺍ ⺌ 半 关 关 送 送	▶ ⻌ (F)

247

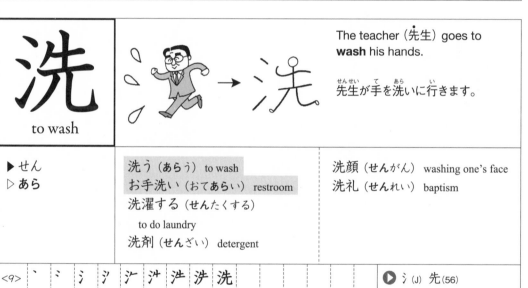

洗
to wash

The teacher（先生）goes to
wash his hands.

先生が手を洗いに行きます。

▶ せん ▷ あら	洗う（あらう）to wash お手洗い（おてあらい）restroom 洗濯する（せんたくする） 　to do laundry 洗剤（せんざい）detergent	洗顔（せんがん）washing one's face 洗礼（せんれい）baptism
<9>	丶 ⺀ ⺡ ⺡ 汁 汁 洪 泙 洗	▶ 氵 (J) 先(56)

248

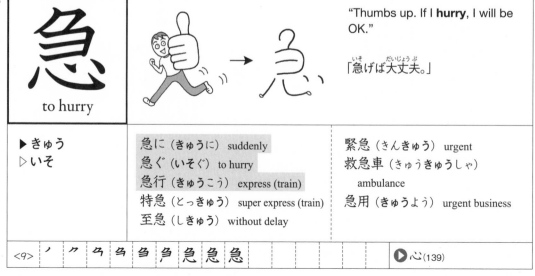

急
to hurry

"Thumbs up. If I **hurry**, I will be
OK."

「急げば大丈夫。」

▶ きゅう ▷ いそ	急に（きゅうに）suddenly 急ぐ（いそぐ）to hurry 急行（きゅうこう）express (train) 特急（とっきゅう）super express (train) 至急（しきゅう）without delay	緊急（きんきゅう）urgent 救急車（きゅうきゅうしゃ） 　ambulance 急用（きゅうよう）urgent business
<9>	⺈ ⺈ 刍 刍 刍 刍 急 急 急	▶ 心(139)

249

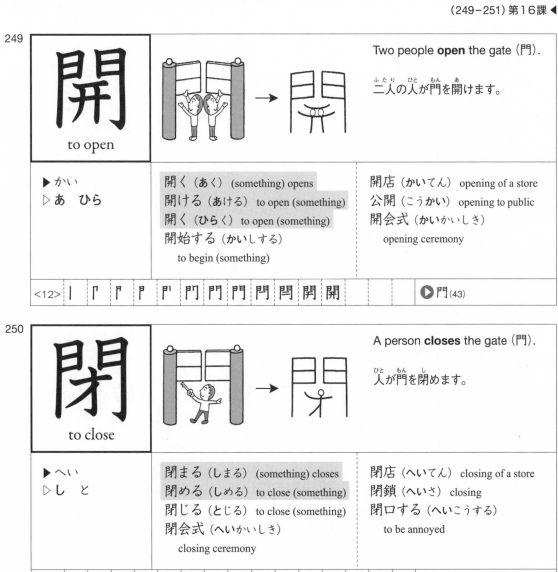

開
to open

Two people **open** the gate (門).

<ruby>二<rt>ふた</rt></ruby>り<ruby>人<rt>ひと</rt></ruby>の<ruby>人<rt>ひと</rt></ruby>が<ruby>門<rt>もん</rt></ruby>を<ruby>開<rt>あ</rt></ruby>けます。

▶ かい
▷ あ　ひら

開く（あく）(something) opens
開ける（あける）to open (something)
開く（ひらく）to open (something)
開始する（かいしする）
　　to begin (something)

開店（かいてん）opening of a store
公開（こうかい）opening to public
開会式（かいかいしき）
　　opening ceremony

<12> 丨 冂 冂 冂 冃 門 門 門 門 閂 閈 開

▶門 (43)

250

閉
to close

A person **closes** the gate (門).

<ruby>人<rt>ひと</rt></ruby>が<ruby>門<rt>もん</rt></ruby>を<ruby>閉<rt>し</rt></ruby>めます。

▶ へい
▷ し　と

閉まる（しまる）(something) closes
閉める（しめる）to close (something)
閉じる（とじる）to close (something)
閉会式（へいかいしき）
　　closing ceremony

閉店（へいてん）closing of a store
閉鎖（へいさ）closing
閉口する（へいこうする）
　　to be annoyed

<11> 丨 冂 冂 冂 冃 門 門 門 閂 閉 閉

▶門 (43)

251

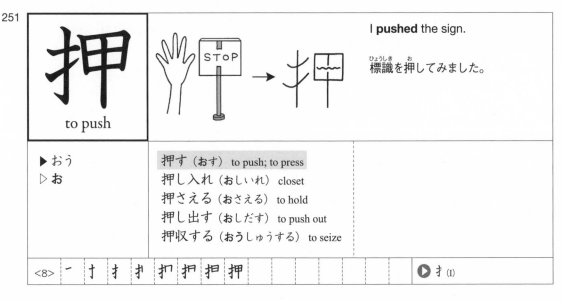

押
to push

I **pushed** the sign.

<ruby>標識<rt>ひょうしき</rt></ruby>を<ruby>押<rt>お</rt></ruby>してみました。

▶ おう
▷ お

押す（おす）to push; to press
押し入れ（おしいれ）closet
押さえる（おさえる）to hold
押し出す（おしだす）to push out
押収する（おうしゅうする）to seize

<8> 一 十 扌 扌 扣 拥 押 押

▶扌 (I)

252 引 to pull

This is a bow (弓) and a string. It is the string that you **pull**.

弓とつるです。引っ張るのは、つるの部分です。

| ▶ いん
▷ ひ　び | 引く（ひく）to pull
引き出し（ひきだし）drawer
引き出す（ひきだす）to withdraw
引っ越す（ひっこす）to move out
引き分け（ひきわけ）drawn match | 割り引き（わりびき）discount
引用（いんよう）citation
引力（いんりょく）gravity |

<4> ¬ コ 弓 引　　▶ 弓(123)

253 思 to think

At a rice field (田), I **think** of a person I love from the heart (心).

田んぼで、心から好きな人のことを思います。

| ▶ し
▷ おも | 思う（おもう）to think
思い出す（おもいだす）to recall
思い出（おもいで）memory
思いがけない（おもいがけない）
　　unexpected | 思いきり（おもいきり）
　　to one's heart's content
不思議な（ふしぎな）mysterious
思想（しそう）thought |

<9> ノ 口 田 田 田 田 思 思 思　　▶ 田(49) 心(139)

254 知 to know

A big (大) mouth (口) **knows** everything.

大きい口の人は、何でも知っています。

| ▶ ち
▷ し | 知る（しる）to know
知らせる（しらせる）to notice
知り合い（しりあい）acquaintance
承知する（しょうちする）to agree
知人（ちじん）acquaintance | 知識（ちしき）knowledge
知性（ちせい）intelligence
知事（ちじ）governor |

<8> ノ ⻏ ⻌ 𠂉 矢 知 知 知　　▶ 矢(194) 大(81) 口(15) ❗ 和(386)

255

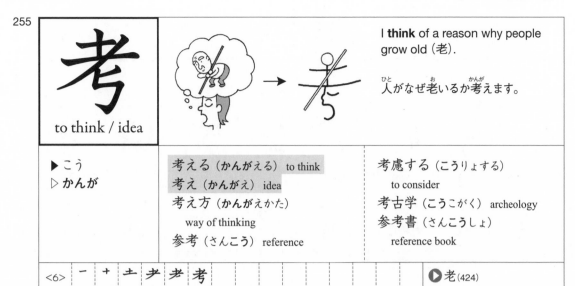

考
to think / idea

I **think** of a reason why people grow old（老）.

人がなぜ老いるか考えます。

▶ こう ▷ かんが	考える（かんがえる） to think 考え（かんがえ） idea 考え方（かんがえかた） 　　way of thinking 参考（さんこう） reference	考慮する（こうりょする） 　　to consider 考古学（こうこがく） archeology 参考書（さんこうしょ） reference book
<6>　一　十　土　耂　耂　考		▶老(424)

256

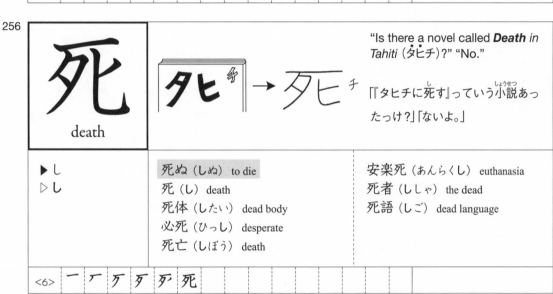

死
death

"Is there a novel called **Death** in Tahiti（タヒチ）?" "No."

『タヒチに死す』っていう小説あったっけ?」「ないよ。」

▶ し ▷ し	死ぬ（しぬ） to die 死（し） death 死体（したい） dead body 必死（ひっし） desperate 死亡（しぼう） death	安楽死（あんらくし） euthanasia 死者（ししゃ） the dead 死語（しご） dead language
<6>　一　厂　歹　歹　死　死		

第 17 課

● この課の漢字

医	始	終	石	研	究	留	有
257	258	259	260	261	262	263	264
産	業	薬	働	員	士	仕	事
265	266	267	268	269	270	271	272

257

医
doctor / medicine

A **doctor** treats the patient wounded with an arrow（矢）.

医者が矢で傷ついた患者を治します。

▶ い

医者（いしゃ）doctor	医師（いし）doctor
医学（いがく）medical science	医薬品（いやくひん）
歯医者（はいしゃ）dentist	medical supplies
医院（いいん）clinic	
医療（いりょう）medical (treatment)	

<7> 一 T F E 至 天 医　　　　▶ 矢(194)

258

始
to begin

When I **began** my speech on a stand（台）, a woman（女）listened.

台の上でスピーチを始めると、女の人が聞きました。

▶ し
▷ はじ

始まる（はじまる）(something) begins	始終（しじゅう）always
始める（はじめる）	書き始める（かきはじめる）
to begin (something)	to start writing
開始する（かいしする）	始発（しはつ）first train of the day
to begin (something)	原始的な（げんしてきな）primitive

<8> く 女 女 女 女 始 始 始　　　　▶ 女(52) 台(185)

259

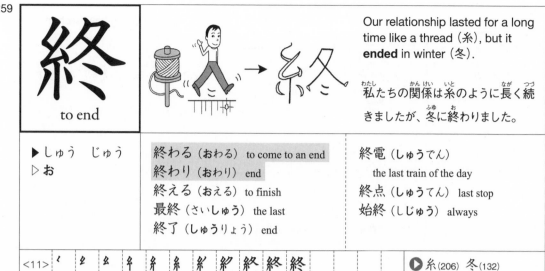

終
to end

Our relationship lasted for a long time like a thread (糸), but it **ended** in winter (冬).

私たちの関係は糸のように長く続きましたが、冬に終わりました。

| ▶ しゅう じゅう
▷ お | 終わる（おわる）to come to an end
終わり（おわり）end
終える（おえる）to finish
最終（さいしゅう）the last
終了（しゅうりょう）end | 終電（しゅうでん）
　　the last train of the day
終点（しゅうてん）last stop
始終（しじゅう）always |

<11> ⟨ ⟨ ⟨ ⟨ ⟨ 糸 糸 紵 終 終 終 ▶ 糸(206) 冬(132)

260

石
stone

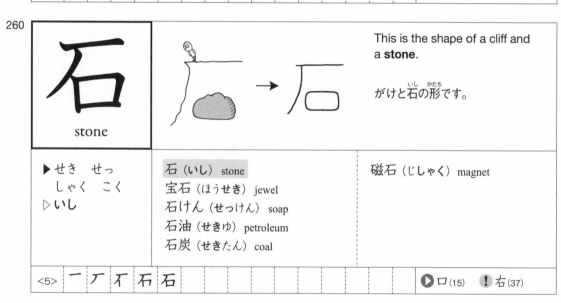

This is the shape of a cliff and a **stone**.

がけと石の形です。

| ▶ せき せっ
　しゃく こく
▷ いし | 石（いし）stone
宝石（ほうせき）jewel
石けん（せっけん）soap
石油（せきゆ）petroleum
石炭（せきたん）coal | 磁石（じしゃく）magnet |

<5> 一 ナ 石 石 石 ▶ 口(15) ！ 右(37)

261

研
to polish

I **polish** a stone (石), sitting on a stool.

台の上に座って石を磨きます。

| ▶ けん
▷ と | 研究（けんきゅう）research
研究者（けんきゅうしゃ）researcher
研究室（けんきゅうしつ）
　　research room | 研究所（けんきゅうじょ／けんきゅうしょ）research institute
研修（けんしゅう）training
研ぐ（とぐ）to sharpen |

<9> 一 ナ 石 石 石 矴 研 研 ▶ 石(260)

262

究
research

→ 究

I have been doing **research** in my house for nine（九）years.

家の中で九年間研究をしています。

▶ きゅう
▷ きわ

研究（けんきゅう）research
研究者（けんきゅうしゃ）researcher
研究室（けんきゅうしつ）
　　research room
究明（きゅうめい）investigation

究極の（きゅうきょくの）ultimate
究める（きわめる）
　　to investigate thoroughly
探究（たんきゅう）inquiry

<7>　丶 宀 宀 宂 究 究 究

▶ 宀（G）九（9）　❗ 空（149）

263

留
to stay

→

I will **stay** in the rice field（田）, and cut rice plants with a knife（刀）.

田んぼにいて、刀で稲を刈ります。

▶ りゅう　る
▷ と

留学する（りゅうがくする）
　　to study abroad
留学生（りゅうがくせい）
　　international student
留守（るす）absence from home

留守番電話（るすばんでんわ）
　　answering machine
留める（とめる）to fasten
書き留め（かきとめ）／書留（*か
　　きとめ）registered mail

<10>　丶 ㇄ ㇒ 卬 卬 卬 卯 留 留 留

▶ 刀（31）田（49）

264

有
to exist

→ 有

The moon（月）does **exist**, but no one can touch it.

月がありますが、触ることができません。

▶ ゆう　う
▷ あ

有名な（ゆうめいな）famous
有る（ある）to exist
有料（ゆうりょう）toll; fee
有利な（ゆうりな）advantageous
有効な（ゆうこうな）valid

有能な（ゆうのうな）talented
有り難い（ありがたい）grateful
有無（うむ）to have or have not

<6>　ノ 𠂇 ナ 冇 有 有 有

▶ 月（18）

265

産
to produce

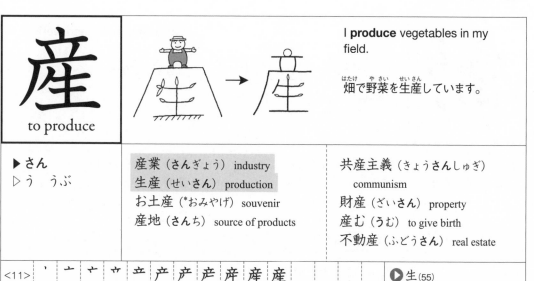

I **produce** vegetables in my field.

畑で野菜を生産しています。
<small>はたけ　やさい　せいさん</small>

▶ さん
▷ う　うぶ

産業（さんぎょう）industry
生産（せいさん）production
お土産（*おみやげ）souvenir
産地（さんち）source of products

共産主義（きょうさんしゅぎ）
　　communism
財産（ざいさん）property
産む（うむ）to give birth
不動産（ふどうさん）real estate

<11> ` 亠 ナ 产 立 产 产 产 产 产 産　▶生 (55)

266

業
business

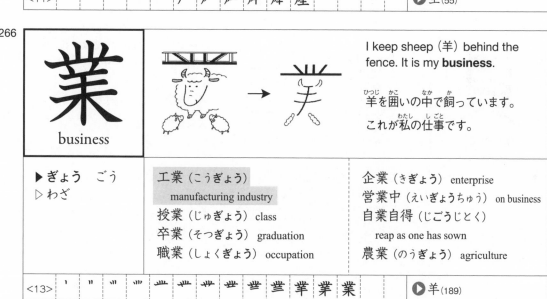

I keep sheep（羊）behind the fence. It is my **business**.

羊を囲いの中で飼っています。
<small>ひつじ　かこ　なか　か</small>
これが私の仕事です。
<small>わたし　しごと</small>

▶ ぎょう　ごう
▷ わざ

工業（こうぎょう）
　　manufacturing industry
授業（じゅぎょう）class
卒業（そつぎょう）graduation
職業（しょくぎょう）occupation

企業（きぎょう）enterprise
営業中（えいぎょうちゅう）on business
自業自得（じごうじとく）
　　reap as one has sown
農業（のうぎょう）agriculture

<13> ` ` ` ` 业 业 业 业 丵 丵 举 業　▶羊 (189)

267

薬
medicine

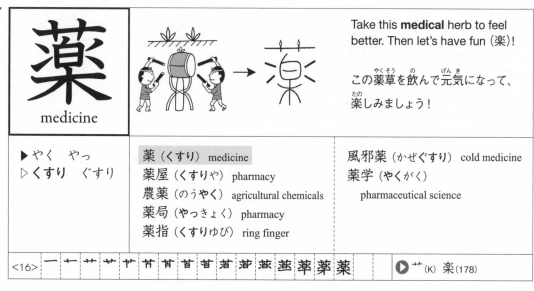

Take this **medical** herb to feel better. Then let's have fun（楽）!

この薬草を飲んで元気になって、
<small>やくそう　の　げんき</small>
楽しみましょう！
<small>たの</small>

▶ やく　やっ
▷ くすり　ぐすり

薬（くすり）medicine
薬屋（くすりや）pharmacy
農薬（のうやく）agricultural chemicals
薬局（やっきょく）pharmacy
薬指（くすりゆび）ring finger

風邪薬（かぜぐすり）cold medicine
薬学（やくがく）
　　pharmaceutical science

<16> 一 十 廾 艹 芍 芍 苩 苩 苩 萡 萡 萞 萞 華 蕐 薬　▶艹(K) 楽 (178)

268 働 to work

People move（動）and **work**.

人が動いて働きます。

▶ どう
▷ はたら　ばたら

働く（はたらく）to work
共働き（ともばたらき）
　　both husband and wife working
働き者（はたらきもの）
　　diligent worker

労働（ろうどう）labor
労働者（ろうどうしゃ）worker
労働組合（ろうどうくみあい）
　　labor union

<13> ノ イ イ 仨 仨 行 伶 伶 俥 俥 俥 働 働

▶ イ (B) 動(242)

269 員 member

A person pays money and gets a **member**ship card.

お金を払って、会員カードを手に入れます。

▶ いん

会社員（かいしゃいん）office worker
店員（てんいん）store clerk
銀行員（ぎんこういん）bank employee
全員（ぜんいん）all members
公務員（こうむいん）civil servant

会員（かいいん）member
満員（まんいん）full to capacity
教員（きょういん）teacher

<10> 丶 冂 冂 尸 阝 阝 目 目 員 員

▶ 口(15) 貝(116) ！買(117) 負(450)

270 士 warrior / samurai

Eleven（十一）samurai, **warriors**.

十一人のさむらい。

▶ し

武士（ぶし）samurai; warrior
博士（はくし／*はかせ）doctor; Ph.D.
修士（しゅうし）master (degree)
弁護士（べんごし）lawyer
紳士（しんし）gentleman

消防士（しょうぼうし）firefighter
会計士（かいけいし）accountant
税理士（ぜいりし）tax accountant

<3> 一 十 士

▶ 十(10) 一(1) ！土(23)

271

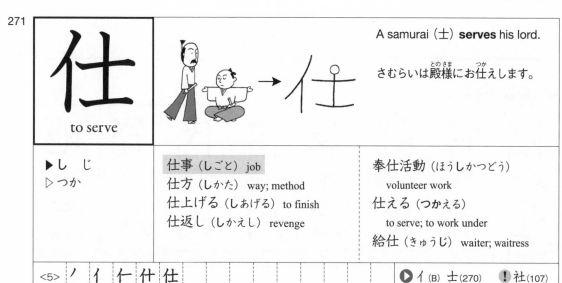

to serve

A samurai（士）**serves** his lord.

さむらいは殿様にお仕えします。

▶し　じ
▷つか

仕事（しごと）job
仕方（しかた）way; method
仕上げる（しあげる）to finish
仕返し（しかえし）revenge

奉仕活動（ほうしかつどう）
　　volunteer work
仕える（つかえる）
　　to serve; to work under
給仕（きゅうじ）waiter; waitress

<5> ノ　イ　仁　什　仕　　　　　　▶イ (B) 士(270)　！社(107)

272

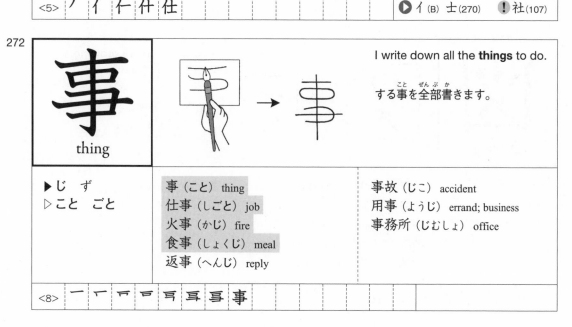

thing

I write down all the **things** to do.

する事を全部書きます。

▶じ　ず
▷こと　ごと

事（こと）thing
仕事（しごと）job
火事（かじ）fire
食事（しょくじ）meal
返事（へんじ）reply

事故（じこ）accident
用事（ようじ）errand; business
事務所（じむしょ）office

<8> 一　ｒ　ｒ　亐　写　写　写　事

第 18 課

●この課の漢字

図	官	館	昔	借	代	貸	地
273	274	275	276	277	278	279	280
世	界	度	回	用	民	注	意
281	282	283	284	285	286	287	288

273

図

drawing

ツ メ → ツ メ

This is someone's **drawing**.
It looks like ツ and メ.

これはだれかがかいた絵（え）です。
「ツ、メ」のように見（み）えます。

▶ と　ず
▷ はか

図書館（としょかん）library
地図（ちず）map
図（ず）chart; diagram
図表（ずひょう）figures and diagrams
合図（あいず）signal; sign

意図（いと）intention
図る（はかる）to plot; to attempt

<7> 丨 冂 冂 冋 冈 図 図 　　　 ▶口 (E)　！区 (312)

274

官

government official

A fat **government official** is in his house.

太（ふと）った役人（やくにん）が家（いえ）の中（なか）にいます。

▶ かん

長官（ちょうかん）director general
外交官（がいこうかん）diplomat
警官（けいかん）police officer
裁判官（さいばんかん）judge
官庁（かんちょう）government office

官僚（かんりょう）government official
器官（きかん）organ

<8> 丶 丷 宀 宀 官 官 官 官 　　　 ▶宀 (G)

275

館
building

Government officials (官) eat (食) in this **building**.

この建物で、役人たちは食事をします。

▶ かん
▷ やかた

図書館（としょかん）library
映画館（えいがかん）movie theater
大使館（たいしかん）embassy
旅館（りょかん）Japanese inn
会館（かいかん）hall

美術館（びじゅつかん）art museum
博物館（はくぶつかん）museum
水族館（すいぞくかん）aquarium
占いの館（うらないのやかた）
　　fortune tellers' mansion

<16> ノ 𠆢 𠆢 今 今 今 食 食 食' 食' 飠 飠 飹 飹 館 館 ▶ 食(70) 官(274)

276

昔
long ago

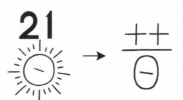

Twenty one days (日) ago is a **long time ago**.

二十一日前は昔です。

▶ せき　じゃく
　しゃく
▷ むかし

昔（むかし）old times
昔話（むかしばなし）old tale
大昔（おおむかし）ancient times
昔日（せきじつ）old days
昔々（むかしむかし）once upon a time

今昔（こんじゃく）the changing times

<8> 一 十 卅 卅 芒 芒 昔 昔 ▶ 十(10) 日(17) ❗音(177)

277

借
to borrow

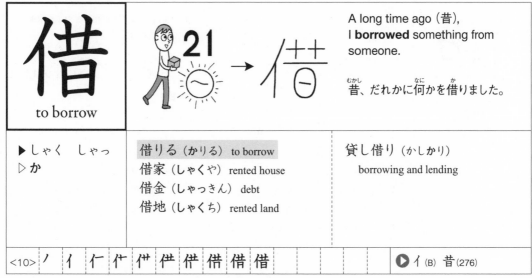

A long time ago (昔), I **borrowed** something from someone.

昔、だれかに何かを借りました。

▶ しゃく　しゃっ
▷ か

借りる（かりる）to borrow
借家（しゃくや）rented house
借金（しゃっきん）debt
借地（しゃくち）rented land

貸し借り（かしかり）
　　borrowing and lending

<10> ノ 亻 亻 亻 㐌 仳 借 借 借 ▶ 亻(B) 昔(276)

278

代
age / to replace

"I will **replace** your position."

「代<ruby>代<rt>か</rt></ruby>わりましょう。」

▶ だい　たい
▷ か　しろ　よ

時代（じだい）age; era	代表（だいひょう）representative
電気代（でんきだい）electricity fee	現代（げんだい）modern days
代わりに（かわりに）instead	代金（だいきん）price; charge
六十年代（ろくじゅうねんだい）60's	身代金（みのしろきん）ransom
十代（じゅうだい）in one's teens	

<5>　ノ　イ　仁　代　代　　　　　　　▶ イ（B）

279

貸
to lend

Instead of（代）him, I will **lend** you money.

<ruby>彼<rt>かれ</rt></ruby>の<ruby>代<rt>か</rt></ruby>わりに<ruby>私<rt>わたし</rt></ruby>がお<ruby>金<rt>かね</rt></ruby>を<ruby>貸<rt>か</rt></ruby>しましょう。

▶ たい
▷ か

貸す（かす）to lend
貸し出し（かしだし）lending out
貸し切り（かしきり）reserved
賃貸マンション（ちんたいマンション）apartment for rent

<12>　ノ　イ　仁　代　代　代　伩　佮　貸　貸　貸　貸　　　▶ 代(278)　貝(116)

280

地
land

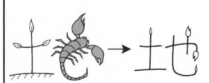

In this **land**, there is a scorpion under the soil（土）.

この<ruby>土地<rt>とち</rt></ruby>には、<ruby>土<rt>つち</rt></ruby>の<ruby>下<rt>した</rt></ruby>にサソリがいます。

▶ ち　じ

地図（ちず）map	意地悪な（いじわるな）mean-spirited
地理（ちり）geography	
地下（ちか）underground	地方（ちほう）region; countryside
地下鉄（ちかてつ）subway	地球（ちきゅう）earth; globe
地震（じしん）earthquake	

<6>　一　十　土　圸　圠　地　　　　　　　▶ 土(23)　！ 池(313)　他(448)

281

世
world

The *hiragana* せ, as in せかい (**world**), is made from this kanji.

せ → せ

「せかい」の「せ」はこの漢字から
作られました。

▶ せ　せい
▷ よ

世界 (せかい) the world
世話 (せわ) care
世紀 (せいき) century
世間 (せけん) the world; society
世代 (せだい) generation

世の中 (よのなか) world; society
世論 (よろん／せろん) public opinion
お世辞 (おせじ) flattery

<5> 一 十 卅 卅 世

282

界
boundary

There is the **boundary** between your rice field (田) and mine.

あなたの田んぼと私の田んぼの間
には、境界があります。

▶ かい

世界 (せかい) the world
限界 (げんかい) limit
境界 (きょうかい) boundary
政界 (せいかい) political world
視界 (しかい) visibility

業界 (ぎょうかい)
　industry; business world

<9> 丨 冂 冂 冊 田 甲 界 界

▶ 田 (49)

283

度
times / degrees

Your hands feel warm when it is 21 **degrees** inside a building.

21 → 度

家の中が二十一度だと、手は温か
いです。

▶ ど　たく　と
▷ たび

一度 (いちど) once
今度 (こんど) near future; next time
三十度 (さんじゅうど) 30 degrees
温度 (おんど) temperature
度々 (たびたび) often

支度する (したくする) to prepare
速度 (そくど) speed
限度 (げんど) limit

<9> 丶 亠 广 广 庐 庐 庐 庌 度

▶ 广 (H) 十 (10) ❗ 席 (475)

284

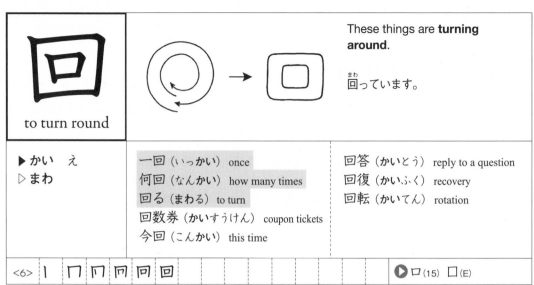

回 to turn round	These things are **turning around**. 回<small>まわ</small>っています。

▶ かい　え
▷ まわ

一回（いっかい）once
何回（なんかい）how many times
回る（まわる）to turn
回数券（かいすうけん）coupon tickets
今回（こんかい）this time

回答（かいとう）reply to a question
回復（かいふく）recovery
回転（かいてん）rotation

<6>　丨　冂　冂　冋　回　回 　　　　　　　　▶ 口 (15)　囗 (E)

285

用 to use	This is the fence that we **use**. 私<small>わたし</small>たちが使<small>つか</small>っているさくです。

▶ よう
▷ もち

用（よう）／用事（ようじ）
　errand; business
用意する（よういする）to prepare
利用する（りようする）to use
用語（ようご）technical term

用紙（ようし）form; sheet
使用する（しようする）to use
費用（ひよう）cost
用いる（もちいる）to use

<5>　丿　冂　月　月　用 　　　　　　　　！ 月 (18)　冊 (439)

286

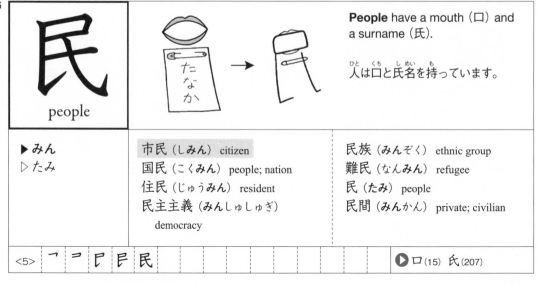

民 people	**People** have a mouth（口）and a surname（氏）. 人<small>ひと</small>は口<small>くち</small>と氏名<small>しめい</small>を持<small>も</small>っています。

▶ みん
▷ たみ

市民（しみん）citizen
国民（こくみん）people; nation
住民（じゅうみん）resident
民主主義（みんしゅしゅぎ）
　democracy

民族（みんぞく）ethnic group
難民（なんみん）refugee
民（たみ）people
民間（みんかん）private; civilian

<5>　⁊　⁒　尸　尸　民 　　　　　　　　▶ 口 (15)　氏 (207)

287

注
to pour

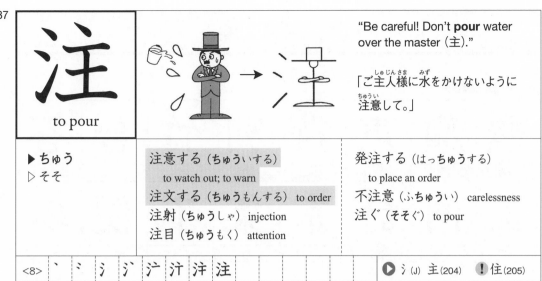

"Be careful! Don't **pour** water over the master (主)."

「ご主人様に水をかけないように注意して。」

▶ ちゅう
▷ そそ

注意する（ちゅういする）
　to watch out; to warn
注文する（ちゅうもんする）to order
注射（ちゅうしゃ）injection
注目（ちゅうもく）attention

発注する（はっちゅうする）
　to place an order
不注意（ふちゅうい）carelessness
注ぐ（そそぐ）to pour

<8> 丶 冫 氵 氵 汼 汼 注 注

▶ 氵 (J) 主(204)　❗ 住(205)

288

意
mind

Listen to the sound (音) of your heart (心) to know your **mind**.

心の音を聞きなさい。自分の気持ちがわかるでしょう。

▶ い

意味（いみ）meaning
注意する（ちゅういする）
　to watch out; to warn
意見（いけん）opinion
用意する（よういする）to prepare

好意（こうい）fondness
意外な（いがいな）unexpected
意思（いし）intention
意地悪な（いじわるな）
　mean-spirited

<13> 丶 亠 ナ 立 产 产 咅 咅 音 音 意 意 意

▶ 音(177)　心(139)

第 19 課

●この課の漢字

頭	顔	声	特	別	竹	合	答
289	290	291	292	293	294	295	296
正	同	計	京	集	不	便	以
297	298	299	300	301	302	303	304

289

頭
head

My **head** looks like a bean (豆).

豆みたいな頭でしょ。

▶ ず　とう　ど
　　と
▷ あたま　かしら

頭（あたま）head
頭痛（ずつう）headache
先頭（せんとう）forefront; top
二頭（にとう）two (big animals)
頭脳（ずのう）brain

頭文字（かしらもじ）the first letter
音頭（おんど）*bon* dance song
店頭（てんとう）shop front

<16> 一 ｢ ｢ 戸 戸 戸 豆 豆 豆 頭 頭 頭 頭 頭 頭 頭　　▶ 豆(237)　自(180)　！顔(290)

290

顔
face

When he takes his hat off his head, you will find scars on his **face**.

頭から帽子を取ると、顔の傷が見えます。

▶ がん
▷ かお　がお

顔（かお）face
笑顔（えがお）smile
洗顔（せんがん）washing one's face
顔つき（かおつき）look on one's face
似顔絵（にがおえ）portrait

<18> ` 亠 十 立 立 产 产 彦 彦 彦 彦 颜 顔 顔 顔 顔 顔 顔　　▶ 自(180)　！頭(289)

291

声
voice

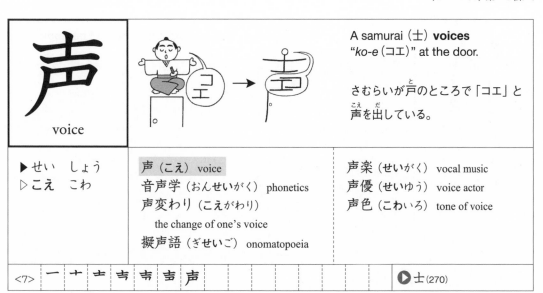

A samurai (士) **voices**
"*ko-e* (コエ)" at the door.

さむらいが戸のところで「コエ」と
声を出している。

▶ せい　しょう
▷ こえ　こわ

声 (こえ) voice
音声学 (おんせいがく) phonetics
声変わり (こえがわり)
　　the change of one's voice
擬声語 (ぎせいご) onomatopoeia

声楽 (せいがく) vocal music
声優 (せいゆう) voice actor
声色 (こわいろ) tone of voice

<7> 一 十 士 吉 吉 吉 声　　　　▶士(270)

292

特
special

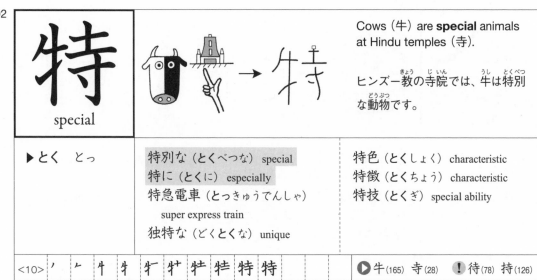

Cows (牛) are **special** animals
at Hindu temples (寺).

ヒンズー教の寺院では、牛は特別
な動物です。

▶ とく　とっ

特別な (とくべつな) special
特に (とくに) especially
特急電車 (とっきゅうでんしゃ)
　　super express train
独特な (どくとくな) unique

特色 (とくしょく) characteristic
特徴 (とくちょう) characteristic
特技 (とくぎ) special ability

<10> ノ 一 十 牛 牛 牜 牪 牥 特 特　　▶牛(165) 寺(28)　！待(78) 持(126)

293

別
to separate

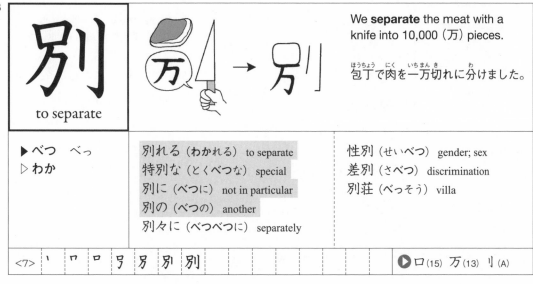

We **separate** the meat with a
knife into 10,000 (万) pieces.

包丁で肉を一万切れに分けました。

▶ べつ　べっ
▷ わか

別れる (わかれる) to separate
特別な (とくべつな) special
別に (べつに) not in particular
別の (べつの) another
別々に (べつべつに) separately

性別 (せいべつ) gender; sex
差別 (さべつ) discrimination
別荘 (べっそう) villa

<7> 丨 冂 口 另 另 別 別　　　　▶口(15) 万(13) 刂(A)

294

竹

bamboo

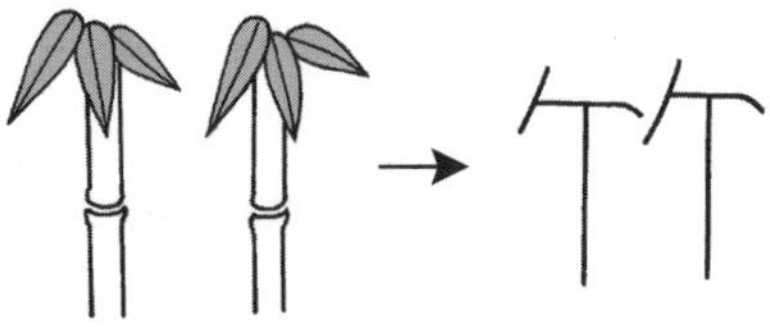

This is the shape of **bamboo**.

竹(たけ)の形(かたち)です。

▶ ちく
▷ たけ

竹（たけ） bamboo
竹の子（たけのこ） bamboo shoot
竹林（ちくりん） bamboo grove

<6>	ノ	𠂉	𠂉丨	𠂉丨ノ	𠂉丨𠂉	竹

295

合

to fit

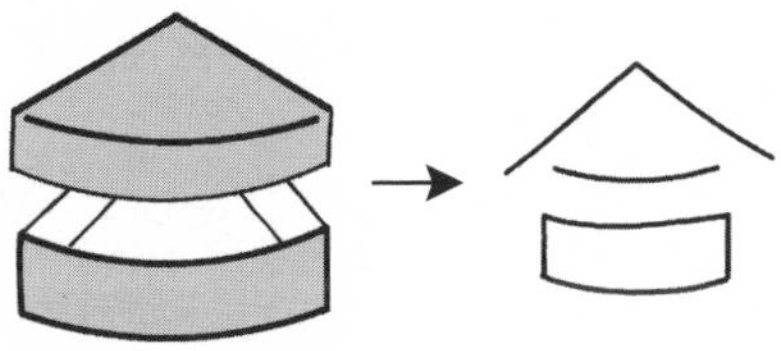

A box and its lid **fit** well.

箱(はこ)とふたは合(あ)っています。

▶ ごう　がっ
　かっ
▷ あ

合う（あう） to fit
試合（*しあい） game; match
間に合う（まにあう） to be in time
都合（つごう） convenience
場合（*ばあい） case

似合う（にあう） to look good
付き合う（つきあう） to date
合宿（がっしゅく） training camp

<6>	ノ	人	亼	亼丨	合	合

▶ 口(15)　! 会(72)　台(183)

296

答

to answer

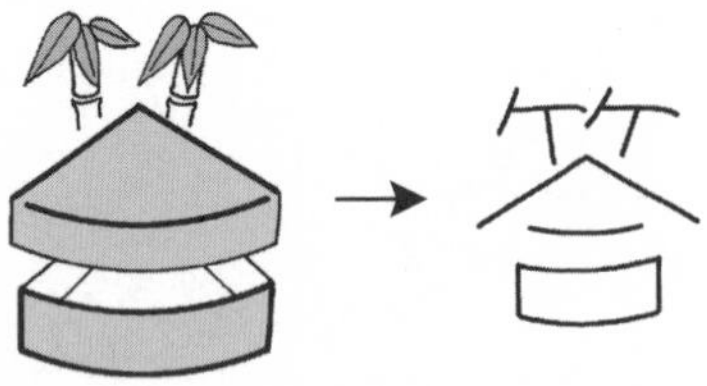

Our **answer** fits（合）like this bamboo（竹）box and its lid.

私(わたし)たちの答(こた)えは、この竹(たけ)の箱(はこ)とふたのように合(あ)いました。

▶ とう
▷ こた

答える（こたえる） to answer
答え（こたえ） answer
答案（とうあん） exam paper
解答（かいとう） answer
回答（かいとう） reply to a question

返答（へんとう） reply

<12>	ノ	𠂉	𠂉丨	𠂉丨ノ	𠂉丨𠂉	⺮	⺮ノ	⺮人	⺮亼	⺮亼一	答	答

▶ 竹(294)　合(295)

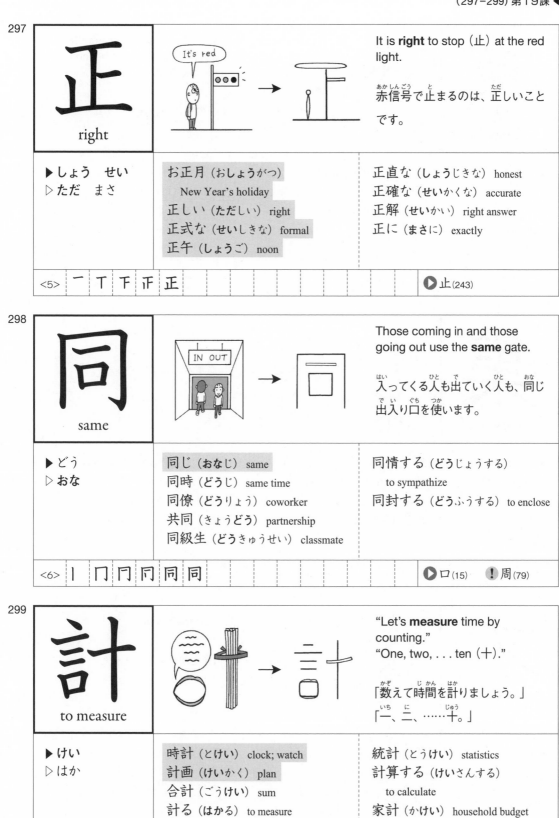

297

正
right

It is **right** to stop (止) at the red light.

赤信号で止まるのは、正しいことです。

▶ しょう　せい
▷ ただ　まさ

お正月 (おしょうがつ)　New Year's holiday
正しい (ただしい)　right
正式な (せいしきな)　formal
正午 (しょうご)　noon

正直な (しょうじきな)　honest
正確な (せいかくな)　accurate
正解 (せいかい)　right answer
正に (まさに)　exactly

<5>　一　丁　下　下　正

▶ 止(243)

298

同
same

Those coming in and those going out use the **same** gate.

入ってくる人も出ていく人も、同じ出入り口を使います。

▶ どう
▷ おな

同じ (おなじ)　same
同時 (どうじ)　same time
同僚 (どうりょう)　coworker
共同 (きょうどう)　partnership
同級生 (どうきゅうせい)　classmate

同情する (どうじょうする)　to sympathize
同封する (どうふうする)　to enclose

<6>　丨　冂　冂　同　同　同

▶ 口(15)　❗ 周(79)

299

計
to measure

"Let's **measure** time by counting."
"One, two, . . . ten (十)."

「数えて時間を計りましょう。」
「一、二、……十。」

▶ けい
▷ はか

時計 (とけい)　clock; watch
計画 (けいかく)　plan
合計 (ごうけい)　sum
計る (はかる)　to measure
会計 (かいけい)　accounting

統計 (とうけい)　statistics
計算する (けいさんする)　to calculate
家計 (かけい)　household budget

<9>　丶　亠　亖　亖　言　言　言　計

▶ 言(75)　十(10)

300

京
capital

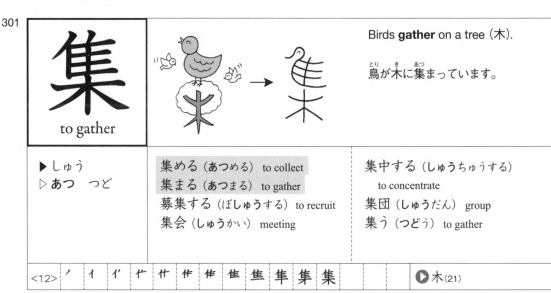

The houses were built on the small（小）hill and it became the **capital**.

丘の上に家が建ち、それが都になりました。

▶ きょう　けい

東京（とうきょう）Tokyo
京子（きょうこ）
　　Kyoko [woman's name]
京都（きょうと）Kyoto

京阪神（けいはんしん）
　Kyoto-Osaka-Kobe
上京する（じょうきょうする）
　to go to Tokyo

<8> 亠 亠 产 古 古 亨 亨 京　　▶ 口(15) 小(82) ! 東(45)

301

集
to gather

Birds **gather** on a tree（木）.

鳥が木に集まっています。

▶ しゅう
▷ あつ　つど

集める（あつめる）to collect
集まる（あつまる）to gather
募集する（ぼしゅうする）to recruit
集会（しゅうかい）meeting

集中する（しゅうちゅうする）
　　to concentrate
集団（しゅうだん）group
集う（つどう）to gather

<12> ノ イ イ 仁 什 作 作 隹 隹 隹 隼 集 集　　▶ 木(21)

302

不
non-

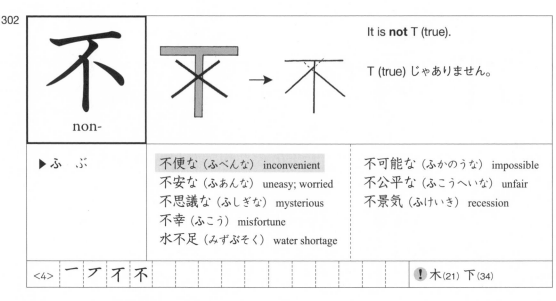

It is **not** T (true).

T (true) じゃありません。

▶ ふ　ぶ

不便な（ふべんな）inconvenient
不安な（ふあんな）uneasy; worried
不思議な（ふしぎな）mysterious
不幸（ふこう）misfortune
水不足（みずぶそく）water shortage

不可能な（ふかのうな）impossible
不公平な（ふこうへいな）unfair
不景気（ふけいき）recession

<4> 一 ア イ 不　　! 木(21) 下(34)

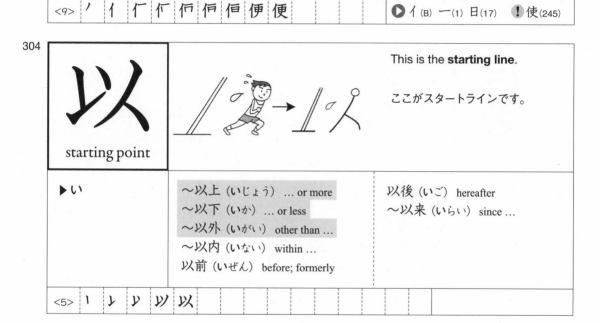

303

便
convenient / mail

If the mail arrives in one day (一日), it is **convenient**.

郵便が一日で届いたら便利ですね。

▶べん　びん
▷たよ

不便な（ふべんな）inconvenient
便利な（べんりな）convenient
郵便局（ゆうびんきょく）post office
便り（たより）letter; news
便所（べんじょ）lavatory

航空便（こうくうびん）airmail
船便（ふなびん）surface mail
便せん（びんせん）letter paper
便（びん）flight

<9> ノ　イ　イ　仁　仟　仟　便　便　便

● イ (B) 一 (1) 日 (17) ❗ 使 (245)

304

以
starting point

This is the **starting line**.

ここがスタートラインです。

▶い

～以上（いじょう）… or more
～以下（いか）… or less
～以外（いがい）other than …
～以内（いない）within …
以前（いぜん）before; formerly

以後（いご）hereafter
～以来（いらい）since …

<5> 丨　丨　以　以　以

第 20 課

● この課の漢字

場	戸	所	屋	堂	都	県	区
305	306	307	308	309	310	311	312
池	発	建	物	品	旅	通	進
313	314	315	316	317	318	319	320

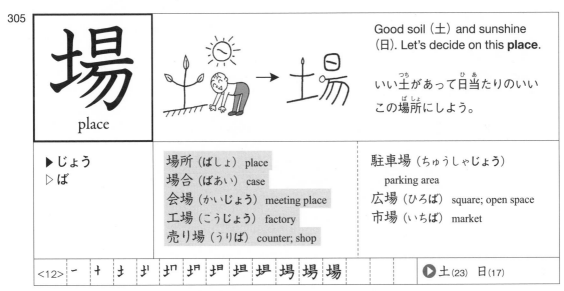

305

場
place

Good soil（土）and sunshine（日）. Let's decide on this **place**.

いい土_{つち}があって日_ひ当_あたりのいい
この場所_{ばしょ}にしよう。

▶ じょう
▷ ば

場所（ばしょ）place
場合（ばあい）case
会場（かいじょう）meeting place
工場（こうじょう）factory
売り場（うりば）counter; shop

駐車場（ちゅうしゃじょう）
　　parking area
広場（ひろば）square; open space
市場（いちば）market

<12> 一 十 土 圹 圯 圯 圯 坦 埸 場 場 場　　　　▶ 土(23) 日(17)

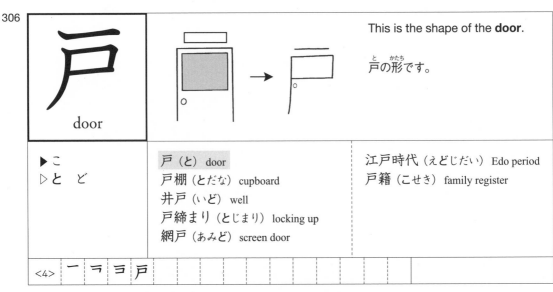

306

戸
door

This is the shape of the **door**.

戸_との形_{かたち}です。

▶ こ
▷ と　ど

戸（と）door
戸棚（とだな）cupboard
井戸（いど）well
戸締まり（とじまり）locking up
網戸（あみど）screen door

江戸時代（えどじだい）Edo period
戸籍（こせき）family register

<4> 一 ラ ヨ 戸

307

所
place

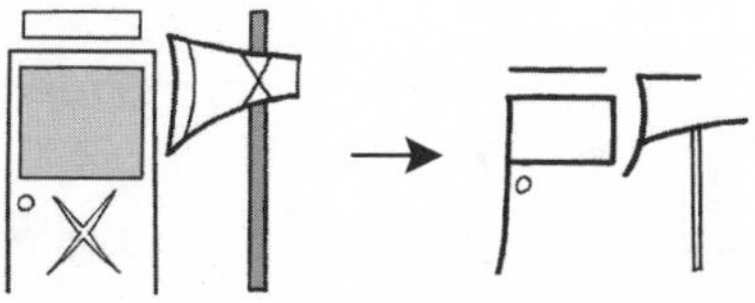

I mark the door（戸）with an ax to indicate it is the **place**.

おので戸に印をつけて、場所がわかるようにします。

▶しょ　じょ
▷ところ　どころ

どんな所（どんなところ）what kind of place
台所（だいどころ）kitchen
住所（じゅうしょ）address
近所（きんじょ）neighborhood
場所（ばしょ）place
事務所（じむしょ）office
市役所（しやくしょ）city hall

<8> 一 ㇇ ヨ 戸 戸 所 所 所

▶戸(306)

308

屋
roof / shop

People need soil（土）and a **roof**.

人は土と屋根が必要です。

▶おく
▷や

本屋（ほんや）bookstore
屋上（おくじょう）rooftop
八百屋（やおや）vegetable shop
部屋（へや）room
床屋（とこや）barber shop
屋根（やね）roof
名古屋（なごや）Nagoya
酒屋（さかや）liquor store

<9> ㇇ コ 尸 尸 层 层 层 屋 屋

▶土(23)　!室(210)

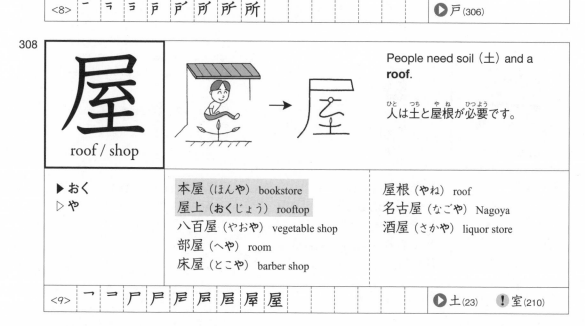

309

堂
hall

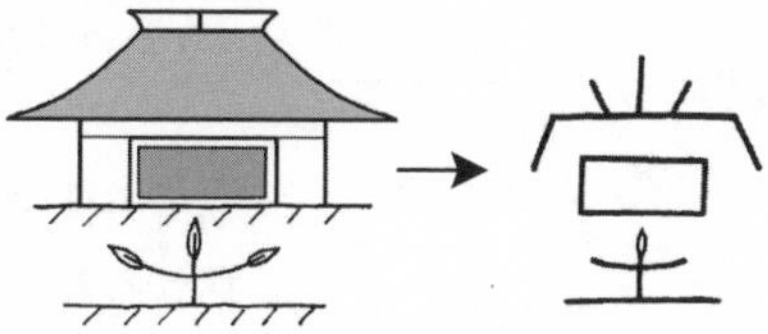

It is a big **hall** on the soil（土）.

土の上の大きな建物です。

▶どう

食堂（しょくどう）cafeteria
講堂（こうどう）lecture hall
堂々と（どうどうと）in a dignified manner
公会堂（こうかいどう）public hall
国会議事堂（こっかいぎじどう）the Diet building

<11> ｜ 〃 ⺌ ⺌ 㐾 㐾 尚 尚 堂 堂 堂

▶口(15)　土(23)　!党(400)

310

都
metropolis

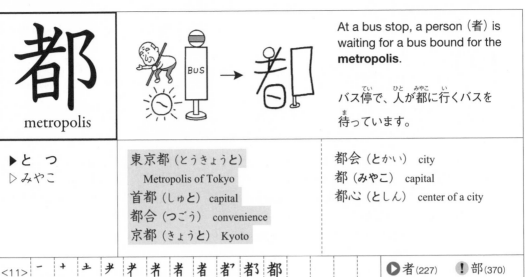

At a bus stop, a person（者）is waiting for a bus bound for the **metropolis**.

バス停で、人が都に行くバスを待っています。

▶ と　つ
▷ みやこ

東京都（とうきょうと）
　　Metropolis of Tokyo
首都（しゅと）capital
都合（つごう）convenience
京都（きょうと）Kyoto

都会（とかい）city
都（みやこ）capital
都心（としん）center of a city

<11> 一 十 土 耂 耂 者 者 者 者³ 都³ 都　　　▶者(227)　！部(370)

311

県
prefecture

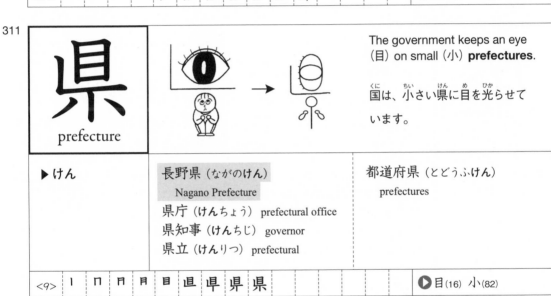

The government keeps an eye（目）on small（小）**prefectures**.

国は、小さい県に目を光らせています。

▶ けん

長野県（ながのけん）
　　Nagano Prefecture
県庁（けんちょう）prefectural office
県知事（けんちじ）governor
県立（けんりつ）prefectural

都道府県（とどうふけん）
　　prefectures

<9> 丨 冂 月 月 目 由 皀 昌 県　　　▶目(16)　小(82)

312

区
zone

This **zone** is divided by three walls and two roads.

この区は三つの壁と二つの道で区切られています。

▶ く

北区（きたく）Kita Ward
区切る（くぎる）to divide
区域（くいき）district
地区（ちく）area
区役所（くやくしょ）ward office

区別する（くべつする）
　　to differentiate
区間（くかん）section

<4> 一 フ ヌ 区　　　！図(273)

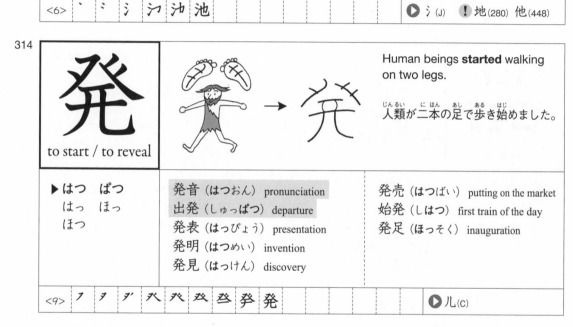

313

池
pond

There is crawfish in the **pond**.

池にザリガニがいます。

▶ ち
▷ いけ

池 (いけ) pond
電池 (でんち) battery
溜め池 (ためいけ) irrigation pond
貯水池 (ちょすいち) reservoir
用水池 (ようすいち) reservoir

<6> 丶 氵 氵 汁 池 池 | ▶ シ (J) ！ 地(280) 他(448)

314

発
to start / to reveal

Human beings **started** walking on two legs.

人類が二本の足で歩き始めました。

▶ はつ　ぱつ
　はっ　ほっ
　ほつ

発音 (はつおん) pronunciation
出発 (しゅっぱつ) departure
発表 (はっぴょう) presentation
発明 (はつめい) invention
発見 (はっけん) discovery

発売 (はつばい) putting on the market
始発 (しはつ) first train of the day
発足 (ほっそく) inauguration

<9> フ 了 了 癶 癶 癶 癶 発 発 | ▶ 儿(C)

315

建
to build

Before **building** it, you must have something to write (書) with and draw up a plan.

建物を建てる前に、書くものを持ち、設計することが大切です。

▶ けん　こん
▷ た　だ

建てる (たてる) to build
建物 (*たてもの) building
建つ (たつ) to be built
建設 (けんせつ) construction
建築 (けんちく) architecture

二階建て (にかいだて) two-story
建国 (けんこく) founding a nation
建立 (こんりゅう)
　building (temples, etc.)

<9> フ ㇕ ㇕ ㇕ 彐 聿 聿 建 建 | ▶ 書(120)

316

		Cows（牛）and foxes are living **things**.
物 thing	🐄 物 → 牜勿	牛_{うし}やきつねは生_いき物_{もの}です。

牛やきつねは生き物です。

▶ ぶつ　もつ ▷ もの	物（もの）thing 食べ物（たべもの）food 飲み物（のみもの）drink 買い物（かいもの）shopping 着物（きもの）kimono	動物（どうぶつ）animal 建物（たてもの）building 果物（くだもの）fruit 荷物（にもつ）baggage

<8>	' ｰ 十 牛 牛 牜 物 物	▶ 牛(165)

317

		This is the shape of three **goods**.
品 goods	□ □ □ → □ □	三_{みっ}つの品物_{しなもの}の形_{かたち}です。

三つの品物の形です。

▶ ひん ▷ しな	品物（しなもの）goods 日用品（にちようひん） 　　daily necessities 製品（せいひん）product 必需品（ひつじゅひん）necessity	作品（さくひん）artistic piece 上品な（じょうひんな）elegant 下品な（げひんな）vulgar 食料品（しょくりょうひん）groceries

<9>	' 口 口 口 品 品 品 品 品	▶ 口(15)

318

		Two people are **traveling**, following the guide with a flag.
旅 travel	🚩 → 方𣎴	二人_{ふたり}の人_{ひと}が旗_{はた}を持_もったガイドの後_{あと}について旅行_{りょこう}しています。

二人の人が旗を持ったガイドの後について旅行しています。

▶ りょ ▷ たび	旅行（りょこう）travel 旅館（りょかん）Japanese inn 旅券（りょけん）passport 旅（たび）journey 一人旅（ひとりたび）traveling alone	旅費（りょひ）travel expense

<10>	' ｰ 方 方 扩 扩 扩 於 旅 旅	▶ 方(136)　！族(195)

319

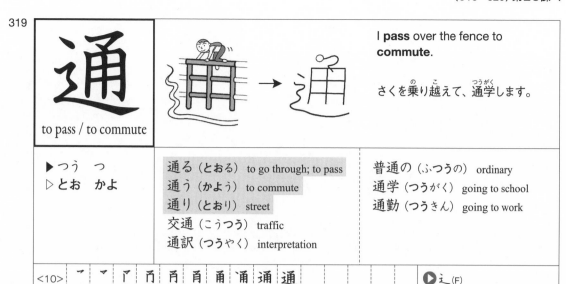

通

to pass / to commute

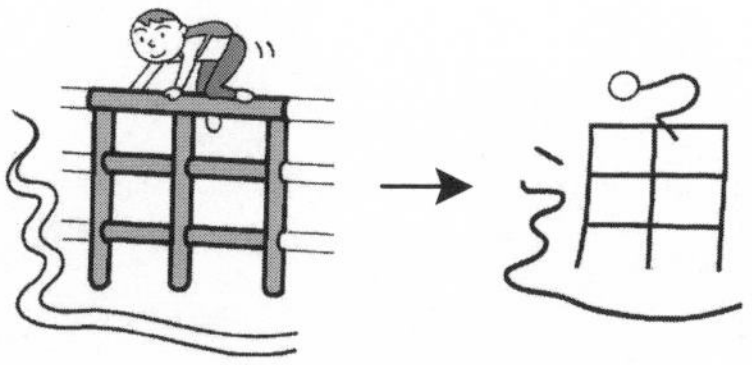

I **pass** over the fence to **commute**.

さくを乗(の)り越(こ)えて、通学(つうがく)します。

▶つう　つ
▷とお　かよ

通る（とおる） to go through; to pass
通う（かよう） to commute
通り（とおり） street
交通（こうつう） traffic
通訳（つうやく） interpretation

普通の（ふつうの） ordinary
通学（つうがく） going to school
通勤（つうきん） going to work

<10> 

辶(F)

320

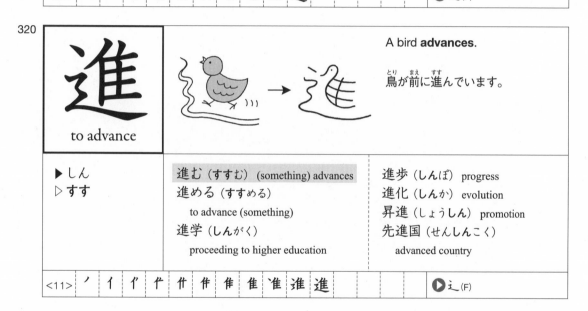

進

to advance

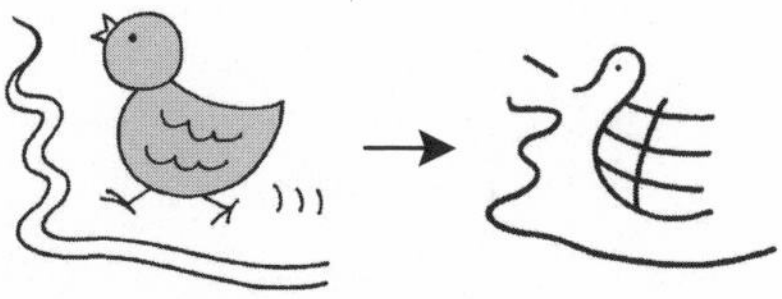

A bird **advances**.

鳥(とり)が前(まえ)に進(すす)んでいます。

▶しん
▷すす

進む（すすむ） (something) advances
進める（すすめる） to advance (something)
進学（しんがく） proceeding to higher education

進歩（しんぽ） progress
進化（しんか） evolution
昇進（しょうしん） promotion
先進国（せんしんこく） advanced country

<11> 

辶(F)

Part 3

第21課 － 第32課

(漢字番号 321-512)

第 21 課

●この課の漢字

丸	熱	冷	甘	汚	果	卵	皿
321	322	323	324	325	326	327	328
酒	塩	付	片	焼	消	固	個
329	330	331	332	333	334	335	336

321

丸
round

I **curl** up myself.

体を丸めています。

▶ がん
▷ まる

丸い（まるい）round
丸（まる）circle
丸める（まるめる）to curl
弾丸（だんがん）bullet

<3> ノ 九 丸　　　▶九(9)

322

熱
heat

I curl up（丸）myself to keep **heat** from escaping.

熱を逃がさないように、体を丸めています。

▶ ねつ　ねっ
▷ あつ

熱い（あつい）hot
熱（ねつ）fever
熱心な（ねっしんな）enthusiastic
熱中する（ねっちゅうする）
　　to be absorbed

熱帯（ねったい）tropics
熱する（ねっする）to heat
加熱（かねつ）heating
熱湯（ねっとう）
　　hot water; boiling water

<15> 一 十 土 尹 尹 赱 幸 坴 刲 執 執 埶 熱 熱 熱　▶土(23) 丸(321) 灬(N)

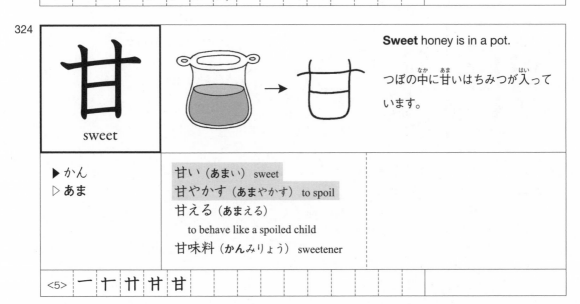

323

冷
to freeze

A person trembles in the **freezing** wind.

冷たい風の中で震えています。

▶ れい
▷ つめ ひ さ

冷たい（つめたい）cold
冷える（ひえる）to become cold
冷やす（ひやす）to chill
冷ます（さます）to cool
冷蔵庫（れいぞうこ）refrigerator

冷房（れいぼう）air conditioner
冷凍する（れいとうする）to freeze
冷静な（れいせいな）calm

<7> 丶 冫 冫 仒 仒 冷 冷

324

甘
sweet

Sweet honey is in a pot.

つぼの中に甘いはちみつが入って
います。

▶ かん
▷ あま

甘い（あまい）sweet
甘やかす（あまやかす）to spoil
甘える（あまえる）
　　to behave like a spoiled child
甘味料（かんみりょう）sweetener

<5> 一 十 廿 甘 甘

325

汚
dirty

A person is drinking **dirty** water.

汚い水を飲んでいます。

▶ お
▷ きたな よご
　けが

汚い（きたない）dirty
汚れる（よごれる）to become dirty
汚す（よごす）to make something dirty
汚染（おせん）pollution
汚れ（よごれ）dirt; spot

汚職（おしょく）corruption
汚れる（けがれる）to become dirty

<6> 丶 冫 冫 汙 汙 汚

⏵ シ (J)

127

326

果 fruit		It is a tree (木) in **fruit**. <ruby>果物<rt>くだもの</rt></ruby>がなっている<ruby>木<rt>き</rt></ruby>です。
▶ か ▷ は	果物（*くだもの）fruit 結果（けっか）result 効果（こうか）effect 果実（かじつ）fruit 果たして（はたして）as it turns out	成果（せいか）accomplishment
<8>　丿　冂　日　日　旦　甲　里　果		▶ 木(21)

327

卵 egg		Let's break an **egg**. <ruby>卵<rt>たまご</rt></ruby>を<ruby>割<rt>わ</rt></ruby>りましょう。
▶ らん ▷ たまご	卵（たまご）egg 卵黄（らんおう）yolk 卵白（らんぱく）egg white 卵焼き（たまごやき）fried egg	
<7>　ノ　匕　匕　匇　卵　卵　卵		

328

皿 plate		A cake is on the **plate**. <ruby>皿<rt>さら</rt></ruby>の<ruby>上<rt>うえ</rt></ruby>にケーキがのっています。
▷ さら　ざら	（お）皿（おさら）plate; dish 灰皿（はいざら）ashtray 紙皿（かみざら）paper plate 大皿（おおざら）big plate 小皿（こざら）small plate	皿洗い（さらあらい）dishwashing
<5>　丨　冂　冊　皿　皿		

329

酒
alcohol

Good water makes good *sake*.

おいしいお酒はいい水からできます。

▶ しゅ
▷ さけ　さか
　　ざか　ざけ

（お）酒（おさけ）　alcohol
酒屋（さかや）　liquor store
日本酒（にほんしゅ）　*sake*
飲酒運転（いんしゅうんてん）
　　　　　　drunk driving

洋酒（ようしゅ）　Western liquor
居酒屋（いざかや）　Japanese-style pub
地酒（じざけ）　locally brewed *sake*

<10>　丶　氵　氵　沪　汀　沂　洒　洒　酒　酒　　▶ シ（J）

330

塩
salt

The food on this plate（皿）is **salty**.

皿の食べ物は塩辛いです。

▶ えん
▷ しお

塩（しお）　salt
塩辛い（しおからい）　salty
食塩（しょくえん）　table salt
塩分（えんぶん）　salt content
塩水（しおみず）　salt water

<13>　一　十　土　圹　圹　圹　圹　圹　坫　塩　塩　塩　　▶ 土(23)　口(15)　皿(328)

331

付
to attach

I **attach** something to a person.

人に何かを付けます。

▶ ふ
▷ つ　づ

付き合う（つきあう）　to date
片付ける（かたづける）　to tidy up
付ける（つける）　to attach
付く（つく）　to stick
日付（*ひづけ）／日付け（ひづけ）　date

受付（*うけつけ）／受け付け（うけつけ）　reception
寄付（きふ）　donation
付録（ふろく）　appendix

<5>　ノ　イ　仁　付　付　　▶ イ（B）　⚠ 村(101)

332

片

one side

This is **one side** of a tree.

木の片側です。

▶へん
▷かた

片付ける（かたづける）to tidy up
片道（かたみち）one way
片方（かたほう）one of a pair
片手（かたて）one hand
片言（かたこと）prattle; baby talk

片寄る（かたよる）to be one-sided
破片（はへん）fragment

<4> ノ 丿 广 片

333

焼

to burn

I **burned** thirty sticks.

30本の棒を焼きました。

▶しょう
▷や

焼く（やく）to burn; to bake
焼ける（やける）
　　to be burned; to be baked
夕焼け（ゆうやけ）sunset
日焼け（ひやけ）sun-tanning

焼き鳥（やきとり）grilled chicken
焼き肉（やきにく）grilled meat
燃焼（ねんしょう）combustion

<12> 丶 丷 丷 火 灯 灶 炷 炷 焼 焼 焼 焼　▶ 火(19) 十(10) 儿(C)

334

消

to turn off / to disappear

The moon（月）**disappeared** into the water.

月が水の中に消えました。

▶しょう
▷け　き

消す（けす）to turn off
消える（きえる）
　　something turns off; to disappear
消化する（しょうかする）to digest
消防署（しょうぼうしょ）fire station

取り消す（とりけす）to cancel
消去する（しょうきょする）to erase

<10> 丶 冫 氵 氵 氵 沪 沪 消 消 消　▶ 氵(J) 月(18)

335

固

hard

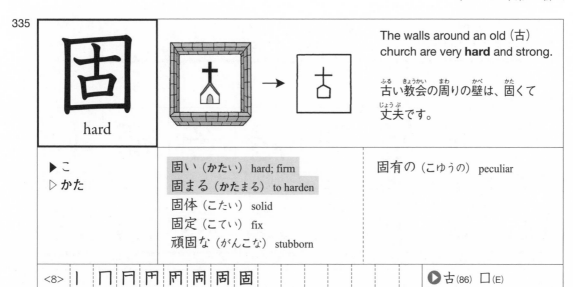

The walls around an old (古) church are very **hard** and strong.

古い教会の周りの壁は、固くて丈夫です。

▶こ
▷かた

固い（かたい） hard; firm
固まる（かたまる） to harden
固体（こたい） solid
固定（こてい） fix
頑固な（がんこな） stubborn

固有の（こゆうの） peculiar

<8> 丨 冂 冃 円 円 両 固 固

▶ 古(86) 囗(E)

336

個

individual

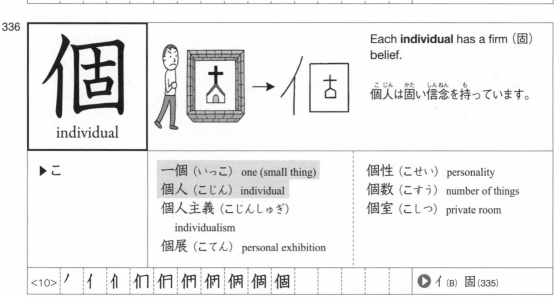

Each **individual** has a firm (固) belief.

個人は固い信念を持っています。

▶こ

一個（いっこ） one (small thing)
個人（こじん） individual
個人主義（こじんしゅぎ）
　individualism
個展（こてん） personal exhibition

個性（こせい） personality
個数（こすう） number of things
個室（こしつ） private room

<10> ノ イ 仆 们 们 倜 個 個 個

▶ イ (B) 固(335)

131

第　22　課

● この課の漢字

笑	泣	怒	幸	悲	苦	痛	恥
337	338	339	340	341	342	343	344
配	困	辛	眠	残	念	感	情
345	346	347	348	349	350	351	352

337

笑
to laugh

A person （人）is **laughing** hard
"*Ke ke* （ケケ）."

人が「ケケ」と大笑いしています。

▶ しょう
▷ わら　え

笑う（わらう）to laugh
笑顔（えがお）smile
ほほ笑む（ほほえむ）to smile
微笑（びしょう）slight smile

爆笑する（ばくしょうする）
　to burst into laughter
苦笑い（にがわらい）bitter smile

<10> ノ ト ヒ ヒ ヒ ケ ケ 竺 竺 笑　　▶ 竹(294) 人(26)

338

泣
to cry

A person is standing （立）and
crying.

立って、泣いています。

▶ きゅう
▷ な

泣く（なく）to cry
泣き声（なきごえ）cry
泣き虫（なきむし）crybaby
嬉し泣き（うれしなき）cry for joy
号泣する（ごうきゅうする）to wail

<8> 丶 冫 冫 冫 氵 氵 汸 泣　　▶ 氵 (J) 立(77)

339

怒
anger

The **angry** woman（女）hit me.

怒った女の人にたたかれました。
(おこ　おんな　ひと)

▶ ど
▷ おこ　いか

怒る（おこる）to be angry
怒り（いかり）anger
怒鳴る（どなる）to shout

<9>　ㄑ　夕　夕　奴　奴　奴　怒　怒　怒

▶ 女(52)　心(139)

340

幸
happy

I have a lot of yen（¥）under the soil（土）. I am very **happy**.

土の下に円（¥）をたくさん持っていて幸せです。
(つち　した　えん　　　　　　　　　　　　も　　しあわ)

▶ こう
▷ しあわ　さいわ
　さち

幸せな（しあわせな）happy
不幸（ふこう）misfortune
幸運（こううん）good fortune
幸い（さいわい）fortunately
幸福な（こうふくな）happy

幸（さち）happiness

<8>　一　十　土　土　幸　幸　幸　幸

▶ 土(23)　十(10)　❗辛(347)

341

悲
sad

My heart（心）is **sad** because he is behind bars.

彼が刑務所に入っているので、
(かれ　けい む しょ　はい)
私の心は悲しいです。
(わたし　こころ　かな)

▶ ひ
▷ かな

悲しい（かなしい）sad
悲しむ（かなしむ）to grieve
悲劇（ひげき）tragedy
悲惨な（ひさんな）miserable

悲観する（ひかんする）
　to be pessimistic

<12>　丿　ヲ　ヲ　ヲ　ヺ　非　非　非　非　悲　悲　悲

▶ 心(139)

342

to suffer

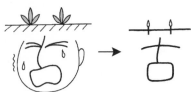

If you eat old (古) grass, you will **suffer**.

古い草を食べたら、苦しくなります。

▶ く
▷ にが　くる

苦い (にがい) bitter
苦手 (にがて) to be weak at
苦しい (くるしい) painful
苦しむ (くるしむ) to suffer
苦痛 (くつう) pain

苦労 (くろう) difficulty
苦情 (くじょう) complaint

<8> 一 十 艹 芐 芐 芐 苦 苦 ▶ 艹 (K) 古 (86) ！若 (423)

343

痛

pain

I pass over the fence of the hospital with **pain**.

痛みを感じながら、病院のさくを越えます。

▶ つう
▷ いた

痛い (いたい) painful
痛み (いたみ) pain
頭痛 (ずつう) headache
苦痛 (くつう) pain
痛み止め (いたみどめ) painkiller

腹痛 (ふくつう) stomachache
腰痛 (ようつう) lower back pain

<12> ` 一 广 广 广 疒 疒 疔 病 病 痛 痛 ▶ 广 (0) ！病 (111)

344

恥

shame

It's a **shame** if you do not listen to the voice from your heart (心).

自分の心の声に耳を傾けないなんて、恥ずべきことです。

▶ ち
▷ は　はじ

恥ずかしい (はずかしい)
to be embarrassed
恥 (はじ) shame
恥ずかしがる (はずかしがる)
to be shy

恥じる (はじる) to be ashamed
恥知らず (はじしらず)
shameless person
羞恥心 (しゅうちしん)
sense of shame

<10> 一 丆 F F 耳 耳 耶 恥 恥 ▶ 耳 (73) 心 (139)

345

配

to deliver

A person kneels down and **delivers** sake (酒).

ひざまずいてお酒を配っています。

▶ ぱい　はい
▷ くば

心配する（しんぱいする）to worry
配る（くばる）to distribute
配達（はいたつ）delivery
支配（しはい）control; rule
配偶者（はいぐうしゃ）spouse

支配人（しはいにん）manager
宅配便（たくはいびん）
　　home delivery service

<10> 一 厂 冂 両 酉 酉 酉 酉 配

▶ 酒(329)

346

困

trouble

We are in **trouble** because there is a big tree (木).

大きな木があるので困っています。

▶ こん
▷ こま

困る（こまる）to be in trouble
困難な（こんなんな）difficult
貧困（ひんこん）poverty
困惑（こんわく）confusion

<7> 丨 冂 冃 用 困 困 困

▶ 木(21) 口(E)

347

辛

painful / spicy

Standing (立) on a pole is **painful**.

棒の上に立つのは辛いです。

▶ しん
▷ から

辛い（からい）spicy
塩辛い（しおからい）salty
香辛料（こうしんりょう）spice
辛抱（しんぼう）patience
辛子（からし）mustard

辛い（*つらい）painful; arduous

<7> 、 亠 十 立 立 立 辛

▶ 立(77) 十(10) ！ 辛(340)

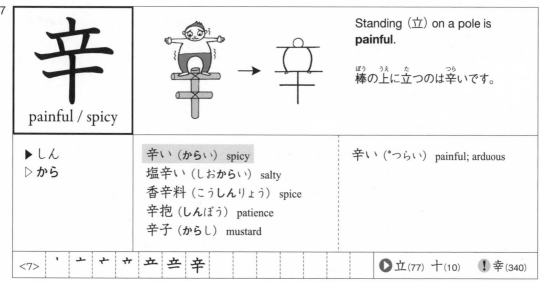

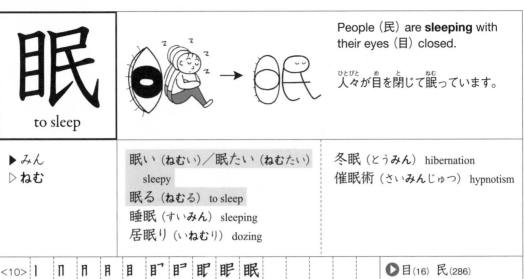

348 眠
to sleep

People（民）are **sleeping** with their eyes（目）closed.

人々が目を閉じて眠っています。

▶ みん
▷ ねむ

眠い（ねむい）／眠たい（ねむたい）
  sleepy
眠る（ねむる）to sleep
睡眠（すいみん）sleeping
居眠り（いねむり）dozing

冬眠（とうみん）hibernation
催眠術（さいみんじゅつ）hypnotism

<10> 丨 冂 冃 冃 目 目 盯 眇 眠 眠

▶ 目(16) 民(286)

---

349 残
to remain

The three（三）people died（死）and only their weapons **remained**.

三人は死んで、武器だけが残りました。

▶ ざん
▷ のこ

残念な（ざんねんな）regrettable
残る（のこる）to remain
残す（のこす）to leave something
残り（のこり）remainder
残業（ざんぎょう）work overtime

残高（ざんだか）account balance
残らず（のこらず）without exception

<10> 一 ア ヲ タ 歺 歼 歼 残 残 残

▶ 死(256) 三(3)

---

350 念
thought

Now（今），I am having **thoughts** of you.

今、あなたのことを考えています。

▶ ねん

残念な（ざんねんな）regrettable
記念（きねん）remembrance
記念日（きねんび）memorial day
信念（しんねん）belief
念願（ねんがん）long-cherished wish

無念（むねん）regret; mortification
概念（がいねん）concept
断念する（だんねんする）to give up

<8> ノ 人 个 今 今 念 念 念

▶ 今(27) 心(139)

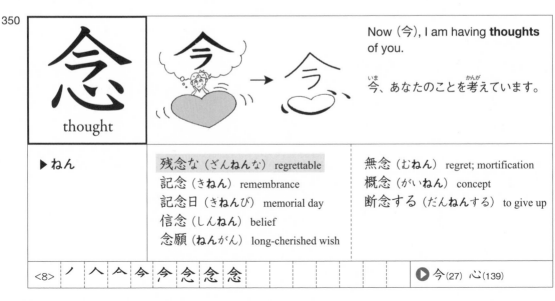

351

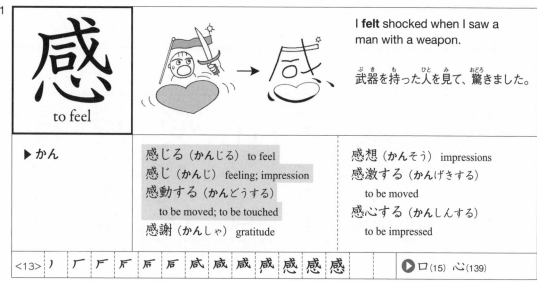

感
to feel

I **felt** shocked when I saw a man with a weapon.

<ruby>武器<rt>ぶき</rt></ruby>を<ruby>持<rt>も</rt></ruby>った<ruby>人<rt>ひと</rt></ruby>を<ruby>見<rt>み</rt></ruby>て、<ruby>驚<rt>おどろ</rt></ruby>きました。

▶ かん

感じる（かんじる）to feel
感じ（かんじ）feeling; impression
感動する（かんどうする）
　　　to be moved; to be touched
感謝（かんしゃ）gratitude

感想（かんそう）impressions
感激する（かんげきする）
　　　to be moved
感心する（かんしんする）
　　　to be impressed

<13> ノ 厂 厂 厃 厉 咸 咸 咸 咸 感 感 感 感　　▶ 口(15) 心(139)

352

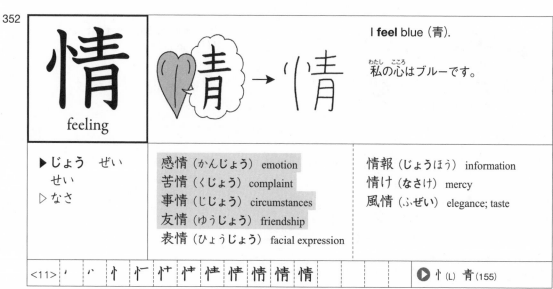

情
feeling

I **feel** blue（青）.

<ruby>私<rt>わたし</rt></ruby>の<ruby>心<rt>こころ</rt></ruby>はブルーです。

▶ じょう　ぜい
　　せい
▷ なさ

感情（かんじょう）emotion
苦情（くじょう）complaint
事情（じじょう）circumstances
友情（ゆうじょう）friendship
表情（ひょうじょう）facial expression

情報（じょうほう）information
情け（なさけ）mercy
風情（ふぜい）elegance; taste

<11> ` ˊ 忄 忄 忄 忄 忄 情 情 情 情　　▶ 忄(L) 青(155)

第　23　課

●この課の漢字

覚	忘	決	定	比	受	授	徒
353	354	355	356	357	358	359	360
練	復	表	卒	違	役	皆	彼
361	362	363	364	365	366	367	368

353

覚

to memorize

We **memorize** what we see （見）in school.

_{がっこう} _み _{おぼ}
学校で見たものを覚えます。

▶ かく
▷ おぼ　さ　ざ

覚える（おぼえる）to memorize
感覚（かんかく）sense
目が覚める（めがさめる）to wake
自覚する（じかくする）to realize
味覚（みかく）the sense of taste

視覚（しかく）the sense of sight
目覚まし時計（めざましどけい）
　　alarm clock

<12> 、　丶　ツ　ツ　ⴀ　ⴀ　ⴀ　ⴀ　ⴀ　ⴀ　覚　覚　　▶見(65)　❗党(400)

354

忘

to forget

I **forgot** to build the wall on the right.

_{みぎがわ} _{かべ} _{つく} _{わす}
右側の壁を作るのを忘れました。

▶ ぼう
▷ わす

忘れる（わすれる）to forget
忘れ物（わすれもの）
　　things left behind
忘れっぽい（わすれっぽい）
　　forgetful

忘年会（ぼうねんかい）
　　year-end party

<7> 、　亠　亡　亡　忘　忘　忘　　　　▶心(139)

355

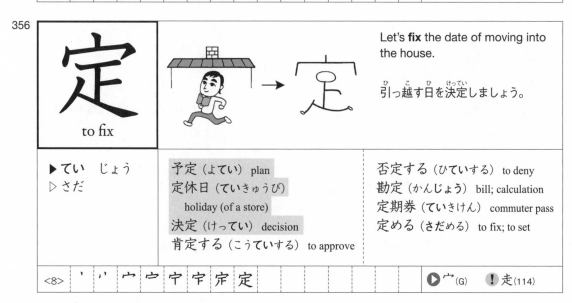

決
to decide

We have **decided** to save water.

節水(せっすい)することに決(き)めました。

▶ けっ　けつ
▷ き

決める（きめる）to decide
決まる（きまる）to be decided
決して（けっして）never
決定（けってい）decision
決心（けっしん）determination

解決（かいけつ）solution
決勝（けっしょう）final match
判決（はんけつ）judgment

<7> 丶 冫 氵 氵ユ 沪 沪 決

▶ 氵(J) 人(26)

356

定
to fix

Let's **fix** the date of moving into the house.

引(ひ)っ越(こ)す日(ひ)を決定(けってい)しましょう。

▶ てい　じょう
▷ さだ

予定（よてい）plan
定休日（ていきゅうび）
　　holiday (of a store)
決定（けってい）decision
肯定する（こうていする）to approve

否定する（ひていする）to deny
勘定（かんじょう）bill; calculation
定期券（ていきけん）commuter pass
定める（さだめる）to fix; to set

<8> 丶 丷 宀 宀 宀 宁 定 定

▶ 宀(G)　! 走(114)

357

比
to compare

Are they both the *katakana* ヒ? Let's **compare** them.

どちらもカタカナの「ヒ」でしょうか？ 比(くら)べてみましょう。

▶ ひ
▷ くら

比べる（くらべる）to compare
比較（ひかく）comparison
比較的（ひかくてき）comparatively
対比（たいひ）contrast
比例（ひれい）proportion

<4> 一 ヒ ヒ 比

! 北(48)

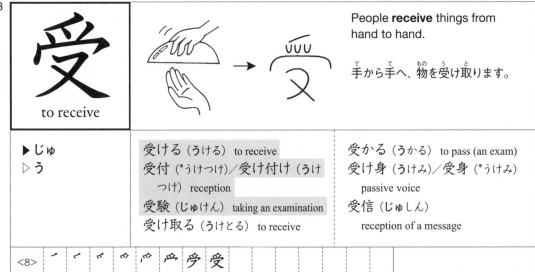

358

受

to receive

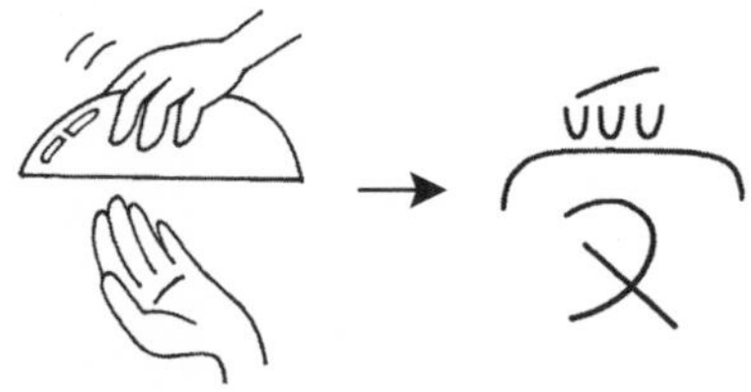

People **receive** things from hand to hand.

手(て)から手(て)へ、物(もの)を受(う)け取(と)ります。

▶ じゅ
▷ う

- 受ける（うける） to receive
- 受付（*うけつけ）／受け付け（うけつけ） reception
- 受験（じゅけん） taking an examination
- 受け取る（うけとる） to receive
- 受かる（うかる） to pass (an exam)
- 受け身（うけみ）／受身（*うけみ） passive voice
- 受信（じゅしん） reception of a message

<8> 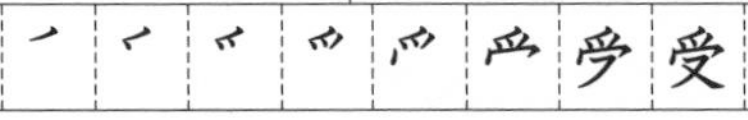

359

授

to instruct

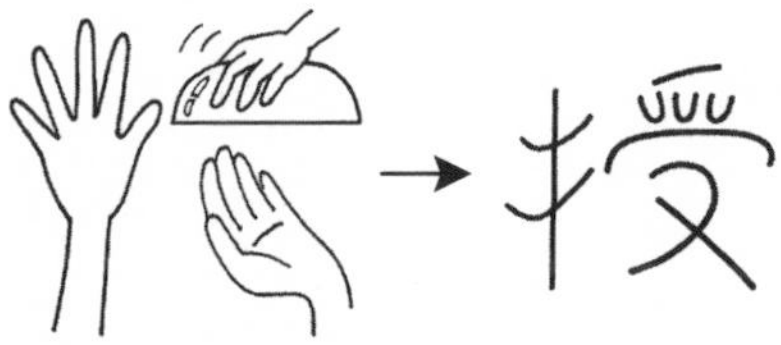

Being **instructed** is like receiving（受）things from someone.

教(おし)えてもらうことは何(なに)かを受(う)け取(と)ることです。

▶ じゅ
▷ さず

- 授業（じゅぎょう） class
- 教授（きょうじゅ） professor
- 授業料（じゅぎょうりょう） tuition
- 授ける（さずける） to confer
- 授かる（さずかる） to be given
- 授受（じゅじゅ） giving and receiving

<11> 

扌(I) 受(358)

360

徒

follower

The **follower** runs（走）on the street.

弟子(でし)が道(みち)を走(はし)っています。

▶ と

- 生徒（せいと） pupil
- 徒歩で（とほで） on foot
- イスラム教徒（イスラムきょうと） Muslim
- キリスト教徒（キリストきょうと） Christian

<10> 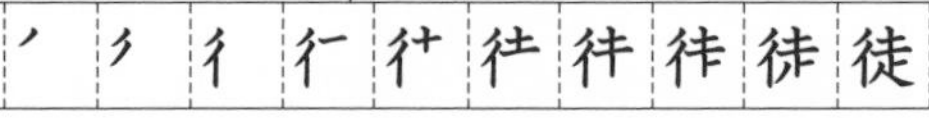

イ(D) 走(114)

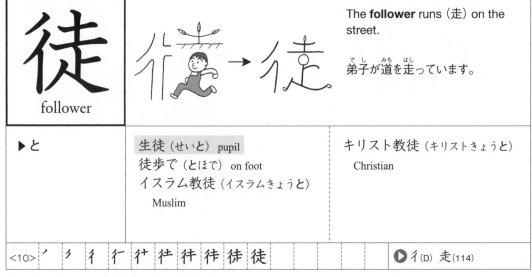

361

練
to elaborate

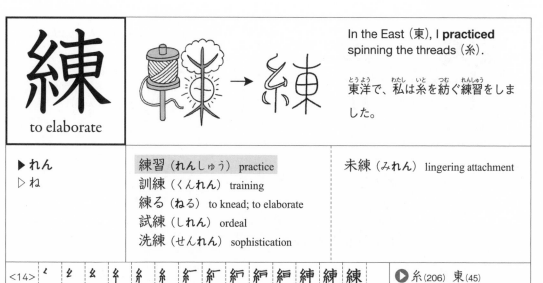

In the East（東）, I **practiced** spinning the threads（糸）.

とうよう わたし いと つむ れんしゅう
東洋で、私は糸を紡ぐ練習をしました。

▶ れん
▷ ね

練習（れんしゅう）practice
訓練（くんれん）training
練る（ねる）to knead; to elaborate
試練（しれん）ordeal
洗練（せんれん）sophistication

未練（みれん）lingering attachment

| <14> | ㇑ | ㇗ | 幺 | 糸 | 糸 | 糸 | 糽 | 紳 | 紳 | 紳 | 緋 | 綀 | 練 | 練 | ▶ 糸(206) 東(45) |

362

復
to repeat

People **repeatedly** walk along the same road every day（日）.

ひと おな みち まいにち ある
人は同じ道を毎日、歩きます。

▶ ふく ふっ
ぷく

復習（ふくしゅう）review
回復（かいふく）recovery
往復（おうふく）lap; both ways
復旧（ふっきゅう）retrieval
復興（ふっこう）rebuilding

復活（ふっかつ）revival
反復（はんぷく）repetition

| <12> | ㇒ | ㇉ | 彳 | 彳 | 犭 | 行 | 行 | 行 | 狛 | 泊 | 復 | 復 | ▶ イ(D) 日(17) |

363

表
to express / surface

She **expresses** her joy because the tree grows well.

き おお そだ よろこ
木が大きく育ったので、喜びを
ひょうげん
表現しています。

▶ ひょう ぴょう
▷ おもて あらわ

表（おもて）surface
表（ひょう）list; table
発表（はっぴょう）presentation
表す（あらわす）to express
表紙（ひょうし）cover page

代表（だいひょう）representative
表情（ひょうじょう）facial expression

| <8> | 一 | 十 | 丰 | 圭 | 声 | 表 | 表 | 表 |

364

卒

to graduate

Ten （十） people （人） **graduated**.

十人の人が卒業しました。
<small>じゅうにん ひと そつぎょう</small>

▶ そつ

卒業（そつぎょう） graduation
卒業式（そつぎょうしき）
　graduation ceremony
卒業生（そつぎょうせい） graduate
大卒（だいそつ） university graduate

卒論（そつろん） graduation thesis
新卒（しんそつ） recent graduate

<8> 　 ` 　 ーー 　 广 　 六 　 ぁ 　 六 　 立 　 卒 | ▶人(26) 十(10)

365

違

different

The streets are complicated.
I think I am on a **different** street.

道が複雑なので、間違えたみたい
<small>みち ふくざつ まちが</small>
です。

▶ い
▷ ちが

違う（ちがう） to differ
間違える（まちがえる）
　to make a mistake
間違い（まちがい） mistake
違い（ちがい） difference

違反（いはん） violation
勘違い（かんちがい）
　misunderstanding
相違（そうい） difference

<13> ` 　 ー 　 立 　 产 　 弃 　 音 　 音 　 音 　 音 　 韋 　 違 　 違 　 違 | ▶ 辶(F)

366

役

duty

My **duty** is to carry a stone.

私の役目は石を運ぶことです。
<small>わたし やくめ いし はこ</small>

▶ やく　えき

役に立つ（やくにたつ） to be useful
市役所（しやくしょ） city hall
役目（やくめ） duty
役者（やくしゃ） actor
役（やく） role

主役（しゅやく） leading character
兵役（へいえき） military service

<7> ` 　 ク 　 彳 　 彳 　 疒 　 役 　 役 | ▶ 彳(D)　 ！ 彼(368) 投(457)

367

皆
everyone

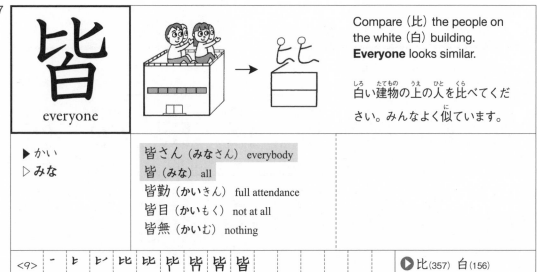

Compare (比) the people on the white (白) building. **Everyone** looks similar.

白い建物の上の人を比べてください。みんなよく似ています。

▶ かい
▷ みな

皆さん（みなさん） everybody
皆（みな） all
皆勤（かいきん） full attendance
皆目（かいもく） not at all
皆無（かいむ） nothing

<9> 一 ト ヒ 比 比 毕 毕 皆 皆

▶ 比(357) 白(156)

368

彼
he

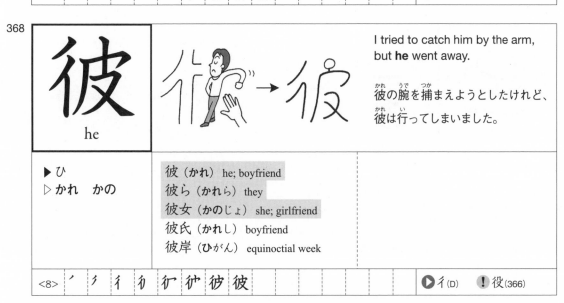

I tried to catch him by the arm, but **he** went away.

彼の腕を捕まえようとしたけれど、彼は行ってしまいました。

▶ ひ
▷ かれ　かの

彼（かれ） he; boyfriend
彼ら（かれら） they
彼女（かのじょ） she; girlfriend
彼氏（かれし） boyfriend
彼岸（ひがん） equinoctial week

<8> ノ ク イ 彳 疒 犴 狩 彼 彼

▶ イ(D)　！役(366)

第 24 課

● この課の漢字

全	部	必	要	荷	由	届	利
369	370	371	372	373	374	375	376
払	濯	寝	踊	活	末	宅	祭
377	378	379	380	381	382	383	384

369

全
all

The king（王）rules **all** on the mountain.

王様は山にある全部の物を統治
しています。

▶ ぜん
▷ まった　すべ

全部（ぜんぶ）all
安全（あんぜん）safety
全国（ぜんこく）whole country
全員（ぜんいん）all members
全く（まったく）entirely

完全な（かんぜんな）perfect
全力（ぜんりょく）all one's might
全て（すべて）all

<6> ノ 入 入 今 全 全　　　　▶ 王(63)　! 金(22)

370

部
section

A person is standing（立）in a **section** where a bus stop is.

バス停のところに、人が立って
います。

▶ ぶ

全部（ぜんぶ）all
部屋（*へや）room
部長（ぶちょう）department head
一部（いちぶ）one part
テニス部（テニスぶ）tennis team

工学部（こうがくぶ）
　department of engineering
大部分（だいぶぶん）most of...

<11> ` 亠 立 立 立 产 咅 咅 咅 部 部　　▶ 立(77) 口(15)　! 都(310)

371

必
surely

I **surely** will win your heart (心).

あなたのハートは必ず射止めて
みせます。

▶ ひつ　ひっ
▷ かなら

必要な（ひつような）necessary
必ず（かならず）surely
必ずしも（かならずしも）not always
必死（ひっし）desperate
必修（ひっしゅう）required

必需品（ひつじゅひん）necessity

<5> 丶 ソ 义 必 必 　｜ ▶ 心(139)

372

要
necessary

A woman (女) keeps
necessary things in her bag.

女の人はかばんに必要な物を入れ
ています。

▶ よう
▷ い　かなめ

要る（いる）to be needed
必要な（ひつような）necessary
重要な（じゅうような）important
不要な（ふような）unnecessary
要求（ようきゅう）demand

要約（ようやく）summary
要するに（ようするに）in short
主要な（しゅような）main
チームの要（チームのかなめ）
　　mainstay of a team

<9> 一 厂 戸 両 両 西 要 要 要 　｜ ▶ 女(52)

373

荷
baggage

I can see grass sticking out of
the **baggage**. What (何) is in it?

その荷物から草が見えます。
中に何が入っていますか。

▶ か
▷ に

荷物（にもつ）baggage
荷造り（にづくり）packing
重荷（おもに）burden
入荷（にゅうか）arrival of goods
出荷（しゅっか）shipping of goods

<10> 一 十 艹 芍 芍 芢 荷 荷 荷 荷 ▶ 艹(K) 何(57)

374

由
because

Don't open this box, **because** something scary may come out.

箱を開けないでください。怖いものが出てくるかもしれませんから。

▶ ゆう　ゆ
　　ゆい
▷ よし

自由（じゆう）freedom
理由（りゆう）reason
パリ経由（パリけいゆ）via Paris
不自由な（ふじゆうな）inconvenient
由来（ゆらい）origin

由緒ある（ゆいしょある）venerable

<5>｜口巾由由　　　　　　　！田(49)　申(481)

375

届
to deliver

A package was **delivered** to my house.

我が家に小包が届けられました。

▷ とど

届ける（とどける）to deliver
届く（とどく）to be delivered
婚姻届（*こんいんとどけ）
　　registration of marriage

欠席届（*けっせきとどけ）
　　registration of absence
届け出る（とどけでる）to report

<8>　フ　コ　尸　尸　尸　吊　届　届　　　　　▶ 由(374)

376

利
profit

We cut ears of rice and make **profits**.

稲を刈り取って利益を得ます。

▶ り
▷ き

便利な（べんりな）convenient
利用する（りようする）to use
利益（りえき）profit
利口な（りこうな）smart
権利（けんり）right

利子（りし）interest
左利き（ひだりきき）left-handed

<7>　丿　二　千　チ　禾　利　利　　　　　▶ 禾(P)　刂(A)

377

払
to pay

I will **pay** money.

私がお金を払います。

▶ ふっ　ふつ
▷ はら

払う（はらう）to pay
支払い（しはらい）payment
払い戻す（はらいもどす）to refund
払い込む（はらいこむ）to pay in

払拭する（ふっしょくする）
　　to sweep away

<5> 一 丁 扌 払 払　　　▶ 扌 (I)　❗私(201)

378

濯
to wash

On what day（曜）do you **wash** your clothes?

何曜日に洗濯しますか。

▶ たく

洗濯する（せんたくする）
　　to do laundry
洗濯物（せんたくもの）laundry
洗濯機（せんたくき）washing machine

<17> ` 氵 氵 氵 氵 氵 氵 沪 沢 沢 沢 沢 沢 沢 沢 濯 濯　　　▶ 氵 (J)　曜(24)

379

寝
to sleep

Two people are **sleeping**.

二人の人が寝ています。

▶ しん
▷ ね

寝る（ねる）to sleep
昼寝（ひるね）nap
寝坊（ねぼう）oversleeping
寝室（しんしつ）bedroom
寝台車（しんだいしゃ）sleeping car

寝言（ねごと）talking in one's sleep

<13> ` 宀 宀 宀 宀 宀 宀 宀 宀 寍 寝 寝　　　▶ 宀 (G)

380

踊
dance

Move your leg（足）and **dance** on a fence!

足を動かして、塀の上で踊りましょう！

▶ よう
▷ おど

踊る（おどる） to dance
踊り（おどり） dance
日本舞踊（にほんぶよう）
　　Japanese dance
盆踊り（ぼんおどり） *Bon* dance

<14> ノ ロ ロ ア 犀 星 星 距 距 跳 踊 踊 踊 踊　▶足(141)

381

活
active

I drink a lot of water and become **active**.

水をたくさん飲んで、元気になります。

▶ かつ　かっ

生活（せいかつ） life
活動（かつどう） activity
活字（かつじ） printing type
活気（かっき） liveliness
活躍する（かつやくする） to be active

活用（かつよう） conjugation
活発な（かっぱつな） lively
食生活（しょくせいかつ）
　　eating habit

<9> ヽ ⺀ ⺌ ⺌ 汼 汗 汗 活 活　▶ 氵(J) 千(12) 口(15)

382

末
end

The tree（木）is at the **end** of its life.

木の命が終わろうとしています。

▶ まつ　ばつ
▷ すえ

週末（しゅうまつ） weekend
月末（げつまつ） the end of a month
年末（ねんまつ） the end of a year
末（すえ） end of a period
末っ子（すえっこ） youngest child

期末試験（きまつしけん）
　　final examination

<5> 一 二 キ 末 末　▶木(21)　！未(175)

383

宅

house

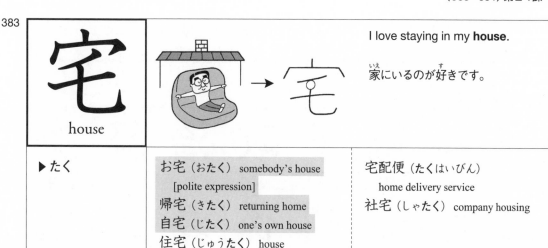

I love staying in my **house**.

家_{いえ}にいるのが好_すきです。

▶ たく

お宅（おたく） somebody's house
　　　 [polite expression]
帰宅（きたく） returning home
自宅（じたく） one's own house
住宅（じゅうたく） house

宅配便（たくはいびん）
　　 home delivery service
社宅（しゃたく） company housing

<6> ＇ 宀 宀 宅 宅 宅

▶ 宀 (G)

384

祭

festival

On the day of **festival**, meat is offered on an altar.

祭_{まつ}りの日_ひには、祭壇_{さいだん}に肉_{にく}が捧_{ささ}げられます。

▶ さい
▷ まつ

祭り（まつり）／祭（*まつり） festival
祭日（さいじつ） national holiday
学園祭（がくえんさい） school festival
夏祭り（なつまつり） summer festival
祭る（まつる） to enshrine

<11> ノ ク タ タ 夕フ 夕又 祭 祭 祭 祭 祭

第 25 課

● この課の漢字

平	和	戦	争	政	治	経	済
385	386	387	388	389	390	391	392
法	律	際	関	係	義	議	党
393	394	395	396	397	398	399	400

385

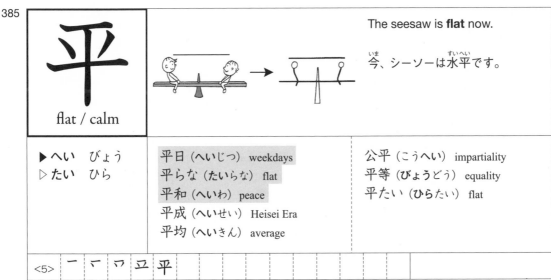

平

flat / calm

The seesaw is **flat** now.

今、シーソーは水平です。

▶ へい　びょう
▷ たい　ひら

平日（へいじつ）weekdays
平らな（たいらな）flat
平和（へいわ）peace
平成（へいせい）Heisei Era
平均（へいきん）average

公平（こうへい）impartiality
平等（びょうどう）equality
平たい（ひらたい）flat

<5> 一 一 一 平 平

386

和

peace / Japan

Japanese-style meals come with rice.

和食にはご飯がついてきます。

▶ わ　お
▷ なご　やわ

平和（へいわ）peace
和食（わしょく）Japanese food
和（わ）harmony
英和辞典（えいわじてん）
　　English-Japanese dictionary

和やか（なごやか）friendly
昭和（しょうわ）Showa Era
和らぐ（やわらぐ）to soften
共和国（きょうわこく）republic

<8> ノ 二 千 千 禾 禾 和 和

▶禾(P) 口(15) ! 私(201) 知(254)

387

戦
war

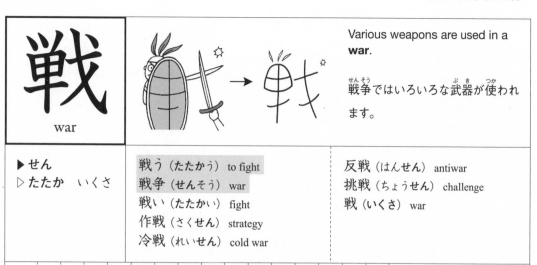

Various weapons are used in a **war**.

<ruby>戦<rt>せん</rt></ruby><ruby>争<rt>そう</rt></ruby>ではいろいろな<ruby>武<rt>ぶ</rt></ruby><ruby>器<rt>き</rt></ruby>が<ruby>使<rt>つか</rt></ruby>われます。

▶ せん
▷ たたか　いくさ

戦う（たたかう） to fight	反戦（はんせん） antiwar
戦争（せんそう） war	挑戦（ちょうせん） challenge
戦い（たたかい） fight	戦（いくさ） war
作戦（さくせん） strategy	
冷戦（れいせん） cold war	

<13> ` ＇ ＂ ＼ ʸ ʸ 当 当 単 単 戦 戦 戦

388

争
conflict

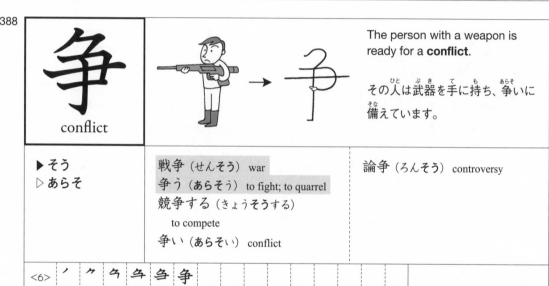

The person with a weapon is ready for a **conflict**.

その<ruby>人<rt>ひと</rt></ruby>は<ruby>武<rt>ぶ</rt></ruby><ruby>器<rt>き</rt></ruby>を<ruby>手<rt>て</rt></ruby>に<ruby>持<rt>も</rt></ruby>ち、<ruby>争<rt>あらそ</rt></ruby>いに<ruby>備<rt>そな</rt></ruby>えています。

▶ そう
▷ あらそ

戦争（せんそう） war	論争（ろんそう） controversy
争う（あらそう） to fight; to quarrel	
競争する（きょうそうする） to compete	
争い（あらそい） conflict	

<6> ノ ク ク 与 争 争

389

政
government

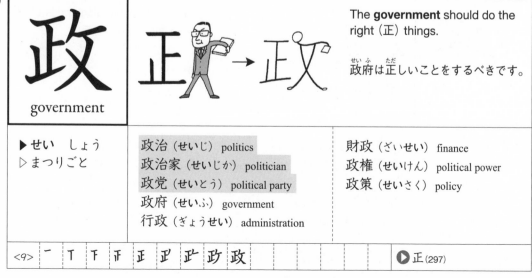

The **government** should do the right（正）things.

<ruby>政<rt>せい</rt></ruby><ruby>府<rt>ふ</rt></ruby>は<ruby>正<rt>ただ</rt></ruby>しいことをするべきです。

▶ せい　しょう
▷ まつりごと

政治（せいじ） politics	財政（ざいせい） finance
政治家（せいじか） politician	政権（せいけん） political power
政党（せいとう） political party	政策（せいさく） policy
政府（せいふ） government	
行政（ぎょうせい） administration	

<9> 一 丁 下 下 正 正 正 政 政　　　▶ 正 (297)

390

治

to govern / to cure

I **govern** the seaside area.

私は海岸地帯を治めています。

▶ じ　ち
▷ なお　おさ

治る（なおる）to be cured
治す（なおす）to cure
政治（せいじ）politics
政治家（せいじか）politician
治める（おさめる）to rule; govern

治療（ちりょう）medical care
治安（ちあん）law and order

<8> ｀　 氵　 氵　 氵　 氵　 治　 治　 治　　　　　　▶ シ (J) 台 (185)

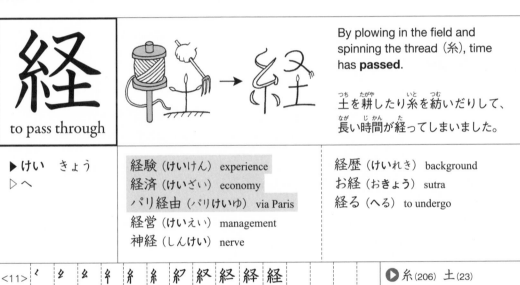

391

経

to pass through

By plowing in the field and spinning the thread（糸）, time has **passed**.

土を耕したり糸を紡いだりして、長い時間が経ってしまいました。

▶ けい　きょう
▷ へ

経験（けいけん）experience
経済（けいざい）economy
パリ経由（パリけいゆ）via Paris
経営（けいえい）management
神経（しんけい）nerve

経歴（けいれき）background
お経（おきょう）sutra
経る（へる）to undergo

<11> く　 乡　 幺　 糸　 糸　 糸　 紀　 紹　 経　 経　 経　　　▶ 糸 (206) 土 (23)

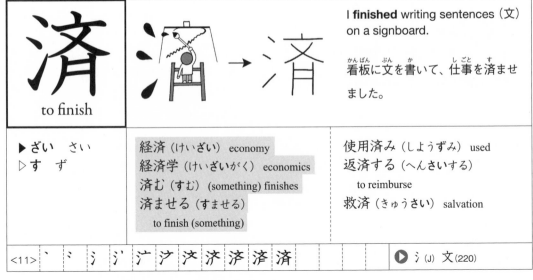

392

済

to finish

I **finished** writing sentences（文）on a signboard.

看板に文を書いて、仕事を済ませました。

▶ ざい　さい
▷ す　ず

経済（けいざい）economy
経済学（けいざいがく）economics
済む（すむ）(something) finishes
済ませる（すませる）to finish (something)

使用済み（しようずみ）used
返済する（へんさいする）to reimburse
救済（きゅうさい）salvation

<11> ｀　 氵　 氵　 氵　 汸　 汸　 済　 済　 済　 済　 済　　　▶ シ (J) 文 (220)

393

法
law / method

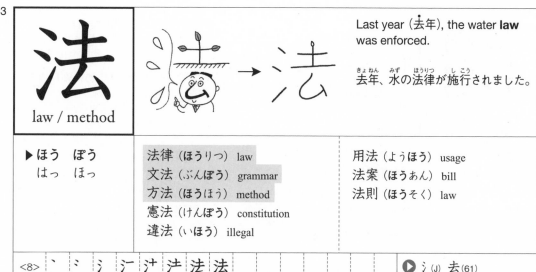

Last year (去年), the water **law** was enforced.

去年、水の法律が施行されました。

▶ ほう　ぽう
　 はっ　ぽっ

法律 (ほうりつ)　law
文法 (ぶんぽう)　grammar
方法 (ほうほう)　method
憲法 (けんぽう)　constitution
違法 (いほう)　illegal

用法 (ようほう)　usage
法案 (ほうあん)　bill
法則 (ほうそく)　law

<8>　丶　冫　氵　氵　汁　汢　法　法

▶ シ (J) 去(61)

394

律
regulation

I wrote (書) down the traffic **regulations**.

交通規則を書きました。

▶ りつ　りち

法律 (ほうりつ)　law
規律 (きりつ)　discipline
戒律 (かいりつ)　commandment
一律に (いちりつに)　uniformly

自律神経 (じりつしんけい)
　　autonomic nerve
律儀な (りちぎな)　conscientious

<9>　ノ　クイ　彳　彳'　律'　彳聿　律聿　律

▶ 彳 (D) 書(120)

395

際
occasion

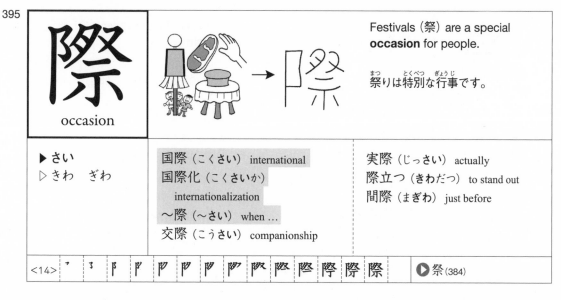

Festivals (祭) are a special **occasion** for people.

祭りは特別な行事です。

▶ さい
▷ きわ　ぎわ

国際 (こくさい)　international
国際化 (こくさいか)
　　internationalization
〜際 (〜さい)　when ...
交際 (こうさい)　companionship

実際 (じっさい)　actually
際立つ (きわだつ)　to stand out
間際 (まぎわ)　just before

<14>　'　了　阝　阝　阝'　阝`　阝`'　阝`'　阝`'　際　陉　陜　際　際

▶ 祭(384)

396

関
to relate

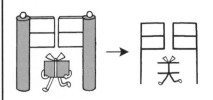

I brought a gift to the gate（門）to have a good **relationship**.

いい関係をつくるために贈り物を門まで持ってきました。

▶ かん
▷ せき　かか

関係（かんけい）relation
国際関係（こくさいかんけい）
　　international relationship
関心（かんしん）interest; concern
関東（かんとう）Kanto area

関西（かんさい）Kansai area
関取（せきとり）*sumo* wrestler
玄関（げんかん）entrance of the house
税関（ぜいかん）customs
関わる（かかわる）to get involved

<14> 亅 厂 厂 門 門 門 門 門 門 門 閇 関 関　▶ 門（43）

397

係
to connect

 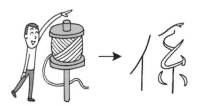

People are **connected** with each other like threads（糸）.

人々は、糸のように結びついています。

▶ けい
▷ かかり　かか

関係（かんけい）relation
国際関係（こくさいかんけい）
　　international relationship
係（かかり）person in charge
係員（かかりいん）someone in charge

人間関係（にんげんかんけい）
　　human relations
無関係（むかんけい）irrelevant
係る（かかる）to be concerned

<9> ノ イ 亻 伫 伫 佟 係 係 係　▶ イ (B) 糸（206）

398

義
righteousness

To fight for our sheep（羊）is **right**!

羊のために戦うことは、正しいことだ！

▶ ぎ

主義（しゅぎ）principle; -ism
民主主義（みんしゅしゅぎ）
　　democracy
社会主義（しゃかいしゅぎ）
　　socialism

講義（こうぎ）lecture
義務（ぎむ）duty
義理（ぎり）obligation
正義（せいぎ）justice
定義（ていぎ）definition

<13> 丶 丷 半 半 半 羊 羊 差 羊 義 義 義　▶ 羊（189）

399

議

discussion

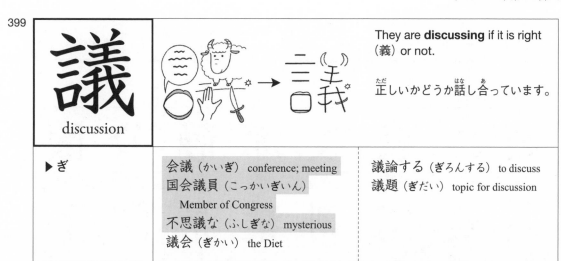

They are **discussing** if it is right
（義）or not.

正^{ただ}しいかどうか話^{はな}し合^あっています。

▶ ぎ

会議（かいぎ）conference; meeting
国会議員（こっかいぎいん）
  Member of Congress
不思議な（ふしぎな）mysterious
議会（ぎかい）the Diet

議論する（ぎろんする）to discuss
議題（ぎだい）topic for discussion

<20> 丶 亠 二 ニ 言 言 言 訂 証 評 詳 詳 詳 詳 詳 議 議 議　▶ 言(75) 義(398)

400

党

(political) party

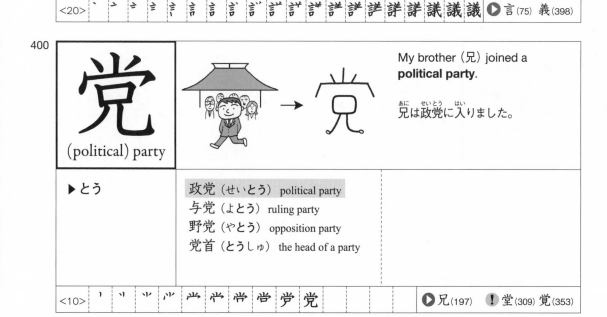

My brother（兄）joined a
political party.

兄^{あに}は政党^{せいとう}に入^{はい}りました。

▶ とう

政党（せいとう）political party
与党（よとう）ruling party
野党（やとう）opposition party
党首（とうしゅ）the head of a party

<10> 丶 丷 丷 丷 尚 尚 尚 党 党 党　　▶ 兄(197) ！ 堂(309) 覚(353)

第 26 課

● この課の漢字

遊	泳	疲	暖	涼	静	公	園
401	402	403	404	405	406	407	408
込	連	窓	側	葉	景	記	形
409	410	411	412	413	414	415	416

401

遊
to play

A child（子）with a flag is going out to **play**.

旗を持った子供が遊びに出かけます。

▶ ゆう　ゆ
▷ あそ

遊ぶ（あそぶ）to play
遊び（あそび）play
遊園地（ゆうえんち）amusement park
周遊（しゅうゆう）excursion

<12>　' 亠 ラ 方 方 扩 扩 斿 斿 斿 遊 遊

▶ 方(136) 子(53) 辶(F)

402

泳
to swim

I **swim** in the water.

水の中を泳ぎます。

▶ えい
▷ およ

泳ぐ（およぐ）to swim
水泳（すいえい）swimming
平泳ぎ（ひらおよぎ）breaststroke
背泳ぎ（せおよぎ）backstroke
競泳（きょうえい）swimming race

<8>　' ' ラ ラ 汀 汀 泳 泳

▶ 氵(J)

403

疲
exhausted

He（彼）was **exhausted** and went to a hospital.

彼は疲れがひどく、病院に行きました。

▶ ひ
▷ つか

疲れる（つかれる）to get tired
疲れ（つかれ）fatigue
疲労（ひろう）fatigue

<10> 　 ` 一 广 广 疒 疒 疒 疒 疲 疲 　 ▶ 广 (0) 彼(368)

404

暖
warm

When you put hands together with your friend（友）, you feel **warm**.

友だちと手を合わせると、暖かいです。

▶ だん
▷ あたた

暖かい（あたたかい）warm
暖める（あたためる）to warm
暖まる（あたたまる）to become warm
暖房（だんぼう）heating
温暖な（おんだんな）warm

暖冬（だんとう）mild winter

<13> | 冂 日 日 日 日 日 日 旷 暖 暖 暖 暖 　 ▶ 日(17) 友(96)

405

涼
cool

The rain **cooled** down the capital（京）.

雨が降って京の都が涼しくなりました。

▶ りょう
▷ すず

涼しい（すずしい）cool
涼む（すずむ）to keep oneself cool
清涼飲料水（せいりょういんりょうすい）soft drink

夕涼み（ゆうすずみ）
cooling oneself in the evening

<11> 　 ` 冫 冫 氵 氵 氵 氵 涼 涼 涼 涼 　 ▶ 氵 (J) 京(300)

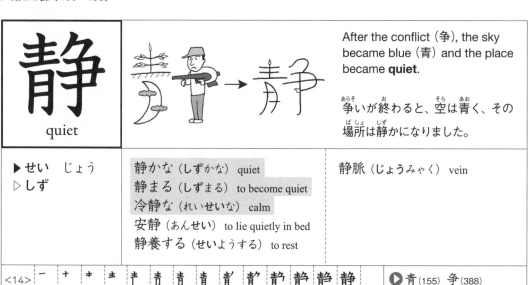

406

静　quiet

▶ せい　じょう
▷ しず

静かな（しずかな）quiet
静まる（しずまる）to become quiet
冷静な（れいせいな）calm
安静（あんせい）to lie quietly in bed
静養する（せいようする）to rest

静脈（じょうみゃく）vein

After the conflict（争）, the sky became blue（青）and the place became **quiet**.

争いが終わると、空は青く、その場所は静かになりました。

<14> 一 十 キ 主 丰 青 青 青 青 静 静 静 静 静　▶ 青(155) 争(388)

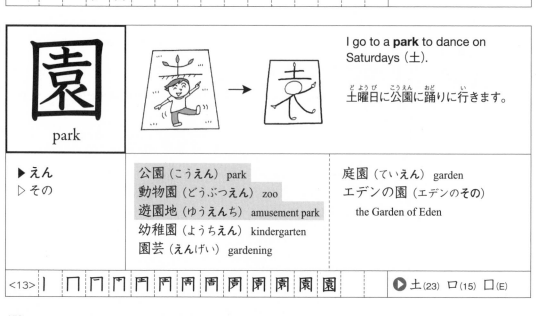

407

公　public

▶ こう
▷ おおやけ

公園（こうえん）park
公平（こうへい）impartiality
公務員（こうむいん）
　　civil servant
公衆（こうしゅう）the public

公立（こうりつ）public (institution)
公の（おおやけの）public; official
公開（こうかい）opening to public

Serving the **public** is a hard job.

公衆のために働くのは大変です。

<4> ノ 八 公 公

408

園　park

▶ えん
▷ その

公園（こうえん）park
動物園（どうぶつえん）zoo
遊園地（ゆうえんち）amusement park
幼稚園（ようちえん）kindergarten
園芸（えんげい）gardening

庭園（ていえん）garden
エデンの園（エデンのその）
　　the Garden of Eden

I go to a **park** to dance on Saturdays（土）.

土曜日に公園に踊りに行きます。

<13> 丨 冂 冂 冃 門 閠 閠 園 園 園 園 園 園　▶ 土(23) 口(15) 口(E)

409

込 crowded

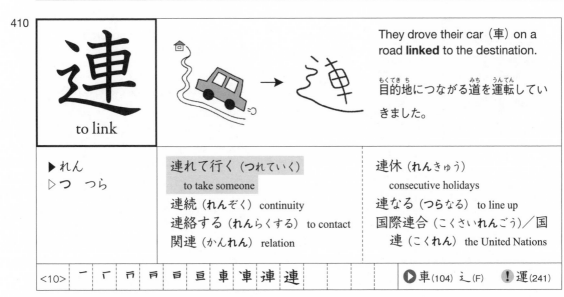

Many people are going in (入).
It must be **crowded** inside.

たくさんの<ruby>人<rt>ひと</rt></ruby>が<ruby>入<rt>はい</rt></ruby>っていきます。
<ruby>中<rt>なか</rt></ruby>はきっと<ruby>込<rt>こ</rt></ruby>んでいるでしょう。

▷ こ　ご

込む (こむ) to get crowded	割り込む (わりこむ) to cut into (a line)
人込み (ひとごみ) crowd	
申し込む (もうしこむ) to apply	思い込む (おもいこむ) to assume
飛び込む (とびこむ) to jump in	
税込み (ぜいこみ) including tax	

<5> ノ　入　`入`　`込`　込　　　　　　　▶入(97)　辶(F)

410

連 to link

They drove their car (車) on a
road **linked** to the destination.

<ruby>目的地<rt>もくてきち</rt></ruby>につながる<ruby>道<rt>みち</rt></ruby>を<ruby>運転<rt>うんてん</rt></ruby>してい
きました。

▶ れん
▷ つ　つら

連れて行く (つれていく) to take someone	連休 (れんきゅう) consecutive holidays
連続 (れんぞく) continuity	連なる (つらなる) to line up
連絡する (れんらくする) to contact	国際連合 (こくさいれんごう)／国連 (こくれん) the United Nations
関連 (かんれん) relation	

<10> 一　厂　冂　冃　冃　亘　車　車　連　連　　　▶車(104)　辶(F)　❗運(241)

411

窓 window / counter

Let's open the **window** of your
heart (心).

<ruby>心<rt>こころ</rt></ruby>の<ruby>窓<rt>まど</rt></ruby>を<ruby>開<rt>あ</rt></ruby>けましょう。

▶ そう
▷ まど

窓 (まど) window	窓側の席 (まどがわのせき) window seat
窓口 (まどぐち) window/counter in a public office	
同窓会 (どうそうかい) class reunion	

<11> ` ` ′　丷　宀　灾　空　空　突　窓　窓　窓　　　▶宀(G)　心(139)

412

側
side

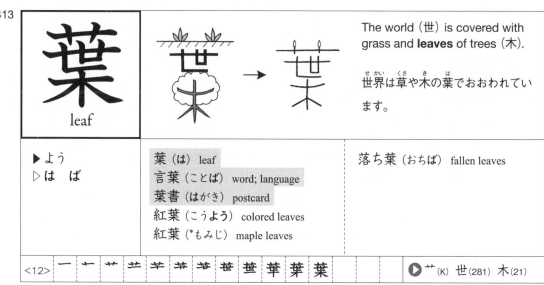

I put money and a knife by my **side**.

お金_{かね}とナイフをそばに置_おきました。

▶ そく
▷ がわ

右側 （みぎがわ） right side
両側 （りょうがわ） both sides
向こう側 （むこうがわ） the other side
側面 （そくめん） side

反対側 （はんたいがわ）
　the opposite side
外側 （そとがわ） outside; exterior
内側 （うちがわ） inside; interior

<11> ノ 亻 亻 亻 亻 侧 侧 侧 俱 側 側 ▶ 亻 (B) 貝 (116) 刂 (A)

413

葉
leaf

The world （世） is covered with grass and **leaves** of trees （木）.

世界_{せかい}は草_{くさ}や木_きの葉_はでおおわれています。

▶ よう
▷ は　ば

葉 （は） leaf
言葉 （ことば） word; language
葉書 （はがき） postcard
紅葉 （こうよう） colored leaves
紅葉 （*もみじ） maple leaves

落ち葉 （おちば） fallen leaves

<12> 一 十 艹 艹 芏 芏 荢 荢 苹 華 葦 葉 ▶ 艹 (K) 世 (281) 木 (21)

414

景
view

On a sunny day （日）, you can get a fine **view** of the capital （京）.

天気_{てんき}のいい日_ひは、京_{きょう}の都_{みやこ}がきれいに見_みえます。

▶ けい

景色 （*けしき） scenery
景気 （けいき） business conditions
不景気 （ふけいき） recession
風景 （ふうけい） scenery
夜景 （やけい） night view

背景 （はいけい） background
光景 （こうけい） sight
景品 （けいひん） free gift; prize

<12> 丿 冂 曰 曰 旦 旱 早 昙 景 景 景 ▶ 日 (17) 京 (300)

415

記
to write down

I **wrote down** what you said.

あなたが言ったことを書き記しました。

▶ き
▷ しる

日記（にっき）diary
暗記する（あんきする）
　　　to learn by heart
記事（きじ）newspaper article
記者（きしゃ）journalist

記入する（きにゅうする）to fill in
記念（きねん）remembrance
記録（きろく）record
記す（しるす）to take notes

<10>　丶　ㄧ　ㄴ　ㄹ　言　言　言　記　記　記　　　▶ 言 (75)

416

形
shape

I am **shaping** something.

何か形を作っています。

▶ ぎょう　けい
▷ かたち　かた

形（かたち）shape
人形（にんぎょう）doll
形容詞（けいようし）adjective
過去形（かこけい）past tense
現在形（げんざいけい）present tense

図形（ずけい）figure
正方形（せいほうけい）square
形見（かたみ）relic; memento

<7>　一　二　チ　开　开　形　形

第 27 課

●この課の漢字

吉	結	婚	共	供	両	若	老
417	418	419	420	421	422	423	424
息	娘	奥	将	祖	育	性	招
425	426	427	428	429	430	431	432

417

吉
good luck

A samurai（士）shouts "**Good luck!**"

さむらいが「幸運を祈る！」と叫び
ます。

▶ きち きつ
きっ

吉（きち）good fortune
大吉（だいきち）very good luck
吉日（きちじつ）lucky day
不吉な（ふきつな）unlucky
吉報（きっぽう）welcome news

吉凶（きっきょう）good or ill luck
吉田さん（*よしださん）
 Mr./Ms. Yoshida

<6> 一 十 士 吉 吉 吉　　　　▶ 士(270) 口(15)

418

結
to tie

I **tied** threads（糸）and made a good luck（吉）charm.

糸を結んで、幸運のお守りを作り
ました。

▶ けっ けつ
▷ むす ゆ

結婚する（けっこんする）to marry
結ぶ（むすぶ）to tie a knot
結果（けっか）result
結論（けつろん）conclusion
結う（ゆう）to tie

結局（けっきょく）after all
団結する（だんけつする）to unite
結構（けっこう）well enough; all right

<12> く 幺 幺 糸 糸 糸 糸 紅 結 結 結　　　　▶ 糸(206) 吉(417)

419

婚
marriage

The woman (女) changed her surname (氏) after her **marriage**.

女の人は結婚後、姓を変えました。

▶ こん

結婚する （けっこんする） to marry
離婚 （りこん） divorce
婚約 （こんやく） engagement
婚約者 （こんやくしゃ） fiancé(e)
既婚 （きこん） married

未婚 （みこん） unmarried
新婚 （しんこん） newly married
求婚する （きゅうこんする）
　　to propose marriage

<11> く　夕　女　女　妒　妒　妖　妖　婚　婚　婚

▶ 女(52)　氏(207)　日(17)

420

共
together

Let's get **together**.

あなたと共に。

▶ きょう
▷ とも

共に （ともに） together
共通 （きょうつう） in common
公共 （こうきょう） public
共感する （きょうかんする）
　　to sympathize

共産主義 （きょうさんしゅぎ）
　　communism
共学 （きょうがく） coeducation
共同 （きょうどう） partnership

<6> 一　十　卄　世　并　共

421

供
offer

We together (共) **offer** you help.

一緒にあなたを助けます。

▶ きょう　く
▷ ども　そな
　とも

子供 （こども） child
供える （そなえる）
　　to offer something to a spirit
供給する （きょうきゅうする）
　　to supply

提供 （ていきょう） offer
試供品 （しきょうひん） sample
お供する （おともする） to accompany
供養 （くよう） memorial service

<8> ノ　イ　仁　什　什　供　供　供

▶ イ (B)　共(420)

422

両
both

A fishmonger is carrying the beam on **both** of his shoulders.

魚屋が両肩にさおを担いでいます。

▶ りょう

両親（りょうしん）parents
両手（りょうて）both hands
両方（りょうほう）both (sides)
両側（りょうがわ）both sides
両替（りょうがえ）exchange (money)

両立する（りょうりつする）
　　to be compatible

<6> 一 一 一 両 両 両

423

若
young

I pick **young** leaves with my right（右）hand.

出たばかりの若葉を右手で摘みます。

▶ じゃく　にゃく
▷ わか　も

若い（わかい）young
若者（わかもの）young people
若々しい（わかわかしい）youthful
若しくは（もしくは）or

若輩（じゃくはい）
　　young and inexperienced person
老若男女（ろうにゃくなんにょ）
　　men and women of all ages

<8> 一 十 艹 サ 艹 若 若 若

▶ 艹(K) 右(37)　! 苦(342) 君(491)

424

老
old age

An **old** man has a cane, and an **old** woman is sitting down.

おじいさんはつえを持って、おばあさんは座っています。

▶ ろう
▷ お　ふ

老人（ろうじん）old people
老いる（おいる）to grow old
老ける（ふける）to grow old
老化（ろうか）aging

老眼（ろうがん）
　　farsightedness due to old age

<6> 一 十 土 耂 耂 老

! 考(255)

425

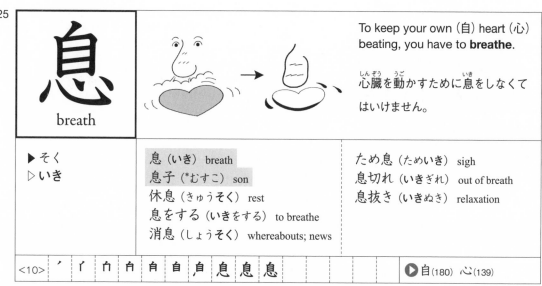

息
breath

To keep your own（自）heart（心）beating, you have to **breathe**.

心臓を動かすために息をしなくてはいけません。
<small>しんぞう・うご・いき</small>

| ▶ そく
▷ いき | 息（いき）breath
息子（*むすこ）son
休息（きゅうそく）rest
息をする（いきをする）to breathe
消息（しょうそく）whereabouts; news | ため息（ためいき）sigh
息切れ（いきぎれ）out of breath
息抜き（いきぬき）relaxation |

<10> ´ ㇒ ㇌ 自 自 自 自 息 息 息 ▶ 自(180) 心(139)

426

娘
daughter

My **daughter** is a good（良）girl（女）.

私の娘はいい子です。
<small>わたし・むすめ・こ</small>

| ▷ むすめ | 娘（むすめ）daughter
一人娘（ひとりむすめ）only daughter
娘婿（むすめむこ）son-in-law | |

<10> く ㇄ 女 女 妒 妒 妇 娘 娘 娘 ▶ 女(52) 良(69)

427

奥
back

I put rice（米）in a big（大）box and store it in the **back**.

米を大きい箱に入れ、奥にしまっておきます。
<small>こめ・おお・はこ・い・おく</small>

| ▶ おう
▷ おく | 奥（おく）inmost; back
奥さん（おくさん）someone's wife
奥歯（おくば）back tooth
奥ゆかしい（おくゆかしい）
　　modest; elegant | 奥行き（おくゆき）
　the depth of a space |

<12> ´ ㇒ ㇌ 内 内 戸 甪 甪 甶 奥 奥 奥 ▶ 米(67) 大(81)

428

将

command

A **commander** is thinking about the future.

しょうぐん しょうらい かんが
将軍が将来について考えています。

▶ しょう

将来（しょうらい） future
将棋（しょうぎ） shogi (Japanese chess)
将軍（しょうぐん） shogun
主将（しゅしょう） captain of a team

<10> 丨 丬 丬 丬 丬 丬 丬 丬 将 将

429

祖

ancestor

People visit their **ancestors'** graves and offer things.

せん ぞ はか い そな
先祖の墓へ行ってお供えをします。

▶ そ ぞ

祖父（そふ） grandfather
祖母（そぼ） grandmother
祖先（そせん） ancestor
祖国（そこく） motherland
先祖（せんぞ） ancestor

祖父母（そふぼ） grandparents
元祖（がんそ） originator
教祖（きょうそ） founder of a religion

<9> 丶 ラ ネ ネ 礻 礻 初 祖 祖　　　▶ ネ (M)

430

育

to grow

I **grew** up, watching the moon (月).

わたし つき み そだ
私は月を見ながら育ちました。

▶ いく
▷ そだ　はぐく

教育（きょういく） education
育てる（そだてる） to raise
育つ（そだつ） to grow
体育（たいいく） physical education
育児（いくじ） nursing

保育（ほいく） child care
飼育する（しいくする）
　　to raise animals
育む（はぐくむ） to cultivate

<8> 丶 亠 𠫓 𠫓 产 育 育 育　　　▶ 月 (18)

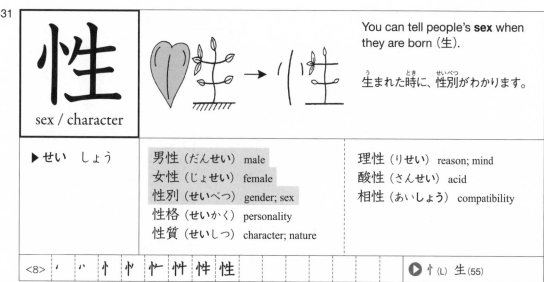

431

性
sex / character

You can tell people's **sex** when they are born（生）。

生まれた時に、性別がわかります。

▶ せい　しょう

男性 （だんせい）　male
女性 （じょせい）　female
性別 （せいべつ）　gender; sex
性格 （せいかく）　personality
性質 （せいしつ）　character; nature

理性 （りせい）　reason; mind
酸性 （さんせい）　acid
相性 （あいしょう）　compatibility

<8>　ノ　ハ　忄　忄　忰　忰　性　性

▶ 忄 (L) 生 (55)

432

招
to invite

I will **invite** you for a meal.

食事に招待します。

▶ しょう
▷ まね

招待する （しょうたいする）　to invite
招く （まねく）　to invite
招き （まねき）　invitation
招待状 （しょうたいじょう）
　　invitation card

<8>　一　十　扌　招　招　招　招　招

▶ 扌 (I) 刀 (31) 口 (15)

第 28 課

● この課の漢字

取	最	初	番	歳	枚	冊	億
433	434	435	436	437	438	439	440
点	階	段	号	倍	次	々	他
441	442	443	444	445	446	447	448

433

取
to take

Don't **take** my ear.

私の耳を取らないでください。

▶ しゅ
▷ と

取る （とる） to take
受け取る （うけとる） to receive
取り出す （とりだす） to take out
取り消す （とりけす） to cancel

取り替える （とりかえる）
　　　　to exchange
聞き取り （ききとり） hearing
取材する （しゅざいする）
　　　　to cover (news)

<8> 一 丁 丆 F E 耳 取 取　　　　▶ 耳 (73)

434

最
utmost

To take （取） the sun （日） is the **most** difficult thing to do.

太陽を手に取ることは最も難しいことです。

▶ さい
▷ もっと

最初 （さいしょ） first
最後 （さいご） last
最近 （さいきん） recently
最高 （さいこう） the best
最低 （さいてい） the lowest

最新 （さいしん） the latest
最も （もっとも） most
最終電車 （さいしゅうでんしゃ）
　　　last train of the day

<12> 丶 冂 冃 日 旦 早 早 昌 昌 昌 最 最　　　　▶ 日 (17) 取 (433)

435

初
first

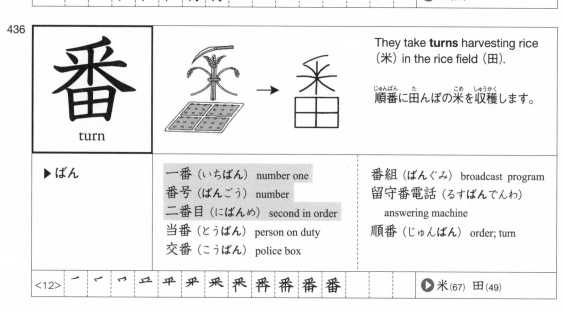

When you make kimono, cut the cloth with a knife (刀) **first**.

着物を作る時は、初めに布を刀で切ります。

▶ しょ
▷ はじ　はつ
　うい　そ

初めは（はじめは）at first
初めて（はじめて）for the first time
最初（さいしょ）first
初級（しょきゅう）introductory
初恋（はつこい）first love

初心者（しょしんしゃ）beginner
初夏（しょか）early summer
初々しい（ういういしい）innocent

<7> 　丶　ラ　ネ　ネ　ネ　初　初　　　　　　　▶ 刀(31)

436

番
turn

They take **turns** harvesting rice (米) in the rice field (田).

順番に田んぼの米を収穫します。

▶ ばん

一番（いちばん）number one
番号（ばんごう）number
二番目（にばんめ）second in order
当番（とうばん）person on duty
交番（こうばん）police box

番組（ばんぐみ）broadcast program
留守番電話（るすばんでんわ）
　　answering machine
順番（じゅんばん）order; turn

<12> 　一　ヘ　ヘ　平　平　平　来　来　番　番　番　▶ 米(67) 田(49)

437

歳
age

Stop (止) asking about my **age**.

私が何歳か聞くのは止めてください。

▶ さい　ざい
　せい

五歳（ごさい）five years old
二十歳（*はたち／にじゅっさい）
　　20 years old
万歳（ばんざい）banzai
お歳暮（おせいぼ）year-end gift

歳月（さいげつ）years
歳入（さいにゅう）revenue
歳出（さいしゅつ）expenditure

<13> 　I　ト　止　止　广　庐　庐　歩　歩　歩　歳　歳　歳　▶ 止(243)

438

枚
sheet of ...

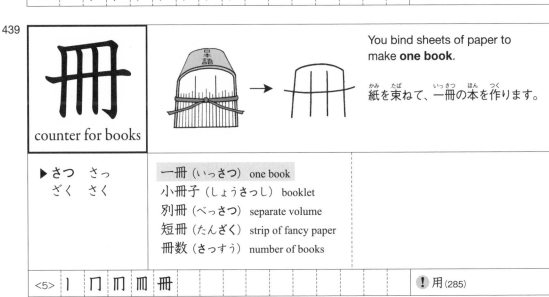

I made this **sheet of** paper from the tree（木）.

木から紙を一枚作りました。

▶ まい

一枚（いちまい） one sheet
枚数（まいすう） number of thin things
二枚目（にまいめ） handsome man

<8> 一 十 才 木 杧 朾 杖 枚

▶ 木(21)

439

冊
counter for books

You bind sheets of paper to make **one book**.

紙を束ねて、一冊の本を作ります。

▶ さつ　さっ
　 ざく　さく

一冊（いっさつ） one book
小冊子（しょうさっし） booklet
別冊（べっさつ） separate volume
短冊（たんざく） strip of fancy paper
冊数（さっすう） number of books

<5> 丨 冂 冊 冊 冊

❗ 用(285)

440

億
hundred million

One **hundred million** people have different minds（意）.

一億人の人はそれぞれ違う意志があります。

▶ おく

一億（いちおく） one hundred million
十億（じゅうおく） one billion
億万長者（おくまんちょうじゃ）
　　billionaire

<15> ノ 亻 亻 仁 仁 俨 倍 倍 億 億 億 億 億

▶ 亻 (B) 意(288)

441

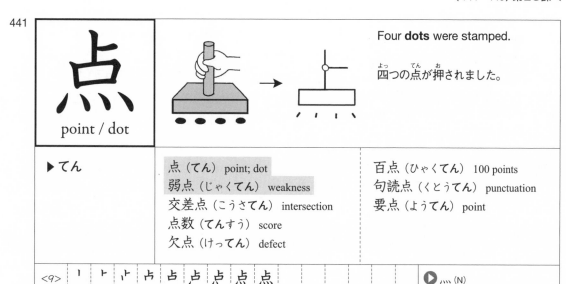

点
point / dot

Four **dots** were stamped.

四つの点が押されました。

▶ てん

点（てん）point; dot
弱点（じゃくてん）weakness
交差点（こうさてん）intersection
点数（てんすう）score
欠点（けってん）defect

百点（ひゃくてん）100 points
句読点（くとうてん）punctuation
要点（ようてん）point

| <9> | 丶 | 十 | 卜 | 占 | 占 | 占 | 点 | 点 | 点 | | | | | | ▶ 灬 (N) |

442

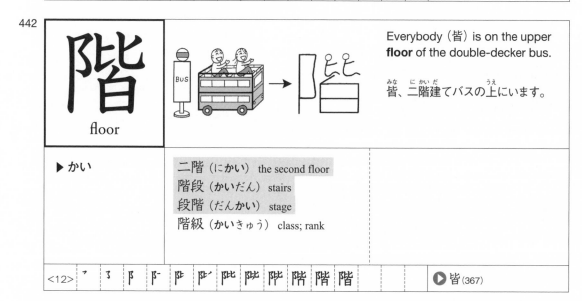

階
floor

Everybody（皆）is on the upper **floor** of the double-decker bus.

皆、二階建てバスの上にいます。

▶ かい

二階（にかい）the second floor
階段（かいだん）stairs
段階（だんかい）stage
階級（かいきゅう）class; rank

| <12> | ⁊ | ㇌ | 阝 | 阝ˉ | 阝ʳ | 阝ʲ | 阝ヒ | 阝比 | 阝比 | 階 | 階 | 階 | | ▶ 皆 (367) |

443

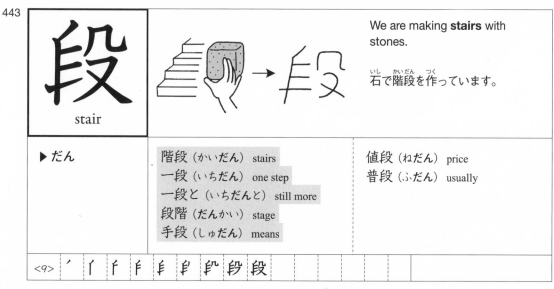

段
stair

We are making **stairs** with stones.

石で階段を作っています。

▶ だん

階段（かいだん）stairs
一段（いちだん）one step
一段と（いちだんと）still more
段階（だんかい）stage
手段（しゅだん）means

値段（ねだん）price
普段（ふだん）usually

| <9> | ´ | 亻 | 𠂉 | 乍 | 𠂢 | 𠂢 | 㲋 | 段 | 段 | | | | | |

444

号
number

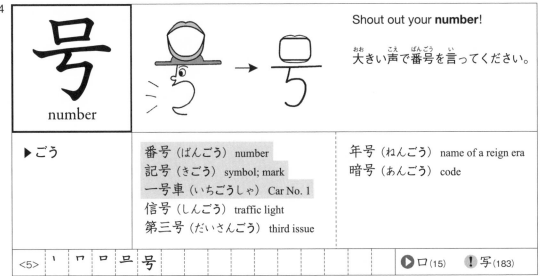

Shout out your **number**!

<ruby>大<rt>おお</rt></ruby>きい<ruby>声<rt>こえ</rt></ruby>で<ruby>番号<rt>ばんごう</rt></ruby>を<ruby>言<rt>い</rt></ruby>ってください。

▶ ごう

番号 (ばんごう) number	年号 (ねんごう) name of a reign era
記号 (きごう) symbol; mark	暗号 (あんごう) code
一号車 (いちごうしゃ) Car No. 1	
信号 (しんごう) traffic light	
第三号 (だいさんごう) third issue	

<5> 丶 冂 口 吕 号   ▶口(15) ! 写(183)

445

倍
double

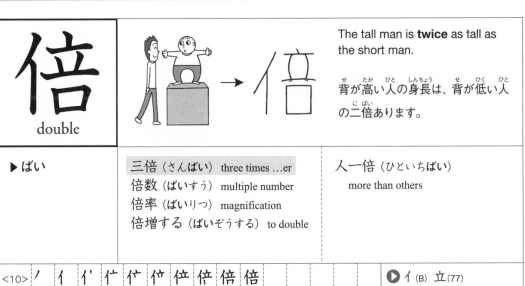

The tall man is **twice** as tall as the short man.

<ruby>背<rt>せ</rt></ruby>が<ruby>高<rt>たか</rt></ruby>い<ruby>人<rt>ひと</rt></ruby>の<ruby>身長<rt>しんちょう</rt></ruby>は、<ruby>背<rt>せ</rt></ruby>が<ruby>低<rt>ひく</rt></ruby>い<ruby>人<rt>ひと</rt></ruby>の<ruby>二倍<rt>にばい</rt></ruby>あります。

▶ ばい

三倍 (さんばい) three times …er	人一倍 (ひといちばい)
倍数 (ばいすう) multiple number	more than others
倍率 (ばいりつ) magnification	
倍増する (ばいぞうする) to double	

<10> ノ イ イ′ 广 伫 佇 位 倍 倍 倍   ▶イ (B) 立(77)

446

次
next

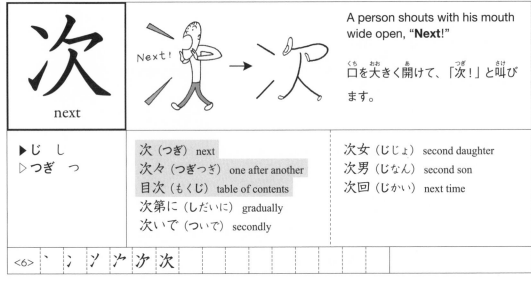

A person shouts with his mouth wide open, "**Next!**"

<ruby>口<rt>くち</rt></ruby>を<ruby>大<rt>おお</rt></ruby>きく<ruby>開<rt>あ</rt></ruby>けて、「<ruby>次<rt>つぎ</rt></ruby>!」と<ruby>叫<rt>さけ</rt></ruby>びます。

▶ じ し
▷ つぎ つ

次 (つぎ) next	次女 (じじょ) second daughter
次々 (つぎつぎ) one after another	次男 (じなん) second son
目次 (もくじ) table of contents	次回 (じかい) next time
次第に (しだいに) gradually	
次いで (ついで) secondly	

<6> 丶 冫 ニ 次 次 次

447

々

symbol of repetition

⟲ → ⟳

This symbol indicates **repetition**.

これは繰り返しを表します。

人々 （ひとびと） people
色々な （いろいろな） various
時々 （ときどき） sometimes
少々 （しょうしょう） a little

先々週 （せんせんしゅう）
    the week before last
別々に （べつべつに） separately
昔々 （むかしむかし） once upon a time

<3> ノ ク 々

448

他

other

→ 伲

I want to have **other** pets, not a scorpion.

サソリじゃなくて、他のペットを飼いたいです。

▶ た
▷ ほか

その他 （そのた／そのほか） others
他の （たの／ほかの） another; other
他人 （たにん） stranger
他動詞 （たどうし） transitive verbs

<5> ノ イ 仂 仲 他

▶ イ (B)   ❗地(280) 池(313)

第 29 課

● この課の漢字

勝	負	賛	成	絶	対	続	辞
449	450	451	452	453	454	455	456
投	選	約	束	守	過	夢	的
457	458	459	460	461	462	463	464

449

勝
to win

月 → 勝

I **won** on Monday（月）, not Tuesday（火）.

勝ったのは火曜日ではなく月曜日です。

▶ しょう ▷ か　かっ 　まさ	勝つ（かつ）to win 勝負（しょうぶ）victory or defeat 勝手に（かってに）arbitrarily 一勝（いっしょう）one win	優勝する（ゆうしょうする） 　to win a victory 決勝（けっしょう）final match 勝る（まさる）to surpass

<12> ノ 刀 月 月 月 肝 胪 胪 胪 胖 勝 勝　　▶ 月(18) 火(19) 力(50)

450

負
to defeat

→ 自

The **defeated** person pays money.

負けた人がお金を払います。

▶ ぶ　ふ ▷ ま　お	負ける（まける）to lose (a game, etc.) 勝負（しょうぶ）victory or defeat 勝ち負け（かちまけ）victory or defeat 負担（ふたん）burden 背負う（せおう）to shoulder	負傷（ふしょう）wound 抱負（ほうふ）aspiration; ambition 負かす（まかす）to defeat

<9> ノ ク 产 冇 角 負 自 負 負　　▶ 貝(116)　！ 頁(269)

451

賛
to praise

We **praised** the husbands（夫）who brought back a big shellfish（貝）.

大きな貝を持ち帰った夫を、皆が賛賛しました。

▶ さん

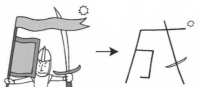
賛成する（さんせいする）to agree
賞賛する（しょうさんする）to praise
賛否（さんぴ）approval or disapproval
絶賛（ぜっさん）great admiration

<15> 一 ニ チ 夫 夫- 夫= 夫+ 夫夫 扶 替 替 替 替 替 賛 ▶ 夫(202) 貝(116) ❗ 質(222)

452

成
to accomplish

I **accomplished** the mission with the weapon.

武器を使って、その使命を成しとげました。

▶ せい　じょう
▷ な

賛成する（さんせいする）to agree
成長（せいちょう）growth
成人（せいじん）adult
成る（なる）to become; to consist of
成績（せいせき）grade

完成（かんせい）completion
成功（せいこう）success
成就する（じょうじゅする）to fulfill

<6> ノ 厂 万 成 成 成

453

絶
to discontinue

This color（色）of the thread（糸）has been **discontinued**.

この色の糸は、もう作られていません。

▶ ぜっ　ぜつ
▷ た

絶対に（ぜったいに）definitely
絶滅（ぜつめつ）extinction
絶えず（たえず）continually
気絶する（きぜつする）to faint
絶望（ぜつぼう）despair

絶える（たえる）to die out

<12> く 幺 幺 幺 糸 糸 糸 紆 絶 絶 絶 絶 ▶ 糸(206) 色(158)

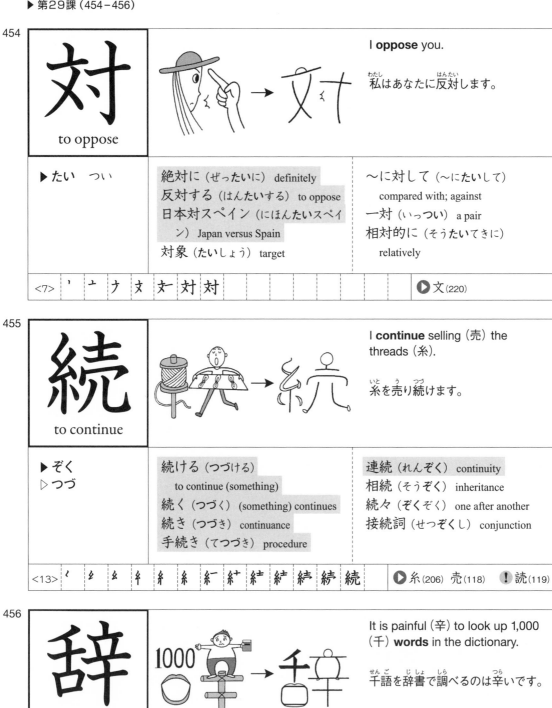

454

対
to oppose

I oppose you.

私はあなたに反対します。

▶ たい　つい

絶対に（ぜったいに） definitely
反対する（はんたいする） to oppose
日本対スペイン（にほんたいスペイン） Japan versus Spain
対象（たいしょう） target

〜に対して（〜にたいして）
　　compared with; against
一対（いっつい） a pair
相対的に（そうたいてきに）
　　relatively

| <7> | ' | 十 | ナ | 文 | 文 | 対 | 対 | | | | | |

▶ 文(220)

455

続
to continue

I continue selling（売）the threads（糸）.

糸を売り続けます。

▶ ぞく
▷ つづ

続ける（つづける）
　　to continue (something)
続く（つづく）（something) continues
続き（つづき） continuance
手続き（てつづき） procedure

連続（れんぞく） continuity
相続（そうぞく） inheritance
続々（ぞくぞく） one after another
接続詞（せつぞくし） conjunction

| <13> | ' | 幺 | 幺 | 牟 | 糸 | 糸 | 糸 | 紅 | 結 | 統 | 続 | 続 |

▶ 糸(206)　売(118)　！読(119)

456

辞
word / to resign

It is painful（辛）to look up 1,000（千）**words** in the dictionary.

千語を辞書で調べるのは辛いです。

▶ じ
▷ や

辞書（じしょ） dictionary
辞める（やめる） to resign
辞典（じてん） dictionary
辞職する（じしょくする） to resign
辞退する（じたいする） to decline

お世辞（おせじ） flattery
辞表（じひょう） letter of resignation

| <13> | ' | ニ | 千 | 手 | 舌 | 舌 | 舌' | 舌゙ | 辞 | 辞゙ | 辞 | 辞 |

▶ 千(12)　口(15)　辛(347)

457

投
to throw

I **throw** a stone with my hands.

手で石を投げます。

▶ とう
▷ な

投げる（なげる）to throw
投票する（とうひょうする）to vote
投書（とうしょ）letter from a reader
投資（とうし）investment
投手（とうしゅ）pitcher

<7> 一 十 扌 扌 扩 抄 投

▶ま(I) ！役(366)

458

選
to choose

Let's **choose** our leader together（共）.

みんなでリーダーを選ぼう。

▶ せん
▷ えら

選ぶ（えらぶ）to choose
選手（せんしゅ）player
選択する（せんたくする）to choose
選挙（せんきょ）election
抽選（ちゅうせん）lottery

当選する（とうせんする）
　to be elected
選挙権（せんきょけん）suffrage

<15> ⺋ ⺋ 尸 尸 尸 巴 巴 ⺊ 哭 巽 巽 巽 巽 選 選

▶共(420) ⻌(F)

459

約
to promise / approximate

Please grab an **approximate** amount of thread（糸）.

適当な量の糸をつかんでください。

▶ やく

約束（やくそく）promise
予約（よやく）reservation
約百人（やくひゃくにん）
　about 100 people
婚約（こんやく）engagement

節約する（せつやくする）
　to economize
契約（けいやく）contract
要約（ようやく）summary

<9> ⺯ ⺯ ⺰ ⺱ 糸 糸 糸 約 約

▶糸(206)

460

束
bundle

He gave me a **bundle** of flowers.

彼が花束をくれました。

▶ そく
▷ たば

約束（やくそく）promise
花束（はなたば）bouquet
束（たば）bundle
束ねる（たばねる）to bind
束縛（そくばく）restraint

<7> 一 厂 冂 市 束 束 束 ! 束(45)

461

守
to protect

This key will **protect** your house.

このかぎが家を守ります。

▶ す　しゅ
▷ まも　もり

留守（るす）absence from home
留守番電話（るすばんでんわ）
　　answering machine
守る（まもる）to protect
保守的（ほしゅてき）conservative

子守歌（こもりうた）lullaby
お守り（おまもり）good-luck charm
守衛（しゅえい）guard

<6> ' ' 宀 宀 守 守 ▶ 宀(G)

462

過
to pass

Please **pass** the big building on the street.

その道の大きな建物を通り過ぎてください。

▶ か
▷ す　あやま

過去（かこ）past
過ぎる（すぎる）to pass
三時過ぎ（さんじすぎ）
　　a few minutes past three o'clock
過ごす（すごす）to spend (time)

過半数（かはんすう）majority
通り過ぎる（とおりすぎる）
　　to pass by
過ち（あやまち）fault

<12> ｜ 冂 冋 冎 冎 咼 咼 咼 咼 渦 渦 過 ▶ 口(15) 辶(F)

463

夢

dream

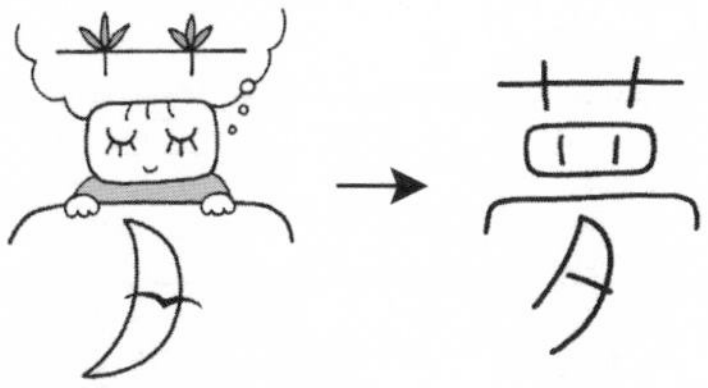

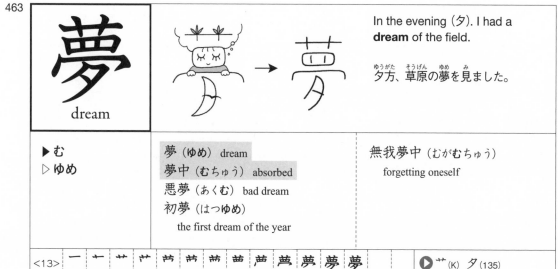

In the evening (夕). I had a **dream** of the field.

夕方（ゆうがた）、草原（そうげん）の夢（ゆめ）を見（み）ました。

▶む
▷ゆめ

夢（ゆめ） dream
夢中（むちゅう） absorbed
悪夢（あくむ） bad dream
初夢（はつゆめ） the first dream of the year

無我夢中（むがむちゅう） forgetting oneself

<13> 

▶ 艹(K) 夕(135)

464

的

target / -ish

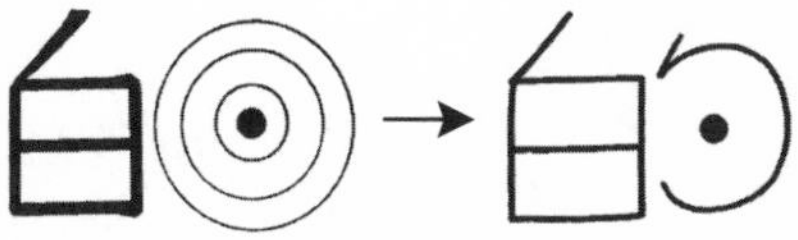

It is a white (白) **target**.

白（しろ）い的（まと）です。

▶てき
▷まと

目的（もくてき） purpose
民主的（みんしゅてき） democratic
社会的（しゃかいてき） social
国際的（こくさいてき） international
積極的（せっきょくてき） positive

消極的（しょうきょくてき） passive
比較的（ひかくてき） comparatively
的（まと） target

<8> 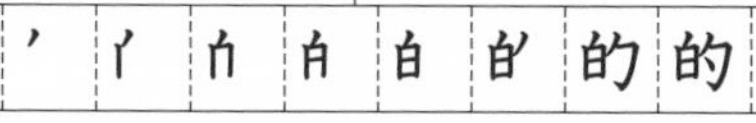

▶ 白(156)

第 30 課

● この課の漢字

飛	機	失	鉄	速	遅	駐	泊
465	466	467	468	469	470	471	472
船	座	席	島	陸	港	橋	交
473	474	475	476	477	478	479	480

465

to fly

Birds **fly** with their wings widely spread.

鳥が羽を広げて飛んでいます。

▶ ひ
▷ と

飛ぶ（とぶ）(something) flies
飛行機（ひこうき）airplane
飛び出す（とびだす）to jump out
飛ばす（とばす）to fly (something)
飛行場（ひこうじょう）airport

飛び込む（とびこむ）to jump in
飛び起きる（とびおきる）
　　to jump out of bed

<9> 乁 飞 飞 飞 飞 飛 飛 飛 飛

466

機

machine / occasion

We used a wooden（木）**machine** to weave the cloth from threads（糸）.

糸から布を織るのに、木の機械を使いました。

▶ き
▷ はた

飛行機（ひこうき）airplane
機会（きかい）opportunity
洗濯機（せんたくき）washing machine
機械（きかい）machine
機能（きのう）function

機嫌（きげん）mood
機関（きかん）organization
危機（きき）crisis
機織り機（はたおりき）loom

<16> 一 十 オ 才 术 杉 杉 柱 柱 拶 榋 榉 榉 機 機 機　　▶木(21) 糸(206)

467

失
to lose

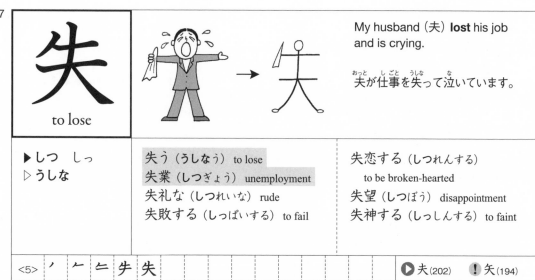

My husband（夫）**lost** his job and is crying.

夫が仕事を失って泣いています。

▶ しつ　しっ
▷ うしな

失う（うしなう）to lose
失業（しつぎょう）unemployment
失礼な（しつれいな）rude
失敗する（しっぱいする）to fail

失恋する（しつれんする）
　　to be broken-hearted
失望（しつぼう）disappointment
失神する（しっしんする）to faint

<5> ノ ⸌ ⸗ 牛 失　　　▶夫(202)　！矢(194)

468

鉄
iron

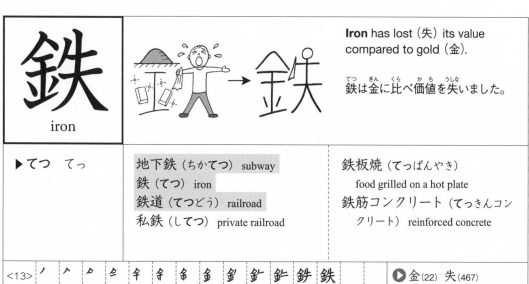

Iron has lost（失）its value compared to gold（金）.

鉄は金に比べ価値を失いました。

▶ てつ　てっ

地下鉄（ちかてつ）subway
鉄（てつ）iron
鉄道（てつどう）railroad
私鉄（してつ）private railroad

鉄板焼（てっぱんやき）
　　food grilled on a hot plate
鉄筋コンクリート（てっきんコン
　クリート）reinforced concrete

<13> ノ 𠂉 ⼇ 𠂤 牟 金 金 釒 鈩 鈢 鉄　　▶金(22) 失(467)

469

速
quick

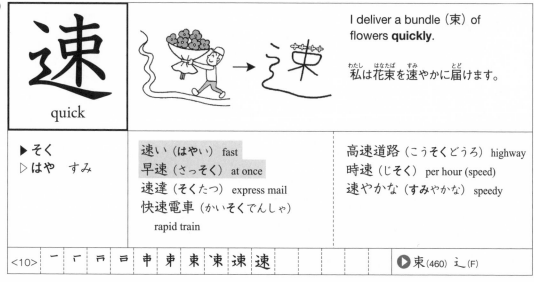

I deliver a bundle（束）of flowers **quickly**.

私は花束を速やかに届けます。

▶ そく
▷ はや　すみ

速い（はやい）fast
早速（さっそく）at once
速達（そくたつ）express mail
快速電車（かいそくでんしゃ）
　rapid train

高速道路（こうそくどうろ）highway
時速（じそく）per hour (speed)
速やかな（すみやかな）speedy

<10> 一 𠂆 𠃍 𦘒 申 束 束 涑 涑 速　　▶束(460) ⻌(F)

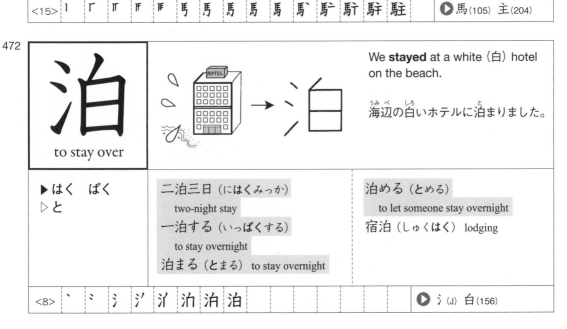

470

遅
late

One of the sheep（羊）rested and came **late**.

羊は休んでいたため、遅れてしまいました。

▶ ち
▷ おそ　おく

遅い（おそい）late; slow
遅れる（おくれる）to be late
遅刻する（ちこくする）to be late
乗り遅れる（のりおくれる）
　　to miss (transportation)

遅れ（おくれ）delay

<12> ⁻ ⁼ ⼫ ⼫ ⼫ ⼫ 屋 屋 屋 遅 遅 遅

▶羊(189) 辶(F) ❗達(492)

471

駐
to stay

The master（主）and his horse（馬）**stay** here.

主人と馬がここにいます。

▶ ちゅう

駐車する（ちゅうしゃする）to park
駐車場（ちゅうしゃじょう）
　　parking area
駐日大使（ちゅうにちたいし）
　　ambassador to Japan

<15> 丨 厂 Ⅱ 厈 厈 馬 馬 馬 馬 馬 馬 駐 駐 駐 駐

▶馬(105) 主(204)

472

泊
to stay over

We **stayed** at a white（白）hotel on the beach.

海辺の白いホテルに泊まりました。

▶ はく　ぱく
▷ と

二泊三日（にはくみっか）
　　two-night stay
一泊する（いっぱくする）
　　to stay overnight
泊まる（とまる）to stay overnight

泊める（とめる）
　　to let someone stay overnight
宿泊（しゅくはく）lodging

<8> 丶 冫 氵 氵 氵 泊 泊 泊

▶氵(J) 白(156)

473

船
ship

He said that this **ship** can accommodate eight (八) people.

この船は八人乗れるそうです。

▶ せん
▷ ふね　ふな

船（ふね）ship
船便（ふなびん）surface mail
風船（ふうせん）balloon
造船（ぞうせん）shipbuilding
客船（きゃくせん）passenger ship

貨物船（かもつせん）cargo ship
船長（せんちょう）captain
船旅（ふなたび）voyage

<11> ＇ 丿 丿 月 月 舟 舟 舟ヽ 舟ヽ 船 船 ｜ ｜ ｜ ｜ ▶ 八(8) 口(15)

474

座
to sit

Two people (人) **sit** on the ground (土).

二人の人が土の上に座ります。

▶ ざ
▷ すわ

座る（すわる）to sit
口座（こうざ）bank account
座席（ざせき）seat
座布団（ざぶとん）
　Japanese-style cushion

座談会（ざだんかい）round-table talk
座敷（ざしき）Japanese-style room

<10> ＇ 亠 广 广 广 庐 庂 座 座 座 ｜ ｜ ｜ ▶ 广(H) 人(26) 土(23)

475

席
seat

There are 21 **seats** in this shop.

この店には21の席があります。

▶ せき

席（せき）seat
出席（しゅっせき）attendance
空席（くうせき）empty seat
欠席（けっせき）absence

客席（きゃくせき）
　passenger/audience seats
着席する（ちゃくせきする）
　to be seated

<10> ＇ 亠 广 广 庐 庐 庐 庐 席 席 ｜ ｜ ▶ 广(H) 十(10) 一(1) ！度(283)

476

島
island

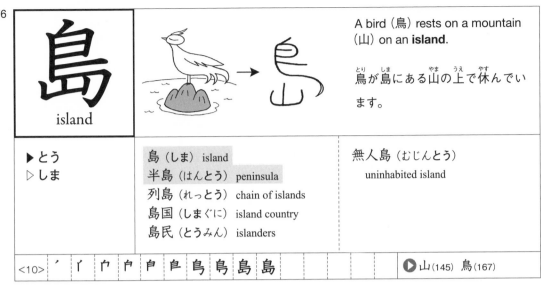

A bird（鳥）rests on a mountain（山）on an **island**.

鳥が島にある山の上で休んでいます。

▶ とう
▷ しま

島（しま）island
半島（はんとう）peninsula
列島（れっとう）chain of islands
島国（しまぐに）island country
島民（とうみん）islanders

無人島（むじんとう）
uninhabited island

<10> ノ イ ウ 戸 户 自 鸟 鸟 島 島　　▶ 山(145) 鳥(167)

477

陸
land

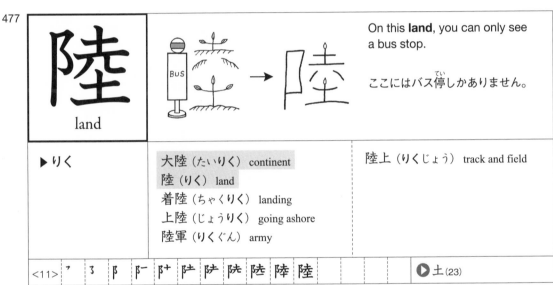

On this **land**, you can only see a bus stop.

ここにはバス停しかありません。

▶ りく

大陸（たいりく）continent
陸（りく）land
着陸（ちゃくりく）landing
上陸（じょうりく）going ashore
陸軍（りくぐん）army

陸上（りくじょう）track and field

<11> ⁷ ³ β β⁻ β⁺ 陜 陸 陸 陸 陸　　▶ 土(23)

478

港
port

Let's get together（共）at the **port**.

みんなで港に集まりましょう。

▶ こう
▷ みなと

空港（くうこう）airport
港（みなと）port
神戸港（こうべこう）Kobe Port
港町（みなとまち）port town

<12> ` ; シ シ⁻ シ⁺ 汁 汫 泮 洪 洪 港 港　　▶ シ (J) 共(420)

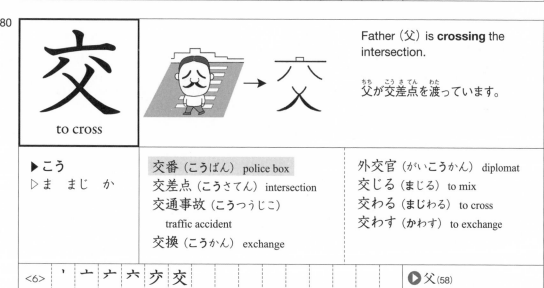

479

橋
bridge

▶ きょう
▷ はし　ばし

橋（はし）bridge
鉄橋（てっきょう）
　　iron bridge; railway bridge
歩道橋（ほどうきょう）
　　pedestrian bridge

つり橋（つりばし）suspension bridge

These are a wooden（木）**bridge** and a building.

木でできた橋と建物です。

<16> 一 十 才 才 木 杧 杧 柈 柈 榰 橋 橋 橋 橋 橋 橋　▶ 木 (21) 口 (15)

480

交
to cross

▶ こう
▷ ま　まじ　か

交番（こうばん）police box
交差点（こうさてん）intersection
交通事故（こうつうじこ）
　　traffic accident
交換（こうかん）exchange

外交官（がいこうかん）diplomat
交じる（まじる）to mix
交わる（まじわる）to cross
交わす（かわす）to exchange

Father（父）is **crossing** the intersection.

父が交差点を渡っています。

<6> 丶 亠 六 六 亦 交　▶ 父 (58)

第 31 課

● この課の漢字

申	神	様	信	調	査	相	談
481	482	483	484	485	486	487	488
案	内	君	達	星	雪	降	直
489	490	491	492	493	494	495	496

481

申
to tell

Thunder **told** me that his name was "Thunder."

雷が「私は雷と申します」と言いました。

▶ しん
▷ もう

申す（もうす）to tell; My name is …
申し上げる（もうしあげる）
　　I humbly tell you
申し込む（もうしこむ）to apply

申し訳ない（もうしわけない）
　　I'm sorry.
申請書（しんせいしょ）
　　application form
申し出る（もうしでる）to offer

<5> 丨 冂 冃 日 申　　　　! 田(49) 由(374)

482

神
god

We offer sacrifice to the thunder **god**.

雷の神様にお供えをします。

▶ じん　しん
▷ かみ　こう
　　かん

神（かみ）／神様（かみさま）god
神社（じんじゃ）shrine
神経（しんけい）nerve
精神（せいしん）mind
神話（しんわ）myth

神道（しんとう）
　　Shinto (religion originated in Japan)
神戸（こうべ）Kobe

<9> 丶 ラ ネ ネ ネ 衤 衤 神 神　　　▶ ネ (M) 申(481)

483

様
situation / Mr.; Ms.

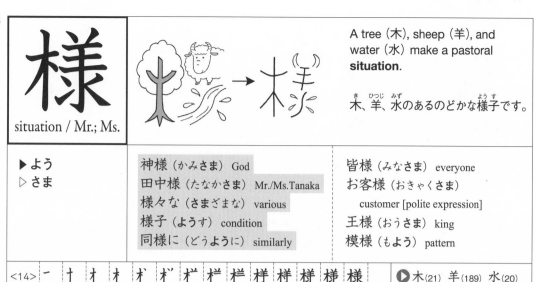

A tree (木), sheep (羊), and water (水) make a pastoral **situation**.

木、羊、水のあるのどかな様子です。

▶ よう
▷ さま

神様 （かみさま） God
田中様 （たなかさま） Mr./Ms.Tanaka
様々な （さまざまな） various
様子 （ようす） condition
同様に （どうように） similarly

皆様 （みなさま） everyone
お客様 （おきゃくさま）
　　customer [polite expression]
王様 （おうさま） king
模様 （もよう） pattern

<14> 一 十 才 オ 栏 栏 栏 栏 栏 栏 様 様 様 様　　▶ 木(21) 羊(189) 水(20)

484

信
to believe

I **believe** what people say (言).

人の言うことを信じます。

▶ しん

信号 （しんごう） traffic light
信じる （しんじる） to believe
自信 （じしん） confidence
信用 （しんよう） trust
信頼 （しんらい） trust

信仰 （しんこう） faith
受信 （じゅしん）
　　reception of a message

<9> ノ イ 仁 广 仁 仁 信 信 信　　▶ イ (B) 言(75)

485

調
to investigate / tone

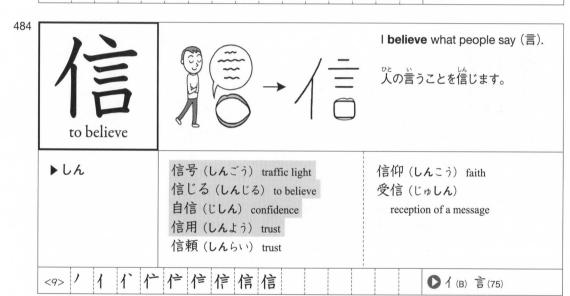

They say (言) they will **investigate** the surroundings (周).

周りを調査すると言っています。

▶ ちょう
▷ しら　ととの

調べる （しらべる） to investigate
強調する （きょうちょうする）
　　to emphasize
調子 （ちょうし） condition
調査 （ちょうさ） investigation

調味料 （ちょうみりょう） seasoning
調節 （ちょうせつ） adjustment
調える （ととのえる） to arrange

<15> 丶 二 三 三 三 言 言 訂 訶 訶 詷 調 調 調　　▶ 言(75) 周(79)

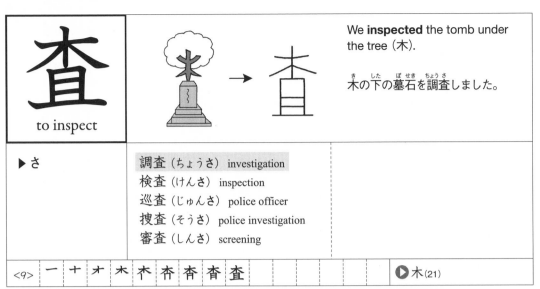

486 | 査 | to inspect

We **inspected** the tomb under the tree（木）.

木の下の墓石を調査しました。

▶ さ

調査（ちょうさ） investigation
検査（けんさ） inspection
巡査（じゅんさ） police officer
捜査（そうさ） police investigation
審査（しんさ） screening

<9> 一 十 オ 木 木 杏 杏 杳 査

▶ 木(21)

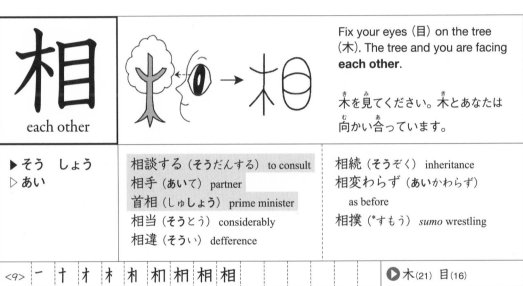

487 | 相 | each other

Fix your eyes（目）on the tree （木）. The tree and you are facing **each other**.

木を見てください。木とあなたは向かい合っています。

▶ そう　しょう
▷ あい

相談する（そうだんする） to consult
相手（あいて） partner
首相（しゅしょう） prime minister
相当（そうとう） considerably
相違（そうい） defference

相続（そうぞく） inheritance
相変わらず（あいかわらず）
　　as before
相撲（*すもう） *sumo* wrestling

<9> 一 十 オ 木 木 朾 相 相 相

▶ 木(21) 目(16)

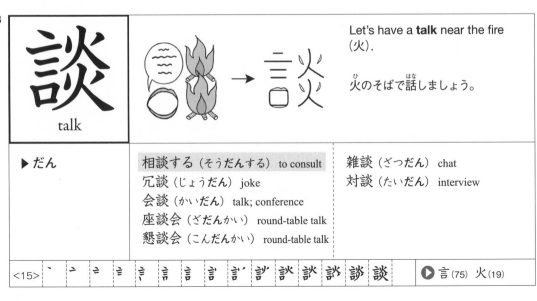

488 | 談 | talk

Let's have a **talk** near the fire （火）.

火のそばで話しましょう。

▶ だん

相談する（そうだんする） to consult
冗談（じょうだん） joke
会談（かいだん） talk; conference
座談会（ざだんかい） round-table talk
懇談会（こんだんかい） round-table talk

雑談（ざつだん） chat
対談（たいだん） interview

<15> 、 二 二 三 言 言 言 言 訁 訬 談 談 談 談 談

▶ 言(75) 火(19)

489

案
plan

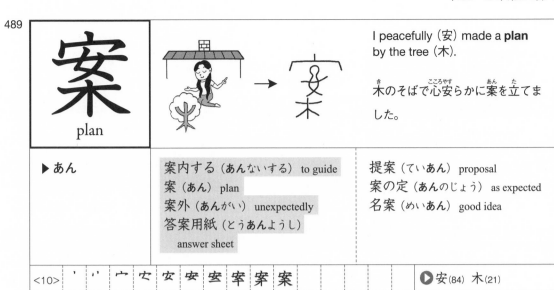

I peacefully (安) made a **plan** by the tree (木).

木のそばで心安らかに案を立てました。

▶ あん

案内する（あんないする）to guide
案（あん）plan
案外（あんがい）unexpectedly
答案用紙（とうあんようし）
answer sheet

提案（ていあん）proposal
案の定（あんのじょう）as expected
名案（めいあん）good idea

<10> ` ' 宀 宀 安 安 安 宰 宰 案 案

▶ 安(84) 木(21)

490

内
inside

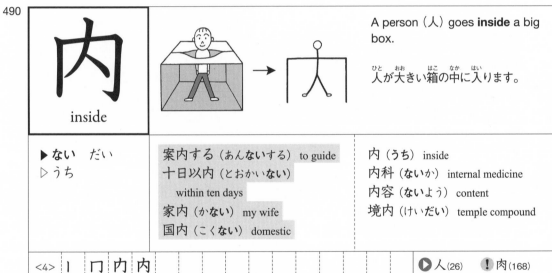

A person (人) goes **inside** a big box.

人が大きい箱の中に入ります。

▶ ない　だい
▷ うち

案内する（あんないする）to guide
十日以内（とおかいない）
within ten days
家内（かない）my wife
国内（こくない）domestic

内（うち）inside
内科（ないか）internal medicine
内容（ないよう）content
境内（けいだい）temple compound

<4> 丨 冂 内 内

▶ 人(26)　! 肉(168)

491

君
lord / you

My **lord** gives orders with the baton and his mouth (口).

王様はつえと口で命令します。

▶ くん
▷ きみ

山本君（やまもとくん）Mr. Yamamoto
君（きみ）you
君主（くんしゅ）ruler

<7> 乛 ⼘ ⺕ 尹 君 君 君

▶ 口(15)　! 若(423)

492

達
to reach

The sheep（羊）carrying soil
（土）finally **reached** its
destination.

土_{つち}を積_つんだ羊_{ひつじ}が、やっと到着_{とうちゃく}しました。

▶ たつ　たっ

友達（*ともだち）friend
私達（*わたしたち）we
速達（そくたつ）express mail
上達する（じょうたつする）
　　　　to improve

配達（はいたつ）delivery
達する（たっする）to reach
発達する（はったつする）to develop
達人（たつじん）expert

<12>　一　十　土　キ　ヰ　去　去　查　幸　峯　達　達

▶ 土(23)　羊(189)　辶(F)　❗遅(470)

493

星
star

Do you think **stars** were born
（生）from the sun（日）？

星_{ほし}は太陽_{たいよう}から生_うまれたと思_{おも}いますか。

▶ せい　じょう
　しょう
▷ ほし　ぼし

星（ほし）star
衛星（えいせい）satellite
星座（せいざ）constellation
星占い（ほしうらない）horoscope
火星（かせい）Mars

惑星（わくせい）planet
流れ星（ながれぼし）shooting star
明星（みょうじょう）Venus

<9>　丿　冂　冂　日　尸　早　早　旱　星

▶ 日(17)　生(55)

494

雪
snow

"Rain（雨）?" "No, touch it, it's
snow."

「雨_{あめ}?」「いいえ、触_{さわ}ってみて。
雪_{ゆき}だよ。」

▶ せつ
▷ ゆき

雪（ゆき）snow
大雪（おおゆき）heavy snow
雪だるま（ゆきだるま）snowman
新雪（しんせつ）fresh snow
降雪（こうせつ）snowfall

雪崩（*なだれ）avalanche
吹雪（*ふぶき）snowstorm

<11>　一　广　广　千　千　零　零　雪　雪　雪

▶ 雨(102)

495

降

to descend

You **get off** at the bus stop.

そのバス停で降ります。

▶ こう
▷ お　ふ　ぶ

降りる（おりる）to get off
降る（ふる）(rain/snow) falls
〜以降（いこう）after …
下降（かこう）descent
降ろす（おろす）to let off

降水量（こうすいりょう）rainfall
飛び降りる（とびおりる）
　　to jump off
土砂降り（どしゃぶり）downpour

<10> ⁊ ⻖ ⻖ ⻖ 阝 阝 降 降 降 降

496

直

fix / direct

"Look! It's broken." "Let's **fix** it!"

「ほら、壊れているよ。」「直そう！」

▶ じき　ちょく
▷ なお　ただ

直す（なおす）to correct; to fix
直る（なおる）to be fixed
正直な（しょうじきな）honest
見直す（みなおす）to take another look
直接（ちょくせつ）direct

直線（ちょくせん）straight line
素直な（すなおな）docile
直ちに（ただちに）immediately

<8> 一 十 广 市 冇 肖 盲 直

▶十(10)　目(16)　！真(184)

第　32　課

●この課の漢字

危	険	拾	捨	戻	吸	放	変
497	498	499	500	501	502	503	504
歯	髪	絵	横	当	伝	細	無
505	506	507	508	509	510	511	512

497

危
dangerous

Look at that stone on the cliff. That person is in **danger**.

がけの上の石を見てください。
危険です。

▶ き
▷ あぶ　あや

危ない（あぶない）dangerous
危険（きけん）danger
危うい（あやうい）dangerous
危害（きがい）harm; injury
危機（きき）crisis

危篤（きとく）critical condition

<6> ノ ク ㇗ ㇗ 产 危

498

険
steep

A person（人）is looking at a **steep** mountain.

人が険しい山を見ています。

▶ けん
▷ けわ

危険（きけん）danger
険しい山（けわしいやま）
　　steep mountain
冒険（ぼうけん）adventure
保険（ほけん）insurance

険悪な（けんあくな）hostile

<11> ＇ ㇇ ㇏ ㇏ ㇏ ㇏ ㇏ ㇏ 険 険　　▶人(26)

499

拾
to pick up

I **picked up** a 10,000-yen bill from a trash can.

ごみ箱から一万円を拾いました。

▶ しゅう　じゅう
▷ ひろ

拾う（ひろう）to pick up
拾得物（しゅうとくぶつ）
　　something found

<9> 一　十　扌　扩　扮　抡　拵　拾　拾

▶ 扌(I) 合(295)　! 捨(500)

500

捨
to throw away

I **throw away** garbage in a trash can on Saturdays（土）.

土曜日にごみを捨てます。

▶ しゃ
▷ す

捨てる（すてる）to throw away
見捨てる（みすてる）to abandon
四捨五入（ししゃごにゅう）
　　rounding off (to the nearest number)

取捨選択（しゅしゃせんたく）
　　sorting out

<11> 一　十　扌　扩　扮　抡　捗　捨　捨　捨　捨

▶ 扌(I) 土(23) 口(15)　! 拾(499)

501

戻
to return

He became big（大）and **returned**. Now he is at the door（戸）.

彼は大きくなって戻り、今、戸の前にいます。

▶ れい
▷ もど

戻る（もどる）to return to (a place)
戻す（もどす）to return (something)
払い戻す（はらいもどす）to refund
取り戻す（とりもどす）to take back
返戻金（へんれいきん）refund

<7> 一　ニ　ヨ　戸　戸　戻　戻

▶ 戸(306) 大(81)

502

吸
to inhale

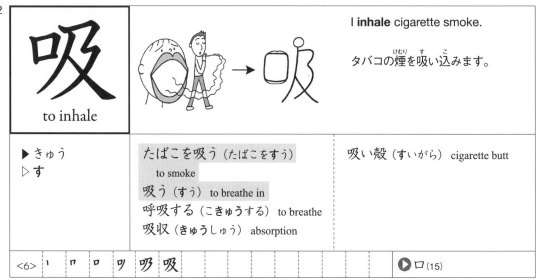

I **inhale** cigarette smoke.

タバコの煙を吸い込みます。

▶ きゅう
▷ す

たばこを吸う（たばこをすう）
　　to smoke
吸う（すう）to breathe in
呼吸する（こきゅうする）to breathe
吸収（きゅうしゅう）absorption

吸い殻（すいがら）cigarette butt

| <6> | ノ | 口 | ロ | 叩 | 吸 | 吸 | | | | | | ▶口(15) |

503

放
to release

We were **released** under the flag.

旗の下で解放されました。

▶ ほう
▷ はな　ばな
　 ほう

放す（はなす）to release
放送（ほうそう）broadcast
開放する（かいほうする）to open
解放する（かいほうする）to release
追放（ついほう）exile

手放す（てばなす）
　　to give up ownership
放射能（ほうしゃのう）radioactivity
放火（ほうか）arson
放る（ほうる）to toss; to leave ~ alone

| <8> | ノ | 亠 | ゥ | 方 | 扩 | 扩 | 放 | 放 | | | | ▶方(136) |

504

変
to change / weird

He is wearing **weird** clothes.

彼は変な服を着ています。

▶ へん
▷ か

変な（へんな）weird
変わる（かわる）(something) changes
変える（かえる）to change (something)
大変（たいへん）very; hard
変化（へんか）change

変更（へんこう）alteration
相変わらず（あいかわらず）
　　as before

| <9> | ノ | 亠 | ナ | 方 | 亦 | 亦 | 亦 | 変 | 変 | | | |

505

歯
tooth

Stop（止）talking, and chew rice（米）well with your **teeth**.

話すのを止めて、歯でごはんをよくかみましょう。

▶ し
▷ は　ば

歯（は）tooth
歯医者（はいしゃ）dentist
虫歯（むしば）decayed tooth
歯磨き（はみがき）
　　brushing one's teeth

歯科（しか）dentistry

<12> 丨 ト l上 l止 l此 l此 l此 l歩 l歯 l歯 l歯 l歯

▶ 止(243) 米(67)

506

髪
hair

My friend（友）has long（長）**hair**.

友達は髪が長いです。

▶ ぱつ　はつ
▷ かみ

髪（かみ）hair
髪の毛（かみのけ）hair
洗髪（せんぱつ）shampoo
散髪（さんぱつ）haircut
髪型（かみがた）hair style

金髪（きんぱつ）blonde
黒髪（くろかみ）black hair
白髪（はくはつ／*しらが）
　　white (grey) hair

<14> 丨 厂 厂 匚 三 長 長 長 髟 髟 髟 髣 髪 髪

▶ 長(93) 友(96)

507

絵
picture

They meet（会）and make an embroidery **picture**.

会って、ししゅうでこの絵を作ります。

▶ かい
▷ え

絵（え）picture
絵本（えほん）picture book
絵の具（えのぐ）paint
絵画（かいが）painting
油絵（あぶらえ）oil painting

墨絵（すみえ）monochrome painting
浮世絵（うきよえ）*ukiyoe*
似顔絵（にがおえ）portrait

<12> く 幺 幺 糸 糸 糸 糹 絵 絵 絵 絵

▶ 糸(206) 会(72)

508

横
beside

The children are playing in a big box **beside** a tree（木）.

子供たちが木の横の箱の中で遊んでいます。

▶ おう
▷ よこ

横（よこ） side; beside
横切る（よこぎる） to cross
横断歩道（おうだんほどう）
　　pedestrian crossing
横断する（おうだんする） to cross

横綱（よこづな） *sumo* grand champion

<15> 一 十 オ 木 木 栏 栏 栏 栏 梏 梏 横 横 横 横　　▶ 木(21)　由(374)

509

当
to hit

An arrow **hit** the target.

矢が的に当たりました。

▶ とう
▷ あ

本当に（ほんとうに） really
当たる（あたる） to be hit
お弁当（おべんとう） lunch box
適当（てきとう） appropriate
当てる（あてる） to hit

当時（とうじ） at that time
担当（たんとう） person in charge
当然（とうぜん） naturally

<6> 丨 丷 丷 当 当 当

510

伝
to convey

Two（二）people **convey** a message.

二人の人がメッセージを伝えます。

▶ でん
▷ つた　つだ

伝える（つたえる） to convey
手伝う（てつだう） to help
伝言（でんごん） message
伝統（でんとう） tradition
宣伝（せんでん） advertisement

伝染（でんせん） infection
伝記（でんき） biography
遺伝子（いでんし） gene

<6> ノ イ 仁 仁 伝 伝　　▶ イ (B)　二(2)

511

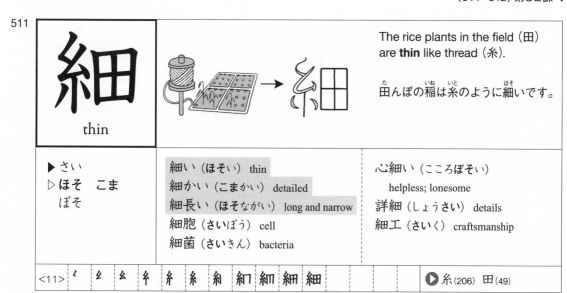

細
thin

The rice plants in the field（田）are **thin** like thread（糸）.

田んぼの稲は糸のように細いです。

▶ さい
▷ ほそ　こま
　 ぼそ

細い（ほそい） thin
細かい（こまかい） detailed
細長い（ほそながい） long and narrow
細胞（さいぼう） cell
細菌（さいきん） bacteria

心細い（こころぼそい）
　 helpless; lonesome
詳細（しょうさい） details
細工（さいく） craftsmanship

<11> ⟨ ⟨ ⟨ ⟨ 幺 糸 糸 糽 紬 細 細　　　▶ 糸(206) 田(49)

512

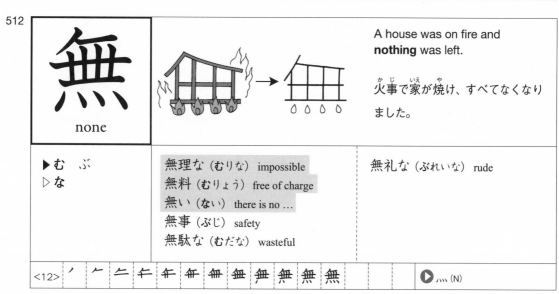

無
none

A house was on fire and **nothing** was left.

火事で家が焼け、すべてなくなりました。

▶ む　ぶ
▷ な

無理な（むりな） impossible
無料（むりょう） free of charge
無い（ない） there is no …
無事（ぶじ） safety
無駄な（むだな） wasteful

無礼な（ぶれいな） rude

<12> ノ 𠂉 ⼆ 午 缶 缶 無 無 無 無 無 無　　　▶ 灬 (N)

画数さくいん（Stroke Count Index）

本書で扱う漢字を画数ごとに並べ、漢字番号を示した。

This index contains all the kanji appearing in this book, arranged by their stroke counts. The entry number of each kanji is also listed.

<1>

一	1

<2>

二	2
七	7
八	8
九	9
十	10
人	26
刀	31
力	50
入	97

<3>

三	3
千	12
万	13
口	15
土	23
上	33
下	34
工	38
女	52
子	53
大	81
小	82
弓	123
夕	135
山	145
川	146
士	270
丸	321
々	447

<4>

五	5
六	6
円	14
日	17
月	18
火	19
水	20
木	21
今	27
分	32
中	35
午	42
父	58
王	63
元	87
少	90
友	96
方	136
心	139
手	140
化	151
天	153
犬	160
牛	165
予	170
切	173
夫	202
氏	207
文	220
太	236
止	243
引	252
不	302
戸	306
区	312
片	332
比	357
公	407
内	490

<5>

四	4
目	16
本	25
半	30
外	36
右	37
左	39
北	48
田	49
生	55
母	59
去	61
立	77
古	86
広	91
出	98
市	99
冬	132
白	156
未	175
写	183
台	185
央	186
矢	194
兄	197
主	204
石	260
仕	271
代	278
世	281
用	285
民	286
正	297
以	304
甘	324
皿	328
付	331
必	371
由	374
払	377
末	382
平	385
込	409
冊	439
号	444
他	448
失	467
申	481

<6>

百	11
寺	28
西	46
先	56
年	60
毎	62
行	66
米	67
会	72
耳	73
安	84
気	88
多	89
早	92
好	95
休	113
虫	124
名	127
色	158
肉	168
自	180
羊	189
糸	206
羽	211
字	214
式	215
光	239
考	255
死	256
有	264
地	280
回	284
竹	294
合	295
同	298
池	313
汚	325
全	369
宅	383
争	388
吉	417
共	420
両	422
老	424
次	446
成	452
守	461
交	480
危	497
吸	502
当	509
伝	510

<7>

男	51
何	57
見	65
来	68
良	69
言	75
町	100
村	101
車	104
社	107
走	114
貝	116
売	118
足	141
体	142
花	152
赤	154
作	174
弟	199
私	201
住	205
近	226
低	232
豆	237
医	257
究	262
図	273
声	291
別	293
冷	327
卵	346
困	347
辛	
忘	354
決	355
役	366
利	376
形	416
初	435
対	454
投	457
束	460
君	491
戻	501

<8>

金	22
門	43
東	45
学	54
国	64
周	79
長	93
明	94
雨	102
店	109
夜	138
林	147
空	149
青	155
味	176
画	188
服	191
姉	198
妹	200
妻	203
英	221
者	227
歩	244

〈8画つづき〉

使 245　押 251　知 254　始 258　事 272　官 274　昔 276　注 287　京 300　所 307　物 316　果 326　固 335　泣 338　幸 340　苦 342　念 350　定 356　受 358　表 363　卒 364　彼 368　届 375　和 386　治 390　法 393　泳 402　供 421　若 423　育 430　性 431　招 432　取 433　枚 438　的 464　泊 472　直 496　放 503

〈9〉

前 40　後 41　南 47　食 70　待 78　持 126　春 129　秋 131　昼 134　首 143　海 150　茶 169　音 177　乗 182　映 187　洋 190　室 210　重 230　風 240　送 246　洗 247　急 248　思 253　研 261　界 282　度 283　計 299　便 303　屋 308　県 311　発 314　品 315　怒 317　皆 339　要 367　活 372　政 381　律 389　係 394　祖 397　点 429　段 441　負 443　約 450　飛 459　神 482　信 484　査 486　相 487　星 493　拾 499　変 504

〈10〉

時 29　高 83　馬 105　校 108　病 111　院 112　起 115　書 120　帰 121　勉 122　夏 130　料 161　真 184　家 193　紙 208　弱 233　留 263　員 269　借 277　特 292　旅 318　通 319　酒 329　消 334　個 336　笑 337　恥 344　配 345　眠 348　残 349　徒 360　荷 373　党 400　疲 403　連 410　記 415　息 425　娘 426　将 428　倍 445　速 469　座 474　席 475　島 476　案 489　降 495

〈11〉

週 80　強 125　黒 157　魚 159　理 162　豚 166　鳥 167　野 171　菜 172　転 181　族 195　教 209　習 212　宿 218　問 223　悪 234　動 242　閉 250　終 259　産 265　堂 309　都 310　進 320　情 352　授 359　部 370　祭 384　経 391　済 392　涼 405　窓 411　側 412　婚 419　船 473　陸 477　雪 494　険 498　捨 500　細 511

〈12〉

間 44　飲 71　買 117　朝 133　晩 137　道 144　森 148　飯 164　着 192　暑 228　寒 229　軽 231　短 238　運 241　開 249　貸 279　答 296　集 301　場 305　焼 333　悲 341　痛 343　覚 353　復 362　遊 401　葉 413　景 414　結 418　奥 427　最 434　番 436　階 442　勝 449　絶 453　過 462　遅 470　港 478　達 492　歯 505　絵 507　無 512

〈13〉

話 76　新 85　電 103　楽 178　漢 213　試 216　遠 225　暗 235　業 266　働 268　意 288　塩 330　感 351　違 365　寝 379　戦 387　義 398　暖 404　園 408　歳 437　続 455　辞 456　夢 463　鉄 468

〈14〉

聞 74　駅 106　銀 110　読 119　語 128　歌 179　説 224　練 361　踊 380　際 395　関 396　静 406　様 483　髪 506

〈15〉

質 222　熱 322　億 440　賛 451　選 458　駐 471　調 485　談 488　横 508

〈16〉

親 196　薬 267　館 275　頭 289　機 466　橋 479

〈17〉

濯 378

〈18〉

曜 24　験 217　題 219　顔 290

〈20〉

議 399

本書に収録されたすべての漢字の読み方を五十音順に並べ、漢字と漢字番号を示した。

This index contains all the kanji readings appearing in this book, arranged in *a-i-u-e-o* order. The kanji for each reading is also listed, along with its entry number.

あ

読み	漢字	番号
ぁ	上	33
ぁ	会	72
ぁ	明	94
ぁ	空	149
ぁ	開	249
ぁ	有	264
ぁ	合	295
ぁ	当	509
あい	相	487
あいだ	間	44
あお	青	155
あか	明	94
あか	赤	154
あき	明	94
あき	秋	131
あく	悪	234
あさ	朝	133
あざ	字	214
あし	足	141
あじ	味	176
あそ	遊	401
あたた	暖	404
あたま	頭	289
あたら	新	85
あつ	暑	228
あつ	集	301
あつ	熱	322
あと	後	41
あに	兄	197
あね	姉	198
あぶ	危	497
あま	雨	102
あま	天	153
あま	甘	324
あめ	雨	102
あめ	天	153
あや	危	497
あやま	過	462
あゆ	歩	244
あら	新	85
あら	洗	247
あらそ	争	388
あらわ	表	363
ある	歩	244
あん	行	66
あん	安	84
あん	暗	235
あん	案	489

い

読み	漢字	番号
い	生	55
い	行	66
い	言	75
い	入	97
い	医	257
い	意	288
い	以	304
い	違	365
い	要	372
いえ	家	193
いか	怒	339
いき	息	425
いく	育	430
いくさ	戦	387
いけ	池	313
いし	石	260
いそ	急	248
いた	痛	343
いち	一	1
いち	市	99
いっ	一	1
いつ	一	1
いつ	五	5
いと	糸	206
いぬ	犬	160
いま	今	27
いもうと	妹	200
いろ	色	158
いん	飲	71
いん	院	112
いん	音	177
いん	引	252
いん	員	269

う

読み	漢字	番号
う	右	37
う	生	55
う	雨	102
う	売	118
う	羽	211
う	有	264
う	産	265
う	受	358
うい	初	435
うえ	上	33
うお	魚	159
うご	動	242
うし	後	41
うし	牛	165
うじ	氏	207
うしな	失	467
うた	歌	179
うち	内	490
うつ	写	183
うつ	映	187
うぶ	産	265
うま	馬	105
うみ	海	150
うわ	上	33
うん	運	241

え

読み	漢字	番号
え	会	72
え	重	230
え	回	284
え	笑	337
え	絵	507
えい	映	187
えい	英	221
えい	泳	402
えき	駅	106
えき	役	366
えら	選	458
えん	円	14
えん	遠	225
えん	塩	330
えん	園	408

お

読み	漢字	番号
お	下	34
お	生	55
お	小	82
お	起	115
お	悪	234
お	押	251
お	終	259
お	汚	325
お	和	386
お	老	424
お	負	450
お	降	495
おう	王	63
おう	央	186

よみ	漢字	ページ
おう	押	251
おう	奥	427
おう	横	508
おお	大	81
おお	多	89
おおやけ	公	407
おく	後	41
おく	送	246
おく	屋	308
おく	奥	427
おく	億	440
おく	遅	470
おこ	怒	339
おこな	行	66
おさ	治	390
おし	教	209
おそ	教	209
おそ	遅	470
おっと	夫	202
おと	音	177
おど	踊	380
おとうと	弟	199
おとこ	男	51
おな	同	298
おぼ	覚	353
おも	主	204
おも	重	230
おも	思	253
おもて	表	363
おや	親	196
およ	泳	402
おん	音	177
おん	遠	225
おんな	女	52

か

よみ	漢字	ページ
か	日	17
か	火	19
か	下	34
か	何	57
か	買	117
か	書	120
か	夏	130
か	化	151
か	花	152
か	歌	179
か	家	193
か	借	277
か	代	278
か	貸	279
か	果	326
か	荷	373
か	勝	449
か	過	462
か	交	480
か	変	504
が	書	120
が	画	188
が	会	72
がい	員	116
かい	海	150
かい	開	249
かい	界	282
かい	回	284
かい	皆	367
かい	階	442
かい	絵	507
がい	外	36
がい	貝	116
かえ	帰	121
がえ	帰	121
かお	顔	290
がお	顔	290
かか	関	396
かか	係	397
かかり	係	397
かく	画	188
かく	覚	353
がく	学	54
がく	楽	178
かさ	重	230
かざ	風	240
かしら	頭	289
かぜ	風	240
かた	語	128
かた	方	136
かた	片	332
かた	固	335
かた	形	416
がた	方	136
かたち	形	416
かたな	刀	31
かっ	合	295
かっ	活	381
かっ	勝	449
かつ	活	381
がっ	学	54
がっ	楽	178
がっ	合	295
がつ	月	18
かど	門	43
かな	金	22
かな	悲	341
かなめ	要	372
かなら	必	371
かね	金	22
かの	彼	368
かみ	上	33
かみ	紙	208
かみ	神	482
かみ	髪	506
がみ	紙	208
かよ	通	319
から	空	149
から	辛	347
からだ	体	142
かる	軽	231
がる	軽	231
かれ	彼	368
かろ	軽	231
かわ	川	146
がわ	川	146
がわ	側	412
かん	間	44
かん	漢	213
かん	寒	229
かん	官	274
かん	館	275
かん	甘	324
かん	感	351
かん	関	396
かん	神	482
がん	元	87
がん	顔	290
がん	丸	321
かんが	考	255

き

よみ	漢字	ページ
き	木	21
き	生	55
き	来	68
き	聞	74
き	気	88
き	起	115
き	帰	121
き	切	173
き	着	192
き	消	334
き	決	355
き	利	376
き	記	415
き	機	466
き	危	497
ぎ	着	192
ぎ	義	398
ぎ	議	399
きた	北	48
きた	来	68
きたな	汚	325
きち	吉	417
きっ	切	173
きっ	吉	417
きつ	吉	417
きみ	君	491
きゅう	九	9
きゅう	休	113
きゅう	弓	123
きゅう	急	248
きゅう	究	262
きゅう	泣	338
きゅう	吸	502
ぎゅう	牛	165

読み	漢字	ページ
きょ	去	61
ぎょ	魚	159
きょう	強	125
きょう	兄	197
きょう	教	209
きょう	京	300
きょう	経	391
きょう	共	420
きょう	供	421
きょう	橋	479
ぎょう	行	66
ぎょう	業	266
ぎょう	形	416
きわ	究	262
きわ	際	395
ぎわ	際	395
きん	金	22
きん	今	27
きん	近	226
ぎん	銀	110

く

読み	漢字	ページ
く	九	9
く	口	15
く	工	38
く	来	68
く	食	70
く	区	312
く	苦	342
く	供	421
くう	空	149
くすり	薬	267
ぐすり	薬	267
くだ	下	34
くち	口	15
ぐち	口	15
くに	国	64
くば	配	345
くび	首	143
くら	暗	235
くら	比	357
くる	苦	342
くるま	車	104
くろ	黒	157
くん	君	491

け

読み	漢字	ページ
け	気	88
け	化	151
け	家	193
け	消	334
け	下	34
げ	外	36
げ	夏	130
げ	兄	197
けい	軽	231
けい	計	299
けい	京	300
けい	経	391
けい	係	397
けい	景	414
けい	形	416
けが	汚	325
けっ	決	355
けっ	結	418
けつ	決	355
けつ	結	418
げつ	月	18
けわ	険	498
けん	間	44
けん	見	65
けん	犬	160
けん	験	217
けん	研	261
けん	県	311
けん	建	315
けん	険	498
げん	間	44
げん	言	75
げん	元	87
げん	験	217

こ

読み	漢字	ページ
こ	木	21
こ	子	53
こ	去	61
こ	来	68
こ	小	82
こ	古	86
こ	戸	306
こ	固	335
こ	個	336
こ	込	409
ご	五	5
ご	後	41
ご	午	42
ご	語	128
ご	込	409
こう	口	15
こう	工	38
こう	後	41
こう	行	66
こう	高	83
こう	広	91
こう	好	95
こう	校	108
こう	光	239
こう	考	255
こう	幸	340
こう	公	407
こう	港	478
こう	交	480
こう	神	482
こう	降	495
ごう	強	125
ごう	業	266
ごう	合	295
ごう	号	444
こえ	声	291
こく	国	64
こく	黒	157
こく	石	260
ごく	国	64
ここの	九	9
こころ	心	139
こころ	試	216
こた	答	296
こっ	国	64
こと	言	75
こと	事	272
ごと	事	272
この	好	95
こま	困	346
こま	細	511
こめ	米	67
ころ	転	181
こわ	声	291
こん	金	22
こん	今	27
こん	建	315
こん	困	346
こん	婚	419
ごん	言	75

さ

読み	漢字	ページ
さ	下	34
さ	左	39
さ	去	61
さ	茶	169
さ	作	174
さ	冷	323
さ	覚	353
さ	査	486
ざ	覚	353
ざ	座	474
さい	西	46
さい	菜	172
さい	切	173
さい	妻	203
さい	祭	384
さい	済	392
さい	際	395
さい	最	434
さい	歳	437
さい	細	511
ざい	西	46
ざい	済	392
ざい	歳	437
さいわ	幸	340
さか	酒	329
ざか	酒	329
さかな	魚	159

読み	漢字	ページ
ざかな	魚	159
さき	先	56
さく	作	174
さく	冊	439
ざく	冊	439
さけ	酒	329
ざけ	酒	329
さず	授	359
さだ	定	356
さち	幸	340
さっ	早	92
さっ	作	174
さっ	冊	439
さつ	冊	439
さま	様	483
さむ	寒	229
さら	皿	328
ざら	皿	328
さん	三	3
さん	山	145
さん	産	265
さん	賛	451
ざん	山	145
ざん	残	349

し

読み	漢字	ページ
し	四	4
し	子	53
し	市	99
し	強	125
し	自	180
し	矢	194
し	姉	198
し	私	201
し	糸	206
し	氏	207
し	紙	208
し	試	216
し	止	243
し	使	245
し	閉	250
し	思	253
し	知	254
し	死	256
し	始	258
し	士	270
し	仕	271
し	次	446
し	歯	505
じ	寺	28
じ	時	29
じ	耳	73
じ	持	126
じ	自	180
じ	字	214
じ	仕	271
じ	事	272
じ	地	280
じ	治	390
じ	次	446
じ	辞	456
しあわ	幸	340
しお	塩	330
しき	色	158
しき	式	215
じき	食	70
じき	直	496
しず	静	406
した	下	34
した	親	196
しち	七	7
しち	質	222
しっ	失	467
しつ	室	210
しつ	質	222
じっ	失	467
じつ	十	10
じつ	日	17
しな	品	317
しま	島	476
しも	下	34
しゃ	車	104
しゃ	社	107
しゃ	写	183
しゃ	者	227
しゃ	捨	500
じゃ	社	107
しゃく	赤	154
しゃく	石	260
しゃく	昔	276
しゃく	借	277
じゃく	着	192
じゃく	弱	233
じゃく	昔	276
じゃく	若	423
しゃっ	借	277
しゅ	手	140
しゅ	首	143
しゅ	主	204
しゅ	酒	329
しゅ	取	433
しゅ	守	461
じゅ	受	358
じゅ	授	359
しゅう	周	79
しゅう	週	80
しゅう	秋	131
しゅう	習	212
しゅう	終	259
しゅう	集	301
しゅう	拾	499
じゅう	十	10
じゅう	中	35
じゅう	住	205
じゅう	重	230
じゅう	終	259
じゅう	拾	499
しゅく	宿	218
しゅっ	出	98
しゅつ	出	98
じゅっ	十	10
しゅん	春	129
しょ	書	120
しょ	暑	228
しょ	所	307
しょ	初	435
じょ	女	52
じょ	所	307
しょう	上	33
しょう	生	55
しょう	小	82
しょう	少	90
しょう	青	155
しょう	声	291
しょう	正	297
しょう	焼	333
しょう	消	334
しょう	笑	337
しょう	政	389
しょう	将	428
しょう	性	431
しょう	招	432
しょう	勝	449
しょう	相	487
しょう	星	493
じょう	上	33
じょう	生	55
じょう	乗	182
じょう	場	305
じょう	情	352
じょう	定	356
じょう	静	406
じょう	成	452
じょう	星	493
しょく	食	70
しょく	色	158
しら	白	156
しら	調	485
しる	記	415
しろ	白	156
しろ	代	278
しん	新	85
しん	心	139
しん	森	148
しん	真	184
しん	親	196
しん	進	320
しん	辛	347
しん	寝	379
しん	申	481
しん	神	482
しん	信	484

じん	人	26	せい	星	493	ぞく	足	141	たか	高	83
じん	神	482	せい	説	224	ぞく	族	195	だか	高	83
			ぜい	情	352	ぞく	続	455	たく	度	283
す			ぜき	夕	135	そそ	注	287	たく	濯	378
す	子	53	せき	赤	154	そだ	育	430	たく	宅	383
す	好	95	せき	石	260	そつ	卒	364	たけ	竹	294
す	主	204	せき	昔	276	そと	外	36	ただ	正	297
す	住	205	せき	関	396	そな	供	421	ただ	直	496
す	済	392	せき	席	475	その	園	408	たたか	戦	387
す	守	461	せき	説	224	そら	空	149	たっ	達	492
す	過	462	せっ	石	260	ぞら	空	149	たつ	達	492
す	捨	500	せっ	切	173	そん	村	101	たの	楽	178
す	吸	502	せつ	説	224				たば	束	460
ず	豆	237	せつ	雪	494	**た**			たび	度	283
ず	事	272	せつ	絶	453	た	田	49	たび	旅	318
ず	図	273	ぜっ	絶	453	た	食	70	たまご	卵	327
ず	頭	289	せん	千	12	た	立	77	たみ	民	286
ず	済	392	せん	先	56	た	多	89	ため	試	216
すい	水	20	せん	川	146	た	手	140	たよ	便	303
すい	出	98	せん	洗	247	た	足	141	たん	反	163
すえ	末	382	せん	戦	387	た	太	236	たん	短	238
すく	少	90	せん	選	458	た	建	315	たん	男	51
すこ	少	90	せん	船	473	た	他	448	だん	暖	404
すす	進	320	ぜん	千	12	た	絶	453	だん	段	443
すず	涼	405	ぜん	前	40	だ	田	49	だん	談	488
すべ	全	369	ぜん	全	369	だ	立	77			
すみ	速	469				だ	出	98	**ち**		
すわ	座	474	**そ**			だ	建	315	ち	千	12
			そそ	反	163	たい	待	78	ち	質	222
せ			そそ	祖	429	たい	大	81	ち	知	254
せ	世	281	そ	初	435	たい	体	142	ち	地	280
せい	西	46	ぞ	祖	429	たい	台	185	ち	池	313
せい	生	55	そう	早	92	たい	太	236	ち	恥	344
せい	青	155	そう	走	114	たい	代	278	ち	治	390
せい	世	281	そう	送	246	たい	貸	279	ち	遅	470
せい	声	291	そう	争	388	たい	平	385	ちい	小	82
せい	正	297	そう	窓	411	たい	対	454	ちか	近	226
せい	情	352	そう	相	487	だい	大	81	ちが	違	365
せい	政	389	そく	足	141	だい	台	185	ちから	力	50
せい	静	406	そく	側	412	だい	弟	199	ちく	竹	294
せい	性	431	そく	息	425	だい	題	219	ちち	父	58
せい	歳	437	そく	束	460	だい	代	278	ちゃ	茶	169
せい	成	452	そく	速	469	だい	内	490	ちゃく	着	192

よみ	漢字	ページ
ちゅう	中	35
ちゅう	虫	124
ちゅう	昼	134
ちゅう	注	287
ちゅう	駐	471
ちょう	長	93
ちょう	町	100
ちょう	朝	133
ちょう	鳥	167
ちょう	重	230
ちょう	調	485
ちょく	直	496
つ		
つ	着	192
つ	都	310
つ	通	319
つ	付	331
つ	連	410
つ	次	446
づ	付	331
つい	対	454
つう	通	319
つう	痛	343
つか	使	245
つか	仕	271
つか	疲	403
つき	月	18
つぎ	次	446
つく	作	174
づく	作	174
つた	伝	510
つだ	伝	510
つち	土	23
つづ	続	455
つど	集	301
つま	妻	203
つめ	冷	323
つよ	強	125
つら	連	410
て		
て	手	140
で	出	98
で	弟	199
てい	体	142
てい	弟	199
てい	低	232
てい	定	356
てき	的	464
てっ	鉄	468
てつ	鉄	468
てら	寺	28
でら	寺	28
てん	店	109
てん	天	153
てん	転	181
てん	点	441
でん	田	49
でん	電	103
でん	伝	510
と		
と	十	10
と	土	23
と	問	223
と	説	224
と	止	243
と	閉	250
と	研	261
と	留	263
と	図	273
と	度	283
と	頭	289
と	戸	306
と	都	310
と	徒	360
と	取	433
と	飛	465
と	泊	472
ど	土	23
ど	度	283
ど	頭	289
ど	戸	306
ど	怒	339
とう	刀	31
とう	東	45
とう	読	119
とう	冬	132
とう	道	144
とう	豆	237
とう	頭	289
とう	答	296
とう	党	400
とう	投	457
とう	島	476
とう	当	509
どう	道	144
どう	動	242
どう	働	268
どう	同	298
どう	堂	309
とお	十	10
とお	遠	225
とお	通	319
とき	時	29
とく	読	119
とく	特	292
どく	読	119
ところ	所	307
どころ	所	307
とし	年	60
とっ	特	292
とど	届	375
ととの	調	485
とも	友	96
とも	共	420
とも	供	421
ども	供	421
とり	鳥	167
とん	豚	166
とん	問	223
な		
な	南	47
な	名	127
な	菜	172
な	泣	338
な	成	452
な	投	457
な	無	512
ない	内	490
なお	治	390
なお	直	496
なか	半	30
なか	中	35
なが	長	93
なご	和	386
なさ	情	352
なつ	夏	130
なな	七	7
なに	何	57
なの	七	7
なま	生	55
なら	習	212
なん	南	47
なん	男	51
なん	何	57
に		
に	二	2
に	荷	373
にい	新	85
にが	苦	342
にく	肉	168
にし	西	46
にち	日	17
にっ	日	17
にゃく	若	423
にゅう	入	97
にょ	女	52
にょう	女	52
にん	人	26
ぬ		
ぬし	主	204
ね		
ね	音	177
ね	練	361
ね	寝	379
ねっ	熱	322

読み	漢字	頁	読み	漢字	頁	読み	漢字	頁	読み	漢字	頁	読み	漢字	頁
ねつ	熱	322	はじ	恥	344	ひ	冷	323	ふ	父	58	ふ	付	331
ねむ	眠	348	はじ	初	435	ひ	悲	341	ふ	夫	202	ふ	老	424
ねん	年	60	ばし	橋	479	ひ	比	357	ふ	風	240	ふ	負	450
ねん	念	350	はず	外	36	ひ	彼	368	ふ	歩	244	ふ	降	495
の			はた	機	466	ひ	疲	403	ふ	不	302	ぶ	分	32
の	飲	71	はたら	働	268	ひ	飛	465				ぶ	夫	202
の	野	171	ばたら	働	268	び	日	17				ぶ	歩	244
の	乗	182	はち	八	8	び	火	19				ぶ	不	302
のこ	残	349	はっ	八	8	び	引	252				ぶ	部	370
のち	後	41	はっ	発	314	ひか	光	239				ぶ	負	450
のぼ	上	33	はっ	法	393	ひがし	東	45				ぶ	降	495
は			はっ	発	314	ひかり	光	239				ぶ	無	512
は	生	55	はつ	初	435	ひく	低	232				ふう	夫	202
は	映	187	はつ	髪	506	ひだり	左	39				ふう	風	240
は	羽	211	ばつ	末	382	ひっ	必	371				ふく	服	191
は	果	326	ぱつ	発	314	ひつ	必	371				ふく	復	362
は	恥	344	ぱつ	髪	506	ひつじ	羊	189				ぷく	復	362
は	葉	413	はな	話	76	ひと	一	1				ふた	二	2
は	歯	505	はな	花	152	ひと	人	26				ぶた	豚	166
ば	馬	105	はな	放	503	ひゃく	百	11				ふっ	復	362
ば	化	151	ばな	花	152	びゃく	百	11				ふっ	払	377
ば	羽	211	ばな	放	503	びゃく	白	156				ふつ	払	377
ば	場	305	はなし	話	76	ぴゃく	百	11				ぶつ	物	316
ば	葉	413	はね	羽	211	ひゃっ	百	11				ふと	太	236
ば	歯	505	はは	母	59	ひょう	表	363				ふな	船	473
はい	入	97	はや	早	92	びょう	病	111				ふね	船	473
はい	配	345	はや	速	469	びょう	平	385				ふみ	文	220
ばい	買	117	ばや	早	92	ぴょう	表	363				ふゆ	冬	132
ばい	売	118	はやし	林	147	ひら	開	249				ふる	古	86
ばい	倍	445	ばやし	林	147	ひら	平	385				ふん	分	32
ぱい	配	345	はら	払	377	ひる	昼	134				ぶん	分	32
はか	図	273	はる	春	129	ひろ	広	91				ぶん	聞	74
はか	計	299	はん	半	30	ひろ	拾	499				ぶん	文	220
はく	白	156	はん	反	163	びろ	広	91				ぷん	分	32
はく	泊	472	はん	飯	164	ひん	品	317				**へ**		
ぱく	泊	472	ばん	万	13	びん	便	303				へ	経	391
はぐく	育	430	ばん	晩	137							へい	病	111
はこ	運	241	ばん	番	436	**ふ**						へい	閉	250
はし	走	114	**ひ**			ふ	父	58				へい	平	385
はし	橋	479	ひ	日	17	ふ	夫	202				べい	米	67
はじ	始	258	ひ	火	19	ふ	風	240				ぺい	病	111
			ひ	引	252	ふ	歩	244				べつ	別	293
						ふ	不	302						

べつ	別	293
へん	片	332
へん	変	504
べん	勉	122
べん	便	303
ほ		
ほ	火	19
ほ	歩	244
ぼ	母	59
ぼ	歩	244
ほう	方	136
ほう	法	393
ほう	放	503
ぼう	忘	354
ぼう	法	393
ほか	外	36
ほか	他	448
ほく	北	48
ぼく	目	16
ぼく	木	21
ぼく	北	48
ほし	星	493
ぼし	星	493
ほそ	細	511
ぼそ	細	511
ほっ	北	48
ほっ	発	314
ほっ	法	393
ほつ	発	314
ほん	本	25
ほん	反	163
ぼん	本	25
ぽん	本	25
ま		
ま	目	16
ま	間	44
ま	待	78
ま	馬	105
ま	真	184
ま	負	450
ま	交	480
まい	毎	62
まい	米	67
まい	妹	200
まい	枚	438
まえ	前	40
まさ	正	297
まさ	勝	449
まじ	交	480
まち	町	100
まつ	末	382
まつ	祭	384
まった	全	369
まつりごと	政	389
まと	的	464
まど	窓	411
まな	学	54
まね	招	432
まめ	豆	237
まも	守	461
まる	円	14
まる	丸	321
まわ	周	79
まわ	回	284
まん	万	13
み		
み	三	3
み	見	65
み	未	175
み	味	176
みぎ	右	37
みじか	短	238
みず	水	20
みずか	自	180
みせ	店	109
みち	道	144
みっ	三	3
みな	皆	367
みなと	港	478
みなみ	南	47
みみ	耳	73
みやこ	都	310
みょう	明	94
みょう	名	127
みん	民	286
みん	眠	348
む		
む	六	6
む	夢	463
む	無	512
むい	六	6
むかし	昔	276
むし	虫	124
むす	結	418
むすめ	娘	426
むっ	六	6
むら	村	101
むろ	室	210
め		
め	目	16
め	女	52
めい	明	94
めい	名	127
めし	飯	164
も		
も	持	126
も	若	423
もう	申	481
もく	目	16
もく	木	21
もち	用	285
もつ	物	316
もっと	最	434
もと	本	25
もと	下	34
もと	元	87
もど	戻	501
もの	者	227
もの	物	316
もり	森	148
もり	守	461
もん	門	43
もん	聞	74
もん	文	220
もん	問	223
や		
や	八	8
や	病	111
や	夜	138
や	野	171
や	家	193
や	矢	194
や	屋	308
や	焼	333
や	辞	456
やかた	館	275
やく	薬	267
やく	役	366
やく	約	459
やしろ	社	107
やす	安	84
やす	休	113
やっ	八	8
やっ	薬	267
やど	宿	218
やま	山	145
やまい	病	111
やわ	和	386
ゆ		
ゆ	行	66
ゆ	由	374
ゆ	遊	401
ゆ	結	418
ゆい	由	374
ゆう	右	37
ゆう	友	96
ゆう	夕	135
ゆう	有	264
ゆう	由	374
ゆう	遊	401
ゆき	雪	494
ゆみ	弓	123
ゆめ	夢	463

よ

よ	四	4
よ	良	69
よ	読	119
よ	夜	138
よ	予	170
よ	代	278
よ	世	281
よう	八	8
よう	曜	24
よう	羊	189
よう	洋	190
よう	用	285
よう	要	372
よう	踊	380
よう	葉	413
よう	様	483
よこ	横	508
よご	汚	325

よし	由	374
よっ	四	4
よる	夜	138
よわ	弱	233
よん	四	4

ら

らい	来	68
らく	楽	178
らん	卵	327

り

り	理	162
り	利	376
りき	力	50
りく	陸	477
りち	律	394
りっ	立	77
りつ	立	77

りつ	律	394
りゅう	立	77
りゅう	留	263
りょ	旅	318
りょう	良	69
りょう	料	161
りょう	涼	405
りょう	両	422
りょく	力	50
りん	林	147

る

る	留	263

れ

れい	冷	323
れい	戻	501
れん	練	361
れん	連	410

ろ

ろう	老	424
ろく	六	6
ろっ	六	6

わ

わ	分	32
わ	話	76
わ	和	386
わか	別	293
わか	若	423
わざ	業	266
わす	忘	354
わたくし	私	201
わたし	私	201
わら	笑	337
わる	悪	234

字形さくいん (Kanji Shape Index)

「Kanji Parts for Kanji Shape Index」に漢字の部分を画数順に並べ、次のページからのリストで、各部分を含む漢字と漢字番号を示した。

The following table, Kanji Parts for Kanji Shape Index, lists 215 kanji parts in stroke-count order. The index starting on the next page groups together all kanji that contain the same kanji part. The entry number of each kanji is also listed.

Kanji Parts for Kanji Shape Index

<2>

No.	Part	No.	Part	No.	Part
1	イ	11	ハ	21	七
2	冫	12	十	22	九
3	亠	13	ナ	23	⺄
4	刂	14	冂	24	丁
5	力	15	凵	25	乂
6	刀	16	人	26	匸
7	匕	17	又	27	メ
8	厶	18	マ	28	ミ
9	儿	19	ク	29	几
10	八	20	ク	30	二

| 31 | 入 | 32 | 厂 |

<3>

No.	Part	No.	Part	No.	Part
33	口	42	寸	51	丷
34	土	43	己	52	⺌
35	女	44	也	53	子
36	弓	45	勹	54	尸
37	彳	46	辶	55	尸
38	忄	47	宀	56	夂
39	扌	48	艹	57	千
40	氵	49	广	58	工
41	阝	50	士	59	幺

60	巾	61	ヨ	62	⺕
63	弋	64	小	65	大
66	夕	67	丸	68	山

<4>

No.	Part	No.	Part	No.	Part
69	方	78	斤	87	王
70	日	79	欠	88	氏
71	木	80	灬	89	五
72	月	81	止	90	中
73	歹	82	⺊	91	父
74	牛	83	主	92	元
75	ネ	84	心	93	止
76	戈	85	戸	94	开
77	攵	86	云	95	卅

96	夫	103	罒	110	化
97	文	104	勿	111	比
98	火	105	廿		
99	反	106	友		
100	内	107	今		
101	予	108	少		
102	廿	109	癶		

<5>

No.	Part	No.	Part	No.	Part
112	矢	123	石	134	央
113	禾	124	白	135	本
114	台	125	古	136	民
115	圣	126	右	137	世
116	主	127	⺍	138	代
117	目	128	生	139	未
118	田	129	可	140	由
119	广	130	去	141	失
120	用	131	冬	142	申
121	穴	132	兄	143	且
122	立	133	市	144	皿

| 145 | 正 | 146 | 皮 | 147 | 四 |

<6>

No.	Part	No.	Part	No.	Part
148	糸	156	米	164	式
149	耳	157	竹	165	色
150	舌	158	毎	166	羊
151	寺	159	先	167	合
152	自	160	交	168	安
153	羽	161	艮	169	吉
154	共	162	虫	170	关
155	百	163	至	171	争
				172	会

<7>

No.	Part	No.	Part	No.	Part
173	言	179	走	185	酉
174	車	180	売	186	辛
175	貝	181	豕	187	束
176	里	182	鳥	188	我
177	見	183	足	189	何
178	良	184	豆		

<8>

No.	Part	No.	Part	No.	Part
190	金	193	隹	196	者
191	僉	194	雨	197	食
192	門	195	周	198	東

199	昔	202	青
200	官	203	奎
201	京	204	固

<9>

No.	Part	No.	Part
205	頁	208	首
206	音	209	重
207	亲		

<10>

No.	Part
210	馬
211	袁

<11>

No.	Part
212	祭
213	動

<13>

No.	Part
214	楽
215	意

1 イ

何 57
休 113
夜 138
体 142
化 151
花 152
作 174
住 205
宿 218
低 232
使 245
働 268
仕 271
借 277
代 278
貸 279
便 303
付 331
個 336
荷 373
係 397
側 412
供 421
億 440
倍 445
他 448
信 484
伝 510

2 冫

病 111
楽 178
羽 211
習 212
弱 233
薬 267
冷 323
痛 343
寝 379
疲 403
将 428
次 446
様 483

3 亠

六 6
立 77
高 83
広 91
市 99
店 109
病 111
方 136
夜 138
族 195
姉 198
主 204
住 205
文 220
産 265
度 283
注 287
意 288
顔 290
京 300
旅 318
泣 338
痛 343
辛 347
忘 354
卒 364
済 392
遊 401
疲 403
涼 405
景 414
育 430
対 454
辞 456
駐 471

座 474
席 475
交 480
放 503
変 504

4 リ

前 40
別 293
利 376
側 412

5 力

力 50
男 51
勉 122
動 242
働 268
勝 449

6 刀

刀 31
分 32
切 173
留 263
招 432
初 435

7 ヒ

北 48
化 151
花 152
死 256
比 357
皆 367
老 424
階 442

8 ム

去 61
会 72
広 91
強 125
転 181
台 185
私 201
室 210
始 258
屋 308
払 377
治 390
法 393
公 407
窓 411
育 430
絵 507
伝 510

9 儿

先 56
見 65
元 87
院 112
売 118
読 119
勉 122
晩 137
親 196
兄 197
説 224
光 239
洗 247
発 314
焼 333
覚 353
党 400
続 455

10 入

金 22
今 27
食 70
飲 71
会 72
銀 110
飯 164
茶 169
験 217
館 275
界 282
合 295
答 296
冷 323
念 350
全 369
鉄 468
険 498
拾 499
捨 500
絵 507

11 八

六 6
八 8
分 32
父 58
貝 116
買 117
真 184
題 219
質 222
寒 229
員 269
貸 279
頭 289
顔 290
公 407
側 412

負 450
選 458
船 473
港 478
横 508

12 十

十 10
千 12
午 42
南 47
古 86
早 92
朝 133
真 184
士 270
仕 271
計 299
焼 333
固 335
個 336
幸 340
苦 342
辛 347
卒 364
辞 456
直 496

13 ナ

右 37
左 39
友 96
有 264
若 423

14 冂

円 14
南 47
周 79
週 80
高 83
市 99
雨 102
病 111
肉 168
用 285
同 298
通 319
痛 343
踊 380
両 422
冊 439
過 462
橋 479
調 485
内 490

15 凵

画 188
歯 505

16 人

火 19
人 26
飲 71
春 129
肉 168
歌 179
央 186
夫 202
験 217
笑 337
卒 364
次 446
座 474
談 488
内 490
険 498

17 又		族	195	売	118	政	389	夫	202	足	141	園	408
友	96	教	209	読	119	枚	438	絵	507	味	176	景	414
反	163	短	238	帰	121	交	480	伝	510	歌	179	記	415
飯	164	知	254	空	149	放	503			台	185	吉	417
服	191	医	257	写	183			31 入		兄	197	結	418
軽	231	旅	318	家	193	26 匚		入	97	問	223	若	423
度	283	塩	330	室	210	医	257	込	409	説	224	招	432
怒	339	復	362	字	214	区	312			遠	225	点	441
受	358	政	389	宿	218			32 厂		豆	237	号	444
授	359	遊	401	寒	229	27 乂		広	91	短	238	倍	445
役	366	枚	438	運	241	気	88	店	109	知	254	辞	456
彼	368	放	503	究	262	図	273	病	111	始	258	過	462
寝	379	無	512	官	274	区	312	反	163	石	260	船	473
経	391			館	275			飯	164	研	261	橋	479
疲	403	20 ク		堂	309	28 ⺡		産	265	員	269	信	484
暖	404	勉	122	覚	353	雨	102	度	283	図	273	調	485
取	433	晩	137	定	356	電	103	顔	290	回	284	談	488
最	434	色	158	受	358	冬	132	痛	343	頭	289	君	491
段	443	魚	159	授	359	料	161	疲	403	別	293	拾	499
投	457	急	248	寝	379	寒	229	座	474	合	295	捨	500
髪	506	争	388	宅	383	終	259	席	475	答	296	吸	502
		静	406	党	400	雪	494	危	497	同	298		
18 マ		負	450	窓	411					計	299	34 土	
予	170	絶	453	続	455	29 几		33 口		京	300	土	23
野	171	危	497	守	461	風	240	四	4	堂	309	寺	28
通	319			夢	463	役	366	口	15	品	317	時	29
冷	323	21 七		案	489	段	443	右	37	塩	330	生	55
痛	343	七	7			投	457	何	57	固	335	先	56
踊	380	切	173	24 丁				国	64	個	336	去	61
々	447			何	57	30 二		言	75	苦	342	待	78
		22 九		行	66	二	2	話	76	困	346	周	79
19 ⼇		九	9	町	100	午	42	周	79	感	351	週	80
午	42	究	262	歌	179	行	66	週	80	違	365	社	107
年	60			荷	373	会	72	高	83	部	370	走	114
毎	62	23 宀				元	87	古	86	荷	373	起	115
気	88	学	54	25 乂		転	181	店	109	踊	380	持	126
海	150	安	84	父	58	矢	194	読	119	活	381	赤	154
作	174	院	112	校	108			名	127	和	386	黒	157
矢	194			教	209			語	128	治	390	室	210
				文	220					議	399	遠	225
										党	400	軽	231
										涼	405		

洗 247
地 280
特 292
場 305
屋 308
堂 309
熱 322
塩 330
幸 340
徒 360
経 391
法 393
園 408
座 474
陸 477
調 485
達 492
捨 500

35
女
女 52
安 84
好 95
姉 198
妹 200
妻 203
始 258
怒 339
要 372
婚 419
娘 426
案 489

36
弓
弓 123
強 125
弟 199
弱 233
引 252

37
彳
後 41
行 66
待 78
徒 360
復 362
役 366
彼 368
律 394

38
忄
情 352
性 431

39
扌
持 126
押 251
授 359
払 377
招 432
投 457
拾 499
捨 500

40
氵
海 150
洋 190
漢 213
洗 247
注 287
池 313
汚 325
酒 329
消 334
泣 338
決 355
濯 378
活 381

治 390
済 392
法 393
泳 402
涼 405
泊 472
港 478

41
阝
院 112
都 310
部 370
際 395
階 442
陸 477
降 495
険 498

42
寸
寺 28
時 29
待 78
村 101
持 126
特 292
付 331
将 428
対 454
守 461

43
己
起 115
配 345
記 415
選 458
港 478

44
也
地 280
池 313
他 448

45
勹
約 459
的 464

46
辶
週 80
道 144
遠 225
近 226
運 241
送 246
通 319
進 320
違 365
遊 401
込 409
連 410
選 458
過 462
速 469
遅 470
達 492

47
宀
安 84
院 112
空 149
家 193
室 210
字 214
宿 218
寒 229
究 262

官 274
館 275
定 356
寝 379
宅 383
窓 411
守 461
案 489

48
艹
花 152
茶 169
菜 172
漢 213
英 221
薬 267
苦 342
荷 373
葉 413
若 423
夢 463

49
广
広 91
店 109
病 111
度 283
痛 343
疲 403
座 474
席 475

50
士
売 118
読 119
士 270
仕 271
声 291
吉 417

51
⺌
光 239
堂 309
消 334
党 400
当 509

52
⺍
学 54
菜 172
覚 353
受 358
授 359
戦 387

53
子
子 53
学 54
好 95
教 209
字 214
遊 401

54
尸
駅 106
昼 134
戸 306
所 307
屋 308
届 375
遅 470

55
夂
後 41

結 418
続 455

51
⺌
光 239
堂 309
消 334
党 400
当 509

56
夕
外 36
多 89
名 127
夕 135
死 256
夢 463

57
千
千 12
話 76
重 230
活 381
辞 456

58
工
工 38
左 39
空 149
式 215
試 216

59
幺
後 41
糸 206
紙 208
終 259
練 361
経 391
係 397
結 418

絶 453
続 455
約 459
機 466
絵 507
細 511

60 巾
市 99
雨 102
帰 121
姉 198
席 475

61 ヨ
曜 24
帰 121
急 248
濯 378
寝 379
雪 494
当 509

62 ヨ
書 120
妻 203
建 315
争 388
律 394
静 406
君 491

63 弋
式 215
試 216
代 278
貸 279

64 小
小 82
少 90
糸 206
紙 208
歩 244
終 259
京 300
県 311
練 361
祭 384
経 391
際 395
係 397
涼 405
景 414
結 418
歳 437
絶 453
続 455
約 459
絵 507
細 511

65 大
大 81
天 153
犬 160
矢 194
族 195
太 236
短 238
知 254
医 257
笑 337
奥 427
戻 501

66 彡
形 416
髪 506

67 丸
丸 321
熱 322

68 山
山 145
島 476

69 方
方 136
族 195
旅 318
遊 401
放 503

70 日
百 11
日 17
曜 24
時 29
間 44
東 45
早 92
明 94
春 129
朝 133
昼 134
晩 137
白 156
音 177
楽 178
映 187
習 212
宿 218
題 219
者 227
暑 228
暗 235
薬 267
借 277
意 288
場 305
都 310
復 362
皆 367
暖 404
景 414
婚 419
最 434
億 440
階 442
的 464
泊 472
星 493

71 木
木 21
本 25
東 45
米 67
新 85
村 101
校 108
休 113
秋 131
林 147
森 148
料 161
菜 172
未 175
楽 178
乗 182
親 196
私 201
薬 267
集 301
果 326
困 346
利 376
末 382
和 386
葉 413
番 436
枚 438
機 466
橋 479
様 483
査 486
相 487
案 489
歯 505
横 508

72 月
月 18
前 40
明 94
朝 133
青 155
豚 166
服 191
有 264
消 334
情 352
静 406
勝 449

73 歹
死 256
残 349

74 牛
牛 165

特 292
物 316

75 ネ
社 107
祖 429
初 435
神 482

76 戈
感 351
戦 387
義 398
議 399
歳 437
成 452
機 466

77 攵
教 209
政 389
枚 438
放 503

78 斤
新 85
質 222
近 226
所 307

79 欠
飲 71
歌 179
次 446

80 灬
馬 105
駅 106
黒 157
魚 159
鳥 167
験 217
熱 322
点 441
無 512

81 止
止 243
歩 244
正 297
踊 380
政 389
歳 437
歯 505

82 耂
教 209
者 227
暑 228
考 255
都 310
老 424

83 主
青 155
情 352
表 363
静 406

84 心
心 139
悪 234

急 248
思 253
意 288
怒 339
悲 341
恥 344
念 350
感 351
忘 354
必 371
窓 411
息 425

85 戸
戸 306
所 307
戻 501

86 云
会 72
転 181
絵 507
伝 510

87 王
王 63
国 64
理 162
主 204
住 205
注 287
全 369
駐 471

88 氏
氏 207
紙 208
低 232

民 286
婚 419

89 五
五 5
語 128

90 中
中 35
虫 124
強 125

91 父
父 58
校 108
交 480

92 元
元 87
院 112

93 止
走 114
起 115
足 141
題 219
定 356
徒 360

94 开
開 249
研 261
形 416

95 丬
年 60
違 365
降 495

96 夫
夫 202
漢 213
賛 451
失 467
鉄 468

97 文
文 220
済 392
対 454

98 火
火 19
秋 131
焼 333
勝 449
談 488

99 反
反 163
飯 164

100 内
肉 168
内 490

101 予
予 170
野 171

102 丑
昔 276
借 277
共 420
供 421
選 458
港 478
横 508

103 爫
菜 172
受 358
授 359
暖 404
将 428

104 勿
場 305
物 316

105 廿
度 283
席 475

106 友
友 96
暖 404
髪 506

107 今
今 27
念 350

108 少
少 90

歩 244

109 殳
役 366
段 443
投 457

110 化
化 151
花 152

111 比
比 357
皆 367

112 矢
矢 194
族 195
短 238
知 254
医 257

113 禾
秋 131
私 201
利 376
和 386

114 台
台 185
始 258
治 390

115 圣
軽 231

経 391

116 主
主 204
住 205
注 287
駐 471

117 目
目 16
見 65
貝 116
買 117
夏 130
首 143
道 144
自 180
真 184
着 192
親 196
題 219
質 222
員 269
貸 279
頭 289
顔 290
県 311
眠 348
覚 353
側 412
息 425
負 450
賛 451
相 487
直 496

118 田
田 49
男 51

町 100
電 103
黒 157
魚 159
理 162
画 188
思 253
留 263
界 282
番 436
細 511

119 广
病 111
痛 343
疲 403

120 用
用 285
通 319
痛 343
踊 380

121 穴
空 149
究 262
窓 411

122 立
立 77
新 85
音 177
乗 182
親 196
暗 235
産 265
意 288
顔 290

泣 338
辛 347
部 370
億 440
倍 445
辞 456

123 石
石 260
研 261

124 白
百 11
白 156
楽 178
習 212
宿 218
薬 267
皆 367
階 442
的 464
泊 472

125 古
古 86
固 335
個 336
苦 342

126 右
右 37
若 423

127 ⺍
学 54
覚 353
受 358

授 359

128 生
生 55
産 265
性 431
星 493

129 可
何 57
歌 179
荷 373

130 去
去 61
法 393

131 冬
冬 132
終 259

132 兄
兄 197
説 224
党 400

133 市
市 99
姉 198

134 央
央 186
映 187
英 221

135 本
本 25
体 142

136 民
民 286
眠 348

137 世
世 281
葉 413

138 代
代 278
貸 279

139 未
未 175
味 176
妹 200

140 由
由 374
届 375
横 508

141 失
失 467
鉄 468

142 申
申 481
神 482

143 且
祖 429
査 486

144 皿
皿 328
塩 330

145 正
正 297
政 389

146 皮
彼 368
疲 403

147 四
四 4
西 46

148 糸
糸 206
紙 208
終 259
練 361
経 391
係 397
結 418
絶 453
続 455
約 459
絵 507
細 511

149 耳
耳 73
聞 74
恥 344
取 433
最 434

150 舌
話 76
活 381
辞 456

151 寺
寺 28
時 29
待 78
持 126
特 292

152 自
夏 130
首 143
道 144
自 180
題 219
頭 289
顔 290
息 425

153 羽
羽 211
習 212

154 共
共 420
供 421

選 458

155 百
百 11
宿 218

156 米
米 67
来 68
料 161
奥 427
番 436
歯 505

157 竹
竹 294
答 296
笑 337

158 毎
毎 62
海 150

159 先
先 56
洗 247

160 交
校 108
交 480

161 艮
良 69
食 70
銀 110

娘 426

162 虫
虫 124
強 125
風 240

163 至
室 210
屋 308

164 式
式 215
試 216

165 色
色 158
絶 453

166 羊
羊 189
洋 190
着 192
業 266
義 398
議 399
遅 470
様 483
達 492

167 合
合 295
答 296
拾 499

168
安
安 84
案 489

169
吉
吉 417
結 418

170
关
送 246
関 396

171
争
争 388
静 406

172
会
会 72
絵 507

173
言
言 75
話 76
読 119
語 128
試 216
説 224
計 299
議 399
記 415
信 484
調 485
談 488

174
車
車 104
転 181
軽 231
運 241
連 410

175
貝
貝 116
買 117
題 219
質 222
員 269
貸 279
頭 289
顔 290
側 412
負 450
賛 451

176
里
黒 157
理 162
野 171

177
見
見 65
親 196
覚 353

178
良
良 69
食 70
娘 426

179
走
走 114
起 115
徒 360

180
売
売 118
読 119
続 455

181
豕
豚 166
家 193

182
鳥
鳥 167
島 476

183
足
足 141
踊 380

184
豆
豆 237
短 238
頭 289

185
酉
酒 329
配 345

186
辛
辛 347
辞 456

187
束
束 460
速 469

188
我
義 398
議 399

189
何
何 57
荷 373

190
金
金 22
銀 110
鉄 468

191
僉
験 217
険 498

192
門
門 43
間 44
聞 74
問 223
開 249
閉 250
関 396

193
隹
曜 24
集 301
進 320
濯 378

194
雨
雨 102
電 103
雪 494

195
周
周 79
週 80
調 485

196
者
者 227
暑 228
都 310

197
食
飲 71
飯 164
館 275

198
東
東 45
練 361

199
昔
昔 276
借 277

200
官
官 274
館 275

201
京
京 300

202
青
青 155
情 352
静 406

203
圥
熱 322
陸 477

204
固
固 335
個 336

205
頁
題 219
頭 289
顔 290

206
音
音 177
暗 235
意 288
億 440

207
亲
新 85
親 196

208
首
首 143
道 144

涼 405
景 414

209
重
重 230
動 242
働 268

210
馬
馬 105
駅 106
験 217
駐 471

211
袁
遠 225
園 408

212
祭
祭 384
際 395

213
動
動 242
働 268

214
楽
楽 178
薬 267

215
意
意 288
億 440

語彙さくいん (Vocabulary Index)

本書に収録されたすべての漢字語彙の読み方を五十音順に並べ、その語彙を収録している漢字と漢字番号を示した。

This index contains all the vocabulary appearing in this book, arranged in *a-i-u-e-o* order. The kanji entry where each word appears is also listed, along with its entry number.

あ

あいかわらず [相変わらず]	相	487
	変	504
あいしょう [相性]	性	431
あいず [合図]	図	273
あいだ [間]	間	44
あいて [相手]	相	487
あいどくしょ [愛読書]	読	119
あう [会う]	会	72
あう [合う]	合	295
あお [青]	青	155
あおい [青い]	青	155
あおしんごう [青信号]	青	155
あおぞら [青空]	青	155
あおもり [青森]	青	155
あか [赤]	赤	154
あかい [赤い]	赤	154
あかじ [赤字]	赤	154
あかちゃん [赤ちゃん]	赤	154
あかるい [明るい]	明	94
あき [秋]	秋	131
あきかぜ [秋風]	秋	131
あきがっき [秋学期]	秋	131
あきらか [明らか]	明	94
あく [空く]	空	149
あく [悪]	悪	234
あく [開く]	開	249
あくま [悪魔]	悪	234
あくむ [悪夢]	夢	463
あける [明ける]	明	94
あける [開ける]	開	249
あげる [上げる]	上	33
あさ [朝]	朝	133
あさいち [朝市]	市	99
あさごはん [朝ご飯]	朝	133
	飯	164

あさって [明後日]	明	94
あさねぼうする [朝寝坊する]	朝	133
あし [足]	足	141
あじ [味]	味	176
あしおと [足音]	足	141
あした [明日]	明	94
あしもと [足元]	元	87
あじわう [味わう]	味	176
あす [明日]	明	94
あそび [遊び]	遊	401
あそぶ [遊ぶ]	遊	401
あたたかい [暖かい]	暖	404
あたたまる [暖まる]	暖	404
あたためる [暖める]	暖	404
あたま [頭]	頭	289
あたらしい [新しい]	新	85
あたる [当たる]	当	509
あつい [暑い]	暑	228
あつい [熱い]	熱	322
あつまる [集まる]	集	301
あつめる [集める]	集	301
あてる [当てる]	当	509
あとで [後で]	後	41
あに [兄]	兄	197
あね [姉]	姉	198
あのかた [あの方]	方	136
あぶない [危ない]	危	497
あぶらえ [油絵]	絵	507
あまい [甘い]	甘	324
あまえる [甘える]	甘	324
あまのがわ [天の川]	川	146
	天	153
あまみず [雨水]	雨	102
あまやかす [甘やかす]	甘	324
あまやどり [雨宿り]	宿	218
あみど [網戸]	戸	306

あめ [雨]	雨	102
あやうい [危うい]	危	497
あやまち [過ち]	過	462
あゆみ [歩み]	歩	244
あらう [洗う]	洗	247
あらそい [争い]	争	388
あらそう [争う]	争	388
あらた [新た]	新	85
あらわす [表す]	表	363
ありがたい [有り難い]	有	264
ある [有る]	有	264
あるく [歩く]	歩	244
あん [案]	案	489
あんいな [安易な]	安	84
あんがい [案外]	案	489
あんきする [暗記する]	暗	235
	記	415
あんごう [暗号]	号	444
あんさつ [暗殺]	暗	235
あんしょうばんごう [暗証番号]	暗	235
あんしんする [安心する]	安	84
	心	139
あんせい [安静]	静	406
あんぜん [安全]	安	84
	全	369
あんてい [安定]	安	84
あんないする [案内する]	案	489
	内	490
あんのじょう [案の定]	案	489
あんらくし [安楽死]	死	256

い

いいわけ [言い訳]	言	75
いいん [医院]	院	112
	医	257
いう [言う]	言	75

いえ［家］	家	193
いか［〜以下］	以	304
いがい［〜以外］	以	304
いがいな［意外な］	外	36
	意	288
いがく［医学］	医	257
いかり［怒り］	怒	339
いき［息］	息	425
いきかえり［行き帰り］	帰	121
いきぎれ［息切れ］	息	425
いきぬき［息抜き］	息	425
いきる［生きる］	生	55
いきをする［息をする］	息	425
いく［行く］	行	66
いくさ［戦］	戦	387
いくじ［育児］	育	430
いけ［池］	池	313
いけばな［生け花］	花	152
いけん［意見］	見	65
	意	288
いご［以後］	以	304
いこう［〜以降］	降	495
いざかや［居酒屋］	酒	329
いし［医師］	医	257
いし［石］	石	260
いし［意思］	意	288
いじする［維持する］	持	126
いしゃ［医者］	者	227
	医	257
いじゅうする［移住する］	住	205
いじょう［〜以上］	以	304
いしょくじゅう［衣食住］	住	205
いじわるな［意地悪な］	悪	234
	地	280
	意	288
イスラムきょうと［イスラム教徒］	徒	360
いぜん［以前］	以	304
いそぐ［急ぐ］	急	248
いたい［痛い］	痛	343
いたみ［痛み］	痛	343
いたみどめ［痛み止め］	痛	343
いち［一］	一	1
いちおく［一億］	億	440
いちがつ［一月］	一	1

	月	18
いちがつなかば［一月半ば］	半	30
いちぎょうめ［一行目］	行	66
いちごうしゃ［一号車］	号	444
いちじ［一時］	一	1
	時	29
いちじかん［一時間］	時	29
いちだん［一段］	段	443
いちだんと［一段と］	段	443
いちど［一度］	度	283
いちにち［一日］	一	1
いちにちめ［一日目］	目	16
いちねん［一年］	年	60
いちねんじゅう［一年中］	中	35
いちば［市場］	市	99
	場	305
いちばん［一番］	一	1
	番	436
いちぶ［一部］	部	370
いちまい［一枚］	枚	438
いちまん［一万］	万	13
いちりつに［一律に］	律	394
いちわ［一羽］	羽	211
いつか［五日］	五	5
いっかい［一回］	回	284
いっかげつ［一か月］	月	18
いっこ［一個］	個	336
いっさい［一切］	切	173
いっさつ［一冊］	冊	439
いっしゅうかん［一週間］	間	44
	週	80
いっしゅうねん［一周年］	周	79
いっしょう［一生］	生	55
いっしょう［一勝］	勝	449
いっせきにちょう［一石二鳥］	鳥	167
いっそく［一足］	足	141
いっちょういっせき［一朝一夕］	夕	135
いつつ［五つ］	五	5
いっつい［一対］	対	454
いっぱくする［一泊する］	泊	472
いっぷたさい［一夫多妻］	妻	203
いっぷん［一分］	一	1
いっぽ［一歩］	歩	244
いっぽん［一本］	本	25

いでんし［遺伝子］	伝	510
いと［糸］	糸	206
いと［意図］	図	273
いど［井戸］	戸	306
いない［〜以内］	以	304
いなか［田舎］	田	49
いぬ［犬］	犬	160
いねむり［居眠り］	眠	348
いはん［違反］	反	163
	違	365
いほう［違法］	法	393
いま［今］	今	27
いみ［意味］	味	176
	意	288
いもうと［妹］	妹	200
いやくひん［医薬品］	医	257
いらい［〜以来］	以	304
いりぐち［入り口／入口］	口	15
	入	97
いりょう［医療］	医	257
いる［要る］	要	372
いれる［入れる］	入	97
いろ［色］	色	158
いろいろな［色々な］	色	158
	々	447
いろえんぴつ［色鉛筆］	色	158
いんしゅうんてん［飲酒運転］	飲	71
	酒	329
いんしょくてん［飲食店］	飲	71
いんよう［引用］	引	252
いんりょうすい［飲料水］	飲	71
いんりょく［引力］	引	252

う

ういういしい［初々しい］	初	435
うえ［上］	上	33
うおいちば［魚市場］	魚	159
うかる［受かる］	受	358
うき［雨季］	雨	102
うきよえ［浮世絵］	絵	507
うけつけ［受付／受け付け］	付	331
	受	358
うけとる［受け取る］	受	358
	取	433

うけみ［受け身／受身］	受	358
うける［受ける］	受	358
うごく［動く］	動	242
うし［牛］	牛	165
うじがみ［氏神］	氏	207
うしなう［失う］	失	467
うしろ［後ろ］	後	41
うた［歌］	歌	179
うたう［歌う］	歌	179
うち［内］	内	490
うちあける［打ち明ける］	明	94
うちがわ［内側］	側	412
うつす［写す］	写	183
うつす［映す］	映	187
うつる［映る］	映	187
うま［馬］	馬	105
うまごや［馬小屋］	馬	105
うまれる［生まれる］	生	55
うみ［海］	海	150
うむ［有無］	有	264
うむ［産む］	産	265
うもう［羽毛］	羽	211
うよく［右翼］	右	37
うらないのやかた［占いの館］	館	275
うりきれる［売り切れる］	売	118
うりば［売り場］	売	118
	場	305
うる［売る］	売	118
うれしなき［嬉し泣き］	泣	338
うれる［売れる］	売	118
うわぎ［上着］	上	33
	着	192
うんがいい［運がいい］	運	241
うんちん［運賃］	運	241
うんてん［運転］	転	181
	運	241
うんてんしゅ［運転手］	転	181
	運	241
うんどう［運動］	運	241
	動	242
うんめい［運命］	運	241

え

え［絵］	絵	507

えいえんの［永遠の］	遠	225
えいが［映画］	映	187
	画	188
えいかいわ［英会話］	英	221
えいがかん［映画館］	映	187
	館	275
えいぎょうちゅう［営業中］	業	266
えいご［英語］	語	128
	英	221
えいこく［英国］	英	221
えいせい［衛星］	星	493
えいぶん［英文］	文	220
えいゆう［英雄］	英	221
えいわじてん［英和辞典］	英	221
	和	386
エーゲかい［エーゲ海］	海	150
えがお［笑顔］	顔	290
	笑	337
えき［駅］	駅	106
えきいん［駅員］	駅	106
えきまえ［駅前］	駅	106
えしゃく［会釈］	会	72
えだまめ［枝豆］	豆	237
エデンのその［エデンの園］	園	408
えどじだい［江戸時代］	戸	306
えのぐ［絵の具］	絵	507
えほん［絵本］	絵	507
えらぶ［選ぶ］	選	458
えん［円］	円	14
えんげい［園芸］	園	408
えんそく［遠足］	足	141
	遠	225
えんだか［円高］	円	14
	高	83
えんぶん［塩分］	塩	330
えんぽう［遠方］	遠	225
えんまん［円満］	円	14
えんやす［円安］	円	14
	安	84
えんりょする［遠慮する］	遠	225

お

おいる［老いる］	老	424
おう［王］	王	63

おうこく［王国］	王	63
おうさま［王様］	王	63
	様	483
おうじ［王子］	王	63
おうしざ［牡牛座］	牛	165
おうしゅうする［押収する］	押	251
おうじょ［王女］	王	63
おうだんする［横断する］	横	508
おうだんほどう［横断歩道］	横	508
おうふく［往復］	復	362
おうべい［欧米］	米	67
おえる［終える］	終	259
おおあめ［大雨］	雨	102
おおい［多い］	多	89
おおうりだし［大売り出し］	売	118
おおきい［大きい］	大	81
おおざら［大皿］	皿	328
おおぞら［大空］	空	149
おおのし［大野氏］	氏	207
おおむかし［大昔］	昔	276
おおや［大家］	大	81
	家	193
おおやけの［公の］	公	407
おおゆき［大雪］	雪	494
おかあさん［お母さん］	母	59
おかね［お金］	金	22
おかねもち［お金持ち］	金	22
	持	126
おがわ［小川］	小	82
おがわさん［小川さん］	川	146
おかん［悪寒］	悪	234
おきゃくさま［お客様］	様	483
おきょう［お経］	経	391
おきる［起きる］	起	115
おく［奥］	奥	427
おくさん［奥さん］	奥	427
おくじょう［屋上］	上	33
	屋	308
おくば［奥歯］	奥	427
おくまんちょうじゃ［億万長者］	億	440
おくゆかしい［奥ゆかしい］	奥	427
おくゆき［奥行き］	奥	427
おくる［送る］	送	246
おくれ［遅れ］	遅	470

おくれる [後れる]	後	41
おくれる [遅れる]	遅	470
おこす [起こす]	起	115
おこなう [行う]	行	66
おこのみやき [お好み焼き]	好	95
おこめ [お米]	米	67
おこる [起こる]	起	115
おこる [怒る]	怒	339
おさえる [押さえる]	押	251
おさけ [お酒]	酒	329
おさめる [治める]	治	390
おさら [お皿]	皿	328
おじ [叔父／伯父]	父	58
おしいれ [押し入れ]	押	251
おしえる [教える]	教	209
おしだす [押し出す]	押	251
おしょうがつ [お正月]	月	18
	正	297
おしょく [汚職]	汚	325
おす [押す]	押	251
おせいぼ [お歳暮]	歳	437
おせじ [お世辞]	世	281
	辞	456
おせん [汚染]	汚	325
おそい [遅い]	遅	470
おそわる [教わる]	教	209
おたく [お宅]	宅	383
おちつく [落ち着く]	着	192
おちば [落ち葉]	葉	413
おちゃ [お茶]	茶	169
おつかい [お使い]	使	245
おっと [夫]	夫	202
おてあらい [お手洗い]	手	140
	洗	247
おてら [お寺]	寺	28
おと [音]	音	177
おとうさん [お父さん]	父	58
おとうと [弟]	弟	199
おとこのこ [男の子]	男	51
	子	53
おとこのひと [男の人]	男	51
おとな [大人]	人	26
	大	81
おともする [お供する]	供	421

おどり [踊り]	踊	380
おどる [踊る]	踊	380
おなじ [同じ]	同	298
おにいさん [お兄さん]	兄	197
おねえさん [お姉さん]	姉	198
おのさん [小野さん]	野	171
おば [叔母／伯母]	母	59
おばけ [お化け]	化	151
おふろ [お風呂]	風	240
おべんとう [お弁当]	当	509
おぼえる [覚える]	覚	353
おまもり [お守り]	守	461
おみやげ [お土産]	土	23
	産	265
おもい [重い]	重	230
おもいがけない [思いがけない]	思	253
おもいきり [思い切り]	思	253
おもいこむ [思い込む]	込	409
おもいだす [思い出す]	出	98
	思	253
おもいで [思い出]	思	253
おもう [思う]	思	253
おもしろい [面白い]	白	156
おもて [表]	表	363
おもに [主に]	主	204
おもに [重荷]	荷	373
おや [親]	親	196
おやこ [親子]	親	196
およぐ [泳ぐ]	泳	402
おりがみ [折り紙]	紙	208
おりる [降りる]	降	495
おろす [下ろす]	下	34
おろす [降ろす]	降	495
おわり [終わり]	終	259
おわる [終わる]	終	259
おんがく [音楽]	音	177
	楽	178
おんしつ [温室]	室	210
おんせいがく [音声学]	声	291
おんだんな [温暖な]	暖	404
おんど [温度]	度	283
おんど [音頭]	頭	289
おんなのこ [女の子]	女	52
	子	53

おんなのひと [女の人]	人	26
	女	52
おんりょう [音量]	音	177

か

かい [貝]	貝	116
かいいん [会員]	員	269
かいが [絵画]	画	188
	絵	507
かいがい [海外]	外	36
	海	150
かいかいしき [開会式]	開	249
かいがら [貝殻]	貝	116
かいかん [会館]	館	275
かいがん [海岸]	海	150
かいぎ [会議]	会	72
	議	399
かいぎしつ [会議室]	室	210
かいきゅう [階級]	階	442
かいきん [皆勤]	皆	367
かいけい [会計]	計	299
かいけいし [会計士]	士	270
かいけつ [解決]	決	355
がいこうかん [外交官]	官	274
	交	480
がいこく [外国]	外	36
	国	64
がいこくご [外国語]	語	128
がいこくじん [外国人]	外	36
かいざいく [貝細工]	貝	116
かいしする [開始する]	開	249
	始	258
かいしめる [買い占める]	買	117
かいしゃ [会社]	会	72
	社	107
かいしゃいん [会社員]	会	72
	員	269
かいじょう [会場]	会	72
	場	305
かいすい [海水]	海	150
かいすいよく [海水浴]	水	20
かいすうけん [回数券]	回	284
かいせつ [解説]	説	224
かいそう [海藻]	海	150

かいそうでんしゃ［回送電車］	送	246
かいぞく［海賊］	海	150
かいそくでんしゃ［快速電車］	速	469
かいだん［階段］	階	442
	段	443
かいだん［会談］	談	488
かいて［買い手］	買	117
かいてん［開店］	開	249
かいてん［回転］	回	284
かいてんずし［回転ずし］	転	181
かいとう［回答］	回	284
	答	296
かいとう［解答］	答	296
がいねん［概念］	念	350
かいふく［回復］	回	284
	復	362
かいほうする［開放する］	放	503
かいほうする［解放する］	放	503
かいむ［皆無］	皆	367
かいもく［皆目］	皆	367
かいもの［買い物］	買	117
	物	316
かいりつ［戒律］	律	394
かいわ［会話］	会	72
	話	76
かう［買う］	買	117
かえり［帰り］	帰	121
かえる［帰る］	帰	121
かえる［変える］	変	504
かお［顔］	顔	290
かおつき［顔つき］	顔	290
かかわる［関わる］	関	396
がか［画家］	画	188
かがく［化学］	化	151
かかり［係］	係	397
かかりいん［係員］	係	397
かかる［係る］	係	397
かきとめ［書き留め／書留］	留	263
かきはじめる［書き始める］	始	258
かく［書く］	書	120
がくえんさい［学園祭］	祭	384
がくしゃ［学者］	学	54
	者	227
がくしゅう［学習］	学	54
	習	212
かくすう［画数］	画	188
がくせい［学生］	学	54
	生	55
がくぶ［学部］	学	54
がくもん［学問］	問	223
がくりょく［学力］	力	50
かけい［家計］	計	299
かこ［過去］	去	61
	過	462
かこう［下降］	降	495
かこけい［過去形］	形	416
かさい［火災］	火	19
かさねる［重ねる］	重	230
かざん［火山］	火	19
	山	145
かし［歌詞］	歌	179
かし［華氏］	氏	207
かじ［火事］	火	19
	事	272
かじ［家事］	家	193
かしかり［貸し借り］	借	277
かしきり［貸し切り］	貸	279
かしだし［貸し出し］	貸	279
かじつ［果実］	果	326
かしゅ［歌手］	手	140
	歌	179
かしらもじ［頭文字］	頭	289
かす［貸す］	貸	279
かぜ［風］	風	240
かぜ［風邪］	風	240
かせい［火星］	火	19
	星	493
かぜぐすり［風邪薬］	薬	267
かせつ［仮説］	説	224
かせん［河川］	川	146
がそ［画素］	画	188
かぞく［家族］	家	193
	族	195
かたい［固い］	固	335
かだい［課題］	題	219
かたがき［肩書き］	書	120
かたこと［片言］	片	332
かたち［形］	形	416
かたづける［片付ける］	付	331
	片	332
かたて［片手］	片	332
かたな［刀］	刀	31
かたほう［片方］	片	332
かたまる［固まる］	固	335
かたみ［形見］	形	416
かたみち［片道］	道	144
	片	332
かたよる［片寄る］	片	332
かたる［語る］	語	128
かちまけ［勝ち負け］	負	450
かつ［勝つ］	勝	449
かっき［活気］	活	381
がっき［楽器］	楽	178
がっこう［学校］	学	54
	校	108
かつじ［活字］	字	214
	活	381
がっしゅく［合宿］	合	295
かってに［勝手に］	勝	449
かつどう［活動］	動	242
	活	381
かっぱつな［活発な］	活	381
かつやくする［活躍する］	活	381
かつよう［活用］	活	381
かてい［家庭］	家	193
かどまつ［門松］	門	43
かない［家内］	家	193
	内	490
かなしい［悲しい］	悲	341
かなしむ［悲しむ］	悲	341
かなづち［金づち］	金	22
かならず［必ず］	必	371
かならずしも［必ずしも］	必	371
かねつ［加熱］	熱	322
かのじょ［彼女］	女	52
	彼	368
かはんすう［過半数］	過	462
かびん［花瓶］	花	152
かふんしょう［花粉症］	花	152
かみ［紙］	紙	208
かみ［神］	神	482
かみ［髪］	髪	506

かみがた［髪型］	髪 506	
かみくず［紙くず］	紙 208	
かみコップ［紙コップ］	紙 208	
かみさま［神様］	神 482	
	様 483	
かみざら［紙皿］	皿 328	
かみのけ［髪の毛］	髪 506	
かもく［科目］	目 16	
かもつせん［貨物船］	船 473	
かよう［通う］	通 319	
かようび［火曜日］	火 19	
	曜 24	
からい［辛い］	辛 347	
からし［辛子］	辛 347	
からだ［体］	体 142	
からっぽ［空っぽ］	空 149	
からて［空手］	空 149	
かりる［借りる］	借 277	
かるい［軽い］	軽 231	
かれ［彼］	彼 368	
かれし［彼氏］	氏 207	
	彼 368	
かれら［彼ら］	彼 368	
かろやかに［軽やかに］	軽 231	
かわ［川］	川 146	
かわあそび［川遊び］	川 146	
かわかみ［川上］	上 33	
かわぎし［川岸］	川 146	
かわしも［川下］	下 34	
かわす［交わす］	交 480	
かわりに［代わりに］	代 278	
かわる［変わる］	変 504	
かんがえ［考え］	考 255	
かんがえかた［考え方］	考 255	
かんがえる［考える］	考 255	
かんかく［感覚］	覚 353	
かんき［寒気］	寒 229	
かんけい［関係］	関 396	
	係 397	
かんげきする［感激する］	感 351	
かんこう［観光］	光 239	
かんこく［韓国］	国 64	
がんこな［頑固な］	固 335	
かんさい［関西］	西 46	

	関 396	
かんじ［漢字］	漢 213	
	字 214	
かんじ［感じ］	感 351	
がんじつ［元日］	元 87	
かんしゃ［感謝］	感 351	
かんじょう［感情］	情 352	
かんじょう［勘定］	定 356	
かんじる［感じる］	感 351	
かんしん［関心］	関 396	
かんしんする［感心する］	心 139	
	感 351	
かんせい［完成］	成 452	
かんぜんな［完全な］	全 369	
がんそ［元祖］	祖 429	
かんそう［感想］	感 351	
かんたい［寒帯］	寒 229	
かんちがい［勘違い］	違 365	
かんちょう［官庁］	官 274	
かんとう［関東］	東 45	
	関 396	
かんどうする［感動する］	動 242	
	感 351	
かんびょうする［看病する］	病 111	
かんぷう［寒風］	寒 229	
かんぶん［漢文］	漢 213	
かんぽうやく［漢方薬］	漢 213	
かんみりょう［甘味料］	甘 324	
かんりょう［官僚］	官 274	
かんれん［関連］	連 410	
かんわじてん［漢和辞典］	漢 213	

き

き［木］	木 21	
きえる［消える］	消 334	
きか［帰化］	帰 121	
きかい［機会］	機 466	
きかい［機械］	機 466	
きがい［危害］	危 497	
ぎかい［議会］	議 399	
きかがく［幾何学］	何 57	
きがるに［気軽に］	軽 231	
きかん［器官］	官 274	
きかん［機関］	機 466	

きき［危機］	機 466	
	危 497	
ききとり［聞き取り］	取 433	
ききとる［聞き取る］	聞 74	
きぎょう［企業］	業 266	
きぎょうする［起業する］	起 115	
きく［聞く］	聞 74	
ぎけい［義兄］	兄 197	
きけん［危険］	危 497	
	険 498	
きげん［起源］	起 115	
きげん［機嫌］	機 466	
きげんぜん［紀元前］	元 87	
きごう［記号］	号 444	
きこえる［聞こえる］	聞 74	
きこく［帰国］	帰 121	
きこん［既婚］	婚 419	
きじ［記事］	記 415	
きしゃ［記者］	者 227	
	記 415	
きしょう［起床］	起 115	
ぎせいご［擬声語］	声 291	
きぜつする［気絶する］	絶 453	
きぞく［貴族］	族 195	
きた［北］	北 48	
ぎだい［議題］	題 219	
	議 399	
きたいする［期待する］	待 78	
きたく［帰宅］	帰 121	
	宅 383	
きたく［北区］	区 312	
きたぐち［北口］	口 15	
	北 48	
きたちょうせん［北朝鮮］	朝 133	
きたない［汚い］	汚 325	
きたやまちょう［北山町］	町 100	
きたやままち［北山町］	町 100	
きたる［来る］	来 68	
きち［吉］	吉 417	
きちじつ［吉日］	吉 417	
きちょうひん［貴重品］	重 230	
きっきょう［吉凶］	吉 417	
きっさてん［喫茶店］	店 109	
	茶 169	

きって [切手]	手	140
	切	173
きっぷ [切符]	切	173
きっぽう [吉報]	吉	417
ぎてい [義弟]	弟	199
きとく [危篤]	危	497
きにいる [気に入る]	気	88
	入	97
きにゅうする [記入する]	記	415
きねん [記念]	念	350
	記	415
きねんび [記念日]	念	350
きのう [機能]	機	466
きふ [寄付]	付	331
きぶん [気分]	分	32
きます [来ます]	来	68
きまつしけん [期末試験]	末	382
きまる [決まる]	決	355
きみ [君]	君	491
ぎむ [義務]	義	398
きむらさん [木村さん]	木	21
きめる [決める]	決	355
きもち [気持ち]	気	88
	持	126
きもの [着物]	着	192
	物	316
ぎもん [疑問]	問	223
きゃくせき [客席]	席	475
きゃくせん [客船]	船	473
きゅう [九]	九	9
きゅうきゅうしゃ [救急車]	車	104
	急	248
きゅうきょくの [究極の]	究	262
きゅうこう [休講]	休	113
きゅうこう [急行]	急	248
きゅうこんする [求婚する]	婚	419
きゅうさい [九歳]	九	9
きゅうさい [救済]	済	392
きゅうじ [給仕]	仕	271
きゅうじつ [休日]	日	17
	休	113
きゅうしゅう [吸収]	吸	502
きゅうそく [休息]	息	425
きゅうどう [弓道]	弓	123
ぎゅうどん [牛丼]	牛	165
きゅうに [急に]	急	248
ぎゅうにく [牛肉]	牛	165
	肉	168
ぎゅうにゅう [牛乳]	牛	165
きゅうにん [九人]	九	9
きゅうねん [九年]	九	9
きゅうびょう [急病]	病	111
きゅうめい [究明]	究	262
きゅうよう [急用]	急	248
きゅうりょう [給料]	料	161
きょう [今日]	日	17
	今	27
きょういく [教育]	教	209
	育	430
きょういん [教員]	員	269
きょうえい [競泳]	泳	402
きょうかい [教会]	教	209
きょうかい [境界]	界	282
ぎょうかい [業界]	界	282
きょうがく [共学]	共	420
きょうかしょ [教科書]	書	120
	教	209
きょうかする [強化する]	強	125
きょうかんする [共感する]	共	420
きょうきゅうする [供給する]	供	421
きょうけんびょう [狂犬病]	犬	160
きょうこ [京子]	京	300
きょうさんしゅぎ [共産主義]	産	265
	共	420
きょうし [教師]	教	209
ぎょうじ [行事]	行	66
きょうしつ [教室]	教	209
	室	210
きょうじゅ [教授]	教	209
	授	359
ぎょうせい [行政]	政	389
きょうせいする [強制する]	強	125
きょうそ [教祖]	祖	429
きょうそうする [競争する]	争	388
きょうだい [兄弟]	兄	197
	弟	199
きょうちょうする [強調する]	強	125
	調	485
きょうつう [共通]	共	420
きょうと [京都]	京	300
	都	310
きょうどう [共同]	同	298
	共	420
きょうみ [興味]	味	176
きょうりょくする [協力する]	力	50
きょうわこく [共和国]	和	386
ぎょかいるい [魚介類]	魚	159
ぎょそん [漁村]	村	101
きょねん [去年]	年	60
	去	61
きよみずでら [清水寺]	寺	28
ぎり [義理]	義	398
キリストきょうと [キリスト教徒]	徒	360
きりつ [規律]	律	394
きりつする [起立する]	起	115
きる [切る]	切	173
きる [着る]	着	192
きろく [記録]	記	415
ぎろんする [議論する]	議	399
きわだつ [際立つ]	際	395
きわめる [究める]	究	262
きをつける [気をつける]	気	88
ぎん [銀]	銀	110
ぎんいろ [銀色]	銀	110
ぎんが [銀河]	銀	110
きんかくじ [金閣寺]	寺	28
きんきゅう [緊急]	急	248
きんぎょ [金魚]	魚	159
ぎんこう [銀行]	行	66
	銀	110
ぎんこういん [銀行員]	員	269
きんし [近視]	近	226
きんしする [禁止する]	止	243
きんじょ [近所]	近	226
	所	307
きんだいてきな [近代的な]	近	226
きんにく [筋肉]	肉	168
きんぱつ [金髪]	髪	506
きんべんな [勤勉な]	勉	122
きんようび [金曜日]	金	22
	曜	24

く

く［九］	九	9
くいき［区域］	区	312
くう［食う］	食	70
くうき［空気］	空	149
くうこう［空港］	空	149
	港	478
くうせき［空席］	席	475
くがつ［九月］	九	9
くかん［区間］	区	312
くぎる［区切る］	区	312
くじ［九時］	九	9
くじょう［苦情］	苦	342
	情	352
くすり［薬］	薬	267
くすりや［薬屋］	薬	267
くすりゆび［薬指］	薬	267
ください［下さい］	下	34
くだもの［果物］	物	316
	果	326
くち［口］	口	15
くちょう［口調］	口	15
くつう［苦痛］	苦	342
	痛	343
くとうてん［句読点］	読	119
	点	441
くに［国］	国	64
くにん［九人］	九	9
くねん［九年］	九	9
くばる［配る］	配	345
くび［首］	首	143
くびになる［首になる］	首	143
くふう［工夫］	工	38
	夫	202
くべつする［区別する］	区	312
くやくしょ［区役所］	区	312
くよう［供養］	供	421
くらい［暗い］	暗	235
クラスのあと［クラスの後］	後	41
くらべる［比べる］	比	357
くる［来る］	来	68
くるしい［苦しい］	苦	342
くるしむ［苦しむ］	苦	342
くるま［車］	車	104

くるまいす［車いす］	車	104
くろ［黒］	黒	157
くろい［黒い］	黒	157
くろう［苦労］	苦	342
くろかみ［黒髪］	髪	506
くろじ［黒字］	黒	157
くろねこ［黒猫］	黒	157
くんしゅ［君主］	君	491
くんれん［訓練］	練	361

け

けいえい［経営］	経	391
けいかく［計画］	画	188
	計	299
けいかん［警官］	官	274
けいき［景気］	景	414
けいけん［経験］	験	217
	経	391
けいご［敬語］	語	128
けいざい［経済］	経	391
	済	392
けいざいがく［経済学］	済	392
けいさんする［計算する］	計	299
けいじどうしゃ［軽自動車］	軽	231
けいそつな［軽率な］	軽	231
けいだい［境内］	内	490
けいと［毛糸］	糸	206
けいば［競馬］	馬	105
けいはんしん［京阪神］	京	300
けいひん［景品］	景	414
けいべつ［軽蔑］	軽	231
けいやく［契約］	約	459
けいようし［形容詞］	形	416
けいれき［経歴］	経	391
げか［外科］	外	36
けがれる［汚れる］	汚	325
けさ［今朝］	今	27
	朝	133
げし［夏至］	夏	130
けしき［景色］	色	158
	景	414
げしゅく［下宿］	宿	218
けしょう［化粧］	化	151
けす［消す］	消	334

けっか［結果］	果	326
	結	418
けっきょく［結局］	結	418
けっこう［結構］	結	418
けっこんしき［結婚式］	式	215
けっこんする［結婚する］	結	418
	婚	419
けっして［決して］	決	355
けっしょう［決勝］	決	355
	勝	449
けっしん［決心］	決	355
けっせき［欠席］	席	475
けっせきとどけ［欠席届］	届	375
けってい［決定］	決	355
	定	356
けってん［欠点］	点	441
げつまつ［月末］	末	382
げつようび［月曜日］	月	18
	曜	24
けつろん［結論］	結	418
けはい［気配］	気	88
げひんな［下品な］	品	317
けわしいやま［険しい山］	険	498
げん［元］	元	87
けんあくな［険悪な］	険	498
けんえんのなか［犬猿の仲］	犬	160
げんかい［限界］	界	282
けんがく［見学］	見	65
げんかん［玄関］	関	396
げんきな［元気な］	元	87
	気	88
けんきゅう［研究］	研	261
	究	262
けんきゅうしつ［研究室］	室	210
	研	261
	究	262
けんきゅうしゃ［研究者］	者	227
	研	261
	究	262
けんきゅうしょ／けんきゅう じょ［研究所］	研	261
げんきん［現金］	金	22
げんごがく［言語学］	言	75
けんこく［建国］	建	315

けんさ [検査]	査	486
げんざいけい [現在形]	形	416
げんしてきな [原始的な]	始	258
けんしゅう [研修]	研	261
げんしょう [減少]	少	90
けんせつ [建設]	建	315
げんだい [現代]	代	278
けんちく [建築]	建	315
けんちじ [県知事]	県	311
けんちょう [県庁]	県	311
げんど [限度]	度	283
けんぶつ [見物]	見	65
けんぽう [憲法]	法	393
けんり [権利]	利	376
けんりつ [県立]	県	311

こ

ご [五]	五	5
こいぬ [子犬]	犬	160
こうい [好意]	好	95
	意	288
こううん [幸運]	幸	340
こうえん [公園]	公	407
	園	408
こうか [校歌]	校	108
	歌	179
こうか [効果]	果	326
こうかい [公開]	開	249
	公	407
こうかいどう [公会堂]	堂	309
こうがく [工学]	工	38
こうがくぶ [工学部]	部	370
こうかん [好感]	好	95
こうかん [交換]	交	480
こうぎ [講義]	義	398
こうきゅう [高級]	高	83
ごうきゅうする [号泣する]	泣	338
こうきょう [公共]	共	420
こうぎょう [工業]	工	38
	業	266
こうくうびん [航空便]	空	149
	便	303
こうけい [光景]	光	239
	景	414

ごうけい [合計]	計	299
こうこう [高校]	高	83
	校	108
こうこうせい [高校生]	高	83
こうこがく [考古学]	古	86
	考	255
こうこく [広告]	広	91
こうざ [口座]	座	474
こうさい [交際]	際	395
こうさてん [交差点]	点	441
	交	480
こうし [子牛]	牛	165
こうじ [工事]	工	38
こうしゃ [校舎]	校	108
こうしゅう [公衆]	公	407
こうじょう [工場]	工	38
	場	305
こうしんりょう [香辛料]	辛	347
こうすい [香水]	水	20
こうすいりょう [降水量]	降	495
こうせつ [降雪]	雪	494
こうせん [光線]	光	239
こうそくどうろ [高速道路]	速	469
こうたいし [皇太子]	太	236
こうちゃ [紅茶]	茶	169
こうちょう [校長]	校	108
こうつう [交通]	通	319
こうつうじこ [交通事故]	交	480
こうてい [高低]	低	232
こうていする [肯定する]	定	356
こうどう [行動]	行	66
こうどう [講堂]	堂	309
ごうとう [強盗]	強	125
こうねつひ [光熱費]	光	239
こうはん [後半]	後	41
こうばん [交番]	番	436
	交	480
こうふくな [幸福な]	幸	340
こうべ [神戸]	神	482
こうへい [公平]	平	385
	公	407
こうべこう [神戸港]	港	478
こうま [子馬]	馬	105
こうむいん [公務員]	員	269

	公	407
こうよう [紅葉]	葉	413
こうりつ [公立]	公	407
こうりょする [考慮する]	考	255
こえ [声]	声	291
こえがわり [声変わり]	声	291
コーヒーまめ [コーヒー豆]	豆	237
こかげ [木陰]	木	21
ごがつ [五月]	五	5
こきゅうする [呼吸する]	吸	502
こくおう [国王]	王	63
こくさい [国際]	国	64
	際	395
こくさいか [国際化]	際	395
こくさいかんけい [国際関係]	関	396
	係	397
こくさいてき [国際的]	的	464
こくさいれんごう [国際連合]	連	410
こくせき [国籍]	国	64
こくない [国内]	国	64
	内	490
こくばん [黒板]	黒	157
こくふくする [克服する]	服	191
こくみん [国民]	民	286
こくりつだいがく [国立大学]	立	77
こくれん [国連]	連	410
ごご [午後]	後	41
	午	42
ここのか [九日]	九	9
ここのつ [九つ]	九	9
こころ [心]	心	139
こころぼそい [心細い]	細	511
こころみる [試みる]	試	216
ごさい [五歳]	五	5
	歳	437
こざかな [小魚]	魚	159
こざら [小皿]	皿	328
ごじ [五時]	五	5
こしつ [個室]	個	336
こじん [個人]	個	336
こじんしゅぎ [個人主義]	個	336
こすう [個数]	個	336
こせい [個性]	個	336
こせき [戸籍]	戸	306

ごぜん［午前］　前　40
　　　　　　　午　42
ごぜんちゅう［午前中］　前　40
　　　　　　　午　42
こたい［固体］　固　335
こだい［古代］　古　86
こたえ［答え］　答　296
こたえる［答える］　答　296
ごちそう［ご馳走］　走　114
こっか［国歌］　歌　179
こっかい［国会］　国　64
　　　　　　　会　72
こっかいぎいん［国会議員］　議　399
こっかいぎじどう［国会議事堂］　堂　309
こづつみ［小包］　小　82
こてい［固定］　固　335
こてん［個展］　個　336
こと［古都］　古　86
こと［事］　事　272
ことし［今年］　今　27
　　　　　　　年　60
ことば［言葉］　言　75
　　　　　　　葉　413
こども［子供］　子　53
　　　　　　　供　421
ことり［小鳥］　鳥　167
こない［来ない］　来　68
ごにん［五人］　五　5
ごねん［五年］　五　5
このみ［好み］　好　95
このむ［好む］　好　95
こばやしさん［小林さん］　林　147
ごはん［ご飯］　飯　164
こひつじ［小羊］　羊　189
こぶた［子豚］　豚　166
ごふん［五分］　分　32
こまかい［細かい］　細　511
こまる［困る］　困　346
こむ［込む］　込　409
こむぎ［小麦］　小　82
（お）こめ［（お）米］　米　67
こめや［米屋］　米　67
こもりうた［子守歌］　守　461
こゆうの［固有の］　固　335

ごらく［娯楽］　楽　178
ころがる［転がる］　転　181
ころぶ［転ぶ］　転　181
こわいろ［声色］　声　291
こんいんとどけ［婚姻届］　届　375
こんかい［今回］　回　284
こんげつ［今月］　月　18
　　　　　　　今　27
こんじゃく［今昔］　昔　276
こんしゅう［今週］　今　27
　　　　　　　週　80
こんだんかい［懇談会］　談　488
こんちゅう［昆虫］　虫　124
こんど［今度］　今　27
　　　　　　　度　283
こんなんな［困難な］　困　346
こんばん［今晩］　今　27
　　　　　　　晩　137
こんや［今夜］　夜　138
こんやく［婚約］　婚　419
こんやく［婚約］　約　459
こんやくしゃ［婚約者］　婚　419
こんりゅう［建立］　立　77
　　　　　　　建　315
こんわく［困惑］　困　346

さ

〜さい［〜際］　際　395
さいあく［最悪］　悪　234
さいえん［菜園］　菜　172
さいきん［最近］　近　226
　　　　　　　最　434
さいきん［細菌］　細　511
さいく［細工］　工　38
　　　　　　　細　511
さいげつ［歳月］　歳　437
さいご［最後］　後　41
　　　　　　　最　434
さいこう［最高］　高　83
　　　　　　　最　434
ざいさん［財産］　産　265
さいし［妻子］　妻　203
さいじつ［祭日］　祭　384
さいしゅう［最終］　終　259

さいしゅうでんしゃ［最終電車］　最　434
さいしゅつ［歳出］　歳　437
さいしょ［最初］　最　434
　　　　　　　初　435
さいしょくしゅぎ［菜食主義］　菜　172
さいしん［最新］　最　434
ざいせい［財政］　政　389
さいてい［最低］　低　232
　　　　　　　最　434
さいにゅう［歳入］　歳　437
さいばんかん［裁判官］　官　274
さいぼう［細胞］　細　511
さいみんじゅつ［催眠術］　眠　348
ざいもく［材木］　木　21
ざいりょう［材料］　料　161
さいわい［幸い］　幸　340
さかな［魚］　魚　159
さかなや［魚屋］　魚　159
さかや［酒屋］　屋　308
　　　　　　　酒　329
さきに［先に］　先　56
さくしゃ［作者］　者　227
さくせん［作戦］　戦　387
さくひん［作品］　作　174
　　　　　　　品　317
さくぶん［作文］　作　174
　　　　　　　文　220
（お）さけ［（お）酒］　酒　329
さげる［下げる］　下　34
ざしき［座敷］　座　474
さずかる［授かる］　授　359
さずける［授ける］　授　359
ざせき［座席］　座　474
さだめる［定める］　定　356
ざだんかい［座談会］　座　474
　　　　　　　談　488
さち［幸］　幸　340
さっか［作家］　作　174
さっすう［冊数］　冊　439
さっそく［早速］　早　92
　　　　　　　速　469
ざつだん［雑談］　談　488
さどう［茶道］　茶　169
ざぶとん［座布団］　座　474

さべつ［差別］	別	293
さまざまな［様々な］	様	483
さます［冷ます］	冷	323
さむい［寒い］	寒	229
さむけ［寒気］	寒	229
さゆう［左右］	右	37
	左	39
さよく［左翼］	左	39
（お）さら［（お）皿］	皿	328
さらあらい［皿洗い］	皿	328
さる［去る］	去	61
さん［三］	三	3
さんがつ［三月］	三	3
さんぎょう［産業］	産	265
ざんぎょう［残業］	残	349
さんこう［参考］	考	255
さんこうしょ［参考書］	考	255
さんさい［三歳］	三	3
さんさい［山菜］	菜	172
さんじ［三時］	三	3
さんじげん［三次元］	元	87
さんじすぎ［三時過ぎ］	過	462
さんじはん［三時半］	半	30
さんじゅうど［三十度］	度	283
ざんしょ［残暑］	暑	228
さんせい［酸性］	性	431
さんせいする［賛成する］	賛	451
	成	452
さんぜん［三千］	千	12
ざんだか［残高］	高	83
	残	349
さんち［産地］	産	265
さんにん［三人］	三	3
	人	26
さんねんせい［三年生］	年	60
ざんねんな［残念な］	残	349
	念	350
さんねんまえ［三年前］	前	40
さんばい［三倍］	倍	445
さんぱつ［散髪］	髪	506
さんぴ［賛否］	賛	451
さんびゃく［三百］	百	11
さんぽする［散歩する］	歩	244
さんぼん［三本］	本	25

| さんりん［山林］ | 山 | 145 |
| | 林 | 147 |

し

し［四］	四	4
し［死］	死	256
じ［字］	字	214
しあい［試合］	試	216
	合	295
しあげる［仕上げる］	仕	271
しあわせな［幸せな］	幸	340
しいくする［飼育する］	育	430
しいる［強いる］	強	125
しいん［子音］	音	177
じいん［寺院］	寺	28
しお［塩］	塩	330
しおからい［塩辛い］	塩	330
	辛	347
しおみず［塩水］	塩	330
しか［歯科］	歯	505
しかい［視界］	界	282
じかい［次回］	次	446
しかえし［仕返し］	仕	271
しかく［視覚］	覚	353
じかくする［自覚する］	覚	353
しかた［仕方］	仕	271
しがつ［四月］	四	4
じかん［時間］	時	29
	間	44
しき［式］	式	215
しきゅう［至急］	急	248
しきょうひん［試供品］	供	421
しけん［試験］	試	216
	験	217
しご［死語］	死	256
じこ［事故］	事	272
じごうじとく［自業自得］	業	266
じこくひょう［時刻表］	時	29
しごと［仕事］	仕	271
	事	272
じざけ［地酒］	酒	329
しじする［支持する］	持	126
ししゃ［死者］	死	256
じしゃく［磁石］	石	260

ししゃごにゅう［四捨五入］	捨	500
しじゅう［始終］	始	258
	終	259
じしゅう［自習］	自	180
	習	212
じしょ［辞書］	書	120
	辞	456
じじょ［次女］	次	446
しじょう［市場］	市	99
じじょう［事情］	情	352
ししょく［試食］	試	216
じしょくする［辞職する］	辞	456
ししょばこ［私書箱］	私	201
じしん［自信］	自	180
	信	484
じしん［地震］	地	280
しずかな［静かな］	静	406
しずまる［静まる］	静	406
しせいかつ［私生活］	私	201
しぜん［自然］	自	180
しそう［思想］	思	253
じそく［時速］	速	469
じぞくする［持続する］	持	126
した［下］	下	34
したい［死体］	死	256
じだい［時代］	時	29
	代	278
じたいする［辞退する］	辞	456
しだいに［次第に］	次	446
したぎ［下着］	着	192
じたく［自宅］	宅	383
したくする［支度する］	度	283
したしい［親しい］	親	196
しち［七］	七	7
しちがつ［七月］	七	7
しちじ［七時］	七	7
しちにん［七人］	七	7
しちふん［七分］	七	7
しちや［質屋］	質	222
しちょう［市長］	市	99
しちょうそん［市町村］	村	101
しつ［質］	質	222
しつぎょう［失業］	失	467
じっけん［実験］	験	217

じっさい［十歳］	十	10	じみ［地味］	味	176	しゅうかん［習慣］	習	212
じっさい［実際］	際	395	しみん［市民］	市	99	しゅうき［周期］	周	79
しっしんする［失神する］	失	467		民	286	しゅうきょう［宗教］	教	209
しっぱいする［失敗する］	失	467	じむしょ［事務所］	事	272	しゅうし［修士］	士	270
じっぷん［十分］	十	10		所	307	しゅうじ［習字］	習	212
	分	32	しめい［氏名］	名	127		字	214
しっぺい［疾病］	病	111		氏	207	じゅうじ［十時］	十	10
しつぼう［失望］	失	467	しめい［使命］	使	245	じゅうしょ［住所］	住	205
しつもん［質問］	質	222	しめきり［締め切り］	切	173		所	307
	問	223	しめる［閉める］	閉	250	じゅうだい［十代］	代	278
しつれいな［失礼な］	失	467	じもと［地元］	元	87	じゅうたく［住宅］	住	205
しつれんする［失恋する］	失	467	しゃかい［社会］	社	107		宅	383
してつ［私鉄］	私	201	しゃかいがく［社会学］	社	107	しゅうだん［集団］	集	301
	鉄	468	しゃかいしゅぎ［社会主義］	社	107	しゅうちしん［羞恥心］	恥	344
してん［支店］	店	109		義	398	しゅうちゅうする［集中する］	集	301
じてん［辞典］	辞	456	しゃかいてき［社会的］	的	464	しゅうてん［終点］	終	259
じてんしゃ［自転車］	車	104	しゃくしょ［市役所］	市	99	しゅうでん［終電］	終	259
	自	180		所	307	じゅうどう［柔道］	道	144
	転	181		役	366	しゅうとくぶつ［拾得物］	拾	499
じどうしゃ［自動車］	車	104	しゃくち［借地］	借	277	しゅうにゅう［収入］	入	97
	自	180	じゃくてん［弱点］	弱	233	じゅうにん［十人］	十	10
	動	242		点	441	じゅうびょう［重病］	病	111
じどうドア［自動ドア］	動	242	じゃくにくきょうしょく			しゅうぶん［秋分］	秋	131
じどうはんばいき［自動販売機］	売	118	［弱肉強食］	弱	233	じゅうぶん［十分］	十	10
しなもの［品物］	品	317	じゃくはい［若輩］	若	423		分	32
じなん［次男］	次	446	しゃくや［借家］	借	277	しゅうへん［周辺］	周	79
しぬ［死ぬ］	死	256	しゃじつしゅぎ［写実主義］	写	183	しゅうまつ［週末］	週	80
しはい［支配］	配	345	しゃしん［写真］	写	183		末	382
しはいにん［支配人］	配	345		真	184	じゅうまん［十万］	万	13
しはつ［始発］	始	258	しゃしんか［写真家］	写	183	じゅうみん［住民］	住	205
	発	314	しゃせい［写生］	写	183		民	286
しはらい［支払い］	払	377	しゃたく［社宅］	宅	383	じゅうやく［重役］	重	230
じびか［耳鼻科］	耳	73	しゃちょう［社長］	長	93	しゅうゆう［周遊］	遊	401
じひょう［辞表］	辞	456		社	107	じゅうような［重要な］	重	230
じぶん［自分］	分	32	しゃっきん［借金］	借	277		要	372
	自	180	しゅい［首位］	首	143	しゅうり［修理］	理	162
しへい［紙幣］	紙	208	しゆう［私有］	私	201	しゅうりょう［終了］	終	259
しぼう［死亡］	死	256	じゅう［十］	十	10	じゅうりょく［重力］	力	50
しま［島］	島	476	じゆう［自由］	自	180	しゅえい［守衛］	守	461
しまい［姉妹］	姉	198		由	374	しゅぎ［主義］	主	204
	妹	200	じゅうおく［十億］	億	440		義	398
しまいとし［姉妹都市］	姉	198	しゅうかい［集会］	集	301	じゅぎょう［授業］	業	266
しまぐに［島国］	島	476	じゅうがつ［十月］	十	10		授	359
しまる［閉まる］	閉	250	しゅうかん［週刊］	週	80	じゅぎょうりょう［授業料］	料	161

		授	359	じょうえいする［上映する］	映	187	しょうちする［承知する］	知	254

しゅくだい［宿題］ 宿 218
題 219
じょうえいする［上映する］ 映 187
しょうかき［消火器］ 火 19
しょうちする［承知する］ 知 254
しようちゅう［使用中］ 使 245
しゅくはく［宿泊］ 宿 218
泊 472
しょうがくきん［奨学金］ 金 22
しょうがくせい［小学生］ 小 82
しょうねん［少年］ 少 90
じょうば［乗馬］ 馬 105
じゅけん［受験］ 験 217
受 358
しょうかする［消化する］ 消 334
しょうがっこう［小学校］ 小 82
校 108
乗 182
しょうばい［商売］ 売 118
しゅご［主語］ 語 128
主 204
じょうかまち［城下町］ 町 100
しょうぎ［将棋］ 将 428
じょうひんな［上品な］ 品 317
しょうぶ［勝負］ 勝 449
負 450
しゅざいする［取材する］ 取 433
しゅしゃせんたく［取捨選択］ 捨 500
じゅじゅ［授受］ 授 359
しゅしょう［首相］ 首 143
相 487
じょうきゃく［乗客］ 乗 182
じょうきょうする［上京する］ 京 300
しょうきょくてき［消極的］ 的 464
しょうきょする［消去する］ 去 61
消 334
じょうぶな［丈夫な］ 夫 202
じょうほう［情報］ 情 352
しょうぼうし［消防士］ 士 270
しょうぼうしょ［消防署］ 消 334
じょうみゃく［静脈］ 静 406
しゅしょう［主将］ 将 428
しゅしょく［主食］ 主 204
しゅじん［主人］ 主 204
じゅしん［受信］ 受 358
信 484
しょうぐん［将軍］ 将 428
じょうげ［上下］ 下 34
しょうご［正午］ 午 42
正 297
しょうめいしょ［証明書］ 明 94
しょうらい［将来］ 来 68
将 428
じょうりく［上陸］ 陸 477
しゅだい［主題］ 主 204
題 219
しょうさい［詳細］ 細 511
しょうさっし［小冊子］ 冊 439
しょうさんする［賞賛する］ 賛 451
しょうりょう［少量］ 少 90
しょうわ［昭和］ 和 386
じょおう［女王］ 王 63
しゅだん［手段］ 段 443
しゅっか［出荷］ 荷 373
じゅっさい［十歳］ 十 10
しょうじきな［正直な］ 正 297
直 496
しょか［初夏］ 夏 130
初 435
しょきゅう［初級］ 初 435
しゅっせき［出席］ 出 98
席 475
しょうしゃ［商社］ 社 107
じょうしゃ［乗車］ 乗 182
じょうしゃけん［乗車券］ 乗 182
じょきょする［除去する］ 去 61
しょくえん［食塩］ 塩 330
しょくぎょう［職業］ 業 266
しゅっぱつ［出発］ 発 314
じゅっぷん［十分］ 十 10
分 32
じょうじゅする［成就する］ 成 452
しょうじょ［少女］ 女 52
少 90
しょくじ［食事］ 食 70
事 272
しゅと［首都］ 首 143
都 310
しょうしょう［少々］ 少 90
々 447
しょくせいかつ［食生活］ 活 381
しょくどう［食堂］ 食 70
堂 309
しゅふ［主婦］ 主 204
しゅみ［趣味］ 味 176
しゅやく［主役］ 役 366
しょうしん［昇進］ 進 320
じょうずな［上手な］ 上 33
手 140
しょくりょうひん［食料品］ 料 161
品 317
しゅような［主要な］ 要 372
しゅわ［手話］ 話 76
しょうずみ［使用済み］ 済 392
しょうする［使用する］ 用 285
じょしがくせい［女子学生］ 子 53
しょしんしゃ［初心者］ 初 435
しゅんかしゅうとう［春夏秋冬］ 春 129
夏 130
秋 131
冬 132
しょうせつ［小説］ 小 82
説 224
しょうそく［消息］ 息 425
しょうたいじょう［招待状］ 招 432
じょせい［女性］ 女 52
性 431
しょちゅうみまい［暑中見舞い］ 暑 228
しょてん［書店］ 店 109
じゅんさ［巡査］ 査 486
じゅんばん［順番］ 番 436
しゅんぶん［春分］ 春 129
しよう［私用］ 私 201
しょうたいする［招待する］ 待 78
招 432
じょうたつする［上達する］ 達 492
じょうだん［冗談］ 談 488
しょどう［書道］ 書 120
道 144
しらが［白髪］ 白 156
髪 506

しらせる [知らせる]	知	254
しらべる [調べる]	調	485
しりあい [知り合い]	知	254
じりつしんけい [自律神経]	律	394
しりつだいがく [私立大学]	私	201
しりょう [資料]	料	161
しりょく [視力]	力	50
しる [知る]	知	254
しるす [記す]	記	415
しれん [試練]	練	361
しろ [白]	白	156
しろい [白い]	白	156
しろくろ [白黒]	白	156
	黒	157
しわす [師走]	走	114
しんか [進化]	化	151
	進	320
しんがく [進学]	進	320
しんかんせん [新幹線]	新	85
しんけい [神経]	経	391
	神	482
しんけいしつ [神経質]	質	222
しんけん [真剣]	真	184
しんこう [信仰]	信	484
しんごう [信号]	号	444
	信	484
じんこう [人口]	口	15
じんこうてき [人工的]	工	38
しんこん [新婚]	婚	419
しんさ [審査]	査	486
しんし [紳士]	士	270
しんしつ [寝室]	寝	379
しんじつ [真実]	真	184
じんじゃ [神社]	社	107
	神	482
しんじる [信じる]	信	484
しんせいしょ [申請書]	申	481
しんせつ [新雪]	雪	494
しんせつな [親切な]	切	173
	親	196
しんせんな [新鮮な]	新	85
しんぞく [親族]	族	195
しんそつ [新卒]	卒	364
しんだいしゃ [寝台車]	寝	379
しんちょう [身長]	長	93
しんとう [神道]	神	482
しんねん [新年]	新	85
しんねん [信念]	念	350
しんぱいする [心配する]	心	139
	配	345
しんぶん [新聞]	聞	74
	新	85
しんぽ [進歩]	歩	244
	進	320
しんぼう [辛抱]	辛	347
しんまい [新米]	米	67
しんや [深夜]	夜	138
しんゆう [親友]	友	96
	親	196
しんよう [信用]	信	484
しんらい [信頼]	信	484
しんりがく [心理学]	心	139
	理	162
しんりん [森林]	林	147
	森	148
しんわ [神話]	神	482

す

ず [図]	図	273
すいえい [水泳]	水	20
	泳	402
すいがら [吸い殻]	吸	502
すいぎゅう [水牛]	牛	165
すいぎん [水銀]	銀	110
すいぞくかん [水族館]	族	195
	館	275
すいでん [水田]	田	49
すいどう [水道]	水	20
すいはんき [炊飯器]	飯	164
すいみん [睡眠]	眠	348
すいようび [水曜日]	水	20
	曜	24
すう [吸う]	吸	502
すうじ [数字]	字	214
すえ [末]	末	382
すえっこ [末っ子]	末	382
すきな [好きな]	好	95
すぎる [過ぎる]	過	462

すくない [少ない]	少	90
ずけい [図形]	形	416
すこし [少し]	少	90
すごす [過ごす]	過	462
すずしい [涼しい]	涼	405
すすむ [進む]	進	320
すずむ [涼む]	涼	405
すすめる [進める]	進	320
ずつう [頭痛]	頭	289
	痛	343
すてる [捨てる]	捨	500
すなおな [素直な]	直	496
ずのう [頭脳]	頭	289
すばやい [素早い]	早	92
ずひょう [図表]	図	273
すべて [全て]	全	369
すませる [済ませる]	済	392
すみえ [墨絵]	絵	507
すみやかな [速やかな]	速	469
すむ [住む]	住	205
すむ [済む]	済	392
すもう [相撲]	相	487
すわる [座る]	座	474

せ

せいか [成果]	果	326
せいかい [政界]	界	282
せいかい [正解]	正	297
せいかく [性格]	性	431
せいがく [声楽]	声	291
せいかくな [正確な]	正	297
せいかつ [生活]	活	381
ぜいかん [税関]	関	396
せいき [世紀]	世	281
せいぎ [正義]	義	398
ぜいきん [税金]	金	22
せいけん [政権]	政	389
せいこう [成功]	成	452
ぜいこみ [税込み]	込	409
せいざ [星座]	星	493
せいさく [政策]	政	389
せいさん [生産]	産	265
せいじ [政治]	政	389
	治	390

せいじか［政治家］	政	389
	治	390
せいしきな［正式な］	式	215
	正	297
せいしつ［性質］	質	222
	性	431
せいしゅん［青春］	春	129
	青	155
せいしょうねん［青少年］	年	60
せいしん［精神］	神	482
せいじん［成人］	成	452
せいせき［成績］	成	452
せいちょう［成長］	成	452
せいと［生徒］	徒	360
せいとう［政党］	政	389
	党	400
せいねん［青年］	青	155
せいひん［製品］	品	317
せいふ［政府］	政	389
せいふく［制服］	服	191
せいふく［征服］	服	191
せいべつ［性別］	別	293
	性	431
せいほうけい［正方形］	形	416
せいもん［正門］	門	43
せいゆう［声優］	声	291
せいよう［西洋］	西	46
	洋	190
せいようする［静養する］	静	406
ぜいりし［税理士］	士	270
せいりょういんりょうすい		
［清涼飲料水］	涼	405
せおう［背負う］	負	450
せおよぎ［背泳ぎ］	泳	402
せかい［世界］	世	281
	界	282
せかいいっしゅう［世界一周］	周	79
せかいじゅう［世界中］	中	35
せき［席］	席	475
せきがいせん［赤外線］	赤	154
せきじつ［昔日］	昔	276
せきじゅうじ［赤十字］	赤	154
せきたん［石炭］	石	260
せきどう［赤道］	赤	154

せきとり［関取］	関	396
せきはん［赤飯］	赤	154
せきゆ［石油］	石	260
せけん［世間］	間	44
	世	281
せけんてい［世間体］	体	142
せだい［世代］	世	281
せっきょうする［説教する］	説	224
せっきょくてき［積極的］	的	464
せっけん［石けん］	石	260
ぜっさん［絶賛］	賛	451
せっし［摂氏］	氏	207
せつぞくし［接続詞］	続	455
ぜったいに［絶対に］	絶	453
	対	454
せっとくする［説得する］	説	224
ぜつぼう［絶望］	絶	453
せつめい［説明］	明	94
	説	224
ぜつめつ［絶滅］	絶	453
せつやくする［節約する］	約	459
せなか［背中］	中	35
せびろ［背広］	広	91
せろん［世論］	世	281
せわ［世話］	話	76
	世	281
せん［千］	千	12
ぜんいん［全員］	員	269
	全	369
せんえん［千円］	千	12
せんがん［洗顔］	洗	247
	顔	290
せんきょ［選挙］	選	458
せんきょけん［選挙権］	選	458
せんげつ［先月］	先	56
ぜんこく［全国］	全	369
せんざい［洗剤］	洗	247
せんじつ［先日］	先	56
せんしゅ［選手］	選	458
せんしゅう［先週］	先	56
	週	80
せんしんこく［先進国］	進	320
せんせい［先生］	生	55
	先	56

せんせんしゅう［先々週］	々	447
せんぞ［先祖］	先	56
	祖	429
せんそう［戦争］	戦	387
	争	388
ぜんたい［全体］	体	142
ぜんだいみもん［前代未聞］	聞	74
せんたくき［洗濯機］	濯	378
	機	466
せんたくする［洗濯する］	洗	247
	濯	378
せんたくする［選択する］	選	458
せんたくもの［洗濯物］	濯	378
せんちょう［船長］	船	473
せんでん［宣伝］	伝	510
せんとう［先頭］	頭	289
せんにん［千人］	千	12
せんねん［千年］	千	12
せんば［千羽］	羽	211
せんぱい［先輩］	先	56
せんぱつ［洗髪］	髪	506
ぜんはん［前半］	半	30
	前	40
ぜんぶ［全部］	全	369
	部	370
せんもん［専門］	門	43
ぜんりょく［全力］	全	369
せんれい［洗礼］	洗	247
せんれん［洗練］	練	361

そ

そうい［相違］	違	365
	相	487
そうこう［走行］	走	114
そうさ［操作］	作	174
そうさ［捜査］	査	486
そうしんする［送信する］	送	246
ぞうせん［造船］	船	473
そうぞく［相続］	続	455
	相	487
そうたいてきに［相対的に］	対	454
そうだんする［相談する］	相	487
	談	488
そうちょう［早朝］	早	92

そうとう［相当］	相	487	だいがく［大学］	学	54	だいめい［題名］	題	219
そうべつかい［送別会］	送	246		大	81	たいよう［太陽］	太	236
そうりょう［送料］	送	246	だいがくいん［大学院］	院	112	たいらな［平らな］	平	385
ぞくぞく［続々］	続	455	だいがくいんせい［大学院生］	院	112	たいりく［大陸］	陸	477
そくたつ［速達］	速	469	だいがくせい［大学生］	大	81	たいわん［台湾］	台	185
	達	492	だいきち［大吉］	吉	417	たうえ［田植え］	田	49
そくど［速度］	度	283	だいきん［代金］	代	278	たえず［絶えず］	絶	453
そくばく［束縛］	束	460	だいく［大工］	工	38	たえる［絶える］	絶	453
そくめん［側面］	側	412	たいけん［体験］	験	217	だえん［楕円］	円	14
そこく［祖国］	祖	429	たいこ［太鼓］	太	236	たかい［高い］	高	83
そしつ［素質］	質	222	だいさんごう［第三号］	号	444	たかめる［高める］	高	83
そせん［祖先］	祖	429	たいし［大使］	使	245	たくはいびん［宅配便］	配	345
そそぐ［注ぐ］	注	287	たいしかん［大使館］	大	81		宅	383
そだつ［育つ］	育	430		使	245	たけ［竹］	竹	294
そだてる［育てる］	育	430		館	275	たけのこ［竹の子］	竹	294
そつぎょう［卒業］	業	266	たいじゅう［体重］	体	142	たしょう［多少］	多	89
	卒	364		重	230	たす［足す］	足	141
そつぎょうしき［卒業式］	卒	364	たいしょう［対象］	対	454	だす［出す］	出	98
そつぎょうせい［卒業生］	卒	364	だいじょうぶ［大丈夫］	夫	202	たすう［多数］	多	89
そつろん［卒論］	卒	364	だいず［大豆］	豆	237	たすうけつ［多数決］	多	89
そと［外］	外	36	だいすきな［大好きな］	大	81	たたかい［戦い］	戦	387
そとがわ［外側］	側	412		好	95	たたかう［戦う］	戦	387
そなえる［供える］	供	421	たいせいよう［大西洋］	西	46	ただしい［正しい］	正	297
そのた［その他］	他	448		洋	190	ただちに［直ちに］	直	496
そのとき［その時］	時	29	たいせつな［大切な］	大	81	たつ［立つ］	立	77
そのほか［その他］	他	448		切	173	たつ［建つ］	建	315
そふ［祖父］	父	58	たいそう［体操］	体	142	だっしょく［脱色］	色	158
	祖	429	だいそつ［大卒］	卒	364	たつじん［達人］	達	492
そふぼ［祖父母］	父	58	たいだん［対談］	談	488	たっする［達する］	達	492
	母	59	たいちょう［体調］	体	142	だっそう［脱走］	走	114
	祖	429	だいどころ［台所］	台	185	たてもの［建物］	建	315
そぼ［祖母］	母	59		所	307		物	316
	祖	429	たいひ［対比］	比	357	たてる［建てる］	建	315
そら［空］	空	149	だいひょう［代表］	代	278	たどうし［他動詞］	他	448
そる［反る］	反	163		表	363	たなかさま［田中様］	様	483
そんちょう［村長］	村	101	たいふう［台風］	台	185	たなかさん［田中さん］	田	49
そんみん［村民］	村	101		風	240	たなばた［七夕］	七	7
			だいぶぶん［大部分］	部	370		夕	135
た			たいへいよう［太平洋］	洋	190	たにん［他人］	他	448
だい［台］	台	185		太	236	たの［他の］	他	448
だい［題］	題	219	たいへん［大変］	変	504	たのしい［楽しい］	楽	178
たいいく［体育］	育	430	たいぼう［待望］	待	78	たのしみ［楽しみ］	楽	178
たいいんする［退院する］	院	112	たいぼく［大木］	木	21	たのしむ［楽しむ］	楽	178
たいおん［体温］	体	142	だいほん［台本］	台	185	たば［束］	束	460

たばこをすう［たばこを吸う］　吸　502
たばねる［束ねる］　束　460
たび［旅］　旅　318
たびたび［度々］　度　283
たぶん［多分］　多　89
たべもの［食べ物］　食　70
　　　　　　　　　　物　316
たべる［食べる］　食　70
たまご［卵］　卵　327
たまごやき［卵焼き］　卵　327
たみ［民］　民　286
たむらさん［田村さん］　村　101
ためいき［ため息］　息　425
ためいけ［溜め池］　池　313
ためす［試す］　試　216
たより［便り］　便　303
たりょう［多量］　多　89
たりる［足りる］　足　141
たんか［短歌］　歌　179
　　　　　　　　　短　238
だんかい［段階］　階　442
　　　　　　　　　段　443
だんがん［弾丸］　丸　321
たんき［短期］　短　238
たんきだいがく［短期大学］　短　238
たんきな［短気な］　短　238
たんきゅう［探究］　究　262
だんけつする［団結する］　結　418
たんご［単語］　語　128
たんざく［短冊］　冊　439
だんしがくせい［男子学生］　男　51
　　　　　　　　　　　　　子　53
だんじき［断食］　食　70
たんしょ［短所］　短　238
たんじょうび［誕生日］　生　55
だんせい［男性］　男　51
　　　　　　　　　性　431
だんたい［団体］　体　142
たんとう［短刀］　刀　31
たんとう［担当］　当　509
だんとう［暖冬］　冬　132
　　　　　　　　　暖　404
だんねんする［断念する］　念　350
たんぺん［短編］　短　238

たんぼ［田んぼ］　田　49
だんぼう［暖房］　暖　404
たんもの［反物］　反　163

ち

ちあん［治安］　治　390
ちいさい［小さい］　小　82
チームのかなめ［チームの要］　要　372
ちか［地下］　地　280
ちかい［近い］　近　226
ちがい［違い］　違　365
ちがう［違う］　違　365
ちかく［近く］　近　226
ちかごろ［近ごろ］　近　226
ちかしつ［地下室］　室　210
ちかてつ［地下鉄］　下　34
　　　　　　　　　地　280
　　　　　　　　　鉄　468
ちかみち［近道］　道　144
ちから［力］　力　50
ちきゅう［地球］　地　280
ちく［地区］　区　312
ちくりん［竹林］　竹　294
ちこくする［遅刻する］　遅　470
ちじ［知事］　知　254
ちしき［知識］　知　254
ちじん［知人］　知　254
ちず［地図］　図　273
　　　　　　　　　地　280
ちせい［知性］　知　254
ちち［父］　父　58
ちちおや［父親］　親　196
ちちのひ［父の日］　父　58
ちばけん［千葉県］　千　12
ちほう［地方］　地　280
ちゃいろ［茶色］　茶　169
ちゃくせき［着席する］　席　475
ちゃくりく［着陸］　陸　477
ちゃどう［茶道］　茶　169
ちゃみせ［茶店］　茶　169
ちゃわん［茶碗］　茶　169
ちゅういする［注意する］　注　287
　　　　　　　　　　　　意　288
ちゅうおう［中央］　央　186

ちゅうおうぐち［中央口］　口　15
ちゅうおうしゅうけん［中央集権］　央　186
ちゅうおうせん［中央線］　央　186
ちゅうがっこう［中学校］　中　35
　　　　　　　　　　　　校　108
ちゅうきゅう［中級］　中　35
ちゅうきんとう［中近東］　近　226
ちゅうこ［中古］　古　86
ちゅうごく［中国］　中　35
　　　　　　　　　　国　64
ちゅうごくご［中国語］　語　128
ちゅうし［中止］　中　35
　　　　　　　　　止　243
ちゅうしゃ［注射］　注　287
ちゅうしゃじょう［駐車場］　車　104
　　　　　　　　　　　　場　305
　　　　　　　　　　　　駐　471
ちゅうしゃする［駐車する］　駐　471
ちゅうしょく［昼食］　食　70
　　　　　　　　　　昼　134
ちゅうしん［中心］　心　139
ちゅうせん［抽選］　選　458
ちゅうとう［中東］　東　45
ちゅうにちたいし［駐日大使］　駐　471
ちゅうねん［中年］　年　60
ちゅうもく［注目］　目　16
　　　　　　　　　注　287
ちゅうもんする［注文する］　注　287
ちょうかん［朝刊］　朝　133
ちょうかん［長官］　官　274
ちょうさ［調査］　調　485
　　　　　　　　　査　486
ちょうし［調子］　調　485
ちょうしょ［長所］　長　93
ちょうじょ［長女］　女　52
ちょうしょく［朝食］　食　70
　　　　　　　　　　朝　133
ちょうせつ［調節］　調　485
ちょうせん［挑戦］　戦　387
ちょうちょう［町長］　町　100
ちょうなん［長男］　男　51
　　　　　　　　　長　93
ちょうほうけい［長方形］　長　93
　　　　　　　　　　　　方　136

ちょうみりょう［調味料］　味 176
　　　　　　　　　　　　　調 485
ちょうみん［町民］　　　町 100
ちょくせつ［直接］　　　直 496
ちょくせん［直線］　　　直 496
ちょすいち［貯水池］　　池 313
ちり［地理］　　　　　　理 162
　　　　　　　　　　　　地 280
ちりょう［治療］　　　　治 390
ちんたいマンション
　［賃貸マンション］　　貸 279

つ

ついたち［一日］　　　　一 1
ついで［次いで］　　　　次 446
ついほう［追放］　　　　放 503
つうがく［通学］　　　　通 319
つうきん［通勤］　　　　通 319
つうやく［通訳］　　　　通 319
つかいふるす［使い古す］古 86
つかう［使う］　　　　　使 245
つかえる［仕える］　　　仕 271
つかれ［疲れ］　　　　　疲 403
つかれる［疲れる］　　　疲 403
つき［月］　　　　　　　月 18
つぎ［次］　　　　　　　次 446
つきあう［付き合う］　　合 295
　　　　　　　　　　　　付 331
つぎつぎ［次々］　　　　次 446
つく［着く］　　　　　　着 192
つく［付く］　　　　　　付 331
つくばし［つくば市］　　市 99
つくる［作る］　　　　　作 174
つける［付ける］　　　　付 331
つごう［都合］　　　　　合 295
　　　　　　　　　　　　都 310
つたえる［伝える］　　　伝 510
つち［土］　　　　　　　土 23
つづき［続き］　　　　　続 455
つづく［続く］　　　　　続 455
つづける［続ける］　　　続 455
つどう［集う］　　　　　集 301
つま［妻］　　　　　　　妻 203
つめたい［冷たい］　　　冷 323

つゆ［梅雨］　　　　　　雨 102
つよい［強い］　　　　　強 125
つよき［強気］　　　　　強 125
つらい［辛い］　　　　　辛 347
つらなる［連なる］　　　連 410
つりいと［釣り糸］　　　糸 206
つりばし［つり橋］　　　橋 479
つれていく［連れて行く］連 410

て

て［手］　　　　　　　　手 140
ていあん［提案］　　　　案 489
ていえん［庭園］　　　　園 408
ていおん［低温］　　　　低 232
ていか［低下］　　　　　低 232
ていぎ［定義］　　　　　義 398
ていきあつ［低気圧］　　低 232
ていきけん［定期券］　　定 356
ていきゅうび［定休日］　休 113
　　　　　　　　　　　　定 356
ていきょう［提供］　　　供 421
ていしする［停止する］　止 243
ていしゅつする［提出する］出 98
ていでん［停電］　　　　電 103
でかける［出かける］　　出 98
てがみ［手紙］　　　　　手 140
　　　　　　　　　　　　紙 208
てがるな［手軽な］　　　軽 231
てきとう［適当］　　　　当 509
でぐち［出口］　　　　　口 15
　　　　　　　　　　　　出 98
てくび［手首］　　　　　首 143
でし［弟子］　　　　　　弟 199
てつ［鉄］　　　　　　　鉄 468
てっきょう［鉄橋］　　　橋 479
てっきんコンクリート
　［鉄筋コンクリート］　鉄 468
てづくり［手作り］　　　作 174
てつだう［手伝う］　　　手 140
　　　　　　　　　　　　伝 510
てつづき［手続き］　　　続 455
てつどう［鉄道］　　　　鉄 468
てっぱんやき［鉄板焼］　鉄 468
てつやする［徹夜する］　夜 138

テニスぶ［テニス部］　　部 370
てばなす［手放す］　　　放 503
（お）てら［（お）寺］　寺 28
でる［出る］　　　　　　出 98
てん［点］　　　　　　　点 441
てんいん［店員］　　　　店 109
　　　　　　　　　　　　員 269
でんえん［田園］　　　　田 49
てんき［天気］　　　　　気 88
　　　　　　　　　　　　天 153
でんき［電気］　　　　　気 88
　　　　　　　　　　　　電 103
でんき［伝記］　　　　　伝 510
でんきだい［電気代］　　代 278
てんきよほう［天気予報］天 153
　　　　　　　　　　　　予 170
でんげん［電源］　　　　電 103
てんこう［転校］　　　　転 181
てんごく［天国］　　　　天 153
でんごん［伝言］　　　　言 75
　　　　　　　　　　　　伝 510
てんさい［天才］　　　　天 153
てんし［天使］　　　　　天 153
　　　　　　　　　　　　使 245
でんし［電子］　　　　　電 103
でんしじしょ［電子辞書］子 53
でんしゃ［電車］　　　　電 103
　　　　　　　　　　　　車 104
てんしょく［転職］　　　転 181
てんすう［点数］　　　　点 441
でんせん［伝染］　　　　伝 510
でんち［電池］　　　　　電 103
　　　　　　　　　　　　池 313
てんちょう［店長］　　　店 109
てんとう［店頭］　　　　頭 289
でんとう［伝統］　　　　伝 510
てんのう［天皇］　　　　天 153
てんもんがく［天文学］　天 153
でんりょく［電力］　　　力 50
　　　　　　　　　　　　電 103
でんわ［電話］　　　　　話 76
　　　　　　　　　　　　電 103

と

と［戸］　　　　　　　　戸 306

とい [問い]	問	223	とうよう [東洋]	東	45	どだい [土台]	土	23
といあわせ [問い合わせ]	問	223		洋	190	とだな [戸棚]	戸	306
とうあん [答案]	答	296	どうように [同様に]	様	483	とち [土地]	土	23
とうあんようし [答案用紙]	案	489	どうりょう [同僚]	同	298	とっきゅう [特急]	急	248
とうかいちほう [東海地方]	東	45	とお [十]	十	10	とっきゅうでんしゃ		
とうぎゅう [闘牛]	牛	165	とおい [遠い]	遠	225	[特急電車]	特	292
どうきゅうせい [同級生]	同	298	とおか [十日]	十	10	とどうふけん [都道府県]	県	311
とうきょう [東京]	東	45	とおかいない [十日以内]	内	490	とどく [届く]	届	375
	京	300	とおく [遠く]	遠	225	とどけでる [届け出る]	届	375
とうきょうえき [東京駅]	駅	106	とおり [通り]	通	319	とどける [届ける]	届	375
とうきょうと [東京都]	都	310	とおりすぎる [通り過ぎる]	過	462	ととのえる [調える]	調	485
どうぐ [道具]	道	144	とおる [通る]	通	319	どなる [怒鳴る]	怒	339
とうけい [統計]	計	299	とかい [都会]	都	310	とばす [飛ばす]	飛	465
どうさ [動作]	作	174	ときどき [時々]	時	29	とびおきる [飛び起きる]	飛	465
とうざい [東西]	西	46		々	447	とびおりる [飛び降りる]	降	495
とうし [投資]	投	457	とく [説く]	説	224	とびこむ [飛び込む]	込	409
とうじ [冬至]	冬	132	とぐ [研ぐ]	研	261		飛	465
とうじ [当時]	当	509	とくぎ [特技]	特	292	とびだす [飛び出す]	飛	465
どうし [動詞]	動	242	どくしゃ [読者]	読	119	とぶ [飛ぶ]	飛	465
どうじ [同時]	同	298		者	227	とほで [徒歩で]	徒	360
とうしゅ [党首]	党	400	どくしょ [読書]	読	119	とまる [止まる]	止	243
とうしゅ [投手]	投	457		書	120	とまる [泊まる]	泊	472
とうしょ [投書]	投	457	とくしょく [特色]	色	158	とまれ [止まれ]	止	243
どうじょうする [同情する]	同	298		特	292	とめる [止める]	止	243
とうぜん [当然]	当	509	とくちょう [特徴]	特	292	とめる [留める]	留	263
とうせんする [当選する]	選	458	どくとくな [独特な]	特	292	とめる [泊める]	泊	472
とうそう [逃走]	走	114	とくに [特に]	特	292	ともだち [友だち／友達]	友	96
どうそうかい [同窓会]	窓	411	とくべつな [特別な]	特	292		達	492
とうちゃく [到着]	着	192		別	293	ともに [共に]	共	420
どうどうと [堂々と]	堂	309	とけい [時計]	時	29	ともばたらき [共働き]	働	268
とうなんアジア [東南アジア]	南	47		計	299	どようび [土曜日]	土	23
とうにゅう [豆乳]	豆	237	とこや [床屋]	屋	308		曜	24
とうばん [当番]	番	436	とざん [登山]	山	145	とり [鳥]	鳥	167
とうひょうする [投票する]	投	457	とし [年]	年	60	とりい [鳥居]	鳥	167
とうふ [豆腐]	豆	237	とし [都市]	市	99	とりかえる [取り替える]	取	433
どうふうする [同封する]	同	298	とじまり [戸締まり]	戸	306	とりけす [取り消す]	消	334
どうぶつ [動物]	動	242	どしゃぶり [土砂降り]	降	495		取	433
	物	316	としょかん [図書館]	書	120	とりだす [取り出す]	取	433
どうぶつえん [動物園]	園	408		図	273	とりにく [鳥肉]	鳥	167
とうほくちほう [東北地方]	東	45		館	275		肉	168
	北	48	とじる [閉じる]	閉	250	とりもどす [取り戻す]	戻	501
とうみん [冬眠]	冬	132	としん [都心]	都	310	どりょく [努力]	力	50
	眠	348	どせい [土星]	土	23	とる [取る]	取	433
とうみん [島民]	島	476	どそくげんきん [土足厳禁]	土	23	とんカツ [豚カツ]	豚	166

どんなところ ［どんな所］	所 307	ならけん ［奈良県］	良 69
とんや ［問屋］	問 223	なる ［成る］	成 452
		なん ［何］	何 57
な		なんかい ［何回］	回 284
ない ［無い］	無 512	なんきょく ［南極］	南 47
ないか ［内科］	内 490	なんじ ［何時］	何 57
ないよう ［内容］	内 490	なんせい ［南西］	西 46
ナイルがわ ［ナイル川］	川 146	なんでも ［何でも］	何 57
なおす ［治す］	治 390	なんど ［何度］	何 57
なおす ［直す］	直 496	なんとう ［南東］	南 47
なおる ［治る］	治 390	なんにん ［何人］	何 57
なおる ［直る］	直 496	なんべい ［南米］	南 47
なか ［中］	中 35		米 67
ながい ［長い］	長 93	なんぼく ［南北］	南 47
ながさ ［長さ］	長 93		北 48
ながの ［長野］	野 171	なんみん ［難民］	民 286
ながのけん ［長野県］	県 311		
ながれぼし ［流れ星］	星 493	**に**	
なきごえ ［泣き声］	泣 338	に ［二］	二 2
なきむし ［泣き虫］	泣 338	にあう ［似合う］	合 295
なく ［泣く］	泣 338	にいがた ［新潟］	新 85
なげる ［投げる］	投 457	にかい ［二階］	階 442
なごや ［名古屋］	屋 308	にがい ［苦い］	苦 342
なごやか ［和やか］	和 386	にかいだて ［二階建て］	建 315
なさけ ［情け］	情 352	にがおえ ［似顔絵］	顔 290
なだれ ［雪崩］	雪 494		絵 507
なつ ［夏］	夏 130	にがつ ［二月］	二 2
なっとう ［納豆］	豆 237	にがて ［苦手］	苦 342
なつふく ［夏服］	夏 130	にがわらい ［苦笑い］	笑 337
なつまつり ［夏祭り］	祭 384	にく ［肉］	肉 168
なつやすみ ［夏休み］	休 113	にくや ［肉屋］	肉 168
	夏 130	にし ［西］	西 46
なな ［七］	七 7	にじ ［二時］	二 2
ななつ ［七つ］	七 7	にじかん ［二時間］	間 44
ななにん ［七人］	七 7	にしぐち ［西口］	西 46
ななふん ［七分］	七 7	にじゅっさい ［二十歳］	二 2
なに ［何］	何 57		歳 437
なにか ［何か］	何 57	にせん ［二千］	千 12
なのか ［七日］	七 7	にだい ［二台］	台 185
なのはな ［菜の花］	菜 172	～にたいして ［～に対して］	対 454
なま ［生］	生 55	にちようび ［日曜日］	日 17
なまえ ［名前］	前 40		曜 24
	名 127	にちようひん ［日用品］	品 317
ならう ［習う］	習 212	にっき ［日記］	日 17

	記 415
にづくり ［荷造り］	荷 373
にっこう ［日光］	光 239
にっぽん ［日本］	日 17
	本 25
にとう ［二頭］	頭 289
にはくみっか ［二泊三日］	泊 472
にばんめ ［二番目］	番 436
にひゃく ［二百］	百 11
にほん ［日本］	日 17
	本 25
にほん ［二本］	本 25
にほんご ［日本語］	本 25
	語 128
にほんしゅ ［日本酒］	酒 329
にほんじん ［日本人］	人 26
にほんたいスペイン ［日本対スペイン］	対 454
にほんとう ［日本刀］	刀 31
にほんぶよう ［日本舞踊］	踊 380
にまいめ ［二枚目］	枚 438
にもつ ［荷物］	物 316
	荷 373
にゅういんする ［入院する］	入 97
	院 112
にゅうか ［入荷］	荷 373
にゅうがくしき ［入学式］	式 215
にゅうがくしけん ［入学試験］	試 216
にゅうがくする ［入学する］	入 97
にゅうもん ［入門］	門 43
にょうぼう ［女房］	女 52
にんき ［人気］	気 88
にんぎょ ［人魚］	魚 159
にんぎょう ［人形］	形 416
にんげん ［人間］	間 44
にんげんかんけい ［人間関係］	係 397
ね	
ねごと ［寝言］	寝 379
ねだん ［値段］	段 443
ねつ ［熱］	熱 322
ねっしんな ［熱心な］	心 139
	熱 322
ねっする ［熱する］	熱 322

ねったい［熱帯］	熱 322	
ねったいぎょ［熱帯魚］	魚 159	
ねっちゅうする［熱中する］	熱 322	
ねっとう［熱湯］	熱 322	
ねぼう［寝坊］	寝 379	
ねむい［眠い］	眠 348	
ねむたい［眠たい］	眠 348	
ねむる［眠る］	眠 348	
ねる［練る］	練 361	
ねる［寝る］	寝 379	
ねんがん［念願］	念 350	
ねんごう［年号］	号 444	
ねんしょう［燃焼］	焼 333	
ねんど［粘土］	土 23	
ねんまつ［年末］	末 382	

の

のうぎょう［農業］	業 266	
のうそん［農村］	村 101	
のうやく［農薬］	薬 267	
のこす［残す］	残 349	
のこらず［残らず］	残 349	
のこり［残り］	残 349	
のこる［残る］	残 349	
のせる［乗せる］	乗 182	
のちほど［後ほど］	後 41	
のはら［野原］	野 171	
のぼる［上る］	上 33	
のみぐすり［飲み薬］	飲 71	
のみもの［飲み物］	飲 71	
	物 316	
のみや［飲み屋］	飲 71	
のむ［飲む］	飲 71	
のりおくれる［乗り遅れる］	遅 470	
のりかえる［乗り換える］	乗 182	
のりもの［乗り物］	乗 182	
のる［乗る］	乗 182	

は

は［葉］	葉 413	
は［歯］	歯 505	
ばあい［場合］	合 295	
	場 305	
はいいろ［灰色］	色 158	
ばいう［梅雨］	雨 102	

はいぐうしゃ［配偶者］	配 345	
はいけい［背景］	景 414	
はいざら［灰皿］	皿 328	
はいしする［廃止する］	止 243	
はいしゃ［歯医者］	者 227	
	医 257	
	歯 505	
ばいしゅうする［買収する］	買 117	
ばいすう［倍数］	倍 445	
ばいぞうする［倍増する］	倍 445	
はいたつ［配達］	配 345	
	達 492	
ばいてん［売店］	店 109	
	売 118	
ばいばい［売買］	買 117	
ばいりつ［倍率］	倍 445	
はいる［入る］	入 97	
はえる［生える］	生 55	
はえる［映える］	映 187	
ばか［馬鹿］	馬 105	
はがき［葉書］	葉 413	
はかせ［博士］	士 270	
はかる［図る］	図 273	
はかる［計る］	計 299	
はぐくむ［育む］	育 430	
はくさい［白菜］	菜 172	
はくし［白紙］	白 156	
はくし［博士］	士 270	
ばくしょうする［爆笑する］	笑 337	
はくちょう［白鳥］	白 156	
	鳥 167	
はくはつ［白髪］	白 156	
	髪 506	
はくぶつかん［博物館］	館 275	
はこぶ［運ぶ］	運 241	
はし［橋］	橋 479	
はじ［恥］	恥 344	
はじしらず［恥知らず］	恥 344	
はじまる［始まる］	始 258	
はじめて［初めて］	初 435	
はじめは［初めは］	初 435	
はじめる［始める］	始 258	
ばしゃ［馬車］	馬 105	
ばしょ［場所］	場 305	

	所 307	
はしる［走る］	走 114	
はじる［恥じる］	恥 344	
はずかしい［恥ずかしい］	恥 344	
はずかしがる［恥ずかしがる］	恥 344	
はずす［外す］	外 36	
はたおりき［機織り機］	機 466	
はたして［果たして］	果 326	
はたち［二十歳］	二 2	
	歳 437	
はたらきもの［働き者］	働 268	
はたらく［働く］	働 268	
はち［八］	八 8	
はちがつ［八月］	八 8	
はちじ［八時］	八 8	
はちにん［八人］	八 8	
はつおん［発音］	音 177	
	発 314	
はつか［二十日］	二 2	
はっけん［発見］	発 314	
はつこい［初恋］	初 435	
はっさい［八歳］	八 8	
ばっし［抜糸］	糸 206	
はっせん［八千］	千 12	
はったつする［発達する］	達 492	
はっちゅうする［発注する］	注 287	
はつばい［発売］	発 314	
はっぴゃく［八百］	八 8	
	百 11	
はっぴょう［発表］	発 314	
	表 363	
はつみみ［初耳］	耳 73	
はつめい［発明］	発 314	
はつゆめ［初夢］	夢 463	
はな［花］	花 152	
はなし［話］	話 76	
はなしあう［話し合う］	話 76	
はなす［話す］	話 76	
はなす［放す］	放 503	
はなたば［花束］	束 460	
はなび［花火］	火 19	
	花 152	
はなみ［花見］	見 65	
	花 152	

はなみず［鼻水］	水	20
はなや［花屋］	花	152
はなよめ［花嫁］	花	152
はね［羽］	羽	211
はね［羽根］	羽	211
はは［母］	母	59
ははおや［母親］	親	196
ははのひ［母の日］	日	17
	母	59
はへん［破片］	片	332
はみがき［歯磨き］	歯	505
はやい［早い］	早	92
はやい［速い］	速	469
はやおくり［早送り］	早	92
はやく［早く］	早	92
はやくち［早口］	早	92
はやし［林］	林	147
はやめる［早める］	早	92
はらいこむ［払い込む］	払	377
はらいもどす［払い戻す］	払	377
	戻	501
はらう［払う］	払	377
パリけいゆ［パリ経由］	由	374
	経	391
はる［春］	春	129
はるがっき［春学期］	春	129
はるまき［春巻］	春	129
はるやすみ［春休み］	春	129
ばん［晩］	晩	137
はんえいする［反映する］	映	187
はんがく［半額］	半	30
ばんぐみ［番組］	番	436
はんけつ［判決］	決	355
ばんけん［番犬］	犬	160
はんこう［反抗］	反	163
ばんごう［番号］	番	436
	号	444
ばんごはん［晩ご飯］	晩	137
	飯	164
ばんこん［晩婚］	晩	137
ばんざい［万歳］	万	13
	歳	437
ばんしゅう［晩秋］	秋	131
はんせい［反省］	反	163
はんせん［反戦］	戦	387
はんたいがわ［反対側］	側	412
はんたいする［反対する］	反	163
	対	454
はんとう［半島］	半	30
	島	476
はんとし［半年］	半	30
ばんねん［晩年］	晩	137
はんのう［反応］	反	163
はんぷく［反復］	復	362
はんぶん［半分］	半	30
	分	32
ひ		
ひ［火］	火	19
ひえる［冷える］	冷	323
ひがえりりょこう［日帰り旅行］	帰	121
ひかく［比較］	比	357
ひかくてき［比較的］	比	357
	的	464
ひがし［東］	東	45
ひがしぐち［東口］	東	45
ひかり［光］	光	239
ひかる［光る］	光	239
ひがん［彼岸］	彼	368
ひかんする［悲観する］	悲	341
ひきだし［引き出し］	引	252
ひきだす［引き出す］	引	252
ひきわけ［引き分け］	引	252
ひく［引く］	引	252
ひくい［低い］	低	232
ひげき［悲劇］	悲	341
ひこうき［飛行機］	飛	465
	機	466
ひこうじょう［飛行場］	飛	465
ひさんな［悲惨な］	悲	341
びじゅつかん［美術館］	館	275
びしょう［微笑］	笑	337
ひしょち［避暑地］	暑	228
ひだり［左］	左	39
ひだりがわ［左側］	左	39
ひだりきき［左利き］	左	39
	利	376
ひだりて［左手］	左	39
ひづけ［日付／日付け］	付	331
ひっこす［引っ越す］	引	252
ひっし［必死］	死	256
	必	371
ひつじ［羊］	羊	189
ひっしゅう［必修］	必	371
ひつじゅひん［必需品］	品	317
	必	371
ひつような［必要な］	必	371
	要	372
ひていする［否定する］	定	356
ひと［人］	人	26
ひといちばい［人一倍］	倍	445
ひときれ［一切れ］	切	173
ひとこと［一言］	言	75
ひとごみ［人込み］	込	409
ひとつ［一つ］	一	1
ひとびと［人々］	々	447
ひとり［一人］	一	1
	人	26
ひとりたび［一人旅］	旅	318
ひとりで［一人で］	人	26
ひとりむすめ［一人娘］	娘	426
ひにく［皮肉］	肉	168
ひゃく［百］	百	11
ひゃくえん［百円］	円	14
ひゃくてん［百点］	点	441
ひゃくまん［百万］	万	13
びゃくや［白夜］	白	156
ひやけ［日焼け］	焼	333
ひやす［冷やす］	冷	323
ひゃっかじてん［百科事典］	百	11
ひゃっかてん［百貨店］	百	11
ひょう［表］	表	363
ひよう［費用］	用	285
びょういん［病院］	病	111
	院	112
びよういん［美容院］	院	112
びょうき［病気］	病	111
ひょうし［表紙］	紙	208
	表	363
びょうじゃく［病弱］	弱	233
びょうしゃする［描写する］	写	183
ひょうじょう［表情］	情	352

	表 363	
びょうどう [平等]	平 385	
ひらおよぎ [平泳ぎ]	泳 402	
ひらがな [平仮名]	名 127	
ひらく [開く]	開 249	
ひらたい [平たい]	平 385	
ひる [昼]	昼 134	
ひるごはん [昼ご飯]	昼 134	
	飯 164	
ひるね [昼寝]	昼 134	
	寝 379	
ひるま [昼間]	昼 134	
ひるやすみ [昼休み]	休 113	
	昼 134	
ひれい [比例]	比 357	
ひろい [広い]	広 91	
ひろう [疲労]	疲 403	
ひろう [拾う]	拾 499	
ひろがる [広がる]	広 91	
ひろさ [広さ]	広 91	
ひろしま [広島]	広 91	
ひろば [広場]	広 91	
	場 305	
ひろめる [広める]	広 91	
びん [便]	便 303	
ひんこん [貧困]	困 346	
びんせん [便せん]	便 303	

ふ

ぶあい [歩合]	歩 244	
ふあんな [不安な]	安 84	
	不 302	
ふうけい [風景]	風 240	
	景 414	
ふうせん [風船]	風 240	
	船 473	
ふうふ [夫婦]	夫 202	
ふうん [不運]	運 241	
ふかのうな [不可能な]	不 302	
ふきつな [不吉な]	吉 417	
ふく [服]	服 191	
ふくしゃ [複写]	写 183	
ふくしゅう [復習]	習 212	
	復 362	

ふくそう [服装]	服 191	
ふくつう [腹痛]	痛 343	
ふけいき [不景気]	不 302	
	景 414	
ふける [老ける]	老 424	
ふこう [不幸]	不 302	
	幸 340	
ふこうへいな [不公平な]	不 302	
ふさい [夫妻]	夫 202	
	妻 203	
ぶし [武士]	士 270	
ぶじ [無事]	無 512	
ふしぎな [不思議な]	思 253	
	不 302	
	議 399	
ふじさん [富士山]	山 145	
ぶしゅ [部首]	首 143	
ふじゆうな [不自由な]	由 374	
ふしょう [負傷]	負 450	
ふじん [夫人]	夫 202	
ふぜい [風情]	情 352	
ぶた [豚]	豚 166	
ぶたい [舞台]	台 185	
ふたえまぶた [二重まぶた]	重 230	
ふたつ [二つ]	二 2	
ぶたにく [豚肉]	豚 166	
	肉 168	
ふたり [二人]	二 2	
	人 26	
ふたん [負担]	負 450	
ふだん [普段]	段 443	
ふちゅうい [不注意]	注 287	
ぶちょう [部長]	長 93	
	部 370	
ふつうの [普通の]	通 319	
ふつか [二日]	二 2	
ふっかつ [復活]	復 362	
ふっきゅう [復旧]	復 362	
ふっこう [復興]	復 362	
ぶっしつ [物質]	質 222	
ぶっしょくする [払拭する]	払 377	
ふとい [太い]	太 236	
ふどうさん [不動産]	産 265	
ふとる [太る]	太 236	

ふなたび [船旅]	船 473	
ふなびん [船便]	便 303	
	船 473	
ふね [船]	船 473	
ふぶき [吹雪]	雪 494	
ふべんな [不便な]	不 302	
	便 303	
ふぼ [父母]	父 58	
	母 59	
ふみ [文]	文 220	
ぶもん [部門]	門 43	
ふゆ [冬]	冬 132	
ふゆやすみ [冬休み]	冬 132	
ふような [不要な]	要 372	
ふりょう [不良]	良 69	
ふる [降る]	降 495	
ふるい [古い]	古 86	
ふるほん [古本]	古 86	
ぶれいな [無礼な]	無 512	
ふろく [付録]	付 331	
ぶんか [文化]	化 151	
	文 220	
ぶんがく [文学]	学 54	
	文 220	
ぶんぽう [文法]	文 220	
	法 393	
ぶんや [分野]	野 171	

へ

へいえき [兵役]	役 366	
へいかいしき [閉会式]	閉 250	
へいきん [平均]	平 385	
へいこうする [閉口する]	閉 250	
べいこく [米国]	米 67	
へいさ [閉鎖]	閉 250	
へいじつ [平日]	平 385	
へいせい [平成]	平 385	
へいてん [閉店]	閉 250	
へいわ [平和]	平 385	
	和 386	
へたな [下手な]	下 34	
	手 140	
べっさつ [別冊]	冊 439	
べっそう [別荘]	別 293	

べつに［別に］　別 293
べつの［別の］　別 293
べつべつに［別々に］　別 293
　　　々 447
へや［部屋］　屋 308
　　　部 370
へる［経る］　経 391
へんか［変化］　化 151
　　　変 504
べんがく［勉学］　勉 122
べんきょうする［勉強する］　勉 122
　　　強 125
へんこう［変更］　変 504
べんごし［弁護士］　士 270
へんさいする［返済する］　済 392
へんじ［返事］　事 272
べんじょ［便所］　便 303
へんとう［返答］　答 296
へんな［変な］　変 504
べんりな［便利な］　便 303
　　　利 376
へんれいきん［返戻金］　戻 501

ほ

ほいく［保育］　育 430
ぼいん［母音］　音 177
ほうあん［法案］　法 393
ほうえいする［放映する］　映 187
ぼうえんきょう［望遠鏡］　遠 225
ほうか［放火］　放 503
ほうげん［方言］　言 75
　　　方 136
ぼうけん［冒険］　険 498
ほうこう［方向］　方 136
ほうしかつどう［奉仕活動］　仕 271
ぼうしする［防止する］　止 243
ほうしゃのう［放射能］　放 503
ほうせき［宝石］　石 260
ほうそう［放送］　送 246
　　　放 503
ぼうそうぞく［暴走族］　走 114
ほうそく［法則］　法 393
ぼうねんかい［忘年会］　忘 354
ほうふ［抱負］　負 450

ぼうふうう［暴風雨］　雨 102
ほうほう［方法］　方 136
　　　法 393
ほうもん［訪問］　問 223
ほうりつ［法律］　法 393
　　　律 394
ほうる［放る］　放 503
ほかの［外の］　外 36
ほかの［他の］　他 448
ほくせい［北西］　西 46
ほくとう［北東］　北 48
ほくべい［北米］　米 67
ほけん［保険］　険 498
ぼご［母語］　母 59
ほこうしゃ［歩行者］　歩 244
ほし［星］　星 493
ほしうらない［星占い］　星 493
ぼしゅうする［募集する］　集 301
ほしゅてき［保守的］　守 461
ほそい［細い］　細 511
ほそながい［細長い］　細 511
ほっかいどう［北海道］　北 48
　　　道 144
　　　海 150
ほっきょく［北極］　北 48
ほっそく［発足］　発 314
ほどう［歩道］　道 144
　　　歩 244
ほどうきょう［歩道橋］　橋 479
ほほえむ［ほほ笑む］　笑 337
ほん［本］　本 25
ぼんおどり［盆踊り］　踊 380
ほんてん［本店］　店 109
ほんとうに［本当に］　当 509
ほんね［本音］　音 177
ほんや［本屋］　屋 308

ま

まいあさ［毎朝］　毎 62
　　　朝 133
まいしゅう［毎週］　毎 62
　　　週 80
まいすう［枚数］　枚 438
まいつき［毎月］　月 18

まいど［毎度］　毎 62
まいとし［毎年］　年 60
　　　毎 62
まいにち［毎日］　日 17
　　　毎 62
まいねん［毎年］　年 60
　　　毎 62
まいばん［毎晩］　毎 62
　　　晩 137
まえ［前］　前 40
まえうりけん［前売り券］　前 40
まかす［負かす］　負 450
まきがい［巻き貝］　貝 116
まぎわ［間際］　際 395
まける［負ける］　負 450
まさに［正に］　正 297
まさる［勝る］　勝 449
まじる［交じる］　交 480
まじわる［交わる］　交 480
まち［町］　町 100
まちあいしつ［待合室］　待 78
　　　室 210
まちあわせる［待ち合わせる］　待 78
まちがい［間違い］　間 44
　　　違 365
まちがえる［間違える］　違 365
まつ［待つ］　待 78
まっか［真っ赤］　赤 154
まっくら［真っ暗］　暗 235
まっくろ［真っ黒］　黒 157
　　　真 184
まっさお［真っ青］　青 155
まっしろ［真っ白］　白 156
　　　真 184
まったく［全く］　全 369
まつばやし［松林］　林 147
まつり［祭り／祭］　祭 384
まつる［祭る］　祭 384
まと［的］　的 464
まど［窓］　窓 411
まどがわのせき［窓側の席］　窓 411
まどぐち［窓口］　口 15
　　　窓 411

まなつ［真夏］	夏	130	
まなぶ［学ぶ］	学	54	
まにあう［間に合う］	間	44	
	合	295	
まねき［招き］	招	432	
まねく［招く］	招	432	
まふゆ［真冬］	冬	132	
まめ［豆］	豆	237	
まもる［守る］	守	461	
まよなか［真夜中］	真	184	
まる［円］	円	14	
まる［丸］	丸	321	
まるい［円い］	円	14	
まるい［丸い］	丸	321	
まるた［丸太］	太	236	
まるめる［丸める］	丸	321	
まわり［周り］	周	79	
まわる［回る］	回	284	
まんいち［万一］	万	13	
まんいん［満員］	員	269	
まんが［漫画］	画	188	
まんぞく［満足］	足	141	
まんなか［真ん中］	真	184	
まんねんひつ［万年筆］	万	13	
まんびき［万引き］	万	13	

み

みえる［見える］	見	65	
みおくる［見送る］	送	246	
みかく［味覚］	覚	353	
みかづき［三日月］	三	3	
みぎ［右］	右	37	
みぎあし［右足］	右	37	
みぎがわ［右側］	右	37	
	側	412	
みぎて［右手］	右	37	
みこん［未婚］	未	175	
	婚	419	
みじかい［短い］	短	238	
みじゅく［未熟］	未	175	
みず［水］	水	20	
みずいろ［水色］	色	158	
みずから［自ら］	自	180	
みずぎ［水着］	水	20	

	着	192	
みすてる［見捨てる］	捨	500	
みずぶそく［水不足］	足	141	
	不	302	
みせ［店］	店	109	
みせいねん［未成年］	未	175	
みせる［見せる］	見	65	
みそ［味噌］	味	176	
みち［道］	道	144	
みっか［三日］	三	3	
	日	17	
みっつ［三つ］	三	3	
みつりん［密林］	林	147	
みてい［未定］	未	175	
みな［皆］	皆	367	
みなおす［見直す］	直	496	
みなさま［皆様］	様	483	
みなさん［皆さん］	皆	367	
みなと［港］	港	478	
みなとまち［港町］	町	100	
	港	478	
みなみ［南］	南	47	
みなみぐち［南口］	南	47	
みのしろきん［身代金］	代	278	
みほん［見本］	見	65	
みまん［未満］	未	175	
みみ［耳］	耳	73	
みみかき［耳かき］	耳	73	
みみなり［耳鳴り］	耳	73	
みめい［未明］	未	175	
みやこ［都］	都	310	
みょうごにち［明後日］	明	94	
みょうじ［名字］	名	127	
	字	214	
みょうじょう［明星］	星	493	
みょうにち［明日］	明	94	
みらい［未来］	未	175	
みる［見る］	見	65	
みれん［未練］	練	361	
みんかん［民間］	民	286	
みんしゅか［民主化］	化	151	
みんしゅく［民宿］	宿	218	
みんしゅしゅぎ［民主主義］	民	286	
	義	398	

みんしゅてき［民主的］	的	464	
みんぞく［民族］	族	195	
	民	286	

む

むいか［六日］	六	6	
むかし［昔］	昔	276	
むかしばなし［昔話］	昔	276	
むかしむかし［昔々］	昔	276	
	々	447	
むがむちゅう［無我夢中］	夢	463	
むかんけい［無関係］	係	397	
むこうがわ［向こう側］	側	412	
むし［虫］	虫	124	
むしあつい［蒸し暑い］	暑	228	
むしば［虫歯］	虫	124	
	歯	505	
むじんとう［無人島］	島	476	
むすこ［息子］	息	425	
むすぶ［結ぶ］	結	418	
むすめ［娘］	娘	426	
むすめむこ［娘婿］	娘	426	
むだな［無駄な］	無	512	
むちゃくちゃ［無茶苦茶］	茶	169	
むちゅう［夢中］	夢	463	
むっつ［六つ］	六	6	
むねん［無念］	念	350	
むほん［謀反］	反	163	
むら［村］	村	101	
むりな［無理な］	理	162	
	無	512	
むりやり［無理矢理］	矢	194	
むりょう［無料］	料	161	
	無	512	

め

め［目］	目	16	
めいあん［名案］	案	489	
めいさく［名作］	作	174	
めいし［名刺］	名	127	
めいし［名詞］	名	127	
めいもん［名門］	門	43	
めがさめる［目が覚める］	覚	353	
めがみ［女神］	女	52	
めざましどけい［目覚まし時計］	覚	353	

めし［飯］	飯 164		
めだつ［目立つ］	立 77		
めったに［滅多に］	多 89		
めやす［目安］	安 84		
めんぼくない／めんもく			
ない［面目ない］	目 16		

も

もうしあげる［申し上げる］	申 481
もうしこむ［申し込む］	込 409
	申 481
もうしでる［申し出る］	申 481
もうしわけない［申し訳ない］	申 481
もうす［申す］	申 481
もうどうけん［盲導犬］	犬 160
もくじ［目次］	目 16
	次 446
もくせい［木星］	木 21
もくてき［目的］	目 16
	的 464
もくようび［木曜日］	木 21
	曜 24
もじ［文字］	字 214
	文 220
もしくは［若しくは］	若 423
もちあげる［持ち上げる］	持 126
もちいる［用いる］	用 285
もちぬし［持ち主］	主 204
もちもの［持ち物］	持 126
もつ［持つ］	持 126
もっとも［最も］	最 434
もどす［戻す］	戻 501
もどる［戻る］	戻 501
もの［物］	物 316
もふく［喪服］	服 191
もみじ［紅葉］	葉 413
もめん［木綿］	木 21
もよう［模様］	様 483
もり［森］	森 148
もりたさん［森田さん］	森 148
もん［門］	門 43
もんく［文句］	文 220
もんだい［問題］	題 219
	問 223

や

や［矢］	矢 194
やおや［八百屋］	八 8
	百 11
	屋 308
やぎ［山羊］	羊 189
やきとり［焼き鳥］	鳥 167
	焼 333
やきにく［焼き肉］	焼 333
やきゅう［野球］	野 171
やく［焼く］	焼 333
やく［役］	役 366
やくがく［薬学］	薬 267
やくしゃ［役者］	役 366
やくそく［約束］	約 459
	束 460
やくにたつ［役に立つ］	立 77
	役 366
やくひゃくにん［約百人］	約 459
やくめ［役目］	役 366
やけい［夜景］	景 414
やける［焼ける］	焼 333
やさい［野菜］	野 171
	菜 172
やしょく［夜食］	夜 138
やじるし［矢印］	矢 194
やしろ［社］	社 107
やすい［安い］	安 84
やすみ［休み］	休 113
やすむ［休む］	休 113
やちん［家賃］	家 193
やっきょく［薬局］	薬 267
やっつ［八つ］	八 8
やど［宿］	宿 218
やとう［野党］	野 171
	党 400
やね［屋根］	屋 308
やま［山］	山 145
やまい［病］	病 111
やまかじ［山火事］	山 145
やまだけ［山田家］	家 193
やまださん［山田さん］	田 49
	山 145
やまでら［山寺］	寺 28

や

やまみち［山道］	山 145
やまもとくん［山本君］	君 491
やまもとさん［山本さん］	本 25
やむ［病む］	病 111
やめる［辞める］	辞 456
やわらぐ［和らぐ］	和 386

ゆ

ゆいしょある［由緒ある］	由 374
ゆう［結う］	結 418
ゆうえんち［遊園地］	遊 401
	園 408
ゆうがた［夕方］	夕 135
	方 136
ゆうかん［夕刊］	夕 135
ゆうこう［友好］	友 96
ゆうこうな［有効な］	有 264
ゆうじょう［友情］	友 96
	情 352
ゆうしょうする［優勝する］	勝 449
ゆうしょく［夕食］	夕 135
ゆうじん［友人］	友 96
ゆうすずみ［夕涼み］	涼 405
ゆうぜい［遊説］	説 224
ゆうそうする［郵送する］	送 246
ゆうだち［夕立］	夕 135
ゆうのうな［有能な］	有 264
ゆうひ［夕日］	夕 135
ゆうびんきょく［郵便局］	便 303
ゆうめいな［有名な］	名 127
	有 264
ゆうやけ［夕焼け］	焼 333
ゆうりな［有利な］	有 264
ゆうりょう［有料］	有 264
ゆき［雪］	雪 494
ゆきだるま［雪だるま］	雪 494
ゆく［行く］	行 66
ゆしゅつ［輸出］	出 98
ゆにゅう［輸入］	入 97
ゆみ［弓］	弓 123
ゆみや［弓矢］	弓 123
ゆめ［夢］	夢 463
ゆらい［由来］	由 374

よ

よあけ［夜明け］	夜	138
よい［良い］	良	69
よう［用］	用	285
よういする［用意する］	用	285
	意	288
ようか［八日］	八	8
ようきゅう［要求］	要	372
ようご［用語］	用	285
ようし［用紙］	用	285
ようじ［用事］	事	272
	用	285
ようしき［洋式］	洋	190
	式	215
ようしゅ［洋酒］	酒	329
ようしょ［洋書］	洋	190
ようしょく［洋食］	洋	190
ようす［様子］	子	53
	様	483
ようすいち［用水池］	池	313
ようするに［要するに］	要	372
ようちえん［幼稚園］	園	408
ようつう［腰痛］	痛	343
ようてん［要点］	点	441
ようび［曜日］	曜	24
ようふう［洋風］	風	240
ようふく［洋服］	洋	190
	服	191
ようほう［用法］	法	393
ようもう［羊毛］	羊	189
ようやく［要約］	要	372
	約	459
よくしつ［浴室］	室	210
よげん［予言］	言	75
	予	170
よこ［横］	横	508
よこぎる［横切る］	横	508
よごす［汚す］	汚	325
よこづな［横綱］	横	508
よごれ［汚れ］	汚	325
よごれる［汚れる］	汚	325
よさん［予算］	予	170
よじ［四時］	四	4
よしださん［吉田さん］	吉	417

よしゅう［予習］	予	170
	習	212
よそく［予測］	予	170
よっか［四日］	四	4
よっつ［四つ］	四	4
よてい［予定］	予	170
	定	356
よとう［与党］	党	400
よなか［夜中］	夜	138
よにん［四人］	四	4
よねんせい［四年生］	四	4
よのなか［世の中］	世	281
よぼう［予防］	予	170
よみかた［読み方］	方	136
よみもの［読み物］	読	119
よむ［読む］	読	119
よやく［予約］	予	170
	約	459
よる［夜］	夜	138
よろん［世論］	世	281
よわい［弱い］	弱	233
よわき［弱気］	弱	233
よわむし［弱虫］	虫	124
よわる［弱る］	弱	233
よん［四］	四	4
よんさい［四歳］	四	4

ら

らいがっき［来学期］	来	68
らいげつ［来月］	月	18
らいしゅう［来週］	来	68
	週	80
らいねん［来年］	年	60
	来	68
らくな［楽な］	楽	178
らんおう［卵黄］	卵	327
らんぱく［卵白］	卵	327

り

りえき［利益］	利	376
りかい［理解］	理	162
りきがく［力学］	力	50
りく［陸］	陸	477
りくぐん［陸軍］	陸	477

りくじょう［陸上］	陸	477
りこうな［利口な］	利	376
りこん［離婚］	婚	419
りし［利子］	利	376
りせい［理性］	性	431
りそう［理想］	理	162
りちぎな［律儀な］	律	394
りっぱ［立派］	立	77
りゆう［理由］	理	162
	由	374
りゅうがくする［留学する］	留	263
りゅうがくせい［留学生］	留	263
りょうがえ［両替］	両	422
りょうがわ［両側］	側	412
	両	422
りょうきん［料金］	金	22
	料	161
りょうけん［猟犬］	犬	160
りょうしん［良心］	良	69
りょうしん［両親］	親	196
	両	422
りようする［利用する］	用	285
	利	376
りょうて［両手］	両	422
りょうほう［両方］	方	136
	両	422
りょうり［料理］	料	161
	理	162
りょうりつする［両立する］	両	422
りょかん［旅館］	館	275
	旅	318
りょけん［旅券］	旅	318
りょこう［旅行］	行	66
	旅	318
りょひ［旅費］	旅	318
りんぎょう［林業］	林	147
りんどう［林道］	林	147

る

るす［留守］	留	263
	守	461
るすばんでんわ［留守番電話］	留	263
	番	436
	守	461

れ

れいせいな［冷静な］	冷	323
	静	406
れいせん［冷戦］	戦	387
れいぞうこ［冷蔵庫］	冷	323
れいとうする［冷凍する］	冷	323
れいぼう［冷房］	冷	323
れっとう［列島］	島	476
れんきゅう［連休］	連	410
れんしゅう［練習］	習	212
	練	361
れんぞく［連続］	連	410
	続	455
れんらくする［連絡する］	連	410

ろ

ろうか［老化］	老	424
ろうがん［老眼］	老	424
ろうじん［老人］	老	424
ろうどう［労働］	働	268
ろうどうくみあい［労働組合］	働	268
ろうどうしゃ［労働者］	働	268

ろうにゃくなんにょ［老若男女］	若	423
ローマじ［ローマ字］	字	214
ろく［六］	六	6
ろくおん［録音］	音	177
ろくがつ［六月］	六	6
ろくじ［六時］	六	6
ろくじゅうねんだい［六十年代］	代	278
ろくにん［六人］	六	6
ろっぴゃく［六百］	六	6
	百	11
ろっぷん［六分］	六	6
ろんそう［論争］	争	388

わ

わ［和］	和	386
わえいじてん［和英辞典］	英	221
わかい［若い］	若	423
わかもの［若者］	者	227
	若	423
わかる［分かる］	分	32
わかれる［別れる］	別	293
わかわかしい［若々しい］	若	423

わくせい［惑星］	星	493
わける［分ける］	分	32
わし［和紙］	紙	208
わしき［和式］	式	215
わしつ［和室］	室	210
わしょく［和食］	和	386
わすれっぽい［忘れっぽい］	忘	354
わすれもの［忘れ物］	忘	354
わすれる［忘れる］	忘	354
わだい［話題］	話	76
	題	219
わたくし［私］	私	201
わたし［私］	私	201
わたしたち［私達］	達	492
わふう［和風］	風	240
わふく［和服］	服	191
わらう［笑う］	笑	337
わりこむ［割り込む］	込	409
わりびき［割り引き］	引	252
わるい［悪い］	悪	234
わるくち／わるぐち［悪口］	悪	234
わるもの［悪者］	悪	234

INTERCULTURAL
COMMUNICATION
IN CONTEXTS

INTERCULTURAL COMMUNICATION IN CONTEXTS

SEVENTH EDITION

Judith N. Martin
Arizona State University

Thomas K. Nakayama
Northeastern University

INTERCULTURAL COMMUNICATION IN CONTEXTS, SEVENTH EDITION

Published by McGraw-Hill Education, 2 Penn Plaza, New York, NY 10121. Copyright © 2018 by McGraw-Hill Education. All rights reserved. Printed in the United States of America. Previous editions © 2013, 2010, and 2006. No part of this publication may be reproduced or distributed in any form or by any means, or stored in a database or retrieval system, without the prior written consent of McGraw-Hill Education, including, but not limited to, in any network or other electronic storage or transmission, or broadcast for distance learning.

Some ancillaries, including electronic and print components, may not be available to customers outside the United States.

This book is printed on acid-free paper.

2 3 4 5 6 7 8 9 LCR 21 20 19 18

ISBN 978-0-07-352393-4
MHID 0-07-352393-3

Chief Product Officer, SVP Products & Markets: *G. Scott Virkler*
Vice President, General Manager, Products & Markets: *Michael Ryan*
Vice President, Content Design & Delivery: *Betsy Whalen*
Managing Director: *David Patterson*
Brand Manager: *Penina Braffman*
Director, Product Development: *Meghan Campbell*
Product Developer: *Jamie Laferrera*
Marketing Manager: *Meredith Leo*
Director, Content Design & Delivery: *Terri Schiesl*
Program Manager: *Jennifer Shekleton*
Content Project Managers: *Lisa Bruflodt, Samantha Donisi-Hamm*
Buyer: *Sandy Ludovissy*
Content Licensing Specialist: *DeAnna Dausener*
Cover Image: *Andrey Prokhorov/Getty Images*
Compositor: *MPS Limited*
Printer: *LSC Communications*

All credits appearing on page or at the end of the book are considered to be an extension of the copyright page.

Library of Congress Cataloging-in-Publication Data

Martin, Judith N., author. | Nakayama, Thomas K., author.
   Interculturalcommunication in contexts / Judith N. Martin, Arizona
   State University, Thomas K. Nakayama, Northeastern University.
   Seventh edition. | New York, NY : McGraw-Hill Education, [2018]
   LCCN 2016052759 | ISBN 9780073523934 (alk. paper)
   LCSH: Intercultural communication. | Cultural awareness. | Multiculturalism.
   LCC HM1211 .M373 2018 | DDC 303.48/2—dc23
   LC record available at https://lccn.loc.gov/2016052759

The Internet addresses listed in the text were accurate at the time of publication. The inclusion of a website does not indicate an endorsement by the authors or McGraw-Hill Education, and McGraw-Hill Education does not guarantee the accuracy of the information presented at these sites.

mheducation.com/highered

The two authors of this book come to intercultural communication from very different backgrounds and very different research traditions. Yet we believe that these differences offer a unique approach to thinking about intercultural communication. We briefly introduce ourselves here, but we hope that by the end of the book you will have a much more complete understanding of who we are.

Judith Martin grew up in Mennonite communities, primarily in Delaware and Pennsylvania. She has studied at the Université de Grenoble in France and has

taught in Algeria. She received her doctorate at the Pennsylvania State University. By background and training, she is a social scientist who has focused on intercultural communication on an interpersonal level and has studied how people's communication is affected as they move or sojourn between international locations. More recently, she has studied how people's cultural backgrounds influence their online communication. She has taught at the State University of New York at Oswego, the University of Minnesota, the University of New Mexico, and Arizona State University. She enjoys gardening, hiking in the Arizona desert, traveling, and Netflix.

Tom Nakayama grew up mainly in Georgia, at a time when the Asian American presence was much less than it is now. He has studied at the Université de Paris and various universities in the United States. He received his doctorate from the University of Iowa. By background and training, he is a critical rhetorician who views intercultural communication in a social context. He has taught at the California State University at San Bernardino and Arizona State University. He has done a Fulbright at the Université de Mons in Belgium. He is now professor of communication studies at Northeastern University in Boston. He lives in Providence, Rhode Island and loves

taking the train to campus. He loves the change of seasons in New England, especially autumn.

The authors' very different life stories and research programs came together at Arizona State University. We have each learned much about intercultural communication through our own experiences, as well as through our intellectual pursuits. Judith has a well-established record of social science approaches to intercultural communication. Tom, in contrast, has taken a nontraditional approach to understanding intercultural communication by emphasizing critical perspectives. We believe that these differences in our lives and in our research offer complementary ways of understanding intercultural communication.

For more than 20 years, we have engaged in many different dialogues about intercultural communication—focusing on our experiences, thoughts, ideas, and analyses—which led us to think about writing this textbook. But our interest was not primarily sparked by these dialogues; rather, it was our overall interest in improving intercultural relations that motivated us. We believe that communication is an important arena for improving those relations. By helping people become more aware as intercultural communicators, we hope to make this a better world for all of us.

Brief Contents

PART I   FOUNDATIONS OF INTERCULTURAL COMMUNICATION 1

Chapter 1   Why Study Intercultural Communication? 2

Chapter 2   The History of the Study of Intercultural Communication 43

Chapter 3   Culture, Communication, Context, and Power 82

Chapter 4   History and Intercultural Communication 121

PART II   INTERCULTURAL COMMUNICATION PROCESSES 165

Chapter 5   Identity and Intercultural Communication 166

Chapter 6   Language and Intercultural Communication 223

Chapter 7   Nonverbal Codes and Cultural Space 273

PART III   INTERCULTURAL COMMUNICATION APPLICATIONS 315

Chapter 8   Understanding Intercultural Transitions 316

Chapter 9   Popular Culture and Intercultural Communication 361

Chapter 10   Culture, Communication, and Intercultural Relationships 395

Chapter 11   Culture, Communication, and Conflict 440

Chapter 12   Striving for Engaged and Effective Intercultural Communication 478

PART I COMMUNICATIONS OF INTERCULTURAL COMMUNICATION 1

Chapter 1 Why Study Intercultural Communication? 2

Chapter 2 The History of the Study of Intercultural Communication 45

Chapter 3 Culture, Communication, Context, and Power 81

Chapter 4 History and Intercultural Communication 121

PART II INTERCULTURAL COMMUNICATION PROCESSES 156

Chapter 5 Identity and Intercultural Communication 158

Chapter 6 Language and Intercultural Communication 217

Chapter 7 Nonverbal Codes and Cultural Spaces 276

PART III INTERCULTURAL COMMUNICATION APPLICATIONS 310

Chapter 8 Understanding Intercultural Transitions 318

Chapter 9 Popular Culture and Intercultural Communication 361

Chapter 10 Cultural Communication and Intercultural Relationships 393

Chapter 11 Culture, Communication, and Conflict 160

Chapter 12 Striving for Engaged and Effective Intercultural Communication 208

Contents

Preface xix
To the Student xxxi

PART I FOUNDATIONS OF INTERCULTURAL COMMUNICATION 1

Chapter 1 *Why Study Intercultural Communication?* 2

The Self-Awareness Imperative 3

The Demographic Imperative 5
Changing U.S. Demographics 5
Changing Immigration Patterns 6

The Economic Imperative 15

The Technological Imperative 19
Technology and Human Communication 19
Access to Communication Technology 24

The Peace Imperative 25

The Ethical Imperative 29
Relativity versus Universality 29
Being Ethical Students of Culture 32

Internet Resources 35

Summary 36

Discussion Questions 37

Activities 37

Key Words 38

References 38

Credits 41

Chapter 2   *The History of the Study of Intercultural Communication*   43

The Early Development of the Discipline   44

Nonverbal Communication   45

Application of Theory   45

An Emphasis on International Settings   45

An Interdisciplinary Focus   46

Perception and Worldview of the Researcher   48

Three Approaches to Studying Intercultural Communication   49

The Social Science Approach   51

The Interpretive Approach   57

The Critical Approach   64

A Dialectical Approach to Understanding Culture and Communication   69

Combining the Three Traditional Paradigms: The Dialectical Approach   69

Six Dialectics of Intercultural Communication   72

Keeping a Dialectical Perspective   74

Internet Resources   75

Summary   75

Discussion Questions   76

Activities   76

Key words   76

References   77

Credits   80

Chapter 3   *Culture, Communication, Context, and Power*   82

What Is Culture?   83

Social Science Definitions: Culture as Learned, Group-Related Perceptions   86

Interpretive Definitions: Culture as Contextual Symbolic Patterns of Meaning, Involving Emotions   87

Critical Definitions: Culture as Heterogeneous, Dynamic, and a Contested Zone   89

What Is Communication?   91

The Relationship Between Culture and Communication   92
How Culture Influences Communication   94
How Communication Reinforces Culture   106
Communication as Resistance to the Dominant Cultural System   109

The Relationship Between Communication and Context   110

The Relationship Between Communication and Power   111

Internet Resources   116

Summary   117

Discussion Questions   117

Activities   118

Key Words   118

References   118

Credits   120

Chapter 4   *History and Intercultural Communication*   121

From History to Histories   123
Political, Intellectual, and Social Histories   124
Family Histories   125
National Histories   126
Cultural-Group Histories   128

History, Power, and Intercultural Communication   129
The Power of Texts   130
The Power of Other Histories   132
Power in Intercultural Interactions   134

History and Identity   134
Histories as Stories   135
Nonmainstream Histories   136

Intercultural Communication and History   147

Antecedents of Contact   148

The Contact Hypothesis   149

Negotiating Histories Dialectically in Interaction   155

Internet Resources   156

Summary   157

Discussion Questions   158

Activities   158

Key words   159

References   159

Credits   162

PART II   INTERCULTURAL COMMUNICATION PROCESSES   165

Chapter 5   *Identity and Intercultural Communication   166*

Thinking Dialectically About Identity   167

The Social Science Perspective   168

The Interpretive Perspective   171

The Critical Perspective   172

Identity Development Issues   176

Minority Identity Development   178

Majority Identity Development   180

Social and Cultural Identities   183

Gender Identity   183

Sexual Identity   186

Age Identity   186

Racial and Ethnic Identities   188

Characteristics of Whiteness   191

Religious Identity   195

Class Identity   197

National Identity   199

Regional Identity   201

Personal Identity 202

Multicultural People 202

Identity, Stereotypes, and Prejudice 208

Identity and Communication 212

Internet Resources 214

Summary 215

Discussion Questions 215

Activities 216

Key words 216

References 217

Credits 221

Chapter 6   *Language and Intercultural Communication* 223

Social Science Perspective on Language 225

Language and Perception 226

Language and Thought: Metaphor 229

Cultural Variations in Communication Style 230

Influence of Interactive Media Use on Language and Communication Style 234

Slang and Humor in Language Use 235

Interpretive Perspective on Language 238

Variations in Contextual Rules 238

Critical Perspective on Language 240

Co-Cultural Communication 240

Discourse and Social Structure 244

The "Power" Effects of Labels 244

Moving Between Languages 247

Multilingualism 247

Translation and Interpretation 251

Language and Identity 255

Language and Cultural Group Identity 255

Code Switching 257

Language Politics and Policies   260

Language and Globalization   263

Internet Resources   266

Summary   267

Discussion Questions   268

Activities   268

Key words   269

References   269

Credits   271

Chapter 7   *Nonverbal Codes and Cultural Space   273*

Thinking Dialectically About Nonverbal Communication: Defining Nonverbal Communication   275
Comparing Verbal and Nonverbal Communication   276
What Nonverbal Behavior Communicates   277

The Universality of Nonverbal Behavior   279
Recent Research Findings   279
Nonverbal Codes   281
Stereotype, Prejudice, and Discrimination   292
Semiotics and Nonverbal Communication   295

Defining Cultural Space   297
Cultural Identity and Cultural Space   298
Changing Cultural Space   303
Postmodern Cultural Spaces   304

Internet Resources   308

Summary   308

Discussion Questions   309

Activities   309

Key Words   309

References   310

Credits   313

PART III   INTERCULTURAL COMMUNICATION APPLICATIONS   315

Chapter 8   *Understanding Intercultural Transitions*   316

Thinking Dialectically About Intercultural Transitions   319

Types of Migrant Groups   321
Voluntary Migrants   321
Involuntary Migrants   323

Migrant–Host Relationships   325
Assimilation   326
Separation   327
Integration   330
Cultural Hybridity   331

Cultural Adaptation   332
Social Science Approach   333
Interpretive Approach   338
Critical Approach: Contextual Influences   347

Internet Resources   353

Summary   353

Discussion Questions   354

Activities   354

Key words   354

References   355

Credits   358

Chapter 9   *Popular Culture and Intercultural Communication*   361

Learning About Cultures Without Personal Experience   363
The Power of Popular Culture   363
What Is Popular Culture?   364

Consuming and Resisting Popular Culture   369

Consuming Popular Culture   369

Resisting Popular Culture   371

Representing Cultural Groups   374

Migrants' Perceptions of Mainstream Culture   376

Popular Culture and Stereotyping   377

U.S. Popular Culture and Power   380

Global Circulation of Images and Commodities   381

Cultural Imperialism   384

Internet Resources   388

Summary   388

Discussion Questions   389

Activities   389

Key Words   390

References   390

Credits   392

Chapter 10   *Culture, Communication, and Intercultural Relationships   395*

Benefits and Challenges of Intercultural Relationships   397

Benefits   397

Challenges   399

Thinking Dialectically About Intercultural Relationships   403

Personal–Contextual Dialectic   404

Differences–Similarities Dialectic   405

Cultural–Individual Dialectic   405

Privilege–Disadvantage Dialectic   406

Static–Dynamic Dialectic   406

History/Past–Present/Future Dialectic   406

Intercultural Relationships   407

Social Science Approach: Cross-Cultural Differences   407

Interpretive Approach: Communicating in Intercultural Relationships 413

Critical Approach: Contextual Influences 428

Internet Resources 432

Summary 432

Discussion Questions 433

Activities 433

Key Words 434

References 434

Credits 437

Chapter II   *Culture, Communication, and Conflict* 440

Characteristics of Intercultural Conflict 443

Ambiguity 443

Language 444

Contradictory Conflict Styles 444

The Social Science Approach to Conflict 446

Cultural Values and Conflict 447

Religion and Conflict 447

Family Influences 449

Intercultural Conflict Styles 451

Gender, Ethnicity, and Conflict Styles 454

Interpretive and Critical Approaches to Social Conflict 455

Social Movements 457

Historical and Political Contexts 458

Managing Intercultural Conflict 461

Dealing with Interpersonal Conflict 461

Mediation 468

Peacebuilding 471

Internet Resources 472

Summary 473

Discussion Questions   474

Activities   474

Key Words   474

References   474

Credits   477

Chapter 12   *Striving for Engaged and Effective Intercultural Communication*   478

The Components of Competence   479

Social Science Perspective: Individual Components   479

Interpretive Perspective: Competence in Contexts   488

Critical Perspective: Competence for Whom?   490

Applying Knowledge About Intercultural Communication   491

Entering into Dialogue   492

Becoming Interpersonal Allies   494

Building Coalitions   496

Social Justice and Transformation   497

Forgiveness   501

What the Future Holds   503

Internet Resources   507

Summary   508

Discussion Questions   508

Activities   509

Key Words   509

References   509

Credits   512

Name Index   I-I

Subject Index   I-9

Preface

THE INCREASING IMPORTANCE OF INTERCULTURAL COMMUNICATION IN A RAPIDLY CHANGING WORLD

While the rise of digital mobile technology has provided instant connectivity to people and cultures that were once distant and isolated, worldwide political and economic uncertainties highlight the increasing importance of intercultural communication. There are now more people displaced from their homelands than ever before—65 million or 34,000 people *per day* fleeing war, droughts, and other calamities (UNHCR Global Trends, 2016). Increasing ethnic and religious tensions and the weak world economy lead us to question the ability of humanity to live peacefully and to doubt the benefits of globalization. How will the expansion of globalization be affected? If the euro fails, what happens to Europe's economy, and what kind of impact will there be on the exchange of products and movement of people around the world? How will economic changes influence where tourists, businesspeople, students, immigrants, and refugees come from and where they go? What languages will be studied, and what is the future role of English in the world? Changes such as these are likely to influence the shape of intercultural communication.

When we look back upon the international and intercultural situation at the time we first began writing this book, we recognize how rapidly the world has changed and how, as a result, these changes have raised even more pressing issues for intercultural communication scholars and practitioners. We could not have predicted that people in the United Kingdom would vote to leave the European Union nor that the United States would still be involved in conflicts in Iraq and Afghanistan after 25 years. The world will continue to change in ways that we cannot predict, but we must face this dynamic world open to new challenges, rather than retreating to ways of life that are rapidly disappearing.

In this climate, the study of intercultural communication takes on special significance, because it offers tools to help us as we grapple with questions about religious and ethnic differences, hate crimes, environmental disasters, and many other related issues. Those who study, teach, and conduct research in intercultural communication face an increasing number of challenges and difficult questions: Are we actually reinforcing stereotypes in discussing cultural differences? Is there a way to understand the dynamics of intercultural communication without resorting to lists of instructions? How do we understand the broader social, political, and historical contexts when we teach intercultural communication? How can we use our intercultural communication skills to help enrich our lives and the lives of those around us? Can intercultural communication scholars promote a better world for all?

Such questions are driven by rapidly changing cultural dynamics—both within the United States and abroad. On the one hand, natural disasters like earthquakes in Chile, Indonesia, Nepal, and elsewhere, flooding in Europe and Sri Lanka and elsewhere, deadly Ebola outbreak in West Africa, and the spread of the Zika virus have elicited a variety of positive responses, including tremendous caring and compassion across intercultural and international divide. On the other hand, the increasing number of terrorist attacks in many countries, the tightening of national borders in response to global migration, conflicts between police and communities of color in the United states, and the racist and hateful content posted on social media exemplify continuing intergroup conflict. These extremes demonstrate the dynamic nature of culture and communication.

We initially wrote this book in part to address questions and issues such as these. Although the foundation of intercultural communication theory and research has always been interdisciplinary, the field is now informed by three identifiable and competing *paradigms,* or "ways of thinking." In this book, we attempt to integrate three different research approaches: (1) the traditional social-psychological approach that emphasizes cultural differences and how these differences influence communication, (2) the interpretive approach that emphasizes understanding communication in context, and (3) the more recent critical approach that underscores the importance of power and historical context to understanding intercultural communication, including postcolonial approaches.

We believe that each of these approaches has important contributions to make to the understanding of intercultural communication and that they operate in interconnected and sometimes contradictory ways. In this seventh edition, we have further strengthened our *dialectical* approach, which encourages students to think critically about intercultural phenomena as seen from these various perspectives.

Throughout this book, we acknowledge that there are no easy solutions to the difficult challenges of intercultural communication. Sometimes our discussions raise more questions than they answer. We believe that this is perfectly reasonable. The field of intercultural communication is changing, but the relationship between culture and communication is as well—because that relationship is, and probably always will be, complex and dynamic. We live in a rapidly changing world where intercultural contact will continue to increase, creating an increased potential for both conflict and cooperation. We hope that this book provides the tools needed to think about intercultural communication, as a way of understanding the challenges and recognizing the advantages of living in a multicultural world.

References

UNHCR Global Trends (2016, June 16). Retrieved June 29, 2016, from https://s3.amazonaws.com/unhcrsharedmedia/2016/2016-06-20-global-trends/2016-06-14-Global-Trends-2015.pdf.

SIGNATURE FEATURES OF THE BOOK

Students usually come to the field of intercultural communication with some knowledge about many different cultural groups, including their own. Their understanding often is based on observations drawn from the Internet, social media, television, movies, books, personal experiences, news media, and other sources. In this book, we hope to move students gradually to the notion of a *dialectical framework* for thinking about cultural issues. That is, we show that knowledge can be acquired in many different ways—through social scientific studies, experience, media reports, and so on—but these differing forms of knowledge need to be seen dynamically and in relation to each other. We offer students a number of ways to begin thinking critically about intercultural communication in a dialectical manner. These include:

- An explicit discussion of differing research approaches to intercultural communication, focusing on both the strengths and limitations of each
- Ongoing attention to history, popular culture, and identity as important factors in understanding intercultural communication
- Student Voices boxes in which students relate their own experiences and share their thoughts about various intercultural communication issues
- Point of View boxes in which diverse viewpoints from news media, research studies, and other public forums are presented
- Incorporation of the authors' own personal experiences to highlight particular aspects of intercultural communication

NEW TO THE SEVENTH EDITION

- To reflect the increasing doubts about the benefits of globalization, we continue to emphasize its importance to intercultural communication. For example, in Chapter 1, we discuss how globalization and related economic recessions influence intercultural communication. In Chapter 8, we provide new examples of the impact of war and terrorism on the continuing worldwide migration and the resulting intercultural encounters.
- The continuing and expanding influence of communication technology in our daily lives is addressed by new material in Chapter 1 acknowledging the increasing (and dialectic) role, negative and positive, of social media in intercultural encounters, and social media examples are interwoven throughout the book.
- Our expanded discussion of the implications of religious identity and belief systems in Chapters 1 and 11 is prompted by continued awareness of the important role religion plays in intercultural communication.
- We continue to emphasize the important roles that institutions play in intercultural contact. In Chapter 8, we address the role of institutions in supporting or discouraging refugees, as well as immigrants and other kinds of intercultural transitions.

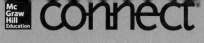

McGraw-Hill Connect®
Learn Without Limits

Connect is a teaching and learning platform that is proven to deliver better results for students and instructors.

Connect empowers students by continually adapting to deliver precisely what they need, when they need it, and how they need it, so your class time is more engaging and effective.

Connect's Impact on Retention Rates, Pass Rates, and Average Exam Scores

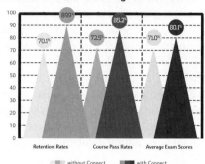

	without Connect	with Connect

73% of instructors who use **Connect** require it; instructor satisfaction **increases** by 28% when **Connect** is required.

Using **Connect** improves retention rates by **19.8%**, passing rates by **12.7%**, and exam scores by **9.1%**.

Analytics

Connect Insight®

Connect Insight is Connect's new one-of-a-kind visual analytics dashboard—now available for both instructors and students—that provides at-a-glance information regarding student performance, which is immediately actionable. By presenting assignment, assessment, and topical performance results together with a time metric that is easily visible for aggregate or individual results, Connect Insight gives the user the ability to take a just-in-time approach to teaching and learning, which was never before available. Connect Insight presents data that empowers students and helps instructors improve class performance in a way that is efficient and effective.

Impact on Final Course Grade Distribution

without Connect		with Connect
22.9%	A	31.0%
27.4%	B	34.3%
22.9%	C	18.7%
11.5%	D	6.1%
15.4%	F	9.9%

Students can view their results for any **Connect** course.

Mobile

Connect's new, intuitive mobile interface gives students and instructors flexible and convenient, anytime–anywhere access to all components of the Connect platform.

Adaptive

THE **ADAPTIVE** **READING EXPERIENCE**
DESIGNED TO TRANSFORM THE WAY STUDENTS READ

More students earn **A's** and **B's** when they use McGraw-Hill Education **Adaptive** products.

SmartBook®

Proven to help students improve grades and study more efficiently, SmartBook contains the same content within the print book, but actively tailors that content to the needs of the individual. SmartBook's adaptive technology provides precise, personalized instruction on what the student should do next, guiding the student to master and remember key concepts, targeting gaps in knowledge and offering customized feedback, and driving the student toward comprehension and retention of the subject matter. Available on tablets, SmartBook puts learning at the student's fingertips—anywhere, anytime.

Over **8 billion questions** have been answered, making McGraw-Hill Education products more intelligent, reliable, and precise.

STUDENTS WANT SMARTBOOK®

95% of students reported SmartBook to be a more effective way of reading material.

100% of students want to use the Practice Quiz feature available within SmartBook to help them study.

100% of students reported having reliable access to off-campus wifi.

90% of students say they would purchase SmartBook over print alone.

95% of students reported that SmartBook would impact their study skills in a positive way.

Mc Graw Hill Education

*Findings based on 2015 focus group results administered by McGraw-Hill Education

www.mheducation.com

Mc Graw Hill Education connect®

The seventh edition of Intercultural Communication in Contexts is now available online with Connect, McGraw-Hill Education's integrated assignment and assessment platform. Connect also offers SmartBook for the new edition, which is the first adaptive reading experience proven to improve grades and help students study more effectively. All of the title's website and ancillary content is also available through Connect, including:

- A full Test Bank of multiple choice questions that test students on central concepts and ideas in each chapter
- An Instructor's Manual for each chapter with full chapter outlines, sample test questions, and discussion topics

CHAPTER-BY-CHAPTER OVERVIEW

Intercultural Communication in Contexts is organized into three parts: Part I, "Foundations of Intercultural Communication"; Part II, "Intercultural Communication Processes"; and Part III, "Intercultural Communication Applications."

Part I, "Foundations of Intercultural Communication," explores the history of the field and presents various approaches to this area of study, including our own.

We begin Chapter 1 with a focus on the dynamics of social life and global conditions as a rationale for the study of intercultural communication. We introduce ethics in this chapter to illustrate its centrality to any discussion of intercultural interaction. In this edition, we have emphasized the importance of social justice and engagement with communities including indigenous and homeless and introduced the notion of cultural humility as an important element in intercultural effectiveness. We have also updated our discussion of the impact of globalization and immigration policies on intercultural encounters.

In Chapter 2, we introduce the history of intercultural communication as an area of study as well as the three paradigms that inform our knowledge about intercultural interactions. We establish the notion of a dialectical approach so that students can begin to make connections and form relationships among the paradigms. We describe and illustrate these approaches through the very relevant case study of the current global migration, including the impacts on the various cultural groups who have left their countries and also on host communities in the destination countries, including the related short- and long-term political implications.

In Chapter 3, we focus on four basic intercultural communication components—culture, communication, context, and power. In this edition, we've updated the Hofstede framework to reflect recent research and included a discussion of cyberspace as a cultural context. We have also provided new examples of interpretive ethnographic research and extended our discussion of the critical impact of social media on cultural resistance.

Chapter 4 focuses on the importance of historical forces in shaping contemporary intercultural interaction. We have added the concept of altered histories to discuss the ways that the past has been retold to serve certain cultural needs and interests. We also highlight the importance of using careful language when communicating about the past, by pointing to an error made by President Obama that soured relations with Poland.

Part II, "Intercultural Communication Processes," establishes the factors that contribute to the dynamics of intercultural communication: identity, language, and nonverbal codes.

Chapter 5, on identity, has extended coverage of religious identity, multicultural identity, and sexual identity (in addition to gender identity). This chapter now includes a deeper exploration of cisgender and transgender identity, and its current status in various cultures. We also introduce the many different terms used to attempt to capture the diversity of gendered and sexual identities. We also discuss microaggression as a communication strategy used to demean another identity in subtle ways.

Chapter 6 addresses language issues, with new examples of slang, the evolution of new Englishes as well as code switching. There are also new discussions of the impact of digital translation tools on language learning and the impact of social media on language and communication styles.

Chapter 7 focuses on nonverbal codes and cultural spaces and includes new examples of cultural variations in nonverbal behavior, including emojis. There is also a discussion of recent research questioning the universality of facial expressions, and examples of nonverbal microaggressions and the implications for intercultural communication.

Part III, "Intercultural Communication Applications," helps students apply the knowledge of intercultural communication presented in the first two parts.

Chapter 8 addresses intercultural transitions. In this edition, we have added more focus on refugees. We have also added a discussion on the problems of integration and assimilation, as well as the issues of working overseas for global businesses.

In Chapter 9, we focus on popular and folk culture and their impact on intercultural communication. We have included new updated examples and an enhanced discussion of how social media is used to shape culture, including Twitter, because of the power of user-generated content.

Chapter 10 explores intercultural relationships. In this edition, we update the discussion of sexuality and intimate relationships in multicultural environments, as well as tensions over these changes, and the implications for intercultural communication.

Chapter 11 emphasizes an integrated approach to intercultural conflict, using the recent riots in London and Paris, as well as global terrorist attacks as case studies. We have expanded the discussion on intractable conflicts and important strategies in peacebuilding, as well as the role of social movements (e.g., Black Lives Matter) in intercultural conflict.

Chapter 12 includes a new discussion of cosmopolitanism as a way to think about and negotiate cultural differences and continues to emphasize practical experience in striving for intercultural competence in everyday encounters.

ACKNOWLEDGMENTS

The random convergence of the two authors in time and place led to the creation of this textbook. We both found ourselves at Arizona State University in the early 1990s. Over the course of several years, we discussed and analyzed the multiple approaches to intercultural communication. Much of this discussion was facilitated by the ASU Department of Communication's "culture and communication" theme.

Department faculty met to discuss research and pedagogical issues relevant to the study of communication and culture; we also reflected on our own notions of what constituted intercultural communication. This often meant reliving many of our intercultural experiences and sharing them with our colleagues.

Above all, we must recognize the fine work of the staff at McGraw-Hill: Jamie Laferrera, Brand Manager; Jasmine Stanton, Editorial Coordinator; Meredith Leo, Marketing Manager; and Lisa Bruflodt, Production Manager and the **ansr**source developmental editing team lead by Anne Sheroff and Poornima H arikumar.

In addition, we want to thank all the reviewers of this and previous editions of *Intercultural Communication in Contexts,* whose comments and careful readings were enormously helpful. They are:

First Edition Reviewers

Rosita D. Albert, *University of Minnesota*

Carlos G. Aleman, *University of Illinois, Chicago*

Deborah Cai, *University of Maryland*

Gail Campbell, *University of Colorado, Denver*

Ling Chen, *University of Oklahoma*

Alberto Gonzalez, *Bowling Green State University*

Bradford "J" Hall, *University of New Mexico*

Mark Lawrence McPhail, *University of Utah*

Richard Morris, *Northern Illinois University*

Catherine T. Motoyama, *College of San Mateo*

Gordon Nakagawa, *California State University, Northridge*

Joyce M. Ngoh, *Marist College*

Nancy L. Street, *Bridgewater State College*

Erika Vora, *St. Cloud State University*

Lee B. Winet, *State University of New York, Oswego*

Gust A. Yep, *San Francisco State University*

Second Edition Reviewers

Eric Akoi, *Colorado State University*

Jeanne Barone, *Indiana/Purdue University at Fort Wayne*

Wendy Chung, *Rider University*

Ellen Shide Crannell, *West Valley College*

Patricia Holmes, *University of Missouri*

Madeline Keaveney, *California State University, Chico*

Mark Neumann, *University of South Florida*

Margaret Pryately, *St. Cloud State University*

Kara Shultz, *Bloomsburg University*

Third Edition Reviewers

Marguerite Arai, *University of Colorado at Colorado Springs*

Rona Halualani, *San José State University*

Piper McNulty, *De Anza College*

Karla Scott, *St. Louis University*

Candace Thomas-Maddox, *Ohio University, Lancaster*

Susan Walsh, *Southern Oregon University*

Jennifer Willis-Rivera, *Southern Illinois State University*

Fourth Edition Reviewers

Sara DeTurk, *University of Texas, San Antonio*

Christopher Hajek, *University of Texas, San Antonio*

Mary M. Meares, *Washington State University*

Kimberly Moffitt, *DePaul University*

James Sauceda, *California State University, Long Beach*

Kathryn Sorrells, *California State University, Northridge*

David Zuckerman, *Sacramento State University*

Fifth Edition Reviewers

Shirene Bell, *Salt Lake Community College*

Lisa Bradford, *University of Milwaukee-Wisconsin*

John Chiang, *State University of New York Oneonta*

Susan DeTurk, *University of Texas at San Antonio*

Charles Elliott, *Cedarville University*

Gayle Houser, *Northern Arizona University*

Tema Oliveira Milstein, *University of New Mexico*

Marc Rich, *California State University, Long Beach*

Sixth Edition Reviewers

Nader Chaaban, *Northern Virginia Community College*

Jenny Gardner, *Bay Path College*

Rachel Alicia Griffin, *Southern Illinois University-Carbondale*

Julia Hagemann, *Drexel University*

Amy N. Heuman, PhD, *Texas Tech University*

Kumi Ishii, *Western Kentucky University*

Meina Lui, *University of Maryland*

Dr. Nina-Jo Moore, *Appalachian State University*

Craig VanGeison, *Saint Charles County Community College*

Nadene Vevea, *North Dakota State University*

MJ Woeste, *University of Cincinnati*

Seventh Edition Reviewers

Julie Chekroun, *Santa Monica College & Cal State University*

Becky DeGreeff, *Kansas State University Polytechnic Campus*

Thomas Green, *Cape Fear Community College*

Rebecca Hall-Cary, *Florida State University*

Kristine Knutson, *University of Wisconsin Eau Claire*

Jerome Kreitzer, *Community College of Vermont*

Grace Leinbach Coggio, *University of Wisconsin-River Falls*

Ines Meyer-Hoess, *The Pennsylvania State University*

Our colleagues and students have provided invaluable assistance. Thanks to our colleagues for their ongoing moral support and intellectual challenges to our thinking. Thanks to our editorial assistants, Dr. Gladys Muasya at Arizona State University and Maggie Williams at Northeastern University. They found relevant scholarship and interesting examples to support and liven up our writing. They were also always cooperative and responsive even when they had their own research projects to complete and academic deadlines to meet. And as always, we owe thanks to our undergraduate students, who continue to challenge us to think about intercultural communication in ways that make sense to their lives.

We thank our families and friends for once again allowing us absences and silences as we directed our energies toward the completion of this revision. We want to acknowledge both Ronald Chaldu and David L. Karbonski, who continue to be supportive of our academic writing projects.

Our international experiences have enriched our understanding of intercultural communication theories and concepts. We thank all of the following people for helping us with these experiences: Tommy and Kazuko Nakayama; Michel Dion and Eliana Sampaïo of Strasbourg, France; Jean-Louis Sauvage and Pol Thiry of the Université de Mons-Hainaut, Belgium; Christina Kalinowska and the Café "Le Ropieur" in Mons, Belgium; Scott and the others at Le BXL in Brussels, Belgium; Emilio, Vince, Jimmy, Gene and the others at the Westbury Bar in Philadelphia; Jerzy, Alicja, Marek, and Jolanta Drzewieccy of Bedzin, Poland; as well as Margaret Nicholson of the Commission for Educational Exchange between Belgium, Luxembourg, and the United States; and Liudmila Markina from Minsk, Belarus. Some research in this book was made possible by a scholarship from the Fulbright Commission and the Fonds National de la Recherche Scientifique in Brussels. We also thank Dr. Melissa Steyn and her students at the Centre for Diversity Studies at the University of the Witswatersrand in Johannesburg, South Africa for their insightful discussions. In addition, we thank the countless others we have met in cafés, train stations, bars, and conferences, if only for a moment of international intercultural interaction.

Other people helped us understand intercultural communication closer to home, especially the staff and students at the Guadalupe Center at South Mountain Community College, and also Dr. Amalia Villegas, Cruzita Mori, and Lucia Madril and family.

In spirit and conceptualization, our book spans the centuries and crosses many continents. It has been shaped by the many people we have read about and encountered. It is to these guiding and inspiring individuals—some of whom we had the good fortune to meet and some of whom we will never encounter—that we dedicate this book. It is our hope that their spirit of curiosity, openness, and understanding will be reflected in the pages that follow.

Many textbooks emphasize in their introductions how you should use the text. In contrast, we begin this book by introducing ourselves and our interests in intercultural communication. There are many ways to think about intercultural interactions. One way to learn more about intercultural experiences is to engage in dialogue with others on this topic. Ideally, we would like to begin a dialogue with you about some of the ways to think about intercultural communication. Learning about intercultural communication is not about learning a finite set of skills, terms, and theories. It is about learning to think about cultural realities in multiple ways. Unfortunately, it is not possible for us to engage in dialogues with our readers.

Instead, we strive to lay out a number of issues to think about regarding intercultural communication. In reflecting on these issues in your own interactions and talking about them with others, you will be well on your way to becoming both a better intercultural communicator and a better analyst of intercultural interactions. There is no endpoint from which we can say that we have learned all there is to know. Learning about communication is a lifelong process that involves experiences and analysis. We hope this book will generate many dialogues that will help you come to a greater understanding of different cultures and peoples and a greater appreciation for the complexity of intercultural communication.

COMMUNICATING IN A DYNAMIC, MULTICULTURAL WORLD

We live in rapidly changing times. Although no one can foresee the future, we believe that changes are increasing the imperative for intercultural learning. In Chapter 1, you will learn more about some of these changes and their influence on intercultural communication.

You stand at the beginning of a textbook journey into intercultural communication. At this point, you might take stock of who you are, what your intercultural communication experiences have been, both online and face-to-face, how you responded in those situations, and how you tend to think about those experiences. Some people respond to intercultural situations with amusement, curiosity, or interest; others may respond with hostility, anger, or fear. It is important to reflect on your experiences and to identify how you respond and what those reactions mean.

We also think it is helpful to recognize that in many instances people do not want to communicate interculturally. Sometimes people see those who are culturally different as threatening, as forcing them to change. They may believe that such people require more assistance and patience, or they may simply think of them as "different." People bring to intercultural interactions a variety of emotional states and attitudes; further, not everyone wants to communicate interculturally. Because of this dynamic, many people have had negative intercultural experiences that influence subsequent intercultural interactions. Negative experiences can range from simple misunderstandings to physical violence. Although it may be unpleasant to discuss such situations, we believe that it is necessary to do so if we are to understand and improve intercultural interaction.

Intercultural conflict can occur even when the participants do not intentionally provoke it. When we use our own cultural frames in intercultural settings, those hidden assumptions can cause trouble. For example, one of our students recounted an experience of conflict among members of an international soccer team based in Spain: "One player from the United States would have nervous breakdowns if practice started at 7:30 p.m., and players arrived late. This individual had been taught that 'five minutes early was ten minutes late.' The Spanish are not ones for arriving on time; to them you get there when you get there, no big deal. The players' 'hidden' differing assumptions about appropriate behavior, time, and timing contributed to the conflict." Intercultural experiences are not always fun. Sometimes they are frustrating, confusing, and distressing.

On a more serious level, we might look at the U.S. military's continued engagement in Iraq and Afghanistan as yet another example of intercultural communication. The subsequent interpretations of and reactions to this presence by different communities of people reflect important differences in our society and in the world at large. Although some people in the United States and abroad see these efforts as attempts to liberate oppressed people and establish democratic governments, others view them as imperialist intervention on the part of the United States. These differing views highlight the complexity of intercultural communication. We do not come to intercultural interactions as blank slates; instead, we bring our identities and our cultures.

IMPROVING YOUR INTERCULTURAL COMMUNICATION

Although the journey to developing awareness in intercultural communication is an individual one, it is important to recognize the connections we all have to many different aspects of social life. You are, of course, an individual. But you have been influenced by culture. The ways that others regard you and communicate with you are influenced largely by whom they perceive you to be. By enacting cultural characteristics of masculinity or femininity, for example, you may elicit particular reactions from others. Reflect on your social and individual characteristics; consider how these characteristics communicate something about you.

Finally, there is no list of things to do in an intercultural setting. Although prescribed reactions might help you avoid serious faux pas in one setting or culture, such lists are generally too simplistic to get you very far in any culture and may cause serious problems in other cultures. The study of communication is both a science and an art. In this book, we attempt to pull the best of both kinds of knowledge together for you. Because communication does not happen in a vacuum but is integral to the many dynamics that make it possible—economics, politics, technology—the ever-changing character of our world means that it is essential to develop sensitivity and flexibility to change. It also means that you can never stop learning about intercultural communication.

PART I

Foundations of Intercultural Communication

CHAPTER I
Why Study Intercultural Communication?

CHAPTER 2
The History of the Study of Intercultural Communication

CHAPTER 3
Culture, Communication, Context, and Power

CHAPTER 4
History and Intercultural Communication

CHAPTER

1

WHY STUDY INTERCULTURAL COMMUNICATION?

CHAPTER OBJECTIVES

After reading this chapter, you should be able to:

1. Identify six imperatives for studying intercultural communication.

2. Describe how technology can impact intercultural interaction.

3. Describe how global and domestic economic conditions influence intercultural relations.

4. Explain how understanding intercultural communication can facilitate resolution of intercultural conflict.

5. Explain how studying intercultural communication can lead to increased self-understanding.

6. Understand the difference among a universalistic, a relativist, and a dialogic approach to the study of ethics and intercultural communication.

7. Identify and describe three characteristics of an ethical student of culture.

THE SELF-AWARENESS IMPERATIVE

THE DEMOGRAPHIC IMPERATIVE
Changing U.S. Demographics
Changing Immigration Patterns

THE ECONOMIC IMPERATIVE

THE TECHNOLOGICAL IMPERATIVE
Technology and Human Communication
Access to Communication Technology

THE PEACE IMPERATIVE

THE ETHICAL IMPERATIVE
Relativity versus Universality
Being Ethical Students of Culture

INTERNET RESOURCES

SUMMARY

DISCUSSION QUESTIONS

ACTIVITIES

KEY WORDS

REFERENCES

*When I was back home [Kuwait], before I came to the United States to go to
college, I knew all about my culture and about my religion. However, I did
not really know what other people from the other world [United States] think
of Middle Eastern people or Muslims in general. So, what I have witnessed
is a lot of discrimination in this country, not only against my race but against
other groups. . . . Yet I understand that not all Americans hate us. I met a lot of
Americans who are cooperative with me and show me love and are interested
to know about my country and culture.*

—Mohamad

*My longest relationship was an intercultural relationship with a guy from
Colombia. We didn't run into very many problems because we were both
culturally open and enthusiastic to learn about each other's traditions and
values. We talked a lot about our backgrounds and really learned to embrace
our differences, as we grew close with each other's families. We both learned
a lot about each other's culture and different philosophies on life. Overall, it
was an extremely rewarding experience.*

—Adrianna

Both Mohamad's and Adrianna's experiences point to the benefits and challenges of
intercultural communication. Through intercultural relationships, we can learn a tremendous amount about other people and their cultures, and about ourselves and our own
cultural background. At the same time, there are many challenges. Intercultural communication can also involve barriers like stereotyping and discrimination. And these
relationships take place in complex historical and political contexts. Mohamad's experience in the United States is probably more challenging today than it would have been
several years ago because of recent political events. An important goal in this book is
how to increase your understanding of the dynamics at work in intercultural interaction.

This book will expose you to the variety of approaches we use to study intercultural communication. We also weave into the text our personal stories to make
theory come alive. By linking theory and practice, we hope to give a fuller picture of
intercultural communication than either one alone could offer.

We bring many intercultural communication experiences to the text. As you
read, you will learn not only about both of us as individuals but also about our views
of intercultural communication. Don't be overwhelmed by the seeming complexity of intercultural communication. Not knowing everything that you would like to
know is very much a part of this process.

Why is it important to focus on intercultural communication and to strive to
become better at this complex pattern of interaction? We can think of at least six
reasons; perhaps you can add more.

THE SELF-AWARENESS IMPERATIVE

One of the most important reasons for studying intercultural communication is the
awareness it raises of our own cultural identity and background. This is also one of
the least obvious reasons. Peter Adler (1975), a noted social psychologist, observes

that the study of intercultural communication begins as a journey into another culture and reality and ends as a journey into one's own culture.

We gain insights in intercultural experiences overseas. When Judith was teaching high school in Algeria, a Muslim country in North Africa, she realized something about her religious identity as a Protestant. December 25 came and went, and she taught classes with no mention of Christmas. Judith had never thought about how special the celebration of Christmas was or how important the holiday was to her. She then recognized on a personal level the uniqueness of this particular cultural practice. Erla, a graduate student from Iceland, notes the increased knowledge and appreciation she's gained concerning her home country:

> *Living in another country widens your horizon. It makes you appreciate the things you have, and it strengthens the family unit. You look at your country from a different point of view. We have learned not to expect everything to be the same as "at home," but if we happen to find something that reminds us of home, we really appreciate it and it makes us very happy. Ultimately we are all very thankful that we had the opportunity to live in another country.*

ethnocentrism A tendency to think that our own culture is superior to other cultures.

However, it is important to recognize that intercultural learning is not always easy or comfortable. Sometimes intercultural encounters makes us aware of our own **ethnocentrism**—a tendency to think that our own culture is superior to other cultures. This means that we assume, subconsciously, that the way we do things is the only way. For example, when Tom first visited France he was surprised to discover that shoppers are expected to greet shopkeepers when entering a small store. Or that French people sometimes ate horsemeat, snails, and very fragrant cheeses. Sometimes Americans think that these foods shouldn't be eaten. This attitude that foods we eat are somehow normal and that people shouldn't eat these other foods is a kind of ethnocentrism. To be surprised or even taken aback by unfamiliar customs is not unexpected; however, a refusal to expand your cultural horizons or to acknowledge the legitimacy of cultural practices different from your own can lead to intergroup misunderstandings and conflict.

What you learn depends on your social and economic position in society. Self-awareness through intercultural contact for someone from a racial or minority group may mean learning to be wary and not surprised at subtle slights by members of the dominant majority—and reminders of their place in society. For example, a Chinese American colleague is sometimes approached at professional meetings by white communication professors who ask her to take their drink order.

If you are white and middle class, intercultural learning may mean an enhanced awareness of your privilege. A white colleague tells of feeling uncomfortable staying in a Jamaican resort, being served by blacks whose ancestors were brought there as slaves by European colonizers. On the one hand, it is privilege that allows travelers like our colleague to experience new cultures and places. On the other hand, one might wonder if we, through this type of travel, are reproducing those same historical postcolonial economic patterns.

Self-awareness, then, that comes through intercultural learning may involve an increased awareness of being caught up in political, economic, and historical systems—not of our own making.

THE DEMOGRAPHIC IMPERATIVE

You have probably observed that your world is increasingly diverse. You may have classes with students who differ from you in ethnicity, race, religion, and/or nationality. College and university student bodies in the United States are becoming increasingly diverse. Statistics show that college enrollment for all racial and ethnic minorities has grown in the past 20 years, especially for Latino students where college enrollment has more than tripled. In fact, for the first time, the rate of Hispanic college enrollment has now surpassed that of whites, and whites make up a smaller proportion of students on campus today than they did 20 years ago, when three out of every four college students were white (Krogstad & Fry, 2014).

Sports are also a very visible part of increasing diversity. The Institute for Diversity and Ethics in Sport issues diversity "grades" for various U.S. American professional and college teams. In the most recent report, the National Basketball Association and Women's National Basketball Association received the highest grades for racial and gender hiring practices; the Major League Baseball organization also received high marks for diversity in administration (office staff, managers, etc.) and now almost 40% of its players are ethnic/racial minorities. In the National Football League 4 of the 12 teams in the 2013 playoffs had either an African American head coach or general manager. College sports are maintaining their diversity, and probably the greatest prospects for expanding opportunities exist in college sports rather than at the professional sport level because of the number of jobs available (Lapcheck, 2013). In addition, team diversity can apparently improve performance. One research study of European soccer teams (with players from almost 50 different nationalities) found that the most linguistically diverse teams had the best winning records (Malesky & Saiegh, 2014).

Changing U.S. Demographics

U.S. **demographics** are changing rapidly and provide another source of increased opportunity for intercultural contact. The 2010 U.S. Census revealed a dramatic increase in ethnic/racial diversity, as racial and ethnic minorities are now growing more rapidly in numbers than whites. The fastest growth is among multiracial Americans, followed by Asians and Hispanics. Non-Hispanic whites make up 63% of the U.S. population; Hispanics make up 17%; blacks, 12.3%; Asians, 5%; and multiracial Americans, 2.4% (Humes, Jones, & Ramirez, 2011). This trend is expected to continue as shown in Figure 1-2 (Passel & Cohn, 2008). In fact, there are now four states—Hawaii, California, New Mexico, and Texas—that are "majority-minority"—where there is no one majority ethnic group, and minority groups account for more than 50% of the population. Nevada and Maryland should gain this status by 2020 (Kayne, 2013; Teixeira, Frey, & Griffin, 2015).

There is increasing diversity in the U.S. workforce as well—representing the diversity in the general population, in race and ethnicity, people with disabilities, and straight, gay, and transgendered individuals (See Figure 1-1). The workforce continues to get older as baby boomers age, and there are also now more women in the workforce. In fact, more women than men are expected to make up the labor force by 2020 (Burns, Barton, & Kerby, 2012).

demographics The characteristics of a population, especially as classified by race, ethnicity, age, sex, and income.

Rapid changes in technology, demographics, and economic forces mean that you are likely to come into contact with many people with diverse backgrounds and experiences. Although many of these communication experiences will be in professional and work situations, many other interactions will be in public and social settings. (© *Esbin-Anderson/The Image Works*)

More women are in the workforce for several reasons. First, economic pressures have come to bear; more women are single parent, and even in two-parent families, it often takes two incomes to meet family expenses. Second, the women's movement of the 1960s and 1970s resulted in more women seeking careers and jobs outside the home.

Changing Immigration Patterns

The second source of demographic change is different immigration patterns. Although the United States has often been thought of as a nation of immigrants, it is also a nation that established itself by subjugating the original inhabitants and

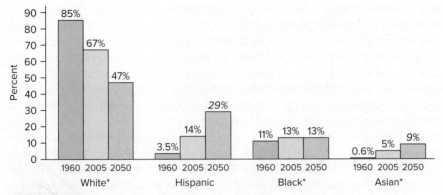

FIGURE 1-2 Population by race and ethnicity, actual and projected: 1960, 2005, and 2050 (% of total).

Source: From J. S. Passel and D'Vera Cohn, *U.S. Population Projections: 2005–2050*, Pew Research Center, 2008, p. 9.

Note: All races modified and not Hispanic (*); American Indian/Alaska Native not shown. See "Methodology." Projections for 2050 indicated by light gray bars.

that prospered to some extent as a result of slave labor. These aspects of national identity are important in understanding contemporary society. Today, immigration has changed the social landscape significantly. First, the foreign-born population continues to rise as a percentage of the total population, up from almost 5% in 1970 to more than 13% in 2013. However, this is still lower than it was during the great migrations in the 1800s and 1900s when most Europeans came to the United States (Zong & Batalova, 2015).

A second change concerns the origin of the immigrants. Prior to the 1970s, most of the immigrants to the United States came from Europe; now the large majority of immigrants are from Asia and Latin America (Zong & Batalova, 2015). We should note, however, that immigration from Mexico has actually decreased in the past 10 years, as more Mexican immigrants returned to Mexico than came to the United States—probably due to the recession in the United States and lack of economic opportunities (Gonzalez-Barrera, 2015). These shifts in patterns of immigration have resulted in a much more racially and ethnically diverse population. It's not hard to see that the United States is becoming more heterogeneous. We address the issue of whites losing majority status in Chapter 5.

Sometimes more **heterogeneous** cultures are contrasted to more **homogeneous** cultures. Instead of thinking of cultures as either heterogeneous or homogeneous, it is more useful to think about cultures as more or less heterogeneous (or more or less homogeneous). Cultures can change over time and become more or less homogeneous. They can also be more heterogeneous than another culture.

This heterogeneity presents many opportunities and challenges for students of intercultural communication. Sometimes tensions can be created by (and be the result of) world events and proposed legislation. After the devastating terror attacks in Paris in November 2015, people and governments had heightened concerns about security threat posed by Middle Eastern refugees moving into Europe. For some,

heterogeneous Difference(s) in a group, culture, or population.

homogeneous Similarity in a group, culture, or population.

this concern translated to anti-immigrant/refugee attitudes and legislation. A Bloomberg Politics poll found that 53% of U.S. Americans didn't want to accept any Syrian refugees at all; 11% more would accept only Christian refugees from Syria (Desilver, 2015); and almost half of Americans said immigrants are a burden because they take jobs, housing, and health care (Krogstad, 2015). President Obama had proposed that the United States take 10,000 Syrian and Iraqi refugees fleeing from war, but the U.S. House of Representatives passed a bill with an overwhelming majority that would suspend this program, and more than half the states' governors stated that Syrian refugees are not welcome in their states (see Point of View, p. 11). While the U.S. Senate eventually blocked the bill, the passage of the House bill and President Trump's travel ban orders reflects the tension and conflict regarding the issue of immigration in the United States (Fantz & Brumfield, 2015; Walsh & Barrett, 2015). Similarly, 26 states have challenged President Obama's executive actions that allowed young adults who were brought to the country illegally to avoid deportation and to apply for work permits (Cohn, 2015). Arizona's Senate Bill 1070 makes it a crime to not carry immigration papers and gives the police broad powers to detain anyone suspected of being in the country illegally (Archibold, 2010). While some feel that these are reasonable measures, others feel that they pave the way for increased prejudice and discrimination against foreigners, particularly those from the Middle East and Latin America.

diversity The quality of being different.

We should also note the potential opportunities in a culturally diverse society. **Diversity** can expand our conceptions of what is possible—linguistically, politically, socially—as various lifestyles and ways of thinking converge. In fact, a growing number of research studies show that being around people who are different can make us more creative, more diligent, and make us work harder, especially for groups that value innovation and new ideas. Specifically, innovative groups and organizations who have gender and racial diversity produce more creative ideas and outperform less diverse groups (Phillips, 2014). However, increased opportunity does not always lead to increased interaction or positive attitudes. While a recent survey found that incoming college students place greater emphasis than earlier cohorts on wanting to help promote racial understanding (41.2% rating it "very important" or "essential" (Eagan et. al., 2016), another study found that college students reported limited contact among racial groups on campus and few students reporting close interracial friendships (Halualani, 2010). In addition, there have been numerous reports of racist incidents on college and high school campuses across the country in recent years. This may be because these students are graduating from high schools that are becoming increasingly more segregated (Orfield & Frankenberg, 2014).

immigrants People who come to a new country, region, or environment to settle more or less permanently. (Compare with **sojourners**, see Chapter 8)

To get a better sense of the situation in the United States today, let's take a look at our history. As mentioned previously, the United States has often been referred to as a nation of **immigrants**, but this is only partly true. When Europeans began arriving on the shores of the New World, an estimated 8 to 10 million Native Americans were already living here. Their ancestors probably began to arrive via the Bering Strait at least 40,000 years earlier. The outcome of the encounters between these groups—the colonizing Europeans and the native peoples—is well known. By 1940, the Native American population of the United States had been reduced to an estimated 250,000.

Today, about 2.9 million Native Americans (from 565 recognized tribes) live in the United States (American Indians by the Numbers, 2011).

African American Immigrants   African Americans represent a special case in the history of U.S. immigration. African Americans did not choose to emigrate but were brought here involuntarily, mainly as slave labor. Many Europeans also emigrated as indentured servants. However, the system of contract servitude was gradually replaced by perpetual servitude, or slavery, almost wholly of Africans. Many landowners wanted captive workers who could not escape and who could not become competitors. They turned to slave labor.

The slave trade, developed by European and African merchants, lasted about 350 years, although slavery was outlawed in Europe long before it was outlawed in the United States. Roughly 10 million Africans reached the Americas, although many died in the brutal overseas passage (Curtin, 1969). Slavery is an important aspect of U.S. immigration history. As James Baldwin (1955) suggested, the legacy of slavery makes contemporary interracial relations in the United States very different from interracial relations in Europe and other regions of the world.

Slavery presents a moral dilemma for many whites even today. A common response is simply to ignore history. Many people assert that because not all whites owned slaves, we should forget the past and move on. For others, forgetting the past is not acceptable. In fact, some historians, like James Loewen, maintain that acknowledging and understanding the past is the only viable alternative in moving forward and making the connection of slavery to the current racial tensions in the United States:

> *Slavery's twin legacies to the present are the social and economic inferiority it conferred upon blacks and the cultural racism it spread throughout our culture. Slavery ended in 1863–65, depending upon where one lived. Unfortunately, racism, slavery's handmaiden, did not. It lives on afflicting all of us today. (Loewen, 2010, p. 159)*

Scholar and theologian Cornel West (1993) agrees that we should begin by acknowledging the historical flaws of U.S. society and recognizing the historical consequences of slavery. However, the United States has several Holocaust museums but no organized, official recognition of the horrors of slavery. Perhaps it is easier for us to focus on the negative events of another nation's history than on those of our own. On the other hand, many U.S. Americans feel that the election of Barack Obama, the first African American president, shows some progress in U.S. race relations. In Chapter 4, we explore the importance of history in understanding the dynamics of intercultural communication.

Relationships with New Immigrants   Relationships between residents and immigrants—between oldtimers and newcomers—have often been filled with tension and conflict. In the 19th century, Native Americans sometimes were caught in the middle of European rivalries. During the War of 1812, for example, Indian allies of the British were severely punished by the United States when the war ended. In 1832, the U.S. Congress recognized the Indian nations' right to self-government, but in 1871, a congressional act prohibited treaties between the U.S. government and Indian tribes. In 1887, Congress passed the Dawes Severalty Act, terminating Native Americans' special relationship with the U.S. government and paving the way for their removal from their homelands.

As waves of immigrants continued to roll in from Europe, the more firmly established European—mainly British—immigrants tried to protect their way of life, language, and culture. As one citizen lamented in 1856,

> *Four-fifths of the beggary and three-fifths of the crime spring from our foreign population; more than half the public charities, more than half the prisons and almshouses, more than half the police and the cost of administering criminal justice are for foreigners. (quoted in Cole, 1998, p. 126)*

The foreigners to which this citizen was referring were mostly from Ireland, devastated by the potato famines, and from Germany, which had fallen on hard economic and political times. Historian James Banks (1991) identifies other anti-immigrant events throughout the nation's history. As early as 1729, an English mob prevented a group of Irish immigrants from landing in Boston. A few years later, another mob destroyed a new Scots-Irish Presbyterian church in Worcester, Massachusetts. In these acts, we can see the **Anglocentrism** that characterized early U.S. history. Later, northern and western European (e.g., German and Dutch) characteristics were added to this model of American culture. Immigrants from southern, central, and eastern Europe (e.g., Italy and Poland) were expected to assimilate into the so-called mainstream culture—to jump into the **melting pot** and come out "American."

In the late 19th and early 20th centuries, a **nativistic** (anti-immigrant) movement propagated violence against newer immigrants. In 1885, 28 Chinese were killed in an anti-Chinese riot in Wyoming; in 1891, a white mob attacked a Chinese community in Los Angeles and killed 19 people; also in 1891, 11 Italian Americans were lynched in New Orleans.

Nativistic sentiment was well supported at the government level. In 1882, Congress passed the Chinese Exclusion Act, officially prohibiting anyone who lived in China from immigrating to this country. In 1924, the Johnson-Read Act and the Oriental Exclusion Act established extreme quotas on immigration, virtually precluding the legal immigration of Asians. According to Ronald Takaki (1989), these two laws "provided for immigration based on nationality quotas: the number of immigrants to be admitted annually was limited to 2% of the foreign-born individuals of each nationality residing in the United States in 1890" (p. 209). The nativistic sentiment increasingly was manifested in arguments that economic and political opportunities should be reserved solely for whites, and not just for native-born Americans.

By the 1930s, southern and eastern European groups were considered "assimilatable," and the concept of race assumed new meaning. All of the so-called white races were now considered one, so racial hostilities could focus on ethnic (nonwhite) groups, such as Asian Americans, Native Americans, and Mexican Americans (Banks, 1991). Sociologist David Roediger (1991) traces how devastating this racialization was, particularly for African Americans. In the growing, but sometimes

Anglocentrism Using Anglo or white cultural standards as the criteria for interpretations and judgments of behaviors and attitudes.

melting pot A metaphor that assumes that immigrants and cultural minorities will be assimilated into the U.S. majority culture, losing their original cultures.

nativistic Extremely patriotic to the point of being anti-immigrant.

Below is the list of states whose governors refused to accept Syrian refugees in the fall of 2015. While they don't legally have the authority to bar refugees from settling within their borders, if they do come they can withhold funds to help them learn English, get job training, or help their children succeed in school. What are some implications for intercultural communication and the encounters between U.S. Americans and other immigrants or foreigners visiting the United States?

Alabama	Illinois	Maine	Nevada	Texas
Arizona	Indiana	Maryland	New Jersey	Wisconsin
Arkansas	Iowa	Massachusetts	North Carolina	Wyoming
Florida	Kansas	Michigan	Ohio	North Dakota
Georgia	Louisiana	Mississippi	South Carolina	South Dakota
Idaho	Maine	Nebraska	Tennessee	Pennsylvania

Source: From A. Fantz and B. Brumfield, "More Than Half the Nation's Governors Say Syrian Refugees Not Welcome," *cnn.com*. Retrieved November 19, 2015, from http://www.cnn.com /2015/11/16/world/paris-attacks-syrian-refugees-backlash/.

fragile, economy of the first half of the 20th century, white workers had an advantage. Although white immigrants received low wages, they had access to better schools and to public facilities, and they were accorded greater public acceptance. People of color often were considered less fit to receive economic benefits and, to some extent, were not considered to be truly American (Foner, 1998).

The notion of the melting pot began to break down as immigrants came in larger numbers from outside of Europe. Although European immigrants were able to melt into white society, other immigrants were barred from doing so. In order to melt into white society, European immigrants were encouraged to assimilate by speaking English only and dropping their culturally specific customs. As part of this melting pot experience, many Americans of European ancestry today do not speak their forebearers' languages, such as German, Dutch, Norwegian, Polish, or Hungarian.

Although the notion of the melting pot could explain European immigrant experiences, the metaphor did not explain other immigrant experiences. Immigrants from Asia, Latin America, and Africa did not simply blend into white society. As we will see in Chapter 4, there are many legal and historical reasons why this did not happen. Some people are critical of the melting pot metaphor, not only because it does not explain the experiences of non-European immigrants, but also because it implies that immigrants should give up their unique cultural backgrounds to become white and American.

Economic conditions make a big difference in attitudes toward foreign workers and immigration policies. During the Depression of the 1930s, Mexicans and Mexican Americans were forced to return to Mexico to free up jobs for white Americans. When prosperity returned in the 1940s, Mexicans were welcomed back as a source of cheap labor. This type of situation is not limited to the United States, but occurs all over the world. For example, Algerian workers are alternately welcomed and rejected in France, depending on the state of the French economy and the demand for imported labor. Guest workers from Turkey have been subjected to similar uncertainties in Germany. Indian workers in Kenya, Chinese immigrants in Malaysia, and many other workers toiling outside their native lands have suffered the vagaries of fluctuating economies and immigration policies. In Chapter 8, we discuss the implications of these migration patterns for intercultural communication.

The tradition of tension and conflict among cultures continues to this day. The conflicts that arise in Southern California exemplify many aspects of the demographic changes in the United States. We can examine on a variety of levels the tensions in Los Angeles among Latinos/as, African Americans, Korean Americans, and European Americans. Some of the conflict is related to different languages, values, and lifestyles. Some African Americans resent the economic success of recent Korean immigrants—a reaction that reflects a typical historical pattern. The conflict may also be due to the pattern of settlement that results in cultural enclaves.

Immigration and Economic Classes   Some of the conflict may be related to the economic disparity that exists among these different groups. To understand this disparity, we need to look at issues of economic class. Most Americans are reluctant to admit that a class structure exists and even more reluctant to admit how difficult it is to move up in this structure. Indeed, most people live their lives in the same economic class into which they were born. And there are distinct class differences in clothing, housing, recreation, conversation, and other aspects of everyday life (Fussell, 1992). For example, the driveways to the homes of the very rich are usually obscured, whereas those of upper-class homes usually are long and curved and quite visible. Driveways leading to middle-class homes, in contrast, tend to go straight into garages.

The myth of a classless society is hardly benign. It not only reinforces middle- and upper-class beliefs in their own superior abilities, but also promotes a false hope among the working class and the poor that they can get ahead. Whereas real-life success stories of upward mobility are rare, fictitious ones abound in literature, film, and television. Studies have shown that U.S. Americans want to believe the myth and seriously underestimate the gap between the rich and not rich. One recent survey showed that the average American believes that the richest 20% owns 59% of the wealth and that the bottom 40% own 9%. The reality is strikingly different and rather grim. The top 20% of U.S. households own more than 84% of the wealth, and the bottom 40% combine for a mere 0.3% (that's right, not 3%, but 0.3%). Most of the recent growth after the recession is going to a tiny segment: 95% of the gains have gone to the richest 1% of people, whose share of overall income is once again close to its highest level in a century. The most unequal country in the rich world is thus becoming even more so (Growing apart, 2013). The Walton family, for example, has more wealth than 42% of American families combined, and the nation's official poverty rate in 2015 was almost 15%, which means there were 46.7 million people in poverty (Fitz, 2015; https://www.census.gov/library/publications/2016 /demo/p60-256.html).

Another recent study asked more than 50,000 people from 40 countries to estimate how much corporate CEOs and unskilled workers earned. Then they asked people how much CEOs and workers *should* earn. The average American estimated that the CEO-to-worker pay-ratio was 30-to-1, and that ideally, it'd be 7-to-1. The reality? The difference between CEO pay and unskilled worker is 354-1. Fifty years ago, it was 20-1. Again, the patterns were the same for all, regardless of age, education, political affiliation, or opinion on inequality and pay. While many Americans acknowledge this gap between rich and poor, few see it as a serious issue (one study reports only 5%). These two studies imply that our apathy about inequality may be due to rose-colored misperceptions (Fitz, 2015). How far do you think income inequality can go before Americans take action to change this situation?

A real consequence of this gap and the number of working poor is lowered economic growth in the nation and less equality of opportunity for the next generation. Measures of social mobility between generations, already lower than in much of Europe, have stagnated. There are real material consequences. For example, the gap in test scores between rich and poor children is 30% to 40% wider than it was 25 years ago, suggesting that rich youngsters are benefiting more than ever from their economic and social advantages (Growing apart, 2013). A recent study showed that the rich even live longer than the poor. Men in the top 1% income bracket live 15 years longer than the poorest 1%. In fact in some parts of the United States, adults with the lowest incomes on average die as young as people in much poorer nations in Africa and Asia (Irwin & Bui, 2016).

This widening gap is partly due to the loss of stable industrial jobs as companies move to cheaper labor markets within the United States and abroad and slow recovery from the recession with wages remaining low. Class and demographic issues also play a role, with racial and ethnic minorities typically hardest hit by economic downturns. The impact of the downturn on household net worth of white, black, and Hispanic families is dramatic. (Net worth is defined as what you have if you subtract your debt from what you own.) According to a recent Pew Research Center analysis of government data, the wealth of white households was 13 times the median wealth of black households in 2013, compared with 8 times the wealth in 2010. The wealth of white households is now more than 10 times the wealth of Hispanic households, compared with 9 times the wealth in 2010 (Kochhar & Fry, 2014).

Religious Diversity   Immigration also contributes to religious diversity, bringing increasing numbers of Muslims, Buddhists, Confucians, Catholics, and others to the United States. The religious composition of the United States is rapidly changing due to a number of factors. According to the U.S. Religious Landscape Survey (2014) done by the Pew Forum on Religion and Public Life, the percentages of Americans who say they believe in God, pray daily, and regularly go to church or other religious services all have declined somewhat in recent years.

I am involved in many different intercultural relationships. The main benefit of these relationships is that it shows other people that there is no reason to fear intercultural relationships. My generation, while more open to intercultural relationships than previous ones, is still hesitant, and I am often the recipient of dirty looks from strangers who disapprove. It is disheartening that people believe there is a difference in races, but the best way to change people's minds is to show them firsthand, which is what I hope to do.

—Katie

The recent decrease in religious beliefs and behaviors is largely attributable to the "nones"—the growing minority of Americans, particularly in the Millennial generation, who say they do not belong to any organized faith. At the same time, the report notes that the vast majority of Americans (77% of all adults) continue to identify with some religious faith (U.S. public becoming less religious, 2015). What do these changes mean to the role of religion in a diverse society? What is the future of religion in the United States? Religious beliefs and practices often play an important role in everyday cultural life. One example is the very different views on abortion, described by our student Tanya:

Pro-choice and pro-lifers have incredibly different worldview lenses. These different lenses they see through are most of the time influenced by religion and social upbringing. The values are different, yet no side is wrong and cannot see through the same worldview lens as their opponents.

These different worldviews can sometimes lead to prejudices and stereotypes. Stereotypes about Islam and Muslims are widespread in the United States and violence against Muslims has increased. Across the country, hate crimes targeting Muslims, their mosques, and businesses have tripled in 2015. Girls wearing hijabs have been harassed, mosques have been defaced and targeted by arsonists, and a New York City shopkeeper, Sarker Haque, was beaten up by a customer shouting anti-Muslim slurs (Siemaszko, 2015). Some say that religious and political leaders use these stereotypes in ways that increase prejudice and discrimination. For example, President Trump's proposals to ban Muslims from traveling to the United States were denounced by many, but one poll showed that more than 70% of Republicans seem to agree with this view (Shebaya, 2015). Political scientist Ali Muzrui (2001) describes Islam as the "ultimate negative 'Other' to the Christian tradition" and laments the rising tide of Islamophobia (fear of Islam and the hostility toward it). He lists the contrasting stereotypes:

Whereas Christianity is supposed to be peace loving, Islam is portrayed as foster- ing holy war (Jihad). Whereas Christianity liberates women, Islam enslaves them. Whereas Christianity is modern, Islam is medieval. Whereas Christianity is for- ward looking, Islam is backward looking. Whereas Christians prefer nonviolence, Muslims easily resort to terrorism. (p. 110)

Muzrui goes on to present evidence to debunk each of these stereotypes. Religious diversity is part of the demographic imperative that challenges us to learn more about intercultural communication.

These increasingly diverse ethnic, racial, economic, and religious groups come into contact mostly during the day in schools, businesses, and other settings, bringing to the encounters different languages, histories, and economic statuses. This presents great challenges for us as a society and as individuals. The main challenge is to look beyond the stereotypes and biases, to recognize the disparities and differences, and to try to apply what we know about intercultural communication. Perhaps the first step is to realize that the melting pot metaphor probably was never viable, that it was not realistic to expect everyone to assimilate into the United States in the same way. Today we need a different metaphor, one that reflects the racial, ethnic, and cultural diversity that truly exists in our country. Perhaps we should think of the United States as a "salad," in which each group retains its own flavor and yet contributes to the whole. Or we might think of it as a "tapestry," with many different strands contributing to a unified pattern.

In any case, the United States is hardly a model of diversity; many countries are far more diverse ethnically. For example, Nigeria has some 200 ethnic groups, and Indonesia has a similar number. Nigeria was colonized by the British, and artificially drawn boundaries forced many different groups into one nation-state, which caused many conflicts. The diverse groups in Indonesia, in contrast, have largely coexisted amiably for many years. Diversity, therefore, does not necessarily lead to intercultural conflicts.

Fortunately, most individuals are able to negotiate day-to-day activities in spite of cultural differences. Diversity can even be a positive force. Demographic diversity in the United States has given us tremendous linguistic richness and culinary variety, varied resources to meet new social challenges, as well as domestic and international business opportunities.

THE ECONOMIC IMPERATIVE

The idea of globalization—the creation of a world market in goods, services, labor, capital, and technology—is shown dramatically in the account of a journalist who asks a Dell computer manager where his laptop is made. The answer? It was codesigned by engineers in Texas and Taiwan; the microprocessor was made in one of Intel's factories in the Philippines, Costa Rica, Malaysia, or China; the memory came from factories in Korea, Germany, Taiwan, or Japan. Other components (keyboard, hard drive, batteries, etc.) were made by Japanese, Taiwanese, Irish, Israeli, or British firms with factories mainly in Asia, and finally, the laptop was assembled in Taiwan (Friedman, 2005).

What is the ultimate impact of globalization on the average person? Some economists defend it, saying the losses are always offset by the gains in cheaper consumer prices. However, many working people, seeing their jobs outsourced to cheap labor in India, China, and Malaysia, feel threatened. There are many blue-collar industrial jobs that have been lost to overseas in the past 10 years but one

Americans, including myself, sometimes have this belief that what we do here in the United States is the best and only way to do things. We put these "cultural blinders" on and are oblivious to any other cultures and/or values. Although American tradition has been and can be a big influence on other markets and business sectors, we are failing to realize that the way we do business is not the basis for all businesses. Most of our international business ventures are failing due to our stubbornness. In the past we felt that we could send someone to Mexico or Japan without any intercultural training and still show them how to do business. How wrong were we?

Today we realize it takes an understanding of others and their beliefs and values to truly gain respect and further our business and personal relationships. Businesses are taking the time and money to train their employees about the new culture that they will be submerged in. People in the past failed because we did not take into account that companies' attitudes and beliefs differed from ours. Good relations with other international businesses can produce a lifelong bond that can create great economic wealth for each country. The companies are not only training their employees for this culture shock but are training their families as well, because they know that without family support, this venture will surely fail. The United States has taken strides to correct their errors of the past and are continuing their efforts to produce intercultural employees, and I hope this trend continues.

—Luis

recent study concludes that as many as 14 million white-collar jobs are also vulnerable to being outsourced offshore—jobs in information technology, accounting, architecture, advanced engineering design, news reporting, stock analysis, and medical and legal services—jobs that generate the bulk of tax revenues that fund our education, health, infrastructure, and social security systems. In fact, the Department of Labor reminds us that the track record for the re-employment of displaced U.S. workers is not good, that more than one in three workers who are displaced remains unemployed, and many of those who are lucky enough to find jobs take major pay cuts (Roberts, 2014).

The world economy has been volatile and seemingly shrinking in recent years. The economic powerhouse, China has seen disastrous economic trends with a plummeting stock market, housing crisis, and a manufacturing slowdown. The most recent growth figures show a drop from 7.7% growth in 2013 and China's slowest growth since 1990. The worry now and the evidence seems to support that a slowing China also lowers growth in other countries (Beech, 2016; Worstall, 2015).

The point is that, to compete effectively in this uncertain global market, Americans must understand how business is conducted in other countries (Varner & Beamer, 2011) (See Figure 1-3). American businesspeople should be able to negotiate deals that are advantageous to the U.S. economy. However, they are not always willing to take the time and effort to do this. For example, most U.S. automobile

FIGURE 1-3   To conduct business successfully in the global marketplace, Americans must understand the principles of intercultural business communication. (© *Goran Bogicevic/123RF*)

manufacturers do not produce automobiles that have right-hand drive, which prevents them from penetrating markets in nations like Japan. Stories abound of U.S. marketing slogans that were inaccurately translated, like Pepsi's "Come alive with the Pepsi Generation," which was translated into Chinese as "Pepsi brings your ancestors back from the grave" or had culturally inappropriate meanings like Ford's marketing the Pinto in Brazil (slang for "small male genitals") or General Motors marketing the Nova in South America (*no va* is Spanish for "*no go*") (Branding so much more, 2011).

Cross-cultural trainers in the United States report that Asian business personnel often spend years in the United States studying English and learning about the country before they decide to establish operations here or invest money. In contrast, many American companies provide little or no training before sending their workers overseas and expect to close business deals quickly, with little regard for cultural idiosyncrasies.

Many management experts have examined other countries' practices for ways to increase U.S. productivity. One such idea was "quality circles," borrowed from the Japanese and now popular in the United States. Another strength demonstrated in many Asian (and European) companies is the belief in effort for its own sake. Employees in many Asian countries work longer hours and sometimes produce better products simply as a result of persistance. This trait also pays off in schools where Asian and European students score higher on standardized math and science exams than do American students (Dillon, 2010).

It will also behoove Americans to research how to do business in the huge emerging market that is 21st-century China. For example, *eBay*, the successful American Ecommerce giant, copied its American model to China and got completely destroyed by local competitor *Taobao*. Why? Because *Taobao* understood that in China, shopping is a social experience and people like talking and even haggling with sellers and building relationships with them. *Taobao* had a chat feature that allowed customers to easily talk to sellers (Custer, 2015). In contrast, Starbucks' decision to change its logo when it entered the Asian markets seems to be successful. Starbucks decided to drop the Starbucks name and the word "coffee" from its logo, giving it a more rounded appearance, which seems to appeal to collectivist consumers—found in China and other Asian countries (Walsh, Winterich, & Mittal, 2010).

Why do so many businesspeople have difficulty succeeding in Chinese and other Asian markets? The reasons involve both differences in business practices and cultural differences between East and West. For example, business dealings in China, as in many Eastern countries, are relationship oriented, and business relationships cannot succeed without respect and harmony, and great importance is placed on *guanxi* or *kuan-hsi* (relationship or connection). Businesses, like eBay, who ignore this are likely to fail. There are other important cultural differences.

For example, contract law is practiced very differently in China. Whereas in the West, the law is the essential set of rules of conduct; the "rules of conduct" in China are the ethics and standards of behavior required in a Confucian society. This means that social pressures rather than legal instruments are used to ensure compliance. Thus, what we might conceptualize as a legal issue may be seen in China as a relationship issue (Varner & Beamer, 2011).

Sometimes there are cultural differences in work ethics. One of our students, Vincent, describes a difference he observed while working as an intern in a manufacturing company:

> When looking back at this internship I can easily see that Mexican workers were more loyal to the company. I constantly noticed that American workers at this company would be walking around talking or smoking while they were supposed to be at their work stations, but the Mexican workers would never leave their stations until it was time for break. This sometimes created problems between Mexicans and other employees because of the differences in work ethics.

We discuss the implications of these types of cultural differences for relationships (Chapter 10) and conflicts (Chapter 11).

Cultural differences in business practices have implications not only when people from different companies do business with each other, but also when people from different cultures work on the same team. One effect of globalization is increasing numbers of international teams—sometimes working as virtual teams and rarely meeting face-to-face. These teams present large challenges in intercultural communication. A Hewlett-Packard project involved a 16-country multilingual virtual team that operated on both sides of the international dateline. The leaders describe the challenges: "Relatively routine tasks, such as scheduling a meeting, become complex and fraught with interpersonal friction when one person's work day begins as another is sitting down to dinner or sound asleep. A simple e-mail exchange frazzles nerves because of cultural misunderstandings" (Snyder, 2003).

Even when employees have good language skills, they naturally interpret written and verbal communication through the filter of their own culture. For example, Israeli workers in the project just described wondered why their U.S. counterparts would sometimes seem upset by e-mail exchanges. It turned out that Israelis, who tend to be rather direct and sometimes blunt, were sending e-mails that seemed rude to their American counterparts. And Americans' e-mails seemed "wishy-washy" to the Israelis. The Americans' requests, with phrases like "Thanks in advance for sending me . . . ," mystified the Israelis who would say, "Thanks for what? I haven't done anything yet." After some cultural training, both sides adapted to the other (Snyder, 2003). In later chapters, we explore the implications of these and other cultural differences in communication practices.

Globalization presents many new issues. Increasingly, **multinational corporations** are moving operations to new locations, often overseas, because of lower labor costs. These business moves have far-reaching implications, including the loss of jobs at closed facilities. Many U.S.-owned companies have established production facilities, known as *maquiladoras*, along the U.S.–Mexican border, where workers produce goods bound mainly for U.S. markets. These companies benefit from lower labor costs, tax breaks, and relaxed environmental regulations. Although Mexican laborers profit from the jobs, there is a cost in terms of environmental hazards. *Maquiladoras* thus present intercultural challenges for Mexicans and U.S. Americans.

> **multinational corporations** Companies that have operations in two or more nations.
>
> *maquiladoras* Assembly plants or factories (mainly of U.S. companies) established on the U.S.-Mexican border and using mainly Mexican labor.

Domestic diversity also requires businesses to be attentive to cultural differences. As the workforce becomes more diverse, many businesses are interested in capitalizing on these differences for economic gain. When businesses foreground cultural diversity in their employment practices, this also has an impact on how they view their customers and how they develop and market new products that appeal to ever-widening consumer bases (Yohn, 2011).

Understanding cultural differences involves not only working with diverse employees, but also recognizing new business markets, developing new products, and so on. From this perspective, diversity is a potentially powerful economic resource if organizations view the challenge as an opportunity. In this sense, then, business can capitalize on diversity.

THE TECHNOLOGICAL IMPERATIVE

Technology and Human Communication

Communication technology is a constant and we do live in the **global village** envisioned so long ago by media expert Marshall McLuhan (1967). We are linked by technology to events in the most remote parts of the world and connected to people we may never meet face-to-face. In any given day, you may text message or snapchat friends about evening plans, post a Facebook message to a relative stationed overseas, participate in a discussion board for one of your courses, send an e-mail message to your professor, and use Google Hangouts for a virtual team project in an Online course. The effects of social media like Facebook and Twitter have

> **global village** A term coined by Marshall McLuhan in the 1960s that refers to a world in which communication technology unites people in remote parts of the world.

far-reaching consequences, and it is important to understand that these technologies can have positive and negative impacts on intercultural encounters. For example, through social media, people were able to receive up-to-the-minute information and connect with friends and family in the immediate aftermath of the devastating Japanese tsunami in January 2011 (Smith, 2011). On the other hand, there was a multitude of vicious racist tweets posted in reaction to the crowning of the first Indian American as Miss America (Cisneros & Nakayama, 2015). Or consider the videos of brutal beheadings of U.S. journalists and others posted by Islamic State militants that shocked and appalled millions and their skillful use of social media to persuade and enlist recruits all around the world. These media videos and messages illustrate the far-reaching negative potential of communication technologies (Internet uproar, 2011; Islamic state says . . . 2014) and some media sites like Facebook and Twitter have increased their efforts to thwart Islamic State's use of their platforms for recruitment and propaganda (Finkle, 2016).

The extent of global connection and communication through social network sites is staggering. For example, Facebook was the first to surpass 1 billion monthly active users, and about 2 billion people now use social network sites Facebook, Instagram, Twitter Tumbler in the United States, VK in the United Kingdom, and Chinese social networks QQ, Qzone and Renren (Facebook is banned by the Chinese government) (https://www.statista.com/statistics/272014/global-social-networks-ranked-by-number-of-users/)

These communication technologies have tremendous implications for intercultural communication. We will focus on five impacts on intercultural communication: (1) information about people and cultures; (2) contact with people who are different from us; (3) contact with people who are similar to us who can provide communities of support; (4) identity, culture, and technology; and (5) differential access to communication technology.

Information about People and Cultures   The Internet provides instant online access to information about other cultures and people and this *should* give us a better understanding of our neighbors and perhaps some motivation to coexist peacefully (Purcell & Rainie, 2014). However, the evidence seems to be to the contrary. According to the Center for Systemic Peace, while conflict between national powers has decreased, societal wars (conflict between groups within a country) have increased (Marshall & Cole, 2014). It would seem that knowledge about others—those we live closest to—does not necessarily lead to better communication. In addition, some evidence shows that we mostly access information that supports our existing views of the world. We will tackle issues like this later.

People also have access to increasing amounts of information about what is happening in their own and other countries. This is especially important in countries where media are government controlled. For example, people in Pakistan and Afghanistan learn more about military actions in their countries by accessing CNN.com than through their local newspapers. In some ways, the Internet has democratized information, in that more people control and disseminate information than ever before. For this reason, leaders in some countries try to limit their citizens' access to information. According to some net watchers, China was the year's worst

Why is it that some languages are more dominant than others on the Internet regardless of the number of native speakers? For example, while there are more Chinese speakers than English speakers, English still retains the number one spot as the most commonly used language among Internet users. According to Internet World Stats, English is number 1 with almost 900 million users, Chinese comes in second with 700 million users, Spanish is third with 250 million users, Arabic 4th with 170 million users, and Portuguese fifth with 130 million users. However, experts note that Asia now has the largest share of Internet users (45%) and if key Asian markets continue to expand their Internet usage Chinese could be expected to overtake English as the #1 Internet language. What are the implications for the future of intercultural communication?

Source: Top 10 Languages Used on the Internet (2016, September 3). Accredited Language Services. Retrieved February 2, 2017 from https://www.accreditedlanguage.com/2016/09/13 /top-10-languages-used-on-the-internet/

abuser of Internet freedom in 2015. For example, in September, the Chinese government censored images of the cartoon character Winnie the Pooh on Sina Weibo, mocking President Xi Jinping in a military parade, shared more than 65,000 times before it was removed. In 2015, Google was almost completely blocked and human rights defenders were jailed for online expression. Other countries like Libya, Ukraine, and France put in place new laws of political censorship—after internal conflicts (*Freedom on the Net*, 2015).

In spite of governments' attempts to limit their citizens' access to online communication, there remains information, world news, and possibilities for interpersonal communication that at the same time both facilitate and hinder intercultural communication.

Contact with People Who Differ Online communication and social media bring us in contact with people we may never meet face-to-face, both in personal (social media, community listservs) and professional encounters (LinkedIn, virtual teams); and many of these people are from different cultural backgrounds. However, such communication across cultures does present unique challenges. For example, some online communication (e.g., e-mail, text messages, tweets) filters out important nonverbal cues.

When we are talking to individuals face-to-face, we use nonverbal information to help us interpret what they are *really* saying—tone of voice, facial expressions, gestures, and so on. The absence of these cues in some mediated contexts (e.g., e-mail, text messages, tweets) makes communication more difficult and can lead to misunderstandings. And these misunderstandings can be compounded when communicating across cultures. For example, a U.S. colleague reports that she was offended when the e-mails she received from colleagues overseas seemed too brief and to the point. She discovered in working in several virtual team projects that her colleagues in some countries (e.g., India) tend to deliver part of their message with silence or nonverbal signs and prefer to communicate face-to-face. With this knowledge, she now uses Skype more to communicate with team members rather than e-mail.

Also, language may be a factor. The people we talk to Online may speak languages different from our own. An interesting situation arose for one of the authors of this book. Tom was on a discussion forum when someone posted a message in Dutch. It was met with a flurry of hostile responses from people protesting the use of an exclusionary language, one most people couldn't read. A discussion ensued about which languages might be acceptable on the network.

The decision reached was that subscribers could post messages in any language as long as there was an English translation. In a subsequent posting, someone from a university in South Africa recommended a book "for those of you who can read Dutch (heh-heh, all four of us)"—an apparent reaction to the exclusionary sentiments of other subscribers. Digital translation apps like Google Translate, Universal Translator, iTranslate can facilitate communication for travelers, businesspeople, and others in everyday intercultural encounters (See Point of View, p. 23). Of course the use of some languages is privileged over others on the Internet. As expert note, if you want to do business online, it's more likely going to be in English, the FIGS languages (French, Italian, German, Spanish), the CJK languages (Chinese, Japanese, Korean), and "the main languages of former colonial empires" (Dutch, Russian, Portuguese) (see Point of View, p. 23).

Linguist András Kornai (2013) cautions that the Internet itself may hasten the demise of many languages—those with fewer speakers or less representation online. Only about 250 languages can be called well established online, and another 140 are borderline. Of the 7,000 languages still alive, perhaps 2,500 will survive, in the classical sense, for another century, and many fewer will make it on to the Internet.

Contact with People Who Are Similar   Social media and other online communication promote contact with people who are very similar to ourselves, with family members, friends, and others who share common interests. We can also turn to online groups for support and community. For example, international students can stay in touch with their local communities, keep up with what's going on at home, and receive emotional support during difficult times of cultural adaptation. According to a recent Pew Center study, more than 60% of Americans who are online say they are better informed now about their friends, their family members, and their neighbors than they were five years ago—due to mobile phone and online technology (Purcell & Rainie, 2014).

diasporic groups
Ethnic and/or national groups that are geographically dispersed throughout the world.

The Internet can also be used to strengthen a sense of identity, as is the case for some **diasporic groups**—ethnic and/or national groups that are geographically dispersed throughout the world, sometimes as refugees fleeing from war, sometimes as voluntary emigrants. A recent study of children of South Asian immigrants found that the Internet plays a major role in creating a sense of community and ethnic identity for these young people. Whereas earlier generations of immigrants were expected to assimilate as quickly as possible into the host culture, the Internet now allows these children of immigrants to connect with other Indian adolescents, discussing religion and issues concerning Indian and immigrant identity. Similar diasporic discussions are

Translation and new technologies have helped bring different bodies of literature to English audiences. For example, Saudi author Raja Al-Sanea, wrote an interesting novel, *Girls of Riyadh*, now in its 7th edition and translated into 23 languages. The novel tells the story of a group of young Saudi women, who use their transcribed emails to communicate with each other every Friday. While they are traditional Saudi women who can't drive a car, drink alcohol, or go to the mall without being accompanied by a male family member, they text, blog, and use the Internet and lead interesting relational lives. While the book has been banned in Saudi Arabia, Al-Sanea says that the work reveals how these women create a "virtual liberating space" allowing some freedom of expression—and how they navigate between this virtual freedom and the more traditional non-virtual spaces of family and society. In fact, there is a now a new language "Arabish" or Arabic Chat Alphabet used by many Saudi youth when communicating on digital devices—unfamiliar to their parents and older relatives. It's a combination of Arabic and English written in the Latin alphabet which evolved because keyboards on mobile devices don't have the Arabic alphabet.

Source: D. Tresilian, the Fun of the Fair. 2008, May 24, *Al-Ahram Weekly*. Retrieved February 2, 2017 from http://www.masress.com/en/ahramweekly/7564.

held in the *Kava Bowl* and the *Kamehameha Roundtable*, online meeting places for the Polynesian diaspora and other people from the Pacific Islands who live in the United States, Australia, and New Zealand (Franklin, 2003). A British e-mail filtering company has been monitoring websites that were categorized as hate and violence sites. In 2000, there were about 2,500 such sites. However, the number of sites that promote hatred against Americans, Muslims, Jews, homosexuals, and people of non-European ancestry, as well as graphic violence, continues to rise. In fact, a recent report by the Simon Wiesenthal Center for Tolerance (2014) estimates that there are now more than 30,000 online hate groups. Social networking is where the biggest growth is happening, particularly on Facebook and YouTube, where hate-filled messages are often packaged in very creative ways. Experts point out that young people are especially vulnerable to racist online flash games, jokes, and general hate-filled information on social networking sites, blogs, and web pages. One of the most recent digital strategies of hate groups is to send out tweets and FB posts from fake accounts, which are supposed to be from minority or protest movements, hijacking the media moments and garnering more recruits. When minority students at the University of Missouri protested, hashtags #Mizzou and #PrayForMizzou spread false Twitter reports that the University of Missouri police was complicit with the Ku Klux Klan and that crosses were being burned on the university lawn—apparently trying to show that overly sensitive antiracist protesters will believe anything and calling for similar campaigns. Twitter banned the username, but the damage had been done (Hawkes, 2016).

Identity, Culture, and Technology   Advances in communication technology lead us to think differently about ourselves and our **identity management**. For example,

identity management The way individuals make sense of their multiple images concerning the sense of self in different social contexts.

23

communication technologies give us more choices in how we express our identities than we typically have in face-to-face interaction. As noted previously, many of the identity cues individuals use to figure out how to communicate with others—such as age, gender, and ethnicity—are filtered out on the Internet. For instance, when you send an e-mail message or post a message, you can choose whether to reveal certain aspects of your identity. The recipients won't know if you are male or female, young or old, and so on—unless you tell them. You can choose which aspects, if any, of your identity you want to reveal. In fact, you can even give false information about your identity.

It is also true that the same lack of nonverbal cues can result in less prejudice and stereotyping in mediated intercultural interaction. Some of these same nonverbal cues that are filtered out (indicators of age, gender, ethnicity, race) are often the basis for stereotyping and prejudice in initial interactions. When these cues are absent, communication may be more open because people cannot use the information to form impressions that often negatively impact communication.

Access to Communication Technology

As we've seen, technology plays a huge role in our everyday lives and often has a lot to do with our success as students and professionals. What would you do if you had no access to communication technology? If you were not able to text-message your friends or could not use your cell phone? Could not e-mail your family? How might you feel in our technology-dominated world? Although communication technologies are a fact of life for millions of people around the world, lack of access to these technologies is a reality for many people. Consider that

- 15% of adult Americans are not online at all, and those living in rural areas, those with annual incomes of less than $25,000, and individuals with disabilities have less online access than others (Rainie, 2015)

- In many countries (South Asia, Africa, and the Middle East), only a fraction of the population has access to computers and the Internet, for example, Internet access in Africa is 29% compared to the worldwide average of about 50% (Internet Statistics for Africa, 2015).

However, digital access now varies little by age, gender, race, and ethnicity in the United States, and many people worldwide have Internet access through smartphones (Horrigan & Duggan, 2015). In fact, a recent study shows that people in South Africa and Nigeria have the same level of cellphone ownership as in America (Winsor, 2015). So the inequity of technology access between "haves" and the "have-nots"—once referred to as the "digital divide," is probably more accurately viewed as a continuum of digital inequalities rather than a divide (Wei, 2012). And there are some inequities, as noted above, related to income, urban-rural location, and physical ability. In addition, those Americans (mostly poor and some ethnic minorities) who have only a smartphone for online access at home have challenges. They are more likely than other users to encounter data-cap limits on smartphone service, frequently have to cancel or suspend service due to financial constraints, and face challenges when it comes to important tasks such as filling out job applications and writing (and reading) documents (Horrigan & Duggan, 2015).

Why do differences in access matter? In order to function effectively in our digital society, people need **cultural capital**, or certain bodies of cultural knowledge and cultural competencies, including the ability to use digital media effectively.

The implications for intercultural communication are enormous. How do people relate to each other when one is information technology rich and the other is not? When there is increasing use of English on the Internet, what happens to those who don't speak English? Can this lead to resentment? Will the increase in communication technology lead to increasing gaps between haves and have-nots? To more misunderstandings?

Recent communication technology has impacted our lives in ways our grandparents could not have imagined and requires that we reexamine even our most basic conceptions of self, others, and culture. As Sherry Turkle (1995) observes, once we take virtuality seriously as a way of life, we need to consider who we are in these virtual relationships and what the connection is between our physical and virtual bodies. What kind of society or societies are we creating when we are so connected in cyberspace but not really present in physical spaces? We check our phones for text messages when eating a meal with friends, for example, not really relationally present with them (Turkle, 2008). We might also examine our own technological use: Who are we in contact with? People who are like ourselves? People who are different? Do we use technology to increase our contact with and understanding of other cultures or merely to hang out with people who are like us? What does this say about us and our identities?

cultural capital certain bodies of cultural knowledge and cultural competencies.

THE PEACE IMPERATIVE

The bottom line seems to be this: Can individuals of different genders, ages, ethnicities, races, languages, socioeconomic statuses, and cultural backgrounds coexist on this planet? (See Figure 1-4.) Both the history of humankind and recent world events lead us not to be very optimistic on this point. The current trend is toward longer, more intra-national protracted conflicts where military or material supports are supplied by foreign powers—fighting "proxy wars"—to warring groups. By mid-2016, 23 countries were experiencing major armed conflicts—mainly in League of Arab States after the invasion of Iraq in 2003 and the Arab Spring upheavals that began in Tunisia in 2011, but in other countries as well (Marshall & Cole, 2014 Backer, Bhavnani & Huth 2016). For example, consider the religious strife between Shia and Sunni Muslims throughout the Middle East and between Kurds and government forces in Iraq and Turkey, the conflict between insurgent rebel groups and the government in Syria—with Russia and the United States backing different factions; the various groups in Libya where there is no central government at the moment, and woven throughout this region, conflict with the Islamic State (ISIS). There are also the conflicts between the government and various drug cartels in Mexico and the Boko Haram and Christian-Muslim conflicts in Nigeria. We could also note the recent tensions and conflicts between refugees/immigrants and the people/governments in Europe, as well as the racial and ethnic tensions in U.S. neighborhoods and recent conflicts between law enforcement and some black communities.

FIGURE I-4   This Iraqi boy looks at shoes and clothes of victims of a car bomb explosion in Baghdad on March I, 2006. The causes of this violence stem from long histories of intercultural conflict and are likely to influence intercultural relations in the future. (© *Akram Saleh/Getty Images*)

colonialism (I) The system by which groups with diverse languages, cultures, religions, and identities were united to form one state, usually by a European power; (2) the system by which a country maintains power over other countries or groups of people to exploit them economically, politically, and culturally.

Some of these conflicts are tied to histories of **colonialism** around the world, whereby European powers lumped diverse groups—differing in language, culture, religion, or identity—together as one state. For example, the division of Pakistan and India was imposed by the British; eventually, East Pakistan declared its independence to become Bangladesh. Nevertheless, ethnic and religious differences in some areas of India and Pakistan continue to cause unrest. And the acquisition of nuclear weapons by both India and Pakistan makes these antagonisms of increasing concern. The tremendous diversity—and accompanying antagonisms—within many former colonies must be understood in the context of histories of colonialism.

Some of the conflicts are also tied to economic disparities and influenced by U.S. technology and media. Many people in the United States see these influences as beneficial, but they also stimulate resistance. Communication scholar Fernando Delgado (2002) explains:

> *Such cultural dominance, though celebrated at home, can spark intercultural conflicts because it inhibits the development of other nations' indigenous popular culture products, stunts their economic development and foists U.S. values and perspectives on other cultures. These effects, in turn, often lead to resentment and conflict. (p. 353)*

STARBUCKS' LOGO REDESIGN COULD PROVE BENEFICIAL TO COMPANY

A recent press release describes why Starbucks' decision to change its logo could be a good move as it expands into Asian markets. It recently dropped both its name and the word "coffee" from its 40-year-old logo in preparation for tripling its locations in China from about 400 to 1,500.

In this release, Rice University Professor of Marketing Vikas Mittal described the interesting results of several studies investigating customers, logos, and brand commitment. He and his coresearchers found that, while Starbucks may have alienated some of their loyal U.S. customers, the redesign will probably attract new consumers in Asian countries like China, India, Taiwan, and Singapore, where consumers tend to be culturally collectivist and interdependent.

Mittal said that removing the lettering gives the logo a more rounded appearance, and his research found that people with collectivistic values, like those in Asia, prefer rounded shapes. In fact, brands in collectivistic countries tend to have a higher percentage of rounded logos when compared to logos in individualistic countries (e.g., the United States), and logos and product shapes that are rounded are more acceptable and embraced in those cultures. The researchers' explanation for Asians' preference for rounded shapes is that these shapes represent harmony, which is consistent with an interdependent view of the world.

Source: J. Stark, "Rice Research Shows Starbucks Logo Redesign Could Prove Beneficial to Company," Press Release, Rice University, January 6, 2011. Retrieved May 25, 2011, from www.media.rice.edu/media/NewsBot.asp?MODE=VIEW&ID=15215&SnID=1521497554.

For example, according to many Canadians, a Canadian cultural identity is almost impossible because of the dominance of U.S. media. This type of cultural domination is very complex. One can see anti-American sentiments in graffiti, newspapers, and Online alongside U.S. influence everywhere—in music, television, film, cars, fast food, and fashion. So resentment, frustration, and disdain from many cultural groups outside the United States can coexist with an amazement at the penetration of U.S. popular culture.

Some of the conflicts have roots in past foreign policies. For example, recent terrors are partly related to the confusing and shifting alliances among the United States, Afghanistan, Syria, and other Arab and Muslim countries. In Afghanistan in the early 1990s, the Taliban seized power in response to the destructive rule of the Northern Alliance, a loose coalition of warlords. The United States had supported the Taliban in the fight against Soviet aggression in the late 1980s and had promised aid in rebuilding their country after the hostilities were over. However, with the withdrawal of Soviet forces and the fall of the Soviet Union, the United States wasn't as concerned about fulfilling its promises to the Afghan nation and withdrew military support. After September 11, the United States once again put troops and support in Afghanistan to fight the Al-Queda-supported Taliban, and once again in 2016, the U.S. withdrew most troops from Afghanistan, having twice promised and then withdrawn support, leaving

Afghan people to deal with the Taliban forces mostly on their own. In addition, U.S. foreign policies toward many Arab countries in the last half century, coupled with open support for Israel, have caused widespread resentment (Kirkpatrick, 2011). Although there is no simple explanation for why terrorists attack the United States, the attacks clearly do not happen in a vacuum. They need to be understood in historical, political, religious, and economic contexts.

It would be naive to assume that simply understanding the issues of intercultural communication would end war and intercultural conflict, but these problems do underscore the need for individuals to learn more about social groups other than their own. (See Figure 1-5.) Ultimately, people, and not countries, negotiate and sign peace treaties. An example of how individual communication styles may influence political outcomes can be seen in the negotiations between Iraqi president Saddam Hussein and representatives of the United States and the United Nations just prior to the Gulf War, in 1990. Many Middle East experts assumed that Hussein was not ready to fight, that he was merely bluffing, using an Arabic style of communication (see Chapter 6). This style emphasizes the importance of animation, exaggeration, and conversational form over content (Slackman, 2006).

However, although communication on the interpersonal level is important, we always need to consider the relationship between individual and societal forces in studying intercultural communication, and that sometimes individuals are born into and caught up in conflicts that they neither started nor chose. With this in mind, communication scholar Benjamin Broome, who has worked with many groups in conflict,

FIGURE I-5   Although this sign is an attempt to reach out to many cultural groups in Boston Harbor by posting in many languages, it does not explain the rationale for the ban and differing views on who "owns" natural resources, health concerns, and other issues facing shellfishing may lead to misunderstanding and conflicts among cultural groups. (*Courtesy © T.K. Takayama*)

including Greek and Turk Cypriots, proposes a comprehensive approach to peace-building. This approach is not just focused on eliminating conflict, but is also an effort to stop all forms of violence and to also promote transformative ways to deal with conflict, including strategies that address personal, relational, and structural (orga-nizational, economic conditions, etc.) levels of interaction. According to Broome, communication, especially facilitated dialogue, plays a key role in the peacebuilding process (Broome, 2013; Broome & Collier, 2012). We will explore this and other approaches to deal with conflict in Chapter 11.

THE ETHICAL IMPERATIVE

Living in an intercultural world presents ethical challenges as well. **Ethics** may be thought of as principles of conduct that help govern the behavior of individuals and groups. These principles often arise from communities' consensus on what is good and bad behavior. Cultural values tell us what is "good" and what "ought" to be good. Ethical judgments focus more on the degrees of rightness and wrongness in human behavior than do cultural values (Johannesen, 1990).

ethics Principles of conduct that help govern behaviors of individuals and groups.

Some judgments are stated very explicitly. For example, the Ten Command-ments teach that it is wrong to steal, tell a lie, commit murder, and so on. Many other identifiable principles of conduct that arise from our cultural experience may be less explicit—for instance, that people should be treated equally and should work hard. Several issues come to mind in a discussion of ethics in intercultural commu-nication. For example, what happens when two ethical systems collide? Although an individual may want to "do the right thing" to contribute to a better society, it is not always easy to know what is "right" in specific situations. Ethical principles are often culture bound, and intercultural conflicts arise from various notions of what is ethical behavior.

One common cross-cultural ethical dilemma involves standards of conduct-ing business in multinational corporations. The U.S. Congress and the Securities and Exchange Commission consider it unethical to make payments to government officials of other countries to promote trade. (Essentially, such payments smack of bribery.) However, in many countries, like China, government officials are paid in this informal way instead of being supported by taxes (Ambler & Witzel, 2000). What, then, is ethical behavior for personnel in multinational subsidiaries?

Relativity versus Universality

In this book, we stress the relativity of cultural behavior—that no cultural pattern is inherently right or wrong. So, is there any universality in ethics? Are any cultural behaviors always right or always wrong? The answers depend on one's perspective. A universalist might try, for example, to identify acts and conditions that most soci-eties think of as wrong, such as murder, theft, or treason. Someone who takes an extreme universalist position would insist that cultural differences are only super-ficial, that fundamental notions of right and wrong are universal. Some religions take universal positions—for example, that the Ten Commandments are a universal

HOW NOT TO SAVE THE WORLD

The good news is that many college students today are highly motivated to do good and make a difference in the world today. They are seeking volunteer opportunities in health care, construction, child care, or other community projects in international locations around the world. However, international service experts have cautioned these volunteers about the pitfalls and potential damage to the host community. Some issues to consider:

- Local institutions may be called on to spend precious time and energy in taking care of the volunteers, providing translation services, transportation, and expenses not covered by the sending institution or trainees.

- Host communities may be hesitant to explicitly address problems that arise as it may be considered impolite and not culturally appropriate to indicate that a volunteer's presence was anything but helpful.

- Volunteers, especially in exotic tourist areas, can be tempted to spend more time as tourists rather than helping out, which reduces their effectiveness.

- Ethical dilemmas are especially challenging for volunteers or trainees in the medical field and include: not being familiar enough with local conditions to recognize serious illnesses, challenges compounded by language barriers, and the inability to understand the meaning of patient's statements. Because of lack of resources in some areas, trainees are thrust into patient-care setting for which they are unprepared. This can result in stress and/or guilt, and place their own health at risk.

Helpful advice for motivated do gooders: As Lisa V. Adams, associate dean for global health and director of the Center for Health Equity at Dartmouth tells her students: "You have succeeded in your academic careers because you are assertive, active learners who are not afraid to ask questions or to push yourselves hard and always deliver an outstanding final product." She then tells them they must *unlearn* all this socialization, and need to "resist the temptation to share every great thought or idea" and instead switch into "listener mode." What may look like easy fixes may "be complicated problems embedded in complex systems" that they can only begin to understand about weeks or months on site (Strauss, 2016).

Source: From J. A. Crump and J. Sugarman, "Ethical Considerations for Short-Term Experiences by Trainees in Global Health," *Journal of American Medical Association*, *300*(12), 1456–1458, 2008. From V. Strauss, "How NOT to save the world: Why U.S. students who go to poor countries to 'do good' often do the opposite," *washingtonpost.com*. Retrieved March 22, 2016, from https://www.washingtonpost.com/news/answer-sheet/wp/2016/03/22/how-not-to-save-the-world-why-u-s-students-who-go-to-poor-countries-to-do-good-often-do-the-opposite/.

code of behavior. But Christian groups often disagree about the universality of the Bible. For example, are the teachings of the New Testament mainly guidelines for the Christians of Jesus's time, or can they be applied to Christians in the 21st century? These are difficult issues for many people searching for ethical guidelines (Johannesen, 1990). The philosopher Immanuel Kant (1949) believed in the universality of moral laws. His well-known "categorical imperative" states that people should act only on maxims that apply universally, to *all* individuals.

The extreme relativist position holds that any cultural behavior can be judged only within the cultural context in which it occurs. This means that only those members of a community can truly judge the ethics of their own members. According to communication scholar William S. Howell (1982),

> *The environment, the situation, the timing of an interaction, human relationships, all affect the way ethical standards are applied. . . . The concept of universal ethics, standards of goodness that apply to everyone, everywhere, and at all times, is the sort of myth people struggle to hold onto. (pp. 182, 187)*

And yet, to accept a completely relativistic position seems to tacitly accept the horrors of Nazi Germany, South African apartheid, or U.S. slavery. In each case, the larger community developed cultural beliefs that supported persecution and discrimination in such extreme forms that worldwide condemnation ultimately resulted (Hall, 1997, p. 23).

Philosophers and anthropologists have struggled to develop ethical guidelines that seem universally applicable but that also recognize the tremendous cultural variability in the world. And many ethical relativists appeal to more natural, humanitarian principles. This more moderate position assumes that people can evaluate cultures without succumbing to ethnocentrism, that all individuals and cultural groups share a fundamental humanistic belief in the sanctity of the human spirit and the goodness of peace, and that people should respect the well-being of others (Kale, 1994).

Communication scholar Bradford J. Hall (1997) reminds us that relativistic and universalistic approaches to ethics should be viewed not as a dichotomy, but rather as a compound of universalism and relativism. All ethics systems involve a tension between the universal and the relative. Although we recognize some universal will toward ethical principles, we may have to live with the tension of not being able to impose our "universal" ethic on others.

A recent suggestion for meeting the ethical imperative is to employ a **dialogical approach** (Evanoff, 2004). The dialogical approach emphasizes the importance of relationships and dialogues between individuals and communities in wrestling with ethical dilemmas. Communication scholar M. J. Collier describes using a critical dialogic approach in working with a national nonprofit that aims to move poor families into financial stability. The organization provides training and resource development with a team approach, matching people in poverty, called Circle Leaders (CLs) with middle-class partners, called Allies. She interviewed CLs and Allies to identify recommendations for successful ethical intercultural interactions in this project. Her approach and interview data confirm the importance of recognizing multilevels involved in moving people from poverty, including the macro levels (social service policies, societal myths about poverty), the meso level (cultural, social class, and

dialogical approach Focuses on the importance of dialogue in developing and maintaining relationships between individuals and communities.

racial differences of individuals partnering in the project) and the micro level (individual interactions among those involved). The CLs emphasized how important it was to acknowledge the social class, racial, ethic, gender, and sometimes religious and political differences involved in these intercultural teams, and that they all are needed to be able to confront and navigate these differences in a collaborative way. They noted that too often the Allies positioned themselves as "teachers" while not actually understanding the realities of being poor, for example, the myths about the "abundance of resources" available for the poor, the difficulty (impossibility) of living on a minimum wage salary, the fear that moving out of poverty might mean losing their family and community. Collier examines her own position as a white, academic researcher and how she can learn through dialogue and critical reflection. She concludes that "critical dialogic reflexivity is particularly useful in building engaged, inclusive, and equitable relationships" that are so essential in creating success in long-term ethical social justice projects (Collier, 2015, p. 221).

The study of intercultural communication not only provides insights into cultural patterns, but also helps us address the ethical issues involved in intercultural interaction. Specifically we should be able to (1) judge what is ethical and unethical behavior given variations in cultural priorities and (2) identify guidelines for ethical behavior in intercultural contexts in which ethics clash.

Being Ethical Students of Culture

Related to the issue of judging cultural patterns as ethical or unethical are the issues surrounding the study of culture. Part of learning about intercultural communication is learning about cultural patterns and cultural identities—our own and others. There are three issues to address here: developing self-reflexivity, learning about others, and acquiring a sense of social justice.

Developing Self-Reflexivity In studying intercultural communication, it is vital to develop **self-reflexivity**—to understand ourselves and our position in society. In learning about other cultures and cultural practices, we often learn much about ourselves. Immigrants often comment that they never felt so much like someone of their own nationality until they left their homeland.

self-reflexivity A process of learning to understand oneself and one's position in society.

Think about it: Many cultural attitudes and ideas are instilled in you, but these can be difficult to unravel and identify. Knowing who you are is never simple; rather, it is an ongoing process that can never fully capture the ever-emerging person. Not only will you grow older but your intercultural experiences will also change who you are and who you think you are. It is also important to reflect on your place in society. By recognizing the social categories to which you belong, and the implications of those categories, you will be in a better position to understand how to communicate. For example, being an undergraduate student positions you to communicate your ideas on specific subjects and in particular ways to various members of the faculty or staff at your school. You might want to communicate to the registrar your desire to change majors—this would be an appropriate topic to address to that person. But you would not be well positioned during an exam to communicate to your chemistry professor your problems with your girl- or boyfriend.

I have spent three years in the United States seeking an education. I am from Singapore, and I believe that in many ways both countries are similar. They are both multicultural. They both have a dominant culture. In the United States the dominant culture is white, and in Singapore it is Chinese.

Coming to the United States has taught me to be more aware of diversity. Even though in Singapore we are diverse, because I was part of the majority there, I didn't feel the need to increase my level of intercultural awareness. In the United States I became a minority, and that has made me feel the need to become more culturally competent.
—Jacqueline

Learning About Others   It is important to remember that the study of cultures is actually the study of other people. Never lose sight of the humanity at the core of the topic. Try not to observe people as if they are zoo animals. Communication scholar Bradford Hall (1997) cautions against using the "zoo approach" to studying culture:

> *When using such an approach we view the study of culture as if we were walking through a zoo admiring, gasping and chuckling at the various exotic animals we observe. One may discover . . . the point that we are as culturally "caged" as others and that they are culturally as "free" as we are. (p. 14)*

Remember that you are studying real people who have real lives, and your conclusions about them may have very real consequences for them and for you. The notion of **cultural humility** is foundational for an ethical stance in learning about others. Being culturally humble means (1) having an awareness of the limitations of one's own cultural background and worldview as well as the limitations of an ability to truly understand the cultural background and experiences of others, and (2) trying to take an "other-oriented" stance in each new intercultural encounter, which includes trying to suppress any readymade cultural assumptions about the other (Gallardo, 2014). Cultural studies scholar Linda Alcoff (1991/1992) acknowledges the ethical issues involved when students of culture try to describe the cultural patterns of others; she recognizes the difficulty of speaking "for" and "about" others who have different lives. Instead, she suggests, students of culture should try to speak "with" and "to" others. Rather than merely describe others from a distance, it's better to engage others in a dialogue about their cultural realities.

cultural humility being aware of one's cultural limitations and taking an "other-oriented approach" in intercultural encounters.

Learn to listen to the voices of others, to cultivate experiential knowledge. Hearing about the experiences of people who are different from you can broaden your ways of viewing the world. Many differences—based on race, gender, sexual orientation, nationality, ethnicity, age, and so on—deeply affect people's everyday lives. Listening carefully as people relate their experiences and their ways of knowing will help you learn about the many aspects of intercultural communication.

Developing a Sense of Social Justice   A final ethical issue involves the responsibility that comes with the acquisition of intercultural knowledge and insights—that this educational experience is not just transformative for the individual but should also benefit the larger society and other cultural groups in the increasingly interdependent world.

Learning about intercultural communication sometimes calls into question the core of our basic assumptions about ourselves, our culture, and our worldviews and challenges existing and preferred beliefs, values, and patterns of behavior. Liliana, a Colombian student, describes such a transformation:

> *When I first came to the States to study and live I was surprised with all the diversity and different cultures I encountered. I realized I came from a country, society, school and group of friends with little diversity. During all the years I lived in Colombia I did not meet more than five people from other countries. Even at my school, there was little diversity—only two students of color among three thousand students. I realized that big difference when I was suddenly sharing a college classroom with students from all over the world, people of all colors and cultures. At the beginning it was difficult getting used to it because of the wide diversity, but I like and enjoy it now and I wish my family and friends could experience and learn as much as I have.*

As you learn about yourself and others as cultural beings, as you come to understand the larger economic, political, and historical contexts in which interaction occurs, is there an ethical obligation to continue learning? We believe that as members of an increasingly interdependent global community, intercultural communication students have a responsibility to educate themselves, not just about interesting cultural differences but also about intercultural conflicts, the impacts of stereotyping and prejudice, and the larger systems that can oppress and deny basic human rights—and to apply this knowledge to the communities in which they live and interact. This is the basis of social justice (Alexander et al., 2014).

For example, how could you apply intercultural communication concepts in situations where gay, lesbian and transgender young people are the targets of bullying? Statistics show that gay and lesbian youth get bullied two to three times more than their heterosexual peers (Berlan, Corliss, Field, Goodman, & Austin, 2010). Why does this happen? What can be done to reduce harassment of this particular cultural group? In the following chapters, you will learn about the causes and patterns of conflict between various cultural groups, the origins and expressions of prejudice and discrimination, as well as strategies for reducing conflict and discrimination. Consider the homeless—another cultural group rarely mentioned by cultural communication scholars—often the target of prejudice and violence. Perhaps increased knowledge about this group and ethical application of intercultural communication principles could lead to better understanding of these individuals and ultimately to less discrimination and prejudice. After working as an advocate for homeless people in Denver, one communication scholar, Professor Phil Tompkins, describes the link between communication skills and social justice. He defines social justice as the "process of communicating, inspiring, advocating, organizing and working with others of similar and diverse organizational affiliations to help all people gain respect and participate fully in society in a way that benefits the community as well as the individual" (Tompkins, 2009). This definition has three important components: (1) communication is central; (2) the outcome of social justice must be beneficial to society, not just the individuals involved; and (3) respect for and participation by all is important. Another research project that fits Tompkins' definition of social justice is communication scholar Uttaran Dutta's (2015) work with indigenous communities in rural India. He, along with the leaders and members of the villages, cocreated a mobile app, using community-designed pictograph icons (requiring no reading or writing) that allowed the villagers (some of whom are illiterate) to access important information regarding local weather, employment, education, and other basic services such as health care. We hope that as you read the following chapters, you will agree with us that learning about intercultural communication also involves ethical application of that knowledge.

What are unethical applications of intercultural communication knowledge? One questionable practice involves people who study intercultural communication in order to proselytize others without their consent. (Some religious organizations conduct Bible study on college campuses for international students under the guise of English language lessons.) Another questionable practice is the behavior of cross-cultural consultants who misrepresent or exaggerate their ability to deal with complex issues of prejudice and racism in brief, one-shot training sessions.

A final questionable practice concerns research on the intercultural communication of U.S. minority groups. A common approach in the United States is for a white tenured faculty member to conduct such research employing graduate and undergraduate students from the minority groups being studied:

> *Minority students are sometimes used as a way to gain immediate access to the community of interest. These students go into communities and the (usually white) professors are spared the intense, time-consuming work of establishing relationships in the community. (Martin & Butler, 2001, p. 291)*

These students are then asked to report their findings to and interpret their community for the faculty member. Unfortunately, doing so can jeopardize their relationship to their community, which may be suspicious of the academic community. The faculty member publishes articles and reaps the tangible rewards of others' hard work—promotions, pay raises, and professional visibility. Meanwhile, the community and the students may receive little for their valuable contributions to this academic work.

We feel there is a concomitant responsibility that goes along with this intercultural knowledge: to work toward a more equitable and fair society and world. We want you to keep in mind this ethical issue as you study the various topics covered in this book. In the final chapter, we'll address this issue again with practical suggestions for meeting this ethical challenge.

INTERNET RESOURCES

www.intercultural.org/
This is the website of a nonprofit organization dedicated to improving intercultural communication. It contains a lot of valuable information aimed at a broad audience, including businesses. The most interesting aspect of the website is that it is full of

actual training materials used by intercultural practitioners in helping their clients develop a greater intercultural proficiency.

www.refintl.org/
This website explores the topic of refugees. Many people consider intercultural communication in the business setting, but intercultural communication due to refugee migrations is actually rather common. The site includes information about many refugee crises including the 220,000 Burundi refugees in Tanzania, many female, and the Myanmar Rohingya refugee crisis where as many as 1,000 people died in the Andaman Sea—because no country would permit them to disembark from their boats. What special intercultural issues are present when considering refugees?

www.kwintessential.co.uk/cultural-services/articles/intercultural
-communication-tips.html
This is a "quick-tip" guide to intercultural communication. There are some good tips on this page, like encouragement to reflect on the practices you engage in while communicating in an intercultural context. It is worth considering that this is the type of information many people use when engaging in intercultural business, and so forth. What types of information or analysis are missing from its list of tips?

SUMMARY

There are six reasons or imperatives for studying intercultural communication:

- The self-awareness imperative involves increasing understanding of our own location in larger social, political, and historical contexts.
- The demographic imperative includes the changing domestic and international migration—raising questions of class and religious diversity.
- The economic imperative highlights issues of globalization and the challenges for increased cultural understanding needed to reach the global market.
- The technological imperative gives us increasing information and increased contact with people who are similar and different from us. Increased use of communication technology also raises questions about identity and access to these technologies.
- The peace imperative involves working through issues of colonialism, economic disparities, and racial, ethnic, and religious differences.
- The ethical imperative calls for an understanding of the universalist, relativist, and dialogic approach to ethical issues.

Being an ethical student of culture involves developing self-reflexivity, learning about others, and developing a sense of social justice and responsibility.

DISCUSSION QUESTIONS

1. How do electronic means of communication (e-mail, the Internet, fax, and so on) differ from face-to-face interactions?
2. How do these communication technologies change intercultural communication interaction?
3. What are some of the potential challenges organizations face as they become more diverse?
4. Why is it important to think beyond ourselves as individuals in intercultural interaction?
5. How do economic situations affect intergroup relations?

ACTIVITIES

1. *Family Tree.* Interview the oldest member of your family you can contact. Then answer the following questions:
   a. When did your ancestors come to the United States?
   b. Where did they come from?
   c. What were the reasons for their move? Did they come voluntarily?
   d. What language(s) did they speak?
   e. What difficulties did they encounter?
   f. Did they change their names? For what reasons?
   g. What were their occupations before they came, and what jobs did they take on their arrival?
   h. How has your family status changed through the generations?

   Compare your family experience with those of your classmates. Did most immigrants come for the same reasons? What are the differences in the various stories?

2. *Intercultural Encounter.* Describe and analyze a recent intercultural encounter. This may mean talking with someone of a different age, ethnicity, race, religion, and so on.
   a. Describe the encounter. What made it "intercultural"?
   b. Explain how you initially felt about the communication.
   c. Describe how you felt after the encounter, and explain why you think you felt as you did.
   d. Describe any challenges in trying to communicate. If there were no challenges, explain why you think it was so easy.
   e. Based on this experience, identify some characteristics that may be important for successful intercultural communication.

KEY WORDS

Anglocentrism (10)
cultural capital (25)
cultural humility (33)
colonialism (26)
demographics (5)
dialogical approach (31)
diasporic groups (22)

diversity (8)
ethics (29)
ethnocentrism (4)
global village (19)
heterogeneous (7)
homogeneous (7)
identity management (23)

immigrants (8)
maquiladoras (19)
melting pot (10)
multinational
    corporations (19)
nativistic (10)
self-reflexivity (32)

REFERENCES

Adler, P. S. (1975). The transition experience: An alternative view of culture shock. *Journal of Humanistic Psychology, 15,* 13–23.

Alcoff, L. (1991/1992). The problem of speaking for others. *Cultural Critique, 20,* 5–32.

Alexander, B. K., Arasaratnam, L. A., Durham, A., Flores, L., Leeds-Hurwitz, W., Mendoza, S. L., & Halualani, R. (2014). Identifying key intercultural urgencies, issues, and challenges in today's world: Connecting our scholarship to dynamic contexts and historical moments. *Journal of International & Intercultural Communication, 7*(1), 38–67.

Ambler, T., & Witzel, M. (2000). *Doing business in China.* New York: Routledge.

American Indians by the Number, US Census Bureau. Retrieved December 26, 2011, from www.infoplease.com/spot/aihmcensus1.html.

Backer D., Bhavnani, R. & Huth, R. (2016). Peace & Conflict 2016. NY: Routledge.

Baldwin, J. (1955). *Notes of a native son.* Boston, MA: Beacon Press.

Banks, J. (1991). *Teaching strategies for ethnic studies.* Needham, MA: Allyn & Bacon.

Beech, H. (2016, March 7). As China's NPC meets, here are four danger signs to watch for in the nation's economy. *Time.com.* Retrieved March 7, 2016, from http://time.com/4249299/china-economy-npc-national-peoples-congress/

Berlan, E. D., Corliss, H. L., Field, A. E., Goodman, E. & Austin, S. B. (2010). Sexual orientation and bullying among adolescents in the Growing Up Today study. *Journal of Adolescent Health, 46*(4), 366–371.

Branding so much more than a name (2011). *Strategic Direction, 27*(3), 6–8.

Broome, B. J. (2013). Building cultures of peace: The role of intergroup dialogue. In J. G. Oetzel & S. Ting-Toomey (Eds.), *Sage handbook of conflict communication: Integrating theory, research, and practice* (2nd ed., pp. 737–762). Los Angeles, CA: Sage.

Broome, B. J., & Collier, M. J. (2012). Culture, communication, and peacebuilding: A reflexive multi-dimensional contextual framework. *Journal of International & Intercultural Communication, 5*(4), 245–269.

Burns, C., Barton, K., & Kerby, S. (2012). The state of diversity in today's workforce. Retrieved March 8, 2016, from https://cdn.americanprogress.org/wp-content/uploads/issues/2012/07/pdf/diversity_brief.pdf

Cisneros, J. D., & Nakayama, T.K. (2015). New media, old racisms: Twitter, Miss America, and cultural logics of race. *Journal of International & Intercultural Communication, 8*(2), 108–127.

Cohn, D. (2015, September 30). How U.S. immigration laws and rules have changed through history. *Pew Research Reports.* Retrieved March 8, 2015, from http://www.pewresearch.org/fact-tank/2015/09/30/how-u-s-immigration-laws-and-rules-have-changed-through-history/

Cole, D. (1998). Five myths about immigration. In P. S. Rothenberg (Ed.), *Race, class, and gender in the United States: An integrated study* (4th ed., pp. 125–129). New York: St. Martin's Press.

Collier, M. J. (2015). Partnering for anti-poverty praxis in circles USA: Applications of critical dialogic reflexivity. Partnering for anti-poverty praxis in Circles USA: Applications of Critical Dialogic Reflexivity. *Journal of International & Intercultural Communication, 8*(3), 208–223.

Curtin, P. D. (1969). *The Atlantic slave trade: A census.* Madison, WI: University of Wisconsin Press.

Custer, C. (2015, May 20). The 3 biggest reasons foreign companies fail in China. *techinasia.com.* Retrieved April 4, 2016, from https://www.techinasia.com/3-biggest-reasons-foreign-companies-fail-china

Delgado, F. (2002). Mass-mediated communication and intercultural conflict. In J. N. Martin, T. K. Nakayama, & L. A. Flores (Eds.), *Readings in intercultural communication* (pp. 351–359). Boston, MA: McGraw-Hill.

Desilver, D. (2015, November 19, 2015). U.S. public seldom has welcomed refugees into country. *Pew Research Reports.* Retrieved March 8, 2016, from http://www.pewresearch.org/fact-tank/2015/11/19/u-s-public-seldom-has-welcomed-refugees-into-country/

Dillon, S. (2010, December 7). Top test scores from Shanghai stun educators. *The New York Times*, p. 1A.

Dutta, U., & Das, S. (2015). Digital divide at the margins: Co-designing information solution to address needs of indigenous populations of rural India. *Communication Design Quarterly, 4*(1), 36–48.

Eagan, K., Stolzenberg, E. B., Bates, A. K., Aragon, M. C., Suchard, M. R., & Rios-Aguilar, C. (2016). *The American freshman: National norms fall 2015.* Los Angeles, CA: Higher Education Research Institute, UCLA.

Evanoff, R. J. (2004). Universalist, relativist, and constructivist approaches to intercultural ethics. *International Journal of Intercultural Relations*, 28, 439–458.

Fantz, A., & Brumfield, B. (2015, November 19). More than half the nation's governors say Syrian refugees not welcome. *CNN.com*. Retrieved March 8, 2016, from http://www.cnn.com/2015/11/16/world/paris -attacks-syrian-refugees-backlash/

Finkle, J. (2016, March 7). Twitter praised for cracking down on use by Islamic State. Reuters.com. Retrieved March 8, 2016, from http://www.reuters.com/article /us-twitter-isis-reportcard-idUSKCN0W9207

Fitz, N. (2015, March 31). Economic inequality: It's far worse than you think. *Scientificamerica.com*. Retrieved March 8, 2015, from http://www.scientificamerican .com/article/economic-inequality-it-s-far-worse-than -you-think/.

Foner, E. (1998). Who is an American? In P. S. Rothenberg (Ed.), *Race, class, and gender in the United States: An integrated study* (4th ed., pp. 84–92). New York: St. Martin's Press.

Franklin, M. I. (2003). I define my own identity: Pacific articulations of 'race' and 'culture' on the Internet. *Ethnicities, 3,* 465–490.

Freedom on the Net 2015. Freedom house. Retrieved March 8, 2016, from https://freedomhouse.org/sites /default/files/FH_FOTN_2015Report.pdf

Friedman, T. L. (2005). The world is flat: *A brief history of the twenty-first century*. New York: Farrar, Straus & Giroux.

Fussell, P. (1992). *Class: A guide through the American status system*. New York: Touchstone Books.

Gallardo, M. (Ed). (2014). *Developing cultural humility: Embracing race, privilege, and power*. Thousand Oaks, CA: Sage.

Gonzalez-Barrera, A. (2015, November 15). More Mexicans leaving than coming to the U.S. *Pew Research Reports*. Retrieved March 8, 2016, from http://www.pewhispanic.org/2015/11/19/more -mexicans-leaving-than-coming-to-the-u-s/

Growing apart. (2013, September 21). *Economist.com*. Retrieved March 8, 2016 from http://www.economist .com/news/leaders/21586578-americas-income-inequality -growing-again-time-cut-subsidies-rich-and-invest

Hall, B. J. (1997). Culture, ethics and communication. In F. L. Casmir (Ed.), *Ethics in intercultural and international communication* (pp. 11–41). Mahwah, NJ: Lawrence Erlbaum.

Halualani, R. T. (2010). Interactant-based definitions of intercultural interaction at a multicultural university. *Howard Journal of Communications, 21*(3), 247–272.

Hawkes, K. (2016, January 5). How the extremist right hijacked 'Star Wars,' Taylor Swift and the Mizzou student protests to promote racism. Southern Poverty Law Center. Retrieved March 8, 2016, from https://www.splcenter.org/hatewatch/2016/01/05 /how-extremist-right-hijacked-%E2%80%98star -wars%E2%80%99-taylor-swift-and-mizzou-student -protests-promote

Horrigan, J., & Duggan, M. (2015, December 15). Home broadband 2015. *Pew Research Report*. Retrieved March 8, 2016, from http://www.pewinternet.org /files/2015/12/Broadband-adoption-full.pdf

Howell, W. S. (1982). *The empathic communicator*. Belmont, CA: Wadsworth.

Humes, K. R., Jones, N. C., & Ramirez, R. R. (2011, March). Overview of race and Hispanic origin: 2010 (*2010 Census Briefs*). United States Census Bureau. Retrieved April 20, 2016, from http://www.census .gov/prod/cen2010/briefs/c2010br-02.pdf

Internet rant causes uproar at UD university (2011, March 27). *VOANews.com*. Retrieved May 6, 2011, from www.voanews.com/english/news/usa/Internet -Rant-Causes-Uproar-at-US-University-118747924 .html.

Internet usage statistics for Africa. (2015, November 15). Retrieved March 8, 2016, from http://www .internetworldstats.com/stats1.htm

Irwin, N., & Bui, Q. (2016, April 11). The rich live longer everywhere. For the poor, geography matters. *nytimes.com*. Retrieved April 20, 2016, from http://www.nytimes.com/interactive/2016/04/11 /upshot/for-the-poor-geography-is-life-and-death .html?_r=1

Islamic says beheads U.S. journalist and holds other (2014, August 19). *Reuters.com*. Retrieved March 8, 2016, from http://www.reuters.com/video/2014/08 /20/islamic-state-says-beheads-us-journalist?videoId =340547198

Johannesen, R. L. (1990). *Ethics in human communication* (3rd ed.). Prospect Heights, IL: Waveland Press.

Kale, D. W. (1994). Peace as an ethic for intercultural communication. In L. Samovar & R. E. Porter (Eds.), *Intercultural communication: A reader* (7th ed., pp. 435–441). Belmont, CA: Wadsworth.

Kant, I. (1949). *Fundamental principles of the metaphysics of morals* (T. Abbott, Trans.). Indianapolis, IN: Library of Liberal Arts/Bobbs-Merrill.

Kayne, E. (2013, June 13). White majority in U.S. gone by 2043. *NBCNews.com*. Retrieved March 6, 2015, from http://usnews.nbcnews.com/_news/2013 /06/13/18934111-census-white-majority-in-us-gone -by-2043?lite

Kirkpatrick, D. D. (2011, May 20). Many in Arab world say Obama's speech doesn't dispel grievances against U.S. *The New York Times*, p. A10.

Kochhar, R., & Fry, R. (2014, December 12). Wealth inequality has widened along racial, ethnic lines since end of Great Recession. *Pew Research Cent*. Retrieved on March 8, 2014, from http://www.pewresearch .org/fact-tank/2014/12/12/racial-wealth-gaps-great -recession/.

Kornai, A. (2013). Digital language death. *Plosone*. Retrieved March 8, 2016, from http://journals .plos.org/plosone/article?id=10.1371/journal .pone.0077056.

Krogstad, J. M. (2015, September 24). What Americans, Europeans think of immigrants. *Pew Research Center*. Retrieved March 8, 2015, from http://www .pewresearch.org/fact-tank/2015/09/24/what-americans -europeans-think-of-immigrants/.

Krogstad, J. M., & Fry, R. (2014, April 24). More Hispanics, blacks enrolling in college, but lag in bachelor's degrees. *Pew Research Center*. Retrieved April 20, 2016, from http://www.pewresearch.org /fact-tank/2014/04/24/more-hispanics-blacks-enrolling -in-college-but-lag-in-bachelors-degrees/.

Lapchick, R. E. (2014). *The 2013 racial and gender report card*. The Institute for Diversity and Ethics in Sport, University of Central Florida, Orlando, FL. Retrieved April 4, 2016, from http://nebula.wsimg.com/728474de 65f7d28b196a0fbb47c05a91?AccessKeyId=DAC3 A56D8FB782449D2A&disposition=0&alloworigin=1

Loewen, J. W. (2010). *Teaching what really happened*. NYC: Teachers College Press.

Malesky, E. J., & Saiegh, S. M. (2014, June 2). Diversity is good for team performance in soccer. *Washingtonpost .com*. Retrieved April 4, 2016, from https://www .washingtonpost.com/news/monkey-cage/wp/2014 /06/02/diversity-is-good-for-team-performance -in-soccer/

Marshall, M. G., & Cole, B. R. (2014). *Global Report 2014: Conflict governance and state fragility*. Vienna: Center for Systemic Peace, from http://www.systemicpeace .org/vlibrary/GlobalReport2014.pdf

Martin, J. N., & Butler, R. L. W. (2001). Toward an ethic of intercultural communication research. In V. H. Milhouse, M. K. Asante, & P. O. Nwosu (Eds.), *Transcultural realities: Interdisciplinary perspectives on cross-cultural relations* (pp. 283–298). Thousand Oaks, CA: Sage.

McLuhan, M. (1967). *The medium is the message*. New York: Bantam Books.

Muzrui, A. (2001). Historical struggles between Islamic and Christian worldviews: An interpretation. In V. H. Milhouse, M. K. Asante, & P. O. Nwosu (Eds.), *Transcultural realities: Interdisciplinary perspectives on cross-cultural relations* (pp. 109–120). Thousand Oaks, CA: Sage.

Orfield, G., & Frankenburg, E. (2014). Increasingly segregated and unequal schools as courts reverse policy. *Educational Administration Quarterly, 50*(5), 718–734.

Passel, J. S., & Cohn, D. V. (2008, February 11). *U.S. populations projections: 2005–2050*. Washington, DC: Pew Research Center.

Phillips, K. W. (2014, October 1). How diversity makes us smarter. *scientificamerican.com*. Retrieved April 23, 2016, from http://www.scientificamerican.com/article /how-diversity-makes-us-smarter/.

Purcell, K., & Rainie, L. (2014, December 8). Americans feel better informed due to the Internet. *Pew Research Reports*. From http://www.pewinternet.org/files/2014 /12/PI_InformedWeb_120814_02.pdf.

Rainie, L. (2015, September 22). Digital divide 2015. *Pew Research Presentation*. Retrieved March 8, 2016, from http://www.pewinternet.org/2015/09/22/digital -divides-2015/.

Roberts, P. C. (2014). The offshore outsourcing of American jobs: A greater threat than terrorism. *Globalresearch.ca*. From http://www.globalresearch .ca/the-offshore-outsourcing-of-american-jobs-a -greater-threat-than-terrorism/18725.

Roediger, D. (1991). *The wages of whiteness: Race and the making of the American working class*. New York: Verso.

Shapiro, T. R. (2016, April 18). Student's racist video spreads online, draws concern at elite private school. *washingtonpost.com*. Retrieved April 20, 2016, from https://www.washingtonpost.com/news/education /wp/2016/04/18/students-racist-video-spreads-online -draws-concern-at-elite-private-school/.

Shebaya, H. (2015, December 13). Trump and Islamo-phobia: discrimination fuels terror. *Opendemocracy .net*. Retrieved March 8, 2016, from https://www .opendemocracy.net/arab-awakening/halim-shebaya /trump-and-islamophobia-discrimination-fuels-terror.

Siemaszko, C. (2015, December 20). Hate attacks on Muslims in U.S. spike after recent acts of terrorism. *nbcnews.com*. Retrieved March 8, 2016, from http:// www.nbcnews.com/news/us-news/hate-attacks-muslims -u-s-spike-after-recent-acts-terrorism-n482456.

Simon Wiesenthal Center. *2014 Report on Digital terrorism and hate*. Retrieved April 17, 2016, from http://www.wiesenthal.com/site/apps/nlnet/content .aspx?c=lsKWLbPJLnF&b=8776547&ct=13928897.

Slackman, M. (2006, August 6). Iranian 101: A lesson for Americans; the fine art of hiding what you mean to say. *The New York Times online*. Retrieved May 24, 2011, from http://query.nytimes.com/gst/fullpage.html?res= 9A04E1DD1E3FF935A3575BC0A9609C8B63.

Smith, C. (2011, March 14). Twitter user statistics show stunning growth. *huffingtonpost.com*. Retrieved May 6, 2011, from www.huffingtonpost.com/2011/03/14 /twitter-user-statistics_n_835581.html.

Snyder, B. (2003, May). Teams that span time zones face new work rules. Stanford Graduate School of Business website: www.gsb.stanford.edu/news/bmag/sbsm0305 /feature_virtual_teams.shtml.

Takaki, R. (1989). *Strangers from a different shore*. New York: Penguin Books.

Teixeira, R., Frey, W. H., & Griffin, R. (2015, February 24). 10 big trends that are transforming America. *Center for American Progress.com*. Retrieved March 8, 2016, from https://www.americanprogress.org/issues /progressive-movement/report/2015/02/24/107261 /states-of-change/.

Tompkins, P. K. (2009). *Who is my neighbor? Communicating and organizing to end homelessness*. Boulder, CO: Paradigm Publishers.

Turkle, S. (2011). *Alone together: Why we expect more from technology and less from each other*. New York: Basic Books.

U.S. public becoming less religious. (2015, November 3). *Pew Research Reports*. Retrieved March 7, 2016, from http://www.pewforum.org/files/2015/11/201.11.03 _RLS_II_full_report.pdf.

Varner, I., & Beamer, L. (2010). *Intercultural communication in the global workplace*. 5th ed. Boston, MA: McGraw-Hill.

Walsh, D., & Barrett, T. (2015, November 19). House passes bill that could limit Syrian refugees. *CNN .com*. Retrieved March 8, 2016, from http://www .cnn.com/2015/11/19/politics/house-democrats-refugee -hearings-obama/.

Walsh, M. F., Winterich, K. P., & Mittal, V. (2010). Do logo redesigns help or hurt your brand? The role of brand commitment. *Journal of Product & Brand Management, 19*(2), 76–84.

Wei, L. (2012). Number matters: The multimodality of Internet use as an indicator of the digital inequalities. *Journal of Computer-Mediated Communication. 17,* 303–318.

West, C. (1993). *Race matters*. Boston, MA: Beacon Press.

Winsor, M. (2015, April 15). African cell phone use: Sub-Saharan Africa sees surge in mobile ownership, study finds. *International Business Time*. Retrieved March 8, 2016, from http://www.ibtimes.com/african -cell-phone-use-sub-saharan-africa-sees-surge-mobile -ownership-study-finds-1883449.

Worstall, T. (2015, January 20). The really bad news about China's economic slowdown. *Forbes.com*. Retrieved March 8, 2016, from http://www.forbes .com/sites/timworstall/2015/01/20/the-really-bad -news-about-chinas-economic-slowdown-and-growth -targets-miss/#47c2c95e7d40.

Yohn, D. L. (2011, May). Leveraging franchisee diversity. *QSRmagazine.com*. Retrieved April 4, 2016, from http://www.qsrmagazine.com/franchising/leveraging -franchisee-diversity.

Zong, J., & Batalova, J. (2015, February 26). Frequently requested statistics on immigrants and immigration in the United States. Migration Policy Institute. Retrieved March 8, 2016, from http://www.migrationpolicy.org /article/frequently-requested-statistics-immigrants -and-immigration-united-states.

communicator." Wadsworth. [page 30, text] J. A. Crump and J. Sugarman, excerpt from "Ethical considerations for short-term experiences by trainees in global health." The Journal of American Medical Association. [page 30, text] V. Strauss, excerpt from "How NOT to save the world: Why U.S. students who go to poor countries to 'do good' often do the opposite." The Washington Post. [page 33, text] Jacqueline, excerpt from "Student Voices: I have spent three years in the United States seeking an education . . . more culturally competent." Original Work; [page 33, text] B. J. Hall, excerpt from "Ethics in intercultural and international communication." Lawrence Erlbaum. [page 34, text] P. K. Tompkins, quote from "Who is my neighbor? Communicating and organizing to end homelessness." Paradigm Publishers. [page 35, text] J. N. Martin and R. L. W. Butler, excerpt from "Transcultural realities: Interdisciplinary perspectives on cross-cultural relations." Sage.

THE HISTORY
OF THE STUDY
OF INTERCULTURAL
COMMUNICATION

THE EARLY DEVELOPMENT OF THE DISCIPLINE
Nonverbal Communication
Application of Theory
An Emphasis on International Settings
An Interdisciplinary Focus

**PERCEPTION AND WORLDVIEW
OF THE RESEARCHER**

**THREE APPROACHES TO STUDYING
INTERCULTURAL COMMUNICATION**
The Social Science Approach
The Interpretive Approach
The Critical Approach

**A DIALECTICAL APPROACH TO
UNDERSTANDING CULTURE AND
COMMUNICATION**
Combining the Three Traditional Paradigms:
    The Dialectical Approach
Six Dialectics of Intercultural Communication
Keeping a Dialectical Perspective

INTERNET RESOURCES

SUMMARY

DISCUSSION QUESTIONS

ACTIVITIES

KEY WORDS

REFERENCES

CHAPTER OBJECTIVES

*After reading this chapter, you
should be able to:*

1. Identify four early foci in the
   development of intercultural
   communication.
2. Describe three approaches to
   the study of intercultural
   communication.
3. Identify the methods used
   within each of the three
   approaches.
4. Explain the strengths and
   weaknesses of each approach.
5. Identify three characteristics
   of the dialectical approach.
6. Explain the strengths of a
   dialectical approach.
7. Identify six intercultural
   communication dialectics.

Now that we've described a rationale for studying intercultural communication, we turn to ways in which the study of intercultural communication is conducted. To understand the contemporary approaches to this discipline, it's important to examine its historical and philosophical foundations. Why should you study how the field of intercultural communication got started? Before answering this question, let us pose a few others: Whom do you think should be regarded as an expert in intercultural communication? Someone who has actually lived in a variety of cultures? Or someone who has conducted scientific studies on how cultural groups differ in values and attitudes? Or someone who analyzes what popular culture (movies, television, magazines, and so on) has to say about a particular group of people?

Consider a related question: What is the best way to study intercultural communication behavior? By observing how people communicate in various cultures? By asking people to describe their own communication patterns? By distributing questionnaires to various cultural groups? Or by analyzing books, videos, movies, and other cultural performances of various groups?

The answers to these questions help determine what kind of material goes into a textbook on intercultural communication. And intercultural communication scholars do not agree on what are the "right" answers to these questions. Thus, these questions and answers have implications for what you will be exposed to in this book and this course. By choosing some types of research (questionnaire, observation data), we may neglect other types (interviews, travel journal, media analysis).

To help you understand why we chose to include the material we did, we describe the origins of the discipline in the United States and the philosophical worldviews that inform the current study and practices of intercultural communication. We then outline three contemporary perspectives that recognize contributions from other disciplines. Finally, we outline our dialectical approach, which integrates the strengths from all three contemporary perspectives.

THE EARLY DEVELOPMENT OF THE DISCIPLINE

worldview Underlying assumptions about the nature of reality and human behavior.

The current study of intercultural communication is influenced in part by how it developed in the United States and in part by the **worldviews,** or research philosophies, of the scholars who pursue it. The roots of the study of intercultural communication can be traced to the post–World War II era, when the United States increasingly came to dominate the world stage. However, government and business personnel working overseas often found that they were ill equipped to work among people from different cultures. The language training they received, for example, did little to prepare them for the complex challenges of working abroad.

In response, the U.S. government in 1946 passed the Foreign Service Act and established the Foreign Service Institute (FSI). The FSI, in turn, hired Edward T. Hall and other prominent anthropologists and linguists (including Ray Birdwhistell and George Trager) to develop "predeparture" courses for overseas workers. Because intercultural training materials were scarce, they developed their own. In so doing, FSI theorists formed new ways of looking at culture and communication. Thus, the field of intercultural communication was born (Martin, Nakayama, & Carbaugh, 2012).

Nonverbal Communication

The FSI emphasized the importance of nonverbal communication and applied linguistic frameworks to investigate nonverbal aspects of communication. These researchers concluded that, just like language, nonverbal communication varies from culture to culture. Edward T. Hall pioneered this systematic study of culture and communication with *The Silent Language* (1959) and *The Hidden Dimension* (1966), which influenced the new discipline. In *The Silent Language,* for example, Hall introduced the notion of **proxemics,** the study of how people use personal space to communicate. In *The Hidden Dimension,* in elaborating on the concept of proxemics, he identified four **distance zones**—intimate, personal, social, and public—at which people interact and suggested that people know which distance to use depending on the situation. He noted that each cultural group has its own set of rules for personal space and that respecting these cultural differences is critical to smooth communication.

Application of Theory

The staff at the FSI found that government workers were not interested in theories of culture and communication; rather, they wanted specific guidelines for getting along in the countries they were visiting. Hall's initial strategy in developing materials for these predeparture training sessions was to observe variations in cultural behavior. At the FSI, he was surrounded by people who spoke many languages and who were from many cultures, so it was a great place to observe and test his theories about cultural differences. For example, he might have observed that Italians tend to stand close to each other when conversing, or that Greeks use lots of hand gestures when interacting, or that Chinese use few hand gestures in conversations. He could then have confirmed his observations by consulting members of different cultural groups. Today, most textbooks in the discipline retain this focus on practical guidelines and barriers to communication.

This emphasis on the application of theory spawned a parallel "discipline" of **cross-cultural training,** which began with the FSI staff and was expanded in the 1960s to include training for students and business personnel. More recently, it has come to include **diversity training,** which facilitates intercultural communication among members of various gender, ethnic, and racial groups, mostly in the corporate or government workplace (Landis, Bennett, Bennett, 2004).

An Emphasis on International Settings

Early scholars and trainers in intercultural communication defined *culture* narrowly, primarily in terms of "nationality." Usually, scholars mistakenly compared

proxemics The study of how people use personal space.

distance zones The area, defined by physical space, within which people interact, according to Edward Hall's theory of proxemics. The four distance zones for individuals are intimate, personal, social, and public. (See also **proxemics.**)

cross-cultural training Training people to become familiar with other cultural norms and to improve their interactions with people of different domestic and international cultures.

diversity training The training meant to facilitate intercultural communication among various gender, ethnic, and racial groups in the United States.

middle-class U.S. citizens with all residents of other nations, and trainers tended to focus on helping middle-class professionals become successful overseas.

One might ask why so few scholars focused on domestic contexts, particularly in the 1960s and 1970s when the United States was fraught with civil unrest. One reason may be the early emphasis of the FSI on helping overseas personnel. Another reason may be that most scholars who studied intercultural communication gained their intercultural experience in international contexts such as the Peace Corps, the military, or the transnational corporation.

An Interdisciplinary Focus

The scholars at the FSI came from various disciplines, including linguistics, anthropology, and psychology. Not surprisingly, in their work related to communication, they drew from theories pertinent to their specific disciplines. Contributions from these fields of study blended to form an integrated approach that remains useful to this day.

Linguists help us understand the importance of language and its role in intercultural interaction. They describe how languages vary in "surface" structure and are similar in "deep" structure. They also shed light on the relationship between language and reality. For example, the **Sapir-Whorf hypothesis,** developed by linguists Edward Sapir and Benjamin Whorf, explores phenomena such as the use of formal and informal pronouns. French and Spanish, for instance, have both formal and informal forms of the pronoun *you.* (In French, the formal is *vous* and the informal is *tu;* in Spanish, the formal is *usted* and the informal is *tu.*) In contrast, English makes no distinction between formal and informal usage; one word, *you,* suffices in both situations. Such language distinctions affect our culture's notion of formality. In Chapter 6, we'll look at some more recent studies that problematize this hypothesis. Linguists also point out that learning a second or third language can enhance our **intercultural competence** by providing insights into other cultures and expanding our communication repertoire.

Anthropologists help us understand the role that culture plays in our lives and the importance of nonverbal communication. Anthropologist Renate Rosaldo (1989) encouraged scholars to consider the appropriateness of cultural study methods, and other anthropologists have followed Rosaldo's lead. They point out that many U.S. and European studies reveal more about the researchers than about their subjects. Further, many anthropological studies of the past, particularly of non-Europeans, concluded that the people studied were inferior. To understand this phenomenon, science writer Stephen Jay Gould (1993) argues that "we must first recognize the cultural milieu of a society whose leaders and intellectuals did not doubt the propriety of racial thinking, with Indians below whites, and blacks below everyone else" (p. 85).

The so-called scientific study of other peoples is never entirely separate from the culture in which the researchers are immersed. In his study of the Victorian era, for example, Patrick Brantlinger (1986) notes that "evolutionary anthropology often suggested that Africans, if not nonhuman or a different species, were such an inferior

Sapir-Whorf hypothesis The assumption that language shapes our ideas and guides our view of social reality. This hypothesis was proposed by Edward Sapir, a linguist, and his student, Benjamin Whorf, and represents the relativist view of language and perception.

intercultural competence The ability to behave effectively and appropriately in interacting across cultures.

'breed' that they might be impervious to 'higher influences'" (p. 201). Consider this famous case, which dates back to the early 19th century:

> *The young African woman was lured to Europe with false promises of fame and fortune. She was paraded naked before jeering mobs. She was exhibited in a metal cage and sold to an animal trainer. When she died in Paris in 1816, she was penniless and friendless among people who derided her as a circus freak.*
>
> *White scientists intent on proving the inferiority of blacks dissected her body, bottled her brain and genitals, wired her skeleton and displayed them in a French museum. That might have been the end of Saartjie Baartman, the young African woman derisively labeled the "Hottentot Venus."*
>
> *[However,] 192 years after she last looked on these rugged cliffs and roaring sea [of South Africa], her remains returned to the land of her birth. In an agreement negotiated after years of wrangling between South Africa and France, her remains were finally removed from the Musée de l'Homme in Paris and flown back home. (Swarns, 2002, p. A28)*

This return of Baartman's remains is part of a larger movement away from a scientific "era when indigenous people were deemed worthy of scientific study, but unworthy of the consideration commonly accorded to whites" (Swarns, 2002, p. A28). Indeed, the conclusions from such studies reveal more about the cultural attitudes of the researchers (e.g., ethnocentrism, racism, sexism) than they do about the people studied. An **interdisciplinary** focus can help us acquire and interpret information in a more comprehensive manner—in ways relevant to bettering the intercultural communication process, as well as producing knowledge.

interdisciplinary Integrating knowledge from different disciplines in conducting research and constructing theory.

Psychologists such as Gordon Allport help us understand notions of stereotyping and the ways in which prejudice functions in our lives and in intercultural interaction. In his classic study *The Nature of Prejudice* (1979), he describes how prejudice can develop from "normal" human cognitive activities such as categorization and generalization. Other psychologists, such as Richard Brislin (1999) and Dan Landis (Landis & Wasilewski, 1999), reveal how variables like nationality, ethnicity, personality, and gender influence our communication.

Whereas the early study of intercultural communication was characterized as interdisciplinary, over time, it became increasingly centered in the discipline of communication. Nevertheless, the field continues to be influenced by interdisciplinary contributions, including ideas from cultural studies, critical theory, and the more traditional disciplines of psychology and anthropology (Martin, Nakayama, & Carbaugh, 2012).

In her historical overview of the ways that "culture" has been viewed in intercultural communication, communication scholar Dreama Moon (2010) noted that how culture is defined determines how it is studied. She also argues for expanding the notion of culture to include the idea of a struggle over power. So while intercultural communication is more firmly rooted in the communication field, the definition of "culture" has expanded to make intercultural communication more interdisciplinary.

As a child, I did not consciously think of myself as a German or as a Norwegian. Since I never viewed myself in terms of my culture, cultural heritage was something with which I never used to identify others. When I communicated with others, the cultural background of the person I was talking with never crossed my mind. To someone who constantly sees racism and prejudice, this situation may seem ideal, but ignoring a person's culture can cause as much harm as judging someone based upon that culture. Knowledge of someone's historical background is necessary when communicating on anything other than a superficial level.

—Andrew

I grew up in northern Minnesota and we were very aware that we were Norwegian and not Swedish. We ate lutefisk and lefse, but we also ate American food. I really don't like lutefisk. My dad belonged to the Sons of Norway, but I think he was more interested in socializing with his friends than insisting that we learned about Norwegian culture. I don't speak Norwegian, but we always knew we were Norwegian. I guess that I mostly feel like an American, and most of the time people probably see me as white.

—Juliann

PERCEPTION AND WORLDVIEW OF THE RESEARCHER

paradigm A framework that serves as the worldview of researchers. Different paradigms assume different interpretations of reality, human behavior, culture, and communication.

perception The process by which individuals select, organize, and interpret external and internal stimuli to create their view of the world.

A second influence on the current study of intercultural communication is the research **paradigm,** or worldview, of the scholars involved. People understand and learn about the world through filtering lenses; they select, evaluate, and organize information (stimuli) from the external environment through **perception.** As Marshal Singer (1987) explains:

> *We experience everything in the world not "as it is"—because there is no way that we can know the world "as it is"—but only as the world comes to us through our sensory receptors. From there, these stimuli go instantly into the "data-storage banks" of our brains, where they have to pass through the filters of our censor screen, our decoding mechanism, and the collectivity of everything we have learned from the day we were born. (p. 9)*

In this sense, all of the information we have already stored in our brains (learning) affect how we interpret new information. Some of our learning and perception is group related. That is, we see the world in particular ways because of the cultural groups (based on ethnicity, age, gender, and so on) to which we belong. These group-related perceptions (worldviews or value orientations) are so fundamental that we rarely question them (Singer, 1998). They involve our assumptions about human nature, the physical and spiritual world, and the ways in which humans should relate to one another. For example, most U.S. Americans perceive human beings as separate from nature and believe that there is a fundamental difference between, say, a human and a rock. However, other cultural groups (Japanese, Chinese, traditional

Native Americans) see humans and human reality as part of a larger physical reality. For them, the difference between a human and a rock is not so pronounced.

The key point here is that academic research is also cultural behavior because research traditions require particular worldviews about the nature of reality and knowledge and particular beliefs about how research should be conducted. For example, researchers studying communication often reflect their own cultural assumptions in their research projects. Asian scholars say that U.S. communication scholars often emphasize individuality and rationality—two strong cultural beliefs held by many U.S. Americans—and ignore human interdependence and feeling in human encounters, important beliefs for many people around the world (Miike, 2007a, 2007b). And these research paradigms are often held as strongly as cultural or spiritual beliefs (Burrell & Morgan, 1988; Kuhn, 1970). There are even examples of intercultural conflicts in which scholars strongly disagree. For example, Galileo was excommunicated from the Catholic Church in the 17th century because he took issue with theologians' belief that the earth was the center of the universe.

More recent examples of the relation between academic research and cultural behavior can be seen in the social sciences. Some communication scholars believe there is an external reality that can be measured and studied, whereas others believe that reality can be understood only as lived and experienced by individuals (Casmir, 1994). Scholars' cultural beliefs and experiences also influence them to focus on particular areas of the world and not others—resulting in extensive research on U.S., European, and Asian communication, but neglecting many others (Africa, South Asia, and the Middle East), resulting in academic "silent zones," where there is little study of cultural communication (Dutta & Martin, 2017). In short, beliefs and assumptions about reality influence research methods and findings, and so also influence what we currently know about intercultural communication.

At present, we can identify three broad approaches, or worldviews, that characterize the study of culture and communication (Gudykunst, 2005a; Hall, 1992). All three approaches involve a blend of disciplines and reflect different worldviews and assumptions about reality, human behavior, and ways to study culture and communication. As you read about each of these approaches, think about what kinds of assumptions concerning "culture" are used in each approach. How we think about "culture" influences how it is studied.

THREE APPROACHES TO STUDYING INTERCULTURAL COMMUNICATION

Three contemporary approaches to studying intercultural communication are: (1) the social science (or functionalist) approach, (2) the interpretive approach, and (3) the critical approach. (See Tables 2-1 and 2-2.) These approaches are based on different fundamental assumptions about human nature, human behavior, and the nature of knowledge. Each one contributes in a unique way to our understanding of the relationship between culture and communication, but each also has limitations. These approaches vary in their assumptions about human behavior, their research goals, their conceptualization of culture and communication, and their preferred

	Social Science (or Functionalist)	Interpretive	Critical
TABLE 2-1 THREE APPROACHES TO INTERCULTURAL COMMUNICATION			
Discipline on which approach is founded	Psychology	Anthropology, sociolinguistics	Various
Research goal	Describe and predict behavior	Describe behavior	Change behavior
Assumption of reality	External and describable	Subjective	Subjective and material
Assumptions of human behavior	Predictable	Creative and voluntary	Changeable
Method of study	Survey, observation	Participant observation, field study	Textual analysis of media
Relationship of culture and communication	Communication influenced by culture	Culture created and maintained through communication	Culture a site of power struggles
Contribution of the approach	Identifies cultural variations; recognizes cultural differences in many aspects of communication but often does not consider context	Emphasizes that communication and culture and cultural differences should be studied in context	Recognizes the economic and political forces in culture and communication; asserts that all intercultural interactions are characterized by power

methodologies. As a student of intercultural communication, you may not see yourself doing research on intercultural communication issues; however, it is important to understand the assumptions behind the scholarship that is being undertaken. Think about the strengths and weaknesses of each assumption and what each approach reveals (and also hides) about other cultures and their communication patterns.

To examine these three approaches, let us start with a situation that illustrates a communication dilemma—the worldwide refugee crisis. You probably know that in the past few years, an unprecedented number of people have fled their homes because of violence or famine—approximately 60 million people are now displaced from their homes, many of whom are refugees (Geiger, 2016). Remember the many stories of people trying desperately to escape the war-ravaged and dangerous existence in their home countries and find refuge in other countries? After leaving their homes with a few possessions, many walked for hundreds, sometimes thousands of miles, and/or risked their lives by crossing in treacherous waters in tiny unsafe boats (in 2016, two children drowned every day on average trying to reach safely in Europe, UNHCR; http://www.unhcr.org/cgi-bin/texis/vtx/home). How were these refugees

TABLE 2-2   THE SIGNIFICANCE OF RESEARCH APPROACHES

Social scientific	This research style emphasizes statistical measures. Understanding quantitative approaches is critical to analyzing data and statistics. These are skills important in any walk of life.
Interpretive	Interpretive approaches emphasize using language to describe human behavior. Understanding interpretive approaches is important to understanding how news is reported, how information is transferred, and how most people make decisions.
Critical	Critical methodologies analyze the large power structures that guide everyday life. Understanding this approach helps students grasp the invisible forces that alter our lives.

welcomed once they arrived safely to foreign countries? News reports tell us that some were welcomed, processed, and given food, shelter, and aid by compassionate citizens and governments. Others were stopped by border fences, government security forces, and even citizens who felt threatened by these waves of foreigners. Still others encountered ambivalent hosts who wanted to be compassionate but were afraid that their neighborhoods and countries were not able to assimilate these vast numbers of newcomers (See Figure 2-1).

These situations provide good examples of intercultural encounters and offer useful insights into how we might think about intercultural communication and how different cultural groups understand (or don't understand) each other. There are a variety of ways that foreigners (migrants) and hosts can interact, and we will explore these in more detail in Chapter 8. But for now, let's analyze these encounters to demonstrate the characteristics of the three approaches to studying intercultural communication—contributions and limitations.

The Social Science Approach

The **social science approach** (also called the **functionalist approach**), popular in the 1980s, is based on research in psychology and sociology. This approach assumes a describable external reality. It also assumes that human behavior is predictable and that the researcher's goal is to describe and predict behavior. Researchers who take this approach often use **quantitative methods,** gathering data by administering questionnaires or observing subjects firsthand.

Social science researchers assume that culture is a **variable** that can be measured. This suggests that culture influences communication in much the same way that personality traits do. The goal of this research, then, is to predict specifically how culture influences communication.

Applications   So how might social science researchers understand the communication issues of those migrants who find themselves in a foreign country, trying to adapt to new ways of thinking and behaving? Social science researchers often

social science approach See **functionalist approach.**

functionalist approach A study of intercultural communication, also called the *social science approach,* based on the assumptions that (1) there is a describable, external reality, (2) human behaviors are predictable, and (3) culture is a variable that can be measured. This approach aims to identify and explain cultural variations in communication and to predict future communication. (Compare with **critical approach** and **interpretive approach.**)

quantitative methods Research methods that use numerical indicators to capture and ascertain the relationships among variables. These methods use survey and observation.

variable A concept that varies by existing in different types or different amounts and that can be operationalized and measured.

FIGURE 2-1   A refugee couple sleeps in the Serbian town of Presevo hoping to cross the border to Hungary. (© *Dimitar Dilkoff and Csaba Segesvari/AFP/Getty Images*)

use theories to predict human behavior. What predictions might be made about intercultural encounters between immigrants and individuals from the host country? One approach might be to investigate how various communication technologies affect cultural adaptation. For example, one study tried to find out whether Muslim migrants' use of Facebook affected their cultural adaptation to the United States. Specifically, the researchers predicted that immigrants' use of Facebook to communicate with other immigrants would impact their rate of adaptation to the United States and their perceptions of America. Perhaps not surprising, they discovered that, over time, these immigrants used Facebook mostly to interact with other Muslims and were also less likely to culturally adapt to the U.S. culture, and more likely to have a negative perception of the United States. They suggest that one reason for this outcome is the negative political and social situation in the United States and the War on Terror where Muslims have been the center of attention. In such a situation, the length of time immigrants spent in the United States led to negative feelings about this country (Croucher & Rahmani, 2015).

However, another similar social science study found slightly different results. Like the previous study, communication researchers Young Yun Kim and Kelly McKay-Semmler (2013) measured Asian and European immigrants' use of social media and e-mail to communicate with people from their own country and also with Americans. They also measured the immigrants' face-to-face contacts with the same two groups. Based on Kim's **integrative theory of adaptation,** they predicted (and found) that the more immigrants communicated with people in the United States (both face-to-face and on social media), the better adapted they were to U.S. culture and the less they communicated with friends and family back home. However, they also found that online connections *did not replace* direct interpersonal communication with U.S. Americans. They stressed the importance for immigrants to be directly and actively engaged with people in the host country as they strive to adapt to the new culture (Kim & McKay-Semmler, 2013). Perhaps the difference in the results for the two studies could be attributed to the difference in the attitudes of the host culture (the United States) toward the two groups of immigrants—Asian and European immigrants who experienced a more welcoming reception versus Muslim immigrants from the Middle East who experienced a less welcoming reception.

Another group of social science researchers predicted that immigrants' degree of acculturation in the United States might influence their perceptions of racial discrimination and their need for social support (Hanasono, Chen, & Wilson, 2014). They surveyed 345 racial minority first-and second-generation immigrants and asked them to report how acculturated they felt to the U.S. society and also their experiences with discrimination (how often they experienced discrimination and how severe were these experiences). They also asked them to describe how likely they were to ask for social support from others to cope with these experiences—for advice or comfort in dealing with these experiences. Interestingly, the researchers found that immigrants who were less acculturated, less integrated into the fabric of U.S. society did express a higher need for social support in dealing with the detrimental effects of discrimination, but they were not likely to seek support! The researchers speculated that they did not ask for support because of language barriers or perhaps because they come from cultures where directly asking for support from others is not socially approved. In any case, the results suggest that there are members of immigrant communities in the United States that need help, and community leaders should find ways to develop resources and programs (e.g., communication workshops) that help less acculturated individuals to find, seek, and receive social support.

All three studies provide insight into intercultural communication between immigrants and people in the host culture. Other contemporary research programs illustrate the social science approach. One such program was headed by the late William B. Gudykunst (2005b), a well-known communication researcher. He proposed the **anxiety uncertainty management (AUM) theory**, which explains the role of anxiety and uncertainty in individuals communicating with host culture members when they enter a new culture. This theory predicts certain optimal levels of uncertainty and anxiety, and how they motivate individuals to engage in successful interaction. This theory is explained further in Chapter 8.

A related social science program is Stella Ting-Toomey's (1985, 2005) **face negotiation theory.** *Face* is the sense of favorable self-worth, and in all cultures people are concerned about saving face. Ting-Toomey suggests that conflict is a face negotiation process in which people often have their face threatened or questioned. She and her colleagues have conducted a number of studies in which they try to identify how cultures differ in conflict style and face concerns (Neuliep & Johnson, 2016). For example, they found that members of individualistic societies like the United States are concerned with saving their own face in conflict situations and so use more dominating conflict resolution styles. In contrast, members of collectivistic cultures, like China, South Korea, and Taiwan, are more concerned with saving the other person's face in conflict situations and use more avoiding, obliging, or integrating conflict resolution styles (Ting-Toomey et al., 1991; Ting-Toomey, 2005). Research also shows that Latino and Asian

anxiety uncertainty management theory The view that the reduction of anxiety and uncertainty plays an important role in successful intercultural communication, particularly when experiencing new cultures.

face negotiation theory The view that cultural groups vary in preferences for conflict styles and face-saving strategies.

Americans in the United States use more avoiding and third-party conflict styles than African Americans and more than do European Americans (Ting-Toomey, Yee-Jung, Shapiro, Garcia, Wright, & Oetzel, 2000).

Another social science research program focuses on cultural differences in conversational strategies. In contrast to AUM, **conversational constraints theory,** developed by Min-Sun Kim (2005), attempts to explain how and why people make particular conversational choices. It suggests five universal conversational constraints, or concerns: (1) clarity, (2) minimizing imposition, (3) consideration for the other's feelings, (4) risking negative evaluation by the hearer, and (5) effectiveness. Kim and her colleagues have discovered that people from individualistic and collectivistic cultures place varying importance on these various conversational concerns. Individualists seem to be most concerned with clarity; collectivists, with concerns about hurting the other's feelings and minimizing imposition. Concerns for effectiveness and avoidance of negative evaluation by others seem to be universally important (Kim, 1994, 2005).

The **communication accommodation theory** is the result of another social science program in which researchers attempted to identify how and when individuals accommodate their speech and nonverbal behavior to others during an interaction. Unlike AUM and conversational constraints theory, communication accommodation theory focuses on adaptation during intercultural interaction. The researchers posited that in some situations individuals change their communication patterns to accommodate others (Gallois, Ogay, & Giles, 2005). Specifically, individuals are likely to adapt during low-threat interactions or situations in which they see little difference between themselves and others. The underlying assumption is that we accommodate when we feel positive toward the other person. For example, when we talk to international students, we may speak more slowly, enunciate more clearly, use less jargon, and mirror their communication. We also may adapt to regional speech. For example, when Tom talks with someone from the South, he sometimes starts to drawl and use words like "'y'all." Of course, it is possible to overaccommodate. For example, if a white American speaks black English to an African American, this may be perceived as overaccommodation.

The **diffusion of innovations theory,** developed by communication scholar Everett Rogers (2003), explains how cultural practices can be changed—largely due to communication. This theory explains why some innovations, like computer technology or the Internet, or certain behaviors, like "safe sex," are accepted by some people and rejected by others. The theory posits that in order for people to accept a new technology, they have to see the usefulness of it and it has to be compatible with their values and lifestyle. Communication also plays a key role; usually people first learn of innovations through impersonal channels—like mass media—but only decide to adopt an innovation later, after asking the opinion or observing the behavior of someone who is known, trusted, or considered an expert—an "opinion leader." If people important to the individual (e.g., peers for adolescents) adopt the innovation first, then the individual is more likely to adopt it. Opinion leaders can also be responsible for innovations *not* diffusing, if they ignore or speak out against an innovation. There seems to be a predictable, over-time pattern for the spread of

conversational constraints theory The view that cultural groups vary in their fundamental concerns regarding how conversational messages should be constructed.

communication accommodation theory The view that individuals adjust their verbal communication to facilitate understanding.

diffusion of innovations theory The view that communication and relationships play important roles in how new ideas are adopted (or not) by individuals and groups.

ONE REFUGEE STORY. *Time* reporter Alex Altman tells the story of one Syrian refugee family.

Altman's account of Faez al Sharaa's story begins with the day Faez thought he was going to die. He was walking to work in Daraa, his hometown in Spring 2013. Daraa was the scene of grisly murders and torture of young and old in the war between President Assad's forces and the antigovernment insurgents. He was suddenly confronted by government army soldiers and with a gun pointed at his head he knew he was going to die. Altman describes how Faez got lucky. An old woman, a stranger to Faez, came running and begged the soldiers to "spare her son." The soldiers relented and he was saved. That day he and his wife decided to flee Syria. He hired a smuggler to carry them to the border, taking some clothes, wedding photos, and a few mementos. Across the border, they landed in a refugee camp of 80,000 in Jordon. They started the long process of trying to get relocated. They were denied entry to Sweden and then Finland.

As Altman notes, Faez was one of the rare lucky ones. After 2 years of waiting in Jordan, he and his wife gained asylum in the United States and now they and their 14-year-old daughter live in Dallas. He got a job at Walmart and is slowly making the mandatory repayments to the U.S. government for their air tickets to the United States.

They are learning English and he says neighbors have been kind. However, he laments the anti-immigrant backlash that has occurred recently in the U.S.— and the restrictions placed on new refugees. As Altman describes the situation in Texas, "With fear spreading and solutions in short supply, the refugees have become a target, even though they are trying to escape violence and move on with their lives." Altman says that Faez himself worries about becoming a target—with some justification. A few days after Altman talked with Faez, armed protesters—some with masks and tactical weapons—gathered in a nearby town: one sign decried the "Islamization of America." Faez said he's been shocked "because America prides itself on diversity. It is a melting pot."

Source: From A. Altman, "A Syrian Refugee Story," *time.com,* November 20, 2015. Retrieved April 20, 2016, from http://time.com/a-syrian-refugee-story/.

an innovation, first to early adopters and then to many more individuals (Singhal & Dearing, 2006).

Many social science studies explain how communication styles vary from culture to culture—often based on **individualistic** versus **collectivistic** values (Gudykunst, 1998). For example, many people in the United States who have strong individualistic tendencies see value in direct communication and self-promotion. In cultures with a more collectivistic orientation such as Japan and China, people are more likely to use an indirect approach (Merkin, Taras, & Steel, 2014). We will discuss more of these cultural differences in communication patterns throughout the rest of the book.

individualistic The tendency to emphasize individual identities, beliefs, needs, goals, and views rather than those of the group. (Compare with **collectivistic**.)

collectivistic The tendency to focus on the goals, needs, and views of the ingroup rather than individuals' own goals, needs, and views. (Compare with **individualistic**.)

Strengths and Limitations   Many of these social science studies have been useful in identifying variations in communication from group to group and specifying psychological and sociological variables in the communication process. However, this approach is limited. Many scholars now realize that human communication is often more creative than predictable and that reality is not just external but also internally constructed. We cannot identify all of the variables that affect our communication. Nor can we predict exactly why one intercultural interaction seems to succeed and another does not (Ting-Toomey, 2010).

Scholars also recognize that some methods in this approach are not culturally sensitive and that researchers may be too distant from the phenomena or people they are researching (Kim, 2012). In other words, researchers may not really understand the cultural groups they are studying (Lu & Gutua, 2014). For example, suppose we conducted a study that compared self-disclosure in the United States and Algeria using the social science perspective. We might distribute Jourard's self-disclosure measure (a common instrument used in U.S. research) to students in both countries. However, we might not realize that the concept of self-disclosure does not translate exactly between the United States and Algeria, and that Algerians and U.S. Americans have different notions of this concept.

To overcome these kinds of problems, social scientists have developed strategies for achieving equivalence of measures. A leading cross-cultural psychologist, Richard Brislin (1999), has written extensively on guidelines for cross-cultural researchers. He has identified several types of equivalencies that researchers should establish, including **translation equivalence** and **conceptual equivalence.** For example, in cross-cultural studies, literal translations are inadequate. To establish translation equivalence, research materials should be translated several times, using different translators. Materials that proceed smoothly through these multiple steps are considered translation equivalent.

translation equivalence The linguistic sameness that is gained after translating and back-translating research materials several times using different translators. (See also **conceptual equivalence**.)

In Chapter 6, we explore issues of translation in more detail and describe some of the impressive improvements being made in machine translation. The European Union has been a major force behind these improvements, as well as in the goals of machine translation (Mark my words, 2007).

While machine translation can be enormously helpful for common phrases and rough drafts, these translations cannot yet do away with humans. Advances are being made rapidly and, as the databases increase, the computer-generated translations will improve.

conceptual equivalence The similarity of linguistic terms and meanings across cultures. (See also **translation equivalence**.)

Researchers can establish conceptual equivalence by ensuring that the notions they are investigating are similar at various levels. For example, problem solving is one aspect of intelligence that may be conceptually equivalent in many cultures. Once this equivalence is established, researchers can identify culture-specific ways in which problem solving is achieved. Another example is communication apprehension or a fear of communicating—viewed negatively in U.S. culture, whereas in Japan, reticence is seen as socially desirable (Gudykunst, 2005). Thus, the construct of reticence is not equivalent between these two groups because U.S. American and Japanese individuals may not view it in the same way. Therefore, when establishing equivalence, researchers need to be careful to determine that the construct is viewed similarly in the cultures being compared (Fletcher et al., 2014). Establishing these equivalencies allows researchers to isolate and describe what distinguishes one culture from another.

The Interpretive Approach

The **interpretive approach** gained prominence in the late 1980s among communication scholars. One interpretive approach, rooted in sociolinguistics, is the **ethnography** of communication (Hymes, 1974). Ethnographers of communication are devoted to descriptive studies of communication patterns within specific cultural groups. Interpretive researchers assume not only that reality is external to humans, but also that humans construct reality. They believe that human experience, including communication, is subjective and human behavior is neither predetermined nor easily predicted.

The goal of interpretive research is to understand and describe human behavior. (Predicting behavior is not a goal.) Whereas the social scientist tends to see communication as influenced by culture, the interpretivist sees culture as created and maintained through communication (Carbaugh, 1996). This type of research uses **qualitative methods** derived from anthropology and linguistics such as field studies, observations, and participant observations. An example is shown in Figure 2-2. (A researcher engaging in **participant observation** contributes actively to the communication processes being observed and studied. The researcher thus is intimately involved in the research and may become good friends with members of the communities he or she is studying.)

Another example of interpretive research is the **rhetorical approach,** also used by critical researchers, perhaps the oldest communication scholarship, dating back to the ancient Greeks. Rhetoricians typically examine and analyze texts or public speeches in the contexts in which they occur.

Cross-cultural psychologists use the terms **etic** and **emic** to distinguish the social science and interpretive approaches (Berry, 1997). These terms were borrowed from linguistics—*etic* from *phonetic* and *emic* from *phonemic*. Social science research usually searches for universal generalizations and studies cultures objectively, with an "outsider's" view; in this way, it is "etic." In contrast, interpretive research usually focuses on understanding phenomena subjectively, from within a particular cultural community or context; in this way, it is "emic." These researchers try to describe patterns or rules that individuals follow in specific contexts. They tend to be more interested in describing cultural behavior in one community than in making cross-cultural comparisons.

Applications   How might an interpretive researcher investigate the communication experiences of immigrants? One possible approach would be to talk with immigrants about their experiences in a foreign country. That is the approach taken by communication scholar Julie Semlak, who conducted two focus groups with African immigrant women living in South Dakota. She and a team of researchers transcribed and analyzed these focus group discussions. They found that these immigrant women expressed conflicting feelings about their interactions with host country individuals and labeled these feelings *dialectics* (more

interpretive approach An approach to intercultural communication that aims to understand and describe human behavior within specific cultural groups based on the assumptions that (1) human experience is subjective, (2) human behavior is creative rather than determined or easily predicted, and (3) culture is created and maintained through communication. (Compare with **critical approach** and **functionalist approach.**)

ethnography A discipline that examines the patterned interactions and significant symbols of specific cultural groups to identify the cultural norms that guide their behaviors, usually based on field studies.

qualitative methods Research methods that attempt to capture people's own meanings for their everyday behavior in specific contexts. These methods use participant observation and field studies.

participant observation A research method where investigators interact extensively with the cultural group being studied.

rhetorical approach A research method, dating back to ancient Greece, in which scholars try to interpret the meanings or persuasion used in texts or oral discourses in the contexts in which they occur.

FIGURE 2-2   One way to study and learn about cultural patterns is to interview other people, which is this woman's approach. What are the strengths and weaknesses of interviewing as a research strategy? (© *Digital Vision/Alamy RF*)

etic A term stemming from *phonetic*. The etic inquiry searches for universal generalizations across cultures from a distance. (Compare with **emic**.)

emic A term stemming from *phonemic*. The emic way of inquiry focuses on understanding communication patterns from inside a particular cultural community or context. (Compare with **etic**.)

about this approach at the end of this chapter). They identified four dialectics: positive-negative (the immigrants described challenges to living in America and at the same time also expressed happiness at being here); acceptance-rejection (a struggle with accepting and/or rejecting elements of American culture); inclusion-exclusion (a desire to be included in local communities and a perceived exclusion from these communities); and real-ideal (struggle between their own lifestyle and the perception of the lifestyles of Americans (Semlak, Pearson, Amundson, & Kudak, 2008).

A similar study also involved focus groups (Korem & Horenczyk, 2015). In this study, researchers asked young immigrants from Ethiopia living in Israel about their experiences and specifically what communication strategies they used to adapt to live there. These young men and women described the differences between Ethiopian and Israeli cultural values and communication preferences. They described their home (Ethiopian) values as a strong emphasis on respect for elders and parents and the total loyalty one has for a friend, "if we are friends, you have to make me feel that I can depend on you no matter what." They also contrasted the strong emphasis on gentleness and reservedness in Ethiopian relationships with the more assertiveness and directness preferred by Israelis. They described how they sometimes emphasized cultural commonalities and sometimes differences in their interactions in the foreign country—depending on the context.

There are many different ways of encountering new cultures: as a tourist, a military family, an immigrant, or a refugee. Think of how each of these individual's experiences create specific intercultural communication challenges:

Last summer my best friend and I visited Paris for the first time. The excitement of finally being in the beautiful city we had been dreaming of left us feeling so happy and grateful. It didn't take long for us to adjust and get into the groove of the way the people of the city communicate and work. Overall, the experience of my first trip to Paris was a very positive one. Being in a culture outside of my own made me realize how big the world really is and how the way we live here in America isn't the only way to live and that there is so much more out there to experience.
    —Elizabeth

As a subculture, my father was in the military. Military families are subject to an entirely different culture from other families as we were unable to have roots in one place due to military transfers every 3 to 4 years. Military families were therefore dependent on each other even more, and we had to learn to make new friends easily and accept change frequently. We were exposed to many different cultures, which required us to be more open and accepting of other people. I believe that my experiences as a military family have allowed me to be a "people person."
    —Carrie

My father is a first-generation Hispanic who was certainly not given an easy start in life. He was raised by his grandparents who did not speak a word of English and constantly experienced economic hardships and challenges. Yet my father found a way to rise above his circumstances and make something of his life; through hard work. My father is the hardest working person I know, and instilled in me the importance and value of an incredible work ethic.
    —Charles

In some situations, they emphasized their commonalities; for example, they tried hard to speak Hebrew without an accent. In other situations, they emphasized that they were different and the uniqueness of their cultural backgrounds, "If there are elements that I like very much in my culture and they don't limit me, I will preserve them" (p. 20). It also depended on whom they are interacting with, as one said, "Next to Israelis, I allow myself to behave more openly. Among Ethiopians I choose my words" although he goes on to say that this "double life" can be "tiresome."

    We can see that immigrants in both studies describe some ambivalence and contradictory feelings in their adaptation experience—on the one hand, recognizing and even embracing their own unique cultural background and values and at the same time, trying out the new values and communication patterns. We see here the challenges of living with two competing sets of values and expectations—a theme we will discuss more in later chapters.

In a third study, interpretive scholars interviewed Turkish immigrants who returned home from living in western Europe (Germany, the Netherlands, or France) (Kunuroglu, Yagmur, van de Vijver, & Kroon, 2015). These researchers asked the returned immigrants about their life back in their home country of Turkey; they recorded, transcribed, and then analyzed the interviews for recurring themes. The immigrants reported that their readaptation in their home country was almost as difficult as their adaptation in the foreign country. Back in Turkey, they found that many of their friends and family did not welcome them with open arms, some were maybe jealous of the immigrants' experiences abroad and many criticized them for being "too foreign" (too German, Dutch, or French)—even though the returned immigrants reported that they hadn't really adapted very much while in the foreign country. That is, many had not learned the host language; they had interacted mainly with other Turks and consumed only Turkish media (newspapers, radio, TV). However, they were still regarded by Turks at home as not being Turkish enough! One returned immigrant from Germany describes the sadness he feels when he is called "almanci" (not-Turkish):

> *"When I hear the word 'almanci', I feel a deep sorrow . . . . . it means someone is 'provincial' and 'mannerless'. I have been exposed to this treatment many times . . . . . one time, I never forget, I was traveling on the very first row in a bus and it was night time. I warned the driver as he had the high beam headlamps on, thinking that the driver on the car ahead of us can be distracted. I asked the driver why he was doing that. And he replied, 'they are almancıs, let them die'." (p. 206).*

There were many children-related issues. The children of these immigrants had grown up in the foreign country and were seen by other Turks as not Turkish. Back at home in Turkey, they had some trouble with the Turkish language and adapting to new school situations. However, some of them said that they also enjoyed some advantages, became popular among their peers at school, having acquired western European cultural and linguistic knowledge/skills, which made them feel positive and special.

As you can see, in contrast to the social science studies that aim to predict aspects of the immigrant experiences, the goal of interpretive researchers is to provide us with in-depth descriptions of experiences, often in the words of the immigrants themselves.

Some interpretive studies investigate the language patterns in many different groups—from the Burundi in Africa, to the Athabascan in northern Canada, to various groups within the United States, such as urban blacks or Cajuns. Other interpretive studies investigate the different communication patterns of one cultural group. For example, communication scholar David Engen (2012) describes the communication patterns of his white working class community. He characterizes the communication style in his home and community as direct, even blunt, and sometimes impassioned and argumentative. It was also pretty functional (no need for abstract language) and there was the role of humor—in ommunication scholar Sarah Amira de la Garza proposes a unique ethnographic methodology in studying cultural practices. It's based on the seasonal cycles of nature (spring, summer, winter, and fall) and honors unique paces and rhythms of the natural world. She admonishes the culture learner to surrender to the process, to become one with the process, the research instrument (González, 2000).

Spring is a time of preparation, which involves self-searching and introspection, opening oneself to the privilege of entering and being welcomed into another culture's life-world.

Summer is the season of immersion into the culture, a challenging and sometime exhausting time, living with uncertainty, discomfort, testing one's limits living in accepting another's way of living. May grieve the loss of the unfamiliar, and yearn for the familiar.

Fall is the harvest season—when the learner begins to understand some of the cultural patterns, a tentative thesis starts to form in answer to the research questions posed, vague, half-shaped insights start to take a coherent shape.

Winter, like summer, is a difficult season, when one wrestles with issues of accountability, how to present one's findings, how to represent the voices of those who graciously shared their lives and cultural knowledge.

Many researchers have used this framework and gained interesting insights into their own and other cultural patterns. For a critical study of the tensions between indigenous child-rearing practices and modernizing influences in a small village in the Copper Canyon of Mexico, see Mendoza (2016).

working class life you laugh to survive. He then describes the shock of discovering the communication norms of the four-year American college classroom: abstract and philosophical, requiring "political correctness" and "proper" English (he vividly recalls saying things like "I seen that" and "I ain't worried about that") and his discomfort at realizing he did not have "the appropriate classroom language and dialogue" (p. 236).

In similar studies, communication scholar Donal Carbaugh (1999) describes the important role of silence and listening in Blackfeet (American Indian) communication; Carbaugh and Berry (2001) describe the tendency of Finns to be rather reserved in communication. More importantly, these scholars show how communication patterns are inextricably tied to cultural identities in these communities.

A number of interpretive scholars have emphasized that descriptions of the communication rules of a given people must be grounded, or *centered,* in their beliefs and values (Alexander et al, 2014; Asante & Miike, 2013). Most scholarly studies of communication are rooted in a European American perspective, and this frame of reference is not necessarily applicable to communication of all cultural groups. For example, Molefi Asante (1987, 2001) developed the framework of **Afrocentricity**

Afrocentricity An orientation toward African or African American cultural standards, including beliefs and values, as the criteria for interpreting behaviors and attitudes.

to apply to studies about African or African American communication. He identifies five cultural themes shared by peoples of African descent:

- A common origin and experience of struggle
- An element of resistance to European legal procedures, medical practices, and political processes
- Traditional values of humaneness and harmony with nature
- A fundamentally African way of knowing and interpreting the world
- An orientation toward communalism

Communication scholars have used this framework to understand various aspects of contemporary African American communication. For example, communication scholar Janice Hamlet (2015) emphasizes the strong creative oral tradition of African Americans, demonstrated in the interactive style of worship in many black congregations. As she describes it, the traditional African American preacher's job is to transform the congregation into an actively participating group, through emotional, often poetic and rhythmic sermons, and the congregation is expected to respond. Responses such as "Amen," "Preach!", "Tell it," or "Go on Pastor" are common and expected during the sermon. This interaction is often referred to as call-response. Hamlet traces this communication tradition historically to the "hush harbors" created by slaves where they could, out of the sight of their owners, enjoy the warmth of their friends and family and vent their emotions by speaking, singing, crying, or shouting.

Similarly, Asian scholars have developed Asiacentric frameworks to study communication of people from Asian cultures. Communication scholar Yoshitaka Miike (2003, 2004) has identified five Asiacentric themes (circularity, harmony, other-directedness, reciprocity, and relationality). Based on these themes, he developed five propositions on human communication. Communication is a process in which

- We remind ourselves of the interdependence and interrelatedness of the universe.
- We reduce our selfishness and egocentrism.
- We feel the joy and suffering of all beings.
- We receive and return our debts to all beings.
- We moralize and harmonize the universe.

From this Asiacentric framework, other scholars are developing specific communication theories, for example, a Chinese model of human relationship development (Chen, 1998) and a Buddhist consciousness-only model of intrapersonal communication (Ishii, 2004).

It is important to remember that scholars like Asante and Miike (2013) are not suggesting that these culture-specific frameworks are superior or should replace the traditional Eurocentric models, only that they are not inferior.

Another important interpretive theory, a communication theory of identity, was developed by Michael Hecht (1993). He argues that communication is a communicative process and our identities emerge in relationships with others and are expressed in core symbols, meaning, and labels. He also contends that there are four identity frames: personal, enacted, relational, and communal. These frames help us interpret reality and understand the social world. We will discuss this theory further in Chapter 5.

Several scholars have used this framework to understand the identities of various cultural groups. For example, Mark Orbe (2004) conducted a recent study investigating how first-generation college students negotiated this identity—using the four frames in Hecht's identity theory. Through interviewing the students, he discovered that their identities as first-generation college students clearly emerged as personal (in the pressure to succeed and in the economic hardships they experienced), enacted, and relational (in their experiences with friends and families, who often give them special attention). However, they did not seem to develop a communal identity—they did not really know or interact with other groups of first-generation college students.

In a later study Urban and Orbe (2010) used this same theoretical framework to explore the identities of a group of immigrants to the United States from many different countries. They found that, while most of the immigrants desired to both fit into their new culture and retain a core of their own cultural identity, they also expressed some struggles with identity gaps between the various layers of identity. One such gap was between their enacted and relational identities. That is, those who had accents or were not white said they tried to *enact* American behaviors, but many Americans would *relate* to them as foreigners. Other immigrants experienced other identity gaps. So they were constantly negotiating their identity in relation to those around them. Urban and Orbe stress that their study demonstrated that immigrants are a very diverse population and highlights the similarities and differences of their experiences in negotiating their identities.

Strengths and Limitations   The utility of the interpretivist approach is that it provides an in-depth understanding of communication patterns in particular communities because it emphasizes investigating communication in context. Thus, for example, we learn more about African American communication in religious contexts and more about U.S. white working class students in classroom contexts than we would by distributing questionnaires with general questions on African American or European American communication.

The main limitation of this approach is that there are few interpretivist studies of *intercultural* communication. Interpretive scholars typically have not studied what happens when two groups come in contact with each other. However, there are some comparative studies, including Charles Braithwaite's (1990) study, which compares rules for silence in 15 different communities, and Hammer and Rogan's (2002) study comparing how Latino and Indochinese view and negotiate conflict with law enforcement officers.

A second limitation is that the researchers often are outsiders to the communities under investigation, which means they may not represent accurately the communication patterns of members of that community. For example, Fred Jandt and Dolores Tanno (2001) recount the dilemma of many marginalized cultural groups who have been studied by outsiders who characterize the group rather erroneously and negatively. A number of scholars, members of these groups, are now trying to rewrite these cultural descriptions. One of these is Tuhiwai Smith (1999), a Maori scholar, who lists the words used to describe her people in anthropological accounts: not civilized, not literate, incapable of inventing, creating, or imagining, and not fully human. After analyzing the impact of these negative labels, she makes arguments for insider research and develops an indigenous research agenda and process—part of a movement by peoples throughout the world who have too long been explained by outsiders and have been offered no opportunity to explain themselves. One of her contributions is a Maori-based code of conduct for ethnographic researchers:

- A respect for people
- Presenting yourself face-to-face
- Look, listen, . . . speak
- Share and host people, be generous
- Do not flaunt your knowledge

Jandt and Tanno conclude that this ethical code should apply to all those who study groups of people who traditionally have been the object of study rather than participants in research.

The Critical Approach

critical approach A metatheoretical approach that includes many assumptions of the interpretive approach but that focuses more on macrocontexts, such as the political and social structures that influence communication. (Compare with **interpretive approach** and **functionalist approach.**)

macrocontexts The political, social, and historical situations, backgrounds, and environments that influence communication.

textual analysis Examination of cultural texts such as media—television, movies, journalistic essays, and so on.

A third approach to the study of intercultural communication includes many assumptions of the interpretive approach. For instance, researchers who use the **critical approach** believe in subjective (as opposed to objective) and material reality. They also emphasize the importance of studying the context in which communication occurs—that is, the situation, background, or environment. However, critical researchers usually focus on **macrocontexts,** such as the political and social structures that influence communication. Critical scholars, unlike most social scientists and interpretivists, are interested in the historical context of communication (see Figure 2-3).

Critical scholars are interested in the power relations in communication. For them, identifying cultural differences in communication is important only in relation to power differentials. In this perspective, culture is, in essence, a battleground—a place where multiple interpretations come together but a dominant force always prevails. The goal of critical researchers is not only to understand human behavior but also to change the lives of everyday communicators. Researchers assume that by examining and reporting how power functions in cultural situations, they can help the average person learn how to resist forces of power and oppression.

Like interpretive scholars, critical scholars also use interviews, focus groups, and rhetorical methods in analyzing encounters between immigrants and host groups. They also use **textual analyses**. That is, they analyze the cultural products such as media (television, movies, journals, and so on) as powerful voices in shaping contemporary culture. Critical scholars try to understand these encounters within a larger cultural struggle that has a much longer history than simply the current interactions. A critical scholar would want to understand the larger political, historical, and economical contexts of intercultural encounters.

FIGURE 2-3   German Chancellor Angela Merkel delivers a speech in December 2015, promising to "tangibly reduce" the number of migrants allowed to enter Germany. How might each of the paradigms study her message and its influence in shaping the response to the challenges of mass migration into Europe? (*Photo by © Thomas Lohnes/Getty Images*)

Applications   For example, one critical study used informal, conversational face-to-face interviews to understand the larger societal contexts of one group of immigrants—Montagnards who settled in North Carolina. The Montagnards come from the Central Highlands of Vietnam and fought with the United States against the Vietnamese government in the 1960s. After the war ended, they were persecuted by the Vietnamese for helping the United States and many fled the country and settled in the United States. In this study, communication scholar Etsuko Kinefuchi (2011) asked a group of Montagnard men to talk about their experiences in coming to the United States and to discuss what place they see as their home and why. In analyzing the interview data, she found that many of the men still thought of Vietnam as home, had strong emotional attachment to the people there and their indigenous land, as one man said, "I'm here, but I'm not really here. My mind is with my people in Vietnam" (p. 235). They also maintained strong ties to the Montagnard immigrant community in the United States. All of them lived close to other Montagnards and socialized almost entirely with other Montagnards, speaking their own language. They found it very difficult to make friends and form relationships with U.S. Americans—the cultural differences seemed insurmountable and they had limited opportunities to interact with Americans. They thought that people in America are too busy, life is too hurried and stressful, and no one has time to talk. Nobody just drops by unannounced to see their friends—a common and cherished practice within their ethnic community. In addition, they felt targeted by prejudice and racism. They were often mistaken for Mexicans and said, "Americans don't seem to like Mexicans" (p. 240), and hey thought this attitude toward Mexicans contributed to the U.S. Americans' indifference toward them.

Unlike social science scholars who usually focus on the immigrants' experience and initiative in adapting to the host culture, critical scholars like Kinefuchi focus on the structural (societal) limitations that prevent the Montagnards from having satisfying interpersonal encounters with Americans. She points out that their "choices" of home and their attachment to their Montagnard community were not only based on their individual preferences, but were also significantly shaped by the (lack of) opportunity for interactions and relationships with U.S. Americans. Most lacked "cultural capital" (e.g., education and English proficiency) that would help them build social networks and facilitate their integration into the mainstream U.S. society, and in addition they were subject to a racialized U.S. society and a racial hierarchy that was in place well before their arrival in the United States. She describes a perpetual contradiction that many immigrants (due to such unequal systems as race, gender, and class) face in the United States: the expectation of assimilation on the one hand and the structural limitations that prevent assimilation on the other. She and other critical scholars question the assumption that immigrants always wish to assimilate or that assimilation or acculturation is a good thing, and urge other scholars to pay more attention to the importance of ethnic communities for immigrant well-being—that these communities can play active roles in helping immigrants (especially refugees) by providing them with emotional, relational, sociocultural, and political anchoring. They stress that when refugees are forced to flee their homes because of abject poverty, political turmoil, ostracism, and/or discrimination, it makes sense for them to resist assimilation into the new and often unwelcoming host culture, that "holding onto one's culture can be (and often is) a source of comfort and strength, a source of rational survival, persistence, and positive self-identity" (Garza & Ono, 2015, p. 281). In addition, retaining certain aspects of one's culture (e.g. language, being bilingual) may facilitate academic success of immigrant youth (McKay-Semmler & Y. Y. Kim, 2014).

A similar study analyzed the stories of foreign domestic helpers in Hong Kong who recounted their intercultural encounters with host culture members—the Hongkongese (Ladegaard, 2013). Most of the women come from the Philippines and out of desperate financial situations, leave their families and migrate to find work in Hong Kong. They report enormous challenges of their immigrant situation. They are paid extremely low wages, have very few legal protections and rights, and are often exploited and even abused by their employees. Ladegaard, like Kinefuchi, suggests that researchers need to pay more attention to the larger sociocultural and political contexts of immigrant-host interaction that allow for and even promote negative stereotyping and prejudice.

Another critical study did just that. This study analyzed the speeches of several right wing leaders in France, the Netherlands, and Belgium to show how the social and political landscape can be manipulated to promote attitudes of distrust and prejudice against immigrants (Mols & Jetten, 2014). Using rhetorical analyses, they found that the speeches conveyed a feeling of collective nostalgia and perceptions of discontinuity to persuade people to take a tougher stance on immigration and refugee asylum-seeking. They accomplished this in a three-step process. First, there were references to the "glorious" past that was contrasted with the current bleak political and economic situation ("we know who's bringing the country down"). In

I think 9/11 is an intercultural issue because what happens in Jerusalem (Palestine) is actually the real definition of terrorism. But people from the West (i.e., the United States, Canada) don't admit that, and the citizens of those countries don't know what's going on in the outside world. They claim that all Arabs are terrorists, but they don't take a minute to discover the truth. Also, in the news, you don't see what actually is going on in the Middle East, and this is just not fair to the Arab communities around the world.
　　—Mohammad

the second part, the speeches suggested that the glorious past was due to toughness against foreigners, and the third part then called for the country to be tough once again—a justification for harsher treatment of migrants and minorities.

Taken together, these various viewpoints emphasize how different migrant groups experience cultural adaptation in a new country and their encounters with host members there. A critical perspective would emphasize the economic, political, and cultural differences among these groups, in understanding their experiences and their reception by host members in the new culture.

An important critical perspective is **postcolonialism,** an intellectual, political, and cultural movement that calls for the independence of colonized states and liberation from colonialist *mentalité,* or ways of thinking. The legacy of this cultural invasion often lasts much longer than the political relationship. "It theorizes not just colonial conditions but why those conditions are what they are, and how they can be undone and redone" (Shome & Hegde, 2002, p. 250).

Postcolonialism is not simply the study of colonialism but the study of how we might deal with that past and its aftermath, which may include the ongoing use of the colonial language, culture, and religion. For example, a study by Marwan Kraidy (2005) explores how youth in Lebanon negotiate their postcolonial identity through their media consumption. Lebanon was colonized at various times by Arabs, Ottomans, and the French, and partly because of this colonial past, Lebanese have access to a wide range of television channels (all Arab satellite channels, some Indian, and the major U.S. and European cable and satellite channels). Kraidy shows how the young people pick and choose specific shows to watch, and then he analyzes how they interpret those shows. He concludes that, because of their colonialist legacy, they gravitate toward Western shows in addition to the Arabic shows, and this media consumption ultimately contributes to their having a **hybrid identity**—an identity comprised of both Western and Arabic elements.

Hybrid identities form in locations where people mix and meld aspects of their cultural life from more than one culture. While Kraidy looked at the case in Lebanon, hybrid identities are emerging in many regions. In his study of the use of Kiswahili as a regional language in East Africa, linguistics professor Benson Oduor Ojwang (2008) points to the colonial past of this part of Africa as a foundation for unification. Kenya, Uganda, and Tanzania, formerly British colonies, are looking for greater cooperation, as they were earlier closer under British colonial rule. Known as East African Cooperation, the former colonies have a colonial past

postcolonialism An intellectual, political, and cultural movement that calls for the independence of colonialized states and also liberation from colonialist ways of thinking.

hybrid identity An identity that is consciously a mixture of different cultural identities and cultural traditions.

that they are using to forge a new postcolonial entity. Kiswahili is emerging as the language on which this new integration might occur, rather than English.

Another example of a critical study is Davin Grindstaff and Kevin DeLuca's (2004) analysis of the media coverage of the kidnapping and execution of Daniel Pearl, a journalist for *The Wall Street Journal,* who was pursuing terrorism leads in Pakistan and was later captured and decapitated, which was videotaped. This videotape becomes a contested site where it "takes on starkly different meanings in the construction of both claims to 'terrorism' and to national identities in both Pakistan and the United States" (p. 306). The struggle between these readings must be contextualized within the larger power relations between Pakistan and the United States.

Grindstaff and DeLuca note that the same week Daniel Pearl was murdered, two Pakistani children were murdered in the United States. The outcry over Pearl and the deafening silence over these children's murders underscores the way that bodies represent national identities and "exacerbates Pakistani anti-Americanism and complicates Pakistani national identity" (2004, p. 316). In contrast, U.S. American discourses about Pearl's murder focus on Pearl as both a hero in the "war on terrorism" *and* an innocent victim. This paradox points to the way that multiple ideological needs are serviced and empowered by this video and its meanings.

A final example of a critical study is Dreama Moon's (1999) investigation of gender and social class communication in the U.S. In her study, Moon analyzed interviews of white women from working-class backgrounds. She discovered that social class is a "marked feature" in the communication practices in academia that restricts upward mobility. Subtle communication practices that reinforce social class differences are not so invisible to women from working-class backgrounds. Moon shows how culture, social class, and communication work together to reproduce the contemporary social structure. She also identifies some strategies used by these women to resist this process of **social reproduction.**

social reproduction
The process of perpetuating cultural patterns.

Strengths and Limitations   The critical approach emphasizes the power relations in intercultural interactions and the importance of social and historical contexts. However, one limitation is that most critical studies do not focus on face-to-face intercultural interaction. Rather, they focus on popular media forms of communication—TV shows, music videos, magazine advertisements, and so on. Such studies, with their lack of attention to face-to-face interactions, may yield less practical results. Thus, for example, although understanding different discourses about racism may give us insights into U.S. race relations, it may not provide individuals with specific guidelines on how to communicate better across racial lines. However, one exception is cocultural theory, presented in Chapter 6, which is used to understand how people's location in a social hierarchy influences their perceptions of reality regarding, among other things, relational issues or problems (Orbe, 1998).

Also, this approach does not allow for much empirical data. For example, Davin Grindstaff and Kevin DeLuca did not measure Pakistani or U.S. American reactions to the decapitation of Daniel Pearl; instead, their essay analyzed the media discourses. Grindstaff and DeLuca's argument rests on the discussions about the videotape of the murder, how it was used, and its influence on these international audiences.

Here are three different student perspectives on the various approaches to studying intercultural communication:

I am an engineer, so I think that hypotheses and research are very important in order to describe and predict a subject. On the other hand, it is important to understand the individual more like a person and not like a number.
　—Liliana

I like the interpretive approach. I think that it is important to understand and to actually get involved hands-on to understand something so important and complicated as intercultural communication. Even though outsiders may never fully be considered an insider, they are better off than neither an insider nor an outsider.
　—Matt

Having three different paradigms allows me to view intercultural communication from three different perspectives. I can then incorporate all three into how I interpret other cultures. I personally like the critical view the most because I agree that often cultural groups are in a power struggle against one another, and that's just human nature.
　—Andrew

A DIALECTICAL APPROACH TO UNDERSTANDING CULTURE AND COMMUNICATION

Combining the Three Traditional Paradigms: The Dialectical Approach

As you can see from our discussion and the list of theories in Table 2-3, there are many different ways to approach the study of intercultural communication. The social science, interpretive, and critical approaches operate in interconnected and sometimes contradictory ways. Rather than advocating any one approach, we propose a **dialectical approach** to intercultural communication research and practice (see also Martin, Nakayama, & Flores, 2002). The dialectical approach emphasizes the processual, relational, and contradictory nature of intercultural communication, which encompasses many different kinds of intercultural knowledge.

First, with regard to the **processual** nature of intercultural communication, it is important to remember that cultures change, as do individuals. For example, the many cultures that constitute the war torn areas of Syria include Syrian Arabs, Syrian Turkmen, Kurds, Armenians, Greeks, Muslims, Christians, Jews, gay, lesbian, and transgendered Syrians, and many other cultural and linguistic groups. Intercultural communication studies provide a static but fleeting picture of these cultural groups. It is important to remember that the adaptation, communication, and other patterns identified are dynamic and ever changing, even if the research studies only provide a snapshot in time.

dialectical approach An approach to intercultural communication that integrates three approaches—functionalist (or social science), interpretive, and critical—in understanding culture and communication. It recognizes and accepts that the three approaches are interconnected and sometimes contradictory.

processual Refers to how interaction happens rather than to the outcome.

69

TABLE 2-3   SUMMARY OF THEORETICAL NOTIONS IN THREE RESEARCH APPROACHES

Social Science	Interpretive	Critical
Anxiety uncertainty management (AUM)	Ethnography of communication	Postcolonial
Integrative theory of adaptation	Afrocentrism	Identity hybridity
Face negotiation		
Conversational constraints	Asiacentrism	Social reproduction
Communication accommodation theory	Communication theory of identity	
Diffusion of innovations	Interpretive theory of identity	

Second, a dialectical perspective emphasizes the relational aspect of intercultural communication study. It highlights the relationship among various aspects of intercultural communication and the importance of viewing these holistically rather than in isolation. The key question becomes, Can we really understand culture without understanding communication, and vice versa? Specifically, can we understand the ways in which different cultural groups respond to forced migration and how they survive without looking at the values, beliefs, and histories of the various cultural groups involved, the cultural institutions that different groups have in place, the relative wealth available to different cultural groups, and so on?

A third characteristic of the dialectical perspective involves holding contradictory ideas simultaneously. This notion may be difficult to comprehend because it goes against most formal education in the United States, which emphasizes dichotomous thinking. Dichotomies such as "good and evil," "arteries and veins," and "air and water" form the core of our philosophical and scientific beliefs. The fact that dichotomies such as "far and near," "high and low," and "long and short" sound complete, as if the two parts belong together, reveals our tendency to form dichotomies (Stewart & Bennett, 1991). One such dichotomy that emerged in American and European public discourse from the mass refugee migration from Syria was "terrorist" and citizen—where many lumped all immigrants into the "terrorist" category and this led to increased anti-immigration attitudes and even to governments closing their borders, and many refugees were then further victimized. However, a dialectical approach requires that we transcend dichotomous thinking in studying and practicing intercultural communication.

Certainly, we can learn something from each of the three traditional approaches, and our understanding of intercultural communication has been enriched by all three.

One of our students described how the three perspectives can be useful in everyday communication:

> *The three paradigms help me understand intercultural communication by giving me insight into how we can work with people. Understanding how to predict communication behavior will make it easier for us to deal with those of other cultures—the social science approach. By changing unfair notions we have [about people from other cultures], we can gain more equality, as in the critical approach. We try to change things. Finally, the interpretive perspective is important so we can see face-to-face how our culture is.*

Combining these approaches, our discussion of the migrant crisis provides us with extensive insight into the problems and challenges of this and other intercultural ventures. Clearly, if we limit ourselves to a specific research orientation, we may fail to see the complexities of contemporary intercultural interaction in contexts. Although this kind of paradoxical thinking is rather foreign to Western minds, it is quite accepted in many Asian cultures. For example, people doing business in China are advised to recognize this dialectical thinking: "It is not possible to overstate the importance of 'and' versus 'or' thinking. It recurs, in various forms, throughout business in China and the Orient as a whole" (Ambler & Witzel, 2000, p. 197).

In fact, research findings can make a difference in the everyday world. From the social science perspective, we can see how specific communication and cultural differences might create differing worldviews, which can help us predict intercultural conflicts. An interpretive investigation gives us an opportunity to confirm what we predicted in a hypothetical social science study. In the case of the current mass migration, a social science study might predict and discover why various groups of citizens have negative attitudes toward immigrants, or what factors lead immigrants to successful adaptation in a new country. An interpretive study might show in-depth how different groups of immigrants experience cultural adaptation and encounters in the new country. A critical approach might focus on the different access to economic, political, and material resources among the cultural groups—such as which cultural groups were or were not welcomed and how these power differentials influenced their intercultural experience.

Employing these different perspectives is similar to photographing something from different angles. No single angle or snapshot gives us the truth, but taking pictures from various angles gives a more comprehensive view of the subject. The content of the photos, of course, to some extent depends on the interests of the photographer. And the photos may contradict one another, especially if they are taken at different times. But the knowledge we gain from any of these "angles" or approaches is enhanced by the knowledge gained from the others.

However, a dialectical approach requires that we move beyond simply acknowledging the contributions of the three perspectives and accept simultaneously the assumptions of all three. That is, we need to imagine that reality can be at once external *and* internal, that human behavior is predictable *and* creative *and* changeable. These assumptions may seem contradictory, but that's the point. Thinking dialectically forces us to move beyond our familiar categories and opens us up to new possibilities for studying and understanding intercultural communication.

Six Dialectics of Intercultural Communication

dialectic (I) A method of logic based on the principle that an idea generates its opposite, leading to a reconciliation of the opposites; (2) the complex and paradoxical relationship between two opposite qualities or entities, each of which may also be referred to as a *dialectic.*

We have identified six **dialectics** that characterize intercultural communication and have woven them throughout this book. Perhaps you can think of other dialectics as you learn more about intercultural communication.

Cultural–Individual Dialectic   Intercultural communication is both cultural and individual, or idiosyncratic. That communication is *cultural* means we share communication patterns with members of the groups to which we belong. For example, Sandra, a fifth-generation Italian American, tends to be expressive, like other members of her family. However, some of her communication patterns—such as the way she gestures when she talks—are completely idiosyncratic (i.e., particular to her and no one else). Consider another example, that of Amelia, who tends to be relationally oriented. Although her role as a woman and the relationships she cultivates in that role are important, being a woman does not completely define her behaviors. In this book, we often describe communication patterns that seem to be related to membership in particular cultural groups. However, it is important to remember that communication for all of us is both cultural and individual. We need to keep this dialectic in mind as we try to understand and develop relationships across cultural differences.

Personal–Contextual Dialectic   This dialectic involves the role of context in intercultural relationships and focuses simultaneously on the person and the context. Although we communicate as individuals on a personal level, the context of this communication is important as well. In some contexts, we enact specific social roles that give meaning to our messages. For example, when Tom was teaching at a Belgian university, he often spoke from the social role of professor. But this role did not correspond exactly to the same role in the United States because Belgian students accord their professors far more respect and distance than do U.S. students. In Belgium, this social role was more important than his communication with the students. In contrast, his communication with students in the United States is more informal.

Differences–Similarities Dialectic   Intercultural communication is characterized by both similarities and differences, in that people are simultaneously similar to and different from each other. In this book, we identify and describe real and important differences between groups of people—differences in values, language, nonverbal behavior, conflict resolution, and so on. For example, Japanese and U.S. Americans communicate differently, just as do men and women. However, there also are many similarities in human experiences and ways of communicating. Emphasizing only differences can lead to stereotyping and prejudice (e.g., that women are emotional or that men are rational); emphasizing only similarities

When I was working in the Philippines there was a privilege–disadvantage dialectic with the general population. My trip got extended for an extra week. I had to go out and buy clothes at a department store in Manila. I did not speak any Filipino so this was a very interesting experience. Knowing that the Filipino people can speak English and Spanish somewhat I knew I would be able to get by. While the prices on the clothes were clearly marked the lady at the register had inflated the price by 1,000 pesos ($20). Knowing what the price should be I had to try to explain the situation to get the price down to the correct level. Americans are envied in the Philippines for what we have. After spending a good amount of time trying to explain my situation the Filipino lady appeared not to understand anything I was saying. I ended up not getting the clothes from her.
 —Bob

In the past African Americans have dealt with a lot of prejudice and discrimination against them. There used to be separate water fountains, bathrooms, seats on a bus, etc., . . . the list could go on. So today when any African Americans come to dine at the restaurant I work at, we try to avoid seating them at the back of the restaurant. Since there has been a complaint, we don't want them to feel as if we are discriminating against them by putting them in a place where they are tucked away. The discrimination that African Americans once felt should not translate over to the present since our society has come so far. Some might say we are giving them special treatment to make African Americans feel equal but I don't see it like that. I see it as a sign of respect and a way of showing the African American culture that the discrimination they once felt should not exist anymore and they are just as equal as anyone else.
 —Jodi

can lead us to ignore the important cultural variations that exist. Therefore, we try to emphasize both similarities and differences and ask you to keep this dialectic in mind.

Static–Dynamic Dialectic This dialectic suggests that intercultural communication tends to be at once static and dynamic. Some cultural and communication patterns remain relatively constant, whereas other aspects of cultures (or personal traits of individuals) shift over time—that is, they are dynamic. For example, as we learned in Chapter 1, anti-immigrant sentiment traditionally has been a cultural constant in the United States, although the groups and conditions of discrimination have changed. Thus, the antagonism against Irish and Italian immigrants that existed at the turn of the 20th century has largely disappeared but may linger in the minds of some people. To understand interethnic communication in the United States today, we must recognize both the static and dynamic aspects of these relations.

History/Past–Present/Future Dialectic   Another dialectic emphasizes the need to focus simultaneously on the past and the present in understanding intercultural communication. On the one hand, we need to be aware of contemporary forces and realities that shape interactions of people from different cultural groups. On the other hand, we need to realize that history has a significant impact on contemporary events. One of our students described how this dialectic was illustrated in a televised panel discussion on race relations:

> *The panelists frequently referred to and talked about the history of different cultural groups in the United States and the present. They also touched on racial conflicts of the past and future possible improvement for certain groups. They were, therefore, communicating in a history/past–present/future dialectical manner. The discussions of past and present were critical to the overall goal of understanding current cultural identity. Without understanding the history of, for example, the slave trade or the Jim Crow laws, can we truly comprehend the African American experience in the United States today? The history of each cultural group plays a major role in the present role of that group.*

Privilege–Disadvantage Dialectic   A dialectical perspective recognizes that people may be simultaneously privileged and disadvantaged, or privileged in some contexts and disadvantaged in others. For example, many tourists are in the position of economic privilege because they can afford to travel, but in their travels, they also may be disadvantaged if they do not speak the local language. We can also be simultaneously privileged and disadvantaged because of gender, age, race, socioeconomic status, and other identities. One of our Asian American colleagues relates how he is simultaneously privileged because he is educated, middle class, and male and disadvantaged because he experiences subtle and overt mistreatment based on his race and accent (Collier, Hegde, Lee, Nakayama, & Yep, 2002, p. 247).

Keeping a Dialectical Perspective

We ask that you keep a dialectical perspective in mind as you read the rest of this book. The dialectics relate in various ways to the topics discussed in the following chapters and are interwoven throughout the text. Keep in mind, though, that the dialectical approach is not a specific theory to apply to all aspects of intercultural communication. Rather, it is a lens through which to view the complexities of the topic. Instead of offering easy answers to dilemmas, we ask you to look at the issues and ideas from various angles, sometimes holding contradictory notions, but always seeing things in processual, relational, and holistic ways.

The dialectical approach that we take in this book combines the three traditional approaches (social science, interpretive, and critical) and suggests four components to consider in understanding intercultural communication: culture, communication, context, and power. Culture and communication are the foreground, and context and power are the backdrop against which we can understand intercultural communication. We discuss these four components in the next chapter.

INTERNET RESOURCES

www.state.gov/m/fsi/
This is the State Department's website for the Foreign Service Institute (FSI). The FSI is the primary mechanism the federal government uses for training individuals to go overseas to serve, in some capacity, as representatives of the U.S. government. Check out the "Youth and Education" link, which has useful information about studying and working abroad and information about how to be a "smart traveler" (preparing travel documents, what to do in emergency situation when traveling abroad, etc.).

www.peacecorps.gov/
This is the home page for the Peace Corps. Volunteering in the Peace Corps is a way that many young people travel overseas and experience different cultures. It is worth considering how traveling abroad is portrayed differently by the Peace Corps and the State Department.

http://www.refugeecouncil.org.au/getfacts/international/journeys/stories/
Refugee stories is website sponsored by the nonprofit Refugee Council of Australia (RCOA), a national umbrella body for more than 200 organizations and over 900 individual members. Read about the various refugee programs sponsored by Australians. Click on "Get the Facts" and read about refugee stories–those who have found a new life in Australia. Click on "News & Events" and compare the national discussion about immigration in Australia to discussions on the same topic in the U.S. media.

SUMMARY

- The field of intercultural communication in the United States began with the establishment of the FSI in 1946.
- This new field was interdisciplinary and pragmatic. It emphasized nonverbal communication in international contexts.
- The perceptions and worldviews of scholars have an impact on the study of intercultural communication and have led to three contemporary approaches: the social science, interpretive, and critical approaches.
- This textbook advocates a dialectical approach that combines these three approaches.
- A dialectical approach emphasizes a processual, relational, and holistic view of intercultural communication, and it requires a balance of contradictory views.
- Intercultural communication is both cultural *and* individual, personal *and* contextual, characterized by differences *and* similarities, static *and* dynamic, oriented to both the present *and* the past, and characterized by both privilege *and* disadvantage.

DISCUSSION QUESTIONS

1. How have the origins of the study of intercultural communication in the United States affected its present focus?

2. How did business and political interests influence what early intercultural communication researchers studied and learned?

3. How have the worldviews of researchers influenced how they studied intercultural communication?

4. How have other fields contributed to the study of intercultural communication?

5. What are the advantages of a dialectical approach to intercultural communication?

ACTIVITIES

1. *Becoming Culturally Conscious.* One way to understand your cultural position within the United States and your own cultural values, norms, and beliefs is to examine your upbringing. Answer the following questions:

   a. What values did your parents or guardians attempt to instill in you?

   b. Why were these values considered important?

   c. What were you expected to do when you grew up?

   d. How were you expected to contribute to family life?

   e. What do you know about your ethnic background?

   f. What was your neighborhood like?

   Discuss your answers with classmates. Analyze how your own cultural position is unique and how it is similar to that of others.

2. *Analyzing Cultural Patterns.* Find a text or speech that discusses some intercultural or cultural issues, and analyze the cultural patterns present in the text. Consider, for example, the "I Have a Dream" speech by Martin Luther King, Jr. (Andrews & Zarefsky, 1992), or Chief Seattle's 1854 speech (Low, 1995).

3. *Analyzing a Film.* View a feature film or a video (e.g., *Chir-raq* or *Brooklyn*) and assume the position of a researcher. Analyze the cultural meanings in the film from each of the three perspectives: social science, interpretive, and critical. What cultural patterns (related to nationality, ethnicity, gender, and class) do you see? What does each perspective reveal? What does each one fail to reveal?

KEY WORDS

Afrocentricity (61)
anxiety uncertainty
   management
   theory (53)
collectivistic (56)

communication
   accommodation
   theory (54)
conceptual
   equivalence (56)

conversational contraints
   theory (54)
critical approach (64)
cross-cultural
   training (45)

dialectic (72)
dialectical approach (69)
diffusion of innovations
  theory (54)
distance zones (45)
diversity training (45)
emic (58)
ethnography (57)
etic (58)
face negotiation
  theory (53)
functionalist
  approach (51)
hybrid identity (67)

individualistic (55)
intercultural competence
  (46)
interdisciplinary (47)
interpretive approach (57)
macrocontexts (64)
paradigm (48)
participant
  observation (57)
perception (48)
postcolonialism (67)
processual (69)
proxemics (45)
qualitative methods (57)

quantitative
  methods (51)
rhetorical
  approach (57)
Sapir-Whorf
  hypothesis (46)
social reproduction (68)
social science
  approach (51)
textual analysis (64)
translation
  equivalence (56)
variable (51)
worldview (44)

REFERENCES

Alexander, B. K., Arasaratnam, L. A.; Flores, L.; Leeds-Hurwitz, W., Mendoza, S. L., Oetzel, J.; Osland, J., Tsuda, Y.; Yin, J., & Halualani, R. (2014). Our role as intercultural scholars, practitioners, activists, and teachers in addressing these key intercultural urgencies, issues, and challenges. *Journal of International and Intercultural Communication, 7*(1), 68–99.

Allport, G. W. (1979). *The nature of prejudice.* Reading, MA: Addison-Wesley.

Ambler, T., & Witzel, M. (2000). *Doing business in China.* New York: Routledge.

Andrews, J. R., & Zarefsky, D. (1992). *Contemporary American voices: Significant speeches in American history, 1945–present* (pp. 78–81). New York: Longman.

Après Katrina, l'Amérique s'interroge sur les failles de son modèle. (2005, September 7). *Le Monde.* www.lemonde.fr/web/imprimer_element/0,40-0@2-3222,50-686407,0.html.

Asante, M. K. (1987). *The Afrocentric idea.* Philadelphia, PA: Temple University Press.

Asante, M. K. (2001). Transcultural realities and different ways of knowing. In V. H. Milhouse, M. K. Asante, & P. O. Nwosu (Eds.), *Transcultural realities: Interdisciplinary perspectives on cross cultural relations* (pp. 71–82). Thousand Oaks, CA: Sage.

Asante, M. K., & Miike, Y. (2013). Paradigmatic issues in intercultural communication studies: An Afrocentric–Asiacentric dialogue. *China Media Research, 9*(3), 1–19.

Berry, J. W. (1997). Preface. In P. R. Dasen, T. S. Saraswathi, & J. W. Berry (Eds.), *Handbook of cross cultural psychology: Vol. 2. Basic processes and human development* (pp. xi–xvi). Boston, MA: Allyn & Bacon.

Braithwaite, C. (1990). Communicative silence: A cross cultural study of Basso's hypothesis. In D. Carbaugh (Ed.), *Cultural communication and intercultural contact* (pp. 321–328). Hillsdale, NJ: Lawrence Erlbaum.

Brantlinger, P. (1986). Victorians and Africans: The genealogy of the myth of the dark continent. In H. L. Gates, Jr. (Ed.), *"Race," writing and difference* (pp. 185–222). Chicago, IL: University of Chicago Press. (Original work published in 1985)

Brislin, R. (1999). *Understanding culture's influence on behavior* (2nd ed.). Belmont, CA: Wadsworth.

Carbaugh, D. (1996). *Situating selves: The communication of social identities in American scenes.* Albany, NY: State University of New York Press.

Carbaugh, D. (1999). "Just listen": "Listening" and landscape among the Blackfeet. *Western Journal of Communication, 63,* 250–270.

Carbaugh, D., & Berry, M. (2001). Communicating history, Finnish and American discourses: An ethnographic contribution to intercultural communication inquiry. *Communication Theory, 11,* 352–366.

Casmir, F. L. (1994). The role of theory and theory building. In F. L. Casmir (Ed.), *Building communication theories* (pp. 7–41). Hillsdale, NJ: Lawrence Erlbaum.

Chen, G.-M. (1998). A Chinese model of human relationship development. In B. L. Hoffer, & J. H. Koo (Eds.), *Cross-cultural communication: East and West in the 90's* (pp. 45–53). San Antonio, TX: Institute for Cross-Cultural Research, Trinity University.

Collier, M. J., Hegde, R. S., Lee, W., Nakayama, T. K., & Yep, G. A. (2002). Dialogue on the edges: Ferment in communication and culture. In M. J. Collier (Ed.), *Transforming communication about culture (International and Intercultural Communication Annual)*, (Vol. 24, pp. 219–280). Thousand Oaks, CA: Sage.

Croucher, S. M., & Rahmani, D. (2015). A longitudinal test of the effects of Facebook on cultural adaptation. *Journal of International and Intercultural Communication, 8*(4), 30–345.

De La Garza, A. T., & Ono, K. (2015). Retheorizing adaptation: Differential adaptation and critical intercultural communication. *Journal of International & Intercultural Communication, 8*(4), 269–289.

Dutta, U., & Martin, J. N. (2017). Theoretical perspectives in intercultural communication. In L. Chen (ed.), *Handbook of Intercultural Communication*. Berlin: Mouton de Gruyter.

Fletcher, C. V., Nakazawa, M., Chen, Y., Oetzel, J. G., Ting-Toomey, S., Chang, S. et al. (2014). Establishing cross-cultural measurement equivalence of scales associated with Face-Negotiation Theory: A critical issue in cross-cultural comparisons. *Journal of International and Intercultural Communication, 7*(2), 148–169.

Gallois, C., Ogay, T., & Giles, H. (2005). Communication accommodation theory. In W. B. Gudykunst (Ed.), *Theorizing about intercultural communication* (pp. 121–148). Thousand Oaks, CA: Sage.

Geiger, A. (2016). 16 striking findings from 2016. Pew Research Report. Retrieved March 17, 2017 from http://www.pewresearch.org/fact-tank/2016/12/21/16-striking-findings-from-2016/.

Gould, S. J. (1993). American polygeny and craniometry before Darwin: Blacks and Indians as separate, inferior species. In S. Harding (Ed.), *The "racial" economy of science: Toward a democratic future* (pp. 84–115). Bloomington, IN: Indiana University Press. (Original work published in 1981)

Grindstaff, D. A., & DeLuca, K. M. (2004). The corpus of Daniel Pearl. *Critical Studies in Media Communication, 21,* 305–324.

Gudykunst, W. B. (1998). Individualistic and collectivistic perspectives on communication: An introduction. *International Journal of Intercultural Relations, 22,* 107–134.

Gudykunst, W. B. (Ed.), (2005a). *Theorizing about intercultural communication*. Thousand Oaks, CA: Sage.

Gudykunst, W. B. (2005b). An anxiety/uncertainty management (AUM) theory of effective communication: Making the mesh of the net finer. In W. B. Gudykunst (Ed.), *Theorizing about intercultural communication* (pp. 281–323). Thousand Oaks, CA: Sage.

Hall, B. J. (1992). Theories of culture and communication. *Communication Theory, 1,* 50–70.

Hall, E. T. (1959). *The silent language.* Garden City, NY: Doubleday.

Hall, E. T. (1966). *The hidden dimension.* Garden City, NY: Doubleday.

Hamlet, J. D. (2015). The reason why we sing: Understanding traditional African American Worship. In A. Gonzaléz, M. Houston & Y-W. Chen (Eds.), *Our voices: Essays in culture, ethnicity and communication* 6th edition. New York: Oxford University Press.

Hammer, M. R., & Rogan, R. G. (2002). Latino and Indochinese interpretive frames in negotiating conflict with law enforcement: A focus group analysis. *International Journal of Intercultural Relations, 26,* 551–576.

Hanasono, L. K., Chen, L., & Wilson, S. R. (2014). Identifying communities in need: Examining the impact of acculturation on perceived discrimination, social support, and coping amongst racial minority members in the United States. *Journal of International and Intercultural Communication, 7*(3). 216–237.

Hecht, M. L. (1993). A research odyssey: Towards the development of a communication theory of identity. *Communication Monographs, 60,* 76–82.

Hymes, D. (1974). *Foundations in sociolinguistics: An ethnographic approach.* Philadelphia, PA: University of Pennsylvania Press.

Ishii, S. (2004). Proposing a Buddhist consciousness-only epistemological model for intrapersonal communication research. *Journal of Intercultural Communication Research, 33,* 63–76.

Jandt, F. E., & Tanno, D. V. (2001). Decoding domination, encoding self-determination: Intercultural communication research processes. *Howard Journal of Communications, 12,* 119–135.

Kim, M.-S. (1994). Cross-cultural comparisons of the perceived importance of conversational constraints. *Human Communication Research, 21,* 128–151.

Kim, M.-S. (2005). Culture-based conversational constraints theory: Individual and culture-level analyses. In W. B. Gudykunst (Ed.), *Theorizing about intercultural communication* (pp. 93–117). Thousand Oaks, CA: Sage.

Kim, M-S. (2012). World peace through intercultural research: From culture of war to a research culture of peace. *International Journal of Intercultural Relations 36*(1), 1–16.

Kim, S-h, Carvalho, J. P., Davis, A. G. & Mullins, A. M. (2011). The view of the border: News framing of the definition, causes, and solutions to illegal immigration. *Mass Communication and Society, 14*(3), 292–314.

Kim, Y. Y., & McKay-Semmler, K. (2013). Social engagement and cross-cultural adaptation: An examination of direct- and mediated interpersonal communication activities of educated non-natives in the United States. *International Journal of Intercultural Relations, 37,* 99–112.

Kinefuchi, E. (2011). Finding home in migration: Montagnard refugees and post-migration identity. *Journal of International and Intercultural Communication. 3*(3), 228–248.

Korem, A., & Horenczyk, G. (2015). Perceptions of social strategies in intercultural relations: The case of Ethiopian immigrants in Israel. *International Journal of Intercultural Relations, 49,* 13–24.

Kraidy, M. M. (2005). *Hybridity, or the cultural logic of globalization.* Philadelphia, PA: Temple University Press.

Kuhn, T. (1970). *The structure of scientific revolutions* (Rev. ed.). Chicago, IL: University of Chicago Press.

Kunuroglu, F., Yagmur, K., van de Vijver, F. J., & Kroon, S. (2015). Consequences of Turkish return migration from Western Europe. *International Journal of Intercultural Relations, 49,* 198–211.

Ladegaard, H. J. (2013). Beyond the reach of ethics and equity? Depersonalisation and dehumanisation in foreign domestic helper narratives. *Language and Intercultural Communication, 13*(1), 44–59.

Landis, D., Bennett, J. M., & Bennett, M. J. (Eds.) (2004). *Handbook of intercultural training.* 3rd ed. (pp. 309–336). Thousand Oaks, CA: Sage.

Landis, D., & Wasilewski, J. H. (1999). Reflections on 22 years of the *International Journal of Intercultural Relations* and 23 years in other areas of intercultural practice. *International Journal of Intercultural Relations, 23,* 535–574.

Low, D. (1995). Contemporary reinvention of Chief Seattle's 1854 speech. *American Indian Quarterly, 19*(3), 407.

Lu, Y., & Gatua, M. W. (2014). Methodological considerations for qualitative research with immigrant populations: Lessons from two studies. *The Qualitative Report, 19,* 1–16, from http://www.nova.edu/ssss/QR/QR19/lu16.pdf

Mark my words. (2007, February 16). *The Economist.* Retrieved May 13, 2008 from www.economist.com/science/displaystory.cfm?story_id=E1_RSNTRJD.

Martin, J. N., Nakayama, T. K., & Carbaugh, D. (2012). The history and development of the study of intercultural communication and applied linguistics. In J. Jackson (Ed.), *The Routledge handbook of intercultural communication.* New York: Routledge.

Martin, J. N., Nakayama, T. K., & Flores, L. A. (2002). A dialectical approach to intercultural communication. In J. N. Martin, T. K. Nakayama, & L. A. Flores (Eds.), *Readings in intercultural communication:*

Experiences and contexts (2nd ed., pp. 3–13). Boston, MA: McGraw-Hill.

McKay-Semmler, K., & Kim, Y. (2014). Cross-cultural adaptation of Hispanic youth: A study of communication patterns, functional fitness, and psychological health. *Communication Monographs, 81*(2), 133–156.

Mendoza, S. L. (2016). Doing "indigenous" enthography as a cultural outsider: Lessons from the Four Seasons. *Journal of International and Intercultural Communication, 9*(2), 140–160

Merkin, R., Taras, V., & Steel, P. (2014). State of the art themes in cross cultural communication research: A systematic and meta-analytic review. *International Journal of Intercultural Relations, 38,* 1–23.

Miike, Y. (2003). Beyond Eurocentrism in the intercultural field: Searching for an Asiacentric paradigm. In W. J. Storosta, & G. M. Chen (Eds.), *Ferment in the intercultural field* (*International and Intercultural Communication Annual,* Vol. 26). Thousand Oaks, CA: Sage.

Miike, Y. (2004). Rethinking humanity, culture and communication: Asiacentric critiques and contributions. *Human Communication, 7,* 69–82.

Miike, Y. (2007a). An Asiacentric reflection on Eurocentric bias in communication theory. *Communication Monographs, 74*(2), 272–278.

Miike, Y. (2007b). Asian contributions to communication theory: An introduction. *China Media Research, 3*(4), 1–6.

Mols, F., & Jetten, J. (2014). No guts, no glory: How framing the collective past paves the way for anti-immigrant sentiments. *International Journal of Intercultural Relations, 43,* 74–86.

Moon, D. (1999). White enculturation and bourgeois ideology: The discursive production of 'good (white) girls'. In T. K. Nakayama, & J. N. Martin (Eds.), *Whiteness: The communication of social identity* (pp. 177–197). Thousand Oaks, CA: Sage.

Moon, D. (2010). Critical reflections on culture and critical intercultural communication. In T. K. Nakayama, & R. K. Halualani (Eds)., *The handbook of critical intercultural communication* (pp. 34–58). Malden, MA: Wiley-Blackwell.

Nakayama, T. K., & Halualani, R. T. (Eds.) (2010). *Handbook of critical intercultural communication.* Malden, MA: Blackwell Publishing.

Neuliep, J. W., & Johnson, M. (2016). A cross-cultural comparison of Ecuadorian and United States face, facework, and conflict styles during interpersonal conflict: An application of face-negotiation theory. *Journal of International & Intercultural Communication, 9*(1), 1–19.

Ojwang, B. O. (2008). Prospects of Kishwahili as a regional language in a socioculturally heterogeneous East Africa. *Journal of International and Intercultural Communication, 1*(4), 327–347.

Orbe, M. (1998). *Constructing co-cultural theory: An explication of culture, power and communication.* Thousand Oaks, CA: Sage.

Orbe, M. P. (2004). Negotiating multiple identities with multiple frames: An analysis of first-generation college students. *Communication Education, 53,* 131–149.

Rogers, E. M. (2003). *Diffusion of innovations.* 5th ed. New York: Free Press.

Rosaldo, R. (1989). *Culture and truth: The remaking of social analysis.* Boston, MA: Beacon Press.

Semlak, J. L., Pearson, J. C., Amundson, N. G., & Kudak, A. D. (2008). Navigating dialectic contradictions experienced by female African refugees during cross-cultural adaptation. *Journal of Intercultural Communication Research, 37*(1), 43–64.

Shome, R., & Hegde, R. (2002). Postcolonial approaches to communication: Charting the terrain, engaging the intersections. *Communication Theory, 12,* 249–270.

Singer, M. R. (1987). *Intercultural communication: A perceptual approach.* Englewood Cliffs, NJ: Prentice-Hall.

Singer, M. R. (1998). Culture: A perceptual approach. In M. J. Bennett (Ed.), *Basic concepts of intercultural communication* (pp. 97–110). Yarmouth, ME: Intercultural Press.

Singhal, A., & Dearing, J. W. (Eds.). (2006). *Communication of innovations: A journey with Ev Rogers.* Thousand Oaks, CA: Sage.

Smith, L. T. (1999). *Decolonizing methodologies: Research and indigenous peoples.* New York: St. Martin's Press.

Stewart, E. C., & Bennett, M. J. (1991). *American cultural patterns: A cross-cultural perspective* (Rev. ed.). Yarmouth, ME: Intercultural Press.

Swarns, R. (2002, May 5). France returns old remains to homeland. *The Arizona Republic,* p. A28.

Ting-Toomey, S. (1985). Toward a theory of conflict and culture. In W. Gudykunst, L. Stewart, & S. Ting-Toomey (Eds.), *Communication, culture and organizational processes* (pp. 71–86). Beverly Hills, CA: Sage.

Ting-Toomey, S. (2005). The matrix of face: An updated face-negotiation theory. In W. B. Gudykunst (Ed.), *Theorizing about intercultural communication* (pp. 71–92). Thousand Oaks, CA: Sage.

Ting-Toomey, S. (2010). Applying dimensional values in understanding intercultural communication. *Communication Monographs, 77*(2), 169–180.

Ting-Toomey, S., Gao, G., Trubisky, P., Yang, Z., Kim, H. S., Lin, S.-L. et al. (1991). Culture, face maintenance, and styles of handling interpersonal conflict: A study in five cultures. *International Journal of Conflict Management, 2,* 275–296.

Ting-Toomey, S., Yee-Jung, K. K., Shapiro, R. B., Garcia, W., Wright, T. J., & Oetzel, J. G. (2000). Ethnic/cultural identity salience and conflict styles in four US ethnic groups. *International Journal of Intercultural Relations, 24,* 47–81.

UNHCR Statistical Online Population Database. United Nations High Commissioner for Refugees (UNHCR). Retrieved April 16, 2017, from www.unhcr.org /statistics/populationdatabase.

Urban, E. L., & Orbe, M. P. (2010). Identity gaps of contemporary US immigrants: Acknowledging divergent communicative experiences. *Communication studies, 61*(3), 304–320.

CREDITS

quote from "The corpus of Daniel Pearl." Critical Studies in Media Communication. [page 69, text] Liliana, excerpt from "Student Voices: I am an engineer, so I think that hypotheses and research are very . . . not like a number." Original Work; [page 69, text] Matt, excerpt from "Student Voices: I like the interpretive approach. I think that it is important . . . neither an insider nor an outsider." Original Work; [page 69, text] Andrew, excerpt from "Student Voices: Having three different paradigms . . . and that's just human nature." Original Work; [page 71, text] T. Ambler and M. Witzel, quote from "Doing business in China." Routledge. [page 73, text] Bob, excerpt from "When I was working in the Philippines there . . . getting the clothes from her." Original Work; [page 73, text] Jodi, excerpt from "In the past African Americans have dealt with . . . just as equal as anyone else." Original Work.

CULTURE, COMMUNICATION, CONTEXT, AND POWER

CHAPTER OBJECTIVES

After you read this chapter, you should be able to:

1. Identify three approaches to culture.
2. Define communication.
3. Identify and describe nine cultural value orientations.
4. Describe how cultural values influence communication.
5. Understand how cultural values influence conflict behavior.
6. Describe how communication can reinforce cultural beliefs and behavior.
7. Explain how culture can function as resistance to dominant value systems.
8. Explain the relationship between communication and context.
9. Describe the characteristics of power.
10. Describe the relationship between communication and power.

WHAT IS CULTURE?
Social Science Definitions: Culture as Learned, Group-Related Perceptions
Interpretive Definitions: Culture as Contextual Symbolic Patterns of Meaning, Involving Emotions
Critical Definitions: Culture as Heterogeneous, Dynamic, and a Contested Zone

WHAT IS COMMUNICATION?

THE RELATIONSHIP BETWEEN CULTURE AND COMMUNICATION
How Culture Influences Communication
How Communication Reinforces Culture
Communication as Resistance to the Dominant Cultural System

THE RELATIONSHIP BETWEEN COMMUNICATION AND CONTEXT

THE RELATIONSHIP BETWEEN COMMUNICATION AND POWER

INTERNET RESOURCES

SUMMARY

DISCUSSION QUESTIONS

ACTIVITIES

KEY WORDS

REFERENCES

In Chapter 2, we touched on the history of intercultural communication studies, examined three theoretical approaches, and outlined an integrated dialectical approach to intercultural communication. In this chapter, we continue our discussion of the dialectical approach and identify four interrelated components or building blocks in understanding intercultural communication: culture, communication, context, and power. As noted previously, culture and communication are the foreground and context and power form the backdrop against which we can understand intercultural communication. First, we define and describe culture and communication. Then we examine how these two components interact with issues of context and power to enhance our understanding of intercultural communication.

WHAT IS CULTURE?

Culture is often considered the core concept in intercultural communication. Intercultural communication studies often focus on how cultural groups differ from one another: Muslims differ from Christians; Japanese differ from U.S. Americans; men differ from women; environmentalists differ from conservationists; pro-lifers differ from pro-choicers; older people differ from young people, and on and on.

Perhaps it is more helpful here to think of the similarities–differences dialectic in trying to understand intercultural communication. That is, we are all similar to *and* different from each other simultaneously (Root, 2013). Humans, regardless of cultural backgrounds, engage in many of the same daily activities and have many of the same wants and desires. We all eat, sleep, love, pursue friendships and romantic relationships and want to be respected and loved by those who are important to us.

And yet some real differences exist between cultural groups. How we pursue these activities varies from culture to culture. Men and women often do not see the world in the same way. Old and young have different goals and dreams. Muslims and Christians have different beliefs, and the old adage "When in Rome do as the Romans do" implies that it is easy simply to adapt to different ways of thinking and behaving, yet anyone who has struggled to adapt to a new cultural situation knows that only the Romans are Romans and only they know how to be truly Romans. The challenge is to negotiate these differences and similarities with insight and skill. First, we need to examine what we mean by the term *culture*.

Culture has been defined in many ways—from a pattern of perceptions that influence communication to a site of contestation and conflict. Because there are many acceptable definitions of culture, and because it is a complex concept, it is important to reflect on the centrality of culture in our own interactions. The late British writer Raymond Williams (1983) wrote that culture "is one of the two or three most complicated words in the English language" (p. 89). And this very complexity indicates the many ways in which it influences intercultural communication (Williams, 1981). Culture is more than merely one aspect of the practice of intercultural communication. How we think about culture frames our ideas and perceptions. For example, if we think that culture is defined by nation-states, then

culture Learned patterns of behavior and attitudes shared by a group of people.

POINT *of* VIEW

In this essay, communication scholar Wen Shu Lee identifies different common uses of the term *culture* and then describes how each definition serves particular interests. She also defends her preferred choice, the sixth definition.

1. Culture = unique human efforts (as different from nature and biology). For example, "*Culture* is the bulwark against the ravages of nature."

2. Culture = refinement, mannerism (as different from things that are crude, vulgar, and unrefined). For example, "Look at the way in which he chows down his food. He has no *culture* at all."

3. Culture = civilization (as different from backward barbaric people). For example, "In countries where darkness reigns and people are wanting in *culture*, it is our mandate to civilize and Christianize those poor souls."

4. Culture = shared language, beliefs, values (as different from language beliefs and values that are not shared; dissenting voices; and voices of the "other"). For example, "We come from the same *culture*, we speak the same language, and we share the same tradition."

5. Culture = dominant or hegemonic culture (as different from marginal cultures). For example, "It is the *culture* of the ruling class that determines what is moral and what is deviant." (This definition is a more charged version of definitions 2, 3, and 4 through the addition of power consciousness.)

6. Culture = the shifting tensions between the shared and the unshared (as different from shared or unshared things). For example, "American *culture* has changed from master/slave, to white only/black only, to antiwar and black power, to affirmative action/multiculturalism and political correctness, to transnational capital and anti-sweatshop campaigns."

Each of these definitions privileges certain interests. Definition 2 privileges high culture and leaves out popular culture. . . . Definition 3 privileges nations that are/were imperialistic, colonizing. . . . Definition 4 privileges a "universal and representative" view of a society, but such a view often represents only a specific powerful group and silences other groups that do not readily share this view. Definition 5 privileges the interaction of the culture authorized by the dominant group/sector/nation—more politically explicit than definitions 2, 3, and 4. Definition 6 is the one I like the most. It is more of a meta view of cultures. It focuses on the "links" between "the shared" and the "little shared." But the sharedness, *the* unshared- ness, *and their* links *remain not only situated but also unstable, shifting, and contested.*

Source: From M. J. Collier, R. Hegde, W. S. Lee, T. Nakayama, and G. Yep, "Dialogue on the edges: Ferment in communication and culture." In M. J. Collier, et al. (Eds.), *Transforming Communication About Culture* (Thousand Oaks, CA: Sage, 2002), pp. 229–230.

TABLE 3-I THREE PERSPECTIVES ON DEFINING CULTURE		
Social Science	**Interpretive**	**Critical**
Culture is:		
Learned and shared	Learned and shared	Heterogeneous, dynamic
Patterns of perception	Contextual symbolic meanings	Site of contested meanings
	Involves emotion	
The relationship between culture and communication:		
Culture influences communication.	Culture influences communication.	Communication reshapes culture.
	Communication reinforces culture.	

Source: From J. N. Martin and T. K. Nakayama, "Thinking Dialectically About Culture and Communication," *Communication Theory, 9* (1999): 5.

communication between a Japanese and an Italian would be intercultural communication because Japan and Italy are different nation-states. However, according to this definition, an encounter between an Asian American from North Carolina and an African American from California would not be intercultural because North Carolina and California are not different nation-states.

We do not advocate a singular definition of culture because any one definition is too restrictive (Baldwin, Faulkner, & Hecht, 2006). A dialectical approach suggests that different definitions offer more flexibility in approaching the topic. We believe that the best approach to understanding the complexities of intercultural communication is to view the concept of culture from different perspectives (see Table 3-1).

By and large, social science researchers focus not on culture per se but on the *influence* of culture on communication. In other words, such researchers concern themselves with communication differences that result from culture. They pay little attention to how we conceptualize culture or how we see its functions. In contrast, interpretive researchers focus more on how cultural contexts influence communication. Critical researchers, for their part, often view communication—and the power to communicate—as instrumental in reshaping culture. They see culture as the way that people participate in or resist society's structure.

Although research studies help us understand different aspects of intercultural communication, it is important to investigate how we think about culture, not simply as researchers but as practitioners as well. We, therefore, broaden our scope to consider different views of culture, especially in terms of how they influence intercultural communication.

Social Science Definitions: Culture as Learned, Group-Related Perceptions

Communication scholars from the social science paradigm, influenced by research in psychology, view culture as a set of learned, group-related perceptions (Hall, 1992). Geert Hofstede (1984), a noted social psychologist, defines culture as "the programming of the mind" and explains his notion of culture in terms of a computer program:

> *Every person carries within him or herself patterns of thinking, feeling, and potential acting which were learned throughout [his or her] lifetime. Much of [these patterns are] acquired in early childhood, because at that time a person is most susceptible to learning and assimilating. (p. 4)*

Hofstede goes on to describe how these patterns are developed through interactions in the social environment and with various groups of individuals—first in the family and neighborhood, then at school and in youth groups, then at college, and so on. Culture becomes a collective experience because it is shared with people who live in and experience the same social environments.

To understand this notion of the collective programming of the mind, Hofstede and other scholars studied organizational behavior at various locations of a multinational corporation; this study is discussed in detail later in the chapter. Social scientists also have emphasized the role of perception in cultural patterns. They contend that cultural patterns of thinking and meaning influence our perceptual process, which, in turn, influence our behavior. Communication scholar Milton Bennett (2013) describes various cultural differences in perceptual styles or how people organize their perceptions. For example, some cultural groups, such as Asian, tend to be more *concrete*, using more description and physical metaphors to capture their perceptions, with heavy emphasis on sensory information (color, shape, size) and feeling—seen in the rich sensory imagery of Japanese haiku (short succinct poetry), Vietnamese films, and Chinese opera. In contrast, other groups, for example, many Northern European cultural groups, tend to be more *abstract*, stressing coherent explanation and historical context of events. U.S. Americans' perceptual style on this continuum is somewhere between these two, emphasizing action-oriented procedures, but that can be tested. He goes on to describe the important implications of these different perceptual styles in everyday workplace encounters. For example, when people from different cultures with different perceptual styles work together, there are predictable problems:

> *Asians are more likely to want information about who exactly is involved and what exactly they want . . . Northern Europeans are more likely to want to know why the action is anticipated and when it was tried before. North Americans are almost exclusively focused on how the action with be implemented—including some determination of the probability of success. (p. 74)*

He describes the resulting conflict from the viewpoints of the various individuals: The Asians seem to ask for endless amounts of detail, the North Americans are impatient and just want to get started and learn from their mistakes, and Northern Europeans are offended by the idea of even discussing making mistakes! (p. 75).

Intercultural communication scholars, who use the social science approach, are most interested in identifying these cultural differences in perception and behavior and then trying to understand how these differences impact communication between individuals with varying backgrounds. We will explore their research findings and insights later in the chapter.

Interpretive Definitions: Culture as Contextual Symbolic Patterns of Meaning, Involving Emotions

Interpretive scholars, influenced by anthropological studies, also view culture as shared and learned; however, they tend to focus on contextual patterns of communication behavior, rather than on group-related perceptions. According to communication scholar Philipsen's (1992) definition, culture refers to "a socially constructed and historically transmitted pattern of symbols, meaning, premises, and rules" (p. 7). Philipsen's approach is through **ethnography of communication**—a common interpretive approach. These scholars look for symbolic meaning of verbal and nonverbal activities in an attempt to understand patterns and rules of communication. This area of study defines cultural groups rather broadly—for example, talk show participants, therapy support groups, and hip hop fans.

Ethnography of communication scholar Donal Carbaugh (2007) suggests that it is best to reserve the concept of culture for patterns of symbolic action and meaning that are deeply felt, commonly intelligible, and widely accessible. Patterns that are deeply felt are sensed collectively by members of the cultural group. Gathering around the coffee machine at work every morning, for example, could be a cultural pattern, but only if the activity holds **symbolic significance** or evokes feelings that extend beyond itself. Then the activity more completely exemplifies a cultural pattern. Suppose that gathering around the coffee machine each morning symbolizes teamwork or the desire to interact with colleagues. To qualify as a cultural pattern, the activity must have the same symbolic significance for all members of the group; they must all find the activity meaningful in more or less the same way. Further, all participants must have access to the pattern of action. This does not mean that they must all use the pattern; it only means the pattern is available to them.

These definitions of culture are influenced by communication ethnographer Dell Hymes's (1972) framework for studying naturally occurring speech in depth and in context. The framework comprises eight elements: scene, participant, end, act sequence, key, instrumentality, norm, and genre. In this sequence, the terms form the acronym *SPEAKING*. The *S*cene is the setting of the communication event. The *P*articipants are the people who perform or enact the event. The *E*nd is the goal of the participants in conversation. The *A*ct sequence is the order of phases during the enactment. The *K*ey is the tone of the conversation. The channel of communication is the *I*nstrumentality. The *N*orms, as you know, are the rules that people follow. And *G*enre is the type or category of talk. By analyzing speech using this descriptive framework, we can gain a comprehensive understanding of the rules and patterns followed in any given speech community.

Culture is not only experienced as perceptions and values, and contextual, but the concept of culture also involves emotions. When we are in our own cultural

ethnography of communication A specialized area of study within communication. Taking an interpretive perspective, scholars analyze verbal and nonverbal activities that have symbolic significance for the members of cultural groups to understand the rules and patterns followed by the groups. (See **interpretive approach** on page 59.)

symbolic significance The importance or meaning that most members of a cultural group attach to a communication activity.

B   ob Marley, the well-known singer–songwriter and musician, was born in a
      rural area of Jamaica to a young, black, Jamaican woman and a white British
      officer during a time in Jamaica when society divided strictly along racial
lines. Marley came to terms with his own racial identity at an early age and resisted
being categorized as white or black:

> In the video biography, "Time Will Tell," Marley was asked whether he
> was prejudiced against white people. He replied, "I don't have preju-
> dice against myself. My father was a white and my mother was black.
> Them call me half-caste or whatever. Me don't dip on nobody's side. Me
> don't dip on the black man's side nor the white man's side. Me dip on
> God's side, the one who create me and cause me to come from black and
> white." Perhaps it was his biracial background that led Marley to write
> songs with a universal message. One of his most profound songs address-
> ing unification, "War," took the words of a speech by Emperor Haile
> Selassie I of Ethiopia and put them to music, "Until the philosophy which
> holds one race superior and another inferior is finally discredited and
> abandoned÷WAR!"

Source: From http://jahworks.org/bob-marley/.

embodied ethnocentrism
Feeling comfortable and familiar in the spaces, behaviors, and actions of others in our own cultural surroundings.

surroundings, we *feel* a sense of familiarity and a certain level of comfort in the space, behavior, and actions of others. We might characterize this feeling as a kind of **embodied ethnocentrism,** which is normal (Bennett & Castiglioni, 2004). (Later on we'll discuss the negative side of ethnocentrism.) This aspect of culture has implications for understanding adaptation to other cultural norms and spaces. That is, the stronger your identification with a particular space/cultural situation, the more difficult it might be to change spaces without experiencing a lot of discomfort—actual psychological and physiological changes. For example, students studying in France described their feelings in coping with the French language. Their self-esteem dropped and they became very self-conscious. Their whole bodies were entrenched in this effort of trying to communicate in French; it was a laborious and involved process that was connected to all aspects of themselves—a feeling of being out of their cultural comfort zone (Kristjánsdóttir, 2009). We should not underestimate the importance of culture in providing us a feeling of familiarity and comfort.

Although the notion of culture as shared, learned group patterns of perception or symbolic behavior has long been the standard in a variety of disciplines, more and more people are beginning to question its utility. They question how much of "culture" is truly shared. For example, one colleague reports that in a class discussion about the definition of culture in which most students were giving the usual definitions, "one student almost indignantly jumped into our discussion and said, 'Do we really have a common culture?'" She then followed with the question "Whose version of a shared and common culture are we talking about?" (Collier, Hegde, Lee, Nakayama, & Yep, 2002, p. 269). Indeed, these are important questions, and so the next section describes an alternative approach to defining culture. (For a challenge to common notions of a "shared" U.S. culture, take the "Test of U.S. Cultural Knowledge" on pages 95–96.)

Critical Definitions: Culture as Heterogeneous, Dynamic, and a Contested Zone

A more recent approach to culture, influenced by cultural studies scholarship, emphasizes the heterogeneity of cultural groups and the often conflictual nature of cultural boundaries. For example, what is the "U.S. American culture"? Is there *an* American culture? How many perceptions, attitudes, and beliefs and behaviors are actually shared among the many diverse people living in the United States? Critical scholars suggest that in emphasizing only the shared aspects of culture, we gloss over the many interesting differences among U.S. Americans. Further, they emphasize that cultural boundaries are often contested and not easily agreed upon. For example, increasing numbers of people have multicultural identities, growing up to negotiate *multiple* cultural realities. Perhaps the best known is President Barack Obama, whose father was an exchange student from Kenya and his mother a U.S. American student. Others include news anchor Soledad O'Brien, whose parents are Irish-Australian and Cuban; American singer Mariah Carey, who is black, Irish, and Venezuelan; and Jamaican singer Bob Marley. There is also Senator Ted Cruz whose mother was born in the United States and father in Cuba. They often resist the many efforts by some to pigeonhole their race/ethnicity, as shown in the Point of View box on p. 90.

This notion of culture as heterogeneous and often conflictual originated with British cultural studies scholars in the 1960s. Cultural studies scholars were fiercely interdisciplinary and dedicated to understanding the richness, complexity, and relevance of cultural phenomena in the lives of ordinary people. This desire to make academic work relevant to everyday life resonated in other fields. Most people, in fact, want to find the connections between what they learn in the classroom and what is occurring in contemporary society. In any case, this movement led to the reconfiguration of the role of the university in society. Cultural studies soon spread from Britain to Australia, Latin America, and other parts of the world. Because of differing cultural and political situations, the specific construction of cultural studies differs from place to place. In the United States, for instance, cultural studies developed mainly within departments of communication (Grossberg, 1993).

You may sense that the concept of culture that emerged from this area of inquiry differs markedly from the concept expressed in social science or even interpretive research. However, it is in agreement with concepts found in recent work in anthropology. Many anthropologists have criticized research that categorizes people and characterizes cultural patterns as set, unchanging, and unconnected to issues of gender, class, and history. Recent anthropological research sees cultural processes as dynamic and fluid that extend across national and regional borders within contexts of history and power (Baldwin et al., 2006). Communication scholars who embrace the critical notions reject notions of culture as fixed,

A recent news report from Phoenix, Arizona, illustrates the cultural struggles concerning who gets to be included as a U.S. American. Which of the three approaches to intercultural communication does this story typify?

On this Arizona State University graduation day, Angelica Hernández should be reflecting on her accomplishments and her future career prospects. Instead, she worries about being deported and not being able to get a job. She has no citizenship papers. "There's my degree but I can't use it as much as I want to get a job, as much as I want to help somewhere or do research, I can't. It's just very unfortunate."

Hernández' mom moved her and her sister to Arizona when Hernández was 9 years old, to be with their dad. "She knew that just having my dad there while growing up was worth the risk of crossing," recalls Hernández. Now she's the "outstanding distinguished senior" in mechanical engineering at ASU—which is what a valedictorian is to other universities. She wears a "Dream Act" button proudly.

"I'm just kind of hoping for the Dream Act to pass and to have those kinds of opportunities," she says. "There is really no place for me to go. They say go back home you don't belong here, but I do belong here, this is home for me."

It's a hot issue. Some sympathize with Angelica, while others think the concept is unfair. . . .

Samantha Kozuch is a recent graduate from the University of Arizona. She and her family immigrated from Australia 10 years ago, and she is now a U.S. citizen. . . . She thinks people shouldn't come into the country illegally, but after watching Angelica's story, Kozuch has sympathy for these dreamers. . . .

Jaime Molera, president of the Arizona School Board and former state superintendent, is a Republican, but on this issue he breaks with some of his colleagues.

"I think its a no brainer. She's an American citizen. She came here not of her own volition, but she was raised through our system, she did what she needed to do, she's been a good citizen, she's been a good student," says Molera. "These are kids that are going to end up at Intel or Microsoft, they're going to end up doing great things, they're going to be great contributors to our tax base . . . they'll be great assets to any community they live in. Their only crime is their parents came here illegally and they were babies."

Source: "Arizona State University valedictorian is an undocumented immigrant. " *Latino.foxnews .com.* May 11, 2011. Retrieved November 1, 2016 from http://latino.foxnews.com/latino/news /2011/05/13/arizona-state-university-valedictorian-undocumented-immigrant/

unchanging, and stable, calling it "seductive" in allowing us "a false sense of security" (Halulalani, 2011, p. 48). Rather, their goal is to dismantle this fixed notion of culture and to pose the following questions:

Can we ever truly know a culture let alone our own? How culture is positioned? Who benefits from specific versions and interpretations of culture? Which power

*forces and structures help to shape and represent culture in these ways? What
does it mean for us in a complex intercultural world? (Halualani, 2011, p. 44).*

Viewing culture as a contested site or zone helps us understand the struggles
of various groups—Native Americans, Asian Americans, Pacific Islanders, African
Americans, Latinos/as, women, gays and lesbians, transgender individuals, working-
class people, and so on—as they attempt to negotiate their relationships and promote
their well-being within U.S. society. By studying the communication that springs from
these ongoing struggles, we can better understand several intercultural concerns. Consider, for example, the DREAM Act (Development, Relief, and Education for Alien
Minors Act) that would allow some undocumented immigrant students who have
grown up in the United States to apply for U.S. citizenship if they attend college or
serve in the U.S. military. The controversies surrounding these and other propositions
illustrate the concerns of many different cultural groups. (See Point of View, p. 93.)

Viewing culture as a contested site opens up new ways of thinking about intercultural communication. After all, the individuals in a given culture are not identical,
which suggests that any culture is replete with cultural struggles. Thus, when we use
terms like *Chinese culture* and *French culture,* we gloss over the heterogeneity, the
diversity, that resides in that culture. Yet the ways in which various cultures are heterogeneous are not the same elsewhere as in the United States, which means it would
be a mistake to map our structure of differences onto other cultures. How sexuality,
ethnicity, gender, and class function in other cultures is not necessarily the same as,
or even similar to, their function in the United States. By viewing any culture as a
contested zone or site of struggle, we can understand the complexities of that culture;
we can become more sensitive to how people in that culture live.

Our dialectical approach, though, enables us to accept and see the interrelatedness of these different views. Culture is at once a shared and a learned pattern of
beliefs and perceptions that are mutually intelligible and widely accessible. It is also
a site of struggle for contested meanings. A dialectic perspective can help facilitate
discussions on conflicting cultural notions (e.g., how to reconcile U.S. patriotism and
instances of anti-Americanism). Our task in taking a dialectical approach is not to say
whose views are right or wrong, but to recognize "the truth in all sides of the conflict
and understanding the ways in which multiple realities constitute the whole of the
cultural quandary" (Cargile, 2005, p. 117).

WHAT IS COMMUNICATION?

The second component, **communication,** is as complex as culture and can be defined
in many different ways. The defining characteristic of communication is meaning,
and we could say that communication occurs whenever someone attributes meaning
to another person's words or actions. Communication may be understood as a "symbolic process whereby reality is produced, maintained, repaired and transformed"
(Carey, 1989, p. 23). The three perspectives emphasize different aspects of this communication process.

For example, the social science perspective emphasizes the various components
of communication: There is a sender/receiver, message, channel, and context. This

communication A sym-
bolic process whereby
reality is produced,
maintained, repaired,
and transformed.

perspective also emphasizes that communication tends to be patterned and therefore can be predicted. This tradition also focuses on the variables, or influences on the communication, like gender, or the nature of a relationship. For example, people in long-term relationships will communicate in a different way from individuals who have recently met, or men and women will tend to communicate in different ways.

The interpretive perspective emphasizes the symbolic, processual nature of communication; the symbolic nature of communication means that the words we speak or the gestures we make have no inherent meaning. Rather, they gain their significance from an agreed-upon meaning. When we use symbols to communicate, we assume that the other person shares our symbol system. Also, these symbolic meanings are conveyed both verbally and nonverbally. Thousands of nonverbal behaviors (gestures, postures, eye contact, facial expressions, and so on) involve shared meaning.

To make things more complicated, each message has more than one meaning; often, there are many layers of meaning. For example, the message *I love you* may mean, "I'd like to have a good time with you tonight," "I feel guilty about what I did last night without you," "I need you to do me a favor," "I have a good time when I'm with you," or "I want to spend the rest of my life (or at least the next few hours) with you." When we communicate, we assume that the other person takes the meaning that we intend. It is more likely, when individuals come from different cultural backgrounds and experiences, that this assumption may be faulty.

The interpretive perspective also emphasizes that the *process* by which we negotiate meaning is dynamic. Communication is not a singular event but is ongoing. It relies on other communication events to make sense. When we enter into communication with another person, we simultaneously take in messages through all of our senses. The messages are not discreet and linear but simultaneous, with blurry boundaries of beginning and end. When we negotiate meaning, we are creating, maintaining, repairing, or transforming reality. This implies that people are actively involved in the communication process. One person cannot communicate alone.

The critical perspective emphasizes the importance of societal forces in the communication process. That is, that all voices and symbols are not equal, but are arranged in a social hierarchy in which some individual characteristics are more highly valued than others; for example, people are more likely to listen carefully to a police officer than to a young child. In addition, powerful social symbols—for example, flags, national anthems, and Disney logos—also communicate meaning nonverbally. Many of these symbols are material as well; that is, they have material consequences in the world. For example, when school children in the United States bring guns to school and kill schoolmates, the symbolism of these acts communicates something, and the acts themselves are material.

THE RELATIONSHIP BETWEEN CULTURE AND COMMUNICATION

The relationship between culture and communication is complex. A dialectical perspective assumes that culture and communication are interrelated and reciprocal. That is, culture influences communication, and vice versa. Thus, cultural groups influence

TEST OF U.S. CULTURAL KNOWLEDGE

This test examines your knowledge of many of the cultures that comprise the contemporary United States.

1. *Lagniappe* is a term used in southern Louisiana for:

   a. Hurricanes
   b. Something free or sometimes a small gift given by a store owner to a customer after a purchase
   c. Inviting someone over for a meal
   d. Helping a friend with home remodeling or yard work

2. What is the name of the dish that features black-eyed peas and rice (although sometimes collards, ham hocks, stewed tomatoes, or other items) and is served in the South, especially on New Year's Day?

   a. Chitlings
   b. Jowls
   c. Hoppin' John
   d. Red rice

3. A very sweet pie made from molasses that originated with the Pennsylvania Dutch:

   a. Mincemeat pie
   b. Sugar pie
   c. Shoofly pie
   d. Lancaster pie

4. Which of the following is *not* the name of a Native American tribe?

   a. Seminole
   b. Apache
   c. Arapaho
   d. Illini

5. The month of Ramadan, a month of fasting for Muslims, ends with which holiday?

   a. Eid ul-Fitr
   b. Allahu Akbar
   c. Takbir
   d. Abu Bakr

6. On June 12 every year, some U.S. Americans celebrate "Loving Day" to commemorate:

   a. Your legal right to love someone of another race
   b. Your legal right to love someone of the same sex
   c. Your legal right to be a single parent
   d. Your legal right to get a divorce

7. The celebration of Buddha's birthday is not held on Christmas, but instead on:

   a. Fourth of July
   b. July 14
   c. Asian Lunar New Year's Day
   d. Hanamatsuri

8. Sometimes viewed as a Scandinavian tortilla, these potato flatcakes are often sold in areas with high Scandinavian American populations:

   a. Lefse
   b. Lutefisk
   c. Aquavit
   d. Fiskepudding

9. This traditional Mexican soup is made mostly from tripe, hominy, and chili:

   a. Tortilla soup
   b. Tomatillo
   c. Chorizo soup
   d. Menudo

10. Like a coconut pudding, this food comes from Hawaii:

    a. Lomi lomi
    b. Poke
    c. Haupia
    d. Kalua

Answers can be found on page 115.

the process by which the perception of reality is created and maintained: "All communities in all places at all times manifest their own view of reality in what they do. The entire culture reflects the contemporary model of reality" (Burke, 1985, p. 11). However, we might also say that communication helps create the cultural reality of a community. Let's see how these reciprocal relationships work.

How Culture Influences Communication

Intercultural communication scholars use broad frameworks from anthropology and psychology to identify and study cultural differences in communication. Two of the most relevant were developed by anthropologists Kluckhohn and Strodtbeck (1961) and by social psychologist Hofstede (1984).

Kluckhohn and Strodtbeck Value Orientations   Researchers Florence Kluckhohn and Fred Strodtbeck studied contemporary Diné (Navaho) and descendants of Spanish colonists and European Americans in the Southwest in the 1950s. They

International students describe the different cultural and communication patterns they encounter in the United States.

A graduate student from India noted the U.S. patterns of greeting. In her native culture people only say hello to those they know. Initially, she was surprised by the frequency with which Americans greet each other; she later became disillusioned:

> *I thought, they are really interested in how I am. Then . . . "I'm fine and how about you?" Then I realized that people are really not interested in the answer. It is just a way of acknowledging you.*

A British student commented on how openly Americans share their religious affiliation.

> *At first, I felt like a bit separated because I didn't quite fit into any. . . . They didn't know quite how to respond to me. I thought, Oh, am I supposed to be religious? Am I going to fit in here?*

A graduate student from Iran noted how Americans are taught to "sell themselves":

> *The job search is another thing in this country that is culturally quite different. . . . In my society, mostly, they ask the professors in the university about efficient people or good students—there is not, you know, no selling yourself. And for the first couple of months I wasn't very successful because I didn't have the experience in selling myself.*

Source: From L. A. Erbert, F. G. Perez, and E. Gareis, "Turning Points and Dialectical Interpretations of Immigrant Experiences in the United States," *Western Journal of Communication, 67,* 113–137, 2003.

emphasized the centrality of **cultural values** in understanding cultural groups. Values are the most deeply felt beliefs shared by a cultural group (see Figure 3-1); they reflect a shared perception of what ought to be, and not what is. Equality, for example, is a value shared by many people in the United States. It refers to the belief that all humans are created equal, even though we must acknowledge that, in reality, there are many disparities, such as in talent, intelligence, or access to material goods.

Intercultural conflicts are often caused by differences in value orientations. For example, some people feel strongly that it is important to consider how things were done in the past. For them, history and tradition help provide guidance. Values often conflict among participants in international assistance projects in which future-oriented individuals show a lack of respect for traditional ways of doing things. And conflicts may be exacerbated by power differentials, with some values privileged over others. Organizational communication scholars have pointed out that many U.S. workplaces reward extremely individualistic relationships and "doing" behaviors at the expense of more collaborative (and equally productive)

cultural values The worldview of a cultural group and its set of deeply held beliefs.

FIGURE 3-1   Holidays are significant ways of enacting and transmitting culture and cultural values across the generations. For example, Kwanzaa is an important holiday for many African Americans. It was established in 1966 by Ron Karenga and lasts seven days—December 26 to January 1—to mark seven important cultural values: unity, self-determination, collective work and responsibility, cooperative economics, purpose, creativity, and faith. What holidays does your family celebrate? What cultural values are being transmitted in those celebrations? (© *Lawrence Migdale/Getty Images*)

work (Buzzanell, 2000). Kluckhohn and Strodtbeck suggested that members of all cultural groups must answer the following important questions:

- What is human nature?
- What is the relationship between humans and nature?
- What is the relationship between humans?
- What is the preferred personality?
- What is the orientation toward time?

According to Kluckhohn and Strodtbeck, there are three possible responses to each question as they relate to shared values. (See Table 3-2.) Kluckhohn and Strodtbeck believed that, although all responses are possible in all societies, each society has one, or possibly two, preferred responses to each question that reflect the predominant values of that society. Religious beliefs, for example, may reinforce certain cultural values. The questions and their responses become a framework for understanding

Values are complex, and in this post, Sang Won describes the negative and positive aspects of the *high power distance* value common in South Korea:

> *In South Korea, teachers get a lot of respect. Students must come to school on their best behavior. It is one of the commitments that they make before they come to school. Also, they do not eat or talk during class to show respect to their teachers. However, there is a negative aspect of being so respectful to their teachers. Sometimes, students do not speak up and say their opinion out of respect for the teacher. Consequently, teachers have to teach them how to speak up for their opinions.*
> —Sang Won

broad differences in values among various cultural groups. Although the framework was applied originally to ethnic groups, we can extend it to cultural groups based on gender, class, nationality, and so on.

The Nature of Human Nature   As the table below shows, there are three possible responses, or solutions, to basic questions about human nature. One solution is a belief in the fundamental goodness of human nature. Legal practices in a society that holds this orientation would emphasize rehabilitating violators of the law; jails and prisons would be seen as places to train violators to rejoin society as contributing citizens. Religions such as Buddhism and Confucianism tend toward this orientation, focusing on improving the natural goodness of humans.

TABLE 3-2 KLUCKHOHN AND STRODTBECK VALUE ORIENTATIONS

	Range of Values		
Human nature	Basically good	Mixture of good and evil	Basically evil
Relationship between humans and nature	Humans dominate	Harmony exists between the two	Nature dominates
Relationships between humans	Individual	Group oriented	Collateral
Preferred personality	"Doing": stress on action	"Growing": stress on spiritual growth	"Being": stress on who you are
Time orientation	Future oriented	Present oriented	Past oriented

Source: From F. Kluckhohn and F. Strodtbeck, *Variations in Value Orientation* (Chicago, IL: Row, Peterson, 1961).

A second solution reflects a perception of a combination of goodness and evil in human nature. Many groups within the United States hold this value orientation, although there has been a shift in views for many U.S. Americans in the past 50 years. With regard to religious beliefs, there is less emphasis on the fundamental evil of humanity, which many European settlers of the Puritan tradition believed (Kohls, 1996). However, the current emphasis seems to be on incarceration and punishment for violators of the law. Given this orientation, not surprisingly, the United States currently has a higher proportion of citizens incarcerated than any other industrialized country (Warmsley, 2015).

According to the third orientation, human nature is essentially evil. Societies that hold this belief would be less interested in rehabilitation of criminals than in punishment. We often have trouble understanding torture or the practice of cutting off hands and other limbs—practices prevalent in many societies in the past—without understanding their orientation to human nature. While he lived in Belgium, Tom was particularly struck by the display of punishments and tortures in the Counts of Flanders Castle in Ghent. Perhaps the key to understanding these cultural practices is an understanding of the Christian view of humans as essentially evil and born in sin.

Relationship Between Humans and Nature   In most of U.S. societies, humans dominate nature. For instance, scientists seed clouds when we need rain, and engineers reroute rivers and build dams to meet the needs for water, recreation, and power. We control births with drugs and medical devices, and we make snow and ice for the recreational pastimes of skiing and skating. Certainly, not everyone in the United States agrees that humans should always dominate nature. Conflicts between environmentalists and land developers often center on disagreements over this value orientation. And, of course, there are variations in how these values play out in different societies. For example, a country like Canada, which generally espouses a "humans over nature" orientation, still seems more concerned with environmental issues than does the United States. As described by a student,

> *Canada is very concerned about protecting their environment, and this is very clear even if you are just traveling through. They are concerned about clean water, clean air and not doing too much logging of their trees, keeping streams free of pollution, etc.*

In societies that believe mainly in the domination of nature over humans, decisions are made differently. Families may be more accepting of the number of children that are born naturally. There is less intervention in the processes of nature, and there are fewer attempts to control what people see as the natural order.

Many Native Americans and Japanese believe in the value of humans living in harmony with nature, rather than one force dominating the other. In this value orientation, nature is respected and plays an integral part in the spiritual and religious life of the community. Some societies—for example, many Arab groups—emphasize aspects of both harmony with and domination of nature. This reminds us that values are played out in very complex ways in any cultural group.

J ohn Engle, a professor of Anglo-American literature and civilization, teaches a course, "French and North African Cultural Patterns," to American students studying in France. Here, he describes how difficult it is for many Americans to accept the notion of cultural difference—a problem that he attributes to their own cultural value of individualism. He says he starts his course with important distinctions between stereotypes and generalizations—pointing out that stereotypes are limiting and dangerous while generalizations can be useful, allowing for individual exceptions while permitting categorization, which is necessary for intelligent analysis. He describes how students resist his way of thinking:

"You can't say that," a student will object when you suggest that, say, the ritualized sit-down dinner or the five-week vacation might tell us something broadly significant about the French attitude toward the present moment. "I know people back home who eat long meals. Everyone is different. You can't generalize like that."

The irony is that in essentially refusing to discuss culture, my students are actually obeying powerful cultural imperatives. For what better manifestation of American mythic individualism is there than the conviction that the basic unit of human society is the autonomous self?

Professor Engle concludes that, while it's really difficult to discuss the topic of cultural patterns with American students who see every story as an individual one, he understands where that impulse comes from. They have been constantly bombarded with messages espousing the virtues of social and economic individualism for the first 20 years of their lives, and "students see no reason to discard this outlook when they go abroad."

Source: From J. Engle, "Culture's Unacknowledged Iron Grip," *Chronicle of Higher Education, 53*(22) (February 2, 2007), B16.

Relationships Between Humans Some cultural groups value individualism, whereas others are more group oriented. The cultural differences pertaining to these values distinguish two types of societies. Individualism, often cited as a value held by European Americans, places importance on individuals rather than on families, work teams, or other groups (Bellah, Madsen, Sullivan, Swidler, & Tipton, 2007). This characteristic is often cited as the most important European American cultural value. As you can see in the Point of View (p. 101), this value is so ingrained in many U.S. Americans that it rarely rises to a conscious level. In contrast, people from more collectivistic societies, like those in Central and South America, Asia, and many Arab societies, place a great deal of importance on extended families and group loyalty. In the United States, this is the case in Amish communities and in some Latino/a and Native American communities. A visitor to Mexico described one example of collectivism in that culture:

> *I remember that in public that children always seem to be accompanied by someone older, usually a family member. People went around in family groups—children with older siblings, grandparents, aunts—not nearly so age-segregated as it is here in the U.S.*

The collateral orientation emphasizes the collectivist connection to other individuals (mostly family members) even after death. This orientation is found in cultures in which ancestors are seen as a part of the family and are influential in decisions even though they are not alive. Examples of this include the Asian practice of maintaining a table in the house to honor their ancestors or the Mexican "Day of the Dead" practice of having a picnic near the graves of the family members and leaving food for them.

Values may also be related to economic status or rural–urban distinctions. In the United States, for example, working-class people tend to be more collectivistic than middle- or upper-class people. Working-class people donate a higher percentage of their time and money to help others (Piff , Kraus, Côté, Cheng, & Keltner , 2010). Historian Roxanne A. Dunbar (1997), who grew up poor in Oklahoma, describes an encounter she had with middle-class individualism while on an extended car trip with her new husband, Jimmy. They passed several stranded motorists, the women sitting in the shade while the men worked on the cars. She was surprised when her husband didn't stop to help:

> *"Why don't we stop?" I asked. No one in my family would ever have passed up a stranded motorist. . . .*
> *"They're hustlers, rob you blind, highway bandits," Jimmy said.*
> *"How do you know?"*
> *"I just know, they use the kids and old people for bait to get you to stop, then rob you, they're transients, fruit pickers, white trash."*
> *I stared at the sad faces as we passed by and tried to see the con artists and criminals behind the masks. But they merely looked familiar, like my own relatives. (p. 83)*

These cultural values may influence patterns of communication. For example, people who value individualism *tend* also to favor direct forms of communication and to support overt forms of conflict resolution. People in collectivistic societies *may* employ less direct communication and more avoidance-style conflict resolution. Of course, sometimes people belong to cultural groups that hold contradictory values. For example, most U.S. work contexts require highly individualistic communication, which may conflict with the collectivistic family or ethnic backgrounds of some workers. Workers may find it hard to reconcile and live with these competing values. Consider the experience of Lucia, a Native American college student. When one of her uncles passed away during the first week of school, she was expected to participate in family activities. She traveled out of state with her family to his home, helped cook and feed other family members, and attended the wake and the funeral. Then her mother became ill, and she had to care for her. Thus,

The cause of the 2013 crash of Asiana Airlines Boeing 777 at San Francisco International Airport may have been partly related to cultural values (e.g., power distance). It crashed on landing and burst into flames killing three passengers and injuring nearly 200. Analysis of the crash placed part of the blame on pilot confusion about the operation of the automatic throttle. However, some experts suggested that another contributing factor may have been the Korean emphasis on authoritarian structure and strong respect for age seniority. According to this hierarchy, copilots are neither encouraged to challenge senior pilots, nor ever speak out of turn. This authoritarian cockpit culture had been identified as a factor in several South Korean airliner crashes in the 1980s and 90s, and Korean transport authorities now maintain that their procedures and hierarchies have been overhauled. However, the pilot that day, a veteran pilot but new to the 777 (and a training captain was in the right seat watching his performance) reported that he did not immediately move to abort the landing when he should have because he felt that only the instructor pilot had that authority.

Source: From "Asiana airlines crash caused by pilot error and confusion, investigators say," *theguardian.com*, June 24, 2014. Retrieved April 21, 2016, from http://www.theguardian.com /world/2014/jun/24/asiana-crash-san-francsico-controls-investigation-pilot.

she missed the first 2 weeks of school. Some of her professors were sympathetic; others were not. As Lucia describes it, she feels almost constantly torn between the demands of her collectivistic family and the demands of the individualistic professors and administration.

Preferred Forms of Activity   The most common "activity value" in the United States is the "doing" orientation, which emphasizes productivity. (Remember the expression "Idle hands are the devil's workshop"?) Employment reward systems reflect this value in that workers often must document their progress (e.g., in numbers of sales made or numbers of clients seen). In general, the highest status is conferred on those who "do" (sports figures, physicians, lawyers), rather than on those who "think" (philosophers, professors, priests).

The "growing" orientation emphasizes spiritual aspects of life. This orientation seems to be less prevalent than the other two, perhaps practiced only in Zen Buddhism and as a cultural motif in the United States in the 1960s (Stewart & Bennett, 1991). Some societies, as in Japan, combine both "doing" and "growing" orientations, emphasizing action and spiritual growth. The third solution is to emphasize "being," a kind of self-actualization in which the individual is fused with the experience. Some societies in Central and South America, as well as in Greece and Spain, exhibit this orientation.

Orientation to Time   Most U.S. cultural communities—particularly European American and middle class—seem to emphasize the future. Consider the practices of depositing money in retirement accounts or keeping appointment books that reach years into the future. Other societies—for example, in Spain or Greece—seem to emphasize the importance of the present, a recognition of the value of living fully in and realizing the potential of the present moment.

Many European and Asian societies strongly emphasize the past, believing that knowledge and awareness of history have something to contribute to an understanding of contemporary life. For example, a U.S. American student in language school in Mexico reported that her professors would always answer questions about contemporary society with an historical reference. For instance, there were regional elections going on at the time. If students asked about the implication of the campaign platform of one of the candidates, the professor would always answer by describing what had happened in the region 50 or 100 years earlier.

Hofstede Value Orientations   Social psychologist Geert Hofstede and colleagues (Hofstede, Hofstede, & Minkov, 2010) extended the work of Kluckhohn and Strodtbeck, based on extensive cross-cultural study of personnel working in IBM subsidiaries in 53 countries. Whereas Kluckhohn and Strodtbeck based their framework on cultural patterns of ethnic communities within the United States, Hofstede and colleagues examined value differences among national societies. Hofstede identified five areas of common problems. One problem type, individualism versus collectivism, appeared in the Kluckhohn and Strodtbeck framework. Although the problems were shared by different cultural groups, solutions varied from culture to culture. As shown in Table 3-3, the problem types are identified as follows:

- Power distance: social inequality, including the relationship with authority
- Femininity versus masculinity: the social implications of having been born male or female
- Ways of dealing with uncertainty, controlling aggression, and expressing emotions
- Long-term versus short-term orientation to life
- Indulgence versus restraint: the subjective feeling of happiness and enjoying life

Hofstede then investigated how these various cultural values influenced corporate behavior in various countries. Let's examine the other problem types more closely.

power distance A cultural variability dimension that concerns the extent to which people accept an unequal distribution of power.

Power distance refers to the extent to which less powerful members of institutions and organizations within a country expect and accept the unequal distribution of power. Denmark, Israel, and New Zealand, for example, value small power distance. Most people there believe that less hierarchy is better and that power should be used only for legitimate purposes. Therefore, the best corporate leaders in those countries are those who minimize power differences. In societies that value high power distance—for example, Mexico, the Philippines, and India—the decision-making process and the relationships between managers and subordinates are more formalized. In addition, people may be uncomfortable in settings in which hierarchy is unclear or ambiguous.

TABLE 3-3 HOFSTEDE VALUE ORIENTATIONS

Power Distance

Low power distance	High power distance
Less hierarchy better	More hierarchy better
e.g., Denmark, Israel, New Zealand	e.g., Mexico, India

Femininity/Masculinity

Femininity	Masculinity
Fewer gender-specific roles	More gender-specific roles
Value quality of life, support for unfortunate	Achievement, ambition, acquisition of material goods
e.g., Denmark, Norway, Sweden	e.g., Japan, Austria, Mexico

Uncertainty Avoidance

Low uncertainty avoidance	High uncertainty avoidance
Dislike rules, accept dissent	More extensive rules, limit dissent
Less formality	More formality
e.g., Great Britain, Sweden, Hong Kong	e.g., Greece, Portugal, Japan

Long-Term/Short-Term Orientation

Short-term orientation	Long-term orientation
Universal guidelines for good and evil	Definition of good and evil depends on circumstances
Prefer quick results	Value perseverance and tenacity
e.g., Western Religions Judaism, Christianity, Islam	e.g., Confucianism, Hinduism, Buddhism

Indulgence/Restraint

Indulgence	Restraint
Relatively free gratification of needs related to enjoying life and having fun	Suppression and regulation of needs related to enjoying life and having fun
Freedom of speech over maintaining order	Maintaining order over freedom of speech
e.g., Mexico, Nigeria, Sweden, Australia	e.g., Russia, Egypt, China, India

Source: From G. Hofsted, G. J. Hofstede, and M. Minkov, *Cultures and Organizations: Software of the Mind,* 3rd ed. (Boston, MA: McGraw-Hill, 2010)

masculinity–femininity value A cultural variability dimension that concerns the degree of being feminine—valuing fluid gender roles, quality of life, service, relationships, and interdependence—and the degree of being masculine—emphasizing distinctive gender roles, ambition, materialism, and independence.

uncertainty avoidance A cultural variability dimension that concerns the extent to which uncertainty, ambiguity, and deviant ideas and behaviors are avoided.

long-term versus short-term orientation A cultural variability dimension that reflects a cultural-group orientation toward virtue or truth. The long-term orientation emphasizes virtue, whereas the short-term orientation emphasizes truth.

indulgence versus restraint A cultural variability dimension that reflects a subjective feeling of happiness. The indulgence orientation emphasizes relatively free gratification of basic and natural human drives related to enjoying life and having fun. Restraint emphasizes suppressing gratification of needs and regulates it by means of strict social norms.

The **masculinity–femininity value** is two-dimensional. It refers to (1) the degree to which gender-specific roles are valued and (2) the degree to which cultural groups value so-called masculine values (achievement, ambition, acquisition of material goods) or so-called feminine values (quality of life, service to others, nurturance, support for the unfortunate). IBM employees in Japan, Austria, and Mexico scored high on the masculine values orientation, expressing a general preference for gender-specific roles, with some roles (e.g., main wage earner) better filled by men and other roles (e.g., homemaker, teacher) by women. In contrast, employees in northern Europe (Denmark, Norway, Sweden, and the Netherlands) tended to rank higher in feminine values orientation, reflecting more gender equality and a stronger belief in the importance of quality of life for all.

Uncertainty avoidance concerns the degree to which people who feel threatened by ambiguous situations respond by avoiding them or trying to establish more structure to compensate for the uncertainty. Societies that have a low uncertainty avoidance orientation (Great Britain, Sweden, Hong Kong, and the United States) prefer to limit rules, accept dissent, and take risks. In contrast, those with a high uncertainty avoidance orientation (Greece, Portugal, and Japan) usually prefer more extensive rules and regulations in organizational settings and seek consensus about goals.

Hofstede's original framework contained only four problem types and was criticized for its predominantly western European bias. In response, a group of Chinese researchers developed and administered a similar, but more Asian-oriented, questionnaire to people in 22 countries around the world (Chinese Culture Connection, 1987). Their questionnaire included ideas related to Confucian-based thinking. In comparing their framework to Hofstede's, they concluded that there was, in fact, a great deal of overlap. Indeed, the three dimensions of individualism—collectivism, power distance, and masculinity–femininity—seem to be universal. However, uncertainty avoidance seems to be more relevant to Western societies. A fifth dimension that emerged from the Asian study and that seems to apply to both Eastern and Western societies is the **long-term versus short-term orientation,** which reflects a society's search for virtue or truth.

Those with a short-term orientation are concerned with possessing the truth (reflected in the Western religions of Judaism, Christianity, and Islam), focusing on quick results in endeavors, and recognizing social pressure to conform. Those with a long-term orientation tend to respect the demands of virtue (reflected in Eastern religions such as Confucianism, Hinduism, Buddhism, and Shintoism); to focus more on thrift, perseverance, and tenacity in whatever they attempt; and to be willing to subordinate themselves to a larger purpose.

Based on recent research by Michael Minkov, one of Hofstede's associates, there is now an additional value dimension, **indulgence versus restraint**. This dimension is related to the *subjective* feelings of happiness. That is, people may not actually *be* happy or healthy but they report that they *feel* happier and healthier. National cultures that are categorized as more indulgent (Mexico, Nigeria, Sweden, Australia) tend to allow relatively free gratification of needs related to enjoying life and having fun. Indulgence orientation is expressed in the importance of having lots of friends (e.g., Facebook), active participation in sports

I recently spent two weeks in Mexico City. It was an amazing experience. The contrast between Phoenix and Mexico City totally blew me away, especially the architecture. I mean, just walking down the street you see buildings all around you that are hundreds of years old. We went to the Basilica of the Virgin of Guadalupe, and our guide showed us the exact hill where Juan Diego supposedly saw the Virgin and brought back roses to prove to the priests that he saw her. The priests then built a church exactly right there because that was what the Virgin told Juan to tell the priests to do. Juan Diego is like a national hero in Mexico, and this place where they built these churches is totally sacred. People come from all over Mexico to this exact place, and it is just so hugely important to them.

We also went to Teotihuacán and Templo Mayor. Both are ancient ruins from the Aztecs. These places were really, really amazing. Our guide pointed out for us places where the Spanish built buildings right on top of the ancient structures. It was their way of winning over the natives, of making the Spanish ways take over the ways of the native people. I realized that this change in architecture conveyed a whole history of different cultures and conquest. I was amazed that as I stood there at Templo Mayor, right in the heart of this huge city, I could literally see hundreds of years of history. And the domination also hit me. The Spanish had to build over the temples and other sacred sites of the Aztecs in order to win the hearts of the people. And they needed to make Juan Diego a national hero and make sacred the spot that he is said to have seen the Virgin of Guadalupe. And in order to make all that real to the people, they had to put it all in the architecture.
　　—Samantha

(not just watching sporting events) and there is less moral regulation. Societies that emphasize restraint (Russia, Egypt and other Islamic countries, China, India) tend to suppress gratification of needs and regulate it by means of strict social norms. Having many friends is reportedly less important, there is more watching of sports but less participation, and a strong work ethic. Countries with a predominant indulgence orientation emphasize freedom of speech over maintaining order; countries with more restraint orientation tend to value maintaining order over allowing freedom of speech.

Limitations of Value Frameworks　　Identifying cultural values helps us understand broad cultural differences, but it is important to remember that not everyone in a given society holds the dominant value (Kirkman, Lone, & Gibson, 2006). We shouldn't reduce individuals to mere stereotypes based on these value orientations. After all, not all Amish or Japanese are group oriented, and not all Americans and Australians are individualistic. Remember that cultures are dynamic and heterogeneous. Although people in small rural communities may be more collectively oriented, or more willing to help their neighbors, we cannot say that people in big cities ignore those around them.

Value heterogeneity may be particularly noticeable in a society that is undergoing rapid change. South Korea, for example, has transformed itself in the past 50 years from a poor, agrarian country into a global economic and technological powerhouse; it is one of the world's largest economies, the world's #1 leader in broadband penetration, and has the most techno-savvy young people in the world. Influenced by Western capitalism and individualism, many young Koreans are now embracing more individualistic values, making their own decisions regarding marriage and career, rather than following their family's wishes—a practice unheard of 50 years ago (Shim, Kim, & Martin, 2008).

Another limitation of value frameworks is that they tend to "essentialize" people. In other words, people tend to assume that a particular group characteristic is the essential characteristic of a given member at all times and in all contexts. However, a recent study found that all Korean women interviewed expressed *both* a strong family orientation *and* a "relational" concept of self as well as a concept of the autonomous or independent self (Shim, Kim, & Martin, 2008). Similarly, researchers who have spent many years in China also observe that the contemporary Chinese "are not either individualist or collective but both at the same time" (Ambler & Witzel, 2000). It is useful to keep these tensions in mind when thinking about cultural groups—that they often reflect a set of dynamic contrasts, rather than a static set of specific characteristics or traits.

The cultural–individual dialectic reminds us that these value orientations exist on a continuum and are all present, to a greater or lesser extent, in all societies. For example, we could characterize the debate about health care in the United States as a struggle between "masculine" and "feminine" value orientations. Those with a "masculine" orientation believe that each person should take care of him- or herself and be free to achieve and to acquire as many material goods as possible. Others, representing a "feminine" position, believe that everyone should sacrifice a little for the good of the whole and that everyone should be assured access to health care and hospitalization.

The differences–similarities dialectic reminds us that although people may differ with respect to specific value orientations, they also may hold other value orientations in common. For example, people may have different views on the importance of individual or group loyalty but share a belief in the essential goodness of human nature and find similarity in religious faith and practice. Finally, a static–dynamic dialectic reminds us that although group-related values tend to be relatively consistent, people are dynamic, and their behavior varies contextually. Thus, they may be more or less individualistic or group oriented depending on the context.

How Communication Reinforces Culture

Culture not only influences communication but also is enacted through, and so is influenced by, communication. Scholars of cultural communication describe how various aspects of culture are enacted in speech communities in situ, that is, in contexts. They seek to understand communication patterns that are situated socially and give voice to cultural identity. Specifically, they examine how the cultural forms and frames (terms, rituals, myths, and social dramas) are enacted through structuring norms of conversation and interaction. The patterns are not connected in a deterministic way to any cultural group (Philipsen, 2002).

Using an ethnography of communication approach, researcher Craig Engstrom (2012) examined how patterns of talk about drinking alcohol shape and reinforce notions of masculinity and gender identity among U.S. college students. He conducted fieldwork, observing and interacting with students in resident halls and other campus locations for more than a year and also conducted extensive interviews with male and female students. He concluded that in order to be seen as a competent communicator in this speech community, male students had to portray drinking as a normal behavior and follow several **communication rules**:

Rule 1: Refer to alcoholic consumption in non-numeric and abstract way, never say exactly how much was drunk (e.g., "I *partied* hard," "At least you got to have *fun*") and one should not ask specifically how much was consumed. However, explicit references "I was drunk" could be said as a way to explain some other unacceptable action, for example, urinating in public, making derogatory references to women. Even nondrinkers would follow this rule and use it to deflect attention or make excuses for some undesirable behavior.

Rule 2: Refer to alcohol positively. One should not make negative statements about alcohol consumption—even when there was clearly an alcohol-related tragedy, for example, when a student got hit by a train because he was drunk and fell on railroad tracks. Conversations instead would point to other possible explanations.

Rule 3: Refer to alcohol consumption as normal. Behavior that seemed out of the ordinary or excessive would be normalized and excused by "normal" alcoholic consumption. Again, this excuse was used for discounting unacceptable behavior even *when students were not drinking*.

Engstrom discusses the role and value of these patterns of talk in the speech community of college students and shows how, by following these communication rules, they could take the emphasis off an embarrassing behavior, or get "off the hook" for questionable behaviors, and maintain and reinforce a cultural identity of masculinity. Illustrating the reciprocal relationship between communication and cultural identity, one feels more masculine when following the rules. This reciprocity is also seen in the consequences for students who do not follow these rules—they may be seen as effeminate or just odd. Engstrom also suggests that his study shows that excessive drinking does not *cause* misconduct; rather, talk about drinking "accounts for" and normalizes such misconduct.

A related approach from cultural communication studies sees culture as **performative**. If we accept this metaphor, then we are not studying any external (cultural) reality. Rather, we are examining how persons enact and represent their culture's worldviews. (See Figure 3-2.) Several Latino/a communication scholars have described, in **autoethnographies** (writing about their own experiences), how they each perform their ethnic identity in various contexts, and they emphasize that being Latino is never just one thing; there are multiple, contingent, and overlapping ways to experience and articulate Latina/o identity (Delgado, 2009). They show us that individuals in the same cultural category (Latino/a) may share some similarities but also view and perform their identities in very different ways.

For example, Hector Amaya (2007) describes how he has "rewritten" himself and performed this identity change through the process of acculturating to upper-middle-class academic life—after coming to the United States as an adult,

communication rules
A systematic pattern of behavior that takes place on a regular basis within a cultural community.

performative Acting or presenting oneself in a specific way so as to accomplish some goal.

autoethnography Research method where writers examine their own life experiences to discover broader cultural insights.

FIGURE 3-2 This photo of tourists watching Aztec dancers in Mexico City reflects an earlier context in which Aztec culture was dominant in Mexico. What role does Aztec culture play in Mexican life today? What does this communicate about the continued vitality of Aztec culture in today's Mexico? (*Courtesy © Jackie Martinez, Arizona State University*)

learning English, and acquiring graduate degrees. He says that every immigrant must answer the question, "What kind of personal characteristics ought I have to be treated ethically by others?" (p. 195). He describes how he deliberately worked very hard to "learn to perform what others (white majority) value as evidence of moral worth" (p. 200), acquiring the necessary mannerisms, and tastes in clothing, food, and art. It is not easy; he says his "brownness" is still often seen as threatening to whites, and he feels he has to dress much better than most white middle-class people in order to get the same treatment they enjoy even when they are dressed in grubbies. He feels he has to pay more attention to clothing brand, to style, and to newness; things he never considered in Mexico.

Karma Chavez, daughter of a Mexican father and a white U.S. mother, describes growing up in rural Nebraska—in contrast to most Latina/os, who mostly live in urban U.S. areas on the two coasts—and what it means to be brown in the beet-growing heartland of the United States. She describes what happened when a meat-packing plant was opened and the *new* brown (Mexican migrant) workers moved into her town in the 1980s. Many whites were not welcoming to this new group—some even moved away. She tried to distance herself from this marginalized group and stressed her (fictionalized) Spanish heritage to her white friends. "Their Brown bodies reflected my family's history. Their Brown bodies, like a spotlight, highlighted our brownness to the Whites we had learned to relate to in ways that concealed our otherness from them. I learned to hide our food, our traditions, and my father. Those parts of me now seemed vulnerably naked in front of everyone's eyes" (Chavez, 2009, p. 170).

As she grew up, she became more conscious of the discrimination and prejudice against Latinos in her rural hometown and, as a scholar, committed to understanding and changing the marginalized position of many Latinas/os. She could never understand why her parents and grandparents never talked about their negative experiences. As a communication scholar now, she studied the situation and describes how the particular rural context, the distances between farms, and the relatively small Latino/a population affected her family's relationships and identity. In contrast to urban areas with large Latino/a populations, rural living—where Latino/as are few and far between—means you probably have to assimilate in order to survive. She concludes: "Latinas/os in rural spaces often lack Latina/o community, and thus lack the resources to resist discrimination or to reshape Brown-White relationships" (p. 173). Like Amaya, she sees that trying to assimilate to whiteness can be an invaluable resource for those who are capable of performing it. She also notes the high price of the assimilation and what it means to lack resources to resist—that her grandparents rarely speak of the discrimination and even violence they experienced in Nebraska. It is simply too painful.

Finally, Fernando Delgado views his performance as a Latino, a little differently from Amaya and Chavez. He describes how he tactically and strategically performs his roles as a Latino teacher, scholar, and administrator in higher education, saying that one is more intentional and deliberate when one's presence is challenged institutionally. He recounts instances of being marginalized as the only Latino in his white Iowan graduate program and later being marginalized by other minority faculty (an African American professor questioned his being listed as a "Faculty of Color," saying that Spanish aristocrats should not be counted toward diversity). He describes times where he deliberately seeks separation (not acculturation), in order to be accepted by Mexican Americans as well as the majority Anglos and acknowledges he is committed to Latina/o politics, straddling *both* majority and minority worlds (which is not always easy): "Uncertainty, reflection, and self-critique often drive the contingent actions that I take because while on the one hand I may risk losing a job, on the other I may risk losing my self" (Delgado, 2009, p. 163).

Each of these three scholars interrogates their own performances of identity and identifies some constraints to those performances; what are some contextual constraints that might inhibit anyone's performances of identity?

Communication as Resistance to the Dominant Cultural System

Resistance is the metaphor used in cultural studies to conceptualize the relationship between culture and communication. Borrowing this metaphor, we can try to discover how individuals use their own space to resist the dominant cultural system. For example, workers can find ways to resist the authority structure of management and extreme competition in many ways, some subtle (e.g., work slowdowns, extending their autonomy) and some more obvious (e.g., whistleblowing) (Mumby, 2005). Working-class clients involved in social services organizations resist the dominant authority structure and try to make relationships and contexts more equitable by breaking some of the rules, or reframing client–social worker relationships (refusing to be treated in demeaning ways) (Tretheway, 1997). Or students may sign their advisors' names on course registration forms, thereby circumventing the university bureaucracy. Social media has dramatically increased the efficiency of resistance. For example, a Facebook post and then a tweet (#blacklivesmatter) after the murder of Trayvon Martin and Michael Brown by white police officers gathered momentum, which led hundreds of protesters from around the country to converge on Ferguson, Missouri (home of Michael Brown) in 2014. Soon thousands joined, showing up at other scenes of police action against unarmed black men, political rallies, and other meetings, communicating their nonviolent resistance against perceived injustices and institutionalized racism (Day, 2015).

Day, a journalist for *the Guardian*, describes the impact of social media on resistance: "A hashtag on Twitter can link the disparate fates of unarmed black men shot down . . . in a way that transcends geographical boundaries and time zones. A shared post on Facebook can organize a protest in a matter of minutes. Documentary photos and videos can be distributed on Tumblr pages and Periscope feeds, through Instagram and Vines. Power lies in a single image. Previously unseen events become unignorable" (Day, 2015). In all these ways of resisting the dominant cultural systems, people find ways to meet their needs and struggle to make relationships and contexts more equitable.

THE RELATIONSHIP BETWEEN COMMUNICATION AND CONTEXT

Context typically is created by the physical/virtual or social aspects of the situation in which communication occurs. For example, communication may occur face-to-face in a classroom, a bar, a church, or in a virtual context online, and people communicate differently depending on the context. You probably communicate differently when hanging out with friends and when talking with your instructor and other students in a classroom. Intercultural communication may be more or less challenging online or face-to-face. For example, communicating via a phone conversation can be more challenging than talking face-to-face when there are language barriers. On the other hand, communicating online through Facebook posts or e-mail may be easier than face-to-face context when language barriers are involved. Perhaps you can think of other examples of how an online context affects intercultural communication.

Context is neither static nor objective, and it can be multilayered. Context may consist of the social, political, and historical structures in which the communication occurs. Not surprisingly, the social context is determined on the societal level. Consider, for example, the controversy over the Calvin Klein underwear ads in the early 1990s that used young adolescents as models: Many critics viewed the ads as equivalent to pedophilia. The controversy took place in a social context in which pedophilia was seen as perverse or immoral. This meant that any communication that encouraged or fed that behavior or perspective, including advertising, was deemed wrong by the majority of observers. However, pedophilia has not been considered wrong in all societies in all periods of history. To interpret the ads adequately, we would have to know something about the current feelings toward and meanings attached to pedophilia wherever the ads were displayed.

The political context in which communication occurs, whether online or face-to-face, includes those forces that attempt to change or retain existing social structures and relationships. For example, consider the actions of BlackLivesMatter protesters described above who chanted "Hands up, don't shoot" (a reference to incidents where black suspects were shot when their hands were supposedly up). In order to understand these communicative actions, we must consider the political context. In this case, the political context would be the ongoing debates over policing policies and practices in communities of color in the United States. In other locales or other eras, the protester's communicative acts would not make sense or might be interpreted in other ways.

We also need to examine the historical context of communication. For example, the meaning of a college degree depends in part on the particular school's reputation. Why does a degree from Harvard communicate a different meaning than a degree from an obscure state university? Harvard's reputation relies on history—the large endowments given over the years, the important persons who have attended and graduated, and so forth.

THE RELATIONSHIP BETWEEN COMMUNICATION AND POWER

Power is pervasive in communication interactions, although it is not always evident or obvious how power influences communication or what kinds of meaning are constructed. We often think of communication between individuals as being between equals, but this is rarely the case (Allen, 2011). As communication scholar Mark Orbe (1998) describes it,

> *In every society a social hierarchy exists that privileges some groups over others. Those groups that function at the top of the social hierarchy determine to a great extent the communication system of the entire society. (p. 8)*

Orbe goes on to describe how those people in power, consciously or unconsciously, create and maintain communication systems that reflect, reinforce, and promote their own ways of thinking and communicating. There are two levels of group-related power: (1) the primary dimensions—age, ethnicity, gender, physical abilities, race, and sexual orientation—which are more permanent in nature and (2) the secondary dimensions—educational background, geographic location, marital status, and socio-economic status—which are more changeable (Loden & Rosener, 1991). The point is that the dominant communication systems ultimately impede those who do not share the systems. The communication style most valued in college classrooms, for example, emphasizes public speaking and competition (because the first person who raises his or her hand gets to speak). Not all students are comfortable with this style, but those who take to it naturally are more likely to succeed.

Power also comes from social institutions and the roles individuals occupy in those institutions. For example, in the classroom, there is temporary inequality, with instructors having more power. After all, they set the course requirements, give grades, determine who speaks, and so on. In this case, the power rests not with the individual instructor but with the role that he or she is enacting.

Rose Weitz, a communication scholar, describes the importance of hair for women in U.S. society in attracting men. Although some writers say that women who use strategies like the "hair flip" in attracting men do so unconsciously and are just blindly obeying cultural rules, her interviews with women reveal that many are acutely aware of the cultural rules and the power of the "flip." Those who cannot participate feel marginalized.

A young white woman:

I have very long hair and use the hair flip, both consciously and unconsciously. When I do it [consciously], I check the room to see if anyone is looking in my direction but never catch a guy's eye first. I just do it in his line of vision. [I] bend over slightly, pretending to get something from a bag or pick something up) so that some of my hair falls in front of my shoulder. Then I lean back and flip my hair out and then shake my head so my hair sways a little.

A young Latino woman:

In Hispanic culture hair is very important for a woman. It defines our beauty and gives us power over men. Now that I cut my hair short, I miss the feeling of moving my hair around and the power it gave me. . . .

The hair flip is especially aggravating for those black women whose hair will not grow long. As one black graduate student explains,

As an African American woman, I am very aware of non–African American women "flipping" their hair. . . . I will speak only for myself here (but I think it's a pretty global feeling for many African American women), but I often look at women who can flip their hair with envy, wishfulness, perhaps regret?, . . . with my "natural" hair, if I run my fingers through it, it's going to be a mess [and won't] gracefully fall back into place.

Source: From R. Weitz, *Rapunzel's Daughters: What Women's Hair Tells Us About Women's Lives* (New York: Farrar, Straus and Giroux, 2004).

Power is dynamic. It is not a simple one-way proposition. For example, students may pay attention to their mobile devices, carry on conversations through instant messages, read Facebook buzzfeeds, Twitter feeds, or engage in other "distracting" behaviors—thus weakening the professor's power over them (Cheong, Shuter, & Suwinyattichaiporn, 2016). They may also refuse to accept a grade and file a grievance with the university administration to have the grade changed. Further, the typical power relationship between instructor and student often is not perpetuated beyond the classroom. However, some issues of power play out in a broader social context (Johnson, 2006). For example, in contemporary society, cosmetic companies have a vested interest in a particular image of female beauty that involves purchasing and using makeup. Advertisements encourage women to feel compelled to participate in this cultural definition. Resistance can be expressed by a refusal to go along with the dominant cultural standards of beauty. Angela, a student from rural Michigan, describes how she resisted the "beauty culture" of her metropolitan university:

> *I came to school, and when I looked around I felt like I was inadequate. I had one of two choices: to conform to what the girls look like here, or to stay the same. I chose to stay true to my "Michigan" self. I felt more confident this way. I still remember looking at all of the blond girls with their fake boobs and black pants, strutting down campus. Four years later, I have a more mature attitude and realized that this culture wasn't for me.*

What happens when someone like Angela decides not to buy into this definition? Regardless of the woman's individual reason for not participating, other people are likely to interpret her behavior in ways that may not match her own reasons. What her unadorned face communicates is understood against a backdrop of society's definitions—that is, the backdrop developed by the cosmetics industry.

Dominant cultural groups attempt to perpetuate their positions of privilege in many ways. However, subordinate groups can resist this domination in many ways too. Cultural groups can use political and legal means to maintain or resist domination, but these are not the only means of invoking power relations. Groups can negotiate their various relations to culture through economic boycotts and strikes, for example, when University of Missouri football players (black and white) refused to play in Fall 2015 to protest the pervasive and casual forms of racism on their campus. Individuals can subscribe (or not subscribe) to specific magazines or newspapers, change TV channels, write letters to government officials, or take action in other ways to change the influence of power.

The disempowered can negotiate power in varied and subtle ways. Tracy's (2000) ethnographic study of organizational communication on cruise ships analyzes the complex, subtle power dynamics between the ship's staff and management. The staff found it very stressful to follow management's mandate to "never say no [to the customers]" and "smile, we are on stage"; they demonstrated their resistance to management by making fun of the guidelines.

Power is complex, especially in relation to institutions or the social structure. Some inequities, such as in gender, class, or race, are more rigid than those created by temporary roles such as student or teacher. The power relations between student and teacher, for example, are more complex if the teacher is a female challenged by male students. We really can't understand intercultural communication without considering the power dynamics in the interaction.

A dialectical perspective looks at the dynamic and interrelated ways in which culture, communication, context, and power intersect in intercultural communication interactions. Consider this example: When Tom first lived in Brussels, he asked for a national train schedule from the information office at one of the train stations. Because he does not speak Dutch, he talked to the agent behind the counter in French. The agent gave Tom a copy of the national train schedule in Dutch. When Tom asked if it was available in French, the man politely apologized, saying that it was the end of the season and there were no more available in French. It was clear to

Many of the Thai managers I spoke with while doing research on American companies in Thailand stressed to me that when working with Thais one needed to be very aware of relationships and the hierarchy in which they exist. A Thai woman I spoke with, who was the secretary to the company's American president, provided this example of the need for attention to the details of relationships:

> *I believe in the United States it is common for a boss to ask the secretary to request some materials from another person or to call people and tell them the boss wants to see them. In the United States, you all look at each other as equals. It is not so important what someone's title is, their age, or time with the company. In Thailand, those things are very important. For example, my boss, who is an American, was always asking me to go call so-and-so and request a meeting or go talk to so-and-so and get some reports from them. By having me do this, the Thais were wondering several things: Why should we deal with her; she is just a secretary, and have I done something wrong that the boss does not want to talk with me? Finally, I got my boss to understand that when he had a request for someone—especially someone who was high-ranking in the company, someone who was much older than me or had been with the company longer than me—I would write a short note to that person, he would sign it, then I would pass the note along. That way, everyone's face was saved, their positions were recognized, and the boss came across as showing that he cared about his personal relationships with everyone. Mind you, I can run over and ask others of my same rank, age, or time with the company for any information or a meeting, but it is important to show respect toward those in high positions.*
> —Chris

Tom that, although both parties followed *la forme de la politesse,* the agent did not want to give him the train schedule in French. Indeed, it was not near the end of the season because he requested the schedule in January and the annual train schedule ran from June 1 to May 23.

From a communication perspective, it might not be at all clear that an intercultural struggle had taken place. None of the traditional signals of conflict were manifested: no raised voices, no harsh words, no curtness. Indeed, the exchange seemed polite and courteous.

From a cultural perspective, however, with various contexts and power differentials in mind, a different view of this intercultural interaction emerges. Belgium is a nation largely divided by two cultures, Flemish and Walloon, although there is a small German-speaking minority in the far eastern part of the country. Belgium is officially trilingual (Dutch, French, German); that is, each language is the official language in its territory. Dutch is the official language in Flanders, and French is the official language in Wallonia, except in the eastern part, where German is the official language. The only part of Belgium that is officially bilingual is the "Brussels-Capital Region."

ANSWERS TO THE TEST OF U.S. CULTURAL KNOWLEDGE

1. The correct answer is B. Lagniappe refers to small freebies or sometimes small gifts given by stores when you purchase something. It is used mostly in southern Louisiana and Mississippi and also along the Gulf Coast.

2. The correct answer is C. Hoppin' John is a New Year's tradition across the South. Normally it is simply rice and black-eyed peas, but it can include other items.

3. The correct answer is C. Shoofly pie, traditionally made from molasses, is a very sweet pie.

4. The correct answer is D. The Illini are a nonexistent tribe used as the mascot of the University of Illinois at Urbana-Champaign.

5. The correct answer is A. Also sometimes just called Eid, this is a 3-day joyous festival that celebrates family, friendship, community, and the Creator. It is a time of reconciliation.

6. The correct answer is A. It marks the anniversary of the Supreme Court ruling in *Loving v. Virginia* that overturned legal barriers to interracial marriage.

7. The correct answer is D. Hanamatsuri (or flower festival) is in the spring and marks a time of renewal and the birthday of Buddha.

8. The correct answer is A. Lefse is made primarily from potatoes.

9. The correct answer is D. Menudo is traditionally served on New Year's Day.

10. The correct answer is C. Haupia is made from coconut milk.

There are many historical contexts to consider here. For example, Brussels is historically a Flemish city, located in Flanders (but near the border with Wallonia). Also, the French language dominated in Belgium from the time it gained independence from the Netherlands in 1830 until the early 20th century when Flemish gained parity.

There are social and economic contexts to consider as well. Since the 1960s, Flanders has been more economically powerful than Wallonia. The Brussels-Capital Region, despite being in Flanders, has become increasingly French speaking; some estimates place the current percentage of francophones at 85% to 90%. And nearly 30% of Brussels' residents are foreigners, most of whom are francophones. The increasing migration of city dwellers to the suburbs has also caused tensions because a number of communes located in Flanders now have a francophone majority.

So, although the Brussels-Capital Region is officially bilingual, this is the site of a number of struggles between French and Dutch. Indeed, as many Walloons told Tom, one does not get a sense of the conflict in Wallonia, but it is evident in Brussels. In the context of the various tensions that existed at the time of Tom's arrival in Belgium, the intercultural conflict at the train station is merely a playing out of much larger issues in Belgian society. Tom's entry into that society, as another francophone foreigner, situated his communication interactions in largely prefigured ways.

Although he later secured a French train schedule, he continued to use the Dutch one so he could learn the Dutch names of many Belgian cities as well. In any case, Tom's experience involved various dialectical tensions: (1) being a francophone foreigner versus a traditional Flemish resident, (2) being in an officially bilingual region versus an increasingly francophone one, (3) recognizing the importance of formality and politeness in French versus the nature of this ancient conflict, (4) having abundant opportunities to learn French versus the lack of opportunities to study Dutch in the United States, and (5) illustrating the economic power of the Flemish in Belgium versus that of the francophones in Brussels. From these dialectical tensions and others, Tom attempted to understand and contextualize his intercultural interaction.

There are no simple lists of behaviors that are key to successful intercultural interaction. Instead, we encourage you to understand the contexts and dialectical tensions that arise in your intercultural communication experiences. In this way, you will better understand the constraints you face in your interactions. You will also come to a better understanding of the culture you are in and the culture you are from. Although the dialectical perspective makes the investigation of culture and communication far more complex, it also makes it far more exciting and interesting and leads to a much richer understanding.

INTERNET RESOURCES

www.geert-hofstede.com
This Geert Hofstede Cultural Dimensions website provides a description of Hofstede's cultural values dimensions and the specific value scores for a variety of countries and regions of the world. For those of you who may be studying, working, or traveling abroad, you may find it useful to compare the values scores of your home culture and host culture to better understand how the two cultures are similar and different according to Hofstede's cultural dimensions.

www.powerofculture.nl/en
The Power of Culture website provides a review of art and cultural expressions, along with information on human rights, education, the environment, emancipation, and democratization. The website provides links to themes, such as cultural exchange and culture, conflict and culture, and ethics, with news stories and articles related to the subject matter.

www.unesco.org/new/en/culture/
This UNESCO Culture Sector website provides links to relevant news and events along with general background information about the changing realm of culture, both regionally and globally. The website also provides links that describe the culture and people from different regions worldwide, such as the Arab states, Latin America, the Caribbean, Europe, and North America.

www.globalvoicesonline.org/
The Global Voices Online website is sponsored by Harvard's Berkman Center for Internet and Society. The site provides blogs, podcasts, photo-sharing sites, and videoblogs from around the world. There is a site search available along with an index of countries and topics. You can select a topic, such as racism or politics, and select the country you wish to read and learn more about in terms of that topic.

SUMMARY

- There are four building blocks to understanding intercultural communication: culture, communication, context, and power.
- Culture can be viewed as
  - Learned patterns of group-related perceptions
  - Contextual symbolic patterns of meaning, involving emotions
  - Heterogeneous, dynamic, and a site of contestation
- Communication is a symbolic process whereby reality is produced, maintained, repaired, and transformed.
- Communication can be viewed as
  - Components of speaker, sender, receiver, message and channel, and variables
  - Symbolic and processual
  - Involving power dynamics
- The relationship between culture and communication is complex:
  - Culture influences communication and is enacted and reinforced through communication.
  - Communication also may be a way of contesting and resisting the dominant culture.
- The context also influences communication: It is the physical (or virtual) and social setting in which communication occurs or the larger political, social, and historical environment.
- Power is pervasive and plays an enormous, although sometimes hidden, role in intercultural interactions.

DISCUSSION QUESTIONS

1. How do definitions of culture influence people's perspectives on intercultural communication?
2. How do the values of a cultural group influence communication with members of other cultural groups?
3. What techniques do people use to assert power in communication interactions?
4. How is culture a contested site?

ACTIVITIES

1. *Cultural Values.* Look for advertisements online or on social media. Analyze the ads to see if you can identify the social values to which they appeal.

2. *Culture: Deeply Felt or Contested Zone?* Analyze the lyrics of songs you listen to and try to identify patterns in the songs. Then think about your own cultural position and discuss which framework—the one proposed by cultural ethnographies (culture as deeply felt) or the one proposed by cultural studies (culture as a contested zone)—more adequately articulates the connection between culture and communication.

KEY WORDS

autoethnography (107)
communication (91)
communication
    rules (107)
cultural values (95)
culture (83)
embodied
    ethnocentrism (88)

ethnography of
    communication (87)
indulgent vs restraint
    orientation (104)
long-term versus short-
    term orientation (104)
masculinity–femininity
    value (104)

performative (107)
power distance (102)
symbolic
    significance (87)
uncertainty
    avoidance (104)

REFERENCES

Allen, B. (2011). *Difference matters: Communicating social identity* (2nd ed.). Long Grove, IL: Waveland Press.

Amaya, H. (2007). Performing acculturation: Rewriting the Latino/a immigrant self. *Text and Performance Quarterly*, 27(3), 194–212.

Ambler, T., & Witzel, M. (2000). *Doing business in China.* New York: Routledge.

Baldwin, J. R., Faulkner S. L., & Hecht, M. L. (2006). A moving target: The illusive definition of culture. In J. R. Baldwin, S. L. Faulkner, M. L. Hecht, & S. L. Lindsley (Eds.), *Redefining culture: Perspectives across the disciplines* (pp. 3–26). Mahwah, NJ: Lawrence Erlbaum Associates.

Bellah, R. N., Madsen, R., Sullivan, W. M., Swidler, A., & Tipton, S. M. (2007). *Habits of the heart: Individualism and commitment in American life.* Berkeley, CA: University of California Press.

Bennett, M. J. (2013). *Basic concepts of intercultural communication: Paradigms, principles, & practices* (2nd ed.) Boston, MA: Nicholas Brealey.

Bennett, M. J., & Castiglioni, I. (2004). Embodied ethnocentrism and the feeling of culture. In D. Landis, J. M. Bennett, & M. J. Bennett (Eds.), *Handbook of intercultural training* (3rd ed., pp. 249–265). Thousand Oaks, CA: Sage.

Berger, Y. (1998, January 7). A bout portant. *Le Soir,* p. 2.

Burke, J. (1985). *The day the universe changed.* Boston, MA: Little, Brown.

Buzzanell, P. M. (ed.) (2000). *Rethinking organizational and managerial communication from feminist perspectives.* Thousand Oaks, CA: Sage.

Carbaugh, D. (2007). Cultural discourse analysis: Communication practices and intercultural encounters. *Journal of Intercultural Communication Research*, 36(3), 167–182

Carey, J. W. (1989). *Communication as culture: Essays on media and society.* Boston, MA: Unwin Hyman.

Cargile, A. (2005). Describing culture dialectically. In W. J. Starosta, & G.-M. Chen (Eds.), *Taking stock in intercultural communication: Where to now?* (pp. 99–123). Washington, DC: National Communication Association.

Chavez, K. (2009). Remapping *Latinidad*: A performance cartography of Latino/a in rural Nebraska. *Text and Performance Quarterly, 29*(2), 165–182.

Cheong, P. H., Shuter, R. & Suwinyattichaiporn, T. (2016). Managing student digital distractions and hyperconnectivity: communication strategies and challenges for professorial authority. *Communication Education, 65*(3), 272–289.

Chinese Culture Connection (1987). Chinese values and the search for culture-free dimensions of culture. *Journal of Cross-Cultural Psychology, 18,* 143–164.

Collier, M. J., Hegde, R. S., Lee, W., Nakayama, T. K., & Yep, G. A. (2002). Dialogue on the edges: Ferment in communication and culture. In M. J. Collier (Ed.), *Transforming communication about culture (International and Intercultural Communication Annual,* vol. 24, pp. 219–280). Thousand Oaks, CA: Sage.

Day, E. (2015, July 19). #Black lives matter: The birth of a new civil rights movement. *Theguardian.com.* Retrieved April 10, 2016, from http://www.theguardian.com/world/2015/jul/19/blacklivesmatter-birth-civil-rights-movement

Delgado, F. (2009). Reflections on being/performing Latino identity in the academy. *Text and Performance Quarterly, 29*(2), 149–164.

Dunbar, R. A. (1997). Bloody footprints: Reflections on growing up poor white. In M. Wray, & A. Newitz (Eds.), *White trash: Race and class in America* (pp. 73–86). New York: Routledge.

Engstrom, C. L. (2012). "Yes . . ., But I Was Drunk": Alcohol references and the (re)production of masculinity on a college campus. *Communication Quarterly, 60*(3), 403–423.

Geertz, C. (1973). *The interpretation of culture.* New York: Basic Books.

Grossberg, L. (1993). Can cultural studies find true happiness in communication? *Journal of Communication, 43*(4), 89–97.

Hall, B. (1992). Theories of culture and communication. *Communication Theory, 1,* 50–70.

Hall, S. (1992). Cultural studies and its theoretical legacies. In L. Grossberg, C. Nelson, & P. Treichler (Eds.), *Cultural studies* (pp. 277–294). New York: Routledge.

Halualani, R. T. (2011). In/visible dimensions: Framing the intercultural communication course through a critical intercultural communication framework. *Intercultural Education, 22*(1), 43–54.

Hofstede, G. (1984). *Culture's consequences.* Beverly Hills, CA: Sage.

Hofstede, G., Hofstede, G. J., & Minkov, M. (2010). *Cultures and organizations: Software of the mind* (Revised and Expanded 3rd ed.). Boston, MA: McGraw-Hill.

Hymes, D. (1972). Models of the interaction of language and social life. In J. Gumperz, & D. Hymes (Eds.), *Directions in sociolinguistics: The ethnography of speaking* (pp. 35–71). New York: Holt, Rinehart & Winston.

Johnson, A. G. (2006). *Privilege, power, and difference* (2nd ed.). Boston, MA: McGraw-Hill.

Kirkman, B. L., Lowe, K. B., & Gibson, C. B. (2006). A quarter century of culture's consequences: A review of empirical research incorporating Hofstede's cultural values framework. *Journal of International Business Studies, 37,* 285–320.

Kluckhohn, F., & Strodtbeck, F. (1961). *Variations in value orientations.* Chicago, IL: Row, Peterson.

Kohls, L. R. (1996). *Survival kit for overseas living.* Yarmouth, ME: Intercultural Press.

Kristjánsdóttir, E. S. (2009). Invisibility dreaded and desired: Phenomenological inquiry of sojourners' cross-cultural adaptation. *Howard Journal of Communications, 20*(2), 129–146.

Loden, M., & Rosener, J. B. (1991). *Workforce American! Managing employee diversity as a vital resource.* Homewood, IL: Business One Irwin.

Martin, J. N., & Nakayama, T. K. (1999). Thinking dialectically about culture and communication. *Communication Theory, 9,* 1–25.

Orbe, M. O. (1998). *Constructing co-cultural theory: An explication of culture, power, and communication.* Thousand Oaks, CA: Sage.

Philipsen, G. (2002). Cultural communication. In W. B. Gudykunst, & B. Mody (Eds.), *Handbook of international and intercultural communication* (2nd ed., pp. 51–67). Thousand Oaks, CA: Sage.

Piff, P. K., Kraus, M. W., Côté, S., Cheng, B. H., & Keltner, D. (2010). Having less, giving more: The influence of social class on prosocial behavior. *Journal of Personality and Social Psychology, 99*(5), 771–784.

Root, E. (2013) Insights into the differences—similarities dialectic in intercultural communication from university students' narratives. *Intercultural Communication Studies, 22*(3), 61–79.

Shim, Y-j., Kim, M-S, & Martin, J. N. (2008). *Changing Korea: Understanding culture and communication.* New York: Peter Lang.

Sobré-Denton, M., & Bardhan, N. (2013). *Cultivating Cosmopolitanism for intercultural communication: Communicating as global citizens.* New York: Routledge.

Stewart, E. C., & Bennett, M. J. (1991). *American cultural patterns: A cross-cultural perspective.* Yarmouth, ME: Intercultural Press.

Tracy, S. J. (2000). Becoming a character for commerce: Emotion labor, self-subordination, and discursive construction of identity in a total institution. *Management Communication Quarterly, 14*(1), 90–128.

Trethewey, A. (1997). Resistance, identity, and empowerment: A postmodern feminist analysis of clients in a human service organization. *Communication Monographs, 64,* 281–301.

Walmsley, R. (2015). *World Prison Population List* (11th ed.) Institute for Criminal Policy Research (ICPR). Retrieved April 10, 2016, from http://www.prisonstudies.org/sites/default/files/resources/downloads/world_prison_population_list_11th_edition.pdf

Williams, R. (1981). The analysis of culture. In T. Bennett, G. Martin, C. Mercer, & J. Woollacott (Eds.), *Culture, ideology and social process: A reader* (pp. 43–52). London: Open University Press.

Williams, R. (1983). *Keywords: A vocabulary of culture and society* (Rev. ed.). New York: Oxford University Press.

CREDITS

HISTORY AND INTERCULTURAL COMMUNICATION

FROM HISTORY TO HISTORIES
Political, Intellectual, and Social Histories
Family Histories
National Histories
Cultural-Group Histories

HISTORY, POWER, AND
INTERCULTURAL COMMUNICATION
The Power of Texts
The Power of Other Histories
Power in Intercultural Interactions

HISTORY AND IDENTITY
Histories as Stories
Nonmainstream Histories

INTERCULTURAL COMMUNICATION
AND HISTORY
Antecedents of Contact
The Contact Hypothesis
Negotiating Histories Dialectically in Interaction

INTERNET RESOURCES

SUMMARY

DISCUSSION QUESTIONS

ACTIVITIES

KEY WORDS

REFERENCES

CHAPTER OBJECTIVES

After reading this chapter, you should be able to:

1. Identify six different types of history.
2. Define "the grand narrative."
3. Explain the relationship between history, power, and intercultural communication.
4. Describe the role of narratives in constructing history.
5. Describe the relationship between history and identity.
6. Identify seven types of hidden histories.
7. Identify four antecedents that influence intercultural contact.
8. Explain the contact hypothesis.
9. Identify eight contact conditions that influence positive attitude change.
10. Describe a dialectic perspective in negotiating personal histories.

> *Americans ignore history, for to them everything has always seemed new under the sun. The national myth is that of creativity and progress, of a steady climbing upward into power and prosperity, both for the individual and for the country as a whole. Americans see history as a straight line and themselves standing at the cutting edge of it as representatives for all mankind. They believe in the future as if it were a religion; they believe that there is nothing they cannot accomplish, that solutions wait somewhere for all problems.*

In writing about the Vietnam War, Frances FitzGerald (1972), a journalist, contrasted the U.S. orientation to history with the Vietnamese cultural orientation. This difference in orientation to the past framed the Vietnam conflict in a very narrow way for the United States. This contrasts greatly with the Vietnamese view of history, especially in the context of their struggles against outside aggression over thousands of years.

You may think it odd to find a chapter about history in a book on intercultural communication. After all, what does the past have to do with intercultural interaction? In this chapter, we discuss how the past is a very important facet of intercultural communication.

The history that we know and our views of that history are very much influenced by our culture. When people of different cultural backgrounds encounter one another, the differences among them can become hidden barriers to communication. However, people often overlook such dynamics in intercultural communication. We typically think of "history" as something contained in history books. We may view history as those events and people, mostly military and political, that played significant roles in shaping the world of today. This chapter examines some of the ways in which history is important in understanding intercultural interaction. Many intercultural interactions involve a dialectical interplay between past and present.

We have found, in the classes we teach, that European American students often want to deemphasize history. "Why do we have to dwell on the past? Can't we all move on?" they ask. In contrast, some other students argue that without history it is impossible to understand who they are. How do these different viewpoints affect the communication among such students? What is the possibility for meaningful communication interactions among them?

On a larger scale, we can see how history influences intercultural interaction in many different contexts. For example, the ongoing conflict between the Israelis and the Palestinians makes little sense without an understanding of the historical relations among the different groups that reside in the area. Historical antagonisms help explain the present-day animosity felt by many Pakistanis toward Indians. Disputes over the Kashmir region, Indian participation in the struggle for independence of Bangladesh, and conflicts over the Himalayas underscore deep-rooted bases for strife.

How we think about the past very much influences how we think about ourselves and others even here in the United States. Judith went to college in southern Virginia after growing up in Delaware and Pennsylvania. She was shocked to encounter the antipathy that her dormitory suitemates expressed toward northerners. The suitemates stated emphatically that they had no desire to visit the North; they felt certain that "Yankees" were unfriendly and unpleasant people.

For Judith, the Civil War was a paragraph in a history book; for her suitemates, that historical event held a more important meaning. It took a while for friendships to develop between Judith and her suitemates. In this way, their interactions demonstrated the present–past dialectic. Indeed, this exemplifies the central focus of this chapter: that various histories contextualize intercultural communication. Taking a dialectical perspective enables us to understand how history positions people in different places from which they can communicate and understand other people's messages.

Earlier in this book, we set forth six dialectical tensions that we believe drive much intercultural interaction. In this chapter, we focus on the history/past–present/ future dialectic. As you will see, culture and cultural identities are intimately tied to history because they have no meaning without history. Yet there is no single version of history; the past has been written in many different ways. For example, your own family has its version of family history that must be placed in dialectical tension with all of the other narratives about the past. Is it important to you to feel positive about who your forebears were and where they came from? We often feel a strong need to identify in positive ways with our past even if we are not interested in history. The stories of the past, whether accurate or not, help us understand why our families live where they do, why they own or lost land there, and so on. We experience this dialectical tension between the past, the present, and the future every day. It helps us understand who we are and why we live and communicate in the ways we do.

In this chapter, we first discuss the various histories that provide the contexts in which we communicate: political, intellectual, social, family, national, and cultural-group histories. We then describe how these histories are intertwined with our various identities, based on gender, sexual orientation, ethnicity, race, and so on. We introduce two identities that have strong historical bases: diasporic and colonial. We pay particular attention to the role of narrating our personal histories. As you read this chapter, think about the importance of history in constructing your own identity and the ways in which the past–present dialectic helps us understand different identities for others in various cultural groups. Finally, we explore how history influences intercultural communication.

FROM HISTORY TO HISTORIES

Many different kinds of history influence our understanding of who we are—as individuals, as family members, as members of cultural groups, and as citizens of a nation. To understand the dialectics in everyday interaction, we need to think about the many histories that help form our different identities. These histories necessarily overlap and influence each other. For example, when Fidel Castro came to power in Cuba in the 1950s, some Cubans left Cuba and came to the United States. Today, the families that departed and those that have stayed

have a complex relationship and a desire to reunite. "When Mr. Obama fulfilled that promise with a policy change in 2009, a rush to Cuba began. Now more than 400,000 Cuban-Americans go annually. When Mr. Castro later signaled a shift of his own, no longer calling exiles gusanos, or worms, [...] the divide between Cuban and Cuban-American, between exile and loyalist, eased further away" (Cave, 2016). Political histories tell the story of that exodus but not necessarily the story of every family, even though many families' histories were very much influenced by that event. Identifying the various forms of historical contexts is the first step in understanding how history affects communication. (See Figure 4-1.)

political histories
Written histories that focus on political events.

intellectual histories
Written histories that focus on the development of ideas.

Political, Intellectual, and Social Histories

Some people restrict their notion of history to documented events. Although we cannot read every book written, we do have greater access to written history. When these types of history focus on political events, we call them **political histories.** Written histories that focus on the development of ideas are often called **intellectual histories.**

Some writers seek to understand the everyday life experiences of various groups in the past; what they document are called **social histories.**

Although these types of history seem more manageable than the broad notion of history as "everything that has happened before now," we must also remember that many historical events never make it into books. For example, the strict laws that forbade teaching slaves in the United States to read kept many of their stories from being documented. **Absent history,** of course, does not mean the people did not exist, their experiences do not matter, or their history has no bearing on us today. To consider such absent histories requires that we think in more complex ways about the past and the ways it influences the present and the future.

Absent history is also the result of concealing the past. One important way that this happens is when the past is deliberately erased or hidden. Until July 2016, the U.S. government had kept 28 pages of the 9/11 Commission's report hidden or unavailable to the public. Under tremendous public pressure, the U.S. government finally released the hidden 28 pages. In contrast, the report that looked into the 1961 Bay of Pigs invasion in Cuba has remained classified and unavailable to the public. Our understanding of the history and the role of the Central Intelligence Agency (CIA) remains a part of hidden history. After so many decades, many people wonder why the role of the U.S. government in this invasion should remain a part of absent history.

Altered history is another way that influences how we see ourselves and others. In altered history, the past is changed to fit particular worldviews and interests. In this sense, history is not a series of facts to be memorized, but a place where the past can be used for present interests and goals. Altered history is not the same as alternative history. Alternative history is a fictional genre in which authors try to speculate on what the world would look like if particular scenarios in the past had happened, for example, the South won the Civil War, Germany and Japan won World War II. Altered history is often presented in textbooks where "There is a constant tension between those who believe that textbooks exist to promote fervent patriotism and those who believe that they exist to promote dispassionate analysis" (Gardner, 2014). Recent textbook controversies have erupted over the ways that the past is portrayed not only in Japanese textbooks, but also Korean, Chinese, German, U.S. American, and Saudi Arabian, among others. Another recent revelation is that the ancient Egyptian pharaoh, Hatshepsut, was one of several early female pharaohs. In 2016, the Egyptian Minister of Antiquities announced recent research that: "In the reign of Thutmosis III, all mentions of her name were erased and all representations of her female figure were replaced by images of a male king, her deceased husband Thutmosis II" (Izadi, 2016). In this case, the past is not erased, but altered to construct a different, gendered view of the pharaohs.

Family Histories

Family histories occur at the same time as other histories but on a more personal level. They often are not written down but are passed along orally from one generation to the next. Some people do not know which countries or cities their families

---

social histories Written histories that focus on everyday life experiences of various groups in the past.

absent history Any part of history that was not recorded or that is missing. Not everything that happened in the past is accessible to us today because only some voices were documented and only some perspectives were recorded.

altered history Sometimes historical events are changed in order to serve particular ideological goals. This communication practice results in a revised history.

family histories Histories of individual families that are typically passed down through oral stories.

emigrated from or what tribes they belonged to or where they lived in the United States. Other people place great emphasis on knowing that their ancestors fought in the Revolutionary War, survived the Holocaust, or traveled the Trail of Tears when the Cherokees were forcibly relocated from the Southeast to present-day Oklahoma. Many of these family histories are deeply intertwined with ethnic-group histories, but the family histories identify each family's participation in these events.

Sometimes, family histories shed some light on well-known figures. In his autobiography, *Dreams From My Father,* Barak Obama recounts his family's history from his mother's family in Kansas and their migration to Hawaii to his father's Kenyan family and his connection to them. Although he did not have much contact with his father's family until after his father passed away, his visit to Kenya thrust him back into that part of his family history. More recently, on a visit to Ireland, Obama went to the town where his forebearer, Falmouth Kearney, a shoemaker, lived before immigrating to the United States in 1850 (Mason & Halpin, 2011). His family history is one of immigration and migration that is one part of U.S. history.

Michelle Obama's family reflects a very different family history that is entwined in another part of the nation's story: slavery. *The New York Times* traced her family history and found: "the more complete map of Mrs. Obama's ancestors—including the slave mother, white father and their biracial son, Dolphus T. Shields—for the first time fully connects the first African-American first lady to the history of slavery, tracing their five-generation journey from bondage to a front-row seat to the presidency" (Swarns & Kantor, 2009). Think about how these family histories inform us and the Obamas about their past, as well as their place in the United States and in the world.

You might talk to members of your own family to discover how they feel about your family's history. Find out, for example, how family history influences their perceptions of who they are. Do they wish they knew more about their family? What things has your family continued to do that your forebears probably also did? Do you eat some of the same foods? Practice the same religion? Celebrate birthdays or weddings in the same way? The continuity between past and present often is taken for granted.

National Histories

national history
A body of knowledge based on past events that influenced a country's development.

The history of any nation is important to the people of that nation. We typically learn **national history** in school. In the United States, we learn about the founding fathers—George Washington, Benjamin Franklin, John Jay, Alexander Hamilton, and so on—and our national history typically begins with the arrival of Europeans in North America in the 16th century.

U.S. citizens are expected to recognize the great events and the so-called great people (mostly men of European ancestry) who were influential in the development of the nation. In history classes, students learn about the Revolutionary War, Thomas Paine, the War of 1812, the Civil War, Abraham Lincoln, the Great Depression, Franklin D. Roosevelt, and so on. They are told stories, verging on myths, that give life to these events and figures. For example, students learn about Patrick Henry's

THE FIRST SLAVERY MUSEUM

The history of slavery is an important part of U.S. history. Why is there no federally funded museum about slavery? One man's approach is to undertake the project himself.

"A nation builds museums to understand its own history and to have its history understood by others, to create a common space and language to address collectively what is too difficult to process individually. Forty-eight years after World War II, the United States Holocaust Memorial Museum opened in Washington. A museum dedicated to the September 11 terrorist attacks opened its doors in Lower Manhattan less than 13 years after they occurred. One hundred and fifty years after the end of the Civil War, however, no federally funded museum dedicated to slavery exists, no monument honoring America's slaves." Thirty-five miles west of New Orleans, along Louisiana's River Road, John Cummings, a wealthy white man, purchased the Whitney Plantation with the goal of telling the story of slavery. Among the plantations along River Road, the *"most conspicuous are those that have been restored for tourists, transporting them into a world of bygone Southern grandeur—one in which mint juleps, manicured gardens, and hoop skirts are emphasized over the fact that such grandeur was made possible by the enslavement of black human beings."* In contrast, the Whitney Plantation has been turned into a museum about slavery. *"What makes slavery so difficult to think about, from the vantage point of history, is that it was both at odds with America's founding values—freedom, liberty, democracy—and critical to how they flourished. The Declaration of Independence proclaiming that "all men are created equal" was drafted by men who were afforded the time to debate its language because the land that enriched many of them was tended to by slaves. The White House and the Capitol were built, in part, by slaves."* Cummings feels that the history of slavery is too important to ignore and notes, *"But just in case you're worried about people getting distracted by the pretty house over there, the last thing you'll see before leaving here will be 60 beheaded slaves."*

Source: From D. Amsden, "Building the first slavery museum in America." *New York Times,* February 26, 2015. Retrieved April 15, 2016, from http://www.nytimes.com/2015/03/01/magazine/building-the-first-slave-museum-in-america.html?_r=0.

"give me liberty or give me death" speech even though the text of the speech was collected by a biographer who "pieced together twelve hundred words from scattered fragments that ear witnesses remembered from twenty years before" (Thonssen, Baird, & Braden, 1970, p. 335). Students also learn about George Washington having chopped down a cherry tree and confessing his guilt ("I cannot tell a lie"), although there's no evidence of this story's truth.

National history gives us a shared notion of who we are and solidifies our sense of nationhood. Although we may not fit into the national narrative, we are expected to be familiar with this particular telling of U.S. history so we can understand the many references used in communication. It is one way of constructing cultural discourses. Yet U.S. students seldom learn much about the histories of other nations and cultures unless they study the languages of those countries. As any student of another language knows, it is part of the curriculum to study not only the grammar and vocabulary of the language but also the culture and history of the people who speak that language.

Judith and Tom both studied French. Because we learned a great deal about French history, we understand references to the *ancien régime* (the political system prior to the French Revolution in 1789), *les Pieds-noirs* (colonial French who returned to France during the struggle for Algerian independence in the mid-20th century), *la Bastille* (the notorious prison), and other commonly used terms. The French have their own national history, centering on the development of France as a nation. For example, French people know that they live in the *Vème République* (or Fifth Republic), and they know what that means within the grand narrative of French history.

When Judith lived in Algeria, her French friends spoke of *les Événements* (the events), but her Algerian friends spoke of *la Libération*—both referring to the war between France and Algeria that led to Algerian independence. When Tom lived in France, he also heard the expression *la Libération,* but here it referred to the end of the German occupation in France during World War II. Historical contexts shape language, which means we must search for salient historical features in communicating across cultural differences.

Cultural-Group Histories

Although people may share a single national history, each cultural group within the nation may have its own history. The history may be obscure (hidden), but it is still related to the national history. **Cultural-group histories** help us understand the identities of various groups.

cultural-group histories The history of each cultural group within a nation that includes, for example, the history of where the group originated, why the people migrated, and how they came to develop and maintain their cultural traits.

Consider, for example, the expulsion of many Acadians from eastern Canada and their migration to and settlement in Louisiana. These historical events are central to understanding the cultural traits of the Cajuns. Their neighbors, the Creoles, have been displaced by a more recent historical event, Hurricane Katrina. It remains unclear how the hurricane will shape Creole culture. "With their geographic underpinnings swept away, many New Orleanians of Creole descent are trying to figure out how best to preserve a community separated from both its birthplace and home base" (Saulny, 2005, p. A13). The forced removal in 1838 of the Cherokees from Georgia to settlements in what eventually became the state of Oklahoma resulted in a 22% loss of the Cherokee population. This event, known as the Trail of Tears, explains much about the Cherokee Nation. The migration in 1846 of 12,000 Latter Day Saints from Nauvoo, Illinois, to the Great Basin region in the western United States was prompted by anti-Mormon attacks. These events explain much about the character of Utah. The northward migration of African Americans in the early part of the 20th century helps us understand the settlement patterns and working conditions in northern cities such as Cleveland, Detroit, Chicago, and New York. These cultural histories are not typically included in our national history, but they are important in the development of group identity, family histories, and contemporary lives of individual members of these cocultures.

I am the fourth generation of females raised in Philadelphia. My great-grandmother raised me until she died, when I was 13. Her mother was a slave who had 19 children. Charlotte, North Carolina, was the place my great-grandmother said she was born. I care because my grandmother had personal information about why blacks should be glad slavery is over. She encouraged my family to make use of all of the benefits of freedom. She always said, "Get an education so you can own something, because we couldn't own anything. We couldn't even go to school." So that is why she moved to the city of Philadelphia. She made getting an education a reward instead of a joke.
—Marlene

I was born and raised in Pakistan, and lived there until I was 7 years old. I remember growing up there very well, but I also remember very well when we moved out of Pakistan. I am basically the first generation in my family to grow up outside of Pakistan. Today most of the immigrants that live in the United States moved here a very long time ago. They have ancestors that came to the United States a long time ago. That is not the case with my family. In addition the immigration to the United States for my family was different in the fact that at first we moved to Canada and then we moved to the United States.
—Waleed

My family immigrated to the United States for a better life. I didn't realize that my family history had so much involvement with the history I learned in class. For instance, my great-grandfather was an orphan who rode the orphan train west from New York until a family chose him and his brother to work on their farm. I also had a member of my family die during WWII, some lived in Chicago during the Chicago Fire, and my great grandpa was a rural mail carrier who used a horse and buggy to deliver the mail. Something I didn't know before was my grandpa, who now works for Burlington Northern, started out as an apprentice telegraph operator. . . . He has come quite far from that!
—William

We prefer to view history as the many stories we tell about the past, rather than one story on a single time continuum. Certainly, the events of families, cultural groups, and nations are related. Even world events are related. Ignorance of the histories of other groups makes intercultural communication more difficult and more susceptible to misunderstandings.

HISTORY, POWER, AND INTERCULTURAL COMMUNICATION

Power is a central dynamic in the writing of history. It influences the content of the history we know and the way it is delivered. Power dictates what is taught and what is silenced, what is available and what is erased. Let's look at what this means.

FIGURE 4-2   Memorial Day services are being held by internees at the Manzanar Internment Camp for U.S. Americans of Japanese ancestry during World War II. Although the U.S. Supreme Court upheld the constitutionality of the internment of U.S. citizens based on their ethnicity, the U.S. government later apologized. (*Courtesy Francis Stewart Gallery/National Park Service*)

The Power of Texts

History is extremely important in understanding identity. Think about all of the stories about the past that you have been taught. Yet, as literature professor Fredric Jameson (1981) notes, although history is not a narrative at all, it is accessible to us only in textual, narrative form. However, people do not have equal access to the writing and production of these texts.

Political texts reflect the disparities of access to political participation in various countries at various times in history. Some languages have been forbidden, making the writing of texts difficult if not impossible. For example, U.S. government Indian schools did not permit Native American children to speak their native languages, which makes it more difficult for people today to understand what this experience was about.

With regard to the language we use to understand history, think about the difference between the terms *internment camp* and *concentration camp*. In 1942, at the height of World War II, after President Franklin Roosevelt signed Executive Order 9066, anyone of Japanese ancestry—whether they were U.S. citizens or not—was rounded up from a restricted zone, including parts of Arizona, Oregon, and Washington and all of California, and placed mostly into 10 camps. (See Figure 4-2.) The U.S. federal government used both terms in the 1940s, but the historical weight of the German concentration camps of the same era, in which millions of Jews perished, often casts a

The internment, or mass imprisonment, of Japanese Americans by the U.S. government in the 1940s has led to much discussion about the right term for these camps. What difference does it make if we call them "concentration camps" or "relocation centers"? This entry from the *Encyclopedia of Japanese American History* provides food for thought.

> **Concentration camps.** *Euphemistically called "relocation centers" by the War Relocation Authority (WRA), the concentration camps were hastily constructed facilities for housing Japanese Americans forcibly removed from their homes and businesses on the West Coast during World War II. Located in isolated areas of the United States on either desert or swampland, the camps were usually surrounded by barbed wire and guarded by armed sentries. Although these sentries were presumably in place to protect the inmates from hostile outsiders, their guns usually pointed into the camps instead of away from them. Most inmates were transported to their camp by train from an assembly center between April and September 1942. In all, over 120,000 Japanese Americans served time in these camps.*

Source: From B. Niiya (Ed.), *Encyclopedia of Japanese American History: An A-to-Z Reference from 1868 to the Present* (New York: Checkmark Books, 2001), p. 142.

shadow over our understanding of the U.S. concentration camps. Denotatively, the use of the term *concentration camp* is correct, but connotatively, it invokes quite different responses. You may wish to keep this in mind as you read Chapter 6, which discusses the importance of language and discourse in intercultural communication.

When U.S. Americans are taught history, they also learn a particular way of looking at the world from their history textbooks. This worldview, as James Loewen (1995) tells us, reinforces a very positive white American identity. In his analysis of history textbooks, he notes, "History is furious debate informed by evidence and reason. Textbooks encourage students to believe that history is facts to be learned" (p. 16). Yet these "facts" are often wrong or portray the past in ways that serve the white American identity. For example, he analyzes the way in which Native Americans are depicted in history texts:

> *Even if no Natives remained among us, however, it would still be important for us to understand the alternatives forgone, to remember the wars, and to learn the unvarnished truths about white–Indian relations. Indian history is the antidote to the pious ethnocentrism of American exceptionalism, the notion that European Americans are God's chosen people. Indian history reveals that the United States and its predecessor British colonies have wrought great harm in the world. We must not forget this—not to wallow in our wrongdoing, but to understand and to learn, that we might not wreak harm again. (p. 136)*

But the prevailing value of teaching history lies not in serving the future but in reinforcing a positive cultural identity for white Americans. How does power function in determining which stories are told and how they are told?

concentration camp A place where governments have interned people from various religious or ethnic groups who usually did not have trials and were not convicted of any crimes.

The relative availability of political texts and the ways that they reflect powerful inequities are reinscribed in the process of writing history. History writing requires documentation and texts and, of course, is limited by what is available. In writing history, we often ask ourselves, "What was important?" without asking, "Important to whom? For what purposes?" Once texts are written, they are available for teaching and learning about the past. But the seeming unity of the past, the linear nature of history, is merely the reflection of a **modernist identity**, grounded in the Western tradition.

modernist identity
The identity that is grounded in the Western tradition of scientific and political beliefs and assumptions—for example, the belief in external reality, democratic representation, liberation, and independent subjects.

grand narrative
A unified history and view of humankind.

The Power of Other Histories

We live in an era of rapid change, which causes us to rethink cultural struggles and identities. It may be difficult for you to envision, but at one time a unified story of humankind—the **grand narrative**—dominated how people thought of the past, present, and future. The grand narrative refers to the overarching, all-encompassing story of a nation or humankind in general. Because of the way it is built, this grand narrative organizes history into an understandable story that leads to some "truths" over other possible conclusions. In the story of humankind, the grand narrative was one of progress and an underlying assumption that developments in science, medicine, and education would lead to progress and better lives. This is no longer the case. French philosopher Jean-François Lyotard (1984) writes:

> *In contemporary society and culture—postindustrial society, postmodern culture—the grand narrative has lost its credibility, regardless of what mode of unification it uses, regardless of whether it is a speculative narrative or a narrative of emancipation. (p. 37)*

More recently, communication scholar Dave Tell (2008) has analyzed how a grand narrative about the murder of Emmett Till arose. Tell argues that an article in *Look* magazine about the murder is key to establishing the narrative of Till's murder, which played an important role in the rise of the civil rights movement.

In the wake of continuous wars and global conflicts, global warming, failed promises of liberation, new diseases such as human immunodeficiency virus (HIV) and bird flu, and other events that challenge what we know and what has changed, the master narrative no longer seems as believable to many. In its place are many other narratives that tell different stories. In the context of intercultural communication, the master narratives of many cultures and nations are also undergoing reconsideration, and many new narratives are emerging.

In her work on the constructions of white identity in South Africa, communication scholar Melissa Steyn (2001) notes how the grand narrative in South Africa served white interests and led to the establishment of **apartheid.** Although racially restrictive laws existed in South Africa for many years, the South African government instituted a rigid framework for regulating race in 1948. This system, apartheid, lasted until it was dismantled from 1990 to 1994, but only after a long struggle against it. Under this apartheid system, everyone was required to register their race in one of four categories: black, white, Indian, and colored. These categories were

apartheid A policy that segregated people racially in South Africa.

The way that Japanese history is taught in Japan has been a source of controversy in Japan and outside of Japan. Because there is no agreement on the events in the 1930s and 1940s, the controversy is unlikely to end anytime soon. However, there are consequences to the absence of coverage, or when they are covered, of this period in history. Think about how any understanding of history is important in creating cultural identities and influencing international relationships.

> *Japanese people often fail to understand why neighboring countries harbor a grudge over events that happened in the 1930s and 40s. The reason, in many cases, is that they barely learned any 20th century history. I myself only got a full picture when I left Japan and went to school in Australia.*
>
> *Without knowing these debates, it is extremely difficult to grasp why recent territorial disputes with China or South Korea cause such an emotional reaction among our neighbors. The sheer hostility shown towards Japan by ordinary people in street demonstrations seems bewildering and even barbaric to many Japanese television viewers.*
>
> *All this has resulted in Japan's Asian neighbors—especially China and South Korea—accusing the country of glossing over its war atrocities.*

Source: From M. Oi, "What Japanese history lessons leave out," *BBC Magazine,* March 14, 2013. Retrieved April 15, 2016, from http://www.bbc.com/news/magazine-21226068.

used to restrict where people could live (e.g., blacks were permitted to live on only 13% of the land, although they constituted 60% of the population), employment, access to public facilities (e.g., hospitals, ambulances, educational institutions), and other aspects of public life. Although they were numerically a minority, whites dominated this social system and accrued most of the benefits of it. To do so, they needed to tell a master narrative in which this system seemed to make sense. It was only under tremendous domestic and international pressure that the system was dismantled (Bureau of African Affairs, 2005; Guelke, 2005; Thompson, 2001). The popular film *Cry Freedom* (Attenborough, 1987), starring Denzel Washington as Steven Biko, a black leader, highlights the struggle and consequences of apartheid. Steyn writes:

> *In drawing on the master narrative, interpreting it and adapting it to the particular circumstances in which they found themselves in the country, whites were able to maintain their advantage as the dominating group that controlled the political, material, and symbolic resources of the country for three centuries. (p. 43)*

By telling and retelling one view of the past, white South Africans were able to create a society in which a white minority dominated.

In place of the grand narrative are revised and restored histories that previously were suppressed, hidden, or erased. The cultural movements making this shift possible are empowering to the cultural identities involved. Recovering various histories is necessary to rethinking what some cultural identities mean. It also helps us rethink the dominant cultural identity.

For example, on June 30, 1960, at the signing of the treaty granting independence to the former Belgian colony of the Congo (formerly Zaire), the king of the Belgians, Baudouin, constructed one way of thinking about the past:

> *All of our thoughts should be turned toward those who founded the African emancipation and after them, those who made the Congo into what it is today. They merit at the same time our admiration and your recognition since it was they who consecrated all of their efforts and even their lives for a grand ideal, bringing you peace and enriching your homeland materially and morally. They must never be forgotten, not by Belgium, not by the Congo. (Quoted in Gérard-Libois & Heinen, 1989, p. 143)*

In response, Patrice Lumumba, who would become prime minister, offered a different view of Belgian colonialism:

> *After eighty years of colonial rule, our wounds are still too fresh and too deep to be chased from our memory. . . . We have known the ironies, the insults, the beatings to which we had to submit morning, noon, and night because we were negroes. Who will forget that they spoke to Blacks with "tu" certainly not because of friendship, but because the honorary "vous" was reserved only for speaking to whites. (p. 147)*

Lumumba's words created a different sense of history. These differences were clear to the people of the time and remain clear today. In this way, the grand narrative of Belgian colonialism has been reconfigured and no longer stands as the only story of the Belgian Congo.

Power in Intercultural Interactions

Power is also the legacy, the remnants of the history that leaves cultural groups in particular positions. We are not equal in our intercultural encounters, nor can we ever be equal. Long histories of imperialism, colonialism, exploitation, wars, genocide, and more leave cultural groups out of balance when they communicate. Regardless of whether we choose to recognize the foundations for many of our differences, these inequalities influence how we think about others and how we interact with them. They also influence how we think about ourselves—our identities. These are important aspects of intercultural communication. It may seem daunting to confront the history of power struggles. Nevertheless, the more you know, the better you will be positioned to engage in successful intercultural interactions.

HISTORY AND IDENTITY

The development of cultural identity is influenced largely by history. In this next section, we look at some of the ways that cultural identities are constructed through understanding the past. Note how different cultural-group identities are tied to history.

PASSING AS WHITE

In the United States, people of color have historically passed or tried to pass as white because of the racial discrimination faced by racial minorities. Today, some Asian Americans are employing the same strategy in an effort to gain admission to a number of elite colleges and universities. For decades, a number of Asian American groups have charged that Harvard, Yale and other elite institutions discriminate against Asian Americans in admissions. Some Asian American organizations have again filed a racial discrimination complaint with the U.S. Department of Education, focusing on Brown, Dartmouth and Yale—all Ivy League institutions (Belkin, 2016). They charge that these institutions have a cap on Asian American admissions and discriminate against high achieving Asian American applicants. Sara Harberson (2015), a former associate dean of admissions at an Ivy League institution, writes: "racial stereotyping is alive and well." She notes that Asian American students are expected to be at the top of their class and have the highest test scores and when they do, they can end up on wait lists or be rejected. In response, some Asian American students do not check the "Asian" box on their applications as a strategy to deal with this situation (Some Asians, 2011). Although no one knows how many Asian American applicants try to pass as white, passing as white is nothing new in the history of the United States due to the racial situation in the past and the present. Will it continue to be necessary in the future?

Source: Belkin, D. (2016, May 23). Asian-American groups seek investigation into Ivy League admissions. *The Wall Street Journal*. Retrieved from http://www.wsj.com/articles/asian-american-groups-seek-investigation-into-ivy-league-admissions-1464026150

Harberson, S. (2015, June 9). Op ed: The truth about 'holistic' college admissions. *Los Angeles Times*. Retrieved from http://www.latimes.com/opinion/op-ed/la-oe-harberson-asian-american-admission-rates-20150609-story.html

Some Asians college strategy: Don't check 'Asian.' (2011, December 4). *USA Today*. Retrieved from http://usatoday30.usatoday.com/news/education/story/2011-12-03/asian-students-college-applications/51620236/1

Histories as Stories

Faced with these many levels or types of history, you might wonder how we make sense of them in our everyday lives. Although it might be tempting to ignore them all and merely pretend to be "ourselves," this belies the substantial influence that history has on our own identities.

According to communication scholar Walter Fisher (1984, 1985), storytelling is fundamental to the human experience. Instead of referring to humans as *Homo sapiens,* Fisher prefers to call them *Homo narrans* because it underscores the importance of narratives in our lives. Histories are stories that we use to make sense of who we are and who we think others are.

It is important to recognize that a strong element in our cultural attitudes encourages us to forget history at times. French writer Jean Baudrillard (1988) observes:

> *America was created in the hope of escaping from history, of building a utopia sheltered from history. . . . [It] has in part succeeded in that project, a project it is still pursuing today. The concept of history as the transcending of a social and political rationality, as a dialectical, conflictual vision of societies, is not theirs, just as modernity, conceived precisely as an original break with certain history, will never be ours [France's]. (p. 80)*

The desire to escape history is significant in what it tells us about how our culture negotiates its relation to the past, as well as how we view the relations of other nations and cultures to their pasts. By ignoring history, we sometimes come to wrongheaded conclusions about others that only perpetuate and reinforce stereotypes. For example, the notion that Jewish people are obsessed with money and are disproportionately represented in the world of finance belies the history of anti-Semitism, whereby Jews were excluded from many professions. The paradox is that we cannot escape history even if we fail to recognize it or try to suppress it.

Nonmainstream Histories

People from nonmainstream cultural groups often struggle to retain their histories. Their are not the histories that everyone learns about in school, yet these histories are vital to understanding how others perceive them and why. These nonmainstream histories are important to the people in these cultural groups, as they may play a significant role in their cultural identities.

hidden histories The histories that are hidden from or forgotten by the mainstream representations of past events.

Nonmainstream histories sometimes stand alongside the grand narrative, but sometimes they challenge the grand narrative. As we saw earlier, some nonmainstream histories are absent histories, as these histories have been lost or are not recoverable. Sometimes these nonmainstream histories are **hidden histories,** as they offer different views on the grand narrative and, therefore, have been suppressed or marginalized in our understanding of the past. Let's look at some of these nonmainstream histories and how these views of the past help us better understand different cultural groups.

ethnic histories The histories of ethnic groups.

racial histories The histories of nonmainstream racial groups.

Racial and Ethnic Histories   Mainstream history has neither the time nor the space nor the inclination to include all **ethnic histories** and **racial histories.** This is especially true given that the histories of cultural groups sometimes seem to question, and even undermine, the celebratory nature of the mainstream national history.

When Tom's parents meet other Japanese Americans of their generation, they are often asked, "What camp were you in?" This question makes little sense outside of its historical context. Indeed, this question is embedded in understanding a particular moment in history, a moment that is not widely understood. Most Japanese

This letter from the president of the United States was sent to all of the surviving Japanese American internees who were in U.S. concentration camps during World War II. In recognizing that there is no way to change mistakes made in the past, what does this letter do? If you were to compose this letter, what would you write? How should we deal with the past to construct better intercultural relations in the future?

THE WHITE HOUSE
WASHINGTON

A monetary sum and words alone cannot restore lost years or erase painful memories; neither can they fully convey our Nation's resolve to rectify injustice and to uphold the rights of individuals. We can never fully right the wrongs of the past. But we can take a clear stand for justice and recognize that serious injustices were done to Japanese Americans during World War II.

In enacting a law calling for restitution and offering a sincere apology, your fellow Americans have, in a very real sense, renewed their traditional commitment to the ideals of freedom, equality, and justice. You and your family have our best wishes for the future.

Sincerely,

GEORGE BUSH
PRESIDENT OF THE UNITED STATES

OCTOBER 1990

Americans were interned in concentration camps during World War II. In the aftermath of the experience, the use of that history as a marker has been important in maintaining cultural identity.

The injustices done by any nation are often swept under the carpet. In an attempt to bring attention to and promote renewed understanding of the internment of Japanese

Americans during World War II, academician John Tateishi (1984) collected the stories of some of the internees. He notes at the outset that

> *this book makes no attempt to be a definitive academic history of Japanese American internment. Rather it tries to present for the first time in human and personal terms the experience of the only group of American citizens ever to be confined in concentration camps in the United States. (p. vii)*

Although not an academic history, this collection of oral histories provides insight into the experiences of many Japanese Americans. Because this historical event demonstrates the fragility of our constitutional system and its guarantees in the face of prejudice and ignorance, it is not often discussed as significant in U.S. history. For Japanese Americans, however, it represents a defining moment in the development of their community.

While Pearl Harbor may feel like a distant historical event, the internment of Japanese Americans has drawn important parallels to the treatment of Muslims after 9/11. Because of the fears that arose after these events, "In recent years, many scholars have drawn parallels and contrasts between the internment of Japanese-Americans after the attack on Pearl Harbor, and the treatment of hundreds of Muslim noncitizens who were swept up in the weeks after the 2001 terror attacks, then held for months before they were cleared of links to terrorism and deported" (Bernstein, 2007). "When a federal judge in Brooklyn ruled last June that the government had wide latitude to detain noncitizens indefinitely on the basis of race, religion or national origin" (Bernstein, 2007), a number of Japanese Americans spoke out against the broad ruling and the parallels it had to their cultural group's historical experience.

Similarly, for Jewish people, remembering the Holocaust is crucial to their identity. Since the Holocaust, survivors and others have insisted on the importance of "never forget" as a way to have the Holocaust make a difference in the contemporary world. Jeff Jacoby (2016), a journalist whose father survived the Holocaust, ponders the future of the "never forget" movement and speculates that:

> *It was always inevitable that the enormity of the Holocaust would recede in public awareness. [...]Accounts of what was done in Treblinka did not prevent mass murder in Cambodia or Bosnia or Rwanda. Holocaust remembrance has not inoculated human beings against treating other human beings with brutality. [...] I have always taken the Holocaust personally, and always will. But the world, I know, will not. Eventually, everything is forgotten. Even the worst crime in history.*

In an effort to keeping the memory of the Holocaust alive, people have built monuments, museums, captured the oral histories and voices of survivors, and worked to document as much as possible. But like other horrors in the past, will the Holocaust also become just another event in history books? What does that mean about how history shapes our present and future?

Ethnic and racial histories are never isolated; rather, they crisscross other cultural trajectories. We may feel as if we have been placed in the position of victim or victimizer by distant historical events, and we may even seem to occupy both of these positions simultaneously. Consider, for example, the position of German American Mennonites during World War II. They were punished as pacifists and

I used to feel very guilty in history classes, learning about the tragedies white Europeans have committed against other races. Even though my ancestors immigrated to the United States after the abolition of slavery and the conflict with Native Americans, I still felt like I was somehow part of this historic problem. It wasn't until one of my upper level courses that the teacher told the class that guilt does not help anything, but awareness and conscious efforts to combat lingering historic problems can make a difference to members of disadvantaged minorities, and this is what matters.
    —Evangeline

When I came to the United States, I was surprised to meet so many Americans who were very proud of their family histories. They knew a lot about the accomplishments of their families over many struggles in the past. I didn't know as much about my family's history; I never really thought much about it and it took me a while to feel comfortable interacting with the American students.
    —Li Wei

I was in Germany for a few hours in April. My boyfriend is Jewish, so lately I have been thinking about how the Holocaust has affected his family. I found myself angry at every German in the airport. I knew that I was placing a ridiculous stereotype on the German people.
    —Angela

yet also were seen as aggressors by U.S. Jews. To further complicate matters, U.S. citizens of German ancestry were not interned in concentration camps, as were U.S. citizens of Japanese ancestry. How we think about being victims and victimizers is quite complex.

French writer Maurice Blanchot, in confronting the horrors of the Holocaust, the devastation of the atom bomb, and other human disasters, redefines the notion of responsibility, separating it from fault. In *The Writing of the Disaster,* Blanchot (1986) asserts,

> *My responsibility is anterior to my birth just as it is exterior to my consent, to my liberty. I am born thanks to a favor which turns out to be a predestination— born unto the grief of the other, which is the grief of all. (p. 22)*

This perspective can help us face and deal with the different positions that history finds for us.

The displacement of various populations is embedded in the history of every migrating or colonizing people. Whether caused by natural disasters such as the drought in the Midwest during the Great Depression of the 1930s or determined by choice, migrations influence how we live today. Native peoples throughout most of the United States were exterminated or removed to settlements in other regions. The state of Iowa, for example, has few Native Americans and only one reservation. The current residents of Iowa had nothing to do with the events in their state's history, but they are the beneficiaries through the ownership of farms and other land. So, although contemporary Iowans are not in a position of fault or blame, they are, through these benefits, in a position of responsibility. Like all of us, their lives are entangled in the web of history from which there is no escape, only denial and silence.

Gender Histories   Feminist scholars have long insisted that much of the history of women has been obliterated, marginalized, or erased. Historian Mei Nakano (1990) notes:

> *The history of women, told by women, is a recent phenomenon. It has called for a fundamental reevaluation of assumptions and principles that govern traditional history. It challenges us to have a more inclusive view of history, not merely the chronicling of events of the past, not dominated by the record of men marching forward through time, their paths strewn with the detritus of war and politics and industry and labor. (p. xiii)*

gender histories The histories of how cultural conventions of men and women are created, maintained, and/or altered.

Although there is much interest in women's history among contemporary scholars, documenting such **gender histories** is difficult because of the traditional restrictions on women's access to public forums, public documents, and public records. Even so, the return to the past to unearth and recover identities that can be adapted for survival is a key theme of writer Gloria Anzaldúa (1987). She presents *la Llorana* (the crying woman) as a cultural and historical image that gives her the power to resist cultural and gender domination. *La Llorana* is well known in northern Mexico and the U.S. southwest. This legend tells the story of a woman who killed her children and who now wanders around looking for them and weeping for them. Her story has been retold in various ways, and Anzaldúa rewrites the tale to highlight the power that resides in her relentless crying. This mythical image gives her the power to resist cultural and gender domination:

> *My Chicana identity is grounded in the Indian woman's history of resistance. The Aztec female rites of mourning were rites of defiance protesting the cultural changes which disrupted the equality and balance between female and male, and protesting their demotion to a lesser status, their denigration. Like la* Llorana, *the Indian woman's only means of protest was wailing. (p. 21)*

Anzaldúa's history may seem distant to us, but it is intimately tied to what her Chicana identity means to her. In a similar vein, transgender history can reconfigure the contemporary cultural context. For example, Susan Stryker (2008) focuses on "the collective political history of transgender social change activism in the United States—that is, on efforts to make it easier and safer and more acceptable for the people who need to cross gender boundaries to be able to do so" (p. 2).

Sexual Orientation Histories   In recounting his experiences as a young man whom the police registered as "homosexual," Pierre Seel (1994) recounts how police lists were used by the Nazis to round up homosexuals for internment. The incarceration

In the face of historical wrongs, there may seem to be little that can be done to correct things that happened in the past. Spain, however, is attempting to make amends for its past by allowing Sephardic Jews (Jews who trace their roots to the Iberian Peninsula) to apply for dual citizenship with a law that came into effect in October 2015.

> *The measure aims to correct what Spain's conservative government calls the "historic mistake" of sending Jews into exile in 1492, forcing them to convert to Catholicism or burning them at the stake.*
>
> *Historians believe at least 200,000 Jews lived in Spain before the Catholic monarchs Isabella and Ferdinand ordered them to convert to the Catholic faith or leave the country. Many found refuge in the Ottoman Empire, the Balkans, North Africa, and Latin America. They risked the death penalty if they returned to Spain.*

Source: From "Spain passes law awarding citizenship to descendants of expelled Jews," *The Guardian*, June 11, 2015. Retrieved April 15, 2016, from http://www.theguardian.com /world/2015/jun/11/spain-law-citizenship-jews.

and extermination of gays, as members of one of the groups deemed "undesirable" by Nazi Germany, is often overlooked by World War II historians. Seel recalls one event in his **sexual orientation history:**

sexual orientation history The historical experiences of gays and lesbians.

> *One day at a meeting in the SOS Racisme [an antiracism organization] room, I finished by getting up and recounting my experience of Nazism, my deportation for homosexuality. I remarked as well the ingratitude of history which erases that which is not officially convenient for it. (p. 162)*
>
> *(Un jour de réunion, dans la salle de SOS Racisme, je finis par me lever et par raconter mon expérience du nazisme, ma déportation pour homosexualité. Je fis également remarquer l'ingratitude de l'histoire qui gomme ce qui ne lui convient pas officiellement.)*

This suppression of history reflects attempts to construct specific understandings of the past. If we do not or cannot listen to the voices of others, we miss the significance of historical lessons. For example, a legislative attempt to force gays and lesbians to register with the police in the state of Montana ultimately was vetoed by the governor after he learned of the law's similarities to laws in Nazi Germany.

The late Guy Hocquenghem (Hocquenghem & Blasius, 1980), a gay French philosopher, lamented the letting go of the past because doing so left little to sustain and nurture his community:

> *I am struck by the ignorance among gay people about the past—no, more even than ignorance: the "will to forget" the German gay holocaust. . . . But we aren't even the only ones who remember, we don't remember! So we find ourselves beginning at zero in each generation. (p. 40)*

How we think about the past and what we know about it help us to build and maintain communities and cultural identities. And our relationships with the past are intimately tied to issues of power. To illustrate, the book *The Pink Swastika: Homosexuality in the Nazi Party* attempts to blame the Holocaust on German gays and lesbians ("Under Surveillance," 1995). This book, in depicting gays and lesbians as perpetrators, rather than victims, of Nazi atrocities, presents the gay identity in a markedly negative light. However, stories of the horrendous treatment of gays and lesbians during World War II serve to promote a common history and influence intercultural communication among gays and lesbians in France, Germany, the Netherlands, and other nations. Today, a monument in Amsterdam serves to mark that history, to help ensure that we remember that gays and lesbians were victims of the Nazi Holocaust as well.

In the United States, Bayard Rustin is often forgotten, despite his enormous contributions to the civil rights movement. "His obscurity stemmed not only from amnesia but also from conscious suppression" (Kennedy, 2003), despite his major role in U.S. history. *The Nation* (2003) observed: "Rustin helped found the Congress of Racial Equality (CORE) and the Southern Christian Leadership Conference (SCLC). He advised Martin Luther King Jr., organized the 1963 March on Washington and wrote several essays that continue to repay close study. Throughout these pursuits, Rustin expressed a gay sexuality for which he was stigmatized as a sexual criminal, a smear that crippled his ability to lead the movements to which he passionately contributed ideas and inspiration."

Abraham Lincoln's sexual history has also been a major point of contention over a number of years (see Table 4-1). Psychologist C. A. Tripp's book *The Intimate World of Abraham Lincoln* once again raised the possibility that the former president's sexual history included men. While we may never know whatever really happened, the concern over this history underscores the way it may influence our national history. The Lincoln case points to the difficulty in understanding this type of history. The words, *homosexual, heterosexual,* and *bisexual* did not exist during Lincoln's era; therefore, those words would not be used to describe his private life. Among other examples, Tripp points to a member of Lincoln's bodyguard, Captain David V. Derickson, who would come over to the White House and sleep in the same bed with Lincoln. Is this evidence for how we might understand this sexual history? On the one hand, it seems odd for Captain Derickson to come to the White House and sleep in the same bed with Lincoln; however, "as many historians have noted, same-sex bed sharing was common at the time and hardly proof of homosexual activities or feelings" (Greenberg, 2005). There is no general agreement about Lincoln's sexual history, but more importantly, the debate over how we should think about Lincoln points to the power of these histories in understanding our national identity.

Diasporic Histories   The international relationships that many racial and ethnic groups have with others who share their heritage and history are often overlooked in intercultural communication. These international ties may have been created by transnational migrations, slavery, religious crusades, or other historical forces. Because most people do not think about the diverse connections people have to other nations

TABLE 4-1   HISTORICAL CONTROVERSY: ABRAHAM LINCOLN'S SEXUALITY

Year	Event	Reaction	Outcome
1924	Carl Sandburg alludes to Lincoln's homosexual tendencies using euphemisms of the day like "streak of lavender."	This claim was not central to Sandburg's work and was widely dismissed.	Lingering questions over Lincoln's sexual history (Nobile, 2005).
1999	Prominent gay activist Larry Kramer claims to have acquired a journal of one of Lincoln's lovers.	Many historians and commentators rail against Kramer and his claim to have found the journal.	Kramer has kept the journal private, but the controversy has lived on (Lloyd, 1999).
2004	C. A. Tripp makes the definitive claim that Lincoln was gay in his 2004 biography.	Controversy erupts over Tripp's objectivity, his research, and the topic.	Most historians continue to claim that Lincoln was heterosexual, while some question this claim (Brookhiser, 2005).
2008	Charles E. Morris publishes an account of Lincoln's sexual history and an analysis of reactions to the topic (Morris, 2008).		

Sources: From P. Nobile, "Broken promises, plagiarism, misused evidence and the new gay Lincoln book published by the Free Press," *The History News Network,* January 10, 2005. Retrieved from http://hnn.us/articles/9514.html; C. Lloyd, "Was Lincoln gay?" *Salon.com,* May 3, 1999. Retrieved from http://www.salon.com/books/it/1999/04/30/lincoln/index.html; R. Brookhiser, "Was Lincoln gay?" *The New York Times,* January 9, 2005. Retrieved from http://query.nytimes.com/gst/fullpage.html?res=9F05E5D61439F93AA35752C0A9639C8B63; C. E. Morris III, "Profile," 2008. Retrieved from http://www.bc.edu/schools/cas/communication/faculty/fulltime/morris.html.

and cultures, we consider these histories to be hidden. In his book *The Black Atlantic,* scholar Paul Gilroy (1993) emphasizes that to understand the identities, cultures, and experiences of African descendants living in Britain and the United States, we must examine the connections between Africa, Europe, and North America.

A massive migration, often caused by war or famine or persecution, that results in the dispersal of a unified group is called a **diaspora.** The chronicles of these events are **diasporic histories.** A cultural group (or even an individual) that flees its homeland is likely to bring some customs and practices to the new homeland. In fact, diasporic migrations often cause people to cling more strongly to symbols and practices that reflect their group's identity. Over the years, though, people become acculturated to some degree in their new homelands. Consider, for example, the dispersal of eastern European Jews who migrated during or after World War II to the United States, Australia, South America, Israel, and other parts of the world. They brought their Jewish culture and eastern European culture with them, but they also adopted new cultural patterns as they became New Yorkers, Australians, Argentinians, Israelis, and so on. Imagine the communication differences among these people over time. Imagine the differences between these groups and members of the dominant culture of their new homelands.

History helps us understand the cultural connections among people affected by diasporas and other transnational migrations. Indeed, it is important that we recognize these relationships. But we must also be careful to distinguish between the ways in which these connections are helpful or hurtful to intercultural communication. For example, some cultures tend to regard negatively those who left their homeland. Thus, many Japanese tend to look down on Japanese Canadians, Japanese Americans, Japanese Brazilians, Japanese Mexicans, and Japanese Peruvians. In contrast, the Irish tend not to look down on Irish Americans or Irish Canadians. Of course, we must remember, too, that many other intervening factors can influence diasporic relationships on an interpersonal level.

Colonial Histories   As you probably know, throughout history, societies and nations have ventured beyond their borders. Because of overpopulation, limited resources, notions of grandeur, or other factors, people have left their homelands to colonize other territories. It is important to recognize these **colonial histories** so we can better understand the dynamics of intercultural communication today.

Let's look at the significance of colonialism in determining language. Historically, three of the most important colonizers were Britain, France, and Spain. As a result of colonialism, English is spoken in Canada, Australia, New Zealand, Belize, Nigeria, South Africa, India, Pakistan, Bangladesh, Zimbabwe, Hong Kong, Singapore, and the United States, among many places in the world. French is spoken in Canada, Senegal, Tahiti, Haiti, Benin, Côte d'Ivoire, Niger, Mali, Chad, and the Central African Republic, among other places. And Spanish is spoken in most of the Western Hemisphere, from Mexico to Chile and Argentina, and including Cuba, Venezuela, Colombia, and Panama.

Many foreign language textbooks proudly display maps that show the many places around the world where that language is commonly spoken. Certainly, it's nice to know that one can speak Spanish or French in so many places. But the maps don't reveal *why* those languages are widely spoken in those regions, and they don't reveal the legacies of colonialism in those regions. For example, the United Kingdom

---

diaspora A massive migration often caused by war, famine, or persecution that results in the dispersal of a unified group.

diasporic histories The histories of the ways in which international cultural groups were created through transnational migrations, slavery, religious crusades, or other historical forces.

colonial histories The histories that legitimate international invasions and annexations.

W hen the Commonwealth of Virginia passed the Racial Integrity Act of 1924, it "didn't just make blacks in Virginia second-class citizens—it also erased any acknowledgment of Indians […]. With a stroke of the pen, Virginia was on a path to eliminating the identity of the Pamunkey, the Mattaponi, the Chickahominy, the Monacan, the Rappahonnok, the Nansemond, and the rest of Virginia's tribes" (Heim, 2015). There are important consequences to the absent history of Indian tribes in Virginia. Until recently, Virginia had no federally recognized Indian tribes. "In order to receive federal recognition, and be eligible for the housing, education, and health-care funding that comes with it, Indian tribes need to meet several criteria heavily weighted to historical documentation" (Heim, 2015). Claiming Pochahontas as one of their ancestors, the Pamunkey tribe worked for decades to make their case for federal recognition. This small tribe initially received federal recognition in July 2015, but that was put on hold as a legal challenge was made to their new status. In February 2016, the challenge was denied and the Pamunkey became Virginia's first and only federally recognized Indian tribe. Given the erasure of Indian history in Virginia, will any other tribes in Virginia be able to gain federal recognition? In what other cases have people been impacted by absent history?

maintains close relations with many of its former colonies, and the queen of England is also the queen of Canada, Australia, New Zealand, and the Bahamas. But some colonial relationships are not close, such as the relationship with Ireland (see Figure 4-3 on page 152). And others are changing, as both Australia and Jamaica are considering ending the British monarch as their heads of state (Botelho & Brocchetto, 2016; McKenzie, 2016).

Other languages have been spread through colonialism as well, including Portuguese in Brazil, Macao, and Angola; Dutch in Angola, Suriname, and Mozambique; and a related Dutch language, Afrikaans, in South Africa. Russian is spoken in the former Soviet republics of Kazakhstan, Azerbaijan, and Tajikistan. In addition, many nations have reclaimed their own languages in an effort to resist the influences of colonialism. For example, today Arabic is spoken in Algeria and Vietnamese is spoken in Vietnam; at one time, French was widely spoken in both countries. And in the recently independent Latvia, the ability to speak Latvian is a requirement for citizenship.

The primary languages that we speak are not freely chosen by us. Rather, we must learn the languages of the societies into which we are born. Judith and Tom, for example, both speak English, although their ancestors came to the United States from non-English-speaking countries. We did not choose to learn English among all of the languages of the world. Although we don't resent our native language, we recognize why many individuals might resent a language imposed on them. Think about the historical forces that led you to speak some language(s) and not others. Understanding history is crucial to understanding the linguistic worlds we inhabit, and vestiges of colonialism are often part of these histories.

Postcolonialism is useful in helping us understand the relationship between history and the present. In struggling with a colonial past, people have devised many ways of confronting that past. As explained in Chapter 2, postcolonialism is not simply the study of colonialism, but the study of how we might deal with that past and its aftermath, which may include the *ongoing* use of the colonial language, culture, and religion. For example, many companies are locating parts of their businesses in India because of the widespread use of English in this former British colony. How should people in India deal with the ongoing dominance of English, the colonizer's language, but also the language of business?

For example, Hispanics or Latinos/as share a common history of colonization by Spain, whether their families trace their origins to Mexico, Puerto Rico, Cuba, and so on. Although Spain is no longer in political control of these lands, how do those who live in the legacy of this history deal with that history? In what ways does it remain important, as a part of this cultural identity, to embrace the colonizer's language (Spanish)? The colonizer's religion (Catholicism)? And are there other aspects of Spanish culture that continue to be reproduced over and over again? Postcolonialism is not simply a call to make a clean break from that colonial past, but "to examine the violent actions and erasures of colonialism" (Shome & Hegde, 2002, p. 250). In this case, that interrogation might even mean reconsidering the category "Hispanic" that incorporates a wide range of groups that share a Spanish colonial history but do not share other histories that constitute their cultures. The legacy of this cultural invasion often lasts much longer than the political relationship.

Socioeconomic Class Histories   Although we often overlook the importance of socioeconomic class as a factor in history, the fact is that economic and class issues prompted many people to emigrate to the United States. The poverty in Ireland in the 19th century, for example, did much to fuel the flight to the United States; in fact, today, there are more Irish Americans than Irish.

Yet it is not always the socioeconomically disadvantaged who emigrate. After the Russian Revolution in 1917, many affluent Russians moved to Paris. Likewise, many affluent Cubans left the country after Castro seized power in 1959. Currently, the U.S. Citizenship and Immigration Services office administers the EB-5 visa program that allows foreign investors to secure permanent residency (a green card) in the United States if they meet certain requirements (creating a new business, creating a certain number of jobs, and investing a certain amount of money). Called the EB-5 Immigrant Investor Program, this visa program is an example of how socioeconomic class can influence international migrations. Many other countries also offer similar programs.

The key point here is that socioeconomic class distinctions are often overlooked in examining the migrations and acculturation of groups around the world. Historically, the kinds of employment that immigrants supplied and the regions they settled were often marked by the kinds of capital—cultural and financial—that they were or were not able to bring with them. These factors also influence the interactions and politics of different groups; for example, Mexican Americans and Cuban Americans, as groups, frequently are at odds with the political mainstream.

Religious Histories   In the past, as well as today, religion is an important historical force that has shaped our planet. Religious conflicts have led to wars, such as
the Christian Crusades nearly a thousand years ago. Religious persecution has also
led to migration of various religious groups to new places. In the United States, one
example of this movement are the Mormons, who left New York, settled in Illinois,
and then left to go to Utah. Many French Huguenots (Protestants), persecuted by
French Catholics, left France to settle primarily in North America, South Africa, and
elsewhere in Europe.

Because many of these religious histories remain controversial, they are viewed
differently, depending on with which side one identifies. Even recent historical
events, and how they are interpreted, can create religious conflict. In August 2010,
a New York City commission approved the construction of a mosque near "Ground
Zero," the site of the former World Trade Center. This created a national controversy
over the proposed mosque and the role of Islam in the attacks on 9/11. For many
Muslims, the 9/11 attackers were extremists, much like the extremists in many other
religions. For many non-Muslims, the 9/11 attackers were acting as Muslims. In a
speech made at a White House dinner, President Obama stated:

> *Now, that's not to say that religion is without controversy. Recently, attention has
> been focused on the construction of mosques in certain communities—particularly
> New York. Now, we must all recognize and respect the sensitivities surrounding
> the development of Lower Manhattan. The 9/11 attacks were a deeply traumatic
> event for our country. And the pain and the experience of suffering by those
> who lost loved ones is just unimaginable. So I understand the emotions that this
> issue engenders. And Ground Zero is, indeed, hallowed ground. But let me be
> clear. As a citizen, and as President, I believe that Muslims have the same right
> to practice their religion as everyone else in this country. (Applause.) And that
> includes the right to build a place of worship and a community center on private
> property in Lower Manhattan, in accordance with local laws and ordinances. This
> is America. And our commitment to religious freedom must be unshakeable. The
> principle that people of all faiths are welcome in this country and that they will
> not be treated differently by their government is essential to who we are.*

In this example, we can see that different views about the role of religion in the
past can create contemporary controversies. Although religious freedom is an important American cultural value, as noted by President Obama, that cultural value can be
in tension with other views on what happened and why on 9/11.

INTERCULTURAL COMMUNICATION AND HISTORY

One way to understand specific relationships between communication and history is
to examine the attitudes and notions that individuals bring to an interaction; these are
the antecedents of contact. A second way is to look at the specific conditions of the
interaction and the role that history plays in these contexts. Finally, we can examine
how various histories are negotiated in intercultural interaction, applying a dialectical perspective to these different histories.

The flying of the Confederate battle flag at the South Carolina capitol building points to the complexities in dealing with the past. History, although it is past, continues to shape contemporary life. The slaughter of nine African American churchgoers in Charleston by a white gunman who wrapped himself in the Confederate flag again raised the issue of flying the flag, but this time, the political decision was made to take it down. The removal of the flag, however, did not erase the conflicted feelings that many South Carolinians have about the Confederacy and the flag. The flag, as a symbol, points to a much more contested history.

> The banishment of perhaps the most conspicuous and polarizing symbol of the Old South from the seat of South Carolina government Friday morning was the culmination of decades of racially charged political skirmishes.
> [...]
> At issue were vexing questions about how a state that was first to secede from the Union—and then later raised the battle flag in 1962 when white Southerners were resisting calls for integration—should honor its Confederate past.
> It was a conversation that seemed like it might never end here, until it was hurried to a resolution by unspeakable horror: the massacre of nine black churchgoers in downtown Charleston last month, and a gathering sense of outrage and offense that was felt even by many white conservatives who had previously supported the flag. The arrest of the alleged gunman, 21-year-old Dylann Roof, who posed proudly with the flag and apparently posted a long racist manifesto online before the massacre, was the flag's final undoing.

Source: From R. Fausset and A. Blinder (2015, July 10), "Era ends as South Carolina lowers Confederate flag," *New York Times.* Retrieved April 16, 2016, from http://www.nytimes.com/2015/07/11/us/south-carolina-confederate-flag.html.

Antecedents of Contact

We may be able to negotiate some aspects of history in interaction, but it is important to recognize that we bring our personal histories to each intercultural interaction. These personal histories involve our prior experience and our attitudes. Social psychologist Richard Brislin (1981) has identified four elements of personal histories that influence interaction.

First, people bring childhood experiences to interactions. For example, both Judith and Tom grew up hearing negative comments about Catholics. As a result, our first interactions with adherents to this faith were tinged with some suspicion. This personal history did not affect initial interactions with people of other religions.

Second, people may bring historical myths to interactions. These are myths with which many people are familiar. The Jewish conspiracy myth—that Jewish people are secretly in control of U.S. government and business—is one example.

Third, the languages that people speak influence their interactions. Language can be an attraction or a repellent in intercultural interactions. For example, many people from the United States enjoy traveling in Britain because English is spoken there. However, these same people may have little desire, or even be afraid, to visit Russia, simply because it is not an English-speaking country.

Finally, people tend to be affected by recent, vivid events. For example, after the terrorist attacks in San Bernardino, Brussels, Paris, and the Boston Marathon, interactions between Arab Americans and other U.S. residents were strained, characterized by suspicion, fear, and distrust. The media's treatment of such catastrophic events often creates barriers and reinforces stereotypes by blurring distinctions between Arabs, Muslims, and Palestinians. Perhaps recent histories, such as the police shootings of African Americans, such as Eric Garner, Michael Brown, Tamir Rice, Sandra Bland, and others, as well as the rise of the Black Lives Matter movement are more influential in our interactions than the hidden or past histories, such as the massacre in 1890 of some 260 Sioux Indians at Wounded Knee in South Dakota or the women's suffrage movement around the turn of the 20th century.

The Contact Hypothesis

The **contact hypothesis** is the notion that better communication between groups of people is facilitated simply by bringing them together and allowing them to interact. Although history does not seem to support this notion, many public policies and programs in the United States and abroad are based on this hypothesis. Examples include desegregation rulings; the prevalence of master-planned communities like Reston, Virginia; and many international student exchange programs. All of these programs are based on the assumption that simply giving people from different groups opportunities to interact will result in more positive intergroup attitudes and reduced prejudice.

contact hypothesis The notion that better communication between groups is facilitated simply by putting people together in the same place and allowing them to interact.

Gordon Allport (1979) and Yehudi Amir (1969), two noted psychologists, have tried to identify the conditions under which the contact hypothesis does and does not hold true. The histories of various groups figure prominently in their studies. Based on these and subsequent studies, psychologists have outlined at least eight conditions that must be met (more or less) to improve attitudes and facilitate intergroup communication (Schwarzwald & Amir, 1996; Stephan & Stephan, 1996). These are particularly relevant in light of increasing diversity in U.S. society in general and the workforce in particular. The eight conditions are as follows:

1. Group members should be of equal status, both within and outside the contact situation. Communication will occur more easily if there is no disparity between individuals in status characteristics (education, socioeconomic status, and so on). This condition does not include temporary inequality, such as in student–teacher or patient–doctor roles. Consider the implications of this condition for relations among various ethnic groups in the United States. How are we likely to think of individuals from specific ethnic groups if our interactions are characterized by inequality? A good example is the interaction between longtime residents and recent immigrants in the

In an April 23, 2012 press release, the White House announced that President Obama would be giving posthumously Jan Karski the Presidential Medal of Freedom. President Obama said:

We must tell our children about how this evil was allowed to happen— because so many people succumbed to their darkest instincts; because so many others stood silent. But let us also tell our children about the Righteous Among the Nations. Among them was Jan Karski—a young Polish Catholic—who witnessed Jews being put on cattle cars, who saw the killings, and who told the truth, all the way to President Roosevelt himself. Jan Karski passed away more than a decade ago. But today, I'm proud to announce that this spring I will honor him with America's highest civilian honor—the Presidential Medal of Freedom.

On May 29, 2012 when the award was made, President Obama said:

Fluent in four languages, possessed of a photographic memory, Jan served as a courier for the Polish resistance during the darkest days of World War II. Before one trip across enemy lines, resistance fighters told him that Jews were being murdered on a massive scale, and smuggled him into the Warsaw Ghetto and a *Polish death camp* to see for himself. Jan took that information to President Franklin Roosevelt, giving one of the first accounts of the Holocaust and imploring to the world to take action.

After President Obama's laudatory remarks on all of the recipients of the Presidential Medal of Honor, an immediate uproar ensued over the use of the term, "Polish death camp." The asterisks are marked on the White House press release, along with an apology for using those words., as they are historically inaccurate. The Polish Prime Minister Donald Tusk explained: "When someone says "Polish death camps," it's as if

Southwest, where Mexican Americans often provide housecleaning, gardening, and similar services for whites. It is easy to see how the history of these two groups in the United States contributes to the lack of equality in interaction, leads to stereotyping, and inhibits effective intercultural communication. But the history of relations between Mexican Americans and whites varies within this region. For example, families of Spanish descent have lived in New Mexico longer than other European-descent families, whereas Arizona has a higher concentration of recent immigrants from Mexico. Intergroup interactions in New Mexico are characterized less by inequality (Stephan & Stephan, 1989).

2. Strong normative and institutional support for the contact should be provided. This suggests that when individuals from different groups come together, positive outcomes do not happen by accident. Rather, institutional encouragement is necessary. Examples include university support for contact between

there were no Nazis, no German responsibility, as if there was no Hitler. That is why our Polish sensitivity in these situations is so much more than just simply a feeling of national pride." In his analysis of the speech, David Frum more directly explains that "the camps were German, German, German: ordered into being by Germans, designed by Germans, fulfilling a German plan of murder." And he concludes: "The medal to Karski was to be part of the process of laying painful memories to rest. It was intended too to strengthen the U.S.–Polish relations that the Obama administration had frayed in pursuit of its "reset" with Russia. Instead, this administration bungled everything: past, present and future." In response, the White House amended the posted speech with: "*Note–the language in asterisks below is historically inaccurate. It should instead have been: 'Nazi death camps in German occupied Poland.' We regret the error."

How we communicate about the past can have tremendous impacts on contemporary and future intercultural relations. It is difficult to know how much damage was caused to U.S.–Polish relations, but this example highlights the importance of thinking about how you communicate about the past.

Sources:

From The White House (2012, April 23), "President Obama announces Jan Karski as a recipient of the Presidential Medal of Freedom." Retrieved from https://www.whitehouse.gov/the-press-office/2012/04/23/president-obama-announces-jan-karski-recipient-presidential-medal-freedo.

From President Obama (2012, May 29), "Remarks by the President at Presidential Medal of Freedom Ceremony. The White House Office of the Press Secretary." Retrieved from https://www.whitehouse.gov/the-press-office/2012/05/29/remarks-president-presidential-medal-freedom-ceremony.

From D. Tusk, quoted in M. Landler (2012, May 30), "Polish premier denounces Obama for referring to a 'Polish death camp,'" New York Times. Retrieved April 16, 2016, from http://www.nytimes.com/2012/05/31/world/europe/poland-bristles-as-obama-says-polish-death-camps.html.

From D. Frum (2012, May 30), "It wasn't a 'gaffe,'" The Daily Beast. Retrieved April 16, 2016, from http://www.thedailybeast.com/articles/2012/05/30/poland-insult.html.

U.S. and international students, or for contact among different cultural groups within the university, and local community support for integrating elementary and high schools. Numerous studies have shown the importance of commitment by top management to policies that facilitate intercultural interaction in the workplace (Brinkman, 1997). Finally, institutional support may also mean government and legal support, expressed through court action.

3. Contact between the groups should be voluntary. This may seem to contradict the previous condition, but it doesn't. Although support must exist beyond the individual, individuals need to feel that they have a choice in making contact. If they believe that they are being forced to interact, as with some diversity programs or affirmative action programs, the intercultural interaction is unlikely to have positive outcomes. For example, an air traffic controller was so incensed by a required diversity program exercise on gender differences that he sued the Department of Transportation for

FIGURE 4-3   Irish dissident Republicans hold a protest close to Dublin Castle as Britain's Queen Elizabeth II made a historic address in Irish toward the end of her second day of her State Visit to Dublin, Ireland, May 18, 2011. The Queen began her speech in Irish by addressing "A hUachtarain agus a chairde." The Queen said it was impossible to ignore the weight of history, as so much of the visit reminds people of the complexity of the history between both countries. She said the relationship had not always been straightforward and that the islands had experienced more than their fair share of heartache, turbulence, and loss. (© *Chris Jackson/Getty Images*)

$300,000 (Erbe & Hart, 1994). A better program design would be to involve all participants from the beginning. This can be done by showing the benefits of an inclusive diversity policy—one that values all kinds of diversity, and not merely that based on gender, for example. Equally important is the mounting evidence of bottom-line benefits of diverse personnel who work well together (Harris, 1997).

4. The contact should have the potential to extend beyond the immediate situation and occur in a variety of contexts with a variety of individuals from all groups. This suggests that superficial contact between members of different groups is not likely to have much impact on attitudes (stereotypes, prejudice) or result in productive communication. For instance, simply sitting beside someone from another culture in a class or sampling food from different countries is not likely to result in genuine understanding of that perszon or appreciation for his or her cultural background (Stephan & Stephan, 1992). Thus, international students who live with host families are much more likely to have positive impressions of the host country and to develop better intercultural communication skills than those who go on "island programs," in which students interact mostly with other foreigners in the host country.

5. Programs should maximize cooperation within groups and minimize competition. For example, bringing a diverse group of students together should not involve pitting the African Americans against the European Americans on separate sports teams. Instead, it might involve creating diversity within teams to emphasize cooperation. Especially important is having a superordinate goal, a goal that everyone can agree on. This helps diverse groups develop a common identity (Gaertner, Dovidio, & Bachman, 1996). For instance, there is a successful summer camp in Maine for Arab and Jewish youths; the camp brings together members of these historically conflicting groups for a summer of cooperation, discussion, and relationship building.

6. Programs should equalize numbers of group members. Positive outcomes and successful communication will be more likely if members are represented in numerical equality. Research studies have shown that being in the numerical minority can cause stress and that the "solo" minority, particularly in beginning a new job, is subject to exaggerated expectations (either very high or very low) and extreme evaluations (either very good or very bad) (Pettigrew & Martin, 1989).

7. Group members should have similar beliefs and values. A large body of research supports the idea that people are attracted to those whom they perceive to be similar to themselves. This means that, in bringing diverse groups of people together, we should look for common ground—similarities based on religion, interests, competencies, and so on. For example, an international group of mothers is working for peace in the Middle East. Although members represent different ethnic groups, they come together with a shared goal—to protect their children from military action between the warring factions in the region.

8. Programs should promote individuation of group members. This means that they should downplay the characteristics that mark the different groups (such

When we look back, we see that many wrongs have been perpetrated against some people for the benefit of others. For those who benefited from the wrongs of the past, how should they address these wrongs? Georgetown University in Washington, D.C. is an example of the complexity of dealing with the past.

[I]n the fall of 1838, no one was spared: not the 2-month-old baby and her mother, not the field hands, not the shoemaker, and not Cornelius Hawkins, who was about 13 years old when he was forced onboard.

Their panic and desperation would be mostly forgotten for more than a century. But this was no ordinary slave sale. The enslaved African Americans had belonged to the nation's most prominent Jesuit priests. And they were sold, along with scores of others, to help secure the future of the premier Catholic institution of higher learning at the time, known today as Georgetown University.

Now, with racial protests roiling college campuses, an unusual collection of Georgetown professors, students, alumni, and genealogists is trying to find out what happened to those 272 men, women, and children. And they are confronting a particularly wrenching question: What, if anything, is owed to the descendants of slaves who were sold to help ensure the college's survival?

[...]

At Georgetown, slavery and scholarship were inextricably linked. The college relied on Jesuit plantations in Maryland to help finance its operations, university officials say. (Slaves were often donated by prosperous parishioners.) And the 1838 sale—worth about $3.3 million in today's dollars—was organized by two of Georgetown's early presidents, both Jesuit priests.

[...]

What has emerged from their research, and that of other scholars, is a glimpse of an insular world dominated by priests who required their

as language, physical abilities, or racial characteristics). Instead, group members might focus on the characteristics that express individual personalities.

This list of conditions can help us understand how domestic and international contexts vary (Gudykunst, 1979). It is easy to see how the history within a nation-state may lead to conditions and attitudes that are more difficult to facilitate. For example, historical conditions between African Americans and white Americans may make it impossible to meet these conditions; interracial interactions in the United States cannot be characterized by equality.

Note that this list of conditions is incomplete. Moreover, meeting all of the conditions does not guarantee positive outcomes when diverse groups of people interact. However, the list is a starting place, and it is important to be able to identify which conditions are affected by historical factors that may be difficult to change and which can be more easily facilitated by communication professionals.

slaves to attend Mass for the sake of their salvation, but also whipped and sold some of them.

[...]

Mismanaged and inefficient, the Maryland plantations no longer offered a reliable source of income for Georgetown College, which had been founded in 1789. It would not survive, Father Mulledy feared, without an influx of cash.

[...]

Father Mulledy promised his superiors that the slaves would continue to practice their religion. Families would not be separated. And the money raised by the sale would not be used to pay off debt or for operating expenses.

None of those conditions were met, university officials said.

Father Mulledy took most of the down payment he received from the sale—about $500,000 in today's dollars—and used it to help pay off the debts that Georgetown had incurred under his leadership.

In the uproar that followed, he was called to Rome and reassigned.

[...]

Meanwhile, Georgetown's working group has been weighing whether the university should apologize for profiting from slave labor, create a memorial to those enslaved, and provide scholarships for their descendants, among other possibilities, said Dr. Rothman, the historian.

"It's hard to know what could possibly reconcile a history like this," he said. "What can you do to make amends?"

Source: From R. L. Swarns (2016, April 16), "272 slaves were sold to save Georgetown. What does it owe their descendants?" *New York Times*. Retrieved April 16, 2016, from http://www.nytimes.com/2016/04/17/us/georgetown-university-search-for-slave-descendants.html?_r=0.

Negotiating Histories Dialectically in Interaction

How can a dialectical perspective help us negotiate interactions, given individual attitudes and personal and cultural histories? How can we balance past and present in our everyday intercultural interactions?

First, it is important to recognize that we all bring our own histories (some known, some hidden) to interactions. We can try to evaluate the role that history plays for those with whom we interact.

Second, we should understand the role that histories play in our identities, in what we bring to the interaction. Communication scholar Marsha Houston (1997) says there are three things that white people who want to be her friends should never say: "I don't notice you're black," "You're not like the others," and "I know how you feel." In her opinion, each of these denies or rejects a part of her identity that is deeply rooted in history.

Sometimes it is unwise to ask people where they are "really from." Such questions assume that they cannot be from where they said they were from, due to racial characteristics or other apparent features. Recognizing a person's history and its link to her or his identity in communication is a first step in establishing intercultural relationships. It is also important to be aware of your own historical blinders and assumptions.

Sometimes the past–present dialectic operates along with the disadvantage–privilege dialectic. The Hungarian philosopher György Lukács wrote a book titled *History and Class Consciousness* (1971), in which he argues that we need to think dialectically about history and social class. Our own recognition of how class differences have influenced our families is very much affected by the past and by the conditions members experienced that might explain whom they married, why they lived where they did, what languages they do and do not speak, and what culture they identify with.

Two dialectical tensions emerge here: (1) between privilege and disadvantage and (2) between the personal and the social. Both of these dialectics affect our view of the past, present, and future. As we attempt to understand ourselves and our situations (as well as those of others), we must recognize that we arrived at universities for a variety of reasons. Embedded in our backgrounds are dialectical tensions between privilege and disadvantage and the ways in which those factors were established in the past and the present. Then there is the dialectical tension between seeing ourselves as unique persons and as members of particular social classes. These factors affect both the present and the future. In each case, we must also negotiate the dialectical tensions between the past and the present, and between the present and the future. Who we think we are today is very much influenced by how we view the past, how we live, and what culture we believe to be our own.

INTERNET RESOURCES

http://americanradioworks.publicradio.org/features/remembering/
The American Radio Works has compiled information and documents relating to segregation in the United States and posted them online. Students can listen to accounts of segregation and retrospective analyses as well as read many detailed accounts. There is also a section that outlines key laws of the Jim Crow era.

http://www.archives.gov/research/genealogy/
The National Archives has set up this webpage to help you research your family history. You can see what kinds of records they hold and how you might go about doing this research.

http://www.discovernikkei.org/en/journal/2016/2/17/building-bridges/
This is a website about the Japanese diaspora in the Western Hemisphere, hence it is available in English, Japanese, Portuguese, and Spanish. The entire website is worth exploring, but this particular page makes important connections between Asian Americans and Arab Americans. It underscores the ways that the United States has

changed and remained the same regarding race, racial profiling and stereotyping, and national security.

http://www.pbs.org/wgbh/pages/frontline/shows/jefferson/true/
This webpage explores the evidence and controversy over the possible sexual relationship between Thomas Jefferson and one of his slaves, Sally Hemmings. Here you can read about the DNA evidence, as well as the reaction from historians and descendants. Here you can see an example of a contested intercultural history and its importance for the contemporary world.

www.ushmm.org/museum/

www.ushmm.org/research/center/

The first web address is for the United States Holocaust Museum. The museum website offers many exhibits related to the Holocaust that are viewable online. The second web address is specifically designed for university students. This section includes a searchable database for tracing Holocaust survivors and archiving information.

SUMMARY

- Multiple histories are important for empowering different cultural identities.
- Multiple histories include:
  - Political histories
  - Intellectual histories
  - Social histories
  - Family histories
  - National histories
  - Cultural-group histories
- Histories are constructed through narrative.
- Hidden histories are those typically not conveyed in a widespread manner and are based on race/ethnicity, gender, sexual orientation, diaspora, colonialism, socioeconomic class, and religion.
- People bring four elements of personal history to intercultural interactions:
  - Childhood experience
  - Historical myths
  - Language competence
  - Memories of recent political events
- Contact hypothesis suggests that simply bringing people from diverse groups together will only work if certain conditions are met:
  - Group members must be of equal status and relatively equal numbers.
  - Contact must be voluntary, extend beyond the superficial, have institutional support, and promote similarity and individuation of group members.
  - There should be maximum cooperation among participants.
- A dialectical perspective helps negotiate histories in intercultural interaction.

DISCUSSION QUESTIONS

1. What are some examples of hidden histories, and why are they hidden?

2. How do the various histories of the United States influence our communication with people from other countries?

3. How do you benefit or have been disenfranchised in the telling of certain histories? How do you take responsibility for the histories from which you benefit?

4. What factors in your experience have led to the development of positive feelings about your own cultural heritage and background? What factors have led to negative feelings, if any?

5. When can contact between members of two cultures improve their attitudes toward each other and facilitate communication between them?

6. How do histories influence the process of identity formation?

7. What is the significance of the shift from history to histories? How does this shift help us understand intercultural communication?

8. Why do some people in the United States prefer not to talk about history? What views of social reality and intercultural communication does this attitude encourage?

ACTIVITIES

1. *Cultural-Group History.* This exercise can be done by individual students or in groups. Choose a cultural group in the United States that is unfamiliar to you. Study the history of this group, and identify and describe significant events in its history. Answer the following questions:

   a. What is the historical relationship between this group and other groups (particularly the dominant cultural groups)?

   b. Are there any historical incidents of discrimination? If so, describe them.

   c. What are common stereotypes about the group? How did these stereotypes originate?

   d. Who are important leaders and heroes of the group?

   e. What are notable achievements of the group?

   f. How has the history of this group influenced the identity of group members today?

2. *Family Histories.* Write a brief personal narrative that tells the story of your family history. This may require additional research or conversations with family members. You may want to focus more on one parent's side, depending

on how much information you can find or which story has more meaning to you. Try and trace this story back to its furthest beginning.

a. How did your family come to live where they currently live?

b. Were there any great historical events that affected them and the decisions they made (e.g., slavery, the Holocaust)?

c. How does this history have meaning for you?

KEY WORDS

absent history (125)
altered history (125)
apartheid (132)
colonial histories (144)
concentration camps (131)
contact hypothesis (149)
cultural-group
   histories (128)

diaspora (144)
diasporic histories (144)
ethnic histories (136)
family histories (125)
gender histories (140)
grand narrative (132)
hidden histories (136)
intellectual histories (124)

modernist identity (132)
national history (126)
political histories (124)
racial histories (136)
sexual orientation
   history (141)
social histories (125)

REFERENCES

Allport, G. (1979). *The nature of prejudice.* New York: Addison-Wesley.

Amir, Y. (1969). Contact hypothesis in ethnic relations. *Psychological Bulletin, 71,* 319–343.

Amsden, D. (2015, February 26). Building the first slavery museum in America. *New York Times,* February 26, 2015. Retrieved April 15, 2016, from http://www .nytimes.com/2015/03/01/magazine/building-the-first -slave-museum-in-america.html?_r=0

Anzaldúa, G. (1987). *Borderlands/La frontera: The new mestiza.* San Francisco, CA: Spinsters/Aunt Lute.

Attenborough, R. (Director). (1987). *Cry Freedom* [Motion picture]. United States: Universal Studios.

Baudrillard, J. (1988). *America* (C. Turner, Trans.). New York: Verso.

Bernstein, N. (2007, April 3). Relatives of interned Japanese-Americans side with Muslims. *The New York Times.* Retrieved May 8, 2008, from www.nytimes .com/2007/04/03/nyregion/03detain.html?pagewanted= 1&sq=muslim&scp=153.

Blanchot, M. (1986). *The writing of the disaster* (A. Smock, Trans.). Lincoln, NE: University of Nebraska Press.

Botelho, G., & Brocchetto, M. (2016, April 15). Jamaica may oust UK's queen as official head of state. *CNN.* Retrieved May 2, 2016, from http://www.cnn .com/2016/04/15/americas/jamaica-queen-elizabeth -marijuana/.

Brinkman, H. (1997). Managing diversity: A review of recommendations for success. In C. D. Brown, C. Snedeker, & B. Sykes (Eds.), *Conflict and diversity* (pp. 35–50). Cresskill, NJ: Hampton Press.

Brislin, R. W. (1981). *Cross cultural encounters: Face to face interaction.* New York: Pergamon.

Bureau of African Affairs. (2005, September). Background note: South Africa. United States Department of State. Retrieved October 30, 2005, from www.state .gov/r/pa/ei/ bgn/2898.htm#history.

Cave, D. (2016, March 26). With Obama visit to Cuba, old battlelines fade. *New York Times.* Retrieved April 16, 2016, from http://www.nytimes .com/2016/03/27/world/americas/with-obama -visit-to-cuba-old-battle-lines-fade.html?login= email&_r=1.

Erbe, B., & Hart, B. (1994, September 16). Employer goes overboard on "gender sensitivity" issue. *The Evansville Courier,* p. A13.

Fausset, R., & Blinder, A. (2015, July 10). Era ends as South Carolina lowers Confederate flag. *New York Times.* Retrieved April 16, 2016, from http://www.nytimes.com/2015/07/11/us/south-carolina-confederate-flag.html.

Fisher, W. (1984). Narration as a human communication paradigm: The case of public moral argument. *Communication Monographs, 51,* 1–22.

Fisher, W. (1985). The narrative paradigm: An elaboration. *Communication Monographs, 52,* 347–367.

FitzGerald, F. (1972). *Fire in the lake: Vietnamese and Americans in Vietnam.* New York: Vintage Books.

Fleischer, A. (2001, September 18). Press briefing by Ari Fleischer. *The White House.* Retrieved May 8, 2008, from www.whitehouse.gov/news/releases/2001/09/20010918-5.html.

Frum, D. (2012, May 30). It wasn't a "gaffe." *The Daily Beast.* Retrieved April 16, 2016, from http://www.thedailybeast.com/articles/2012/05/30/poland-insult.html.

Gaertner, S. L., Dovidio, J. F., & Bachman, B. A. (1996). Revisiting the contact hypothesis: The induction of a common ingroup identity. *International Journal of Intercultural Relations, 20,* 271–290.

Gardner, W. (2014, January 11). History textbook wars cross borders. *Japan Times.* Retrieved April 15, 2016, from http://www.japantimes.co.jp/opinion/2014/01/11/commentary/world-commentary/history-textbook-wars-cross-borders/"http://www.japantimes.co.jp/opinion/2014/01/11/commentary/world-commentary/history-textbook-wars-cross-borders/#.VxFC2yMrLk9.

Gérard-Libois, J., & Heinen, J. (1989). *Belgique-Congo, 1960.* Brussels: Politique et Histoire.

Gilroy, P. (1993). *The Black Atlantic: Modernity and double consciousness.* New York: Verso.

Greenberg, D. (2005, January 14). The gay emancipator? *Slate.* Retrieved May 8, 2008, from www.slate.com/id/2112313/.

Gudykunst, W. B. (1979). Intercultural contact and attitude change: A review of literature and suggestions for future research. *International and Intercultural Communication Annual, 4,* 1–16.

Guelke, A. (2005). *Rethinking the rise and fall of apartheid: South Africa and world politics.* New York: Palgrave Macmillan.

Harris, T. E. (1997). Diversity: Importance, ironies, and pathways. In C. D. Brown, C. Snedeker, & B. Sykes (Eds.), *Conflict and diversity* (pp. 17–34). Cresskill, NJ: Hampton Press.

Heim, J. (2015, July 1). How a long-dead white supremacist still threatens the future of Virginia's Indian tribes. *The Washington Post.* Retrieved April 15, 2016, from https://www.washingtonpost.com/local/how-a-long-dead-white-supremacist-still-threatens-the-future-of-virginias-indian-tribes/2015/06/30/81be95f8-0fa4-11e5-adec-e82f8395c032_story.html?postshare=4041435865010465.

Hocquenghem, G., & Blasius, M. (1980, April). Interview. *Christopher Street, 8*(4), 36–45.

Houston, M. (1997). When Black women talk with White women: Why dialogues are difficult. In A. González, M. Houston, & V. Chen (Eds.), *Our voices: Essays in ethnicity, culture, and communication* (2nd ed., pp. 187–194). Los Angeles, CA: Roxbury.

Izadi, E. (2016, April 23). A new discovery sheds light on ancient Egypt's most successful female pharaoh. *The Washington Post.* Retrieved May 1, 2016, from https://www.washingtonpost.com/world/a-new-discovery-sheds-light-on-ancient-egypts-most-successful-female-pharaoh/2016/04/23/946b7976-0983-11e6-a12f-ea5aed7958dc_story.html.

Jacoby, J. (2016, May 1). 'Never forget' the world said of the Holocaust. But the world is forgetting. *The Boston Globe.* Retrieved May 2, 2016, from https://www.bostonglobe.com/opinion/2016/04/30/never-forget-world-said-holocaust-but-world-forgetting/59cUqLNFxylkW7BDuRPgNK/story.html.

Jameson, F. (1981). *The political unconscious: Narrative as a socially symbolic act.* Ithaca, NY: Cornell University Press.

Kennedy, R. (2003, September 11). From protest to patronage. *The Nation.* Retrieved May 8, 2008, from www.thenation.com/doc/20030929/kennedy.

Kothari, G. (1995). Where are you from? In G. Hongo (Ed.), *Under Western eyes: Personal essays from Asian America* (pp. 151–173). New York: Anchor Books/Doubleday.

Loewen, J. W. (1995). *Lies my teacher told me: Everything your American history textbook got wrong.* New York: Touchstone.

Lukács, György. (1971). *History and class consciousness: Studies in Marxist dialectics* (R. Livingstone, Trans.). Cambridge, MA: MIT Press.

Lyotard, J.-F. (1984). *The postmodern condition: A report on knowledge* (G. Bennington & B. Massumi, Trans.). Minneapolis, MN: University of Minnesota Press.

Mason, J., & Halpin, P. (2011, May 23). Obama visits family roots in Ireland. Reuters. Retrieved May 30, 2011, from www.reuters.com/article/2011/05/23/us-obama-ireland-idUSTRE74M09F20110523.

McGrory, B. (2011, May 11). Centuries of interruption and a history rejoined. *The Boston Globe,* pp. A1, A9.

McKenzie, S. (2016, January 25). Will Australia ditch the queen? *CNN.* Retrieved May 2, 2016, from http://www.cnn.com/2016/01/25/asia/australia-republic -debate-leaders-queen/index.html.

Nakano, M. (1990). *Japanese American women: Three generations, 1890–1990.* Berkeley and San Francisco, CA: Mina Press/National Japanese American Historical Society.

Obama, B. H. (2010, August 13). Remarks by the President at Iftar Dinner. Office of the Press Secretary, White House. Retrieved June 11, 2011, from www.whitehouse.gov/the-press -office/2010/08/13/remarks-president-iftar -dinner-0.

Obama, B. H. (2012, May 29). Remarks by the President at Presidential Medal of Freedom Ceremony. *The White House Office of the Press Secretary.* Retrieved from https://www.whitehouse.gov/the-press-office /2012/05/29/remarks-president-presidential-medal -freedom-ceremony.

Oi, M. (2013, March 24). What Japanese history lessons leave out. *BBC Magazine,* March 14, 2013. Retrieved April 15, 2016, from http://www.bbc.com/news /magazine-21226068.

Pettigrew, T. F., & Martin, J. (1989). Organizational inclusion of minority groups: A social psychological analysis. In J. P. VanOudenhoven, & T. M. Willemsen (Eds.), *Ethnic minorities: Social psychological per- spectives* (pp. 169–200). Amsterdam/Lisse: Swets & Zeitlinger.

Saulny, S. (2005, October 11). Cast from their ancestral home, Creoles worry about culture's future. *The New York Times,* p. A13.

Schwarzwald, J., & Amir, Y. (1996). Guest editor's intro- duction: Special issue on prejudice, discrimination and conflict. *International Journal of Intercultural Relations, 20,* 265–270.

Sciiutto, J., Browne, R. & Walsh, D. (2016, July 15). Congress releases secret "28 pages" on alleged Saudi 9/11 ties. *CNN.* Retrieved October 2, 2016, from http://www.cnn.com/2016/07/15/politics/congress -releases-28-pages-saudis-9-11/

Seel, P., with Bitoux, J. (1994). *Moi, Pierre Seel, déporté homosexual.* Paris: Calmann-Lévy.

Shaffer, M. (2002, June 9). Navajos protest national status for Old Spanish Trail. *The Arizona Republic,* pp. B1, B8.

Shome, R., & Hegde, R. (2002). Postcolonial approaches to communication: Charting the ter- rain, engaging the intersections. *Communication Theory, 12,* 249–270.

Spain passes law awarding citizenship to descendants of expelled Jews. (2015, June 11). *The Guardian.* Retrieved April 15, 2016, from http://www.theguardian .com/world/2015/jun/11/spain-law-citizenship -jews

Stephan, C. W., & Stephan, W. G. (1989). Antecedents of intergroup anxiety in Asian Americans and Hispanic Americans. *International Journal of Intercultural Relations, 13,* 203–216.

Stephan, C. W., & Stephan, W. G. (1992). Reducing intercultural anxiety through intercultural contact. *International Journal of Intercultural Relations, 16,* 89–106.

Stephan, W. G., & Stephan, C. W. (1996). *Intergroup relations.* Boulder, CO: Westview Press.

Steyn, M. (2001). *"Whiteness just isn't what it used to be": White identity in a changing South Africa.* Albany, NY: State University of New York Press.

Stryker, S. (2008). *Transgender history.* Berkeley, CA: Seal Press.

Swarns, R. L. & Kantor, J. (2009, October 7). In First Lady's roots, a complex path from slavery. *The New York Times.* Retrieved May 30, 2011, from www.nytimes.com/2009/10/08/us/politics/08 -genealogy.html?_r=3.

Swarns, R. L. (2016, April 16). 272 slaves were sold to save Georgetown. What does it owe their descen- dants? *New York Times.* Retrieved April 16, 2016, from http://www.nytimes.com/2016/04/17/us /georgetown-university-search-for-slave-descendants. html?_r=0.

Tateishi, J. (1984). *And justice for all: An oral history of the Japanese American detention camps.* New York: Random House.

Tell, D. (2008). The "shocking story" of Emmett Till and the politics of public confession. *Quarterly Journal of Speech, 94,* 156–178.

The White House. (2012, April 23). President Obama announces Jan Karski as a recipient of the Presiden- tial Medal of Freedom. https://www.whitehouse .gov/the-press-office/2012/04/23/president-obama -announces-jan-karski-recipient-presidential-medal -freedo.

Thompson, L. (2001). *A history of South Africa* (3rd ed.). New Haven, CT: Yale University Press.

Thonssen, L., Baird, A. C., & Braden, W. W. (1970). *Speech criticism* (2nd ed.). New York: Ronald Press.

Tripp, C. A. (2004). *The intimate world of Abraham Lincoln.* New York: Free Press.

Tusk, D. (quoted in Landler, M.) (2012, May 30). Polish premier denounces Obama for referring to a 'Polish death camp.' *New York Times.* Retrieved April 16, 2016, from http://www.nytimes.com/2012/05/31 /world/europe/poland-bristles-as-obama-says-polish -death-camps.html.

Under surveillance. (1995, December 26). *The Advocate,* p. 14.

U.S. Citizenship and Immigration Services. (n.d.) EB-5 Immigrant Investor Program. *Department of Homeland Security.* Retrieved from https://www.uscis.gov/eb-5.

Will, G. (2016, April 15). Histories that shouldn't be secret. *The Washington Post.* Retrieved April 16, 2016, from https://www.washingtonpost.com/opinions/histories-that-shouldnt-be-secret/2016/04/15/9fa6bdbe-0262-11e6-b823-707c79ce3504_story.html.

CREDITS

Freedom" from *The White House* (April 23, 2012). The White House is Public Domain and does not require permission. [page 150–151, text] President Obama, excerpt from "Remarks by the President at Presidential Medal of Freedom Ceremony" from *The White House Office of the Press Secretary* (May 29, 2012). [page 150–151, text] D. Tusk quoted in M. Landler, excerpt from "Polish premier denounces Obama for referring to a 'Polish death camp'" from *New York Times* (May 30, 2012). [page 151, text] D. Frum, excerpt from "It wasn't a 'gaffe'" from *The Daily Beast* (May 30, 2012). [page 153, text] D. Frum, quote from "It wasn't a 'gaffe'" from *The Daily Beast* (May 30, 2012). [page 154–155, text] R. L. Swarns, excerpt from "272 slaves were sold to save Georgetown. What does it owe their descendants?" from *New York Times* (April 16, 2016).

PART II

Intercultural Communication Processes

CHAPTER 5
Identity and Intercultural Communication

CHAPTER 6
Language and Intercultural Communication

CHAPTER 7
Nonverbal Codes and Cultural Space

CHAPTER

5

IDENTITY AND INTERCULTURAL COMMUNICATION

CHAPTER OBJECTIVES

After reading this chapter, you should be able to:

1. Identify three communication approaches to identity.
2. Define identity.
3. Describe phases of minority identity development.
4. Describe phases of majority identity development.
5. Identify and describe nine social and cultural identities.
6. Identify characteristics of whiteness.
7. Describe phases of multicultural identity development.
8. Explain the relationship among identity, stereotyping, and prejudice.
9. Explain the relationship between identity and communication.

THINKING DIALECTICALLY ABOUT IDENTITY
The Social Science Perspective
The Interpretive Perspective
The Critical Perspective

IDENTITY DEVELOPMENT ISSUES
Minority Identity Development
Majority Identity Development

SOCIAL AND CULTURAL IDENTITIES
Gender Identity
Sexual Identity
Age Identity
Racial and Ethnic Identities
Characteristics of Whiteness
Religious Identity
Class Identity
National Identity
Regional Identity

PERSONAL IDENTITY

MULTICULTURAL PEOPLE

IDENTITY, STEREOTYPES, AND PREJUDICE

IDENTITY AND COMMUNICATION

INTERNET RESOURCES

SUMMARY

DISCUSSION QUESTIONS

ACTIVITIES

KEY WORDS

REFERENCES

Now that we have examined some sociohistorical contexts that shape culture and communication, let us turn to a discussion of identity and its role in intercultural communication. Identity serves as a bridge between culture and communication. It is important because we communicate our identity to others, and we learn who we are through communication. It is through communication—with our family, friends, and others—that we come to understand ourselves and form our identity. Issues of identity are particularly important in intercultural interactions.

Conflicts can arise, however, when there are sharp differences between who we think we are and who others think we are. For example, many Muslims, like Omar Alnatour, feel that: "As a Muslim, I am tired of condemning terrorist attacks being carried out by inherently violent people who hijack my religion. [...] Above it all, I am tired of having to repeatedly say that Muslims are not terrorists" (2015). In this case, his Muslim identity and who he thinks he is do not always match with what others think about him and Muslim identity. This conflict lies at the heart of Islamophobia, as there is an unfounded, irrational fear of Muslims when people from many religions kill others for political reasons. When Sadiq Khan was elected mayor of London in 2016, he became the first Muslim mayor of a European Union capital. His election may signal a shift away from fear of Muslims and an acceptance of Muslim identity in Britain.

In this chapter, we describe a dialectical approach to understanding identity, one that encompasses three communication approaches: social science, interpretive, and critical. We then explore the important role language plays in understanding identity and how minority and majority identities develop. We then turn to the development of specific aspects of our social and cultural identity including those related to gender, race or ethnicity, class, religion, and nationality. We describe how these identities are often related to problematic communication—stereotypes, prejudice, and discrimination. We also examine an increasingly important identity—that of multicultural individuals. Finally, we discuss the relationship between identity and communication.

THINKING DIALECTICALLY ABOUT IDENTITY

Identity is a core issue for most people. It is about who we are and who others think we are. How do we come to understand who we are? And how do we communicate our identity to others? A useful theory is that of **impression management**—how people present themselves and how they guide the impression others form of them (Goffman, 1959). Some scholars suggest that individuals are constantly performing "spin control" campaigns to highlight their strengths and virtues while also attempting "damage control" by minimizing deficiencies (Tedeschi, Lindskold, & Rosenfeld, 1985; Rosenfeld and Giaclone, 1991). As we will see, individuals cannot control others' impressions completely, as those we interact with also play an important role in how our identities develop and are expressed.

What are the characteristics of identity? In this section we use both the static–dynamic and the personal–contextual dialectics in answering this question.

There are three contemporary communication perspectives on identity (see Table 5-1). The social science perspective, based largely on research in psychology, views the self in a relatively static fashion in relation to the various cultural

identity The concept of who we are. Characteristics of identity may be understood differently depending on the perspectives that people take—for example, social science, interpretive, or critical perspectives.

impression management theory The ways by which individuals attempt to control the impressions others have of them.

TABLE 5-1 THREE PERSPECTIVES ON IDENTITY AND COMMUNICATION		
Social Science	Interpretive	Critical
Identity created by self (by relating to groups)	Identity formed through communication with others	Identity shaped through social, historical forces
Emphasizes individualized, familial, and spiritual self (cross-cultural perspective)	Emphasizes avowal and ascribed dimensions	Emphasizes contexts and resisting ascribed identity

communities to which a person belongs: nationality, race, ethnicity, religion, gender, and so on. The interpretive perspective is more dynamic and recognizes the important role of interaction with others as a factor in the development of the self. Finally, the critical perspective views identity even more dynamically—as a result of contexts quite distant from the individual. As you read this chapter, keep in mind that the relationship between identity and intercultural interaction involves both static and dynamic elements and both personal and contextual elements.

The Social Science Perspective

The social science perspective emphasizes that identity is created in part by the self and in part in relation to group membership. According to this perspective, the self is composed of multiple identities, and these notions of identity are culture bound. How, then, do we come to understand who we are? That depends very much on our cultural background. According to Western psychologists like Erik Erikson, our identities are self-created, formed through identity conflicts and crises, through identity diffusion and confusion (Erikson, 1950, 1968). Occasionally, we may need a moratorium, a time-out, in the process. Our identities are created not in one smooth, orderly process but in spurts, with some events providing insights into who we are and long periods intervening during which we may not think much about ourselves or our identities.

Cross-Cultural Perspectives   In the United States, young people are often encouraged to develop a strong sense of identity, to "know who they are," to be independent and self-reliant, which reflects an emphasis on the cultural value of individualism. However, this was not always the case, and even today in many countries there is a very different, more collectivist notion of self. Min-Sun Kim (2002), a communication scholar, traces the evolution of the individualistic self. Before 1500, people in Europe as well as in most other civilizations lived in small cohesive communities, with a worldview characterized by the interdependence of spiritual and material phenomena. With the beginning of the industrial revolution in the 1600s came the notion of the world as a machine; this mechanistic view extended to living organisms and has had a profound effect on Western thought. It taught people to think of themselves as isolated egos—unconnected to the natural world and society in general. Thus, according to Kim, a person in the West came to be understood as "an individual entity with a separate existence independent

Identities are not simply a matter of how we personally identify. Identities are also how others and social institutions value or devalue certain identities. How cultures feel about various identities can change over time. How we live together with people of different identities is always negotiated. After the mass shooting in an Orlando gay nightclub in 2016, former President Obama asked U.S. Americans not to fall into demonizing and attacking those U.S. Americans with Muslim identities. He attempts to shape how we live together with identity differences:

> We hear language that singles out immigrants and suggests that entire religious communities are complicit in violence. Where does this stop? The Orlando killer, one of the San Bernardino killers, the Fort Hood killer—they were all U.S. citizens.
>
> Are we going to start treating all Muslim Americans differently? Are we going to start subjecting them to special surveillance? Are we going to start discriminating against them because of their faith? We've heard these suggestions during the course of this campaign. Do Republican officials actually agree with this? Because that's not the America we want. It doesn't reflect our democratic ideals. It won't make us more safe; it will make us less safe—fueling ISIL's notion that the West hates Muslims, making young Muslims in this country and around the world feel like no matter what they do, they're going to be under suspicion and under attack. It makes Muslim Americans feel like they're government is betraying them. It betrays the very values America stands for.
>
> We've gone through moments in our history before when we acted out of fear—and we came to regret it. We've seen our government mistreat our fellow citizens. And it has been a shameful part of our history.
>
> [...]
>
> Our diversity and our respect for one another, our drawing on the talents of everybody in this country, our making sure that we are treating everybody fairly—that we're not judging people on the basis of what faith they are or what race they are, or what ethnicity they are, or what their sexual orientation is—that's what makes this country great. That's the spirit we see in Orlando. That's the unity and resolve that will allow us to defeat ISIL. That's what will preserve our values and our ideals that define us as Americans. That's how we're going to defend this nation, and that's how we're going to defend our way of life.

Source: President Obama (2016, June 14). Remarks by the president after counter-ISIL meeting. *The White House.* Retrieved from https://www.whitehouse.gov/the-press-office/2016/06/14/remarks -president-after-counter-isil-meeting

of place in society" (Kim, 2002, p. 12). In contrast, people in many other regions of the world have retained the more interdependent notion of the self.

Cross-cultural psychologist Alan Roland (1988) has identified three universal aspects of identity present in all individuals: (1) an individualized identity,

(2) a familial identity, and (3) a spiritual identity. Cultural groups usually emphasize one or two of these dimensions and downplay the other(s). Let's see how this works. The **individualized identity** is the sense of an independent "I," with sharp distinctions between the self and others. This identity is emphasized by most groups in the United States, where young people are encouraged to be independent and self-reliant at a fairly early age—by adolescence.

individualized identity The sense of self as independent and self-reliant.

In contrast, the **familial identity,** evident in many collectivististic cultures, stresses the importance of emotional connectedness to and interdependence with others. For example, in many African and Asian societies, and in some cultural groups in the United States, children are encouraged and expected to form strong, interdependent bonds, first with the family and later with other groups. As one of our students explains,

familial identity The sense of self as always connected to family and others.

> to be Mexican American is to unconditionally love one's family and all it stands for. Mexican-Americans are an incredibly close-knit group of people, especially when it comes to family. We are probably the only culture that can actually recite the names of our fourth cousins by heart. In this respect our families are like clans, they go much further than the immediate family and very deep into extended families. We even have a celebration, Dia de los Muertos (Day of the Dead), that honors our ancestors.

In these societies, educational, occupational, and even marital choices are made by individuals with extensive family guidance. The goal of the developed identity is not to become independent from others but rather to gain an understanding of and cultivate one's place in the complex web of interdependence with others.

In addition, the understanding of the familial self may be more connected to others and situation bound. According to studies comparing North Americans' and East Asians' senses of identity, when asked to describe themselves, the North Americans give more abstract, situation-free descriptions ("I am kind," "I am outgoing," "I am quiet in the morning"), whereas East Asians tend to describe their memberships and relationships to others rather than themselves ("I am a mother," "I am the youngest child in my family," "I am a member of a tennis club") (Cross, 2000).

spiritual identity Identification with feelings of connectedness to others and higher meanings in life.

The third dimension is the **spiritual identity,** the inner spiritual reality that is realized and experienced to varying extents by people through a number of outlets. For example, the spiritual self in India is expressed through a structure of gods and goddesses and through rituals and meditation. In Japan, the realization of the spiritual self tends more toward aesthetic modes, such as the tea ceremony and flower arranging (Roland, 1988).

Clearly, identity development does not occur in the same way in every society. The notion of identity in India, Japan, and some Latino/a and Asian American groups emphasizes the integration of the familial and the spiritual self but very little of the more individualized self.

This is not to say there is not considerable individuality among people in these groups. However, the general identity contrasts dramatically with the predominant mode in most U.S. cultural groups, in which the individualized self is emphasized and there is little attention to the familial self. However, there may be some development of the spiritual self among devout Catholic, Protestant, Jewish, or Muslim individuals.

Groups play an important part in the development of all these dimensions of self. As we are growing up, we identify with many groups, based on gender, race, ethnicity, class, sexual orientation, religion, and nationality (Tajfel, 1981, 1982).

And depending on our cultural background, we may develop tight or looser bonds with these groups (Kim, 2002). By comparing ourselves and others with members of these groups, we come to understand who we are. Because we belong to various groups, we develop multiple identities that come into play at different times, depending on the context. For example, in going to church or temple, we may highlight our religious identity. In going to clubs or bars, we may highlight our sexual orientation identity. Women who join social groups exclusive to women (or men who attend social functions just for men) are highlighting their gender identity.

Communication scholar Ting-Toomey (1993, 2005) argues in her **identity negotiation theory** that cultural variability influences our sense of self and ultimately influences how successful we are in intercultural interactions. Her argument goes like this: Individuals define themselves in relation to groups they belong to due to the basic human need for security and inclusion. At the same time, humans also need differentiation from these same groups. Managing relationships to these various groups involves boundary regulation and working through the tension between inclusion and differentiation and can make us feel secure or vulnerable. How we manage this tension influences the coherent sense of self (identity)—individuals who are more secure are more open to interacting with members of other cultures. When people feel good about themselves and the groups to which they belong, they are more successful in intercultural interactions. However, as we will see in the next section, identities are formed not just by the individual but also through interactions with others.

identity negotiation theory A theory that emphasizes the process of communicating one's own desired identities while reinforcing or resisting others' identities as the core of intercultural communication.

The Interpretive Perspective

The interpretive perspective builds on the notions of identity formation discussed previously but takes a more dynamic turn. That is, it emphasizes that identities are negotiated, co-created, reinforced, and challenged though communication with others; they emerge when messages are exchanged between persons (Hecht, Warren, Jung, & Krieger, 2005; Ting-Toomey, 2005). This means that presenting our identities is not a simple process. Does everyone see you as you see yourself? Probably not. To understand how these images may conflict, the concepts of avowal and ascription are useful.

Avowal is the process by which individuals portray themselves, whereas **ascription** is the process by which others attribute identities to them. Sometimes these processes are congruent. In June 2015, the racial identity of Rachel Dolezal, former president of the local NAACP chapter in Spokane, Washington and former instructor at Eastern Washington University, became a site of contestation. She notes that: "If somebody asked me how I identify, I identify as black. Nothing about whiteness describes who I am" (qtd. in McGreal, 2015). While her avowed racial identity is black, her parents and society identify her as white. When her parents revealed that they are white, the reaction was strong: "Some white people painted Dolezal as mentally unstable, on the grounds that no normal white person would choose to call themselves black. But it was the wave of rage and mockery from the African American community that really stung" (McGreal, 2015). Many people felt betrayed by the conflict between her avowed identity and her ascribed identity.

avowal The process by which an individual portrays himself or herself.

ascription The process by which others attribute identities to an individual.

Different identities are emphasized depending on the individuals we are communicating with and the topics of conversation. For example, in a social conversation with someone we are attracted to, our gender or sexual orientation identity is probably more important to us than other identities (ethnicity, nationality). And our communication is probably most successful when the person we are talking with confirms the identity we think is most important at the moment. In this sense, competent intercultural communication affirms the identity that is most salient in any conversation (Collier & Thomas, 1988). For example, if you are talking with a professor about a research project, the conversation will be most competent if the interaction confirms the salient identities (professor and student) rather than other identities (e.g., those based on gender, religion, or ethnicity).

How do you feel when someone does not recognize the identity you believe is most salient? For example, suppose your parents treat you as a child (their ascription) and not as an independent adult (your avowal). How might this affect communication? One of our students describes how she feels about the differences between black identity and African American identity:

> *I think my identity is multifaceted. In some spaces I am Black. In others I am African American. In very few, I am both. This is both due to the connotations associated with the words and also the location I am in. In social spaces, I identify myself as being black because in my eyes the word "black" is associated with hip hop culture, Black Power, and more recently, Black Lives Matter, topics that I believe appropriate to discuss in social settings. However, the term African American seems more proper. To me it is just a description of a person from a continent I've never stepped foot on. "African American" is an ascribed identity as opposed to my black avowed identity.*

core symbols The fundamental beliefs that are shared by the members of a cultural group. *Labels,* a category of core symbols, are names or markers used to classify individual, social, or cultural groups.

Central to the interpretive perspective is the idea that our identities are expressed communicatively—in core symbols, labels, and norms. **Core symbols** (or cultural values) tell us about the fundamental beliefs and the central concepts that define a particular identity. Communication scholar Michael Hecht and his colleagues (Hecht, 1998; Hecht, Jackson, & Ribeau, 2003) have identified the contrasting core symbols associated with various ethnic identities. For example, core symbols of African American identity may be positivity, sharing, uniqueness, realism, and assertiveness. Individualism is often cited as a core symbol of European American identity. Core symbols are not only expressed but also created and shaped through communication. Labels are a category of core symbols; they are the terms we use to refer to particular aspects of our own and others' identities—for example, *African American, Latino, white,* or *European American.*

Finally, some norms of behavior are associated with particular identities. For example, women may express their gender identity by being more concerned about safety than men. They may take more precautions when they go out at night, such as walking in groups. People might express their religious identity by participating in activities such as going to church or Bible study meetings.

The Critical Perspective

Like the interpretive perspective, the critical perspective emphasizes the dynamic nature of identities, but in addition, it emphasizes the contextual and often conflictual

FIGURE 5-1 We have many different identities—including gender, ethnicity, age, religion, and sexuality—that we express in different ways at different times. Celebrations are one way to highlight identity. Here, Sikhs in the northern Indian city of Chandigarh light candles in a temple to celebrate Diwali. Diwali marks the age-old culture of India and celebrates knowledge and the vanquishing of ignorance. (© *AP Photo/Aman Sharma*)

elements of identity development. This perspective pays particular attention to the societal structures and institutions that constrain identities and are often the root of injustice and oppression (Collier, 2005).

Contextual Identity Formation   The driving force behind a critical approach is the attempt to understand identity formation within the contexts of history, economics, politics, and discourse. To grasp this notion, ask yourself, How and why do people identify with particular groups and not others? What choices are available to them?

We are all subject to being pigeonholed into identity categories, or contexts, even before we are born. (See Figure 5-1.) Many parents ponder a name for their unborn child, who is already part of society through his or her relationship to the parents. Some children have a good start at being, say, Jewish or Chicana before they are even born. We cannot ignore the ethnic, socioeconomic, or racial positions from which we start our identity journeys.

The identities that others may ascribe to us are socially and politically determined. They are not constructed by the self alone. We must ask ourselves what drives the construction of particular kinds of identities. For example, the label "heterosexual" is a relatively recent one, created less than a hundred years ago (Katz, 1995). Today, people do not hesitate to identify themselves as "heterosexuals." A critical perspective insists on the constructive nature of this process and attempts to identify the social forces and needs that give rise to these identities.

These contextual constraints on identity are also reflected in the experience of a Palestinian woman who describes her feelings of not having a national "identity" as represented by a passport—because of political circumstances far beyond her control:

> *I am Palestinian but I don't have either a Palestinian passport or an Israeli passport. . . . If I take the Palestinian passport, the Israeli government would prevent me from entering Jerusalem and Jerusalem is a part of my soul. I just can't NOT enter it. And of course I'm not taking an Israeli passport, so . . . I get frustrated when I talk to people WITH identity, especially Palestinians with Israeli identity. I just get like kind of offended because I think they're more comfortable than me. (Collier, 2005, p. 243)*

Resisting Ascribed Identities   When we invoke such discourses about identity, we are pulled into the social forces that feed the discourse. We might resist the position they put us in, and we might try to ascribe other identities to ourselves. Nevertheless, we must begin from that position in carving out a new identity.

French philosopher Louis Althusser (1971) uses the term **interpellation** to refer to this process. He notes that we are pushed into this system of social forces:

> *by that very precise operation which I have called interpellation or hailing, and which can be imagined along the lines of the most commonplace everyday police (or other) hailing: "Hey you there!" . . . Experience shows that the practical telecommunication of hailings is such that they hardly ever miss their man: verbal call or whistle, the one hailed always recognizes that it is really him who is being hailed. And yet it is a strange phenomenon, and one which cannot be explained solely by "guilt feelings." (p. 163)*

interpellation The communication process by which one is pulled into the social forces that place people into a specific identity.

This hailing process that Althusser describes operates in intercultural communication interactions. It establishes the foundation from which the interaction occurs. For example, occasionally someone will ask Tom if he is Japanese, a question that puts him in an awkward position. He neither holds Japanese citizenship, nor has he ever lived in Japan. Yet the question probably doesn't mean to address these issues. Rather, the person is asking what it means to be "Japanese." How can Tom reconfigure his position in relation to this question?

The Dynamic Nature of Identities   The social forces that give rise to particular identities are never stable but are always changing. Therefore, the critical perspective insists on the dynamic nature of identities. For example, the emergence of the European Union has given new meaning to the notion of being "European" as an identity. This larger political context can reshape many identities. For example, the

When Katya Cengel, a Rwandan tour guide, was hired by a white American photographer to show him around Rwanda and Uganda, he recognized his own stereotypes of white people when the photographer tried to leave him without paying about $1000. His surprise was based on his notions of white people. How much of this image is the result of colonization? How much is due to his limited contact with white people? How widespread is white privilege around the world?

> *When I was a child, we were taught only good things about white people: mzungus are always on time, mzungus always treat people fairly, mzungus are to be trusted. […] I had this image that all white people were perfect.*

Source: K. Cengel, "A sudden breach in Uganda," *The New York Times Magazine,* April 15, 2016. Retrieved from http://www.nytimes.com/2016/04/17/magazine/a-sudden-breach-in-uganda.html?rref=collection%2Fsectioncollection%2Fmagazine&action=click&contentCollection=magazine&region=stream&module=stream_unit&version=latest&contentPlacement=30&pgtype=sectionfront

recent influx of refugees into Germany has changed how Germans think of their country, their culture, and their place in the world:

> **In the past** *five years, as the number of people displaced worldwide by conflict and persecution has reached a level not seen since the end of World War II, many Germans have expressed pride that their nation—which unleashed the violence that prompted the earlier mass flight—has now become a beacon of safety and opportunity for imperiled and dispossessed people around the world. The degree to which many Germans embraced this new identity became exceedingly clear last summer, when Hungary tried to stop the mass of Germany-bound migrants traveling through the country by cutting off their access to trains. Migrants stranded outside Budapest's Keleti train station chanted: "Germany! Germany!" And within days, roughly a thousand of them had set out on foot from Hungary and across Austria to Germany, some of them holding posters of the German chancellor, Angela Merkel. Merkel, fearing chaos, should she turn the migrants away, instead sent German trains to pick them up, a decision she later called a "humanitarian imperative." As migrants arrived at Munich's central station, local residents greeted them with cheers and applause. Some handed out chocolate and balloons. Germans spoke of their strong Willkommenskultur, or "Welcome Culture," and German politicians portrayed the warm reception as a moral achievement, a further step toward redefining modern Germany as a benevolent nation that has moved beyond the ignominy of its ultranationalist past* (Angelos, p. 43).

While these refugees may change German culture and identity, Germans are also changing German culture and identity as they demonstrated that many of them embrace their "Welcome Culture."

Aside from these larger contexts for identity, identities are also dynamic on the individual level because of someone's own experiences. One of our students explains how his personal identity has changed over the past few years:

I will say I am 100% Chinese, but after I came abroad, studying in the United States for a couple of years, learning a different language, interacting with international students, and assimilating into this new environment for quite a while, I feel my self-identity is changed a little, as part of me did have to integrate into this new culture.

It is important to remember that identities—whether national, cultural or personal—are always changing.

For another example, look at the way that identity labels have changed from "colored" to "Negro" to "black" to "Afro-American" to "African American." Although the labels seem to refer to the same group of people, the political and cultural identities of those so labeled are different. The term "Negro" was replaced by "Black" during the civil rights movement in the 1960s because it stood for racial pride, power, and rejection of the status quo. "Black is beautiful" and "Black power" became slogans during this time. In the late 1980s, Black leaders proposed that "Black" be replaced with "African American," saying that this label would provide African Americans a cultural identification with their heritage and ancestral homeland. The changes in these labels have worked to strengthen group identity and facilitate the struggle for racial equality (Smith, 1992). Currently, both terms are used—depending on people's preference—and "Black" is preferred by some because it shows commonality with people of African descent who are not U.S. American (e.g., Caribbean Islanders) (Sigelman, Tuch, & Martin, 2005; Why Black . . . , 2008).

IDENTITY DEVELOPMENT ISSUES

People can identify with a multitude of groups: gender, age, religion, nationality, to name only a few. How do we come to develop a sense of identities? As we noted earlier, our identities develop over a period of time and always through interaction with others. How an individual's identity develops depends partly on the relative position or location of the identity within the societal hierarchy. Some identities have a higher position on the social hierarchy. For example, a heterosexual identity has a more privileged position than a homosexual identity; a Christian religious identity is generally more privileged than a Jewish or Muslim religious identity in the United States. To distinguish among the various positions, we label the more privileged identities "majority identities" and label the less privileged "minority identities." This terminology refers to the relative dominance or power of the identity position, not the numerical quantity.

Social science researchers have identified various models that describe how minority and majority identities develop. (See Table 5-2.) Although the models center on racial and ethnic identities, they may also apply to other identities, such as class, gender, or sexual orientation (Ponterotto & Pedersen, 1993). It is also important to remember that, as with any model, these represent the experience of many people, but the stages are not set in stone. Identity development is a complex process; not everyone experiences these phases in exactly the same way.

TABLE 5-2 MAJORITY, MINORITY, AND BIRACIAL IDENTITY DEVELOPMENT STAGES

Minority	Majority	Biracial
1. Unexamined identity • Lack of exploration of ethnicity • Acceptance of majority group values • Positive attitudes toward the majority group • Lack of interest in issues of ethnicity	1. Unexamined identity • Lack of exploration of ethnicity • Acceptance of majority group values • Positive attitudes toward the majority group • Lack of interest in issues of ethnicity	1. May cycle through three stages of identity development • Awareness of differences and resulting dissonance • Awareness that they are different from other children • Sense that they don't fit in anywhere
2. Conformity • Internalization of dominant group norms; desire for assimilation into this group • Negative attitudes toward themselves and their groups until an experience causes them to question the dominant culture attitudes	2. Acceptance • Internalization of a racist ideology (passive or active acceptance) • The key point is that individuals are not aware that they have been programmed to accept this worldview.	2. Struggle for acceptance • May feel that they need to choose one race or another
3. Resistance and separatism • Growing awareness that not all dominant values are beneficial to minorities • Often triggered by negative events • Blanket endorsement of one's group's values and attitudes • Rejection of dominant group values and norms	3. Resistance • Moving from blaming minority members for their situations and beginning to blame their own dominant group	3. Self-acceptance and self-assertion
4. Integration • Ideal outcome of identity development—achieved identity • Strong sense of their own group identity and an appreciation for other cultural groups	4. Redefinition • Nonacceptance of society's definition of white • Able to see positive aspects of being white • Becoming comfortable with being in dominant group	
	5. Integration • Ideal outcome of identity development—achieved identity • Strong sense of their own group identity and an appreciation for other cultural groups	

Some people spend more time in one phase than do others; individuals may experience the phases in different ways, and not everyone reaches the final phase.

Minority Identity Development

In general, minority identities tend to develop earlier than majority identities. For example, straight people tend to not think about their sexual orientation identity often, whereas gay people are often acutely aware of their sexual orientation identity being different from the majority and develop a sense of sexual orientation identity earlier than people who are straight. Similarly, while whites may develop a strong ethnic identity, they often do not think about their racial identity, whereas members of racial minority groups are aware of their racial identities at an early age (Ferguson, 1990).

minority identity
A sense of belonging to a nondominant group.

Minority identity often develops in the following stages (as shown in Table 5-2):

Stage 1: Unexamined Identity   This stage is characterized by the lack of exploration of identity, be it racial, ethnic, sexual orientation, gender, or whatever. At this stage, individuals may simply lack interest in the identity issue. As one African American woman put it: "Why do I need to learn about who was the first black woman to do this or that? I'm just not too interested." Or minority group members may initially accept the values and attitudes of the majority culture, expressing positive attitudes toward the dominant group and negative views of their own group. Gay young people may try very hard to act "straight" and may even participate in "gay bashing."

Stage 2: Conformity   This stage is characterized by the internalization of the values and norms of the dominant group and a strong desire to assimilate into the dominant culture. Individuals in this phase may have negative, self-deprecating attitudes toward both themselves and their group. As one young Jewish woman said: "I tried very hard in high school to not let anyone know I was Jewish. I'd talk about Christmas shopping and Christmas parties with my friends even though my parents didn't allow me to participate at all in any Christmas celebration."

Individuals who criticize members of their own ethnic or racial group may be given negative labels such as "Uncle Tom" or "oreo" for African Americans, "banana" for Asian Americans, "apple" for Native Americans, and "Tio Taco" for Chicanos. Such labels condemn attitudes and behaviors that support the dominant white culture. This stage often continues until they encounter a situation that causes them to question prodominant culture attitudes, which initiates the movement to the next stage.

Stage 3: Resistance and Separatism   Many kinds of events can trigger the move to the third stage, including negative ones such as encountering discrimination or name-calling. A period of dissonance, or a growing awareness that not all dominant group values are beneficial to minorities, may also precede this stage.

International students sometimes develop their national identity as a minority identity when they study overseas. Dewi, an Indonesian student, reported that when she first arrived in the United States, she thought little of her national identity (because this was a majority identity in *her* country). She told everyone she thought the United States was the greatest place and really tried hard to use American slang,

My father is American and my mother is Singaporean. I grew up in Singapore and identify more with my Asian side. However, since my father is white, Singaporeans do not see me as a fellow Singaporean but as a foreigner. It has been difficult to deal with my multiracial identity because I don't see myself as 100% American or 100% Singaporean. In Singapore, the country I identify more with, Singaporeans see me as a foreigner. Having moved to America for college, Americans do not identify me as an American either.
    —Lauren

Whenever I tell people that I am Canadian, one of the first things they ask is if I can speak French. I have even had people start speaking French to me right away. I think they realize once I look at them with big bug eyes that no, I am not fluent in French, and that only a select portion of the Canadian population can speak French.
    —Ainsley

dress American, and fit in. After several experiences with discrimination, she moved to a more separate stage where she only socialized with other Indonesian or other international students for a time. For writer Ruben Martinez (1998), a defining moment was when he was rather cruelly rejected by a white girl whom he had asked to dance at a high school prom:

> *I looked around me at the dance floor with new eyes: Mexicans danced with Mexicans, blacks with blacks, whites with whites. Who the hell did I think I was? Still, it would take a while for the gringo-hater in me to bust out. It was only a matter of time before I turned away from my whiteness and became the ethnic rebel. It seemed like it happened overnight, but it was the result of years of pentup rage in me.* (p. 256)

Sometimes the move to this phase happens because individuals who have been denying their identity meet someone from that group who exhibits a strong identity. This encounter may result in a concern to clarify their own identity. So the young woman who was ashamed of being Jewish and tried hard to act "Christian" met a dynamic young man who was active in his synagogue and had a strong Jewish faith. Through their relationship she gained an appreciation of her own religious background, including the Jewish struggle for survival throughout the centuries. As often happens in this stage, she wholeheartedly endorsed the values and attitude attributed to the minority (Jewish) group and rejected the values and norms associated with the dominant group—she dropped most of her Christian friends and socialized primarily with her Jewish friends.

This stage may be characterized by a blanket endorsement of one's group and all the values and attitudes attributed to the group. At the same time, the person may reject the values and norms associated with the dominant group.

Stage 4: Integration   According to this model, the ideal outcome of the identity development process is the final stage—an achieved identity. Individuals who have reached this stage have a strong sense of their own group identity (based on gender, race, ethnicity, sexual orientation, and so on) and an appreciation of other cultural groups. In this stage, they come to realize that racism and other forms of oppression occur, but they try to redirect any anger from the previous stage in more positive ways. The end result is individuals with a confident and secure identity characterized by a desire to eliminate all forms of injustice, and not merely oppression aimed at their own group.

> *Brenda: I had a hard time accepting my "old age identity." And for a while, I didn't even want to be around younger people. However, now I realize there will always be some discrimination against older women. We're really just invisible. I walk into a store and if there is anyone younger and more attractive, salespeople will often look right though me. However, I accept that this is the way our society is. And I can enjoy being around younger people now—I love their energy and their optimism. And I know that there are positive things about being older. Like, many things I just don't worry about anymore.*

> *Jack: I have a very diverse ethnic background. I am 50% Armenian, 25% Italian, and 25% Irish. Throughout my childhood, people were only surprised when I mentioned I had Irish ethnicity. Due to the other ethnicities I have a darker skin tone, I realized that people had judged my ethnicity based on my physical appearance. Once explaining my interesting family history and ethnic background, people said it was interesting that I come from multiple different ethnicities and it made me feel unique and happy to have such a diverse background.*

Majority Identity Development

majority identity A sense of belonging to a dominant group.

Rita Hardiman (1994, 2003), educator and pioneer in antiracism training, presents a model of **majority identity** development that has similarities to the model for minority group members. Although she intended the model to represent how white people develop a sense of healthy racial identity, it can also be helpful in describing how other majority identities develop—straight sexual orientation, Christian religious identity, male gender identity, middle-class identity, and so on. Again, remember that majority identity, like minority identity, develops through a complex process. And this model—unlike some other identity development models—is prescriptive. In other words, it outlines the way some scholars think a majority identity *should* develop, from accepting societal hierarchies that favor some identities and diminish others to resisting these inequities.

Hardiman (1993, 2004) outlines the following five stages:

Stage 1: Unexamined Identity This first stage is the same as for minority identities. In this case, individuals may be aware of some physical and cultural differences, but they do not fear the other or think much about their own identity. There is no understanding of the social meaning and value of gender, sexual orientation, religion, and so on. Although young boys may develop a sense of what it means to be a male by watching their fathers or other males, they are not aware of the social consequences of being born male over female. Those with majority identities, unlike those with minority identities, may stay in this stage for a long time.

Stage 2: Acceptance   The second stage represents the internalization, conscious or unconscious, of a racist (or otherwise biased) ideology. This may involve passive or active acceptance. The key point is that individuals are not aware that they have been programmed to accept this worldview.

In the passive acceptance stage, individuals have no conscious identification with being white, straight, male, and so forth. However, they may hold some assumptions based on an acceptance of inequities in the larger society. In general, the social hierarchy is experienced as "normal" for the dominant group, and they may view minority groups as being unduly sensitive and assume that if the minority members really wanted to change their lot in life they could. Here are some possible assumptions.

Being male in this stage may involve the following (sometime unconscious) assumptions:

- Men and women may be different, but they are basically equal. Kyle, a student, tells us, "I never heard so much whining from 'feminists' until I came to college. Frankly, it is a little much. Although women may have faced barriers in the past, that's in the past. Women can pretty much do whatever they want in society today. If they want to be doctors, lawyers, police officers, firefighters, or anything else, they just need to set their minds to it and do it."
- If women really want to make it professionally, they can work as hard as men work and they will succeed.

Being straight may involve these assumptions:

- Gay people choose to be gay.
- Gay people whine a lot, unfairly, about discrimination. There is no recognition of the many privileges given to those who are straight.
- Gay people put their gayness in straight people's faces. At this stage there is no recognition of the vast societal emphasis on heterosexuality.

Being white may involve these assumptions:

- Minority groups are culturally deprived and need help to assimilate.
- Affirmative action is reverse discrimination because people of color are being given opportunities that whites don't have.
- White culture—music, art, and literature—is "classical"; works of art by people of color are folk art or "crafts."
- People of color are culturally different, whereas whites have no group identity or culture or shared experience of racial privilege.

Individuals in this stage usually take one of two positions with respect to interactions with minorities: (1) They avoid contact somewhat with minority group members or (2) they adopt a patronizing stance toward them. Both positions are possible at the same time.

In contrast, those in the active acceptance stage are conscious of their privileged position and may express their feelings of superiority collectively (e.g., join male-only clubs). Some people never move beyond this phase—whether it is characterized by passive or active acceptance. And if they do, it is usually a result of a number of cumulative events. For example, Judith gradually came to realize that her two nieces, who are sisters—one of whom is African American and one of whom is white—had very different experiences growing up. Both girls lived in middle-class neighborhoods, both were honor students in high school, and both went to Ivy League colleges. However, they often had very different experiences. On more than one occasion, the African American girl was followed by security while shopping; she also was stopped several times by police while driving her mother's sports car. Her white sister never had these experiences. Eventually, awareness of this reality prodded Judith to the next stage.

This model recognizes that it is very difficult to escape the societal hierarchy that influences both minority and majority identity development because of its pervasive, systemic, and interlocking nature. The hierarchy is a by-product of living within and being impacted by the institutional and cultural systems that surround us.

Stage 3: Resistance   The next stage represents a major paradigm shift. It involves a move from blaming minority members for their condition to naming and blaming their own dominant group as a source of problems. This resistance may take the form of passive resistance, with little behavioral change, or active resistance—trying to reduce, eliminate, or challenge the institutional hierarchies that oppress. In reference to one's own identity, this stage is often characterized by embarrassment about one's own privileged position, guilt, shame, and a need to distance oneself from the dominant group.

> Our student, Kayla, says: *I was raised as a Christian, so I was never taught to question our beliefs. Since I've left home, I have met gay and lesbian students and I no longer understand why my church has such a problem with homosexuality. I get angry and sometimes I speak out when I'm at home and my parents get upset, but I don't want to stand around and let bigots take over my church. I have begun to question my Christian values, as I no longer know if they are compatible with my sense of right and wrong.*

Stage 4: Redefinition   In the fourth stage, people begin to refocus or redirect their energy toward redefining their identity in a way that recognizes their privilege and works to eliminate oppression and inequities. They realize that they don't have to accept uncritically the definitions of being white, straight, male, Christian, U.S. American that society has instilled in them. For example, Nick tells us, "As a straight white guy, I often find myself in social situations in which people feel free to make offhand remarks or jokes that are somewhat racist, heterosexist, or sexist. They assume that I would agree with them, since I'm not a minority, gay, or a woman, but I don't. I am happy to be who I am, but this doesn't mean that being a straight white man means I need to be racist, sexist, or homophobic. I am proud to be who I am, but I don't think that means I have to put down others."

Stage 5: Integration   As in the final stage of minority identity development, majority group individuals now are able to internalize their increased consciousness and integrate their majority identities into all other facets of their identity. They not only recognize their identity as white but also appreciate other groups. This integration affects other aspects of social and personal identity, including religion and gender.

Hardiman (2003) acknowledges that this model is rather simplistic in explaining the diverse experiences of people. It does not acknowledge the impact of diverse environments and socialization processes that influence how people experience their dominant identities or the realities of interlocking identities.

Systems of privilege are complicated; this is one reason why people can belong to a privileged category and not feel privileged. You may have several identities that are more privileged and several that are less privileged. So, for example, a middle-class white lesbian, benefiting from and yet unaware of the privileges of race or class, may think that her experience of sexual orientation and gender inequality enables her to understand what she needs to know about other forms of privilege and oppression. Or a straight working-class white man may be annoyed at the idea that his sexual orientation, whiteness, and maleness somehow gives him access to privilege. As a member of the working class, he may feel insecure in his job, afraid of being outsourced, downsized, and not at all privileged (Johnson, 2001).

To make it more complicated, our multiple identities exist all at once in relation to one another. People never see us solely in terms of race or gender or nationality—they see us as a complex of identities. So it makes no sense to talk about the experience of one identity—being white, for example—without looking at other identities. A dialectical perspective helps here in avoiding falling into the trap of thinking we are or are not privileged. Most of us are both.

SOCIAL AND CULTURAL IDENTITIES

People can identify with a multitude of groups. This section describes some of the major types of groups.

Gender Identity

We often begin life with gender identities. When newborns arrive in our culture, they may be greeted with clothes and blankets in either blue for boys or pink for girls. To establish a **gender identity** for the newborn, visitors may ask if the baby is a boy or a girl. Many people identify with the gender that they were born into biologically. This means that there are men who identify as male, feel male, and were born into male bodies. This kind of gender identification is called **cisgender.** Cisgendered people can also be called cismales or cisfemales.

What it means to be a man or a woman in our society is heavily influenced by cultural notions. For example, some activities are considered more masculine or more feminine. Thus, whether people hunt or sew or fight or read poetry can transform the ways that others view them. Similarly, the programs that people watch on television—soap operas, football games, and so on—affect how they socialize with others, contributing to gendered contexts.

gender identity The identification with the cultural notions of masculinity and femininity and what it means to be a man or a woman.

cisgender A person whose gender identity matches the biological sex that she or he was born into.

As culture changes, so does the notion of what we idealize as masculine or feminine. Cultural historian Gail Bederman (1995) observes,

Even the popular imagery of a perfect male body changed. In the 1860s, the middle class had seen the ideal male body as lean and wiry. By the 1890s, however, an ideal male body required physical bulk and well-defined muscles. (p. 15)

In this sense, the male body, as well as the female body, can be understood not in its "natural" state but in relation to idealized notions of masculinity and femininity. To know that this man or that woman is particularly good looking requires an understanding of the gendered notions of attractiveness in a culture.

Our notions of masculinity and femininity change continually, driven by commercial interests and other cultural forces. For example, there is a major push now to market cosmetics to men. However, advertisers acknowledge that this requires sensitivity to men's ideas about makeup:

Unlike women, most men don't want to talk about makeup, don't want to go out in public to shop for makeup and don't know how to use makeup. The first barrier is getting men to department stores or specialty shops to buy products. (Yamanouchi, 2002, p. D1)

Our expression of gender not only communicates who we think we are but also constructs a sense of who we want to be. Initially, we learn what masculinity and femininity mean in our culture. Communication scholar Julia T. Wood (2005) has identified feminine and masculine themes in U.S. society. These are the femininity themes: appearance still counts, be sensitive and caring, accept negative treatment by others, and be a superwoman. The masculinity themes are don't be female, be successful, be aggressive, be sexual, and be self-reliant. Masculinity themes are often the opposite of what it means to be a woman or a gay man. According to Wood, U.S. American men are socialized first and foremost that, being a man is about *not* being a woman. Then, through various media, we monitor how these notions shift and negotiate to communicate our gendered selves to others.

Consider, for example, the contemporary trend in the United States for women to have very full lips. If one's lips are not naturally full, there is always the option of getting collagen injections or having other body fat surgically inserted into the lips. In contrast, our Japanese students tell us that full lips are not considered at all attractive in Japan. The dynamic character of gender reflects its close connection to culture. Society has many images of masculinity and femininity; we do not all seek to look and act according to a single ideal. At the same time, we *do* seek to communicate our gendered identities as part of who we are.

Gender identity is also demonstrated by communication style. For example, women's communication style is often described as supportive, egalitarian, personal, and disclosive, whereas men's is characterized as competitive and assertive (Wood, 2005). However, these differences may be more perception than fact. Results of recent research suggest that women's and men's communication styles are more similar than they are different (Canary & Hause, 1993; Pennebaker, Mehl, & Niederhoffer, 2003). And yet these stereotypes of gender differences persist, maybe partly because of the stereotypical depictions of men and women in magazines, on television, and in movies

Identity terms for gender and sexualities are rapidly changing to meet the diversity of how people experience these identities. There is no comprehensive list that remains fixed and stable, as people are identifying in a myriad of ways to meet different needs. Facebook, for example, allows people to self-identify their gender in an open manner, without preset categories. However, some of the widely used terms are listed in a glossary assembled by the University of Wisconsin LGBT Campus Center:

> *https://lgbt.wisc.edu/documents/Trans_and_queer_glossary.pdf and
> another helpful list was put together by Sam Killermann and Meg Bolger
> of the Safe Zone Project and is located at: http://itspronouncedmetrosexual
> .com/2013/01/a-comprehensive-list-of-lgbtq-term-definitions/*

There are differences between the two lists that underscores the dynamic and complex character of these identities. For example:

> *Androsexual/Androphilic – (adj) attraction to men, males, and/or masculinity Gynesexual/Gynephilic – (adj; pronounced "guy-nuh-seks-shu-uhl")
> attracted to woman, females, and/or femininity*

These two terms do not appear on the Wisconsin list, whereas: **Agender (Also Non-gender):** not identifying with any gender, the feeling of having no gender, does not appear on the Safe Zone Project list.

Explore both lists and see how many of these terms and identities are familiar or unfamiliar to you.

Transgender refers to identification with a gender that differs from the biologically assigned gender at birth. Like cisgendered people, transgendered people can identify with any of a number of sexual identities. Thus, if someone is transgendered, it does not mean that this person is gay or lesbian. They may identify as heterosexual or some other sexual identity. Some countries recognize transgender people; others do not. Some countries include transgender or third gender (identifying as neither male nor female) in their national census forms. Recently, for example, "Nepal's Central Burueau of Statistics is giving official recognition to gay and transgender people" (Shrestha, 2011). Also, in the 2011 census, India gave respondents the choice of a third gender in the census questions about gender. The third gender has roots in Indian culture: "The transgender community, which has long hoped for more social acceptance, is being given an 'other' option under gender apart from 'male' and 'female.' The results will give India a firm count for its 'third-gender' hijra community—the origins of which go back millennia to a time when transsexual, eunuch and gays held a special place in society backed by Hindu myths of their power to grant fertility" (Daigle, 2011). The official count of the census revealed about 490,000 "people identified themselves as belonging to the third gender, despite the fact that the census counting happened well before the Supreme Court order gave legal recognition to the third gender in April" of 2014 (Nagarajan, 2014).

transgender Identification with a gender that does not match one's biological gender

In contrast, the most recent U.S. Census in 2010 gave two gender choices—male and female—so there is no national census data on the number of people who identify as transgender. However, attitudes may be changing as activists continue to work on these issues, prominent media figures, such as Laverne Cox from *Orange is the New Black,* and political battles over the status of transgendered people emerge, such as North Carolina's HB 2, among other states. The future of transgendered identity is contested in the United States and transgendered identity may gain more recognition.

However, what it means to be feminine and masculine are not stable, clear-cut identity categories. Rather, these notions are created, reinforced, and reconstructed by society through communication and overlap with our other identities.

Sexual Identity

sexual identity One's identification with various categories of sexuality.

Sexual identity refers to one's identification with various categories of sexuality. You are probably most familiar with heterosexual, gay or lesbian, and perhaps bisexual categories; however, sexual identity categories vary from culture to culture and have been variously viewed throughout history (Foucault, 1988). Also, views on sexual identities differ in various historical contexts. Same-sex activities were not always looked down upon, pedophilia was accepted in some eras and cultures, and on the occasions when children were born with both male and female sexual organs, they were not necessarily operated on or forced to be male or female (Foucault, 1988).

Our sexual identities influence our consumption, which television shows we watch, which magazines we read, which Internet sites we visit. Some assume a certain level of public knowledge about sexual identities or stereotypes; for example, *Glee, Modern Family,* and *Grey's Anatomy* assumed viewers were familiar with stereotypes of gays. What are some cultural products that assume knowledge of heterosexual culture?

Official recognition of gay, lesbian, and transgender people varies around the world. As people begin to communicate more openly about sexuality, new and emerging sexual identities have been emerging. On the one hand, there are many countries where same-sex activities are illegal with some having the death penalty. On the other hand, some countries embrace same-sex relationships and allow public, legal recognition of same-sex marriages.

Age Identity

age identity The identification with the cultural conventions of how we should act, look, and behave according to our age.

As we age, we also play into cultural notions of how individuals our age should act, look, and behave; that is, we develop an **age identity.** As we grow older, we sometimes look at the clothes displayed in store windows or advertised in newspapers and magazines and feel that we are either too old or too young for that "look." These feelings stem from an understanding of what age means and how we identify with people that age.

Some people feel old at 30; others feel young at 40 or 50. Nothing inherent in age tells us we are young or old. Rather, our notions of age and youth are all based on cultural conventions. The United States is an age-conscious society. One of the first things we teach children is to tell their age. And children will proudly tell their age, until about the mid-20s on, when people rarely mention their age. In contrast, people older than 70 often brag about their age. Certain ages have special significance in some cultures.

I am half Qatari and half Emirati. My father comes from Qatar; my mother is from Dubai, although they are in some complicated way related (it is normal for people in the gulf to marry their cousins). My father's side of the family originates back to Saudi Arabia, a specific tribe (al-Gahtani). The tribe eventually expanded and began migrating around the gulf, to Bahrain, then to Dubai, and lastly to Qatar. I still have family in those areas; my grandfather is the only one who migrated to Qatar. In general, this is a typical story for anyone who is from the gulf. Arabian families are quite big in numbers, are related to other bigger families, and have family all over the gulf, but usually originating from Saudi Arabia—that I would say is the typical structure or format of an Arabian background.

—Najla

Latino families sometimes celebrate a daughter's 15th birthday with a *quinceañera* party—marking the girl's entry into womanhood. Some Jewish families celebrate with a bat mitzvah ceremony for daughters and a bar mitzvah for sons on their 13th birthday (Allen, 2004). These same cultural conventions also suggest that it is inappropriate to engage in a romantic relationship with someone who is too old or too young.

Our notions of age often change as we grow older ourselves. When we are quite young, someone in college seems old; when we are in college, we do not feel so old. Yet the relative nature of age is only one part of the identity process. Social constructions of age also play a role. Different generations often have different philosophies, values, and ways of speaking. For example, recent data show that today's college freshmen are more liberal politically and more interested in volunteer work and civic responsibility than were Gen Xers. Scholars who view generations as "cultural groups" say that these characteristics make them similar to the World War I generation—politically curious and assertive and devoted to a sense of personal responsibility (Sax, Lindholm, Astin, Korn, & Mahoney, 2001).

Different generations often have different philosophies, values, and ways of speaking (Strauss & Howe, 1997). For example, recent data show that the millennium generation (or Gen Y, those born between 1982–2001) are more diverse and globally oriented and more knowledgeable about computers and technology than any preceding generation. They are also more optimistic, more committed to contributing to society and more interested in life balance between work and play than the previous, Gen X, group (those born between 1961–1981) (Strauss & Howe, 2006). This also is reflected in the way they learn and work (multitasking, use of multimedia, etc.).

In 2016, it was predicted that Millennials surpassed Baby Boomers as the largest generation in the United States (Fry, 2016). Aside from the demographic dominance of this group, Jen Mishory, executive director of a national millennial research and advocacy organization, argues against the stereotype that Millennials are lazy. She argues that her generation has had to do more with less (due to the financial situation that they grew up in, declining wages for millennial workers, etc.), face large student loan debt, contribute to charitable causes, and demonstrate tremendous fortitude. She says that: "In the end, the fact remains: We're a generation that does more with less, while thinking about our own futures and trying to build a better tomorrow for those around us" (2016).

Sometimes these generational differences can lead to conflict in the workplace. For example, young people who entered the job market during the "dot .com" years have little corporate loyalty and think nothing of changing jobs when a better opportunity comes along. This can irritate baby boomer workers, who emphasize the importance of demonstrating corporate loyalty, of "paying one's dues" to the establishment while gradually working one's way "up the corporate ladder" (Howe & Strauss, 2007). Although not all people in any generation are alike, the attempt to find trends across generations reflects our interest in understanding age identity.

Racial and Ethnic Identities

racial identity Identifying with a particular racial group. Although in the past racial groups were classified on the basis of biological characteristics, most scientists now recognize that race is constructed in fluid social and historical contexts.

Racial Identity   Race consciousness, or **racial identity,** is largely a modern phenomenon. In the United States today, the issue of race is both controversial and pervasive. It is the topic of many public discussions, from television talk shows to talk radio. Yet many people feel uncomfortable talking about it or think it should not be an issue in daily life. Perhaps we can better understand the contemporary issues if we look at how the notion of race developed historically in the United States.

Current debates about race have their roots in the 15th and 16th centuries, when European explorers encountered people who looked different from themselves. The debates centered on religious questions of whether there was "one family of man." If so, what rights were to be accorded to those who were different? Debates about which groups were "human" and which were "animal" pervaded popular and legal discourse and provided a rationale for slavery. Later, in the 18th and 19th centuries, the scientific community tried to establish a classification system of race based on genetics and cranial capacity. However, these efforts were largely unsuccessful.

Most scientists have abandoned a strict biological basis for classifying racial groups, especially in light of recent genetic research. To date, researchers have found only 55 genes out of almost 3 million that differentiate various groups. Their conclusions about the implications of their research: "All in all, the school of thought which holds that humans, for all their outward variety, are a pretty homogenous species received a boost" ("Human races or human race," 2008, p. 86). Rather than adhere to the rather outdated notion of a biological basis for racial categorization, most scholars hold a social science viewpoint—agreeing that racial categories like white and black are constructed in social and historical contexts.

Several arguments refute the physiological basis for race. First, racial categories vary widely throughout the world. In general, distinctions between white and black are fairly rigid in the United States, and many people become uneasy when they are unable to categorize individuals. In contrast, Brazil recognizes a wide variety of intermediate racial categories in addition to white and black. These variations indicate a cultural, rather than a biological, basis for racial classification (Omi & Winant, 2001). Terms like *mulatto* and *Black Irish* demonstrate cultural classifications; terms like *Caucasoid* and *Australoid* are examples of biological classification.

Second, U.S. law uses a variety of definitions to determine racial categories. A 1982 case in Louisiana reopened debates about race as socially created rather than biologically determined. Susie Phipps applied for a passport and discovered that under Louisiana law she was black because she was $1/32$ African (her great-grandmother had been a slave). She then sued to be reclassified as white. Not only did she consider herself white, inasmuch as she grew up among whites, but was also married to a white man. And because her children were only $1/64$ African, they were legally white. Although she lost her lawsuit, the ensuing political and popular discussions persuaded Louisiana lawmakers to change the way the state classified people racially. It is important that the law was changed, but this legal situation does not obscure the fact that social definitions of race continue to exist (Hasian & Nakayama, 1999).

A third example of how racial categories are socially constructed is illustrated by their fluid nature. As more and more southern Europeans immigrated to the United States in the 19th century, the established Anglo and German society tried to classify these newcomers (Irish and Jewish, as well as southern European) as nonwhite. However, this attempt was not successful because, based on the narrower definition, whites might have become demographically disempowered. Instead, the racial line was drawn to include all Europeans, and people from outside of Europe (e.g., immigrants from China) were designated as nonwhite (Roediger, 2005). We intentionally use the term *nonwhite* here to highlight the central role of *whiteness* in defining racial identity in the United States.

Racial categories, then, are based to some extent on physical characteristics, but they are also constructed in fluid social contexts. It probably makes more sense to talk about racial *formation* than racial *categories,* thereby casting race as a complex of social meanings rather than as a fixed and objective concept. How people construct these meanings and think about race influences the ways in which they communicate.

Ethnic Identity   In contrast to racial identity, **ethnic identity** may be seen as a set of ideas about one's own ethnic group membership. It typically includes several dimensions: (1) self-identification, (2) knowledge about the ethnic culture (traditions, customs, values, and behaviors), and (3) feelings about belonging to a particular ethnic group. Ethnic identity often involves a shared sense of origin and history, which may link ethnic groups to distant cultures in Asia, Europe, Latin America, or other locations.

Having an ethnic identity means experiencing a sense of belonging to a particular group and knowing something about the shared experience of group members. For instance, Judith grew up in an ethnic community. She heard her parents and relatives speak German, and her grandparents made several trips back to Germany and talked about their German roots. This experience contributed to her ethnic identity.

For some U.S. residents, ethnicity is a specific and relevant concept. They see themselves as connected to an origin outside the United States—as Mexican American, Japanese American, Welsh American, and so on—or to some region prior to its being absorbed into the United States—Navajo, Hopi, and so on. As one African American student told us, "I have always known my history and the history of my people in this country. I will always be first African American and then American. Who I am is based on my heritage." For others, ethnicity is a vague concept. They see themselves as "American" and reject the notion of **hyphenated Americans.** One of our students explains:

> *I don't necessarily identify with my ethnicity. I am Italian American and Irish American but I am three or more generations removed from when either side immigrated to the United States. I also don't look noticeably Italian or Irish.*

ethnic identity
(1) A set of ideas about one's own ethnic group membership and (2) a sense of belonging to a particular group and knowing something about the shared experience of the group.

hyphenated Americans U.S. Americans who identify not only with being U.S. citizens but also as being members of ethnic groups.

I still tell people that I am half Irish and half Italian, but the only time I really connect and identify with my ethnic heritage is for holidays and for certain traditional meals or styles of cooking.

We will discuss the issues of ethnicity for white people later.

What, then, does *American* mean? Who defines it? Is there only one meaning, or are there many different meanings? It is important to determine what definition is being used by those who insist that we should all simply be "Americans." If one's identity is "just American," how is this identity formed, and how does it influence communication with others who see themselves as hyphenated Americans (Alba, 1985, 1990; Carbaugh, 1989)?

Racial Versus Ethnic Identity   Scholars dispute whether racial and ethnic identity are similar or different. Some suggest that ethnic identity is constructed by both selves and others but that racial identity is constructed solely by others. They stress as well that race overrides ethnicity in the way people classify others (Cornell & Hartmann, 1998). The American Anthropological Association has suggested that the U.S. government phase out use of the term *race* in the collection of federal data because the concept has no scientific validity or utility.

On the one hand, discussions about ethnicity tend to assume a "melting pot" perspective on U.S. society. On the other hand, discussions about race as shaped by U.S. history allow us to talk about racism. If we never talk about race, but only about ethnicity, can we consider the effects and influences of racism?

Bounded Versus Dominant Identities   One way to sort out the relationship between ethnicity and race is to differentiate between bounded and dominant (or normative) identities (Frankenburg, 1993; Trinh, 1986/1987). Bounded cultures are characterized by groups that are specific but not dominant. For most white people, it is easy to comprehend the sense of belonging in a bounded group (e.g., an ethnic group). Clearly, for example, being Amish means following the *ordnung* (community rules). Growing up in a German American home, Judith's identity included a clear emphasis on seriousness and very little on communicative expressiveness. This identity differed from that of her Italian American friends at college, who seemed much more expressive.

However, what it means to belong to the dominant, or normative, culture is more elusive. *Normative* means "setting the norm for a society." In the United States, whites clearly are the normative group in that they set the standards for appropriate and effective behavior. Although it can be difficult for white people to define what a normative white identity is, this does not deny its existence or importance. It is often not easy to see what the cultural practices are that link white people together. For example, we seldom think of Thanksgiving or Valentine's Day as white holidays.

Our sense of racial or ethnic identity develops over time, in stages, and through communication with others. These stages seem to reflect our growing understanding of who we are and depend to some extent on the groups we belong to. Many ethnic or racial groups share the experience of oppression. In response, they may generate attitudes and behaviors consistent with a natural internal struggle to develop a strong sense of group identity and self-identity. For many cultural groups, these strong identities ensure their survival.

Characteristics of Whiteness

What does it mean to be white in the United States? What are the characteristics of a white identity? Is there a unique set of characteristics that define whiteness, just as other racial identities have been described?

It may be difficult for most white people to describe exactly what cultural patterns are uniquely white, but scholars have tried to do so. For example, scholar Ruth Frankenburg (1993) says that whiteness may be defined not only in terms of race or ethnicity but also as a set of linked dimensions. These dimensions include (1) normative race privilege, (2) a standpoint from which white people look at themselves, others, and society, and (3) a set of cultural practices (often unnoticed and unnamed). More recently, communication scholar Dreama Moon has argued that white identity is a process of becoming white through a process of social pressure and control "utilized in White communities to produce the next generation of 'white-thinking' Whites" (2016, p. 299). Much of this pressure to be "white" in a particular way comes from family and friends, as well as observing public performances of whiteness.

Normative Race Privilege   Historically, whites have been the normative (dominant) group in the United States and, as such, have benefited from privileges that go along with belonging to the dominant group (see Point of View on page 192). However, not all whites have power, and not all have equal access to power. In fact, at times during U.S. history, some white communities were not privileged and were viewed as separate, or different, if not inferior. Examples include the Irish and Italians in the early 20th century and German Americans during World War II. And as scholars point out, the memory of marginality outlasts the marginality. For example, memories of discrimination may persist in the minds of some Italian Americans although little discrimination exists today. There also are many white people in the United States who are poor and so lack economic power.

There is an emerging perception that being white no longer means automatic privilege, particularly as demographics change in the United States and as some whites perceive themselves to be in the minority. This has led some whites to feel threatened and "out of place." A Chicago college professor tells the story of how her white students thought that 65% of the population near their university was African American; they perceived themselves to be in the minority and based their estimate on their observations and anecdotes. When she corrected them, they were stunned. In fact, according to the 2000 U.S. Census, the percentage of blacks in Chicago was only 37% (Myers, 2003, p. 130). Students' perceptions affected their sense of identity, which, in turn, can affect intercultural communication.

Some white young people today are very aware of their whiteness (Frankenburg, 2001). Further, they believe that being white is a liability, that they are sometimes prejudged as racist and blamed for social conditions they personally did not cause, and that they are denied opportunities that are unfairly given to minority students. One of our white students describes this feeling:

> *When I was trying to get into college I had to fight for every inch. I didn't have a lot of money to go to school with, so to get a scholarship was of great importance to me. So I went out and bought a book titled* The Big Book of Scholarships.

Identities can be valued and devalued in different ways in different cultures. The African American rap artist and poet Saul Williams, who now lives in Paris, France, explains how African American identity functions differently in France than in the United States:

If you want to know, as a black American, what white privilege feels like, you needn't endure the laborious process of donning a wig and sitting to have gummy makeup applied to your face by a professional.
No, you only need a passport.
[...]
An American passport is a magical piece of paper. It will allow you entry into a country where Nina Simone lyrics are used to teach the national language, where Christmas is synonymous with James Brown, where John Cassavetes and Kristen Stewart are prized as cinematic treasures. That country, of course, is France.
[...]
"Hey, if you want to experience white privilege, hop on a plane and go anywhere with your American passport and you will experience American privilege and you'll be able to understand exactly what it's like to have certain doors opened for you and back rooms opened for you and privileges given to you just as a result of what happens when you open your mouth and people realize where you're from."
[...]
Williams recounted how his black American friends would come to visit him in Paris. They had questions reflective of decades of personal experiences living in an environment where an undercurrent of hostility toward blackness lurks ever-present. The baggage they brought with them was a special sort of skepticism, fueled by feeling like a lessee of one's place in your own country, even when the Constitution and your birth certificate guarantee a slice of the mortgage.

Source: From S. N. McDonald (2015, September 23), "American in Paris: Saul Williams critiques his home country from the outside looking in," *The Washington Post.* Retrieved May 4, 2016, from https://www.washingtonpost.com/news/arts-and-entertainment/wp/2015/09/23/american-in -paris-saul-williams-critiques-his-home-country-from-the-outside-looking-in/

Ninety percent of the scholarships that this book contained didn't apply to me. They applied to the so-called minorities. . . . I think this country has gone on so long with the notion that white equals wealth or with things like affirmative action, that it has lost sight of the fact that this country is not that way any longer.

In addition, because of corporate downsizing and the movement of jobs overseas in recent decades, increasing numbers of middle-aged white men have not achieved the degree of economic or professional success they had anticipated. They sometimes blame their lack of success on immigrants who will work for less or on the increasing numbers of women and minorities in the workplace. In these cases, whiteness is not invisible; it is a salient feature of the white individuals' identities.

The point is not whether these perceptions are accurate. Rather, the point is that identities are negotiated and challenged through communication. People act on their perceptions, not on some external reality. As the nation becomes increasingly diverse and whites no longer form a majority in some regions, there will be increasing challenges for all of us as we negotiate our cultural identities.

How can whites in the United States incorporate the reality of not belonging to a majority group? Will whites find inclusive and productive ways to manage this identity change? Or will they react in defensive and exclusionary ways?

One reaction to feeling outnumbered and being a "new member" of an ethnic minority group is to strengthen one's own ethnic identity. For example, white people may tend to have stronger white identities in those U.S. states that have a higher percentage of nonwhites (e.g., Mississippi, South Carolina, Alabama). In these states, the white population traditionally has struggled to protect its racial privilege in various ways. As other states become increasingly less white, we are beginning to see various moves to protect whiteness.

Although it had been discussed for a while, the U.S. Census Bureau predicted in 2015 that the United States population would become majority-minority in 2044. In other words, non-Hispanic whites would become a minority with less than 50% of the population. Charles Gallagher, a sociologist who studies white identity, notes: "We went from being a privileged group to all of a sudden becoming whites, the new victims . . . You have this perception out there that whites are no longer in control or the majority. Whites are the new minority group" (quoted in Blake, 2011). Although they are not numerically a minority group, their experiences may be shaping what white identity means. Tim Wise, a writer, says: "For the first time since the Great Depression, white Americans have been confronted with a level of economic insecurity that we're not used to. It's not so new for black and brown folks, but for white folks, this is something we haven't seen since the Depression" (quoted in Blake, 2011). Fears about the loss of white America drive much of this discussion. Yet, as a Vassar College professor prefers to see it: "This moment was not the end of white America; it was not the end of anything. It was a bridge, and we crossed it" (Hsu, 2009).

A Standpoint from Which to View Society   Opinion polls reveal significant differences in how whites and blacks view many issues, including President Obama. For example, a Pew Research Center study conducted one year after President Obama's election found that blacks were more likely to view President Obama as black (55%) rather than mixed race (34%). For whites, the responses were reversed: 53% of whites saw President Obama as mixed race and 24% as black. When asked if opposition to Obama's policies is racially motivated, 52% of blacks thought so, whereas only 17% of whites felt that way. And since the election of President Obama, blacks and whites feel that blacks are better off than five years ago (see Figure 5-2), but a 10 percentage point difference remains ("Blacks upbeat about black progress, prospects," 2010).

A Set of Cultural Practices   Is there a specific, unique "white" way of viewing the world? As noted previously, some views held consistently by whites are not necessarily shared by other groups. And some cultural practices and core symbols (e.g., individualism) are expressed primarily by whites and significantly less by members of minority groups. We need to note here that not everyone who is white shares all

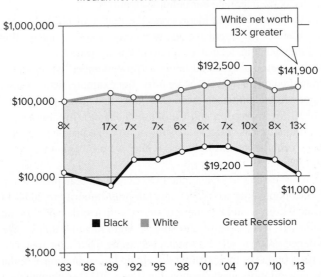

Wealth Gap Between Blacks and Whites Grew after Great Recession

Median net worth of households, in 2013 dollars

Note: Blacks and whites include only non-Hispanics. Chart scale is logarithmic; each gridline is ten times greater than the gridline below it. Great Recession began December 2007 and ended June 2009.

FIGURE 5-2   As you can see from this Pew Research Center graph, the wealth gap between white households and black households has increased and the net worth of white households is now 13 times greater than black households. Why has this gap been increasing, rather than decreasing?

Stepler, R. (2016, June 27). Five key takeaways about views of race and inequality in America. *Pew Research Center.* Retrieved from http://www.pewresearch.org/fact-tank/2016/06/27/key -takeaways-race-and-inequality/

cultural practices. (See Figure 5-3.) For example, recent immigrants who are white, but not born in the United States, may share in the privilege accorded to all white people in the United States. However, they might not necessarily share in the viewpoints or the set of cultural practices of whites whose families have been in the United States for many generations. It is important to remember that some whites may identify fairly strongly with their European roots, especially if their families are more recent immigrants and they still have family members in Europe; other whites may not feel any connection to Europe and feel completely "American." These cultural practices are most clearly visible to those who are not white, to those groups who are excluded (Bahk & Jandt, 2004). For example, in the fairy tale of Snow White, the celebration of her beauty—emphasizing her beautiful, pure white skin— is often seen as problematic by people who are not white.

White culture is difficult to define. White people do not often think of some of their activities as white cultural practices, such as sunbathing, a common leisure activity among many white people. Not all cultural groups place a high value on suntans. In this photo, a Chinese man holds an umbrella to shield his wife from the sun as she takes a photo of her parents at Tiananmen Square. In this culture, darker skin, particularly on a woman, is seen as more negative than light skin. Gender and racial identities function together to place a low cultural value on suntanning. (© *Andrew Wong/Reuters/Corbis*)

Religious Identity

Religious identity can be an important dimension of many people's identities, as well as an important site of intercultural conflict. Religious identity often is conflated with racial or ethnic identity, which makes it difficult to view religious identity simply in terms of belonging to a particular religion. For example, when someone says, "I am Jewish," does it mean that he practices Judaism? That he views Jewish identity as an ethnic identity? Or when someone says, "She has a Jewish last name," is it a statement that recognizes religious identity? With a historical view, we can see Jews as a racial group, an ethnic group, and a religious group.

Drawing distinctions among various identities—racial, ethnic, class, national, and regional—can be problematic. For example, Italians and Irish are often viewed as Catholics, and Episcopalians are frequently seen as belonging to the upper classes. Issues of religion and ethnicity have come to the forefront in the war against Al-Qaeda and other militant groups. Although those who carried out the attacks against the Pentagon and the World Trade Center were Muslims and Arabs, it is hardly true that all Muslims are Arabs or that all Arabs are Muslims (Feghali, 1997).

religious identity
A sense of belonging to a religious group.

Religious differences have been at the root of contemporary conflicts from the Middle East to Northern Ireland, and from India and Pakistan to Bosnia-Herzegovina. In the United States, religious conflicts caused the Mormons to flee the Midwest for Utah in the mid-19th century. More recently, religious conflicts have become very real for some Arab Americans as the U.S. government presses the war against terrorism, with many of those people subject to suspicion if not persecution. And militant Muslims in the Middle East and elsewhere see their struggle against the United States as a very serious endeavor and are willing to die for their religious beliefs.

In the United States, we often believe that people should be free to practice whatever religion they wish. Conflicts arise, however, when the religious beliefs of some individuals are imposed on others who may not share those beliefs. For example, some Jews see the predominance of Christmas trees and Christian crosses as an affront to their religious beliefs. The influence of religious identities on Americans' attitudes was evidenced in 2007 during Mitt Romney's (a Mormon politician) presidential campaign. A research study found that bias against Mormons was significantly more intense than bias against either African Americans or women and that bias against Mormons was even more pronounced among conservative Evangelicals (Luo, 2007; "New Vanderbilt . . . ," 2007).

People in some religions communicate and mark their religious differences by their clothing. For example, Hassidic Jews wear traditional, somber clothing, and Muslim women are often veiled according to the Muslim guideline of female modesty. Of course, most religions are not identified by clothing. For example, you may not know if someone is Buddhist, Catholic, Lutheran, or atheist based upon the way he or she dresses. (See Figure 5-4.) Because religious identities are less salient, everyday interactions may not invoke religious identity.

FIGURE 5-4 You might not know someone's religious identity, except for certain religious observances, like Ash Wednesday for some Christians. (© *Sean Gardner/Getty Images*)

Class Identity

We don't often think about socioeconomic class as an important part of our identity. Yet scholars have shown that class often plays an important role in shaping our reactions to and interpretations of culture. For example, French sociologist Pierre Bourdieu (1987) studied the various responses to art, sports, and other cultural activities of people in different French social classes. According to Bourdieu, working-class people prefer to watch soccer, whereas upper-class individuals like tennis, and middle-class people prefer photographic art, whereas upper-class individuals favor less representational art. As these findings reveal, class distinctions are real and can be linked to actual behavioral practices and preferences.

English professor Paul Fussell (1992) shows how similar signs of **class identity** operate in U.S. society. According to Fussell, the magazines we read, the foods we eat, and the words we use often reflect our social class position. At some level, we recognize these class distinctions, but we consider it impolite to ask directly about a person's class background. Therefore, we may use communication strategies to place others in a class hierarchy. Unfortunately, these strategies don't always yield accurate information. For example, people may try to guess your class background by the foods you eat. Some foods are seen as "rich folk's food"—for instance, lamb, white asparagus, brie, artichokes, goose, and caviar. Do you feel as if you are revealing your class background if you admit that these foods are unfamiliar to you? Perhaps not admitting your unfamiliarity is a form of "passing," of representing yourself as belonging to a group you really don't belong to. Another strategy that people may use to guess a person's class background is to ask where that person did her or his undergraduate work.

Most people in the United States recognize class associations even as they may deny that such class divisions exist. What does this apparent contradiction indicate? Most importantly, it reveals the complexities of class issues, particularly in the United States. We often don't really know the criteria for inclusion in a given social class. Is membership determined by financial assets? By educational level? By profession? By family background? These factors may or may not be indicators of class.

Another reason for this apparent contradiction is that people in the majority or normative class (the middle class) tend not to think about class, whereas those in the working class are often reminded that their communication styles and lifestyle choices are not the norm. David Engen (2004), a communication scholar, describes his own experience of entering college from a working-class background and feeling like he had entered a new culture. For one thing, the working-class communication style he was accustomed to was very different from the proper English required in his classes. "I vividly recall coming to college saying things such as 'I seen that,' 'I ain't worried about that' and 'that don't mean nothing to me.' I am glad my professors and friends helped me acquire a language that allowed me to succeed in mainstream American society" (p. 253). And the philosophical conversations expected in class were a challenge. As he describes it, working-class communication is about getting things done, very different from the abstract conversations he was expected to participate in—designed to broaden perspective rather than to accomplish any particular task. In this respect, class is like race. For example, terms like *trailer trash*

class identity A sense of belonging to a group that shares similar economic, occupational, or social status.

Higher education is another area where income inequality influences admissions to more selective colleges and universities. A recent study (Giancola & Kahlenberg, 2016) found that, in the past ten years, the number of low-income students with high academic achievements were not enrolling at elite institutions has not really increased or changed, despite lots of rhetoric and interest in doing so. They conclude that "these young people have enormous potential, yet are by passed by a system that honors legacy and wealth more than hard work and talent" (p. 37).

As you think about your own experience in the college admissions process, what kinds of structural policies led you to your college or university? Aside from how this affects you personally, how does the current situation impact our society? When very bright students are not able to attend top institutions, is our society losing out on their potential to do great things in the future for all of us? How much mobility is there in the United States, not only in higher education, but also in society more generally?

Source: Giancola, J. & Kahlenberg, R. D. (2016). *True merit: Ensuring our brightest students have access to our best colleges and universities.* Available at http://www.jkcf.org/assets/1/7/JKCF_True _Merit_Report.pdf

and *white trash* show the negative connotations associated with people who are not middle class (Moon & Rolison, 1998).

A central assumption of the American dream is that, with hard work and persistence, individuals can improve their class standing, even in the face of overwhelming evidence to the contrary. And the American dream seems alive and well. An estimated 94% of Americans still think that "people who work full time should be able to earn enough to keep their families out of poverty" (Allen, 2004, p. 105).

The American dream, however, has come under serious scrutiny in the wake of the Great Recession. Recent poll data show a huge swing in how people feel about their children doing better than them. In 1999, "two thirds of Americans predicted that children would grow up to have it better than their parents," but recent polls show that almost 63% of Americans now feel that their children won't be better off than them (Cillizza, 2014). The American dream does not have the same pull as it did in previous eras.

Perhaps this has led to a rethinking of class identity, advanced in part by social movements, such as the Occupy Wall Street movement, from the more traditional class structure into two categories: the 1% and the 99%. Public debates about income inequality may change how we think about class identity in the future.

Recent reports indicate that the mortality rates for white Americans has been dramatically increasing, while every other group is seeing a decline. In addition, "a new analysis from the Commonwealth Fund suggests there's more to the story. The report, by David Squires and David Blumenthal, notes that between 1999 and 2014, mortality rates in the United States rose for white Americans aged 22 and 56.

Before that, death rates had been falling by nearly 2 percent each year since 1968" (Khazan, 2016). Squires and Blumenthal think that the reason behind this increasing mortality rate is economic: "They have lower incomes, fewer are employed, and fewer are married" (quoted in Khazan, 2016). Others have speculated that it is also due to the emphasis on individualism in American culture where one's successes and failures are individual, rather than societal.

The point is that although class identity is not as readily apparent as, say, gender identity, it still influences our perceptions of and communication with others. Race, class, and sometimes gender identity are interrelated. For example, statistically speaking, being born African American, poor, and female increases one's chances of remaining in poverty (Mishel, Bernstein, & Allegretto, 2006). But, of course, race and class are not synonymous. There are many poor whites, and there are increasing numbers of wealthy African Americans. In this sense, these multiple identities are interrelated but not identical.

National Identity

Among many identities, we also have a **national identity,** which should not be confused with racial or ethnic identity. Nationality, unlike racial or ethnic identity, refers to one's legal status in relation to a nation. Many U.S. citizens can trace their ethnicity to Latin America, Asia, Europe, or Africa, but their nationality, or citizenship, is with the United States.

national identity
National citizenship.

Although national identity may seem to be a clear-cut issue, this is not the case when the nation's status is unclear. For example, bloody conflicts erupted over the attempted secession in the mid-1800s of the Confederate States of America from the United States. Similar conflicts erupted in more recent times when Eritrea tried to separate from Ethiopia, and Chechnya from Russia. Less bloody conflicts that involved nationhood led, in the former Czechoslovakia, to the separation of Slovakia and the Czech Republic. The former Yugoslavia was broken up into a number of smaller countries, but the terrible conflicts ensued.

Calls for independence and nationhood continue to emerge around the world. In 2014, Scotland voted to remain in the United Kingdom and not become an independent nation. Flanders and Wallonia continue to struggle to remain united as Belgium. Yet, calls for independence for Catalonia from Spain continue to put pressure on Madrid. Independence movements exist around the world, but their strength and viability come and go throughout different eras. Sometimes nations disappear from the political map but persist in the social imagination and eventually reemerge, such as Poland, Ukraine, Latvia, Lithuania, and Estonia.

More recently, the annexation of Crimea by Russia from Ukraine has meant that many people have had to negotiate new relationships with their national identities. Crimea is a peninsula in the Black Sea that was part of Ukraine, but was annexed by Russia in 2014. Although most of the international community recognizes Crimea as part of Ukraine, Russia is in control of the peninsula. For some people, the change in national status from Ukraine to Russia has been a good one. "Oleg Zubkov was born in Russia but studied in Kiev and is married to a Ukrainian. He said he previously had the warmest feelings toward Ukraine,

National identities are complex creations that are influenced by many factors. When the United States was founded, a sense of belonging to a larger collectivity needed to be created. One way to do this was the creation of stories, such as George Washington chopping down the cherry tree, or Betsy Ross sewing the first flag. But creating these narratives is not the only influence in building national identity. Benedict Anderson (1983) is famous for his work on understanding national identity as what he called "imagined communities." People feel a connection with others of their nation. Communication plays an important role in constructing national identity, especially at particular events, for example, the Olympics.

In their study of the role of sports in developing a national identity, Doupona Topič, & Coakley (2010) focused on the case of Slovenia which gained its independence in 1991 from Yugoslavia. As a new nation, Slovenia was interested in using sports to help develop its new national identity and communicate it to the world. As every nation has its own history, the case of Slovenia may be quite different from older nations such as a Japan or India. As you think about your own national identity, what role do sports play in promoting and reinforcing that identity? Are some sports or sporting events more important than others in communicating your national identity?

Source: Anderson, B. (1983). *Imagined communities: Reflections on the origin and spread of nationalism.* New York: Verso.
Doupona Topič, M., & Coakley, J. (2010). Complicating the relationship between sport and national identity: the case of post-socialist Slovenia. *Sociology of sport journal.* 27(4), 371–389.

but that nationalist slogans during the Maidan revolution and the sight of Lenin statues being pulled down across Ukraine led him to throw his weight behind the Russian annexation" (Guardian reporter & Walker, 2016). Although he is frustrated by the Russian bureaucracy, he is happy to be part of Russia. In contrast, a journalist, "Anna Andriyevskaya cannot go home. If she does, she will be arrested for inciting separatism and face a jail term of five years. Skype is her main connection to her homeland of Crimea, where her family and friends have remained two years after Russia's annexation of the region previously tied to Ukraine. They, too, face threats from the Russian government, she said" (Tomkiw, 2016). Although she is a native of Crimea, she moved to Kiev after she was put on a list of journalists for reporting about corruption. She cannot visit her parents or her homeland as she could be jailed for her journalistic reports. Thus, "The annexation has divided families, with some staying in Crimea to safeguard their property and others moving to Ukraine, unwilling to take Russian passports" (Tomkiw, 2016). As this example shows, some people in Crimea have strong feelings and prefer to be Russians and others have strong feelings in another direction and prefer to be Ukrainians.

National identity can also play out in nonconflict contexts. The Swedish Tourist Association, to mark the 250th anniversary of Sweden's abolishing censorship, set up a telephone number where anyone worldwide can call and speak directly to a Swede. The tourist association says, "Call today and get connected to a random Swede, anywhere in Sweden and talk about anything you want" (Davidson, 2016). The calls to the telephone number are randomly routed to Swedes who have signed up to answer the calls. In this context, those answering the calls are representatives of Sweden and Swedish national identity. The tourist association has no control over what people ask and talk about. Yet, the calls are asking about Sweden, Swedish culture, and Swedish everyday life.

In sum, people have various ways of thinking about nationality, and they sometimes confuse nationality and ethnicity. Thus, we have overheard students asking minority students, "What is your nationality?" when they actually meant, "What is your ethnicity?" This confusion can lead to—and perhaps reflects—a lack of understanding about differences between, say, Asian Americans (ethnic group) and Asians (nationality groups). It can also tend to alienate Asian Americans and others who have been in the United States for several generations but are still perceived as foreigners.

Regional Identity

Closely related to nationality is the notion of **regional identity.** Many regions of the world have separate, but vital and important, cultural identities. The Scottish Highlands is a region of northern Scotland that is distinctly different from the Lowlands, and regional identity remains strong in the Highlands.

regional identity
Identification with a specific geographic region of a nation.

Here in the United States, regional identities remain important, but perhaps less so as the nation moves toward homogeneity. Southerners, for example, often view themselves, and are viewed by others, as a distinct cultural group. Similarly, Texas advertises itself as "A Whole Other Country," promoting its regional identity. Although some regional identities can fuel national independence movements, they more often reflect cultural identities that affirm distinctive cuisines, dress, manners, and language. These identities may become important in intercultural communication situations. For example, suppose you meet someone who is Chinese. Whether the person is from Beijing, Hong Kong, or elsewhere in China may raise important communication issues. After all, Mandarin is not understood by Cantonese speakers, although both are dialects of the Chinese language. Indeed, there are many dialects in China, and they certainly are not understood by all other Chinese speakers.

One fairly recent variation in regional identities has to do with the degree of diversity within certain parts of the United States. Data from the 2000 census reveal that the South and the West are the most diverse, along with the coastal Northeast. The Midwest, in contrast, with a few exceptions, remains relatively homogenous (Brewer & Suchan, 2001, pp. 22–23). In addition, the overwhelming majority of multiracial individuals (67%) live in the South and the West (pp. 87–89). What are the implications for identity and intercultural communication? It could mean that people in these areas have more opportunities for understanding and practicing intercultural communication and so benefit from the diversity. Or they may withdraw into their own groups and protect their racial and ethnic "borders."

PERSONAL IDENTITY

personal identity
Who we think we are
and who others think
we are.

Many issues of identity are closely tied to our notions of self. Each of us has a **personal identity,** which is the sum of all our identities, but it may not be unified or coherent. A dialectical perspective allows us to see identity in a more complex way. We are who we think we are; at the same time, however, contextual and external forces constrain and influence our self-perceptions. We have many identities, and these can conflict. For example, according to communication scholar Victoria Chen (1992), some Chinese American women feel caught between the traditional values of their parents' culture and their own desire to be Americanized. From the parents' point of view, the daughters are never Chinese enough. From the perspective of many people within the dominant culture, though, it is difficult to relate to these Chinese American women simply as "American women, born and reared in this society" (p. 231). The dialectical tension related to issues of identity for these women reveals the strain between feeling obligated to behave in traditional ways at home and yet holding a Western notion of gender equality. A dialectical perspective sees these contradictions as real and presenting challenges in communication and everyday life.

Our personal identities are important to us, and we try to communicate them to others. We are more or less successful depending on how others respond to us. We use the various ways that identity is constructed to portray ourselves as we want others to see us.

MULTICULTURAL PEOPLE

Multicultural people, a group currently dramatically increasing in number, are those who live "on the borders" of two or more cultures. They often struggle to reconcile two very different sets of values, norms, worldviews, and lifestyles. Some are multicultural as a result of being born to parents from different racial, ethnic, religious, or national cultures or they were adopted into families that are racially different from their own family of origin. Others are multicultural because their parents lived overseas and they grew up in cultures different from their own, or because they spent extended time in another culture as an adult, or married someone from another cultural background. Let's start with those who are born into biracial or multiracial families. Some contemporary examples of multiracial individuals include Barack Obama, Carmelo Anthony, Derek Jeter, Freddie Prinze Jr., Jordin Sparks, Mariah Carey, Norah Jones, Tiger Woods, and Vanessa Williams (multiracial celebrities).

According to the 2010 Census, the United States has almost 9 million multiracial people—that is, people whose ancestry includes two or more races (Saulny, 2011). This number has increased about 32% from the 2000 Census, which was the first time people were given the option of selecting several categories to indicate their racial identities. This rapidly growing segment of our population must be understood in its historical context. The United States has a long history of forbidding miscegenation (the mixing of two races). The law sought not to prevent *any* interracial marriage but to protect "whiteness";

interracial marriage between people of color was rarely prohibited or regulated (Root, 2001). Thus, in 1957, the state of Virginia ruled the marriage of Mildred Jeter (African American and Native American heritage) and Peter Loving (white) illegal. The couple fought to have their marriage legalized for almost 10 years. Finally, in 1967, the Supreme Court ruled in their favor, in *Loving v. Virginia,* overturning 200 years of antimiscegenation legislation.

As shown in Table 5-2, the development of racial identity for the children of parents like the Lovings is a fluid process of complex transactions between the child and the broader social environment (Nance & Foeman, 2002). Whereas majority and minority identities seem to develop in a fairly linear fashion, biracial children may cycle through three stages: (1) awareness of differentness and resulting dissonance, (2) struggle for acceptance, and (3) self-acceptance and self-assertion. And as they mature, they may experience the same three phases with greater intensity and awareness.

In the first stage, multiracial children realize that they are different from other children—they may feel that they don't fit in anywhere. Tiffany, whose mother is white and father is black, describes her experience:

> *Growing up I had kids make fun of me because they said I did not know what color I was. That really hurt me as a kid because even at a young age, I started questioning my own race.*

At the next stage, struggle for acceptance, multiracial adolescents may feel that they have to choose one race or the other—and indeed this was Tiffany's experience:

> *During my teenage years I still was a little confused about my race because I would only choose one side. When people asked me what color I was I would tell them I was black because I was embarrassed about being mixed. I was afraid of not being accepted by the black community if I said I was mixed. . . . I would go around telling people that I am black and would get mad if someone said I was white. I never thought about being mixed with both black and white.*

After being torn between the two (or more) races, multiracial individuals may reach the third stage, of self-acceptance and self-assertion. Tiffany describes how this happened for her:

> *I can recall a time when I had to spend Christmas with my mother's side of the family. This was the first time I met her side of the family and I felt myself being scared. Honestly, I have never been around a lot of white people, and when I was there I realized that I am mixed and this is who I am and I cannot hide it anymore. . . . From then on I claimed both sides.*

And she goes on to demonstrate her self-acceptance and self-assertion:

> *Being mixed is wonderful, and most importantly, being mixed taught me many things especially growing up. It taught me how to be strong, not to worry about what other people think and to just be myself. It also taught me not to like only one color and that all colors are beautiful. My race made me who I am today. I am strong and I know my race. I no longer have to deny what my race is or who I am.*

As you might imagine, many positive aspects are associated with having a biracial identity. In one recent study, the majority of biracial respondents "did not express feelings of marginality as suggested by traditional theories of bicultural identity. Instead, these youth exhibited a clear understanding and affiliation with both groups' cultures and values" (Miller, Watling, Staggs, & Rotheram-Borus, 2003, p. 139). Later in the chapter, we will discuss further the important role that multicultural people can play in intercultural relations. Biracial or multiracial identities can be more complex, depending on the racial configuration involved. Sociologist Richard Alba (2015) explains: "About 60 percent of multiracial Americans who have some black ancestry reported discrimination by restaurants or other businesses, and 40 percent reported being unfairly stopped by the police." In contrast, "adults from mixed white and Asian backgrounds feel they have more in common with whites than they do with Asians; almost half have friendship circles that are mostly made up of whites; and two-thirds live in mostly white neighborhoods." The various racial configurations and how people respond in various contexts point to the complexities of multiracial identity—in the United States and around the world.

But multiracial identity can also be more complex. Korean adoptees who were adopted by white families do not seem to have had an easy reconciliation of these identities. In the Hongdae section of Seoul, South Korea: "The neighborhood is also a popular spot for the approximately 300 to 500 adoptees who have moved to South Korea—primarily from the United States but also from France, Denmark and other nations. Most lack fluency in the language and possess no memories of the country they left when they were young. But they are back, hoping for a sense of connection—to South Korea, to their birth families, to other adoptees" (Jones, 2015, p. 32). The rejection that they felt in the United States and elsewhere was due to acceptance: "In a 2009 survey of adult adoptees by the Donaldson Adoption Institute, more than 75 percent of the 179 Korean respondents who grew up with two white parents said they thought of themselves as white or wanted to be white when they were children. Most also said they had experienced racial discrimination, including from teachers. Only a minority said they felt welcomed by members of their own ethnic group" (Jones, 2015, p. 34). Some reported having parents who dismissed the racism that their children experienced or couldn't discuss race and white privilege with their children. In other words, the complexities of interracial families, racial identities, in the context of racism and racial thinking can create complex family relationships as we can see in the case of interracial adoptions. Not all international adoptions end badly, but some do and we should acknowledge the complexity of race and racism as larger contexts for understanding identities and identity development.

In addition to multicultural identities based on race and ethnicity, there are multicultural identities based on religion, sexual orientation, or other identities. For example, children growing up with a Jewish and a Christian parent may feel torn between the two and follow some of the same identity development phases as biracial children—where they feel different, forced to choose between one or the other. Teresa says, "My father is Mexican American and my mother is white, so I have a Latino last name. When I was younger, some kids would tease me with racial slurs about Mexicans. My mother totally didn't understand and just said that I should ignore them, but my father understood much better. He faced the same taunting as a child in Indiana." A straight child of gay parents may have similar feelings of needing to negotiate between straight and gay worldviews.

Individuals develop multicultural identities for other reasons. For example, **global nomads** (or **third-culture kids**—TCKs) grow up in many different cultural contexts because their parents move around a lot (e.g., missionaries, international business employees, and military families). According to a recent study, these children have unique challenges and unique opportunities. They move an average of about eight times, experience cultural rules that may be constraining (e.g., in cultures where children have less freedom), and endure periods of family separation. At the same time, they have opportunities not provided to most people—extensive travel, living in new and different places around the world. As adults they settle down and often feel the need to reconnect with other global nomads (easier now through technologies such as the Internet) (Ender, 2002). President Barack Obama is a good example of a global nomad—his father was an African exchange student and his mother a U.S. American college student. He spent his childhood first in Hawaii and then in Indonesia when his mother and his Indonesian stepfather moved there. Like many TCKs, he was separated from his family during high school when he returned to Hawaii to live with his grandparents. His stepsister credits his ability to understand people from many different backgrounds to his many intercultural experiences as a child and adolescent—like many global nomads, these experiences "gave him the ability to . . . understand people from a wide array of backgrounds. People see themselves in him . . . because he himself contains multitudes" ("Obama's sister talks about his childhood," 2008).

Children of foreign-born immigrants may also develop multicultural identities. Foreign-born immigrants in the United States represent one of the fastest-growing segments—almost a third of the current foreign-born population arrived in the United States since 1990. These include refugees from war zones like Syria and Iraq and migrants who come to the United States to escape dire economic conditions. They often struggle to negotiate their identities, torn between family expectations and their new American culture. Melanie, a student of ours, is not a refugee but is an example of a TCK. Having lived in a number of countries, she explains how she feels:

> As a global nomad, I am grateful for all of the experiences I was lucky enough to experience a lot from a young age; however, the downfall for me is that I have a little bit of many cultures and identities. I have never stopped for long enough to learn about one culture or identity because it was constantly changing. I was born in Argentina and my family has kept a lot of Argentine traditions but I know very little about Argentine history and my Spanish has slowly worsened. I grew up in France where I developed my family identity as I was surrounded with family but I didn't associate myself as a "French" person. I lived in New Zealand for 10 years where I learned a lot about the history and social norms but I was missing my family identity.

global nomads (third-culture kids) People who grow up in many different cultural contexts because their parents relocated.

Tom, another student of ours, explains the complexity of communicating who he is:

I was born in South Africa and lived there for the first two years of my life. Then my family moved to New Jersey. In the seventh grade, I went across the pond to boarding school in North Yorkshire, England. After I explain where I'm from, people always ask me which country I identify most closely with. Honestly that's a tough question. There are so many aspects and habits in my life which I've taken away with me from every individual culture that I have integrated into what I feel a strong connection to each.

In contrast, Anna, another student, who was born in Russia, does not feel that she is really Russian because of her international experiences:

I have always strongly disliked the question, "where are you from?" What do you mean by that? Are you asking me where I was born, or where I have lived throughout my life? I could tell you where I was born, but that does not necessarily mean that I feel any connection to that place or that I strongly identify with that particular city. I have always had a tough time truly defining who I am. However, I do believe that identity is not static; it constantly evolves and changes. My identity is made up of the cultures that I have been exposed to throughout my life. Every place that I have lived in has shaped me into the person I am today. The interaction that I have had with individuals from different backgrounds have also influenced my identity. I do not consider myself Russian. In fact, I consider myself Russian-Swedish-American, as strange as that may sound.

All of these students have negotiated their identities in various cultural and national contexts. Multicultural identities can be quite complex, but are becoming increasingly common in an era of globalization.

A final category of multicultural people includes those who have intense intercultural experiences as adults—for example, people who maintain long-term romantic relationships with members of another ethnic or racial group or who spend extensive time living in other cultures. Miguel tells us, "My father is an American, but my mother is from Chile. Because they divorced when I was young and my father returned to the United States, I spent a lot of time traveling back and forth and learning to adapt to two different cultures and languages. I don't feel completely Chilean or American, but I feel like I am both. I have family and friends in both places and I feel connected in different ways."

We will discuss these multicultural identities more in Chapter 8, "Understanding Intercultural Transitions." All multicultural people may feel as if they live in cultural margins, struggling with two sets of cultural realities: not completely part of the dominant culture but not an outsider, either.

Social psychologist Peter Adler (1974) describes the multicultural person as someone who comes to grips with a multiplicity of realities. This individual's identity is not defined by a sense of belonging; rather, it is a new psychocultural form of consciousness. Milton Bennett (1993) describes how individuals can develop an "ethnorelative" perspective based on their attitudes toward cultural difference. The first, and most ethnocentric, stage involves the denial or ignoring of difference. The next stage occurs when people recognize difference but attach negative meaning to it. A third stage occurs when people minimize the effects of difference—for example, with statements like "We're really all the same under the skin" and "After all, we're all God's children." Bennett recognizes that minority and majority individuals may experience these phases differently. In addition, minority individuals usually skip the first phase. They don't have the option to deny difference; they are often reminded by others that they are different.

The remainder of the stages represent a major shift in thinking—a paradigm shift—because positive meanings are associated with difference. In the fourth phase (acceptance), people accept the notion of cultural difference; in the fifth phase (adaptation), they may change their own behavior to adapt to others. The final phase (integration) is similar to Peter Adler's (1974) notion of a "multicultural person."

According to Adler, multicultural individuals may become **culture brokers**—people who facilitate cross-cultural interaction and reduce conflict, which we'll discuss in more detail in Chapter 12. For example, TCKs/global nomads often develop resilience, tolerance, and worldliness, characteristics essential for successful living in an increasingly diverse and global social and economic world (Ender, 1996). And, indeed, there are many challenges and opportunities today for multicultural people, who can reach a level of insight and cultural functioning not experienced by others. One of our students, who is Dutch (ethnicity) and Mexican (nationality), describes this:

culture brokers
Individuals who act as bridges between cultures, facilitating cross-cultural interaction and conflict.

> *Being the makeup I am to me means I come from two extremely proud cultures. The Dutch in me gives me a sense of tradition and loyalty. The Mexican side gives me a rich sense of family as well as closeness with not only my immediate family, with my aunts, uncles, and cousins as well. My unique mix makes me very proud of my identity. To me it means that I am proof that two parts of the world can unite in a world that still believes otherwise.*

However, Adler (1974) also identifies potential stresses and tensions associated with multicultural individuals:

They may confuse the profound with the insignificant, not sure what is really important.

They may feel multiphrenic, fragmented.

They may suffer a loss of their own authenticity and feel reduced to a variety of roles.

They may retreat into *existential absurdity. (p. 35)*

Communication scholar Janet Bennett (1993) provides insight into how being multicultural can be at once rewarding *and* challenging. She describes two types of multicultural individuals: (1) *encapsulated marginals,* who become trapped by their own marginality and (2) *constructive marginals,* who thrive in their marginality.

Encapsulated marginals have difficulty making decisions, are troubled by ambiguity, and feel pressure from both groups. They try to assimilate but never feel comfortable, never feel "at home." In contrast, constructive marginal people thrive in their marginal existence and, *at the same time,* they recognize the tremendous challenges. They see themselves (rather than others) as choice makers. They recognize the significance of being "in between," and they are able to make commitments within the relativistic framework. Even so, this identity is constantly being negotiated and explored; it is never easy, given society's penchant for superficial categories. Writer Ruben Martinez (1998) describes the experience of a constructive marginal:

> *And so I can celebrate what I feel to be my cultural success. I've taken the far-flung pieces of myself and fashioned an identity beyond that ridiculous, fraying old border between the United States and Mexico. But my "success" is still marked by anxiety, a white noise that disturbs whatever raceless utopia I might imagine. I feel an uneasy tension between all the colors, hating and loving them all, perceiving and speaking from one and many perspectives simultaneously. The key word here is "tension": nothing, as yet, has been resolved. My body is both real and unreal, its color both confining and liberating. (p. 260)*

IDENTITY, STEREOTYPES, AND PREJUDICE

stereotypes Widely held beliefs about a group of people.

model minority A stereotype that characterizes all Asians and Asian Americans as hardworking and serious and so a "good" minority.

The identity characteristics described previously sometimes form the basis for stereotypes, prejudice, and racism. We will see in the next chapter that these can be communicated verbally, nonverbally, or both. The origins of these have both individual and contextual elements. To make sense out of the overwhelming amount of information we receive, we necessarily categorize and generalize, sometimes relying on **stereotypes**—widely held beliefs about some group. Stereotypes help us know what to expect from others. They may be positive or negative. For example, Asian Americans have often been subjected to the positive **model minority** stereotype, which characterizes all Asians and Asian Americans as hardworking and serious. This stereotype became particularly prevalent in the United States during the civil rights movement of the 1960s and 1970s. At that time, Asian Americans were seen as the "good" minority—in contrast to African Americans, who were often confrontative and even militant in their fight for equality.

Even positive stereotypes can be damaging in that they create unrealistic expectations for individuals. Simply because someone is Asian American (or pretty, or smart) does not mean that he or she will excel in school or be outgoing and charming. Stereotypes become particularly detrimental when they are negative and are held rigidly. Research has shown that, once adopted, stereotypes are difficult to discard. In fact, people tend to remember information that supports a stereotype but may not retain information that contradicts it (Hamilton, Sherman, & Ruvolo, 1990).

We pick up stereotypes in many ways, including from the media. In TV shows and movies, older people often are portrayed as needing help, and Asian Americans, African Americans, or Latinos/as rarely play leading, assertive roles. Current research also shows that although obvious negative stereotypes of Native American Indians are less common in the media, they are still commonly represented in print media as degraded outsiders, often "corrupt, alcoholic and doomed objects of pity" (Miller & Ross, 2004, p. 255) or as either the "good" or "bad" Indians. Communication scholar Bishetta D. Merritt (2000) analyzes portrayals of African American women on television shows and decries the lack of multidimensional roles. She identifies the kinds of roles that perpetuate stereotypes:

> *Portrayals that receive little or no attention today are the background characters that merely serve as scenery on television programs. These characters include the homeless person on the street, the hotel lobby prostitute, or the drug user making a buy from her dealer. They may not be named in the credits or have recurring roles, but their mere appearance can have an impact on the consciousness of the viewer and, as a result, an impact on the imagery of the African American women. (p. 52)*

We may learn stereotypes from our families and peers. One student described how she learned stereotyping and prejudice from her classmates:

> *One of my earliest experiences with a person ethnically diverse from me was when I was in kindergarten. A little girl in my class named Adelia was from Pakistan. I noticed that Adelia was a different color from me, but I didn't think it was a bad thing. I got along with her very well. We played the same games, watched the same cartoons, and enjoyed each other's company. Soon I discovered that my other friends didn't like Adelia as much as I did. They didn't want to hold hands with her, and they claimed that she was different from us. When I told them that Adelia was my friend, they didn't want to hold hands with me either. They started to poke fun at me and excluded me from their games. This hurt me so much that I stopped playing with Adelia, and I joined my friends in avoiding her. As a result, Adelia began to resent me and labeled me prejudiced.*

Stereotypes can also develop out of negative experiences. If we have unpleasant encounters with people, we may generalize that unpleasantness to include all members of that group, whatever group characteristic we focus on (e.g., race, gender, or sexual orientation). This was demonstrated repeatedly after the attacks of September 11, 2001. Many people of Middle Eastern descent became victims of stereotyping, particularly when traveling. Although we do not know how often such events happen, stereotypes and prejudice can work together to thwart the everyday workings of airlines. Recently, a University of Pennsylvania faculty member who was flying from Philadelphia to Syracuse, New York was questioned about the writing he was doing, as a woman became concerned about him and asked to be rebooked on another flight. She left the plane and the flight was delayed over two hours as her concerns were investigated. The professor Guido Menzio is Italian. "That's right: He's Italian, not Middle Eastern, or whatever heritage usually gets ethnically profiled on flights these days" (Rampell, 2016). His writing was not Arabic, but mathematical equations relevant to his work as an economist. The U.S. Department of Homeland Security does ask all of us, "If you see something, say

I fell in love with a first-generation Mexican American. It took many arguments and lots of time before he was accepted into my family. Once everyone saw what an incredible person Gabe is, I think they favored him more than me. . . . He and I had been together for a year and a half and the time had come for me to meet his family. I was extremely nervous because his parents spoke only Spanish and I only spoke English. How was I going to communicate with my boyfriend's family? To my surprise, this was the least of my worries. When we were introduced, I thought his parents were going to faint. I am "white." I am not the same race as this family, and they resented my having a relationship with their son. I must be very naive, but I never thought prejudices would be directed toward me. This was quite an eye-opener for me. . . .

Unfortunately, Gabriel's sisters spoke English. They made quite a point to be rude and neglect me in every conversation they had. I felt terrible. Before I knew it, Gabe's sister, Amelia, pulled me into her room. She began explaining to me how I would never be part of their family. Because I was not of Hispanic descent, I was not worthy to be with her brother. She went on to tell me that her parents hated me. . . . This was really difficult for me to swallow. This family hated me because of something I have absolutely no control over, my race.

I sat there, not sure of what to say or do. I was so hurt and upset, I stood up and yelled. I told her that this is the problem with society. Why, when we have a chance to change what we hate, do we resist? How can we consciously continue doing these things? Basically, the same countless arguments I had with my parents, I had with Gabe's sister. Whatever happened in that room was the most rewarding experience. We continued discussing the problem. By the end of the conversation, we were such good friends. Shortly after that, Gabe's family felt like my family.

The slight taste of prejudice I felt has to be minimal compared to other people's experiences. I am thankful I was fortunate enough to have such an experience early in my life. I honestly have to admit, Amelia changed me for the better.

—Jennifer

something," and they tell us that: "So if you see something you know shouldn't be there—or someone's behavior that doesn't seem quite right—say something. Because only you know what's supposed to be in your everyday" (Department of Homeland Security, n.d.). This system relies on people seeing things that don't seem right, which can play into stereotypes and prejudice against certain groups. A dialectical approach asks us to balance our concerns about odd behaviors of others with the recognition that we may be engaging in racial or ethnic profiling.

Because stereotypes often operate at an unconscious level and so are persistent, people have to work consciously to reject them. First, they must recognize the stereotype, and then they must obtain information to counteract it. This is not easy because, as noted previously, we tend to "see" behavior that fits our stereotypes and to ignore that which doesn't. For example, if you think that most women are bad drivers, you will tend to notice when a female motorist makes a mistake but to ignore bad male driving. To undo this stereotype, you have to be very vigilant and do something that isn't "natural"—to be very conscious of how you "see" and categorize bad driving and to note bad driving by both males and females.

Prejudice is a negative attitude toward a cultural group based on little or no experience. It is a prejudgment of sorts. Whereas stereotypes tell us what a group is like, prejudice tells us how we are likely to feel about that group (Newberg, 1994). Scholars disagree somewhat on the origins of prejudice and its relationship to stereotyping. Prejudice may arise from personal needs to feel positive about our own groups and negative about others, or it may arise from perceived or real threats (Hecht, 1998). Researchers Walter Stephan and Cookie Stephan (1996) have shown that tension between cultural groups and negative previous contact, along with status inequalities and perceived threats, can lead to prejudice. One communicative practice in which people express their prejudices is called **microaggressions**. Microaggressions "are subtle insults (verbal, nonverbal, and/or visual) directed toward people of color, often automatically or unconsciously" (Solórzano, Ceja, & Yosso, 2000, p. 60). Although the term "microaggression" was initially used to describe behavior directed against African Americans decades ago, it has been expanded to include aversive behavior directed against other identities, including gender, sexuality, and disability. Unlike other more explicit expressions of prejudice, such as hate crimes, cross burnings, explicit use of racial (or other) terms, microaggressions are subtle, but serve to communicate prejudice against particular cultural groups.

Why do people hold prejudices? Psychologist Richard Brislin (1999) suggests that just as stereotyping arises from normal cognitive functioning, holding prejudices may serve understandable functions. These functions may not excuse prejudice, but they do help us understand why prejudice is so widespread. He identifies the following four such functions:

1. The utilitarian function. People hold certain prejudices because they can lead to rewards. For example, if your friends or family hold prejudices toward certain groups, it will be easier for you simply to share those attitudes, rather than risk rejection by contradicting their attitudes.

2. The ego-defensive function. People hold certain prejudices because they don't want to believe unpleasant things about themselves. For example, if either of us (Judith or Tom) is not a very good teacher, it will be useful for us to hold negative stereotypes about students, such as that they are lazy and don't work hard. In this way, we can avoid confronting the real problem—our lack of teaching skills. The same kind of thing happens in the workplace: It is easier for people to stereotype women and minorities as unfit for jobs than to confront their own lack of skill or qualifications for a job.

prejudice An attitude (usually negative) toward a cultural group based on little or no evidence.

microaggression Subtle insults directed toward cultural groups often unconsciously.

3. The value-expressive function. People hold certain prejudices because they serve to reinforce aspects of life that are highly valued. Religious attitudes often function in this way. Some people are prejudiced against certain religious groups because they see themselves as holding beliefs in the one true God, and part of their doctrine is the belief that others are wrong. For instance, Judith's Mennonite family held prejudices against Catholics, who were viewed as misguided and wrong. This may also be operating today as some U.S. Americans search for validation of prejudices again Muslims. A more extreme example involves the atrocities committed against groups of people by others who want to retain the supposed values of a pure racial stock (e.g., "ethnic cleansing" by Serbs against Muslims in the former Yugoslavia).

4. The knowledge function. People hold certain prejudices because such attitudes allow them to organize and structure their world in a way that makes sense to them—in the same way that stereotypes help us organize our world. For example, if you believe that members of a certain group are flaky and irresponsible, then you don't have to think very much when meeting someone from that group in a work situation. You already know what they're like and so can react to them more automatically.

Prejudices can serve several of these functions over the life span. Thus, children may develop a certain prejudice to please their parents (utilitarian) and continue to hold the prejudice because it helps define who they are (value-expressive). Brislin (1999) points out that many remedial programs addressing the problem of prejudice fail because of a lack of recognition of the important functions that prejudice fulfills in our lives. Presenting people with factual information about groups addresses only one function (knowledge) and ignores the more complex reasons that we hold prejudices. Prejudice and stereotypes can also lead to *acts* of discrimination, which will be discussed in Chapter 7.

IDENTITY AND COMMUNICATION

Identity has a profound influence on intercultural communication processes. We can employ some of the dialectics identified in earlier chapters to illuminate this relationship. First, we can use the individual–cultural dynamic to examine the issues that arise when we encounter people whose identities we don't know. In intercultural communication interactions, mistaken identities are often exacerbated and can create communication problems.

Sometimes we assume knowledge about another person's identity based on his or her membership in a particular cultural group. When we do so, we are ignoring the individual aspect. Taking a dialectical perspective can help us recognize and balance both the individual and the cultural aspects of another's identity. This perspective can guide the ways that we communicate with that person (and conceivably with others). "The question here is one of identity: Who am I perceived to be when I communicate with others? . . . My identity is very much tied to the ways in which others speak to me and the ways in which society represents my interests" (Nakayama, 2000, p. 14).

I would have to say that the most important identity to me is being Pakistani and being a Muslim. My religion and culture are both very important to me. I have not really had too many experiences in which I thought that my identity was not being affirmed. However, there have been some minor experiences that I have faced. We all know that after that incident, Muslims really got a bad name. People used to associate all Muslims with being terrorists. During that time, that seemed to be the subject of discussion in every single class.

I remember in one of my classes, a guy said that all Muslims are terrorists. That really hurt me and I took offense to that. I spoke up and said that if you are not a Muslim then you have no right to say that. I said that if you are not a Muslim, then you really do not know what it means to be one, and you do not know the true values and beliefs of the religion. I am a practicing Muslim, and I know my religion very well, and I know that the religion of Islam does not teach anything but to love one another. I did not care if someone did not believe me because everyone is entitled to their own opinion, but my main purpose was to say that it was wrong for the guy to say something that big about a whole group of people. It would be best if people could keep comments like that to themselves. If the guy just kept that comment to himself, it would not have hurt him and it would have not hurt me for sure. That was one time, that I thought that my identity was not being affirmed. But other than that, most people that I have come across and most people who I tell that I am a Muslim do not react with any sort of hostility. That makes me feel really good and accepted in a society in which most people are not Muslims.

—Shazim

Think about the assumptions you might make about others based on their physical appearance. What do you "know" about people if you know only that they are from, say, the South, or Australia, or Pakistan? Perhaps it is easier to think about the times that people have made erroneous assumptions about you based on limited information—assumptions that you became aware of in the process of communication. Focusing solely on someone's nationality, place of origin, education, religion, and the like, can lead to mistaken conclusions about the person's identity.

Another way to understand how we communicate our identities comes from the study of performance. Although we can look at someone's individual performance of identity to better understand how they understand who they think they are, we can also look at cultural performance to understand cultural identities.

One part of U.S. history often hidden is the horrific practice of lynching. Yet we must acknowledge that lynching was a widespread and common practice in U.S. culture, and we can often be confused when we see many of the perpetrators smiling in these photos because it seems incomprehensible that they were not horrified by this event.

Performance studies scholar Kirk Fuoss (1999) suggests that a performance perspective can help us better understand how people can participate in these atrocities and the purpose of these lynchings for the perpetrators. For example, Fuoss argues that lynching in the United States functioned as a cultural performance that served to reinforce a particular kind of racial order for those who participated in or heard about the lynching. Lynchings took place outside of the legal system, and therefore a belief in the evilness of the victim substituted for a proof or evidence of guilt. This inversion of right and wrong served to relieve the group identity of the lynchers from their own evil behavior. These murders reflect aspects of our culture that have deep historical roots. By examining these performative acts, we can begin to see what they communicate to others and the kinds of social order they encourage. Thus, lynchings are a public act that serve to communicate the positions of various cultural groups in society. It is important to remember that performances not only are artistic and interesting but can also be horrific. In both cases, performances of identity can offer insights into our culture.

Now let's turn to the static–dynamic dialectic. The problem of erroneous assumptions has increased during the information age, due to the torrent of information about the world and the dynamic nature of the world in which we live. We are bombarded daily with information from around the globe about places and people. This glut of information and intercultural contacts has heightened the importance of developing a more complex view of identity.

Given the many identities that we all negotiate for ourselves in our everyday interactions, it becomes clear how our identities and those of others make intercultural communication problematic. We need to think of these identities as both static and dynamic. We live in an era of information overload, and the wide array of communication media only serves to increase the identities we must negotiate. Consider the relationships that develop via e-mail, for example. Some people even create new identities as a result of online interactions. We change who we are depending on the people we communicate with and the manner of our communication. Yet we also expect some static characteristics from the people with whom we communicate. We expect others to express certain fixed qualities; these help account for why we tend to like or dislike them and how we can establish particular communication patterns with them. The tensions that we feel as we change identities from e-mail to telephone to mail to fax and other communication media demonstrate the dynamic and static characters of identities.

Finally, we can focus on the personal–contextual dialectic of identity and communication. Although some dimensions of our identities are personal and remain fairly consistent, we cannot overlook the contextual constraints on our identity.

INTERNET RESOURCES

http://www.whitenessproject.org

https://www.facebook.com/whitenessproject
Whitney Dow's Whiteness Project is an ongoing project to interview whites about being white. The project has a webpage with the interviews posted in which whites

speak about being white. There is also a Facebook page, if you are interested in reading what others are discussing about the interviews or adding your own comments.

http://pewforum.org/
The Pew Forum on Religion and Public Life website provides research, news, and discussions regarding topics related to religious identity, for example, college students' beliefs about religion, the role of religion in debates on gay marriage, science education, politics, and so forth. The site also provides religious demographic profiles for different countries.

www.pbs.org/race/001_WhatIsRace/001_00-home.htm
This website provided by PBS is a comprehensive exploration of myths and constructions of race. It has some interesting interactive links, such as "Sorting People," which allows a person to categorize pictures of people based on contemporary U.S. racial categories and then see how the government would classify the pictures. It also provides a "race timeline"—how the notion of race developed through history.

www.intermix.org.uk/word_up/index.asp
This British web page was developed to benefit mixed-race families and multiracial individuals. It contains news stories about Mariah Carey, Halle Berry, Craig David, and other multiracial celebrities.

SUMMARY

There are three approaches to identity: social science, interpretive, and critical.

- A dialectical view of identity emphasizes that identities are both static (as described by the social science perspective) and dynamic (described by the interpretive and critical perspectives), as well as personal and contextual.
- Identities also develop in relation to minority and majority group membership.
- Identities are multiple and reflect gender, sexuality, age, race, ethnicity, religion, class, nationality, regionality, and other aspects of our lives.
- Increasing numbers of multicultural people live "on the borders" between two or more cultures—based on race, ethnicity, religion, and nationality.
- Identity characteristics sometimes form the basis for stereotypes and prejudice.
- Communication plays an important role in identity—identities are formed and expressed through communication.

DISCUSSION QUESTIONS

1. How do our perceptions of our own cultural identity influence our communication with others?
2. What are some ways in which we express our identities?
3. How does being white affect one's experience in the United States?

4. What are the roles of avowal and ascription in the process of identity formation?

5. What are some of the ways in which members of minority cultures and members of majority cultures develop their cultural identities?

ACTIVITIES

1. *Stereotypes in Your Life.* List some of the stereotypes you have heard about U.S. Americans. Then answer the following questions:

   a. How do you think these stereotypes developed?

   b. How do they influence communication between U.S. Americans and people from other countries?

2. *Stereotypes in Prime-Time TV.* Watch four hours of television during the next week, preferably during evening hours when there are more commercials. Record the number of representatives of different identity groups (ethnic, racial, gender, age, class, and so on) that appear in the commercials; also record the role that each person plays. Answer the following questions:

   a. How many different groups were represented?

   b. What groups were most represented? Why do you think this is so?

   c. What groups were least represented? Why do you think this is so?

   d. What differences (if any) were there in the roles that members of the various groups played? Did one group play more sophisticated or more glamorous roles than others?

   e. In how many cases were people depicted in stereotypical roles—for example, African Americans as athletes, or women as homemakers?

   f. What stereotypes were reinforced in the commercials?

   g. What do your findings suggest about the power of the media and their effect on identity formation and intercultural communication? (Think about avowal, ascription, and interpellation.)

3. *Communication of White Identity.* Go to the website http://stuffwhitepeoplelike .com/. This website parodies the stereotypes of white people, and by extension, the stereotyping of other groups. Read through a number of these entries, and then be ready to discuss how whiteness, racism, stereotyping, and identity function in society.

KEY WORDS

age identity (186)	core symbols (172)	global nomads (third-
ascription (171)	culture brokers (207)	culture kids) (205)
avowal (171)	ethnic identity (189)	hyphenated Americans
class identity (197)	familial identity (170)	(189)
cisgender (183)	gender identity (183)	identity (167)

identity negotiation
theory (171)
impression management
theory (167)
individualized identity (170)
interpellation (174)
majority identity (180)

microaggression (211)
minority identity (178)
model minority (208)
national identity (199)
personal identity (202)
prejudice (211)
racial identity (188)

regional identity (201)
religious identity (195)
sexual identity (186)
spiritual identity (170)
stereotypes (208)
third-culture kids (205)
transgender (185)

REFERENCES

Adler, P. (1974). Beyond cultural identity: Reflections on cultural and multicultural man. *Topics in culture learning* (vol. 2, pp. 23–40). Honolulu: East-West Center.

Alba, R. D. (1985). The twilight of ethnicity among Americans of European ancestry: The case of Italians. *Ethnic and Racial Studies, 8,* 134–158.

Alba, R. D. (1990). *Ethnic identity: The transformation of white America.* New Haven, CT: Yale University Press.

Alba, R. (2015, June 11). The myth of a white minority. *The New York Times.* Retrieved May 3, 2016, from http://www.nytimes.com/2015/06/11/opinion/the-myth-of-a-white-minority.html?_r=0

Allen, B. (2004). *Difference matters: Communicating social identity.* Waveland Press.

Alnatour, O. (2015, December 9). Muslims are not terrorists: A factual look at terrorism and Islam. *The World Post.* Retrieved May 5, 2016, from http://www.huffingtonpost.com/omar-alnatour/muslims-are-not-terrorist_b_8718000.html.

Althusser, L. (1971). Ideology and ideological state apparatuses (notes toward an investigation). In B. Brewster (Trans.), *Lenin and philosophy and other essays* (pp. 134–165). London: NLB.

Angelos, J. (2016, April 10). Becoming European. *The New York Times Magazine,* pp. 40–47, 54, 57, 59.

Bahk, C. M., & Jandt, F. E. (2004). Being white in America: Development of a scale. *The Howard Journal of Communications, 15,* 57–68.

Bederman, G. (1995). *Manliness and civilization: A cultural history of gender and race in the United States, 1880–1917.* Chicago, IL: University of Chicago Press.

Bennett, J. M. (1993). Cultural marginality: Identity issues in intercultural training. In R. M. Paige (Ed.), *Education for the intercultural experience* (pp. 109–136). Yarmouth, ME: Intercultural Press.

Bennett, M. J. (1993). Towards ethnorelativism: A developmental model of intercultural sensitivity. In R. M. Paige (Ed.), *Education for the intercultural experience* (pp. 21–72). Yarmouth, ME: Intercultural Press.

Bernstein, J., & Mishel, L. (2007, September 3). Economy's gains fail to reach most workers' paychecks. Economic Policy Institute Briefing Paper #195. Retrieved February 18, 2008, from www.epi.org/content.cfm/bp195.

Blake, J. (2011, March 4). Are whites racially oppressed? CNN. Retrieved June 9, 2011, from www.cnn.com/2010/US/12/21/white.persecution/index.html?hpt=T2.

Bourdieu, P. (1987). *Distinction: A social critique of the judgment of taste* (R. Nice, Trans.). Cambridge, MA: Harvard University Press.

Brewer, C. A., & Suchan, T. A. (2001). *Mapping Census 2000: The geography of U.S. diversity* (U.S. Census Bureau, Census Special Reports, Series CENSR/01-1). Washington, DC: U.S. Government Printing Office.

Brislin, R. (1999). *Understanding culture's influence on behavior* (2nd ed.). Belmont, CA: Wadsworth.

Canary, D. J., & Hause, K. S. (1993). Is there any reason to research sex difference in communication? *Communication Quarterly, 41,* 129–144.

Carbaugh, D. (1989). *Talking American: Cultural discourse on* Donahue. Norwood, NJ: Ablex.

Cengel, K. (2016, April 15). A sudden breach in Uganda. *The New York Times Magazine.* From http://www.nytimes.com/2016/04/17/magazine/a-sudden-breach-in-uganda.html?rref=collection%2Fsectioncollection%2Fmagazine&action=click&contentCollection=magazine&region=stream&module=stream_unit&version=latest&contentPlacement=30&pgtype=sectionfront

Chen, V. (1992). The construction of Chinese American women's identity. In L. F. Rakow (Ed.), *Women making meaning* (pp. 225–243). New York: Routledge.

Cillizza, C. (2014, June 5). Is the American Dream dead? *The Washington Post.* Retrieved May 3, 2016, from https://www.washingtonpost.com/news/the-fix/wp/2014/06/05/is-the-american-dream-dead/

Collier, M. J. (2005). Theorizing cultural identification: Critical updates and continuing evolution. In W. B. Gudykunst (Ed.), *Theorizing about intercultural communication* (pp. 235–256). Thousand Oaks, CA: Sage.

Collier, M. J., & Thomas, M. (1988). Cultural identity: An interpretive perspective. In Y. Y. Kim & W. B. Gudykunst (Eds.), *Theories in intercultural communication* (pp. 99–122). Newbury Park, CA: Sage.

Cornell, S., & Hartmann, D. (1998). *Ethnicity and race: Making identities in a changing world.* Thousand Oaks, CA: Pine Forge Press.

Cross, S. E. (2000). What does it mean to "know thyself" in the United States and Japan?: The cultural construction of the self. In T. J. Owens (Ed.), *Self and identity through the life course in cross-cultural perspective* (pp. 159–180). Stamford, CT: JAI Press.

Davidson, H. (2016, April 8). Sweden launches phone a random Swede hotline—but don't ask about the chef. *The Guardian.* Retrieved May 8, 2016, from http://www.theguardian.com/world/2016/apr/08/sweden-launches-phone-a-random-swede-hotline-but-dont-mention-the-chef.

Department of Homeland Security. (n.d.). If you see something, say something. Retrieved May 8, 2016, from https://www.dhs.gov/see-something-say-something.

Ehrenreich, B. (2001). *Nickel and dimed: On (not) getting by in America.* New York: Metropolitan Books.

Ehrenreich, B. (2005). *Bait and switch: The (futile) pursuit of the American Dream.* New York: Metropolitan Books.

Ender, M.D. (1996). Recognizing healthy conflict: The postmodern self. *Global Nomad Perspectives Newletter, 4*(1), 12–14.

Ender, M. G. (2002). Beyond adolescence: The experiences of adult children of military parents. In M. G. Ender (Ed.), *Military brats and other global nomads* (pp. 83–100). Westport, CT: Praeger.

Engen, D. (2004). Invisible identities: Notes on class and race. In A. Gonzalez, M. Houston, & V. Chen (Eds.), *Our voices: Essays in culture, ethnicity and communication* (pp. 250–255). Los Angeles, CA: Roxbury.

Erikson, E. (1950). *Childhood and society.* New York: Norton.

Erikson, E. (1968). *Identity: Youth and crisis.* New York: Norton.

Feghali, E. (1997). Arab cultural communication patterns. *International Journal of Intercultural Relations, 21,* 345–378.

Ferguson, R. (1990). Introduction: Invisible center. In R. Ferguson, M. Gever, T. M. Trinh, & C. West (Eds.), *Out there: Marginalization and contemporary cultures* (pp. 9–14). New York and Cambridge: New Museum of Contemporary Art/MIT Press.

Foucault, M. (1988). *History of sexuality* (R. Hurley, Trans.). New York: Vintage Books.

Frankenburg, R. (1993). *White women, race matters: The social construction of whiteness.* Minneapolis: University of Minnesota Press.

Frankenberg, R. (2001). The mirage of an unmarked whiteness. In B. B. Rasmussen, E. Klineberg, I. J. Nexica, & M. Wray (Eds.), *The making and unmaking of whiteness* (pp. 72–96). Durham, NC: Duke University Press.

Fry, R. (2016, April 25). Millennials overtake Baby Boomers as America's largest generation. *Pew Research Center.* Retrieved May 3, 2016, from http://www.pewresearch.org/fact-tank/2016/04/25/millennials-overtake-baby-boomers/.

Fuoss, K. W. (1999). Lynching performances, theaters of violence. *Text and Performance Quarterly, 19,* 1–37.

Fussell, P. (1992). *Class: A guide through the American status system.* New York: Touchstone Books. (Original work published 1979)

Gallager, C. A. (1994). White construction in the university. *Review, 1/2,* 167–187.

Goffman, E. (1959). *The presentation of self in everyday life.* Garden City, New York: Doubleday.

Guardian reporter, & Walker, S. (2016, January 19). No regrets over Ukraine split, but Crimeans want more love from Russia. *The Guardian.* Retrieved May 8, 2016, from http://www.theguardian.com/world/2016/jan/19/crimeans-still-tigerish-over-split-with-ukraine.

Hall, S. (1985). Signification, representation, ideology: Althusser and the poststructuralist debates. *Critical Studies in Mass Communication, 2,* 91–114.

Hamilton, D. L., Sherman, S. J., & Ruvolo, C. M. (1990). Stereotype-based expectancies: Effects on information processing and social behavior. *Journal of Social Issues, 46,* 35–60.

Hardiman, R. (1994). White racial identity development in the United States. In E. P. Salett & D. R. Koslow (Eds.), *Race, ethnicity and self: Identity in multicultural perspective* (pp. 117–142). Washington, DC: National MultiCultural Institute.

Hardiman, R. (2003). White racial identity development in the United States. In E. P. Salett & D. R. Koslow (Eds.), *Race, ethnicity and self* (2nd ed., pp. 117–136). Washington, DC: National MultiCultural Institute.

Hargittai, E. (2007). Whose space? Differences among users and non-users of social network sites. *Journal of Computer-Mediated Communication, 13*(1), article 14. Retrieved February 18, 2008, from http://jcmc.indiana.edu/vol13/issue1/hargittai.html.

Hasian, M., Jr., & Nakayama, T. K. (1999). Racial fictions and cultural identity. In J. Sloop & J. McDaniels (Eds.), *Treading judgment.* Boulder, CO: Westview Press.

Hecht, M. L. (1998). Introduction. In M. L. Hecht (Ed.), *Communicating prejudice* (pp. 3–23). Thousand Oaks, CA: Sage.

Hecht, M. L., Jackson, R. L. III, & Ribeau, S. A. (2003). *African American communication: Exploring identity and culture* (2nd ed.). Mahwah, NJ: Lawrence Erlbaum.

Hecht, M. L., Warren, J. R., Jung, E., & Krieger, J. L. (2005). A communication theory of identity: Development, theoretical perspective and future directions. In W. B. Gudykunst (Ed.), *Theorizing about intercultural communication* (pp. 257–278). Thousand Oaks, CA: Sage.

Howe, N., & Strauss, W. (2007). The next 20 years: How customer and workforce attitudes will evolve. *Harvard Business Review, 85*(7–8), 41.

Hsu, H. (2009, January/February). The end of white America? *The Atlantic.* Retrieved June 9, 2011, from www.theatlantic.com/magazine/archive/2009/01/the-end-of-white-america/7208/.

Human races or human race? *The Economist, 386*(8566), 86.

Jones, M. (2015, January 14). Why a generation of adoptees is returning to South Korea. *The New York Times Magazine,* pp. 30–37, 51.

Katz, J. (1995). *The invention of heterosexuality.* New York: Dutton.

Khazan, O. (2016, January 29). Why are so many middle-aged white Americans dying? *The Atlantic.* Retrieved May 7, 2016, from http://www.theatlantic.com/health/archive/2016/01/middle-aged-white-americans-left-behind-and-dying-early/433863/.

Kim, M.-S. (2002). *Non-western perspectives on human communication.* Thousand Oaks, CA: Sage.

Kohut, A., et al. Blacks upbeat about black progress, prospect: A year after Obama's election. (2010, January 12). *Pew Research Center.* Retrieved June 9, 2011, from http://pewsocialtrends.org/files/2010/10/blacks-upbeat-about-black-progress-prospects.pdf.

Leonard, M. F. (2004). Struggling for identity: Multiethnic and biracial individuals in America. In A. Gonzalez, M. Houston, & V. Chen (Eds.), *Our voices* (pp. 228–239). Los Angeles, CA: Roxbury.

Leonhardt, D. (2011, May 24). Top colleges, largely for the elite. *The New York Times.* Retrieved June 9, 2011, from www.nytimes.com/2011/05/25/business/economy/25leonhardt.html?_r=1.

Luo, M. (2007, December 6). Crucial test for Romney in speech on his religion. *The New York Times.* Retrieved February 4, 2008, from www.nytimes.com.

Martinez, R. (1998). Technicolor. In C. C. O'Hearn (Ed.), *Half and half: Writers on growing up biracial + bicultural* (pp. 245–264). New York: Pantheon Books.

McDonald, S. N. (2015, September 23). American in Paris: Saul Williams critiques his home country from the outside looking in. *The Washington Post.* Retrieved May 4, 2016, from https://www.washingtonpost.com/news/arts-and-entertainment/wp/2015/09/23/american-in-paris-saul-williams-critiques-his-home-country-from-the-outside-looking-in/.

McGreal, C. (2015, December 13). Rachel Dolezal: 'I wasn't identifying as black to upset people. I was being me.' *The Guardian.* Retrieved May 1, 2016, from http://www.theguardian.com/us-news/2015/dec/13/rachel-dolezal-i-wasnt-identifying-as-black-to-upset-people-i-was-being-me.

Mehl, M. R., & Pennebaker, J. W. (2003). The sounds of social life: A psychometric analysis of students' daily social environments and natural conversations. *Journal of Personality and Social Psychology, 84,* 857–870.

Merritt, B. D. (2000). Illusive reflections: African American women on primetime television. In A. Gonzalez, M. Houston, & V. Chen (Eds.), *Our voices: Essays in culture, ethnicity and communication* (3rd ed., pp. 47–53). Los Angeles, CA: Roxbury.

Miller, A., & Ross, S. D. (2004). They are not us: Framing of American Indians by the *Boston Globe. Howard Journal of Communications, 15,* 245–259.

Miller, R. L., Watling, J. R., Staggs, S. L., & Rotheram-Borus, M. J. (2003). Growing up biracial in the United States. In E. P. Salett, & D. R. Koslow (Eds.), *Race, ethnicity and self* (2nd ed., pp. 139–168). Washington, DC: National MultiCultural Institute.

Mishel, L., Bernstein, J., & Allegretto, S. (2006). *The state of working America 2006/2007.* An Economic Policy Institute Book. Ithaca, NY: ILR Press, an imprint of Cornell University Press.

Mishory, J. (2016, May 5). How millennials earn success with struggle. *CNN.* Retrieved May 3, 2016, from http://www.cnn.com/2016/05/05/opinions/millennials-have-grit-mishory/index.html.

Moon, D. G., & Rolison, G. L. (1998). Communication of classism. In M. L. Hecht (Ed.), *Communicating prejudice* (pp. 122–135). Thousand Oaks, CA: Sage.

Moon, D. (2016). "Be/coming" White and the myth of White ignorance: Identity projects in White communities. *Western Journal of Communication, 80*(3): 282–303.

Morin, R. (2001, July 11). Misperceptions cloud whites' view of blacks. *The Washington Post,* p. A01.

Multiracial celebrities. (n.d.). *Blackfix.com.* Retrieved May 24, 2011, from www.blackflix.com/articles/multiracial.html.

Myers, K. (2003). White fright: Reproducing white supremacy through casual discourse. In A. W. Doane & E. Bonilla-Silva (Eds.), *White out: The continuing significance of racism* (pp. 129–144). New York: Routledge.

Nagarajan, R. (2014, May 30). First count of third gender in census: 4.9 lakh. *The Times of India.* Retrieved May 3, 2016, from http://timesofindia.indiatimes.com/india/First-count-of-third-gender-in-census-4-9-lakh/articleshow/35741613.cms.

Nakayama, T. K. (2000). Dis/orienting identities: Asian Americans, history, and intercultural communication. In A. González, M. Houston, & V. Chen (Eds.), *Our voices: Essays in ethnicity, culture, and communication* (3rd ed., pp. 13–20). Los Angeles, CA: Roxbury.

Nance, T. A., & Foeman, A. K. (2002). On being biracial in the United States. In J. N. Martin, T. K. Nakayama, & L. A. Flores (Eds.), *Readings in intercultural communication: Experiences and contexts* (pp. 53–62). Boston: McGraw-Hill.

New Vanderbilt scientific poll reveals intense bias against Mormons (2007, December 4). Retrieved February 18, 2008, from www.vanderbilt.edu/news/releases?.

Newberg, S. L. (1994). Expectancy-confirmation processes in stereotype-tinged social encounters: The moderation of social goals. In M. P. Zanna & J. M. Olson (Eds.), *Ontario symposium on personality and social psychology: Vol 7. The psychology of prejudice* (pp. 103–130). Hillsdale, NJ: Lawrence Erlbaum.

Obama's sister talks about his childhood. (2008, February14). *CBSNews.com.* Retrieved May 1, 2008, from www.cbsnews.com/stories/2008/02/14/politics/main3831108.shtml.

Omi, M., & Winant, H. (1998). Racial formation. In P. S. Rothenberg (Ed.), *Race, class and gender in the United States* (pp. 26–35). New York: St. Martin's Press.

Omi, M., & Winant, H. (2001). Racial formation. In P. S. Rothenberg (Ed.), *Race, class and gender in the United States* (pp. 11–21). New York: Worth.

Pennebaker, J. W., Mehl, M. R., & Niederhoffer, K. G. (2003). Psychological aspects of natural language use: Our words, our selves. *Annual Review of Psychology, 54,* 547–577.

Pew Research Center for the People & the Press. (2005, September 8). Huge racial divide over Katrina and its consequences. *News release.* Available from http://people-press.org/reports/pdf/255.pdf.

Pew Research Center for the People & the Press. (2007 May). Muslim Americans: Middleclass and mostly mainstream. Report available at http://pewresearch.org/assets/pdf/muslim-americans.pdf.

Phinney, J. S. (1993). A three-stage model of ethnic identity development in adolescence. In M. E. Bernal & G. Knight (Eds.), *Ethnic identity* (pp. 61–79). Albany, NY: State University of New York Press.

Ponterotto, J. G., & Pedersen, P. B. (1993). *Preventing prejudice* (Chaps. 4 & 5). Newbury Park, CA: Sage.

Roediger, D. R. (2005). *Working toward whiteness: How America's immigrants became white.* New York: Basic Books.

Roland, A. (1988). *In search of self in India and Japan: Towards a cross-cultural psychology.* Princeton, NJ: Princeton University Press.

Root, M. P. P. (2001). *Love's revolution: Interracial marriage.* Philadelphia, PA: Temple University Press.

Rosefeld, P., & Giaclone, R. A. (1991). From extreme to the mainstream: Applied impression management in organization. In R. A. Giaclone & P. Rosenfeld (Eds.), *Applied impression management: How image making affects managerial decision making.* Newbury Park, CA: Sage.

Saulny, S. (2011, March 24). Census data presents rise in multiracial population of youths. *The New York Times.* Retrieved May 24, 2011, from.nytimes.com/2011/03/25/us/25race.html.

Sigelman, L., Tuch, S. A., & Martin, J. K. (2005). What's in a name? Preference for "Black" versus "African American" among Americans of African descent. *Public Opinion Quarterly, 69,* 429–438.

Smith, T.W. (1992). Changing racial labels: From "Colored" to "Negro" to "Black" to "African American." *Public Opinion Quarterly, 56*(4), 496–514.

Solórzano, D., Ceja, M., & Yosso, T. (2000). Critical race theory, racial microaggressions, and campus racial climate: The experiences of African American college students. *Journal of Negro Education,* 69 (1/2): 60–73.

Stephan, W., & Stephan, C. (1996). Predicting prejudice: The role of threat. *International Journal of Intercultural Relations, 20,* 409–426.

Strauss, W., & Howe, N. (1997). *The fourth turning: American Prophecy.* New York: Broadway Books.

Strauss, W., & Howe, N. (2006). *Millennials and the pop culture.* Great Falls, VA: LifeCourse Associates.

Tajfel, H. (1978). Social categorization, social identity and social comparison. In H. Tajfel (Ed.), *Differentiation between social groups* (pp. 61–76). London: Academic Press.

Tajfel, H. (1981). *Human categories and social groups.* Cambridge: Cambridge University Press.

Tajfel, H. (1982). *Social identity and intergroup relations.* Cambridge: Cambridge University Press.

Tanno, D. (2000). Names, narratives, and the evolution of ethnic identity. In A. González, M. Houston, & V. Chen (Eds.), *Our voices: Essays in ethnicity, culture, and communication* (3rd ed., pp. 25–28). Los Angeles, CA: Roxbury.

Tedeschi, J. T., Lindskold, S., & Rosenfeld, P. (1985). *Introduction to social psychology.* St. Paul, MN: West.

Ting-Toomey, S. (1993). Communication resourcefulness: An identity negotiation perspective. In R. Wiseman & J. Koester (Eds.), *Intercultural communication.* Newbury Park, CA: Sage.

Ting-Toomey, S. (2005). Identity negotiation theory: Crossing cultural boundaries. In W. B. Gudykunst (Ed.), *Theorizing about intercultural communication* (pp. 211–233). Thousand Oaks, CA: Sage.

Tomkiw, L. (2016, March 19). Russia-Ukraine conflict: Two years after Crimea annexation, region is a "black hole" for human rights. *International Business Times.* Retrieved May 8, 2016, from http://www.ibtimes.com/russia-ukraine-conflict-two-years-after

-crimea-annexation-region-black-hole-human
-2338629.

Trinh, T. M. (1986/1987). Difference: A special third world women issue. *Discourse, 8.*

U.S. Census Bureau (2015, March 3). New Census Bureau report analyzes U.S. population projections. Retrieved May 3, 2016, from https://www.census.gov /newsroom/press-releases/2015/cb15-tps16.html.

Why Black and not African American? (20 April 2007). Retrieved February 16, 2008, from http://

theangryblackwoman.wordpress.com/2007/04/20 /why-black-and-not-african-american/.

Witteborn, S. (2004). Of being an Arab woman before and after September 11: The enactment of communal identities in talk. *Howard Journal of Communications, 15,* 83–98.

Wood, J. T. (2005). *Gendered lives: Communication, gender and culture* (6th ed.). Belmont, CA: Wadsworth.

Yamanouchi, K. (2002, May 19). Cosmetic companies market products aimed at men, *Arizona Republic,* p. D1.

CREDITS

[page 167, text] O. Alnatour, quote from "Muslims are not terrorist: A factual look at terrorism and Islam." from *The World Post* (December 9, 2015). [page 169, text] President Obama (2016, June 14). Remarks by the president after counter-ISIL meeting. *The White House.* [page 168–169, text] M.-S. Kim, quote from *Non-western perspectives on human communication.* Sage. [page 169–170, text] A. Roland, excerpt from *In search of self in India and Japan: Towards a cross-cultural psychology.* Princeton University Press. [page 170, text] S. E. Cross, quote from "What does it mean to "know thyself" in the United States and Japan?: The cultural construction of the self" in *Self and identity through the life course in cross-cultural perspective,* edited by T. J. Owens. JAI Press. [page 171, text] C. McGreal, quote from "Rachel Dolezal: 'I wasn't identifying as black to upset people. I was being me'" from *The Guardian* (December 13, 2015). [page 174, text] M. J. Collier, excerpt from "Theorizing cultural identification: Critical updates and continuing evolution" in *Theorizing about intercultural communication,* edited by W. B. Gudykunst. Sage. [page 174, text] L. Althusser, excerpt from "Ideology and ideological state apparatuses (notes toward an investigation)" in *Lenin and philosophy and other essays,* (trans.). B. Brewster. NLB. [page 175, text] J. Angelos, excerpt from "Becoming European" from *The New York Times Magazine* (April 10, 2016): 40–47, 54, 57, 59. [page 175, text] K. Cengel, excerpt from "A Sudden Breach in Uganda" from *The New York Times Magazine* (April 15, 2016). [page 179, text] R. Martinez, excerpt from "Technicolor" in *Half and half: Writers on growing up biracial 1 bicultural,* edited by C. C. O'Hearn. Pantheon Books. [page 179, text] Lauren, excerpt from "Student Voice: My father is American . . . an American either." Original work; [page 179, text] Ainsley, excerpt from "Student Voice: Whenever I tell . . . can speak French." Original work; [page 180, text] Jack, excerpt from "I have a very diverse ethnic background." Original work.; [page 180–183, text] R. Hardiman, excerpt from "White racial identity development in the United States" in *Race, ethnicity and self: Identity in multicultural perspective,* edited by E. P. Salett & D. R. Koslow. National MultiCultural Institute. [page 180–183, text]

R. Hardiman, excerpt from "White racial identity development in the United States" in *Race, ethnicity and self,* edited by E. P. Salett & D. R. Koslow. National MultiCultural Institute. [page 184, text] G. Bederman, excerpt from *Manliness and civilization: A cultural history of gender and race in the United States, 1880–1917.* University of Chicago Press. [page 184, text] K. Yamanouchi, excerpt from "Cosmetic companies market products aimed at men" from *Arizona Republic* (May 19, 2002): D1. [page 187, text] R. Fry, quote from "Millennials overtake Baby Boomers as America's largest generation" from *Pew Research Center* (April 25, 2016). [page 187, text] W. Strauss, and N. Howe, quote from *Millennials and the pop culture.* LifeCourse Associates. [page 188, text] The Economist, quote from "Human races or human race?" from *The Economist.* [page 191, text] D. Moon, quote from ""Be/coming" White and the myth of White ignorance: Identity projects in White communities" from *Western Journal of Communication* (2016): 282–303. [page 192, text] S. N. McDonald, excerpt from "American in Paris: Saul Williams critiques his home country from the outside looking in" from *The Washington Post* (September 23, 2015). [page 193, text] J. Blake, quote from "Are whites racially oppressed?" from *CNN* (March 4, 2011). [page 193, text] J. Blake, quote from "Are whites racially oppressed?" from *CNN* (March 4, 2011). [page 193, text] H. Hsu, quote from "The end of white America?" from *The Atlantic* (January/February, 2009). [page 197, text] D. Engen, quote from "Invisible identities: Notes on class and race" in *Our voices: Essays in culture, ethnicity and communication,* edited by A. Gonzalez, M. Houston, and V. Chen. Roxbury. [page 198, text] B. Allen, quote from *Difference matters: Communicating social identity.* Waveland Press. [page 198, text] J. Giancola & R. D. Kahlenberg, excerpt from *True merit: ensuring our brightest students have access to our best colleges and universities.* Jack Kent Cooke Foundation [page 198, text] C. Cillizza, quote from "Is the American Dream dead?" from *The Washington Post* (June 5, 2014). [page 198–199, text] O. Khazan, quote from "Why are so many middle-aged white Americans dying?" from *The Atlantic* (January 29, 2016). The Atlantic. [page 200, text] Guardian reporter and S. Walker, quote from "No regrets over Ukraine split, but Crimeans want more love from Russia" *The Guardian* (January 19, 2016). [page 200, text] L. Tomkiw, quote from "Russia-Ukraine conflict: Two years after Crimea annexation, region is a "black hole" for human rights" from *International Business Times* (March 19, 2016). [page 201, text] H. Davidson, quote from "Sweden launches phone a random Swede hotline—but don't ask about the chef" from *The Guardian* (April 8, 2016). [page 202, text] V. Chen, quote from "The construction of Chinese American women's identity" in *Women making meaning*, edited by L. F. Rakow. Routledge. [page 204, text] R. L. Miller, J. R. Watling, S. L. Staggs, and M. J. Rotheram-Borus, quote from "Growing up biracial in the United States" in *Race, ethnicity and self*, edited by E. P. Salett and D. R. Koslow. National MultiCultural Institute. [page 204, text] R. Alba, quote from "The myth of a white minority" from *The New York Times* (June 11, 2015). [page 204, text] M. Jones, quote from "Why a generation of adoptees is returning to South Korea" from *The New York Times Magazine* (January 14, 2015): 30–37, 51. [page 205, text] Quote from Obama's sister talks about his childhood from *CBSNews.com* (February 14, 2008). [page 207, text] P. Adler, excerpt from "Beyond cultural identity: Reflections on cultural and multicultural man" in *Topics in culture learning*. East-West Center. [page 208, text] R. Martinez,

excerpt from "Technicolor" in *Half and half: Writers on growing up biracial 1 bicultural*, edited by C. C. O'Hearn. Pantheon Books. [page 209, text] A. Miller, and S. D. Ross, quote from "They are not us: Framing of American Indians by the Boston Globe" from *Howard Journal of Communications* (2004): 245–259. [page 209, text] B. D. Merritt, excerpt from "Illusive reflections: African American women on primetime television" in *Our voices: Essays in culture, ethnicity and communication*, edited by A. Gonzalez, M. Houston, and V. Chen. Roxbury. [page 210, text] Jennifer excerpt from "Students Voices: I fell in love . . . me for the better." Original work; [page 211, text] D. Solórzano, M. Ceja, and T. Yosso, quote from "Critical race theory, racial microaggressions, and campus racial climate: The experiences of African American college students" from *Journal of Negro Education* (2000): 60–73. [page 211–212, text] R. Brislin, excerpt from *Understanding culture's influence on behaviour, Second Edition*. Wadsworth. [page 212, text] T. K. Nakayama, quote from "Dis/orienting identities: Asian Americans, history, and intercultural communication" in *Our voices: Essays in ethnicity, culture, and communication*, edited by A. González, M. Houston, and V. Chen. Roxbury. [page 213, text] Shazim, excerpt from "Students Voices: I would have . . . are not Muslims." Original work;

LANGUAGE AND INTERCULTURAL COMMUNICATION

SOCIAL SCIENCE PERSPECTIVE ON LANGUAGE
Language and Perception
Language and Thought: Metaphor
Cultural Variations in Communication Style
Influence of Interactive Media Use on Language
   and Communication Style
Slang and Humor in Language Use

INTERPRETIVE PERSPECTIVE ON LANGUAGE
Variations in Contextual Rules

CRITICAL PERSPECTIVE ON LANGUAGE
Co-Cultural Communication
Discourse and Social Structure
The "Power" Effects of Labels

MOVING BETWEEN LANGUAGES
Multilingualism
Translation and Interpretation

LANGUAGE AND IDENTITY
Language and Cultural Group Identity
Code Switching

LANGUAGE POLITICS AND POLICIES

LANGUAGE AND GLOBALIZATION

INTERNET RESOURCES

SUMMARY

DISCUSSION QUESTIONS

ACTIVITIES

KEY WORDS

REFERENCES

CHAPTER OBJECTIVES

After reading this chapter, you should be able to:

1. Discuss the four components of language.
2. Explain the nominalist, relativist, and qualified relativist positions on language and perception.
3. Describe the role of metaphor in understanding intercultural communication.
4. Identify cultural variations in communication style.
5. Give examples of variations in contextual rules.
6. Explain the power of labels.
7. Understand the challenges of multilingualism.
8. Explain the difference between translation and interpretation.
9. Understand the phenomenon of code switching and interlanguage.
10. Discuss the complexities of language policies.

I communicate with my friends around the world, like my friends from Germany and from Venezuela—I keep in touch with them by e-mail, Facebook, and sometimes Skype. For the most part, I feel English is a power language, since a lot of people speak English or at least know it somewhat. So when I am speaking with my friends on e-mail or Facebook, they can understand me, but there are a lot of times when I talk with them, I have to use basic English because they don't understand some words, especially slang. Another thing is my friends from Venezuela are only three hours ahead of us but my German friends are eight hours ahead, and they are usually online only at night (their time) after they finish their school work and dinner—which is the middle of the night for me. Here in America it seems that everyone is online all the time.

—Monica

As our student, Monica discovered, language is a central element in intercultural communication, whether face-to-face or online. There are often challenges, like understanding slang, and the issue of power is always present—why does Monica use English rather than German or Spanish in communicating with her friends? In online communication, timing and time zones can also be a challenge. Online communication and other communication technologies highlight another important challenge of language—it is constantly changing. Consider the words that have become part of English (and other languages): tweet, retweet, hashtag, emoticon, troll, and sexting *[le tweet, le hashtag* (or *le mot-clic),* émoticône, and troller (to troll) in French]. In addition, social media, like twitter, make us think carefully about language efficiency—how to communicate our idea in 140 characters (minus the usernames) or less?

How can we begin to understand the important role of language in intercultural communication in today's world, with more people on the move and technological connectivity to every corner of the earth? First, the sheer number of languages spoken in the world today, approximately 7,000 is staggering. Experts estimate that 800 languages are spoken in New York City alone. How can people possibly communicate given all these different languages? Is intercultural communication easier online or face-to-face? Do we use language differently online? What are the difficulties in interpreting and translating? Should everyone learn a second or third language? In this chapter, we focus on language-related issues in verbal communication processes; the next chapter focuses on the nonverbal elements.

The social science approach generally focuses on individual aspects of language in relation to intercultural communication, the interpretive approach focuses on contextual uses of language practices, and the critical approach emphasizes the relations between discourse and power. This chapter uses a dialectical perspective to explore how language works dynamically in intercultural contexts. With the personal–contextual dialectic, we can consider not only how language use operates on an individual level but also how it is influenced by context. We also use the static–dynamic dialectic to distinguish between language and discourse, to identify the components of language, and to explore the relationship among language, meaning, and perception. Although it may seem that the components of language are static, the *use* of language is a dynamic process.

In this chapter, we also explore cultural variations of language and some of the barriers presented by these variations. Then we discuss the relationship between language and power, and between language and identity, and examine issues of multilingualism, translation, and interpretation. Finally, we look at language and identity, language policies and politics, and globalization.

SOCIAL SCIENCE PERSPECTIVE ON LANGUAGE

The social science perspective focuses on the individual aspects of language use: the components of language, language perception and thought, the way cultural groups use language in different ways, and the barriers presented by these variations. The study of linguistics is just one of many ways to think about language, and this study provides us with a useful foundation for our exploration of language in intercultural communication. As shown in Table 6-1, linguists generally divide the study of language into four parts: semantics, syntactics, phonetics, and pragmatics.

Pragmatics is probably the most useful for students of intercultural communication because it focuses on actual language use—what people do with language—the

TABLE 6-1   THE COMPONENTS OF LANGUAGE

Component	Definition	Example
Semantics	The study of meaning—how individual words communicate the meanings we intend.	Think about the word *chair.* Do we define *chair* by its shape? By its function? Does a throne count as a chair? How about a table we sit on? Is this a chair?
Syntactics	The study of the structure, or grammar—the rules for combining words into meaningful sentences. Order of words is important.	"The red car smashed into the blue car" has different meaning than "The blue car smashed into the red car."
Pragmatics	The study of how meaning is constructed in relation to receivers, how language is actually used in particular contexts in language communities.	Saying "that's an awesome outfit" has different meanings depending on the context. It could be mocking, flirting, or just descriptive.
Phonetics	The study of the sound system of language—how words are pronounced, which units of sounds (phonemes) are meaningful for a specific language and which sounds are universal. (See Figure 6-1.)	French has no equivalent sound of English *th;* Japanese has a sound which is between *r* and *l.*

MODERN LANGUAGES PROBABLY ORIGINATED IN AFRICA

As described here, recent research suggests that all modern human languages may have originated in Africa. Isn't it interesting that as humans, our languages connect us all on the one hand and, on the other, is often what divides us and prevents us from communicating and understanding each other?

After studying the phonemes (sounds) in languages around the world, Dr. Quentin D. Atkinson, an evolutionary psychologist from New Zealand concluded that all modern languages originate from the same place—Southern Africa. He discovered that a language area uses fewer phonemes the farther that early humans had to travel from Africa to reach it. That is, as early humans began to migrate from southern Africa, it affected the number of distinct sounds that got used. Using mathematical modeling he found that the greater the distance from Africa, the fewer number of phonemes were detected in the languages spoken. So, for example, while some African languages have more than 100 sounds, English has about 45. Hawaiian, even farther from Africa, has only 13.

He concludes that this linguistic origin diversity parallels genetic origin diversity—as scientists have also suggested that human species originated in Southern Africa.

Sources: From Q. D. Atkinson, "Phonemic diversity supports a serial founder effect model of language expansion in Africa," *Science,* 332 (April 15, 2011), 346–349; www.neatorama.com /tag/quentin-d-atkinson/.

focus of this chapter. People around the world speak many different languages and some scholars think that the particular language we speak influences how we see the world. Before we address the question of how to reduce language barriers in intercultural communication, we need to ask the following questions: Do speakers of Japanese, Chinese, Arabic, and other languages actually perceive the world differently, depending on the particular language they speak? Or do we all experience the world in the same way but have different ways of expressing our experiences? We tackle these questions in the next section.

Language and Perception

The question of how much of our perception is shaped by the particular language we speak is at the heart of the "political correctness" debate. We can address these questions from two points of view: the nominalist and the relativist.

nominalist position
The view that perception is not shaped by the particular language one speaks. (Compare with **relativist position** and **qualified relativist position**.)

The Nominalist Position   According to the **nominalist position,** perception is not shaped by the particular language we speak. Language is simply an arbitrary "outer form of thought." Thus, we all have the same range of thoughts, which we express in different ways with different languages. This means that any thought can

My co-worker, Nam, who moved to the US from Vietnam with his parents when he was a child, talked with me about his difficulties with learning English. He indicated that he learned English about 10 years ago and that the first difficulty he encountered while learning English was the way we structure our words while forming sentences. He indicated to me that in English we have more "continuous tense" sentences compared to Vietnamese or Chinese. For example, the straight translation of Vietnamese to English without the reordering of words would turn "The phone rang while I was taking a bath" into "I had a bath when the phone rang."
—Jason

be expressed in any language, although some may take more or fewer words. The existence of different languages does not mean that people have different thought processes or inhabit different perceptual worlds. After all, a tree may be an *arbre* in French and an *arbol* in Spanish, but we all perceive the tree in the same way.

The Relativist Position According to the **relativist position,** the particular language we speak, especially the structure of that language, determines our thought patterns, our perceptions of reality, and, ultimately, important cultural components (see Figure 6-1). This position is best represented by the Sapir-Whorf hypothesis. As you may recall from Chapter 2, this hypothesis was proposed by Edward Sapir (1921), a linguist, and his student, Benjamin Whorf (1956), based on linguistic research they conducted in the 1930s and 1940s on Native American languages. According to the Sapir-Whorf hypothesis, language defines our experience. For example, there are no possessives (*his/her/our/your*) in the Diné (Navajo) language; we might conclude, therefore, that the Diné think in a particular way about the concept of possession. Another example is the variation in verb forms in English, Spanish, and French. In English and Spanish, the present continuous verb form is frequently used; thus, a student might say, "I am studying" or *"Estoy estudiando."* A French speaker, in contrast, would use the simple present form, *"J'étudie."* The Sapir-Whorf hypothesis suggests that, based on this variation in verb form, French, English, and Spanish speakers may think differently about movement or action. Variations in formal and informal forms raises similar issues. Consider that English speakers do not distinguish between a formal and an informal you (as in German, with *du* and *Sie,* or in Spanish, with *tu* and *usted*). In Japanese, formality is not simply noted by you; it is part of the entire language system. Nouns take the honorific "o" before them, and verbs take more formal and polite forms. Thus, *"Doitsu-go ga dekimasen"* [I—or you, he, she, we, they—don't speak German] is more polite and formal than *"Doitsu-go ga dekinai."* Does this mean that English, German, and Spanish speakers think about formality and informality differently?

Another frequently cited example involves variation in color vocabulary. The Diné use one word for blue and green, two words for two different colors of black, and one word for red; these four words form the vocabulary for primary colors in

relativist position The view that the particular language individuals speak, especially the structure of the language, shapes their perception of reality and cultural patterns. (Compare with **nominalist position** and **qualified relativist position.**)

FIGURE 6-1   Language is an important aspect of intercultural communication. The particular symbols used in any language are arbitrary and communicate meaning only when used in particular contexts. (© *David Rubinger/Getty Images*)

Diné culture. The Sapir-Whorf hypothesis suggests that English and Diné speakers perceive colors differently. Other examples of variations in syntax and semantics reflect differences in perception.

As a final example, note that some languages are gendered and others are not. Thus, in English you could tell your friend, "I had dinner with a neighbor last night," and the friend would not know if the neighbor was male or female. However, if you were speaking French, you would have to indicate the gender of your neighbor: *voisine* (female) or *voisin* (male). The same is true for the many other "gendered" languages, including Spanish, German, and Russian. In these languages, not only are people gendered, but also inanimate objects—the clock, the bridge, the chair, and so forth—are all either masculine or feminine. And while speakers of gendered languages obviously know that inanimate objects do not really have biological sex, the Sapir-Whorf hypothesis would suggest that using gendered language can shape the feelings and associations speakers have concerning objects around them. For example, when French and Spanish speakers were asked to assign human voices to some cartoon objects (e.g., a fork) in a recent study, the French thought the fork *(la forchette)* should speak in a male voice; the Spanish thought it should be a man's because fork in Spanish is masculine *(el tenedor)* (Deutscher, 2010). However, in another study researchers asked German speakers about their associations with gendered nouns (e.g., lady liberty, godfather, death) and found no strong evidence to support linguistic relativity (Bender, Beller, & Klauer, 2016).

The Sapir-Whorf hypothesis has had tremendous influence on scholarly thinking about language and its impact on everyday communication. It questions the basic assumption that we all inhabit the same perceptual world, the same social reality.

However, the Sapir-Whorf hypothesis has been critiqued by a number of studies that challenge the connection between language and how we think (Deutscher, 2010). For example, if according to Sapir-Whorf, language structures thought, then language must precede and only subsequently influence thought. This raises the question whether it is possible to think without language. Studies of children's **language acquisition** seem to suggest that language and thought are so closely related that it is difficult to conclude that one initiates influence over the other—not supporting the Sapir-Whorf hypothesis.

language acquisition The process of learning language.

Findings from studies of cross-cultural differences in language suggest similar conclusions. The question here is, do different language groups perceive the world completely differently? For example, one study focused on the Munduruku people who live in isolated rural areas in Brazil. Their language has few words to describe geometrical or spatial concepts and they had no rules or compasses. Sapir-Whorf hypothesis would predict that they would have limited understanding of angles and spatial distances. However, when they were shown three actual containers (one was hiding an object) and then a diagram of three containers in a triangle with one container identified as holding a hidden object, they could identify which of the containers on the ground hid the object—with about the same accuracy as American subjects. So they understood right angles and parallelism and could use distance and angles to locate a hidden object—even though they had none of these words in their language (Dehaene, Izard, Pica, & Spelke, 2006).

Given these and findings from other studies, most contemporary language experts advocate a middle ground, the **qualified relativist position,** suggesting that while not a "prison," the language habits that our culture has instilled in us from the time we first learn to speak probably does shape our orientation to the world and the people and objects we encounter (Deutscher, 2010). This view allows for more freedom than the Sapir-Whorf hypothesis. As you read the research findings that follow, you may see the wisdom of the qualified relativist position.

qualified relativist position A moderate view of the relationship between language and perception. Sees language as a tool rather than a prison (compare with nominalist position and relativist position).

Language and Thought: Metaphor

One way of thinking about the relationship between language and thought is to look at metaphors. A *metaphor* is an expression where a word (or words) is used outside of its normal conventional meaning to express a *similar* concept (Lakoff, 1992). For example, "you are my sunshine." Although an individual cannot literally *be* sunshine, comparing someone to sunshine expresses a particular positive meaning. Experts used to think that metaphors are about language, or literary writing, not useful for understanding everyday speech. A famous cognitive scientist and linguist George Lakoff disagrees and proposes that metaphors are part of thinking, one way we organize our thoughts, in everyday living. In fact, metaphors are "a major and indispensable part of our ordinary conventional way of conceptualizing the world, and that our everyday behavior reflects our metaphorical understanding of experience" (p. 203).

Understanding a culture's metaphors, then, helps us understand something about the culture itself. Consider the English metaphor of likening love to a journey: *Our relationship has hit a dead-end street. Look how far we've come. It's been a long, bumpy road. We can't turn back now. We're at a crossroads. We may have to go our separate ways. The relationship isn't going anywhere. We're spinning our wheels. Our relationship is off the track.* These are ordinary, everyday English expressions. They are not poetic, nor are they necessarily used for special rhetorical effect, but for *reasoning about* our relationships (Lakoff, 1992, p. 205).

Metaphors can also be a useful way to understand other cultures. Some metaphors are universal, like the metaphor of an angry person as a pressurized container, for example (Kövecses, 2005). Consider these English phrases: "His pent-up anger *welled up* inside him. Billy's just *blowing off* steam. He was *bursting* with anger. When I told him *he just exploded.*" Other languages have similar expressions. The universality of the metaphor may rest in the universal human physiology—since physical bodily changes actually occur when we are angry (blood pressure rises, pulse rate increases, temperature rises). Metaphors may focus on different parts of the body; the Japanese, for example, have a number of metaphors that refer to the belly—where emotions are thought to rest. In contrast, U.S. Americans and Chinese tend to refer to the heart as the source of emotions (My heart is breaking; his heart swelled with pride).

In English, metaphors for happiness seem to center on a feeling of being up, light, fluid in a container (She was floating on air, bursting with happiness). However, the Chinese have a metaphor that does not exist in English—that happiness is flowers in the heart. Experts suggest that metaphors reflect cultural beliefs and values; in this case, the metaphor reflects the more restrained Chinese communication style, while the English metaphor of "happiness is being off the ground" reflects the relatively expressive English communication style (Kövecses, 2005, p. 71). See Point of View (p. 231) for cross-cultural examples of happiness metaphors appearing in advertising.

Cultural Variations in Communication Style

What else do we need to understand in order to reduce the language and verbal barriers in intercultural communication? In addition to cultural differences in metaphor use, social science scholars also identify differences in the way people use language in everyday conversations. By this, we mean that even if people are

high-context communication A style of communication in which much of the information is contained in the contexts and nonverbal cues rather than expressed explicitly in words. (Compare with **low-context communication**.)

low-context communication A style of communication in which much of the information is conveyed in words rather than in nonverbal cues and contexts. (Compare with **high-context communication**.)

Because we live in a more global world, think about the impact of language differences in hospital emergency rooms, as well as other everyday situations such as those involving fire departments, police departments, and so on. How can we ensure adequate services for everyone? Consider the following incidents, witnessed by journalist Nina Bernstein.

A Spanish-speaking construction worker with a severely injured leg was brought to an emergency room at St. Vincent's Staten Island Hospital. Since the interpreter was on lunch break, the worker's seven-year-old cousin tried to interpret and had to tell the worker that an amputation was necessary. The child said he wasn't even sure if the doctors meant the toe or foot had to be amputated! It turns out that the worker had come to the E.R twice before, but unable to communicate his symptoms in English, he was rudely dismissed and returned home. Finally, when he came back for the third time, the foot was full of gangrene and the toe had to be amputated. After the surgery, other patients were asked to translate the doctor's instructions for the worker's post operative care.

Another patient in the same hospital, a pregnant immigrant from Mexico, had serious complications and was asked to sign a consent form for emergency surgery. She understood the doctor to say the surgery was necessary to "save the baby", and so she consented—only to wake up after the surgery and told she had had a hysterectomy and was now childless and sterile.

Source: Nina Bernstein, "Language barrier called health hazard in E.R.," *The New York Times,* April 21, 2005, p. B1.

speaking the same language, there can be misunderstandings due to differences in communication style.

Communication style combines both language and nonverbal communication. It is the **metamessage** that contextualizes how listeners are expected to receive and interpret verbal messages. A primary way in which cultural groups differ in communication style is in a preference for high- versus low-context communication. A **high-context communication** style is one in which "most of the information is either in the physical context or internalized in the person, while very little is in the coded, explicit, transmitted part of the message" (Hall, 1976, p. 79). This style of communication emphasizes understanding messages without direct verbal communication. People in long-term relationships often communicate in this style. For example, one person may send a meaningful glance across the room at a party, and his or her partner will know from the nonverbal clue that it is time to go home.

In contrast, in **low-context communication,** the majority of meaning and information is in the verbal code. This style of communication, which emphasizes explicit verbal messages, is highly valued in many settings in the United States. Interpersonal communication textbooks often stress that we should not rely on nonverbal, contextual information. It is better, they say, to be explicit and to the point, and not to leave things ambiguous. However, many cultural groups around the world value high-context

communication style The metamessage that contexualizes how listeners are expected to accept and interpret verbal messages.

metamessage The meaning of a message that tells others how they should respond to the content of our communication based on our relationship to them.

communication. They encourage children and adolescents to pay close attention to contextual cues (body language, environmental cues), and not simply the words spoken in a conversation (Gudykunst & Matsumoto, 1996).

William Gudykunst and Stella Ting-Toomey (2003) identify two major dimensions of communication styles: direct versus indirect and elaborate versus understated.

Direct Versus Indirect Styles   This dimension refers to the extent to which speakers reveal their intentions through explicit verbal communication and emphasizes low-context communication. A direct communication style is one in which verbal messages reveal the speaker's true intentions, needs, wants, and desires. An indirect style is one in which the verbal message is often designed to camouflage the speaker's true intentions, needs, wants, and desires (Gudykunst, Ting-Toomey, & Chua, 1988). Most of the time, individuals and groups are more or less direct depending on the context.

Many English speakers in the United States favor the direct speech style as the most appropriate in most contexts. This is revealed in statements like "Don't beat around the bush," "Get to the point," and "What exactly are you trying to say?" Although "white lies" may be permitted in some contexts, the direct style emphasizes honesty, openness, forthrightness, and individualism.

However, some cultural groups prefer a more indirect style, with the emphasis on high-context communication. Preserving the harmony of relationships has a higher priority than being totally honest. Thus, a speaker might look for a "soft" way to communicate that there is a problem in the relationship, perhaps by providing contextual cues (Bello et al., 2010; Park & Guan, 2009). Some languages have many words and gestures that convey the idea of "maybe." For example, three Indonesians studying in the United States were invited by their advisor to participate in a cross-cultural training workshop. They did not want to participate, nor did they have the time. But neither did they want to offend their professor, whom they held in high regard. Therefore, rather than tell him they couldn't attend, they simply didn't return his calls and didn't show up at the workshop.

An international student from Tunisia told Judith and Tom that he had been in the United States for several months before he realized that if someone was asked for directions and didn't know the location of the place, that person should tell the truth instead of making up a response. He explained that he had been taught that it was better to engage in conversation, to give *some* response, than to disappoint the person by revealing he didn't know.

Different communication styles are responsible for many problems that arise between men and women and between persons from different ethnic groups. These problems may be caused by different priorities for truth, honesty, harmony, and conflict avoidance in relationships. In addition, online communication tends to be fairly low context and direct. For example, written text messages and social media posts can't reveal emotions as well as face-to-face conversations. Individuals who prefer high-context and/or more indirect communication may use more emoticons or higher context platforms (e.g., Skype). We'll discuss the impact of interactive media later in the chapter.

Elaborate Versus Understated Styles   This dimension of communication styles refers to the degree to which talk is used. The elaborate style involves the use of rich, expressive language in everyday talk. For example, the Arabic language has many metaphorical expressions used in everyday speech. In this style, a simple assertive statement means little; the listener will believe the opposite.

In contrast, the understated style values succinct, simple assertions, and silence. Amish people often use this style of communication. A common refrain is, "If you don't have anything nice to say, don't say anything at all." Free self-expression is not encouraged. Silence is especially appropriate in ambiguous situations; if one is unsure of what is going on, it is better to remain silent.

The exact style falls between the elaborate and the understated, as expressed in the maxim "Verbal contributions should be no more or less information than is required" (Grice, 1975). The exact style emphasizes cooperative communication and sincerity as a basis for interaction.

In international negotiations, visible differences in style can contribute to misperceptions and misunderstandings. For example, if we look at two speeches concerning the Libyan conflict in the spring of 2011, we can see striking differences in the styles used by President Barack Obama and Libyan leader Muammar Gaddafi. In February 2011, there was an uprising of many Libyan people against Gaddafi (see Figure 6-2). Gaddafi responded by severe reprisals against the protestors. Obama made the decision to send U.S. troops along with other North Atlantic Treaty Organization (NATO) forces to stop Gaddafi's forces, and on March 28, 2011, Obama explained U.S. plans in a speech to the American people in a direct and dispassionate manner:

We knew that if we waited one more day, Benghazi—a city nearly the size of Charlotte—could suffer a massacre that would have reverberated across the region and stained the conscience of the world.

FIGURE 6-2   Libyans in the capital city of Tripoli celebrate after toppling their government in summer 2011. (© *Francisco Leong/AFP/Getty Images*)

It was not in our national interest to let that happen. I refused to let that happen. And so nine days ago, after consulting the bipartisan leadership of Congress, I authorized military action to stop the killing and enforce UN Security Council Resolution 1973. We struck regime forces approaching Benghazi to save that city and the people within it. We hit Gaddafi's troops in neighboring Ajdabiya, allowing the opposition to drive them out. We hit his air defenses, which paved the way for a No Fly Zone. We targeted tanks and military assets that had been choking off towns and cities and we cut off much of their source of supply. And tonight, I can report that we have stopped Gaddafi's deadly advance. (www.newstatesman.com/north-america/2011/03 /gaddafi-libyan-military-united)

Gaddafi addressed his people in a long, 75-minute speech, full of metaphors, and in a more indirect and elaborated style:

I am bigger than any Rank, I am a Revolutionary, I am the Bedouin from oasis that brought victory to enjoy it from generation to generation. Libya will remain at the top and will lead Africa and South America. We cannot hinder the process of this revolution from these greasy rats and cats. I am paying the price for staying here and my grandfather, Abdus Salam Bomanyar, who fell a martyr in 1911. I will not leave the country and I will die as a martyr in the end. The remains of my father, grandfather and my uncle Sheikh Saadi in the cemetery of Neder is the proof. I will not leave these righteous remains. Saddam says that freedom cannot enjoy the shadow of these trees unless we planted these trees and we watered it with our blood. https://docs.google.com /document/d/10dy5oLJY2QL7k2VuwKonUpSgCUX-_9ATQ-134Xka9fs /edit?hl=en&pref=2&pli=1#

While some analysts were quick to point out that Gaddafi is prone to extreme language and not held in high regard by many Arab leaders, other experts point to the particular challenges of the Arab language as it is spoken today. The classical form of the Arabic language (that based on the Qur'an), while rich and poetic, is actually nobody's mother tongue. Each Arab country region has its own local dialect, making communication within the Arab world a distinct challenge. A former British ambassador to Libya notes that Gaddafi's personal speaking style is often unintelligible to anyone who doesn't speak the Libyan dialect and clearly reflects his Bedouin background—where elaborated speech is commonplace, people talk for hours at a time, and Gaddafi's speeches regularly go on for three or four hours at a stretch (Miles, 2011).

Influence of Interactive Media Use on Language and Communication Style

Some experts wonder about the influence of communication technologies on communication style. In general, e-mail, text messaging, and especially Twitter emphasize low-context, direct and understated written communication. In these media, precision, efficiency, and making sure that the meaning is clearly conveyed are priorities. Do the prevalence of these social media platforms worldwide ultimately promote and lead to more direct, low-context, understated communication style regardless of our cultural background? Probably not, for several reasons. First, interactive media provide increasing opportunities to provide contextual information along with our words; we add emoticons, emojis, and stickers to our texts as well as photos and videos in order to convey more emotional meanings to our messages. Second, not everyone adopts or uses all available technologies. Business experts report that in many countries where high-context, indirect communication is preferred, even though digital communication is prevalent and available (and used in marketing), business people prefer face-to-face contact or telephone (especially for initial contacts) or use Skype and teleconferencing more than e-mail and text messaging in order to incorporate more contextual information (http://www.aperianglobal.com). In many countries, voicemail and texting are still not popularly used in business contexts. For example, in Kenya, many people have cell phones, young people use social media, and financial transaction via mobile phones is common. However, most Kenyans prefer written communication and face-to-face communication versus virtual communication in business contexts especially when dealing with serious issues. Government transactions require written communication on a hard copy, delivered and signed for (Virtual communication in Kenya, 2016). Similarly, while China is a big telecom market (1.1 billion WeChat accounts (http://expandedramblings.com/index.php/wechat -statistics/)), and the majority of its population use the internet, technology has not replaced face-to-face communication. This is still an essential piece to developing and maintaining interpersonal relationships, especially in business: "Even a face-to-face meeting isn't the whole requirement. It can take several in-person meetings before trust and confidence is established" (Alexander, 2014).

Moreover, people may adopt the technologies to their own style. For example, high-context communicators may use Skype rather than e-mail because video and audio allow for more contextual cues. According to the results of one study, Japanese blog users used "significantly more" emojis than American personal blog writers and blog comment contributors. The emoticons reflected cultural themes such as language play, cute culture, and politeness strategies, creating a more harmonious online environment. These results seem consistent with low- and high-context communication styles in North America and Japan, respectively (Kavanaugh, 2015). In addition to highlighting cultural differences in language, interactive media also have an enormous impact on slang and humor, discussed in the following section.

Slang and Humor in Language Use

Another cultural variation in language use that can present barriers is slang. According to language expert Tom Dalzell (2005), slang is generally wittier and cleverer than standard language. It's inventive and creative and serves an important function—it establishes a sense of community identity among its users, often in opposition to standard language users. Slang, then, can be perceived as a barrier to those outside the language group. Dalzell suggests that the cultural groups most likely to produce slang in a society are the young, the powerless, sports participants, and criminals.

Slang is particularly important for youth cultures; it's almost imperative to invent slang that belongs to each generation and is unintelligible to parents and other adults. The whole point of slang is to keep your language separate, but using social media means that one can make a video or a Vine. The link goes viral and soon 2 billion people are using the word, but the slang may not endure. Social media have really "shortened the shelf life" of slang. It is not only created more quickly due to social media and technology, but also goes out of style faster because once a new slang word reaches a wider audience, it loses its value (Social media speeds up language evolution, 2015).

International students struggle to learn slang (see Point of View, p. 237), as well as parents and grandparents who are mystified by the language of their children. What makes it particularly challenging is the fact that slang is dynamic and can be fleeting: here today, gone tomorrow, largely due to social media influence. A recent poll found that 86% of British parents think their teenagers speak an entirely different language. They are mystified by FOMO, Bae, ICYMI, and TBT and are probably using terms now considered outdated by the young (e.g., TXT, TTYL, ROFL, and GR8) (English language is changing faster than ever, 2015).

Communication accommodation theory (CAT) suggests that there is an optimum use of slang by an outsider accommodating to the slang of a particular culture. Using too much slang, or using it in inappropriate contexts, can sound awkward to the "native" listener, like when your parents try to use your slang or foreign students use lots of slang, but make mistakes in grammar and pronunciation.

Humor can be another cultural language variation that presents challenges, even when two cultural groups speak the same language. For example, some say that British humor is nuanced and subtle and often relies on irony, while American humor tends to be more obvious and straightforward—much like U.S. Americans themselves. However, these differences don't seem to present much of a barrier— comedy TV sitcoms have been adapted between the two countries for many years (e.g., *The Office*) (Emma, 2009).

Trying to use humor in a foreign language can be really challenging because the basis of humor is so often linked to particular cultural experiences (or history). For example, understanding Chinese sarcasm requires a thorough understanding of Chinese history and politics; sarcasm is often used in a very subtle way to criticize someone (often politicians) without losing face. So one way to mock present politicians is by criticizing an ancient Chinese emperor who was evil because he killed scholars and oppressed the peasants. A foreigner might not get the true humor (sarcasm) at all, but Chinese listeners would understand (www.quora.com/How-is-Chinese-sarcasm-different -from-Western-sarcasm). The best advice to cultural outsiders or language learners is to use humor and slang fairly sparingly, if at all.

Another type of humor that presents a barrier in intercultural communication is humor at the expense of another. For example, individuals sometimes mock another's accent or language use—a situation encountered by one of our students, Alejandro:

I am extremely proud of my Mexican heritage, and I usually feel offended when my identity is not respected. I have a slight accent and occasionally

K nowing another language isn't necessarily enough to communicate well. Consider all the slang used by speakers in every language. Here's some U.S. American slang from a website for students trying to learn English (and these are just the A's and B's of the alphabet)!

Abs

BAE

Benjamins

To be bent on doing something

Bling

Bogus

Booty

To be broke

Paul Kerswill, professor of sociolinguistics at York University, says that a new dialect, "Multicultural London English" is emerging among the young there, a mixture of cockney, ex-colonial English (Pakistan, Nigeria, etc.), West Indian (Jamaica, etc.), and standard English. This new style is due to lots of contact between youths from different ethnic backgrounds (high migration rates from 1950s onward) in low-income neighborhoods with few opportunities for interaction with wider, mainstream communities.

Some common words:

blud: friend

ends: neighborhood

bare: very

cotch: relax

Sources: From "Cool American English." Retrieved May 27, 2016, from http://www .coolamericanenglish.com/american-english-slang.php; E. Sinmaz (2013, November 10), "Is this the end of Cockney?" *dailymail.com*. Retrieved May 27, 2016, from http://www.dailymail.co.uk /news/article-2498152/Is-end-Cockney-Hybrid-dialect-dubbed-Multicultural-London-English -sweeps-country.html

when I go out and mispronounce something people crack jokes. They think that it is all in good humor but it can be offensive.

As he goes on to say, it's especially hurtful because the humor usually reflects (and perpetuates) negative stereotypes:

People connect too many stereotypes to Hispanics; society must learn to stop stereotyping minorities. When this happens then everyone can truly be united and respected, without preconceived notions based off a person's race.

These different uses of language communicate different things to their culturally disparate audiences. As they also demonstrate, it is not easy to interpret language use from other people's perspectives.

Taking a dialectical perspective, though, should help us avoid stereotyping specific groups (such as Arabic or English speakers) in terms of communication style. We should not expect any group to use a particular communication style all the time. Instead, we might recognize that style operates dynamically and is related to context, historical forces, and so on. Furthermore, we might consider how tolerant we are when we encounter others who communicate in very different ways and how willing or able we are to alter our own style to communicate better.

INTERPRETIVE PERSPECTIVE ON LANGUAGE

The interpretive perspective focuses on an in-depth understanding of communication use in context and how communication practices may vary from one cultural context to another.

Variations in Contextual Rules

A dialectical perspective reminds us that the particular communication style we use may vary from context to context. Think of the many contexts in which you communicate during the day—classroom, family, work, and so on—and about how you alter your communication to suit these contexts. You may be more direct with your family and less direct in classroom settings. Similarly, you may use high-context informal communication in interaction with friends and more low-context formal with your professors. These same cultural variations can apply to written communication. You probably write in more formal language when communicating with professors by e-mail than when texting to your friends.

Many research studies have examined the rules for the use of socially situated language in specific contexts. They attempt to identify contexts and then "discover" the rules that apply in these contexts for a given speech community. For example, several studies examined gender differences in the interpersonal communication "rules" of text messaging for men and women in India. In a first study, researchers discovered that in contrast to men, women tended to send and receive text messages mostly when they were alone (Shuter & Chattopadhyay, 2010). In a second study, through in-depth interviews, Indian women reported receiving negative reactions from parents, extended family members, husbands, and male friends when sending or reading text messages in their presence. In addition, they reported being subjected to "Eve Teasing," a form of interpersonal harassment by males who observed them text messaging. The study also revealed the creative strategies used by Indian women to deal with these limitations placed on them by others: storing phone numbers of male friends under female names, erasing all text messages daily, communicating through social networking sites (SNSs) rather than texting. The study concludes that these differential "textiquettes" (text messaging rules) for women and men in India reflect the unequal power relations between men and women in India, and that women texting represents a threat to male patriarchy (Shuter, 2012).

A related study examined the communication patterns involved in the common practice of "nagging" in U.S. American family contexts (Boxer, 2002). Nagging (repeated requests by one family member to another) usually concerns household chores and is often a source of conflict. More importantly, the communication practice seems to be related to issues of gender, power, and control. To be more specific, men are rarely perceived as the naggers; in this study, only six of the seventy sequences involved men nagging women. The researcher suggests that this is because they are perceived as having more power and, therefore, able to successfully request and gain compliance from another family member without resorting to nagging. This also means that children can have power (if they refuse to comply with a request despite lacking status), and parents can lack power despite having status. If our styles constrain how we request and respond to requests, then by nagging we lose power. Without power we are forced into nagging, and so it seems a vicious cycle.

Another study examines communication patterns in the Australian elementary school classroom, specifically "teacher talk" and how teachers dominate through their questioning of students, which makes up a large part of the student-teacher interaction (Gale & Cosgrove, 2004). These researchers, through analysis of very specific teacher-student exchanges, explore the power dynamics revealed in this questioning, as the teacher maintains her position of power as she gives the student a series of questions to which (she) already knows the answers. In this particular instance, the focus of the questions is concerned with eliciting responses from the student that the teacher then examines for their grammatical and pronunciation accuracy in a rather demeaning way. The researchers find that this particular type of "teacher talk" devalues and disempowers the students because of the focus on the "wrong" words they say, rather than values and empowers because of what they do know—taking away their confidence as speakers. In summary, they show how, in a classroom, many things teachers say—by virtue of their position—would be deemed completely "out of line" if said by students, by virtue of their position. This might never be stated explicitly, but is learned through what is commonly referred to as schooling's "hidden curriculum" (Gale & Cosgrove, 2004). These studies show, through in-depth contextual analysis, that what we do with words affects many of our important relationships.

Other studies compare communication styles used by two different speech communities. For example, researchers have examined how communication style varies from generation to generation. They suggest that millennials (those born between 1982 and 2001) tend to be polite, prefer electronic communication, are not as skilled at face-to-face communication because they are more used to technical ways of communicate, like visual pictures in language, and prefer action-oriented communication. Gen Xers, a little older, are comfortable with more direct and informal communication and like immediate communication and results. In comparison, the older generation, Baby Boomers, communicates in a direct and diplomatic fashion, prefers face-to-face communication but can use digital communication. These communication style differences have caused some conflicts and business experts have written extensively on how to manage multigenerational workplaces (Boogaard, 2015; Goudreau, 2013).

People communicate differently in different speech communities. Thus, the context in which the communication occurs is a significant part of the meaning. Although we might communicate in one way in one speech community, we might change our communication style in another. Understanding the dynamics of various speech communities helps us see the range of communication styles.

CRITICAL PERSPECTIVE ON LANGUAGE

A critical perspective on language suggests that, in order to use language effectively in intercultural encounters, we need to understand the role of power and power differentials in these encounters. Recall that discourse refers to language in use. This means that all discourse is social. The language used—the words and the meanings that are communicated—depends not only on the context but also on the social relations that are part of that interaction. For example, bosses and workers may use the same words, but the meanings communicated are not always the same. A boss and a worker may both refer to the company personnel as a "family." To the boss, this may mean "one big happy family," whereas to a disgruntled employee, it may mean a "dysfunctional family." To some extent, the disparity is related to the inequality between boss and worker, to the power differential.

In Chapter 2, we introduced communication accommodation theory. There are different ways that people accommodate or resist accommodating, depending on the situation. One such theory that encompasses various approaches is co-cultural communication, which we examine next.

Co-Cultural Communication

The co-cultural communication theory, proposed by communication scholar Mark Orbe (1998), describes how language works between dominant and nondominant groups—or **co-cultural groups.** Groups that have the most power (whites, men, heterosexuals) consciously or unconsciously formulate a communication system that supports their perception of the world. This means that co-cultural group members (ethnic minorities, women, gays) must function in communication systems that often do not represent their experiences. Nondominant groups thus find themselves in dialectical struggles: Do they try to adapt to the dominant communication style, or do they maintain their own styles? Women in large male-dominated corporations often struggle with these issues. Do they adapt a male corporate style of speaking, or do they assert their own style?

There seem to be three general answers to the question of how co-cultural groups can relate to the more powerful (dominant) groups: They can communicate nonassertively, assertively, or aggressively. Within each of these communication postures, co-cultural individuals may emphasize assimilation—trying to become like the dominant group—or they can try to accommodate and adapt to the dominant group. They can also try to remain separate from the dominant groups as much as possible. These three sets of orientations result in nine types of communication strategies (Table 6-2). The strategy chosen depends on many things, including preferred outcome, perceived costs and rewards, and context.

co-cultural groups
Nondominant cultural groups that exist in a national culture, such as African American or Chinese American.

TABLE 6-2 CO-CULTURAL COMMUNICATION ORIENTATIONS			
	Nonassertive	**Assertive**	**Aggressive**
Assimilation	Emphasize commonalities	Extensive preparation	Dissasociating
	Developing positive face	Overcompensating	Mirroring
	Censoring self	Manipulating stereotypes	Strategic distancing
	Averting controversy	Bargaining	Ridiculing self
Accomodation	Increasing visibility	Communicating self	Confronting
	Dispelling stereotypes	Intragroup networking	Gaining advantage
		Using liaisons	
		Educating others	
Separation	Avoiding	Exemplifying strengths	Attacking
	Maintaining interpersonal barriers	Embracing stereotypes	Sabotaging others

Source: From M. Orbe, & T. Roberts, "Co-Cultural Theorizing: Foundations, Applications & Extensions," *Howard Journal Of Communications*, *23*(4), 2012: 295–296.

The point here is that there are both costs and benefits for co-cultural members when they choose which of these strategies to use. Because language is structured in ways that do not reflect their experiences, they must adopt some strategy for dealing with the linguistic framework. For example, if Mark wants to refer to his relationship with Kevin, does he use the word *boyfriend, friend, roommate, husband, partner,* or some other word? If Mark and Kevin are married he might choose to refer to Kevin as his husband in some contexts; in others (e.g. Thanksgiving dinner with disapproving family, or at work) he may choose a different term, depending on how he perceives costs and benefits in each situations. Let's look at how these strategies might work, and the costs and the benefits of each.

Assimilation Strategies The three assimilation strategies are nonassertive, assertive, and aggressive. Some co-cultural individuals tend to use nonassertive assimilation strategies. These strategies emphasize trying to fit and be accepted by the dominant group. Such strategies might emphasize commonalities ("I'm not that different"), be self-monitoring ("I'd better be careful about what I say in this organization to make sure I don't offend those in power"), and, above all, avoid controversy. There are potential costs to this approach because these co-cultural individuals may feel they cannot be honest about themselves and may also feel uncomfortable reinforcing the dominant group's worldview and power.

The second assimilation strategy is assertive assimilation. Co-cultural individuals taking this strategy may downplay co-cultural differences and try to fit into the existing structures. Unlike the nonassertive assimilation strategy, this individual will try to fit in but also let people know how she or he feels from time to time. However, this strategy can promote an us-versus-them mentality, and some people find it difficult to maintain this strategy for very long.

Aggressive assimilation strategies emphasize fitting in, and co-cultural members who take this approach can go to great lengths to prove they are like members of the dominant group. Sometimes this means distancing themselves from other members of their co-culture, mirroring (dressing and behaving like the dominant group), or self-ridiculing. The benefit of this strategy is that the co-cultural member is not seen as "typical" of members of that co-culture. The cost may entail ridicule from members of that co-culture who may accuse this individual of acting white, thinking like a man, or "straight." Thus, these strategies involve constantly negotiating position with the dominant group while being isolated from one's own co-cultural group.

Accommodation Strategies   Nonassertive accommodation strategies emphasize blending into the dominant culture but tactfully challenging the dominant structure to recognize co-cultural practices. For example, a Jewish co-worker may want to put up a menorah near the company's Christmas tree as a way of challenging the dominant culture. By gently educating the organization about other religious holidays, the co-cultural member may be able to change their presumptions about everyone celebrating Christmas. Using this strategy, the co-cultural individual may be able to influence group decision making while still showing loyalty to the larger organization's goals. The cost of this strategy may be that others feel that she or he is not pushing hard enough to change larger structural issues in the organization. Also, this strategy does not really promote major changes in organizations to make them more inclusive and reflective of the larger society.

Assertive accommodation strategies try to strike a balance between the concerns of co-cultural and dominant group members. These strategies involve communicating self, doing intragroup networking, using liaisons, and educating others. For example, Asian American co-workers may share information about themselves with their co-workers, but they also share information about words that are offensive, such as *Oriental* and *slope*.

Aggressive accommodation strategies involve moving into the dominant structures and then working from within to promote significant changes—no matter how high the personal cost. Although it may seem as if co-cultural workers who use these strategies are confrontational or self-promoting, they also reflect a genuine desire to work with and not against dominant group workers. For example, a disabled co-worker may consistently remind others that facilities need to be more accessible, such as door handles, bathrooms that can accommodate wheelchairs, and so on. Co-cultural members with this orientation may periodically use assertive as well as aggressive accommodation strategies and so may be perceived as genuinely committed to the larger group's good. In this way, they reap the benefits of being perceived positively by the dominant group and also have an impact on the organization. However, co-cultural members who consistently use aggressive accommodating strategies may find themselves alienated from both other co-cultural members and from dominant group colleagues for being too confrontational.

Separation Strategies   Nonassertive separation strategies are often used by those who assume that some segregation is part of everyday life in the United States. Generally, people live, work, learn, socialize, and pray with those who resemble them. This is generally easier for the dominant group than for co-cultural members. Some co-cultural individuals regard segregation as a natural phenomenon but also use subtle communication practices to maintain separation from the dominant group. Perhaps the most common strategy is simply avoiding interactions with dominant group members whenever possible. Thus, gay people using this orientation may spend their social time with other gay people. Or women may prefer to use professional women's services (having a female doctor, dentist, and attorney) and socialize with other women. The benefit of this approach is that co-cultural members do not have to deal with any negative feelings or stereotypes about their group, but the cost is that they cannot network and make connections with those in power positions.

Assertive separation strategies reflect a conscious choice to maintain space between dominant and co-cultural group members. Typical strategies might include stressing strengths and embracing stereotypes. One of the benefits of this approach, like the nonassertive separation strategy, is that it promotes co-cultural unity and self-determination. The cost, however, is that co-cultural group members must try to survive without having access to resources controlled by the dominant group.

Aggressive separation strategies are used by those for whom co-cultural segregation is an important priority. These strategies can include criticizing, attacking, and sabotaging others. The benefit of this approach for co-cultural members is that it enables them to confront pervasive, everyday, assumed discriminatory practices and structures. The cost may be that the dominant group retaliates against this open exposure of the presumed way of doing things.

Again, when confronted with various situations, dominant and co-cultural group members need to think carefully about how they wish to respond. There are benefits and costs to all of the decisions made. Although dominant group members are likely to be less harmed than co-cultural group members, everyone may suffer in the end. If Miguel is "cut out of the loop" at work and not told about an important meeting that affects his job, how should he handle this situation? He could pursue an assertive accommodation strategy and remind his co-workers that he needs to be included by pointing out when he is excluded. This could work and produce a more inclusive work environment, or the exclusion may continue because he is ignored. Or he could adopt a more aggressive accommodation strategy and meet with the manager and insist he be included. What are the costs and benefits of this approach? There are no easy answers, but it is important to consider what verbal communication strategy you may want to use when interacting in intercultural communication situations.

Discourse and Social Structure

Just as organizations have particular structures and specific positions within them, societies are structured so that individuals occupy social positions. Differences in **social positions** are central to understanding intercultural communication. For one thing, not all positions within the structure are equivalent; everyone is not the same. When men whistle at an attractive woman walking by, it has a different force and meaning than if women were to whistle at a man walking by.

Power is a central element, by extension, of this focus on social position. For instance, when a judge in court says what he or she thinks *freedom of speech* means, it carries much greater force than when a neighbor or a classmate gives an opinion about what the phrase means. When we communicate, we tend to note (however unconsciously) the group membership and positions of communication participants. To illustrate, consider the previous example. We understand how communication functions, based on the group membership of the judge (as a member of the judicial system) and of the neighbors and classmates; we need to know nothing about their individual identities.

Groups also hold different positions of power in the social structure. Because intercultural contact occurs between members of different groups, the positions of the groups affect communication. Group differences lend meaning to intercultural communication because, as noted previously, the concept of differences is key to language and the semiotic process.

The "Power" Effects of Labels

We often use labels to refer to other people and to ourselves. Labels, as signifiers, acknowledge particular aspects of our social identity. For example, we might label ourselves or others as "male" or "female," indicating sexual identity. Or we might say we are "Canadian" or a "New Englander," indicating a national or regional identity. The context in which a label is used may determine how strongly we feel about the label. On St. Patrick's Day, for example, someone may feel more strongly about being an Irish American than about being a woman or a student or a Texan.

Sometimes people feel trapped or misrepresented by labels. They might complain, "Why do we have to have labels? Why can't I just be me?" These complaints belie the reality of the function of discourse. It would be nearly impossible to communicate without labels. People rarely have trouble when labeled with terms they agree with—for example, "man," "student," "Minnesotan," or "Australian." Trouble arises, however, from the use of labels that they don't like or that they feel describe them inaccurately. Think about how you feel when someone describes you using terms you do not like.

social positions The places from which people speak that are socially constructed and thus embedded with assumptions about gender, race, class, age, social roles, sexuality, and so on.

Growing up in Pakistan, my first languages were Urdu and Gujarati and learning English was a struggle when I came to the U.S. Grammar was especially difficult for me and I would often say things like "I ranned there" or "I supposed" (I was supposed to). One of the things one can do when trying to speak with someone who does not speak English fluently is be sensitive and not treat them like they're dumb. When I first came to America people would talk to me very loudly as if I were completely incapable of understanding.
—Amir

My native language is Spanish. Since I was a little kid, I've been learning English so I already knew the language when I moved to the U.S. However, even to this day, I have trouble understanding slang. I feel uncomfortable when situations arise where I don't understand what is being said because of slang. . . . I think that when speaking with someone from another culture, specifically with someone who speaks (American) English as a second language, one must be more considerate toward that person's needs; e.g., speaking slower, repeating oneself if necessary, explaining and/or avoiding slang terms.
—Sergio

Labels communicate many levels of meaning and establish particular kinds of relationships between speaker and listener. Sometimes people use labels to communicate closeness and affection for others. Labels like "friend," "lover," and "partner" communicate equality. Sometimes people intentionally invoke labels to establish a hostile relationship. Labels like "white trash" and "redneck" intentionally communicate inequality. Sometimes people use labels that are unintentionally offensive to others.

Many times, these labels are spoken without any knowledge or understanding of their meanings, origin, or even current implications and can demonstrate prejudicial feelings (Cruz-Jansen, 2002). For example, many descendants of Spanish-speaking people living in the United States reject the term "Hispanic" since it was a term mandated by the U.S. government and never used by the people themselves. In fact, in a recent survey, 71% said that "Hispanics" in the United States encompass many different cultures. Reflecting this notion, 51% said they prefer to use their family's country of origin as an ethnic label (e.g., Mexican or Cuban) and 21% said they use the term "American" most often (Taylor, Lopez, Martinez, & Velasco, 2012). Similarly, "Oriental" is a term rejected by many Asians and Asian Americans, and "homosexual" communicates negative characteristics about the speaker and establishes distance between the speaker and listener. Similarly, many indigenous people reject the term "Native American"—saying that it is only used by white people—preferring their more specific tribal name or the terms "American Indian" or "Indian." Many prefer "First Nations" people—to underscore the fact that tribes are in fact nations, recognized by the U.S.

government (Yellow Bird, 1999). And you can probably think of many other labels ("bitch," "ho," "faggot," etc.) that are sometimes casually uttered that could be considered offensive by the targeted group.

Discourse is tied closely to social structure, so the messages communicated through the use of labels depend greatly on the social position of the speaker. If the speaker and listener are close friends, then the use of particular labels may not lead to distancing in the relationship or be offensive. But if the speaker and listener are strangers, then these same labels might invoke anger or close the lines of communication. Cultures change over time, as do languages. It is important that you stay aware of these changes as much as possible so you do not unintentionally offend others. Regardless of the intentions of the speaker, negative labels can work in small but powerful ways: Each utterance works like a grain of sand in sedimentary rock or like one roll of snowball going down a hill—small in itself but said over and over serves to reproduce systems of sexism, racism, homophobia, and the like.

Furthermore, if the speaker is in a position of power, then he or she has potentially an even greater impact. For example, when politicians use discourse that invokes racist, anti-Semitic, or other ideologies of intolerance, many people become concerned because of the influence they may have. These concerns were raised in 2016 over anti-immigrant, anti-Semitic, anti-Islam comments by many of the leaders of the growing right-wing populism in Europe, for example, Austria's Norbert Hofer of the Freedom party, France's Marine Le Pen of the National Front, Poland's Pawel Kukiz, and others (Troianovski, 2016). Similar concerns have arisen over the political discourse of presidential candidates Donald Trump and Ted Cruz that openly and explicitly voice anti-Muslim and anti-immigrant views (Ayala, 2016). Of course, political office is not the only powerful position from which to speak. Fundamentalist Christian leaders have caused concern with their antigay discourse, and celebrities like actor Mel Gibson and designer John Galliano have been criticized for racist, sexist, and anti-Semitic discourse.

Judith and Tom collaborated on a study about reactions to labeling. We asked white students which of the following they preferred to be called: white, Caucasian, white American, Euro-American, European American, Anglo, or WASP. They did not favor such specific labels as "WASP" or "European American" but seemed to prefer a more general label like "white." We concluded that they probably had never thought about what labels they preferred to be called. As we noted in Chapter 5, the more powerful aspects of identity seem to go unnoticed; for many people, whiteness just "is," and the preferred label is a general one that does not specify origin or history. Individuals from powerful groups generally do the labeling of others; they themselves do not get labeled (Martin, Krizek, Nakayama, & Bradford, 1996). For example, when men are asked to describe their identities, they often forget to specify gender as part of their identity. Women, in contrast, often include gender as a key element in their identity. This may mean that men are the defining norm and that women exist in relation to this norm. We can see this in the labels we use for men and women and for people of color. We rarely refer to a "male physician" or a "white physician," but we do refer to a "female doctor" or a "black doctor."

MOVING BETWEEN LANGUAGES

Multilingualism

Why do some people choose to learn foreign languages and others do not? Given the choice, some people, particularly in the United States, do not feel the need to learn a second language. They assume that most people they encounter either at home or abroad will be able to speak English (see Figure 6-3). Or perhaps they feel they have been successful so far without learning another language, so why start now? If the need arises in a professional context, they can always hire an interpreter. In fact, a recent survey of Canadian and U.S. professionals concluded that a foreign language was not essential in doing business abroad and that language was *not* that crucial. However, international business experts pointed out that the conclusions of this study were probably premature; first, the professionals surveyed were mono-lingual and would probably not advocate for fluency in a foreign language and also

FIGURE 6-3 French/English stop sign.
(© *T. K. Nakayama*)

Harumi Befu, emeritus professor at Stanford University, discusses the consequences of English domination for monolingual Americans.

Instead of language enslavement and intellectual imperialism, however, one more often is told of the benefit of learning a second language, such as English. For example, non-native English speakers can relativize their own language and appreciate each language on its own terms. It was Goethe who said that one who does not know a foreign language does not know his/her own language. . . .

Thanks to the global dominance of their country, American intellectuals have acquired the "habitus" (Bourdieu) of superiority, whereby they exercise the license of expressing their thoughts in English wherever they go instead of showing respect to locals through expending efforts to learn their language. This privileged position, however, spells poverty of the mind.

For their minds are imprisoned in a single language; they are unable to liberate their minds through relativizing English. In short, other things being equal, monolingual Americans (not all Americans are monolingual) are the most provincial and least cosmopolitan among those who traffic in the global interlinguistic community—a price they pay for the strength of the country backing them.

Source: From H. Befu, "English Language Intellectual Imperialism and Its Consequences," *Newsletter: Intercultural Communication, 37* (Intercultural Communication Institute, Kanda University of International Studies, Japan), June 2000, p. 1.

did not include anyone whose native language wasn't English. Further, they did not examine the implications of monolingualism in a competitive global environment (Varner & Beamer, 2011).

While the advantage of being an English speaker may make it easier for Americans to travel overseas, there may be some downsides. As shown in the Point of View on p. 248, one professor thinks that a being monolingual makes American less cosmopolitan and more provincial—compared to others we're competing against in the current global economy. The fact is that a person who only knows one language may be understood by others, if the language is commonly spoken (like English) as a foreign language, but that person can never understand what others are saying in their own languages and will always have to rely on translators and are more likely to misunderstand what others are saying. Perhaps more importantly, such people miss the opportunity to learn about a culture. As we have described it, language and culture are so inextricably intertwined that to learn a new language is to gain insight into another culture and another world. Acclaimed author Benedict Anderson (2016), who spoke many languages and was a renowned authority on nationalism, said, "It is important to keep in mind that to learn a language is not simply to learn a linguistic means of communication. It is also to learn the way of thinking and feeling of people who speak and write a language that is different from ours. It is to learn the history and culture underlying their thoughts and emotions and so to learn to empathize with them" (Anderson, 2016). Language acquisition studies have shown that it is nearly impossible for individuals to learn the language of a group of people they dislike. For instance, Tom was talking to a student about meeting the program's foreign language requirement. The student said, "I can't take Spanish. I'm from California." When Tom said that he did not understand what she meant, she blurted that she hated Mexicans and wouldn't take Spanish under any circumstances. As her well-entrenched racism suggested, she would indeed never learn Spanish.

While some learn a foreign language in order to compete in global markets or to navigate the increasingly global village, more personal imperatives also drive people to learn languages. For example, while our student Katarina already speaks three languages (English, Spanish, and Serbian), she is not satisfied with this. She says, "With an expanding world, Americans have to be more aggressive in their pursuit of cultural knowledge. I feel that learning a fourth language, specifically Chinese, would greatly benefit me in my job prospects as well as in my ability to communicate with more of the world."

Many people use foreign languages to escape from a legacy of oppression in their own languages. Consider the case of Sam Sue (1992), a Chinese American born and raised in Mississippi, who explains his own need to alter his social reality—often riddled by stigmatizing stereotypes—by changing the way he speaks:

> *Northerners see a Southern accent as a signal that you're a racist, you're stupid, or you're a hick. Regardless of what your real situation is. So I reacted to that by adapting the way I speak. If you talked to my brother, you would definitely know he was from the South. But as for myself, I remember customers telling my dad, "Your son sounds like a Yankee." (p. 4)*

Among the variations in U.S. English, the southern accent unwittingly communicates many negative stereotypes. Escaping into another accent is, for some, the only way to escape the stereotypes.

People who speak two languages are often called **bilingual;** people who speak more than two languages are considered **multilingual.** Rarely do bilinguals speak both languages with the same level of fluency. More commonly, they prefer to use one language over another, depending on the context and the topic. Sometimes entire nations are bilingual or multilingual. Belgium, for example, has three national languages (Dutch, German, and French), and Switzerland has four (French, German, Italian, and Romansh). The United States has a growing number of bilinguals and multilinguals. According to a recent report, the number of people who spoke a language other than English has more than doubled in the last three decades. The 10 most popular languages in the United States are:

bilingual The ability to speak two languages fluently or at least competently.

multilingual The ability to speak more than two languages fluently or at least competently.

1. Spanish
2. Chinese
3. Tagalog

4. Vietnamese

5. French

6. German

7. Korean

8. Arabic

9. Russian

10. Italian (https://www.alsintl.com/blog/top-10-languages/)

On either the individual or the national level, multilinguals must engage in language negotiation. That is, they need to work out, whether explicitly or implicitly, which language to use in a given situation. These decisions are sometimes clearly embedded in power relations. For example, French was the court language during the reign of Catherine the Great in 18th-century Russia. French was considered the language of culture, the language of the elite, whereas Russian was considered a vulgar language, the language of the uneducated and the unwashed. Special-interest groups in many U.S. states, especially Arizona and California, have attempted to pass laws declaring English the official language. These attempts reflect a power bid to determine which language will be privileged.

Sometimes a language is chosen as a courtesy to others. For example, Tom joined a small group going to see the fireworks display at the Eiffel Tower on Bastille Day one year. (Bastille Day is a French national holiday, celebrated on July 14, to commemorate the storming of the Bastille prison in 1789 and the beginning of the French Revolution.) One woman in the group asked, "*Alors, on parle français ou anglais?*" ["Are we speaking French or English?"]. Because one man felt quite weak at English, French was chosen as the language of the evening.

An interesting linguistic phenomenon known as **interlanguage** has implications for the teaching and learning of other languages. Interlanguage refers to a kind of communication that emerges when speakers of one language are speaking in another language. The native language's semantics, syntactics, pragmatics, and phonetics often overlap into the second language and create a third way of communicating. For example, many English-speaking female students of German might say, "*Ich bin ein Amerikanerin,*" which is incorrect German but is structured on the English way of saying, "I am an American." The correct form is "*Ich bin Amerikanerin.*" The insertion of "*ein*" reveals the English language overlap.

In his work on moving between languages, Tom has noted that this creation of other ways of communicating can offer ways of resisting dominant cultures. He notes that "the powerful potential of translation for discovering new voices can violate and disrupt the systemic rules of both languages" (Nakayama, 1997, p. 240). He gives the example of "*shiros,*" which is used by some Japanese Americans to refer to whites. *Shiro* is the color white, and adding an *s* at the end is the English grammatical way to pluralize words. Tom explains,

> *Using the color for people highlights the overlay of the ideology of the English language onto Japanese and an odd mixing that probably would not make*

interlanguage A kind of communication that emerges when speakers of one language are speaking in another language. The native language's semantics, syntactics, pragmatics, phonetics, and language styles often overlap and create a third way of communicating.

sense to people who speak only English or Japanese, or those who do not live in the spaces between them. (p. 242n)

Different people react differently to the dialectical tensions of a multilingual world. Some work hard to learn other languages and other ways of communicating, even if they make numerous errors along the way. Others retreat into their familiar languages and ways of living. The dialectical tensions that arise over different languages and different systems of meaning are played out around the world. But these dialectical tensions never disappear; they are always posing new challenges for intercultural communicators.

Translation and Interpretation

Because no one can learn all of the languages in the world, we must rely on translation and interpretation—two distinct but important means of communicating across language differences. The European Union (EU), for example, has a strict policy of recognizing all of the languages of its constituent members. Hence, many translators and interpreters are hired by the EU to help bridge the linguistic gaps.

Translation generally refers to the process of producing a written text that refers to something said or written in another language. The original language text of a translation is called the **source text;** the text into which it is translated is the **target text.**

Interpretation refers to the process of verbally expressing what is said or written in another language. Interpretation can either be simultaneous, with the interpreter speaking at the same time as the original speaker, or consecutive, with the interpreter speaking only during the breaks provided by the original speaker.

As we know from language theories, languages are entire systems of meaning and consciousness that are not easily rendered into another language in a word-for-word equivalence. The ways in which different languages convey views of the world are not equivalent, as we noted previously. Consider the difficulty involved simply in translating names of colors. The English word *brown* might be translated as any of these French words, depending on how the word is used: *roux, brun, bistre, bis, marron, jaune,* and *gris* (Vinay & Darbelnet, 1977, p. 261).

Issues of Equivalency and Accuracy   Some languages have tremendous flexibility in expression; others have a limited range of words. The reverse may be true, however, for some topics. This slippage between languages is both aggravating and thrilling for translators and interpreters. Translation studies traditionally have tended to emphasize issues of **equivalency** and accuracy. That is, the focus, largely from linguistics, has been on comparing the translated meaning with the original meaning. However, for those interested in the intercultural communication process, the emphasis is not so much on equivalence as on the bridges that people construct to cross from one language to another.

Many U.S. police departments are now hiring officers who are bilingual because they must work with a multilingual public. In Arizona, like many other states, Spanish

translation The process of producing a written text that refers to something said or written in another language.

source text The original language text of a translation. (See also **target text.**)

target text The new language text into which the original language text is translated. (See also **source text.**)

interpretation The process of verbally expressing what is said or written in another language.

equivalency An issue in translation, the condition of being equal in meaning, value, quantity, and so on.

These students describe the best strategies for communicating with someone who is trying to learn a foreign language:

I think it's important to be patient with people. When I was in Tanzania trying to learn Swahili and trying to not use English, everyone was so helpful. Every time I made a mistake they would correct me in a positive way. They would not be rude or judge how bad it was. This was very constructive for me. It helped me have a positive outlook that I really could learn the language.
—Rachel

It's important to speak in short, simple sentences in the beginning. For example when I was visiting my Aunt Josephina (from Mexico), usually around the holidays when lots of cooking is involved, I would tend to ask her, "Can I help you with that?" rather than something longer like, "Would you rather I help cook or should I just wait and do the dishes after?" A longer sentence with multiple questions usually wound up with a questionable smile, where I would have to then reword the question. Second, I also find that "using visual aids to support what you are saying—for example, write down key words or numbers, or use simple gestures"—is an incredibly important suggestion for successful communication. In mine and my aunt's case, this usually included hand gestures such as pointing specific things out which then she was usually able to put together what I was saying or asking after. And third, of course, speaking slowly and being patient with the person you are speaking to who is not fluent in English. Showing frustration is only going to embarrass or degrade the person who you are speaking to and ultimately leads them to pull back and stop communicating all together.
—Carrie

is a particularly important language. Let's look at a specific case in which a police detective for the Scottsdale (Arizona) Police Department explained an unusual phrase:

Detective Ron Bayne has heard his share of Spanish phrases while on the job. But he recently stumped a roomful of Spanish-speaking police officers with an unusual expression.

A suspect said, "Me llevaron a tocar el piano" [They took me to play the piano].

"I knew it couldn't mean that," said Bayne, a translator for the Scottsdale Police Department. "But I had no idea what it really meant." (Meléndez, 2002, p. B1)

This slang term, popular with undocumented aliens, highlights the differences between "street" Spanish and classroom Spanish. It also points to the importance

Translation can create amusing and interesting intercultural barriers. Consider the following translation experiences:

- When McDonald's brought its big Mac to France, it translated to the name "Gros mec" which actually means "big pimp"
- Frank Perdue's Chicken hit Spanish markets, its tagline "It takes a strong man to make a tender chicken" to "it takes an aroused man to make a chicken affectionate"
- Coors' "Turn it loose" campaign in Spain was translated to "you will suffer from diarrhea"
- Clairol didn't realize when it marketed its "Mist Stick" curling iron in Germany that "mist" is slang for manure in German
- Schweppes campaign tried to sell Italian consumers "toilet water" instead of "tonic water"
- Hunt-Wesson introduced its baked beans in French Canada as "Gros Jos" not realizing that's slang for "big breasts"
- KFC mistakenly translated its "Finger-lickin good" tagline to "eat your fingers off" in Chinese
- "Got Milk" campaign was less successful among Latinos since the literal translation was "Are you lactating?"

Source: From K. Weinmann (2011, October 17), "13 Slogans that got hilarious when they were lost in translation." Available at http://www.businessinsider.com/13-hilarious-slogans-lost-in -translation-2011-10.

of context in understanding meaning. In this context, we know that the police did not take a suspect to play a piano. Instead, this suspect was saying that the police had fingerprinted him. The varieties of expression in Spanish reflect social class and other differences that are not always communicated through translation or interpretation.

Yet the context for interpreters and translators must also be recognized. The need for Spanish speakers in the U.S. Southwest represents only the tip of the "linguistic iceberg." The continuing "war on terror" has created another need for translators and interpreters who are fluent in Arabic, Farsi, Urdu, Punjabi, Pashto, and Dari. The changing context for intelligence work has changed the context for translators and interpreters as well, to say nothing of the languages that are highly valued. These issues, although beyond the scope of equivalency and accuracy, are an important part of the dynamic of intercultural communication.

The Role of the Translator or Interpreter   We often assume that translators and interpreters are "invisible," that they simply render into the target language whatever they hear or read. The roles that they play as intermediaries, however, often regulate how they render the original. Tom believes that it is not always appropriate to translate everything that one speaker is saying to another, in exactly the same way, because the potential for misunderstanding due to cultural differences might be too great. Translation is more than merely switching languages; it also involves negotiating cultures. Writer Elisabeth Marx (1999) explains,

> *It is not sufficient to be able to translate—you have to comprehend the subtleties and connotations of the language. Walter Hasselkus, the German chief executive of Rover, gave a good example of this when he remarked: "When the British say that they have a 'slight' problem, I know that it has to be taken seriously." There are numerous examples of misunderstandings between American English and British English, even though they are, at root, the same language. (p. 95)*

It might be helpful to think of translators and interpreters as cultural brokers who must be highly sensitive to the contexts of intercultural communication.

We often assume that anyone who knows two languages can be a translator or an interpreter. Research has shown, however, that high levels of fluency in two languages do not necessarily make someone a good translator or interpreter. The task obviously requires the knowledge of two languages. But that's not enough. Think about all of the people you know who are native English speakers. What might account for why some of them are better writers than others? Knowing English, for example, is a prerequisite for writing in English, but this knowledge does not necessarily make a person a good writer. Because of the complex relationships between people, particularly in intercultural situations, translation and interpretation involve far more than linguistic equivalence, which traditionally has been the focus.

With the continued growth and progression of machine translation tools such as Google Translate, many people wonder if we soon will no longer need to teach foreign languages in schools. Language educators think not, and give several reasons: (1) Instant translators aren't always accurate, as you probably already know. (2) Instant translation ignores context, so the sarcastic comment you mean to be a joke is put through an instant translator, the translation might come across as serious or even offensive—distorting your meaning. (3) Of course, instant translation tools do not know all the idioms and slang of most languages, so if you try looking for a "cool" or "chill" restaurant, you might end up at a place that blasts air conditioning. (4) Machine translation is inconvenient—what if you don't have access to Online tools? How can you have a conversation if you have to keep typing or saying every sentence into your phone? (https://www.alsintl.com/blog/will-instant-translators-make-foreign-language-teaching-obsolete/)

The field of translation studies is rapidly becoming more central to academic inquiry as it moves from the fringes to an area of inquiry with far-reaching consequences for many disciplines. These developments will have a tremendous impact on how academics approach intercultural communication. Perhaps intercultural communication scholars will begin to play a larger role in the developments of translation studies.

LANGUAGE AND IDENTITY

In the previous chapter, we discussed cultural identity and its complexities. One part of our cultural identity is tied to the language(s) that we speak. As U.S. Americans, we are expected to speak English. If we travel to Nebraska, we assume the people there speak English. When we travel around the world, we expect Russians to speak Russian, Koreans to speak Korean, and Indonesians to speak Indonesian. But things get more involved, as we noted in Chapter 4, when we consider why Brazilians speak Portuguese, Congolese speak French, and Australians speak English. The relationship between language and culture becomes more complicated when we look at the complexity of cultural identities at home and abroad.

Language and Cultural Group Identity

When Tom was at the Arizona Book Festival recently, a white man held up a book written in Chinese and asked Tom what it was about. "I don't read Chinese," Tom replied. "Well, you should," he retorted and walked away. Two assumptions seem to be at work here: (1) Anyone who looks Asian must be Chinese and (2) Asian Americans should be able to speak their ancestral languages. This tension has raised important identity questions for Asian Americans. Writer Henry Moritsugu (1992), who was born and raised in Canada and who later immigrated to the United States, explains:

> There is no way we could teach our children Japanese at home. We speak English. It wasn't a conscious effort that we did this. . . . It was more important to be accepted. . . . I wish I could speak the language better. I love Japanese food. I love going to Japanese restaurants. Sometimes I see Japanese groups enjoying themselves at karaoke bars . . . I feel definitely Western, more so than Asian. . . . But we look Asian, so you have to be aware of who you are. (p. 99)

The ability to speak another language can be important in how people view their group membership.

Many Chicana/os also have to negotiate a relationship to Spanish, whether or not they speak the language and 76% of Latinos ages 18–33 say they speak only English at home or "very well" (Krogstad, 2016). Communication scholar Jacqueline Martinez (2000) explains:

> It has taken a long time for me to come to see and feel my own body as an ethnic body. Absent the capacity to express myself in Spanish, I am left to reach for less tangible traces of an ethnic self that have been buried under layers of assimilation into Anglo culture and practice. . . . Yet still there is a profoundly important way in which, until this body of mine can speak in Spanish, gesture in a "Spanishly" way, and be immersed in Spanish-speaking communities, there will remain ambiguities about its ethnic identification. (p. 44)

Although some people who migrate to the United States retain the languages of their homelands, many other U.S. American families no longer speak the language of their forebears. Historically, bilingualism was openly discouraged in the

Given the globalization and the increasing prominence of English as the global language, how does this affect English speakers and their place in world that is increasingly diverse? Professor Christof Demont-Heinrich conducted research to answer this question, asking English-speaking students from the United States and non-English speakers from a Danish University whether it was important to learn a second language. He found that:

1. Most Danish students thought they should learn English and most American students thought they SHOULD learn another language but didn't really see it as necessary; a few were adamant that no American should need to know a foreign language—because of the prevalence of English as worldwide language. They agreed with the Danish students that non-English speakers SHOULD learn English.

2. However, some thought it was just rude to "always expect someone to speak English and not attempt to learn their language." "It's unfortunate that English has become so globalized, because it seems to have made Americans lazy and allowed them to take their privilege for granted." "As we continue to believe this, the world will become less and less diverse and so much more boring." "There was almost a 'wistful regret'".

Demont-Heinrich concludes that the dominance of English is both a privilege and disadvantage in a way. The global language order's lack of equality cuts in multiple directions; it forces "multilingual opportunity" on some and denies it to others. What do you think?

Source: From C. Demont-Heinrich, "Linguistically Privileged and Cursed? American University Students and the Global Hegemony of English." *World Englishes, 29*(2) (2010): 281–298.

United States. Writer Gloria Anzaldúa (1987) recalls how she was discouraged from speaking Spanish:

> *I remember being caught speaking Spanish at recess—that was good for three licks on the knuckles with a sharp ruler. I remember being sent to the corner of the classroom for "talking back" to the Anglo teacher when all I was trying to do was tell her how to pronounce my name. If you want to be American, speak "American." If you don't like it, go back to Mexico where you belong. (p. 53)*

Even today we often hear arguments in favor of making English the official language of the nation. The interconnections between cultural identity and language are indeed strong.

Another intersection between identity and language occurred in 2006, when a controversy arose over the release by some Latino pop stars of a Spanish version of the U.S. national anthem ("Star Spangled Banner"), with somewhat different lyrics ("The time has come to break the chains"), called *Nuestro Himno* (Our Anthem). For the song's producer and singers, it was about trying to help engage immigrants, as a tribute to the United States. For others, the national anthem was a symbol of unity that should be sung only in English. Here we see the importance of contexts. What many people don't know is that the national anthem was translated into Spanish (and many other languages) by the Bureau of Education and has been available in those languages since 1919—with no controversy until the issue becomes related to the current immigration debate (Goldstein, 2006).

What about the challenges facing cultural groups whose languages are nearing extinction? Although millions of people speak Chinese, Japanese, and Spanish, some languages are spoken by only a handful of people. Consider that every 14 days, one of the world's nearly 7,000 languages "dies." Linguists say that each language is a unique lens, a unique way of viewing the world, and they are increasingly concerned about what is being lost when a language goes extinct. What knowledge is lost forever? In Tuvan (spoken in Republic of Tuva, in southern Siberia), for example, the past is always spoken of as ahead of one, and the future is behind one's back. It makes total sense if you think of it in a Tuvan sort of way: If the future were ahead of you, wouldn't it be in plain view? When language disappears so does significant aspects of cultural diversity. "The disappearance of a language deprives us of knowledge no less valuable than some future miracle drug that may be lost when a species goes extinct. Small languages, more than large ones, provide keys to unlock the secrets of nature, because their speakers tend to live in proximity to the animals and plants around them, and their talk reflects the distinctions they observe" (Rymer, 2012). One of the last speakers of Chemehuevi, a native American language, Johnny Hill, Jr., says of his language, "It's like a bird losing feathers. You see one float by, and there it goes—another word gone. I speak it inside my heart" (http://ngm.nationalgeographic.com/2012/07/vanishing-languages/johnson-photography).

Many Native American tribes are currently working to save their tribal languages, but they face enormous challenges. Yet it is their culture and identity that are at risk.

The languages we speak and the languages others think we should speak can create barriers in intercultural communication. Why might some U.S. Americans assume that someone whose ancestors came from China continues to speak Chinese, while someone whose ancestors came from Germany or Denmark is assumed to no longer speak German or Danish? Here, again, we can see how identity, language, and history create tensions between who we think we are and who others think we are.

Code Switching

Code switching is a technical term in communication that refers to the phenomenon of changing languages, dialects, or even accents. People code switch for several reasons, as shown in Point of View (p. 262).

Linguistics professor Jean-Louis Sauvage (2002) studied the complexity of code switching in Belgium, which involves not only dialects but languages as well. He explains the practical side of code switching:

> *For example, my house was built by a contractor who sometimes resorted to Flemish subcontractors. One of these subcontractors was the electrician. I*

code switching A technical term in communication that refers to the phenomenon of changing languages, dialects, or even accents.

spoke Dutch to him but had to use French words when I referred to techni-
cal notions that I did not completely understand even in French. This was not
a problem for the electrician, who knew these terms in Dutch as well as in
French but would have been unable to explain them to me in French. (p. 159)

Given the complex language policies and politics in Belgium, code switching takes on particularly important political meaning. Who code switches and who does not is a frequent source of contestation.

In her work on code switching of black women, communication scholar Karla Scott (2013) discusses how choice of language style is often strategic as black women in predominantly white environments are called on to constantly "shift" between white and black vernacular style, "changing outward behavior, attitude, and tone, and adopting an alternate pose or voice—without thinking" (p. 315). Through discussions in focus groups with 30 black women, she found that their primary communicative goals were to dispel stereotypes and be seen as competent. This often involves code switching, as one participant describes it, "In communicating with people, I work very hard at using code switching. So I talk proper English that I learned in school, especially in the classroom or around people I attend school with. And I'm learning to avoid certain behaviors, such as resting my hand on my hip or roll my eyes, when in certain environments" (Scott, 2013, p. 320).

There are similar examples of code switching between English and Spanish, as increasing numbers of U.S. Americans speak both languages—18 million now according to the U.S. Census (Silverstein, 2007). Scholar Holly Cashman (2005) investigated how a group of bilingual women code switched during a game of *lotería* (Mexican bingo). She makes the point that code switching does not just demonstrate linguistic competence but, as in Scott's (2000) study, also communicates important information about ethnic identities and social position. Throughout the game, the women's choices to speak Spanish and/or English demonstrated various identifications and social places. When they preferred to speak Spanish, they were identifying inclusively with both English and Spanish speakers. In correcting other's language choices, they were also identifying as not just bilingual, but as arbiters of the spoken language. And in rejecting others' corrections of their language use, they were also asserting certain identifications, as when one woman in refusing another's correction of her Spanish "categorizes herself as 'Chicana,' bringing about a bilingual, oppositional social identity, and rejecting the social structures previously talked into being" (p. 313).

This discussion of code switching and language settings brings up the question of how does a bilingual person decide which language to speak in a setting where there are multiple languages spoken? Is it rude to switch between two languages when some people in the room only understand one language? As our student Liz describes (in the following Student Voices box), this is not always an easy question to answer. A helpful theory here is communication accommodation theory (CAT), discussed in Chapter 2. As you might remember, this theory posits that in some situations individuals change their communication patterns to accommodate others—depending on the situation and the attitude of the speaker toward other people. So, for example, if the situation is a neutral one and the speaker feels positively toward

Is it rude to code switch between languages when someone in the room only understands one of the languages?

Growing up in a household that predominately spoke Spanish was challenging when I brought friends over. Not everyone in my family spoke English and not all of my friends spoke Spanish. For as long as I can remember, my father expected me to translate everything that my friends and I said when family members were around us, even if they were not a part of the conversation. My father instilled the importance of respecting people around me by ensuring that everyone was included in the conversation, and to be sensitive to those around me who do not understand the language by giving them a general idea of what was being said.

As I have gotten older, I wonder when is it appropriate to switch languages when someone in the room does not understand the language being spoken. The first time that I really thought about this was when I attended a dinner at a friend's house. All of the people, excluding myself, were from Serbia. When one of the guests realized that I did not speak Serbian, she said, "Oh, so we will have to speak English all night?" My immediate reaction was that I did not think that everyone had to adjust to my needs. After all, this was their time to share food and conversations in their language.

However, I recently went Salsa dancing with a friend who did not speak Spanish. Knowing that most of the people around us were bilingual, I asked people if they could speak in English so that we did not exclude my friend. Most people would start speaking in English, but then break out into conversations in Spanish, which frustrated me. I ended up interpreting conversations for him and felt bad that he was excluded from the conversation. As I apologized to him, my friend said, "Don't feel bad. It is my fault that I do not speak Spanish."

Reflecting on these situations, I wondered when is it appropriate to code switch between languages when someone in the room only understands one of the languages? Why did I not think it was offensive in a situation where I was the one who did not understand and offensive when it was a friend of mine who did not?

—Liz

others, they will more likely accommodate others. This seems to be the case in Liz's family. Her father instructed her to accommodate everyone in the situation. Liz's experience at a recent party was different. Here, the Serbian speakers did not want to accommodate Liz. At the Salsa party, she tried to accommodate everyone, but it was difficult and her friends did not follow her lead. What is important to remember is that the outcome of accommodation is usually a positive feeling. However, in some situations (like high threat) speakers may not want to accommodate, may even want to accentuate their linguistic differences, or perhaps, as in Liz's Salsa party experience, the effort of accommodating is too challenging.

LANGUAGE POLITICS AND POLICIES

Nations can enact laws recognizing an official language, such as French in France or Irish in Ireland (despite the fact that more Irish speak English than Irish). Some nations have multiple official languages. For instance, Canada has declared English and French to be the official languages. Here in the United States, there is no official national language, although English is the de facto national language. Yet the state of Hawai'i has two official languages, English and Hawaiian. Other U.S. entities have also declared official languages, such as Guam (Chamorro and English), New Mexico (English and Spanish), and Samoa (English and Samoan). Laws or customs that determine which language is spoken where and when are referred to as **language policies.** These policies often emerge from the politics of language use. As mentioned previously, the court of Catherine the Great of Russia used not Russian but French, which was closely tied to the politics of social and economic class. The history of colonialism also influences language policies. Thus, Portuguese is the official national language of Mozambique, and English and French are the official national languages of Cameroon. (See Figure 6-4.)

language policies
Laws or customs that determine when and where which language will be spoken.

Language policies are embedded in the politics of class, culture, ethnicity, and economics. They do not develop as a result of any supposed quality of the language itself. There are different motivations behind the establishment of language policies that guide the status of different languages in a place. Sometimes nations decide on a national language as part of a process of driving people to assimilate into the national culture. If the state wishes to promote assimilation, language policies that encourage everyone to speak the official language and conduct business in that language are promoted. One such group, U.S. English, Inc., has been advocating for the establishment of English as the official language of the United States.

Sometimes nations develop language policies as a way of protecting minority languages so these languages do not disappear. Welsh in Wales is one example, but Irish in Ireland and Frisian in Germany and the Netherlands are legally protected languages. Some language policies recognize the language rights of its citizens wherever they are in the nation. One example of this is Canada (English and French). Another is Kenya (Swahili and English). Government services are available in either language throughout the nation.

Other language policies are governed by location. In Belgium, Dutch (Flemish) is the official language in Flanders in the north part of the country. French is the official language in Wallonia in the South, and German is the official language in the Eastern Cantons bordering Germany. Thus, if you are boarding a train to go from Antwerp to Liège, you would need to look for "Luik" in the Antwerp train station. When you returned to the train station in Liège to go back, you would look for the train to "Anvers." The signs would not be posted in both languages, except in the Brussels-capital region (the only bilingual part of the nation).

FIGURE 6-4   Tensions between English and French speakers—shown by this photo taken near Montreal's Olympic Stadium—have led to the creation of language policies in Quebec. Some U.S. states have attempted to implement language policies as "English-only" laws. Do these language policies reduce or exacerbate intercultural communication problems? Why do some languages face more difficulty in their survival than others? (© *T. K. Nakayama*)

In Quebec, Canada, Law 101—passed in the early 1980s—required all Quebec students to attend French-speaking schools (unless their parents went to an English-speaking school in Quebec). So lots of immigrants from all over the world, few of whom spoke French, were required to attend French-speaking schools. Years later, these former students talked about this experience and how this law is changing Quebec. It's creating a more multicultural identity in contrast to previous years when most immigrants would choose English, leaving French to be spoken only by a small, relatively isolated group (Roy, 2007).

Sometimes language policies are developed with language parity, but the implementation is not equal. In Cameroon, for example, English and French are both official languages, although 247 indigenous languages are also spoken. Although Germany was the initial colonizer of Cameroon, Britain and France took over in 1916—with most of the territory going to France—and these "new colonial masters then sought to impose their languages in the newly acquired territory" (Echu, 2003, p. 34). At independence in 1960, French Cameroon established French as its official language and English became the official language in the former British Cameroon areas once they joined together to form Cameroon. Once united in 1961, Cameroon established both languages as official languages. Because French speakers are far more numerous than English speakers, "French has a de facto dominance over English in the areas of administration, education and the media. In fact, it is not an exaggeration to say that French influence as expressed in language, culture and

National Public Radio recently conducted an informal survey, asking people about their experiences in code switching. The survey revealed five primary motivations for code switching:

1. *Lizard brains* take over. Sometimes people just switch to another language or accent without thinking about it. One young Japanese American woman described an experience she had while visiting relatives in Japan. They all went to a popular Japanese horror house and she got so frightened, she dropped her fluent Japanese and started screaming in English (much to the amusement of staff and her relatives).

2. To fit in. People often code switch to talk and act more like those around them. A Spanish teacher in Nashville who picked up the Southern, African American English dialect of his students forgot to switch to standard English when his boss asked him if he had forgotten to return a book and the teacher replied, "Nah, you flaugin' bruh, I put that on your desk yesterday."

3. To get something. People in the service industry report that a Southern accent is a "surefire way to get tips," and almost everyone working in their restaurant starts using "you' all" from day one. Also, an American woman living in Ireland discovered she got better prices as a shopper if she talked in the local Irish accent.

4. To say something in secret. A U.S. woman reported that she and a friend would speak French to each other on their train commute in Chicago if they wanted to comment on other passengers. One day they commented on how good looking a fellow commuter was and he answered in perfect French, "Merci."

5. To help convey a thought. Sometimes only a particular word in a particular language will get the point across. An example was given of staff at a bilingual school. Since nonprofit fundraising is a very American idea, the French speakers tend to switch to English when that's the topic. Similarly, when discussing technology topics—if they learn about a particular software product in English, it's hard to discuss it in the other language.

Source: From M. Thompson, "Five reasons why people code-switch." *NPR Blog—CodeSwitch: Race and Identity* Remixed, April 13, 2013. From http://www.npr.org/sections/codeswitch /2013/04/13/177126294/five-reasons-why-people-code-switch.

political policy prevails in all domains" (p. 39). So although Cameroon is officially bilingual, French dominates in nearly all domains because most of the people are French speakers. Thus, "what appears to be a language policy for the country is hardly clearly defined, in spite of the expressed desire to promote English-French bilingualism and protect the indigenous languages" (p. 44). European colonialism has left its mark in this African nation, and the language policy and language realities remain to be worked out.

We can view the development of language policies as reflecting the dialectical tensions between the nation's history and its future, between the various language communities, and between economic and political relations inside and outside the nation. Language policies can help resolve or exacerbate these tensions.

LANGUAGE AND GLOBALIZATION

In a world in which people, products, and ideas can move easily around the globe, rapid changes are being made in the languages spoken and learned. Globalization has sparked increased interest in some languages while leaving others to disappear, and with increasing language hybridity, has called into question stability, purity, and authenticity of language (Kramsch, 2014). In addition, communication technologies, along with globalization, have tremendous impact on how languages are used (and misused). Let's look more closely now at these impacts.

Linguists estimate that half of the world's 6,000 languages of today will be gone within the next century. Some language loss, like species loss, is natural and predictable. No language exists forever. Languages are disappearing more quickly today for various reasons. Sometimes, small, unindustrialized communities are forced to choose between their language and participation in the larger world—due to global economic pressures. East Africans speak Swahili; many feel they need to speak English. On the other hand, disappearing languages can make a comeback. Cornish (a language spoken in southwestern England) disappeared in 1777 when the last speaker died. Recently, working from old written documents, descendents of Cornish speakers began to learn the language and speak it; now there are more than 2,000 Cornish speakers. Modern Hebrew is another example. For centuries, it was a religious and scholarly language; in the late 19th century, it was revived in Palestine and is now taught in the schools and is the common language of Israeli citizens (Ostler, 2000).

Media and communication technologies also have made a dramatic impact on language use. In small communities, children gain from them a knowledge of the world that doesn't come from their elders. Children are less interested in the traditional language. Consider how e-mail and text messaging have changed written language practices. Experts say that language is not just about meaning but has far-reaching social and political impact. For example, as discussed earlier, it can present intergenerational communication challenges for parents and children.

Global forces can sometimes produce other changes in language use, like producing a new dialect—the *multicultural London English,* which is emerging among the young in England and replacing the traditional cockney. (See Point of View, p. 237.) Language educators also note the impact of online communication on language learners: "On the Internet people no longer observe a strict separation between languages; comprehensibility, online trumps, accuracy, and appropriateness." The Internet and online exchanges expose students to the real world of linguistic hybridity (Kramch, 2014, p. 300).

The dream of a common international language has long marked Western ways of thinking. Ancient Greeks viewed the world as filled with Greek speakers or those who were *barbaroi* (barbarians). The Romans attempted to establish Latin and Greek, which led to the subsequent establishment of Latin as the learned language of Europe. Latin was eventually replaced by French, which became the **lingua franca** of Europe. More recently, English has become the lingua franca of international communication.

lingua franca A commonly shared language that is used as a medium of communication between people of different languages.

Many native English speakers are happy with the contemporary status of the language. They feel much more able to travel around the world, without the burden of having to learn other ways of communicating, given that many people around the world speak English. Having a common language also facilitates intercultural communication, but it can also create animosity among those who must learn the other's language. Dominique Noguez (1998) explains:

> *In these language affairs, as in many other moral or political affairs—toler-ance, for example—is the major criteria for reciprocity. Between comparable languages and equal countries, this must be: I speak and learn your language and you speak and learn mine. Otherwise, it's sadomasochism and company— the sadist being simply the one with the gall to say to another: "I am not speaking your language, therefore speak mine!" This is what Anglo-Saxons have been happily doing since at least 1918. (p. 234)*
>
> *(En ces affaires de langue, comme en bien d'autres affaires morales ou politiques—la tolérance, par exemple—le critère majeur, c'est la réciprocité. Entre langues comparables et pays égaux, ce devrait être: je parle et enseigne votre langue et vous parlez et enseignez la mienne. Autrement, c'est sadomas-ochisme et compagnie—le sadique étant tout simplement celui qui l'aplomb de declarer à l'autre: "Je ne parle pas votre langue, parlez donc la mienne!" C'est ce que font, avec assez de bonheur, les Anglo-Saxons depuis au moins 1918.)*

What is the relationship between our four touchstones and this contemporary linguistic situation? That is, how do culture, communication, power, and context play out in the domination of English? First, the intimate connections between language and culture mean that the diffusion of English is tied to the spread of U.S. American culture around the world. Is this a new form of colonialism? If we consider issues of power, what role does the United States play in the domination of English on the world scene? How does this marginalize or disempower those who are not fluent in English in intercultural communication? What kinds of resentment might be fostered by forcing people to recognize their disempowerment?

In what intercultural contexts is it appropriate to assume that others speak English? For English speakers, this is a particularly unique context. Latvians, for example, cannot attend international meetings and assume that others will speak Latvian; and Albanians will have difficulty transacting international trade if they assume that others know their language.

This brings up the question of what languages U.S. Americans should be studying in order to communicate better with others in global contexts. For many years, the most studied languages in high schools and colleges in the United States were French, Spanish, and German. However, some suggest that, in order for the United States to remain a key player on the global stage, its citizens should be studying Chinese and Arabic. Experts observe that China is very close

Colonial histories have influenced how people communicate. In Brazil, colonialists developed their own language to communicate across the many indigenous communities they colonized. Although imposed by colonists, today this general language is used to resist domination by Portuguese. How does a language serve political ends? What are the politics of speaking English in the world today?

When the Portuguese arrived in Brazil five centuries ago, they encountered a fundamental problem: the indigenous peoples they conquered spoke more than 700 languages. Rising to the challenge, the Jesuit priests accompanying them concocted a mixture of Indian, Portuguese and African words they called "língua geral," or the "general language," and imposed it on their colonial subjects.

Elsewhere in Brazil, língua geral as a living, spoken tongue died off long ago. But in this remote and neglected corner of the Amazon where Brazil, Colombia and Venezuela meet, the language has not only managed to survive, it has made a remarkable comeback in recent years. . . .

Two years ago, in fact, Nheengatú, as the 30,000 or so speakers of língua geral call their language, reached a milestone. By vote of the local council, São Gabriel da Cachoeira became the only municipality in Brazil to recognize a language other than Portuguese as official, conferring that status on língua geral and two local Indian tongues.

As a result, Nheengatú, which is pronounced neen-gah-TOO and means "good talk," is now a language that is permitted to be taught in local schools, spoken in courts and used in government documents. People who can speak língua geral have seen their value on the job market rise and are now being hired as interpreters, teachers and public health aides. . . .

"Nheengatú came to us as the language of the conqueror," explained Renato da Silva Matos, a leader of the Federation of Indigenous Organizations of the Rio Negro. "It made the original languages die out" because priests and government officials punished those who spoke any language other than Portuguese or Nheengatú.

But in modern times, the language acquired a very different significance. As the dominion of Portuguese advanced and those who originally imposed the language instead sought its extinction, Nheengatú became "a mechanism of ethnic, cultural and linguistic resistance," said Persida Miki, a professor of education at the Federal University of Amazonas.

Source: From L. Rohter, "Language born of colonialism thrives again in Amazon," *The New York Times*, August 28, 2005, p. A6.

to overtaking United States as the predominant actor in the major power system (Kissane, 2005).

In his study of the developing use of English in Switzerland, Christof Demont-Heinrich (2005) focused on Switzerland in global and local contexts, cultural and national identity issues, power, and communication. The nation recognizes four national languages—French, German, Italian, and Romansh. Three of these are recognized as official languages—German, French, and Italian—which means that all national government materials are available in the three official languages. Some of the power differences among these language communities are reflected in the demographics from the 2000 Census in which "63.9% of respondents named German, 19.5% listed French, 6.6% claimed Italian, and 0.5% named Romansh as their first language" (p. 72). In this context, English has become more influential, not only among the banking and financial sectors but increasingly in "consumer and pop culture" (p. 74). Recently, at the initiation of the Zürich canton, a proposal was made to allow English to be the first foreign language taught in school (rather than one of the national languages), and eight other German-speaking cantons quickly aligned themselves with this idea. The Swiss Conference of Cantonal Ministers of Education decided that by 2012 all Swiss students must study two foreign languages, but only one must be a national language. Given the value of English in the global economy and the use of English to communicate with other Swiss, one can see why there would be support for the Zürich position. Given the importance of Swiss national identity and their multilingual identity that is shaped by the languages spoken by other Swiss, one can also see why some French-speaking politicians preferred a policy where one of the other national languages would be the first foreign language. Zürich and other cantons are now proposing a ballot initiative that would "require just one foreign language to be taught, ideally English, at the primary school level" (p. 76), which would leave the other national language to be taught in secondary school. Demont-Heinrich concludes by noting that Romansh is likely headed for linguistic extinction, but what will happen to Switzerland? Can Swiss national identity be maintained with English? And what about the world? "Can such a colossal human social order sustain the diverse forms of human linguistic expression" (p. 81), or must humanity reduce its linguistic expression to a few dominant languages that facilitate economic trade? In the era of globalization, where economic growth is driven by external relations and trade, should we be studying Chinese?

INTERNET RESOURCES

http://anthro.palomar.edu/language/default.htm
This web resource is an interactive guide to understanding the relationships between language and culture. The site contains very interesting information on a variety of language topics. It also includes audio files that highlight regional differences in pronunciation and dialect and flash cards to test your mastery of the material.

www.us-english.org/
www.lsadc.org/
These two websites contain very different views on the "English-only" issue in the United States. The group U.S. English is a strong advocate for English-only within the United States. Its website contains lots of information about the group's legislative activities and political agenda. The second website is the home page of the Linguistic Society of America. This group was not formed to counter

English-only policies, but it is a strong advocate of a multilingual society. The group's statement on language rights can be found at www.smo.uhi.ac.uk/saoghal /mion-chanain/LSA_statement.txt.

https://www.babelfish.com/
This website is an example of one of the ways that technology is changing translation. The "Babel" feature, which can be added to web content, translates from a great number of languages to a great number of languages. A similar feature is also available in the Online Community of Second Life. What opportunities and challenges does automated translation present for intercultural communication?

SUMMARY

- The social science approach focuses on individual aspects of language. The interpretive approach focuses on contextual aspects of language. The critical approach emphasizes the role of power in language use.

- There are different positions on the relationship between language and our perceptions. The nominalist position feels that our perception is not shaped by the language we speak. The relativist position argues that our perception is determined by the language we speak. The qualified relativist position argues that language influences how we perceive.

- Communication styles can be high context or low context, more direct or indirect, or more elaborate or understated.

- Interactive media influences language use and communication style in several ways.

- Slang and humor are two additional variations in language use.

- Co-cultural groups may use one of three orientations to dealing with dominant groups—assimilation, accommodation, or separation. Within each of these approaches are nonassertive, assertive, and aggressive strategies. Each of these strategies comes with benefits and costs to the co-cultural individual.

- We use language from our social positions, and the power of our language use and labels comes from that social position.

- People have various reasons for learning or not learning new languages.

- People can be bilingual or multilingual, and they may engage in code switching or changing languages in different situations, depending on the contexts.

- Translation refers to expressing what was said in another language in a written text. Interpretation is the same process but is oral rather than written.

- Language policies are instituted with different goals. Sometimes language policies are meant to encourage assimilation into a language and national identity. Sometimes language policies are meant to provide protection to minority languages. Sometimes language policies regulate language use in different parts of a nation.

- Globalization, along with technology, has affected how languages are used or not used. Globalization has meant that English has not only become more important worldwide but also has created other intercultural communication conflicts.

DISCUSSION QUESTIONS

1. Why is it important for intercultural communication scholars to study both language and discourse?

2. What is the relationship between our language and the way we perceive reality?

3. What are some cross-cultural variations in language use and communication style?

4. In what ways do social media and online communication affect language use and communication style?

5. What aspects of context influence the choice of communication style?

6. What does a translator or an interpreter need to know to be effective?

7. Why is it important to know the social positions of individuals and groups involved in intercultural communication?

8. Why do some people say that we should not use labels to refer to people but should treat everybody as individuals? Do you agree?

9. Why do people have such strong reactions to language policies, as in the "English-only" movement?

10. In what ways is the increasing and widespread use of English around the world both a positive and a negative change for U.S. Americans?

ACTIVITIES

1. *Regional Language Variations.* Meet in small groups with other class members and discuss variations in language use in different regions of the United States (accent, vocabulary, and so on). Identify perceptions that are associated with these variations.

2. *"Foreigner" Labels.* Meet in small groups with other class members and generate a list of labels used to refer to people from other countries who come to the United States—for example, "immigrants" and "aliens." For each label, identify a general connotation (positive, negative, mixed). Discuss how connotations of these words may influence our perceptions of people from other countries. Would it make a difference if we referred to them as "guests" or "visitors"?

3. *Values and Language.* Although computer-driven translations have improved dramatically over earlier attempts, translation is still intensely cultural. Communication always involves many layers of meaning, and when you move between languages, there are many more opportunities for misunderstanding. Try to express some important values that you have (e.g., freedom of the press) on this website, and see how they are retranslated in five different languages: www.tashian.com/multibabel/.

KEY WORDS

bilingual (249)
co-cultural groups (240)
code switching (257)
communication
    style (231)
equivalency (251)
high-context
    communication (230)
interlanguage (250)

interpretation (251)
language
    acquisition (229)
language policies (260)
lingua franca (264)
low-context
    communication (230)
metamessage (231)
multilingual (249)

nominalist position (226)
qualified relativist
    position (229)
relativist position (227)
social positions (244)
source text (251)
target text (251)
translation (251)

REFERENCES

Alexander, D. (2014, March 29). *Quora.com*. Retrieved May 30, 2016, from https://www.quora.com/Why-are-face-to-face-in-person-meetings-so-important-when-doing-business-in-China.

Anderson, B. (2016). *A life beyond boundaries: A memoir*. Brooklyn, NY: Verso.

Anzaldúa, G. (1987). *Borderlands/la frontera: The new mestiza*. San Francisco: Spinsters/Aunt Lute.

Ayala, C. (2016, May 27). Latino celebrities rally against Trump, Rubio, and Cruz for anti-immigrant fear-mongering. *dallasnews.com*. Retrieved May 27, 2016, from http://trailblazersblog.dallasnews.com/2016/02/latino-celebrities-rally-against-trump-rubio-and-cruz-for-anti-immigrant-stances.html/.

Barthes, R. (1980). *Elements of semiology* (A. Lavers & C. Smith, Trans.). New York: Hill & Wang. (Original work published 1968).

Befu, H. (2000, June). English language intellectual imperialism and its consequences. *Newsletter: Intercultural Communication, 37* (Intercultural Communication Institute, Kanda University of International Studies, Japan), p. 1.

Bello, R. S., Brandau-Brown, F. E., Zhang, S., & Ragsdale, J. D. (2010). Verbal and nonverbal methods for expressing appreciation in friendships and romantic relationships: A cross-cultural comparison. *International Journal of Intercultural Relations, 34,* 294–302.

Bender, A., Beller, S., & Klauer, K. C. (2016). Lady Liberty and Godfather Death as candidates for linguistic relativity? Scrutinizing the gender congruency effect on personified allegories with explicit and implicit measures. *The Quarterly Journal of Experimental Psychology, 69*(1), 48–64.

Boogaard, K. (2015, August 27). Mixing Millenials and Baby Boomers in the workplace melting pot. *officeninjas.com*. Retrieved May 27, 2016, from http://officeninjas.com/2015/08/27/mixing-millennials-and-baby-boomers-in-the-workplace-melting-pot/.

Boxer, D. (2002). Nagging: The familial conflict arena. *Journal of Pragmatics, 34,* 49–61.

Cashman, H. (2005). Identities at play: Language preference and group membership in bilingual talk in interaction. *Journal of Pragmatics, 37,* 301–315.

Cruz-Janzen, M. (2002). Lives on the crossfire: The struggle of multiethnic and multiracial Latinos for identity in a dichotomous and racialized world. *Race, Gender & Class, 9*(2), 47–62.

Dazell, T. (2005). Sez who? The power of slang. *PBS.org*. Retrieved June 4, 2011, from www.pbs.org/speak/words/sezwho/slang/.

Dehaene, S., Izard, V., Pica, P., & Spelke, E. (2006). Core knowledge of geometry in an Amazonian indigene group. *Science, 311,* 381–384.

Demont-Heinrich, C. (2005). Language and national identity in the era of globalization: The case of English in Switzerland. *Journal of Communication Inquiry, 29,* 66–84.

Desnoes, E. (1985). The death system. In M. Blonsky (Ed.), *On signs* (pp. 39–42). Baltimore, MD: Johns Hopkins University Press.

Deutscher, G. (2010). *Through the language glass: Why the world looks different in other languages*. New York: Metropolitan Books.

Echu, G. (2003). Coping with multilingualism: Trends in the evolution of language policy in Cameroon. *PhiN, 25,* 31–46. Available at http://web.fuberlin.de/phin/phin25/p25t2.htm#ech99b.

Emma (2009, October). English humour vs. American humor—Is there a difference? *LEXOPHILES.com*. Retrieved June 4, 2011, from www.lexiophiles.com/english/english-humour-vs-american-humor-is-there-a-difference.

English language is changing faster than ever, research reveals (2015, May 1). *telegaph.co.uk.com*. Retrieved May 30, 2016, from http://www.telegraph.co.uk/news/newstopics/howaboutthat/11574196/new-forms-of

-social-media-terms-which-parents-do-not-understand
.html.

Gale, T., & Cosgrove, D. (2004). "We learnt that last week": Reading into the language practices of teachers. *Teachers and Teaching: Theory and Practice, 10*(2), 125–134.

Goldstein, D. (2006, May 6). National anthem in other languages? Heard this before. *Seattle Times.* Retrieved April 28, 2008, from http://seattletimes.nwsource.com/html/nationworld/2002975852_anthem06.html.

Goudreau, J (2016). How to communicate in the new multigenerational office. forbes.com. Retrieved May 27, 2016, from http://www.forbes.com/sites/jennagoudreau/2013/02/14/how-to-communicate-in-the-new-multigenerational-office/#f68656150d8d.

Grice, H. (1975). Logic and conversation. In P. Cole & J. Morgan (Eds.), *Syntax and semantics: Vol. 3. Speech acts.* New York: Academic Press.

Gudykunst, W. B., & Matsumoto, Y. (1996). Cross-cultural variability of communication in personal relationships. In W. B. Gudykunst, S. Ting-Toomey, & T. Nishida (Eds.), *Communication in personal relationships across cultures* (pp. 19–56). Thousand Oaks, CA: Sage.

Gudykunst, W. B., Ting-Toomey, S., & Chua, E. (1988). *Culture and interpersonal communication.* Newbury Park, CA: Sage Publications.

Gudykunst, W. B., & Ting-Toomey, S. (2003). *Communicating with strangers: An approach to intercultural communication* (4th ed.). New York: McGraw-Hill.

Hall, E. T. (1976). *Beyond culture.* Garden City, NY: Doubleday.

Hill, P., & Van Zyl, S. (2002). English and multilingualism in the South African engineering workplace. *World Englishes, 21*(1), 23–35.

Jameson, F. (1972). *The prisonhouse of language.* Princeton, NJ: Princeton University Press.

Karlson, D. (2005, December 2). Swastika on sign unnerves residents. *The Cape Codder.* From www.townonline.com/brewster/localRegional/view.bg?articleid=382002&format=&page=1.

Kavanaugh, B. (2015). A contrastive analysis of American and Japanese online communication: A study of UMC function and usage in popular personal weblogs. Thesis from Kohoku University. From http://ir.library.tohoku.ac.jp/re/bitstream/10097/59657/1/150325-Kavanagh-169-1.pdf.

Kissane, D. (2005). 2015 and the rise of China: Power cycle analysis and the implications for Australia. *Security Challenges, 1*(1), 105–121.

Kövecses, Z. (2005). *Metaphor in culture: Universality and variation.* Cambridge: Cambridge University Press.

Kramsch, C. (2014). Teaching foreign languages in an era of globalization: Introduction. *The Modern Language Journal, 98*(1), 296—311.

Krogstad, J. M. (2016, April 20). Rise in English proficiency among U.S. Hispanics is driven by the young. *Pew Research.* Retrieved May 26, 2016, from http://www.pewresearch.org/fact-tank/2016/04/20/rise-in-english-proficiency-among-u-s-hispanics-is-driven-by-the-young/.

Lakoff, G. (1989). Some empirical results about the nature of concepts. *Mind & Language, 4,* 103–129.

Lakoff, G. (1992). The contemporary theory of metaphor. In Ortony, A. (Ed.), *Metaphor and thought* (2nd ed.) (pp. 202–251). New York: Cambridge University Press.

Martin, J. N., Krizek, R. L., Nakayama, T. K., & Bradford, L. (1996). Exploring whiteness: A study of self-labels for White Americans. *Communication Quarterly, 44,* 125–144.

Martinez, J. (2000). *Phenomenology of Chicana experience and identity: Communication and transformation in praxis.* Lanham, MD: Rowan & Littlefield.

Marx, E. (1999). *Breaking through culture shock.* London: Nicholas Brealey.

Meléndez, M. (2002, April 7). Police try to connect, reach out in Spanish. *The Arizona Republic,* p. B1.

Miles, O. (2011, February 24). How Gaddafi's words get lost in translation. *BBC News Africa.* Retrieved June 2, 2011, from www.bbc.co.uk/news/world-africa-12566277?print=true.

Moritsugu, H. (1992). To be more Japanese. In J. F. J. Lee (Ed.), *Asian Americans* (pp. 99–103). New York: New Press.

Nakayama, T. K. (1997). Les voix de l'autre. *Western Journal of Communication, 61*(2): 235–242.

Noguez, D. (1998). *La colonisation douce: Feu la langue française, carnets, 1968–1998.* Paris: Arléa.

Orbe, M. P. (1998). *Constructing co-cultural theory: An explication of culture, power, and communication.* Thousand Oaks, CA: Sage.

Orbe, M. P., & Roberts, T. L. (2012). Co-Cultural Theorizing: Foundations, applications & extensions. *Howard Journal Of Communications, 23*(4), 293–311.

Ostler, R. (2000). Disappearing language of the 6000 languages still on earth, 90 percent could be gone by 2100. *BNET.* Retrieved June 3, 2011, from http://findarticles.com/p/articles/mi_m0GER/is_2000_Spring/ai_61426207/pg_2/?tag=mantle_skin;content.

Park, H. S., & Guan, X. (2009). Cross-cultural comparison of verbal and nonverbal strategies of apologizing. *Journal of International and Intercultural Communication, 2*(1), 66–87.

Roy, J-H. (2007, September 15). *Les enfants de la loi 101* (Children of Law 101). *L'actualite, 32*(14), 34–50.

Rymer, R. (2012, July). Vanishing languages. *National Geographic.com.* Retrieved May 26, 2016, from http://ngm.nationalgeographic.com/2012/07/vanishing-languages/rymer-text.

Sapir, E. (Ed.). (1921). *Language: An introduction to the study of speech.* New York: Harcourt, Brace & World.

Saussure, F. de. (1966). In C. Bally & A. Sechehaye (Eds), *Course in general linguistics* (W. Baskin, Trans.). New York: McGraw-Hill.

Sauvage, J.-L. (2002). Code-switching: An everyday reality in Belgium. In J. N. Martin, T. K. Nakayama, & L. A. Flores (Eds.), *Readings in intercultural communication: Experiences and contexts* (2nd ed., pp. 156–161). New York: McGraw-Hill.

Scott, K. D. (2000). Crossing cultural borders: "Girl" and "look" as markers of identity in Black women's language use. *Discourse & Society, 11*(2): 237–248.

Shuter, R. When Indian women text message; culture, identity and emerging interpersonal norms of new media. In P. H. Cheong, J. N. Martin, & L. P. Macfadyen (Eds.), *New media and intercultural communication.* New York: Peter Lang.

Shuter, R., & Chattopadhyay, S. (2010). Emerging interpersonal norms of text messaging in India and the United States. *Journal of Intercultural Communication Research, 39*(2), 121–145.

Silverstein, S. (2007, November 12). Biding their tongues. *Los Angeles Times,* p. A1.

Social media speeds up language evolution. (2015, May).

languagemagazine.com. Retrieved May 30, 2016, from http://languagemagazine.com/?page_id=123684.

Taylor, P., Lopez, M. H., Martinez , J. H., & Velasco, G. (2012). When labels don't fit: Hispanics and their views of identity. *Pew Hispanic Center.* Retrieved May 12, from http://www.pewhispanic.org /files/2012/04/PHC-Hispanic-Identity.pdf.

Troianovski, A. (2016, May 19). Europe's populist politicians tap into deep seated frustration. *wsj.com.* Retrieved May 27, 2016, from http://www.wsj.com /articles/europes-populist-politicians-win-voters -hearts-1463689360.

Vinay, J. P., & Darbelnet, J. (1977). *Stylistique comparée du français et de l'anglais: Méthode de traduction.* Paris: Marcel Didier.

Virtual communication in Kenya. *learning.aperianglobal. com.* Retrieved May 30, 2016, from http://learning. aperianglobal.com/web/globesmart/locale/topic.cfm? topicid=E4177268C037B7C6A8E6ACA660495393.

West, F. (1975). *The way of language: An introduction.* New York: Harcourt Brace Jovanovich.

Whorf, B. L. (1956). *Language, thought and reality.* Cambridge, MA: MIT Press.

Yellow B. M. (1999). What we want to be called. *American Indian Quarterly, 23*(2), 1–20.

CREDITS

obsolete?" (May 9, 2016). Accredited Language Services. [page 255, text] H. Moritsugu, excerpt from "To be more Japanese" in *Asian Americans*, edited by J. F. J. Lee. New Press. [page 256, text] C. Demont-Heinrich, excerpt from "Linguistically privileged and cursed? American university students and the global hegemony of English" from *World Englishes* (2010): 281–298. [page 255, text] J. Martinez, excerpt from *Phenomenology of Chicana experience and identity: Communication and transformation in praxis.* Rowan & Littlefield. [page 256, text] G. Anzaldúa, excerpt from *Borderlands/la frontera: The new mestizo.* Spinsters/Aunt Lute. [page 257, text] R. Rymer, quote from "Vanishing languages" from *National Geographic* (July, 2012). [page 257–258, text] J.-L. Sauvage, excerpt from "Code-switching: An everyday reality in Belgium" in *Readings in intercultural communication: Experiences and contexts, Second edition,* edited by J. N. Martin, T. K. Nakayama, and L. A. Flores. McGraw-Hill. [page 259, text] Liz, excerpt from "Students Voices: Growing up in a . . . mine who did not?" Original work; [page 258, text] K. D. Scott, quote from "Crossing cultural borders: "Girl" and "look" as markers of identity in Black women's language use"

from *Discourse & Society* (2000): 237–248. [page 262, text] M. Thompson, excerpt from "Five reasons why people code-switch" from *NPR Blog—CodeSwitch: Race and Identity Remixed* (April 13, 2013). NPR Blog—CodeSwitch: Race and Identity Remixed. [page 261, text] G. Echu, quote from "Coping with multilingualism: Trends in the evolution of language policy in Cameroon" from *PhiN* (2003): 31–46. [page 263, text] C. Kramsch, quote from "Teaching foreign languages in an era of globalization: Introduction" from *The Modern Language Journal* (2014): 296–311. [page 264, text] D. Noguez, excerpt from *La colonisation douce: Feu la langue française, carnets, 1968–1998.* Arléa. [page 248, text] H. Befu, excerpt from "English Language Intellectual Imperialism and Its Consequences" from *Newsletter: Intercultural Communication* (June 2000): 1. [page 265, text] L. Rohter, excerpt from "Language born of colonialism thrives again in Amazon" from *The New York Times* (August 28, 2005): A6. [page 266, text] C. Demont-Heinrich, quote from "Language and national identity in the era of globalization: The case of English in Switzerland" from *Journal of Communication Inquiry* (2005): 66–84.

NONVERBAL CODES AND CULTURAL SPACE

THINKING DIALECTICALLY ABOUT
NONVERBAL COMMUNICATION:
DEFINING NONVERBAL COMMUNICATION
Comparing Verbal and Nonverbal Communication
What Nonverbal Behavior Communicates

THE UNIVERSALITY OF NONVERBAL BEHAVIOR
Recent Research Findings
Nonverbal Codes
Stereotype, Prejudice, and Discrimination
Semiotics and Nonverbal Communication

DEFINING CULTURAL SPACE
Cultural Identity and Cultural Space
Changing Cultural Space
Postmodern Cultural Spaces

INTERNET RESOURCES

SUMMARY

DISCUSSION QUESTIONS

ACTIVITIES

KEY WORDS

REFERENCES

CHAPTER OBJECTIVES

After reading this chapter, you should be able to:

1. Understand how verbal and nonverbal communication differ.
2. Discuss the types of messages that are communicated nonverbally.
3. Identify cultural universals in nonverbal communication.
4. Explain the limitations of some cross-cultural research findings.
5. Define and give an example of cross-cultural differences in facial expressions, prox-emics, gestures, eye contact, paralanguage, chronemics, and silence.
6. Discuss the relation-ship between nonverbal communication and power.
7. Define cultural space.
8. Describe how cultural spaces are formed.
9. Explain why it is important to understand cultural spaces in intercultural communication.
10. Understand the differences between the modernist and postmodern views of cultural spaces.

Nonverbal elements of cultural communication are highly dynamic and play an important role in understanding intercultural communication. Our Kenyan student Gladys describes a nonverbal mis-step when she first arrived in the United States:

> *Back at home women love touching and patting each other's hair as a way of admiring it. When I moved to the United States, there was this lady who attended the same church we did. The lady was fairly friendly and even talked of inviting me to her apartment. She had long blonde hair. One day, I made the mistake of patting her hair as a way of admiring how long it was. She was so mad at me, and that occurrence strained our relationship which never recovered. Since then I became afraid of patting anyone's hair again.*

Consider expected spatial distance. A colleague recently observed that walking on the sidewalks in England, she found herself frequently bumping into oncoming pedestrians—and figured out it was because people tend to walk on the same side of the pavement as they drive on the road. So walking in England, as they approached her and she steps to her left, they step to their right.

While the consequences for these encounters may be a bit awkward, in some other instances, understanding nonverbal communication can be a key to survival. A news story described how nonverbal behaviors at military checkpoints in Baghdad played an important role in the safety and security of Iraqi civilians. Military investigators asked U.S. soldiers if they had shot at women and children in cars at checkpoints, and one soldier answered, "Yes." Asked why, he replied, "They didn't respond to the signs [we gave], the presence of troops or warning shots. Basically, we were at a checkpoint, we had two Arabic signs that said to turn around or be shot. Once [they passed] . . . the first sign, they fired a warning shot. If they passed the second sign, they shot the vehicle. Sometimes it bothers me. What if they couldn't read the signs?" (Smith & Tyson, 2005).

You may never need to know the right nonverbal behavior to pass through a military checkpoint (see Figure 7-1), but you certainly will find yourself in many intercultural communication situations and cultural spaces. Your own nonverbal communication may create additional problems and, if the behaviors are inappropriate for the particular cultural space, may exacerbate existing tensions. In other cases, your use of nonverbals might reduce tension and confusion.

The first part of this chapter focuses on the importance of understanding nonverbal aspects of intercultural communication. We can examine nonverbal communication in terms of the personal–contextual and the static–dynamic dialectics. Although nonverbal communication can be highly dynamic, personal space, gestures, and facial expressions are fairly static patterns of specific nonverbal communication codes. These patterns are the focus of the second part of this chapter. Finally, we investigate the concept of cultural space and the ways in which cultural identity is shaped and negotiated by the cultural spaces (home, neighborhood, and so on) that people occupy.

There are no guidebooks for reading everyday nonverbal behaviors, and nonverbal communication norms vary from culture to culture; therefore, we believe it is useless to list nonverbals to memorize. Instead, it will be more beneficial for you to learn the framework of nonverbal communication and cultural spaces so you can tap into the nonverbal systems of whatever cultural groups become relevant to your life. Understanding communication is a matter of understanding how to think

FIGURE 7-1   Nonverbal behaviors at military checkpoints in Iraq play an important role in the safety and security of Iraqi civilians. (© *Wathiq Khuzaie/Getty Images*)

dialectically about *systems* of meaning, and not discrete elements. Nonverbal intercultural communication is no exception.

THINKING DIALECTICALLY ABOUT NONVERBAL COMMUNICATION: DEFINING NONVERBAL COMMUNICATION

In this chapter, we discuss two forms of communication beyond speech. The first includes facial expression, personal space, gestures, eye contact, paralanguage, use of time, and conversational silence. (What is not said is often as important as what is spoken.) The second includes the cultural spaces that we occupy and negotiate. **Cultural spaces** are the social and cultural contexts in which our identity forms—where we grow up and where we live (not necessarily the physical homes and neighborhoods, but the cultural meanings created in these places).

   In thinking dialectically, we need to consider the relationship between the nonverbal behavior and the cultural spaces in which the behavior occurs, and between the nonverbal behavior and the verbal message. Although there are patterns to nonverbal behaviors, they are not always culturally appropriate in all cultural spaces. Remember, too, that some nonverbal behaviors are cultural, whereas others are idiosyncratic, that is, peculiar to individuals.

cultural space The particular configuration of the communication that constructs meanings of various places.

Comparing Verbal and Nonverbal Communication

Recognizing Nonverbal Behavior   Both verbal and nonverbal communication are symbolic, communicate meaning, and are patterned—that is, they are governed by contextually determined rules. Societies have different nonverbal languages, just as they have different spoken languages. However, some differences between nonverbal and verbal communication codes have important implications for intercultural interaction.

Let's look at some examples of these differences. The following incident occurred to Judith when she was new to Algeria, where she lived for a while. One day she stood at her balcony and waved to one of the young Algerian teachers, who was walking across the school yard. Several minutes later, the young teacher knocked on the door, looking expectantly at Judith, as if summoned. Because Judith knew that it was uncommon in Algeria for men to visit women they didn't know well, she was confused. Why had he come to her door? Was it because she was foreign? After a few awkward moments, he left. A few weeks later, Judith figured it out. In Algeria (as in many other places), the U.S. "wave" is the nonverbal signal for "come here." The young teacher had assumed that Judith had summoned him to her apartment. As this example illustrates, rules for nonverbal communication vary among cultures and contexts.

Let's consider another example. Two U.S. students attending school in France were hitchhiking to the university in Grenoble for the first day of classes. A French motorist picked them up and immediately started speaking English to them. They wondered how he knew they spoke English. Later, when they took a train to Germany, the conductor walked into their compartment and berated them in English for putting their feet on the opposite seat. Again, they wondered how he had known that they spoke English. As these examples suggest, nonverbal communication entails more than gestures—even our appearance can communicate loudly. The students' appearance alone probably was a sufficient clue to their national identity. One of our students explains:

> *When I studied abroad in Europe, London more specifically, our clothing as a nonverbal expression was a dead giveaway that we were from America. We dressed much more casual, wore more colors, and had words written on our T-shirts and sweatshirts. This alone said enough; we didn't even have to speak to reveal that we were Americans.*

As these examples also show, nonverbal behavior operates at a subconscious level. We rarely think about how we stand, what gestures we use, and so on. Occasionally, someone points out such behaviors, which brings them to the conscious level. Consider one more example, from our student Suzanne:

> *I was in Macedonia and I was traveling in a car, so I immediately put on my seat belt. My host family was very offended by this because buckling my seat belt meant I didn't trust the driver. After that I rode without a seat belt.*

When misunderstandings arise, we are more likely to question our verbal communication than our nonverbal communication. We can search for different ways to explain verbally what we mean. We can also look up words in a dictionary or ask someone to explain unfamiliar words. In contrast, it is more difficult to identify nonverbal miscommunications or misperceptions.

I have a couple of good friends who are deaf, and it is evident that body language, eye contact, and visual communication are far more important in our conversations than between two hearing people. I found that both of my friends, who lived very close to me, would much rather stop by my house than call me on the relay. I can see the cultural implications of space and distance. We keep in touch mostly by using e-mail. It's funny because the e-mails that I get from those guys have more commonly used slang words than most of my hearing friends use. The question is: Do my friends understand the slang, make it a part of their language, and create a sign for it, or do they know the words through somewhat of a verbal exchange with the hearing?

—Andrea

Learning Nonverbal Behavior   Although we learn rules and meanings for language behavior in grammar and language arts lessons, we learn nonverbal meanings and behaviors by more implicit socialization. No one explains, "When you talk with someone you like, lean forward, smile, and touch the person frequently, because that will communicate that you really care about him or her." In many contexts in the United States, such behaviors communicate immediacy and positive meanings (Ray & Floyd, 2006). But how is it interpreted if someone does not display these behaviors?

Sometimes, though, we learn strategies for nonverbal communication. Have you ever been told to shake hands firmly when you meet someone? You may have learned that a limp handshake indicates a weak person. Likewise, many young women learn to cross their legs at the ankles and to keep their legs together when they sit. These strategies combine socialization and the teaching of nonverbal codes.

Coordinating Nonverbal and Verbal Behaviors   Generally our nonverbal behaviors reinforce our verbal behaviors. For example, when we shake our heads and say "no," we are reinforcing verbal behavior, and not surprisingly, consistency between verbal and nonverbal behaviors usually translates into perceptions of credibility and positive first impressions (Weisbuch, Ambady, Clark, Achor, & Weele, 2010). However, nonverbal behaviors can also contradict our verbal communication. If we tell a friend, "I can't wait to see you," and then don't show up at the friend's house, our nonverbal behavior is contradicting the verbal message. Because nonverbal communication operates at a less conscious level, we tend to think that people have less control over their nonverbal behavior. Therefore, we often think of nonverbal behaviors as conveying the "real" messages.

What Nonverbal Behavior Communicates

Although language is an effective and efficient means of communicating explicit information or content, every communication also conveys **relational messages**—information on how the talker wants to be understood and viewed by the listener.

relational messages Messages (verbal and nonverbal) that communicate how we feel about others.

These messages are communicated not by words, but through nonverbal behavior, including facial expressions, eye gaze, posture, and even our tone of voice (Bello, Brandau-Brown, Zhang, & Ragsdale, 2010). Nonverbal behavior also communicates **status** and power. For example, a supervisor may be able to touch subordinates, but it is usually unacceptable for subordinates to touch a supervisor. Broad, expansive gestures are associated with high status; conversely, holding the body in a tight, closed position communicates low status (Bente, Heuschner, Al Issa, & Blascovich, 2010).

status The relative position an individual holds in social or organizational settings.

In addition, nonverbal behavior communicates **deception**. However, this is not easy and researchers have spent years trying to identify behaviors that clearly indicate deception. Some thought there were particular behaviors (e.g., avoiding eye contact or touching or rubbing the eyes), others think that deception is communicated by fairly idiosyncratic behaviors and inconsistency in an individual's behaviors. The most recent research reveals that it is possible, but extremely time consuming, to identify deceptive behaviors. Communication researcher Burgoon and her team (2014) used sophisticated computer-assisted behavioral observation tools and found that in a U.S. sample, deceivers were more redundant and less creative in their speech and used more illustrator gestures in efforts to redirect the conversation in particular ways and also used more lip adaptors—(biting, pursing, crunching, or licking lips). To make it more complicated, it appears that other cultural groups may have different ways of communicating deception (Vrij, Granhag, & Mann, 2010). One study showed that Jordanian students agreed with U.S. American students about some behaviors signaling deception (shifting posture, hesitation, and speech rates). However, they identified additional behaviors (e.g., blinking, touching body, gestures, and blushing) (Al-Simadi, 2000). These research findings and others like these have high-stakes consequences. Trained nonverbal experts watching Russian diplomat's nonverbal cues led to the discovery of a bug at the State Department, and watching Saddam Hussein's body language during speeches he had given predicted his invasion of Iran. America has spent $900 million since 2007 trying to read the body language of passengers in airports (James Bond's body language, 2015).

deception The act of making someone believe what is not true.

Most nonverbal communication about affect, status, and deception happens at an unconscious level. For this reason, it plays an important role in intercultural interactions. Both pervasive and unconscious, it communicates how we feel about each other and about other cultural groups.

A useful theory in understanding nonverbal communication across cultures is **expectancy violations theory.** This theory suggests that we have expectations (mostly subconscious) about how others should behave nonverbally in particular situations. When these expectations are violated (e.g., when someone stands too close to us), we will respond in specific ways. If an act is unexpected and interpreted negatively, for example, when someone stands too close to us at a religious service, we tend to regard the person and the relationship rather negatively. However, if the act is unexpected and interpreted positively (e.g., an attractive person stands close at a party), we will probably regard the relationship rather favorably. In fact, more favorably than if someone stands the exact "expected" distance from us at a religious service or party. Because nonverbal communication occurs at a subconscious level, our negative or positive feelings toward someone may be due to the fact that they violated our expectations—without our realizing it (Burgoon, 1995; Floyd, Ramirez, & Burgoon, 2008).

expectancy violations theory The view that when someone's nonverbal behavior violates our expectations, these violations will be perceived positively or negatively depending on the specific context and behavior.

THE UNIVERSALITY OF NONVERBAL BEHAVIOR

Most traditional research in intercultural communication focuses on identifying cross-cultural differences in nonverbal behavior. How do culture, ethnicity, and gender influence nonverbal communication patterns? How universal is most nonverbal communication? Research traditionally has sought to answer these questions.

As we have observed in previous chapters, it is neither beneficial nor accurate to try to reduce individuals to one element of their identity (gender, ethnicity, nationality, and so on). Attempts to place people in discrete categories tend to reduce their complexities and lead to major misunderstandings. However, we often classify people according to various categories to help us find universalities. For example, although we may know that not all Germans are alike, we may seek information about Germans in general to help us communicate better with individual Germans. In this section, we explore the extent to which nonverbal communication codes are universally shared. We also look for possible cultural variations in these codes that may serve as tentative guidelines to help us communicate better with others.

Recent Research Findings

Research investigating the universality of nonverbal communication has focused on four areas: (1) the relationship of human behavior to that of primates (particularly chimpanzees), (2) nonverbal communication of sensory-deprived children who are blind or deaf, (3) facial expressions, and (4) universal functions of nonverbal social behavior.

Chimpanzees and humans share many nonverbal behaviors. For example, both exhibit the eyebrow flash—a slight raising of the eyebrow that communicates recognition—one of the most primitive and universal animal behaviors. Primates and humans also share some facial expressions, and recent research reveals another gesture shared by chimps and humans—the upturned palm, meaning "gimme." Chimps have been observed using it in the wild and in captivity, to ask other chimps to share food, for help in a fight, or to request a grooming session (Pollick, Jeneson, & de Waal, 2008). Some nonhuman primates also communicate status through nonverbal means. Chimps display their rank in the social hierarchy by a "pant-grunt" greeting along with a crouching or bobbing motion. Baboons display status by a "wahoo" sound (Weisbuch & Ambady, 2008). There do seem to be compelling parallels between specific facial expressions and gestures displayed by human and nonhuman primates, universally interpreted to hold similar meanings. However, it still remains true that communication among nonhuman primates, like chimps and monkeys, appears to be less complex than among humans (Preuschoft, 2000).

Studies have also compared the facial expressions of children who were blind with those of sighted children and found many similarities. Even though the children who were blind couldn't see the facial expressions of others to mimic them, they still made the same expressions. This suggests some innate, genetic basis for these behaviors (Galati, Sini, Schmidt, & Tinti, 2003).

Indeed, many cross-cultural studies support the notion of some universality in nonverbal communication, particularly in **facial expressions.** Several facial

facial expressions
Facial gestures that convey emotions and attitudes.

gestures seem to be universal, including the eyebrow flash just described, the nose wrinkle (indicating slight social distancing), and the "disgust face" (a strong sign of social repulsion). It is also possible that grooming behavior is universal (as it is in animals), although it seems to be somewhat suppressed in Western societies (Schiefenhovel, 1997). For many years, scientists assumed that at least six basic emotions—happiness, sadness, disgust, fear, anger, and surprise—were communicated by similar facial expressions in most societies (Ekman, 2003). However, as explained in the following section, these assumptions are now being questioned as the result of more research.

Recent research on the universality of nonverbal behavior has also focused on how some nonverbal behavior fills universal human social needs for promoting social affiliation or bonding. For example, according to this research, laughter is not just a message about the positive feeling of the sender but an attempt to influence others, to make them feel more positive toward the sender. Similarly, the social purpose of mimicry—when interaction partners adopt similar postures, gestures, and mannerisms—is to create an affective or social bond with others. Researchers point out that people in all cultures use these nonverbal behaviors to influence others, and over time, these behaviors that contributed to positive relationships were favored and eventually became automatic and nonconscious (Montepare, 2003; Patterson, 2003).

Although research may indicate universalities in nonverbal communication, some variations exist. The evoking stimuli (i.e., what causes the nonverbal behavior) may vary from one culture to another. Smiling, for example, is universal, but what prompts a person to smile may be culture specific. Similarly, there are variations in the rules for nonverbal behavior and the contexts in which nonverbal communication takes place. For example, people kiss in most cultures, but there is variation in who kisses whom and in what contexts. When French friends greet each other, they often kiss on both cheeks but never on the mouth. Friends in the United States usually kiss on greeting only after long absence, with the kiss usually accompanied by a hug. The rules for kissing also vary along gender lines.

Finally, it is important to look for larger cultural patterns in the nonverbal behavior, rather than trying simply to identify all of the cultural differences. Researcher David Matsumoto (2006) suggests that although cultural differences in nonverbal patterns are interesting, noting these differences is not sufficient. Studying and cataloging every variation in every aspect of nonverbal behavior would be an overwhelming task. Instead, he recommends studying nonverbal communication patterns that vary with other cultural patterns, such as values.

For example, recent research links cultural patterns of individualism and collectivism to differences in facial cues and ultimately to different uses of emoticons on Twitter (Park, Baek, & Cha, 2014). Previous research found that individualistic cultural groups tend to emphasize the self and are trained to express their feeling through explicit cues, whereas those from collectivistic culture are taught to suppress personal feelings, conveying them indirectly through more subtle cues. It is not surprising then that recent studies show that people from individualist cultures focus more on the mouth muscles when reading emotions and collectivists more on the subtle, less easily controlled muscles surrounding the eyes. Since emoticons are expressions of feeling, researchers predicted that individualist and collectivists might use and

In a recent essay, Steven M. Croucher, a communication scholar, identified reasons given by Muslim women for wearing the hijab (Islamic veil/headscarf). This information was based on interviews with 42 women living in France—following the passing of a 2004 law banning the hijab in French public schools. What do you think are some implications for intercultural communication in societies implementing bans against hijabs?

1. The hijab and Muslim heritage: The women explained that wearing the hijab helped integrate their multicultural identity. They identified as French and also with their country of origin (e.g., Algeria, Tunisia, Morocco) and as Muslim women. As one woman said—growing up hearing a hijab has taught her Islamic and Algerian values in France.

2. The hijab as security in public: The word for "to shield" in Arabic is "hijaba" and many of the women talked about how the hijab provides "a shroud of protection," that they could move easily and comfortably within it, shielded from staring at their bodies—and feeling that people then saw their "real" identity as a religious person.

3. Relationship with Muhammad and the community. Women also talked about how wearing the hijab made them feel closer to Muhammad—akin to a marriage relationship—similar to wearing a wedding ring. Also, that it represents a transformation from a women into a mother within their community. It "helps me show my virtue and be a good example for my community" (p. 207).

4. Protest against the French government: In response to the French ban, many women wear the hijab as a silent protest and an expression of unity with other Muslim women. In fact, some said that before the ban, they only saw themselves as French and Muslim, and now have a stronger feeling of being Muslim and more respect for the hijab.

Source: From S. M. Croucher, "French-Muslims and the Hijab: An Analysis of Identity and the Islamic Veil in France," *Journal of Intercultural Communication Research, 37*(3); (2008): 199–213.

evaluate emoticons differently. And this is exactly what they found, after analyzing almost 2 billion tweets from 54 million users in 78 countries over 3.5 years. People in East Asian countries tended to use the vertical emoticons "^_ ^"—emphasizing the eyes, while emoticons from people in the West used the horizontal emoticon : :) (Park et al., 2014).

Nonverbal Codes

Physical Appearance Physical appearance is an important nonverbal code. It includes physical characteristics like height, weight, and body shape, as well as personal grooming (including body hair, clothing choices) and personal artifacts such as jewelry, glasses, and backpacks/briefcases/purses.

Of course, physical attractiveness is dynamic and variable—beauty is in the eye of the beholder, to some extent (Swami et al., 2010). However, are there any universal measures of attractiveness? Do different cultures have different standards for beauty? It turns out that two aspects of beauty seems to be present in many cultures: (1) There is more emphasis on female attractiveness than male and (2) men consistently express stronger preferences for attractive mates than women (Gottschall, 2008).

Research shows that the notion of female attractiveness varies from culture to culture: Preferences for different body weights in Malaysia and Britain varied with socioeconomic status, and body shape played a relatively minor role. In a study comparing Britain and Japan, the Japanese participants found smaller-bodied women more attractive than the British participants, and in general, preferred small-headed and longer-legged women—the so-called *hattou shin* beauty (Swami, Caprario, & Tovée, 2006). Our Japanese students tell us that generally, Japanese find thinner lips more attractive than do U.S. Americans.

A study comparing notions of male physical attractiveness in Britain and Greece found that waist-to-chest ratio (WCR) was the most important indicator of male physical attractiveness to women in both countries; however, Greek women showed a preference for smaller men—a lower WCR and smaller overall body weight—than did the British women (Swami et al., 2007).

Some experts have argued that the importance of body shape to physical attractiveness may vary according to gender roles in particular cultural settings: Where traditional sex roles prevail, people prefer "traditional" body shapes (V-shaped for men, hour-glass for women). This seems to be true to some degree. In one study, the Portuguese (Portugal is more of a sex-role-stereotyped European country) were more likely to prefer traditional, "curvaceous" females and V-shaped male bodies when compared to the Danish (Denmark is a less sex-role-stereotyped European country). The Danes preferred thinner, angular shapes (with small hips) for both males and females (Swami et al., 2006).

How do clothing choices and artifacts like purses and backpacks figure in? We might argue that these can be individual choices that express elements of one's personality and affiliation with particular social groups—for example, goth clothing versus jock or preppie. Some clothing may reflect religious affiliation and expressions of religious identity, as we discussed in Chapter 5 (see Figure 7-2). For example, some orthodox Jewish women cover their heads at all times with scarves or hats; some of Judith's relatives wear prayer bonnets that cover the head and "cape" dresses (modest, shirtwaist dresses with an extra layer of material designed to deemphasize the female shape); Muslim women in many countries wear the Islamic hijab (headscarf) or burqa (sheet-like covering of the entire body with only eyes showing.) (See Point of View on p. 281.) As you might expect, women have various reasons for their clothing choices. Sometimes these choices conflict with secular society or norms in other cultures. For example, First Lady Michelle Obama caused some controversy when she (deliberately) wore black trousers and a long patterned jacket, and most importantly no head scarf, when she accompanied her husband on a presidential visit to Saudi Arabia, where women must cover their hair in public and must wear niqabs (head scarves) (Ridge, 2015). In 2010, the French parliament made it illegal

FIGURE 7-2 Muslim women in many countries wear the Islamic burqa as an expression of religious identity. (© *Royalty-Free/Corbis*)

for Muslim women to wear the full veil, a law supported by a majority of French citizens, and there are similar sentiments in Britain (Thompson, 2011). Bans have also been proposed in Italy, the Netherlands, and Belgium. Most U.S. Americans are not in favor, and some suggest that values of tolerance and religious freedom should prevail—banning the burqa in very limited contexts (schools, courts) where faces need to be seen (Banning the burqa a bad idea, 2010). Some compare the ban to the French requiring Jews to wear a Star of David during World War II, emphasizing the underlying intolerance and prejudice (Zaretsky, 2010), which will be discussed later in this chapter. The context and people involved may call for different choices. During Iranian President Rouhani's 2016 trip to Europe where he made $18 billion worth of business deals, the Italians decided to cover some of their famous nude statues during his visits to art museums, in deference to Rouhani's strict theocratic sensibilities. They placed plywood boxes and panels around the nudes to obscure them from the president's vision, or at least in photo-ops (Tharoor, 2016).

Facial Expressions   As noted earlier, there have been many investigations of the universality of facial expressions. During the past 60 years, psychologist Paul Ekman and colleagues, through extensive and systematic research, have maintained that there are six basic emotions expressed through universal facial expressions: happiness, sadness, disgust, surprise, anger, and fear. However, using more sophisticated computer-generated digital measurement, recent research found that the six basic emotions suggested earlier held true for Western Caucasians. However, East Asians showed less distinction, and more overlap between emotional categories, particularly for surprise, fear, disgust, and anger, specifically showing "signs of emotional intensity with the eyes, which are under less voluntary control than the mouth, reflecting restrained facial behaviors as predicted by the literature" (Jack, Garrod, Yub, Caldarac & Schyns, 2012, p. 7242). So this research refutes the notion that human emotion is universally represented by the same set of six distinct facial expression signals and early research probably neglected expressions of shame, pride, or guilt, fundamental emotions in East Asian societies.

Secondly, it turns out many facial expressions do not express one emotion, but several (e.g., happily surprised, sadly disgusted, etc). One recent project photographed 230 volunteers making faces in response to verbal cues ("you got some great unexpected news") and then analyzed the resulting 5,000 images and identified 21 distinct facial expressions of emotions (Du, Tao, & Martinez, 2014).

While a smile may signal a universally positive emotion, there are cultural variations in how much and how often people are expected to smile. Recent studies show that eastern Europeans tend to smile less than western Europeans, and North Americans tend to smile more often than any other cultural group. Communication experts suggest that these differences stem from deeply held cultural preferences involving friendliness and sincerity. America is a "culture of affirmation," where friendliness reigns and people should be happy, or at least appear to be happy. In comparison, French, German, and eastern European cultures place a strong emphasis on sincerity and presenting one's feelings "truthfully," so people are expected to smile only when they are truly feeling happy. In fact, someone who smiles a lot is seen as a bit loony or perhaps insincere; after all, who is truly happy all the time? In most cultures women tend to smile more than men, probably reflecting the social expectations that women are supposed to be more affiliative and communal, and smiling is a way to express these attributes (Szarota, 2010).

Proxemics Unlike facial expressions, the norms for personal space seem to vary considerably from culture to culture. As you may recall from Chapter 2, proxemics is the study of how people use various types of space in their everyday lives: fixed feature space, semifixed space, and informal space. Fixed feature space is characterized by set boundaries (divisions within an office building); semifixed feature space is defined by fixed boundaries such as furniture. Informal space, or personal space, is characterized by a personal zone or "bubble" that varies for individuals and circumstances. The use of each of these spatial relationships can facilitate or impede effective communication across cultures; the area that humans control and use most often is their informal space.

Are there cultural variations in how people use personal space? A recent study of personal distances in six countries did find some cultural differences as well as some universals (Høgh-Olesen, 2008). First, the universal norms: We tend to place ourselves further away when we are standing near to more than one stranger, we narrow down our personal space when we are in control of our own "territory" (personal space) and expand it when we arrive in someone else's territory. Now for the cultural variations—you probably know from personal experience that when someone stands too close to you or too far in conversation, you tend to feel uncomfortable and may even move to shorten or widen the space. The same study found that people from

Our Kenyan student Gladys describes an interesting nonverbal cultural tradition:

At home (Kenya), when you invite a visitor/friend in your house you have to escort him/her out of your house to their car or walk them a short distance to the bus stop. Failure to do that may be interpreted that their visit was not appreciated. When I came to the U.S., I continued with the same tradition, and thought, visitors have to be escorted. But surprisingly, most of my visitors did not mind being escorted. At first, I insisted on escorting them, but my husband informed me that it was not the norm in U.S.

Northern countries of Greenland, Finland, and Denmark systematically kept larger distances between them and their conversational partner than did Italians, Indians, and Cameroonians. These results support Edward Hall's 1966 observations about personal space. Hall distinguished contact cultures from noncontact cultures. He described **contact cultures** as those societies in which people stand closer together while talking, engage in more direct eye contact, use face-to-face body orientations more often while talking, touch more frequently, and speak in louder voices. He suggested that societies in South America and southern Europe are contact cultures, whereas those in northern Europe, the United States, and the Far East are **noncontact cultures**—in which people tend to stand farther apart when conversing, maintain less eye contact, and touch less often. Subsequent research seems to confirm Hall's observations.

Of course, many other factors besides regional culture determine how far we stand from someone. Gender, age, ethnicity, context, and topic all influence the use of personal space. In fact, some studies have shown that regional culture is perhaps the least important factor. For example, in many Arab and Muslim societies, gender may be the overriding factor, because unmarried men and women rarely stand close together, touch each other, or maintain direct eye contact. In contrast, male friends may stand very close together, kiss on the cheek, and even hold hands—reflecting loyalty, great friendship, and, most important, equality in status, with no sexual connotation (Fattah, 2005; Khuri, 2001).

Gestures   Gestures, perhaps even more so than personal space, vary greatly from culture to culture (see Figure 7-3). The consequences for this variation can be quite dramatic, as former First Lady Michele Obama discovered when she threw her arm around Her Majesty The Queen and shocked the Queen and the British media. One of the classic British rules of contact is that you never touch the Queen.

Researcher Dane Archer (1997) describes his attempt to catalog the various gestures around the world on video. He began this video project with several hypotheses: First, that there would be great variation, and this he found to be true. However, more surprising, his assumption regarding the existence of some universal gestures or at least some universal *categories* of gestures (e.g., every culture must have an obscene gesture) was not confirmed.

contact cultures Cultural groups in which people tend to stand close together and touch frequently when they interact—for example, cultural groups in South America, the Middle East, and southern Europe. (See **noncontact cultures**.)

noncontact cultures Cultural groups in which people tend to maintain more space and touch less often than people do in contact cultures. For instance, Great Britain and Japan tend to have noncontact cultures. (See **contact cultures**.)

285

FIGURE 7-3   In many Asian countries, the traditional greeting is a bow. The depth of the bow signals the status relationship of the two individuals. (© *Andersen Ross/Blend Images LLC RF*)

He gathered his information by visiting English as a Second Language classes and asking international students to demonstrate gestures from their home cultures, resulting in the documentary *A World of Gestures: Culture and Nonverbal Communication.* He drew several conclusions from his study: First, that gestures and their meanings can be very subtle. His work "often elicited gasps of surprise, as ESL students from one culture discovered that what at first appeared to be a familiar gesture actually means something radically different in another society" (p. 87). For example, in Germany, and many other European cultures, the gesture for "stupid" is a finger on the forehead; the American gesture for "smart" is nearly identical, but the finger is held an inch to the side, at the temple. Similarly, the American raised thumb gesture of "way to go" is a vulgar gesture, meaning "sit on this" in Sardinia and "screw you" in Iran.

Second, Archer emphasizes that gestures are different from many other nonverbal expressions in that they are accessible to conscious awareness—they can be explained, illustrated, and taught to outsiders. Finally, as noted earlier, he had

SHAKE HANDS? OR BOW?

Handshakes and bows are important nonverbal greetings around the world. In many Asian countries, the traditional greeting is a bow. It does not signal subservience, but rather humility and respect. The most important guideline here is to observe the other's bow carefully and try to bow to the same depth. The depth of the vow signals the status relationship of the two individuals. Too deep a bow will be seen as ingratiating, too shallow a bow will seem arrogant. In many countries now, particularly in a business context, people may combine the bow and handshake: a slight bow or nod accompanied with a handshake.

Handshakes can vary in frequency and firmness. Some Europeans shake hands at each encounter during the day and may spend as much as 30 minutes a day shaking hands. Here are some guidelines:

Germans:	Firm, brisk, and frequent
French:	Light, quick, and frequent
Latin American:	Firm and frequent
North America:	Firm and infrequent, compared to France and Latin America
Arabs:	Gentle, repeated and lingering (may place hand over heart after)
Koreans:	Moderately firm
Most other Asians:	Very gentle and infrequent

Sources: From R. E. Axtell, *Essential Do's and Taboos: Complete Guide to International Business and Leisure Travel* (Hoboken, NJ: John Wiley & Sons, 2007), p. 20; T. Morrison and W. A. Conaway, *Kiss, Bow, Shake Hands* (Avon, MA: Adams Media, 2006).

assumed there would be some universal categories—a gesture for "very good," a gesture for "crazy," an obscene gesture. Not so. A number of societies (e.g., the Netherlands, Norway, Switzerland) have no such gesture. In the end, he concludes that through making the video, "We all acquired a deeply enhanced sense of the power, nuances, and unpredictability of cultural differences" (p. 87). And the practical implication of the project was to urge travelers to practice "gestural humility"—assuming that the familiar gestures of our home culture will not mean the same things abroad and also "that we cannot infer or intuit the meaning of any gestures we observe in other cultures" (p. 80).

Eye Contact   **Eye contact** often is included in proxemics because it regulates interpersonal distance. Direct eye contact shortens the distance between two people, whereas less eye contact increases the distance. Eye contact communicates meanings about respect and status and often regulates turn-taking.

eye contact A nonverbal code, eye gaze, that communicates meanings about respect and status and often regulates turn-taking during interactions.

Patterns of eye contact vary from culture to culture. In many societies, avoiding eye contact communicates respect and deference, although this may vary from context to context. For many U.S. Americans, maintaining eye contact communicates that one is paying attention and showing respect.

When they speak with others, most U.S. Americans look away from their listeners most of the time, looking at their listeners perhaps every 10 to 15 seconds. When a speaker is finished taking a turn, he or she looks directly at the listener to signal completion. However, some cultural groups within the United States use even less eye contact while they speak. For example, some Native Americans tend to avert eye gaze during conversation.

paralinguistics The study of vocal behaviors include voice qualities and vocalization.

Paralinguistics   **Paralinguistics** refers to the study of paralanguage—vocal behaviors that indicate *how* something is said, including speaking rate, volume, pitch, and stress. Saying something very quickly in a loud tone of voice will be interpreted differently from the same words said in a quieter tone of voice at a slower rate. There are two types of vocal behavior—voice qualities and vocalizations (Alberts, Nakayama, & Martin, 2007).

voice qualities The "music" of the human voice, including speed, pitch, rhythm, vocal range, and articulation.

Voice qualities—or the nontechnical term, tone of voice—mean the same thing as vocal qualities. Voice qualities include speed, pitch, rhythm, vocal range, and articulation; these qualities make up the "music" of the human voice. There do appear to be some universal meanings for particular vocal qualities. A recent study found that vocalizations (e.g., screams, laughter, tone of voice showing disgust, fear) communicating the six basic emotions were recognized equally by two dramatically different cultural groups: European native English speakers and residents of remote, culturally isolated Namibian villages. The researchers conclude that some emotions are psychological universals, shared by all humans. Furthermore, these emotions can be communicated by vocal signals that can be broadly interpreted across cultures that do not share language or culture (Bänziger, Patel, & Scherer, 2014; Sauter, Eisner, Ekman, & Scott, 2010). We all know people whose voice qualities are widely recognized. For example, the voice of actor Fran Drescher, who starred in the TV sitcom *The Nanny,* has been frequently remarked upon. Her trademark whiny chuckle and nasal voice allow her to be recognized no matter where she is. Speakers also vary in how they articulate sounds, that is, how distinctly they pronounce individual words and sounds. We tend not to notice these paralinguistic features unless someone articulates very precisely or very imprecisely. Paralinguistics often lead people to negatively evaluate speakers in intercultural communication contexts even when they don't understand the language. For example, Chinese speakers often sound rather musical and nasal to English speakers; English speakers sound rather harsh and guttural to French speakers.

vocalizations The sounds we utter that do not have the structure of language.

Vocalizations are the sounds we utter that do not have the structure of language. Tarzan's yell is one famous example. Vocalizations include vocal cues such as laughing, crying, whining, and moaning as well as the intensity or volume of one's speech. They also include sounds that aren't actual words but that serve as fillers, such as "uh-huh," "uh," "ah," and "er." The paralinguistic aspects of speech serve a variety of communicative functions. They reveal mood and emotion; they also allow us to emphasize or stress a word or idea, create a distinctive identity, and (along with gestures) regulate conversation. Paralanguage can be a confusing factor in intercultural communication. For example, Europeans interpret the loudness of Americans as aggressive behavior, while Americans might think the British are secretive because they talk quietly. The amount of silence in conversations and also the speaking rate differ among cultures. For instance, the Finnish and Japanese are comfortable having pauses in their conversations, while most U.S. Americans are seen to talk rapidly and are pretty uncomfortable with silences.

Chronemics   **Chronemics** concerns concepts of time and the rules that govern its use. There are many cultural variations regarding how people understand and use time. Edward Hall (1966) distinguished between monochronic and polychronic time orientation. People who have a **monochronic** concept of time regard it as a commodity: Time can be gained, lost, spent, wasted, or saved. In this orientation, time is linear, with one event happening at a time. In general, monochronic cultures value being punctual, completing tasks, and keeping to schedules. Most university staff and faculty in the United States maintain a monochronic orientation to time. Classes, meetings, and office appointments start when scheduled; faculty members see one student at a time, hold one meeting at a time, and keep appointments except in the case of emergency. Family problems are considered poor reasons for not fulfilling academic obligations—for both faculty and students.

> **chronemics** The concept of time and the rules that govern its use.

> **monochronic** An orientation to time that assumes it is linear and is a commodity that can be lost or gained.

In contrast, in a **polychronic** orientation, time is more holistic, and perhaps more circular: Several events can happen at once. Many international business negotiations and technical assistance projects falter and even fail because of differences in time orientation. For example, U.S. businesspeople often complain that meetings in the Middle East do not start "on time," that people socialize during meetings, and that meetings may be canceled because of personal obligations. Tasks often are accomplished *because* of personal relationships, not in spite of them. International students and business personnel observe that U.S. Americans seem too tied to their schedules; they suggest that U.S. Americans do not care enough about relationships and often sacrifice time with friends and family to complete tasks and keep appointments.

> **polychronic** An orientation to time that sees it as circular and more holistic.

Silence   Cultural groups may vary in the degree of emphasis placed on silence, which can be as meaningful as language (Acheson, 2007). One of our students recalls his childhood:

> *I always learned while growing up that silence was the worst punishment ever. For example, if the house chore stated clearly that I needed to take the garbage out, and I had not done so, then my mother would not say a word to me. And I would know right away that I had forgotten to do something.*

In most U.S. American contexts, silence is not highly valued. Particularly in developing relationships, silence communicates awkwardness and can make people feel uncomfortable. According to scholar William B. Gudykunst's (1985, 2005) uncertainty reduction theory, the main reason for communicating verbally in initial interactions is to reduce uncertainty. In U.S. American contexts, people employ active uncertainty reduction strategies, such as asking questions. However, in many other

Giving gifts seems to be a universal way to please someone, if the gift is appropriate. One colleague of mine, Nishehs, once tried to impress our boss, Joe. Nishehs brought a well-wrapped gift to Joe when they first met with each other in person. Joe was indeed pleased as he received the gift from Nishehs, but his smile faded away quickly right after he opened the gift. Joe questioned Nishehs angrily, "Why is it green?" Shocked and speechless, Nishehs murmured, "What's wrong with a green hat?"

The miscommunication resulted from the cultural differences between them. Nishehs is an Indian, whereas Joe is Chinese. For the Chinese, a green hat means one's wife is having an extramarital affair.
—Chris

cultural contexts, people reduce uncertainty using more passive strategies—for example, remaining silent, observing, or perhaps asking a third party about someone's behavior.

In many communities, silence is not simply associated with uncertainty. Silence also is associated with social situations in which a known and unequal distribution of power exists among participants (Braithwaite, 1990).

Recently, scholar Covarrubias (2007) points out that some of the early investigations of silence in American Indian communities did not fully value the communicative importance of silence in these and other cultures. She now encourages communication scholars to rethink the way they view silence, to see it not "as an absence, but, rather, as a fullness of opportunity for being and learning" (p. 270) and perhaps ask what American Indian perspectives can contribute to our knowledge of communication, "particularly to the much underengaged and much needed inquiry into the worlds humans create within silence?" (p. 271)

Recent research has found similar patterns in other cultures. For example, researchers have described the *Asaillinen* (matter-of-fact) verbal style among Finnish people that involves a distrust of talkativeness as "slickness" and a sign of unreliability (Carbaugh & Berry, 2001; Sajavaara & Lehtonen, 1997). Silence, for Finns, reflects thoughtfulness, appropriate consideration, and intelligence, particularly in public discourse or in educational settings like a classroom. In an ethnographic study investigating this communication pattern, Wilkins (2005) reports two excerpts from interviews that illustrate this pattern—one interview with a Finnish student and one with an American student:

Excerpt 1

Finnish Student: I have been to America.

Wilkins: Can you tell me what the experience was like?

Student: The people and the country were very nice.

Wilkins: Did you learn anything?

Student: No.

Wilkins: Why not?

Student: Americans just talk all the time.

Excerpt 2

Wilkins: Do you like Finland?

American Student: Oh yes, I like it a lot.

Wilkins: How about the people?

Student: Sure, Finns are very nice.

Wilkins: How long have you been at the university?

Student: About nine months already.

Wilkins: Oh, have you learned anything?

Student: No, not really.

Wilkins: Why not?

Student: Finns do not say anything in class.

In addition to a positive view of silence, nonverbal facial expressions in the *Asaillinen* style tend to be rather fixed—and expressionless. The American student, of course, did not have the cultural knowledge to understand what can be accomplished by thoughtful activity and silence. Similarly, a Russian student in one of our classes recounts that one of the "traditions" that Russians have before they leave for the airport, or any road trip, is "to sit down and be silent for about 30 seconds." Her U.S. American boyfriend found this extremely strange, but has adapted: "ever since I explained it to him, he always makes sure that we sit down and are silent before we head to the airport."

Scholars have reported similar views on talk and silence in Japanese and Chinese cultures influenced by Confucianism and Taoism. Confucius rejected eloquent speaking and instead advocated hesitancy and humble talk in his philosophy of the ideal person (Chang, 1997; Kim, 2001). As one of our Taiwanese students told us, "In America, sometimes students talk about half the class time. Compared to my classes in Taiwan, if a student asked too many questions or expressed his/her opinions that much, we would say that he or she is a show-off."

In a recent review of scholarly research on silence, communication scholar Kris Acheson (2007) acknowledges that silence in the United States has often been associated with negative, unhealthy relationships, or with disempowerment, for example, when women and/or minorities feel their voices are not heard. However, she tells us that increasingly U.S. Americans recognize the positive and sometimes powerful uses of silences in certain contexts. For example, nurses and doctors are encouraged to honor silent patients and learn to employ silence in their ethical care; young people are advised to seek out silence in their lives for the sake of health and sanity, to even noiseproof their homes in an attempt to boost health. In business contexts, sometimes keeping quiet is the best strategy and talking too much can kill a business deal. In education, teachers can create a space for understanding rather than counterarguments by asking for silent reflection after comments or performances. Finally, she admits that in some contexts, like politics and law, silence is still seen as completely negative; for example, pleading the Fifth equates silence with guilt, and silence by politicians is often viewed as too much secrecy.

Stereotype, Prejudice, and Discrimination

As noted previously, one of the problems with identifying cultural variations in non-verbal codes is that it is tempting to overgeneralize these variations and stereotype people. For example, researchers in the early 1970s identified certain nonverbal behaviors associated with African Americans—"getting and giving skin," the ritualistic handshakes (Black Power handshake), the stance and strutting walk of pimps and "players," and the "Afro-style" hairdo (Cook, 1972; Kochman, 1972). Since then, these nonverbal behaviors have been used to stereotype all blacks—still seen in pop culture images on television and film. However, a recent study showed that black students now acknowledged a few of the behaviors, not exactly as described 40 years ago and always context-dependent. That is, there are still some ritualistic handshakes and touching [e.g., the "pound" or "brother-man hug" (gripping right hands and pulling other into half-embrace)]—but not carried out with intensity or high frequency. They acknowledged that they sometimes strutted (males) or "walked sexy" (females)—but the walks and posture were always context-dependent. Choice of grooming style was now not so much about showing a connection to Africa but more of an individual expression (Green & Stewart, 2011).

In any case, we would be wise to be careful about generalizations. Cultural variations are tentative guidelines that we can use in intercultural interaction. They should serve as examples, to help us understand that there is a great deal of variation in nonverbal behavior. Even if we can't anticipate how other people's behavior may differ from our own, we can be flexible when we do encounter differences in how close someone stands or how she or he uses eye contact or conceptualizes time.

While explicit racial slurs are less common today, a series of recent studies showed that bias (both negative and positive) is demonstrated through subtle facial expressions and body language in popular television programs. They also showed that the more viewers watched shows that had pro-white nonverbal bias, the more biased viewers became—even though they could not consciously identify the biased behaviors they had seen in the programs. Overall, the findings suggest that these "hidden" patterns of biased nonverbal behavior influence bias among viewers (Weisbuch, Pauker, & Ambady, 2009). These same researchers conducted similar studies regarding nonverbal biases toward slim women (see Point of View, p. 293).

Prejudice is often based on nonverbal aspects of behavior. That is, the negative prejudgment is triggered by physical appearance or behavior. For example, prejudice is sometimes expressed toward Muslim women who wear the hijab, or toward men from the Middle East or South Asia wearing turbans, or even toward people who appear to belong to a particular ethnic group. The following news report of violence toward two Mexican nationals, attacked because of their skin color, underscores the importance of physical appearance in prejudice. One victim, attacked by assailants yelling "white power," was

> *surrounded by five men who punched and kicked him in the face, putting boots to him, while he was being held down—to the point of unconsciousness. Another man who came to his aid was similarly attacked. (Burack, 2011)*

UNSPOKEN CULTURAL INFLUENCE: EXPOSURE TO AND INFLUENCE OF NONVERBAL BIAS

Researcher Max Weisbuch and his colleagues hypothesized that nonverbal behavior plays a subtle but powerful role in communicating and perpetuating positive and negative bias. One set of studies looked at positive nonverbal bias toward slim women.

STUDY 1

The first study examined nonverbal bias, especially toward slim women. They selected 18 popular national television programs, and took clips of interactions where there were a range of slim and heavy women. They eliminated the slim or heavy character in each clip and the audio—so all that could be seen were the nonverbal reactions of other characters to the "target" female character.

These clips were shown to judges (people who had not seen the show, so they wouldn't have preexisting knowledge of the characters). The judges then rated the degree to which other characters demonstrated positive nonverbal behaviors toward the unseen female characters.

Results: The results showed that slim female characters elicited more favorable nonverbal responses than did heavier female characters.

STUDY 2

The second study examined the extent to which individual differences in media exposure to nonverbal bias could account for body-related attitudes, beliefs, and behavior. Researchers asked women to complete a survey asking about their favorite television shows and various attitudes.

Results: Women who saw more television shows with pro-slim nonverbal bias also (1) desired smaller body size, (2) demonstrated a prejudice against fat people, and (3) indicated a fear of becoming fat.

SUMMARY

To summarize, these and other studies show:

1. Millions of young women are regularly exposed to nonverbal bias.
2. Nonverbal bias can account for substantial variance in young women's body-related beliefs, attitudes, and behavior.
3. Widespread exposure to nonverbal bias can partially account for regional trends in unhealthy dieting behavior.

For these reasons, the researchers argue that nonverbal bias—at least with regard to one type of social characteristic—is likely to play an important role in the formation of culturally shared beliefs, attitudes, and behavior.

Source: From M. Weisbuch and N. Ambady, "Unspoken Cultural Influence: Exposure to and Influence of Nonverbal Bias," *Journal of Personality and Social Psychology*, 96(6); 2009: 1104–1119.

As in many instances of hate crimes, the victim's appearance was more significant than his specific cultural heritage. From these kinds of experiences with prejudice, victims can often spot prejudicial behavior and people with surprising accuracy. In an interesting study, blacks were able to detect prejudiced people (identified previously by objective survey measurement) after only 20 seconds of observation, with much higher accuracy than whites (Richeson & Shelton, 2005). Victims may also then develop imaginary "maps" that tell them where they belong and where they are likely to be rejected. They may even start to avoid places and situations in which they do not feel welcome (Marsiglia & Hecht, 1998). Can you identify places you've been where you or others were not welcome?

discrimination
Behaviors resulting from stereotypes or prejudice that cause some people to be denied equal participation or rights based on cultural-group membership, such as race.

Stereotyping or prejudice can lead to overt nonverbal actions to exclude, avoid, or distance and are called **discrimination.** Discrimination may be based on race (racism), gender (sexism), or any of the other identities discussed in Chapter 5. It may range from subtle, nonverbal behavior such as lack of eye contact or exclusion from a conversation, to verbal insults and exclusion from jobs or other economic opportunities, to physical violence and systematic exclusion. To see how exclusion and avoidance can be subtle, consider all the communication choices people can make that affect whether other people feel welcome or valued or like outsiders who don't belong (Johnson, 2017):

- Whether we look at people when we talk with them

- Whether we smile at people when they walk into the room or stare as if to say "What are you doing?" or stop the conversation with a hush they have to wade through to be included in the smallest way

- Whether we listen and respond to what people say, or drift away to someone or something else; whether we talk about things they know about, or stick to what's peculiar to the "in-group"

- Whether we acknowledge people's presence, or make them wait as if they weren't there; whether we avoid touching their skin when giving or taking something; how closely we watch them to see what they're up to

As described in Chapter 5, more assertive expressions are called "microaggressions": brief subtle denigrating messages sent by well-intentioned people who are unaware of the hidden messages being communicated. While these messages may be sent verbally ("You speak good English."—said to an Asian American whose family is been in the States for 100 years), many times they're sent nonverbally (clutching one's purse more tightly) or environmentally (symbols like the confederate flag or using American Indian mascots). Such communications are usually outside the level of conscious awareness of perpetrators. Often people who send these messages believe they are acting with the best of intentions and would be aghast if someone accuses them of committing microaggressions. Psychologist Derald Wing Sue's research suggest that most people have unconscious biases and prejudices that leak out in many interpersonal situations and decision points. While these microaggressions may seem somewhat trivial taken one at a time, the cumulative results of constant and continuing (almost daily) microaggressions have a tremendous impact on the targets of these messages: they assail self-esteem, produce anger and frustration, deplete psychic energy, lower feelings of well being and worthiness, produce physical health problems, and even shorten life expectancy (Sue, 2010).

Discrimination may be interpersonal, collective, or institutional. In recent years, interpersonal racism is expressed subtly and indirectly as well as more overtly, but also more persistent. Equally persistent is institutionalized or collective discrimination whereby individuals are systematically denied equal participation in society or equal access to rights in informal and formal ways (Maluso, 1995).

An example of institutionalized discrimination can be evidenced in hiring practices where resumes (and applicants) with "foreign" or "non-white" names are routinely rejected, leading some applicants to "whiten" their resumes. This entails eliminating language in resumes that reveals race. Recently researchers tested the effect of whitened resumes. They created two sets of resumes, one whitened and the other not, and randomly sent them in response to 1,600 job postings in 16 U.S. cities. They found that whitened resumes were twice as likely to get callbacks—a pattern that held even for companies that emphasized diversity.

"The most troubling part is that we saw the same kind of rates for employers who said that they were pro-diversity [in job postings] and the ones that didn't mention it," said Kang. "Employers are sending signals, that students are picking up on, that this is a safe place where you can use your real name and real experiences. But [the students] are not being rewarded at all. The statements the employers are putting out there aren't really tied to any real change in the discriminatory practices" (Lam, 2016).

Semiotics and Nonverbal Communication

The study of **semiotics,** or semiology, offers a useful approach to examining how different signs communicate meaning. While semiotics is often used for analyzing language/discourse, we find it more useful in analyzing nonverbals and cultural spaces. A particularly useful framework comes from literary critic Roland Barthes (1980). In his system, **semiosis** is the production of meaning and is constructed through the interpretation of **signs**—the combination of signifiers and signified. **Signifiers** are the culturally constructed arbitrary words or symbols we use to refer to something else, the **signified.** For example, the word *man* is a signifier that refers to the signified, an adult male human being.

Obviously, *man* is a general signifier that does not refer to any particular man. The relationship between this signifier and the sign (the meaning) depends on how the signifier is used (e.g., as in the sentence, "There is a man sitting in the first chair on the left.") or on our general sense of what *man* means. The difference between the signifier *man* and the sign rests on the difference between the word *man* and the meaning of that word. At its most basic level, *man* means an adult human male, but the semiotic process does not end there. *Man* carries many other layers of meaning. *Man* may or may not refer to any particular adult male, but it provides a concept that you can use to construct particular meanings based on the way the sign *man* functions. What does *man* mean when someone says, "Act like a real man!"

semiotics The analysis of the nature of and relationship between signs.

semiosis The process of producing meaning.

signs In semiotics, the meanings that emerge from the combination of the signifiers and signifieds.

signifiers In semiotics, the culturally constructed arbitrary words or symbols that people use to refer to something else.

signified In semiotics, anything that is expressed in arbitrary words or signifiers.

What do you have in mind when you think of the term *man?* How do you know when to use this signifier (and when not to use it) to communicate to others? Think of all of the adult males you know. How do they "fit" under this signifier? In what ways does the signifier reign over their behaviors, both verbal and nonverbal, to communicate particular ideas about them? We are not so much interested in the discrete, individual signifiers, but rather the ways that signifiers are combined and configured. The goal is to establish entire systems of semiosis and the ways that those systems create meaning. Semiotics allows us one way to "crack the codes" of another cultural framework.

The use of these semiotic systems relies on many codes taken from a variety of contexts and places: economic institutions, history, politics, religion, and so on. For example, when Nazi swastikas were spray-painted on Jewish graves in a town outside Budapest, Hungary in 2015, the message they communicated relied on semiotic systems from the past. The history of the Nazi persecution of Jews during World War II is well known: The power behind the signifier, the swastika, comes from that historical knowledge and the codes of anti-Semitism that it invokes to communicate its message. Relations from the past influence the construction and maintenance of intercultural relations in the present. Semiotics is a useful tool for examining the various ways that meaning is created in advertisements, clothing, tattoos, and other cultural artifacts. Semioticians have been attentive to the context in which the signifiers (words and symbols) are placed to understand which meanings are being communicated. For example, wearing certain kinds of clothes in specific cultural contexts may communicate unwanted messages, as shown in the Student Voices box. The meanings can vary from culture to culture. For example, in China, the color red symbolizes good luck and celebration; in India, it denotes purity; however, in South Africa, red is the color of mourning. In Egypt, yellow is the color of mourning; and in Japan, yellow symbolizes courage (Kyrnin, 2008). In the United States, black clothing can hold various meanings depending on the context: in some high schools, black is considered to denote gang membership; an elegant black dress is suitable for a formal dinner event but probably has a different meaning if worn by a bride's mother at her wedding.

Yet cultural contexts are not fixed and rigid. Rather, they are dynamic and fleeting, as Marcel Proust (1981) noted in writing about Paris in *Remembrance of Things Past:*

> *The reality that I had known no longer existed. It sufficed that Mme Swann did not appear, in the same attire and at the same moment, for the whole avenue to be altered. The places we have known do not belong only to the world of space on which we map them for our own convenience. None of them was ever more than a thin slice, held between the contiguous impressions that composed our life at that time; the memory of a particular image is but regret for a particular moment; and houses, roads, avenues are as fugitive, alas, as the years. (p. 462)*

As this excerpt shows, there is no "real" Paris. The city has different meanings at different times for different people, and for different reasons. For example, executives of multinational corporations moving into Paris see the city quite differently from immigrants arriving in Paris for personal reasons. Remember the tremendous unrest in the suburbs of Paris in 2011? Therefore, to think about cultural contexts as dynamic means that we must often think about how they change and in whose interests they change.

DEFINING CULTURAL SPACE

At the beginning of this book, we provided some background information about where we grew up. Our individual histories are important in understanding our identities. As writer John Preston (1991) explains, "Where we come from is important to who we are" (p. xi). There is nothing in the rolling hills of Delaware and Pennsylvania or the red clay of Georgia that biologically determined who Judith and Tom are. However, our identities are constructed, in part, in relation to the cultural milieu of the Mid-Atlantic region or the South. Each region has its own histories and ways of life that help us understand who we are. Our decision to tell you where we come from was meant to communicate something about who we think we are. So, although we can identify precisely the borders that mark out these spaces and make them real, or material, the spaces also are cultural in the ways that we imagine them to be.

The discourses that construct the meanings of cultural spaces are dynamic and ever changing. For example, the Delaware that Judith left behind and the Georgia that Tom left behind are not characterized by the same discourses that construct those places now. In addition, the relationship between those cultural spaces and our identities is negotiated in complex ways. For example, both of us participated in other, overlapping cultural spaces that influenced how we think about who we are. Thus, just because someone is from, say, Rhode Island or Samoa or India does not mean that his or her identity and communication practices are reducible to the history of those cultural spaces.

What is the communicative (discursive) relationship between cultural spaces and intercultural communication? Recall that we define cultural space as the particular configuration of the communication (discourse) that constructs meanings of various places. This may seem like an unwieldy definition, but it underscores the complexity of cultural spaces. A cultural space is not simply a particular location that has culturally constructed meanings. It can also be a metaphorical place from which we communicate. We can speak from a number of social locations, marked on the "map of society," that give added meaning to our communication. Thus, we may speak as parents, children, colleagues, siblings, customers, Nebraskans, and a myriad of other "places." All of these are cultural spaces.

Cultural Identity and Cultural Space

Home   Cultural spaces influence how we think about ourselves and others. One of the earliest cultural spaces we experience is our home. As noted previously, nonverbal communication often involves issues of status. The home is no exception. As English professor Paul Fussell (1983) notes, "Approaching any house, one is bombarded with class signals" (p. 82). Fussell highlights the semiotic system of social class in the American home—from the way the lawn is maintained, to the kind of furniture within the home, to the way the television is situated. These signs of social class are not always so obvious from all class positions, but we often recognize the signs.

Even if our home does not reflect the social class to which we aspire, it may be a place of identification. We often model our own lives on the patterns from our childhood homes. Although this is not always the case, the home can be a place of safety and security. African American writer Bell Hooks (1990) describes the "feeling of safety, of arrival, of homecoming" when as a child she would arrive at her grandmother's house, after passing through the scary white neighborhood with "those white faces on porches staring down at us with hate" (p. 42).

Home, of course, is not the same as the physical location it occupies or the building (the house) at that location. Home is variously defined in terms of specific addresses, cities, states, regions, and even nations. Although we might have historical ties to a particular place, not everyone has the same relationship between those places and their own identities. Indeed, the relationship between place and cultural identity varies. Writer Steven Saylor (1991), who grew up in Texas but moved to San Francisco, describes his ambivalent feelings when returning home to Texas, "Texas is home, but Texas is also a country whose citizenship I voluntarily renounced" (p. 119).

The discourses surrounding Texas and giving meaning to Texas no longer "fit" Saylor's sense of who he is or wants to be. We all negotiate various relationships to the cultural meanings attached to the particular places or spaces we inhabit. Consider writer Harlan Greene's (1991) relationship to his hometown in South Carolina:

> *I often think longingly of my hometown of Charleston. My heart beats faster and color rushes to my cheek whenever I hear someone mentioning her; mirages rise up, and I am as overcome and drenched in images as a runner just come from running. I see the steeples, the streets, the lush setting. (p. 55)*

Despite his attachment to Charleston, Greene does not believe that Charleston feels the same way toward him. He explains, "But I still think of Charleston; I return

Many cities abound with multiple cultural spaces. In this photo, several different cultural contexts are adjacent and emphasize the increasing significance of multiculturalism. How would people in this urban place experience cultural spaces differently from people who live in less diverse cultural spaces? How might it influence their intercultural communication patterns? (© *Robert Brenner/PhotoEdit*)

to her often and always will. I think of her warmly. I claim her now, even though I know she will never claim me" (p. 67).

The complex relationships we have between various places and our identities resist simplistic reduction. These three writers—hooks, Saylor, and Greene—have negotiated different sentiments toward "home." In doing so, each demonstrates the complex dialectical tensions that exist between identity and location.

Neighborhood   One significant type of cultural space that emerged in U.S. cities in the latter 19th and early 20th centuries was the ethnic or racial neighborhood. (See Figure 7-4.) Historical studies show, however, that the ethnic neighborhoods of the European immigrants were rarely inhabited by only one ethnic group, despite memories to the contrary. According to labor historian D. R. Roediger (2005), even the heart of Little Italy in Chicago was 47% non-Italian, and "No single side of even one square block in the street between 1890 and 1930 was found to be 100% Italian. . . . The percentage of Russians, Czechs, Italians and Poles living in segregated neighborhoods ranged from 37% to 61%" (p. 164). However, this type of real segregation was reserved for the African Americans—where 93% of African Americans lived in ghettos. By law and custom, and under different political pressures, some cities developed segregated neighborhoods. Malcolm X (Malcolm X & Haley, 1964), in his autobiography, tells of the strict laws that governed where his family could live after their house burned down:

> *In those days Negroes weren't allowed after dark in East Lansing proper. There's where Michigan State University is located; I related all of this to an audience of students when I spoke there in January, 1963. . . . I told them how East Lansing harassed us so much that we had to move again, this time two miles out of town, into the country. (pp. 3–4)*

The legacy of "white-only" areas pervades the history of the United States and the development of its cultural geography. The segregation of African Americans was not accidental. Beginning in 1890 until the late 1960s (when fair-housing laws were passed), whites in America created thousands of whites-only towns, commonly known as "sundown towns," a reference to the signs often posted at their city limits that warned, as one did in Hawthorne, California, in the 1930s: "Nigger, Don't Let the Sun Set on YOU in Hawthorne." In fact, historian J. Loewen (2005) claims that, during that 70-year period, "probably a majority of all incorporated places [in the United States] kept out African Americans."

Neighborhoods exemplify how power influences intercultural contact. Thus, some cultural groups defined who got to live where and dictated the rules by which other groups lived. These rules were enforced through legal means and by harassment. For bell hooks and Malcolm X, the lines of segregation were clear and unmistakable.

In San Francisco, different racial politics constructed and isolated Chinatown. The boundaries that demarcated Chinatown—the acceptable place for Chinese and Chinese Americans to live—were strictly enforced through violence. Newly arrived immigrants were sometimes stoned as they left the piers and made their way to Chinatown or those who wandered into other neighborhoods could be attacked by "young toughs" who amused themselves by beating Chinese (Nee & Nee, 1974, p. 60).

In contrast to Malcolm X's exclusion from East Lansing, the Chinese of San Francisco were forced to live in a marked-off territory. Yet we must be careful not to confuse the experience of Chinese in San Francisco with the experiences of all Chinese in the United States. For example, newly arrived Chinese immigrants to Savannah, Georgia were advised to live apart from each other. They were told of the whites' distrust of Chinatowns in San Francisco and New York. So no Chinatown developed in Savannah (Pruden, 1990).

Nor should we assume that vast migrations of Chinese necessarily led to the development of Chinatowns in other cities around the world. The settlement of Chinese immigrants in the 13th Arrondissement of Paris, for example, reflects a completely different intersection between cultures: "There is no American-style Chinatown [*Il n'y a pas de Chinatown à la américaine*]" in Paris (Costa-Lascoux & Yu-Sion, 1995, p. 197).

Within the context of different power relations and historical forces, settlement patterns of other cultural groups created various ethnic enclaves across the U.S. landscape. For example, many small towns in the Midwest were settled by particular European groups. Thus, in Iowa, Germans settled in Amana, Dutch in Pella, and Czechs and Slovaks in Cedar Rapids. Cities, too, have their neighborhoods, based on settlement patterns. South Philadelphia is largely Italian American, South Boston

EIGHT MILE ROAD

Sometimes called Detroit's mini Berlin Wall, sometimes called the Wailing Wall, this seemingly innocent looking wall in Joe Louis Park does little to betray its shameful past.

After World War I, some black residents of Detroit moved into a then rural and vacant area near the intersection of Wyoming and Eight Mile. In 1940, a developer sought to build homes for middle income whites in a nearby area. However, the Federal Housing Administration's policies of that era precluded their approving loans in racially mixed areas. To secure FHA approval, this developer put up a wall six feet high, one foot in width and one half mile in length, to clearly demark the white and black areas. His wall led the FHA to approve loans for his project.

Built in 1940, this wall presaged the racial divisions that have come to be symbolized by Eight Mile Road. (© *Clayton Sharrard/PhotoEdit, Inc.*)

Source: From http://detroityes.com/webisodes/2002/8mile/021106-04-8mile-berlin-wall.htm.

is largely Irish American, and Overtown in Miami is largely African American. Although it is no longer legal to mandate that people live in particular districts or neighborhoods based on their racial or ethnic backgrounds, the continued existence of such neighborhoods underscores their historical development and ongoing functions. This is especially true in Detroit, Michigan—one of the most segregated metropolitan region in the country—where the eight-mile road was made famous by the title and the location of the film starring Detroit hip-hop artist Eminem. The eight-mile, eight-lane road separates one city that is 91% white from the other that is overwhelmingly African American (Mullins, 2015). (See the Point of View box on the preceding page.) Economics, family ties, social needs, and education are some factors in the perpetuation of these cultural spaces.

Similar spaces exist in other countries as well. Remember the terrorist attacks in Paris in November 2015? A number of terrorists came from the same Brussels neighborhood, Molenbeek. There is a relationship between place and human relations, as one expert described Molenbeek as one of the segregated suburbs, isolated from the wider Belgium society, where "there are problems with failed integration, socioeconomic problems, and crime that can be exploited for the jihadists" (Robins-Early, 2016).

The relationships among identity, power, and cultural space are quite complex. Power relations influence who (or what) gets to claim who (or what), and under what conditions. Some subcultures are accepted and promoted within a particular cultural space, others are tolerated, and still others may be unacceptable. Sometimes residents fight to keep their neighborhood from being changed by powerful outsiders. This is the case in Boyle Heights, a low-income Latino community of small shops, mariachis, and taco stands that is the last holdout to L.A. gentrification. Property values are skyrocketing and posters offering cash for homes are there. The residents fear that the new money and outsiders will drive up rents, drive out residents, and erase their communal Chicano identity. They have organized and their hardline tactics included harassing an opera company's performance in a park with shouts, whistles, and a brass band. Masked activists stalked a group of visitors on an educational walking tour and ordered them to leave the neighborhood. Of course there is some ambivalence, as development might bring improvements but as one said, "Make it all shiny, great. But then what? The gringos will come" (Carroll, 2016). Identifying with various cultural spaces is a negotiated process that is difficult (and sometimes impossible) to predict and control. The key to understanding the relationships among culture, power, people, and cultural spaces is to think dialectically.

Regionalism   Ongoing regional and religious conflicts, as well as nationalism and ethnic revival, point to the continuing struggles over who gets to define whom. Such conflicts are not new, though. In fact, some cultural spaces (such as Jerusalem) have been sites of struggle for many centuries.

regionalism Loyalty to a particular region that holds significant cultural meaning for that person.

Although regions are not always clearly marked on maps of the world, many people identify quite strongly with particular regions. **Regionalism** can be expressed in many ways, from symbolic expressions of identification to armed conflict. Within the United States, people may identify themselves or others as southerners, New Englanders, and so on. In Canada, people from Montreal might identify more strongly with the province of Quebec than with their country. Similarly, some Corsicans might feel a need to negotiate their identity with France. Sometimes people fly regional flags, wear particular kinds of clothes, celebrate regional holidays, and participate in other cultural activities to communicate their regional identification. However, regional expressions are not always simply celebratory, as the conflicts in Kosovo, Chechnya, Eritrea, Tibet, and Northern Ireland indicate.

National borders may seem straightforward, but they often conceal conflicting regional identities. To understand how intercultural communication may be affected by national borders, we must consider how history, power, identity, culture, and context come into play. Only by understanding these issues can we approach the complex process of human communication.

Changing Cultural Space

Chapter 8 discusses in greater detail the intercultural experiences of those who traverse cultural spaces and attempt to negotiate change. In this chapter, however, we want to focus on some of the driving needs of those who change cultural spaces.

Travel　We often change cultural spaces when we travel. Traveling is frequently viewed as an unimportant leisure activity, but it is more than that. In terms of intercultural communication, traveling changes cultural spaces in ways that often transform the traveler. Changing cultural spaces means changing who you are and how you interact with others. Perhaps the old saying "When in Rome, do as the Romans do" holds true today as we cross cultural spaces more frequently than ever.

On a recent trip to Belgium, Tom flew nonstop on British Airways from Phoenix to London and then on to Brussels. Because the entire flight was conducted in English, Tom did not have a sense of any transition from English to French. Unlike flying the now defunct Sabena (Belgian National Airlines) from the United States to Belgium, flying British Airways provided no cultural transition space between Arizona and Belgium. Thus, when he got off the plane in Brussels, Tom experienced a more abrupt cultural and language transition, from an English environment to a Flemish/French environment.

However, globalization and cyberspace can change the way we experience changing cultural spaces. In recent travels, Judith and Tom are struck by the similarities of big cities around the world. Shopping areas in Shanghai, Las Vegas, and Capetown have the same upscale shops: Prada, Louis Vuitton, Tommy Hilfiger, etc. with the same upscale products. In traversing these spaces one can forget that he/she is not at home. Experts also caution that cyberspace may be changing the way we experience travel. Writer Frank Bruin describes his recent experience of being in Shanghai in his hotel room, watching a season of "The Wire" he had downloaded before he left home. He finally leaves his hotel room and ventures outside but "haunted by how tempting it was to stay put and to look down at our mobile devices instead of up at the world around us and how easily we can now travel the globe in a thoroughly customized cocoon." He calls it "traveling without seeing" (Bruni, 2013). Do you alter your communication style when you encounter travelers who are not in their traditional cultural space? Do you assume they should interact in the ways prescribed by your cultural space? These are some of the issues that travel raises.

Migration　People also change cultural spaces when they relocate. Moving, of course, involves a different kind of change in cultural spaces than traveling. In traveling, the change is fleeting, temporary, and usually desirable; it is something that

This student explains her difficulty in knowing when she is in Japan as she moves through the airport and onto the airplane. How are these cultural spaces different from national borders?

Whenever I am at LAX [Los Angeles International Airport] on the way back to Japan, my sense of space gets really confused. For example, I fly into LAX from Phoenix, and as I line up at the Korean Air check-in counter, I see so many Asian-looking people (mostly Japanese and Koreans). Then, as I proceed, getting past the stores (e.g., duty-free shops) and walk farther to the departure gate, I see a lot less Americans and, eventually and practically, NOBODY but Asian-looking people (except for a very limited number of non-Asian-looking passengers on the same flight). So, when I wait at the gate, hearing Japanese around me, I get confused—"Where am I? Am I still in the U.S.? Or am I already back in Japan?" This confusion gets further heightened when I go aboard and see Japanese food served for meals and watch a Japanese film or TV program on the screen. So, to me, arriving at the Narita International Airport is not the moment of arriving in Japan. It already starts while I am in the U.S. This is just one of the many examples of postmodern cultural spaces that I have experienced in my life.
—Sakura

travelers seek out. However, people who migrate do not always seek out this change. For example, in recent years, many people have been forced from their strife-torn homelands in Rwanda and in Bosnia and have settled elsewhere. Many immigrants leave their homelands simply so they can survive. But they often find it difficult to adjust to the change, especially if the language and customs of the new cultural space are unfamiliar.

Even within the United States, people may have trouble adapting to new surroundings when they move. Tom remembers that when northerners moved to the South they often were unfamiliar with the custom of banks closing early on Wednesday or with the traditional New Year's Day foods of black-eyed peas and collards. Ridiculing the customs of their new cultural space simply led to further intercultural communication problems.

Postmodern Cultural Spaces

postmodern cultural spaces Places that are defined by cultural practices—languages spoken, identities enacted, rituals performed—and that often change as new people move in and out of these spaces.

Space has become increasingly important in the negotiation of cultural and social identities, and so to culture more generally. As Leah Vande Berg (1999) explains, scholars in many areas "have noted that identity and knowledge are profoundly spatial (as well as temporal), and that this condition structures meaningful embodiment and experience" (p. 249). **Postmodern cultural spaces** are places that are defined by cultural practices—languages spoken, identities enacted, rituals performed—and they often change as new people move in and out of these spaces.

Imagine being in a small restaurant when a large group of people arrives, all of whom are speaking another language. How has this space changed? Whose space is it? As different people move in and out of this space, how does the cultural character change?

In his study of listening among the Blackfeet, Donal Carbaugh (1999) reports that listening is intimately connected to place as a cultural space. It is both a physical location and a cultural phenomenon. Through his cultural informant, Two Bears, Carbaugh notes that

> in his oral utterance to us about "listening," in this landscape, he is com-
> menting about a non-oral act of listening to this landscape. This nonverbal
> act is itself a deeply cultural form of action in which the Blackfeet persona
> and the physical place become intimately linked, in a particularly Blackfeet
> way. (p. 257)

But these places are dynamic, and "listening" is not limited to fixed locations: "Some kinds of places are apparently more appropriate for this kind of Blackfeet 'listening' than are others, although—according to Two Bears—'just about any-where' might do" (p. 257). Physical place, in this sense, can become a cultural space in that it is infused with cultural meanings. Think about how the same physical place might have a different meaning to someone from a different cultural group. Scholar Bryce Peake (2012) does just that. He examines the relationship between listening, cultural identity, and power negotiation in the British overseas territory of Gibraltar. He describes the interrelationships of the language soundscapes of English, Spanish, and Llanito—a local Gibraltarian creole of Spanish, Genoese, Hebrew, English, Maltese, and Arabic, particularly as demonstrated on a day of the British nationalistic parade. Llanito allows Gibraltarians to imagine themselves as a buffer between Spanish and British—a soundscape that "can be listened to in such a way that sounds like Spanish to the uninformed, and signifies 'not British' to Gibraltarians." In the frictions between the British-ness and Spanish-ness of Gibraltarians, Main Street on parade is a site where listening is used as a means to reproduce the strategies by which power is maintained and operationalized. "In this way, Gibraltarians speak into existence the spaces in which they speak; the codes they use—Llanito, Spanish, or English-both simultaneously construct spaces in particular ways, while being intimately affected by and tied to other noises within the soundscape—all of which are intimately tied to the construction and performance of the self" (p. 187).

Another set of postmodern spaces that are quite familiar are those on interactive media. There are MMORPG's (massively multiplayer online role-playing games), virtual worlds like Second Life, Onverse, Smallworlds, and Habbo where people meet in real time and interact primarily for recreational purposes. As we discussed in Chapter 1, there are other media spaces like blogs and online discussion groups where people meet for fun, to gain information, or experience a supportive community (e.g., heart patients, transgender people, ethnic communities). Of course there are more than 2 billion people who now use social networking sites such as Facebook, Instagram, and Tumbler in the United States, VKontakte, Qzone, Renren, etc. Some scholars question the effect on relationships of so much time spent in these

RACE AND TECHNOLOGY TRENDS

A recent report by the Pew Internet & American Life Project shows that although disparities in access have been greatly reduced, there are some differences between the way blacks and whites use cultural spaces of social media. Research specialist Aaron Smith outlines three trends:

1. ***The Internet and broadband population have become more diverse over the last decade, although key disparities do remain.*** *Specifically, African Americans have made huge gains in Internet access and now Blacks and Whites are very similar in their access to the Internet—except for older blacks who are less likely to to have access.*

2. ***Access to the digital world is increasingly moblile.*** *Blacks and Whites now have parity when it comes to owning cellphones and smartphones, but Blacks are are more likely to have internet access on smartphone than broadband at home.*

3. ***Social networking site access is identical among white and black internet users*** *but African Americans have higher levels of Twitter use than whites, especially younger black users. Also Blacks are much more likely than whites to use social media for conversations about race and to keep politically engaged.*

Source: From "African Americans and Technology Use," Pew Research Center's Internet & American Life Project, January 6, 2014. Retrieved November 16, 2016, from http://www .pewinternet.org/2014/01/06/african-americans-and-technology-use/.

cultural spaces. While these sites offer opportunities for connection, learning and support, and empowerment, results of one study suggest the longer someone spends on Facebook, the worse their mood gets (Kross, 2013). The reasons may be jealousy that comes from constant comparisons (my friends are having such good times, traveling to exotic places, parties I'm not invited to, etc.)

In addition, they can be hostile cultural places of harassment and exclusion. As we mentioned in Chapter 1, gay, lesbian, and transgendered individuals are much more likely to be the targets of bullying than straight individuals. Women gamers and game developers have been subjected to severe harassment by male gamers, violent threats, and rampant misogyny (#gamergate) (Dougherty & Isaac, 2016). In addition, some experts suggest that the new digital divide may be between those who have and don't have access to the new "shared, collaborative, and on-demand" economy, of Uber and Lyft ride sharing, Airbnb and HomeAway home sharing, and crowdfunding sites. These appear to be used mostly by the educated, urban, and young (under age 45) (Smith, 2016).

Early researchers thought that people who spent a lot of time in online communication were less socially skilled, substituting online communication for "real" face-to-face communication. Actually, as it turns out, the average user of a social networking site has more close friends and is half as likely to feel socially isolated as the average person; in addition, people who use mobile phones and instant messaging also have, on average, more friends. Further, Twitter users are more racially diverse than users of other mainstream SNSs (Hampton et al., 2012).

The fluid and fleeting nature of cultural space stands in sharp contrast to the 18th- and 19th-century notions of space, which promoted land ownership, surveys, borders, colonies, and territories. No passport is needed to travel in the postmodern cultural space because there are no border guards. The dynamic nature of postmodern cultural spaces underscores its response to changing cultural needs. The space exists only as long as it is needed in its present form.

Postmodern cultural spaces are both tenuous and dynamic. They are created within existing places, without following any particular guide. There is no marking off of territory, no sense of permanence, or official recognition. The postmodern cultural space exists only while it is used. An example of the postmodern cultural spaces is the classroom building at the Technical University of Denmark. The rooms and walls are fluid, can be moved to accommodate the needs of any particular day's activities—classes, meetings, study groups, and a digital neon sign on the outside of the building notes the particular rooms and room numbers that will be in use that day.

The ideology of fixed spaces and categories is currently being challenged by postmodernist notions of space and location. Phoenix, for example, which became a city relatively recently, has no Chinatown, or Japantown, or Koreatown, no Irish district, or Polish neighborhood, or Italian area. Instead, people of Polish descent, for example, might live anywhere in the metropolitan area but congregate for special occasions or for specific reasons. On Sundays, the Polish Catholic Mass draws many people from throughout Phoenix. When people want to buy Polish breads and pastries, they can go to the Polish bakery and also speak Polish there. Ethnic identity is only one of several identities that these people negotiate. When they desire recognition and interaction based on their Polish heritage, they can meet that wish. When they seek other forms of identification, they can go to places where they can be Phoenix Suns fans, or community volunteers, and so on. Ethnic identity is neither the sole factor nor necessarily the most important one at all times in their lives.

The markers of ethnic life in Phoenix are the urban sites where people congregate when they desire ethnic cultural contact. At other times, they may frequent different locations in expressing aspects of their identities. In this sense, the postmodern urban space is dynamic and allows people to participate in the communication of identity in new ways (Drzewiecka & Nakayama, 1998).

Cultural spaces can also be metaphorical, with historically defined places serving as sources of contemporary identity negotiation in new spaces. In her study of academia, Olga Idriss Davis (1999) turns to the historical role of the kitchen in African American women's lives and uses the kitchen legacy as a way to rethink the university. She notes that "the relationship between the kitchen and the Academy [university] informs African American women's experience and historically interconnects their struggles for identity" (p. 370). In this sense, the kitchen is a metaphorical cultural space that is invoked in an entirely new place, the university. Again, this postmodern cultural space is not material but metaphoric, and it allows people to negotiate their identities in new places.

INTERNET RESOURCES

http://nonverbal.ucsc.edu/
This website provided by the University of California–Santa Cruz allows students to explore and test their ability to read and interpret nonverbal communication. The site provides videos that examine nonverbal codes, including personal space and gestures, to better understand cross-cultural communication.

http://webdesign.about.com/od/color/a/bl_colorculture.htm
This Web page is dedicated to providing information pertaining to the color symbolism that exists throughout different cultures. Its purpose is to allow Web page designers to understand how their usage of color might be interpreted by different groups and world regions. The page also provides informative links on how gender, age, class, and current trends also play a factor in the meaning of color.

SUMMARY

- Nonverbal communication differs from verbal communication in two ways: It is more unconscious and learned implicitly.
- Nonverbal communication can reinforce, substitute for, or contradict verbal communication.
- Nonverbal communication communicates relational meaning, status, and deception.
- Research investigating the universality of nonverbal behaviors includes comparison of primate behavior, behavior of deaf/blind children, cross-cultural studies, and search for universal social needs filled by nonverbal behaviors.
- Nonverbal codes include physical appearance, facial expressions, eye contact, gestures, paralanguage, chronemics, and silence.
- Sometimes cultural differences in nonverbal behaviors can lead to stereotyping of others and overt discrimination.
- Cultural space influences cultural identity and includes homes, neighborhoods, regions, and nations.
- Two ways of changing cultural spaces are travel and migration.
- Postmodern cultural spaces, like cyberspace, are tenuous and dynamic.

DISCUSSION QUESTIONS

1. How does nonverbal communication differ from verbal communication?
2. What are some of the messages that we communicate through our nonverbal behaviors?
3. Which nonverbal behaviors, if any, are universal?
4. How do our cultural spaces affect our identities?
5. What role does power play in determining our cultural spaces?
6. What is the importance of cultural spaces to intercultural communication?
7. How do postmodern cultural spaces differ from modernist notions of cultural space?

ACTIVITIES

1. *Cultural Spaces.* Think about the different cultural spaces in which you participate (clubs, churches, concerts, and so on). Select one of these spaces and describe when and how you enter and leave it. As a group, discuss the answers to the following questions:

   a. Which cultural spaces do many students share? Which are not shared by many students?

   b. Which cultural spaces, if any, are denied to some people?

   c. What factors determine whether a person has access to a specific cultural space?

2. *Nonverbal Rules.* Choose a cultural space that you are interested in studying. Visit this space on four occasions to observe how people there interact. Focus on one aspect of nonverbal communication (e.g., eye contact or proximity). List some rules that seem to govern this aspect of nonverbal communication. For example, if you are focusing on proximity, you might describe, among other things, how far apart people tend to stand when conversing. Based on your observations, list some prescriptions about proper (expected) nonverbal behavior in this cultural space. Share your conclusions with the class. To what extent do other students share your conclusions? Can we generalize about nonverbal rules in cultural spaces? What factors influence whether an individual follows unspoken rules of behavior?

KEY WORDS

chronemics (289)	eye contact (287)	noncontact cultures (285)
contact cultures (285)	expectancy violations	paralinguistics (288)
cultural space (275)	theory (278)	polychronic (289)
deception (278)	facial expressions (279)	postmodern cultural
discrimination (294)	monochronic (289)	spaces (304)

regionalism (302)
relational messages (277)
semiosis (295)
semiotics (295)

signified (295)
signifiers (295)
signs (295)
status (278)

vocalizations (288)
voice qualities (288)

REFERENCES

Acheson, C. (2007). Silence in dispute. In C. S. Beck (Ed.), *Communication Yearbook 31* (pp. 2–59), New York: Lawrence Erlbaum Associates.

Alberts, J. K., Nakayama, T. K., & Martin, J. N. (2007). *Human communication in society*. Boston, MA: Allyn-Bacon.

Al-Simadi, F. A. (2000). Jordanian students' beliefs about nonverbal behaviors associated with deception in Jordan. *Social Behavior and Personality, 28*(5), 437–442.

Andersen, P. A., Hecht, M. L., Hoobler, G. D., & Smallwood, M. (2002). Nonverbal communication across cultures. In W. B. Gudykunst & B. Mody (Eds.), *Handbook of international and intercultural communication* (2nd ed., pp. 89–106). Thousand Oaks, CA: Sage.

Archer, D. (1997). Unspoken diversity: Cultural differences in gestures. *Qualitative Sociology, 20,* 79–105.

Banning the burqa a bad idea . . . whose time may soon come in parts of Europe. (2010, May 15). *Economist, 395*(8682), 16–18.

Bänziger, T., Patel, S., & Scherer, K. R. (2014). The role of perceived voice and speech characteristics in vocal emotion communication. *Journal of Nonverbal Behavior, 38,* 31–52.

Bello, R. S., Brandau-Brown, F. E., Zhang, S., & Ragsdale, J. D. (2010). Verbal and nonverbal methods for expressing appreciation in friendships and romantic relationships: A cross-cultural comparison. *International Journal of Intercultural Relations, 34,* 294–302.

Bente, G., Heuschner, H., Al Issa, A., & Blascovich, J. J. (2010). The others: Universals and cultural specificities in the perception of status and dominance from nonverbal behavior. *Consciousness and Cognition, 19*(3), 762–777

Boyd, D. (2007). Why youth (heart) social network sites: The role of networked publics in teenage social life. In D. Buckingham (Ed.), *Youth, identity, and digital media* (MacArthur Foundation Series on Digital Learning). Cambridge, MA: MIT Press.

Braithwaite, C. A. (1990). Communicative silence: A cross-cultural study of Basso's hypothesis. In D. Carbaugh (Ed.), *Cultural communication and intercultural contact* (pp. 321–327). Hillsdale, NJ: Lawrence Erlbaum.

Bruni, F. (2013, September 2). Traveling without seeing. *www.nytimes.com.* Retrieved May 27, 2016, from http://www.nytimes.com/2013/09/03/opinion/bruni -traveling-without-seeing.html?_r=0.

Burack, A. (2011, March 18). District Attorney George Gascón says hate crimes on the rise in San Francisco. *San Francisco Examiner online.* Retrieved August 30, 2011, from www.sfexaminer.com/local/crime /2011/03/district-attorney-gasc-n-says-hate-crimes -rise-san-francisco.

Burgoon, J. K. (1995). Cross-cultural and intercultural applications of expectancy violations theory. In R. L. Wiseman (Ed.), *Intercultural communication theory* (International and Intercultural Communication Annual, vol. 19, pp. 194–214). Thousand Oaks, CA: Sage.

Burgoon, J., Proudfoot, J., Schuetzler, R., & Wilson, D. (2014). Patterns of nonverbal behavior associated with truth and deception: Illustrations from three experiments. *Journal of Nonverbal Behavior, 38*(3), 325–354.

Carbaugh, D. (1999). "Just listen": "Listening" and landscape among the Blackfeet. *Western Journal of Communication, 63*(3), 250–270.

Carbaugh, D., & Berry, M. (2001). Communicating history, Finnish and American discourses: An ethnographic contribution to intercultural communication inquiry. *Communication Theory, 11,* 352–366.

Carroll, R. (2016, April 19). "Hope everyone pukes on your artisanal treats": Fighting gentrification, LA-style. *www.theguardian.com.* Retrieved May 27, 2016, from http://www.theguardian.com/us-news/2016/apr/19 /los-angeles-la-gentrification-resistance-boyle-heights.

Chang, H. (1997). Language and words: Communication in the analects of Confucius. *Journal of Language and Social Psychology, 16,* 107–131.

Checkpoints: Baghdad's Russian Roulette. (2007, September 5). Institute for War and Peace Reporting. Retrieved March 17, 2008, from www.iwpr.net/?p =icr&s=f&o=337693&apc_state=henficr337691.

Chu, V. (2013, November 25). The 10 worst diplomatic faux pas by famous politicians. *www.Listverse .com.* Retrieved April 16, 2016, from http://listverse .com/2013/11/25/the-10-worst-diplomatic-faux-pas -by-famous-politicians/.

Cooke, B. (1972). Nonverbal communication among Afro-Americans: An initial classification. In T. Kochman (Ed.), *Rappin' and stylin' out: Communication in urban Black America* (pp. 32–64). Urbana, IL: University of Illinois Press.

Costa-Lascoux, J., & Yu-Sion, L. (1995). *Paris-XIIIe, lumières d'Asie.* Paris: Éditions Autrement.

Covarrubias, P. (2007). (Un)Biased in Western theory: Generative silence in American Indian communication. *Communication Monographs, 74*(2), 265–271.

Croucher, S. M. (2008). French-Muslims and the hijab: An analysis of identity and the Islamic veil in France. *Journal of Intercultural Communication Research, 37*(3), 199–213.

Davis, O. I. (1999). In the kitchen: Transforming the academy through safe spaces of resistance. *Western Journal of Communication, 63*(3), 364–381.

Dougherty, C. & Isaac, M. (2016, March 3). SCSW addresses online harassment of women in gaming. *www.nytimes.com.* Retrieved May 30, 2016, from http://www.nytimes.com/2016/03/14/technology/sxsw-addresses-online-harassment-of-women-in-gaming.html?_r=0.

Drzewiecka, J. A., & Nakayama, T. K. (1998). City sites: Postmodern urban space and the communication of identity. *Southern Communication Journal, 64,* 20–31.

Du, S., Tao, Y, & Martinez, A. M. (2014). Compound facial expressions of emotion. *Proceedings of the National Academy of Sciences, 111*(15), 1454–1462.

Ekman, P. (2003). *Emotions revealed: Recognizing faces and feelings to improve communication and emotional life.* New York: Times Books.

Fattah, H. M. (2005, May 1). Why Arab men hold hands. *The New York Times,* Week in Review, 2.

Fisher, M. L. & Voracek, M. (2006). The shape of beauty: Determinants of female physical attractiveness. *Journal of Cosmetic Dermatology, 5*(2), 190–194.

Floyd, K., Ramirez, A., & Burgoon, J. K. (2008). Expectancy violations theory. In L. K. Guerrero, J. A. DeVito, & M. L. Hecht (Eds.), *The nonverbal communication reader: Classic and contemporary readings* (3rd ed., pp. 503–510). Prospect Heights, IL: Waveland.

Fussell, P. (1983). *Class.* New York: Ballantine Books.

Galati, D., Sini, B., Schmidt, S., & Tinti, C. (2003). Spontaneous facial expressions in congenitally blind and sighted children aged 8–11. *Journal of Visual Impairment and Blindness, 97,* 418–428.

Gottschall, J. (2008). The "beauty myth" is no myth. *Human Nature, 19*(2), 174–188.

Green, D. M., & Stewart, F. R. (2011). African American students' reactions to Benjamin Cooke's "Nonverbal communication among Afro-Americans: An initial classification." *Journal of Black Studies, 42*(3), 389–401.

Greene, H. (1991). Charleston, South Carolina. In J. Preston (Ed.), *Hometowns: Gay men write about where they belong* (pp. 55–67). New York: Dutton.

Gudykunst, W. B. (1985). A model of uncertainty reduction in intergroup encounters. *Journal of Language and Social Psychology, 4,* 79–98.

Gudykunst, W. B. (2005). An anxiety/uncertainty management (AUM) theory of effective communication: Making the mesh of the net finer. In W. B. Gudykunst (Ed.), *Theorizing about intercultural communication* (pp. 281–323). Thousand Oaks, CA: Sage.

Hall, E. T. (1966). *The hidden dimension.* New York: Anchor Books.

Hampton, K. N., Goulet, L. S., Marlow, C., & Rainie, L. (2012). Why most Facebook uers get more than they give. Retrieved November 16, 2016, from http://www.pewinternet.org/2012/02/03/why-most-facebook-users-get-more-than-they-give/

Høgh-Olesen, H. (2008). Human spatial behaviour: The spacing of people, objects, and animals in six cross-cultural samples. *Journal of Cognition & Culture, 8*(3/4), 245–280.

hooks, b. (1990). *Yearning: Race, gender, and cultural politics.* Boston, MA: South End Press.

Jack, R. E., Garrod, O. G. B., Yub, H., Caldarac. R, & Schyns, P. G. (2012). Facial expressions of emotion are not culturally universal. *Proceedings of the National Academy of Sciences, 109*(19), 7241–7244.

James Bond's body language. (2015, January 24). *The Economist, 414*(8922), p. 24.

Johnson, A. (2017). *Privilege, power and difference,* (3rd ed.). New York: McGraw-Hill.

Kim, M.-S. (2001). *Non-Western perspectives on human communication.* Thousand Oaks, CA: Sage.

Kross, E., Verduyn, P., Demiralp, E., Park, J., Lee, D. S., Lin, N., Shablack, H., Jonides, J., & Ybarra, O. (2013). Facebook use predicts decline in subjective well-being in young adults. *PLOS One, 8*(8): e69841.

Khuri, F. I. (2001). *The body in Islamic culture.* London: Saqi Books.

Kochman, T. (Ed.). (1972). *Rappin' and stylin' out: Communication in urban Black America.* Urbana, IL: University of Illinois Press.

Kyrnin, J. Color symbolism chart by culture. Retrieved March 3, 2008, from http://webdesign.about.com/od/color/a/bl_colorculture.htm.

Lam, B (2016). When resumes are made "whiter" to please potential employers. *the atlantic.com.* Retrieved April 16, 2016, from http://www.theatlantic.com/business/archive/2016/03/white-resume-diversity/475032.

Loewen, J. (2005). *Sundown towns: A hidden dimension of American racism.* New York: New Press.

Malcolm X, & Haley, A. (1964). *The autobiography of Malcolm X.* New York: Grove Press.

Maluso, D. (1995). Shaking hands with a clenched fist: Interpersonal racism. In B. Lott & D. Maluso (Eds.), *The social psychology of interpersonal discrimination* (pp. 50–79). New York: Guilford.

Marsiglia, F. F., & Hecht, M. L. (1998). Personal and interpersonal interventions. In M. L. Hecht (Ed.), *Communicating prejudice* (pp. 287–301). Thousand Oaks, CA: Sage.

Matsumoto, D. (2006). Culture and nonverbal behavior. In V. Manusov & M. Patterson (Eds), *The Sage handbook of nonverbal communication* (pp. 219–235). Thousand Oaks, CA: Sage.

Montepare, J. M. (2003). Evolution and nonverbal behavior: Adaptive social interaction strategies. *Journal of Nonverbal Behavior, 27,* 141–143.

Nee, V. G., & Nee, B. D. B. (1974). *Longtime Californ': A documentary study of an American Chinatown.* Boston, MA: Houghton Mifflin.

Park, H. S. & Guan, X. (2009). Cross-cultural comparison of verbal and nonverbal strategies of apologizing. *Journal of International and Intercultural Communication, 2*(1), 66–87.

Park J, Baek, Y., & Cha, M. (2014). Cross-cultural comparison of nonverbal cues in emoticons on Twitter: Evidence from big data analysis. *Journal of Communication, 64*(2), 333–354.

Patterson, M. L. (2003). Commentary: Evolution and nonverbal behavior: Functions and mediating processes. *Journal of Nonverbal Behavior, 27,* 201–207.

Peake, B. (2012). Listening, language and colonialism on Main Street, Gibraltar. *Communication and Critical/Cultural Studies, 9*(3), 171–191.

Pollick, A. S., Jeneson, A., & de Waal, F. B. M. (2008). Gestures and multimodal signaling in bonobos. In T. Furuichi & J. Thompson (Eds.), *Bonobos: Behaviour, ecology, and conservation.* New York: Springer.

Preston, J. (1991). Introduction. In J. Preston (Ed.), *Hometowns: Gay men write about where they belong* (pp. xi–xiv). New York: Dutton.

Preuschoft, S. (2000). Primate faces and facial expressions. *Social Research, 67,* 245–271.

Proust, M. (1981). *Swann in love: Remembrance of things past* (C. K. S. Moncrieff & T. Kilmartin, Trans.). New York: Vintage.

Pruden, G. B., Jr. (1990). History of the Chinese in Savannah, Georgia. In J. Goldstein (Ed.), *Georgia's East Asian connection: Into the twenty-first century: Vol. 27. West Georgia College studies in the social sciences* (pp. 17–34). Carrollton, GA: West Georgia College.

Ray, G. B., & Floyd, K. (2006). Nonverbal expressions of liking and disliking in initial interaction: Encoding and decoding perspectives. *Southern Communication Journal, 71*(1), 45–65.

Richeson, J., & Shelton, J. N. (2005). Brief report: Thin slices of racial bias. *Journal of Nonverbal Behavior, 29,* 75–86.

Ridge, S. (2015, January 29). Make no mistake: Michelle Obama's Saudi Arabia headscarf snub was deliberate and brilliant. *www.telegraph.co.uk.com.* Retrieved April 16, 2016, from http://www.telegraph.co.uk/women/womens-politics/11376192/Michelle-Obamas-Saudia-Arabia-headscarf-snub-was-deliberate.html.

Robins-Early, N. (2016, March 23). Why focusing on Brussels' Molenbeek neighborhood misses the point about terrorism. *www.huffingtonpost.com.* Retrieved May 27, 2016, from http://www.huffingtonpost.com/entry/brussels-attack-isis_us_56f2db1ce4b02c402f6616d0.

Roediger, D. R. (2005). *Working toward whiteness: How America's immigrants became white.* New York: Basic Books, 2005.

Running for cover. (2010, May 15). *Economist, 395*(8682), 66–67.

Sajavaara, K., & Lehtonen, J. (1997). The silent Finn revisited. In A. Jaworski (Ed.), *Silence: Interdisciplinary perspectives* (pp. 263–283). New York: Mouton de Gruyter.

Sauter, D. A., Eisner, F., Ekman, P., & Scott, S. K. (2010). Cross-cultural recognition of basic emotions through nonverbal emotional vocalizations. *Proceedings of the National Academy of Sciences of the United States of America, 107*(6), 2408–2412.

Saylor, S. (1991). Amethyst, Texas. In J. Preston (Ed.), *Hometowns: Gay men write about where they belong* (pp. 119–135). New York: Dutton.

Schiefenhovel, W. (1997). Universals in interpersonal interactions. In U. Segerstråle & P. Molnár (Eds.), *Nonverbal communication: Where nature meets culture* (pp. 61–79). Mahwah, NJ: Lawrence Erlbaum.

Shannon, M. L., & Stark, C. P. (2003). The influence of physical appearance on personnel selection. *Social Behavior & Personality: An International Journal, 31*(6), 613–624.

Smith, A. (2016, May 19). Shared, collaborative and on demand: The new digital economy. *www.pewinternet.org.* Retrieved May 30, 2016, from http://www.pewinternet.org/2016/05/19/the-new-digital-economy/.

Smith, R. J., & Tyson, A. S. (2005, March 7). Shootings by U.S. at Iraq checkpoints questioned page. *Washington Post,* p. A01. Retrieved March 17, 2008, from www.washingtonpost.com/wp-dyn/articles/A12507-2005Mar6.html.

Sniffen, M. J. (2005, August 24). Race disparity seen during traffic stops. The Associated Press News Service.

Sudip, M. (2004, January 26). A hairy situation. *Newsweek,* p. 12.

Sue, D. W. (2010). *Microaggressions in everyday life: Race, gender, and sexual orientation.* New York: John Wiley & Sons.

Suomi, S. J. (1988). Nonverbal communication in nonhuman primates: Implications for the emergence of culture. In U. Segerstråle & P. Molnár (Eds.), *Nonverbal communication: Where nature meets culture* (pp. 131–150). Mahwah, NJ: Lawrence Erlbaum.

Swami, V., Caprario, C., & Tovée, M. J. (2006). Female physical attractiveness in Britain and Japan: A cross-cultural study. *European Journal of Personality, 20,* 69–81.

Swami, V., Smith, J., Tsiokris, A., Georgiades, C., Sangareau, Y., Tovée, M. J., & Furnham, A. (2007). Male physical attractiveness in Britain and Greece: A cross-cultural study. *Journal of Social Psychology, 147*(1), 15–26.

Swami, V., Furnham, A., Chamorro-Premuzic, T., Akbar, K., Gordon, N., Harris, T., Finch, J., & Tovée, M. J. (2010). More than just skin deep? Personality information influences men's ratings of the attractiveness of women's body sizes. *Journal of Social Psychology, 150*(6), 628–647.

Szarota, P. (2010). The mystery of the European smile: A comparison based on individual photographs provided by Internet users. *Journal of Nonverbal Behavior, 34*(4), 249–256.

Teske, J. A. (2002). Cyberpsychology, human relationships and our virtual interiors. *Zygon, 37,* 677–700.

Tharoor, I. (2016, January 26). Italy covers up nude marble statues for Iranian president's visit. *www .washingtonpost.com.* Retrieved May 27, 2016, from https://www.washingtonpost.com/news/worldviews /wp/2016/01/26/italy-covers-up-nude-marble-statues -for-iranian-presidents-visit/.

Thompson, H. (2011, April 4). Two thirds Brits want burqa ban. *Yougov.com.* Retrieved August 5, 2011, from http://today.yougov.co.uk/life/two-thirds-brits -want-burqa-ban.

Traub, J. (2016, April 4). The dark history of defending the "Homeland". *www.nytimes.com.* Retrieved May 31, 2016, from http://www.nytimes.com/2016/04/10 /magazine/the-dark-history-of-defending-the-home-land.html?_r=1.

Vande Berg, L. R. (1999). An introduction to the special issue on "spaces." *Western Journal of Communication, 63*(3), 249.

Vrij, A., Granhag, P. A., & Mann, S. (2010). Good liars. *Journal of Psychiatry & Law, 38*(1/2), 77–98.

Weisbuch, M., Ambady, N., Clarke, A. L., Achor, S., & Weele, J. V-V. (2010). On being consistent: The role of verbal–nonverbal consistency in first impressions. *Basic & Applied Social Psychology, 32*(3), 261–268.

Weisbuch, M., & Ambady, N. (2009). Unspoken cultural influence: Exposure to and influence of nonverbal bias. *Journal of Personality and Social Psychology, 96*(6), 1104–1119.

Weisbuch, M., Pauker, K., & Ambady, N. (2009, December 18). The subtle transmission of race bias via televised nonverbal behavior. *Science, 326*(5960), 1711–1714.

Wilkins, R. (2005). The optimal form: Inadequacies and excessiveness within the *Asiallinen* [matter of fact] nonverbal style in public and civic settings in Finland. *Journal of Communication, 55,* 383–401.

Yang, P. (2010). Nonverbal gender differences: Examining gestures of university-educated Mandarin Chinese speakers. *Text & Talk, 30*(3), 333–357.

Zaretsky, R. (2010, September 17). Uncovering the French ban on veils. *Chronicle of Higher Education, 57*(4), B4–B5.

CREDITS

[page 274, text] R. J. Smith and A. S. Tyson, quote from "Shootings by U.S. at Iraq checkpoints questioned page" from *Washington Post* (March 7, 2005): A01. [page 276, text] One of our students, excerpt from "When I studied abroad … we were Americans." Original work; [page 276, text] Our student Suzanne, excerpt from "I was in Macedonia … without a seat belt." Original work; [page 277, text] Andrea, excerpt from "Student Voices: I have a couple … with the hearing?" Original work; [page 277, text] G. B. Ray and K. Floyd, quote from "Nonverbal expressions of liking and disliking in initial interaction: Encoding and decoding perspectives" from *Southern Communication Journal* (2006): 45–65. [page 281, text] S. M. Croucher, excerpt from "French-Muslims and the Hijab: An Analysis of Identity and the Islamic Veil in France" from *Journal of Intercultural Communication Research* (2008): 199–213. [page 281, text] S. M. Croucher, quote from "French-Muslims and the Hijab: An Analysis of Identity and the Islamic Veil in France" from *Journal of Intercultural Communication Research* (2008): 199–213. [page 282, text] J. Gottschall, excerpt from "The "beauty myth" is no myth" from *Human Nature* (2008): 174–188. [page 284, text] R. E. Jack, O. G. B. Garrod, H. Yub, R. Caldarac, and P. G. Schyns, quote from "Facial expressions of emotion are not culturally universal" from *Proceedings of the National Academy of Sciences* (2012): 7241–7244. [page 285, text] Our Kenyan student Gladys, excerpt from "Student Voice: At home (Kenya), when you … norm in U.S." Original work; [page 287, text] D. Archer, quote from "Unspoken diversity: Cultural differences in gestures" from *Qualitative Sociology* (1997): 79–105. [page 287, text] R. E. Axtell, excerpt from *Essential Do's and Taboos: Complete guide to international business and leisure travel.* John Wiley & Sons. [page 287, text] T. Morrison & W. A. Conaway, excerpt from *Conaway, Kiss, Bow, shake hands*. Adams Media. [page 289, text] One of our students, excerpt from "I always learned … to do something" Original work; [page 290, text] P. Covarrubias, quote from "(Un)Biased in Western theory: Generative silence in American Indian communication" from *Communication Monographs* (2007): 265–271. [page 290, text] Chris, excerpt from "Student Voice: Giving gifts seems … an extramarital affair." Original work; [page 291, text] One of our Taiwanese students, quote from "In America, sometimes … is a show-off." Original work; [page 292, text] A. Burack, excerpt from "District Attorney George Gascón says hate crimes on the rise in San Francisco" from San Francisco Examiner online (March 18, 2011). San Francisco Examiner online. [page 293, text] M. Weisbuch, and N. Ambady, excerpt from "Unspoken cultural influence: Exposure to and influence of nonverbal Bias" from *Journal of Personality and Social Psychology* (2009): 1104–1119. [page 295, text] B. Lam, quote from "When resumes are made "whiter" to please potential employers" from *the atlantic.com* (April 16, 2016). [page 296, text] Adriana, excerpt from "Student Voices: A close friend I used … person my friend was." Original work; [page 297, text] M. Proust, excerpt from *Swann in love: Remembrance of things past*. Vintage. [page 297, text] J. Preston, quote from "Introduction" in *Hometowns: Gay men write about where they belong*, edited by J. Preston. Dutton. [page 298, text] P. Fussell, quote from *Class*. Ballantine Books. [page 298, text] B. Hooks, quote from *Black looks: Race and representation*. [page 298, text] S. Saylor, quote from "Amethyst, Texas" in *Hometowns: Gay men write about where they belong*, edited by J. Preston. Dutton. [page 298, text] H. Greene, excerpt from "Charleston, South Carolina" in *Hometowns: Gay men write about where they belong*, edited by J. Preston. [page 299, text] D. R. Roediger, quote from *Working toward whiteness: How America's immigrants became white*. Basic Books. [page 300, text] X. Malcolm & A. Haley, excerpt from *The autobiography of Malcolm X*. Grove Press. [page 300, text] J. Loewen, quote from *Sundown towns: A hidden dimension of American racism*. New Press. [page 300, text] V. G. Nee & B. D. B. Nee, excerpt from *Longtime Californ': A documentary study of an American Chinatown*. Houghton Mifflin. [page 300, text] G. B. Pruden Jr., "History of the Chinese in Savannah, Georgia" in *Georgia's East Asian connection: Into the twenty-first century: Vol. 27*, edited by J. Goldstein. West Georgia College. [page 300, text] J. Costa-Lascoux and L. Yu-Sion, quote from *Paris-XIIIe, lumières d'Asie*. Éditions Autrement. [page 301, text] Excerpt from Detroityes LLC. [page 302, text] N. Robins-Early, quote from "Why focusing on Brussels' Molenbeek neighborhood misses the point about terrorism" from *huffingtonpost.com* (March 23, 2016). [page 302, text] R. Carroll, quote from "Hope everyone pukes on your artisanal treats": Fighting gentrification, LA-style" from *theguardian.com* (Apri 19, 2016). [page 303, text] F. Bruni, quote from "Traveling without seeing" from *nytimes.com* (September 2, 2013). [page 304, text] L. R. Vande Berg, quote from "An introduction to the special issue on 'spaces.'" from *Western Journal of Communication* (1999): 249. [page 304, text] Sakura, excerpt from "Student voices: Whenever I am at LAX [Los Angeles International … that I have experienced in my life." Original work; [page 305, text] D. Carbaugh, excerpt from "Just listen": "Listening" and landscape among the Blackfeet" from *Western Journal of Communication* (1999): 250–270. [page 305, text] B. Peake, quote from "Listening, language and colonialism on Main Street, Gibraltar" from *Communication and Critical/Cultural Studies* (2012): 171–191. [page 306, text] A. Smith, excerpt from "African Americans and Technology Use" from *Pew Research Center's Internet & American Life Project* (January 6, 2014). Pew Research Center's Internet & American Life Project. [page 307–308, text] O. I. Davis, quote from "In the kitchen: Transforming the academy through safe spaces of resistance." *Western Journal of Communication* (1999): 364–381.

PART III

Intercultural Communication Applications

CHAPTER 8
Understanding Intercultural Transitions

CHAPTER 9
Popular Culture and Intercultural
Communication

CHAPTER 10
Culture, Communication, and Intercultural
Relationships

CHAPTER 11
Culture, Communication, and Conflict

CHAPTER 12
Striving for Engaged and Effective
Intercultural Communication

CHAPTER

8

UNDERSTANDING INTERCULTURAL TRANSITIONS

CHAPTER OBJECTIVES

After reading this chapter, you should be able to:

1. Describe a dialectical approach to cultural transitions.
2. Identify four types of migrant groups.
3. Define cultural adaptation.
4. Identify three approaches to understanding cultural adaptation.
5. Identify individual characteristics that may influence how people adapt.
6. List outcomes of the adaptation process.
7. Define and describe the occurrence of culture shock.
8. Describe the reentry process and how it differs from adaptation to a host culture.
9. Describe a phenomenological approach to understanding cultural adaptation.
10. Describe how the adaptation process is influenced by contextual elements.
11. Explain how different approaches to adaptation are related to cultural identity.
12. Discuss the effect on the identity of living on the border and making multiple returns.

THINKING DIALECTICALLY ABOUT INTERCULTURAL TRANSITIONS

TYPES OF MIGRANT GROUPS
Voluntary Migrants
Involuntary Migrants

MIGRANT–HOST RELATIONSHIPS
Assimilation
Separation
Integration
Cultural Hybridity

CULTURAL ADAPTATION
Social Science Approach
Interpretive Approach
Critical Approach: Contextual Influences

INTERNET RESOURCES

SUMMARY

DISCUSSION QUESTIONS

ACTIVITIES

KEY WORDS

REFERENCES

In Chapter 7, we discussed how we define and move through various cultural spaces. In this chapter, we look more specifically at how we move between cultural contexts. People may travel for work, study, or adventure, or in response to political or other events. Consider the following migration stories:

My name is Valdimir. At first when I emigrate[d] to the United States . . . [from Mexico] I had many struggles . . . I did not know anybody here, did not have enough money for rent, a place to live, and pay for food; I did not understand and speak English. . . . After two weeks I got a job and my life changed; I started to earn money and rented a place to live. Then I saw that it is important to learn English, and two months later I started school. (From http://www.otan .us/webfarm/emailproject/grace.htm)

I studied abroad in Greece during my first semester freshmen year. I found it a bit shocking that so many natives spoke English, and for example, at stores people would even try to speak Greek with me. The Greeks are very kind people and I really appreciated how they live in the moment. They sit at dinner for hours chatting about life. Because of their relaxed nature, I became more appreciative of the present and have tried to instill this quality into my life even now that I am back home in the United States.

—Bakari

I had no choice. I could no longer live in Syria. Of course I knew that escaping with the help of smugglers was a matter of life or death. Nonetheless, they provide the means of reaching Europe.

In Damascus, I had long been dead anyhow. Every morning, I bade farewell to my family not knowing whether I would return again in the evening. [...] I think it is up to each person to decide and ultimately, only fate will determine the success of their journey. Any European or international activities against the smugglers have no bearing on the situation: people in need will always find a way to flee. I would do it again at any time, because in Damascus, I was long dead.

—Alaa Houd

Source: From A. Houd with D. Hodali, "I could no longer live in Syria," *Deutsche Welle,* August 15, 2015. Retrieved June 2, 2016, from http://www.dw.com/en/i-could-no-longer -live-in-syria/a-18680302.

Throughout history people have traveled across cultural boundaries for many different reasons. According to experts, there have been three great waves of global migration. The first wave was motivated by a search for resources and military conquest and lasted into the 16th century. The second, illustrated by Tamara's great-grandparents' arrival in the United States, was dominated by the European migration into poorer "empty territories" of the new world and led to the colonization of Africa, Asia, and America; it lasted until the middle of the 20th century. Valdimir's story illustrates the third wave. This wave—reversing the European colonization from the poorer countries of Asia, Africa, and South America to the richer ones in the postwar period—is more complex and multidimensional (Tehranian, 2004, p. 20).

According to the International Organization for Migration, (World Migration Report 2015), "[t]here are an estimated 232 million international migrants" (p. 2). People leave their countries for many reasons, including wars and famine (Iraq, Somalia, South Sudan, and Syria). In addition, millions of global nomads are roaming around the world as transnational corporate or government employees, guest workers, refugees, tourists, or study-abroad students, like Bakari (see Figure 8-1). According to the most recent census, the U.S. Census Bureau estimates that almost 40 million people in the United States were foreign-born (Grieco et al., 2012). And there are internal migrations—where people move from one place to another within national boundaries—often for the same reasons: for better economic opportunities or because of war or famine. The International Organization for Migration (2015) reported that there are an estimated "740 million internal migrants" (p. 2).

Perhaps you can look at your own family and think about your migration history. Perhaps your ancestors came to the United States in the second wave, from western Europe in the 1800s, or perhaps in the third wave, from Europe, Asia, or Latin or South America. Perhaps you've had a global nomad experience of studying abroad or living abroad as an exchange student.

REFUGEES AND THE PRESIDENT

As a leading recipient of refugees, the United States policy on refugees has been very welcoming. As the U.S. Department of State notes: "The United States is proud of its history of welcoming immigrants and refugees. The U.S. refugee resettlement program reflects the United States' highest values and aspirations to compassion, generosity and leadership. Since 1975, Americans have welcomed over 3 million refugees from all over the world." Unlike immigrants, refugees are long term or short-term, involuntary migrants. They were forced to flee their own countries from fear of persecution. While the overwhelming number of refugees are eventually able to return to their home countries, a very small number are resettled in third countries. The United States accepts about two-thirds of the small number of people who move to third countries. The policy in refugees is set by the U.S. president. Under President Obama, the 2017 resettlement target was increased by more than 30% to 110,000 (Amos, 2016).

The election of Donald Trump to the U.S. presidency has led to significant changes. During his campaign, he suggested that refugees might be terrorists who "could be a better, bigger more horrible version than the legendary Trojan horse ever was" and "who knows, maybe it's ISIS" (qtd. in Chanoff, 2016). As president, his executive orders have made enormous changes in refugee policy. Despite his attempts to link terrorism to refugees, terrorist attacks have not been instigated by refugees. However, the communication about refugees has changed and those changes has already impacted the movement of these involuntary migrants.

Sources: Amos, D. (2016, November 15). For refugees and advocates, an anxious wait for clarity on Trump's policy. *NPR*. Retrieved from http://www.npr.org/sections/parallels/2016/11/15/502010346/for-refugees-and-advocates-an-anxious-wait-for-clarity-on-trumps-policy

Chanoff, S. (2016, August 16). Trump, refugees and the truth. *The Boston Globe*. Retrieved from https://www.bostonglobe.com/opinion/2016/08/16/trump-refugees-and-truth/6m9eGxlS2ZnaS4yVhr7RhN/story.html

U.S. Department of State. (n.d.) Refugee admissions. Available at https://www.state.gov/j/prm/ra/

THINKING DIALECTICALLY ABOUT INTERCULTURAL TRANSITIONS

Understanding the process of adaptation in intercultural transitions depends on several dialectical tensions. Unfortunately, there are no easy answers. Think about how the privilege–disadvantage dialectic structures some kinds of intercultural transitions. For example, businesspeople who live abroad while working for transnational corporations often are economically privileged: They receive additional pay, housing relocation money, and so on. They also meet many people through work and can afford to travel in their new host location. In contrast, refugees often lack financial resources in their new host location, which may have been chosen out of sheer

RENOUNCING CITIZENSHIP

Although the number of emigrants is very small compared to the number of immigrants to the United States, "the number of Americans renouncing U.S. citizenship has gone up, up 560% from its Bush administration high" (Wood, 2016). There are probably many reasons why people decide to give up U.S. citizenship, but some point to the citizenship-based taxation system in which U.S. citizens must file and pay U.S. taxes, wherever they live, and often pay U.S. taxes on top of the taxes already paid in their country of residence. The only other country with citizenship-based taxes is Eritrea (Newlove, 2016).

Whatever reasons people may have for renouncing their U.S. citizenship, this transition to a new national identity can have an affective aspect. The emotional aspect of cultural transition points to the importance of cultural and national identity. Jane who will be going to the U.S. embassy to renounce her citizenship says, "It's not going to be easy at all. It's the last thing I ever thought of doing. I'm very proud of being an American. It's what I am when I look in the mirror. If it weren't for Fatca (the Foreign Account Tax Compliance Act) and the decision by the bank, I'd never be doing this. Never ever. It's just breaking me in half" (quoted in Newlove, 2016). Donna-Lane who lives in Switzerland decided to renounce her U.S. citizenship as her bank told her they would close her account as an American, despite also holding Swiss citizenship. She says: "I renounced my U.S. citizenship in 2011. After I did it, I was so emotional that I threw up outside the embassy. During my renunciation, I broke down. It was like getting a divorce" (Why expats are ditching, 2014).

Sources: From R. Newlove, "Why expat Americans are giving up their passports," *BBC News,* February 9, 2016. Retrieved June 10, 2016, from http://www.bbc.com/news/35383435.

"Why expats are ditching their U.S. passports," *CNN Money,* March 10, 2014. Retrieved June 10, 2016, from http://money.cnn.com/gallery/pf/2014/03/10/expat-taxes-citizenship/index.html.

From R. W. Wood, "Record numbers renounce their U.S. citizenship," *Forbes,* February 6, 2016. Retrieved June 10, 2016, from http://www.forbes.com/sites/robertwood/2016/02/06/record-numbers-renounce-their-u-s-citizenship/#5309c077a6e6.

necessity. They may have few opportunities to meet other people, travel in their new homeland, or purchase basic necessities. In this way, they may not view their new environment in the same way as a more privileged migrant. These dialectical differences shape the intercultural migrant's identity and the changes that this identity undergoes.

We might also invoke the personal–contextual dialectic. Often, in adapting to new cultural contexts, people may find themselves challenged to be culturally competent by behaving in ways that may be contradictory to their personal identities. For example, a Muslim woman may feel that she can't wear her chador in certain U.S. contexts and thus can't express her religious identity. The dialectic calls for a balance between the individual and contextual demands.

What can we learn about cultural transitions from these particular intercultural experiences? Why are some transitions easy for some people and more difficult for others? Why do some people choose to adapt and others resist adaptation? What can we learn about culture and communication from these experiences?

We begin this chapter by discussing four groups of travelers (migrants), and using a dialectical approach, we describe five ways in which migrants and hosts can relate. Then we turn our attention to the individual experience of dealing with cultural adaptation and describe three social science models of adaptation: the AUM model, the transition model, and the integrated theory of communication and cultural adaptation model. Interpretive approaches follow, which focus more on in-depth analysis and description of cultural adaptation, including culture shock and the reentry shock process. Finally, employing a critical lens, we describe the contextual elements (social institutions and political, historical, and economic structures) that influence cultural adaptation.

TYPES OF MIGRANT GROUPS

A dialectical perspective requires that we examine intercultural transitions on both a personal and a contextual level (Berry, 1992). On the personal level, we can look at individual experiences of adapting to new cultural contexts. But we also can examine the larger social, historical, economic, and political contexts in which these personal transitions occur. To understand cultural transitions, we must simultaneously consider both the individual migrant groups and the contexts in which they travel.

Migration may be long term or short term and voluntary or involuntary. A **migrant** is an individual who leaves the primary cultural contexts in which he or she was raised and moves to a new cultural context for an extended period. For instance, exchange-students' sojourns are relatively short term and voluntary, and these transitions occur within a structured sociopolitical context. In contrast, the experience of being forced to relocate because of an unstable sociopolitical context would make the sojourn a long-term one. Cultural transitions may vary in length and in degree of voluntariness. We can identify four types of migrant groups based on these criteria. (See Table 8-1.)

migrant An individual who leaves the primary cultural context in which he or she was raised and moves to a new cultural context for an extended time. (See also **immigrant** and **sojourners**.)

Voluntary Migrants

There are two groups of voluntary travelers: sojourners and immigrants. **Sojourners** are those travelers who move into new cultural contexts for a limited time and a

sojourners People who move into new cultural contexts for a limited period of time and for a specific purpose, such as for study or business.

TABLE 8-I FOUR TYPES OF MIGRANT GROUPS		
Motivation for Migration	**Short-Term Duration**	**Long-Term Duration**
Voluntary	Sojourners	Immigrant
Involuntary (Forced)	Short-term refugee	Long-term refugee

specific purpose. They are often people who have freedom and the means to travel. This includes international students who go abroad to study and technical assistance workers, corporate personnel, and missionaries who go abroad to work for a specific period. Some domestic sojourners move from one region to another within their own country for a limited time to attend school or work (e.g., Native Americans who leave their reservations).

immigrants People who come to a new country, region, or environment to settle more or less permanently.

Another type of voluntary traveler is the **immigrant,** first discussed in Chapter 1. Families who voluntarily leave one country to settle in another exemplify this type of migrant. Although many U.S. Americans believe that most immigrants come to the United States in search of freedom, the truth is that the primary reason people come to the United States is to join other family members; two other primary reasons are for employment and to escape from war, famine, or poverty. There is often a fluid and interdependent relationship between the countries that send and those that receive immigrants. Countries like the United States welcome some working immigrants, even issuing special visas and developing programs (e.g., the *bracero* program of the 1940s between the United States and Mexico) during times of economic prosperity. Currently, "Canada and the United States have 5% of the world's people and almost a quarter of the world's migrants" (Martin, 2013, p. 4). Voluntary migration has been influenced by restrictive immigration laws of various countries. In the United States, there were laws that barred various racial and ethnic groups, as well as sex workers, gays and lesbians, and many others group. Recently, foreigners who contracted HIV were similarly "told to leave the United States" (James, 2010). Today, many countries give preference to some migrants over others. For example, "Canada uses a point system to favor the entry of young and better-educated foreigners who speak English or French, while two-thirds of U.S. immigrants arrive because they have relatives in the United States" (Martin, 2013, p. 5). Similarly, "Australia and New Zealand select most of their immigrants on the basis of point systems that award points to individuals for being young, knowing English, and having skills" (Martin, 2013, p. 14). Sometimes voluntary migrants can gain permanent residency or citizenship, but sometimes they are given temporary nonimmigrant status. One example of this type of status is the H-1B visa in the United States, which is given to workers in certain occupations, including biotechnology, medicine, and other knowledge occupations.

There are two kinds of migrant labor: cheap manual labor and highly skilled intellectual labor. Newly industrializing countries need trained labor for routine and repetitive tasks, and also newly rich countries and individuals are in need of domestic services. Increasing numbers of immigrant workers are women. Because they are often more reliable than men, they are increasingly doing manual work and employed as domestics. Ehrenreich and Hochschild (2003) label this recent pattern of female migration a "worldwide gender revolution" in their book *Global Woman.* They describe how millions of women from poor countries in the south (Philippines, Sri Lanka, and India) migrate to do the "women's work" of the north (North America, Europe, and the Middle East)—work that middle- and upper-class women are no longer able or willing to do. For example, Mexican and Latin

American women are the domestics for U.S. women; Asian migrant women work in British homes; North African women work in French homes; Turkish women in German homes; Filipinas work in Spain, Italy, and Greece; and Filipino, Indian, and Sri Lankan women travel to Saudi Arabia to work. Ehrenreich and Hochschild raise many issues concerning this migration, one of which is who is taking care of the nanny's children. Most of these women leave their own children to care for the children of their employer.

More and more people are moving temporarily. Overseas study options are increasing, and today some 40% of Australia's skilled migrants are drawn from the overseas student cohort, with similar trends in Canada, the United States, and Europe. A core principle of the 27 countries who belong to the European Union (EU) is "freedom of movement," meaning that an EU national may travel to another EU member state and live, study, or work on an equal basis with native-born residents. For example, a French worker who applies for a job at Volkswagen in Germany must be treated just like a German applicant and can complain if a private employer discriminates in favor of local workers (Martin & Zürcher, 2008).

Involuntary Migrants

As shown in Table 8-1, two types of migrants move involuntarily: **long-term refugees** and **short-term refugees.** According to the United Nations High Commissioner for Refugees (UNHCR), in 2015 an estimated 65 million people worldwide were forced to flee their homes. As involuntary migrants, they "were forcibly displaced worldwide as a result of persecution, conflict, generalized violence, or human rights violations" (p. 8). The top countries hosting refugees were Turkey, Pakistan, Lebanon, Iran, and Ethiopia. This is the first time that "Turkey became the largest refugee-hosting country worldwide" (p. 9). The top countries where refugees come from are Syria, Afghanistan, and Somalia.

Some of these refugees seek asylum or refugee status in other countries and, if successful, they become long-term refugees. Some countries received more claims than others: "With 274,700 asylum claims, the Russian Federation was the world's largest recipient of new individual applications, followed by Germany (173,100), the United States of America (121,200), and Turkey (87,800)" (p. 10).

In 2015 there were also an estimated 38.2 million internally displaced people (IDPs), the highest number recorded by the UNHCR. IDPs are people who are refugees within their own countries, due to conflicts, war, famine, or natural disasters. Of these, the UNHCR is assisting and protecting 32.3 million. The largest number of IDPs is in Syria, followed by Colombia, Iraq, and the Democratic Republic of the Congo (p. 35).

Many refugees want to return home, but due to the recent global situation, only 126,800 returned to their country of origin, which "is the lowest number recorded since 1983" (p. 42). As the UNHCR notes, "war and the general political insecurity witnessed around the world in recent years have contributed to the prevailing trends" (p. 42). As the situation worldwide changes, these trends will also be impacted.

long-term refugees
People who are forced to relocate permanently because of war, famine, and oppression.

short-term refugees
People who are forced for a short time to move from their region or country.

IMMIGRATION STORIES

There are many online sites where immigrants and refugees tell their stories. As long-term voluntary migrants, immigrant stories share some similarities and differences from refugees who are long-term and short-term involuntary migrants. The University of Minnesota has an Immigration History Research Center. One of their projects is to create digital stories from recent immigrants and refugees. Listen to some of the stories at: http://cla.umn.edu/ihrc/research/immigrant -stories

The United Nations High Commission for Refugees (UNHCR) also hosts a site with refugee stories. Listen to some of these stories at: http://stories.unhcr.org/us

There are many more website with stories of migrants (voluntary and involuntary). As you listen to their stories, what do we learn from their experiences? What kinds of intercultural lessons might we learn?

One of our students, Naida, describes how her family fled Bosnia to become refugees and then immigrants in the United States:

> *During the year 1992, civil war erupted in my home country, Bosnia. Overnight my life shifted from a peaceful existence to fear, persecution, and anxiety. My family and I were forcefully taken to a concentration camp, where we witnessed the blind rage of mankind expressed through physical and mental abuses, humiliation, destruction, rapes, and killings. Six months later, we were among the 5,000 people released. We returned home to fight for simple survival. At the age of 16, I found myself spending my days planning ways for my family to escape. My family and I were again forced from our home and experienced three years of uncertainty, fear and anger. The life we knew and had taken for granted was abruptly changed by others' political agendas. Having our basic human rights violated was the experience that literally changed my life.*

Her family was eventually rescued by the International Red Cross in 1995 and transported to Phoenix, Arizona.

There are also cases of domestic refugees who are forced, for short or indefinite periods, to move within a country. Examples include the Japanese Americans sent to internment camps during World War II; the Cherokees forcibly removed in 1838 from their own nation, New Echota, to Oklahoma (the devastating Trail of Tears); and the Mormons, who fled the East and eventually settled in Utah and elsewhere in the West. Populations also relocate temporarily because of natural disasters, such as hurricanes or floods. This mass migration of refugees presents complex issues for intercultural communication, pointing to the importance of the relationship between the migrants and their host cultures.

MIGRANT–HOST RELATIONSHIPS

The relationships between immigrants and their hosts are very complex, and understanding these relationships requires a dialectical approach. International migration is usually a carefully considered individual or family decision (see Figure 8-2). The major reasons to migrate can involve economic and/or noneconomic reasons and complex push–pull (dialectical) factors. An economic migrant may be encouraged to move by a host employer recruiter—pulling him or her to migrate, or a push factor might be lack of jobs in the home country. Migrants crossing borders for noneconomic reasons may be moving to escape persecution—a push factor. One of the most important noneconomic motivations for crossing national borders is family unification—a pull factor for family migration (Martin & Zürcher, 2008). Once in the host country, the migrant may face a range of reactions from people there. For example, in Arizona and many other states, business interests depend on cheap labor provided by Mexican immigrants; the general

FIGURE 8-2   U.S. Customs inspectors check trunks of cars and they approach U.S. border from Canada Int'l Peace Bridge Buffalo, NY.
(© Joe Traver/Liaison Agency/Getty Images)

economy also depends on dollars spent by immigrants. At the same time, citizens may fear the consequences of rising illegal immigration and the pressure on the medical, social, and educational systems. The immigrants may be simultaneously accepted and rejected, privileged and disadvantaged, and relationships may be both static and dynamic. These relationships have implications for intercultural as described in the research studies discussed in Chapter 2.

Migrant–host relationships exist in multiple tensions: The migrants want to cherish and retain their own culture as well as value their host culture. The host culture also may be motivated to accept or reject the new migrants. When migrants value the host culture more than their own, they assimilate. When migrants value their heritage culture more than the host, they separate. When migrants value both the host and their heritage culture, they integrate. Of course, we must also consider the reception of the host culture toward the migrants. Scholars point out that many migrant experiences do not fit neatly into one of these types—migrants may shift from one to the other depending on the context—resulting in cultural hybridity (Rosenau, 2004). Let's examine each of these relationships more closely.

Assimilation

assimilation A type of cultural adaptation in which an individual gives up his or her own cultural heritage and adopts the mainstream cultural identity. (See **cultural adaptation.**)

In an **assimilation** mode, the individual does not want to maintain an isolated cultural identity but wants to maintain relationships with other groups in the new culture. The migrant is more or less welcomed by the new cultural hosts. When this course is freely chosen by everyone, it creates the archetypal "melting pot." The central focus in assimilation is not on retaining one's cultural heritage. Many immigrant groups, particularly those from Europe, follow this mode of adapting in North America. For them, assimilating may not require adjusting to new customs. The same religions dominate, eating practices (the use of forks, knives, and spoons) are the same, and many other cultural practices (clearly originated in Europe) are already familiar. However, when the dominant group forces assimilation, especially on immigrants whose customs are different from those of the host society, it creates a "pressure cooker." This mode of relating often entails giving up or losing many aspects of the original culture, including language. One of our students, Rick, describes the process:

> I am Mexican American and I grew up in a household where we took part in cultural events, but we never discussed why we did them. I am always asked if I know how to speak Spanish. I guess people ascribe this to my appearance. My parents speak Spanish fluently, as well as English, but they never taught my siblings or myself because they did not want us to have any problems when we entered school, as they did.

Some people question why immigrants need to give up so much to assimilate. As one of our students said, "Why must we lose our history to fit into the American way of life? I suppose that, because race is such a sensitive issue in our country, by not discussing culture and race we feel it makes the issue less volatile." A recent study of African Americans and Hispanic Americans showed the effects of society's pressure on groups to assimilate. According to the study, the more experiences people had with ethnic or racial discrimination (on the job, in public settings, in housing, and in dealings with police), the less importance they assigned to maintaining their own cultural heritage. This suggests that heavy doses of discrimination can discourage retention of immigrants' original cultural practices (Ruggiero, Taylor, & Lambert, 1996).

In contrast, the integration and assimilation process can be difficult and complicated for some migrants. When people move from one cultural environment to another, most people understand the need to change some of their cultural views. Two examples in Arizona highlight the problem of not adjusting to the new cultural environment. In 2012, Aiya Altameemi was beaten by her family after "leaving her high school with a young man." The mother told police "she hit her daughter because she 'was speaking to a male subject and her Iraq culture states a female is not allowed to be having contact with males because females are not allowed to have boyfriends'" (Schwartz, 2012).

In 2011, Faleh Hassan Almaleki was convicted and sent to prison for more than 34 years after killing his own daughter. According to police, he "believed his daughter had become 'too Westernized' and had abandoned 'traditional' Iraqi values" (Iraqi immigrants gets 34 years, 2011). In both cases, the family members were upset that their daughters were not following Iraqi culture, despite not living in an Iraqi cultural environment.

It should be noted, however, that the inability to adjust to a new cultural environment is not common and that: "The Council on American-Islamic Relations in Washington, D.C., has said such cases are isolated instances that occur sporadically and are widely chastised by the American Muslim community" (Schwartz, 2012). Again, we see a dialectical relationship between assimilation and resistance to assimilation. The advantages and disadvantages of various aspects of assimilation must always be kept in mind.

Separation

There are two forms of **separation.** The first is when migrants choose to retain their original culture and avoid interaction with other groups. This is the mode followed by groups like the Amish, who came to the United States from Europe in the 18th century. They maintain their own way of life and identity and avoid prolonged contact with other groups. Many strict religious groups actively resist the influence of the dominant society. The Amish, for example, do not participate in U.S. popular culture; they don't have televisions or radios, go to movies, or read mainstream newspapers or books. An important point here is that these groups choose separation, and the dominant society respects their choice.

More recently, the 2010 census shows increasing residential segregation. Despite the overall increasing diversity of the U.S. population, "The average non-Hispanic white person continues to live in a neighborhood that looks very different from neighborhoods where the average black, Hispanic and Asian live. Average whites in metropolitan America live in a neighborhood that's 74% white" (El Nasser, 2010). As laws barring various racial or ethnic groups

separation A type of cultural adaptation in which an individual retains his or her original culture while interacting minimally with other groups. Separation may be initiated and enforced by the dominant society, in which case it becomes segregation.

FIGURE 8-3 These migrant farm workers are picking grapes. How does their socioeconomic status influence their intercultural encounters? (© *Ingram Publishing RF*)

from living in certain areas have been struck down, the desire to live in separate neighborhoods may explain this phenomenon. Not only might the minority cultural group choose to live separately, but the dominant cultural group might also choose to live mostly among others of their group. An important point here is that these groups *choose* separation, and the dominant society respects, or accepts, their choice.

segregation The policy or practice of compelling groups to live apart from each other.

However, if such separation is initiated and enforced by the dominant society, the condition constitutes a second type of separation, **segregation** (see Figure 8-3). Many cities and states in the United States historically had quite restrictive codes that dictated where members of various racial and ethnic groups could and could not live. For example, Oregon passed legislation in 1849 excluding blacks from the state; it was not repealed until 1926 (Henderson, 1999, p. 74). You may recall the excerpt in Chapter 7 from Malcolm X's autobiography in which he notes that his family could not live in East Lansing, Michigan, because it was for whites only. An example of de facto segregation is the practice of redlining, in which banks refuse loans to members of particular ethnic groups. This practice was explicitly practiced by the U.S. Federal Housing Authority (FHA) and has perpetuated ethnic segregation.

Native American reservations are another example of segregation: These tribes were forced to give up their ancestral lands and live on a designated parcel of land away from the rest of U.S. society. Jewish ghettos in Europe also have a long history of segregation.

Does this French paradox of assimilation (erasure of differences) versus nondiscrimination (respect for differences) function in other nations? How about the United States?

One of the interesting aspects of immigration in France is that it high-lights the tension between integration and antidiscrimination. Like other countries, France has at times been in the business of soliciting immigrants, but not just any immigrants. Of course, as we saw with Australia, a country can't just pick and choose its immigrants, unless it has the will and the capacity to fiercely enforce its borders against irregular migration. And so France, in recognition of this reality and with its high degree of cultural self-regard, adopted an aggressive stance on integration. Patrick Simon, the head of France's National Institute for Demographic Studies, explained that by the 2005 "inte-gration contract," would-be immigrants were checked on "integration skills" such as knowledge of French values and norms, and linguistic proficiency. Integration was thereby not just an abstract concept or a vague policy goal: it was a selection criterion. "The idea is to produce invisibility," said Mr Simon, "invisibility so equality will be reached."

But there is an implicit contradiction between integration, says Mr Simon, and the antidiscrimination provisions France has also adopted. Integration aims to try to change immigrants, to make them the same as other French people; antidiscrimination rules are meant to change the system, to accommodate people who aren't the same. This mixed message from the state has contributed to the tensions that are apparent over, for example, whether women should be allowed to wear the burqa in public. And homogeneity is harder for some groups to achieve than others. Mr Simon said that in his research, surveys had found that although most foreign-born French people say that they feel French, fully half of the racial minorities—people from Africa, the French Caribbean, and Arabs—said that they do not feel that other people see them as French.

Source: From E. G. Austin, "Immigration: The French Paradox and the British Backlash," *The Economist,* May 24, 2011. Retrieved June 3, 2011, from www.economist.com/blogs /democracyinamerica/2011/05/immigration_1.

Segregation is not uniquely American. Under apartheid in South Africa, racial segregation was the established legal norm. Today in Israel we find that: "Segrega-tion of Jews and Arabs in Israel of 2010 is almost absolute. For those of us who live here, it is something we take for granted. But visitors from abroad cannot believe their eyes: segregated education, segregated businesses, separate entertainment ven-ues, different languages, separate political parties . . . and of course, segregated hous-ing" (Sulitzeanu, 2010). The case of Israel highlights the complexity of these terms, because there is little effort and desire to integrate on both sides. Hence, both types of separation can work together in establishing how we live.

Some people, realizing they have been excluded from the immigrant advancement version of the melting pot by legal or informal discriminatory practices, in turn promote a separate mode of relating to the host culture. They may demand group rights and recognition but not assimilation.

Integration

integration A type of cultural adaptation in which individuals maintain both their original culture and their daily interactions with other groups. (See also **cultural adaptation**.)

Integration occurs when migrants have an interest both in maintaining their original culture and language and in having daily interactions with other groups. This differs from assimilation; in that it involves a greater interest in maintaining one's own cultural identity. Immigrants can resist assimilation in many ways—for example, by insisting on speaking their own language in their home. One immigrant from Ghana, Meri, describes her home:

> *English was spoken only in the presence of people who could not communicate in any of our languages (Ga or Twi). It wasn't as if my parents forbade me to speak English, but if I addressed either of them in English, the response I got was always in Ga. . . . My mother still insists upon conversing with me in Ga. When it appeared as though I was losing fluency, she became adamant and uncompromising about this; in her mind, to forget one's mother tongue was to place the final sever in the umbilical cord. I do believe that she was right, but over the years I have praised and cursed her for this. (quoted in O'Hearn, 1998, p. 102)*

Meri also describes how her family participated in other aspects of American life, such as enjoying American music: "We listened to reggae, calypso, high life, jazz and sometimes R&B. We listened to country music—Kenny Rogers and Willie Nelson" (p. 103).

Other immigrants, like Asian Indians in the United States, maintain a strong sense of their ethnic identity by celebrating Indian holidays like Navarātrī, the Hindu festival that celebrates cosmic good over evil. Communication scholar Radha Hegde (2000) describes how these kinds of celebrations

> *provide a connection and sense of affirmation to immigrants, playing an important part in the process of redefining selfhood and establishing a sense of community in the new environment. . . . To immigrants like myself, these are opportunities to enjoy being Indian and to savor the colors, clothes, tastes, and sounds of a home left behind. (p. 129)*

Migrant communities can actively resist assimilation in many ways. They may refuse to consume popular culture products (TV, radio, movies) or the fashions of the host society, often for many generations. In any case, integration depends on the openness and willingness of those in the dominant society to accept and accommodate somewhat the cultures of others. For example, an interesting debate is occurring in the multicultural city of Liverpool, England. There are currently 122 ethnic support groups, from the Afro-Caribbean lunch club to a forum for Chinese diabetics, and local state-funded "faith schools" can select students according to their religious background. However, when the town was considering "women only" nights at the local swimming pools (in deference to the religious traditions of local Muslims), city officials published guidelines to restrict using public money on projects that "might unnecessarily keep people apart." The challenge for host and immigrant groups is to find the balance of "integration," somewhere between segregation and assimilation ("The search for social glue," 2008).

Cultural Hybridity

Migrants and their family often combine these different modes of relating to the host society—at times assimilating, other times integrating, and still other times separating, forming a cultural hybridity relationship with the host culture. They may desire economic assimilation (via employment), linguistic integration (bilingualism), and social separation (marrying someone from the same group and socializing only with members of their own group), producing not the "melting pot" society where everyone was supposed to try to become the same, but rather a "salad" society, where each group retains a distinctive flavor but blends together to make up one great society. Different societies are taking different approaches. (See Point of View on the French approach to integration, p. 329.)

Many people in today's world who consider themselves the product of many cultures, not easily fitting into any of the categories, are also cultural hybrids. Consider the case of Virginia:

> *I was born in Argentina, my entire family is Argentinean, and culturally I have been raised Argentinean. Yet at age four I moved out of Argentina and only returned on vacations. I grew up in Panama until I was thirteen and then moved to California. So where does that leave me? I speak perfect English and Spanish. Physically, I can pass as Californian, Panamanian, or Argentinean. I know many people who are in my same situation. In a sense, we identify with each other. We have created our own territory, imagined, but a territory nonetheless.*

In some families, individual members choose different paths of relating to the larger culture. This can cause tensions when children want to assimilate and parents prefer a more integrative mode.

One of the more difficult aspects of adaptation involves religion. How do immigrants pass on their religious beliefs to their children in a host country with very different religious traditions? Or should they? Aporva Dave, an honors student at Brown University, was curious about this question and conducted (along with another student) a study as an honors thesis. He interviewed members of South Asian Indian families that, like his own, had immigrated to the United States. He was curious about how strictly the parents followed the Hindu religion, how strongly they wanted their children to practice Hinduism in the future, and how the children felt about following the religious practices of their parents. In general, as expected, the children had a tendency to move away from the traditional practices of Hinduism, placing more emphasis on Hindu values than on Hindu practices (e.g., prayer).

Although many of the parents themselves prayed daily, most were more concerned that their children adopt the morals and values of Hinduism. The parents seemed to understand that assimilation requires a move away from strict Hindu practices. Most viewed Hinduism as a progressing, "living" religion that would change but not be lost. And many spoke of Hinduism as becoming more attractive as a religion of the future generation.

However, the study also revealed that children raised in the same house could have very different attitudes toward adaptation and religion. For example, two sisters who participated in the study were raised with "moderately" religious parents who worship weekly, read religious articles, and spend much time thinking about God. One sister followed the traditions of the parents: She prays every day, spends time reading religious scriptures, and is committed to marrying a Hindi. The other sister does not practice Hinduism and places emphasis on love in making a marriage decision. These kinds of differences can sometimes make communication difficult during the adaptation process.

As individuals encounter new cultural contexts, they have to adapt to some extent. This adaptation process occurs in context, varies with each individual, and is circumscribed by relations of dominance and power in so-called host cultures. Let's look more closely at this process.

CULTURAL ADAPTATION

cultural adaptation
A process by which individuals learn the rules and customs of new cultural contexts.

Cultural adaptation is the long-term process of adjusting to and finally feeling comfortable in a new environment (Kim, 2001, 2005). How one adapts depends to some extent on the host environment—whether it is welcoming or hostile. There are three communication approaches to studying cultural adaptation, and they vary in the degree to which they emphasize individual or contextual/environmental influences in the adaptation process. A dialectical perspective incorporates both the individual and the contextual. As shown in Table 8-2, the social science approach emphasizes the role of personal characteristics of the migrant; the interpretive focuses on the experience of the migrant in the adaptation context; the critical explores the role of larger contexts that influence cultural adaptation: social institutions and history, politics, and economic structures.

TABLE 8-2 CONTRIBUTIONS OF THREE APPROACHES TO CULTURAL ADAPTATION

Social Science	Interpretive	Critical
Role of individual migrant characteristics and background; theories of culture shock and reentry shock; outcomes of adaptations	In-depth analysis of adaptation experience	Importance of history, politics, and societal structures in migrant adaptation and identity

Social Science Approach

The social science approach focuses on the individual in the adaptation process, individual characteristics and background of the migrant, and the individual outcomes of adaptation. It includes three models: the anxiety and uncertainty management (AUM) model, the transition model, and the integrative model.

Individual Influences on Adaptation   Many individual characteristics—including age, gender, preparation level, and expectations—can influence how well migrants adapt (Ward, 1996). But there is contradictory evidence concerning the effects of age and adaptation. On the one hand, younger people may have an easier time adapting because they are less fixed in their ideas, beliefs, and identities. Because they adapt more completely, though, they may have more trouble when they return home. On the other hand, older people may have more trouble adapting because they are less flexible. However, for that very reason, they may not change as much and so have less trouble when they move back home (Kim, 2001).

Level of preparation for the experience may influence how migrants adapt, and this may be related to expectations. Many U.S. sojourners experience more culture shock in England than in other European countries because they expect little difference between life there and life here in the United States (Weissman & Furnham, 1987). In contrast, sojourners traveling to cultures that are very different expect to experience culture shock. The research seems to show that overly positive and overly negative expectations lead to more difficulty in adaptation; apparently, positive but realistic or slightly negative expectations prior to the sojourn are best (Martin, Bradford, & Rohrlich, 1995).

Anxiety and Uncertainty Management Model   Communication theorist William Gudykunst (1995, 1998, 2005) stresses that the primary characteristic of relationships in intercultural adaptation is ambiguity. The goal of effective intercultural communication can be reached by reducing anxiety and seeking information, a process known as **uncertainty reduction.** There are several kinds of uncertainty. **Predictive uncertainty** is the inability to predict what someone will say or do. We all know how important it is to be relatively sure how people will respond to us. **Explanatory uncertainty** is the inability to explain why people behave as they do. In any interaction, it is important not only to predict how someone will behave but also to explain why the person behaves in a particular way. How do we do this? Usually, we have prior knowledge about someone, or we gather more information about the person. One of our students, Linda, describes her interactions with a Swedish exchange student:

> *I remember feeling very uncomfortable and unsure about how to communicate with her. . . . I can remember asking simple questions about her hobbies, her family, and why she wanted to be a foreign exchange student. Basically, I was seeking to reduce my own uncertainty so that I could better predict her behavior. . . . The experience was a very positive one.*

Migrants also may need to reduce the anxiety that is present in intercultural contexts. Some level of anxiety is optimal during an interaction. Too little anxiety may

uncertainty reduction The process of lessening uncertainty in adapting to a new culture by seeking information.

predictive uncertainty A sense of uncertainty that stems from the inability to predict what someone will say or do.

explanatory uncertainty In the process of cultural adaptation, uncertainty that stems from the inability to explain why people behave as they do. (See **cultural adaptation.**)

convey that we don't care about the person, and too much causes us to focus only on the anxiety and not on the interaction. One student recalls her anxiety about communicating during a visit to Italy: "Once I decided to let go of my anxiety and uncertainty, I was much better at assessing behavior and attitudes [of Italians] and thereby increasing my understanding of aspects of the Italian culture."

This model assumes that to communicate effectively we will gather information to help us reduce uncertainty and anxiety. How do we do this? The theory is complicated; however, some general suggestions for increasing effectiveness are useful. The theory predicts that the most effective communicators (those who are best able to manage anxiety and predict and explain others' behaviors) (1) have a solid self-concept and self-esteem, (2) have flexible attitudes (a tolerance for ambiguity, empathy) and behaviors, and (3) are complex and flexible in their categorization of others (e.g., able to identify similarities and differences and avoid stereotypes). The situation in which communication occurs is important in this model. The most conducive environments are informal, with support from and equal representation of different groups. Finally, this model requires that people be open to new information and recognize alternative ways to interpret information.

Of course, these principles may operate differently according to the cultural context; the theory predicts cultural variability. For example, people with more individualistic orientations may stress independence in self-concepts and communities; self-esteem may become more important in interactions. Individualists also may seek similarities more in categorizing.

The Transition Model   Culture shock and adaptation have been viewed as a normal part of human experience, as a subcategory of transition shock. Janet Bennett (1998), a communication scholar, suggests that culture shock and adaptation are just like any other "adult transition." Adult transitions include going away to college for the first time, getting married, and moving from one part of the country to another. These experiences share common characteristics and provoke the same kinds of responses.

All transition experiences involve change, including some loss and some gain, for individuals. For example, when people marry, they may lose some independence, but they gain companionship and intimacy. When international students come to the United States to study, they leave their friends and customs behind but find new friends and new ways of doing things.

Cultural adaptation depends in part on the individual. Each person has a preferred way of dealing with new situations. Psychologists have found that most individuals prefer either a "flight" or a "fight" approach to unfamiliar situations. Each of these approaches may be more or less productive depending on the context. Migrants who prefer a **flight approach** when faced with new situations tend to hang back, get the lay of the land, and see how things work before taking the plunge and joining in. Migrants who take this approach may hesitate to speak a language until they feel they can get it right, which is not necessarily a bad thing. Taking time out from the stresses of intercultural interaction (by speaking and reading in one's native language, socializing with friends of similar background, and so on) may be appropriate. Small periods of "flight" allow migrants some needed rest from

flight approach
A strategy to cope with a new situation, being hesitant or withdrawn from the new environment. (Compare with **fight approach**.)

Is the use of the term "expat" reserved for white people? This provocative question was initially problematized by Christopher DeWolf, a Canadian living in Hong Kong. He observed that: "It's strange to hear some people in Hong Kong described as expats, but not others. Anyone with roots in a Western country is considered an expat. But the distinction is muddied among Hong Kong's deeply entrenched Southeast Asian community. Filipino domestic helpers are just guests, even if they've been here for decades. Mandarin-speaking mainland Chinese are rarely regarded as expats, but they are certainly not locals. By contrast, a native Cantonese speaker earns an automatic right to belong, even if she spent most of her life in Sydney or Vancouver."

Mawuna Remarque Koutonin explains that "expat" functions in a more directly racial way, writing that: "Expat is a term reserved exclusively for western white people going to work abroad. Africans are immigrants. Arabs are immigrants. Asians are immigrants. However, Europeans are expats because they can't be at the same level as other ethnicities. They are superior. Immigrants is a term set aside for 'inferior races.'"

Koutonin's piece created an interesting discussion in a number of places. As you might expect, not everyone agreed with him. Some tried to make a distinction between those who work in another country (expats) and those who are moving to live in another country permanently (immigrants). How careful are you in the use of these terms in your communication? How careful are other people? Are Mexicans who work in the United States most often referred to as "immigrants" or "expats"? How are other groups referred in everyday communication, as well as in the media?

Source: From C. DeWolf, "In Hong Kong, just who is an expat, anyway?" *The Wall Street Journal*, December 29, 2014. Retrieved June 9, 2016, from http://blogs.wsj.com/expat/2014/12/29/in-hong-kong-just-who-is-an-expat-anyway/.

From M. R. Koutonin, "Why are white people expats when the rest of us are immigrants?" *The Guardian*, March 13, 2015. Retrieved June 9, 2016, from http://www.theguardian.com/global-development-professionals-network/2015/mar/13/white-people-expats-immigrants-migration.

the challenges of cultural adaptation. However, getting stuck in the "flight" mode can be unproductive. For example, some U.S. students abroad spend all of their time with other American students and have little opportunity for intercultural learning.

A second method, the **fight approach,** involves jumping in and participating. Migrants who take this approach use the trial-and-error method. They try to speak the new language, don't mind if they make mistakes, jump on a bus even when they aren't sure it's the right one, and often make cultural gaffes. For example, Bill, a U.S. exchange teacher in France, took this approach. His French was terrible, but he would speak with anyone who would talk to him. When he and his wife first arrived in their town late at night, he went to the Hôtel de Ville (City Hall) and asked for a room! His wife, Jan, was more hesitant. She would speak French only when

fight approach
A trial-and-error approach to coping with a new situation. (Compare with **flight approach**.)

she knew she could get the grammar right, and she would study bus schedules for hours rather than risk getting on the wrong bus or asking a stranger. Getting stuck in the "fight" mode can also be unproductive. Migrants who take this approach to the extreme tend to act on their surroundings with little flexibility and are likely to criticize the way things are done in the new culture.

Neither of these preferences for dealing with new situations is inherently right or wrong. Individual preference is a result of family, social, and cultural influences. For example, some parents encourage their children to be assertive, and others encourage their children to wait and watch in new situations. Society may encourage individuals toward one preference or the other. A third alternative is the "flex" approach, in which migrants use a combination of productive "fight" or "flight" behaviors. The idea is to "go with the flow" while keeping in mind the contextual elements. Hostile contexts (such as racism or prejudice) may encourage extreme responses, but a supportive environment (tolerance) may encourage more productive responses.

The Integrative Model   The three approaches discussed so far concentrate on the psychological feelings of migrants, on how comfortable they feel. What role does communication play in the adaptation process? For an answer, we turn to a model of adaptation developed by communication scholar Young Yun Kim (2001, 2005). Kim suggests that adaptation is a process of stress, adjustment, and growth. As individuals experience the stress of not fitting in with the environment, the natural response is to seek to adjust. This process of adjustment represents a psychic breakdown of previously held attitudes and behaviors—ones that worked in original cultural contexts. This model fits very well with our dialectical approach in its emphasis on the interconnectedness of individual and context in the adaptation process.

Adaptation occurs through communication. That is, the migrant communicates with individuals in the new environment and gradually develops new ways of thinking and behaving. In the process, the migrant achieves a new level of functioning and acquires an intercultural identity. Of course, not everyone grows in the migrant experience. Some individuals have difficulty adapting to new ways. According to the cognitive dissonance theorists of the 1950s, individuals typically have three options when confronting ideas or behaviors that do not fit with previously held attitudes: They can (1) reject the new ideas, (2) try to fit them into their existing frameworks, or (3) change their frameworks (Festinger, 1957).

Communication may have a double edge in adaptation: Migrants who communicate frequently in their new culture adapt better but also experience more culture shock. Beulah Rohrlich and Judith Martin (1991) conducted a series of studies of U.S. American students living abroad in various places in Europe. They discovered that those students who communicated the most with host culture members experienced the most culture shock. These were students who spent lots of time with their host families and friends in many different communication situations (having meals together, working on projects together, socializing, and so on). However, these same students also adapted better and felt more satisfied with their overseas experience than the students who communicated less. Along the same lines, communication scholar Stephanie Zimmerman (1995) found that international students who interacted most often with U.S. American students were better adapted than those who interacted less.

Another dimension of communication is the important role of social support. When migrants leave their home countries they are deprived of important others who endorse their sense of self. When feelings of helplessness and inadequacy arise during the cultural adaptation, **social support** from friends can play an important role in helping the newcomer reduce stress, clarify uncertainty, and increase a sense of identity and self-esteem (Adelman, 1988). However, the social support system needs to include individuals both from the home culture and from the host culture. For example, studies show that international students' relationships with host culture members and also with other international students lead to better adjustment in general (Kashima & Loh, 2006).

social support Ties with other people that play a significant part in mediating psychological health over time.

Dan Kealey (1996), who worked for many years with the Canadian International Development Agency, conducted studies of overseas technical assistance workers in many different countries. Kealey and his colleagues tried to understand what characterized effective workers and less effective workers. They interviewed the Canadian workers, their spouses, and their host country co-workers. They discovered that the most important characteristics in adaptation were the interpersonal communication competencies of the workers.

In one study, Kealey (1989) found that those who communicated more in the host country experienced a greater degree of culture shock and had more initial difficulty in adapting to the new country. These people also were rated by their host country co-workers as more successful. As with the student sojourners, for these workers, communication and adaptation seem to be a case of "no pain, no gain." Intercultural interaction may be difficult and stressful but ultimately can be highly rewarding.

Outcomes of Adaptation   Much of the early research on cultural adaptation concentrated on a single dimension. More recent research emphasizes a multidimensional view of adaptation and applies best to voluntary transitions. There are at least three aspects, or dimensions, of adaptation: (1) psychological health, (2) functional fitness, and (3) intercultural identity (Kim, 2001). Again, we must note that these specific aspects are dialectically related to the contexts to which individuals adapt.

Part of adapting involves feeling comfortable in new cultural contexts. **Psychological health** is the most common definition of adaptation, one that concentrates on the emotional state of the individual migrant (Berry, Kim, Minde, & Mok, 1987). Obviously, the newcomer's psychological well-being will depend somewhat on members of the host society. As mentioned previously, if migrants are made to feel welcome, they will feel more comfortable faster. But if the host society sends messages that migrants don't really belong, psychological adjustment becomes much more difficult.

psychological health The state of being emotionally comfortable in a cultural context.

Achieving psychological health generally occurs more quickly than the second outcome, **functional fitness,** which involves being able to function in daily life in many different contexts (Ward, 1996). Some psychologists see adaptation mainly as the process of learning new ways of living and behaving (Ward, Bochner, & Furnham, 2001).

functional fitness The ability to function in daily life in many different contexts.

That is, they view the acquisition of skills as more important than psychological well-being. They have tried to identify areas of skills that are most important for newly arrived members of a society to acquire. Specifically, newcomers to a society should learn the local rules for politeness (e.g., honesty), the rules of verbal communication style (e.g., direct, elaborate), and typical use of nonverbal communication (e.g., proxemic behavior, gestures, eye gaze, facial expressions).

Obviously, this outcome of becoming functionally fit takes much longer and also depends on the cooperation of the host society. Newcomers will become functionally fit more quickly if host members are willing to communicate and interact with them. Even so, it takes most migrants a long time to function at an optimal level in the new society.

intercultural identity
Identity based on two or more cultural frames of reference.

Another potential outcome of adaptation is the development of an **intercultural identity,** a complex concept. Social psychologist Peter Adler (1975) writes that the multicultural individual is significantly different from the person who is more culturally restricted. One student describes her change in identity after living abroad for a year:

> *The year I studied abroad in France was crucial to developing my identity. Not only was I interacting among French people, but I also dealt with intercultural relations among other international students and American exchange students. I developed a new identity of myself and braved a complete transformation of self. All my intercultural experiences have helped me to become a more competent and understanding person.*

The multicultural person is neither a part of nor apart from the host culture; rather, this person acts situationally. But the multicultural life is fraught with pitfalls and difficulty. Multicultural people run the risk of not knowing what to believe or how to develop ethics or values. They face life with little grounding and lack the basic personal, social, and cultural guidelines that cultural identities provide.

Interpretive Approach

The interpretive approach focuses on in-depth descriptions of the adaptation process, often employing a phenomenological approach (see Table 8-2). Scholars using this approach explore the essential structures of lived experience through careful and systematic analysis of interview data and participant observation. Although the social science approach tends to see the adaptation experience in terms of stable categories like phases and variables like age, gender, and so on, that affect adaptation, an interpretive approach emphasizes the complex and continuous nature of cultural adaptation. To understand this process, researchers generally employ qualitative research methods—like interviewing and focus groups. There are three such interpretive models: the U-curve model, W-curve model, and phenomenological model.

U-curve theory
A theory of cultural adaptation positing that migrants go through fairly predictable phases—excitement/anticipation, shock/disorientation, adjustment—in adapting to a new cultural situation.

U-Curve Model   Many theories describe how people adapt to new cultural environments. The pattern of adaptation varies depending on the circumstances and the migrant, but some commonalities exist. The most common theory is the **U-curve theory** of adaptation. This theory is based on research conducted by a Norwegian sociologist, Sverre Lysgaard (1955), who interviewed Norwegian students studying in the United States. He was interested in understanding the experience of cultural adaptation. His results have been confirmed by many other subsequent studies and have been applied to many different migrant groups.

The main idea is that migrants go through fairly predictable phases in adapting to a new cultural situation. They first experience excitement and anticipation, followed by a period of shock and disorientation (the bottom of the U curve); then they gradually adapt to the new cultural context. Although this framework is simplistic and does not represent every migrant's experience, most migrants experience these general phases at one time or another.

Anticipation: The first phase is the anticipation or excitement phase. When a migrant first enters a new cultural context, he or she may be excited to be in the new situation and only a little apprehensive. This was the case for Helga María, who moved from Iceland to the United States so that her mother could attend graduate school in Florida. She describes the excitement of moving to the United States:

> *The travel date finally arrived. My grandma cried as we walked toward our gate at the airport, but I still felt as if we were just going on a long, fun vacation. . . . I remember how huge the supermarket was, the first time we went buying groceries. Every aisle had more and more food and I wanted to taste all the different types of candy and cakes. Even the bread was different, so soft and it felt like a pillow.*

Although moving was mostly fun for Helga María, someone adapting to a new job in a new region of the country may experience more apprehension than excitement during the first part of the transition. The same would be true for, say, an international student from East Africa who experiences prejudice in the first months at a U.S. college, or for refugees who are forced to migrate into new cultural contexts.

Culture Shock: The second phase, culture shock, happens to almost everyone in intercultural transitions. Individuals face many challenges of transition in new cultural contexts. **Culture shock** is a relatively short-term feeling of disorientation, of discomfort due to the unfamiliarity of surroundings, and the lack of familiar cues in the environment. Kalvero Oberg, the anthropologist who coined the term *culture shock,* suggests it is like a disease, complete with symptoms (excessive hand washing, irritability, and so on). If it is treated properly (that is, if the migrant learns the language, makes friends, and so on), the migrant can "recover," or adapt to the new cultural situation and feel at home (Oberg, 1960).

culture shock A relatively short-term feeling of disorientation and discomfort due to the lack of familiar cues in the environment.

Although most individuals experience culture shock during the period of transition to a new culture, they are less likely to experience it if they maintain separateness because culture shock presumes cultural contact. For instance, military personnel who live abroad on U.S. bases and have very little contact with members of the host society often experience little culture shock. However, in more recent military operations (e.g., Iraq and Afghanistan), soldiers are having much more contact with civilians, experiencing strong culture shock and some negative outcomes—searching homes without the presence of a male head of household and males conducting body searches of females—very inappropriate behavior in these Muslim contexts. Almost all migrants who cross cultural boundaries, whether voluntarily or not, experience culture shock. Training before encountering a new culture can help with a smoother transition. For example, incidents of disrespect by American soldiers suggest a need for cultural training and better cultural understanding, since "issues of ethnocentrism and analytical bias can affect tactical, operations, and strategic success" (Chandler 2005, p. 21). High-ranking military personnel have also emphasized that U.S. advisors need to understand the Iraqi perspective by being trained in "general knowledge of the history of the Middle East with a specific focus on the development of Islam and Arab history—which are not the same thing . . . they need to understand the overlapping and competing spheres of influence at play in this complex culture . . . to see the informal networks behind the formal bureaucracy . . . to more effectively comprehend and influence the behavior of the Iraqi counterparts. . . ." (Allardice & Head, 2008).

For many individuals, long-term adaptation is not easy. Some people actively resist assimilation in the short term. For example, many students from Muslim countries, especially females, often continue to wear traditional clothing while living in the United States, thus actively resisting participating in U.S. popular culture. Others resist assimilation in the long term, as is the case with some religious groups, like the Amish and the Hutterites. Some would like to assimilate but are not welcome in the new culture, as is the case with many immigrants to the United States from Latin America. And some people adapt to some aspects of the new culture but not to others.

For Helga María, culture shock happened pretty quickly:

After a few weeks, when my school started, the heat became rather tiring. I could hardly be outside for more than five minutes without looking like I just came out of the shower. . . . I walked around from class to class feeling almost invisible. Thankfully, I could understand some of what people were saying, but not communicate back to them.

For Helga María's mother, Erla, it was even harder:

The first semester in Pensacola was one of the hardest in our lives. . . . I missed my colleagues, my work, and my family at home. I felt so ignorant, unintelligent, and old when I first started. I walked from one building to another, between classes. I kept my mouth shut, and when I tried to speak, the southern instructors often didn't understand what I was trying to say. This was awful. . . . Maybe my friends were right after all; I was being crazy and selfish. But here we were, and not about to give up.

Not everyone experiences culture shock when they move to a new place. For example, migrants who remain isolated from the new cultural context may experience minimal culture shock. As noted previously, U.S. military personnel, as well as diplomatic personnel, often live in compounds overseas where they associate mainly with other U.S. Americans and have little contact with the indigenous cultures. Similarly, spouses of international students in the United States sometimes have little contact with U.S. Americans. In contrast, corporate spouses may experience more culture shock because they often have more contact with the host culture: placing children in schools, setting up a household, shopping, and so on.

STRATEGIES FOR FACILITATING GROWTH

Communication scholar Shelly Smith provides the following strategies to help sojourners gain maximum benefits from long-term living, working, or studying abroad:

1. *When your cultural assumptions are challenged, try to suspend judgment until you understand the reasons for your reaction. Reactions can be emotional and intense. When it is hardest to be rational, it is important to stop, take a deep breath and figure out why you feel as you do.*

2. *Try to remember that not all values are created equal. Many differences can be accepted, embraced, and enjoyed over time but others remain inviolable. . . . Being able to engage in mindfulness allows you to understand it's a personal choice . . . and OK that others embrace behaviors you cannot.*

3. *Be willing to engage the culture. Genuine interest, curiosity, and a willingness to take risks involves the possibility of making mistakes and looking foolish . . . but it's inevitable and OK.*

4. *Keep a sense of humor. The mistakes one makes will make the best stories later and if you can laugh at yourself, adjustment becomes much easier.*

5. *Be patient. Adjusting to a new culture takes time and happens in increments.*

6. *It's OK to temporarily retreat and embrace your emotions. All sojourners experience moments of anger, frustration, confusion, and occasionally even contempt. It's better to take a break than explode needlessly in front of your hosts.*

7. *Remember that successful adaptation involves identity change that will affect your reentry. Take account of how you changed and what you've learned and this will help you explain your experiences to others back home, making reentry a little easier.*

Source: From S. Smith, "The Cycle of Cross-Cultural Adaptation and Reentry." In J. Martin, T. K. Nakayama, and L. A. Flores (Eds.), *Readings in Intercultural Communication* (Boston: McGraw-Hill, 2002), pp. 253–255.

During the culture shock phase, migrants like Helga María and her family may experience disorientation and a crisis of identity. Because identities are shaped and maintained by cultural contexts, experiences in new cultural contexts often raise questions about identities. For example, Judy, an exchange teacher in Morocco, thought of herself as a nice person. Being nice was part of her identity. But when she experienced a lot of discipline problems with her students, she began to question the authenticity of her identity. When change occurs to the cultural context of an identity, the conditions of that identity also change.

Adjustment: The third phase in Lysgaard's model is adjustment, in which migrants learn the rules and customs of the new cultural context. As Erla says,

"After the first semester, we started adapting pretty well. My daughters made new friends and so did my husband and I. I got used to studying, and started looking at it as any other job. My daughters learned how to speak English very well." Like Helga María, Erla, and the rest of their family, many migrants learn a new language, and they figure out how much of themselves change in response to the new context. Remember Naida, the immigrant from Bosnia? After several years here in the States, she, too, has adapted. But she also acknowledges that life here still has its challenges:

> I need to be thankful that I have a stable and peaceful life, a roof over my head, and food to eat. Unlike in some other parts of the world, here I have the opportunity to educate myself, and to make things better, and I must take advantage of it and appreciate it. I should know. I also know that I am going to experience many setbacks, disappointments, and emotional crises in my life, but I want to look forward, beyond that and learn.

However, this phase may be experienced very differently if the sociopolitical context is not conducive to individual adaptation. This was the experience of Maria and her sister, who migrated from Greece to Germany:

> Unfortunately, I am also the victim of discrimination at the moment. I am applying for a job here in Germany, and although I have finished the German university with an excellent grade and I have the permission to work here, I always get rejected because of my nationality! All the other students from my university have already found a job, only because they are German!! The same experience I had in the UK. And I was only looking for a temporary job!! . . . I think that a cultural adaptation will only take place if we all first learn to respect one another!!

Although the U curve seems to represent the experiences of many short-term sojourners, it may be too simplistic for other types of migrants (Berry, 1992). A more accurate model represents long-term adaptation as a series of U curves. Migrants alternate between feeling relatively adjusted and experiencing culture shock; over the long term, the sense of culture shock diminishes.

W-Curve Model   When migrants return home to their original cultural contexts, the same process of adaptation occurs and may again involve culture, or reentry, shock depicted by the W-curve model (Gullahorn & Gullahorn, 1963). Sometimes this adaptation is even more difficult because it is so unexpected. Coming home, we might think, should be easy. However, students who return home from college, businesspeople who return to corporate headquarters after working abroad, and Native Americans who return to their nations all notice the difficulty of readjusting (Martin & Harrell, 2004).

Scholars refer to this process as the **W-curve theory** of adaptation because sojourners seem to experience another U curve: the anticipation of returning home, culture shock in finding that it's not exactly as expected, and then gradual adaptation (Storti, 2001). Other terms for the process of readapting to one's home culture include: *reverse culture shock, reentry shock,* and *repatriation.* Recall Helga María

W-curve theory A theory of cultural adaptation that suggests that soujourners experience another U curve upon returning home. (See **U-curve theory** and **sojourners**.)

lobal businesses often want to send employees on international assignments to gain valuable insights and experiences that will benefit their businesses, but the execution of those plans is not always smooth. On the one hand, many companies see that: "Employees with international experience become an even greater asset to their organization. International assignments can help increase cultural literacy, facilitate the mastery of foreign languages, expand the professional network, and broaden perspective" (Vorhauser-Smith, 2013). But, on the other hand, not all companies are prepared in predeparture and repatriation (the reentry process) to profit from these experiences. A 2015 Ernst & Young report notes that "74.5% of survey respondents [global businesses] said they need more insights about the tax, immigration and social security risks associated with their global mobility programs." Also, the repatriation process does not always leverage the new talents and insights of returning employees as 41% returned to their same positions and 16% quit within two years of their return, an increase from 11% in 2012 (Alsop, 2014). While employees may encounter culture shock when they move to another country and another culture, they can also experience reentry shock when they return to their home country and corporation. Repatriation, or the reentry process, can pose particular challenges as businesses can change a lot while the employee has been away—sometimes organizations are reorganized, bosses and other employees may have changed, or corporation may have been acquired by another company with a very different corporate culture. Given what we know about intercultural transitions, culture shock, and reverse culture shock, how can intercultural communication help global businesses with international assignments?

Source: From R. Alsop, "When expats return home, what's next? *BBC,* January 16, 2015. Retrieved June 10, 2016, from http://www.bbc.com/capital/story/20140115-returning-expat-discontent.

From Ernst & Young, "Data makes mobility work: EY 2015 global mobility effectiveness survey." From http://www.ey.com/Publication/vwLUAssets/EY-global-mobility-effectiveness-survey-2015-executive-summary/$File/EY-global-mobility-effectiveness-survey-2015-executive-summary.pdf.

From S. Vorhauser-Smith, "Global mobility: A win-win for you and your employer." *Forbes,* October 31, 2013. Retrieved June 10, 2016, from http://www.forbes.com/sites/sylviavorhausersmith/2013/10/31/global-mobility-a-win-win-for-you-and-your-employer/#31353b05779c.

migrated from Iceland to Florida with her family. She returned home to Iceland for a short visit and found it was not what she expected:

> We were all pretty excited about going back and seeing our friends and family again. We kind of expected everything to be the same, but it wasn't. My sister and I still talked English to each other. Even when I talked my own language, people said I had an American accent. I never thought that could happen. Being there, I felt more like a visitor, instead of it being my home country.

There are two fundamental differences between the first and second U curves, related to issues of personal change and expectations (Martin, 1984). In the initial curve or phase, the sojourner is fundamentally unchanged and is experiencing new cultural contexts. In the reentry phase, the sojourner has changed through the adaptation process and has become a different individual. The person who returns home is not the same person who left home. Helga María's mother, Erla, describes how much she had changed as a result of her sojourn in the United States and how these changes affected her reentry to Iceland:

> *Surprisingly, I felt like a stranger in my own country; everything seemed so small, the streets, houses, road signs, and I saw my home city in a completely new light. And when I tried to describe all these wonderful, dreadful, amazing, beautiful, and funny things that I had experienced, it seemed like my family and friends weren't interested. Whatever bliss I might have had was quickly blown away, and I felt that I didn't fit into my own culture. I realized that I had changed and so had my previous friends. . . . This was quite a shock for me.*

International students who return home also talk about how their friends and families expect them to be a little different (more educated) but basically the same as before they went off to school (Martin, 1986). This lack of interest on the part of friends and family can be especially detrimental for corporations that send employees overseas. The home corporation often does not take advantage of the knowledge and skills that returnees have acquired during their overseas assignments. Rather, employees in the home office often expect the returnees to fit back in, as if the overseas assignment had never happened (Black & Gregersen, 1999).

Like other sojourners and migrants, the reentry for military personnel can be very stressful, even more stressful than deployment. For example, the website for reservists and their families has extensive information to facilitate the homecoming, including the importance of communication, transitional health care benefits, reemployment rights, as well as emotional issues associated with a reunion. The Army Reserve Child, Youth & School Services unit has information on returning soldiers and the reactions of military children at different ages (Army Reserve Child, Youth & School Services, 2016).

Returnees also need to recognize that the cultural context of reentry is different from being overseas. Depending on how long the person was away, political figures, popular culture, family, technology, and even language may have changed. For instance, when Tom's father went to Japan for the first time, a Japanese taxi driver said to him, "I don't know where you are from, but you have been away for a long, long time." Tom's father had never been to Japan before, so the taxi driver was responding to his use of Japanese. Many words in the Japanese language have changed from the 19th century when Tom's family immigrated to the United States, but many now archaic words and structures remain in use by Japanese speakers in the United States.

Sojourners who leave their countries during times of political upheaval and return when peace is reestablished may have to contend with the ambivalence many of those who stayed have toward those who left. In this excerpt, a Lebanese woman describes her feelings toward a friend who had left during the civil war but who has now returned:

> *When you tried to be one of us again, the dominant expression on your face was pity, for everyone who'd stayed here. As you moved you clasped people to you, then touched their faces, then held them again, as if you were saying,*

"I know what you're suffering." Why were you so sure that those who stayed were the only ones suffering? (Al-Shaykh, 1995, p. 8)

Phenomenological Model   Using a **phenomenological approach,** Chen (2000) interviewed Chinese international students and described in depth how they *experienced and made sense* of the adaptation process. She describes three phases: taking things for granted, making sense of new patterns, and coming to understand new information.

phenomenological approach A research approach that seeks in-depth explanations of human experiences.

In the first phase, migrants realize that their assumptions are wrong and need to be altered. Chen describes the experiences of one of the students she interviewed, Mr. An. He was arriving in the middle of the night at his new U.S. university, but he wasn't worried. In China, student housing is always arranged for by university officials. However, in conversations on the plane with a friendly seatmate named Alice, he began to realize that his expectations of having a place to stay were probably a mistake. He was grateful when Alice offered her home. Mr. An explained, "Alice said she could put me up for the night, that I could live in her house until I found a place. . . . I was surprised but also very grateful" (Chen, 2000, p. 221).

In the second stage, migrants slowly begin to make sense of new patterns, through communication experiences. The first step in making sense for Mr. An took place the next day when he went to the International Students Office. A clerk handed him a map and told him to find his own housing. Although he had heard that people in the United States were individualistic and independent, this cultural pattern was now a living experience for him. The dorms were full, but Mr. An learned how to seek alternatives. He explained how he began to make sense of the experience: "I started to better understand the meaning of independence. I felt I really understood America and was overjoyed [to find] there was a Chinese Student Association on campus. This meant that maybe I could get help from them" (p. 224).

As migrants begin to make sense of their experiences and interactions in new cultural contexts, they come to understand them in a more holistic way. This enables them to fit the new information into a pattern of cultural understanding. Again, this happens through communication with members of the host country and others who implicitly or explicitly explain the new cultural patterns. Mr. An stayed in touch with Alice for a while, but this changed over time. He explained:

> *One day I realized I had not called Alice in a long time, then it occurred to me that she rarely called me; I was the one who usually made the calls. . . . I just didn't get around to calling her again, but now I don't feel guilty about it. She didn't seem to mind one way or the other. I've learned that many Americans are ready to help others, but never see them again afterwards. (p. 226)*

At that point, Mr. An understood the U.S. cultural emphasis on helpful intervention, and he was able to make sense of his friendship with Alice—as a momentary helping relationship. As Chen notes, "Coming to a tentative understanding is the last stage in a cycle of sense-making. . . . In the long run, however, this new perspective will never be completely fulfilled by one's accumulation of knowledge" (p. 227). As Chen points out, there are always more sense-making cycles.

When I first arrived in Belgium, I watched a lot of TV. I always liked to watch TV before I left the United States, so it was a good way for me to learn French. And it was certainly a lot easier and less painful than trying to talk with Belgians. I always hated that pained look they got on their faces when I would screw up the language in my halting speech.
    —Jesse

In a more recent study, Kristjánsdóttir (2009) explored the adaptation experience of a group of undergraduate chemistry majors who worked in French chemistry labs during their summer break. Using a phenomenological approach, she interviewed the students several times before they left, during their sojourn in France, and after they returned to the States. Her findings reflect the embodied, visceral experience of their cultural adaptation—specifically in struggles with the language, their experience of their national and ethnic identity, and their acquired knowledge.

The students described vividly their struggles with the language, how the inability to speak French made their stay in France difficult and how their inability to "read" the social context added to the stress of being misunderstood. One student said, "I feel kind of stupid." Others talked about feeling alone and isolated because no one seemed to want to interact with them. As Kristjánsdóttir describes it, "Due to the language barrier, their embodied relation to the world became problematic. Their self-esteem dropped and they became very self-conscious about themselves. Their whole bodies were entrenched in this effort of trying [to communicate] in French. For the students, it was a laborious and involved process that was connected to all aspects of themselves, being, human sensibilities, and human existence."

The students' experience of their national and ethnic identity was also important in their adaptation process and is described as an experience of feeling invisibility and visibility. Specifically, the white students found that they were often disliked just because they were from the United States—adding stress in the adaptation process. They sometimes feared to talk, knowing their accent would reveal their nationality, and so they would often choose to remain "invisible." They described the experience as a "feeling of being suffocated" because of their Americanness and then a feeling of being extremely visible and standing out when they spoke. Because of their whiteness, they experienced both invisibility and visibility.

In contrast, the students of color did not have the option of experiencing invisibility, and they described their feeling of "standing out" and being extremely visible all the time. They felt their race/ethnicity was adding another layer of stress, of not fitting in the French cultural space. Their "differentness" was apparent even before they opened their mouths to speak, although their nationality might not be entirely obvious. One African American student said, "People are going to look at you . . . they might stare, if they see me looking, and all of a sudden they stare at you all the time." This caused him to feel very uneasy, especially when he was sharing a table with someone at a restaurant or at the university cafeteria. The other students of color described similar experiences.

Having lived through the experience of being rejected enabled the white students to understand a little how it feels to belong to a minority group in the United States. The students' bodily experience of not having a voice in society and the feeling of being invisible created a new embodied relation to their Americanness. Learning about the French value system aided them in erasing stereotypes they used to have about the French people being lazy. The students' intercultural experience of living in France was eye opening; they not only learned about a new culture but, more importantly, learned about themselves as persons and their home culture of the United States.

These interpretive phenomenological studies help flesh out the social science studies—helping us understand the visceral, embodied experience of cultural adaptation, as shown in Table 8-2.

Mass media also play a role in helping sojourners and immigrants adapt. Radio, television, movies, and so on, are powerful transmitters of cultural values and readily accessible as sources of socialization for newcomers. The mass media may play an especially important role in the beginning stages of adaptation. When sojourners or immigrants first arrive, they may have limited language ability and limited social networks. Listening to the radio or watching TV may be the primary source of contact at this stage, one that avoids negative consequences of not knowing the language (Nwanko & Onwumechili, 1991).

Critical Approach: Contextual Influences

The critical approach reminds us that cultural adaptation depends on the context. Some contexts are easier to adapt to than others, and some environments are more accepting. Young Yun Kim (2001) writes about the receptivity of the host environment and the degree to which the environment welcomes newcomers. She maintains that in a country like Japan, which emphasizes homogeneity, people may be less welcoming toward outsiders than in less homogeneous settings, as in many contexts in the United States. Communication scholar Satoshi Ishii (2001) explains the ambivalent feelings of contemporary Japanese toward foreigners and traces their historical roots: "Since ancient times the Japanese have consistently held not positive–negative dichotomous feelings but the conventional welcome–nonwelcome and inclusion–exclusion ambivalence in encountering and treating . . . strangers" (p. 152). Similarly, many Muslim societies tend to be fairly closed to outsiders. In these societies, the distinction between ingroup (family and close friends) and outgroup (everyone else) is very strong.

Institutional, Political, and Class Influences   Local institutions, like schools, religious institutions, and social service agencies, can facilitate or hinder immigrants' adaptation. For example, schools can help immigrant children adapt by offering language classes to bring them up to speed. In the United States today, there are approximately 3.5 million schoolchildren with limited English ability, and most are concentrated in a small number of schools. Some regions offer language programs; however, many are cutting their bilingual programs as part of the English-only movement. In Arizona, for example, Proposition 203 banned bilingual education

In some Muslim countries, for example, Afghanistan and Saudi Arabia, women are required to wear a burqa or niqab. In others, such as Tunisia and Turkey, laws prevent wearing the hijab in government buildings, schools, and universities. In April 2011, France became the first non-Muslim majority country to ban the wearing of full-face covering veils. France is home to an estimated 5 million Muslims, more than any other western European nation. Yet, "When the law went into effect, it was estimated that fewer than 2,000 women wore the full veil." Proponents of the law says it is important as part of the French approach to *"vivre ensemble"* (living together) and encourages people to assimilate. Five years after that law went into effect, not everyone thinks it has led to a more cohesive society. Opponents say that the law was targeting something that wasn't a social problem and that "most of the women who wear niqabs nowadays live in the suburbs and have chosen to wear them as an act of defiance" and "others don't necessarily have a religious motivation at all" but want to express their opposition (Cigainero, 2016).

More recently, diplomatic and economic relations between France (and many other nations) have opened up again with Iran. As a result, Air France has resumed flights to Iran (which were stopped in 2008) and requires that its female employees wear veils. The airline tells women to "wear a head scarf and a wide and long garment to conceal their forms" (quoted in Stack, 2016). This led to an uproar and eventually the airline made wearing the head coverings optional.

Source: From J. Cigainero, "Five years into ban, burqa divide widens in France," *Deutsche Welle,* April 10, 2016. Retrieved June 10, 2016, from http://www.dw.com/en/five-years-into-ban-burqa -divide-widens-in-france/a-19177275.

L. Stack, "Air France faces backlash over veil policy on route to Iran," *The New York Times,* April 5, 2016. Retrieved June 10, 2016, from http://www.nytimes.com/2016/04/06/world/europe /air-france-veil-policy-iran.html?_r=0.

and required schools to use mostly English immersion to teach children with limited English proficiency (Gonzalez, 2005). Some schools are working hard to mainstream these students, reaching out to parents and community leaders to ease the students' linguistic and social adaptation (Reid, 2005). Others are leading the fight to cut such programs. In Australia, children of undocumented parents have been removed from school and placed in detention (Sedgman, 2005). Similar situations occur in the United States (Garcia, 2005). More recently, Alabama passed a strict law that requires schools to check the immigration status of students. Many parents pulled their children from schools to avoid drawing attention to them (Alabama, 2011).

Religious institutions can also play an important role in assisting immigrants. Many churches, synagogues, and mosques delivered aid to the victims of Hurricane Katrina. Muslims in the United States have a long tradition of assisting new immigrants financially and socially, through local mosques and civic organizations (Bahadur, 2005). Religious institutions, in turn, can be revitalized by immigrants. For example, a Baptist church in St. Paul, Minnesota, reached out to immigrants from Myanmar,

When I moved to Arizona from San Francisco to go to school, it was a big shock. I was used to seeing many different kinds of people—Asian Americans, African Americans. At my new university in Phoenix, almost everyone is white. And I was treated differently in Phoenix than I was at home. I often got passed by at the supermarket while the clerk waited on someone who was white. Some of the children who lived in my apartment complex followed me one day, yelling, "Chink, Chink, Chinaman."
    —Lois

providing them accommodations and airport pickups. People in the church bring donations of food and clothes. The downtown church, with dwindling membership, has been revitalized with the new immigrants (Pratik, 2005). Synagogues in South Florida have been revitalized by Russian immigrants who fled Russia and the religious oppression there (Collie, 2005). Today, religious organizations are working very closely with many governments to help refugees resettle in their new countries (Ralston, 2010).

But religious institutions do not always play facilitative roles in migrant transitions. Many Christian organizations in the United States, Canada, and Australia victimized indigenous children by requiring them to attend church schools far away from their homes in an attempt to "drum their native culture from their psyches," where they were often abused and maltreated. Fortunately, some churches have tried to redress these abuses.

The relative status and power of sojourners and host groups also influence adaptation. Several recent studies have found that Asian, African, and Latino students in the United States report experiences of discrimination and hostility based on their race/ethnicity while white international students report very few such experiences. These difficulties make it very difficult to adapt to a new country and range from being ignored to verbal insults, confrontation, and even physical assaults—in a variety of contexts, both in and outside the classroom, by peers, faculty, and members of the local community (Lee & Rice, 2007; Poyrazli & Lopez, 2007).

The authors of the studies point to the institutional accountability for international student satisfaction and, ultimately, for positive relations with potential future students in the internationals' home countries:

> *We recommend that members of the educational community be made aware of this issue and their responsibility in creating intellectual environments that foster cross-national acceptance and learning . . . [and] that guidelines concerning teaching and working with international students be articulated so that administrators and faculty are aware of their responsibility in providing a safe and welcoming environment for international students (Lee & Rice, p. 405.)*

Similarly, it can be difficult for women to adapt in many contexts because of their relatively lower status.

Class issues often enter into the picture. Sometimes immigrant workers are seen as necessary but are not really welcomed into the larger society because of their class (which is often fused with racial differences). And sometimes the discrimination and class issues result in conflict between recent migrants and emigrants from the same country who have been in the host country for a long time. For example, Mexicans have come in increasing numbers to work in the carpet plants in the Southeast and in the meatpacking plants in the Midwest. This has led to tension between those Latinos/as, who have worked hard to achieve harmony with whites and to attain middle-class status, and the newcomers, who are usually poor and have lower English proficiency. The older Latinos/as feel caught between the two—ridiculed by whites for not speaking English correctly and now by recently arrived Mexicans for mangling Spanish. This resentment between old and new immigrants has always been present in America—from the arrival of the first Europeans.

However, there is an upside to the arrival of these new immigrants. Journalist Arian Campo-Flores (2001), writing about the relationships between these two groups in one Midwest town, observes:

> *Cultural collisions can be as enriching as they are threatening. . . . Older Chicanos have learned to adjust, too. In fact many say that the fresh infusion of Hispanic culture brought by immigrants has revitalized their identity as Latinos. Their girls are celebrating* quinceaneras, *the equivalent of "sweet 16" parties. They're singing to their departed relatives at the cemetery. They've resuscitated their language . . . both communities have recognized that their complexions will become only more richly hued. And Chicanos, who in a way are the arbiters between what the towns used to be and what they've become, are uniquely qualified to lead. (p. 51)*

The United States is not the only country grappling with an influx of new workers. When Germany needed low-cost laborers, the country brought in many Turkish guest workers, but these immigrants were not necessarily welcomed into German society. Citizenship and other signs of entry into German society were not easily obtainable, and many immigrants (or those perceived to be immigrants) were victims of violent attacks. In fact, all over Europe, people of color, and especially recent immigrants seem to be facing increasing trends in racism that make life more difficult than it is for the average citizen in any of these countries (Akwani, 2006). The recent influx of immigrants and refugees in Europe presents increasing intercultural communication challenges.

Which groups of migrants do you think have a positive image in the United States? Which groups do you think have a negative image? Which groups of international students do you think U.S. students would want to meet and socialize with? Which groups would students not want to meet? The stereotypes of various cultural groups should make it easy for you to sense which groups would face resistance from U.S. Americans in trying to adapt to U.S. culture.

Identity and Adaptation   How individual migrants develop multicultural identities depends on three issues. One is the extent to which migrants want to maintain their own identity, language, and way of life compared to how much they want to become part of the larger new society. Recall that the immigrant–host culture relationship can be played out in several ways. Immigrants to the United States often are encouraged to "become American," which may entail relinquishing their former cultural identity. For example, Mario and his family emigrated from Mexico to Germany when Mario's father took a new job. Mario and his siblings have taken different paths with respect to their relationship to Mexican culture. Mario, the oldest child, has tried to keep some Mexican traditions. His brother, who was very young when the family migrated to Germany, did not learn to speak Spanish at home but is now trying to learn it in college.

The second issue that affects how migrants develop multicultural identities is the extent to which they have day-to-day interactions with others in the new society. Some migrants find it painful to deal with the everyday prejudices that they experience and so retreat to their own cultural groups.

The third issue that affects how migrants relate to their new society involves the ownership of political power. In some societies, the dominant group virtually dictates how nondominant groups may act; in other societies, nondominant groups are largely free to select their own course. For instance, Tom learned that when his mother first went to grammar school she had to pick an "American name" because her own name "was too hard to pronounce." As a first grader, she chose the name "Kathy" because she thought it sounded pretty. This kind of forced assimilation reflects the power of dominant groups over nondominant groups. In this case, *American* means "English" or "British," even though we are a nation of emigrants from all parts of the world. Looking at how migrants deal with these identity issues in host culture contexts can help us understand different patterns of contact (Berry, 1992).

Living on the Border   As international migration increases and more and more people travel back and forth among different cultures, the lines between adaptation and reentry become less clear (Onwumechilia, Nwosu, Jackson, & James-Huges, 2003). More and more people are living on the border physically, making frequent trips between countries, or living on the border psychologically between bicultural identities.

The experience of living on the border was described by anthropologist Victor Turner (1969) as the experience of **liminality.** According to Turner, liminal people are "threshold people"; they are neither "here nor there," they are "betwixt and between various cultural positions . . . frequently likened to death, to being in the womb, to invisibility, to bisexuality" (p. 95). The trend calls for a new view of cultural boundaries and adaptation.

> *The emerging "interethnic identity" is a special kind of mindset that promises greater fitness in our increasingly interfaced world. It represents a continuous struggle of searching for the authenticity in self and others within and across ethnic groups. . . . A particular emphasis has been placed on the possibility of identity development from a monoethnic identity to a more interethnic identity, from a categorical identity to a more flexible and inclusive identity of individuated and universalized self-other orientation. (Kim, 2006, pp. 292, 295)*

This **transnationalism** calls into question comforting notions like nation-states, national languages, and coherent cultural communities. People who move back and forth

liminality The experience of being between two or more cultural positions.

transnationalism The activity of migrating across the borders of one or more nation-states.

multicultural identity
A sense of in-betweenness that develops as a result of frequent or multiple cultural border crossings.

between cultural worlds often develop a **multicultural identity,** as discussed in Chapter 5. Denis, an international student from France, describes this transnational experience:

> *I have been living outside my home country for several years now, and it seems that the returns home are not as hard as they were in the past. . . . I have learned to just take things as they come and become nonjudgmental regarding people's actions and behaviors. . . . to be able to step back and also realize that in most interactions problems are rarely with the people who live in a country, but rather they are within your own framework of beliefs and behaviors that you have to mentally put aside in order to see the other culture or your own.*

Communication scholar Radha Hegde (1998) uses the metaphor of swinging on a trapeze to describe the immigrant's experience of vacillating between the cultural patterns of the homeland and the new country. Writer Gloria Anzaldúa (1999) also stresses the fluidity and the active roles that individuals must take when living on the borders. She thinks that we need to resist being placed in set categories—like "Chicano/a" or "black" or "Asian American." She also insists that all our identities are in flux and interact with each other. Anzaldúa herself is Chicana, gay, and female. She describes how she has struggled to reconcile the indigenous with the Spanish, the male with the female, and her rather patriarchal Catholic upbringing with her spiritual and sexual identity. The result is the "mestiza"—a person who has actively confronted the negative aspects of identity, such as being silenced as a woman in a patriarchal Mexican-Catholic context, and then constructed a provisional identity:

> *The new* mestiza *copes by developing a tolerance for contradictions, a tolerance for ambiguity. She learns to be an Indian in Mexican culture, to be Mexican from an Anglo point of view. She learns to juggle cultures. She has a plural personality, she operates in a pluralist mode—nothing is thrust out, the good the bad and the ugly, nothing rejected, nothing abandoned. Not only does she sustain contradictions, she turns the ambivalence into something else. (p. 101)*

This "something else" is the construction of her own historical legacy, a transformation that involves facing her fear of change. Once she accomplishes her personal inner journey, she comes to recognize her multiple identities. In her writing, she demonstrates the many facets of her many identities—writing in several languages (Spanish, English, and Nuhuatl), and in prose (the academic) and poetry (the artistic and spiritual):

> *I will no longer be made to feel ashamed of existing. I will have my voice: Indian, Spanish, white. I will have my serpent's tongue—my woman's voice, my sexual voice, my poet's voice. I will overcome the tradition of silence. (p. 81)*

Technological developments have made global travel much easier, and we can change cultural contexts as never before. Yet the movement between cultures is never as simple as getting on a plane (Clifford, 1992). David Mura (1991), a

Japanese American from the Midwest, went to live in Japan and wrote about his experiences there:

> *Japan helped me balance a conversation which had been taking place before I was born, a conversation in my grandparents' heads, in my parents' heads, which, by my generation, had become very one-sided, so that the Japanese side was virtually silenced. My stay helped me realize that a balance, which probably never existed in the first place, could no longer be maintained. In the end, I did not speak the language well enough; I did not have enough attraction to the culture. In the end, the society felt to my American psyche too cramped, too well defined, too rule-oriented, too polite, too circumscribed. I could have lived there a few more years if I had had the money and the time, but eventually I would have left.*

The entanglements of history, identity, language, nonverbal communication, and cultural spaces are all salient concerns for understanding these global movements.

INTERNET RESOURCES

www.migrationpolicy.org

"The Migration Policy Institute is an independent, nonpartisan, nonprofit think tank in Washington, D.C. dedicated to analysis of the movement of people worldwide." Their webpage has a wealth of information on migration.

www.interchangeinstitute.org/html/about.htm
This website offers advice, information, and support for transitioning to the United States. It provides insights on the migration experience and also describes the types of support systems that are available for migrants and travelers.

www.arfp.org
This Army Reserve Family Programs Online page provides various links that offer services for army personnel and their families. Among these links you will find the "Army Family Action Plan" and "Child and Youth Services." It provides extensive information and guidelines for both returning soldiers and their families to facilitate the often stressful time of homecoming and reunion.

http://immigrants.mndigital.org/exhibits/show/immigrantstories-exhibit/page01
Immigrant Stories at the Immigration History Research Center at the University of Minnesota. Listen to some of the stories of people who have immigrated to Minnesota.

SUMMARY

- A dialectical perspective on transitions reveals the tension between the individual and societal level of cultural adaptation.
- The four types of migrants are sojourners, immigrants, short-term refugees, and long-term refugees.

- There are four modes of migrant–host relationships: assimilation, separation, integration, and hybridity.
- A social science approach to adaptation emphasizes individual influences and outcomes and includes the AUM model, the transition model, and the integrative model.
- An interpretive approach emphasizes the lived experience and includes the U-curve theory, the W-curve theory, and phenomenological studies.
- A critical approach emphasizes the contextual influences on adaptation: social institutions, and political, historical, and economic structures.
- Cultural identity and adaptation are related in many ways.
- Those who live "on the borders" often develop multicultural identities.

DISCUSSION QUESTIONS

1. Why does culture shock occur to people who make cultural transitions?
2. Why are adaptations to cultures difficult for some people and easier for others?
3. What is the role of communication in the cultural adaptation process?
4. How do relations of power and dominance affect adaptation?
5. What factors affect migration patterns?
6. What dialectical tensions can you identify in the process of adapting to intercultural transitions?

ACTIVITIES

Culture Shock. Meet with other students in your class in small groups and explore your own experiences of cultural adaptation. Find out how many students experienced culture shock during the first year of college in terms of the three phases of the U-curve model. What did it feel like? How many experienced culture shock when traveling abroad? How about reentry shock? If there are differences in students' experience, explore why these differences exist. Are they related to differences in individual experience? In contexts?

KEY WORDS

assimilation (326)	flight approach (334)	liminality (351)
cultural adaptation (332)	functional fitness (337)	long-term refugees (323)
culture shock (339)	immigrants (322)	migrant (321)
explanatory	integration (330)	multicultural identity (352)
uncertainty (333)	intercultural	phenomenological
fight approach (335)	identity (338)	approach (345)

predictive uncertainty (333)

psychological health (337)

segregation (328)

separation (327)

short-term refugees (323)

social support (337)

sojourners (321)

transnationalism (351)

U-curve theory (338)

uncertainty reduction (333)

W-curve theory (342)

REFERENCES

Adelman, M. B. (1988). Cross-cultural adjustment: A theoretical perspective on social support. *International Journal of Intercultural Relations, 12,* 183–204.

Adler, P. (1975). The transition experience: An alternative view of culture shock. *Journal of Humanistic Psychology, 15,* 13–23.

Akwani, O. (2006, June 10). Racism against blacks is a growing trend in Europe. Global News Digest. Retrieved March 28, 2008, from http://imdcontentnew .searchease.com/villages/global/civil_human_equal _rights/RacismagainstBlacksinEurope.asp.

Alabama. (2011, September 30). Many immigrants pull children from schools. *The New York Times.* Retrieved January 17, 2012, from www.nytimes.com/2011/10/01 /us/alabama-many-immigrants-pull-children-from -schools.html.

Allardice, R. R., & Head, K. (2007, Winter). The coalition Air Force Transition Team. *Air & Space Power Journal.* Retrieved April 2, 2008, from www.airpower .maxwell.af.mil/airchronicles/apj/apj07/win07 /allardice.html.

Alsop, R. (2015, January 16). When expats return home, what's next? *BBC.* Retrieved June 10, 2016, from http://www.bbc.com/capital/story/20140115-returning -expat-discontent.

Al-Shaykh, H. (1995). *Beirut blues.* New York: Anchor Books.

Anzaldúa, G. (1999). *Borderlands/La frontera: The new mestiza* (2nd ed.). San Francisco: Aunt Lute Press.

Army Reserve Child, Youth & School Services (website). Retrieved June 18, 2016, from https://www.arfp.org /pdfs/Military%20Kids%20Homecoming%20and%20 Reunion%202014.pdf.

Bahadur, G. (2005, August 7). Muslims here balance between two cultures. *Philadelphia Inquirer,* p. B01.

Bennett, J. M. (1998). Transition shock: Putting culture shock in perspective. In M. J. Bennett (Ed.), *Basic concepts in intercultural communication: Selected readings* (pp. 215–224). First published in 1977, in N. C. Jain (Ed.), *International and Intercultural Communication Annual, 4,* 45–52.

Berry, J. W. (1992). Psychology of acculturation: Understanding individuals moving between two cultures. In R. W. Brislin (Ed.), *Applied cross cultural psychology* (pp. 232–253). Newbury Park, CA: Sage.

Berry, J. W., Kim, U., Minde, T., & Mok, D. (1987). Comparative studies of acculturative stress. *International Migration Review, 21,* 491–511.

Black, J. S., & Gregersen, H. B. (1999). *So you're coming home.* San Diego, CA: Global Business.

Campo-Flores, A. (2001, September 18). Brown against brown. *Newsweek,* pp. 49–51.

Chandler, J. V. (2005). *Why culture matters: An empirically-based pre-deployment training program.* Masters Thesis, Naval Postgraduate School.

Chen, L. (2000). How we know what we know about Americans: How Chinese sojourners account for their experiences. In A. González, M. Houston, & V. Chen (Eds.), *Our voices: Essays in culture, ethnicity and communication* (3rd ed., pp. 220–227). Los Angeles, CA: Roxbury.

Cigainero, J. (2016, April 10). Five years into ban, burqa divide widens in France. *Deutsche Welle.* Retrieved June 10, 2016, from http://www.dw.com/en/five -years-into-ban-burqa-divide-widens-in-france /a-19177275.

Clifford, J. (1992). Traveling cultures. In L. Grossberg, C. Nelson, & P. Treichler (Eds.), *Cultural studies* (pp. 96–116). New York: Routledge.

Collie, T. (2005, October 30). Rediscovering Judaism: Synagogues, religious schools are booming as Russian Jews reclaim their culture. *South Florida Sun-Sentinel,* p. 3J.

Danquah, M. N.-A. (1998). Life as an alien. In C. C. O'Hearn (Ed.), *Half + half.* New York: Pantheon Books.

DeWolf, C. (2014, December 29). In Hong Kong, just who is an expat, anyway? *The Wall Street Journal.* Retrieved June 9, 2016, from http://blogs.wsj.com /expat/2014/12/29/in-hong-kong-just-who-is-an-expat -anyway/.

Doyle, M. W. (2004). The challenge of worldwide migration. *Journal of International Affairs, 57* (2), 1–5.

Duff-Brown, B. (2005, November 24). Canada, Aboriginals discuss redress plan. Associated Press News Service.

Ehrenreich, B., & Hochschild, A. R. (2003). Introduction. In B. Ehrenreich & A. R. Hochschild (Eds.), *Global woman: Nannies, maids, and sex workers* (pp. 1–14). New York: Metropolitan Books.

El Nasser, H. (2010, December 20). Census data show "surprising" segregation. *USA Today.* Retrieved June 2, 2011, from www.usatoday.com/news/nation /census/2010-12-14-segregation_N.htm.

Ernst & Young (2015). Data makes mobility work: EY 2015 global mobility effectiveness survey. From http://www .ey.com/Publication/vwLUAssets/EY-global-mobility -effectiveness-survey-2015-executive-summary/$File /EY-global-mobility-effectiveness-survey-2015 -executive-summary.pdf.

Facts and figures (n.d.). *International Organization for Migration.* Retrieved May 7, 2011, from www.iom .int/jahia/Jahia/pid/241.

Festinger, L. (1957). *A theory of cognitive dissonance.* Stanford, CA: Stanford University Press.

Gonzalez, D. (2005, October 12). Language gap grows. Studies: Schools face increased challenges. *Arizona Republic,* p. B1.

Grieco, E. M., & Trevelyan, E. N. (2010). Place of birth of foreign-born population: 2009. *American Community Service Briefs.* Retrieved May 7, 2011, from www .census.gov/prod/2010pubs/acsbr09-15.pdf.

Grieco, E. M., et al. (2012, May). The Foreign-born population in the United States: 2010. Washington, D.C.: United States Census Bureau, US Department of Commerce. From https://www.census.gov/prod/2012pubs /acs-19.pdf.

Gudykunst, W. B. (1995). Anxiety uncertainty management (AUM) theory: Current status. In R. L. Wiseman (Ed.), *Intercultural communication theory* (pp. 8–58). Newbury Park, CA: Sage.

Gudykunst, W. B. (1998). Applying anxiety/uncertainty management (AUM) theory to intercultural adjustment training. *International Journal of Intercultural Relations, 22,* 187–227.

Gudykunst, W. B. (2005). An anxiety/uncertainty management (AUM) theory of effective communication: Making the mesh of the net finer. In W. B. Gudykunst (Ed.), *Theorizing about intercultural communication* (pp. 281–323). Thousand Oaks, CA: Sage.

Gullahorn, J. T., & Gullahorn, J. E. (1963). An extension of the U-curve hypothesis. *Journal of Social Issues, 19,* 33–47.

Hegde, R. S. (1998). Swinging the trapeze: The negotiation of identity among Asian Indian immigrant women in the United States. In D. V. Tanno & A. González (Eds.), *Communication of identity across cultures* (pp. 34–55). Thousand Oaks, CA: Sage.

Hegde, R. S. (2000). Hybrid revivals: Defining Asian Indian ethnicity through celebration. In A. González, M. Houston, & V. Chen (Eds.), *Our voices: Essays in culture, ethnicity and communication* (3rd ed., pp. 133–138). Los Angeles, CA: Roxbury.

Henderson, M. (1999). *Forgiveness: Breaking the chain of hate.* Wilsonville, OR: Book-Partners.

Houd, A. with Hodali, D. (2015, August 15). "I could no longer live in Syria." *Deutsche Welle.* Retrieved June 2, 2016, from http://www.dw.com/en/i-could-no -longer-live-in-syria/a-18680302.

Immigrants in their own words: 100 stories (2015, March 25). *The Guardian.* Retrieved June 10, 2016, from HYPERLINK "http://www.theguardian.com /commentisfree/ng-interactive/2015/mar/24/immigrants -in-their-own-words-100-stories" \l "list"; http://www .theguardian.com/commentisfree/ng-interactive/2015 /mar/24/immigrants-in-their-own-words-100-stories#list.

International Organization for Migration (2015). World migration report 2015. Geneva: International Organization for Migration. From http://publications.iom.int /system/files/wmr2015_en.pdf.

Iraqi immigrant gets 34 years for killing "too Westernized" daughter (2011, April 16). *CNN.* Retrieved June 10, 2016, from http://www.cnn.com/2011 /CRIME/04/15/arizona.honor.killing/.

Ishii, S. (2001). The Japanese welcome-nonwelcome ambivalence syndrome toward Marebito (Ijin) Gaijin strangers: Its implications for intercultural communication research. *Japan Review, 13,* 145–170.

James, S. (2010, March 19). With ban on H.I.V. immigrants now history, relief and revision. *The New York Times.* Retrieved June 10, 2016, from http://www .nytimes.com/2010/03/19/us/19sfmetro.html.

Kashima, E. S., & Loh, E. (2006). International students' acculturation: Effects of international, conational, and local ties and need for closure. *International Journal of Intercultural Relations, 30,* 471–486.

Kealey, D. J. (1989). A study of cross-cultural effectiveness: Theoretical issues, practical applications. *International Journal of Intercultural Relations, 13,* 387–427.

Kealey, D. J. (1996). The challenge of international personnel selection. In D. Landis & R. S. Bhagat (Eds.), *Handbook of intercultural training* (2nd ed., pp. 81–105). Thousand Oaks, CA: Sage.

Kim, M.-S. (2002). Models of acculturative communication competence: Who bears the burden of adaptation? In *Non-western perspectives on human communication* (pp. 141–154). Thousand Oaks, CA: Sage.

Kim, Y. Y. (2001). *Becoming intercultural: An integrative theory of communication and cross-cultural adaptation.* Thousand Oaks, CA: Sage.

Kim, Y. Y. (2005). Adapting to a new culture: An integrative communication theory. In W. B. Gudykunst (Ed.), *Theorizing about intercultural communication* (pp. 375–400). Thousand Oaks, CA: Sage.

Kim, Y. Y. (2006). From ethnic to interethnic: The case for identity adaptation and transformation. *Journal of Language and Social Psychology, 25*(3), 283–300.

Kim, Y. Y., & Gudykunst, W. B. (Eds.). (1988). *Cross cultural adaptation: Current approaches.* International and Intercultural Communication Annual 11. Newbury Park, CA: Sage.

Koutonin, M. R. (2015, March 13). Why are white people expats when the rest of us are immigrants? *The Guardian.* Retrieved June 9, 2016, from http://www.theguardian.com/global-development-professionals-network/2015/mar/13/white-people-expats-immigrants-migration.

Kristjánsdóttir, E. S. (2009). Invisibility dreaded and desired: Phenomenological inquiry of sojourners' cross-cultural adaptation. *Howard Journal of Communications, 20*(22).

Lee, J. J., & Rice, C. (2007). Welcome to America? International student perceptions of discrimination, *Higher Education, 53,* 381–409.

Lysgaard, S. (1955). Adjustment in a foreign society: Norwegian Fulbright grantees visiting the United States. *International Social Science Bulletin, 7,* 45–51.

Martin, J. N. (1984). The intercultural reentry: Conceptualizations and suggestions for future research. *International Journal of Intercultural Relations, 8,* 115–134.

Martin, J. N. (1986). Communication in the intercultural reentry: Student sojourners' perceptions of change in reentry relationships. *International Journal of Intercultural Relations, 10,* 1–22.

Martin, J. N., Bradford, L., & Rohrlich, B. (1995). Comparing predeparture expectations and post-sojourn reports: A longitudinal study of U.S. students abroad. *International Journal of Intercultural Relations, 19,* 87–110.

Martin, J. N., & Harrell, T. (2004). Intercultural reentry of students and professionals: Theory and practice. In D. Landis, J. M. Bennett, & M. J. Bennett (Eds.), *Handbook of intercultural training* (3rd ed., pp. 309–336). Thousand Oaks, CA: Sage.

Martin, P. (2013). The Global Challenge of Managing Migration, *Population Bulletin* 68, no. 2. From http://www.prb.org/pdf13/global-migration.pdf.

Mather, M. (2007). Education and occupation separates two kinds of immigrants in the United States. Population Reference Bureau. Retrieved March 28, 2008, from www.prb.org/Articles/2007/Education AndOccupationSeparatesUSImmigrants.aspx.

Mead, J. C. (2003, September 28). In Island's wealthiest area, backlash against the poorest. *The New York Times,* Section 14LI, p. 1.

Mura, D. (1991). *Turning Japanese: Memoirs of a sansei.* New York: Anchor Books.

Newlove, R. (2016, February 9). Why expat Americans are giving up their passports. *BBC News.* Retrieved June 10, 2016, from http://www.bbc.com/news/35383435.

Numbers. (2008, February 4). *Time,* p. 18.

Nwanko, R. N., & Onwumechili, C. (1991). Communication and social values in cross-cultural adjustment. *Howard Journal of Communications, 3,* 99–111.

Oberg, K. (1960). Cultural shock: Adjustment to new cultural environments. *Practical Anthropology, 7,* 177–182.

O'Hearn, C. C. (ed). (1998). *Half and Half: Writers on growing up biracial and bicultural.* New York: Pantheon Books.

Omelaniuk, I., & Weiss. T. L. (2005). Introduction. In I. Omelaniuk (Ed.), *World migration 2005: Costs and benefits of international migration* (pp. 13–22). Geneva, Switzerland: International Organization for Migration.

Onwumechilia, C., Nwosu, P. O., Jackson, R. L., & James-Huges, J. (2003). In the deep valley with mountains to climb: Exploring identity and multiple reacculturation. *International Journal of Intercultural Relations, 27,* 41–62.

Poyrazli, S., & Lopez, M. D. (2007). An exploratory study of perceived discrimination and homesickness: A comparison of international students and American students. *Journal of Psychology, 141*(3), 263–280.

Pratik, J. (2005, May 15). Refugees renew church. *St. Paul Pioneer Press,* p. C1.

Ralston, J. (2010, July 28). Refugees and the role of religious groups. *Australian Broadcasting Corporation.* Retrieved January 17, 2012, from www.abc.net.au/religion/articles/2010/07/28/2966921.htm.

Reid, B. (2005, November 10). Options are available for students, parents: Finding the right fit for English learners. *Arizona Republic,* p. B3.

Rohrlich, B., & Martin, J. N. (1991). Host country and reentry adjustment of student sojourners. *International Journal of Intercultural Relations, 15,* 163–182.

Rosenau, J. N. (2004). Emergent spaces, new places, and old faces: Proliferating identities in a globalizing world. In J. Friedman & S. Randeria (Eds.), *Worlds on the move: Globalization, migration and cultural security* (pp. 23–62). New York: I. B. Tauris.

Ruggiero, K. M., Taylor, D. M., & Lambert, W. E. (1996). A model of heritage culture maintenance. *International Journal of Intercultural Relations, 20,* 47–67.

Santos, B. (2004). Transnational third world. In J. Friedman & S. Randeria (Eds.), *Worlds on the move: Globalization, migration and cultural security* (pp. 293–318). New York: I. B. Tauris.

Schwartz, D. (2012, November 6). Iraqis spared jail time in Arizona for abusing female relative. *Chicago Tribune.* Retrieved June 10, 2016, from http://articles.chicagotribune.com/2012-11-06/business/sns-rt-usa-arizonairaqil1e8m6i7i-20121106_1_faleh-hassan-almaleki-iraqi-immigrant-jail-time.

Search for social glue. (2008, February 23). *The Economist, 386*(8568), 74.

Sedgman, J. M. (2005, March 16). Children removed from schools by immigration officials. *The World Today, ABC Online.* Accessed at www.abc.net.au/cgi-bin/common/printfriendly.pl?www.abc.net.au/worldtoday/content/2005/s1324795.htm.

Stack, L. (2016, April 5). Air France faces backlash over veil policy on route to Iran. *The New York Times.* Retrieved June 10, 2016, from http://www.nytimes.com/2016/04/06/world/europe/air-france-veil-policy-iran.html?_r=0.

Sulitzeanu, A. B. (2010, November 1). Segregation of Jews and Arabs in 2010 is almost absolute. *Salem (OR), News.* Retrieved June 2, 2011, from http://salem-news.com/articles/november012010/israel-apartheid-abs.php.

Sullivan, K. (1997, December 6). "White" Australia in identity crisis: Many fear Asian immigrants are taking away jobs, culture. *Washington Post,* p. A1.

Tehranian, M. (2004). Cultural security and global governance: International migration and negotiations of identity. In J. Friedman & S. Randeria (Eds.), *Worlds on the move: Globalization, migration and cultural security* (pp. 3–22). New York: I. B. Tauris.

Telles, E. E., & Ortiz, V. (2008). *Generations of exclusion: Mexican Americans, assimilation, and race.* New York: Russell Sage Foundation.

Turner, V. W. (1969). *The ritual process.* Chicago, IL: Aldine.

UNHCR Statistical Yearbook 2009, United Nations High Commissioner for Refugees. Retrieved May 7, 2011, from www.unhcr.org/4ce532ff9.html.

UNHCR (2015). *UNHCR Statistical Yearbook 2014.* Geneva, Switzerland: UNHCR, 2015. From http://www.unhcr.org/en-us/statistics/country/566584fc9/unhcr-statistical-yearbook-2014-14th-edition.html.

Vanderpool, T. (2002, April 2). Lesson no. 1: Shed your Indian identity. *Christian Science Monitor,* p. 14.

Vorhauser-Smith, S. (2013, October 31). Global mobility: A win-win for you and your employer. *Forbes.* Retrieved June 10, 2016, from "http://www.forbes.com/sites/sylviavorhausersmith/2013/10/31/global-mobility-a-win-win-for-you-and-your-employer/" \l "31353b05779c" http://www.forbes.com/sites/sylviavorhausersmith/2013/10/31/global-mobility-a-win-win-for-you-and-your-employer/#31353b05779c.

Ward, C. (1996). Acculturation. In D. Landis & R. S. Bhagat (Eds.), *Handbook of intercultural training* (2nd ed., pp. 125–147). Thousand Oaks, CA: Sage.

Ward, C., Bochner, S., & Furnham, A. (2001). *The psychology of culture shock* (2nd ed.). East Sussex: Routledge. (Simultaneously published in the United States by Taylor & Francis, Philadelphia, PA.)

Weissman, D., & Furnham, A. (1987). The expectations and experiences of a sojourning temporary resident abroad: A preliminary study. *Human Relations, 40,* 313–326.

Why expats are ditching their U.S. passports. (2014, March 10). *CNN Money.* Retrieved June 10, 2016, from http://money.cnn.com/gallery/pf/2014/03/10/expat-taxes-citizenship/index.html.

Witte, K. (1993). A theory of cognitive and negative affect: Extending Gudykunst and Hammer's theory of uncertainty and anxiety reduction. *International Journal of Intercultural Relations, 17,* 197–216.

Wood, R. W. (2016, February 6). Record numbers renounce their U.S. citizenship. *Forbes.* Retrieved June 10, 2016, from HYPERLINK "http://www.forbes.com/sites/robertwood/2016/02/06/record-numbers-renounce-their-u-s-citizenship/" \l "5309c077a6e6" http://www.forbes.com/sites/robertwood/2016/02/06/record-numbers-renounce-their-u-s-citizenship/#5309c077a6e6.

Zimmerman, S. (1995). Perceptions of intercultural communication competence and international student adaptation to an American campus. *Communication Education, 44,* 321–335.

CREDITS

[page 322, text] P. Martin, quote from "The global challenge of managing migration" from *Population Bulletin* (2013). [page 325, text] Excerpt from "Immigrants in their own words: 100 stories" from *The Guardian* (March 25, 2015). [page 321, text] UNHCR, quote from "UNHCR Statistical Yearbook 2014" from *UNHCR* (2015). [page 324, text] Quote from "Immigrants in their own words: 100 stories" from *The Guardian* (March 25, 2015). [page 325, text] Quote from "Immigrants in their own words: 100 stories" from *The Guardian* (March 25, 2015). [page 327, text] D. Schwartz, quote from "Iraqis spared jail time in Arizona for abusing female relative" from *Chicago Tribune* (November 6, 2012). [page 327, text] Quote from "Iraqi immigrant gets 34 years for killing "too Westernized" daughter" from *CNN* (April 16, 2011). [page 327, text] H. El Nasser, quote from "Census data show"surprising" segregation" from *USA Today* (December 20, 2010). [page 329, text] A. B. Sulitzeanu, quote from "Segregation of Jews and Arabs in 2010 is almost absolute" from *Salem News* (November 1, 2010). [page 329, text] E. G. Austin, excerpt from "Immigration: The French Paradox and the British Backlash" from *The Economist* (May 24, 2011). [page 330, text] C. C. O'Hearn, quote from *Half and half: Writers on growing up biracial 1 bicultural*. Pantheon Books. [page 330, text] R. S. Hegde, excerpt from "Hybrid revivals: Defining Asian Indian ethnicity through celebration" in *Our voices: Essays in culture, ethnicity and communication*, edited by A. González, M. Houston, and V. Chen. Roxbury. [page 335, text] C. DeWolf, excerpt from "In Hong Kong, just who is an expat, anyway?" *The Wall Street Journal* (December 29, 2014). [page 335, text] M. R. Koutonin, excerpt from "Why are white people expats when the rest of us are immigrants?" from *The Guardian* (March 13, 2015). [page 335, text] C. DeWolf, quote from "In Hong Kong, just who is an expat, anyway?" *The Wall Street Journal* (December 29, 2014). [page 335, text] M. R. Koutonin, quote from "Why are white people expats when the rest of us are immigrants?" *The Guardian* (March 13, 2015). [page 336, text] L. Festinger, excerpt from *A theory of cognitive dissonance*. Stanford University Press. [page 336, text] Y. Y. Kim, excerpt from *Becoming intercultural: An integrative theory of communication and cross-cultural adaptation*. Sage. [page 340, text] J. V. Chandler, quote from *Why culture matters: An empirically-based pre-deployment training program*. Naval Postgraduate School. [page 340, text] R. R. Allardice, and K. Head, quote from "The coalition Air Force transition team" from *Air & Space Power Journal*. (Winter, 2007). [page 343, text] S. Smith, excerpt from "The cycle of cross-cultural adaptation and reentry" in *Readings in intercultural communication,* edited by J. Martin, T. K. Nakayama, and L. A. Flores. McGraw-Hill. [page 343, text] R. Alsop, excerpt from "When expats return home, what's next?" *BBC* (January 16, 2015). [page 343, text] Ernst & Young, excerpt from "Data makes mobility work: EY 2015 global mobility effectiveness survey" from *Ernst & Young* (2015). [page 343, text] S. Vorhauser-Smith, excerpt from "Global mobility: A win-win for you and your employer" from *Forbes* (October 31, 2013). [page 343, text] S. Vorhauser-Smith, quote from "Global mobility: A win-win for you and your employer" from *Forbes* (October 31, 2013). [page 343, text] Ernst & Young, quote from "Data makes mobility work: EY 2015 global mobility effectiveness survey" from *Ernst & Young* (2015). [page 343–344, text] H. Al-Shaykh, excerpt from *Beirut blues*. Anchor Books. [page 345, text] L. Chen, quote from "How we know what we know about Americans: How Chinese sojourners account for their experiences" in *Our voices: Essays in culture, ethnicity and communication*, edited by A. González, M. Houston, & V. Chen. Roxbury. [page 345, text] L. Chen, quote from "How we know what we know about Americans: How Chinese sojourners account for their experiences" in *Our voices: Essays in culture, ethnicity and communication*, edited by A. González, M. Houston, & V. Chen. Roxbury. [page 345, text] L. Chen, excerpt from "How we know what we know about Americans: How Chinese sojourners account for their experiences" in *Our voices: Essays in culture, ethnicity and communication*, edited by A. González, M. Houston, & V. Chen. Roxbury. [page 346, text] Jesse, excerpt from "Students Voices: When I first arrived . . . in my halting speech." Original work; [page 346, text] E. S. Kristjánsdóttir, quote from "Invisibility dreaded and desired: Phenomenological inquiry of sojourners' cross-cultural adaptation" from *Howard Journal of Communications* (2009). [page 347, text] S. Ishii, quote from "The Japanese welcome-nonwelcome ambivalence syndrome toward Marebito (Ijin) Gaijin strangers: Its implications for intercultural communication research" from *Japan Review* (2001): 145–170. [page 348, text] J. Cigainero, excerpt from "Five years into ban, burqa divide widens in France" from *Deutsche Welle* (April 10, 2016). [page 348, text] L. Stack, excerpt from "Air France faces backlash over veil policy on route to Iran" from *The New York Times* (April 5, 2016). [page 348, text] J. Cigainero, quote from "Five years into ban, burqa divide widens in France" from *Deutsche Welle* (April 10, 2016). [page 348, text] L. Stack, quote from "Air France faces backlash over veil policy on route to Iran" *The New York Times* (April 5, 2016). [page 349, text] Lois, excerpt from "When I moved to . . . Chink, Chinaman." Original work; [page 349, text] B. Duff-Brown, quote from "Canada, Aboriginals discuss redress plan" from *Associated Press News Service* (November 24, 2005). [page 349, text] J. J. Lee, and C. Rice, excerpt from "Welcome to America? International student perceptions of discrimination" from *Higher Education* (2007): 381–409. [page 350, text] A. Campo-Flores, excerpt from "Brown against brown" from *Newsweek* (September 18, 2001): 49–51. [page 351, text] V. W. Turner, quote from *The ritual process*. Aldine. [page 351, text] Y. Y. Kim, excerpt from "From ethnic to interethnic: The case for identity adaptation and transformation" from *Journal of Language and Social Psychology* (2006): 283–300. [page 352, text] G. Anzaldúa, quote from *Borderlands/ La frontera: The new mestizo, Second edition*. Aunt Lute Press. [page 353, text] D. Mura, excerpt from *Turning Japanese: Memoirs of a sansei*. Anchor Books.

POPULAR CULTURE AND INTERCULTURAL COMMUNICATION

LEARNING ABOUT CULTURES WITHOUT PERSONAL EXPERIENCE
The Power of Popular Culture
What Is Popular Culture?

CONSUMING AND RESISTING POPULAR CULTURE
Consuming Popular Culture
Resisting Popular Culture

REPRESENTING CULTURAL GROUPS
Migrants' Perceptions of Mainstream Culture
Popular Culture and Stereotyping

U.S. POPULAR CULTURE AND POWER
Global Circulation of Images and Commodities
Cultural Imperialism

INTERNET RESOURCES

SUMMARY

DISCUSSION QUESTIONS

ACTIVITIES

KEY WORDS

REFERENCES

CHAPTER OBJECTIVES

After reading this chapter, you should be able to:

1. Differentiate between high and low culture.
2. Discuss the importance of popular culture as a public forum.
3. Identify the four characteristics of popular culture.
4. Identify some patterns of how people consume popular culture.
5. Identify some ways that people resist popular culture.
6. Describe some of the ways that popular culture influences how people understand another culture.
7. Explain the role of popular culture in stereotyping.
8. Explain how the global movement of popular culture influences people around the world.
9. Discuss the concerns of some governments about the influence of foreign media in their countries.

In February 2016, Beyoncé released a new music video and song, "Formation," shortly before she was to perform in the Super Bowl halftime show. She also performed this song at Super Bowl 50 during the halftime show. After its release, the ensuing discussion about her video underscored the various interpretations of it to serve very different ends. The video itself is:

> *Bookended by the flooding of the city of New Orleans after 2005's Hurricane Katrina—and by which the city's black residents were disproportionately affected—and a black child in a hoodie dancing opposite a police line and a quick cut to graffiti words "stop shooting us," Beyoncé morphs into several archetypical southern black women (McFadden, 2016).*

The imagery invoked images of the racialized experience of Hurricane Katrina, the Black Lives Matter movement, and more about blackness and black politics. This video created quite a reaction as "she is one of those stars of color who until now has been beyond race for the mainstream audience" (France, 2016). Some celebrated and embraced Beyoncé's video, while others were upset by it. Saturday Night Live created a short piece, "The Day Beyonce Turned Black," that showed white people panicking when they realized that Beyonce is black and unable to understand her music.

The response to the video was not limited to the realm of popular culture. For example, "U.S. Representative Peter King (R-Long Island) released a statement which referred to Beyoncé as 'a gifted entertainer' but took issue with her 'pro-Black Panther and anti-cop video'" (Ex, 2016). Javier Ortiz, the president of the Miami Fraternal Order of Police, declared that "The fact that Beyoncé used this year's Super Bowl to divide Americans by promoting the Black Panthers and her antipolice message shows how she does not support law enforcement" (quoted in Chokshi, 2016). This police organization called for a nationwide boycott of her shows. A number of police unions discussed boycotting off-duty security work during her concerts, including Tampa, Nashville, and Raleigh. While not all thought that was the right approach to communicating their unhappiness with the video, a group called "Proud of the Blues" sent out a call for a protest at the NFL headquarters in New York City to express their unhappiness that they allowed Beyoncé to perform during the Super Bowl. On the day and time of the protest, only "a handful of Beyonce supporters gathered in Manhattan to fend off an anti-Beyonce protest that never happened" (Bonesteel, 2016).

The visibility of the Super Bowl, coupled with the attention given to her video by Saturday Night Live and other venues, boosted "Beyoncé's new 'Formation' single which zoomed straight to No. 1 on the real-time Billboard + Twitter Trending 140 chart shortly after its release on February 6" (Caulfield, 2016) and earned her "over $100 million in ticket sales" (France, 2016) for her concerts. This visibility means that the issues raised by her video reach a very large audience with very different interpretations of it. The video brings a number of cultural tensions into public discussions on the Internet, newspapers, magazine, and other outlets.

LEARNING ABOUT CULTURES
WITHOUT PERSONAL EXPERIENCE

As discussed in Chapter 8, people can experience and learn about other cultures by traveling to and relocating and living in other regions. But there will always be many places around the world that we have not visited and where we have not lived. How do we know about places we have never been? Much of what we know probably comes from popular culture—the media experience of films, television, music, videos, books, and magazines that most of us know and share. How does this experience affect intercultural communication?

The Power of Popular Culture

Neither Tom nor Judith has ever been to Nigeria, India, Russia, or Venezuela. Yet both of us hold tremendous amounts of information about these places from the news, movies, TV shows, advertisements, and more. The kind and quality of information we all have about other places are influenced by popular culture. But the views that the media portray supplement the information we get from other sources. For example, audiences who watch the movie *Restrepo* are likely to be familiar with the military mission in Afghanistan, even if they have not been in military service there. In this sense, popular culture is pervasive.

The complexity of popular culture is often overlooked. People express concern about the social effects of popular culture—for example, the influence of television violence on children, the role of certain kinds of music in causing violent behavior by some youths, and the relationship between heterosexual pornography and violence against women. Yet most people look down on the study of popular culture, as if this form of culture conveys nothing of lasting significance. So, on the one hand, we are concerned about the power of popular culture; on the other, we don't look on popular culture as a serious area of academic research. This inherent contradiction can make it difficult to investigate and discuss popular culture. More recently, communication scholars are turning their attention to the power of videos posted on the Internet that are designed to persuade people to join ISIS (the Islamic State of Iraq and Syria). For example, in their work, Samuel P. Perry and Jerry M. Long (2016) analyzed the rhetorical appeals made in the "Operation Rabi bin Amir" campaign. They found that the videos focused on turning an actual event into a mythic construction of martyrdom as a way to recruit people to ISIS. More work on the power of popular communication may be forthcoming in the current environment.

As U.S. Americans, we are in a unique position in relationship to popular culture. Products of U.S. popular culture are well known and circulate widely on the international market. The popularity of U.S. movies such as *Star Wars* and *The Hunger Games;* U.S. music stars such as Lady Gaga and Katy Perry; and U.S. television shows such as *The Big Bang Theory, NCIS,* and *Empire* create an uneven flow of texts between the United States and other nations. Scholars Elihu Katz and Tamar Liebes (1987) have noted the "apparent ease with which American television

I was on my way to Rome from Newark last summer. Since I took the Polish Airlines, I had to make a stopover in Warsaw. During my first morning in Warsaw, I got up, took a shower, and turned on the TV, just out of curiosity to see what was showing. I guess I expected to hear Polish, some local news and dramas, etc.

The first thing that jumped at me from the TV screen was Ricky Martin! Then followed Destiny's Child! I was shocked! U.S. popular culture really is everywhere! And I thought I already knew that! But I didn't expect it, all the way in Poland.

—Mina

programs cross cultural and linguistic frontiers. Indeed, the phenomenon is so taken for granted that hardly any systematic research has been done to explain the reasons why these programs are so successful" (p. 419).

In contrast, U.S. Americans are rarely exposed to popular culture from outside the United States. Exceptions to this largely one-way movement of popular culture include pop music stars who sing in English, such as Wyclef Jean (Haitian), Shakira (Colombian), and Enrique Iglesias (Spanish). Consider how difficult it is to find foreign films or television programs throughout most of the United States. Even when foreign corporations market their products in the United States, they almost always use U.S. advertising agencies—collectively known as "Madison Avenue." The apparent imbalance of cultural texts globally not only renders U.S. Americans more dependent on U.S.-produced popular culture but also can lead to cultural imperialism, a topic we discuss later in this chapter.

The study of popular culture has become increasingly important in the communication field. Although intercultural communication scholars traditionally have overlooked popular culture, we believe that it is a significant influence in intercultural interaction.

What Is Popular Culture?

The 19th-century essayist and poet Matthew Arnold, who expressed concern about protecting civilization, defined *culture* as "the best that has been thought and said in the world"—a definition that emphasizes quality. In this context, many Western societies distinguish "high culture" from "low culture."

High culture refers to those cultural activities that are often the domain of the elite or the well-to-do: ballet, symphony, opera, great literature, and fine art. These activities sometimes are framed as *international* because supposedly they can be appreciated by audiences in other places, from other cultures, in different time periods. Their cultural value is seen as transcendent and timeless. To protect these cultural treasures, social groups build museums, symphony halls, and theaters. In fact, universities devote courses, programs, and even entire departments to the study of aspects of high culture.

In opposition to high culture is low culture, which refers to the activities of the nonelite: music videos, game shows, professional wrestling, stock car racing, graffiti art, TV talk shows, and so on. Traditionally, low-culture activities have been seen as unworthy of serious study—and so of little interest to museums or universities. The cultural values embedded in these activities were considered neither transcendent nor timeless.

The elitism reflected in the distinction between high and low culture points to the tensions in Western social systems. In recent decades, however, this distinction has begun to break down. Rapid social changes propelled universities to alter their policies and also have affected how we study intercultural communication. For example, the turbulent 1960s brought to the university a powerful new interest in ethnic studies, including African American studies and women's and gay and lesbian issues. These areas of study did not rely on the earlier distinctions between high and low culture. Rather, they contributed to a new conceptual framework by arguing for the legitimacy of other cultural forms that traditionally would have been categorized as low culture but were now framed as **popular culture.** Because of this elitist view of culture, the distinction between "high culture" and "low culture" has led to low culture being reconceptualized as popular culture. Barry Brummett (1994), a contemporary rhetorician, offers the following definition: "Popular culture refers to those systems or artifacts that most people share and that most people know about" (p. 21). According to this definition, television, music videos, YouTube, Disney, advertising, soap operas, and popular magazines are systems of popular culture. In contrast, the symphony and the ballet do not qualify as popular culture because most people cannot identify much about them unless they have studied them.

So, popular culture often is seen as populist—including forms of contemporary culture that are made popular by and for the people. John Fiske (1989), professor of communication arts, explains:

> To be made into popular culture, a commodity must also bear the interests of the people. Popular culture is not consumption, it is culture—the active process of generating and circulating meanings and pleasures within a social system: culture, however industrialized, can never be adequately described in terms of the buying and selling of commodities. (p. 23)

In his study of popular Mexican American music in Los Angeles, ethnic studies professor George Lipsitz (1990) highlights the innovative, alternative ways that marginalized social groups are able to express themselves. In this study, he demonstrates how popular culture can arise by mixing and borrowing from other cultures: "The ability of musicians to learn from other cultures played a key role in their success as rock-and-roll artists" (p. 140). The popular speaks to—and resonates from—the people, but it does so through multiple cultural voices. Lipsitz continues:

> The marginality of Chicano rock-and-roll musicians has provided them with a constant source of inspiration and a constant spur toward innovation that gained them the attention of mainstream audiences. But this marginal sensibility amounts to more than novelty or personal eccentricity; it holds legitimacy and power as the product of a real historical community's struggle with

popular culture A new name for *low culture,* referring to those cultural products that most people share and know about, including television, music, videos, and popular magazines.

oppression. . . . As Chicano musicians demonstrate in their comments about their work, their music reflects a quite conscious cultural politic that seeks inclusion in the American mainstream by transforming it. (p. 159)

Intercultural contact and intercultural communication play a central role in the creation and maintenance of popular culture. Yet, as Lipsitz points out, the popular is political and pleasurable, which further complicates how we think about popular culture.

There are four significant characteristics of popular culture: (1) It is produced by culture industries, (2) it differs from **folk culture,** (3) it is everywhere, and (4) it fills a social function. As Fiske (1989) points out, popular culture is nearly always produced within a capitalist system that sees the products of popular culture as commodities that can be economically profitable. (See Table 9-1.) They are produced by what are called **culture industries.** The Disney Corporation is a noteworthy example of a culture industry because it produces amusement parks, movies, cartoons, and a plethora of associated merchandise.

More recently, communication scholars Joshua Gunn and Barry Brummett (2004) have challenged the second point that there is an important difference between folk culture and popular culture. They suggest, "We write as if there is a fundamental difference between a mass-produced and mass-marketed culture and a more authentic 'folk' culture or subculture. Such a binary is dissolving into a globally marketed culture. A few remaining pockets of folk culture remain here and there: on the Sea Islands, in Amish country, in departments of English. The rest of folk culture is now 50% off at Wal-Mart" (p. 707). In the new context of globalization, whatever happened to folk traditions and artifacts? Have they been unable to escape being mass-produced and marketed around the globe? Where would you look

folk culture Traditional and nonmainstream cultural activities that are not financially driven.

culture industries Industries that produce and sell popular culture as commodities.

TABLE 9-I   DISTINCTIONS AMONG HIGH CULTURE, FOLK CULTURE, AND POPULAR CULTURE

Type	Definition	Who Knows It?	What Does It Look Like?
High culture	Elite aristocratic expressions of culture	Rich members of the political establishment	Opera, classic sculpture, symphony performances
Folk culture	Traditional and nonmainstream cultural activities that are not financially driven	Most cultural groups, but especially middle-class groups	Folk music
Popular culture	Ever-present cultural products designed for profitable consumption	Almost everyone in a social group	Mainstream music, movies, television, romance novels

FIGURE 9-1   Shakira is a multilingual Colombian singer whose songs have hit the charts in many countries, including Turkey and the United States. She exemplifies non-U.S. popular culture making an impact internationally. (© *Miriam Alster/epa/Corbis*)

for folk culture today? Whatever happened to traditional folk dancing, quilting bees, and other forms of folk culture?

Popular culture is ubiquitous. We are bombarded with it, every day and everywhere. On average, U.S. Americans watch more than 40 hours of television per week. Movie theaters beckon us with the latest multimillion-dollar extravaganzas, nearly all U.S. made. Radio stations and music TV programs blast us with the hottest music groups performing their latest hits. (See Figure 9-1.) And we are inundated with a staggering number of advertisements and commercials daily. Much of this consumption of popular culture happens on smartphones and tablets today, rather than exclusively on radios and televisions, as it once was.

It is difficult to avoid popular culture. Not only is it ubiquitous but it also serves an important social function. How many times have you been asked by friends and family for your reaction to a recent movie or TV program? Academicians Horace Newcomb and Paul Hirsch (1987) suggest that television serves as a cultural forum for discussing and working out our ideas on a variety of topics, including those that emerge from the programs themselves. Television, then, has a powerful social function—to serve as a forum for dealing with social issues.

In their study on the early tweets after Michael Brown was shot and killed by officer Darren Wilson in Ferguson, Missouri, Sarah Jackson and Brooke Foucault Welles studied how Twitter and the hashtag #Ferguson shaped discussion on race, policing, and social justice. In analyzing the tweets, they identified "the most influential crowdsourced elite in the Ferguson network, with over two and half times as many retweets and mentions as the next closest elite, was an African American woman using the Twitter handle @AyoMissDarkSkin" (p. 405). @AyoMissDarkSkin was in the neighborhood when Michael Brown was shot and tweeted out two photos of the scene with the text: "Ferguson police just executed an unarmed 17 yr old boy who was walking to the store. Shot him 10 times smh. (12:48 PM-(Aug 2014)." Jackson and Foucault Welles contrast her tweet with the tweet from the *St. Louis Post Dispatch:*

> *The discourse of this tweet immediately frames Brown as the innocent ('unarmed' 'boy') victim of extreme violence ('executed' 'Shot him 10 times') and communicates an effective response ('smh'- Shaking My Head—generally used to indicate disgust or incredulousness). This discursive work stands in sharp contrast to a tweet sent two hours later by the only media outlet to achieve crowdsourced elite status on day one, local mainstream newspaper the St. Louis Post Dispatch (@stltoday). @stltoday reported: "Fatal shooting by Ferguson police prompts mob reaction" (p. 405).*

The use of Twitter to provide and produce a counter discourse to the elite discourse of the newspaper opens an arena for various publics to come to understand what happened in Ferguson and what it means. Aside from the mainstream media reports on Ferguson, Twitter and its followers can offer alternative interpretations from marginalized publics. Hence, "the technological architecture of Twitter becomes an important tool for subverting traditional citizen–state power structures, enabling counterpublics to drive national conversations" (p. 413).

In a similar study, communication scholars Dreama Moon and Tom Nakayama (2005) analyzed newspaper accounts of the murder of Arthur "J. R." Warren in West Virginia. Although the small town where he was murdered did not have a local paper, they found that the media coverage did highlight significant differences in how African Americans, gays and lesbians, and white heterosexual residents experienced and perceived life there. Through the media, African Americans and gays and lesbians were able to offer an alternative view that differed from the dominant view of idealized small-town life. Again, newspapers served as a forum for discussion of this tragic event and related aspects of everyday life and community in this small West Virginia town.

In contrast, not all popular culture serves to open forums for public deliberation. In his study of the "Pro Football and the American Spirit" exhibit, communication scholar Michael Butterworth examined this exhibit at the Pro Football Hall of Fame in Canton, Ohio. This exhibit was meant to travel and has been on display in other locations. This exhibit connects football with militarism. It connects various wars with what was happening in the NFL and the role of the NFL. It not only highlights the sacrifices of veterans affiliated with football, including Pat Tillman, but also shuts down public deliberation about militarism and war. Rather than challenging the history and role of military conflicts, the exhibit ends up "about war itself, about constituting and conditioning citizens to accept the necessity and normalcy of war, and about extending and celebrating a culture of militarism" (2016, p. 255). In this analysis, popular culture reduces the arena of contemporary democratic deliberation.

The ways that people negotiate their relationships to popular culture are complex, and it is this complexity that makes understanding the role of popular culture in intercultural communication so difficult. Clearly, we are not passive recipients of this deluge of popular culture. We are, in fact, quite active in our consumption of or resistance to popular culture, a notion that we turn to next.

CONSUMING AND RESISTING POPULAR CULTURE

Consuming Popular Culture

Faced with this onslaught of **cultural texts,** people negotiate their ways through popular culture in quite different ways. Popular culture texts do not have to win over the majority of people to be "popular." People often seek out or avoid specific forms of popular culture. For example, romance novels are the best-selling form of literature, but many readers have no interest in such books. Likewise, whereas many people enjoy watching soap operas or professional wrestling, many others find no pleasure in those forms of popular culture.

cultural texts Popular culture messages whether television shows, movies, advertisements, or other widely disseminated messages.

Stuart Hall's (1980) encoding/decoding model might be helpful here. Hall is careful to place "meaning" at several stages in the communication process, so that it is never fixed but is always being constructed within various contexts. Thus, in his model, he places **encoding**—or the construction of textual meaning by popular culture institutions—within specific social contexts. **Decoding**—the interpretation of the text's meaning by receivers—is performed by various audiences in different social contexts, whose members have different interests at stake. In this way, the meaning(s) of various popular culture texts can be seen as negotiated throughout the communication process. The "real meaning" of any popular culture text cannot simply be located in either the senders or the receivers. Although this model may seem to suggest tremendous unpredictability in popular culture, people do not create just any meaning out of these texts. We are always enmeshed in our social identities, which help guide our interpretations as decoders. Encoders, in turn, rely on these larger identity formations to help them fashion their texts to sell to particular markets. (See Figure 9-2.)

encoding The process of creating a message for others to understand.

decoding The process of interpreting a message.

For example, communication scholars Rae Lynn Schwartz-Dupre and Shelby Scott (2015) studied how people interpreted the wearing of the *kufiyya,* a scarf made of checkered material. It is often considered a traditional Palestinian headdress that has taken on a number of different meanings in the contemporary context. They note that the *kufiyya* is worn "by both male and female Palestinian protesters, promoted by style junkies (such as Sting, Sara Jessica Parker, Justin Timberlake, Snoop Dogg, and Kate Moss), and rejected by right-wing conservatives (notably Fox News' Michelle Malkin)" (p. 335). They found that the decoding of this piece of clothing was influenced by whether it was seen as a statement on Palestinian pride and the conflict with Israel, post-9/11 politics and views on terrorism, as well as the *kufiyya* as a global fashion piece.

There is some unpredictability in how people navigate popular culture. After all, not all men enjoy watching football, and not all women like to read romance novels.

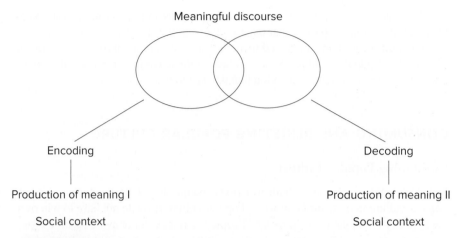

Meaningful discourse

Encoding

Decoding

Production of meaning I

Production of meaning II

Social context

Social context

FIGURE 9-2   Stuart Hall's encoding/decoding model. Try to use this model to discuss how different people might arrive at different interpretations of your favorite TV show.

reader profiles
Portrayals of reader-ship demographics prepared by magazines.

However, some profiles emerge. Advertising offices of popular magazines even make their **reader profiles** available to potential advertisers. These reader profiles portray what the magazine believes its readership "looks" like. Although reader profiles do not follow a set format, they generally detail the average age, gender, individual and household incomes, and so on of their readership. The reader profile for *Vogue,* for example, will not look like the reader profile for *Esquire.*

Each magazine targets a particular readership and then sells this readership to advertisers. The diversity of the U.S. American population generates very different readerships among a range of magazines, in several ways. Let's explore some of the ways this diversity is played out in the magazine market.

How Magazines Respond to the Needs of Cultural Identities   A wide range of magazines respond to the different social and political needs of groups with different cultural identities. You may already be familiar with magazines geared toward a male or a female readership. But many other kinds of magazines serve important functions for other cultural groups. For example, *Ebony* is one of many magazines that cultivate an African American readership. Similar magazines exist for other cultural identities. *People en Español,* published by Time, Inc. targets a Latino/a audience; *The Advocate* claims to be the national newsmagazine for gays and lesbians. These magazines offer information and viewpoints that are generally unavailable in other magazines. They function as a discussion forum for concerns that mainstream magazines often overlook. They also tend to affirm, by their very existence, these other cultural identities, which sometimes are invisible or are silenced in the mainstream culture.

In addition, many non-English-language newspapers circulate among readers of specific ethnic groups, serving the same functions as the magazines just mentioned. However, because their production costs are low, they are better able to survive and reach their limited readerships. For instance, newspapers printed in Cantonese, Spanish, Vietnamese, Japanese, French, Korean, Arabic, Polish, Russian, and other languages reach non-English-speaking readers in the United States.

How Readers Negotiate Consumption   Readers actively negotiate their way through cultural texts such as magazines—consuming those that fulfill important cultural needs and resisting those that do not. Hence, it is possible to be a reader of magazines that reflect various cultural configurations; that is, someone might read several women's magazines and Spanish-language newspapers and magazines, as well as *Newsweek* and *Southern Living*.

Cultural Texts Versus Cultural Identities   We must be careful not to conflate the magazines with the cultural identities they are targeting. After all, many publications offer different points of view on any given topic. Thus, there is no single, unified "Asian American position" on immigration reform or any "Latino position" on affirmative action. Rather, there can be a preponderance of opinions on some issues. These often are played out through popular culture forums.

People come together through cultural magazines and newspapers to affirm and negotiate their relationships with their cultural identities. In this way, the texts resemble cultural spaces, which we discussed in Chapter 7. However, magazines are but one example of how popular culture can function. Not all popular culture texts are easily correlated to particular cultural groups. Think about the various TV programs, movies, mass-market paperbacks, and tabloids that flood our everyday lives. The reasons that people enjoy some over others cannot easily be determined. People negotiate their relationships to popular culture in complex ways.

Resisting Popular Culture

Sometimes people actively seek out particular popular culture texts to consume; other times they resist cultural texts. But resistance to popular culture is a complex process. Avoiding certain forms of popular culture is one kind of resistance, but resistance can occur in a variety of ways.

Let's look at some examples of how people resist popular culture. In 2012, the first of the *Hunger Games* movies was released. Some people began to resist the casting of Amandla Stenber as Rue and Dayo Okeniyi as Thresh. Despite Suzanne Collins, the author of the novel, describing both of these characters as having "dark brown skin," some people resisted "who took to Twitter to complain that the parts should not have been played by black actors" (Bull, 2012). One of the tweets indicated that the tweeter was not going to consume this text: "EWW, rue is black?? I'm not watching" or another pointed to how skin color influenced how the text is read: "Kk call me racist but when I found out rue was black her death wasn't as sad #ihatemyself" (quoted in Bull, 2012).

When one person tweeted: "Awkward moment when Rue is some black girl and not the little blonde innocent girl you picture" (quoted in Holmes, 2012), a fan of the *Hunger Games* believes that "mentality is probably very widespread" and we have to ask "how the heroes in our imaginations are white until proven otherwise, a variation on the principle of innocent until proven guilty that, for so many minorities, is routinely upended" (Holmes, 2012). For some consumers of popular culture, the racial composition of characters is important to them.

For others, the racial implications of the popular culture texts can influence their resistance. *Star Wars* ignited a discussion of race and resistance when Melissa Harris-Perry, a former television host on MSNBC, explained her reading of Darth Vader: "While he was black he was terrible and bad, awful and used to cut off white men's hand, and didn't actually claim his son. But as soon as he claims his son, goes over to the good, takes off his mask and he is white—yes, I have many feelings about that" (quoted in Sheperd, 2015). Others, like Peter Roff, a contributing editor to U.S. News & World Report, disagrees. He denies that Darth Vader is black, but is only dressed in black as an old Hollywood practice: "This is in fact nothing more than an old movie cliche. The good guys wear the white hats and the bad guys wear the black ones—which is how you could tell them apart in the old westerns in the days before Technicolor" (2015). This dispute underscores the complexity of the encoding/decoding process. There are many influences that generate different interpretations. These interpretations can cause people to consume or resist particular popular culture texts.

Complicating the complexity of popular culture resistance was yet another response to *Star Wars: The Force Awakens* that began prior to its release in 2015—a call for a boycott of the movie. One tweet explained: "#BoycottStarWarsVII because it is anti-white propaganda promoting #whitegenocide" (quoted in Griggs, 2015). A number of people used the hashtag #whitegenocide to call for a boycott of the movie. The relationship between white genocide and this film may not be obvious at first glance, but The #BOYCOTTSTARWARSVII campaign accused the film makers of a "hidden black and jewish agenda to erase white people from popular culture and then, by extension, society" (Kyriazis, 2015). Also, many of the tweets were upset that John Boyega, a black actor, plays Finn, a stormtrooper.

These examples highlight the complexity of the encoding and decoding process and its relationship to the consumption and resistance of particular popular culture texts. Resistance to popular culture tends to express a concern about how others are going to be impacted by the popular culture representations.

Indeed, people often resist particular forms of popular culture by refusing to engage in them. For example, some people feel the need to avoid television and even decide not to own televisions. Some people refuse to go to movies that contain violence or sexuality because they do not find pleasure in such films. In this case, these kinds of conscious decisions are often based on concerns about the ways that cultural products should be understood as political.

Resistance to popular culture can also be related to social roles. Likewise, some people have expressed concern about the supposedly homophobic or racist

FIGURE 9-3   This display outside a movie theater in Moscow is promoting the *Star Wars* film. Prior to the release of *Star Wars: The Force Awakens*, boycotts were called from people who were concerned that the film is anti-white and expressed concern that one of the stormtroopers is not white.

ideologies embedded in Disney films such as *Aladdin* (Boone, 1995). *Aladdin* plays into Western fears of homosexuality and the tradition of projecting those concerns on Arab culture. Resistance stems mainly from concerns about the representation of various social groups. Popular culture plays a powerful role in how we think about and understand other groups. The Disney film *Pocahontas* was criticized for its rewriting of the European encounters with Native Americans. According to communication scholars Derek Buescher and Kent Ono (1996), this film "helps audiences unlearn the infamous history of mass slaughter by replacing it with a cute, cuddly one" (p. 128).

Sometimes resistance is targeted at the profits of popular culture corporations. For example, in Iraq, many Iraqis buy pirated DVDs of U.S. films. These pirated DVDs are sold on the black market and the U.S. film corporations do not earn profits from these sales. Milad Tareq, 21, who runs the Option CDs shop, explains that "The best-pirated movies come from Malaysia. Among the more popular movies in the Iraqi capital are those starring Robert DeNiro, Tom Hanks or Julia Roberts," (Sabah, 2006). While this kind of resistance may be oriented toward the store owner making a profit rather than undercutting the U.S. film corporations, these sales both spread U.S. popular culture, as well as hurt the potential profits of the filmmakers.

HOW POWERFUL IS POPULAR CULTURE?

Bob Jones University, located in Greenville, South Carolina, describes itself as a "Christian liberal arts higher education institution." The *Student Handbook* continues to include concerns about the use of popular culture and its effects. The university "encourages students to honor the Lord in how they spend their time and to carefully consider the desensitizing effects of excessive exposure to popular entertainment, even if the content itself is not objectionable." The *Student Handbook* outlines more specifically what this means in a number of popular culture venues. It bans listening to or using "Rock, Pop, Country, Jazz, Electronic/Techno, Rap/Hip Hop, or the fusion of any of these genres" and "because of the sensual nature of many of its forms, dancing is not permitted." Students are not allowed to watch movies on campus but, in private homes, students are permitted to watch G-rated movies. Similarly, television viewing is not allowed on campus, including shows, movies, or sports broadcasts. The policy also bans some kinds of periodicals, "such as *Esquire, GQ, People, Entertainment, Yahoo Magazine, Men's Fitness*, and *ESPN*."

You can read more about these guidelines and others in the *Student Handbook* which is posted online. The consequences for violating these rules are also explained there. What do you think about this approach to dealing with the popular culture environment? Is popular culture powerful enough to influence how people view the world?

REPRESENTING CULTURAL GROUPS

As noted at the beginning of this chapter, people often are introduced to other cultures through the lens of popular culture. These introductions can be quite intimate, in ways that tourists may not experience. For example, movies may portray romance, familial conflict, or a death in the family; the audience experiences the private lives of people they do not know, in ways that they never could simply as tourists.

Yet we must also think about how these cultural groups are portrayed through that lens of popular culture. Not everyone sees the portrayal in the same way. For example, you may not think that the TV shows *Blue Bloods* and *Two and a Half Men* represent quintessential U.S. American values and lifestyles. But some viewers may see it as their entree into how U.S. Americans (or perhaps European Americans) live.

In a social science study on television coverage of affirmative action and African Americans, communication researchers Alexis Tan, Yuki Fujioka, and Gerdean Tan (2000) found that more negative coverage increased negative stereotypes about African Americans. However, they also found that "positive TV portrayals did not lead to positive stereotypes, nor did they influence opinions" (p. 370). They conclude that

A Belgian student describes his first impressions on arriving in the United States:

When I first landed at JFK Airport, I felt like I was going crazy. When I was younger, I only knew about America through television, radio, books, and movies. Even if people don't like America, it is still like a dream-land because it is a place where everything is big, where movies are made, especially police movies. American movies are very well made, with special effects, and so the first time I saw the real America, it was like in the movies. The police in the airport were like cowboys, wearing sunglasses, big mustaches, with badges everywhere and they were big and unafraid, like cowboys. You must respect the customs lines, and all the rules are very strict.

When we left the airport to go to Manhattan, we saw really poor neighborhoods near the airport. I wondered, is America really so poor with small houses? The houses look like they are made of wood and flimsy, unlike the brick ones in Belgium. Once you cross into Manhattan, however, you understand that in America you either have money or you don't. There are majestic cities and poverty; you can get lots of money or nothing. It is another way of living. In Belgium, you do not have to struggle so much for money. Once you have a job in Belgium, there are lots of job protections. In Belgium, if you want to live, you don't have to work.

—Christophe

"negative portrayals are remembered more than positive portrayals, are more arousing and therefore are more influential in the development of stereotypes" (p. 370). Given this dynamic, it is clear how TV news coverage can continue to marginalize and reinforce negative stereotypes, even if the reports also present positive information about minority groups.

In a more recent social science study, Mary Beth Oliver and her colleagues (2004) examined news readers' memories of racial facial features of people in the news. They presented one of four different kinds of news stories—nonstereotyped, stereotyped/noncrime, nonviolent crime, and violent crime—with the same photograph of the individual in the story. Participants were asked to recall this individual's facial features on a computer screen. They conclude, in part, that "[w]hen the stories pertained to crime, Afrocentric features were significantly more pronounced than the actual photograph depicted, whereas when the stories were unrelated to crime, the selected features did not differ significantly from the photograph actually seen" (p. 99). They suggest that certain topics might activate stereotypes and thus influence how these news stories are interpreted.

Migrants' Perceptions of Mainstream Culture

Ethnographers and other interpretive scholars have crossed international and cultural boundaries to examine the influence of popular culture. In an early study, Elihu Katz and Tamar Liebes (1987) set up focus groups to see how different cultural groups perceived the popular 1980s TV drama *Dallas:*

> *There were ten groups each of Israeli Arabs, new immigrants to Israel from Russia, first and second generation immigrants from Morocco, and kibbutz members. Taking these groups as a microcosm of the worldwide audience of* Dallas, *we are comparing their readings of the program with ten groups of matched Americans in Los Angeles. (p. 421)*

Katz and Liebes found that the U.S. Americans in Los Angeles were much less likely to perceive *Dallas* as portraying life in the United States. In contrast, the Israelis, Arabs, and immigrants were much more inclined to believe that this television show was indeed all about life in the United States. Katz and Liebes note, "What seems clear from the analysis, even at this stage, is that the non-Americans consider the story more real than the Americans. The non-Americans have little doubt that the story is about 'America'; the Americans are less sure" (p. 421). The results of this study are not surprising, but we should not overlook what they tell us about the intercultural communication process. We can see that these popular culture images are often more influential in constructing particular ways of understanding other cultural groups than our own. Notably, "Dallas" is being resurrected and a new version of the series is set to appear in 2012.

Another study (Lee & Cho, 1990) that focused on immigrants to the United States yielded similar results. The researchers asked female Korean immigrants why they preferred watching Korean TV shows (which they had to rent at the video store) instead of U.S. programs. The respondents stated that, because of the cultural differences, the Korean shows were more appealing. Yet, as one respondent noted:

> *I like to watch American programs. Actors and actresses are glamorous and the pictures are sleek. But the ideas are still American. How many Korean women are that independent? And how many men commit incest? I think American programs are about American people. They are not the same as watching the Korean programs. But I watch them for fun. And I learn the American way of living by watching them. (p. 43)*

Here, both consumption of and resistance to U.S. television are evident. This woman uses U.S. television to learn about the U.S. American "way of living," but she prefers to watch Korean shows because they relate to her cultural identity. As she says, "I like the Korean programs because I get the sense of what's going on in my country" (p. 43).

The use of popular culture to learn about other cultures should not be surprising. After all, many teachers encourage their students to use popular culture in this manner, not only to improve their language skills but also to learn many of the nuances of another culture. When Tom was first studying French, his French

> *Whenever I go to China, people always ask me, "Is America like what we see on TV?" They want to know if everyone owns a gun, if we eat at McDonald's everyday, and if it's as wild and free as it's portrayed in cinema. For those who have never traveled to America, they base their perception on what they see through media. I politely laugh and tell them they can't believe everything they read and see.*
>
> —Shanyu

professor told the students that *Le dernier métro* (*The Last Metro*), a film by director François Truffaut, was playing downtown. The point, of course, was to hear French spoken by natives. But Tom remembers being amazed at the subtle references to anti-Semitism, the treatment of lesbianism, and the film's style, which contrasted sharply with that of Hollywood films.

Popular Culture and Stereotyping

In what ways does reliance on popular culture create and reinforce stereotypes of different cultures? As we noted at the outset of this chapter, neither author has had the opportunity to travel all over the world. Our knowledge about other places, even places we have been, is largely influenced by popular culture. For people who do not travel and who interact in relatively homogeneous social circles, the impact of popular culture may be even greater.

Film studies scholar Richard Dyer (1993) tells us that

> *the effectiveness of stereotypes resides in the way they invoke a consensus. . . . The stereotype is taken to express a general agreement about a social group, as if that agreement arose before, and independently of, the stereotype. Yet for the most part it is from stereotypes that we get our ideas about social groups. (p. 14)*

Dyer makes an important observation that stereotypes are connected to social values and social judgments about other groups of people. These stereotypes are powerful because they function to tell us how "we" value and judge these other groups.

Many familiar stereotypes of ethnic groups are represented in the media. Scholar Lisa Flores (2000) describes the portrayal of a diverse group of high school students in the television show *Matt Waters*. Flores focuses her analysis on Angela, a Puerto Rican student. According to Flores, there is a strong theme of assimilation at work in this show. She notes:

> *to follow the seeming logic of this assimilationist politics requires an initial belief in the goal of a single, unified American culture expressed in a harmonious community such as that found within the* Matt Waters *community. The assimilationist perspective also mandates an assumption that ethnic minorities cannot maintain*

> *cultural difference except in rejection of all of dominant or mainstream society.* (pp. 37–38)

She turns to Chicana feminism to show how we can resist these popular culture representations.

African American women also traditionally have been portrayed stereotypically on TV, especially in the 1950s and 1960s, when the roles they held were secondary (e.g., as domestics). Scholar Bishetta Merritt (2000) also reminds us of the African American female characters who often appear as background scenery: the person buying drugs, the homeless person on the sidewalk, the hotel lobby prostitute. Merritt points out that these women still project images, even if they aren't the focus:

> *If the majority of black women the television audience is exposed to are homeless, drug-addicted, or maids, and if viewers have no contact with African American women other than through television, what choice do they have but to believe that all women of this ethnic background reflect this television image? . . . It is, therefore, important, as the twenty-first century approaches and the population of this country includes more and more people of color, that the television industry broaden the images of African American women to include their nuances and diversity. (p. 53)*

CAPTAIN AMERICA

When *Captain America: The First Avenger* was released in cinemas in 2011, it did quite well at the box office its opening weekend. Earning $65.8 million, this film bumped *Harry Potter and the Deathly Hollows Part 2* from its first place finish the previous weekend. The film is set during World War II, and Captain America's enemies are Nazis. Although the film is fiction and focuses on a super-hero, any film has to be attentive to historical contexts and also take liberties to ensure the narrative is enticing. So, people in a film set in the 1950s should not be surfing the Internet or chatting on smart phones. In the case of Captain America, a discussion began about the liberties taken about social relations. As Robin Quivers notes: "A woman leads men in combat and even takes part in some of the fighting. Later, when Captain America puts together his own little group of commandos, the crew includes an African American and a Japanese American." These characters defy historical contexts for both gender and race. Indeed, there were no integrated fighting units in the U.S. military at that time. In what ways is this historical revision of the past a good or a bad influence on intercultural relations? Is it helpful to pretend that our past was more open to gender and racial difference than it really was? Or should we be concerned about historical revisionism in popular culture?

Sources: From C. M. Blow, "My very own Captain America," *The New York Times,* July 29, 2011. Retrieved August 23, 2011, from www.nytimes.com/2011/07/30/opinion/blow-my-very-own-captain-america.html?scp=1&sq=captain%20america&st; S. Bowles, " 'Captain America' unseats 'Potter' at box office," *USA Today,* July 24, 2011. Retrieved August 23, 2011, from www.usatoday.com/life/movies/news/2011-07-24-captain-america_n.htm; C. DeVega, "Captain America: The first avenger's dishonest and cowardly racial politics," AlterNet, July 23, 2011. Retrieved August 23, 2011, from http://blogs.alternet.org/speakeasy/2011/07/23/captain-america-the-first-avengers-dishonest-and-cowardly-racial-politics/; R. Quivers, "Captain America's USA," *Huffington Post,* August 1, 2011. Retrieved August 23, 2011, from www.huffingtonpost.com/robin-quivers/captain-americas-usa_b_915142.html.

In her more recent study of local news coverage of Freaknik, an annual African American spring break event in Atlanta that ended in 2000, communication scholar Marian Meyers (2004) studied the ways that the violence perpetrated by African American men on African American women was represented. She found that the media coverage brought together issues of race, class, and gender and therefore tended to identify the perpetrators as nonstudent local trouble-makers rather than as students. The news coverage also "minimizes the serious-ness of the violence and portrays its victims primarily as stereotypic Jezebels who provoke male violence through their own behavior" (p. 96). The contin-ued use of this sexualized stereotype for African American women displaces responsibility for what happened from the male perpetrators to the women who were attacked.

What about those ethnic groups that simply don't appear except as infrequent stereotypes—for example, Native Americans and Asian Americans? How do these stereotypes influence intercultural interaction? Do people behave any differently if they don't hold stereotypes about people with whom they are interacting? Two communication researchers, Valerie Manusov and Radha Hegde (1993), investigated these questions in a study in which they identified two groups of college students: those who had some preconceived ideas about India (which were fairly positive) and those who didn't. Manusov and Hegde asked all of the students to interact, one at a time, with an international student from India who was part of the study.

When the students with preconceptions talked with the Indian student, they interacted differently from those who had no expectations. Specifically, students from the former group relied less on small talk, covered more topics, and asked fewer questions within each topic. Overall, their conversations were more like those between people who know each other. The students with the preconceptions also were more positive about the conversation.

What can we learn from this study? Having some information and positive expectations may lead to more in-depth conversations and positive outcomes than having no information. But what happens when negative stereotypes are present? It is possible that expectations are fulfilled in this case too.

For example, in several studies at Princeton University, whites interviewed both white and black "job applicants" who were actually part of the study and were trained to behave consistently, no matter how interviewers acted toward them. The interviews were videotaped. The interviewers clearly behaved differently toward blacks: Their speech deteriorated, they made more grammatical errors, they spent less time, and they showed fewer "immediacy" behaviors— that is, they were less friendly and less outgoing. In a second study, interviewers were trained to be either "immediate" or "nonimmediate" as they interviewed white job applicants. A panel of judges watched the videotapes and agreed that those applicants interviewed by the "nonimmediate" interviewer performed less well and were more nervous. This suggests that the African American applicants in the first study never had a chance: They were only reacting to the nonimmediate behavior of the interviewers. Mark Snyder (1998) summarizes: "Considered together, the two investigations suggest that in interracial encounters, racial stereotypes may constrain behavior in ways to cause both blacks and whites to behave in accordance with those stereotypes" (p. 455).

U.S. POPULAR CULTURE AND POWER

One of the dynamics of intercultural communication that we have highlighted throughout this text is power. In considering popular culture, we need to think about not only how people interpret and consume popular culture but also how these popular culture texts represent particular groups in specific ways. If people largely view other cultural groups through the lens of popular culture, then we need to think about the power relations that are embedded in these popular culture dynamics.

FIGURE 9-4   James Dean remains a popular cultural icon in the United States and abroad. This 1996 photo shows that one of his films, *East of Eden*, continues to play in Tokyo. How does Dean's popularity in Japan contrast with the absence of a similarly popular Japanese male star in the United States? What might explain this disparity? Think about the issues of cultural imperialism raised in this chapter. (*Courtesy T. K. Nakayama*)

Global Circulation of Images and Commodities

As noted previously, much of the internationally circulated popular culture is U.S. popular culture. U.S.-made films, for example, are widely distributed by an industry that is backed by considerable financial resources. Some media scholars have noted that the U.S. film industry earns far more money outside the United States than from domestic box office receipts (Guback, 1969; Guback & Varis, 1982). This situation ensures that Hollywood will continue to seek overseas markets and that it will have the financial resources to do so. The film, *Batman v. Superman: Dawn of Justice*, received relatively negative reviews from movie critics. Some critics saw the production of the film as largely driven by a need for Warner Bros. to increase their revenues. Prior to its release, Warner Bros. estimated that it would "bring in $100 million to $140 million domestically and an additional $200 million" internationally (Sakoui, 2016, p. 22). Will the strategy of focusing on super heroes work for the studio? Or are audiences less interested in more super hero movies? In any case, the studio hopes to make more money from overseas sales than sales in the United States. (See Figure 9-4.)

Many other U.S. media are widely available outside the United States, including television and newspapers. For example, MTV and CNN are broadcast

POINT *of* VIEW

We are shaped by a variety of influences, and popular culture is among those influences. While it is difficult to know how much popular culture shapes our worldviews, some studies have been done on body image in different cultures. For example, "Asian men show less dissatisfaction with their bodies than males in the United States and Europe, according to a Harvard study. This may explain why anabolic steroid abuse is much less prevalent in places like Taiwan than in the United States, Europe, and Australia." Also, "Black and Asian women generally have a more positive body-image than Caucasian women" while "A study of Mexican immigrants in America found that those who had immigrated after the age of 17 were less affected by the prevailing super-thin ideal than those who were 16 or younger when they came to the U.S." A more recent study of body image found that European Americans generally have a more negative body image than Hispanic/Latina/Latinos with women having a more negative image than men. It is difficult to make a direct correlation to the influence of popular culture, but with the images of beauty (not necessarily evenly distributed across the racial/ethnic diversity of the population), are some groups affected more than others?

Sources: From N. Ceballos and N. Czyzewska, "Body Image in Hispanic/Latino vs. European American Adolescents: Implications for Treatment and Prevention of Obesity in Underserved Populations," *Journal of Health Care for the Poor and Underserved, 21*(3) (2010): 823–838; W. J. Cromie (2005, February 10), "Male body image: East doesn't meet west. Harvard Gazette." Retrieved September 12, 2011, from http://news.harvard.edu/gazette/2005/02.10/11-bodyimage .html; K. Fox, "Mirror, mirror: A summary of research findings on body image," *Social Issues Research Centre*, 1997 Retrieved September 11, 2011, from www.sirc.org/publik/mirror.html.

internationally. And the *International Herald Tribune,* published by *The New York Times,* is widely available in some parts of the world. The implications of the dominance by U.S. media and popular culture have yet to be determined, although you might imagine the consequences. India produces more films than the United States but makes less money in box office receipts. (See the Point of View box on page 386.)

Not all popular culture comes from the United States. For example, James Bond is a British phenomenon, but the famous character has been exported to the United States. In their study of the popularity of the Bond series, scholars Tony Bennett and Janet Woollacott (1987) note that in the Bond film *A License to Kill* "the threat to the dominance of white American male culture is removed not by a representative of that culture, and certainly not by a somewhat foppish English spy, but by the self-destruction of the forces ranged against it" (pp. 293–294). Here, a British character becomes a hero for U.S. and international audiences through the U.S. film industry. It is not always easy to know what is and what is not U.S. popular culture.

Recently, the Korean Wave (*Hallyu*) has demonstrated the profitability of South Korean popular culture. This popular culture phenomenon has "become a

FIGURE 9-5   South Korean actor Bae Yong Joon is shown arriving at the Tokyo airport with thousands of fans awaiting his arrival. He is a very popular television drama star who is part of the Korean Wave. The Korean Wave highlights how non-U.S. popular culture can circulate and become very marketable in other parts of the world. (© AP Photo/Katsumi Kasahara)

rallying cry within Korea for the perceived success of its cultural industries in Asia" (J. Kim, 2007, p. 48). *The Korea Times* reports that "according to the Ministry of Culture, Sports and Tourism, the nation exported about $1.4 billion worth of entertainment products last year" (S.-Y. Kim, 2008). While primarily popular in Asia, *Hallyu* has even made the city of Chuncheon a popular tourist destination, as the local drama "*Winter Sonata*" (2002) gained popularity abroad (S.-Y. Kim, 2008, see Figure 9-5).

Key to this South Korean phenomenon, however, is the global circulation of popular culture. Thus, "Hallyu is a term that can *only* be applied to a cultural product once it has been exposed to foreign audiences. In other words, not every Korean drama, film or pop song, no matter how popular in Korea, will be labeled Hallyu—only those that have been exported and done so successfully" (J. Kim, 2007, pp. 49–50). The focus of *Hallyu,* however, is on "Asian rather than global domination" (p. 55). In their analysis of *Hallyu*, communication researchers Kent Ono and Jungmin Kwon (2013) point to YouTube as "an essential medium for the transnational distribution of certain media products" (p. 210). In any case, the international circulation of Korean popular culture has important implications for the production of Asian standards of beauty and relationships, as well as international trade.

Much popular culture that is expressed in non-English languages has a difficult time on the global scene. Although Céline Dion, who sings in English, has been able to reach a worldwide audience, a fellow French Canadian, Garou, who sings in French, has not reached the same level of notoriety. Still, Garou (Pierre Garand) is extremely popular in the francophone world. Have you ever heard of Garou? To reach a worldwide audience, must he sing in English? Garou released his next CD, *Reviens,* in 2003 and decided that because of "the generosity of his French-speaking public . . . [the album] would be written and sung in French" (www.garouland.com/Reviens/english/bio_08.html). What does this tell us about popular culture? What does it tell us about the unequal power relations that are evident in popular culture? How does it influence how we think about the world?

Cultural Imperialism

It is difficult to measure the impact of the U.S. and Western media and popular culture on the rest of the world, but we do know that we cannot ignore this dynamic. The U.S. government in the 1920s believed that having U.S. movies on foreign screens would boost the sales of U.S. products because the productions would be furnished with U.S. goods. The government thus worked closely with the Hays Office (officially, the Motion Picture Producers and Distributors of America) to break into foreign markets, most notably in the United Kingdom (Nakayama & Vachon, 1991).

media imperialism
Domination or control through media.

electronic colonialism
Domination or exploitation utilizing technological forms.

cultural imperialism
Domination through the spread of cultural products.

Discussions about **media imperialism, electronic colonialism,** and **cultural imperialism,** which began in the 1920s, continue today. The interrelationships among economics, nationalism, and culture make it difficult to determine with much certainty how significant cultural imperialism might be. The issue of cultural imperialism is complex because the definition is complex. In his survey of the cultural imperialism debates, scholar John Tomlinson (1991) identifies five ways of thinking about cultural imperialism: (1) as cultural domination, (2) as media imperialism, (3) as nationalist discourse, (4) as a critique of global capitalism, and (5) as a critique of modernity (pp. 19–23). Tomlinson's analysis underscores the interrelatedness of issues of ethnicity, culture, and nationalism in the context of economics, technology, and capitalism—resources that are distributed unevenly throughout the world. To understand the concerns about cultural imperialism, therefore, it is necessary to consider the complexity of the impact of U.S. popular culture. (See Table 9-2.) There is no easy way to measure the impact of popular culture, but we should be sensitive to its influences on intercultural communication. Let's look at some examples.

Some governments have become concerned about the amount of popular culture coming into their countries. The French government, for example, has expressed dismay about the domination of the English-language broadcasting of CNN because it feels it projects a view of the world it does not share. In order to challenge this view, the French are launching their own international broadcasting network to present their views on the world. Although informally referred to as

TABLE 9-2 U.S. INTERNATIONAL POP CULTURE INFLUENCE

Product	Destination	Impact
Avatar		Number I film of all time at the box office. It earned more than $760 million in the United States, but almost $2.8 billion worldwide (boxofficemojo).
Captain America		This film did well overseas despite concerns that it was too patriotic about the United States. Although the studio offered the alternative title, "The First Avenger," only three countries distributed it under that name: Russia, South Korea, and Ukraine (McClintock).
The film industry	Nigeria	Nigeria's film industry is the second largest as it produces more films annually than the United States, but less than India. Known as "Nollywood," its films are shown across Africa.

Sources: From "All time box office. Retrieved September 24, 2011, from http://boxofficemojo.com/alltime/; P. McClintock, "Box office shocker: 'Captain America' earns more overseas than in U.S," *The Hollywood Reporter,* September 14, 2011. Retrieved September 24, 2011, from www.hollywoodreporter.com/news/box-office-shocker-captain-america-235464; N. Onishi, "Nigeria's booming film industry redefines African life," *The New York Times,* February 18, 2016. Retrieved June 10, 2016, from http://www.nytimes.com/2016/02/19/world/africa/with-a-boom-before-the-cameras-nigeria-redefines-african-life.html?_r=0.

"CNN à la française," this new "channel would promote a vision of a 'multipolar' world that is not dominated by one superpower, such as the United States" (Louet, 2005). Known as France 24, it broadcasts in French, English, and Arabic. Although it has limited availability in the United States, it can be viewed online. It aims to compete with other international broadcasters, including CNN, BBC, Deutsche Welle, Al Jazeera, and NHK World.

In a study on this tension between global networks and local networks, Jonathan Cohen (2005) examined the situation in Israel. He looked at Israel's 99 channels and identified six different ways that these channels function in the global and local environment. He then noted, "Foreign television is often thought to be harmful because it separates people from their national communities" (p. 451), but he warned that we should not so easily view foreign television in this way. He doesn't think it is yet clear that watching U.S. television shows "like *Sex and the City* or *The Apprentice* weakens viewers' connections to Israeli culture or

POINT *of* VIEW

STRUGGLES OVER CULTURE THROUGH FILM

Although we are inundated with Hollywood films, Hollywood, the U.S. film industry, is not the world's largest producer of film every year. Instead, India produces more films worldwide than any other country. Following India is Nigeria, the second largest film producer. Nigeria's film industry is sometimes called "Nollywood." With about 2500 films produced every year, it far exceeds the number produced by Hollywood which is typically under 1000 films per year.

In contrast to the number of films produced, many in the film business have turned their attention to China, as the amount of money to be made there is considerable. China, of course, is interested in promoting its own film industry, but Hollywood is interested in increasing its Chinese revenue. In the coming years, it will be interesting to see what happens in China. Will the Chinese film industry produce films that Chinese movie goers want to see? Or will Hollywood be able to produce films that Chinese consumers will pay to see?

Aside from the economic considerations alone, what difference does it make which national film traditions dominate the cinema screens worldwide? How do movies promote cultural values and ways of viewing the world? How might different cultural notions of romance, friendship, family obligations, heroism, and other issues be different in various national cinemas? It's also important to ask how familiar you are with other national film traditions? How often do you watch films from countries other than your own? Why or why not?

Sources: McPhillips, D. (2016, February 29). Inside Nigeria's prolific film industry. *U.S. News & World Report*. Retrieved from http://www.usnews.com/news/best-countries/articles/2016-02-29/inside-nigerias-prolific-film-industry; Williams, H. (2016, September 18). Rising in the east. *CBS News*. Retrieved from http://www.cbsnews.com/news/60-minutes-china-film-industry-booming-2/

strengthens them by providing a stark contrast to viewers' lives" (p. 451). Think back to Stuart Hall's encoding and decoding model. Cohen is emphasizing that we cannot assume people who watch certain shows will decode them in any particular way. The influence of media is more complex than a simple imposition of meaning from abroad.

Sometimes the Western images are imported and welcomed by the ruling interests in other countries. For example, the government of the Ivory Coast in West Africa has used foreign (mostly French) media to promote its image of a "new" Ivoirien cultural identity. The government purchased a satellite dish that permits 1,400 hours of French programming annually, which represents 77% of all programming. But it has been criticized by many for borrowing heavily from the Western media—for inviting cultural imperialism:

> *While television, as mirror, sometimes reflects multiple Ivoirien cultures, the latter are expected to acquiesce to a singular national culture in the image of*

Some people seek out foreign films; others avoid them. In choosing either response to foreign films, are you choosing films based on the narrative or the subtitles?

I do not like foreign films because I have a hard time understanding what is going on even with the subtitles. I can't understand a lot of the humor in foreign movies. I also don't think that all languages translate to English exactly, and it makes it hard to understand these movies.
—Elizabeth

Foreign films seem to paint a picture that rings more true to me than Hollywood films. In Hollywood films, there seems to be recurring themes: the strong man, the materialistic woman, heterosexuality, white stars with a token minority. They seldom get a role free of the most ridiculous stereotypes. The foreign independent films seem to have more diversity, more balance, a better depiction of the world.
—Sam

the Party, which is also synonymous with a Western cultural image. . . . The cultural priority is openness for the sake of modernization in the quest of the Ivoirien national identity. (Land, 1992, p. 25)

In another take on globalization, communication scholar Radhika Parameswaran (2004) undertook a textual analysis of Indian newspaper and magazine coverage of India's six Miss Universe and Miss World titleholders. In the context of a global economy, these women are upheld as role models who are ordinary women who worked hard to become a beauty queen while maintaining their national identities. Noting that "the therapeutic vocabulary of the beauty queen as role model, a recent construct of liberal individualism in South Asia, induces amnesia and insulates middle class citizens from the contradictions that such individualized discourses of empowerment can conceal. . . . [G]lobalization's ideologies of prosperity in India offer no recourse for the vast majority of poor citizens to attain even the humble ordinariness of the middle class consumer who desires the status of the global beauty queen" (p. 367). By asking what social functions these narratives serve, this critical study argues that they serve the more elite segments of society in India.

In all of these examples, popular culture plays an enormous role in explaining relations around the globe. It is through popular culture that we try to understand the dynamics of other cultures and nations. Although these representations are problematic, we also rely on popular culture to understand many kinds of issues: the conflict in Kashmir between India and Pakistan, the sex abuse scandals in the Catholic Church, the conflict in the West Bank between Israelis and Palestinians, and global warming. For many of us, the world exists through popular culture.

INTERNET RESOURCES

http://culturalpolitics.net/popular_culture
This website has links to other materials, articles, and a bibliography of resources. It is run by a professor at Washington State University. It has sections on class, gender, sexuality, censorship, race/ethnicity, cultural imperialism, and popular culture.

www.npr.org/sections/pop-culture
National Public Radio hosts a Web page devoted to identifying and commenting on popular culture trends. This resource is not specifically about intercultural issues, but these issues are covered. The website is a good mix of information and political commentary for students doing research on emerging popular culture issues.

www.wsu.edu/~amerstu/pop/race.html#articles
Washington State University hosts this Web resource. This website is a compilation of academic and popular press articles related to the intersection of popular culture and race. It contains direct links to articles, a directory of other websites, and a useful bibliography.

www.mediaed.org/cgi-bin/commerce.cgi?key=402&preadd=action
This is the Web resource for the bell hooks video on *Cultural Criticism and Transformation,* a 1997 edited interview with cultural critic bell hooks. The video is not available in its full form online (though sections are available on www.Youtube.com/), but this site does contain related articles and a section for comments.

SUMMARY

- We learn about other cultures through popular culture.
- Popular culture is popular because of its wide dissemination and easy access to many people.
- Popular culture is produced by culture industries, is not folk culture, is ubiquitous, and serves social functions.
- Popular culture can serve as a public forum.
- Cultural texts are not the same as cultural identities.
- People can seek out or resist popular culture.
- Cultural groups are often represented in ways that can play into stereotypes.
- Migrants can learn about other cultures through popular culture.

- The United States still dominates global production of popular culture, but other nations produce significant amounts that are important locally.
- Concerns about cultural imperialism need to be considered.

DISCUSSION QUESTIONS

1. Why do people select some popular culture forms over others?
2. How do the choices you make about what forms of popular culture to consume influence the formation of your cultural identity?
3. What factors influence culture industries to portray cultural groups as they do?
4. How does the portrayal of different cultural groups by the media influence intercultural interactions with those groups?
5. What stereotypes are perpetuated by U.S. popular culture and exported to other countries?
6. How do our social roles affect our consumption of popular culture?
7. What strategies can people apply to resist popular culture?

ACTIVITIES

1. *Popular Culture.* Meet with other students in small groups and answer the following questions:
   a. Which popular culture texts (magazines, TV shows, and so on) do you watch or buy? Why?
   b. Which popular culture texts do you choose *not* to buy or watch? Which do you *not* like? Why?
   c. Think about and discuss why people like some products compared to others. (For example, do they support our worldview and assumptions?)
2. *Ethnic Representation in Popular Culture.* For a week, keep a log of the TV shows you watch. Record the following information for each show and discuss in small groups:
   a. How many different ethnic groups were portrayed in this show?
   b. What roles did these ethnic groups have in the show?
   c. What ethnic groups were represented in the major roles?
   d. What ethnic groups were represented in the minor roles?

e. What ethnic groups were represented in the good-guy roles?

f. What ethnic groups were represented in the bad-guy roles?

g. What types of roles did women have in the show?

h. What intercultural interaction occurred in the show?

i. What was the outcome of the interaction?

j. How do the roles and interactions support or refute common stereotypes of the ethnic groups involved?

KEY WORDS

cultural imperialism (384)
cultural texts (369)
culture industries (366)
decoding (369)

electronic colonialism (384)
encoding (369)
folk culture (366)

media imperialism (384)
popular culture (365)
reader profiles (370)

REFERENCES

Arseneault, M. (2001, December 15). Il chante avec les loups. *L'actualité,* pp. 76–82.

Bennett, T., & Woollacott, J. (1987). *Bond and beyond: The political career of a popular culture hero.* New York: Methuen.

Bob Jones University (n.d.). Mission statement. Retrieved June 10, 2016, from http://www.bju.edu /about/mission-statement.php.

Bob Jones University (2015). Student handbook 15–16. Retrieved June 10, 2016, from http://www.bju.edu /life-faith/student-handbook.pdf.

Bonesteel, M. (2016, February 16). No one showed up to the anti-Beyonce rally at NFL headquarters. *The Washington Post.* Retrieved June 13, 2016, from https://www.washingtonpost.com/news/early-lead /wp/2016/02/16/no-one-showed-up-to-the-anti -beyonce-rally-at-nfl-headquarters/?tid=a_inl.

Boone, J. A. (1995). Rubbing Aladdin's lamp. In M. Dorenkamp & R. Henke (Eds.), *Negotiating lesbian and gay subjects* (pp. 149–177). New York: Routledge.

Brummett, B. (1994). *Rhetoric in popular culture.* New York: St. Martin's Press.

Buescher, D. T., & Ono, K. A. (1996). Civilized colonialism: *Pocahontas* as neocolonial rhetoric. *Women's Studies in Communication, 19,* 127–153.

Bull, S. (2012, March 30). The Hunger Games hit by racism row as movie fans tweet vile slurs over casting of black teen actress as heroine Rue. *Daily Mail.* Retrieved June 10, 2016, from http://www.dailymail .co.uk/news/article-2122714/The-Hunger-Games-hit -racism-row-movie-fans-tweet-vile-slurs-casting-black -teen-actress-heroine-Rue.html.

Butterworth, M. L. (2012). Militarism and memorializing at the Pro Football Hall of Fame. *Communication and Critical/Cultural Studies, 9*(3): 241–258.

Caulfield, K. (2016, February 6). Beyonce's "Formation" hits no. 1 on Billboard + Twitter Trending 140 chart. *Billboard.* Retrieved June 13, 2016, from http://www .billboard.com/articles/columns/chart-beat/6867196 /beyonce-formation-number-1-billboard-twitter -trending-140.

Chokshi, N. (2016, February 19). Boycott Beyoncé's "Formation" tour, police union urges. *The Washington Post.* Retrieved June 13, 2016, from https://www.washingtonpost.com/news /post-nation/wp/2016/02/19/boycott-beyonces -formation-world-tour-police-union-urges/?utm _term=.8d088db2e086.

Cohen, J. (2005). Global and local viewing experiences in the age of multichannel television: The Israeli experience. *Communication Theory, 15,* 437–455.

Dyer, R. (1993). *The matter of images: Essays on representations.* New York: Routledge.

Ex, K. (2016, February 10). Why are people suddenly afraid of Beyonce's black pride? *Billboard.* Retrieved June 13, 2016, from http://www.billboard.com/articles/columns/pop/6873899/beyonce-formation-essay.

Fiske, J. (1989). *Understanding popular culture.* New York: Routledge.

Flores, L. (2000). Challenging the myth of assimilation: A Chicana feminist perspective. In M. J. Collier (Ed.), *Constituting cultural difference through discourse* (pp. 26–46). International and Intercultural Communication Annual 12. Thousand Oaks, CA: Sage.

France, L. R. (2016, February 24). Why the Beyoncé controversy is bigger than you think. *CNN.* Retrieved June 10, 2016, from http://www.cnn.com/2016/02/23/entertainment/beyonce-controversy-feat/.

Griggs, B. (2015, October 21). Internet trolls call new "Star Wars" movie "anti-white." *CNN.* Retrieved June 10, 2016, from http://www.cnn.com/2015/10/20/entertainment/star-wars-trailer-boycott-anti-white-feat/.

Guback, T. (1969). *The international film industry: Western Europe and America since 1945.* Bloomington: Indiana University Press.

Guback, T., & Varis, T. (1982). *Transnational communication and cultural industries.* Paris: UNESCO.

Gunn, J., & Brummett, B. (2004). Popular culture after globalization. *Journal of Communication, 54,* 705–721.

Hall, S. (1980). Encoding/decoding. In S. Hall, D. Hobson, A. Lowe, & P. Willis (Eds.), *Culture, media, language.* London: Hutchinson.

Holmes, A. (2012, March 30). White until proven black: Imagining race in Hunger Games. *The New Yorker.* Retrieved June 10, 2016, from http://www.newyorker.com/books/page-turner/white-until-proven-black-imagining-race-in-hunger-games.

Jackson, S. J., & Foucault W. B. (2016). #Ferguson is everywhere: initiators in emerging counterpublic networks, *Information, Communication & Society, 19*:3, 397–418, DOI: 10.1080/1369118X.2015.1106571.

Katz, E., & Liebes, T. (1987). Decoding *Dallas:* Notes from a cross-cultural study. In H. Newcomb (Ed.), *Television: The critical view* (4th ed., pp. 419–432). New York: Oxford University Press.

Kim, J. (2007). Why does Hallyu matter? The significance of the Korean Wave in South Korea. *Critical Studies in Television, 2,* 47–59.

Kim, S.-Y. (2008, May 5). Korean wave "Hallyu" abroad waning. *The Korea Times.* Retrieved May 15, 2008, from www.koreatimes.co.kr/www/news/special/2008/05/180_23641.html.

Kyriazis, S. (2015, December 10). Star Wars John Boyega attacks "RACIST" comments that the film is ANTI-WHITE. *Express.* Retrieved June 10, 2016, from http://www.express.co.uk/entertainment/films/625689/john-boyega-star-wars-racist-white-genocide.

Land, M. (1992). Ivoirien television, willing vector of cultural imperialism. *Howard Journal of Communications, 4,* 10–27.

Lee, M., & Cho, C. H. (1990, January). Women watching together: An ethnographic study of Korean soap opera fans in the U.S. *Cultural Studies, 4*(1), 30–44.

Lipsitz, G. (1990). *Time passages: Collective memory and American popular culture.* Minneapolis, MN: University of Minnesota Press.

Louet, S. (2005, November 30). "French CNN" seen operational by end of 2006. Reuters Business Channel. Retrieved from December 3, 2005, from http://today.reuters.com/business/newsArticle.aspx?type=media&storyID=nL30762703.

Manusov, V., & Hegde, R. (1993). Communicative outcomes of stereotype-based expectancies: An observational study of cross-cultural dyads. *Communication Quarterly, 41,* 338–354.

McFadden, S. (2016, February 8). Beyoncé's Formation reclaims black Americas narrative from the margins. *The Guardian.* Retrieved June 10, 2016, from http://www.theguardian.com/commentisfree/2016/feb/08/beyonce-formation-black-american-narrative-the-margins.

Merritt, B. D. (2000). Illusive reflections: African American women on primetime television. In A. González, M. Houston, & V. Chen (Eds.), *Our voices* (3rd ed., pp. 47–53). Los Angeles, CA: Roxbury.

Meyers, M. (2004). African American women and violence: Gender, race, and class in the news. *Critical Studies in Media Communication, 21,* 95–118.

Moon, D. G., & Nakayama, T. K. (2005). Strategic social identities and judgments: A murder in Appalachia. *Howard Journal of Communications, 16,* 1–22.

Nakayama, T. K., & Vachon, L. A. (1991). Imperialist victory in peacetime: State functions and the British cinema industry. *Current Research in Film, 5,* 161–174.

Newcomb, H., & Hirsch, P. M. (1987). Television as a cultural forum. In H. Newcomb (Ed.), *Television: The critical view* (4th ed., pp. 455–470). New York: Oxford University Press.

Oliver, M. B., Jackson, R. L., Moses, N. N., & Dangerfield, C. L. (2004). The face of crime:

Viewers' memory of race-related facial features of individuals pictured in the news. *Journal of Communications, 54,* 88–104.

Onishi, N. (2016, February 18). Nigeria's booming film industry redefines African life. *The New York Times.* Retrieved June 10, 2016, from http://www.nytimes.com/2016/02/19/world/africa/with-a-boom-before-the-cameras-nigeria-redefines-african-life.html?_r=0.

Ono, K. A., & Kwon, J. (2013). Re-worlding culture? YouTube as K-pop interlocutor. In Y. Kim (Ed.), *The Korean Wave: Korean Media Go Global* (pp. 199–214). New York: Routledge.

Parameswaran, R. (2004). Global queens, national celebrities: Tales of feminine triumph in post-liberalization India. *Critical Studies in Media Communication, 21,* 346–370.

Perry, S. P., & Long, J. M. (2016). "Why would anyone sell paradise?": The Islamic State in Iraq and the making of a martyr. *Southern Communication Journal, 81*(1): 1–17.

Roff, P. (2015, December 14). Vader is just Vader. *US News & World Report.* Retrieved June 10, 2016, from http://www.usnews.com/opinion/blogs/peter-roff/articles/2015-12-14/msnbcs-racist-darth-vader-star-wars-idea-is-ludicrous.

Sabah, Z. (2006, January 19). Pirated DVDs among hottest items on Iraqi shelves. *USA Today.* Retrieved May 15, 2008, from www.usatoday.com/news/world/iraq/2006-01-19-iraq-dvds_x.htm#.

Sakoui, A. (2016, March 28–April 3). Are Batman and Superman strong enough to lift Warner Bros.? *Bloomberg Businessweek,* pp. 22–23.

Schwartz-DuPre, R. L., & Scott, S. (2015). Postcolonial globalized communication and rapping the *Kufiyya. Communication, Culture & Critique, 8*(3): 335–355.

Shepherd, J. (2015, December 16). Star Wars is racist because Darth Vader is "a black guy", MSNBC's Melissa Harris Perry suggests. *Independent.* Retrieved June 10, 2016, from http://www.independent.co.uk/arts-entertainment/films/news/msnbcs-melissa-harris-perry-implies-star-wars-is-racist-because-darth-vader-is-a-black-guy-a6775406.html.

Snyder, M. (1998). Self-fulfilling stereotypes. In P. Rothenburg (Ed.), *Race, class and gender in the United States* (4th ed., pp. 452–457). New York: St. Martin's Press.

Tan, A., Fujioka, F., & Tan, G. (2000). Television use, stereotypes of African Americans and opinions on affirmative action: An affective model of policy reasoning. *Communication Monographs, 67*(4), 362–371.

Tomlinson, J. (1991). *Cultural imperialism.* Baltimore, MD: Johns Hopkins University Press.

CREDITS

241–258. [page 369, text] R. L. Schwartz-DuPre, and S. Scott, quote from "Postcolonial globalized communication and rapping the Kufiyya" *Communication, Culture & Critique* (2015): 335–355. [page 371, text] A. Holmes, quote from "White until proven black: Imagining race in Hunger Games" from *The New Yorker* (March 30, 2012). [page 372, text] J. Shepherd, quote from "Star Wars is racist because Darth Vader is "a black guy", MSNBC's Melissa Harris Perry suggests" from *Independent* (December 16, 2015). [page 372, text] B. Griggs, quote from "Internet trolls call new "Star Wars" movie "anti-white." from *CNN* (October 21, 2015). [page 372, text] S. Kyriazis, excerpt from "Star Wars John Boyega attacks "RACIST" comments that the film is ANTI-WHITE" from *Express* (December 10, 2015). [page 373, text] D. T. Buescher, and K. A. Ono, quote from "Civilized colonialism: Pocahontas as neocolonial rhetoric" from *Women's Studies in Communication* (1996): 127–153. [page 373, text] Z. Sabah, quote from "Pirated DVDs among hottest items on Iraqi shelves" from *USA Today* (January 19, 2006). [page 375, text] Christophe, excerpt from "Students Voices: When I first … have to work." Original work; [page 374, text] A. Tan, F. Fujioka, and G. Tan, quote from "Television use, stereotypes of African Americans and opinions on affirmative action: An affective model of policy reasoning" *Communication Monographs* (2000): 362–371. [page 375, text] M. B. Oliver, R. L. Jackson, N. N. Moses, and C. L. Dangerfield, quote from "The face of crime: Viewers' memory of race-related facial features of individuals pictured in the news" from *Journal of Communications* (2004): 88–104. [page 376, text] E. Katz, and T. Liebes, excerpt from "Decoding Dallas: Notes from a cross-cultural study" in *Television: The critical view*, edited by H. Newcomb. Oxford University Press. [page 376, text] M. Lee, and C. H. Cho, excerpt from "Women watching together: An ethnographic study of Korean soap opera fans in the U.S." from *Cultural Studies* (January 1990): 30–44. [page 376, text] M. Lee, and C. H. Cho, quote from "Women watching together: An ethnographic study of Korean soap opera fans in the U.S." from *Cultural Studies* (January 1990): 30–44. [page 377, text] R. Dyer, excerpt from *The matter of images: Essays on representations*. Routledge. [page 377–378, text] L. Flores, excerpt from "Challenging the myth of assimilation: A Chicana feminist perspective" in *Constituting cultural difference through discourse*, edited by Mary Jane Collier. Sage. [page 377, text] Shanyu, excerpt from "Whenever I go to … read and see." Original work; [page 378, text] B. D. Merritt, excerpt from "Illusive refl ections: African American women on primetime television" in *Our voices*, edited by

A. González, M. Houston, and V. Chen. Roxbury. [page 378, text] Excerpt from "Bigots Who Rock: An ADL List of Hate Music Groups" from *Anti-Defamation League* (2011). [page 378, text] J. Salamon, excerpt from "Television review; on the fringe of rock 'n' roll, music with a heart full of hatred" *The New York Times* (February 18, 2002). [page 378, text] Excerpt from "Bigots Who Rock: An ADL List of Hate Music Groups" from *Anti-Defamation League* (2011). [page 379, text] M. Meyers, quote from "African American women and violence: Gender, race, and class in the news" from *Critical Studies in Media Communication* (2004): 95–118. [page 379, text] C. M. Blow, excerpt from "My very own Captain America" from *The New York Times* (July 29, 2011). [page 379, text] S. Bowles, excerpt from "'Captain America' unseats 'Potter' at box office," from *USA Today* (July 24, 2011). [page 379, text] C. DeVega, excerpt from "Captain America: The first avenger's dishonest and cowardly racial politics," from *AlterNet* (July 23, 2011). [page 379, text] R. Quivers, excerpt from "Captain America's USA," from *Huffington Post* (August 1, 2011). [page 380, text] M. Snyder, quote from "Self-fulfilling stereotypes" in *Race, class and gender in the United States*, edited by P. Rothenburg. St. Martin's Press. [page 381, text] A. Sakoui, quote from "Are Batman and Superman strong enough to lift Warner Bros.?" from *Bloomberg Businessweek* (March 28–April 3, 2016): 22–23. [page 382, text] T. Bennett, and J. Woollacott, quote from *Bond and beyond: The political career of a popular culture hero*. Methuen. [page 383, text] J. Kim, quote from "Why does Hallyu matter? The significance of the Korean Wave in South Korea" from *Critical Studies in Television* (2007): 47–59. [page 383, text] S.-Y. Kim, quote from "Korean wave "Hallyu" abroad waning" *The Korea Times* (May 5, 2008). [page 383, text] K. A. Ono, and J. Kwon, quote from "Re-worlding culture? YouTube as K-pop interlocutor" in *The Korean wave: Korean media go global*, edited by Y. Kim. Routledge. [page 382, text] N. Ceballos, and N. Czyzewska, excerpt from "Body image in Hispanic/Latino vs. European American Adolescents: Implications for treatment and prevention of obesity in underserved populations" from *Journal of Health Care for the Poor and Underserved* (2010): 823–838. [page 382, text] W. J. Cromie, excerpt from "Male body image: East doesn't meet west" from *Harvard Gazette* (February 10, 2005). Harvard Gazette. [page 382, text] K. Fox, excerpt from "Mirror, mirror: A summary of research findings on body image" from *Social Issues Research Centre* (1997). [page 385, text] J. Cohen, quote from "Global and local viewing experiences in the age of multichannel television: The Israeli experience" from

Communication Theory (2005): 437–455. [page 386–387, text] M. Land, excerpt from "Ivoirien television, willing vector of cultural imperialism" *Howard Journal of Communications* (1992): 10–27. [page 386, text] Elizabeth, excerpt from "I do not like foreign . . . understand these movies." Original work; [page 386, text] Sam, excerpt from "Foreign films . . . depiction of the world." Original work; [page 387, text] R. Parameswaran, quote from "Global queens, national celebrities: Tales of feminine triumph in post-liberalization India" from *Critical Studies in Media Communication* (2004): 346–370.

CULTURE, COMMUNICATION, AND INTERCULTURAL RELATIONSHIPS

BENEFITS AND CHALLENGES OF INTERCULTURAL RELATIONSHIPS
Benefits
Challenges

THINKING DIALECTICALLY ABOUT INTERCULTURAL RELATIONSHIPS
Personal–Contextual Dialectic
Differences–Similarities Dialectic
Cultural–Individual Dialectic
Privilege–Disadvantage Dialectic
Static–Dynamic Dialectic
History/Past–Present/Future Dialectic

INTERCULTURAL RELATIONSHIPS
Social Science Approach: Cross-Cultural Differences
Interpretive Approach: Communicating in Intercultural Relationships
Critical Approach: Contextual Influences

INTERNET RESOURCES

SUMMARY

DISCUSSION QUESTIONS

ACTIVITIES

KEY WORDS

REFERENCES

CHAPTER OBJECTIVES

After reading this chapter, you should be able to:

1. Identify three benefits and three challenges to intercultural relationships.
2. Describe six dialectics of intercultural relationships.
3. Identify three approaches to understanding intercultural relationships.
4. Describe some cultural differences in the notion of friendship.
5. Describe cultural differences in relational development.
6. Describe "turning points" in intercultural friendships.
7. Explain the frequency of intercultural dating today.
8. Identify challenges of intercultural marriages.
9. Identify four interaction styles in intercultural marriages.
10. Identify and describe characteristics of gay and lesbian friendships.
11. Describe how institutional, historical, or political contexts can facilitate or hinder intercultural relationships.

In the early 1990s, John Arthur and Jim Obergefell met and began a same-sex relationship in the State of Ohio. At the time, Ohio did not allow same-sex marriages. In 2013, the U.S. Supreme Court ruled in *United States v. Windsor* that the federal government, including the Internal Revenue Service, had to recognize same-sex marriages that took place where it was legal; Arthur and Obergefell decided to get married in another state. Because John Arthur was suffering from ALS (Lou Gehrig's disease), they needed to fundraise the money to fly a medical flight to another state and get married. They chose Maryland and were married there. Three months and 11 days later, Arthur died and Obergefell asked to have himself listed as Arthur's husband on the death certificate. Because Ohio did not recognize same-sex marriages at all, the State of Ohio refused and a court battle ensued (Rosenwald, 2015). In *Obergefell v. Hodges*, the U.S. Supreme Court ruled that, under the 14th Amendment to the U.S. Constitution, all states had to allow and recognize same-sex marriages (Yoshino, 2015).

The *Obergefell* decision has wide-ranging effects on how our society considers same-sex relationships. Prior to this ruling, 36 states and the District of Columbia recognized same-sex marriages. Because the U.S. federal government now recognizes same-sex marriages, this decision changes how these couples are treated by the Internal Revenue Service, the Social Security Administration, and other government agencies. It also impacts how same-sex couples are regarded as immigrants, refugees, and other legal categories established by the government.

We may not often think about how our personal relationships might be impacted by national laws, but we must realize that not all relationships hold the same status around the world. By the time the United States legalized same-sex marriages nationwide, many other countries had already done so, including Argentina, Belgium, Brazil, France, Greenland, Iceland, the Netherlands, New Zealand, Norway, South Africa, Sweden, United Kingdom, and Uruguay. At the same time, there are ten countries with the death penalty for homosexuality: Afghanistan, Iran, Mauritania, Nigeria, Qatar, Saudi Arabia, Somalia, Sudan, the United Arab Emirates, and Yemen (Bearak & Cameron, 2016) and many more where homosexuality is illegal.

Despite the *Obergefell* ruling, many in the United States have resisted same-sex marriage. In 2016, "at least 11 and possibly 15 counties in Alabama" have closed their marriage license offices and were not issuing marriage licenses to any couples (Broverman, 2016). Kim Davis, the Rowan County clerk in Kentucky, became famous for her refusal to issue marriage licenses to same-sex couples based upon her religious beliefs. Yet many other states are enacting laws to allow discrimination against lesbian, gay, bisexual, and transgender (LGBT) people. The American Civil Liberties Union keeps a list of these bills being considered by various states and updates it every Wednesday to stay abreast of all of the changes. The list is located at: https://www.aclu.org/anti-lgbt-religious -exemption-legislation-across-country?redirect=anti-lgbt-religious-refusals-legislation -across-country. What does this climate do for our understanding of all kinds of relationships and their status around the world? While there are many challenges to any relationship, intercultural and international relationships often face even more difficulties, but there are rewards from these relationships as well.

How do we develop relationships with people who differ from us in terms of age, ethnicity, religion, class, or sexual orientation? Think about friends who differ from you in any of these ways. How did you get to know them? Are these relationships any different from those that are characterized by similarity? Why do we develop relationships with some people and not with others? There seems to be some truth to *both* adages "Birds of a feather flock together" and "Opposites attract."

What is the role of communication in intercultural relationships? And how do contexts (social, historical, political) influence our relationships? In this chapter, we explore the benefits and challenges of intercultural relationships, examine how relationships develop over time, and identify some cultural differences in relational development and maintenance. Throughout the chapter, we emphasize a dialectical perspective on intercultural relationships—both friendship and romantic. Contextual issues exist along with individual relational issues, so for each of these topics we'll examine contextual issues.

There are increasing opportunities to meet people from other cultures through the Internet and increasing cultural diversity in many schools and workplaces, yet in a recent study college students reported limited contact with people from different cultural backgrounds (Halualani, 2010). In surveys, young people repeatedly say they are open to intercultural romantic relationships, yet one recent study showed there is still some resistance to intimate interracial relationships (Djamba & Kimuna, 2014).

Why do some people get involved in intercultural relationships and others not? Why do some intercultural relationships seem to flourish and others not? We think the answer lies in a dialectic: Although individual style and preference may play a large role, the contexts in which people meet and interact have much to contribute to the viability of intercultural friendships and romantic relationships. That is, social, religious, and educational contexts may promote *or* discourage intercultural relationships. Historical and political contexts also play a big role. For example, it was only 50 years ago that it was illegal for whites and African Americans to marry (Root, 2001). This, no doubt, is part of the reason that rates of interracial dating and marriage are the lowest among these two groups when compared to rates for other ethnic and racial groups (Martin, Bradford, Drzewiecka, & Chitgopekar, 2003). Who we choose to befriend is determined both by our individual preferences *and* by social, religious, and political contexts.

In this chapter, we first examine the benefits and challenges of intercultural relationships. Then we describe six dialectics as a way of thinking about intercultural friendships and intercultural romantic relationships. Then we present the contributions of three communication perspectives on intercultural relationships—starting with the social science approach that emphasizes cross-cultural comparisons of relational notions. We then move to the interpretive perspective that has contributed in-depth information about various types of intercultural relationships, and finally we discuss the critical approach that emphasizes the role of context in determining who we form relationships with and how these relationships develop.

BENEFITS AND CHALLENGES OF INTERCULTURAL RELATIONSHIPS

Benefits

Most people have a variety of **intercultural relationships** that may feature differences in age, physical ability, gender, ethnicity, class, religion, race, or nationality. The potential rewards and opportunities in these relationships are tremendous. The

intercultural relationships Relationships that are formed between individuals from different cultures.

key to these relationships often involves maintaining a balance between differences and similarities. One example is the relationship between Judith and a Chicana colleague. When they first met, they thought they had little in common, coming as they did from very different ethnic and cultural backgrounds. But once they found commonality in their academic work, they discovered that they actually had a great deal in common. For instance, both come from large religious families, both have parents who contributed a great deal to their communities, and both are close to their older sisters and their nieces. Through the relationship, they also have learned a lot about each other's different worlds.

The benefits of such relationships include (1) acquiring knowledge about the world, (2) breaking stereotypes, and (3) acquiring new skills. You can probably think of a lot more. In intercultural relationships, we often learn specific information about unfamiliar cultural patterns and languages. Nancy, an undergraduate student, describes how she learned about culture and religion through her relationship with her boyfriend:

> *My family and I are Buddhists; however, we are not very religious. We still celebrate the holidays and traditions, but we do not attend the temple often. Anyway, my boyfriend, being Catholic, asked me to go to his church for an Easter celebration one year. I decided to go because I am an open person and not restricted to believing in just one religion. Anyhow, I went to his church, and I must say it was a good learning experience and a fun one, too. I was glad that I went to see what "Catholics" do to celebrate Easter.*

A romance or a close intercultural friendship may be the vehicle through which we learn something about history. Jennifer, a student in one of our classes, told us how she learned more about the Holocaust from her Jewish friends and about #blacklivesmatter from her African American friends. These are examples of **relational learning**—learning that comes from a particular relationship but generalizes to other contexts. Relational learning is often much more compelling than knowledge gained from books, classes, and so on. And once we develop one close intercultural relationship, it becomes much easier to form others. (See Figure 10-1.)

relational learning Learning that comes from a particular relationship but generalizes to other contexts.

Intercultural relationships can open all kinds of opportunities and new ways of seeing the world. Ingrid, a student of ours, says that she grew up in a mostly African American/Latina(o) community, but made new friends once she came to college. She says: "as time went by, I started to notice that I didn't see that many black people on campus. One of my close friends was white and the other two, Middle Eastern. When I told this to my friends at home I was told that I needed more black friends, but this wasn't true at all. These friendships have allowed me to learn and experience things I wouldn't have, if I only hung out with people who looked like me. I wouldn't have learned how to write my name in Arabic or learned to swear in Italian. If I hadn't attempted to form these relationships, a summer in Dubai, Qatar, or Bahrain wouldn't have been imaginable."

We often learn how to do new things in intercultural relationships. Through her friendships with students in the United States and abroad, Judith has learned to make *paella* (a Spanish dish) and *nopalitos con puerca* (a cactus-and-pork stew), to play bridge in French, and to downhill ski. Through intercultural relationships, newcomers to a society can acquire important skills. All of these potential benefits can lead

FIGURE 10-1 College students often benefit from the experience of forming intercultural relationships. Through these relationships, we can learn about other cultural groups, as well as gain additional insight into our own cultural backgrounds. How often do you come into contact with people who are different from you? How often do you seek out intercultural friendships? (© *Chuck Savage/Corbis RF*)

to a sense of interconnectedness with others and can establish a lifelong pattern of communication across differences. We also hope that it helps us become better intercultural communicators.

Challenges

Intercultural relationships are unique in several ways, and as such present particular challenges. By definition, they are characterized by cultural differences in communication style, values, and perceptions. The dissimilarities probably are most prominent in the early stages of relational development when people tend to exchange less personal information. However, if some commonality is established and the relationship develops beyond the initial stages, these cultural differences may have less of an impact because all relationships become more idiosyncratic as they move to more intimate stages. There seems to be an interplay of both differences and similarities in intercultural relationships. The differences are a given, and the challenge can be to discover and build on the similarities—common interests, activities, beliefs, or goals.

Negative stereotyping often comes into play in intercultural relationships. As we discussed in Chapter 5, stereotypes are a way of categorizing and processing information but are detrimental when they are negative and are held rigidly. Sometimes people must work to get information that can counteract the stereotype.

In 1967, the U.S. Supreme Court ruled in *Loving v. Virginia* that laws prohibiting interracial marriages were unconstitutional. Despite the change in the law, attitudes about interracial marriages have not always changed as quickly. How might negative attitudes about interracial and same-sex marriages change toward acceptance?

In 2016, a Mississippi couple were forced to move out of an RV park because they were in an interracial marriage. Erica Dunahoo who is Hispanic and Native American is married to Stanley Hoskins who is African American. She recounts what happened in Tupelo, a small city in the northeastern part of the state:

> *"He was real nice," she said. "He invited me to church and gave me a hug. I bragged on him to my family."*
>
> *The next day, she said, Baker telephoned her and said, "Hey, you didn't tell me you was married to no black man."*
>
> *She said she replied that she didn't realize it was a problem.*
>
> *"Oh, it's a big problem with the members of my church, my community and my mother-in-law," she quoted him as saying. "They don't allow that black and white shacking."*
>
> *"We're not shacking. We're married," she replied.*
>
> *"Oh, it's the same thing," she quoted him as replying.*

When he was asked if he would rent the RV space to another interracial couple, Gene Baker, the owner of the park, said: "I'm closing it down, and that solves the problem."

Source: From J. Mitchell, "Mississippi RV park owner evicts interracial couple," *The Clarion-Ledger,* April 5, 2016. Retrieved July 19, 2016, from http://www.clarionledger.com/story /news/2016/04/02/mississippi-rv-park-owner-evicts-interracial-couple/82469086/.

Navita Cummings James (2000), a communication scholar, describes the beliefs and stereotypes about white people passed along to her from her family:

- Whites can be violent and treacherous.
- Whites have an inferiority complex that compels them to "put down" blacks and other minorities.
- White men are arrogant, and white women are lazy.
- "Good" whites are the exception.

More importantly, James goes on to describe how she did not let these stereotypes become "an intellectual prison of my self identity or beliefs about Whites" (p. 45). Through intercultural relationships and effort, her beliefs evolved and the stereotypes diminished. She learned that race is not a predictor of intelligence but that income and opportunities are. She learned that all people, regardless of color, deserve to be treated with dignity and respect. And she made definite choices about

As I worked to break the barrier of acquaintance with whites, there were many uncomfortable moments. Once, I had to explain that even though I appreciate history, I wasn't really interested in going to a Civil War reenactment. I've had to tell friends that I'm a bit uncomfortable going to certain restaurants or spas where I've never seen a nonwhite customer. The toughest have come when discussing racially charged situations and events. Yes, I recently told a friend, black parents really do teach their sons about wearing hoodies when walking in white neighborhoods.

Reflecting back, I first nurtured these relationships by being careful to always present myself in a manner that would convince my white friends that "blacks are no different from whites." But with age comes more confidence and authenticity. I no longer "take care of" my white friends by aligning my thoughts and experiences with what they might want to hear or what I think they can handle. Instead, we work and struggle to understand each other—as friends should. [. . .]

Each conversation moved us forward because each was wrapped in the kind of trust that only comes with friendship. Together, we expand our worldviews, challenge our assumptions, and sharpen our thinking.

I hope we become better people as well. That's what friends are for.

Source: From D. L. Plummer, "Why I have white friends," *The Boston Globe*, February 4, 2015. Retrieved July 19, 2016, from http://www.bostonglobe.com/magazine/2015/02/04/why-have -white-friends/RvkIgg5CXYtwza9mOcpmNI/story.html?event=event12.

how to relate to others and to cultivate a variety of friends, and not merely African Americans.

Another challenge in intercultural relationships involves the anxiety that people often experience initially. Some anxiety is present in the early stages of any relationship, but the anxiety is greater in intercultural relationships. Anxiety arises from concern about possible negative consequences. We may be afraid that we'll look stupid or that we'll offend someone because we're unfamiliar with that person's language or culture. Differences in age do not usually evoke such anxiety, but differences in physical ability, class, or race are likely to—at least initially. For example, a student describes his experience of being on a soccer team with players from Kenya, Jamaica, Egypt, and Mexico:

In our first meeting, we were to get acquainted with everyone and introduce ourselves. At the end of the meeting, we all stood around talking—reducing anxiety. Eventually, our conversations were directed toward self-disclosure and relating our experiences. I believe this helped me prepare for more experiences along this line.

The level of anxiety may be higher if one or both parties have negative expectations based on a previous interaction or on stereotypes (Stephan & Stephan, 1992).

Communication plays a key role in intercultural relationships. These intercultural relationships can change who you are and how you see the world. Our student Jessica went to New Zealand:

What an amazing experience. Not only did I get to stay with a family that had three girls, one my age, but I also learned about the Maoris, the first people to inhabit New Zealand. I developed a lifelong relationship with my host family and relished learning the difference and similarities between our cultures. I have fond memories of sitting up late at night drinking tea, not coffee, with my New Zealand mother. We would talk for hours. This was a powerful learning experience.

Although my experiences have for the most part been overseas, I feel they have opened a window for me. My worldview has gone from just me to phenomenally huge. I see things from other people's point of view; I actually try to see things in a different light. I have my experiences with people from other cultures to thank.

—Jessica

In contrast, intercultural interactions in which one or both parties have few negative expectations and no negative prior contact probably have less anxiety.

Writer Letty Cottin Pogrebin (1987) emphasizes that intercultural relationships take more "care and feeding" than do those relationships between people who are very similar. Intercultural relationships are often more work than in-group relationships. A lot of the work has to do with explaining—explaining to themselves, to each other, and to their respective communities.

First, in some way, conscious or unconscious, we ask ourselves, What is the meaning of being friends with someone who is not like me? Am I making this friend out of necessity, for my job, or because everyone I'm around is different from me in some way? Am I making this friend because I want to gain entry into this group for personal benefit? Because I feel guilty?

Second, we explain to each other. This is the process of ongoing mutual clarification, one of the healthiest characteristics of intercultural relationships. It is the process of learning to see from the other's perspective. For example, Judith discovered that, even when she thought she was being very indirect with her Japanese students, they still thought she was being rather direct. In this way, Judith came to understand that others can interpret events and conversation in very different ways.

Third, people who cross boundaries often have to explain this to their respective communities. Thus, your friends may question your close relationship with someone who is much older or is of a different ethnicity. This may be especially true for those who date someone from a different culture. For example, one of our students tells how her friend terminated an intercultural relationship because of her parents' attitudes:

My friend started dating this guy casually. The relationship was going great but when she found out that he was not Jewish, she felt the need to end it because she knew it could never become serious. When I asked her why, she said it wasn't about the relationship itself but because her parents would not approve a non-Jewish partner and approval from her parents is more important to her.

Historically, the biggest obstacles to boundary-crossing friendships have come not from minority communities, but from majority communities (McCullough, 1998). Those in the majority (e.g., whites) have the most to gain by maintaining social inequality and are less likely to initiate boundary-crossing friendships. In contrast, minority groups have more to gain. Developing intercultural relationships can help them survive—economically, professionally, and personally.

Finally, in intercultural relationships, individuals recognize and respect the differences. In these relationships, we often have to remind ourselves that we can never know exactly what it's like to walk in another person's shoes. Furthermore, those in the majority group tend to know less about those in minority groups than vice-versa. As Pogrebin (1992) stated, "Mutual respect, acceptance, tolerance for the faux pas and the occasional closed door, open discussion and patient mutual education, all this gives crossing friendships—when they work at all—a special kind of depth" (p. 318). Perhaps this is especially true of interracial relationships in the United States. Pat, an African American woman, describes the importance of honesty and openness in her relationship with her friend Rose, who is white:

"Rose is one of the few White women that I have an honest, direct relationship with. . . . She is very aware that I am a Black woman and she is a White woman. . . . I care about her very deeply. . . . And I am committed to our friendship and I respect her a whole lot. . . . I like her values. I like how she thinks about people, about nature, her integrity and her principles. . . . It is her willingness to make race her issue." (quoted in McCullough, 1998, p. 193)

THINKING DIALECTICALLY ABOUT INTERCULTURAL RELATIONSHIPS

Researcher Leslie A. Baxter (1993) suggests that a dialectical model explains the dynamics of relationships. She and her colleagues have identified several basic dialectical tensions in relationships: novelty–predictability, autonomy–connection, and openness–closedness (Baxter & Montgomery, 1996). That is, we can simultaneously feel the need to be both connected and autonomous in relationships with our parents, friends, and romantic partners. We may also feel the need simultaneously for novelty and predictability and the need to be open and yet private in our relationships. According to one study, Taiwanese students in close relationships experience these same dialectical tensions (Chen, Drzewiecka, & Sias, 2001). We can extend the notion of dialectical tensions to encompass the entire relational sphere (Chen, 2002; Martin, Nakayama, & Flores, 2002). Let's see how each of these dialectics work.

Personal–Contextual Dialectic

Intercultural relationships are both personal and contextual. There are aspects of the relationship that are personal—consistent from situation to situation—but context also plays a huge role in how intercultural relationships are developed and maintained. For example, are there contexts where you would be more or less comfortable in an intercultural relationship? How do your family, your church, your religious friends react to intercultural relationships? Studies have shown that the number-one predictor of whether individuals engage in intercultural dating is the diversity of their social networks—that is, if you are in contexts where there is diversity, it is more likely you will meet and go out with people from other ethnic/racial backgrounds (Clark-Ibanez & Felmlee, 2004).

Even who we are attracted to is largely determined by cultural contexts. Notions of attractiveness are defined for us and reinforced by what we see on TV and film and in other media. The standard of beauty for American women seems to be white and blond, and at least one study states that 90% of models in U.S. women's magazines are white (Frith, Shaw, & Cheng, 2005). This trend was noticed by one of our in the summer of 2015:

> *I stopped by an airport newsstand and was struck by the similarity of the covers on the popular magazines displayed there (e.g.,* Vanity Fair, Cosmopolitan, Self*). Out of the 24 magazines, 19 had a white model with long blond hair on their covers! Two magazines had Caucasian brunettes, and two covers featured nonwhite women (one was Jennifer Lopez, the other Oprah Winfrey—on the cover of her* O *magazine).*

At the same time, Asian and Asian American women are often portrayed in popular culture texts and discourses as erotic, exotic, and submissive and thus highly attractive to white men (Root, 2001). One young man, Shane, described his attraction to Asian women:

> *I think they're so exotic. Really, what concerns me about the girl is the eyes, and Asian women have beautiful eyes, the form and the shape of them. It's a plus for me. I had another Asian girlfriend before. And I like their skin color, tannish, not just white, white, white. A girl with color. It's just different; it's more sexual, it's not just like plain Jane. ("Talking About Race," 2000, p. 59)*

This kind of attraction has spawned an entire business of mail-order Asian brides. Communication scholar Rona Halualani (1995) analyzed how these businesses perpetuate and market stereotypes of Asian women as idealized wives—submissive, sexual, and eager to please men. In contrast, Asian men are often stereotyped in ways that downplay their masculinity (Eng, 2001).

Of course, we all want to believe we choose our relational partners outside of the influences of these social discourses. We all want to believe we fell in love with this man or this woman because he or she is "special." Yet if we want to understand the problems and dynamics of intercultural communication, we must be attentive to these large contextual discourses about racial and sexual identities and realize there is the tension of both personal and contextual forces in any intercultural relationship.

Differences–Similarities Dialectic

According to the **similarity principle,** we tend to be attracted to people who we perceive to be similar to ourselves, and evidence indicates that this principle works for many cultural groups (Osbeck & Moghaddam, 1997; Tan & Singh, 1995). Finding people who agree with our beliefs confirms our own beliefs and provides us with **cognitive consistency** (if we like ourselves, we'll probably like others who share our views). In fact, we may explicitly seek partners who hold the same beliefs and values because of deep spiritual, moral, or religious conviction. In intercultural relationships, in contrast, we may be attracted to persons who are somewhat different from ourselves. The differences that form the basis of attraction may involve personality traits and may contribute to complementarity or balance in the relationship. An introverted individual may seek a more outgoing partner, or a spendthrift may be attracted to an individual who is more careful with money. Some individuals are attracted to people simply because they have a different cultural background. Intercultural relationships present intriguing opportunities to experience new ways of living in and looking at the world.

Most of us seek a balance between novelty and predictability in our relationships. Research shows that the most successful relationships have a balance of differences and similarities (Luo & Klohnen, 2005). In intercultural relationships especially, it is important to consider differences and similarities at the same time. Tamie, a student from Japan, explains how this dialectic works in her relationship with her roommate/friend Hong-Ju, a Korean graduate student:

> We are both women and about the same age—30. Both of us are pursuing a Ph.D. degree and aspire to become successful professional scholars and educators. When we cook in our apartment, there are several common foods (e.g., rice, dried seaweed) while our eating styles may be different (e.g., Hong-Ju's cooking tends to include more spicy food than mine). We also share some common cultural values (e.g., importance of respect for elders). Yet Hong-Ju is married (a long-distance marriage), and I am single. Finally, we both consider ourselves as "not so typical" Korean or Japanese women. Hong-Ju's long-distance marriage and my staying single even in my 30s are usually considered as nontraditional in our respective countries. Eventually, this "nontraditional-ness" creates in both of us a shared and proud sense of identity and bond.

Cultural–Individual Dialectic

Communication in intercultural relationships is both cultural and individual, that is, idiosyncratic. We have described various cultural differences that exist in value orientations, in both nonverbal and verbal communication. Although we have provided some generalizations about how various cultural groups differ, it is important to remember that communication is both cultural and individual. Tamie describes how she deals with this cultural–individual dialectic in her classroom teaching:

> I have become very aware of cultural differences between U.S. classrooms and Japanese classrooms. In terms of my teaching style, I have noticed myself

similarity principle A principle of relational attraction suggesting that individuals tend to be attracted to people they perceive to be similar to themselves.

cognitive consistency Having a logical connection between existing knowledge and a new stimulus.

delivering the course content in a more linear, straightforward, fast-paced manner than I would in Japan. Therefore, there is definitely a certain cultural expectation that I am aware of as I teach in the U.S. However, I am also aware that there are unique individual styles and preferences among U.S. students— some students are outspoken and comfortable in speaking up; others take more time before speaking up, as they reflect and think more holistically. So this cultural–individual dialectic is always at work in my intercultural teaching experience here in the U.S.

Privilege–Disadvantage Dialectic

We have stressed the importance of (and the difficulty of understanding) power and power differentials in intercultural relationships. People may be simultaneously privileged and disadvantaged, or privileged in some contexts and disadvantaged in others. For example, Laura, a bilingual university student, feels at a greater advantage in settings in which conversations take place in Spanish and English than she does in all-English settings. Her friends who speak only English probably feel the opposite. People in more powerful positions in particular need to be sensitive to power differentials, which may be less obvious to them.

Static–Dynamic Dialectic

This dialectic suggests that people and relationships are constantly in flux, responding to various personal and contextual dynamics. Intercultural relationships are no different in this regard. When Judith first met her friend Patricia (a third-generation, Mexican American, older student), Patricia was single and had just transferred to Arizona State University from a community college. At that time, both were living alone (Judith was in a commuter marriage), but both were close to their families. Patricia is now married, has a daughter, and has almost completed her graduate education. In this context, Judith and Patricia cannot respond to each other as the people they were five years ago but must respond to each other as they are now. Changes occur very slowly sometimes, but we need to remind ourselves that relationships are both static and dynamic.

History/Past–Present/Future Dialectic

Rather than trying to understand relationships by examining the relational partners alone, it is helpful to consider the contexts in which relationships occur. Often, this means the historical context. As noted in Chapter 4, cultural groups have different relationships with each other; some of these relationships are more positive and others more negative. For example, the historical and continuing hostility between the United States and Cuba means that each cultural group has fewer opportunities to meet people from the other nation and thus fewer opportunities to develop relationships. One student, John, gives his views on the past–present dialectic:

I don't feel as if people should feel guilty about what their family, ethnic group, or country did in the past, but they should definitely empathize with those their ancestors have hurt, understand what they did, understand the implications of what they did, and understand how the past (whether we have ties to it or not) greatly affects the present.

INTERCULTURAL RELATIONSHIPS

As with other topics, there are three communication approaches to studying intercultural relationships, and each makes a unique contribution to our understanding of how we develop and maintain relationships across differences. The social science approach identifies cross-cultural differences in how relationships are defined, initiated, and developed. The interpretive approach explores in depth the nature of these relationships and the role communication plays. The critical approach emphasizes the influence of various contexts—institutional, political, and historical—in facilitating and/or discouraging the development and maintenance of intercultural relationships.

Social Science Approach: Cross-Cultural Differences

The social science approach identifies various cross-cultural differences in relationships—including notions of friendships and the initiation and development of relationships.

Differences in Notions of Friendship   What are the characteristics of a friend? How do notions of friendship vary across cultures? To some people, a friend is someone to see or talk with occasionally, someone to do things with—go to a movie, discuss interests, maybe share some problems. This person might be one of many friends. If the friend moves away, the two people might eventually lose contact, and both might make new friends. Other people, however, view friendship much more seriously. For them, a friendship takes a long time to develop, includes many obligations (perhaps lending money or doing favors), and is a lifelong proposition.

Friendships are seen in very different ways around the world. For example, in most Western cultures, these relationships are seen as mostly voluntary and spontaneous, in contrast to family or work relationships. Although our friendships may be more constrained than we think (we do form relationships with people who are often very similar to ourselves), nonetheless, we enter into them voluntarily (Bell & Coleman, 1999).

Cultural differences in notions about friendships are related to ideas discussed earlier—ideas about identity and values. In societies that stress values like individualism and independence, as is the case in most Western cultures, it makes sense to view friendship and romance as voluntary relationships. However, people who view the self always in relation to others—that is, collectivists—hold a notion of friendship that is also less individual oriented and less spontaneous (Carrier, 1999). For example, in China, where the value of collectivism is very strong, friendships are long term and involve obligations:

> *The meaning of friendship itself differs from the American version. Chinese make few casual, short-term acquaintanceships as Americans learn to do*

so readily in school, at work, or while out amusing themselves. Once made, however, Chinese friendships are expected to last and to give each party very strong claims on the other's resources, time and loyalty. (Gates, 1987, p. 6)

guanxi A Chinese term for relational network

Friendship in China cannot be understood without attention to an important related concept, ***guanxi***—"relationships of social connection built on shared identities such as native place, kinship or attending the same school" (Smart, 1999, p. 120). It is through *guanxi* that things get done (e.g., jobs acquired or bureaucratic snafus resolved), often "through the back door." Although "connections" are important in the United States, they are not viewed in so positive a light. In the United States, we prefer to believe that we earned our jobs through our own hard work, perseverance, skills, and intelligence—without anyone else's help. This is a reflection of individualism in the U.S. culture. In China, in contrast, being able to get something done through connections, or *guanxi,* is seen as very positive, and so these relationships are purposefully cultivated. *Guanxi* is not the same thing as friendship, but friendship provides an acceptable base on which *guanxi* can be built (Smart, 1999).

This emphasis in China on cultivating close relationships, filled with obligations (and always open to *guanxi*), can be a bit overwhelming to people from Western cultures, but it can also be rewarding. A prominent journalist, Fox Butterfield (1982), who spent many years in China, describes these rewards:

Friendship in China offered assurances and an intimacy that we have abandoned in America; it gave the Chinese psychic as well as material rewards that we have lost. We ourselves did feel close to the Wangs [their Chinese friends], but as Westerners, the constant gift giving and obligations left us uneasy. (p. 47)

Differences in Relational Development   Cultural differences often come into play in the very beginning stages of relational development, in initial interactions. Different cultural rules govern how to regard strangers. In some cultural communities, all strangers are viewed as sources of potential relationships; in others, relationships can develop only after long and careful scrutiny. For example, in traditional German Mennonite society, strangers, especially those outside the religious group, are regarded with suspicion and not as potential friends. In contrast, many U.S. Americans are known to disclose personal information in very public contexts. One international student observes:

One thing that was very different from what I was used to in Iceland was that people, even people that I didn't know at all, were telling me their whole life stories, or so it felt like. Even some women at the checkout line at the supermarket were talking about how many times they had been married or divorced or about the money they had, which, in my culture, we are not used to just telling anyone about.

The renowned communication scholar Dean Barnlund (1989), along with his colleagues, found many differences in relational development in their students in Japanese and U.S. colleges. Students in both countries were asked about

SOME INTERESTING CULTURAL VARIABLES IN RELATIONSHIPS

Brazil: To be invited to a Brazilian's home is an honor. Guests are expected to stay for many hours rather than stop for a brief visit.

China: Face-saving is extremely important in China. Chinese always avoid embarrassing situations and help one another save face and retain self-respect.

France: When French greet people, they tend to be formal. Titles such as Monsieur, Madame, and Mademoiselle are often used. If they know the person, they may give the traditional kiss by the cheek/air.

Spain: The Spanish often invite guests to their home out of courtesy. One should wait until the host insists to accept the invitation.

Germany: Germans tend to be formal. They do not use first names unless they know the person very well.

Egypt: Always use titles such as Doctor or Professor to address these professionals.

Kenya: The Kenyan socialize at the end of the meal, not before the meal.

Greece: Avoid overpraising any item in a Greek home because the host may feel obligated to present it as a gift later.

Source: From M. Mancini, *Selling Destinations: Geography for the Travel Professional,* 4th ed. (Clifton Park, NY: Thomson/Delmar Learning, 2003).

---

their interactions with strangers and friends and about their views on friendship and more intimate relationships. The U.S. American students were more open and receptive to strangers; they talked to strangers in many different contexts—perhaps at a bus stop, in line at the grocery store, or in classes. In contrast, the Japanese students talked to significantly fewer strangers than did U.S. Americans over the same period.

More recently, communication scholar Pei-Wen Lee studied intercultural friendships that arise in a third culture, a culture that is not home to either of the friends. She notes that "the third cultural context serves as a significant backdrop with rules, norms, and events to which the intercultural dyad can relate and refer during their interactions" (2008, p. 66). The influence of a third culture complicates the **stage model** for intercultural friendships but can serve as a useful background for building these friendships.

> **stage model** The view that relationships develop in predictable phases over time.

Friendships As relationships develop in **intimacy,** friends share more personal and private information.

Over a half century ago, Kurt Lewin (1948), a renowned psychologist, conducted a classic cross-cultural study in self-disclosure whose findings still hold true today. Lewin proposed that the personal/private self can be modeled as three concentric circles representing three areas of information we share with others. The first circle is

> **intimacy** The extent of emotional closeness.

In some societies, the development of relationships is intricately related to issues of status and formality. Communication scholar Wintilo Garcia explains how these issues are expressed in Mexican Spanish.

> *The Mexican use of the Spanish words* tu *and* usted *signals the immediacy and status of the relational partners.* Tu *is the informal application of the pronoun* you. *It is common that individuals refer to their friends, family members, or children by this form of the word. The word* usted *is the formal form of the pronoun* you. *Cultural norms and rules require individuals to use this form when addressing new acquaintances, older people, professional (white-collar) people, and people who possess some sort of power. . . . In Mexico, as relationships become more intimate, the form of address changes. This often occurs over time where people who were once referred to by* usted *will later be referred to by* tu. *. . . Usually this transformation is initiated by the person who holds a perceived higher class. This is reasonable because high class individuals are perceived to possess more power in the relationship. In Mexico, the usual request phrase from the high class player is* tuteame *(interpreted as* you *"tu" me), which implies a desire for relational equality. In order for this request to be fulfilled, relational players must negotiate the pattern of communication. . . . For example, if a student normally addresses professors by the title* Doctor G *and* Doctor T, *it implies a status and class difference. In general, to change this form of address, the professor must initiate the request.*

Source: From W. Garcia, "Respeto: A Mexican Base for Interpersonal Relationships," in *Communication in Personal Relationships Across Cultures,* edited by W. B. Gudykunst, S. Ting-Toomey, and T. Nishida (Thousand Oaks, CA: Sage, 1996), pp. 137–155.

an outer boundary that includes superficial information about ourselves and our lives— our general interests, our daily life, and so on. The middle circle includes more personal information—perhaps our life history, our family background, and so on. Then there is the inner core, which includes very personal and private information, some of which we share with no one. These spheres of information may correspond with the phases in relational development. Thus, in the exploratory stage, people exchange some personal information, and in the stability phase, they may disclose more intimate information.

According to Lewin, there is the most variation in the extent to which the outer area is more or less permeable. For example, for many European Americans, the outer boundary is highly permeable; they may disclose a wide range of relatively superficial information with many people, even those they don't know well, in many contexts. The middle, or second, area is less permeable; this information is shared with fewer people and in fewer contexts. And information in the inner area is shared with very few. In contrast, for many other cultural and ethnic groups, the outer boundary is

I f you do develop a friendship or romantic relationship with someone from another culture, it can be important for both partners to explain some of each person's cultural practices to avoid unnecessary conflict. However, oftentimes we are not always aware that our behavior is culturally specific and not more universal. Our student, Anna, explains one of these cultural behaviors that her boyfriend learned to accommodate:

> I am Russian and I am currently in a relationship with a German. Even though we have both lived in different countries throughout our childhoods and have developed relatively global mindsets, there are certain aspects of each other's culture that we still find strange. As a Russian, I have always been extremely superstitious, which is a prevalent trait in the Russian population, particularly among females. One of the "traditions" that Russians have before they leave for the airport, or any road trip, is to sit down and be silent for about 30 seconds. My boyfriend witnessed this firsthand and found it extremely strange. But once I explained it to him, he always makes sure we sit down and are silent before we head to the airport.

much more closed. International students in the United States often remark that U.S. students seem superficial. That is, U.S. students welcome interaction with strangers and share information of a superficial nature—for example, before class or at a party. When some international students experience this, they assume they are moving into the exploratory "friend" phase (the middle circle), only to discover that the U.S. student considers the international student to be merely an acquaintance. A student from Singapore explains:

> I learned in the first couple months that people are warm yet cold. For example, I would find people saying "Hi" to me when I'm walking on campus or asking me how I am doing. It used to make me feel slighted that even as I made my greeting back to them, they were already a mile away. Then when real interaction occurs—for example, in class—somehow I sense that people tend to be very superficial and false. Yet they disclose a lot of information—for example, talking about personal relationships, which I wasn't comfortable with. I used to think that because of such self-disclosure you would share a special relationship with the other person, but it's not so because the same person who was telling you about her personal relationship yesterday has no idea who you are today. Now I have learned to not be offended or feel slighted by such incidents.

It's probably more accurate to say that what most people in the world consider simply a "friend" is what a U.S. American would consider a "close friend." A German student explains that in Germany people are hardly able to call somebody a friend, even if they have known that person for more than a year. Only if they have a "special emotional relationship" can they call the person a friend (Gareis, 1995, p. 128). For most U.S. Americans, the "special emotional relationship" is reserved for a so-called good or close friend.

Mary Jane Collier conducted a study with these three groups and Asian Americans in which she investigated conversational rules in close friendships (Collier, 1996). Again, she found many similarities in how these groups thought about close friendship. However, she also found some differences. For instance, Latino/a, Asian American, and African American students said that it took, on average, about a year to develop a close friendship; European Americans felt that it took only a few months. She also found differences in what each group thought was important in close friendships: "Latinos emphasized relational support, Asian Americans emphasized a caring, positive exchange of ideas, African Americans emphasized respect and acceptance and Anglo [European] Americans emphasized recognizing the needs of individuals" (p. 315). Clearly, such distinctions affect how people of different cultural groups develop friendships.

In their recent study, Hotta and Ting-Toomey (2013) found that time was an important element in the friendship decisions of international students. Although many U.S. American students did not recognize the importance of time in developing friendships, the international students felt that they did or did not have enough time to develop friendships with the U.S. American students. Many felt that they were in the United States for a limited time and made friendship decisions based upon how much time they had before going home.

romantic relationships Intimate relationships that comprise love, involvement, sharing, openness, connectedness, and so on.

Romantic Relationships   Some intimate relationships develop into **romantic relationships.** Several studies have compared the development of these types of intimate relationships across cultures. For example, communication researcher Gao Ge (1991) compared romantic heterosexual relationships among Chinese and U.S. American young people. Based on interviews with students about their romantic relationships, she identified common themes of openness, involvement, shared nonverbal meanings, and relationship assessment. However, there were some variations between the two groups. The U.S. American students emphasized the importance of physical attraction, passion, and love, which Gao interprets as a reflection of a more individualistic orientation. In contrast, the Chinese students stressed the importance of their partners' connectedness to their families and other relational connections, reflecting a more collectivistic orientation.

In another study, Gao (2001) compared intimacy, passion, and commitment in Chinese and U.S. American heterosexual romantic relationships. Based on her previous research and on cultural values, she predicted that intimacy and passion would be higher for U.S. couples, given that passion and intimacy are more individually centered relationship goals. She also predicted that commitment—a more collectivistic relational value—would be higher for Chinese couples. She found that passion *was* significantly higher in U.S. American couples than in Chinese couples but that the amount of intimacy and commitment did not vary cross culturally. This may mean that intimacy is a universal dimension of romantic relationships, but the finding about commitment is more puzzling. Gao speculates that this finding may be related to the fact that all the couples in her study were in advanced stages of serious relationship, at which time commitment is more universally expected. Her hypothesis about commitment may have applied to couples in earlier stages in their relationships.

This was confirmed in a similar study comparing North American, Japanese, and Russian beliefs about romantic love. In this study, North Americans emphasized romantic love, passionate love, and love based on friendship more than the Japanese or Russians. Other, more collectivistic cultural groups emphasized the acceptance of the potential mate by family members and commitment over romantic or passionate love (Sprecher et al., 1994).

Research on the development of romantic relationships in the United States has focused on the importance of the individual's autonomy. Togetherness is important as long as it doesn't interfere too much with a person's freedom. Being open, talking things out, and retaining a strong sense of self are seen as specific strategies for maintaining a healthy intimate relationship. This emphasis on autonomy—trying to balance the needs of two "separate" individuals—in relationships can be difficult. Also, extreme individualism makes it challenging for either partner to justify sacrificing or giving more than she or he is receiving. All of this leads to fundamental conflicts in trying to reconcile personal freedom with relational obligations (Dion & Dion, 1988). In fact, one study found that people who held extremely individualistic orientations experienced less sense of love, care, trust, and physical attraction toward their partners in romantic relationships (Dion & Dion, 1991). These problems are less common in collectivistic societies.

Interpretive Approach: Communicating in Intercultural Relationships

Now that we have considered the contributions of the social science research, let's turn our attention to more in-depth examination of how we communicate across cultural differences. As we've noted, intercultural relationships may be very similar to intracultural relationships. However, there may be some unique characteristics that can guide our thinking about communicating in these relationships.

Based on interviews with U.S. and Japanese students who were friends, researcher Sandra Sudweeks and colleagues (1990) identified competence, similarity, involvement, and turning points as characterizing important aspects of intercultural relationships. For example, the students talked about the importance of linguistic and cultural competence. At first, language was a common issue. Even when people speak the same language, they sometimes have language difficulties that can prevent relationships from flourishing. The same holds true for cultural information. Dissimilarity may account for the initial attraction, but these students mentioned the importance of finding some *similarity* in their relationships that transcended the cultural differences. For example, they looked for a shared interest in sports or other activities. Or they were attracted by similar physical appearance, lifestyle, or attitude. Sometimes shared religious beliefs can help establish common bonds (Graham, Moeai, & Shizuru, 1985).

Relationships take time to develop; students interviewed by Sudweeks and colleagues mentioned how important it was that the other person make time for the relationship. This is one aspect of involvement. Intimacy of interaction is another element, as are shared friendship networks. According to the study, sharing the same friends is more important for Japanese students than for U.S. American students because the Japanese students had left their friendships behind.

Finally, the students mentioned significant occurrences that were related to perceived changes in the relationship—turning points that moved the relationship forward or backward. For example, asking a friend to do a favor or to share an activity might be a turning point. The students remarked that if the other person refused, the relationship often didn't develop beyond that point. However, a turning point of understanding—**self-disclosure**—may move the relationship to a new level.

Another communication scholar, Brenda J. Allen (2000), gives us an example of a turning point. She describes her relationship across sexual orientation lines with a colleague in her department:

> *We found that we had similar ideas about issues, activities and improvement on our own critical thinking skills in the classroom. . . . [We] were both baby boomers from the Midwest, only months apart in age. We also came from lower-class families, and religion played a strong role in our childhood. (p. 179)*

Allen describes the turning point in their relationship when her friend revealed that she was gay: "As a heterosexual I had never before given much thought to sexual orientation or gays 'coming out of the closet.' Thanks to Anna, I have become far more sensitive and enlightened" (p. 180).

The process of dealing with differences, finding similarities, and moving beyond stereotypes and prejudice is summed up by a U.S. American student talking about her relationship with a Singaporean friend:

> *"We just had different expectations, different attitudes in the beginning, but at the end we were so close that we didn't have to talk about it. . . . After we erased all prejudices, that we thought the other person has to be different, after we erased that by talking, we just understood each other." (quoted in Gareis, 1995, p. 136)*

Intercultural Work Relationships   For many people, work is the place where they encounter the most diversity—working with people from different religions, generations, language backgrounds, ethnicity, races, and nationality. These encounters may be face-to-face or mediated—through telephone or computer. Understanding this diversity is especially important as organizations move from an assimilationist perspective ("Hire the quota and let them assimilate to us") to a more integrative perspective. One leading diversity expert refers to the latter as "foxhole diversity," the view that if the enemy is all around, you need people in the foxhole with you to support you; you need to cut through the superfluous and think about what skills and expertise your foxhole colleagues really need to possess as job requirements, not just what you'd prefer. We may prefer that our co-workers look like us and have the same language and religious background, but these preferences are not the same as the requirements for the job (Chozick, 2005). And more and more organizations are seeing the bottom-line payoff for a truly diverse workforce in a global economy—moving beyond concerns of women and minorities to concerns of generational differences, the pressures on gays and lesbians who have to hide part of their lives, and challenges in incorporating disabled workers (Hymowitz, 2005).

self-disclosure Revealing information about oneself.

So the challenge in the workplace is to get along with people who may be very different, and some of the work relationships may turn into friendships, as one of our students reported:

At my job in the Memorial Union, I work with students of all ethnicities, races, and nationalities. At first I was kind of intimidated, but I've found that I've got to know some of them, since work issues always provide an easy topic to discuss and some of the discussions have led to more socializing. While I can't say these are among my closest friends, I probably wouldn't have had the chance to meet so many different people if I weren't working at this job.

Power, of course, often comes into play because most work relationships are within a hierarchy. There are subordinate–superior relationships and peer relationships, and the nature of the relationship constrains the interaction. If your boss tells you your hairstyle violates company policy, that's one thing. If your office mate, your company peer, tells you the photos on your desk offend her, that's something else. There is more room for negotiation and discussion.

It is difficult when race, ethnicity, and class are all part of the hierarchy—as is common in the tourist and restaurant business. The experience of one of our students is quite common:

In the restaurant where I work, all the servers (like me) are female and white, and all the busboys and kitchen help are Latino, who mostly speak Spanish, and the two bosses are white males—who make everyone speak English when they're around. I kind of like to practice my Spanish a little in talking with the Latino workers, and I have a pretty good relationship with them. Some of the other servers really refuse to speak Spanish.

Because there is a hierarchy, the busboys and kitchen help must speak English—even if the server can speak Spanish whenever she feels like practicing her Spanish.

Intercultural Relationships Online   As we noted in Chapter 1, more and more people are using new technologies to communicate. The first and perhaps the most important impact of new communication technologies, particularly for young people, is the opportunities they provide for developing and maintaining relationships. Through social networking sites (SNSs) like Facebook and Instagram e-mail, mobile messaging apps like Snapchat, and Twitter, we can stay in touch with old friends, maintain almost constant contact with current friends, and find new friends. By some accounts, people spend more time on SNSs than any other online activity (Hampton, Goulet, Rainie, & Purcell, 2011; Zickuhr, 2010).

These new media technologies present us with enormous opportunities to communicate and develop relationships with people who are very different from us. We can communicate with people in other countries as easily as talking to our next-door neighbors. One of our students, Mariana, described her experience of getting to know Charlotte, a Finnish student, during a virtual team project in one of her classes:

Although we're separated by oceans and many miles, we share the same daily activities and understand each other quite well. What I enjoyed most about this experience was that even after this project, Charlotte and I will be friends. We've already contacted each other on Facebook and sent messages. Besides focusing on the course project, I've gotten to know a lot about my partner's studies in school and her personal life.

This increased use of social media also leads us to speculate how online relationships differ from offline relationships and whether it is easier or more difficult to communicate across cultures online. The answers to these questions seem to be dialectical. Online communication is both similar to and different from offline relationships, and communication technologies like the Internet and social media both facilitate and inhibit the development of intercultural relationships. For example, some online communication (e-mail, instant messages, text messages) facilitates intercultural encounters in that it filters out much of the information we base first impressions on—physical attractiveness, gender, age, and race. While we may find it helpful to have information about people's characteristics, this information also sometimes causes prejudice and discrimination. For example, when Mariana and Charlotte communicated during the class project, they didn't know each other's height, race, or age—unless they chose to tell each other. Thus, some of our new media interactions may be freer of the tendency to stereotype or discriminate against someone based on those physical characteristics. People can develop solid online relationships, not based on physical attributes or attractiveness, and by the time online friends meet in person, these **line of sight** data don't matter much; the result can be close, lasting relationships (McKenna, Green, & Gleason, 2002). Of course, this doesn't really address the problem of prejudices based on physical appearance. As scholar Radhika Gajjala points out,

line of sight Information about other people's identity based upon visible physical characteristics.

Why should it be wonderful for women and colored people to be able to hide who they are and to be able to disguise their gender, race, and culture in favor of passing as Caucasian? Why must we be ashamed of being women or colored or both? What's wrong with being colored? What's wrong with being a woman? (p. 84)

A number of studies show that online relationships are very similar to offline relationships; they conclude that using new communication technologies do not weaken relationships, nor do they act as poor substitutes for face-to-face contact. Instead, individuals use various media to connect with different social networks (Boase, 2008). For example, people use mobile phones to stay in contact with people they already know well, and they use social media (Facebook, Twitter) to expand and maintain their social networks—getting to know, or reestablishing "dormant" relationships—and more and more, they are using SNSs to stay in touch with local friends (Hampton, Goulet, Rainie, & Purcell, 2011; Kim, Kim, Park, & Rice, 2007).

How does online communication affect existing relationships? It allows us to be in almost constant contact. In a recent book, media expert Sherry Turkle (2011) challenges us to reexamine our assumptions about technology being the answer to intimacy and connections. She thinks that, although we are constantly in contact with each other—in fact, *tethered* to our technology—we sometimes choose technologies that merely substitute for human intimacy. She offers these examples as proof: Adults would rather e-mail, co-workers would rather leave voicemail messages, and teenagers would rather text. These technologies give us control over our relationships and actually distance us from others; as she puts it, "Technology makes it easy to communicate when we wish and to disengage at will" (p. 13). It's supposedly an efficient way to manage our time and relationships in our busy, hectic lives. As an example of how these new technologies can affect intergenerational relationships, Turkle (2011) describes the experience of Ellen, working in Paris, who used Skype to connect with her grandmother in Philadelphia. Twice a week they would talk for an hour. But, unbeknownst to her grandmother, Ellen was multitasking during the conversation—typing away on her keyboard answering e-mails. So it wasn't a *real* connection because Ellen wasn't really present. And Ellen reportedly felt guilty about her actions.

Communication scholar Ping Yang (2012) investigated intercultural online communication of college students and discovered that their encounters could be described by several dialectics. One dialectic was digital privilege/marginalization. The students reported that they experienced some privilege in these online encounters because of the fluidity and flexibility of online identities, as well as the suspension of prejudgment based on nonverbal cues. This was particularly true for ethnic and racial minority students. According to Claudia, "Interaction online is somewhat anonymous [and this] can be an advantage. Since people don't know [what] the person they are talking to looks like, it is harder to make a judgment based on their ethnicity or how they look." Although e-mails, computer, and the Internet play a vital role in the lives of many U.S. students, those from other cultural groups or world regions may not enjoy the same opportunity and comfort levels using them.

Another dialectic was trust/suspicion. The students explained that the use of some linguistic symbols and special cues facilitated the expression of their cultural selves. One student, Lisa, explained that she uses Yiddish phrases when conversing with Jewish peers online and that creates a bond and trust. At the same time, students described how online communication could also hinder the way they expressed who they were and sometimes created a climate of suspicion. As one student, Lena, said, "it's difficult to fully trust that they tell you about themselves to be true;" another said that in chat rooms, "it is easy to polish, overstate, or fake one's identity in these places," thus leading to some suspicion in online encounters (Yang, 2012, p. 119).

Language differences also create a dialectic for online interaction and intercultural relationships—both facilitating and hindering intercultural communication. The asynchronicity of some online communication allows nonnative speakers more time to compose a message and to decode and respond than is true to face-to-face interaction— thus facilitating communication. However, at the same time, language differences can lead to possible misunderstanding of specific words and phrases and humor online can often be misunderstood—thus inhibiting intercultural communication.

Understanding humor in a language often requires a sophisticated understanding of subtle nuances; irony, sarcasm, and cynicism in online communication across cultures should be approached with great caution (St. Amant, 2002). And when humor is misunderstood, it often takes complicated explanations to clarify, as one communication professor discovered:

> *One of the classmates in my online course made a remark, meant to be*
> *slightly sarcastic and humorous, about one of the group projects he was*

involved in for our course. However, the remark was perceived by some of the international members of his group to be in poor taste. Some thought it very rude and insulting. Others just found it childish. It took almost half the semester to figure out what had gone wrong, why the remark was misunderstood and to get things back on a good footing. I can't imagine it would have taken even half that long if the interaction had been face-to-face instead of on the Internet.

Sometimes problems caused by language differences are exacerbated because one or both interactants may not be aware of the problem, because confusion or misunderstanding is generally shown nonverbally—by a quizzical look or a raised eyebrow. Online communicators may have to work a little harder to make sure they understand each other and to give the other some leeway in expressing different cultural values and communication styles.

What happens when low-context and high-context communicators interact online? Because e-mail and text messages filter out almost all contextual cues (tone of voice, eye gaze, facial expression, etc.), scholars speculate that conversations between low- and high-context communicators might be difficult online (Olaniran, 2012). The low-context communicator might be very comfortable being direct about feelings and opinions, whereas the high-context communicator might feel rather constrained by online communication. When misunderstandings occur, it might be especially difficult to identify the source of misunderstanding and resolve it (Snyder, 2003).

For example, a Korean colleague who teaches at an American university reported that she often feels constrained in e-mail conversations with her U.S. colleagues. Having a preference for high-context communication, she finds the direct, low-context style of her colleagues a bit off-putting. This is especially true when they discuss sensitive issues through e-mail, and her colleagues ask her to give an explicit opinion that might conflict with others' opinions. She reports that she sometimes doesn't respond to these e-mail messages or tries to carry on the discussion with them face-to-face where contextual, nonverbal cues are available to her.

Another possible issue for high- and low-context communication differences concerns identity information. For many high-context cultures, background information of the speaker is part of the contextual information needed to understand and respond to a message, and, as we explained earlier, in text-based online encounters, the cues essential for determining identity (age, status, etc.) and context-related expectations are missing. The lack of identity and contextual cues may cause individuals in some cultures to be reluctant to engage in online communication. As St. Amant (2012, p. 82) explains:

Such hesitation seems particularly acute in high-context cultures where knowing how to communicate effectively is connected to knowing what that specific context/setting is. Without the cues commonly used to identify persons in—and thus the context of—a given situation, individuals from such cultures tend to remain silent. Such silence, in turn, can limit the sharing of essential information out of concern that doing so might violate expectations of credible communication in that context. (p. 82)

Of course, being reserved or quiet in online encounters can have implications for how one is perceived—particularly by those with low-context communication preferences. St. Amant goes on to explain that these factors are particularly problematic for intercultural relationships in global business settings because more organizations are using online media and virtual teams in internationally distributed projects.

Finally, the Internet can also be an important influence in cultural adaptation and helping new arrivals establish friendships in their new country. In their study of children who immigrated from the former Soviet Union to Israel, Elias and Lemish (2009) found that the Internet helped the children to integrate into Israeli life. The Internet helped these children bridge the gap between their former lives and friends and helped them learn new language skills, as well as make new friends in Israel. The Internet helped them with language and culture issues. The Internet allows these children to develop hybrid identities as they remain connected with their friends and culture of origin, while also developing new identities and friends in Israel. They quote a 16-year-old who said, "It is outstanding that we have the internet. Thanks to whoever created it—it helps me survive" (p. 549).

Intercultural Dating   Why do people date others from different cultural backgrounds? Probably for the same reasons we form any intercultural relationship. We are attracted to them, and the relationship offers benefits—increased knowledge about the world and the breaking of stereotypes. This has been the experience of Peiting, a Tawainese American dating Paul, a Danish exchange student: "Dating Paul offers me this whole new perspective of life as a Caucasian and a Dane." Also, she encounters ideas that differ from those of most of her U.S. American friends: "We'll talk for hours about American films, about Danish government, even about variations in our countries attitudes toward drinking" (quoted in Russo, 2001).

Several decades ago, researcher Phillip E. Lampe (1982) investigated interethnic dating among students attending a college in Texas. He discovered that the reasons students gave for dating within and outside their own ethnic group were very similar: They were attracted to the other person, physically and/or sexually. In contrast, the reasons students gave for not dating someone within or outside their own ethnic group were very different. The main reason for not dating *within* the ethnic group was lack of attraction. However, the reasons for not dating *outside* the ethnic group were not having an opportunity to do so and not having thought about it. Lampe interpreted this distinction in responses as reflecting the social and political structure of U.S. American society. That is, most individuals, by the time they reach adolescence, have been taught that it is better to date within one's ethnic and racial group and probably have had very little opportunity to date interethnically.

Have things changed since Lampe's study? It does seem that they have, that U.S. Americans today are much more open to intercultural relationships. For example, in one survey, 77% of those surveyed stated that it's all right for blacks and whites to date each other—up from 48% who felt this way in 1987. The young are the most accepting; 91% of people questioned who were born after 1976 said that interracial dating is acceptable—compared to 50% of the oldest generation (Taylor, Funk, & Craighill, 2006). This survey showed that attitudes are more tolerant, but do people's behaviors match their attitudes? The results of our own study show that, in some instances,

MARRIAGE AGE

In 2015, Spain raised the minimum age at which someone can be married from 14 to 16 years old. The minimum age for marriage varies around the world. While many cultures celebrate marriage as an important cultural ritual and rite of passage, not all marriages are the result of two adults wanting to spend their lives together. The U.K.-based organization, Girls Not Brides, advocates against child marriages, which they see as destroying the lives of these girls. You can read more about their views and activities at http://www.girlsnotbrides.org/.

More recently, the issue of age and marriage arose again in Afghanistan when a young girl, Zahra, was married off as a girl:

> *When her mother was paralyzed and her father decided to marry again, Zahra, then around 11 years old, became part of the dowry, according to her father's accounts to reporters. Then, about two years later, as a sixth grader, she was married off.*
>
> *Last week, Zahra arrived at the central hospital in Ghor with burns over 90 percent of her body. She died six days later, on Saturday, in a Kabul hospital. She was four months pregnant, and she was 14 years old, her father said (Mashal, 2016).*

The debates over the circumstances of her death, her age of marriage, her consent, as well as the status of females in Afghan culture remain at the center of this case. Around the world, there are many cultural differences in how marriage is viewed. How old should people be before they can be married? Do you know the minimum age of marriage where you live? What is the purpose of marriage? What role should the family play in marriage decisions?

Source: From A. Greenberg, "Spain has finally made it illegal for 14-year olds to get married," *Time,* July 24, 2015. Retrieved July 19, 2016, from http://time.com/3970710/spain-marriage-age-of-consent-europe/; M. Mashal, "Clash of values emerges after Afghan child bride burns to death," *New York Times,* July 18, 2016. Retrieved July 21, 2016, from http://www.nytimes.com/2016/07/19/world/asia/afghanistan-zahra-child-marriage.html?_r=0.

patterns of intercultural dating have not changed a great deal and confirm that individual dating experiences and societal contexts are still closely related (Martin, Bradford, Chitgopekar, & Drzewiecka, 2003). Like Lampe's respondents, about 60% of our respondents said they had dated interculturally, with Mexican Americans doing so more frequently than African Americans or whites. Many of the remaining 40% gave the same reasons as respondents in Lampe's study for not dating interculturally: They had no desire or no opportunity. So, even though Lampe's study was conducted in the early 1980s, the same conditions seem to hold, at least in some parts of the United States, particularly for African Americans and whites. The reality remains that most Americans live, go to school, and worship in segregated groups (Logan, Stults, & Farley, 2004). And this was certainly true in our study, as 80% of the white students said they grew up in all-white neighborhoods.

Although polygamy is legal in a number of countries worldwide, it is not legal in the United States. And in some countries, such as Australia and Germany, same-sex couples cannot get married, but they can register for domestic partnerships. The United States Citizenship & Immigration Services (USCIS) do not recognize polygamous marriages, not domestic partnerships, even if they are legal in the country where they occurred. In their policy manual, the USCIS says that they do not recognize various kinds of marriages for naturalization purposes including polygamous marriages and domestic partnerships, "even if valid in the place of celebration." How might these rules impact who can and cannot become U.S. citizens?

Source: From USCIS, Marriage and martial union for naturalization purposes, Vol. 12, Chapter 2. Current as of June 22, 2016. Retrieved July 21, 2016, from https://www.uscis.gov/policymanual /HTML/PolicyManual-Volume12-PartG-Chapter2.html.

We also found that the social context and past experiences were a strong influence on whether young people dated interculturally. Not surprisingly, those who did date interculturally were more likely to have grown up in ethnically diverse neighborhoods and to have more ethnically diverse acquaintances and friends. In addition, they came from families in which other family members had dated interculturally. This suggests that family attitudes play a big role. Indeed, other studies confirm that families often instill negative attitudes regarding interracial friendships or romantic relationships (Moore, 2000). And these attitudes are learned at a very young age. As Derryck, a young black child said, when asked about his relationship with his white friend, "Black and white kids can be friends with each other, if you're in the same class. But they can't get married, because they don't match. They can't have a kid together" ("Talking About Race," 2000, p. 47). Interracial friendships may be more accepted in elementary school, but they are less accepted in teenage years (Graham & Cohen, 1997).

Finally, whether individuals date interculturally may also depend on the region of the country in which they grow up. A study conducted in California, for example, showed a slightly higher incidence of intercultural dating there than we found in our study (Tucker & Mitchell-Kernan, 1995). As the 2010 census shows, there is more diversity in the West and Southwest. Given what we know about the influence of context on interpersonal relationships, we would expect more diverse schools and neighborhoods, and thus more opportunity for intercultural contact in these areas.

There are other factors that do not clearly explain intercultural dating patterns. In a recent study of Internet personal ads, Shauna Wilson and her colleagues (2007) found that blacks who knew they did or did not want children were more willing to date other blacks than blacks who were unsure if they wanted children. Also, blacks in the West were less willing to date other blacks than those living in other parts of the country. Also, black smokers were less willing to date other blacks. It isn't clear how these variables are related to intercultural dating. They call for more research to better understand these patterns.

FIGURE 10-2 In this photo, an American man and Indonesian woman are getting married. How might living in the United States or living in Indonesia shape their relationship? How might living in a third culture, such as Argentina or India, influence their marriage? (© *McGraw-Hill Education/ Christopher Kerrigan, photographer*)

Permanent Relationships In spite of substantial resistance to intercultural (especially interracial) romantic relationships, increasing numbers of people are marrying across racial and ethnic lines, so much so that scholar Maria P. P. Root (2001) says we are in the midst of a "quiet revolution." Who is most likely to intermarry in the United States? According to Root, women (except for black women) intermarry more than men. Also, older rather than younger people tend to intermarry, except where similar-size groups live in proximity to one another. For example, in Hawaii, California, and Arizona, younger persons are more likely to intermarry. In addition, later generations of immigrants have higher rates of intermarriage than earlier ones. (See Figure 10-2.)

Why are the rates of intermarriage so low for certain groups? The answer has to do with various contextual issues related to gender and social status. For example, there are fewer objections to Asian American–white than to black–white marriages. Gender stereotypes come into play in that Asian women are, even now, viewed as traditionally feminine, subservient, and obedient, as well as petite—making them attractive as partners for white men. This has led to increasing numbers of Asian American women intermarrying. The same is true for Latinas and Native American women, but not black women. As Root observes, blackness for them still has caste connotations, which means they are partnered in intermarriages less than any other group. White women, in contrast, intermarry more frequently.

Most people describe their reasons for intermarriage in terms of romantic love. Mariel, a 24-year-old Chicana raised in a suburb of Los Angeles, reflected on what influenced her decision to marry her black husband and how fortunate she was that her family approved.

> *I was really active in* La Raza *and feel committed to my people, so I always thought I would marry a Chicano guy. I love my older brothers and even thought I might marry one of their friends. When I went away to college. . . . I was just exposed to so many people. My political ideals didn't change. But I met my husband in my second year. He was very supportive of my commitments. We just started doing things together, studying, talking, going to parties. He fit in well with my friends and I liked his friends. It was like we would go to parties and there were all sorts of people there and I'd find I always had more in common with him than just about anyone in a room. We had really good talks. And music. We both loved music and movies. So one thing led to another. I tried to talk myself out of my feelings for him, thinking I should just keep it as good friends, but then I thought, "Shouldn't the man I marry be my best friend?" My family liked him. I mean, like, if my brothers didn't like him, this would have been real hard. They have a lot of influence on me even though I make up my own mind. We talked a lot about what it meant to marry someone different than your own cultural background. But I realized I didn't have to give up my commitment to my people. We believed in the same issues. Now it might have been different if he was white. I'm not sure how that would have gone over.*

Source: From M. P. P. Root, *Love's Revolution: Interracial Marriage* (Philadelphia, PA: Temple University Press, 2001), pp. 7–8.

The larger social discourses on interracial relationships should not be ignored. Columnist Hoyt Sze (1992) notes:

> *Naturally, people outmarry [marry outside their racial group] for love. But we must ask ourselves how much of this love is racist, unequal love. Unfortunately, interracial love is still inextricably linked to colonialism. How else does one explain the disproportional rates at which Asian American women and African American men marry out? Is it just a coincidence that the mainstream media objectify the same groups as "exotic-erotic" playthings? I know that Asian American men and African American women aren't fundamentally lacking in attractiveness or desirability. (p. 10)*

If we try to understand romantic love only on the interpersonal level, how might we explain the high rates of outmarriage by some groups and not others?

In any case, the current trend to intermarry may change things. As the rates of intermarriage continue to increase, these families will produce more children who challenge the current race and gender stereotypes, and the structural barriers to inter-marriage will be eroded (Lee & Edmonston, 2005). As Root (2001) observes, "Inter-marriage has ripple effects that touch many people's lives. It is a symbolic vehicle through which we can talk about race and gender and reexamine our ideas about race" (p. 12). And the fact is that younger people do have more tolerant attitudes about intermarriage. Although intermarriage will not solve all intercultural problems, the increasing numbers of multicultural people will have a positive impact.

What are the major concerns of couples who marry interculturally? One study compared experiences of inter- and intracultural couples. Their concerns, like those of dating couples, often involved dealing with pressures from their families and from society in general. An additional issue involved raising children. Sometimes these concerns are intertwined. Although many couples are concerned with raising children and dealing with family pressures, those in intercultural marriages deal with these issues to a greater extent. They are more likely to disagree about how to raise the children and are more likely to encounter opposition and resistance from their families about the marriage (Graham, Moeai, & Shizuru, 1985).

Writer Dugan Romano (1997) interviewed couples in which one spouse came from another country to identify challenges of these international marriages. Some are common problems faced by most couples, including friends, politics, finances, sex, in-laws, illness and suffering, and children. But some issues are exacerbated in these intercultural marriages; these involve values, eating and drinking habits, gender roles, attitudes regarding time, religion, place of residence, stress, and ethnocentrism.

Of course, every husband and wife develop their own idiosyncratic way of relating to each other, but intercultural marriage poses consistent challenges. Romano also points out that most couples have their own systems for working out the power balance in their relationships, for deciding who gives and who takes. She identifies four styles of interaction: submission, compromise, obliteration, and consensus. Couples may adopt different styles depending on the context.

The **submission style** is the most common. In this style, one partner submits to the culture of the other partner, abandoning or denying his or her own. The submission may occur in public, whereas in private life the relationship may be more balanced. Romano points out that this model rarely works in the long run. People cannot erase their core cultural background, no matter how hard they try.

In the **compromise style,** each partner gives up some of his or her culturally bound habits and beliefs to accommodate the other person. Although this may seem fair, it really means that both people sacrifice things that are important to them. For example, the Christian who gives up having a Christmas tree and celebrating Christmas for the sake of a Jewish spouse may eventually come to resent the sacrifice.

In the **obliteration style,** both partners deal with differences by attempting to erase their individual cultures. They may form a new culture, with new beliefs and habits, especially if they live in a country that is home to neither of them. This may seem to be the only way for people whose backgrounds are completely irreconcilable to survive. Because it's difficult for people to completely cut themselves off from their own cultural backgrounds, obliteration is not a viable long-term solution.

---

submission style A style of interaction for an intercultural couple in which one partner yields to the other partner's cultural patterns, abandoning or denying his or her own culture. (Compare with **compromise style, consensus style,** and **obliteration style.**)

compromise style A style of interaction for an intercultural couple in which both partners give up some part of their own cultural habits and beliefs to minimize cross-cultural differences. (Compare with **consensus style, obliteration style,** and **submission style.**)

obliteration style A style of interaction for an intercultural couple in which both partners attempt to erase their individual cultures in dealing with cultural differences. (Compare with **compromise style, consensus style,** and **submission style.**)

The style that is the most desirable, not surprisingly, is the **consensus style,** which is based on agreement and negotiation. It is related to compromise in that both partners give and take, but it is not a trade-off; rather, it is a win-win proposition. Consensus may incorporate elements of the other models. On occasion, one spouse might temporarily "submit" to the other's culture or temporarily give up something to accommodate the other. For example, while visiting her husband's Muslim family, a Swiss wife might substantially change her demeanor, dressing more modestly and acting less assertive. Consensus requires flexibility and negotiation. Romano stresses that couples who are considering permanent international relationships should prepare for the commitment by living together, spending extended time with the other's family, learning the partner's language, studying the religion, and learning the cuisine. The couple should also consider legal issues like their own and their children's citizenship, finances and taxation, ownership of property, women's rights, and divorce.

consensus style
A style of interaction for an intercultural couple in which partners deal with cross-cultural differences by negotiating their relationship. (Compare with **compromise style, obliteration style,** and **submission style.**)

Sexualities and Intimate Relationships   Most of the discussion so far was derived from research on heterosexual friendships and romantic relationships. Much less information is available about gay and lesbian relationships. What we do know is that these relationships are a fact of society: homosexuality has existed in every society and in every era (Chesebro, 1981, 1997).

What we know about gay and lesbian relationships is often in contrast to the "model" of heterosexual relationships. Gay and lesbian relationships may be intracultural or intercultural. Although there are many similarities between gay/lesbian and straight relationships, they may differ in several areas, including the roles of same-sex friendships and cross-sex friendships and the relative importance of friendships.

Same-sex friendship relationships may have different roles for gay and straight males in the United States. Typically, U.S. males are socialized toward less self-expression and emotional intimacy. Most heterosexual men turn to women for emotional support; often, a wife or female romantic partner, rather than a same-sex friend, is the major source of emotional support.

This was not always the case in the United States, and it is not the case today in many countries, where male friendship often closely parallels romantic love. In India, for example, "men are as free as women to form intimate friendships with revelations of deep feelings, failures, and worries and to show their affection physically by holding hands" (Gareis, 1995, p. 36). Same-sex friendships and romantic relationships both may involve expectations of undying loyalty, deep devotion, and intense emotional gratification (Hammond & Jablow, 1987). This seems to be true as well for gay men, who tend to seek emotional support from gay male friendships (Sherrod & Nardi, 1988). However, this differentiation doesn't seem to hold for straight women and lesbians, who more often seek intimacy through same-sex friendships. That is, they seek intimate friendships with women more than with men.

There is frequently a clear distinction between "lover" and "friend" for both gays and lesbians similar to the "incest taboo" among a family of friends (Nardi, 1992, p. 114). Close friendships may play a more important role for gays than for straights. Gays and lesbians often suffer discrimination and hostility from the straight world

(Nakayama, 1998), and they often have strained relationships with their families.
For these reasons, the social support from friends in the gay community can play a
crucial role. Sometimes friends act as family. As one young man explains:

> *"Friends become part of my extended family. A lot of us are estranged from
> our families because we're gay and our parents don't understand or don't
> want to understand. That's a separation there. I can't talk to them about my
> relationships. I don't go to them; I've finally learned my lesson: family is out.
> Now I've got a close circle of good friends that I can sit and talk to about any-
> thing. I learned to do without the family." (quoted in Nardi, 1992, p. 110)*

Many of the issues in heterosexual romantic relationships apply to gay/lesbian
couples as well. However, some relational issues, especially those pertaining to permanence and relational dissolution, are unique to gay partners.

In more than 20 countries, including the United States, same-sex marriage is
legal nationwide, as we noted at the outset of this chapter. These changes in the status of same-sex marriages influence the development, legal benefits, and protections
of these relationships. Same-sex relationships, like heterosexual relationships, are
profoundly influenced by the cultural contexts in which they occur. For example,
Vietnam does not stipulate that marriage must be between members of the opposite
sex ("Mariage Vietnamien Lesbien," 1998), and King Sihanouk has supported gay
marriages in Thailand ("Cambodian King Backs Gay Marriage," 2004). In countries where same-sex marriage is not legal, some offer other kinds of recognition,
including "partnerships," "civil unions," etc. For example, Australia, Germany,
Switzerland, and a number of other countries do not allow same-sex marriages, but
offer alternative types of legal recognition of these relationships. However, in many
places in the world, the social contexts are much more problematic for gay partners
in permanent relationships.

Regardless of one's position on the desirability of gay and lesbian marriage,
it is important to understand the implications for same-sex relationships, which
include issues of dissolution. However, a recent study from the Williams Institute at UCLA has found that same-sex couples are less likely to divorce than
opposite-sex couples. The report observed that: "The average divorce rate for
same-sex couples was just 1.1% annually, compared to an annual average of
2% divorce rate for heterosexual couples. When data sets were expanded to

include dissolutions by same-sex couples in any type of legally recognized relationship (including civil unions and domestic partnerships), the rate increased to 1.6% annually—still lower than the average rate of heterosexual divorces" (Brydum, 2014). This study did not explain why same-sex couple divorced less frequently than heterosexual couples; it focused on compiling the quantitative data.

Feelings about gays and lesbians are very high, making same-sex relationships difficult, if not impossible. In Cameroon, homosexuality is a crime, and there have been a number of arrests of gay men. In this country, gay men risk a prison term of five years, because same-sex activities are unlawful (Cameroun, 2011). Even more repressive than Cameroun is the Islamic State of Iraq and Syria (ISIS) which has reportedly killed more than 25 men suspected of being gay. Reports from the Syrian Observatory for Human Rights have reported: "Six have been stoned to death, three killed from direct shooting to the head and 16 thrown from high-rise buildings. Those that survived the fall, the group added, were then stoned on the streets below by scores of bystanders. Two of those killed were under 18" (Cowburn, 2016). As we noted at the outset of the chapter, a number of other countries have the death penalty for homosexuality. Under these conditions, same-sex relationships are undertaken with great risk, as the anti-gay attitudes are institutionalized under the law.

SEXUAL ORIENTATION LAWS IN THE WORLD - RECOGNITION

ILGA, THE INTERNATIONAL LESBIAN, GAY, BISEXUAL, TRANS AND INTERSEX ASSOCIATION

RECOGNITION

Marriage 22 States	
Equal (almost equal) substitute to marriage 19 States	
Clearly inferior substitute to marriage 6 States	

Joint Adoption [26 States]

Second parent adoption [33 States]

Source: from Carroll, Aengus, "ILGA Report," *State-Sponsored Homophobia: a World Survey of Sexual Orientation Laws: Criminalisation, Protection and Recognition*, June, 2016.

Map: Source: Adapted from "ILGA Report," *State-Sponsored Homophobia: a World Survey of Sexual Orientation Laws: Criminalisation, Protection and Recognition*, June, 2016. Coordinated by Carroll, Aengus and Sabbadini, Renato. Designed by: Enoki, Eduardo

Critical Approach: Contextual Influences

It is important to consider intercultural relationships in the contexts in which they emerge—whether the contexts are supportive or whether they discourage intercultural relationships. Let's examine several of these contextual influences: family and neighborhood, educational and religious institutions, and historical and political contexts.

Family and Neighborhood Contexts   According to Dodd and Baldwin (2002), the first place we learn about communication adaptability and receptivity—how to respond to those who are different and how to respond to new situations—is in the family. Did your family encourage you to seek out intercultural relationships? Did your parents have a culturally diverse set of friends? And some types of relationships are more accepted than others. For example, parents may encourage children to develop friendships across religious, racial, and class lines but discourage romantic relationships with members of these same groups. Parents often play an important role in who their children date—particularly for daughters. In a recent study, it was found that women were much more likely than men to mention pressure from family members as a reason that interethnic dating would be difficult. As one Latina said:

> It would be hard . . . because my parents wouldn't agree with it and neither would my Hispanic friends. They've all told me not to mix blood. Stay with your own. (Clark-Ibanez & Felmlee, 2004, p. 300)

Even more important than what parents say is what they do. In this same study, it was the diversity of parents' friendship network, not the parents' attitudes, that determined the likelihood of the child's dating interethnically. Those whose parents had diverse friends were more likely to date interethnically than those whose parents had less diverse friends.

In some parts of the world, intercultural relationships are not unusual. In fact, it might be unusual not to engage in them. Lauren, a student of ours, explains:

> Having grown up in a multiracial household and in Singapore, a very diverse country, I view having intercultural relationships as something very natural and normal. However, since I have been in the United States, I realized that intercultural relationships are not always the norm, and some people explicitly do not look for intercultural relationships. This struck me as odd because ever since I can remember, intercultural relationships were completely normal and it was not something that people would explicitly point out or try to avoid.

Relationships are influenced by families, as well as the larger social context in which we live. The diversity of one's neighborhood also has a great influence on whether one forms intercultural friendships. Here, the proximity principle comes into play. That is, we are more likely to be attracted to and form relationships with those we see often. How diverse was your childhood neighborhood?

Religious and Educational Contexts   Institutions like schools and churches/synagogues can play a huge part in promoting or discouraging intercultural friendships. It was not that long ago that some colleges banned interracial dating, and an often

There are a number of dating websites, some with smartphone apps, that market themselves as helping people find international romantic relationships. Cupid Media, an Australian-based company, owns a number of websites that promote international relationships, including AsianDating.com, Filipinocupid.com, and Thailovelinks.com. There are similar websites for gay men, including gaydar .net, a British-based company, which boasts members from over 140 countries.

What do you think about this approach to developing international relationships? It may be easier, but is it better to meet people overseas through these websites or is it better to live abroad and learn the language and culture, while meeting people? Do these websites reinforce stereotypes about various groups of people, for example, Asian women? Would you use these websites to meet people in other countries?

quoted statistic is that the most segregated hour of the week is Sunday morning—when Christians are in church. At the same time, religious institutions can provide much-needed support. One interracial couple found support by participating in a series of workshops for interracial families sponsored by their church:

> *I think that being in this community helps us a lot . . . being in interracial family workshops, those kind of things; . . . it's an injection for us and that we value. And being able to expose ourselves to different types of interracial families. . . . I feel very interested and involved and somewhat knowledgeable and interested in the various adoption controversies that are going on and noticing again in this community the various levels of interracial activity. (Rosenblatt, Karis, & Powell, 1995, p. 271)*

According to some research findings, it appears that *integrated* religious institutions and educational institutions provide the best opportunities for intercultural friendships and the best environment to improve attitudes about interracial marriage (Johnson & Jacobson, 2005). For example, a study of six California State University campuses found that the students on these campuses interacted equally, in interracial and intraracial encounters (Cowan, 2005). These campuses are very diverse; no one ethnic or racial group is a majority. On the other hand, neighborhoods and work contexts do not seem to provide opportunities for the *type* of contact (intimate, friendly, equal status interaction) that clearly facilitates intercultural friendships (Johnson & Jacobson, 2005). Having ethnically varied friends has more of an influence on the propensity to engage in an interethnic romance than does being in a diverse social environment in general. "The role of friends is particularly important, perhaps because an individual is most likely to be introduced to a partner by a common friend, and because social approval from one's friends is a potent predictor of relationship stability" (Clark-Ibanez & Felmlee, 2004, p. 301).

Historical and Political Contexts As noted in Chapter 4, history is an important context for understanding intercultural interactions and relationships. Many U.S. men in military service during various wars have returned to the United States with wives

429

whom they met and married while stationed abroad. And many of the servicemen who experienced such intercultural relationships argued successfully against miscegenation laws, or laws that prohibited interracial marriages.

An example of the role that history and politics can play in intercultural communication can be seen in the experiences of William Kelly (2006), a communication scholar who lived in Japan for many years. He recounts his experiences when he first went to Japan to teach English 25 years ago. There were few U.S. Americans in Japan, and they were treated with great deference. In retrospect, he realizes that he was quite arrogant in his view of the Japanese:

> *I expected Japanese to assimilate to my culture. I also felt superior to them. Due to their culture, I believed that Japanese would never reach the goals of individual freedom, rational thought in daily life and speaking English like a U.S. American. Therefore they would always remain aspiring U.S. Americans, not capable of achieving equality. (p. 15)*

His relationship with the Japanese can best be understood in the context of the history of U.S.–Japanese relations. As we learned in Chapter 1, Asians in the United States were treated very badly in the late 18th and early 19th centuries. (Remember the Oriental Exclusion Act of 1882 as well as the Johnson-Read Act of 1924, which severely restricted Japanese immigration to the United States.) Then came World War II and the internment of Japanese Americans, followed by the U.S. occupation of Japan. As a result, in the 1960s, 1970s, and 1980s, although the Japanese deferred to U.S. economic and political superiority, there was restrained resentment, and sometimes outright racism, toward U.S. Americans living in Japan. For example, in the 1980s, U.S. Americans in Japan could not enter certain establishments, obtain loans, or have the same jobs as Japanese. This example reveals the importance of the material and the symbolic realm in understanding culture. Kelly explains:

> *It was the material conditions of white U.S. power and privilege that led me to assume a stance of superiority in relation to the Japanese people I encountered. The communication grooves that I unthinkingly entered when I began living in Japan were the outcome of a colonial relationship between the United States and Japan. (p. 15) Japanese racial discrimination against whites has often been*

a defensive measure to keep members of a powerful nation within well-defined spheres. The goal has been to maintain a private area of Japanese people where the overbearing Western presence was absent and where Japanese could be "themselves." (pp. 16–17)

Over the years, Kelly developed a different way of relating to Japanese. This came about primarily as a result of his encounters with U.S. Americans in Japan who were truly respectful of the Japanese. They learned Japanese, had many Japanese friends, and tried to adapt to the Japanese way of life—thereby achieving a more equal power balance. Eventually, he says, he was able to reach a level of understanding that accepted both similarities and differences between Japan and the United States. Kelly points out that his efforts to communicate with Japanese people in a truly respectful manner were assisted by the diminishing of the unequal power relations between the United States and Japan:

By the 1990s, there were many Japanese who had experienced the West that were no longer so positive about Westerners, and especially Americans. They expected white people to learn the Japanese language and communicate in a more Japanese way. . . . Many Japanese had gone overseas to work or study and there was less of an inferiority complex among Japanese towards white Americans. European Americans had been very gradually losing their place of privilege. (p. 18)

All this points to the effect of power on hierarchical relations of communication. Although power does not determine communication patterns in any simple causal sense, it does have an impact on the direction communication takes within intercultural relations. Although U.S.–Japanese communication is still affected in numerous ways by the legacy of the U.S. occupation of Japan, increased economic power has given the Japanese people a new sense of pride.

There are other examples of how colonial histories framed relationships. The British, for example, constructed myriad intercultural relationships, recognized or not, within the lands they colonized. Writer Anton Gill (1995), in his book *Ruling Passions,* discusses various ways in which the colonialists tried to engage in or to avoid intercultural relations, as well as the legacy of interracial children left in their wake. He was concerned with British social policies in the colonies, particularly as they related to offspring, who were often unwanted and abandoned.

The dialectical tension rests, on the one hand, in the social, political, and economic contexts that make some kinds of intercultural relationships possible and, on the other hand, in the desires and motives of the partners involved. There are no easy explanations for whom we meet, when we meet them, and under what conditions we might have a relationship. Different cultural groups have different demographics, histories, and social concerns. Scholar Harry Kitano and his colleagues (1984) discuss some of these issues for Asian Americans. Scholars Robert Anderson and Rogelis Saenz (1994) apply the demographics of Mexican American communities to argue for the importance of larger structural factors—such as proximity—in understanding interracial marriage.

INTERNET RESOURCES

www.lovingday.org/
This website is dedicated to the legal histories of interracial relationships. There is an interactive map of the United States that gives a visual feel for interracial legislation. The site contains stories of interracial couples and their trials and triumphs. Most importantly, the site works to promote June 12 as "Loving Day" in commemoration of the 1967 decision in *Loving* v. *Virginia* that formally legalized interracial marriage.

www.npr.org/templates/story/story.php?storyId=10184979
This is an NPR podcast about negotiating intercultural relationships. The experts provide practical advice with an academic foundation for couples dealing with the tribulations of intercultural issues. The podcast is part of a series of NPR productions revolving around culture.

https://www.uscis.gov/family/same-sex-marriages
The U.S. Citizenship and Immigration Services has laws that regulate international relationships (whether marriage, adoption, family members, etc.) This Web page answers many questions that may affect people in these relationships.

https://www.hrw.org/news/2016/04/13/dispatches-presumed-gay-and-paying-it
-your-life-russia
This report covers the anti-gay violence in Russia. How do different societies create conditions that make gay relationships difficult or impossible? Should others respect these conditions as cultural differences? Or should others pressure these nations to change?

SUMMARY

- Through relationships, we acquire specific and general knowledge, break stereotypes, and acquire new skills.

- Special challenges of intercultural relationships include coping with differences, tending to stereotype, dealing with anxiety, and having to explain ourselves to others.

- There are six dialectics of intercultural relationships: personal–contextual, differences–similarities, cultural–individual, privilege–disadvantage, static–dynamic, and history/past–present/future.

- There are three communication approaches to understanding intercultural relationships: social science, interpretive, and critical.

- The social science approach emphasizes the individual role in relationships and identifies various cross-cultural differences in notions of friendship and how relationships are developed and maintained.

- The interpretive perspective provides in-depth descriptions of various types of intercultural relationships.

- Intercultural relationships often include competence, similarity, involvement, and turning points.
- Online relationships are both similar to and different from RL (real-life) relationships. Language and communication-style differences can be exacerbated in online communication.
- Relationships at work are characterized by hierarchy and sometimes varying attitudes toward power.
- In gay and lesbian relationships, friendship and sexual involvement are not mutually exclusive.
- Intercultural dating and marriage are increasingly common; however, interracial relationships are still often disapproved of by families and by society.
- Intercultural marriages face challenges of family and societal disapproval and issues of child rearing.
- The critical perspective emphasizes the role of institutions, politics, and history in intercultural relationships.
- Family, schools, and religious institutions can either hinder or discourage intercultural relationships.

DISCUSSION QUESTIONS

1. What are some of the benefits of intercultural relationships?
2. What factors contribute to our forming relationships with some people and not with others?
3. How is the development of intercultural relationships different from that of intracultural relationships?
4. What challenges do intercultural couples face when they decide to make their relationships permanent?
5. What are the advantages of taking a dialectical perspective on intercultural relationships?

ACTIVITIES

1. *Intercultural Relationships.* List all of your friends to whom you feel close. Identify any friends on the list who are from other cultures. Answer the following questions, and discuss your answers with other class members.
   a. Do people generally have more friends from their own culture or from other cultures? Why?
   b. In what ways are intercultural friendships different from or similar to friendships with people from the same culture?
   c. What are some reasons people might have for not forming intercultural friendships?

2. *Friendship Dialectics.* Choose one friend who is different from you. Describe a situation or situations in which you experienced the dialectics discussed in this chapter. (*Hint:* Think of the ways in which the two of you are both similar and different—age, gender, background, interests, personality, and so on. Think of the ways your relationship has both changed and stayed the same—attitudes, experiences, interests, and so on.)

KEY WORDS

cognitive consistency (405)

compromise style (424)

consensus style (425)

guanxi (408)

intercultural relationships (397)

intimacy (409)

line of sight (416)

obliteration style (424)

relational learning (398)

romantic relationships (412)

self-disclosure (414)

similarity principle (405)

stage model (409)

submission style (424)

REFERENCES

Allen, B. J. (2000). Sapphire and Sappho: Allies in authenticity. In A. Gonzalez, M. Houston, & V. Chen (Eds.), *Our voices: Essays in culture, ethnicity and communication* (3rd ed., pp. 179–183). Los Angeles, CA: Roxbury.

Anderson, R. N., & Saenz, R. (1994). Structural determinants of Mexican American intermarriage, 1975–1980. *Social Science Quarterly, 75*(2), 414–430.

Barnlund, D. S. (1989). *Communication styles of Japanese and Americans: Images and reality.* Belmont, CA: Wadsworth.

Baxter, L. A. (1993). The social side of personal relationships: A dialectical perspective. In S. Duck (Ed.), *Social context and relationships* (pp. 139–165). Newbury Park, CA: Sage.

Baxter, L. A., & Montgomery, B. (1996). *Relating: Dialogues and dialectics.* New York: Guilford Press.

Bearak, M., & Cameron, D. (2016, June 16). Here are the 10 countries where homosexuality may be punishable by death. *The Washington Post.* Retrieved July 19, 2016, from https://www.washingtonpost.com/news/worldviews/wp/2016/06/13/here-are-the-10-countries-where-homosexuality-may-be-punished-by-death-2/.

Bell, S., & Coleman, S. (1999). The anthropology of friendship: Enduring themes and future possibilities. In S. Bell & S. Coleman (Eds.), *The anthropology of friendship* (pp. 1–20). New York: Berg.

Boase, J. (2008). Personal networks and the personal communication system. *Information, Communication & Society, 11*(4), 490–508.

Broverman, N. (2016, January 20). At least 11 Alabama counties refuse to comply with marriage equality. *The Advocate.* Retrieved July 19, 2016, from http://www.advocate.com/marriage-equality/2016/1/20/least-11-alabama-counties-refuse-comply-marriage-equality.

Brydum, S. (2004, December 13). Report: Same-sex couples less likely to divorce. *The Advocate.* Retrieved July 19, 2016, from http://www.advocate.com/politics/marriage-equality/2014/12/13/report-same-sex-couples-less-likely-divorce

Butterfield, F. (1982). *Alive in the bitter sea.* Toronto: Bantam Books.

Cambodian king backs gay marriage. (2004, February 20). BBC News. Accessed at http://news.bbc.co.uk/2/hi/asia-pacific/3505915.stm.

Cameroun: Quatre nouvelles arrestations pour homosexualité. *Têtu.* Retrieved September 10, 2011, from www.tetu.com/actualites/international/cameroun-quatre-nouvelles-arrestations-pour-homosexualite-20060.

Carrier, J. G. (1999). People who can be friends: Selves and social relationships. In S. Bell & S. Coleman (Eds.), *The anthropology of friendship* (pp. 21–28). New York: Berg.

Chen, L. (2002). Communication in intercultural relationships. In W. B. Gudykunst & B. Mody (Eds.), *Handbook of international and intercultural communication* (pp. 241–258). Thousand Oaks, CA: Sage.

Chen, T. C.-C., Drzewiecka, J. A., & Sias, P. M. (2001). Dialectical tensions in Taiwanese international student friendships. *Communication Quarterly, 49,* 57–66.

Chesebro, J. W. (Ed.). (1981). *Gayspeak: Gay male and lesbian communication.* New York: Pilgrim Press.

Chesebro, J. W. (1997). Ethical communication and sexual orientation. In J. M. Makau & R. C. Arnett (Eds.), *Communication ethics in an age of diversity* (pp. 126–154). Bloomington, IL: University of Illinois Press.

Chozick, A. (2005, November 14). Beyond the numbers. *Wall Street Journal,* p. R4.

Clark-Ibanez, M. K., & Felmlee, D. (2004). Interethnic relationships: The role of social network diversity. *Journal of Marriage and Family, 66,* 229–245.

Collier M. J. (1996). Communication competence problematics in ethnic friendships. *Communication Monographs, 63,* 314–346.

Cowburn, A. (2016, January 5). ISIS has killed at least 25 men in Syria suspected of being gay, group claims. *Independent.* Retrieved July 19, 2016, from http://www.independent.co.uk/news/world/middle-east/isis-has-killed-at-least-25-men-in-syria-suspected-of-being-gay-group-claims-a6797636.html.

Dion, K. K., & Dion, K. L. (1991). Psychological individualism and romantic love. *Journal of Social Behavior and Personality, 6,* 17–33.

Dion, K. L., & Dion, K. K. (1988). Romantic love: Individual and cultural perspectives. In R. Sternberg & M. Barnes (Eds.), *The psychology of love* (pp. 264–289). New Haven, CT: Yale University Press.

Djamba, Y. K. & Kimuna, S. R. (2014). Are Americans really in favor of interracial marriage? *Journal of Black Studies, 45,* 528–544.

Dodd, C. H., & Baldwin, J. R. (2002). The role of family and macrocultures in intercultural relationships. In J. N. Martin, T. K. Nakayama, & L. A. Flores (Eds.), *Readings in intercultural communication* (2nd ed., pp. 279–289). Boston, MA: McGraw-Hill.

Elias, N., & Lemish, D. (2009). Spinning the web of identity: The roles of the internet in the lives of immigrant adolescents. *New Media & Society, 11*(4), 533–551. doi: 10.1177/1461444809102959.

Eng, D. L. (2001). *Racial castration: Managing masculinity in Asian America.* Durham, NC: Duke University Press.

Fahrenthold, D. A. (2005, October 2). Connecticut's first same-sex unions proceed civilly. *The Washington Post,* p. A3.

Fiebert, M. S., Nugent, D., Hershberger, S. L., & Kasdan, M. (2004). Dating and commitment choices as a function of ethnicity among American college students in California. *Psychological Reports, 94,* 1293–1300.

Frith, K., Shaw, P., & Cheng, H. (2005). The construction of beauty: A cross-cultural analysis of women's magazine advertising. *Journal of Communication, 55,* 56–70.

Gajjala, R. (2004). Negotiating cyberspace/negotiating RL. In A. Gonzalez, M. Houston, & V. Chen (Eds.), *Our voices: Essays in culture, ethnicity and communication* (4th ed., pp. 63–71). Los Angeles, CA: Roxbury.

Gao, G. (1991). Stability of romantic relationships in China and the United States. In S. Ting-Toomey & F. Korzenny (Eds.), *Cross-cultural interpersonal communication* (pp. 99–115). Newbury Park, CA: Sage.

Gao, G. (2001). Intimacy, passion, and commitment in Chinese and U.S. American romantic relationships. *International Journal of Intercultural Relations, 25,* 329–342.

Gareis, E. (1995). *Intercultural friendship: A qualitative study.* Lanham, MD: University Press of America.

Gates, H. (1987). *Chinese working-class lives.* Ithaca, NY: Cornell University Press.

Gill, A. (1995). *Ruling passions: Sex, race and empire.* London: BBC Books.

Graham, J. A., & Cohen, R. (1997). Race and sex factors in children's sociometric ratings and friendship choices. *Social Development, 6,* 355–372.

Graham, M. A., Moeai, J., & Shizuru, L. S. (1985). Intercultural marriages: An intrareligious perspective. *International Journal of Intercultural Relations, 9,* 427–434.

Greenberg, A. (2015, July 24). Spain has finally made it illegal for 14-year olds to get married. *Time.* Retrieved July 19, 2016, from http://time.com/3970710/spain-marriage-age-of-consent-europe/.

Gudykunst, W. B., & Matsumoto, Y. (1996). Cross-cultural variability of communication in personal relationships. In W. B. Gudykunst, S. Ting-Toomey, & T. Nishida (Eds.), *Communication in personal relationships across cultures* (pp. 19–56). Thousand Oaks, CA: Sage.

Haualani, R. T. (1995). The intersecting hegemonic discourses of an Asian mail-order bride catalog: Pilipina "oriental butterfly" dolls for sale. *Women's Studies in Communication, 18*(1), 45–64.

Hammond, D., & Jablow, A. (1987). Gilgamesh and the Sundance Kid: The myth of male friendship. In H. Brod (Ed.), *The making of masculinities: The new men's studies* (pp. 241–258). Boston, MA: Allen & Unwin.

Hampton, K. N., Goulet, L. S., Rainie, L., & Purcell, K. (2011). Social networking sites and our lives. Pew Internet & American Life Project. Retrieved July 22, 2011, from www.pewinternet.org/Reports/2011/Technology-and-social-networks.aspx.

Harris, T. M., & Kalbfleisch, P. J. (2000). Interracial dating: The implications of race for initiating a romantic relationship. *Howard Journal of Communications, 11,* 49–64.

Hotta, J., & Ting-Toomey, S. (2013). Intercultural adjustment and friendship dialectics in international students: A qualitative study. *International Journal of Intercultural Relations, 37*(5): 550–566.

Hymowitz, C. (2005, November 14). The new diversity. *Wall Street Journal,* pp. R1, R3.

Jacobson, C. K., & Johnson, B. R. (2006). Interracial friendship and African Americans' attitudes toward interracial marriage. *Journal of Black Studies, 36,* 570–584.

James, N. C. (2000). When Miss America was always white. In A. González, M. Houston, & V. Chen (Eds.), *Our voices: Essays in culture, ethnicity and communication* (3rd ed., pp. 42–46). Los Angeles, CA: Roxbury.

Johnson, B. R., & Jacobson, C. K. (2005). Context in contact: An examination of social settings on Whites' attitudes toward interracial marriage, *Journal of Social Psychology, 68,* 387–399.

Kelly, W. E. (2006). Applying a critical metatheoretical approach to intercultural relations: The case of U.S.–Japanese communication. *China Media Research, 2*(4), 9–21.

Kim, H., Kim, G. J., Park, H. W., & Rice, R. E. (2007). Configurations of relationships in different media: FtF, email, instant messenger, mobile phone, and SMS. *Journal of Computer-Mediated Communication, 12,* 1183–1207.

Kitano, H. H. L., Yeung, W.-T., Chai, L., & Hatanaka, H. (1984). Asian-American interracial marriage. *Journal of Marriage and the Family, 56,* 179–190.

Lampe, P. (1982). Interethnic dating: Reasons for and against. *International Journal of Intercultural Relations, 6,* 115–126.

Lee, P.-W. (2008). Stages and transitions of relational identity formation in intercultural friendship: Implications for Identity Management Theory. *Journal of International and Intercultural Communication, 1,* 51–69.

Lee, S. M., & Edmonston, B. (2005). New marriages, new families: U.S. racial and Hispanic intermarriage. *Population Bulletin, 60*(2), 3–36.

Lewin, K. (1948). Some social psychological differences between the United States and Germany. In G. Lewin (Ed.), *Resolving social conflicts.* New York: Harper.

Logan, J. R., Stults, B. J., & Farley, R. (2004). Segregation of minorities in the Metropolis. *Demography, 41,* 1–22.

Luo, S., & Klohnen, E. C. (2005). Assortative mating and marital quality in newlyweds: A couple-centered approach. *Journal of Personality and Social Psychology, 88,* 301–326.

McKenna, K. Y. A., Green, A. S., & Gleason, M. E. J. (2002). Relationship formation on the Internet: What's the big attraction? *Journal of Social Issues, 58,* 9–31.

Mariage vietnamien lesbien. (1998, May). *Illico,* 32–33.

Martin, J. N., Bradford, L. J., Drzewiecka, J. A., & Chitgopekar, A. S. (2003). Intercultural dating patterns among young white U.S. Americans: Have they changed in the past 20 years? *Howard Journal of Communications, 14,* 53–73.

Martin, J. N., Nakayama, T. K., & Flores, L. A. (2002). A dialectical approach to intercultural communication. In J. N. Martin, T. K. Nakayama, & L. A. Flores (Eds.), *Readings in intercultural communication* (2nd ed., pp. 3–13). Boston, MA: McGraw-Hill.

Mashal, M. (2016, July 18). Clash of values emerges after Afghan child bride burns to death. *New York Times.* Retrieved July 21, 2016, from http://www.nytimes.com/2016/07/19/world/asia/afghanistan-zahra-child-marriage.html?_r=0.

McCullough, M. W. (1998). *Black and White women as friends: Building cross-race friendships.* Cresskill, NJ: Hampton Press.

McKenna, K. Y. A., Green, A. S., & Gleason, M. E. J. (2002). Relationship formation on the Internet: What's the big attraction? *Journal of Social Issues, 58,* 9–31.

Mercer, K. (1994). *Welcome to the jungle.* New York: Routledge.

Moore, R. M. (2000). An exploratory study of interracial dating on a small college campus. *Sociological Viewpoints, 16,* 46–64.

Nakayama, T. K. (1998). Communication of heterosexism. In M. L. Hecht (Ed.), *Communication of prejudice* (pp. 112–121). Thousand Oaks, CA: Sage.

Nardi, P. M. (1992). That's what friends are for: Friends as family in the gay and lesbian community. In K. Plummer (Ed.), *Modern homosexualities: Fragments of lesbian and gay experience* (pp. 108–120). New York: Routledge.

Olaniran, B. A. (2012). Exploring cultural challenges in e-learning. In P. H. Cheong, J. N. Martin, & L. P. Macfadyen (Eds.), *New media and intercultural communication: Identity, community and politics* (pp. 61–74). New York: Peter Lang.

Osbeck, L. M., & Moghaddam, F. M. (1997). Similarity and attraction among majority and minority groups in a multicultural context. *International Journal of Intercultural Relations, 21,* 113–123.

Plummer, D. L. (2015, February 4). Why I have white friends. *The Boston Globe.* Retrieved July 19, 2016, from http://www.bostonglobe.com/magazine/2015/02/04/why-have-white-friends/RvkIgg5CXYtwza9mOcpmNI/story.html?event=event12.

Pogrebin, L. C. (1987). *Among friends.* New York: McGraw-Hill.

Pogrebin, L. C. (1992). The same and different: Crossing boundaries of color, culture, sexual preference, disability, and age. In W. B. Gudykunst & Y. Y. Kim (Eds.), *Readings on communicating with strangers* (pp. 318–336). New York: McGraw-Hill.

Romano, D. (1997). *Intercultural marriage: Promises and pitfalls* (2nd ed.). Yarmouth, ME: Intercultural Press.

Root, M. P. P. (2001). *Love's revolution: Interracial marriage.* Philadelphia, PA: Temple University Press.

Rosenblatt, P. C., Karis, T. A., & Powell, R. D. (1995). *Multiracial couples: Black and white voices.* Thousand Oaks, CA: Sage.

Rosenwald, M. S. (2015, April 6). How Jim Obergefell became the face of the Supreme Court gay marriage case. *The WashingtonPost.* Retrieved July 7, 2016, from "https://www.washingtonpost.com/local/how-jim-obergefell-became-the-face-of-the-supreme-court-gay-marriage-case/2015/04/06/3740433c-d958-11e4-b3f2-607bd612aeac_story.html" \l "comments" https://www.washingtonpost.com/local/how-jim-obergefell-became-the-face-of-the-supreme-court-gay-marriage-case/2015/04/06/3740433c-d958-11e4-b3f2-607bd612aeac_story.html#comments.

Russo, R. (2001, February 9). Intercultural relationships flourish despite differences. *The (Georgetown) Hoya.*

Sherrod, D., & Nardi, P. M. (1988). *The nature and function of friendship in the lives of gay men and lesbians.* Paper presented at the annual meeting of the American Sociological Association, Atlanta.

Shibazaki, K., & Brennan, K. (1998). When birds of a different feathers flock together: A preliminary comparison of intra-ethnic and inter-ethnic dating relationships. *Journal of Social and Personal Relationships, 15,* 248–256.

Smart, A. (1999). Expression of interest: Friendship and *quanxi* in Chinese societies. In S. Bell & S. Coleman (Eds.), *The anthropology of friendship* (pp. 119–136). New York: Berg.

Snyder, G. (2003, May). Teams that span time zones face new work rules. Stanford Business. Website of Stanford Graduate School of Business. Accessed at www.gsb.stanford.edu/news/bmag/sbsm0305/feature_virtual_teams.shtml.

Sprecher, S., Aron, A., Hatfield, E., Cortese, A., Potapova, E., & Levitskaya, A. (1994). Love: American style, Russian style, and Japanese style. *Personal Relationships, 1,* 349–369.

St. Amant, K. (2012). Culture, context, and cyberspace: Rethinking identity and credibility in international virtual teams. In P. H. Cheong, J. N. Martin, & L. P. Macfadyen (Eds.), *New media and intercultural communication: Identity, community and politics* (pp. 75–92). New York: Peter Lang.

St. Amant, K. (2002). When cultures and computers collide: Rethinking computer-mediated communication according to international and intercultural communication expectations. *Journal of Business and Technical Communication, 16,* 196–214.

Stephan, W., & Stephan, C. (1992). Reducing intercultural anxiety through intercultural contact. *International Journal of Intercultural Relations, 16,* 89–106.

Sudweeks, S., Gudykunst, W. B., Ting-Toomey, S., & Nishida, T. (1990). Developmental themes in Japanese–North American relationships. *International Journal of Intercultural Relations, 14,* 207–233.

Sze, H. (1992, July 24). Racist love. *Asian Week,* pp. 10, 24.

Talking about race. (2000, July 16). *New York Times Magazine,* special issue (How Race Is Lived in America).

Tan, D., & Singh, R. (1995). Attitudes and attraction. *Personality and Social Psychology Bulletin, 21,* 975–986.

Taylor, P., Funk, C., & Craighill, P. (2006). Guess who's coming to dinner?: 22% of Americans have a relative in a mixed-race marriage. Pew research report. Retrieved December 12, 2008, from http://pewsocialtrends.org/assets/pdf/interracial.pdf.

Tucker, M. B., & Mitchell-Kernan, C. (1995). Social structure and psychological correlates of interethnic dating. *Journal of Social and Personal Relationships, 12,* 341–361.

Turkle, S. (2011). *Alone together: Why we expect more from technology and less from each other.* New York: Basic Books.

Wang, W. (2015, June 12). Interracial marriage: Who is marrying "out." Fact Tank. *Pew Research Center.* Retrieved July 19, 2016, from http://www.pewresearch.org/fact-tank/2015/06/12/interracial-marriage-who-is-marrying-out/.

Wilson, S. B., McIntosh, W. D., & Insana, S. P., II. (2007). Dating across race: An examination of African American Internet personal advertisements. *Journal of Black Studies, 37,* 964–982.

Yancy, G. (2002). Who interracially dates: An examination of the characteristics of those who have interracially dated. *Journal of Comparative Family Studies, 33,* 177–190.

Yang, P. (2012). Who am I in virtual space? A dialectical approach to students' online identity expression. In P. H. Cheong, J. N. Martin, & L. P. Macfadyen (Eds.), *New media and intercultural communication: Identity, community and politics* (pp. 109–122). New York: Peter Lang.

Yoshino, K. (2015). A new birth of freedom?: Obergefell v. Hodges. *Harvard Law Review, 129*, 147–179.

Zickuhr, K. (2010, December 16). *Generations 2010*. Pew Internet & American Life Project. Retrieved July 23, 2011, from www.pewinternet.org/Reports/2010/Generations-2010.aspx.

CREDITS

[page 396, text] N. Broverman, quote from "At least 11 Alabama counties refuse to comply with marriage equality" from *The Advocate* (January 20, 2016). [page 400, text] J. Mitchell, excerpt from "Mississippi RV park owner evicts interracial couple" from *The Clarion-Ledger* (April 5, 2016). [page 400, text] N. C. James, quote from "When Miss America was always white" in *Our voices: Essays in culture, ethnicity and communication*, edited by A. González, M. Houston, and V. Chen. Roxbury. [page 401, text] D. L. Plummer, excerpt from "Why I have white friends" from *The Boston Globe* (February 4, 2015). [page 402, text] Jessica, excerpt from "Students Voices: What an amazing experience. . . cultures to thank." Original work; [page 402, text] L. C. Pogrebin, quote from "The same and different: Crossing boundaries of color, culture, sexual preference, disability, and age" in *Readings on communicating with strangers*, edited by W. B. Gudykunst and Y. Y. Kim. McGraw-Hill. [page 403, text] M. W. McCullough, quote from Black and *White women as friends: Building cross-race friendships*. Hampton Press. [page 404, text] Excerpt from *Talking about race*. New York Times Magazine, special issue (How Race Is Lived in America). [page 407–408, text] H. Gates, excerpt from *Chinese working-class lives*. Cornell University Press. [page 408, text] A. Smart, quote from "Expression of interest: Friendship and quanxi in Chinese societies" in *The anthropology of friendship*, edited by S. Bell and S. Coleman. Berg. [page 408, text] F. Butterfield, excerpt from *Alive in the bitter sea*. Bantam Books. [page 409, text] M. Mancini, excerpt from *Selling destinations: Geography for the travel professional, Fourth Edition*. Thomson/Delmar Learning. [page 410, text] Garcia Wintilo, excerpt from "Respeto: A Mexican base for interpersonal relationships" in *Communication in personal relationships across cultures*, edited by W. B. Gudykunst, S. Ting-Toomey, and T. Nishida. Sage. [page 412, text] M. J. Collier, quote from "Communication competence problematics in ethnic friendships" from *Communication Monographs* (1996): 314–346. [page 414, text] B. J. Allen, quote from "Sapphire and Sappho: Allies in authenticity" in *Our voices: Essays in culture, ethnicity and communication*, edited by A. Gonzalez, M. Houston, and V. Chen. Roxbury. [page 412, text] E. Gareis, quote from *Intercultural friendship: A qualitative study*.

University Press of America. [page 416, text] R. Gajjala, quote from "Negotiating cyberspace/negotiating RL" in Our voices: *Essays in culture, ethnicity and communication*, edited by A. Gonzalez, M. Houston, and V. Chen. Roxbury. [page 417, text] S. Turkle, quote from *Alone together: Why we expect more from technology and less from each other*. Basic Books. [page 417–418, text] K. St. Amant, quote from "Culture, context, and cyberspace: Rethinking identity and credibility in international virtual teams" in *New media and intercultural communication: Identity, community and politics*, edited by P. H. Cheong, J. N. Martin, and L. P. Macfadyen. Peter Lang. [page 419, text] R. Russo, quote from *Intercultural relationships flourish despite differences*. The (Georgetown) Hoya. [page 420, text] A. Greenberg, excerpt from "Spain has finally made it illegal for 14-year olds to get married" from *Time* (July 24, 2015). [page 420, text] M. Mashal, excerpt from "Clash of values emerges after Afghan child bride burns to death" from *New York Times* (July 18, 2016). [page 421, text] Quote from *Talking about race*. New York Times Magazine, special issue (How Race Is Lived in America). [page 421, text] USCIS, excerpt from *Marriage and martial union for naturalization purposes*. uscis.gov. [page 422, text] M. P. P. Root, quote from *Love's revolution: Interracial marriage*. Temple University Press. [page 424, text] M. P. P. Root, quote from *Love's revolution: Interracial marriage*. Temple University Press. [page 423, text] M. P. P. Root, quote from *Love's revolution: Interracial marriage*. Temple University Press. [page 425, text] E. Gareis, quote from *Intercultural friendship: A qualitative study*. University Press of America. [page 426, text] P. M. Nardi, quote from "That's what friends are for: Friends as family in the gay and lesbian community" in *Modern homosexualities: Fragments of lesbian and gay experience*, edited by K. Plummer. Routledge. [page 426, text] Kamilla, quote from "Students Voices: When I came to the United States. . . Here it is not like this." Original Work; [page 426–427, text] S. Brydum, quote from "Report: Same-sex couples less likely to divorce" from *The Advocate* (December 13, 2004). [page 427, text] A. Cowburn, quote from "ISIS has killed at least 25 men in Syria suspected of being gay, group claims" from *Independent* (January 5, 2016). [page 428, text] M. K. Clark-Ibanez, and D. Felmlee, quote from "Inter ethnic relationships: The role of social network diversity" from *Journal of Marriage and Family* (2004): 229–245. [page 429, text] P. C. Rosenblatt, T. A. Karis, and R. D. Powell, excerpt from *Multiracial couples: Black and white voices*. Sage. [page 429, text] M. K. Clark-Ibanez, and D. Felmlee, quote from "Inter ethnic relationships: The role of social network diversity" from Journal of Marriage and Family (2004): 229–245. [page 430–431, text] W. E. Kelly, quote from "Applying a

critical metatheoretical approach to intercultural relations: The case of U.S.–Japanese communication" from *China Media Research* (2006): 9–21. [page 430, text] —Bakari, excerpt from "Students Voices: I have a very good friend who is studying . . . factors in its success." Original Work; [page 430–431, text] W. E. Kelly, quote from "Applying a critical metatheoretical approach to intercultural relations: The case of U.S.–Japanese communication" from *China Media Research* (2006): 9–21.

CHAPTER

11

CULTURE, COMMUNICATION, AND CONFLICT

CHAPTER OBJECTIVES

After reading this chapter, you should be able to:

1. Define and describe characteristics of intercultural conflict.

2. Be able to discuss three approaches—social science, interpretive, and critical—to studying conflict.

3. Be able to identify five types of interpersonal conflict.

4. Explain the role of cultural values, family influences, gender, and ethnicity in interpersonal conflict.

5. Be able to discuss some of the contexts that contribute to social conflict.

6. Explain some strategies for dealing with conflict.

7. Be able to distinguish productive from destructive conflict.

8. Describe characteristics and advantages of mediation.

CHARACTERISTICS OF INTERCULTURAL CONFLICT
Ambiguity
Language
Contradictory Conflict Styles

THE SOCIAL SCIENCE APPROACH TO CONFLICT
Cultural Values and Conflict
Religion and Conflict
Family Influences
Intercultural Conflict Styles
Gender, Ethnicity, and Conflict Styles

INTERPRETIVE AND CRITICAL APPROACHES TO SOCIAL CONFLICT
Social Movements
Historical and Political Contexts

MANAGING INTERCULTURAL CONFLICT
Dealing with Interpersonal Conflict
Mediation
Peacebuilding

INTERNET RESOURCES

SUMMARY

DISCUSSION QUESTIONS

ACTIVITIES

KEY WORDS

REFERENCES

The need to understand intercultural conflict seems more important now than ever. One thing we can be sure of is that conflict is inevitable. Conflicts are happening all around the world, as they always have, and at many different levels: interpersonal, social, national, and international. For example, at the interpersonal level, friends or romantic partners may disagree about their relationship between themselves or with friends and family. Interpersonal conflicts can be intergenerational. You may disagree with your parents about where to attend college, or what you spend your money on, or where to live in the summer. These conflicts can have varying outcomes. Intergenerational conflicts can occur in the workplace. For example, experts say that Baby Boomers, Generation Y and Millennials have different characteristics and sets of work-life values that can clash. While Boomers tend to be work-obsessed, Millennials are demanding flexible schedules that allow them to pursue an active life away from the office. Boomers tend to like autonomy, while Millennials want more direction and enjoy collaboration. GenY perceive Boomers as "micromanagers" perhaps because Boomers tend be competitive, logical, and efficient (Koeppel, 2011). These conflicts can make the workplace uncomfortable and challenging. Intergenerational conflicts can have more serious outcomes. Kenji, a Japanese American student from Alabama, had conflicts with her dad—with more serious consequences. When he found out she was gay, he threw her out of the house and still refuses to see her (Kramer, 2011).

Conflicts can also happen on a societal level. For example, various groups in the United States engage in conflict based on deeply held value differences; some feel that health care is a right that should be afforded to everyone for the good of the society in general, and others feel that it is an individual privilege that each person is responsible to obtain. As we've noted earlier, there are also strong feelings that lead to societal conflict around immigration issues. Some U.S. Americans believe that children of undocumented immigrants should not have access to educational opportunities (e.g., scholarships, internships) that are typically reserved for U.S. citizens—that doing so only rewards the illegal actions of their parents. Others believe that these children and young people should not be denied opportunities because of the actions of their parents (see Figure 11-1, p. 448).

An example of international conflict is seen in the tensions between the United States, Russia, and their allies, played out in the proxy war in Syria. While the war in Syria began as a civilian protest against the repressive Assad government in 2011, it quickly escalated into a proxy war with international, competing interests fighting their battles in Syria. The Assad regime retaliated against civilians, with military support from Iran and another long-time powerful ally, Russia—who wanted to weaken the anti-Assad Islamist groups they have fought in their own soil in Chechnya. On its part, the United States, along with Saudi Arabia, and Turkey, wants to prevent Russia, a long-time adversary, from determining the outcome in this important region. Another nuance—Turkey is conflicted in its support because the United States is allied with Kurdish fighters—a group Turkey has viewed as terrorist for many years. As discussed earlier, the human consequences of this complicated conflict have been devastating, with hundreds of thousands of lives lost and millions displaced (al-Masri, 2015).

Conflicts in one country can spill over into another, evidenced by the thousands of refugees from Syria (and Iraq and Afghanistan) fleeing to nearby and even distant countries, where they often encounter more violence and conflict. These conflicts have even reached the United States as individuals supporting the various Middle East factions have attacked civilians here—at the Boston Marathon in 2013, at a social services agency holiday party in San Bernardino in 2015 and at a nightclub in Orlando, Florida in 2016.

As you can see from these examples, conflict is not simply a matter of disagreement. Conflict among cultural groups can escalate into tragedies that stretch across generations and continents. Russia and the United States, Turkey and Russia, Iran and Saudi Arabia, all have complicated historical relationships. Conflicts are often complex and layered. One conflict may have interpersonal, political, and international dimensions, dramatically seen, for example, in recent clashes between migrants and residents in many European countries.

Social media can exacerbate conflict at all levels, from nasty Tweets and retweets to sophisticated ISIS Internet recruitment, in which citizens in any country can be radicalized at any time. For example, Yemeni-American Al-Qaeda leader al-Awlaki has been described as the "bin Laden of the Internet" with a blog, a Facebook page, the Al-Qaeda magazine *Inspire*, and many YouTube videos. Even though he was killed in 2011, his lectures, sermons, and other video messages are still easily found and have inspired a number of terrorist attackers in the United States and abroad, including Dzhokhar and Tamerlan Tsarnaev of the 2013 Boston Marathon bombing and two of the Paris *Charlie Hebdo* attackers (Berger, 2015; Madhani, 2010). On the other hand, some experts suggest that online communication can help resolve conflicts (see the Point of View box on page 445). How can people overcome conflict and put it behind them? How can families and individuals restore relationships after hurtful interpersonal conflict? There are no easy answers to these questions, but we must consider them as part of our understanding of intercultural conflict.

Understanding intercultural conflict is especially important because of the relationship between culture and conflict. That is, cultural differences can cause conflict; once conflict occurs, cultural backgrounds and experience influence how individuals deal with it. Culture can shape what people consider valuable (like moral and religious beliefs) and worth fighting for; it can shape official positions taken and interpretations of others' actions. Sometimes conflicts arise not due to differences in values or morals, but just because someone is "different." For example, a recent report found that men in the military were often being bullied, even raped, because they were different in some way (in accent or from a particular region of the country) (Duell, 2011). Or consider that the targets of bullying and harassment in high school and college campuses often differ from the majority of students in some way. On the other hand, there are many reasons for conflicts, and serious disagreements or even violence can arise between people who are very similar in background (e.g., family members) or who share similar cultural traditions (Greek and Turkish Cypriots). We need to say upfront that intercultural conflict is an extremely complex topic.

As with other topics in this textbook, we use our tripartite framework (social science, interpretive, and critical) to examine and understand intercultural conflict. The social science approach focuses on how cultural differences cause conflict and influence the management of the conflict, primarily on the interpersonal level. The other two approaches—interpretive and critical—focus more on intergroup relationships and on cultural, historical, and structural elements as the primary sources of conflict. These three approaches emphasize different aspects of the individual–contextual dialectic and the need to view conflict on all three levels: the interpersonal, societal, and international.

We first define what we mean by conflict and intercultural conflict and then describe each of the three approaches. We conclude the chapter with practical suggestions for understanding and improving our intercultural conflict skills.

CHARACTERISTICS OF INTERCULTURAL CONFLICT

Conflict is usually defined as involving a perceived or real **incompatibility** of goals, values, expectations, processes, or outcomes between two or more **interdependent** individuals or groups. The complexity of intercultural conflict can be seen in the current debate, discussed in previous chapters, on whether or not Muslim women should be allowed to wear veils in public. This has been a major issue in France, where a no-veil policy has been instituted. In the United States, the issue gained national attention over the question of whether women could wear veils while driving or posing for their driver's license photo. These conflicts have roots in the history of Christian–Muslim relations and U.S./French–Arab/Muslim countries relations—histories characterized by domination on the part of the United States and colonization on France's part and by hostility and resentment on the part of some Muslims and Arabs. There are also gender issues involved. Some political leaders see the veil as a symbol of oppression of women, while others, including some women, see it as a symbol of religious devotion (Croucher, 2013).

The point here is that there is no reason to seek a single source for conflict. By taking a dialectical approach to thinking about conflict, you can see how various forces—economic, social, political, religious—may all play different roles at different times. Yet, when confronted with such conflicts, how should society respond? How should you respond?

What are the characteristics of **intercultural conflict?** How does intercultural conflict differ from other kinds of conflict? One unique characteristic is that intercultural conflicts tend to be more ambiguous than intracultural conflict. Other characteristics involve language issues and contradictory conflict styles.

conflict The interference between two or more interdependent individuals or groups of people who perceive incompatible goals, values, or expectations in attaining those ends.

incompatibility Incapable of existing harmoniously.

interdependent Mutually dependent.

intercultural conflict Conflict between two or more cultural groups.

Ambiguity

While some conflicts are seen unambiguously as conflicts by parties involved (e.g., Israelis and Palestinians), this and many other conflicts are seen in very different ways by the individuals and groups involved. For example, when 49 people were murdered in an Orlando, Florida nightclub in June 2016, there were varying views of the causes and proposed solutions. Some saw it as a hate crime—caused by the gunman's anti-gay prejudice. Some saw it as a clash of cultures and religions, United States (Christianity) and Islam, and refused to acknowledge the anti-gay element. Others saw it as an attack on freedom of all individuals. Still others saw it primarily as the actions of a deranged individual with a history of mental illness and unresolved anger issues. The proposed solutions to the conflict—more gun control legislation, more protection/rights for gay Americans, or legislation to restrict immigration of Muslims to the United States—depended on one's view of the cause (Healey, 2016).

In some interpersonal contexts, individuals may not even agree there is a conflict. A student, Tabbetha, reported an ongoing conflict at work with one of her co-workers, an older gentleman, in the customer service department. She thinks the co-worker doesn't like her very much and they frequently disagree about how to handle certain customer complaints. Part of the problem is that she doesn't really get what is going on between them—she's not sure if it's her age, her gender, or if he's having a bad time in his personal life, and so she is not sure how to handle the situation.

Language

Issues surrounding language may be important to intercultural conflict. One student, Stephanie, described a situation that occurred when she was studying in Spain. She went to an indoor swimming pool with her host family sisters. Being from Arizona, she was unaccustomed to swimming in such cold water, so she went outside to sunbathe. Her "sisters" asked her why she didn't swim with them. Stephanie explains:

> At that point I realized they thought I should really be with them. . . . I didn't know how to express myself well enough to explain to them. . . . I tried, but I don't think it worked very well. So I just apologized. . . . I did basically ignore the conflict. I would have dealt with it, but I felt I did not have the language skills to explain myself effectively, so I did not even try. . . . That is why I had such a problem, because I could not even express what I would have liked to.

When individuals don't know the language well, it is very difficult to handle conflict effectively. At the same time, silence is not always a bad thing. Sometimes it provides a "cooling off" period, allowing things to settle down. Depending on the cultural context, silence can be very appropriate.

Contradictory Conflict Styles

Intercultural conflict also may be characterized by a combination of orientations to conflict and conflict management styles. Communication scholar Sheryl Lindsley

Communication expert Yair Amichai-Hamburger thinks that the Internet can play a useful role in de-escalating or resolving intercultural conflict for discordant groups. He shows how these Internet characteristics help meet several of the conditions necessary for reducing negative intergroup attitudes (as discussed in the Contact Hypothesis in Chapter 4). He also stresses that it is important that these intercultural Internet meetings are facilitated by a skilled supervisor, to ensure the involvement and commitment of participants.

- The Internet is a great status leveler. If the online contact does not involve video, it's impossible to know whether the others are wearing Rolexes or Walmart watches, are attractive or not, or possess any other nonverbal cues that trigger prejudice or bias.

- The Internet also allows people to generalize from positive interactions with individuals "others" to the entire group, as members may tag the group identity to a participant after positive contributions, thus affecting the whole perception of the "other group."

- Internet contact can mean less anxiety—often a factor in conflict situations, allowing people to meet from a place where they feel comfortable, for example, their own living room.

- Internet encounters are cheaper and easier to organize.

Source: From Y. Amichai-Hamberger, "How we can use the Internet to resolve intergroup conflict," *psychologytoday.com*, June 6, 2013. Retrieved from https://www.psychologytoday.com/blog/the -social-net/201306/how-we-can-use-the-internet-resolve-intergroup-conflict.

(1999) interviewed managers in *maquiladoras*—sorting or assembly plants along the Mexican–U.S. border—and found many examples of conflict. For example, Mexican managers thought that U.S. managers were often rude and impolite in their dealings with each other and the workers. The biggest difference between U.S. Americans and Mexicans was in the way that U.S. Americans expressed disagreement at management meetings. One Mexican manager explained:

> When we are in a meeting together, the U.S. American will tell another manager, "I don't like what you did." . . . Mexicans interpret this as a personal insult. They have a difficult time understanding that U.S. Americans can insult each other in this way and then go off and play golf together. . . . Mexicans would be polite, perhaps tell the person in private, or make a suggestion, rather than confronting. (quoted in Lindsley, 1999, p. 158)

As Lindsley points out, the conflict between the Mexican and U.S. American managers in their business meetings needs to be understood as a dialectical and "layered" process in which individual, dyadic, societal, and historical forces are recognized.

POINT *of* VIEW

Why are some cultures more prone to conflicts, whereas others have a low incidence of conflict? Anthropologist Marc Howard Ross (2011) spent many years investigating this question in many different countries. He concludes that in some cultures, conflict tends to be minimized and dealt with constructively; in other cultures, conflicts abound. What makes the differences?

Ross thinks that the reasons are both structural and psychocultural (child-rearing practices, socialization, cultural values). He finds that low-conflict societies share common characteristics: interpersonal practices that build security and trust, a preference for joint problem solving, and a strong link between individual and communities. He describes how Norway exemplifies a low-conflict society.

Norwegians are socialized to avoid conflict, learning early in life that overt aggression is unacceptable and emotional self-control over negative feelings is important. In fact, Norway has a national policy to combat bullying and violence in schools and requires peer mediation and conflict resolution education in all public schools (Johannessen, 2007). There are few aggressive models in the popular culture—newspapers do not sensationalize crime, television features little violence and no boxing, and films are controlled. For example, *E.T.* was considered too violent for children under age 12 (Ross, 1993). In addition, there are high levels of parental nurturance and supervision.

There are also extensive "moralnets"—people who provide support to individuals in times of need, such as extended family, friends, and neighbors. A strong collective sense of responsibility is expressed in a variety of ways, including an emphasis on equality, attentiveness to community norms, and conformity and participation. Norway's low rate of violence predictably explained the horror felt by Norwegians after the senseless murder of children at a summer camp in July 2011 by an anti-immigrant gunman and does suggest that even in very peace-loving countries, individuals can deviate from the cultural norm (Zhang, 2011).

Sources: From M. H. Ross, *The culture of conflict: Interpretations and interests in comparative perspective.* (New Haven, CT: Yale University Press, 1993a); M. H. Ross, "Reflections on the Strengths and Limitations to Cross-Cultural Evidence in the Study of Conflict and Its Mitigation," *Cross-Cultural Research, 45*(1), (2011), 82–96.

THE SOCIAL SCIENCE APPROACH TO CONFLICT

Perhaps if everyone agreed on the best way to view conflict, there would be less of it. But the reality is that different orientations to conflict may result in more conflict. In this section, which takes a social science approach, we identify cultural influences in approaches to conflict, different types of conflict, and different strategies and tactics for responding to conflict.

A key question is this: Is open conflict good or bad? That is, should conflict be welcomed because it provides opportunities to strengthen relationships? Or should it be avoided because it can only lead to problems for relationships and groups? Another key question is this: What is the best way to handle conflict when it arises? Should individuals talk about it directly, deal with it indirectly, or avoid it? Should emotions be part of the conflict resolution? Are expressions of emotions viewed as showing commitment to resolving the conflict at hand? Or is it better to be restrained and solve problems by rational logic rather than emotional expressiveness? Also consider the following questions: How do we learn how to deal with conflict? Who teaches us how to solve conflicts when they arise? How we answer all of these questions depends in large part on our cultural background and the way we were raised.

Cultural Values and Conflict

One general way to understand cultural variations in intercultural conflict resolution is to look at how cultural values influence conflict management. Face negotiation theory links cultural values to facework and conflict styles (Ting-Toomey, 2013). **Facework** refers to specific communication strategies we use to "save" our own or another person's face and is a universal concept; how we "do" facework varies from culture to culture and influences conflict styles. Communication scholar Ting-Toomey and her colleagues have conducted a number of studies showing that people from individualistic societies tend to be more concerned with saving their own face than another person's, so they tend to use more direct conflict management styles (Ting-Toomey & Oetzel, 2002).

> **facework** Communication strategies used to "save" our own or someone else's "face," or public image.

In contrast, people from collectivistic societies tend to be more concerned with preserving group harmony and with saving the other person's face (and dignity) during conflict. They may use a less direct conversational style; protecting the other person's face and making him or her look good is considered a skillful facework style. These face concerns lead them to use a more accommodating conflict style (Ting-Toomey & Oetzel, 2002). However, some evidence indicates that not all collectivistic societies prefer indirect ways of dealing with conflict. How someone chooses to deal with conflict in any situation depends on the type of conflict and the relationship she or he has with the other person (Cai & Fink, 2002; Ting-Toomey & Oetzel, 2013). For example, Kaori, a Japanese student, recounted a conflict she had with her U.S. American friend, Mara, when the two were working together on a sorority project. Mara seemed to take a very competitive, individualistic approach to the project, saying things like, "I did this on the project," or referring to it as "my project." Kaori became increasingly irritated and less motivated to work on the project. She finally said to Mara, "Is this your project or our project?" Mara seemed surprised, tried to defend herself, and eventually apologized; the two women then continued to work on the project and put the conflict behind them. This example is supported by a study that showed that while Japanese young people said they would avoid conflict with strangers or acquaintances, like Kaori, they were more willing to deal openly with conflict and work through conflicts with ingroup members like close friends (Cole, 1996).

Religion and Conflict

Religious differences also can be an important source of conflict. Religious beliefs are often a source of very strongly held views that can cause conflict with others who may not share those views. For example, in 2015 an evangelical Christian baker in Colorado argued that he should not have to provide services to same-sex couples

FIGURE II-I Four student "Dreamers" walked I500 miles from Florida to Washington, D.C. to advocate for the Dream Act. If passed, this legislation would allow immigrant children who were brought into the country before they were I6 and meet several other criteria (e.g., have completed high school), to earn citizenship after finishing two years of college or military service. (© *Sarah L. Volsin/The Washington Post/Getty Images*)

(e.g., bake a wedding cake). However, the court rejected this argument, saying the religious beliefs cannot be used as an excuse to discriminate (Gershman & Audi, 2015). In this case, religious differences are the source of the conflict. While not all people read the Bible in the same way, these religious differences can influence how people view their civic responsibilities and how we should appropriately respond.

Nearby in Utah, conflicts between Mormons and non-Mormons are not uncommon. Some Protestants declare Mormon religion as not truly Christian. Other conflicts center on the historically anti-gay stance of the Mormon church and its financial support of legislation banning gay marriages (McKinley & Johnson, 2008). While church leaders have reportedly softened their anti-gay rhetoric, they recently made it clear that Mormons in same-sex marriage are considered nonbelievers and could be excommunicated. This led to hundred of Mormons personally carrying their letters of resignation to the Salt Lake City Temple (Duara, 2015).

However, religious conflicts are not always nonviolent. Throughout European history, for example, the persecution of Jews often has been violent; recall, for instance, the atrocities of the Inquisition and the Holocaust. Religious conflicts between Catholics and Protestants also have been a mainstay of the conflict in Northern Ireland. Perhaps the most recent religious conflicts are those between Christian and Muslim and two factions of Muslims—the Shia and the Sunni—in the Middle East.

TYPES OF CONFLICT

There are many different types of conflict, and we may manage these types in different ways. Communication scholar Mark Cole (1996) conducted interviews with Japanese students about their views on conflict and found most of the same general categories as those identified in the United States. These categories include the following:

- *Affective conflict* occurs when individuals become aware that their feelings and emotions are incompatible. For example, suppose someone finds that his or her romantic love for a close friend is not reciprocated. The disagreement over their different levels of affection causes conflict.

- A *conflict of interest* describes a situation in which people have incompatible preferences for a course of action or plan to pursue. For example, one student described an ongoing conflict with an ex-girlfriend: "The conflicts always seem to be a jealousy issue or a controlling issue, where even though we are not going out anymore, both of us still try to control the other's life to some degree. You could probably see that this is a conflict of interest." Another example of a conflict of interest is when parents disagree on the appropriate curfew time for their children.

- *Value conflict,* a more serious type, occurs when people differ in ideologies on specific issues. For example, suppose Mario and Melinda have been dating for several months and are starting to argue frequently about their religious views, particularly as related to abortion. Melinda is pro-choice and has volunteered to do counseling in an abortion clinic. Mario, a devout Catholic, is opposed to abortion under any circumstances and is very unhappy about Melinda's volunteer work. This situation illustrates value conflict.

- *Cognitive conflict* describes a situation in which two or more people become aware that their thought processes or perceptions are incongruent. For example, suppose Marissa and Derek argue frequently about whether Marissa's friend Jamal is paying too much attention to her; Derek suspects that Jamal wants to have a sexual encounter with Marissa. Their different perceptions of the situation constitute cognitive conflict.

- *Goal conflict* occurs when people disagree about a preferred outcome or end state. For example, suppose Bob and Ray, who have been in a relationship for 10 years, have just bought a house. Bob wants to furnish the house slowly, making sure that money goes into the savings account for retirement, whereas Ray wants to furnish the house immediately, using money from their savings. Bob's and Ray's individual goals are in conflict with each other.

Family Influences

Most people deal with conflict in the way they learned while growing up—their default style. A primary influence is our family background; some families prefer a particular conflict style, and children come to accept this style as normal. For example, the family

Conflicts arise for many reasons. Religion is a common cause of conflict in intercultural relationships. Note how this student dealt with religious differences in her marriage:

I just recently got married. I am Caucasian, and my husband is Hispanic. He comes from a large, traditional family. My family background does not include many specific traditions. His family is very religious, and I grew up virtually without religion. When I became pregnant, his family told me that the baby would be baptized Catholic and raised Catholic. They also told me that they did not view our marriage as being legitimate (because we were not "married in God's eyes," that is, the Catholic Church). This was hard for me to deal with at first. I felt that I was being pressured to become someone I wasn't. But I agreed to go to church and learn Catholicism.
—Stacy

may have settled conflict in a direct, engaging manner, with the person having the strongest argument (or the biggest muscle) getting his or her way, and preserving his or her own self-esteem, rather than helping the other person "save face." Or, we may prefer to sacrifice our own self-esteem in order to preserve the relationship.

Sometimes, people try very hard to reject the conflict styles they saw their parents using. For example, suppose that Maria's parents avoided open conflict and never discussed what was bothering them. Their children learned to avoid conflict and become very uncomfortable when people around them use a more expressive style of conflict management. Maria has vowed she will never deal with conflict that way with her own children and has tried very hard to use other ways of dealing with conflicts when they do arise in her family. It is important to realize that people deal with conflict in a variety of ways and may not have the same reasons for choosing a certain style (Koerner & Fitzpatrick, 2006).

Family conflict can also arise from generational differences in immigrant families that reflect intercultural differences. In western Europe, Muslim immigrant girls are sometimes punished by their families for being too Western. For example, Samina Younis' parents immigrated to England from Pakistan before she was born and she was brought up in a strict Muslim household. One of her sisters put up a poster of a popular boy band in her bedroom, and "When Dad saw it, he ripped it down and beat her. My parents saw it as a sign she was getting ideas that weren't traditionally Muslim and may bring shame on the family. . . . We weren't allowed to watch most TV programs. I wasn't even allowed to speak to male teachers at school as they said it was shameful so I'd get into trouble for not answering my teachers. We weren't allowed to speak to Western girls at all, so we never did any activities outside the house like Brownies or dance classes."

Other immigrant families may have conflicts over arranged marriages, dating, and other cultural expectations that may highlight differences between the country of origin and the new homeland.

Intercultural Conflict Styles

Given cultural background and values as well as family influences, how do people specifically respond to conflict situations? Conflict expert Mitchell Hammer (2005) has systematically investigated this topic and proposes a four-style framework, based on two primary dimensions (direct/indirect and emotional expressiveness/restraint). Let's see how this works.

Direct and Indirect Conflict Approaches   This **direct/indirect approach** to conflict is similar to the direct/indirect language dimension we discussed in Chapter 6. There it was applied specifically to language use, whereas here it represents a broader conflict resolution approach. Some cultural groups think that conflict is fundamentally a good thing; these groups feel that it is best to approach conflict very directly, because working through conflicts constructively results in stronger, healthier, and more satisfying relationships. Similarly, groups that work through conflict can gain new information about members or about other groups, defuse more serious conflict, and increase group cohesiveness (Putnam, 2006).

direct approach A view that the best way to deal with conflict is to use precise and specific language.

indirect approach A view that best way to approach conflict is to use vague and nonspecific language.

People who take this approach concentrate on using very precise language. While they may not always feel comfortable with face-to-face conflict, they think that it's important to "say what's on your mind" in a conflict situation. The goal in this approach is to articulate the issues carefully and select the "best" solution based on an agreed-upon set of criteria. However, many cultural groups view conflict as ultimately destructive for relationships and do not think that a direct approach to conflict resolution is useful. For example, many Asian cultures, reflecting the influence of Confucianism and Taoism, and some religious groups in the United States see conflict as disturbing the peace. For instance, most Amish think of conflict not as an opportunity for personal growth, but as a threat to interpersonal and community harmony. When conflict does arise, the strong spiritual value of **pacifism** dictates a nonresistant response—often avoidance or dealing with conflict very indirectly (Kraybill, 2001).

pacifism Opposition to the use of force under any circumstances.

Also, these groups think that when members disagree they should adhere to the consensus of the group rather than engage in conflict. In fact, members who threaten group harmony may be sanctioned. One writer gives an example of a man from the Maori culture in New Zealand who was swearing and using inappropriate language in a public meeting:

> *A woman went up to him, laying her hand on his arm and speaking softly. He shook her off and continued. The crowd now moved back from him as far as possible, and as if by general agreement, the listeners dropped their gaze to their toes until all he could see was the tops of their heads. The speaker slowed, faltered, was reduced to silence, and then sat down. (Augsburger, 1992, p. 80)*

These people tend to approach conflict rather indirectly. They concentrate on the meaning that is "outside" the verbal message and tend to be very careful to protect the "face" of the person with whom they disagree. They may emphasize vagueness and ambiguity in language and often rely on third parties to help resolve disagreements. The goal in this approach is to make sure that the relationship stays intact during the disagreement. For example, they may emphasize the past history of the disputants and try to build a deeper relationship that involves increased obligation toward each other.

Emotional Expressiveness/Restraint Approaches   A second broad approach to conflict management concerns the role of emotion in conflict. People who value intense and overt displays of emotions during discussion of disagreement rely on the **emotionally expressive approach.** They think it is better to show emotion during disagreement than to hide or suppress feelings; that is, they show emotion through expressive nonverbal behavior and vocalization. They also think that this outward display of emotions means that one really cares and is committed to resolving the conflict. In fact, one's credibility is based on the ability to be expressive.

On the other hand, people who believe in the **restraint approach** think that disagreements are best discussed in an emotionally calm manner. For these people, it's important to control and internalize one's feelings during conflict and to avoid nonverbal emotion. They are uncomfortable with emotional expression and think that such expressions may hurt others. People who use this approach think that relationships are made stronger by keeping one's emotions in check and protecting the "face" or honor of the other person. Credibility is demonstrated by maintaining tight control over one's emotions.

These two approaches to conflict resolution reflect different underlying cultural values involving identity and preserving self-esteem and "face." In the more individualistic approach that sees conflict as good, the concern is with individuals preserving their own dignity. The more communal approach espoused by both Amish and Asian cultures and by many other collectivist groups is more concerned with maintaining harmony in interpersonal relations and preserving the dignity of others. For example, in classic Chinese thought, social harmony is the goal of human society at all levels—individual, family, village, and nation (Oetzel, Arcos, Mabizela, Weinman, & Zhang, 2006).

It is possible to combine these approaches and come up with four different conflict resolution styles that seem to be connected to various cultural groups: the discussion style, the engagement style, the accommodating style, and the dynamic style (Hammer, 2005).

The **discussion style** combines the direct and emotionally restrained approaches and emphasizes a verbally direct approach for dealing with disagreements—to "say what you mean and mean what you say." People who use this style are comfortable expressing disagreements directly but prefer to be emotionally restrained. This style is often identified as the predominant style preferred by many white Americans, as well as by Europeans, Australians, and New Zealanders

The **engagement style** emphasizes a verbally direct and confrontational approach to dealing with conflict. This style views intense verbal and nonverbal expression of emotion as demonstrating sincerity and willingness to engage intensely to resolve conflict. It has been linked to some African Americans and southern Europeans (France, Greece, Italy, Spain), as well as to some people from Russia and the Middle East (Israel). This approach is captured in the Russian proverb, "After a storm, fair weather; after sorrow, joy."

The **accommodating style** emphasizes an indirect approach for dealing with conflict and a more emotionally restrained manner. People who use this style may be ambiguous and indirect in expressing their views, thinking that this is a way to ensure that the conflict "doesn't get out of control." This style is often preferred by American Indians, Latin Americans (Mexicans, Costa Ricans), and Asians. This style may best be expressed by the Swahili proverb, "Silence produces peace, and peace produces safety," or by the Chinese proverb, "The first to raise their voice loses the argument." In this style, silence and avoidance may be used to manage

---

emotionally expressive approach A view that the best way to deal with conflict is by overt displays of feeling.

restraint approach A view that the best way to deal with conflict is by hiding or suppressing feelings and emotion.

discussion style combines the direct and emotional restrained approaches to conflict.

engagement style combines the direct and emotional expressive approaches to conflict.

accommodating style combines the indrect and emotional restrained manner.

conflict. For example, the Amish would prefer to lose face or money rather than escalate a conflict, and Amish children are instructed to turn the other cheek in any conflict situation, even if it means getting beat up by the neighborhood bully.

Individuals from these groups also use **intermediaries**—friends or colleagues who act on their behalf in dealing with conflict. For example, a Taiwanese student at a U.S. university was offended by the People's Republic of China flag that her roommate displayed in their room. The Taiwanese student went to the international student advisor and asked him to talk to the U.S. American student about the flag. People who think that interpersonal conflict provides opportunities to strengthen relationships also use **mediation**, but mainly in formal settings (lawyers, real estate agents, therapists), which we will discuss later in the chapter. It is often difficult for people who are taught to use the discussion or engaging style to see the value in the accommodating style or in nonviolent approaches. They see indirectness and avoidance as a sign of weakness. However, millions of people view conflict as primarily "dysfunctional, interpersonally embarrassing, distressing and as a forum for potential humiliation and loss of face" (Kim, 2002, p. 63). With this view of conflict, it makes much more sense to avoid direct confrontation and work toward saving face for the other person.

The **dynamic style** uses an indirect style of communicating along with a more emotionally intense expressiveness. People who use this style may use strong language, stories, metaphors, and third-party intermediaries. They are comfortable with more emotionally confrontational talk and view credibility of the other person grounded in their degree of emotional expressiveness. This style may be preferred by Arabs in the Middle East.

Cautions About Stereotyping   As with any generalization, however, it must be remembered that all conflict resolution styles can be found in any one cultural group, and while cultural groups tend to prefer one style over another, we must be careful not to stereotype. Also, these cultural differences may depend on a number of factors, including (1) whether regions have been historically homogeneous and isolated from other cultures, (2) the influence of colonization, and (3) the immigration history of different cultural groups. For example, there is much more African influence in the Caribbean (compared to Central and Latin America), resulting in a more direct and emotionally expressive approach (engagement style) than in Mexico—where people maintain a more indirect and emotionally restrained approach (accommodation style). And there is great variety within the cultures on the African continent, accounting for tremendous variation in conflict resolution styles (Hammer, 2005).

It is also important to recognize that people deal with conflict in a variety of ways for a variety of reasons. Conflict specialists William Wilmot and Joyce Hocker (2010) warn that we should not think of preferred styles as static and set in stone. Rather, they suggest that purely individual styles really do not exist because we are each influenced by others in interaction. Therefore, our conflict management styles are not static across settings and relationships (see the Student Voices box on the next page). For example, people may use a discussion style at work and accommodating style at home, or they may use an accommodating style at work and an engagement style at home. And they may use different styles with different partners. For instance, with co-workers, individuals may tend to collaborate and work through conflict issues in a more direct way; with the boss, they may

intermediary In a formal setting, a professional third party, such as a lawyer, real estate agent, or counselor, who intervenes when two parties are in conflict. Informal intermediaries may be friends or colleagues who intervene.

mediation The act of resolving conflict by having someone intervene between two parties.

dynamic style combines the indirect and emotional expressive approaches to conflict.

When I was back home in Singapore, my parents never really taught me about how to deal with conflict. I was never encouraged to voice my opinions, and, I guess because I'm a girl, sometimes my opinions are not highly valued. I think society also taught me to maintain harmony and peace, and that meant avoiding conflict. I practiced silence and had to learn quietly to accept the way things are at school and especially at work.

When I first came to the United States, I tried to be more vocal and to say what was on my mind. But even then I would restrain myself to a point where I couldn't help it any longer, and then I would try to come across as tactfully as possible. I used to think about when I was back in Singapore, when I dealt with conflict in such a way: If I could not remove the situation, then I would remove myself from the situation. But now, after learning to be more independent, more vocal, and more sure of myself, I know that I can remain in the situation and perhaps try to resolve some if not all of it.
—Jacqueline

tend to employ more accommodating strategies. In addition, our styles often change over the course of a conflict and over the life span. For example, individuals who tend to avoid and accommodate may learn the benefits of engaging and working through conflicts.

Gender, Ethnicity, and Conflict Styles

Our gender and ethnicity may influence how we handle conflict. Some research shows that men and women do tend to behave in stereotypical ways in some contexts: Men using a more engagement conflict style, whereas women use a more accommodating style (Brewer, Mitchell, & Weber, 2002; Cai & Fink, 2002; Davis, Capobianco, & Kraus, 2010). This may reflect the fact that in many cultures, women are socialized to focus on relationships and to be more accommodating and indirect in their interaction, while men are socialized to be more competitive. However, it may be that these gender behaviors are context-specific. Some research shows that the pattern may be reversed in heterosexual, romantic relationships—women tend to engage in more negative (competitive) conflict strategies, and men tend to avoid conflict with their romantic partners (Messman & Mikesell, 2000).

Ethnicity may also influence conflict style. At least one study showed that Asian and Latino Americans tended to use accommodating and third-party conflict styles more than African Americans and that Asian Americans also tended to use more accommodating conflict tactics than European Americans (Ting-Toomey et al., 2000).

The relationship among ethnicity, gender, and conflict management is even more complex. In their study of African American and European American women's views on workplace conflict, communication scholars Lynn Turner and Robert Shuter (2004) found that African American women viewed workplace conflict more negatively, more passively, and with less optimism about a positive resolution than European American women.

At my work, I have learned to be somewhat of a "chameleon" in adapting to different cultural styles of conflict. I supervise a number of workers, a mixture of collectivists and individualists—some from Mexico, Mexican Americans, and white U.S. Americans. I have learned to play to each person's cultural style, soften them up for my suggestions on how to solve the conflict. With the collectivists, people from Mexico, it takes a little time for them to open up to me. I have to build a relationship before they start to resolve the conflict. Since I've figured this out, they have been more cooperative with me in dealing with conflict issues. With the individualists, they come right out and tell me what's wrong, but I still play to their emotional style and make them feel comfortable, calm them down so that we can move on with the resolution process.
—Mike

It is important to remember that, whereas ethnicity and gender may be related to ways of dealing with conflict, it is inappropriate (and inaccurate) to assume that any one person will behave in a particular way because of his or her ethnicity or gender.

INTERPRETIVE AND CRITICAL APPROACHES TO SOCIAL CONFLICT

Both the interpretive and critical approaches tend to emphasize the social, cultural, and historical aspects of conflict. In these perspectives, conflict is far more complex than the ways that interpersonal conflict is enacted. It is deeply rooted in cultural differences in these contexts. Further, a dialectical perspective requires a more complex consideration of types and contexts of conflict.

Social conflict arises from unequal or unjust social relationships. Consider, for example, the recent uprisings of immigrant youths in Europe. In 2005, 2007, and again in 2012, rioting of young people erupted in Paris, cars were torched, and buildings burned (Le Paris flambé, 2007; Fellag, 2014). In the summer of 2011 and again in 2016, young people in London, England rioted with widespread looting and destruction to property (Armored police, 2016; Beckford, Hughes, Gardham, & Whitehead, 2011). How do we understand this conflict? A social science approach may view the conflicts as stemming from cultural differences (generational, ethnic, racial, religious), and these differences certainly play a role.

For example, some experts say it's just hooliganism pure and simple: young undisciplined looters lashing out against society. And some point out the religious element, describing the conflict as rooted in Islamic discontent with the West, particularly in France, because many of the rioters come from Islamic backgrounds. And in both France and England, many of the rioters were ethnic and racial minorities. However, the interpretive and critical perspectives suggest that we look beyond cultural differences to economic, political, and historical contexts and underscore the point that disputes are often more complicated than they first appear. We can invoke the various dialectics to illuminate the complexity of this conflict.

> *I used to work part-time in a restaurant. One time, a large group of German tourists visited the restaurant and had a long leisurely meal. When I gave them the bill, they protested, thinking I had added a 15% tip to the bill because they were tourists, not realizing that it was company policy when serving large groups. Even though I was pretty angry, I was much more accommodating when dealing with this group in the restaurant (maybe because they were foreigners) than I would have been in a more social context. I thought the tourists were rude, but I tried to practice good listening skills and took more of a problem-solving approach than I would have otherwise.*
> —Nikki

The rioting in both England and France started with those economically marginalized in society (i.e., the common denominator in both countries): the perpetrators come from poor neighborhoods. Sociologist Nora Fellag (2014) suggests that the riots, more than anything, revealed "the ongoing isolation and alienation of minorities who continue to be excluded from the resources that necessarily lead to greater equality and integration into larger society [. . .], clustered in the banlieues (suburbs) of big cities with poor housing, limited job opportunities and underfunded, overcrowded and academically inferior schools, remain largely marginalized and have great difficulty achieving upward mobility" (pp. 3–4).

In addition to economic marginalization, many ethnic and racial minorities feel excluded from French and English society. Unlike the United States and Canada, where there is an expression (not always realized) that anyone can become American or Canadian, immigrants in France, particularly of African heritage, can never really become French; they remain forever on the societal periphery.

Fellag (2014) argues that the problem lies in the French constructing the North Africans always with a religious "Muslim" label, "the tendency of policy-makers and citizens to rhetorically and systematically categorize French Magrehibis [citizens from North Africa] as 'Muslims'—a title not without real consequences. . . . Paradoxically, 'native' Algerians of Jewish backgrounds were granted full French citizenship upon Algerian independence, but not those of Islamic origin" (pp. 7–8). While immigrants in the United States have generally more easily assimilated into the larger U.S. society, tensions between communities of color and police and anti-immigrant attitudes, particularly directed at Muslims, have led some to question our ability to realize a peaceful multicultural society.

For these reasons, the rioting points to deep social and cultural conflict. In England and France, officials had warned of tensions in many neighborhoods; as long as these cultural groups remain marginalized, alienated, and largely unemployed, these cultural conflicts are likely to continue.

Some believe this kind of violence is one of the few ways that society can be provoked into interrogating social inequities and begin the long process of changing any society. There are no easy solutions to these conflicts. In England and France, there have been some attempts to change the economic and cultural conditions underlying the social conflict, including renovating neglected neighborhoods and trying to connect with local Muslim leaders. U.S. Federal Bureau of Investigation (FBI) agents are also engaging with community and religious leaders (imams) in U.S. Muslim neighborhoods like Dearborn, Michigan—to decrease chances of disaffected youth from becoming radicalized and to send messages of acceptance and inclusion (Hirsch, 2016). However, there are other forces at work. After several terrorist attacks in 2015, the French government extended emergency powers, outlawed any public demonstrations, made more than a thousand raids, detained many people, and are even surveilling many Muslims who are not terrorists. Likewise, some in the United States are calling for restricting the civil liberties of U.S. Muslims (e.g., tracking, surveillance; Chan, 2015). The point here is that there is no reason to seek a single source for conflict. In a sense, then, the economic contexts, the cultural identities and belongingness, and the political and religious contexts all work together to shape these conflicts. By taking a dialectical approach to thinking about these riots, you can see how these various forces—economic, social, political, religious—may all play different roles simultaneously.

Social Movements

Some conflict may be motivated by a desire to bring about social change. In **social movements**, individuals work together to bring about social change. They often use confrontation as a strategy to highlight the injustices of the present system. So, for example, when African American students in Greensboro, North Carolina, sat down at white-only lunch counters in the 1960s, they were pointing out the injustices of segregation. Although the students were nonviolent, their actions drew a violent reaction that, for many people, legitimized the claims of injustice. The women's suffrage movement of the early 20th century is another example of a social movement, a mass effort to win women the right to vote in the United States. Many similar contemporary social movements give meaning to conflicts. These include movements against racism, sexism, and homophobia and movements in support of animal rights, the environment, free speech, and civil rights.

social movements
Organized activities in which individuals work together to bring about social change.

College campuses are likely locations for much activism, and a 2016 survey of college students found that 8.5% of all students (and 16% of black students) said there was a "very good chance" they would participate in a protest while in college. These numbers were the highest ever recorded since the survey began in 1967 and the report goes on to say that in more than 50 schools, "student protesters made demands to right what they see as historic wrongs—demands for greater faculty diversity, new courses, public apologies, administrators' oustings." The tactics included hunger strikes, boycotts, walkouts, marches, occupying administrative offices, as well as social media strategies. Much of the protests focused on racist incidents including fraternity parties where members are invited to dress up and "go back to da hood," offensive statues (and building names) on campus honoring 19th century white supremacists and pro-slavery graduates/benefactors (Dickey, 2015; Spinella, 2016).

Many interpersonal conflicts arise and must be understood against the backdrop of large-scale social movements designed to change contemporary society. For example, Jacqueline, from Singapore, is annoyed by U.S. Americans who comment on how well she speaks English because English is her first language even though she is ethnically Chinese. She used to say nothing in response; now sometimes she retorts, "So is yours," reflecting her struggle against the stereotype that Asians cannot speak English.

In this context, the social movement against racism gives meaning to the conflict that arises for Jacqueline.

There is, of course, no comprehensive list of existing social movements. They arise and dissipate, depending on the opposition they provoke, the attention they attract, and the strategies they use. As part of social change, social movements need confrontation to highlight the perceived injustice.

Confrontation, then, can be seen as an opportunity for social change. In arguing for a change, Dr. Martin Luther King, Jr. (1984) emphasized the importance of nonviolent confrontation:

> *Nonviolent resistance is not a method for cowards; it does resist. . . . [It] does not seek to defeat or humiliate the opponent, but to win his friendship and understanding. The nonviolent resister must often express his protest through noncooperation or boycotts, but he realizes that these are not ends themselves; they are merely means to awaken a sense of moral shame in the opponent. (pp. 108–109)*

Although nonviolence is not the only form of confrontation employed by social movements, its use has a long history—from Mahatma Gandhi's struggle for India's independence from Britain, to the civil rights struggle in the United States, including Black Lives Matter, to the struggle against apartheid in South Africa. In each case, images of violent responses to nonviolent protesters tended to legitimize the social movements and delegitimize the existing social system. For example, in the resistance to apartheid in South Africa, when the government reacted with brutal force to strikes and boycotts, this led to condemnation and economic punishment by the international community. "Nonviolent power did not by itself bring down the curtain on white rule, but it discredited the regime's authority" (Ackerman & Duvall, 2000, p. 367). More recently, some images of police in military gear confronting peaceful protestors in Ferguson, Missouri and Baton Rouge, reacting against police killings of black men, were also powerful (see Figure 11-2).

Some social movements have also used violent forms of confrontation. Groups such as Action Directe in France, the Irish Republican Army, Earth First, and independence movements in Corsica, Algeria, Kosovo, and Chechnya have all been accused of using violence. As a result, they tend to be labeled as terrorists rather than mere protesters. Even the suggestion of violence can be threatening to the public. For example, in 1964, Malcolm X (1984) spoke in favor of civil rights: "The question tonight, as I understand it, is 'The Negro Revolt and Where Do We Go From Here?' or 'What Next?' In my little humble way of understanding it, it points toward either the ballot or the bullet" (p. 126). Malcolm X's rhetoric terrified many U.S. Americans, who then refused to give legitimacy to his movement. To understand communication practices such as these, it is important to study their social contexts. Social movements highlight many issues relevant to intercultural interaction.

Historical and Political Contexts

Most of us recall the childhood saying "Sticks and stones may break my bones, but words will never hurt me." In fact, we know that derogatory words can be a powerful source of conflict. The force that many derogatory words carry comes from their historical usage

FIGURE 11-2   Young woman confronts highly armed police in nonviolent protest against police killings of black men in Baton Rouge, Louisiana. (© *AP Photo/Max Becherer*)

and the history of oppression to which they refer. As we noted in Chapter 4, much of our identity comes from history. It is only through understanding the past that we can understand what it means to be members of particular cultural groups. For example, understanding the history of Ireland helps give meaning to Irish American identity.

In Kyrgyzstan, a nation in Central Asia, conflicts between the Uzbeks and the Kyrgyz (two different ethnic groups) broke out in 2010. These ethnic conflicts took place in Osh, which is a part of the fertile Fergana Valley, near the Uzbekistan border. Ethnic clashes are not new to this area, but "the clashes are the worst ethnic violence to hit southern Kyrgyzstan since 1990, when several hundred people were killed. Kyrgyzstan was then part of the Soviet Union, which sent in troops to quell the unrest" (Demytrie, 2010).

The historical context is an important part of understanding this conflict. The Fergana Valley is inhabited primarily by Uzbeks, Krygyz, and Tajiks. This fertile valley has been culturally diverse for thousands of years and has seen the influx of peoples from Europe and Asia. More recently, under the Soviet Union, the valley was divided by the establishment of three Soviet Socialist Republics: Uzbekistan, Tajikistan, and Krygyzstan, whose borders split the valley but did not follow along the lines where the ethnic groups lived. Once the Soviet Union collapsed, and the republics became independent, the ethnic composition of these new nations became more significant. Because of this history, "the valley remains an ethnic patchwork, and minority enclaves, like that of the Uzbeks in Osh, have been scenes for violence" (Schwirtz, 2010).

So the violence that broke out between the two ethnic groups in 2010 was embedded in a long history of tensions between these ethnic groups—tensions that go back hundreds of years, but which have been exacerbated by creating national borders and independent nations that put various ethnic groups together in imbalanced ways. The thousands of refugees and the many people who died in the conflict create a new history that will be difficult to easily overcome in the future. Indeed, some observers believe that there is an even larger political context that prevents a more responsible government from arising in Kyrgyzstan: "outside powers, particularly Russia and China, who covet the region's extensive natural resources of natural gas and hydro power, and the United States, with its base in Kyrgyzstan, show little interest in fostering more responsible rule" (Tran, 2010).

These dynamics are at work all around the world. Historical antagonisms become part of cultural identities and practices that place people in positions of conflict. Whether in the Middle East, Northern Ireland, Rwanda, Uganda, Nigeria, Sri Lanka, East Timor, Kosovo, or Chechnya, these historical antagonisms lead to various forms of conflict. (See Figure 11-3.)

FIGURE 11-3 Elderly Kyrgyz man casts his ballot at polling station in the capital Bishkek in October 2011. Krygyzstan held presidential elections that the West had urged should be free and fair to add legitimacy to a new leadership installed after a "People's Revolution" in March. (© *Vyacheslav Oseledko/AFP/Getty Images*)

When people witness conflict, they often assume that it is caused by personal issues between individuals. By reducing conflict to the level of interpersonal interaction, we lose sight of the larger social and political forces that contextualize these conflicts. People are in conflict for reasons that extend far beyond personal communication styles.

MANAGING INTERCULTURAL CONFLICT

Given all the variations in how people deal with conflict, and the historical, political elements of intercultural conflict, what are the strategies for effective conflict management/resolution? While there are no easy answers, this section provides some useful strategies for both individuals and groups. We first provide some strategies for dealing with interpersonal conflict and also outline characteristics of productive and destructive approaches to conflicts for both individuals and groups (see the Point of View box on page 462). In the final part of the chapter, we describe additional strategies for dealing with difficult conflicts: Mediation and Peacebuilding.

Dealing with Interpersonal Conflict

In searching for effective strategies for dealing with interpersonal conflict, we can apply the principles of dialectics; sometimes, we may need to step back and show self-restraint. Occasionally, though, it may be more appropriate to assert ourselves and not be afraid of strong emotion. Here, we offer seven suggestions for dealing with interpersonal conflict:

1. Stay centered and do not polarize.
2. Maintain contact.
3. Recognize the existence of different styles.
4. Identify your preferred style.
5. Be creative and expand your style repertoire.
6. Recognize the importance of conflict context.
7. Be willing to forgive.

Let's look at these guidelines in more detail.

Stay Centered and Do Not Polarize   It's important to move beyond traditional stereotypes and either-or thinking. Try not to view other's motives as simple and antagonistic and your own as complex and reasonable. Try to be open to a third alternative perspective that might bring you to a mutually acceptable solution.

The parties involved must practice self-restraint. It's okay to get angry, but it's important to move past the anger and to refrain from acting out feelings. For example, Jenni and her co-worker both practiced self-restraint and stayed centered in a recent disagreement about religion. Jenni explains,

> *My friend is a devout Catholic, and I am a devout Mormon. She asked me about where we get some of our doctrine and how it relates to the Bible. We never*

One way to think about conflict across cultures is in terms of what is more or less successful—conflict management or resolution. Scholar David Augsburger suggests that productive conflict is different from destructive conflict in the following ways. Can you think of times when you have experienced productive or destructive intercultural conflict?

In Productive Conflict, Individuals or Groups

- Narrow conflict to specifics, in terms of definition, scope, and issues involved in conflict
- Limit conflict to original issue
- Trust leadership that stresses mutually satisfactory outcomes
- Promote cooperative processes: perceived similarity, trust, flexibility, open communication

In Destructive Conflict, Individuals or Groups

- Escalate and broaden conflict from the original problem, bringing in unrelated issues
- Polarize around leadership that is single-minded and militant
- Encourage competitive atmosphere: coercion, deception, suspicion, and rigidity

We should note that longstanding conflict situations—where there is a history of violence and extensive grievances on both sides—call for more complex strategies (e.g., mediation, peacebuilding) discussed later in the chapter.

Source: From D. Augsburger, *Mediation across cultures* (Louisville, KY: Westminster/John Knox press, 1992).

---

really solved our differences, but compromised and "agreed to disagree." This was necessary to keep our friendship and respect as co-workers. I felt bad that she couldn't see the points I was coming from. I do think it turned out for the best, though, because we don't feel tension around each other.

Maintain Contact This does not mean that the parties have to stay in the conflict situation—sometimes it's necessary to step away for a while. However, the parties should not cut off the relationship. Rather, they should attempt a dialogue rather than isolate themselves from each other or engage in fighting. **Dialogue** differs from conversation in that it assumes the transformative power of speaking and being understood; it involves listening and speaking, not to persuade, but to clarify—even to clarify and truly understand an opposing viewpoint. Quality dialogue is attentive, careful, and full of feeling (Wilmot & Hocker, 2010).

Dialogue is possible only between two persons or two groups whose power relationship is more or less in balance. Dialogue offers an important opportunity to come to a richer understanding of intercultural conflicts and experiences.

dialogue Conversation that is slow, careful, full of feeling, respectful, and attentive.

id you know that the third Thursday of October is Conflict Resolution Day? In many conflicts, mediation can be helpful in reaching a solution or compromise. This is an international celebration organized by the Association for Conflict Resolution.

Reproduced with permission from the Association for Conflict Resolution (ACR). www.ACRnet.org.

Our student Cameron experienced an intercultural conflict in an accounting class in which his maintaining contact paid off. He was placed in a group with three Japanese students who were all friends. He recalls:

Right from the beginning things were quite awkward; their mathematics abilities far exceeded mine. After only two days, they had met twice without me and completed part of the assignment. I had been left out of the decision-making process.

Rather than avoiding the problem, however, he decided to invite them all over to his house to talk about the project. Everyone was able to loosen up and discuss what had gone wrong, and the conflict was handled productively: "Although I was unhappy with the way things went during the earlier parts of the project, the end result was three new acquaintances and an A in accounting."

Recognize the Existence of Different Styles   Conflict is often exacerbated because of the unwillingness of partners to recognize management style differences. The heart of the question is how to reconcile these different styles, particularly when dealing with difficult issues like interracial relations, gay and lesbian rights, abortion rights, and so on. One approach is to "maintain civility," stressing that when contentious issues arise, it's most productive to be polite, respectful, and maybe even avoid direct confrontation. As we've discussed earlier, this approach would be very accepted among many cultural groups. However, some Western scholars contend that this emphasis on civility actually constructs barriers to productive understanding and reinforces the very inequality and injustice it portends to address (Mayo, 2002; Mindell, 1995). Mayo says that civility works precisely because it maintains the distance it initially appears to bridge—and is not the way people build close relations. For example, if gay and lesbian students or other minority students complain about homophobia on campus, they may be seen being "uncivil"—making an issue of something that, in polite society, ought to be ignored. Mayo and others advocate a more direct, expressive style—suggesting that we should not be afraid of "incivility" and anger, rather it is in moments of listening to and giving space to angry voices that conflicts can be resolved and hurt feelings soothed (Mindell, 1995).

An example that illustrates these different styles occurred during a Diversity, Racism, and Community meeting in Compton, Los Angeles. There were many diverse community groups in attendance and the atmosphere was tense, when a middle age white man spoke confidently and gently about all the experience he had with multicultural groups and how he did not like anger. A young black man said he thought the white man didn't know what he was talking about. The white man ignored him and finally the black man stood up and spoke vehemently about his experiences of discrimination in the local community and his disappointments at not being listened to. The white man turned his body away, repeatedly saying he was open to anyone but refusing to talk to an "angry" person.

The multiracial facilitating team pointed out the contrasting assumptions underlying the behavior of the two men: different conflict styles and perceptions. The white man thinking that one needs to be calm to debate, the black man perceiving the white's man style (civility and calmness) as communicating a hidden message: don't upset me about issues that aren't mine. The engaging style demonstrated by the black man was that one can be emotional and rational in dealing with conflict, and, in fact, one *should* be emotional about topics one really cares about (Mindell, 1995).

This particular combination of differing but complementary styles often results in damaged relationships and frozen agendas—the rational/avoiding–emotional/confronting "dance." Other combinations may be problematic but less overtly damaging. For example, two people with assertive emotional styles may understand each other and know how to work through the conflict. Likewise, things can work if both people avoid open conflict, particularly in long-term committed relationships (Pike & Sillars, 1985). Jointly avoiding conflict does not necessarily mean that it goes away, but it may give people time to think about how to deal with the conflict and talk about it.

Identify Your Preferred Style   Although people may change their way of dealing with conflict based on the situation and the type of conflict, most tend to use the same style in most situations. For example, Tom and Judith both prefer an avoiding style. If we are pushed into conflict or feel strongly that we need to resolve a particular issue, we can speak up for ourselves or for others. However, we both prefer more indirect means of dealing with current and potential conflicts. We often choose to work things out on a more personal, indirect level.

It is also important to recognize which conflict styles "push your conflict button." Some styles are more or less compatible; it's important to know which styles are congruent with your own. If you prefer a more confronting style and you have a disagreement with someone like Tom or Judith, it may drive you crazy.

Be Creative and Expand Your Style Repertoire   If a particular way of dealing with conflict is not working, be willing to try a different style. Of course, this is easier said than done. As conflict specialists William Wilmot and Joyce Hocker (2010) explain, people often seem to get "frozen" into a conflict style. For example, some people consistently deny any problems in a relationship, whereas others consistently escalate small conflicts into large ones.

There are many reasons for getting stuck in a conflict management style, according to Wilmot and Hocker. The style may have developed during a time when the person felt good about himself or herself—when the particular conflict management style worked well. Consider, for example, the high school athlete who develops an aggressive style on and off the playing field, a style that people seem to respect. A limited repertoire may be related to gender differences. Some women get stuck in an avoiding style, whereas some men get stuck in a confronting style. A limited repertoire also may come from cultural background—a culture that encourages confronting conflict or a culture (like Judith's and Tom's) that rewards avoiding conflict. A combination of these reasons is the likely cause of getting stuck in the use of one conflict management style. For example, even though Tom and Judith prefer an avoiding style, we have occasionally found it effective to be more assertive and direct in intercultural conflicts in which the dominant communication style was more confrontational.

In most aspects of intercultural communication, adaptability and flexibility serve us well—and conflict communication is no exception. This means that there is no so-called objective way to deal with conflict. Many times, as in other aspects of relationships, it's best simply to listen and not say anything. One strategy that mediators use is to allow one person to talk for an extended time while the other person listens.

Recognize the Importance of Conflict Context   As noted earlier in this chapter, it is important to understand the larger social, economic, political, and historical contexts that give meaning to many types of conflict. Conflict arises for many reasons, and it is misleading to think that all conflict can be understood within the interpersonal context alone.

For example, when one student, George, went home for a family reunion, everyone seemed to be talking about their romantic relationships, spouses, children, and so on. When George, who is gay, talked about his own partner, George's uncle asked why gay people had to flaunt their lifestyle. George reacted angrily. The conflict was not simply between George and his uncle; it rests in the social context that accepts straight people talking frequently and openly about their relationships but that does not validate the same discussion of romantic relationships from gay people. The same talk is interpreted differently because of the social context.

People often act in ways that cause conflict. However, it is important to let the context explain the behavior as much as possible. Otherwise, the behavior may not make sense. Once you understand the contexts that frame the conflict, whether cultural, social, historical, or political, you will be in a better position to understand and conceive of the possibilities for resolution. For example, Savina, who is white, was shopping with her friend Lashieki. The employee at the cash register referred to someone as "that black girl," and Lashieki, who is African American, demanded, "Why did they have to refer to her as that black girl?" Lashieki's response can only be understood by knowing something about the context of majority–minority relations in the United States. That is, whites are rarely referred to by color, whereas people of color are often defined solely on the basis of race.

Be Willing to Forgive A final suggestion for facilitating conflict is to consider forgiveness. This means letting go of—not forgetting—feelings of revenge.

Teaching forgiveness between estranged individuals is as old as recorded history; it is present in every culture and is part of the human condition. In fact, recent research suggests that both revenge and forgiveness are instinctual and universal among humans and both have developed as adaptive mechanisms in human evolution (McCullough, 2008).

At the same time, forgiveness is also a basic human instinct that has also served humans well. And it is not always bad to retaliate when someone has done us a great wrong . . . but not helpful to hold a grudge forever. At a very fundamental level, forgiveness ensures that we get along with both family and close friends and helps establish and maintain cooperative relationships with nonrelatives, and, overall, forgiveness is the best strategy for human beings in the long term—it can deliver freedom from fear and freedom to resume normal, peaceful relations. In fact, it is in our self-interest to forgive. Psychologists point out that blaming others and feeling resentment lead to a victim mentality and may actually lead to stress, burnout, and physical problems. Forgiveness, on the other hand, can lead to improved physical health (Waldron & Kelley, 2008).

As cooperation on a group level evolve, revenge and forgiveness are not on opposite sides, they are on the same team. You can't be easy-going all the time, you can't be vengeful and spiteful all of the time. . . . "In social dilemmas that pit the short-term gains of selfishness against the long-term gains of cooperation, evolution favors the organism that can be vengeful when necessary, that can forgive when necessary, and that has the wisdom to know the difference" (p. 87).

There are several models of forgiveness—most include an acknowledgement of feelings of hurt and anger and a need for healing (Zhang, Ting-Toomey, Oetzel, &

Zhang, 2015). Communication scholars Vince Waldron and Doug Kelley (2008) propose a dialectical approach to forgiveness, particularly applicable because forgiveness is a complex process, often with many contradictions. They identify four dialectical tensions: (1) remembering versus forgetting (it may be good to forget the transgression while, at the same time in some relationships, it may be productive to remember so as not to get involved in repeat of conflict), (2) heart versus mind (tension between strong emotional response to conflict and sometimes needing to engage a more intellectual, cognitive approach to forgiveness), (3) trust versus risk (forgiveness is sometimes a process of rebuilding trust and reducing future relational risk; and (4) mercy versus justice (perhaps the most fundamental dialectic; trying to let go of hostile feelings, extending mercy to the transgressor and, at the same time, a letting go of a desire for revenge and retribution).

In a dialectical forgiveness loop, forgiveness is seen as socially constructed and based in communication. If someone is in a stressed relationship, he or she can create actions and behaviors that make forgiveness seem real, balancing these dialectical tensions; then he or she can communicate this to the other person, enabling the relationship to move forward. It is easier to forgive when one can see the offender as someone who is careworthy, valuable and safe and when the vengeful impulse has been satisfied to some degree, perhaps knowing that an offender has been punished. So an important part of apologizing and asking for forgiveness may be making compensation, ensuring some measure of restorative justice.

The importance of compensation in preventing violent revenge and encouraging forgiveness can't be overstated. Cross-cultural studies of premodern cultures found that many had developed compensation strategies and forgiveness rituals for quelling revenge, which often included accepting "blood money" as an alternative to killing a murderer or one of his or her relatives, as well as compensations and gift exchanges (McCullough, 2008). Restorative justice conferences as part of the forgiveness process can play an important role in the criminal justice system. They are extremely effective at reducing the desire for revenge and fostering forgiveness and "give people the chance to process the traumatic experience and talk to their offenders in a safe nonthreatening way" (McCullough, 2008, p. 177). "The restorative justice movement is another great example of an institution that brings out people's best selves in the aftermath of conflict and violence . . . it works because it enables people to use their evolved moral intuitions to address the pain of crime in the mega-societies in which most of us live . . ." (pp. 179–180).

Civil wars that end in forgiveness and reconciliation have four processes: redefine affected people's identities, implement countless small actions, process of public "truth," justice short of revenge (legal consequences, amnesty, reparations) (McCullough, 2008). An example of forgiveness on a national level involves the National Sorry Day and the Journey of Healing, which serve to acknowledge and apologize for the wretched treatment of Aboriginals by non-Aboriginal Australians. Another example is the Truth and Reconciliation Commission in South Africa, formed to investigate and facilitate the healing of racial wounds as a result of apartheid. The committee hears stories of the atrocities that were committed, but the ultimate goal is forgiveness, not revenge (see the Point of View box on page 469). So how do we escape the historical, political, and social forces that entrap us in conflict and work

FIGURE II-4   The Garden of Remembrance in Freedom Park, South Africa provides an opportunity to reflect on the past, but more importantly, to see possibilities for a better future. (© *Jeremy Jowell/Moonshine Media/Africa Media Online/The Image Works*)

toward a more peaceful society and world? Earlier in the chapter, we outlined some strategies for dealing with interpersonal conflict. Let's now turn our attention to several other responses to conflict situations.

Mediation

Sometimes two individuals or groups cannot work through conflict on their own. They may request an intermediary, or one may be assigned to intervene (Donohue, 2006). In some societies, these third parties may be rather informal. In Western societies, though, they tend to be built into the legal and judicial system. For example, lawyers or counselors may act as mediators to settle community or family disputes.

Contemporary Western mediation models often ignore cultural variations in conflict processes. Fortunately, more scholars and mediators are looking at other cultural models that may work better in intercultural conflicts. Augsburger (1992) suggests that the culturally sensitive mediator engages in conflict transformation (not conflict resolution or conflict management). The conflict transformer assists disputants to think in new ways about the conflict—for example, to transform attitudes by redirecting negative perceptions. This requires a commitment by both parties to treat each other with goodwill and mutual respect. Of course, this is often much easier said than done. Behavior can be transformed by limiting all action to collaborative behavior; this can break the negative cycle but requires a commitment to seek a noncoercive process of negotiation even when there has been intense provocation. For example, in the recent Northern Ireland agreement, orgiveness is often complicated, as we can see two cases outlined below. The first example illustrates the difficulty of individual forgiveness, the second is an example of a national attempt at forgiveness and healing.

Raymond Douglas was brutally raped as a youth by a parish priest. The priest was never brought to justice and still lives free of any legal consequence. Douglas thinks that in order for forgiveness to be effective, it requires the full and active participation of the person to be forgiven, in the form of repentance:

> *"Without that essential component, the extending of premature forgiveness is not just futile but positively harmful to the perpetrator . . . an invitation to go on offending rather than doing the necessary work of restitution. . . . and self-rehabilitation. The only forgiveness I am able to offer without his partici-pation is in the original narrow sense of the word, the voluntary giving-up of the right to collect on a debt owed. I renounce any claim of revenge. I do not want him to experience harm as I was harmed, now or in the future. . . . but I do not have the power to restore to him the quality of full humanity from which he has voluntarily and disastrously cut himself off by his action; he alone does. To gain true forgiveness, he needs true repentance." (pp. 98–99)*

A plaque at the new Freedom Park in Pretoria, South Africa titled "Willingness to Forgive" describes the goal of the Truth and Reconciliation Committee (TRC) but also reveals a realistic acknowledgment of its limitations:

> *"The hope was that in uncovering the layers of truth about our brutal past the country should share the pain of the victims and a sense of a common history would be created. Many victims in their willingness to forgive their perpetrators were able to reclaim their dignity and say, this is what it means to be human. But there were others who were strongly opposed to the perpetrators receiving amnesty, some of whom were dissatisfied with the reparations they received and many who did not have the opportunity to give testimony of the TRC and continue to feel betrayed. Although the TRC was a unique and necessary process that made perpetrators account-able for their actions, it could not have been expected to heal the deep wounds of the violent past alone."*

mediation resulted in commitment by most people to change the vision of Northern Ireland, in spite of horrendous provocation on the part of some extremists.

Traditional societies often use mediation models based on nondirect means. The models vary but share many characteristics. Although North American mediation tends to be more formal and structured, involving direct confrontation and commu-nication, most traditional cultural models are more communally based, with involve-ment by trusted leaders. Indirect communication is preferred in order to permit individuals to save face. In addition, the process is more dynamic, directed toward resolving tension in the community—the responsibility of the disputants to their larger community is central (Augsburger, 1992, p. 204).

onflict specialist David Augsburger identifies six key Western assumptions—conflict myths—and notes their inadequacies in intercultural settings.

1. *People and problems can be separated cleanly; interests and positions can be distinguished sharply.* In most cultures of the world, equal attention must be given to both person and problem, to relationship and goals and to private interests as well as public positions if a creative resolution is to be reached.

2. *Open self-disclosure is a positive value in negotiations. An open process of public data shared in candid style is assumed necessary for trust.* "Open covenants, openly arrived at," Woodrow Wilson insisted, as did Harry Truman, were the basis for setting up the United Nations. However, the real negotiation is done in corridors or behind closed doors, and is announced publicly when agreements have been reached. Virtually nothing of any substance is agreed on in the official public UN debates.

3. *Immediacy, directness, decisiveness, and haste are preferred strategies in timing.* The Western valuation that time is money can press the negotiator to come to terms prematurely. Many different cultures find that the best way to reach an agreement is to give the matter sufficient time to allow adjustments to be made, accommodations to emerge, and acceptance to evolve and emerge. Believing that "time is people," they are in less haste to reach closure.

4. *Language employed should be reasonable, rational, and responsible.* In some cultures, deprecative language, extreme accusations and vitriolic expressions are used as a negotiating power tactic.

5. *No is no and yes is yes (an affirmation is absolute, a negation final).* In some cultures, one does not say no to an offer; requests are not phrased to elicit negations; when an offer is affirmed, the real meanings are weighed and assessed carefully.

6. *When an agreement is reached, implementation will take care of itself as a logical consequence.* The agreements negotiated may mean different things to parties in a reconciliation. Built-in processes, ongoing negotiations, open channels for resolving problems as they arise in ongoing interpretation, and circumstances that would warrant renegotiation are all useful elements for ensuring ongoing success.

Source: From D. Augsburger, *Conflict Mediation Across Cultures* (Louisville, KY: Westminster/John Knox Press, 1992), pp. 206–208.

Augsburger provides the example of mediation in the Gitksan Nation, in northwest British Columbia, where mediation of disputes begins with placement of the problem "in the middle of the table." Everyone involved—including those in authority and the witnesses—must make suggestions in a peaceful manner until they come to a decision all can live with. Even conflicts ending in murder are resolved in this consensus-oriented fashion. For instance, "land would be transferred as compensation to help deal with the pain of the loss. The murderer might be required to give up his or her name and go nameless for a period to show respect for the life taken" (p. 213). Eventually, however, the land or anything else that was given up would be returned, "when the pain has passed and time has taken care of the grief" (p. 213). Augsburger points out that this traditional communal approach to mediation is based on collectivistic beliefs that make individualistic solutions to conflicts unacceptable.

Contemporary mediators have learned some lessons from the traditional non-Western models, and mediation is used increasingly in the United States and other countries to resolve conflicts. Mediation is advantageous because it relies on the disputing parties' active involvement in and commitment to the resolution. Also, it represents the work of all involved, so it's likely to be more creative and integrative. Finally, mediation is often cheaper than adversarial legal resolution (Wilmot & Hocker, 2010).

Peacebuilding

Some of the conflicts described in this chapter involve longstanding and violent intergroup conflicts that have lasted for decades, often between ethnic or religious groups within the same geographic area (e.g., Palestinians and Israelis, Sunni and Shia Muslims in Iraq and other countries, Hindus and Muslims in India, Serbs and Croats in former Yugoslavia, Greeks and Turks in Cyprus). These conflicts, where neighbors or sometimes members of the same family are on different sides of the conflict, are particularly horrific and have devastating psychological effects—often enduring for generations.

Experts stress that these types of longstanding "intractable" conflicts require special communication processes and a reframing of the problem and the enemy. For example, communication scholar Don Ellis (2015) suggests that, in "fierce entanglements" the other side should not be considered as an enemy that needs to be destroyed, but as an adversary that needs to be engaged. In addition, both sides need to reframe the problems such that solutions require interdependence and engagement in "reasonable and skilled disagreement" (p. xi). Thus, communication is essential and needs to take place at all levels, from informal intercultural community dialogue groups to high-level government negotiation and diplomacy (Broome & Collier, 2012; Oetzel, Dhar, & Kirschbaum, 2007).

After years of working with these types of conflicts, communication scholar Benjamin Broome has developed a particularly effective approach for improving these difficult situations—**facilitated intergroup dialogue** (Broome, 2004). As we described earlier, dialogue differs from conversation, in that it focuses on the *power* of speaking and being understood; it involves listening and speaking, not to persuade, but to clarify—with a goal of truly understanding an opposing viewpoint.

Intergroup dialogue is one of several strategies of **peacebuilding**, (working toward equilibrium and stability in a society so that new disputes do not escalate into violence and war). The idea behind the facilitated intergroup dialogue, and peacebuilding, is that government leaders alone cannot negotiate a true peace in these types of conflict. Rather, the general population and civic leaders must also be

facilitated intergroup dialogue A peace-bilding approach, involving civic leaders and general public, focused on listening and speaking, not to persuade but to clarify

peacebuilding Working toward equilibrium and stability in a society so that new disputes do not escalate into violence and war.

involved. Dr. Broome has conducted countless dialogue workshops and programs in the United States and all over the world—particularly on the small island of Cyprus where Cypriot Turks and Greeks have been in (often violent) conflict for years (Broome & Hatay, 2006; Broome, 2003).

The facilitated intergroup dialogue process usually begins with bringing together members from the two sides—persons, often community leaders, who are interested in working toward peace. Sometimes presentations are made by each party describing their view of the conflict. Then a three-phase systematic dialogue, an exchange of ideas and perceptions, is conducted—facilitated by an impartial third party expert, like Ben Broome. The first step involves analyzing the current situation that affects peacebuilding efforts, the second is building a collective vision for the future, and finally developing a specific action plan to achieve peaceful collaboration. Each phase is carefully facilitated with the goal that each side really listens to and tries to understand the opposing side's views. As you can image achieving a vision and plan that everyone agrees to in situations where both sides feel tremendously hurt and victimized by the other is not easy!

In spite of these challenges, Broome and others who use this peacebuilding approach have seen success in reducing intergroup conflict and note that it's very important for facilitators to acknowledge the power relations and relative privilege or lack thereof of each group and also the role of strong emotion in conflict situations (Collier & Broome, 2012).

INTERNET RESOURCES

http://www.icsinventory.com/
www.youtube.com/watch?v=s3-Zmj3sTt8&feature=related
The first link is to a website of a for-profit consulting firm, based on Dr. Mitch Hammer's work in intercultural conflict resolution. The website describes the research results and validation studies that led to the development of the Intercultural Conflict Styles inventory, as well as a list of relevant resources and also organizations that have used the program. The second link is a presentation about the conflict resolution program explained on the first website.

http://mediationchannel.com/
This is a great blog maintained by conflict mediation professional Diane Levin. The blog has interesting entries on new media items like *Cool Stuff on the Web, Self Awareness Tools,* and *Police Officer's Dilemma* (a video game that tests the effect of racial bias on decisions to shoot). Browse the website for a variety of mediation guides founded in good academic literature. There is even a section with advice in case you want to pursue a career in conflict mediation!

www.mideastweb.org/timeline.htm
The whole Mideast website contains valuable information about conflict and progress in the Middle East. However, this timeline is especially valuable in trying to understand the context of current conflicts. Information here details key

moments in the Arab-Israeli conflict from over 3,000 years ago to the present. Many of these events and issues form an invisible context for current conflicts and negotiations. It is worth considering what histories inform other cultural conflicts around the world.

www.usip.org/mediation/index.html
This is the website of the U.S. Institute of Peace. Its focus is on international policy. There are a lot of great resources on this site, including reviews of practitioners and detailed descriptions of the group's efforts in hotspots like Iraq and Haiti. Within the site, www.usip.org/library/ is an organized and useful compilation of resources for researchers.

SUMMARY

- Conflict is defined as involving a perceived or real incompatibility of goals, values, expectations, processes, or outcomes between two or more interdependent individuals or groups.

- Intercultural conflict may be characterized by ambiguity, language issues, and contradictory conflict management styles.

- The social science approach focuses on how cultural differences cause conflict and influence the management of the conflict, primarily on the interpersonal level.

- The five types of conflict are affective conflict, conflict of interest, value conflict, cognitive conflict, and goal conflict.

- There are four intercultural conflict styles—discussion, engagement, accommodating, and dynamic.

- The choice of conflict style may be impacted by cultural values, family influences, gender, and ethnicity.

- Interpretive and critical approaches to conflict emphasize intergroup and social conflict and emphasize contexts of conflict.

- Social movements are one approach to social change and often involve conflict or confrontation.

- Conflict can be productive or destructive.

- Some strategies for conflict resolution include staying centered, maintaining contact, recognizing the existence of different conflict management styles, identifying a preferred style, being creative and expanding one's conflict style repertoire, recognizing the importance of conflict context, and being willing to forgive.

- Transforming methods of mediation are commonly used in many cultures.

- Peacebuilding is a strategy of working toward equilibrium and stability in a society so that new disputes do not escalate into violence and war.

DISCUSSION QUESTIONS

1. How can a dialectical perspective be applied to intercultural conflict situations?

2. Why is it important to understand the context in which intercultural conflict occurs?

3. How are conflict strategies used in social movements?

4. How does an attitude of forgiveness facilitate conflict resolution?

5. What are some general suggestions for dealing with intercultural conflict?

ACTIVITIES

Cultures in Conflict. For this assignment, work in groups of four. As a group, select two countries or cultural groups that are currently in conflict or that have historically been in conflict. In your group, form two pairs. One pair will research the conflict from the perspective of one of the two cultural groups or countries; the other pair will research the conflict from the perspective of the other group or country. Use online and community resources (including interviews with members of the culture if possible). Outline the major issues and arguments. Explore the role of cultural values and political, economic, and historical contexts that may contribute to the conflict. Be prepared to present an oral or written report of your research.

KEY WORDS

accommodating style (452)	engagement style (452)	facilitated intergroup
conflict (443)	facework (447)	dialogue (471)
dialogue (462)	incompatibility (443)	mediation (453)
direct approach (451)	indirect approach (451)	pacifism (451)
discussion style (452)	intercultural	peacebuilding (471)
dynamic style (453)	conflict (443)	restraint approach (452)
emotionally expressive	interdependent (443)	social movements (457)
approach (452)	intermediary (453)	

REFERENCES

Ackerman, P. & Duvall, J. (2000). *A force more powerful: A century of nonviolent conflict.* London: Palgrave McMillan, p. 367.

al-Masri, A. (2015, March 14), Syria: Proxy war, not civil war. *middleeastmonitor.com.* Retrieved June 13, 2016, from https://www.middleeastmonitor.com/20150314 -syria-proxy-war-not-civil-war/

Armored police with dogs and helicopters reported quelling "riots" in London's Barking (2016, June 19). *rt.com.* Retrieved July 16, 2016, from https://www.rt.com/uk /347315-london-barking-riots-police-helicopter/.

Augsburger, D. (1992). *Conflict mediation across cultures.* Louisville, KY: Westminster/John Knox Press.

Balmforth, R. (2008, February 20). Seven under investigation for Paris suburb riots. *Reuters.* Retrieved, May 10, 2008, from www.reuters.com/article/worldNews /idUSL2077366820080220?pageNumber=1&virtual BrandChannel=0.

Beckford, M., Hughes, M., Gardham, D., & Whitehead, T. (2011, August 7). Tottenham riots: police let gangs run riot and loot. telegraph.co.uk. Retrieved November 25, 2016, from http://www.telegraph.co.uk/news/uknews /crime/8687540/Tottenham-riots-police-let-gangs-run -riot-and-loot.html

Berger, P. (2015, January 12). The American who inspires terror from Paris to the U.S, *cnn.com.* Retrieved June 13,

2016 from http://www.cnn.com/2015/01/11/opinion/bergen-american-terrorism-leader-paris-attack/index.html.

Brewer, N., Mitchell, P., & Weber, N. (2002). Gender role, organizational status, and conflict management styles. *The International Journal of Conflict Management, 13*(1), 78–94.

Broome, B. J. (2004). Reaching across the dividing line: Building a collective vision for peace in Cyprus. *International Journal of Peace Research, 41*(2), 191–209.

Broome, B. J. (2003). Responding to the challenges of third-party facilitation: Reflections of a scholar-practitioner in the Cyprus conflict. *Journal of Intergroup Relations, 26*(4), 24–43.

Broome, B. J., & Collier, M. J. (2012). Culture, communication, and peacebuilding: A reflexive multi-dimensional contextual framework. *Journal of International and Intercultural Communication, 5*(4), 245–269.

Broome, B. J., & Hatay, J. (2010). In J. Oetzel and S. Ting-Toomey (eds), *Handbook of Conflict Communication* (pp. 627–662). Thousand Oaks, CA: Sage Publications.

Cai, D. A., & Fink, E. L. (2002). Conflict style differences between individualists and collectivists. *Communication Monographs, 69,* 67–87.

Chan, S. (2015, November 29). France uses sweeping powers to curb climate protests but clashes erupt. *nytimes.com.* Retrieved June 22, 2016, from http://www.nytimes.com/2015/11/30/world/europe/france-uses-sweeping-powers-to-curb-climate-protests-but-clashes-erupt.html.

Cole, M. (1996). *Interpersonal conflict communication in Japanese cultural contexts.* Unpublished dissertation, Arizona State University, Tempe.

Collier, M. J. (1991). Conflict competence within African, Mexican, and Anglo American friendships. In S. Ting-Toomey & F. Korzenny (Eds.), *Cross-cultural interpersonal communication* (pp. 132–154). Newbury Park, CA: Sage.

Croucher, S. M. (2013). Integrated Threat Theory and acceptance of immigrant assimilation: An analysis of Muslim immigration in Western Europe. *Communication Monograph, 80*(1), 46–62.

Davis, M., Capobianco, S., & Kraus, L. (2010). Gender differences in responding to conflict in the workplace: Evidence from a large sample of working adults. *Sex Roles, 63*(7/8), 500–514.

Demytrie, R. (2010 June 13). Tens of thousands flee ethnic violence in Krygyzstan. *BBC News.* Retrieved August 26, 2011, from www.bbc.co.uk/news/10304165. www.bbc.co.uk/news/10304165.

Dickey, J. (2016, May 31). The revolution on America's campuses. *time.com.* Retrieved June 23, 2016, from http://time.com/4347099/college-campus-protests/.

Donohue, W. A. (2006). Managing interpersonal conflict: The mediation promise. In J. G. Oetzel & S. Ting-Toomey (Eds.), *The Sage handbook of conflict communication: Integrating theory, research, and practice* (pp. 211–234). Thousand Oaks, CA: Sage Publications.

Duara, N. (2015, November 14). In protest over gay rights, Mormons give up their church membership. *latimes.com.* Retrieved July 16, 2016, from http://www.latimes.com/nation/la-na-mormons-gays-resignation-20151114-story.html.

Duell, M. (2011, April 4). "I was in middle of the viper's pit." *Dailymail.co.uk.* Retrieved August 30, 2011, from www.dailymail.co.uk/news/article-1373270/Male-male-sexual-assault-soldiers-increases-Greg-Jeloudov-reports-gang-rape.html.

Ellis, D. G. (2015). Fierce entanglements: *Communication and ethnopolitical conflict.* NYC: Peter Lang.

Ellis, D. G. (2010). Intergroup conflict. In C.R. Berger, M.E. Roloff, & D.R. Roskso-Ewoldsen (Eds.), *Handbook of communication science,* (pp. 291–308). Thousand Oaks, CA: Sage.

Fellag, N. (2014). The Muslim label: How French North Africans have become "Muslims" and not "Citizens." *Journal on Ethnopolitics and Minority Issues in Europe, 13*(4), 1–25.

Gershman, J., & Audi, T. (2015, Aug 13). Court rules baker can't refuse to make wedding cake for gay couple. *wsj.com.* Retrieved April 28, 2016, from http://www.wsj.com/articles/court-rules-baker-cant-refuse-to-make-wedding-cake-for-gay-couple-1439506296.

Hammer, M. R. (2005). The Intercultural Conflict Style Inventory: A conceptual framework and measure of intercultural conflict approaches. *International Journal of Intercultural Relations, 29,* 675–695.

Healey, P. (2016, June 14). After massacre at Orlando gay club, an arrray of opinion about motive and meaning. *nytimes.com.* Retrieved June 22, 2016, from http://www.nytimes.com/2016/06/14/us/politics/shooting-reaction.html?_r=0.

Henderson, M. (1999). *Forgiveness: Breaking the chain of hate.* Wilsonville, OR: Book-Partners.

Hirsch, M. (2016, March 24). Inside the FBI's secret Muslim network. Politico.com. Retrieved June 22, 2016, from http://www.politico.com/magazine/story/2016/03/fbi-muslim-outreach-terrorism-213765.

Johannessen, H. (2007). Norway's commitment to conflict resolution education. *Conflict Resolution Quarterly, 25*(1), 93–100.

Kim, M-S. (2002). *Non-Western perspectives on human communication.* Thousand Oaks, CA: Sage.

King, M. L., Jr. (1984). Pilgrimage in nonviolence. In J. C. Albert & S. E. Albert (Eds.), *The sixties papers: Documents of a rebellious decade* (pp. 108–112). New York: Praeger. (Original work published 1965)

Koeppel, D. (2011, November 11). Workplace conflict heats up. *thefiscaltimes.com*. Retrieved April 28, 2016, from http://www.thefiscaltimes.com/Articles /2011/11/11/Gen-Y-vs-Boomers-Workplace-Conflict -Heats-Up.

Koerner, A. F., & Fitzpatrick, M. A. (2006). Family conflict communication. In J. G. Oetzel & S. Ting-Toomey (Eds.), *The Sage handbook on conflict communication: Integrating theory, research, and practice* (pp. 159–183). Thousand Oaks, CA: Sage.

Kramer, S. (2011, May 20). "Coming out": Gay teenagers, in their own words. *The New York Times online*. Retrieved August 23, 2011, from www.nytimes.com /2011/05/23/us/23out.html?_r=1.

Kraybill, D. (2001). *The riddle of Amish culture*. Baltimore, MD: Johns Hopkins University Press.

Le Paris flambé. (2007, November 29). *The Economist*. Retrieved May 11, 2008, from www.economist.com /world/europe/displaystory.cfm?story_id=10225005.

Lindsley, S. L. (1999). A layered model of problematic intercultural communication in U.S.-owned *maquiladoras* in Mexico. *Communication Monographs, 66*, 145–167.

Madhani, A. (2010, August 24). Cleric al-Awlaki dubbed 'bin Laden of the Internet'. *Usatoday.com*. Retrieved June 13, 2016, from http://usatoday30.usatoday.com /news/nation/2010-08-25-1A_Awlaki25_CV_N.htm.

Malcolm X. (1984). The ballot or the bullet. In J. C. Albert & S. E. Albert (Eds.), *The sixties papers: Documents of a rebellious decade* (pp. 126–132). New York: Praeger. (Original work published 1965)

Mayo, C. (2002). The binds that tie: Civility and social difference. *Educational Theory*, 53(2), 169–180.

McCullough, M. E. (2008). *Beyond revenge: The evolution of the forgiveness instinct*. San Francisco, CA: Jossey-Bass.

McKinley, J., & Johnson, K. (2008, November 14). Mormons tipped scale in ban on gay marriage. *New York Times*. Retrieved September 7, 2012, from http:// www.nytimes com/2008/11/15/us/politics/15marriage .html?pagewanted=all.

Messman, S. J., & Mikesell, R. I. (2000). Competition and interpersonal conflict in dating relationships. Communication Reports, *13*, 21–34.

Mindell, A. (1995). *Sitting in the fire: Large group transformation using conflict and diversity*. Portland, OR: Lao Tse Press.

Neill, C. (2012, September 7). "I fled in just the clothes I was wearing": How one Muslim woman escaped arranged marriage. mirror.co.uk. Retrieved July 18, 2016, from http://www.mirror.co.uk/news/real-life -stories/shafilea-ahmed-murder-how-i-escaped-1327180.

Oetzel, J. G., Arcos, B., Mabizela, P., Weinman, A. M., & Zhang, Q. (2006). Historical, political, and spiritual factors of conflict: Understanding conflict perspectives and communication in the Muslim world, China, Colombia, and South Africa. In J. G. Oetzel & S. Ting-Toomey (Eds.), *The Sage handbook on conflict communication: Integrating theory, research, and practice* (pp. 549–575). Thousand Oaks, CA: Sage.

Oetzel, J., Dhar, S., & Kirschbaum, K. (2007). Intercultural conflict from a multilevel perspective: Trends, possibilities, and future directions. *Journal of Intercultural Communication Research, 36*(3), 183–204.

Pike, G. R., & Sillars, A. L. (1985). Reciprocity of marital communication. *Journal of Social and Personal Relationships, 2,* 303–324.

Putnam, L. L. (2006). Definitions and approaches to conflict and communication. In J. G. Oetzel & S. Ting-Toomey (Eds.), *The Sage handbook on conflict communication: Integrating theory, research, and practice* (pp. 1–32). Thousand Oaks, CA: Sage.

Rennie, D. (2011, August 2011). Bagehot: The transportation option. *The Economist, 400* (8747), 54.

Ross, M. H. (2011). Reflections on the strengths and limitations to cross cultural evidence in the study of conflict and its mitigation. *Cross-Cultural Research, 45*(1), 82–96.

Ross, M. H. (1993). *The culture of conflict: Interpretations and interests in comparative perspective*. New Haven, CT: Yale University Press.

Schwirtz, M. (2010, June 13). Ethnic rioting ravages Kyrgyzstan. *The New York Times*. Retrieved August 26, 2011, from www.nytimes.com/2010/06/14/world/asia /14kyrgyz.html.

Spinella, S. (2015, November 19). Protests against racism on campuses spread nationally. *Dailycampus.com*. Retrieved on June 24, 2016, from http://dailycampus .com/stories/2015/11/18/protests-against-racism-on -college-campuses-extend-nationally.

Ting-Toomey, S. (2013). Face negotiation conflict theory. In K. Keith (Ed.), *The Encyclopedia of Cross-Cultural Psychology* (pp. 535–537). Hoboken, NJ: Wiley-Blackwell Publishers.

Ting-Toomey, S., & Oetzel, J. G. (2013). Culture-based situational conflict model: An update and expansion. In J. G. Oetzel & S. Ting-Toomey (Eds.), The Sage Handbook of Conflict Communication (2nd ed., pp. 763–789). Los Angeles, CA: Sage.

Ting-Toomey, S., & Oetzel, J. G. (2002). Cross-cultural face concerns and conflict styles: Current status and future directions. In W. B. Gudykunst & B. Mody (Eds.), *Handbook of international and intercultural communication* (2nd ed., pp. 141–163). Thousand Oaks, CA: Sage.

Ting-Toomey, S., Yee-Jung, K. K., Shapiro, R., Garcia, W., Wright, T. J., & Oetzel, J. G. (2000). Ethnic/cultural identity salience and conflict styles in four U.S. ethnic groups. *International Journal of Intercultural Relations, 24,* 47–81.

Tran, M. (2010, June 14). War in Kyrgyzstan: What is causing the violence? *The guardian*. Retrieved August 26, 2011, from www.guardian.co.uk/world /2010/jun/14/kyrgyzstan-conflict-background.

Turner, L. H., & Shuter, R. (2004). African American and European American women's visions of workplace conflict: A metaphorical analysis. *Howard Journal of Communications, 15,* 169–193.

Waldron, V. R., & Kelley, D. L. (2008). *Communicating forgiveness*. Thousand Oaks, CA: Sage.

Wilmot, W. W., & Hocker, J. L. (2010). *Interpersonal conflict* (8th ed.). New York: McGraw-Hill.

Zhang H. (2011, July 27). Norwegians filled with "Oslove." *ChinaDaily.com*. Retrieved August 25, 2011, from www.chinadaily.com.cn/cndy/2011-07/27/content _12989357.htm.

Zhang, Q., Ting-Toomey, S., Oetzel, J.G., & Zhang, J. (2015). The emotional side of forgiveness: A cross-cultural investigation of the role of anger and compassion and face threat in interpersonal forgiveness and reconciliation. *Journal of International and Intercultural Communication 8*(4), 311–320.

CREDITS

[page 445, text] Y. Amichai-Hamberger, excerpt from "How we can use the internet to resolve intergroup conflict" from *psychologytoday.com* (June 6, 2013). [page 445, text] S. L. Lindsley, quote from "A layered model of problematic intercultural communication in U.S.-owned maquiladoras in Mexico" from *Communication Monographs* (1999): 145–167. [page 446, text] M. H. Ross, excerpt from *The culture of conflict: Interpretations and interests in comparative perspective*. Yale University Press. [page 446, text] M. H. Ross, excerpt from "Reflections on the strengths and limitations to cross-cultural evidence in the study of conflict and its mitigation" from *Cross-Cultural Research* (2011): 82–96. [page 450, text] Stacy, excerpt from "Students Voices: I just recently got married. I am Caucasian . . . and learn Catholicism." Original Work; [page 451, text] D. Augsburger, excerpt from *Conflict mediation across cultures*. Westminster/John Knox Press. [page 453, text] M-S. Kim, quote from *Non-Western perspectives on human communication*. Sage. [page 454, text] Jacqueline, excerpt from "Students Voices: When I was back home in Singapore, my parents . . . if not all of it." Original Work; [page 455, text] Mike, excerpt from "Students Voices: At my work, I have learned to be somewhat . . . the resolution process." Original Work; [page 456, text] Nikki, excerpt from "Students Voices: I used to work part-time in a restaurant . . . I would have otherwise." Original Work; [page 456, text] N. Fellag, quote from "The Muslim label: How French North Africans have become "Muslims" and not "Citizens."" from *Journal on Ethnopolitics and Minority Issues in Europe* (2014): 1–25. [page 458, text] P. Ackerman & J. Duvall, J., quote from "*force more powerful: A century of nonviolent conflict*". Palgrave McMillan. [page 458, text] X. Malcolm, quote from "The ballot or the bullet" in *The sixties papers: Documents of a rebellious decade*, edited by J. C. Albert, and S. E. Albert. Praeger (Original work published 1965). [page 459, text] R. Demytrie, quote from "Tens of thousands flee ethnic violence in Krygyzstan" from *BBC News* (June 13, 2010). [page 459, text] M. Schwirtz, quote from "Ethnic rioting ravages Kyrgyzstan" from *The New York Times* (June 13, 2010). [page 460, text] M. Tran, quote from "War in Kyrgyzstan: What is causing the violence?" from *The Guardian* (June 14, 2010). [page 462, text] D. Augsburger, excerpt from *Mediation across cultures*. Westminster/John Knox press. [page 461–462, text] Jenni, excerpt from "My friend is a devout Catholic, and I am a devout Mormon . . . because we don't feel tension around each other." Original Work; [page 463, text] Figure from *Association for Conflict Resolution (ACR)*. [page 466, text] V. R. Waldron, and D. L. Kelley, quote from *Communicating forgiveness*. Sage. [page 467, text] M. E. McCullough, quote from *Beyond revenge: The evolution of the forgiveness instinct*. Jossey-Bass. [page 468 text] David W. Augsburger, quote from *Conflict Mediation across Cultures*. The Westminster Press/John Knox Press, www.wjkbooks.com; [page 469–470, text] David W. Augsburger, quote from *Conflict Mediation across Cultures*. The Westminster Press/John Knox Press, www .wjkbooks.com.

12

STRIVING FOR ENGAGED AND EFFECTIVE INTERCULTURAL COMMUNICATION

CHAPTER OBJECTIVES

After reading this chapter, you should be able to:

1. Identify and describe four individual components of competence.
2. Explain how various contexts influence individual intercultural competence.
3. Describe the importance of applying knowledge about intercultural communication.
4. Describe the various ways one can enter into intercultural dialogue.
5. Identify strategies for building coalitions across cultures.
6. Understand the relationship between social justice and intercultural competence.
7. Identify and describe specific strategies for working for social justice.
8. Explain the role of forgiveness in intercultural communication.
9. Identify several challenges for future intercultural communication.

THE COMPONENTS OF COMPETENCE
Social Science Perspective: Individual Components
Interpretive Perspective: Competence in Contexts
Critical Perspective: Competence for Whom?

APPLYING KNOWLEDGE ABOUT INTERCULTURAL COMMUNICATION
Entering into Dialogue
Becoming Interpersonal Allies
Building Coalitions
Social Justice and Transformation
Forgiveness

WHAT THE FUTURE HOLDS

INTERNET RESOURCES

SUMMARY

DISCUSSION QUESTIONS

ACTIVITIES

KEY WORDS

REFERENCES

Now that we are nearing the end of our journey through this textbook, you might ask, How do you really know whether you are a good intercultural communicator? We have covered a lot of topics and discussed some ideas that will help you be a better communicator. But you can't learn how to be a good communicator merely by reading books. Just as in learning to be a good public speaker or a good relational partner, it takes experience. In this chapter, we want to leave you with some specific ideas and suggestions for improving your skills in communicating across cultures.

We can approach intercultural competence in several ways. We begin this chapter with the social science approach, identifying specific components of competence: motivation, knowledge, attitudes, behaviors, and skills. We then turn to interpretive and critical approaches, emphasizing the contextual issues in competence. Finally, we continue our dialectical perspective, combining individual and contextual elements to offer specific suggestions for improving intercultural relations by building alliances and coalitions across cultures.

THE COMPONENTS OF COMPETENCE

What are the things we have to know, the attitudes and behaviors, to make us competent communicators? Do we have to be motivated to be good at intercultural communication? Intercultural communication scholars have been investigating these questions for many years (Chen & Starosta, 1996; Chen, 2014). Scholars taking a social science perspective have identified four basic components, or building blocks, of intercultural competence: motivation, knowledge, attitudes, and behaviors. We present these components here because we think they serve as a useful starting point. However, interpretive and critical scholars remind us that we need to contextualize these components and examine their usefulness in our contemporary global world (Collier, 2005; Sorrells, 2014). We need to ask ourselves, Who came up with these components? Are they applicable to everyone? For example, if a group of Native American scholars came up with guidelines for what it takes to be interculturally competent, would these guidelines apply to other cultural groups? Do the same competencies work in every context? Again, it is useful to remember our dialectical perspective. Intercultural communication competence may rely on individual competence, but context is also important. Let's look first at the individual components.

Social Science Perspective: Individual Components

Motivation   Perhaps the most important dimension of communication competence is **motivation.** If we aren't motivated to communicate with others, it probably doesn't matter what other skills we possess. We can't assume that people always want to communicate. This is a difficult idea to wrestle with, especially for those of us who have dedicated our lives to studying and understanding intercultural communication. And yet, motivation is an important aspect of developing intercultural competence.

motivation As an individual component of intercultural communication competence, the desire to make a commitment in relationships, to learn about the self and others, and to remain flexible.

Why might people not be motivated to engage in intercultural communication? One reason is that members of large, powerful groups often think they don't need to know much about other cultures; there is simply no incentive. In contrast, people from less powerful groups have a strong incentive to learn about and interact with more powerful groups. For example, female managers in corporations are motivated to learn about and adjust to the dominant male norms, Latinos/as are motivated to learn European American norms, and visitors overseas are motivated to learn about and adjust to the norms of foreign cultures. The survival of these less powerful groups often depends on members' motivation to succeed at intercultural interaction (Johnson, 2017).

Sometimes people can *become* motivated to learn about other cultures and to communicate interculturally. For example, the increasing levels of violence between religious and ethnic groups worldwide have motivated people to reach out to those in other cultures. For example, "Combatants for Peace" is a group of Palestinian and Israeli soldiers who previously "saw each other only through gun sights" but came to believe that conflict cannot be solved by military means. Following principles of nonviolence, they now organize activities, tours, lectures, and events for both Israeli and Palestinian audiences, with the goals of better understanding of the other group through active dialogue and ultimately reducing violence and conflict. The largest event, attended by thousands, is the annual Israeli-Palestinian Memorial Day service, where they remember the victims of the conflict on both sides, and, in their words, "take the burden of the conflict upon ourselves in an attempt to avert the next victims" (Vision, 2016).

A second reason that people aren't motivated is because intercultural communication can be uncomfortable. As discussed previously, anxiety, uncertainty, and fear are common aspects of intercultural interactions. And yet, moving out of our "communication comfort zone" often leads to insights into other individuals, groups, and cultures. One of our students, Jayla, explains:

> *I think that you learn the most by traveling and/or making a conscious effort to interact with those in another culture or nation or race. Especially being thrust outside of your "comfort zone" will force you to see the diverse beauty and differences in other cultures.*

Sometimes people do not address delicate intercultural issues out of fear—fear of being isolated from friends and family members who may be prejudiced and not motivated themselves. In one study, college students said they censored their communication in class discussions about race because they were afraid their comments would be taken as offensive, racist, or ignorant; they were afraid of being attacked or yelled at, and they didn't want to be perceived as "trying to prove" they weren't racist (Harris, Miller, & Trego, 2004). This fear, and the resulting silences, have huge costs to us as individuals and for our society. Individually, when we are not motivated to reach out across cultural divides, we suffer from distorted perception (we don't really know how individuals from other cultures may view us or a particular situation) and a lack of personal growth. On the societal level, when we are not motivated to embrace other cultures and other ways of thinking and behavior, our organizations suffer from a loss of productivity and human potential (not everyone gets the opportunity to contribute ideas; Kivel, 2011).

The following anecdote illustrates how complicated intercultural communication can be. It concerns a well-intentioned individual trying to be sensitive to one group (Native Americans) but inadvertently ignoring the feelings and sensibilities of another (Japanese).

I participated in a week-long cross-cultural seminar last summer in which the participants were from a mix of domestic and international cultural groups. On the first day, as an icebreaker, we took turns introducing the person to the left. There were several international students, including an older Japanese woman, who had a little trouble with English. She introduced her partner in halting English but made only one mistake; she said that her partner (a white American woman) was "Native American." She meant to say that her partner was born in America, but her English wasn't quite fluent.

Immediately, one of the other members of the group raised her hand and said, "I have an ouch," and proceeded to tell the group how important it was that we be honest and tell others when things were bothering us. She said, further, that it bothered her that this woman had been called a Native American when she was not. She emphasized how important it was that people be labeled accurately. She meant well. But the Japanese woman was mortified. She was embarrassed about her English to begin with, and she was really embarrassed at being singled out as being incorrect in her language. She did not say anything at the time. None of the rest of us in the group knew how distressed she was. As soon as the session was over, she went to the workshop leaders and asked to be transferred out of the group.
—Mary

Third, motivation is lacking in contexts in which historical events or political circumstances have resulted in communication breakdowns. For example, it is understandable, given the history of animosity in the Middle East, that Israeli and Arab students would not be motivated to communicate with each other. It is also understandable why a Serbian student would not want to room with a Croatian student, or why a Greek Cypriot would not want to forge a friendship with a Turkish Cypriot, given that these two ethnic communities have been engaged in one of the most protracted international disputes of all time.

To use an example closer to home, many blacks and whites in the United States are not motivated to forge friendships with each other. One recent study found that 75% of whites have no non-white friends, and the authors of the study suggested that it is the racial segregation of neighborhoods and religious institutions in America that lead to limited interracial friendships (Ingraham, 2014). However, another study, investigating the interracial interaction and friendship patterns of 3,000 undergraduates in 28 institutions found that even at large, diverse colleges and universities, white students engaged in much less racial interaction and friendship than did students of color (Bowman & Park, 2014). The researchers also found that students who participated in religious and ethnic student organizations were less likely to form interracial friendships and white students who joined a fraternity or sorority were less likely to have interracial friendships. This is probably because participation in these organizations (ethnic, Greek, and religious) tend to foster tight-knit social bonds and close same-race friendships—limiting motivation to form interracial friendships. Other experts suggest that limited black–white friendship is due to "white habitus"—an "oblivion about the racial components of their own socialization" and shared negative views toward non-whites (they are lazy, complain too much about racism and discrimination)—created by whites' segregation and isolation from minorities. (Bonilla-Silva & Embrick, 2007, p. 325).

The point here is that it doesn't matter how good a communicator you are if you are not motivated to use those communication skills. For some people, the first step in developing intercultural communication competence may be to examine their motivation to reach out to others who are culturally different.

Aside from reasons that motivation might be decreased, we should also think about the ways that motivation might be increased. Motivation can also be increased by personal and international circumstances. If we think dialectically about motivation, motivation is not only about low motivation, but also high motivation. On a personal level, for example, if a German person marries a Japanese person and they choose to live in Osaka, the German should be highly motivated to communicate effectively in Japanese culture. The German should learn the Japanese language, culture, and all of the various things that we've pointed to in this book. In a sense, this is culture specific, as the German would neither be as motivated to learn Russian, Greek, Indonesian, or Arabic, nor learn how to communicate effectively in these other cultures.

Knowledge   The **knowledge** component comprises various cognitive aspects of communication competence; it involves what we know about ourselves and others and about various aspects of communication. Perhaps most important is **self-knowledge**—knowing how you may be perceived as a communicator and what your strengths and weaknesses are. How can you know what these are?

Acquiring self-knowledge is a long and sometimes complicated process. It involves being open to information coming in many different ways. A white student describes her growing awareness of what it means to be white in the United States after listening to Chicano and African American guest speakers:

> *They each spoke about their experiences that they have had [with others pre-judging them]. . . . We discover our white identity by listening to others. We hear these hardships that they have had to endure and we realize that we never have had to experience that. You learn a lot about yourself that way. . . . By listening to our guests speak today, I realized that sometimes other ethnicities might not view my culture very highly.*

We often don't know how we're perceived because we don't search for this information or because there is not sufficient trust in a relationship for people to reveal such things. **Other-knowledge,** or knowledge about how other people think and behave, will also help you be a more effective communicator. However, learning

knowledge As an individual component of intercultural communication competence, the quality of knowing about oneself (i.e., one's strengths and weaknesses), others, and various aspects of communication.

self-knowledge Related to intercultural communication competence, the quality of knowing how one is perceived as a communicator, as well as one's strengths and weaknesses.

other-knowledge Related to intercultural communication competence, knowledge about how people from other cultures think and behave that will also help you be a more effective communicator.

about others in only abstract terms can lead to stereotyping. It is often better to learn through relational experience, as this student did:

> *My friend Jack told me a couple of years ago that he was gay, and we have had many discussions on . . . what it means to be gay. A few years ago I didn't take a stance on whether it was right or wrong to be gay, and if anyone made a joke I would laugh. Now that I gained experience from Jack, I respect his way of life and would always support him. This point is valid because the more one experiences things with other people from different backgrounds, the more one will be able to respect and understand other people.*

Of course, we can't know everything about all cultures or develop relationships with people from all cultural groups, so it's important to develop some general knowledge about cultural differences. For example, in this book, we have described cultural variations in both verbal and nonverbal communication. To avoid stereotyping, perhaps it is better simply to be aware of the range in thought and behavior across cultures, and not to assume that because someone belongs to a particular group, he or she will behave in a particular way.

Linguistic knowledge is another important aspect of intercultural competence. Awareness of the difficulty of learning a second language helps us appreciate the extent of the challenges that sojourners and immigrants face in their new cultural contexts. Also, knowing a second or third language expands our communication repertoire and increases our empathy for culturally different individuals. For example, as Judith struggles through her conversational Spanish class, she is reminded again of how difficult it is to accomplish ordinary things in a second language. And when she sits in class and worries that the instructor might call on her, she is reminded of the anxiety of many international students and immigrants trying to navigate a new country and language.

linguistic knowledge Knowledge of other languages besides one's native language or of the difficulty of learning a second or third language.

Attitudes   Many **attitudes** contribute to intercultural communication competence, including tolerance for ambiguity, empathy, and nonjudgmentalism.

Tolerance for ambiguity refers to the ease in dealing with situations in which much is unknown. Whether we are abroad or at home, interacting with people who look different from us and who behave in ways that are strange to us requires a tolerance for ambiguity. When Judith was studying Spanish in Mexico recently, she was struck by the range of attitudes of her fellow students from the United States. Some seemed very tolerant of the classroom procedures in Mexico, but others seemed to want the classes to be run as they would be in the States.

attitudes An individual's dispositions or mental sets. As a component of intercultural communication competence, attitudes include tolerance for ambiguity, empathy, and nonjudgmentalism.

Tolerance for ambiguity is one of the most difficult things to attain. As mentioned previously, people have a natural preference for predictability; uncertainty can be disquieting. Nick, an exchange student in Mexico, discusses how tolerance and language ability are particularly important—and problematic—in stressful situations:

tolerance for ambiguity The ease with which an individual copes with situations in which a great deal is unknown.

> *I had lost my wallet in the marketplace and asked my wife to wire money to me. I couldn't figure out which Western Union location (there are many) I was supposed to go to to pick up my money. I finally went to the central post office, only to be told that my money had been delivered somewhere else—and I couldn't understand where. I was frustrated, tired and worried—and my language skills were deteriorating rapidly! Fortunately, I pulled myself together, tried to be patient, and joked with*

In his book *Last Watch of the Night*, Paul Monette points out that it is important to recognize the many forms of intolerance most of us experience as we grow up. This excerpt is from a speech he gave at the Library of Congress during National Book Week. The writer he refers to, Urvashi Vaid, is a lesbian who has written about issues of tolerance. Think about how the intolerance around you may affect you and how difficult it is sometimes to be tolerant of the many diversities you encounter.

Most of our families do the very best they can to bring us up whole and make us worthy citizens. But it's a very rare person who manages to arrive at adulthood without being saddled by some form of racism or sexism or homophobia. It is our task as grownups to face those prejudices in ourselves and rethink them. The absolute minimum we can get out of such a self-examination is tolerance, one for another. We gay and lesbian people believe we should be allowed to celebrate ourselves and give back to the larger culture, make our unique contributions—but if all we get is tolerance, we'll take it and build on it.

We don't know what history is going to say even about this week, or where the gay and lesbian revolution is going to go. But we are a revolution that has come to be based very, very strongly on diversity. We have to fight like everyone else to be open in that diversity; but I love Urvashi Vaid's idea that it's not a matter of there being one of each on every board and every faculty and every organization. It's a matter of being each in one. You'll pardon my French, but it's not so hard to be politically correct. All you have to do is not be an ——.

Source: From P. Monette, *Last Watch of the Night* (New York: Harcourt Brace, 1994), pp. 122–123.

---

the postal workers. It took six hours to get my money, but by the end of the day, I had my money and had made some new friends at the post office!

empathy The capacity to "walk in another person's shoes."

Empathy refers to the ability to know what it's like to "walk in another person's shoes." Empathic skills are culture bound. We cannot really view the world through another person's eyes without knowing something about his or her experiences and life. To illustrate, suppose a U.S. American and a Japanese have been introduced and are conversing. The Japanese responds to the U.S. American's first remark with a giggle. The U.S. American feels pleasurable empathic sensations and makes an impulsive comment, indicating a congenial, accepting reaction. However, the Japanese observer now feels intensely uncomfortable. What the U.S. American doesn't realize is that the giggle may not mean that the Japanese is feeling pleasure. Japanese often giggle to indicate embarrassment and unease. In this case, the U.S. American's "empathy" is missing the mark. In this sense, empathy is the capacity to imagine oneself in another role, within the context of one's cultural identity.

Intercultural communication scholars have attempted to come up with a more culturally sensitive view of empathy. For example, Ben Broome (1991, 1993) stresses that to achieve empathy across cultural boundaries, people must forge strong relationships and strive for the creation of shared meaning in their interpersonal encounters. Because this is difficult to achieve when people come from very different cultural backgrounds, Broome suggests that this shared meaning must be seen as both provisional and dynamic, that understanding is not an all-or-nothing proposition. In addition, cross-cultural empathy must integrate both thinking and feeling—we must try to understand not only what others *say* (content) but also how they *feel* (empathy). Finally, he reminds us that to achieve cross-cultural empathy, we must seek to understand the context of both others' lived experiences and the specific encounters.

Magoroh Maruyama (1970), an anthropologist-philosopher, agrees that achieving cross-cultural empathy and trying to see the world exactly as the other person sees is very difficult. She describes the process as **transpection,** a postmodern phenomenon that often involves trying to learn foreign beliefs, assumptions, perspectives, and feelings in a foreign context. Transpection, then, can be achieved only with practice and requires structured experience and self-reflection.

transpection
Cross-cultural empathy.

Communication scholar Milton Bennett (2013) suggests a "Platinum Rule" ("Do unto others as *they themselves* would have done unto them") instead of the Golden Rule ("Do unto others as *you* would have done unto you") (p. 213). This, of course, requires movement beyond a culture-bound sympathy or empathy for others.

Achieving **nonjudgmentalism** is much easier said than done. We might like to think that we do not judge others according to our own cultural frames of reference, but it is very difficult not to do so. One of our colleagues recalls being at a university meeting at which a group of Icelandic administrators and a group of U.S. American faculty were discussing implementing a study-abroad exchange program. The Icelandic faculty were particularly taciturn, and our colleague wanted to lighten up the meeting a little. Eventually, however, she realized that the taciturnity probably reflected different norms of behavior. She had unknowingly judged the tenor of the meeting based on her own style of communication.

nonjudgmentalism
Free from evaluating according to one's own cultural frame of reference.

The **D.I.E. exercise** is helpful in developing a nonjudgmental attitude (Wendt, 1984). It involves making a distinction between description (D), interpretation (I), and evaluation (E) in the processing of information. Descriptive statements convey factual information that can be verified through the senses (e.g., "There are 25 chairs in the room" and "I am 5-feet tall"). Interpretive statements attach meaning to the description (e.g., "You must be tired"). Evaluative statements clarify how we feel about something (e.g., "When you're always tired, we can't have any fun together"). Only descriptive statements are nonjudgmental.

D.I.E. exercise A device that helps us determine if we are communicating at a descriptive, interpretive, or evaluative level. Only descriptive statements are nonjudgmental.

This exercise can help us recognize whether we are processing information on a descriptive, interpretive, or evaluative level. Confusing the different levels can lead to misunderstanding and ineffective communication. For example, if I think a student is standing too close to me, I may interpret the behavior as "This student is pushy," or I may evaluate it as "This student is pushy, and I don't like pushy students." However, if I force myself to describe the student's behavior, I may say to myself, "This student is standing 8 inches away from me, whereas most students stand farther away." This observation enables me to search for other (perhaps cultural) reasons for the behavior. The student may be worried about a grade and may be anxious to get some questions answered. Perhaps the student is used to standing closer to people than I am. Or perhaps the student really is pushy.

It is impossible to always stay at the descriptive level. But it is important to know when we are describing and when we are interpreting. Most communication is at the interpretive level. For example, have you ever been set up for a blind date and asked for a description of the person? The descriptions you might get (e.g., tall, dark, handsome, nice, kind, generous) are not really descriptions; rather, they are interpretations that reflect individual and cultural viewpoints (Wendt, 1984).

Behaviors and Skills Behaviors and skills are another component of intercultural competence. What are the most competent behaviors? Are there any universal behaviors that work well in all cultural contexts? At one level, there probably are. Several communication scholars have attempted to identify universal behaviors including interaction involvement (e.g., active listening skills), behavioral flexibility, respect for the other person, and message skills (Arasaratnam, Banerjee, & Dembek, 2010; Chen, 2014). Some of these general behaviors seem applicable to many cultural groups and contexts. Notably, these skills become problematic when we try to apply them in specific ways. For example, being respectful works well in all intercultural interactions, and many scholars identify this particular skill as important (Collier, 1998). Notably, how one expresses respect behaviorally may vary from culture to culture and from context to context. For example, European Americans show respect by making direct eye contact, whereas some Native Americans show respect by avoiding eye contact. We address the importance of context more fully in the next section.

It is not enough to know how competent behaviors vary from culture to culture, one needs to be able to put that knowledge into practice by demonstrating those behaviors appropriately. Let's see how this works. In one study, Mitch Hammer and his colleagues evaluated the effectiveness of a cross-cultural training program for Japanese and U.S. American managers in a joint venture (a steel company) in Ohio. One goal was to determine if the managers' intercultural communication skills had improved significantly. The research team used a general behavioral framework of communication competence that included the following dimensions: immediacy, involvement, other orientation, interaction management, and social relaxation (Hammer, Martin, Otani, & Koyama, 1990). The two groups (Japanese managers and U.S. American managers) rated these dimensions differently. The U.S. Americans said that the most important dimension was involvement (how expressive one is in conversation), whereas the Japanese managers said that the other orientation (being tuned in to the other person) was most important. The researchers also judged how well each group of managers adapted to the other group's communication style. They videotaped the interaction and asked Japanese raters to judge the U.S. American managers on how well they adapted to the Japanese style, and vice versa. For example, good interaction management for the Japanese meant initiating and terminating interaction and making sure everyone had a chance to talk; for U.S. Americans, it meant asking opinions of the Japanese, being patient with silence, and avoiding strong disagreement and assertive statements. As this example shows, intercultural communication competence

---

unconscious incompetence When one communicates without adapting their communication style and not thinking about why it may not be effective.

conscious incompetence When one is aware that interaction is not going well, but doesn't understand why.

conscious competence When one is aware that interaction is going well and understands why.

unconscious competence When interaction is going well, but one doesn't have to think about why, as the various aspects of intercultural communication are being used unconsciously.

William Howell (1982), a renowned intercultural scholar, investigated how top CEOs made decisions. He found, to his surprise, that they did not follow the analytic process prescribed in business school courses—analysis of cost, benefits, and so on. Rather, they made decisions in a very holistic way. Howell emphasized that intercultural communication is similar, that only so much can be gained by conscious analysis, and that the highest level of communication competence requires a combination of holistic and analytic thinking. He identified four levels of intercultural communication competence: (1) unconscious incompetence, (2) conscious incompetence, (3) conscious competence, and (4) unconscious competence.

Unconscious incompetence is the "be yourself" approach, in which we are not conscious of differences and do not need to act in any particular way. Sometimes this works. However, being ourselves works best in interactions with individuals who are very similar to us. In intercultural contexts, being ourselves often means that we're not very effective and don't realize our ineptness.

At the level of **conscious incompetence,** people realize that things may not be going very well in the interaction, but they are not sure why. Most of us have experienced intercultural interactions in which we felt that something wasn't quite right but couldn't quite figure out what it was. This describes the feeling of conscious incompetence.

As instructors of intercultural communication, we teach at a conscious, intentional level. Our instruction focuses on analytic thinking and learning. This describes the level of **conscious competence.** Reaching this level is a necessary part of the process of becoming a competent communicator. Howell would say that reaching this level is necessary but not sufficient.

Unconscious competence is the level at which communication goes smoothly but is not a conscious process. You've probably heard of marathon runners "hitting the wall," or reaching the limits of their endurance. Usually, inexplicably, they continue running past this point. Communication at the unconscious competent level is like this. This level of competence is not something we can acquire by consciously trying to. It occurs when the analytic and holistic parts are functioning together. When we concentrate too hard or get too analytic, things don't always go easier.

You've probably had the experience of trying unsuccessfully to recall something, letting go of it, and then remembering it as soon as you're thinking about something else. This is what unconscious competence is—being well prepared cognitively and attitudinally, but knowing when to "let go" and rely on your holistic cognitive processing.

means being able to exhibit or adapt to different kinds of behaviors, depending on the other person's or group's cultural background.

While it is useful to acquire knowledge about how competent behaviors vary from culture to culture, as in the cross-cultural training program just described, this analytical knowledge may not be sufficient. A renowned communication scholar, William Howell, suggested that the most competent intercultural communicators are not only those who consciously acquire knowledge, but who also strive for an "unconscious competence" (see Point of View box above).

GLOBAL KIDS

Parents often try to raise their children to be prepared to meet the challenges of the contemporary era. As we move into a more global economy, is the United States raising children who are multilingual and able to work and live in international, multicultural environments? According to the U.S. State Department, there were 125,907,176 valid U.S. passports in 2015 (https://travel.state.gov/content/passports /en/passports/statistics.html) out of a total population of about 324 million (*www .census.gov*). This means about 39% of U.S. Americans have an active passport.

Today, some parents want to raise global children—children who are comfortably multilingual and multicultural—by raising them in other countries. Some send their children to immersion schools, where they learn another language and culture. Others move overseas so that their children are raised with and comfortable in another culture and language. Jim Rogers moved his family from New York City to Singapore so that his children would be fluent in Mandarin. He says, "I'm trying to prepare my children for the future, for the 21st century. I'm trying to prepare them as best I can for the world as I see it" (quoted in Miller, p. 48). When Clifford Levy was stationed in Moscow, he sent his three children to a Russian school. Although they did not speak Russian at first, they quickly learned Russian and Russian culture. This decision made all the difference in their Russian experiences: "Their fluency and familiarity with the culture unlocked doors everywhere. On a long train ride to Estonia, they befriended a middle-aged construction executive and his wife, a doctor, who were from southern Russia. The couple set out black bread, pickled vegetables and smoked fish for the kids, and everyone sat there snacking and chatting for hours" (Levy).

How well prepared are you to be a global citizen in the 21st century? As you see the changes happening around you in the world economy, how would you raise your children differently from how you were raised?

Sources: From C. J. Levy, "My family's experiment in extreme schooling," *The New York Times*, September 2011. Retrieved September 24, 2011, from www.nytimes.com/2011/09/18/magazine/my -familys-experiment-in-extreme-schooling.html?pagewanted=1&_r=1&sq=russian school& st=cse&scp=3; L. Miller, "How to raise a global kid," *Newsweek*, July 25, 2011, pp. 48–50.

Interpretive Perspective: Competence in Contexts

As we have stressed throughout this book, an important aspect of being a competent communicator is understanding the context in which communication occurs. Intercultural communication happens in many contexts. An interpretive perspective reminds us that a good communicator is sensitive to these contexts. (See Figure 12-1.)

Consider how definitions for competence may vary from one cultural context to another. In one research project we asked European American and Latino students to identify nonverbal behaviors that they thought would be competent in various contexts. The Latino students placed importance on approachability behaviors (e.g., smiling, laughing, pleasant facial expression) in *task* contexts. In contrast, non-Latino students reported that it was more important to exhibit these behaviors in *social* contexts

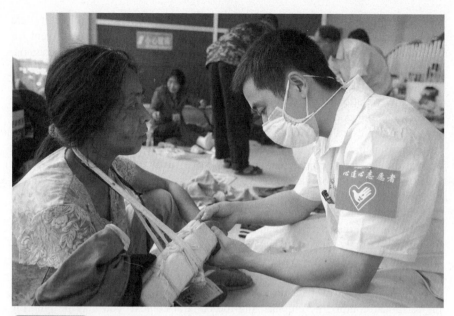

FIGURE 12-1   Intercultural competence in medical contexts may involve getting to know the cultural identities of patients—taking time to understand cultural barriers and showing interest in the patient's cultural background. (© *Ryan Pyle/Getty Images*)

(Martin, Hammer, & Bradford, 1994). These results probably reflect the importance in the Latino community of establishing personal rapport with those they work with (e.g., smiling, laughing), which sets a good "atmosphere." In contrast, non-Latino white cultural patterns often include a strong distinction between work and social relationships. Laughing and smiling—behaviors that typically communicate liking—are expected in pleasant social situations; however, one need not like a person one works with and therefore, in a task situation, it is not necessarily important to smile, laugh, and so forth in order to accomplish a joint task.

Another study examined intercultural communication competence in medical contexts (Rosenberg, Richard, Lussier, & Abdool, 2006). Using the framework described earlier (motivation, attitudes, behaviors), researchers examined (through observation and in-depth interviews) the degree to which the Canadian physicians were competent in their intercultural communication with immigrant patients. They found that intercultural competence in this context involved getting to know the cultural identities of their patients, something that most physicians did not think was essential in their job. Those physicians who were most competent took time to understand cultural barriers, showed interest in patient's cultural background, realized that some medical practices might not be culturally appropriate, and identified a similarity between themselves and their patients. Their patients described their satisfaction with these physicians, saying, "She knows me; she knows my family" or "She's a woman too, so she can understand" (p. 244).

What about intercultural communication competence in contexts? As we've discussed in earlier chapters, the lack of nonverbal cues (behaviors that communicate a liking and positive attitude toward the other and that establish one's identity) are absent in some online communication. Perhaps this requires slightly different (or additional) skills—especially involving issues of identity and language expression. First, consider how different cultures value identity expression. For example, some cultural groups place high importance on knowing the identity of a person before entering into relationships. Since much of our identity is expressed nonverbally (how we look and our conversational style), online conversations pose challenges. Identity is also expressed verbally, through communication style and humor (not always easily translatable across cultures and particularly difficult in cyberspace). Identity expression may involve bragging—not viewed positively in all cultures (St. Amant 2012). A final note about language—online contexts can actually facilitate communication between persons not sharing a native language, since they have more time to interpret and understand the other (the text/words are durable), as well as time to phrase their own messages (Osman & Herring, 2007). It is probably a good idea to use humor sparingly, since it is even more difficult to translate in online conversations and is viewed in different ways in various cultures.

We have emphasized that *many* contexts can influence intercultural communication. For instance, by focusing only on the historical context, you may overlook the relational context; by emphasizing the cultural context, you may be ignoring the gender or racial contexts of the intercultural interaction; and so on. It may seem difficult to keep all of these shifting contexts in mind. However, by analyzing your own intercultural successes and failures, you will come to a better understanding of intercultural communication.

Another aspect of context is the communicator's position within a speech community. Reflect on your own social position in relation to various speech communities and contexts. For example, if you are the only woman in a largely male environment or the only person of color in an otherwise white community, you may face particular expectations or have people project motivations onto your messages. Recognizing your own relation to the speech community and the context will help you better understand intercultural communication.

Critical Perspective: Competence for Whom?

A critical perspective reminds us that individuals' competence must be viewed within larger political, economic, and historical forces. As you know by now, all intercultural encounters—whether on an interpersonal level of two culturally different college friends, or an intergroup context where two ethnic groups live together in a neighborhood or on an international/global nation state encounter—take place within overlapping social, political, and historical contexts. Thus, as communication scholar Kathryn Sorrells (2014) notes, a "multifocal attention" is required for understanding intercultural competence in the 21st century (p. 151). That is, we need to recognize the impacts of macro-level, geopolitical dynamics, cultural identities, and histories on interpersonal interactions and vice versa—micro-level communication and conflict style also impact intergroup relations and geopolitical negotiation.

For example, characteristics of effective communication for women in the United States have changed dramatically in the last 50 years. In the 1960s, an "effective" female communicator was expected to be rather passive (both verbally and nonverbally), indirect, and nurturing. Assertive women met with disapproval and sanctions. Today, the "effective" female is expected to behave rather differently from this. As the 21st century unfolds, there is a broader range of acceptable behaviors that define competence for females. They may be unassertive in some contexts, but they are also free, and even expected, to be more assertive in many contexts. Similarly, effective black communicators in the 1960s were expected to be nonassertive in verbal and nonverbal style. Blacks like Muhammad Ali who went against these expectations were severely sanctioned. In short, we need to understand that notions of communication competence depend on specific social, political, and historical contexts.

Critical scholars also emphasize the role of power differentials and pose the question of who gets to set the standards and define communication competence: "Competence and acceptance from whom? Who decides the criteria? Who doesn't? Competent or acceptable on the basis of what social and historical context?" (Collier, 1998, p. 142). They question the early communication competence research conducted by white U.S. researchers using data from white U.S. respondents and noted that individuals of historically marginalized identities (women, ethnic/racial minorities, gays)—no matter their demonstrating "competent" behaviors as defined by traditional measures of competence—in some contexts are never viewed as competent (Willis, 2011; Yep, 2000). Later research based on data from a variety of ethnic and racial groups expanded the definition and concept of competence to include issues of stereotyping, powerlessness, and authenticity. The point is that powerful groups are not likely to focus on these issues and yet they must be taken into consideration when trying to understand the dimensions of competence. For example, African Americans report that they use stronger, more assertive, aggressive, and divergent strategies not identified in previous competence studies in order to be effective in interethnic interactions (Martin, Hecht, Moore, & Larkey, 2001).

Regarding the problematizing of "competence," consider the goals of intercultural interaction: Why do we want to be competent? Because we enjoy interacting with individuals whose backgrounds are different from our own? Is it because we want to sell products, or because we want to convert people to our religion? Because we want to change the world? Or bring about social justice? It is worth examining our own and others' goals in intercultural encounters and to ask whose interests are being served.

These are important questions raised by the critical perspective that force us to rethink intercultural communication competence. Indeed, you now have the skills to push your own thinking about intercultural communication—both strengths and weaknesses—as they help and hinder your ability to communicate.

APPLYING KNOWLEDGE ABOUT INTERCULTURAL COMMUNICATION

Now that we have taken you down the path of intercultural communication, we would like to conclude with specific suggestions for becoming better intercultural communicators. Our dialectical approach recognizes the important role of individual skills *and* contextual constraints in improving intercultural relations. The dialectical perspective also emphasizes the relational aspects of intercultural communication. Perhaps the first step in applying our knowledge to intercultural communication is to recognize the connectedness of humans and the importance of dialogue.

A comprehensive approach to competence that does this is the notion of **cosmopolitan communication** (CC) (Sobré-Denton, 2011; Sobré-Denton & Bardhan, 2013). CC emphasizes many of the elements we've described: empathy, openness, compassion, mutuality, and also stresses the role of power differentials. At the core is an assumption that part of being human is recognizing our interconnectedness with other humans, including those who may be culturally different—who should not be viewed as distant or as a menace, but as one with us. Our moral obligation, then, is to extend them empathy and kindness, not as something we "bestow" on them but as an imperative, if humankind is going to survive. Thus, CC views cultural differences as important, not as obstacles to be surmounted, but as challenges to work through that offer potential growth and transformation to all as ethical global citizens. The way to work through these challenges is by the process of dialogue and also action—in joining with others to address historically and newly emerging power inequities (addressed later) (Sobré-Denton & Bardhan, 2013).

cosmopolitan communication A notion of ethically working with and through cultural differences and power inequities to achieve understanding, intercultural growth, mutuality, and social and global justice through critical self-transformation.

Entering into Dialogue

To recognize and embrace our connectedness even to people who are different from us, we have to engage in true dialogue. A central notion of dialogue is sharing and reciprocity. Communication scholars Starosta and Chen (2005) suggest that a focus on mutual *listening,* instead of talking, forms the core of successful intercultural dialogue. How to do this? A "sharing of narratives" is one metaphor:

> *We come to the world with a master narrative that explains what things are, which ones count for what, what is good or bad about them, and we "braid" these accounts of fact and value into a somewhat coherent personal web of meaning. (p. 277)*

Starosta and Chen go on to suggest that a good intercultural listener exchanges narrative accounts to expand his or her repertoire of possibilities in explaining the world—and this interest and skill is built on a foundation of openness, curiosity, and empathy.

An Eastern model of listening is also useful here. Japanese scholar Ishii (1984) models intercultural communication as listening. In this model, the effective intercultural communicator, sensitive to the other, thinks *carefully* before speaking and delivers a message that is never threatening or condemnatory and one that appears open to multiple possible interpretations. The listener hears the message, considers it, reconsiders it, trying on different possible interpretations—trying to understand the speaker's possible intent. When the listener believes she has understood the point being made, she frames a response, again in a nonthreatening manner. You can see that ambiguity is a feature of such listening, which may seem contradictory to other guidelines for competent communication that extol being clear and concise. Perhaps this points to a dialectical view. Intercultural dialogue may have to be clear *and* somewhat ambiguous.

There are many small interventions we might make in everyday life to change what we take for granted. Note how this student has learned to use intercultural relationships as a part of her antiracism struggle.

I am beginning to see the long-term benefits of intercultural relationships: acquiring knowledge about the world, breaking stereotypes, and acquiring new skills. I did not have any stereotypes of Brazilians before I met Anna, but I tell all my family and friends about her, so if any of them had any prior stereotypes, they may think differently now. I have also found that when you are friends with a person of a different culture, it tends to promote some sort of peace and unity in some small way. If I am with someone of a different culture, people are less likely to make racial remarks of any kind in front of them. For example, a co-worker of mine often tells jokes about gay or black people in front of workers that are white and seemingly heterosexual. When I bring a friend into work or go out with work friends that are of a different culture (Spanish, Ukrainian, or Brazilian), he will not tell these jokes. Although my friends are not even of the culture that he makes fun of, I think he is not sure of how his jokes will go over with people he sees as being "ethnic." Regardless, the jokes stop, and that is a step toward preventing racial discrimination.
—Michele

But how can we *really* hear the voices of those who come from cultures very different from our own—and especially those who have not been heard from? As you think about all the messages you hear every day, the most obvious voices and images are often the most privileged. To resist the tendency to focus only on the loudest, most obvious voices, we should strive for "harmonic discourse." This is discourse in which all voices "retain their individual integrity, yet combine to form a whole discourse that is orderly and congruous" (Stewart, 1997, p. 119).

Any conciliation between cultures must reclaim the notion of a voice for *all* interactants. In intercultural contexts, there are two options for those who feel left out—exit or expression. When people feel excluded, they often simply shut down, physically or mentally abandoning the conversation. When this happens, their potential contributions—to some decision, activity, or change—are lost. Obviously, the preferred alternative is to give voice to them. People's silence is broken when they feel that they can contribute, that their views are valued. And those who have historically been silenced sometimes need an invitation. Or those who have a more reserved conversation style may need prompting, as was the case with this traveler from Finland:

I was on a business trip in England with some colleagues. We visited universities, where we were shown different departments and their activities. The presenters spoke volubly, and we, in accordance with Finnish speaking rules, waited for our turn in order to make comments and ask questions. However, we never got a turn; neither had we time to react to the situations.

In sum, one way to become a more competent communicator is to work on "dialogue" skills by trying to engage in true dialogue. It's important to work on speaking and listening skills. A second way is to become interpersonal allies with people from other cultures.

Becoming Interpersonal Allies

The dialectical approach involves becoming allies with others for better intergroup relations. But we need a new way to think about multiculturalism and cultural diversity—one that recognizes the complexities of communicating across cultures and that addresses power issues. Otherwise, we can get stuck within a competitive framework: If we win something, the other person or group loses, and we can *only* win if others lose. This kind of thinking can make us feel frustrated and guilty.

The goal is to find a way in which we can achieve equitable unity despite holding many different and contradictory truths, a unity based on conscious coalition, a unity of affinity and political kinship, in which we all win.

intercultural alliances Bonds between individuals or groups across cultures characterized by a shared recognition of power and the impact of history and by an orientation of affirmation.

How can we do this? We first identify what **intercultural alliances** might look like. Communication scholar Mary Jane Collier (2002, 2014, and 2015) has identified characteristics of intercultural alliances and described examples in a variety of cultural contexts. The first characteristic of allies has to do with understanding power and privilege. Intercultural allies recognize and try to understand how ethnic, gender, and class difference lead to power, and try to manage these power issues. For example, in Chapter 1 we described one of Collier's (2015) projects in a nonprofit organization where members of poor families and middle-class community members worked together as allies to move the families out of poverty. She describes how difficult it was for many to acknowledge the social class, racial, ethnic, gender, and sometimes religious and political differences involved in these intercultural teams, and that they all needed to be able to confront and navigate these differences in a collaborative way.

In their study of college students, Chesler, Peet, and Sevig (2003) described how difficult it is for whites to understand power issues in interracial relationships. Their findings are based on interviews with white college students. They found that most students came to college with little experience in interracial relations and were generally unaware or held negative attitudes toward racial issues, or even saw themselves as victims, as described by one young man:

> *I think white males have a hard time because we are constantly blamed for being power-holding oppressors, yet we are not given many concrete ways to change. Then we just feel guilty or rebel. (p. 227)*

Through educational and personal experiences, some did come to understand privilege, but it is often a difficult process. As we discussed in Chapter 5, it involves a phase of feeling guilty and paralyzed. As one student described it, "I was horribly liberal-guilt ridden, paralyzed, I was totally blowing every little minor interaction that I had with people of color way out of proportion. . . . I saw how hard it was for me to stop doing that and start being more productive" (p. 227).

Being on two different sides of the power issue can challenge individuals in intercultural relationships. For example, Eleanor, an African American woman,

My roommate is from Poland; we are allies. We have similar traits in common. We also study the same major. Having the same course of study really helps us understand one another as it takes a certain type of personality to be successful. Understanding what it takes to be a good intercultural ally is indeed a learning process. There are many things that my Polish roommate does that I disagree with. But because he is from another culture I learn to understand what makes him unique and different. I have shared many meals with his extended family and even had him translate a Polish television show. I have met and enjoy being around his Polish friends.
    —David

and her friend Mairead, who is white, describe how they negotiate this issue in their own relationship. Often the only African American participating in discussions of race, Eleanor says she gets tired of "educating white girls" about racism. Mairead recognizes the problem of unwittingly saying or doing racist things and "hurting my friend." This is not merely a matter of benign faux pas, but is an ongoing source of oppression for black women, something with far deeper implications than simply saying the right thing in a social situation involving equals (McCullough, 1998, p. 83). Eleanor sometimes needs to withdraw from her white friends to restore herself. For her part, Mairead recognizes that she needs to educate herself about issues of racism. And the two women realize that negotiating time-out from a friendship or time to work on personal issues alone is one aspect of intercultural friendship in a racially segregated society.

A second component of intercultural alliances has to do with the impact of history: Intercultural friends recognize that people from historically powerful groups view history differently than do those who belong to less powerful groups. As we learned in Chapter 4, history often plays an important part in intercultural interactions. One of our colleagues describes how she and her friend Michael had very different views on history:

> *I was always amazed at how often my friend Michael talked about his relatives' experience during the Holocaust—even though his family wasn't directly involved. He was constantly told as he was growing up that prejudice against Jews could easily lead to another holocaust—and that he always had to be vigilant against anti-Semitism. For me, not being Jewish, I used to get impatient with him, but after learning more about the history and getting to know Michael better, I realize that this is an important part of who he is, and I've actually learned a lot from him about the experiences of a group of people that I knew little about. And I appreciate that side of him better.*

History also plays a part in black–white relationships. We're often struck by how, in discussions about race in our classes, white students go to great lengths to affirm that they aren't racist, often telling stories about friends and family members—who, unlike them, are racist. They seem to want to be absolved of past or present responsibilities where race was concerned. And whites expect persons of color to communicate in ways that are friendly, comfortable, and absolving. In this case, true dialogue for whites involves a genuine commitment to listening, to not being defensive, and to recognizing the historical contexts that impact us all. True intercultural friends accept rather than question others' experiences, particularly when historical inequities and power issues are involved. They recognize the importance of historical power differentials and affirm others' cultural experiences even when this calls into question their own worldviews.

The third component of intercultural alliances has to do with orientations of affirmation. Intercultural friends value and appreciate differences and are committed to the relationship even when they encounter difficulties and misunderstandings. For example, our student Shara comes from a cultural background that emphasizes commitment to family and family obligations. Her wife Kati has very little contact with her parents and siblings. They aren't estranged; they just aren't close. Kati would like to spend time with Shara on holidays, but Shara always spends holidays with her family, who live in another state. This issue has caused tension between the two over the years. But they each realize that these different values are important aspects of their identities. And in complex and dialectical ways, they learn from each other. Shara sometimes envies Kati for her relative freedom and lack of family obligations. But she also feels sorry for Kati that she doesn't have the kind of family support to back her up when she needs help. Similarly, Kati envies Shara's relationships with her large extended family and all the activities and help they provide. But she also sometimes feels sorry for Shara that she never seems to have any time for herself.

Building Coalitions

As we have emphasized throughout this book, many identities and contexts give meaning to who you really are. That is, your identities of gender, sexual orientation, race, region, religion, age, social class, and so on gain specific meaning and force in different contexts. Coalitions can arise from these multiple identities. There are many good examples, such as the Seeds of Peace project (see page 501), which brings together Jewish and Palestinian young people to work toward peace and harmony. Other local coalitions work to promote dialogue between blacks and whites, and between gays and straights.

Some contexts that arise in the future may cause you to rethink many of your identities. The rhetoric that people use to mobilize coalitions may speak to you in various ways. As you strive to build better intercultural relations, you may need to transcend some of your identities, or you may reinforce other identities. These shifting identities allow you to build coalitions among seemingly different peoples, to foster positive intercultural relationships for a better world.

Coalitions, which are built of multiple identities, are never easy to build. In the process, you may find that some of your own identities feel neglected or injured. Part of the process is the commitment to work through these emotional blows, rather than simply withdrawing to the safety of older identities. Work your way to a richer, more meaningful life by navigating between safety and stability, and change.

Social Justice and Transformation

As we near the end our journey, we would like to refer back to our ethical challenge in the first chapter—the responsibility that comes with the acquisition of intercultural knowledge and insights. As we noted then, this educational experience is not just transformative for you, the individual, but should also benefit the larger society and other cultural groups in the increasingly interdependent world.

The first step in working for social justice is acknowledging that oppression and inequities exist—as we have tried to point out, cultural differences are not just interesting and fascinating, they exist within a hierarchy in which some are privileged and set the rules for others (Allen, 2010; Sorrells, 2014).

Social inequities are sometimes manifested in work contexts. For example, workplace bullying—the ill treatment and hostile behavior toward people at work—has recently become a topic of interest to organizational communication scholars. Bullying behaviors range from the most subtle, even unconscious, incivilities to the most blatant, intentional emotional abuse and in some instances are targeted at others explicitly based on race/ethnicity. One study explored the connection between workplace bullying and racism for Asian Americans, African Americans, Latinos, and whites (Fox & Stallworth, 2005). The researchers found that while laws and norms no longer condone overtly racist behaviors, the workplace provides many opportunities for "subtle, even unconscious manifestations of racism, including neglect, incivility, humor, ostracism, inequitable treatment and other forms of 'micro-aggression'" (p. 439). Their results showed that experiences with general bullying were similar (and surprisingly frequent) across the four racial/ethnic groups; 97% of the respondents had experienced some type of general bullying. Members of the three ethnic minority groups reported higher instances of bullying based on race/ethnicity than whites. Many of the reported incidents involved a supervisor or occurred with the knowledge of supervisors. The instances were often subtle, seemingly relatively innocuous behaviors by themselves, but when delivered incessantly, the cumulative effects on the victims are of an unimaginable magnitude, leading to a general decrease in confidence in the organization and lack of confidence in the possibility of addressing or resolving the issues.

Starosta and Chen (2005) point out that intercultural listening should be followed by application. Dialogue should ultimately set things right that have been wrong. Good listening "promotes intercultural and interracial harmony, the amelioration of poverty, the introduction of justice, and mutual respect and harmony" (p. 282).

Johnson (2017) gives the following very concrete suggestions for working toward social justice and personal transformation:

1. Acknowledge that trouble exists. There are many obstacles to doing this. Many involved in oppression—those at the top—deny it, trivialize, call it something else, or blame those who are oppressed.

2. Pay attention. We have given you many suggestions for how to "pay attention," including intercultural listening. Johnson points out that there is a great deal of literature available representing many marginalized "voices," but these are rarely heard. For this reason, he suggests it is a good idea not to rely on the

In outlining specific ways in which white people can fight racism, Paul Kivel lists questions they can ask to better understand specific contexts in which they live and work.

WORKPLACE

1. *What is the gender, race and class composition in your workplace? Which groups hold which positions?*

2. *Who, by race, gender and class, has the power to make decisions about hiring, firing, wages and working conditions in your workplace? Who gets promoted and who doesn't?*

3. *Is hiring non-discriminatory? Are job openings posted and distributed? Do they attract a wide variety of applicants? Are certain groups excluded? Does the diversity of your workplace reflect the diversity of the wider community?*

4. *Are there "invisible" workers, people who cook, clean or do maintenance, for example, who are not generally noticed or paid well?*

5. *What is the racial composition of the people who actually own your workplace? Who makes money from the profits of your work?*

RELIGION

1. *What is your religious upbringing?*

2. *What did you learn about people of color in Sunday school or sermons? About Jewish people?*

3. *Was your religious community all white? Was the leadership of your religious organization all white?*

media for meaningful analysis of social oppression and inequalities—there is little money to be made from the stories of the powerless. While the media often give play to people of color who criticize affirmative action, or women who criticize feminism, there is little attention given to serious discussions of gender and violence, or class and race issues.

3. Do something. The more you pay attention to privilege and oppression, the more you'll see opportunities to do something.

Make noise, be seen. Stand up, volunteer, speak out, write letters, sign petitions, show up. Every oppressive system feeds on silence.

Find little ways to withdraw supports from paths of least resistance. You can start with yourself—by not laughing at racist or heterosexist jokes, or objecting to others' jokes.

I remember the first time I met my sister's boyfriend and he made a disparaging reference to gay people, I knew I had to say something. I objected in a

4. *What attitudes were expressed about people of color through discussion of missionary work, charity or social problems?*

5. *What do you know about the history of resistance to racism in your religious denomination?*

HOME AND FAMILY

1. *Were people of color and racism talked about in your childhood home? Think about particular incidents when it was. Was there tension around it? What was the general tone? Who initiated discussions and who resisted them?*

2. *Was there silence in your home on issues of racism or anti-Semitism? What did you learn from the silence?*

3. *As a child, what stories, TV shows or books influenced you the most in your attitudes about people of color? What do you carry with you from that exposure?*

4. *Talk with your partner, housemates and friends about [racial] issues. Notice the whiteness of your surroundings out loud to family and friends. This needn't be done aggressively or with great anger. You don't need to attack other people. Ask questions, notice things out loud, express your concerns and give other people room to think about and respond to what you say.*

5. *If you did a room-by-room assessment of your home today, would you find a diversity of images and items? If the answer is no, what do you and other family members lose because of that lack? How does it contribute to racial prejudice and discrimination?*

Source: From P. Kivel, *Uprooting Racism: How White People Can Work for Racial Justice* 3rd ed. (Gabriola Island, BC: New Society Publishers, 2011), pp. 242, 269, 303.

nice way, and we ended up talking for hours. I think he had just never thought about it very much and we're good friends to this day, although we disagree on almost every political and social issue!

Dare to make people feel uncomfortable, beginning with yourself. Ask your professors how many people of color are on the college's communication faculty. Ask why administrators at your children's schools are white men and why the teachers and secretaries are women. You might think this doesn't make much difference, but it can. . . . And discomfort is unavoidable. One student describes her discomfort: "I love movies, and now I point out all the instances of racist and homophobic humor in movies. My friends think I'm nuts, but they humored me, and now they're starting to point them out to me."

Actively promote change in how systems are organized around privilege. (See the Point of View box beginning on page 498 with Kivel's lists of questions to ask in the workplace, in houses of worship, and within the home and family.)

I n response to a massive public outcry, the city of Chicago created a task force to examine the relations between African Americans and the Chicago police. The Police Accountability Task Force released its official report in April 2016. *The New York Times* editorial board concludes: "No one who is even passingly familiar with the history of the Chicago Police Department can claim to be surprised by a new report showing that the department is plagued by systemic racism and operates with utter disregard for the lives of the black citizens whom it batters, maims, and kills" (Editorial Board, 2016). The report itself challenges the police department and the city toward changes: "Reform is possible if there is a will and a commitment. But where reform must begin is with an acknowledgment of the sad history and present conditions that have left the people totally alienated from the police, and afraid for their physical and emotional safety. And while many individuals and entities have a role to play, the change must start with CPD. CPD cannot begin to build trust, repair what is broken and tattered unless—from the top leadership on down—it faces these hard truths, acknowledges what it has done at the individual and institutional levels, and earnestly reaches out with respect. Only then can it expect to engage the community in a true partnership" (p. 20).

Sources: Editorial Board, (2016, April 14), "The sins of the Chicago police laid bare," *New York Times,* April 14, 2016. Retrieved August 8, 2016, from http://www.nytimes.com/2016/04/15/opinion/the-sins-of-the-chicago-police-laid-bare.html. Police Accountability Task Force (2016, April), *Recommendations for Reform: Restoring Trust between the Chicago Police and the Communities they serve.* Retrieved from https://chicagopatf.org/wpcontent/uploads/2016/04/PATF_Final_Report_4_13_16-1.pdf.

Don't keep it to yourself. Work with other people—build interpersonal alliances and build coalitions, as discussed earlier. Join organizations dedicated to change the systems that produce privilege and oppression. Most college and university campuses have student organizations that work on issues of gender, race, and sexual orientation. A list of such organizations follows.

National Association for the Advancement of Colored People (NAACP)

National Organization for Women (NOW)

National Conference for Community and Justice

National Gay and Lesbian Task Force

The Southern Poverty Law Center

The National Organization of Men against Sexism

National Urban League

community engagement Active engagement with communities to improve the lives of those in that particular group, by working together.

There are also many opportunities on the Internet where people can participate in online dialogues, gain insights into many different global cultures, and work for social justice. See the Internet Resources, section at the end of this chapter.

One important area where intercultural communication can be productively applied is **community engagement.** Many different organizations are interested in community engagement, such as the Centers for Disease Control, to advance their organizational missions (see the Point of View box on CDC community engagement on page 503).

Forgiveness

Sometimes the cultural divide simply seems too huge. Sometimes there are grievances perpetrated by one cultural group upon another or by one individual on another that are so brutal as to make the suggestions listed above sound hollow and idealistic. What can we say to the parents of Kayla Jean Mueller, a U.S. aid worker who was brutally killed by ISIS in 2015? She had devoted her life to helping refugee children in Syria's ongoing civil war through a Danish humanitarian organization. Or to Pauline Mitchell, the mother of Fred Martinez, a Native American who was brutally murdered because he was *nadleeh* (a Native American term meaning "two spirited—with spirit of both male and female"). His mother described the horror of his death: "He'd been chased, beaten with a rock. He had been left to bleed, with a fractured skull, alone in the dark in a little canyon. . . ."

We would like to return to the notion of forgiveness we introduced in Chapter 11. Although limited and problematic, forgiveness is an option for promoting intercultural understanding and reconciliation. As we noted, forgiveness is more than a simple rite of religious correctness; it requires a deep intellectual and emotional commitment during moments of great pain. It also requires a letting go, a moving on, a true transformation of spirit.

McCullough poses the question: "So if you set out to build 'the forgiving society' a society in which forgiveness flourishes and revenge is ever more infrequent what sorts of conditions and institutions would you need to put in place? And what kind of society would you end up with?" (p. 180). His answer is strongly related to the contact hypothesis that we discussed in Chapter 4. That is, leaders must construct conditions of contact among groups that lead to decategorization and recategorization, opportunities to develop intimate positive knowledge of each other, and provide superordinate goals that foster cooperation. For example, the Seeds of Peace program, started about 15 years ago, is trying to encourage the right kinds of contact. Seeds of Peace is a summer camp where adolescents from warring groups and countries are chosen by their education ministries on the basis of their leadership potential to participate in the camp. The entire agenda is structured around activities that help campers "develop durable friendships with people from the other side, appreciation and respect for the concerns that keep the conflict going and firm conviction that a peaceful and respectful coexistence is possible" (p. 200). The goal is simple: by building up a reserve of new positive experiences, these young leaders can use them as a sort of psychological buffer to help them undo the vicious ingroup–outgroup revenge that they will return to after camp.

The Amish are another group of people that try very hard to foster a life of forgiveness and peaceful relations—persecuted to the point of extinction in Europe in the 17th century, they came to America and settled. As Michael McCullough describes it, the Amish had 400 years to prepare their response to what happened on October 2, 2006, when a gunman entered a one-room Amish schoolhouse in Nickel Mines, Pennsylvania, sent the young male students and adults out of the school, tied up 10 girl students and then shot and killed five, wounded five more, and then shot himself. As soon as it happened, those in the community who knew the Amish well, told reporters at the scene that the Amish would find a way to forgive the killer. As Mennonite scholar Donald Kraybill, describes it, "the blood was hardly dry on the bare, board floor of the West Nickel Mines School when Amish parents sent words of forgiveness to the family of the killer who had executed their children" (Kraybill, 2006, C01).

Amish aren't the only ones; many famous proponents of peace and forgiveness—Martin Luther King, Jr., Mahatma Ghandi, Desmond Tutu—are motivated by deep religious beliefs concerning forgiveness. However, the link between religion and forgiveness is tricky. As Michael McCullough (2008) points out, religion can motivate forgiveness (as described earlier), but also revenge and hateful attitudes. In one study, people who made frequent donations to their churches (a measure of devoutness) administered higher levels of shock to their provokers than did the infrequent donors, even when statistically controlling for age, gender, and other measures of religious behavior (Greer, Berman, Varan, Bobrycki, & Watson, 2005). A recent poll investigating Americans' views on immigrants found that religiously unaffiliated Americans hold the most positive views of immigrants, and in contrast, white evangelical Protestants stand out as the only religious community in which a majority (53%) believe that immigrants present a threat to traditional American customs and values (Cooper, Cox, Lienesch, & Jones, 2016).

Perhaps a useful way to look at the role of religions is to see them as strong viable forces—capable of great good and also violence. "Religions are here for the foreseeable future and religious groups are going to keep doing exactly what they please, largely shaped by their perceptions of their self-interest. . . . We can either ignore religion's power to shape forgiveness and revenge to our peril or else we can try to understand that power and work with it. . . . We shouldn't let misplaced optimism cause us to expect anything more, but we shouldn't let unwarranted pessimism cause us to strive for anything less" (McCullough, 2008, p. 223).

The future of our world may well rest on our ability to control revenge and promote forgiveness. As we suggested in Chapter 11, scholar McCullough is convinced that we humans have an instinct for both, but is optimistic because we are an adaptive species. We have proved that we can adapt quickly to respond to challenges in the environment; we have also shown that we can learn to do the right thing—to learn where and when to seek revenge and when to forgive—by watching those who demonstrate forgiveness—leaders, teachers, parents—and finally, we are cooperative creatures and "we've already organized into very large groups called nation-states, perhaps the next evolutionary transition will result in a lasting bond of cooperation among the world's nations" (p. 234). We must believe that it is possible "as the bad people of the world get angrier, more organized and better funded, we really do have to worry about what the desire for revenge might be capable of doing to our world" (p. 225).

The Centers for Disease Control and Prevention (CDC) have identified core principles of their community engagement. As you have seen throughout the course of this book, intercultural understanding requires a wide range of knowledge about cultural groups, from history to politics to cultural patterns. This approach connects well with the experience of the CDC. For example, they note:

> *Become knowledgeable about the community in terms of its economic conditions, political structures, norms and values, demographic trends, history, and experience with engagement efforts. Learn about the community's perceptions of those initiating the engagement activities.*

It is important to note that they ask that you be self-reflexive about the image of your group in that community. As we noted earlier, intercultural communication is not simply about studying others.

Another principle focuses on understanding cultural diversity:

> *All aspects of community engagement must recognize and respect community diversity. Awareness of the various cultures of a community and other factors of diversity must be paramount in designing and implementing community engagement approaches.*

If you find yourself with a community engagement project, it will require that you pull together all of your intercultural communication skills. You may find the complete CDC guidelines to be helpful.

Source: From Centers for Disease Control and Prevention, *Principles of Community Engagement*, 2nd ed. (Atlanta, GA: CDC/ATSDR Committee on Community Engagement, June 2011). Retrieved September 24, 2011, from www.atsdr.cdc.gov/communityengagement/pdf/PCE_Report _508_FINAL.pdf.

WHAT THE FUTURE HOLDS

Predicting the future is impossible, of course, but we can be sure that the world that we live in tomorrow will be very different from the world we live in today. We live in a rapidly changing world. Although terrorist attacks are not new, they are increasing and continue to hit more and more countries. From Indonesia, Pakistan, and Iraq to Belgium, Canada, France, and the United States, terrorist attacks have impacted how we live everyday and how world events influence us. They also point to how interconnected we are with others whose cultural values and goals are quite different from ours.

The global economic situation continues to change. In 2016, the United Kingdom voted to leave the European Union (EU), as we noted earlier in this book. Known as Brexit, the details on what this means for Britain and for Europe remain to be worked out. However, in the immediate aftermath of the vote, the British pound lost value and the United Kingdom fell to the sixth largest world economy as the French took fifth place (Cockburn, 2016). Will Britain's economy continue to fall in the rankings and size? What will happen to the British pound? Will the border between Ireland and Northern Ireland be more closed? Will other European nations also want to leave the EU in the coming years? Or will more countries want to join the EU?

Rapidly falling oil prices have also increased instability in some parts of the world. The food shortages and unrest in Venezuela and the falling Russian ruble (and economy) are all related to falling petroleum prices. Nigeria, Iran, Iraq, Libya, Algeria, Saudi Arabia, and oil-producing countries are taking an economic hit. In contrast, oil-importing countries such as India, Japan, and European nations are seeing some economic relief from these lower prices. Although there is some debate over the relationship between oil prices and international relations, these low prices can impact foreign relations. Harold James (2016) of Princeton University notes that low prices "can also serve as a barometer—warning of approaching geopolitical storms." He adds that: "The leaders of oil-producing countries are already busy concocting narratives explaining their country's misfortunes" which involves largely blaming the United States. Ian Bremmer (2016), a political scientist, worries even more about Saudi Arabia when he writes: "While Venezuela may wake up to find its house on fire, Saudi Arabia, a declining power at the heart of an increasingly combustible region, risks burning down its neighbors' houses too."

While no one can predict the future, this instability resulted in the shooting down of a Russian fighter jet over Turkey in November 2015. Russia's military action in Syria (next to Turkey) led to the jet flying into Turkish airspace. As a result, Russia banned tourism to Turkey. In the summer of 2016, Russia lifted the ban after talks with Turkey. Along with terrorist attacks, Russia's ban hit the tourism industry hard: "It was Turkey's 10th consecutive monthly fall in arrivals, the longest streak of year-on-year declines in statistics that span a decade" (Biryukov, 2016). The point here is that these economic relations can impact intercultural relations, as fewer Russians and Turks had intercultural contact with a tourism ban.

Although predictions differed in when China would become the world's largest economy and the United States would fall to second, there was wide agreement of the inevitability of that happening. However, the slowing Chinese economy has delayed when that would happen, as "for the first time in almost a decade, China has lost ground in catching up with the U.S. economy" (*Bloomberg News,* 2016). What will happen when China overtakes the United States? How will U.S. Americans, and others, react? What other changes are we facing in the future?

The U.S. military remains a huge force overseas. U.S. American soldiers are stationed around the world, dwarfing the military presence of others: "Despite recently closing hundreds of bases in Iraq and Afghanistan, the United States still maintains nearly 800 military bases in more than 70 countries and territories abroad—from giant "Little Americas" to small radar facilities. Britain, France, and Russia, by contrast, have about 30 foreign bases combined" (Vine, 2015). Although not the primary reason for their assignment overseas, U.S. soldiers can play important roles in foreign relations as cultural ambassadors. Culturally insensitive soldiers can also wreak havoc on the image of the U.S. abroad. After a U.S. military base worker was arrested following the murder of a 20-year-old

Japanese woman, one of the biggest protests against the U.S. military bases in Okinawa took place in June 2016. The governor of Okinawa said, "The [Japanese] government . . . must understand that Okinawa residents should not suffer any more from the burden of the bases" (quoted in McCurry, 2016). Anger toward the United States has erupted in the Philippines, South Korea, and other locations from smaller crimes such as bar brawls to rape and murder of local people. These incidents do not enhance intercultural relations. In order to help its personnel do a better job overseas, the U.S. military has distributed cultural guides (see Point of View on page 507).

At the same time, people continue to work toward fixing injuries caused by cultural differences in the past. For example, in August 2016, the president of Taiwan, Tsai Ing-wen, apologized to the 16 recognized indigenous tribes: "For 400 years, every regime that has come to Taiwan has brutally violated the rights of indigenous peoples through armed invasion and land seizure" (quoted in Chan, 2016). Taiwan is not alone in trying to come to terms with its past.

In Belgium, the Royal Museum for Central Africa was closed in 2013 to undergo renovation and it plans to reopen later in 2017. The renovation is not simply to the building, but "will extend to the contents of this place of memory, where Belgium's colonial past will be addressed capably and openly" (Royal Museum for Central Africa). Belgium has been widely criticized for its colonial past, as well as the way that past has been treated in the museum (and elsewhere). Communication scholars Marouf Hasian, Jr. and Rulon Wood (2010) have analyzed the ways that the museum, which had been built to celebrate colonialism, has attempted to deal with that often brutal and horrific past. Australia instituted National Sorry Day to apologize to the indigenous children who were taken from their homes and raised with a different culture and language (see Figure 12-2). In the United States, a number of states have apologized for slavery, including Virginia, Maryland, North Carolina, Alabama, Florida, Tennessee, and a few others.

In addition to dealing with the distant past, sometimes it is necessary to deal with the recent past. One of the most famous recent attempts to deal with the past has been the Truth and Reconciliation Commission in South Africa. After the ending of apartheid in South Africa, the commission was set up to hear the truth about Apartheid and the ways the commission can foster reconciliation. This approach to dealing with the very recent past stands in sharp contrast to the Nuremberg trials after the collapse of Nazi Germany. In both cases, atrocities were committed. Which approach is the best way to deal with those who perpetrated the atrocities? Should the focus be on the crimes committed and punishments ensue, as in Nuremberg? Or should the focus be on an honest confrontation with the truth about what happened with a focus on reconciliation and amnesty for some, as in South Africa? Which approach makes most sense to you in shaping a more peaceful future?

How we and others face or do not face past events, how they help us understand the ways that history has changed all of us, and what we can do to face these past injustices are important in rebuilding intercultural relations and intercultural understanding. It also reshapes who we think we are which can be a frightening journey for some.

FIGURE 12-2   In February 2008, Australian Prime Minister Kevin Rudd formally apologized to the "stolen generations," the thousands of indigenous children who were forcibly removed from their families and communities between 1910 and 1970, as part of a government "assimilation" program. These children were placed in foster homes and institutions, resulting in many being sexually abused and/or forced into unpaid labor. Rudd said, "In saying we are sorry, and deeply sorry, we remind ourselves that each generation lives in ignorance of the long-term consequences of its actions." How might forgiveness function to overcome this horrible chapter in Australian history? (© *William West/AFP/Getty Images*)

There are no easy answers to what the future holds. But it is important to think dialectically about these issues, to see the dialectical tensions at work throughout the world. For example, a fractured, fragmented Europe is in dialectical tension with a unified Europe. We can see the history/past–present/future dialectic at work here. The fragmented Europe returns to its historical roots, but the unified Europe represents a forward-looking attempt to deal with the global economy. As a unifying force, a global economy also creates fragmentation.

The task of this book has been to help you begin to think dialectically, to begin to see the many contradictions and tensions at work in the world. Understanding these contradictions and tensions is key to understanding the events themselves. We acknowledge that there are no easy answers to the challenge of intercultural communication, but we hope we have given you the groundwork to begin your own intercultural journeys.

Continue to push yourself to see the complexities of life, and you will have taken an important step toward successful intercultural communication. Have the confidence to engage in intercultural communication, but be aware that there is always more to learn.

INTERCULTURAL TRAINING FOR U.S. AMERICAN SOLDIERS IN AFGHANISTAN

This writer lists suggestions U.S. soldiers are given to help them avoid negative encounters with Afghan citizens.

- *Do not walk in front of someone at prayer.*
- *Do not ask a Muslim if he is a Sunni or Shiite.*
- *Identify, show respect to, and communicate with elders. Work with elders to accomplish your mission.*
- *Do not unnecessarily humiliate men by forcing them onto the ground in front of their families.*
- *Males may never ask a man about his wife, daughters, or sisters. Females can.*
- *Do not yell or use profanity. It is a sign of weakness, poor upbringing, and lack of discipline.*
- *When a guest, do not focus complimentary comments on your host's possessions, as he/she will feel culturally obligated to give them to you.*
- *Do not stare at women, touch them, or try to shake a woman's hand (unless she extends her hand first).*
- *Do not react negatively if Afghan men kiss, embrace, or hold hands. This is polite behavior in Afghan society.*
- *Speak about your families. Afghans like to know you have them.*
- *If you are eating something, offer to share.*
- *Dress modestly. Do not wear shorts. Men should not go shirtless.*

Source: From E. Schmitt, "A man does not ask a man about his wife," *The New York Times,* January 8, 2006, Section 4, p. 7.

INTERNET RESOURCES

http://friendshiptrougheducation.org/ptpi.htm
This website, People to People International, which started after September 11, 2001 provides many resources for cyber dialogue and educational collaboration, primarily for elementary and high school children. Students can get pen pals and work on collaborative projects.

www.ciee.org
The Council on International Educational Exchange (CIEE) offers information about overseas study and work programs (including volunteering and teaching) for young people on its website, with resources for individuals, employers, communities, and educational institutions.

www.laetusinpraesens.org/links/webdial.php
This website links to different kinds of dialogue groups (intercultural, interfaith, etc.); resources on how to start such groups; and articles, books, and frameworks for understanding and implementing dialogue groups.

www.globalexchange.org/
The website of Global Exchange, a membership-based international human rights organization "dedicated to promoting social, economic, and environmental justice around the world," provides news on current global issues, organizes "reality tours" that take participants on education tours to various regions of the world, and offers opportunities to get involved in efforts to build international partnerships and affect change.

www.culturelink.org/dbase/links.html
Culturelink lists worldwide cultural "E-resources" on its site. They include intergovernmental organizations, national institutions, research institutions, art organizations, and publications.

http://www.international.gc.ca/cil-cai/index.aspx?lang=eng
The government of Canada hosts the Centre for Intercultural Learning. There are resources for different kinds of audiences, for example, government employees, human relations workers, and international teams.

SUMMARY

- Intercultural communication competence is both individual and contextual.
- Social science research has identified four individual components of intercultural communication: motivation, attitudes, behaviors, and skills.
- The levels of competence are unconscious incompetence, conscious incompetence, conscious competence, and unconscious competence.
- Interpretive and critical perspectives emphasize the importance of contextual constraints on individual intercultural competence.
- Applying knowledge about intercultural communication includes entering into dialogue, becoming interpersonal allies, building coalitions, and working for social justice and personal transformation.
- Forgiveness is an option when transgression of one cultural group on another is too brutal to understand.
- The future holds global challenges for intercultural communication in political, military, and economic contexts.

DISCUSSION QUESTIONS

1. In what ways is the notion of intercultural competence helpful? In what ways is it limiting?
2. How can you be an interpersonal ally? How do you know if you are being an ally?

3. How might you better assess your unconscious competence and unconscious incompetence?

4. How might the European Union affect the United States?

5. How does your own social position (gender, class, age, and so on) influence your intercultural communication competence? Does this competence change from one context to another?

ACTIVITIES

1. *Global Trends and Intercultural Communication.* Identify and list global trends that are likely to influence intercultural communication in the future. Reflect on the contexts and dialectics that might help you better understand these trends.

2. *Roadblocks to Communication.* Identify and list some of the biggest roadblocks to successful intercultural communication in the future. In what ways will the increasingly global economy be a positive or negative factor in intercultural communication?

3. *Strategies for Becoming Allies.* In a dialogue with someone who is culturally different from you, generate a list of ways that each of you might become an ally of the other. Note the specific communication strategies that will help you become each other's allies.

KEY WORDS

attitudes (483)

community engagement (500)

conscious competence (486)

conscious incompetence (486)

cosmopolitan communication (492)

D.I.E. exercise (485)

empathy (484)

intercultural alliances (494)

knowledge (482)

linguistic knowledge (483)

motivation (479)

nonjudgmentalism (485)

other-knowledge (482)

self-knowledge (482)

tolerance for ambiguity (483)

transpection (485)

unconscious competence (486)

unconscious incompetence (486)

REFERENCES

Allen, B. J. (2010). *Difference matters: Communicating social identity* (2nd ed.). Long Grove, IL: Waveland Press.

Arasaratnam, L., Banerjee, S., & Dembek, K. (2010). The integrated model of intercultural communication competence (IMICC): Model test. *Australian Journal of Communication, 37*(3), 103–116.

Bennett, M. J. (2013). Overcoming the Golden Rule: Sympathy and empathy. In M. J. Bennett (Ed.), *Basic concepts in intercultural communication: Selected readings* (pp. 191–214). London: Nicholas Brealey.

Biryukov, A. (2016, June 29). Putin ends Russian tourism ban to Turkey after Erdogan talks. *Bloomberg Businessweek.* Retrieved August 8, 2016, from http://www.bloomberg.com/news/articles/2016-06-29/putin-lifts-ban-on-russian-tourism-to-turkey-after-erdogan-talks.

Bloomberg News. (2016, January 29). China stumbles in race to pass U.S. as world's biggest economy. *Bloomberg Businessweek.* Retrieved August 8, 2016, from http://www.bloomberg.com/news/articles/2016-01-29/china-stumbles-in-race-to-pass-u-s-as-world-s-biggest-economy.

Bonilla-Silva, E., & Embrick, D. (2007). "Every Place Has a Ghetto . . .": The significance of Whites' social and residential segregation. *Symbolic Interaction, 30*(3), 323–345.

Bowman, N. A., & Park, J. J. (2014). Interracial contact on college campuses: Comparing and contrasting predictors of cross-racial interaction and interracial friendship. *Journal of Higher Education, 85*(5), 660–690.

Bremmer, I. (2016, January 21). Saudi Arabia will be the big loser from plunge in oil prices. *Time.* Retrieved August 8, 2016, from http://time.com/4188317/saudi -arabia-will-be-the-big-loser-from-the-plunge-in-oil -prices/.

Broome, B. J. (1991). Building shared meaning: Implications of a relational approach to empathy for teaching intercultural communication. *Communication Education, 40,* 235–249.

Broome, B. J. (1993). Managing differences in conflict resolution: The role of relational empathy. In D. J. D. Sandole & H. van der Merwe (Eds.), *Conflict resolution theory and practice: Integration and application* (pp. 97–111). Manchester, England: Manchester University Press.

Chan, R. (2016, August 1). Taiwan's president apologizes to indigenous people for centuries of abuse. *Time.* Retrieved August 5, 2016, from http://time.com /4433719/taiwan-president-tsai-ing-wen-apologizes -to-indigenous-people/.

Chen, G.-M. (2005). A model of global communication competence. *China Media Research 1*(1), 3–11.

Chen, G. M. (2014). Intercultural communication competence: Summary of 30-year research and directions for future study. In X. D. Dai & G. M. Chen (Eds.), *Intercultural communication competence: Conceptualization and its development in cultural contexts and interactions* (pp. 14–40). Newcastle, UK: Cambridge Scholars Publishing.

Chen, G.-M., & Starosta, W. J. (1996). Intercultural communication competence: A synthesis. In B. R. Burleson (Ed.), *Communication yearbook, 19* (pp. 353–383). Thousand Oaks, CA: Sage.

Chesler, M. A., Peet, M., & Sevig, T. (2003). Blinded by whiteness: The development of white college students' racial awareness. In A. W. Doane & E. Bonilla-Silva (Eds.), *White out: The continuing significance of racism* (pp. 215–230). New York: Routledge.

Cockburn, H. (2016, July 6). France overtakes Britain as world's fifth largest after Brexit fears hit markets. *The Independent.* Retrieved August 8, 2016, from http:// www.independent.co.uk/news/uk/home-news/france -britain-uk-world-s-fifth-largest-economy-brexit-eu -referendum-a7123761.html.

Collier, M. J. (1998). Researching cultural identity: Reconciling interpretive and postcolonial perspectives. In D. V. Tanno & A. González (Eds.), *Communication and identity across cultures* (pp. 122–147). Thousand Oaks, CA: Sage.

Collier, M. J. (2002). Intercultural friendships as interpersonal alliances. In J. N. Martin, T. K. Nakayama, & L. A. Flores (Eds.), *Readings in intercultural communication: Experiences and contexts* (pp. 301–310). Boston, MA: McGraw-Hill.

Collier, M. J. (2014). *Community engagement and intercultural praxis: Dancing with difference across diverse contexts.* New York: Peter Lang.

Collier, M. J. (2015). Partnering for anti-poverty praxis in Circles, USA: Applications for critical dialogic reflexivity. *Journal of International & Intercultural Communication, 8*(3), 208–223.

Cooper, B., Cox, D., Lienesch, R., & Jones, R. P. (2016, March 29). How Americans view immigrants, and what they want from immigration reform: Findings from the 2015 American Values Atlas. *prri.org.* Retrieved August 5, 2016, from http://www.prri.org/research /survey-americans-view-immigrants-want-immigration -reform-findings-2015-american-values-atlas/.

Editorial Board. (2016, April 14). The sins of the Chicago police laid bare. *New York Times.* Retrieved August 8, 2016, from http://www.nytimes.com/2016/04/15/opinion /the-sins-of-the-chicago-police-laid-bare.html.

Fox, S., & Stallworth, L. E. (2005). Racial/ethnic bullying: Exploring links between bullying and racism in the U.S. workplace. *Journal of Vocational Behavior, 66,* 438–456.

Greer,T., Berman, M., Vara, V., Bobrycki, L., & Watson, S. (2005). We are a religious people; we are a vengeful people. *Journal of the Scientific Study of Religion, 44,* 45–57.

Hammer, M. R., Martin, J. N., Otani, M., & Koyama, M. (1990, March). *Analyzing intercultural competence: Evaluating communication skills of Japanese and American managers.* Paper presented at the First Annual Intercultural and International Communication Conference, California State University, Fullerton.

Harris, T. M, Miller, A. N., & Trego, A. (2004). A co-cultural examination of community building in the interracial communication classroom. *Journal of Intergroup Relations, 31,* 39–63.

Hasian, M. A., Jr., & Wood, R. (2010). Critical museology, (post)colonial communication, and the gradual mastering of traumatic pasts at the Royal Museum for Central Africa (RMCA). *Western Journal of Communication, 74*(2): 128–149.

Howell, W. S. (1982). *The empathic communicator.* Belmont, CA: Wadsworth.

Ingraham, C. (2014, August 25). Three quarters of whites don't have any non-white friends. Retrieved from https://www.washingtonpost.com/news/wonk /wp/2014/08/25/three-quarters-of-whites-dont-have -any-non-white-friends/.

Ishii, S. (1984). *Enryo-sasshi* communication: A key to understanding Japanese interpersonal relations. *Cross Currents, 11,* 49–58.

James, H. (2016, February 5). How is cheaper oil affecting global stability? *The World Economic Forum.* Retrieved August 8, 2016, from https://www.weforum.org/agenda /2016/02/how-is-cheaper-oil-affecting-global-stability/.

Johnson, A. G. (2017). *Privilege, power, and difference* (3rd ed.). New York: McGraw-Hill.

Kivel, P. (2011). *Uprooting racism: How white people can work for racial justice* (3rd ed). Gabriola Island, BC: New Society Publishers.

Kraybill, D. B. (2006, October 8). Forgiving is woven into life of Amish. Op Ed page, *The Philadelphia Inquirer,* p. C01. Retrieved August 28, 2008, from http://infoweb.newsbank.com.ezproxy1.lib.asu.edu /iw-search/we/InfoWeb?p_product=AWNB&p _theme= aggregated5&p_action=doc&p_docid= 11A70D2BE9EAD1D8&d_ place=PHIB&f_ subsection= sCURRENTS&f_issue=2006-10-08&f_ publisher=.

Martin, J. N., Hammer, M. R., & Bradford, L. (1994). The influence of cultural and situational contexts on Hispanic and non-Hispanic communication competence behaviors. *Communication Quarterly, 42,* 160–179.

Martin, J. N., Hecht, M. L., Moore, S., & Larkey, L. (2001). An African American perspective on conversational improvement strategies. *Howard Journal of* Communications, *12,* 1–28.

Maruyama, M. (1970). *Toward a cultural futurology.* Paper presented at the annual meeting of the American Anthropological Association, published by the Training Center for Community Programs, University of Minnesota, Minneapolis.

McCullough, M. E. (2008). *Beyond revenge: The evolution of the forgiveness instinct.* San Francisco, CA: Jossey-Bass.

McCullough, M. W. (1998). *Black and White women as friends: Building cross-race friendships.* Cresskill, NJ: Hampton Press.

McCurry, J. (2016, June 19). Thousands protest at U.S. bases in Okinawa after Japanese woman's murder. *The Guardian.* Retrieved August 8, 2016, from https:// www.theguardian.com/world/2016/jun/19/thousands -protest-at-us-bases-on-okinawa-after-japanese-womans.

Osman, G., & Herring, S. (2007). Interaction, facilitation, and deep learning in cross-cultural chat: A case study. *Internet and Higher Education, 10,* 125–141.

Police Accountability Task Force. (2016, April). *Recommendations for Reform: Restoring Trust between the Chicago Police and the Communities they serve.* Retrieved from https://chicagopatf.org/wpcontent /uploads/2016/04/PATF_Final_Report_4_13_16-1.pdf.

Rosenberg, E., Richard, C., Lussier, M-T., & Abdool, S. N. (2006). Intercultural communication competence in family medicine: Lessons from the field. *Patient Education and Counseling, 61*(2), 236–245.

Royal Museum for Central Africa. (n.d.) Why renovate? Retrieved April 6, 2017 from http://www.africamuseum .be/renovation/renovate.

Ruth, J. L. (2007). *Forgiveness: A legacy of the West Nickel Mines Amish School.* Scottdale, PA: Herald Press.

Schmitt, E. (2006, January 8). A man does not ask a man about his wife. *The New York Times,* Section 4, p. 7.

Sobré-Denton, M. (2011). The emergence of cosmopolitan group cultures and its implications for cultural transition: A case study of international student support group. *International Journal of Intercultural Relations, 35,* 79–91.

Sorrels, K. (2014). Intercultural praxis: Transforming intercultural communication competence for the 21st century. In X-d. Dai & G. M. Chen (Eds.), Intercultural communication competence: Conceptualization and its development in cultural contexts and interactions (pp. 144–169). Newcastle, UK: Cambridge Scholars Publishing.

Spitzberg, B. H. & Changnon, G. (2009). Conceptualizing intercultural competence. In D. K. Deardorff, (Ed). The Sage handbook of intercultural competence (pp. 2–64), Thousand Oaks, Ca: Sage.

St.Amant, K. (2012). Culture, context, and cyberspace: Rethinking identity and credibility in international virtual teams. In P. H. Cheong, J. N. Martin & L. P. Macfadyen (eds). New media and intercultural communication: Identity,community and politics (pp. 75–92). New York: Peter Lang.

Starosta, W. J., & Chen, G.-M. (2005). Intercultural listening: Collected reflections, collated refractions. In W. J. Starosta & G.-M. Chen (Eds.), *Taking stock in intercultural communication: Where to now?* (pp. 274–285). Washington, D.C.: National Communication Association.

Stewart, L. P. (1997). Facilitating connections: Issues of gender, culture, and diversity. In J. M. Makau & R. C. Arnett (Eds.), *Communication ethics in an age of diversity* (pp. 111–125). Chicago, IL: University of Illinois Press.

Touraine, A., Dubet, F., Hegedus, Z., & Wieviorka, M. (1981). *Le pays contre l'Etat: Luttes occitanes.* Paris: Editions du Seuil.

Vine, D. (2015, July/August). Where in the world is the U.S. military? *Politico.* Retrieved August 8, 2016, from http://www.politico.com/magazine/story/2015/06/us -military-bases-around-the-world-119321.

Vision (2016). Combatants for Peace. Retrieved August 5, 2016, from http://cfpeace.org/about-us/our-vision/.

Wendt, J. (1984). D.I.E.: A way to improve communication. *Communication Education, 33,* 397–401.

Willis, P. (2011). Laboring in silence: Young lesbian, gay, bisexual, and queer-identifying workers' negotiations of the workplace closet in Australian organizations. *Youth & Society, 43*(3), 957–981.

Yep, G. A. (2000). Encounters with the other: Personal notes for a reconceptualization of intercultural communication competence. *The CATESOL Journal, 12*(1), 117–144.

CREDITS

[page 480, text] Vision, quote from "Combatants for peace" from *cfpeace.org* (2016). [page 480, text] Jayla, excerpt from "I think that you learn the most by traveling . . . differences in other cultures." Original Work; [page 481, text] Mary, excerpt from "Students Voices: I used to work part-time in a restaurant . . . I would have otherwise." Original Work; [page 482, text] E. Bonilla-Silva, and D. Embrick, quote from " "Every Place Has a Ghetto. . .": The significance of Whites' social and residential segregation" from *Symbolic Interaction* (2007): 323–345. [page 484, text] Paul Monette, excerpt from *Last watch of the night.* Harcourt Brace. [page 488, text] C. J. Levy, excerpt from "My family's experiment in extreme schooling" from *The New York Times* (September 2011). [page 488, text] L. Miller, excerpt from "How to raise a global kid" from *Newsweek* (July 25, 2011): 48–50. [page 489, text] E. Rosenberg, C. Richard, M-T. Lussier, and S. N. Abdool, quote from "Intercultural communication competence in family medicine: Lessons from the field" from *Patient Education and Counseling* (2006): 236–245. [page 492, text] W. J. Starosta, and G.-M. Chen, quote from "Intercultural listening: Collected refl ections, collated refractions" in *Taking stock in intercultural communication: Where to now?*, edited by W. J. Starosta, and G.-M. Chen. National Communication Association. [page 493, text] L. P. Stewart, quote from "Facilitating connections: Issues of gender, culture, and diversity" in *Communication ethics in an age of diversity*, edited by J. M. Makau, and R. C. Arnett. University of Illinois Press. [page 493, text] Michele, excerpt from "Students Voices: I am beginning to see the long . . . racial discrimination." Original Work; [page 494, text] M. A. Chesler, M. Peet, and T. Sevig, quote from "Blinded by whiteness: The development of white college students' racial awareness" in *White out: The continuing significance of racism*, edited by A. W. Doane, and E. Bonilla-Silva. [page 495, text] David, excerpt from "Students Voices: My roommate is from Poland . . . Polish friends." Original Work; [page 497, text] S. Fox, and L. E. Stallworth, quote from "Racial/ethnic bullying: Exploring links between bullying and racism in the US workplace" *Journal of Vocational Behavior* (2005): 438–456. [page 497, text] W. J. Starosta, and G.-M. Chen, quote from "Intercultural listening: Collected reflections, collated refractions" in *Taking stock in intercultural communication: Where to now?*, edited by W. J. Starosta, and G.-M. Chen. National Communication Association. [page 498–499, text] Paul Kivel, excerpt from *Uprooting Racism: How white people can work for racial justice, Third edition published 2011.* Paul Kivel. [page 501, text] M. E. McCullough, quote from *Beyond revenge: The evolution of the forgiveness instinct.* Jossey-Bass. [page 502, text] D. B. Kraybill, quote from "Forgiving is woven into life of Amish" from *The Philadelphia Inquirer* (October 8, 2006): p. C01. [page 502, text] M. E. McCullough, quote from *Beyond revenge: The evolution of the forgiveness instinct.* Jossey-Bass. [page 503, text] Centers for Disease Control and Prevention, excerpt from *Principles of community engagement, Second edition.* CDC/ATSDR Committee on Community Engagement. [page 505, text] J. McCurry, quote from "Thousands protest at U.S. bases in Okinawa after Japanese woman's murder." from *The Guardian* (June 19, 2016). [page 505, text] R. Chan, quote from "Taiwan's president apologizes to indigenous people for centuries of abuse" from *Time* (August 1, 2016). [page 505, text] Royal Museum for Central Africa, quote from "Why renovate?" from *africamuseum.be* (2013). [page 507, text] E. Schmitt, excerpt from "A man does not ask a man about his wife," from *The New York Times* (January 8, 2013): p. 7.

Name Index

Abdool, S. N., 489
Acheson, C., 289, 291
Achor, S., 277
Ackerman, P., 458
Adams, Lisa V., 30
Adelman, M. B., 337
Adler, P. S., 3–4, 206, 207, 338
Akwani, O., 350
Alba, R. D., 190, 204
Alberts, J. K., 288
Alcoff, L., 33
Alexander, B. K., 34, 62
Alexander, D., 235
Al Issa, A., 278
Allardice, R. R., 340
Allegretto, S., 199
Allen, B., 111, 187, 198
Allen, B. J., 414, 497
Allport, G. W., 47, 149
Almaleki, Faleh Hassan, 327
al-Masri, A., 441
Alnatour, O., 167
Al-Shaykh, H., 345
Al-Simadi, F. A., 278
Alsop, R., 343
Altameemi, Aiya, 327
Althusser, L., 174
Altman, A., 55
Amaya, H., 107
Ambady, N., 277, 279, 292, 293
Ambler, T., 29, 71, 106
American Indians by the
    Numbers, 9
Amichai-Hamberger, Y., 445
Amir, Y., 149
Amos, D., 319
Amsden, D., 127
Amundson, N. G., 57–58
Anderson, B., 200, 248–249

Anderson, R. N., 431
Andrews, J. R., 76
Andriyevskaya, Anna, 200
Angelos, J., 175
Anzaldúa, G., 140, 256, 352
Arasaratnam, L., 486
Archer, D., 285
Arcos, B., 452
Army Reserve Child, Youth &
    School Services, 344
Arnold, Matthew, 364
Arthur, John, 396
Asante, M. K., 61–62
Atkinson, Q. D., 266
Attenborough, R., 133
Audi, T., 448
Augsburger, D., 451, 462, 468,
    469–471
Austin, E. G., 329
Austin, S. B., 34
Axtell, R. E., 287
Ayala, C., 246

Bachman, B. A., 153
Baek, Y., 280, 281
Bahadur, G., 348
Bahk, C. M., 194
Baird, A. C., 127
Baldwin, J., 9
Baldwin, J. R., 85, 89, 428
Banerjee, S., 486
Banks, J., 10
Bänziger, T., 288
Bardhan, N., 492
Barnlund, D. S., 408–409
Barrett, T., 8
Barthes, R., 295
Barton, K., 5
Batalova, J., 7

Baudrillard, J., 136
Baxter, L. A., 403
Beamer, L., 16, 18, 248
Bearak, M., 396
Beckford, M., 455
Bederman, G., 184
Beech, H., 16
Befu, H., 248
Belkin, D., 135
Bell, S., 407
Bellah, R. N., 99
Beller, S., 229
Bello, R. S., 232, 278
Bender, A., 229
Bennett, J. M., 45, 207, 334
Bennett, M. J., 45, 70, 86, 88,
    101, 206–207, 485
Bennett, T., 382
Bente, G., 278
Berger, P., 442
Berlan, E. D., 34
Berman, M., 502
Bernstein, J., 199
Bernstein, N., 138, 231
Berry, J. W., 57, 321, 337,
    342, 351
Berry, M., 61, 290
Biryukov, A., 504
Black, J. S., 344
Blake, J., 193
Blanchot, M., 139
Blascovich, J. J., 278
Blasius, M., 141
Blinder, A., 148
Bloomberg News, 504
Blow, C. M., 379
Blumenthal, D., 198–199
Boase, J., 416
Bob Jones University, 374

Bobrycki, L., 502
Bochner, S., 337
Bonesteel, M., 362
Bonilla-Silva, E., 482
Boogaard, K., 239
Boone, J. A., 373
Botelho, G., 145
Bourdieu, P., 197
Bowles, S., 379
Bowman, N. A., 481
Boxer, D., 239
Braden, W. W., 127
Bradford, L., 246, 333, 488–489
Bradford, L. J., 397, 420
Braithwaite, C., 63, 290
Brandau-Brown, F. E., 278
Brantlinger, P., 46–47
Bremmer, I., 504
Brewer, C. A., 201
Brewer, N., 454
Brinkman, H., 151
Brislin, R., 47, 56, 211, 212
Brislin, R. W., 148
Brocchetto, M., 145
Brookhiser, R., 143
Broome, B. J., 28–29, 471, 472,
    484–485
Broverman, N., 396
Brumfield, B., 8, 11
Brummett, B., 365, 366
Bruni, F., 303
Brydum, S., 427
Buescher, D. T., 373
Bui, Q., 13
Bull, S., 371
Burack, A., 292
Bureau of African Affairs, 133
Burgoon, J. K., 278
Burke, J., 94
Burns, C., 5
Butler, R. L. W., 35
Butterfield, F., 408
Butterworth, M. L., 368
Buzzanell, P. M., 96

Cai, D. A., 447, 454
Caldarac, R., 284
Cameron, D., 396

Campo-Flores, A., 350
Canary, D. J., 184
Capobianco, S., 454
Caprario, C., 282
Carbaugh, D., 45, 47, 57, 61, 87,
    190, 290, 305
Carey, J. W., 91
Cargile, A., 91
Carrier, J. G., 407
Carroll, R., 302
Cashman, H., 258
Casmir, F. L., 49
Castiglioni, I., 88
Caulfield, K., 362
Cave, D., 124
Ceballos, N., 382
Ceja, M., 211
Cengel, K., 175
Centers for Disease Control and
    Prevention, 503
Cha, M., 280, 281
Chan, R., 505
Chan, S., 457
Chandler, J. V., 340
Chang, H., 291
Chanoff, S., 319
Chattopadhyay, S., 238
Chavez, K., 108–109
Chen, G. M., 62, 479, 486,
    492, 497
Chen, L., 53, 345, 403
Chen, T. C. C., 403
Chen, V., 202
Cheng, B. H., 100
Cheng, H., 404
Cheong, P. H., 112
Chesebro, J. W., 425
Chesler, M. A., 494
Chinese Culture Connection, 104
Chitgopekar, A. S., 397, 420
Cho, C. H., 376
Chokshi, N., 362
Chozick, A., 414
Chua, E., 232
Cigainero, J., 348
Cillizza, C., 198
Cisneros, J. D., 20
Clark, A. L., 277

Clark-Ibanez, M. K., 397, 404,
    428, 429
Clifford, J., 352
Coakley, J., 200
Cockburn, H., 504
Cohen, J., 385–386
Cohen, R., 421
Cohn, D., 8
Cohn, D. V., 5, 7
Cole, B. R., 20, 25
Cole, D., 10
Cole, M., 447, 449
Coleman, S., 407
Collie, T., 349
Collier, M. J., 29, 31–32, 74, 84, 88,
    172, 173, 174, 412, 471, 479,
    486, 491, 494
Cooper, B., 502
Corliss, H. L., 34
Cornell, S., 190
Cosgrove, D., 239
Costa-Lascoux, J., 300
Côté, S., 100
Covarrubias, P., 290
Cowburn, A., 427
Cox, D., 502
Craighill, P., 419
Cromie, W. J., 382
Cross, S. E., 170
Croucher, S. M., 52,
    281, 443
Crump, J. A., 30
Cruz-Janzen, M., 245
Curtin, P. D., 9
Custer, C., 18
Czyzewska, N., 382

Dalzell, T., 235–236
Darbelnet, J., 251
Davidson, H., 201
Davis, M., 454
Davis, O. I., 307
Day, E., 110
Dearing, J. W., 55
Dehaene, S., 229
De La Garza, A. T., 66
Delgado, F., 26, 107, 109
DeLuca, K. M., 68

Dembek, K., 486
Demont-Heinrich, C., 256
Demytrie, R., 459
Desilver, D., 8
Deutscher, G., 229
DeVega, C., 379
de Waal, F. B. M., 279
DeWolf, C., 335
Dhar, S., 471
Dickey, J., 457
Dillon, S., 17
Dion, K. K., 413
Dion, K. L., 413
Dodd, C. H., 428
Donohue, W. A., 468
Dougherty, C., 306
Doupona Topič, M., 200
Dovidio, J. F., 153
Drzewiecka, J. A., 307, 397,
    403, 420
Du, S., 284
Duara, N., 448
Duell, M., 442
Duff-Brown, B., 349
Duggan, M., 24
Dunbar, R. A., 100
Dutta, U., 35
Duvall, J., 458
Dyer, R., 377

Eagan, K., 8
Echu, G., 261
Edmonston, B., 424
Ehrenreich, B., 322
Eisner, F., 288
Ekman, P., 280, 283, 288
Elias, N., 419
Ellis, D. G., 471
El Nasser, H., 327
Embrick, D., 482
Emma, 236
Ender, M. D., 207
Eng, D. L., 404
Engen, D., 60, 197
Engle, J., 99
Engstrom, C. L., 107
Erbe, B., 153
Erbert, L. A., 95

Erikson, E., 168
Ernst & Young, 343
Evanoff, R. J., 31
Ex, K., 362

Fantz, A., 8, 11
Farley, R., 420
Farrell, E., 397
Fattah, H. M., 285
Faulkner, S. L., 85, 89
Fausset, R., 148
Feghali, E., 196
Fellag, N., 455, 456
Felmlee, D., 397, 404,
    428, 429
Ferguson, R., 178
Festinger, L., 336
Field, A. E., 34
Fink, E. L., 447, 454
Finkle, J., 20
Fisher, W., 135
Fiske, J., 365, 366
Fitz, N., 13
FitzGerald, F., 122
Fitzpatrick, M. A., 450
Fletcher, C. V., 57
Flores, L., 377
Flores, L. A., 69, 403
Floyd, K., 277, 278
Foeman, A. K., 203
Foner, E., 11
Foucault, M., 186
Foucault Welles, B.,
    367–368
Fox, K., 382
Fox, S., 497
France, L. R., 362
Frankenburg, E., 8
Frankenburg, R., 190, 191
Franklin, M. I., 23
Freedom on the Net, 21
Frey, W. H., 5
Friedman, T. L., 15
Frith, K., 404
Frum, D., 151
Fry, R., 5, 13, 187–188
Fujioka, F., 374
Funk, C., 419

Fuoss, K. W., 214
Furnham, A., 333, 337
Fussell, P., 12, 197, 298

Gaertner, S. L., 153
Gajjala, R., 416
Galati, D., 279
Gale, T., 239
Gallager, C. A., 193
Gallardo, M., 33
Gallois, C., 54
Gao, G., 412–413
Garcia, W., 54, 410
Gardham, D., 455
Gardner, W., 125
Gareis, E., 95, 412, 414, 425
Garrod, O. G. B., 284
Gates, H., 407–408
Gérard-Libois, J., 134
Gershman, J., 448
Giaclone, R. A., 167
Giancola, J., 198
Gibson, C. B., 105
Giles, H., 54
Gill, A., 431
Gilroy, P., 144
Gleason, M. E. J., 416
Goffman, E., 167
Goldstein, D., 257
Gonzalez, D., 348
Gonzalez-Barrera, A., 7
Goodman, E., 34
Gottschall, J., 282
Goudreau, J., 239
Gould, S. J., 46
Goulet, L. S., 415, 416
Graham, J. A., 421
Graham, M. A., 413, 424
Granhag, P. A., 278
Green, A. S., 416
Green, D. M., 292
Greenberg, A., 420
Greenberg, D., 142
Greene, H., 298
Greer, T., 502
Gregersen, H. B., 344
Greico, E. M., 318
Grice, H., 233

Griffin, R., 5
Griggs, B., 372
Grindstaff, D. A., 68
Grossberg, L., 89
Growing apart, 12, 13
Guan, X., 232
Guback, T., 381
Gudykunst, W. B., 49, 53, 55, 56, 154, 232, 289, 333
Guelke, A., 133
Gullahorn, J. E., 342
Gullahorn, J. T., 342
Gunn, J., 366
Gutua, M. W., 56

Haley, A., 299
Hall, B. J., 31, 33
Hall, E. T., 45, 49, 231, 285, 289
Hall, S., 369, 370
Halpin, P., 126
Halualani, R. T., 8, 404
Hamilton, D. L., 208
Hamlet, J. D., 62
Hammer, M. R., 63, 451, 452, 453, 486, 488–489
Hammond, D., 425
Hampton, K. N., 307, 415, 416
Hanasono, L. K., 53
Harberson, S., 135
Hardiman, R., 180, 183
Harrell, T., 342
Harris, T. E., 153
Harris, T. M., 480
Hart, B., 153
Hartmann, D., 190
Hasian, M., Jr., 189, 505
Hatay, J., 472
Hause, K. S., 184
Hawkes, K., 23
Head, K., 340
Healey, P., 444
Hecht, M. L., 62–63, 85, 89, 171, 172, 211, 294, 491
Hegde, R., 67, 146, 330, 352, 380
Hegde, R. S., 74, 84, 88
Heim, J., 145

Heinen, J., 134
Henderson, M., 328
Herring, S., 490
Heuschner, H., 278
Hirsch, M., 457
Hirsch, P. M., 367
Hochschold, A. R., 322
Hocker, J. L., 453, 462, 465, 471
Hocquenghem, G., 141
Hodali, D., 317
Hofstede, G., 86, 94
Høgh-Olesen, H., 284
Holmes, A., 372
hooks, b., 298
Horenczyk, G., 58
Horrigan, J., 24
Hotta, J., 412
Houd, A., 317
Houston, M., 155
Howe, N., 187, 188
Howell, W. S., 31, 487
Hsu, H., 193
Hughes, M., 455
Humes, K. R., 5
Hymes, D., 57, 87
Hymowitz, C., 414

Ingraham, C., 481
International Organization for Migration, 318
Internet Statistics for Africa, 24
Irwin, N., 13
Isaac, M., 306
Ishii, S., 62, 347, 492
Izadi, E., 125
Izard, V., 229

Jablow, A., 425
Jack, R. E., 284
Jackson, R. L., III, 172, 351
Jackson, S. J., 367–368
Jacobson, C. K., 429
Jacoby, J., 138
James, H., 504
James, N. C., 399–400
James, S., 322
James-Huges, J., 351

Jameson, F., 130
Jandt, F. E., 63–64, 194
Jeneson, A., 279
Jetten, J., 66
Johannesen, R. L., 29, 31
Johannessen, H., 446
Johnson, A., 294
Johnson, A. G., 112, 480, 497–498
Johnson, B. R., 429
Johnson, K., 448
Johnson, M., 53
Jones, M., 204
Jones, N. C., 5
Jones, R. P., 502
Jung, E., 171

Kahlenberg, R. D., 198
Kale, D. W., 31
Kant, I., 31
Kantor, J., 126
Karis, T. A., 429
Kashima, E. S., 337
Katz, E., 363–364, 376
Katz, J., 174
Kavanaugh, B., 235
Kayne, E., 5
Kealey, D. J., 337
Kelley, D. L., 466, 467
Kelly, W. E., 430–431
Keltner, D., 100
Kennedy, R., 142
Kerby, S., 5
Khazan, O., 199
Khuri, F. I., 285
Kim, G. J., 416
Kim, H., 416
Kim, J., 383
Kim, M. S., 54, 56, 106, 168–169, 171, 291, 453
Kim, S. Y., 383
Kim, U., 337
Kim, Y. Y., 52, 66, 332, 333, 336, 337, 347, 351
Kinefuchi, E., 65–66
King, M. L., Jr., 458
Kirkman, B. L., 105
Kirkpatrick, D. D., 28

Kirschbaum, K., 471
Kissane, D., 265
Kitano, H. H. L., 431
Kivel, P., 480, 498–499
Klauer, K. C., 229
Klohnen, E. C., 405
Kluckhohn, F., 94–95, 96, 97, 102
Kochhar, R., 13
Kochman, T., 292
Koeppel, D., 441
Koerner, A. F., 450
Kohls, L. R., 98
Korem, A., 58
Kornai, A., 22
Koutonin, M. R., 335
Kövecses, Z., 230
Koyama, M., 486
Kraidy, M. M., 67
Kramer, S., 441
Kramsch, C., 263
Kraus, L., 454
Kraus, M. W., 100
Kraybill, D., 451, 502
Krieger, J. L., 171
Kristjánsdóttir, E. S., 88, 346
Krizek, R. L., 246
Krogstad, J. M., 5, 8
Kroom, S., 60
Kross, E., 306
Kudak, A. D., 57–58
Kuhn, T., 49
Kunuroglu, F., 60
Kwon, J., 383
Kyriazis, S., 372
Kyrnin, J., 296

Ladegaard, H. J., 66
Lakoff, G., 230
Lam, B., 295
Lambert, W. E., 327
Lampe, P., 419
Land, M., 386–387
Landis, D., 45, 47
Lapchick, R. E., 5
Larkey, L., 491
Lee, J. J., 349

Lee, M., 376
Lee, P. W., 409
Lee, S. M., 424
Lee, W., 74, 84, 88
Lehtonen, J., 290
Lemish, D., 419
Levy, C. J., 488
Lewin, K., 409, 410
Liebes, T., 363–364, 376
Lienesch, R., 502
Lindskold, S., 167
Lindsley, S. L., 444–445
Lipsitz, G., 365–366
Lloyd, C., 143
Loden, M., 111
Loewen, J. W., 9, 131, 300
Logan, J. R., 420
Loh, E., 337
Long, J. M., 363
Lopez, M. D., 349
Lopez, M. H., 245
Louet, S., 385
Low, D., 76
Lowe, K. B., 105
Lu, Y., 56
Lukács, György, 156
Luo, M., 196
Luo, S., 405
Lussier, M. T., 489
Lyotard, J. F., 132
Lysgaard, S., 339

Mabizela, P., 452
Madhani, A., 442
Madsen, R., 99
Malcolm X, 299, 300, 458
Malesky, E. J., 5
Maluso, D., 295
Mancini, M., 409
Mann, S., 278
Manusov, V., 380
Mark my words, 56
Marshall, M. G., 20, 25
Marsiglia, F. F., 294
Martin, J., 153
Martin, J. K., 176
Martin, J. N., 35, 45, 47, 49, 69, 85, 106, 246, 288, 333, 336,

342, 343, 397, 403, 420, 486, 488–489, 491
Martin, P., 322
Martinez, A. M., 284
Martinez, J., 255
Martinez, J. H., 245
Martinez, R., 179, 208
Maruyama, M., 485
Marx, E., 254
Mashal, M., 420
Mason, J., 126
Matsumoto, D., 280
Matsumoto, Y., 232
Mayo, C., 464
McClintock, P., 385
McCullough, M. E., 466, 467, 495, 501–502
McCullough, M. W., 403
McCurry, J., 505
McDonald, S. N., 192
McFadden, S., 362
McGreal, C., 171
McKay-Semmler, K., 52, 66
McKenna, K. Y. A., 416
McKenzie, S., 145
McKinley, J., 448
McLuhan, M., 19
McPhillips, D., 386
Mehl, M. R., 184
Meléndez, M., 252
Mendoza, S. L., 61
Merkin, R., 55
Merritt, B. D., 209, 378
Messman, S. J., 454
Meyers, M., 379
Miike, Y., 49, 61, 62
Mikesell, R. I., 454
Miles, O., 234
Miller, A., 209
Miller, A. N., 480
Miller, L., 488
Miller, R. L., 204
Minde, T., 337
Mindell, A., 464
Mishel, L., 199
Mishory, J., 187–188
Mitchell, J., 400
Mitchell, P., 454

Mitchell-Kernan, C., 421
Mittal, V., 18
Moeai, J., 413, 424
Moghaddam, F. M., 405
Mok, D., 337
Mols, F., 66
Monette, P., 484
Montepare, J. M., 280
Montgomery, B., 403
Moon, D., 47, 68, 191
Moon, D. G., 198, 368
Moore, R. M., 421
Moore, S., 491
Moritsugu, H., 255
Morris, C. E., III, 143
Mura, D., 352–353
Muzrui, A., 14–15
Myers, K., 191

Nagarajan, R., 186
Nakano, M., 140
Nakayama, T. K., 20, 45, 47, 69,
    74, 84, 85, 88, 189, 212, 246,
    250, 288, 307, 368, 403, 426
Nance, T. A., 203
Nardi, P. M., 425, 426
Nee, B. D. B., 300
Nee, V. G., 300
Neuliep, J. W., 53
Newberg, S. L., 211
Newcomb, H., 367
Newlove, R., 320
Niederhoffer, K. G., 184
Niiya, B., 131
Nobile, P., 143
Noguez, D., 264
Nwanko, R. N., 347
Nwosu, P. O., 351

Obama, B. H., 151, 169
Oberg, K., 339
Oetzel, J., 452, 471
Oetzel, J. G., 54, 447,
    466–467
Ogay, T., 54
O'Hearn, C. C., 330
Oi, M., 133
Ojwang, B. O., 67–68

Olaniran, B. A., 418
Oliver, M. B., 375
Omi, M., 188
Onishi, N., 385
Ono, K., 66
Ono, K. A., 373, 383
Onwumechili, C., 347
Onwumechilia, C., 351
Orbe, M. P., 63, 68, 111,
    240, 241
Orfield, G., 8
Orge, M. P., 63
Osbeck, L. M., 405
Osman, G., 490
Ostler, R., 263
Otani, M., 486

Parameswaran, R., 387
Park, H. S., 232
Park, H. W., 416
Park, J., 280, 281
Park, J. J., 481
Passel, J. S., 5, 7
Patel, S., 288
Patterson, M. L., 280
Pauker, K., 292
Peake, B., 305
Pearson, J. C., 57–58
Pedersen, P. B., 176
Peet, M., 494
Pennebaker, J. W., 184
Perez, F. G., 95
Perry, S. P., 363
Pettigrew, T. F., 153
Pew Research Center for the
    People & the Press, 194, 306
Philipsen, G., 87, 106
Phillips, K. W., 8
Pica, P., 229
Piff, P. K., 100
Pike, G. R., 465
Plummer, D. L., 401
Pogrebin, L. C., 402, 403
Police Accountability Task Force,
    Chicago, 500
Pollick, A. S., 279
Ponterotto, J. G., 176
Powell, R. D., 429

Poyrazli, S., 349
Pratik, J., 349
Preston, J., 297
Preuschoft, S., 279
Proust, M., 296–297
Pruden, G. B., Jr., 300
Purcell, K., 20, 24, 415, 416
Putnam, L. L., 451

Quivers, R., 379

Ragsdale, J. D., 278
Rahmani, D., 52
Rainie, L., 20, 24
Ralston, J., 349
Ramirez, A., 278
Ramirez, R. R., 5
Ranie, L., 415, 416
Ray, G. B., 277
Reid, B., 348
Ribeau, S. A., 172
Rice, C., 349
Rice, R. E., 416
Richard, C., 489
Richeson, J., 294
Ridge, S., 282
Roberts, P. C., 16
Roberts, T. L., 241
Robins-Early, N., 302
Roediger, D., 10
Roediger, D. R., 189, 299
Roff, P., 372
Rogan, R. G., 63
Rogers, E. M., 54
Rohrlich, B., 333, 336
Rohter, L., 265
Roland, A., 169–170
Rolison, G. L., 198
Romano, D., 424
Root, E., 83
Root, M. P. P., 203, 397, 404,
    422, 423, 424
Rosaldo, R., 46
Rosefeld, P., 167
Rosenau, J. N., 326
Rosenberg, E., 489
Rosenblatt, P. C., 429
Rosener, J. B., 111

Rosenfeld, P., 167
Rosenwald, M. S., 396
Ross, M. H., 446
Ross, S. D., 209
Rotheram-Borus, M. J., 204
Roy, J. H., 261
Royal Museum of Central Africa, 505
Ruggiero, K. M., 327
Russo, R., 419
Ruvolo, C. M., 208
Rymer, R., 257

Sabah, Z., 373
Saenz, R., 431
Saiegh, S. M., 5
Sajavaara, K., 290
Sakoui, A., 381
Salamon, J., 378
Sapir, E., 227
Saulny, S., 128, 202
Sauter, D. A., 288
Sauvage, J. L., 257–258
Saylor, S., 298
Scherer, K. R., 288
Schiefenhovel, W., 280
Schmidt, S., 279
Schmitt, E., 507
Schwartz, D., 327
Schwartz-DuPre, R. L., 369
Schwarzwald, J., 149
Schwirtz, M., 459
Schyns, P. G., 284
Scott, K. D., 258
Scott, S., 369
Scott, S. K., 288
Sedgman, J. M., 348
Seel, P., 140–141
Semlak, J. L., 57–58
Sevig, T., 494
Shapiro, R. B., 54
Shaw, P., 404
Shebaya, H., 14
Shelton, J. N., 294
Shepherd, J., 372
Sherman, S. J., 208
Sherrod, D., 425
Shim, Y-j., 106

Shizuru, L. S., 413, 424
Shome, R., 67, 146
Shuter, R., 112, 238, 239, 454
Sias, P. M., 403
Siemaszko, C., 14
Sigelman, L., 176
Sillars, A. L., 465
Silverstein, S., 258
Simon Wiesenthal Center for Tolerance, 23
Singer, M. R., 48
Singh, R., 405
Singhal, A., 55
Sini, B., 279
Sinmaz, E., 237
Slackman, M., 28
Smart, A., 408
Smith, A., 306
Smith, C., 20
Smith, R. J., 274
Smith, S., 341
Smith, Tuhiwai, 64
Smith, T. W., 176
Snyder, B., 18
Snyder, G., 418
Snyder, M., 380
Sobré-Denton, M., 492
Solórzano, D., 211
Sorrels, K., 479, 491, 497
Spelke, E., 229
Spinella, S., 457
Sprecher, S., 413
Squires, D., 198–199
Stack, L., 348
Staggs, S. L., 204
Stallworth, L. E., 497
St. Amant, K., 417, 418–419, 490
Stark, J., 27
Starosta, W. J., 479, 492, 497
Steel, P., 55
Stephan, C. W., 149, 150, 153, 211, 401
Stephan, W. G., 149, 150, 153, 211, 401
Stepler, R., 194
Stewart, E. C., 70, 101
Stewart, F. R., 292
Stewart, L. P., 493

Steyn, M., 132
Strauss, V., 30
Strauss, W., 187, 188
Strodtbeck, F., 94–95, 96, 97, 102
Stryker, S., 140
Stults, B. J., 420
Suchan, T. A., 201
Sudweeks, S., 413
Sue, D. W., 294–295
Sue, S., 249
Sugarman, J., 30
Sulitzeanu, A. B., 329
Sullivan, W. M., 99
Suwinyattichaiporn, T., 112
Swami, V., 282
Swarns, R., 47
Swarns, R. L., 126, 155
Swidler, A., 99
Szarota, P., 284
Sze, H., 424

Tajfel, H., 170
Takaki, R., 10
Tan, A., 374
Tan, D., 405
Tan, G., 374
Tanno, D. V., 63–64
Tao, Y., 284
Taras, V., 55
Tateishi, J., 138
Taylor, D. M., 327
Taylor, P., 245, 419
Tedeschi, J. T., 167
Tehranian, M., 317
Teixeira, R., 5
Tell, D., 132
Tharoor, I., 283
Thomas, M., 172
Thompson, H., 283
Thompson, L., 133
Thompson, M., 262
Thonssen, L., 127
Ting-Toomey, S., 53, 54, 56, 171, 232, 412, 447, 454, 466–467
Tinti, C., 279
Tipton, S. M., 99

Tomkiw, L., 200
Tomlinson, J., 384
Tompkins, P. K., 34–35
Tovée, M. J., 282
Tracy, S. J., 113
Tran, M., 460
Trego, A., 480
Trethewey, A., 109
Trinh, T. M., 190
Tripp, C. A., 142, 143
Troianovski, A., 246
Tuch, S. A., 176
Tucker, M. B., 421
Turkle, S., 25, 416–417
Turner, L. H., 454
Turner, V. W., 351
Tusk, D., 151
Tyson, A. S., 274

UNHCR Statistical Online
    Population Database, 50–51
United Nations High Commissioner
    for Refugees, 323
Urban, E. L., 63
U.S. Census Bureau, 193
U.S. Citizenship and Immigration
    Services, 421
U.S. Department of Homeland
    Security, 209–210
U.S. Department of State, 319

Vachon, L. A., 384
Vande Berg, L. R., 304
van de Vijver, F. J., 60
Varan, V., 502
Varis, T., 381
Varner, I., 16, 18, 248

Velasco, G., 245
Vinay, J. P., 251
Vine, D., 504
Vision, 480
Vorhauser-Smith, S., 343
Vrij, A., 278

Waldron, V. R., 466, 467
Walmsley, R., yy
Walsh, D., 8
Walsh, M. F., 18
Ward, C., 333, 337
Warmsley, R., 98
Warren, J. R., 171
Wasilewski, J. H., 47
Watling, J. R., 204
Watson, S., 502
Weber, N., 454
Weele, J. V.-V., 277
Wei, L., 24
Weinman, A. M., 452
Weinmann, K., 253
Weisbuch, M., 277, 279,
    292, 293
Weissman, D., 333
Weitz, R., 112
Wendt, J., 485, 486
West, C., 9
Whitehead, T., 455
White House, The, 151
Whorf, B. L., 227
Wilkins, R., 290
Williams, H., 386
Williams, R., 83
Willis, P., 491
Wilmot, W. W., 453, 462,
    465, 471

Wilson, S. B., 421
Wilson, S. R., 53
Winant, H., 188
Winsor, M., 24
Winterich, K. P., 18
Wise, T., 193
Witte, K., 334
Witzel, M., 29, 71, 106
Wood, J. T., 184
Wood, R., 505
Wood, R. W., 320
Woollacott, J., 382
World Migration Report, 318
Worstall, T., 16
Wright, T. J., 54

Yagmur, K., 60
Yamanouchi, K., 184
Yang, P., 417
Yee-Jung, K. K., 54
Yellow Bird, B. M., 246
Yep, G. A., 74, 84, 88, 491
Yohn, D. L., 19
Yoshino, K., 396
Yosso, T., 211
Yub, H., 284
Yu-Sion, L., 300

Zarefsky, D., 76
Zaretsky, R., 283
Zhang, H., 446
Zhang, J., 466–467
Zhang, Q., 452, 466–467
Zhang, S., 278
Zickuhr, K., 415
Zimmerman, S., 337
Zong, J., 7

Subject Index

absent history, 125
abstract communication, 86
acceptance stage of identity
    development, 181–182, 203
access
    to communication technology,
        24–25
    to information, 20–21
accommodating style of conflict
    resolution, 452–453
accommodation strategies for
    communication, 242–243
achievement gap, 13
activity values, 101
adaptation, individual influences
    on, 333
adjustment phase of U-curve theory
    of adaptation, 341–342
affective conflict, 449
Afghanistan
    child marriages in, 420
    conflict in, 27–28
    military personnel in, 339–340,
        507
African Americans
    call-response interaction
        of, 62
    characteristics of effective
        communication for, 491
    Chicago Police Department
        and, 500
    cultural spaces of social media
        and, 306
    identity labels for, 176
    as immigrants, 9
    passing as white, 135
    racialization and, 10–11
    segregation of, 299–300, 301, 328

stereotypes of, 209
    women, and kitchens,
        307–308
    women, in popular culture,
        378–379
Afrocentricity, 61–62
age identity, 186–188
aggressive accommodation
    strategies for communication,
        242–243
aggressive assimilation strategies
    for communication, 242
aggressive separation strategies for
    communication, 243
Aladdin (movie), 373
alcohol, talk about drinking, 107
Algeria, 4
Allies, 31–32
allies, interpersonal, becoming,
        494–496
Al-Qaeda, videos of, 442
altered history, 125
alternative history, 125
ambiguity
    conflict and, 443–444
    tolerance for, 483–484
American Civil Liberties Union,
        396
American dream, 198
American Radio Works, 156
Amish and forgiveness,
        501–502
Anglocentrism, 10
antecedents of contact,
        148–149
anticipation phase of U-curve
    theory of adaptation, 339
Anti-Defamation League, 378

anti-immigrant/refugee attitudes
    and legislation, 8, 10, 11,
        66–67, 246
anti-Semitism, 246
anxiety in intercultural
    relationships, 401–402
anxiety uncertainty management
    theory, 53, 333–334
apartheid in South Africa,
        132–133, 329
Army Reserve Family Programs
    website, 353
Asaillinen verbal style in Finland,
        290–291
ascription, 171–172
Asiacentricity, 62
Asiana Airlines crash, 101
Asian Americans, as model
    minority, 208
Asians, stereotypes of, 404,
        422
assertive accommodation strategies
    for communication, 242
assertive assimilation strategies for
    communication, 242
assertive separation strategies for
    communication, 243
assimilation
    melting pot metaphor of, 10
    migrants and, 326–327
    resistance to, 330–331
assimilation strategies for
    communication, 241–242
Association for Conflict
    Resolution, 463
asylum claims of refugees, 323
attitude dimension of communication
    competence, 483–486

Australia, National Sorry Day in, 505

authoritarian culture, 101

autoethnographies, 107

autonomy in romantic relationships, 413

Avatar (movie), 385

avowal, 171–172

awareness stage of identity development, 203

Baartman, Saartjie, 47

Baby Boomers, 441

Baker, Gene, 400

beauty culture, 112–113, 404

behaviors and skills component of communication competence, 486–487

"being" orientation, 101

Belgium
  culture of, 113–116
  Royal Museum for Central Africa in, 505
  segregation in, 302

beliefs and communication, 153

Beyoncé, "Formation," 362

bias in nonverbal behavior, 292–295

Biko, Steven, 133

bilingualism, 250, 251–253, 258–260

biracial identity, 177, 202–204

Birdwhistell, Ray, 44

The Black Atlantic (Gilroy), 144

body image, 382

Bond (James) movies, 382

border, living on, 351–353

boundary-crossing friendships, 402–403

bounded identity, 190

bows, 287

Boyega, John, 372

Brown, Michael, 367–368

bullying
  of gay and lesbian adolescents, 34
  in workplace, 497

business people. *See also* workforce; workplace

cultural awareness of, 16–18
repatriation process for, 343, 344

Cameroon, homosexuality in, 427

Canada
  U.S. media in, 27
  value orientations in, 98

Captain America: The First Avenger (movie), 379, 385

Carey, Mariah, 89

Centers for Disease Control and Prevention, 503

Centre for Intercultural Learning, 508

CEOs
  decision making process of, 487
  pay of, 13

child marriages, 420

children
  global, 488
  sensory-deprived, nonverbal behaviors of, 279
  third-culture (TCKs), 205–206, 207

China
  censorship in, 21
  economy of, 16, 504
  film industry of, 386
  friendships in, 407–408
  U.S. businesses in, 17–18

Chinese, segregation of, 300

Chinese Exclusion Act of 1882, 10, 430

Chinese language, 21

chronemics, 289

Circle Leaders (CLs), 31–32

cisgender, 183

citizenship, renouncement of, 320

civility, maintaining, 464

civil war, ending in forgiveness, 468

class. *See* socioeconomic class

class identity, 197–199

class structure and immigration, 12–13

clothing
  decoding, 369
  of Muslim women, 281, 348
  as nonverbal expression, 276, 282–283

coalitions, building, 496

co-cultural groups and communication, 240–244

cocultural theory, 68

code switching, 257–260, 262

cognitive conflict, 449

cognitive consistency, 405

collective programming of mind, culture as, 86

collectivistic cultures
  conflict in, 447
  defined, 55–56
  nonverbal communication in, 281–282
  relationships within, 99–100

college enrollment, diversity of, 5

Collins, Suzanne, 371

colonial histories, 144–146, 265

colonialism
  of Belgium, 505
  defined, 26
  electronic, 384–387
  intercultural relationships and, 431

communication. *See also* communication style; competence in intercultural communication; context; dialectics of intercultural communication; ethnography of communication; language; nonverbal communication
  applying knowledge about, 491–492
  approaches to study of, 49–51
  attitude dimension of competence in, 483–486
  behaviors and skills dimension of competence in, 486–487
  co-cultural groups and, 240–244
  culture and, 92, 94
  defined, 91–92
  development of, 44–47

communication (*continued*)
  identity and, 212–214
  in intercultural relationships, 402
  intergroup, facilitation of, 149–151, 153–154
  knowledge dimension of competence in, 482–483
  levels of competence in, 487
  motivation dimension of competence in, 479–482
  power and, 111–114
  as reinforcing culture, 106–109
  as resistance to dominant culture, 109–110
  social context for, 110, 488–489
  technology and, 19–25
  value orientations in, 94–97, 100–101
communication accommodation theory, 54, 236, 258–260
communication in intercultural relationships
  online, 415–419
  overview, 413–414
  workplace, 414–415
communication rules, 107
communication style
  cultural variations in, 230–234
  dialectical approach to, 238
  gender identity and, 184
  interactive media use and, 234–235
community engagement, 500–501, 503
competence in intercultural communication
  becoming interpersonal allies, 494–496
  building coalitions, 496
  components of, 479
  critical approach to, 490–491
  entering into dialogue, 492–494
  forgiveness, 501–502
  interpretive approach to, 488–490
  social justice and transformation, 497–501

social science approach to, 479–487
compromise style in intercultural marriages, 424
concentration camps, 130–131, 150–151
conceptual equivalence, 56–57
concrete communication, 86
conflict. *See also* conflict management
  ambiguity and, 443–444
  characteristics of, 443
  colonialism and, 26
  destructive, 462
  economic disparity and, 26–27
  ethnic, 12
  family influences on, 449–450
  foreign policy and, 27–28
  historical and political contexts for, 458–461
  interpretive and critical approaches to, 455–461
  intra-national, 25
  language and, 444
  orientations to, 444–445
  overview, 441–443
  productive, 462
  religious, 195–196, 447–448, 450
  social movements and, 457–458
  social science approach to, 446–455
  styles of, 451–455
  types of, 449
  values and, 447
conflict management
  forgiveness and, 469
  interpersonal conflict, 461–468
  mediation, 468–471
  overview, 461
  peacebuilding, 471–472
conflict myths, 470
conflict of interest, 449
Conflict Resolution Day, 463
conflict transformation, 468–469
conformity stage of identity development, 178
Congo, history of, 134

conscious competence, 486, 487
conscious incompetence, 486, 487
consensus style in intercultural marriages, 425
constructive marginals, 207–208
consumption of popular culture, 369–371
contact
  with people who are similar, 22–23
  with people who differ, 21–22
contact cultures, 285
contact hypothesis, 149–151, 153–154, 445
contested site or zone, culture as, 90–91
context
  communication and, 110–111, 153
  for communication competence, 488–490
  conflict and, 465–466
contextual identity formation, 173–174
contextual language rules, 238–240
conversational constraints theory, 54
conversational rules in friendships, 412
cooperation and communication, 153
core symbols, 172
cosmopolitan communication, 492
Council on International Educational Exchange, 507
Crimea, annexation of, by Russia, 199–200
critical approach
  applications of, 65–68
  to communication, 92
  to competence in intercultural communication, 490–491
  to cultural adaptation, 332, 347–353
  to culture, 85, 89–91
  to identity, 168, 172–176
  to intercultural conflict, 443, 455–461

critical approach (*continued*)
  to intercultural relationships,
    428–431
  to language, 240–246
  overview, 49–51, 64
  strengths and limitations of, 68
  theories of, 70
cross-cultural consultants,
    17, 35
cross-cultural differences, social
    science approach to, 407–413
cross-cultural perspectives on
    identity, 168–171
cross-cultural research, guidelines
    for, 56
cross-cultural training
  competent behaviors and,
    486–487
  as discipline, 45
  for military personnel, 507
Cruz, Ted, 89, 246
Cuba, 123–124
cultural adaptation
  critical approach to, 332,
    347–353
  Internet and, 419
  interpretive approach to, 332,
    338–347
  overview, 332
  social science approach to,
    332–338
cultural capital, 25, 66
cultural-group histories,
    128–129
cultural-group identity
  language and, 255–257
  in popular culture, 374–380
cultural humility, 33
cultural hybridity, 331–332
cultural identity and magazines,
    370–371
cultural imperialism, 384–387
cultural-individual dialectic
  identity and, 212–213
  in intercultural relationships,
    405–406
  overview, 72
  value orientations and, 106

cultural practices, whiteness as set
    of, 193–194
cultural spaces
  changing, 303–304
  cultural identity and, 298–303
  defined, 275
  overview, 297–298
  postmodern, 304–308
cultural texts, 369, 371
cultural values, 95–97
culture. *See also* popular culture;
    value orientations
  common uses of term, 84
  communication and, 92, 94,
    106–109
  communication style and,
    230–234
  critical approach to, 89–91
  defined, 45–46, 47, 83, 85
  dominant, communication as
    resistance to, 109–110
  interpretive approach to,
    87–89
  normative, 190
  perspectives on defining, 85
  social science approach to,
    86–87
culture brokers, 207
culture industries, 366
Culturelink website, 508
culture shock, 334, 339–341
Cupid Media, 429

dating, intercultural, 203, 397, 400,
    419–421
Dave, Aporva, 331–332
Davis, Kim, 396
Dawes Severalty Act of 1887, 10
deception, 278
decoding, 369, 370
de la Garza, Sarah Amira, 61
demographic imperative, 5–15
demographics
  defined, 5
  U.S., as changing, 5–6
description, interpretation, evaluation
    (D.I.E.) exercise, 485–486
development of identity

majority, 180–183
minority, 178–180
overview, 176–178
dialectical approach. *See also*
    dialectics of intercultural
    communication
  to communication and power,
    113–116
  to communication competence,
    491–492, 491–502
  to communication style, 238
  to culture, 85, 91
  to forgiveness, 467
  to history, 155–156
  to identity, 210, 212–213
  to intercultural relationships, 397,
    403–407
  to intercultural transitions,
    319–321
  keeping in mind, 74
  to motivation for communication,
    482
  to nonverbal communication,
    275–278
  overview, 57–59, 69–72, 506
  to research, 69–74
dialectics of intercultural
    communication
  cultural-individual, 72, 106,
    212–213, 405–406
  differences-similarities, 72–73,
    83, 106, 405
  history/past-present/future, 74,
    123, 406–407, 506
  personal-contextual, 72, 156, 214,
    320, 404
  privilege-disadvantage, 74, 156,
    319–320, 406, 417
  static-dynamic, 73, 106, 167–168,
    214, 406
dialogical approach to ethical
    imperative, 31–32
dialogue, 462, 471–472, 492–494
diasporic groups, 23–24
diasporic histories, 142, 144
dichotomous thinking, 70
D.I.E. (description, interpretation,
    evaluation) exercise, 485–486

differences-similarities dialectic, 72–73, 83, 106
  in intercultural relationships, 405
diffusion of innovations theory, 54–55
digital inequality, 24–25
digital translation apps, 22
Diné (Navajo) language, 227–228
direct communication style, 232
direct conflict approach, 451, 464
discrimination
  assimilation and, 327
  nonverbal behaviors and, 294–295
  religious, 447–448
discussion style of conflict resolution, 452
Disney Corporation, as culture industry, 366
distance zones, 45
diversity
  defined, 8
  demographics of, 5
  global, 15
  religious, 13–15
  in workplace, 414–415
diversity training, 45. *See also* cross-cultural training
"doing" orientation, 101
Dolezal, Rachel, 171
dominant identity, 190
Douglas, Raymond, 469
DREAM Act, 90, 91
Dreams From My Father (Obama), 126
Drescher, Fran, 288
Dunaboo, Erica, 400
dynamic, identity as, 174–176
dynamic style of conflict resolution, 453

EB-5 Immigrant Investor Program, 146
eBay, 17–18
economic classes of immigrants, 12–13. *See also* socioeconomic class
economic imperative, 15–19

economics
  attitudes toward immigrants and, 11–12
  conflict and, 26–27
  global, 503–504, 506
educational context for intercultural relationships, 428–429
ego-defensive function of prejudice, 211
Eight Mile Road, Detroit, 301–302
elaborate communication style, 232–233
electronic colonialism, 384–387
elitism and culture, 364–365
embodied ethnocentrism, 88
emic, 57, 58
emotionally expressive approach to conflict, 452
emotions and culture, 87–88
empathy, 484–485
encapsulated marginals, 207–208
encoding, 369, 370
engagement style of conflict resolution, 452
England
  economy of, 503–504
  rioting in, 455–456
Engle, John, 99
English language, dominance of, 248, 256, 264
equality, as value, 95
equivalency of translation, 252
ethical imperative, 29–35
ethics
  defined, 29
  of workplace, 18
ethnic diversity, 5
ethnic histories, 136–140
ethnic identity, 189–190. *See also* African Americans; Latinas/os; Native Americans
ethnicity and conflict styles, 454–455
ethnic profiling, 209–210
ethnocentrism
  defined, 4
  embodied, 88

ethnography of communication
  cultural practice research and, 61
  defined, 87
  as interpretive approach, 57
  talk about drinking alcohol, 107
ethnorelative perspective, 206–207
etic, 57, 58
European Union (EU), 503–504
expat, use of term, 335
expectancy violations theory, 278
explanatory uncertainty, 333
eye contact, 287–288

Facebook, 19–20
face negotiation theory, 53–54, 447
facework, 447
facial expressions, 279–280, 283–284
facilitated intergroup dialogue, 471–472
familial identity, 170
family context
  for conflict, 449–450
  for intercultural relationships, 428
  racism and, 499
family histories, 125–126
fear and communication competence, 480
female migration, 322–323
femininity/masculinity value, 103, 104, 106
femininity themes, 184
Ferguson, Brown shooting in, 367–368
fight approach of migrants, 335–336
Finland, silence in, 290–291
fixed feature space, 284
flight approach of migrants, 334–335
folk culture, 366–367
football and militarism, 368
Foreign Account Tax Compliance Act, 320
Foreign Service Institute (FSI), 44, 46, 75

forgiveness
   communication competence and,
      501–502
   conflict management, 466–468,
      469
France
   banning of veiling of Muslim
      women in, 348
   culture of, 4
   immigrants in, 329
   international broadcasting
      network in, 384–385
   rioting in, 455–457
   students living in, 346–347
friendship
   boundary-crossing, 402–403
   interracial, 481–482, 495–496
   intimacy and, 409–412
   views of, 407–408
FSI (Foreign Service Institute),
   44, 46, 75
functional fitness and adaptation,
   337–338
functionalist approach, 49–57

Gaddafi, Muammar, communication
   style of, 233, 234
Garou, 384
gays and lesbians. *See also*
   homosexuality
   adolescents, bullying of, 34
   in Nazi Germany, 140–142
   sexuality and intimacy in
      intercultural relationships,
      425–427
Geert Hofstede Cultural
   Dimensions website, 116
gender. *See also* women
   conflict styles and, 454–455
   physical attractiveness and,
      282–283
   social class communication
      and, 68
gender histories, 140
gender identity, 183–186
generational differences and age
   identity, 186–188
Gen X, 187, 240

Gen Y (Millennials), 187–188,
   240, 441
Georgetown University, 154–155
Germany
   Nuremberg trials in, 505
   refugees in, 174–175
   Turkish guest workers in, 350
gestures, 285–287
Ghandi, Mahatma, 502
Global Exchange website, 508
globalization
   economic imperative and,
      15–19
   language and, 263–266
   of popular culture, 381–384
global kids, 488
global nomads (third-culture kids or
   TCKs), 205–206, 207
global village, 19
Global Voices Online website, 117
goal conflict, 449
grand narrative, 132–133
Great Recession, 198
group identity, 170–171
"growing" orientation, 101
guanxi, 18, 408

hair flip, 112
Hall, Edward T., 44, 45
Hallyu (Korean Wave), 382–383
handshakes, 287
Haque, Sarker, 14
Harberson, Sara, 135
harmonic discourse, 493
Harris-Perry, Melissa, 372
"hate music," 378
Hernández, Angelica, 90
heterogeneous cultures, 7–8,
   89–91
The Hidden Dimension (Hall), 45
hidden histories, 136
high-context communication, 230,
   231–232, 418
high culture, 364, 366
higher education and income
   inequality, 198
Hill, Johnny, Jr., 257
historical context

for communication, 111,
   490–491
for intercultural conflict,
   458–461
for intercultural relationships,
   429–431
for interpersonal allies, 495–496
for motivation for communication,
   481–482
historical revisionism in popular
   culture, 379
history. *See also* nonmainstream
   histories
   cultural-group, 128–129
   dialectical approach to, 155–156
   family, 125–126
   influence of, 122–123
   intercultural communication and,
      147–156
   national, 126–128
   political, intellectual, and social,
      124–125
   power and, 129–134
   as stories, 135–136
   types of, 123–124
history/past-present/future dialectic
   culture, cultural identity, and, 123
   in Europe, 506
   in intercultural relationships,
      406–407
   overview, 74
Holocaust, 138
home, 298–299
homogeneous cultures, 7
homosexuality. *See also* gays and
   lesbians
   death penalty for, 396, 427
   marriage and, 396, 425–427
hooks, bell, *Cultural Criticism and
   Transformation* interview, 388
host communities and volunteers,
   30
human nature, views of, 97–98
humans
   relationship between nature
      and, 98
   relationships between, 99–101
humor, 236–238, 417–418

Hunger Games movies, casting for, 371–372
hybrid identity, 67–68
hyphenated Americans, 189–190

identity
  age, 186–188
  biracial, 177, 202–204
  bounded and dominant, 190
  communication and, 212–214
  communication theory of, 62–63
  contextual identity formation, 173–174
  critical approach to, 172–176
  cross-cultural perspectives on, 168–171
  cultural, 298–303, 370–371
  cultural adaptation and, 350–351
  cultural-group, 255–257, 374–380
  culture and, 192
  defined, 167–168
  development of, 176–183
  dialectical approach to, 210, 212–213
  disaporic groups and, 22–23
  as dynamic, 174–176
  ethnic, 189–190
  expression of, 490
  gender, 183–186
  group, 170–171
  history and, 131, 134–136
  hybrid, 67–68
  individualized, 169–170
  intercultural, 338
  interpretive approach to, 171–172
  language and, 255–260
  magazines and, 370–371
  modernist, 132
  multicultural, 89, 202–208, 331–332, 351–352
  multiple, and building coalitions, 496
  national, 199–201
  online communication and, 418
  performance perspective on, 213–214
  personal, 202
  prejudice and, 208, 211–212

racial, 188–189, 190
regional, 201
religious, 4, 195–196
sexual, 186
social science approach to, 168–171
socioeconomic class, 197–199
spiritual, 170
static-dynamic dialectic and, 214
stereotypes and, 208–212
transgender, 185–186
whiteness, 191–194
identity management, 23–24
identity negotiation theory, 171
IDPs (internally displaced people), 323
immigrants
  adaptation of, and use of social media, 52–53
  African American, 9
  defined, 8
  dialectics and, 57–59
  distrust of and prejudice against, 66–67
  EB-5 Immigrant Investor Program, 146
  economic classes of, 12–13
  family conflict and, 450
  to France, 329
  to Germany, 174–175
  to Hong Kong, 66
  Montagnards of Vietnam, 65–66
  multicultural identity of children of, 205–206
  origin of, 7
  performative culture and, 108
  readaptation to home country, 60
  relationships between residents and, 9–12
  religion of, 13–15
  religious individuals and views of, 502
  social support for, 53
  from Syria, 8, 11, 55, 71
  undocumented, 90, 91
  as voluntary migrants, 322
  white, 194

Immigration History Research Center, 324, 353
immigration patterns, as changing, 6–15
impression management, 167
income inequality and higher education, 198
incompatibility and conflict, 443
India
  beauty queen narrative in, 387
  film industry of, 382, 386
  text messaging in, 238–239
indirect communication style, 232
indirect conflict approach, 451
individualistic cultures
  conflict in, 447
  defined, 55
  nonverbal communication in, 281–282
  relationships within, 99–100
  romantic relationships in, 413
individualized identity, 169–170
individuation of group members, 153–154
Indonesia, diversity in, 15
indulgence/restraint value, 103, 104–105
informal space, 284
information about people and cultures, access to, 20–21
institutional influences on adaptation, 347–348
integration of migrants, 330–331
integration stage of identity development, 179–180, 182–183
integrative model of adaptation, 336–337
integrative theory of adaptation, 52
intellectual histories, 124–125
interactive media use, influence of, on language and communication style, 234–235
Interchange Institute, 353
intercultural communication. *See* communication
intercultural competence, 46
intercultural conflict. *See* conflict

Intercultural Conflict Styles
    inventory, 472
intercultural identity, 338
intercultural interactions, power
    in, 134
intercultural relationships. *See*
    relationships
intercultural transitions. *See*
    transitions
interdependence and conflict, 443
interdisciplinary study, 47
intergenerational conflict, 441
interlanguage, 250
intermediaries, 453
internally displaced people
    (IDPs), 323
international conflict, 441
Internet. *See also* social media
    conflict and, 445
    cultural adaptation and, 419
    languages of, 21
internment camps for Japanese
    Americans, 130–131, 136–138
interpellation, 174
interpersonal allies, becoming,
    494–496
interpersonal conflict management
    context in, 465–466
    forgiveness, 466–468
    maintaining contact, 462–464
    staying centered, 461–462
    style repertoires, 464–465
interpretation of language, 251–254
interpreters, role of, 253–254
interpretive approach
    applications of, 57–63
    to communication, 92
    to competence in intercultural
        communication, 488–490
    to cultural adaptation, 332,
        338–347
    to culture, 85, 87–89
    to identity, 168, 171–172
    to intercultural conflict, 443,
        455–461
    to intercultural relationships,
        413–427
    to language, 238–240

overview, 49–51
strengths and limitations of,
    63–64
theories of, 70
interracial relationships. *See also*
    relationships
    dating and marriage, 203, 397,
        400, 419–421
    friendship, 481–482, 495–496
    stereotypes in, 380
intimacy
    friendship and, 409–412
    intercultural relationships and,
        425–427
involuntary migrants, 323–324
Iraq
    checkpoints in, 274
    culture shock of military in,
        339–340
    pirated DVDs in, 373
ISIS (Islamic State)
    homosexuality and, 427
    videos posted by, 20, 363
Islamophobia, 14
Israel
    "Combatants for Peace" group
        in, 480
    communication in, 19
    foreign television in, 385–386
Ivory Coast, French programming
    in, 386–387

Japan, history of, 133
Japanese Americans
    attitudes toward, 430–431
    internment of, 130–131, 136–138
Jeter, Mildred, 203
Jews
    anti-Semitism and, 246
    Holocaust and, 138
    in Spain, 141
Johnson-Read Act of 1924,
    10, 430
Joon, Bae Yong, 383

Karski, Jan, 150–151
Kerswill, Paul, 237
Khan, Sadiq, 167

King, Martin Luther, Jr., 502
King, Peter, 362
knowledge dimension of
    communication competence,
    482–483
knowledge function of prejudice,
    212
Korean Wave *(Hallyu),*
    382–383
Kyrgyzstan, ethnic conflict in,
    459–460

labels, 244–246
labor, migrant, 322–323, 325
language. *See also* translation
    acquisition of, 229, 249
    colonial histories and, 265
    colonialism and, 144–146
    communication style, culture,
        and, 230–234
    conflict and, 444
    critical perspective on,
        240–246
    culture and, 113–116
    discourse, social structure,
        and, 244
    extinction of, 257, 263
    globalization and, 263–266
    identity and, 255–260
    interactive media use and,
        234–235
    of Internet, 21
    interpretive perspective on,
        238–240
    multilingualism, 247–251
    online communication and, 22,
        417–418, 490
    overview, 224–225
    perception and, 226–229
    phenomenological model of
        adaptation and, 346–347
    politics and, 260–263
    Sapir-Whorf hypothesis, 46
    slang, humor, and, 235–238
    social science approach to,
        225–226
    thought and, 229–230
    translation of literature, 23

language policies, 260–263
Last Watch of the Night
 (Monette), 484
Latinas/os
 gender histories and, 140
 language, colonization, and, 146
 new immigrants and, 350
 in rural communities,
  marginalization of, 108–109
Lebanon, postcolonial identity
 in, 67
Lee, Wen Shu, 84
Levy, Clifford, 488
liminality, 351
Lincoln, Abraham, sexual history
 of, 142, 143
line of sight data, 416
lingua franca, 264
linguistic knowledge, 483
listening
 cultural space and, 305
 mutual, 492–493
long-term refugees, 323–324
long-term/short-term orientation,
 103, 104
Loving, Peter, 203
Loving Day website, 432
Loving v. Virginia, 203, 400
low-conflict societies, 446
low-context communication,
 230, 231–232, 418
low culture, 365
Lumumba, Patrice, 134
lynching, 213–214

machine translation, 254
macrocontexts, 64
magazines and cultural identity,
 370–371
majority identity, development of,
 177, 180–183
maquiladoras, 19, 445
Marley, Bob, 88, 89
marriage
 intercultural, 422–425
 interracial, 203, 397, 400
 minimum age for, 420
 polygamy, 421

same-sex, 396, 426–427,
 447–448
Martinez, Fred, 501
masculinity themes, 184
mass media and cultural
 adaptation, 347
Matt Waters (television show),
 377–378
media imperialism, 384–387
mediation, 453, 468–471
Mediation Channel website, 472
medical context for
 communication, 489
melting pot metaphor, 10–11
Mennonites, German American,
 138–139
Menzio, Guido, 209
"mestiza," 352
metamessage, 231
metaphor, 229–230
Mexico
 as collectivistic culture, 100
 immigrants from, 7, 11–12
microaggressions, 211, 294, 497
Mideast website, 472–473
migrants. *See also* immigrants
 defined, 321
 involuntary, 323–324
 perceptions of mainstream culture
  of, 376–377
 relationships with hosts, 325–332
 voluntary, 321–323
migration. *See also* migrants;
  transitions
 changing cultural spaces and,
  303–304
 diasporic histories and, 142, 144
 overview, 318
 stories of, 317
Migration Policy Institute, 353
militarism and football, 368
military personnel
 as cultural ambassadors,
  504–505
 culture shock of, 339–340
 intercultural relationships of,
  429–430
 intercultural training for, 507

reentry shock of, 344
Millennials (Gen Y), 187–188,
 240, 441
minority identity, development of,
 177, 178–180
miscegenation, 202
Mitchell, Pauline, 501
Mittal, Vikas, 27
MMORPGs, 305–306
model minority stereotype, 208
modernist identity, 132
monochronic concept of time, 289
"moralnets," 446
Mormons, 196, 448
motivation dimension of
 communication competence,
 479–482
Mueller, Kayla Jean, 501
multicultural identity, 89, 202–208,
 331–332, 351–352
multifocal attention, 490
multilingualism, 247–251
multinational corporations, 19, 27, 29
Muslims
 adaptation of, and use of
  Facebook, 52–53
 societal conflict and, 455–457
 stereotypes of, 14–15
 terror attacks and, 138, 147, 167,
  169, 209
 women, clothing of, 281,
  282–283, 348

nagging, 239
National Archives, 156
national histories, 126–128
national identity, 199–201
National Public Radio, 388
Native Americans
 in history texts, 131
 language of, 227–228, 257
 listening, cultural space, and, 305
 population of, 8–9
 right to self-government of, 9–10
 segregation of, 328
 silence in communities of, 290
 stereotypes of, 209
 in Virginia, 145

nativistic movement, 10, 11. *See also* anti-immigrant/refugee attitudes and legislation
nature, relationship between humans and, 98
The Nature of Prejudice (Allport), 47
Nazi Germany, gays in, 140–142
neighborhood, 299–300, 302
neighborhood context for intercultural relationships, 428
net worth, 13
Nickel Mines school shooting, 502
Nigeria
  diversity in, 15
  film industry of, 385, 386
nominalist position, 226–227
nonassertive accommodation strategies for communication, 242
nonassertive assimilation strategies for communication, 241–242
nonassertive separation strategies for communication, 243
noncontact cultures, 285
nonjudgmentalism, 485–486
nonmainstream histories
  colonial, 144–146
  diasporic, 142, 144
  gender, 140
  racial and ethnic, 136–140
  religious, 147
  sexual orientation, 140–142, 143
  socioeconomic class, 146
nonverbal codes
  chronemics, 289
  eye contact, 287–288
  facial expressions, 283–284
  gestures, 285–287
  paralinguistics, 288–289
  physical appearance, 281–283
  proxemics, 284–285
  silence, 289–291
nonverbal communication. *See also* nonverbal codes
  dialectical approach to, 275–278
  errors in, 274
  Foreign Service Institute training and, 45

framework of, 274–275
learning, 277
online communication and, 21–22
recognizing, 276
relational messages of, 277–278
research on, 279–281
semiotics and, 295–297
stereotypes, prejudice, discrimination, and, 292, 294–295
universality of, 279, 280
nonviolence and social movements, 458
normative culture, 190
normative race privilege, 191–193
Norway, as low-conflict society, 446
numerical equality and intergroup communication, 153

Obama, Barack
  communication style of, 233–234
  Dreams From My Father, 126
  as global nomad, 205
  on Karski, 150–151
  multicultural identity of, 89
  on Muslim Americans, 169
  as president, 9
  refugees and, 8, 319
  on religion, 147
Obama, Michelle, 126, 282, 285
Obergefell, Jim, 396
Obergefell v. Hodges, 396
obliteration style in intercultural marriages, 424
O'Brien, Soledad, 89
oil prices, 504
Okeniyi, Dayo, 371
online communication
  conflict and, 442
  as cultural space, 305–307
  intercultural relationships and, 415–419
  language and, 490
Oriental Exclusion Act of 1924, 10
orientations of affirmation, 496

Ortiz, Javier, 362
other-knowledge, 482–483

pacifism, 451
Palestine, Israel "Combatants for Peace" group in, 480
Pamunkey tribe, 145
paradigms, research, 48–49
paralinguistics, 288–289
participant observation, 57
passports, active, 488
peacebuilding, 471–472
Peace Corps, 75
peace imperative, 25–29
Pearl, Daniel, 68
People to People International website, 507
perception
  language and, 226–229
  in research, 48–49
performance perspective on identity, 213–214
performative, culture as, 107–109
personal-contextual dialectic
  identity and, 167–168, 214
  in intercultural relationships, 404
  intercultural transitions and, 320
  overview, 72
  past-present dialectic and, 156
personal histories, 148–149
personal identity, 202
personal space, 284–285
Pew Forum on Religion and Public Life, 215
phenomenological model of adaptation, 345–347
Phipps, Susie, 189
Phoenix, ethnic life in, 307
physical appearance, as nonverbal code, 281–283
Platinum Rule, 485
Pocahontas (movie), 373
political context
  for communication, 111
  for intercultural conflict, 458–461
  for intercultural relationships, 429–431

political context (*continued*)
for motivation for
communication, 481–482
political histories, 124–125
politics and language, 260–263
polychronic concept of time, 289
polygamy, 421
popular culture
consuming, 369–371
cultural groups represented in,
374–380
defined, 364–367
historical revisionism in, 379
overview, 362
power of, 363–364, 380–387
resisting, 371–373
ubiquity of, 367–369
postcolonialism, 67–68, 146
postmodern cultural spaces, 304–308
power
communication and, 111–114
communication competence
and, 491
cultural adaptation and, 349, 351
cultural space, identity, and, 302
history and, 129–134
in intercultural relationships, 431,
494–496
of popular culture, 363–364,
380–387
social positions and, 244
in work relationships, 415
power distance, 102, 103
Power of Culture website, 116
predictive uncertainty, 333
prejudice
development of, 47
identity and, 208, 211–212
nonverbal behaviors and, 292,
294–295
primates, nonverbal behaviors
of, 279
privilege
awareness of, 4, 494
majority identity development
and, 181–183
normative race privilege,
191–193

privilege-disadvantage dialectic
digital, 417
in intercultural relationships, 406
intercultural transitions and,
319–320
overview, 74
past-present dialectic and, 156
processual, 69
proxemics, 45, 284–285
psychological health and
adaptation, 337

qualitative methods, 57
quantitative methods, 51

racial diversity, 5
racial histories, 136–140
racial identity, 188–189, 190
Racial Integrity Act of 1924,
Virginia, 145
racialization, 10–11
racial profiling, 209–210
racism
Chicago Police Department
and, 500
education about, 495
fighting, 498
reader profiles, 370
redefinition stage of identity
development, 182
Refugee Council of Australia, 75
refugees. *See also* anti-immigrant/
refugee attitudes and legislation
in Germany, 174–175
as involuntary migrants, 323–324
from Syria, 8, 11, 55, 71, 442
U.S. policy on, 8, 319
worldwide crisis of, 50–51
regional identity, 201
regionalism, 302–303
relational development, differences
in, 408–409
relational learning, 398
relational messages, 277–278
relationships. *See also* dating,
intercultural; friendship;
interracial relationships; marriage
benefits of, 397–399

challenges of, 399–403
critical approach to, 428–431
dating, 419–421
dialectical approach to, 403–407
interpretive approach to, 413–427
overview, 396–397
power in, 431, 494–496
romantic, 411, 412–413,
421–425, 429
sexuality and intimacy, 425–427
social science approach to,
407–413
relativist position, 227–228
relativity of cultural behavior, 29,
31–32
religion. *See also* Muslims
conflict and, 447–448, 450
cultural hybridity and, 331–332
forgiveness and, 502
identity and, 4
of immigrants, 13–15
proselytizing, 35
racism and, 498–499
religious context for intercultural
relationships, 428–429
religious histories, 147
religious identity, 195–196
religious institutions and adaptation,
348–349
repatriation process, 342–345
research
approaches to, 49–51
critical approach to, 64–68
dialectical approach to, 69–74
interpretive approach to, 57–64
Maori-based code of conduct
for, 64
on minority groups, 35
perception and worldview in,
48–49
social science approach to, 49–57
residential separation, 327–328
resistance
to ascribed identity, 174
to assimilation, 330–331
communication as, 109–110
to dominant culture, 112–113
to popular culture, 371–373

resistance and separatism stage of identity development, 178–179
Resistance Records, 378
resistance stage of identity development, 182
restorative justice, 467
restraint approach to conflict, 452
reverse culture/reentry shock, 342–345
revised and restored histories, 133–134
rhetorical approach, 57
rioting in France and England, 455–457
Rogers, Jim, 488
romantic (intercultural) relationships, 411, 412–413, 421–425, 429
Romney, Mitt, 196
Ruling Passions (Gill), 431
Russia
  annexation of Crimea by, 199–200
  anti-gay violence in, 432
  Syria and, 441
  Turkey and, 504

Sanea, Raja Al-, 23
Sapir-Whorf hypothesis, 46, 227–229
Seeds of Peace project, 496, 501
segregation, 299–300, 301, 302, 328–330. *See also* apartheid in South Africa
self-awareness imperative, 3–4
self-disclosure, 414
self-knowledge, 482
self-reflexivity, 32
self-restraint and interpersonal conflict, 461–462
semifixed feature space, 284
semiosis, 295
semiotics and nonverbal communication, 295–297
sensory-deprived children, nonverbal behaviors of, 279
separation strategies
  for communication, 243–244

for migrants, 327–330
sexual identity, 186
sexuality in intercultural relationships, 425–427
sexual orientation histories, 140–142
Sharaa, Faez al, 55
shared, culture as, 88–89
short-term refugees, 323–324
signified, 295
signifiers, 295
signs, 295
silence, 289–291
The Silent Language (Hall), 45
"silent zones," academic, 49
similarity principle, 405
slang, 235–236, 237
slavery
  apologies for, 505
  Georgetown University and, 154–155
  history of, 127
  immigration and, 9
smiling, 284
social class. *See* socioeconomic class
social construction of racial categories, 188–189
social context for communication, 110, 488–489
social histories, 125
social justice, 33–35, 497–501
social media
  Brown shooting and, 367–368
  conflict and, 442
  hate messages on, 23
  immigrant adaptation and use of, 52–53
  impact of, on resistance, 110
  in India, 238–239
  intercultural relationships through, 415–419
  language, communication style, and, 234–235, 264
  race, and uses of cultural spaces of, 306
  slang and, 236
social movements, 457–458

social positions, 244
social reproduction, 68
social science approach
  applications of, 51–55
  to communication, 91–92
  to competence in intercultural communication, 479–487
  to cultural adaptation, 332–338
  to culture, 85, 86–87
  to identity, 168–171
  to intercultural conflict, 443, 446–455
  to intercultural relationships, 407–413
  to language, 225–226
  overview, 49–51
  strengths and limitations of, 56–57
  theories of, 70
social support
  in gay community, 426
  for immigrants, 53, 337
societal conflict, 441, 455–456
socioeconomic class
  collectivism and, 100
  cultural adaptation and, 350
  histories, 146
  identity and, 197–199
  sojourners, 321–322, 333, 341
source text, 251
South Africa
  apartheid in, 132–133, 329
  Truth and Reconciliation Commission in, 467, 469, 505
South Carolina, Confederate battle flag in, 148
South Korea
  adoptees from, 204
  value heterogeneity in, 106
Spain, Sephardic Jews in, 141
spatial distance, 274
speech
  communication rules for, 107
  framework for studying, 87
speech communities, 238–240, 490
spiritual identity, 170
sports
  diversity of, 5

sports (*continued*)
national identity and, 200
stage model for intercultural
friendships, 409
standpoint from which to view
society, whiteness as, 193
Starbucks, logo of, 18, 27
Star Wars movies, casting for, 372
static-dynamic dialectic
identity and, 167–168, 214
in intercultural relationships, 406
overview, 73
value orientations and, 106
status
communication and, 149–150
cultural adaptation and, 349
nonverbal behavior and, 278
relational development and, 410
Stenber, Amandla, 371–372
stereotypes
of accents, 249
of African American women,
378–379
of Asians, 404
of conflict resolution styles,
453–454
generalizations compared to, 99
identity and, 208–212
in intercultural interaction, 47
in intercultural relationships,
399–401
of Muslims, 14–15
nonverbal behaviors and, 292,
294–295
popular culture and, 377–380
television and, 374–375
stories, histories as, 135–136
struggle for acceptance stage
of identity development,
203
submission style in intercultural
marriages, 424
support for intergroup
communication, 150–151
Swedish Tourist Association,
200–201
Switzerland, language in, 265–266
symbolic significance, 87

Syria
refugees from, 8, 11, 55,
71, 442
war in, as proxy war, 441

Taiwan, indigenous people of, 505
Taobao, 18
target text, 251
task context for communication,
488–489
"teacher talk," 239
technological imperative, 19–25
technology. *See* social media
temporary migration, 323
terror attacks
explanations for, 28
Muslims and, 167, 169
of 9/11, 125, 138, 147, 209
in Paris, 7–8
personal histories and, 149
social media and, 442
Test of U.S. Cultural Knowledge,
93–94
textbooks, altered history in, 125
texts, power of, 130–132
textual analyses, 64
Thai culture, 114
third-culture kids (TCKs or global
nomads), 205–206, 207
thought and language, 229–230
time orientation, 101–102, 289
tolerance for ambiguity, 483–484
Trager, George, 44
transformation, personal, working
toward, 497–501
transgender identity, 185–186
transition model of adaptation,
334–336
transitions. *See also* cultural
adaptation; migration
dialectical approach to, 319–321
migrant-host relationships,
325–332
overview, 317–318
types of migrant groups,
321–324
translation
defined, 251

in health care settings, 231
intercultural, errors in, 253
issues of, 251–253
technology and, 22, 23
translation equivalence, 56
translators, role of, 253–254
transnationalism, 351–352
transpection, 485
travel and changing cultural
spaces, 303
Trump, Donald, 246, 319
trust-suspicion dialectic, digital,
417
Tsarnaev, Dzhokhar and
Tamerlan, 442
Turkey, tourism industry in, 504
Tutu, Desmond, 502

U-curve theory of adaptation,
338–341
uncertainty avoidance, 103, 104
uncertainty reduction, 333
unconscious competence,
486, 487
unconscious incompetence, 486,
487
understated communication style,
232–233
UNESCO Culture Sector
website, 116
unexamined stage of identity
development, 178, 180–181
United Nations High Commission
for Refugees, 324
United States Holocaust Museum,
157
United States v. Windsor, 396
universality of cultural behavior,
29, 31
U.S. Citizenship and Immigration
Services, 432
U.S. Institute of Peace, 473
utilitarian function of
prejudice, 211

Vaid, Urvashi, 484
value-expressive function of
prejudice, 212

value orientations
    on activity, 101
    among national societies, 102–105
    on human nature, 97–98
    on humans and nature, 98–99
    limitations of framework,
        105–106
    overview, 94–97
    on relationships between humans,
        99–101
    on time, 101–102
values. *See also* value orientations
    communication and, 153
    conflict and, 447, 449
variable, 51
violence and social movements, 458
vocalizations, 288–289
voice for all, 493
voice qualities, 288
voluntary contact, 151, 153
voluntary migrants, 321–323
volunteering, 30

Warren, Arthur, murder of, 368
W-curve theory of adaptation,
    342–345
wealth gap, 12–13, 194

Weitz, Rose, 112
white, passing as, 135
"white habitus," 482
whiteness, characteristics of,
    191–194
Whiteness Project, 214–215
whites
    as expats, 335
    mortality rates for, 198–199
Williams, Saul, 192
women
    African American, and kitchens,
        307–308
    African American, in popular
        culture, 378–379
    attractiveness of, 282
    characteristics of effective
        communication for, 490–491
    gender histories, 140
    hair flip by, 112
    Muslim, clothing of, 281,
        282–283, 348
    as voluntary migrants, 322–323
workforce. *See also* business
        people
    contact hypothesis and, 149–151,
        153–154

displaced workers, 15–16
diversity of, 5–6, 19
ethics of, 18
workplace
    bullying in, 497
    conflict in, 445
    ethics of, 18
    intercultural relationships in,
        414–415
    racism in, 498
    value orientations in,
        95–96
A World of Gestures
    (documentary), 286
worldviews
    defined, 44
    in research, 48–49
The Writing of the Disaster
    (Blanchot), 139

Younis, Samina, 450

"zoo approach" to study of
    culture, 33
Zubkov, Oleg, 199–200